COBBETT'S

CYCLOPEDIC SURVEY OF

CHAMBER MUSIC

VOLUME I

A—H

COBBETT'S
CYCLOPEDIC SURVEY OF
CHAMBER MUSIC

Compiled and edited by

WALTER WILLSON COBBETT

With supplementary material edited by

COLIN MASON

SECOND EDITION

VOLUME I

A–H

LONDON

OXFORD UNIVERSITY PRESS

NEW YORK TORONTO

Oxford University Press, Ely House, London W. 1

GLASGOW NEW YORK TORONTO MELBOURNE WELLINGTON
CAPE TOWN SALISBURY IBADAN NAIROBI LUSAKA ADDIS ABABA
BOMBAY CALCUTTA MADRAS KARACHI LAHORE DACCA
KUALA LUMPUR SINGAPORE HONG KONG TOKYO

FIRST PUBLISHED 1929

SECOND EDITION 1963
REPRINTED 1964, 1965, and 1969

PRINTED IN GREAT BRITAIN

TO

SIR HUGH ALLEN

K.C.V.O., M.A., D.Mus.

HEATHER PROFESSOR OF MUSIC IN THE
UNIVERSITY OF OXFORD
DIRECTOR OF THE
ROYAL COLLEGE OF MUSIC

Always a steadfast friend

NOTE TO THE SECOND EDITION

THIRTY-THREE years after its original publication, *Cobbett's Cyclopedic Survey* is still the major work in its field, rivalled in scope and authority only by the collected works of Altmann. Since the last copies were sold in 1946, there have been frequent demands for a reprint or a new edition. The present re-issue, consisting of a photographic reprint of the original two volumes, with an additional one to bring the survey up to date, is a compromise between the two. Except for a handful of small amendments made in Cobbett's text, compiled by Nicolas Slonimsky, and the insertion of symbols in the margin (see below), the original two volumes are exactly as they were. An account of the scope of the new volume will be found in its Preface.

July 1962. COLIN MASON.

The symbols in the margin of Vols. I and II have the following significance:

* A reference to the composer concerned is to be found in Vol. III.
† An entry is to be found in the list of *Additions and corrections to dates given in the original edition* in Vol III.

PREFACE

AS this book claims to be of a pioneer nature, a few words as to its origin and genesis will not be out of place. From time to time friends have assured me that a book devoted to a complete survey of the world's chamber music would be welcomed by the art-loving community, and some of them, in a spirit of amiable optimism, went so far as to suggest that I was indicated for this very laborious task, partly by my life-long experience as a player, and partly because I had already made what may be described as a trial trip, when I edited the publication entitled *Chamber Music*, presented each month during three and a half years (1913–16) to subscribers to the periodical then known as the *Music Student*. Whereupon I made the counter-suggestion that other men more competent than I should be approached, but was met with the retort that all of them were too full of engagements to undertake so engrossing a task, and that other weighty reasons of a financial nature, which I need not particularize, also prevented them stepping in. Thus I found myself faced with a momentous decision. I must either take it on, with all its risks and responsibilities, or resign myself to seeing postponed till the Greek Kalends the issue of a book the need of which was almost painfully apparent to those students and men of letters who, wishing to refer to points of interest connected with chamber music, were unable to spare the time necessary for consulting the numerous books which contain merely sporadic references to the subject. The alternative was distasteful, and so I made my decision—possibly not a very wise one when my age is considered, for I was born as long ago as 11 July 1847. Nor am I an artist by profession; but misgivings on that score were dispelled by my professional friends, who one and all were of the opinion that whenever 'room music' is the subject of discussion the amateur may be regarded as one of the protagonists whose views are of considerable interest. He is represented here by my own articles, my addenda to those of my contributors, and various *obiter dicta* from my pen embodying the amateur's point of view, and (exception being made of the article on *The Chamber Music Life*, which is avowedly autobiographical) to be regarded as expressing, not so much my own individuality, as that of the amateur as type.

I hope that the presence—unusual in a cyclopedic work—of reviews, and essays on abstract subjects, tend to make the book more readable, and that my policy of ignoring those prejudices of race, nationality, and school, which menace the best interests of art, will be cordially endorsed by readers in every country.

For the purposes of this book, the word 'chamber music' has been taken to cover ensemble music suited for playing in a room, without ripieno parts, and extending from duos to nonets. An article on orchestral chamber music has been included, as being germane to the subject, whilst the following genres have been excluded: solo pieces of all kinds, piano sonatas, piano ensemble works (four hands—two pianos), romances, cavatinas *et hoc genus omne*, and music of the kind known as 'teaching material'.

Biography is limited for the most part to birth-dates of composers and occasional references to nationality, whilst, with rare exceptions, MS. works are ignored.

The lacunae, the errata, the omissions inevitable in the first edition of a pioneer work will, no doubt, be discovered in due course, and if a note of them is sent by sympathetic readers to the Oxford University Press, Amen House, Warwick Square, London, E.C. 4, as contributions to a possible appendix, I shall be grateful. Meantime, I can assure them that all dates have been verified with meticulous care, but they will please bear in mind that we of the staff are human, contributors are human, and the authors of one or two of the older books of reference—less than human! The musical world owes much to such a writer as Fétis. His *Biographie universelle des musiciens* is a marvel of painstaking research; but alas! it is full of inaccuracies and should never have been attempted by a single writer. The *Complément et Supplément* to Fétis's great work, by Arthur Pougin, is more accurate, but contains far less information on chamber music. Vidal's famous book has many good features. A catalogue is given of works for strings only, with publisher's names and dates of publication, the illustrations are of the finest, and the binding super-excellent; but it contains only a fraction of the information one asks from such a book. A much more solid writer is Eitner (*Quellen-Lexikon*), who has placed all interested in musical research under a great obligation. The like may be said of the various modern works to which I have occasionally referred. One of them (*Grove's Dictionary*) has emulated Vidal in the splendour of the illustrations included in the latest edition. Dent's *Dictionary* has also been of service, and *Riemann* has proved, as ever, a sterling book of reference.

It has been found impossible with certitude to couple with ancient works the name of the publisher, many of the older houses being long since defunct, and the connexion with modern houses impossible to trace. This applies particularly to Paris publishers[1] (though it may be noted that works published by Richault are generally re-issued by Costallat), and to a less extent those of Vienna. In some cases the publishers' names (e.g. Sieber and Pleyel) are of purely historic interest, the works being unobtainable in modern editions. We must be reconciled to the inevitable obsolescence of certain compositions.

Acknowledgement is due (1) to my staff, including Mr. M. Drake-Brockman, my present assistant editor (and translator), and Mr. H. A. Scott, who held that position in earlier days; to Miss Eileen Colles, who has read the proofs, and to Mr. Edwin Evans, who has represented the Oxford Press in our deliberations; (2) to Mr. Frank Salisbury, who painted the picture reproduced in the frontispiece specially for this book (it was exhibited at the Royal Academy in 1926;[2] (3) to publishers and others who have given me useful information from time to time; (4) and finally to my collaborators, the list of whom includes the *élite* of the world's musicologists. The contributions received in the earliest days were from the pens of Monsieur Vincent d'Indy, principal of the Paris Schola Cantorum, Professor Dr. Altmann of Berlin, and Professor Donald F. Tovey of Edinburgh. Then followed articles sent by the distinguished contributors listed below. By deliberately choosing writers whom I knew to be, either by nationality or proclivity, in sympathy with the subjects treated, I have succeeded in avoiding the type of criticism, the destructive type, which ill becomes a book of this kind. At the same time I have indicated no line of thought to contributors, and have left each, with his individual leanings, to work for the glory of chamber music. Some favour a generous amplitude of phrase, others adopt more concise methods; their diversity of temperament leading to occasional discrepancies in the length of their contributions. This is a difficulty felt by all compilers of books of this kind, who find it far from easy to preserve a just relation between the merit of the composer and the space devoted to discussion of his works.

With regard to the lists of works given at the head of each article on the individual composers, they do not profess to be exhaustive, especially in the case of older or forgotten composers, but a careful selection has been made of works likely to be of interest to players, and the means of obtaining fuller information are indicated as far as possible. The key, opus number, and date (of composition or publication, or both) have been given wherever possible, but in this connexion errors are unavoidable, especially in the case of works which are not readily obtainable to-day.

34 Avenue Road, London, N.W. 8. 11 *July* 1928. EDITOR.

[1] In reading through *Fétis* (published 1863) we found the names of over 100 publishers in Paris alone, and some of these were continually changing, e.g. Imbault=Javet; La Chevardière=Leduc. There exists no reliable source from which copies of these old works are to be obtained.—Ed.

[2] Omitted from the 1962 edition.

INTRODUCTION

BY SIR HENRY HADOW

IF we are asked, 'What is Chamber Music?', within the currently accepted range of the term, the only possible answer is that of St. Augustine—'Si non rogas intelligo'. All terms of art seem incapable of exact definition; those of music perhaps less than any other, in proportion as its vocabulary has been more fluid; we cannot comprise within a formula what the sixteenth century meant by a Madrigal, or the seventeenth by an Oratorio, or the eighteenth by a Symphony. And this is natural enough, for music has grown up gradually and flexibly in the course of human experience. Its discoveries have been quite as often empiric as scientific, and its terminology has been obliged to follow a bewildering variety of discovery and invention. At the same time we know roughly what the term implies, what kinds of work we may expect to find in the programme of a chamber concert, and it is on this principle of division rather than that of definition that our expectation is based. It is therefore quite intelligible that Mr. Cobbett should adopt his own classification of the works included in this Cyclopedia. If he includes one kind and omits another, it is with fair warning, and only a very peevish critic will object to a method of selection which leaves us, after all, confronted with such lavish abundance.

The same law of empirical growth in music renders it also impossible to determine within approximate accuracy the beginnings of this kind of composition. It may well have grown up spontaneously, almost unconsciously. Where a few musicians were gathered together, one would probably start a tune and the others join in from sheer friendliness, and it is most probable that this was not confined to vocal music, but extended in some degree to instrumental as well. It must be remembered that the harpsichord, in one or other of its forms, may be dated back at least to the time of the *Minnesinger*, and it is highly probable that the company gathered round its keyboard was not of listeners only, but of participants joining in an artless consort of sweet sounds with any resources of voice or instrument which they happened to have at hand. This, no doubt, like most early history, is conjectural. The records of musical practice do not become very clear or coherent until the sixteenth century, but there, at any rate, we have a record of the double practice which is beyond dispute. There are still in evidence polyphonic compositions which are designated as suitable either for singing or playing: 'Buone da cantare e suonare' in Orlando di Lasso—apt for viols and voices in some of our English madrigalists; and the explanation of these must either be that the instrumental versions were first written as supports for the voices and then allowed separate treatment, or that they were both devised as independent and alternative to one another. At any rate, by the end of the sixteenth century instrumental forces were beginning definitely to claim autonomy, and their ranks were reinforced by the lutenists (one Elizabethan composer wrote a hunting scene for the lute), and by the very interesting and diverse works which were being composed for the keyed instruments. Towards the end of his life Byrd seems to have carried this instrumental autonomy a stage farther on its road. In some of his later madrigals, as Dr. Fellowes has shown us, the voice parts have independent accompaniments; the famous string sextet, published in the volume of psalms, songs and sonnets in 1611, departs altogether from the current madrigalian structure, and anticipates in tiny embryo the forms of chamber composition which were to prevail in later generations.

Indeed, it is difficult to see how this side of the art could have advanced much farther without a change in its material resources. The viols, whose soft and beautiful tone is now being restored to us by the piety of scholars, were limited in range, compass, and expression; they stood to their successors in something of the same relation as tempera to oil, and in the greater opportunity which seems to be afforded in the new discoveries, they fell gradually into disuse. Thomas Mace at the end of the seventeenth century could exclaim against the 'scoulding violins' which were invading his favourite fields of composition with noise and turbulence, but the advance was irresistible; the greatest of all musical instruments was not to be denied, and by the end of the seventeenth century its reign was assured. At the same time there were gradual improvements in the structure and tone of the keyed instruments; the two forces came into alliance, and so, with Corelli and his contemporaries in Italy and Purcell in England, the forms of concerted chamber music began definitely to take shape and dignity. Two points may here be noted. First, that the harpsichord, which as the solo instrument had come to a high pitch of virtuosity, was in these concerted pieces chiefly relegated to the humble position of accompanist, and indeed had often no greater independence than the deciphering of figured harmony. Secondly, that these sonatas were commonly written for violins and a bass, and that the viola was rather disdainfully omitted. At most, it might find recognition among the attendant crowd in the chamber music of this time; it was not regarded as a principal character. For the former of these, no better reason can be given than the timidity with which early musical composition approached new problems, and the innate conservatism with which it usually treated them. The latter may, perhaps, be explained by the incompetence of the viola players in those early days. The days of Paganini and Berlioz were still far off. As yet the viola seems to have been often entrusted to the less agile executants among the violins; and, even when it found its place in the orchestra, was often set to the menial office of doubling the bass parts.

Among the instrumental forms classified at that time, two of the most important were the sonate da chiesa and the sonate da camera, made accessible to us by abundant instances from Corelli. They were set for much the same kinds of performer—two violins and a 'cello, reinforced in the chamber sonatas by a harpsichord, and in the church sonatas by an organ and sometimes an archlute. Structurally, they followed a conventional scheme of four movements—alternately slow and fast—with this difference, that the church sonatas were chiefly based on the graver and more dignified forms of prelude and fugal canzona, and the chamber sonatas on the lighter measures of the dance tunes which were already beginning to link together into suites. Even here the distinction does not apply to the finale, which in both alike was usually a cheerful and irreverent jig, setting a custom which has injuriously affected more than one branch of composition. Beside these forms was that of the concerto grosso—a concertino of the usual three soloists and a chorus of ripieno strings and continuo—which may be said to have traversed the very narrow frontier between music for the chamber and that for public display.

Another stage was reached in the generation after Corelli. Among the many gifts with which Handel and Bach enriched the art of music, one of the most conspicuous was their experiment in the varieties of instrumental colour. This may be illustrated not only by the obbligati which so frequently accompany the songs in Handel's operas and Bach's cantatas, and which show an astonishing sense both of the beauty of colours and of the fitness of their combination: it greatly affected also the quality and method of instrumental writing and through this of subsequent chamber music. Handel's so-called oboe concertos, for example, require for soloists two each of violins, 'cellos, oboes, flutes, and bassoons, with an obbligato harpsichord, and surround this large company with a corresponding number of forces from the 'concerto grosso'. Bach's Brandenburg concertos, written, no doubt, for a specially constituted band, are too well known to need more than the bare catalogue: the first requires, apart from strings, three oboes, two horns, and a bassoon; the second has four soloists—violin, flute, oboe, and trumpet; the fourth has three, two violins and a flute, and they are woven far more closely into the general texture than had been possible in the seventeenth century. No doubt we should classify them as chamber compositions, but it cannot be too clearly remembered that as yet the differentiation was not established, and that the fields of display were determined more by accident and circumstance than by design. At any rate, the application of these methods to the series of chamber-forces was made forthwith by the most gifted and the most neglected of Bach's sons. The charge that Friedemann Bach was idle and intemperate affords us no reason for disregarding the work that stands to his credit; and in this are included a string quartet (perhaps the first ever written, but the dates are uncertain); trios for two flutes and a bass, and for oboe, bassoon and bass; and if Bitter is right, a sextet for two horns, clarinet, violin, viola, and 'cello, of which the freshness, the charm, and the humour reach out friendly hands to Joseph Haydn (*see* Bitter's account of the instrumental compositions, *C. P. E. und W. F. Bach und deren Brüder*, ii. 230 *seq.*, especially 260–1). It is fair to add that some scholars are now attributing this last work to John Christian Bach, and that the question is still under dispute.

W. F. Bach and Haydn were contemporaries for half a century; by the time that the older man died, the younger had long been acclaimed as the first composer in Europe. With Haydn, the history of chamber music, as we understand it at the present day, may be said to take definite form and substance. It is significant that during forty prolific years he wrote nearly all his instrumental music for the service of the house of Esterhazy, and that his field of action was not the church or the theatre, but the salon. His early symphonies were composed for a tiny band of virtuosi, and therefore approximate in method and character to the composition of chamber music; he showed a special predilection for the strings; he had at disposal a set of first-rate performers with almost unlimited opportunities of rehearsal; and he found in the string quartet his most natural and congenial means of expression. He has left us eighty-three examples; for purity and simplicity of emotion, for transparency of style, for skill so mastered that it has become second nature, and for copious and delightful melody they still remain in their kind unsurpassed.

The Viennese period was the golden age of chamber music, and of its dynasty Haydn was the acknowledged founder. It was he who 'first taught Mozart how to write a quartet'; his later work undoubtedly affected the early compositions of both Beethoven and Schubert; he stood at the fountain-head of one of the most fertilizing streams in all artistic history. Mozart shows traces of the influence all through his last decade—from the six famous quartets which were its firstfruits to the series of quintets which some regard as the crown and climax of his career. Beethoven's debt was more concerned with points of structure: his temperament was alien to that of Haydn, and he soon broke loose from discipleship; by Schubert's time the doors of the new generation were opening, and it is noticeable that all the best of his chamber works were written during the last five years of his life.

With the death of Schubert the great tradition of chamber music came temporarily to a close. For various reasons, mainly of history and environment, the so-called Romantic composers were less in sympathy with this kind of composition: they approached music from other angles, they pursued other artistic ideals. Berlioz left no piece of chamber music in any form; Chopin's one example is an early work of no serious account; Liszt never entered this field except as editor; Schumann, who adventured across it, as he did across every other, is so hasty and unequal that despite some pages of supreme genius his work is beginning to fade from the canvas. Mendelssohn, who had more of the classical spirit than his neighbours, wrote some very pleasant chamber works, for instance the octet, the canzonet in G minor, and the first movement of the quintet in B♭, but even Mendelssohn seems to chafe at the limitations of his medium and to call at times for the more sonorous aid of the orchestra. The real renascence of chamber composition was made by Brahms, to whom by temper, by training, and by outlook it was especially sympathetic: the heir of Beethoven and Schubert who has abundantly and nobly used his inheritance. And after Brahms, Dvořák; and Borodin and Tchaikovsky; and Franck and Fauré and Debussy and Ravel and Florent Schmitt; and our own Elgar and Vaughan Williams; and the younger composers whom it would be here invidious to particularize, but who are carrying on this work with such enthusiasm and distinction.

One of the most encouraging signs of the times is the growing prevalence of interest in chamber music. For one reason, its problems are such as require special skill and concentration; there is no kind of music in which it is more difficult to write a masterpiece, for there is none where the composer retires so intimately to the very centre and fastness of his art. Here is no adventitious aid from trappings or pageantry or the shock of dramatic emotion; it is an art as pure as sculpture and as enduring. Again, it is, among all forms of music, the happiest in presentation; the ideal conditions for hearing it imply comfort and ease and an undisturbed content. To many of us its very name recalls the memory of a musical club—an arm-chair, a pipe, and a quartet playing the first Rasoumovsky—and not all the splendours of Bayreuth or the Gewandhaus lie so near to our affections. And for a third reason, it seems to fall most readily within the comprehension of the average music-lover. There is enough volume of tone to fill the ear without overcharging it: there is enough variety of texture to excite interest without distracting it; we can hear what every voice is saying and so follow both its part in the dialogue and its bearing on the general plot. No other form of music has such power to engage our attention and to keep it unflagging till the end; no other can delight our senses with such exquisite beauty of sound, or display so clearly to our intelligence the intricacies and adventures of its design. We have but to think of Haydn's *Emperor* or Schubert's octet, or the clarinet quintets of Mozart and Brahms, or Beethoven's 'harp' quartet, or the cavatina, or the finale of the quartet in A minor; to those of us who have lived with music, these are far more than the memory of pleasant experiences: they are as the faces of friends, they have become an integral part of our lives. This is not to belittle or disparage the statelier forms of music: to them be all love and honour; but when we have paid our tribute to them and received their royal gifts in exchange, we may find on our return home something that lies even more intimately round our hearts.

A comprehensive study of chamber music has hitherto been seriously hampered for want of organized material. There is plenty of information, but it has been scattered among biographies and text-books and general dictionaries of music; the field has been so wide, and the quarry so elusive, that we have had little to show for our labour at the day's end. Even now there is a great opportunity for some historian who should undertake a comparative survey of these forms, who should regard them with what the philosophers call a 'synoptic' view, and should gather into a coherent scheme their several ideals, methods, and resources. For such a work Mr. Cobbett's Cyclopedia will be invaluable. It is, so far as I know, the first systematic attempt to collect in orderly arrangement all the relevant facts which bear upon its theme; it has drawn upon a wide range of expert knowledge and opinion, it has every prospect of being a definitive and permanent contribution to the literature of music. 'Nos liquorem bibimus et propinamus,' says Bacon in a convivial mood, 'ex infinitis confectum uvis, iisque maturis et tempestivis.' Mr. Cobbett has invited us to no less opulent a banquet and no less generous a vintage.

CONTRIBUTORS

Abert, Hermann
Aldrich, Richard
Altmann, Wilhelm
Antcliffe, Herbert
Aveling, Claude

Bartoš, Josef
Baumann, Émile
Bedford, Herbert
Belaiev, V. M.
Best, Edith Oldham
Betti, Adolfo
Blom, Eric
Boughton, Rutland
Boult, Adrian
Brod, Max
Broman, Sten
Brown, James

Calvocoressi, M. D.
Casella, A.
Cesari, Gaetano
Clarke, Rebecca
Colles, H. C.
Corder, Frederick
Cox, Cynthia
Crabtree, C. M.
Curjel, H.

Davies, Dorothy
Davies, Fanny
Decsey, Ernst
Dent, E. J.
Dolmetsch, Arnold
Downes, Olin
Drake-Brockman, M.
Dubrucq, Edward
Dunhill, T. F.
Dyke, Spencer

Eccles, W.
Eggar, Katharine
Engel, Carl
Evans, Edwin

Farjeon, Harry
Felber, Rudolf
Fellowes, E. H.
Ferroud, P. O.
Fife, Stella B.
Findeisen, N.
Fitzgibbon, H. M.

Fleury, Louis
Fox Strangways, A. H.

Gaillar, J.
Gatti, Guido M.
Goddard, Scott
Godet, R.
Goldberg, A. L.
Goodwin, Amina
Grace, Harvey
Gray, Cecil
Greville, Ursula
Grew, Sydney

Hadow, Sir W. H.
Hay, Frederick
Henkel, Lily
Henley, W.
Henry, Leigh
Howells, Herbert
Hull, A. Eaglefield

d'Indy, Vincent
Isler, Ernst

James, Ivor
Jeanson, Gunnar
Jeffries, L. Stanton
Jirák, K. B.

Kahl, Willi
Kendall, Katharine
Klein, Herman
Korchinska, Maud C.
Kornstein, Egon F.

Labey, Marcel
Landré, Willem
Lazar, F.
Leichtentritt, Hugo
Lespinasse, Pierre
Lockspeiser, Edward
Lourié, Arthur

Mackenzie, Sir A. C.
Mackenzie, Compton
Maitland, J. A. Fuller
Mangeot, André
Mann, Adolph
Meadmore, W. S.
Migot, Georges
Mitson, W. J.
Morales, Pedro G.
Moulin, Léon

Newmarch, Rosa

Olof, Victor
Organ, E. W.

Pijper, Willem
Pincherle, Marc
Piriou, Adolphe
Prunières, Henry
Pulver, Jeffrey

Reed, W. H.
Rice, E. T.
Richards, H. W.

Sabaneiev, L.
Saint-Foix, Georges de
Schiedermair, Ludwig
Schmitt, Florent
Scholes, P. A.
Scott, Cyril
Scott, Hugh Arthur
Scott, Marion M.
Shepherd, Arthur
Sieurin, Marguérite
Sondheimer, R.
Šourek, O.
Speed, Clarisse
Steinhard, Erich
Štěpán, Václav
Straeten, E. van der
Systermans, Georges

Talbot, Rev. G. Surtees
Terry, C. Sanford
Tovey, Donald F.
Trend, J. B.
Tuthill, Burnet C.

Ulfrstad, M. M.

Veselý, Richard

Wadham, D.
Wal, Antoon de
Waldbauer, E. and Imre
Walker, Ernest
Walthew, R. H.
Watson, Victor
Wellesz, Egon
Whitehouse, H. V.
Williams, R. Vaughan
Woollett, H.

TRANSLATORS

Atkinson, Mrs. C. F.
Bonavia, F.
Brath, J.
Calvocoressi, M. D.

Castelli, M.
Cobbett, W. W.
Drake-Brockman, M.
Heming, Mrs.

Newmarch, Mrs. Rosa
Pring, S. W.
Thorburn, Miss
Whyte, F.

ABBREVIATIONS

Allgemeine Musik-Zeitung	*Allg. Mus. Z.*
Altmann's *Chamber Music Literature*: a catalogue of works which have appeared since 1841 (3rd edn. 1923)	*Altmann.*
Altmann's *Handbuch für Streichquartettspieler*	*Handbuch.*
Bote & Bock	B. & B.
Breitkopf & Härtel	B. & H.
British Broadcasting Company	B.B.C.
Cobbett's Cyclopedic Survey	*Cyclopedia.*
Cobbett's *Musical Supplement*, a series of articles dealing with chamber music, edited or written by W. W. Cobbett and presented to readers of the *Music Student*, June 1913—Nov. 1916	*Music Supplement.*
Denkmäler Deutscher Tonkunst	D.D.T.
Denkmäler der Tonkunst, Bavaria	D.T.B.
Denkmäler der Tonkunst in Österreich	D.T.Ö.
Dent's *Dictionary of Modern Music and Musicians*	*Dent.*
Eitner's *Quellen-Lexicon*	*Q.-L.*
Fétis's *Biographie universelle*	*Fétis.*
Grove's Dictionary of Music and Musicians	*Grove.*
Guildhall School of Music	G.S.M.
Musical Section of the State Publishing Dept.	Mus. Sect. State Publ. Dept.
National Gramophone Society	N.G.S.
Pougin's *Complément et Supplément* to Fétis's *Biographie universelle*	*Pougin.*
Riemann's *Lexicon*	*Riemann.*
Ries & Erler	R. & E.
Royal Academy of Music	R.A.M.
Royal College of Music	R.C.M.
Russian Musikverein	R.M.V.
Society for the Publication of American Music	S.P.A.M.
Stainer & Bell	S. & B.
Vidal's *Les Instruments à Archet*	*Vidal.*

CYCLOPEDIA OF CHAMBER MUSIC

A. A request for the 'A' is the invariable prelude to a séance of chamber music. I will therefore start this Cyclopedia with a brief reference to the question of pitch.

After sixty years of experience, I have formed the very definite opinion that, in purely string music, the most satisfactory tone is produced by tuning the instruments to the diapason normal, i.e. A=435 (or C=517), at 59° Fahr. This opinion is shared by most of the chamber music players with whom I have forgathered during that time. Whatever is accomplished in the matter of the standardization of pitch, string players will tend to favour the course which gives the best tonal results, and these are obtained by tuning pianos to the diapason normal.

Trouble, however, arises when wind instruments join the ensemble. They are so constructed as to be only playable at a higher pitch, say A=439, and it follows that strings and piano are compelled to come into line. Very apropos and very interesting is a recent move of the American music industry, which, with characteristic practicality, has decided to stabilize pitch by adopting as a standard A=440 (C 528); and it is not a little curious that Dr. Pole, in his admirable article in *Grove* on this subject, records that in 1834 a 'Congress of Physicists' held at Stuttgart 'adopted a proposal by Scheibler to fix the A at 440 (C 528), the self-same standard.

The sum of it all is that A=435 is the ideal chamber music pitch for strings, and A=440 the ideal compromise for wind and strings combined, or wind and piano. Thus, the excessive acuteness of a higher pitch and the sombreness of a lower are avoided. EDITOR.

† ABACO, EVARISTA FELICE DALL', 1675–1742, director of the concerts of Victor Emmanuel of Bavaria. An old composer in whom there is an evident revival of interest, shown in the many modern republications of his works. These consist of works for three or four stringed instruments with figured bass, as well as solo sonatas and trios. Most are published by B. & H., but there is a suite (sonata da camera), pf, 2 v, vc, reissued by Augener-Schott. A biographical notice and a number of works are in the *D.T.B.* Original publications are in *Riemann* and *Fétis*. EDITOR.

ABBIATÈ, L., director of the Music School at Monaco.

Quartet, str, F	op. 8	Enoch, 1901.
Sonata, pf, vc, g mi	—	,, —
Suite, pf, vc	,, 5	Leduc, 1903.
Suite (after Heine's Intermezzo), pf, vc, d mi	,, 16	,, 1907.

† ABEL, KARL FRIEDRICH, 1725–1787.

Famous player on and composer for the viola da gamba. He was a pupil of Bach at Leipzig, and himself a teacher and a composer of chamber music, most of which is now obsolete (v. *Q.-L.*). Dr. Pearce, in the course of a lecture at Trinity College of Music, introduced a trio for strings and organ containing 'an anticipation of a favourite device of Beethoven'.

Vidal mentions thirty string quartets. The six quartets, op. 14, written in collaboration with Christian Bach ('English' Bach) are set for flute or oboe instead of first violin. *Vidal* also gives six trios for violin, viola, and 'cello, and twelve for two violins and 'cello.

EDITOR.

ABERT, JOHANN JOSEPH, 1832–1915, German Capellmeister.

Quartet, str, A	op. 25	Hofmeister, 1864.

J. J. Abert was the father of our contributor, Hermann Abert, whose recent death we have to deplore. Dr. Altmann gives a touching account of the son's enthusiasm for his father's work—the quartet above mentioned—and himself warmly recommends it to dilettante players, describing it as touched with Mendelssohnian influence, but not without original features of its own. EDITOR.

† ACHRON, JOSEPH, b. 1886, Polish violinist and composer, at present resident in New York.

Suite en style ancien,	op. 21	Johansen, 1911.
Suite en style moderne	,, 22	,, ,,
Sonata	,, 29	Belaiev, 1914.
Suite bizarre, d mi	,, 41	U.E., 1924.

As a violinist, Joseph Achron showed remarkably precocious talent, taking his first lesson at the age of five. He was taught successively by Lotto in Warsaw (1894–9) and Auer in Petrograd (1899–1904). Later, he became identified with work done in company with Michael Gniessin, Alex. Krein, and others, which helped to shape the course taken by Hebrew folk-song, now a quite individual form of the art.

His first important post was as leader of the chamber music class of the Kharkov Conservatorium in 1915, but his subsequent activities took, perforce, the form of military service, and included painful experiences in two revolutions. In November 1922 he gave a farewell concert of his own works before leaving for Berlin, and since 1 January 1925 has lived in New York.

Of the three suites mentioned above, the *Suite bizarre* is the most important. It bears a supplementary title, *Cycle des rhythmes*, and consists of a series of grotesqueries written for virtuoso violinists. The sonata, which has been played by Jascha Heifetz with success, is of more universal interest. My colleague in sonata playing, Mr. Adolph Mann, who has made a special study of this work, writes on it as follows:

'From the very outset, this fine work shows its freedom from purely technical accomplishment. It epitomizes the aspirations of a dreamer of that race to whom belong such great figures as Mendelssohn, Heine, and Spinoza, or, to name the composer's more immediate musical affinity, Carl Goldmark. Ignoring some slight evidences of Achron's Slav upbringing, which peer occasionally through his scheme, we seem to be face to face, in the first movement, with a powerful orator recalling, in epic form, mighty and heroic ventures, and, in the second movement, *Hirtenliebe*, in close touch with those primitive tendencies lying deep hidden in the soul of the successors of the pastoral folk who were the progenitors of the Jewish race. The latter movement, it may be noted, was founded on an eight-bar melody sung by a shepherd in the composer's hearing.

Notwithstanding the disparity of subject-matter, this movement is not only in complete accord with the earlier movement (in fact, the process of the work as a whole—its scale, in an architectural sense —is one of its most noteworthy points) but constitutes in itself a perfect gem of characterization. In an interludium (6/4 time) the composer devotes a brief space to urbane considerations, while in the final movement the imaginative tendencies of his race assume their sway in all their Oriental intensity. Such is the outline of a work which might be a history in brief of a great people, and one devoid of either pessimism or rancour. Its date is significant enough—Petersburg, April 1910.'

With the tone and spirit of Mr. Mann's notice I am in complete sympathy. The time seems ripe for comment upon the startling pre-eminence in this century of Jewish artists in string music, the leading interpreters of which are mainly of Hebrew descent. In his day, Joseph Joachim preferred to be known as a man of culture apart from all ethnical considerations, an attitude I imagine to be that of many prominent violinists at the present moment. How this prominence came about is a problem which I do not pretend to solve, but I venture to throw out a few suggestions. I will spare the reader the usual Biblical references. Every one knows that in ancient times music, for reasons not unrelated to orthodox religion, enjoyed more consideration than the other arts. There are echoes of the psalmody of Solomon's temple to be heard in the latter-day synagogue, where Jewish youth hears the canticles sung with a fervour which is infectious, the violin students among them finding in the most sensitive of all instruments a vehicle for the expression of emotion kindled by song. Thus may the 'sweet singers' have influenced the players of Israel. Another suggestion, and that which I am inclined to favour most, is that the pronounced taste for house music which exists among Jewish families of the better class has had considerable influence in promoting a love for string music among the younger members of the household. Sport is not, as elsewhere, a paramount interest. Musical appreciation begins, as Achron's did, almost in infancy (he was said to have developed an ear for music when only two years old!). And it must be admitted that Jewish parents are the first to foster musical talent in their children, and that the discipline to which certain great violinists were subject in early youth is one of the sources of their greatness.

Something is also to be said of the influence of warm Oriental blood on the temperament, and of the brilliant financial possibilities of violin playing, but such subjects are not within the scope of this review. EDITOR.

ACOUSTICS. The chamber music player is frequently preoccupied with problems of acoustics, unsolved as yet by the expert physicist. Though fortified by his advice, our architects are no nearer than they were a century ago to designing, with any certainty, a room or concert hall that may be relied upon as good for sound. This is a question of paramount importance to the stringed instrument player in private life, for the room in which he plays is as much a part of his instrument as the violin he holds in his hand, with which it co-operates in giving shape and amplitude to the sound waves set in motion by his bow. Before taking a house or flat, the chamber musician, if he is wise, will take heed of the acoustic properties of the room he proposes to devote to music. His musical well-being is at stake. The importance of the question to public performers of chamber music is no less evident. The success of the famous 'Pops' was largely owing to the fine acoustic properties of St. James's Hall, the disappearance of which, to make way for a restaurant, is a national misfortune.

Another unsolved problem is that of the aggravating break in the voice of the violin, known as the 'wolf'. This jarring note is to be found in many an instrument of the highest class. E. J. Payne, in *Grove*, speculates upon the cause of the trouble, which is all, at present, that any of us can do. I recollect a conversation I once had with the late Béla Szepessy, a competent luthier in his day. He maintained stoutly that there was but one explanation to be given. 'It was a question', he said, 'of faulty thickness in the wood of the instrument.' A friend of his, a 'cellist, overhearing the conversation, corroborated this. He played us a 'wolf' note upon his 'cello; then, pointing out a certain spot upon the table of the instrument, asked me to increase the thickness by pressing it with the fingers. This I did, and the 'wolf' note disappeared. Another experiment was less convincing. I placed a mute upon my own Guarneri violin, an instrument which normally betrays no trace whatever of 'wolfiness', and asked Béla to listen to the F on the G string. He did so, and heard the note break badly (so badly that it is necessary, when playing this note upon this violin, con sordino, to use the D string). Thus the theory of faulty thickness is not entirely explanatory. The acoustician familiar with the wonders of wireless and gramophone is yet powerless to help us poor fiddlers to get rid of this abominable scourge. If he were moved to make string instruments the subject of intensive study, he would find much to surprise and fascinate him.

The notes known as harmonics (flageolets) are positively weird. Here is a violin passage in Brahms's sextet in G:

To produce the bottom A the first finger has to be lifted, but the nodal point having been touched, the harmonic A, an octave higher, is heard instead of the open string. Strangest of all is the effect of playing on a violin string with loose hair (see also PONTICELLO). There is no division of the string into aliquot parts, or nodal points, yet various overtones are discernible. Paganini is said to have used this device, and if so, it is not surprising that he was reputed a wizard; but so uncertain is the articulation of these harmonics, and so faint the sounds, that the story borders on the incredible.

Another acoustical question about which much could be written is that of the effect of atmosphere upon the tone quality and responsiveness of stringed instruments. My friend Mr. Adolfo Betti, of the Flonzaley Quartet, has told me of the inconvenience caused by the changes of climate experienced during their concert tours, especially when passing through the great continent of America from one zone to another. In one town the air in the concert hall may be hot and clammy, in another cold and dry, the effect of these variations on the strings being disastrous, whilst the violin itself requires different treatment every time. Even the change from hall to hall is disconcerting, so various are different buildings in their acoustic properties. For instance, in the Æolian Hall, New York, the performers cannot hear each other play in certain parts of the platform, whilst in other parts the acoustics are perfect. An artist requires to be thrice an artist to contend with such difficulties, and we amateurs are full of admiration for the professional players who are able so valiantly to rise superior to them.

A word is to be said on the relation of violin making to acoustics, the craft being intimately associated with the early beginnings of chamber music. The art and the craft, indeed, have ever gone hand in hand, each reacting upon the other. Once more I have to record the failure of the acoustician to give any help that counts. Nearly three hundred years have elapsed since the violin came into being, after an evolution which dates we know not how many centuries back; this triumph of the empirical may be followed by a triumph of the scientific; the wildly improbable of to-day may become the *fait accompli* of to-morrow. With the co-operation of the expert acoustician of the future, violins equal in tone to Stradivari's best may yet be made for five pounds apiece, but such a consummation is not yet in sight.

EDITOR.

ADAIEVSKY, ELLA VON, b. 1846, Russian composer, pupil of Rubinstein.

	Composed.	
Sonata (*Greek*), pf, cl (or v), c mi	1880	Tischer & Jägenberg, 1913.

Good, as Greek atmosphere, and musically effective, if shortened by judicious cuts.

†ADELBURG, AUGUST VON, 1830–1873, Hungarian violinist.

Quartet, str, E	op. 12	Kahnt, 1864.
,, ,, a mi	,, 16	,, 1863.
,, ,, E flat	,, 17	,, 1863.
,, ,, D	,, 18	,, 1863.
,, ,, B flat	,, 19	,, 1864.
Sonata, pf, v, g mi	,, 7	,, 1857.
,, ,, ,, d mi	,, 10	Leuckart, 1860.

Adelburg's quartets are what might be expected from an expert violinist. The first fiddle dominates throughout. The quartet, op. 19, is inscribed 'composé sous les ruines de l'acropole d'Athènes'. It is a work in which fancy has full play, but it is not written in true chamber music style.

ADLER, GEORG, b. 1806, Austrian composer.

Sonata, pf, v	op. 3	Haslinger.

AESCHBACHER, KURT, German composer.

Trio, pf, v, vc, D	op. 2	Süddeutscher Musik-V., 1914.

AFANASIEV, NICOLAI JAKOVLEVITCH, 1821–1898, Russian composer.

Double quartet, str, D	Rahter, 1875.
Quartet (*The Volga*), str, A	Simrock, 1866.

Afanasiev was a violinist, but devoted himself to composition in his later years. His string quartet took the first prize in 1860 at a competition organized by the Russian Musical Society. As the title indicates, songs of the Volga boatmen are incorporated in the quartet, of which an analysis is to be seen in the *Handbuch* of Dr. Altmann, who writes that it is, above all, pleasant to play ('gern gespielt'). This remark applies to a long line of Russian quartets of which this was the first.

It will be seen that Mr. Findeisen, in his article on RUSSIAN CHAMBER MUSIC, speaks of three quintets by Afanasiev, 'two of which are for strings, and the third and last, *Italia*, for piano and strings'. EDITOR.

AGNEL, E., French composer.

Trio (*Pastoral*), pf, v, vc	op. 1	Costallat.
Trio, pf, ob, vc, (also pf, v, vla; or pf, v, vc), D	,, 2	,,

†AGNIEZ, Emil, German composer.

Suite (in Waltz form), pf, vc, g mi		B. & H., 1893.

AGOGIC (French, *agogique*), a term used in modern music to imply increase of movement without increase of tempo—a change from quavers to semiquavers, or duplets to triplets, &c.; generally, too, there is a sense of increased animation. For Agogic Accent *v. Grove*.

†AGOSTINI, Muzio, b. 1875, Italian composer.

Quartet, str		
Trio (Prize work, Paris, 1904), pf, v, vc, F	op. 17	Schmidt, 1911.
Sonata, pf, v	,, 46	Pizzi, 1923.

AGRELL, Johann Joachim, 1701–1765, Swedish composer, court musician at Cassel in 1723.

Cited by Niecks as one of the early initiators of the modern sonata. For works *v. Fétis*.

AHN-CARSE, A. von. *v.* Carse.

†AKIMENKO, Feodor Stepanovitch, b. 1876, Russian composer, pupil of Balakirev and Rimsky-Korsakov.

Trio, v, vla, vc, c mi	op. 7	Belaiev, 1899.
Sonata, pf, v, d mi	,, 32	Jurgenson, 1905.
,, ,, ,, G	,, 38bis	,, 1911.
,, pf, vc, D	,, 37	,, *c.* 1908.

Akimenko's compositions fall into two groups. During the first period he was very much under Russian influences (especially Scriabin's, as shown by his *Poème Lyrique*, op. 20); later, it was chiefly modern French music that influenced him.

The string trio belongs to the first period, and is praiseworthy for the quality of the instrumental writing. It is altogether regular in form.

The first violin sonata has a few noteworthy peculiarities, and deserves to be considered as the best of Akimenko's chamber works. It is in three movements. The very beginning of the introduction to the first movement, with its progressions in ninths, shows how profoundly the composer's musical psychology differs from that of the actual disciples of the so-called 'new-Russian' school. Yet, in the working-out section, there are sharp, characteristically Russian seconds which hail straight from Borodin.

The second movement consists of interesting variations on a slow, grim theme, first given out by the violin in octaves. The finale is written partly in the style of Little Russian dance-tunes, Little Russia being the composer's native country.

The second violin sonata is somewhat drier and more abstract. Like the first, it is in three movements; and again elements suggesting dance-tunes appear in the finale.

The 'cello sonata is less interesting. From the point of view of harmonic writing, as well as from that of emotion, it is decidedly inferior to the first violin sonata. The second subject of the first movement, pastoral in character, is repeated immoderately. The second movement—an elegant, but otherwise insignificant waltz—emphatically suggests Tchaikovsky, or perhaps Arensky. The finale consists of variations on a rather commonplace theme.

V. M. Belaiev.

†ALALEONA, Domenico, b. 1881, Italian composer.

Six *Canzoni italiane*, str. quartet	Ricordi.

Alaleona is an important figure in contemporary Italian music. In his *Canzoni italiane* he has tried to 'reconstruct a basis for instrumental music which shall be genuinely Italian'. (*Dent.*)

ALARD, Delphin, 1815–1888, distinguished French violinist.

Quartet, str, b mi	op. 8	Costallat.
Grand duo concertant, pf, v, b mi	,, 25	B. & H., 1851.

Duets, 2 v, opp. 22, 23, 27, issued by various publishers (Schott, U.E., Herold, Dessauer, B. & H.).

Alard succeeded Baillot at the Paris Conservatoire, among his pupils being Pablo de Sarasate. He composed much chamber music, of which only the duets are interesting. Alard is, perhaps, best known by his editions of old violin sonatas.

Editor.

†ALARY, Georges, French composer.

Sextet, str, F	op. 35	Hamelle.
Fantasy quintet, 2v, 2vla, vc	—	Durdilly, 1897.
Quartet, str, e mi	,, 5	Hamelle.
,, ,, F	,, 14	Hamelle.
,, ,, g mi	,, 25	Leduc.
,, no. 5, str, a mi	—	Hayet, 1916.
,, no. 6, str, E flat	—	,, 1917.
Quintet, pf, 2v, vla, vc, D	,, 45	Durdilly, 1898.
Quintet, no. 2, pf, 2v, vla, vc	—	Hayet, 1911.
Quartet, pf, v, vla, vc	,, 12	Hamelle.

ALBERT, Boubée.

Trio, pf, v, vc, B	op. 33	Zimmermann.

Composer of a trio in D major dedicated to H.R.H. the Princess Louise, then Marchioness of Lorne, afterwards Duchess of Argyll, and published in London during the time when Jul. Heinr. Zimmermann had a branch there. The trio is simple and fairly melodious, but without originality. Though otherwise conforming strictly to precedent, it has one remarkable feature in that the scherzo has for trio a waltz which has almost the character of a 'best-seller' of the ball-room.

EDWIN EVANS.

†ALBERT, EUGEN FRANCIS CHARLES D', b. 1864, famous pianist.

Quartet, str, a mi	B. & B., 1888.
,, ,, E flat	,, ,, 1893.

d'Albert has written but little chamber music, most of his works being in the larger dramatic forms. But, unlike most opera composers, his dramatic bent is by no means reflected in his chamber music, which represents merely an episode in the total amount of his work. Still, his two quartets are in the true chamber music style, which is concerned rather with inner feeling than with outward effect.

THE FIRST QUARTET, op. 7, begins with a very expressive and passionate first subject, accompanied by chords on second violin and viola, the bass maintaining the tonic and gradually moving chromatically downwards. A transition leads to the second subject, in C. This is announced by the viola, and continues in triple counterpoint with the two violins; it then appears as principal voice in the first violin. The development of the first subject is short; it opens very calmly with an augmentation of the theme, and is planned as a single progression to the climax. The recapitulation follows; here the second subject appears in A major in the upper part, while the two remaining counterpoints have changed places.

The emotional slow movement, in F, opens with an introduction of five bars; this begins on the 'cello, the other instruments gradually joining in; the first violin then delivers the vigorous principal theme on the G string. This introduction leads to a middle section in A flat; and now the first violin takes up a new strain, to which the second violin voices an expressive counterpoint, accompanied by soft, syncopated chords from viola and 'cello. The dialogue gradually becomes livelier, and mounts to a climax, after which the tonic key is restored, together with the opening mood. The principal theme appears in the 'cello in its upper register, its continuation being then taken over successively by the viola and the two violins. Shortly before the close, a reminiscence of the middle section appears, again followed by the five-bar introduction which ends the movement.

A joyous humour is apparent in the charming scherzo in A minor, which takes the form of a rapid waltz, with a further increase of speed in the A major middle section. After the melancholy of the preceding movement, the scherzo with its piquant rhythms and delightful instrumental effects proves doubly charming. The finale, a theme with variations, likewise contains some interesting features, but must be designated as the weakest part of the composition.

THE SECOND QUARTET, op. 11, is artistically of greater value. Although the introductory movement makes no great impression, it gives promise which is fulfilled by the excellent scherzo, in which all the instruments are muted. It is very witty, full of rhythmic subtleties and harmonic artifices, yet keeps on a thoroughly diatonic basis. Rhythmically, it resembles the scherzo of the first quartet, but is of greater artistic value. The two violins begin with a legato quaver passage in thirds, interspersed with a few pizzicati by viola and 'cello; this rhythm prevails throughout the movement, and is only interrupted at short intervals by other rhythms, chiefly in the middle section. It gives the impression of a merry dance of elves; this mood is reflected in the degree of force employed—mainly *p*, increased only once to *f*—and in the effective alternation of the bars of 3/4, 2/4, 5/4, 6/8. This movement may be pronounced the best of the entire composition; it is not only happily inspired, but well constructed and treated instrumentally in genuine quartet style. In the last two movements the fine manipulation of the parts is worthy of note; the composer here endeavours to make them as independent as possible and not mere ripieni, his intentions being mostly successfully carried out. The finale combines technical and artistic excellences with impressive effect, and brings the composition to a satisfactory conclusion.

d'Albert's two quartets open no new paths, the composer consciously following the classical traditions, nevertheless, they have enriched the literature of chamber music by reason of their high artistic level and fine technical qualities.

RUDOLF FELBER.

†ALBERT, HEINRICH, contemporary German composer.

Has composed noteworthy works for guitar, and edited an important series of chamber works with guitar by old masters, published by Wilhelm Zimmermann (formerly Julius Heinrich Zimmermann).

ALBRECHTSBERGER, JOHANN GEORG, 1736–1809, famous Austrian theoretician and composer.

Modern republications:

Quintet, 3 v, vla, vc, C	*D.T.Ö.*, B. & H., 1909.
Four quartets, str, A flat, D, A, F (scores only)	,, ,, ,, 1909.

and some duets for violin and 'cello.

One of Albrechtsberger's titles to fame is the fact of his having been Beethoven's teacher at Vienna in 1794–5. He was a famous contrapuntist, teacher, and organist, and formed several other distinguished pupils, Hummel among the number. Albrechtsberger took extreme pains with his wayward pupil (Beethoven), who considered that the lessons had been of the greatest value to him. Albrechtsberger's own opinion was very different. He told another pupil that Beethoven had learnt nothing, and would never do anything in decent style. But as discipline, the teaching of this learned contrapuntist may have been salutary.

Albrechtsberger held the post of court organist at Vienna, and in 1792 he became director of music at St. Stephen's. He was held in the greatest esteem by all the chief musicians of his time. He wrote a great mass of chamber music, including a very large number of string quartets and quintets. Among the former were forty-four 'fugal quartets'. Very little of this great mass of music was published, twenty-seven works only out of a total of two hundred and sixty-one works of all descriptions. A list of Albrechtsberger's chief works is to be found in *Fétis* and in *Q.-L.* M. DRAKE-BROCKMAN.

[Six of Albrechtsberger's 'fugal quartets' were published. The first three of these are prefaced by a prelude in the (minor) key of the fugue which follows. Of the quartets republished in the *D.T.Ö.*, the editor, Dr. Oskar Kapp, writes that these compositions, in spite of their obvious conservatism and the frequent insignificance of the musical matter, cannot be dismissed as mere antiquarian literature. Their importance in the history of the development of sonata form is too great.
EDITOR.]

ALESSANDRESCO, ALFRED. *v.* ROUMANIAN COMPOSERS.

†ALEXANDER FRIEDRICH, Landgrave of Hesse, b. 1863, pupil of Joachim, Bruch, and Fauré.

Quartet, str, C	op. 1	B. & H., 1890.
„ „ c mi	—	„ „ —
Trio, pf, cl, horn, A	„ 3	Simrock, 1897.
Sonata, pf, vc, g mi	„ 12	B. & H., 1911.

Alexander Friedrich's achievements in the realm of chamber music are remarkable, considering that he has been blind since early childhood. He studied under the most famous teachers of his time, and his music, which is written in classic vein, shows that he profited by their instruction. EDITOR.

ALEXANDROV, ANATOL NIKOLAIEVITCH, b. 1888, Russian composer, studied at the Moscow Conservatorium under Zhilyaev, S. Taneiev, and Vassilenko.

Quartet, str, G, op. 7, composed 1916, Mus. Sect. State Publ. Dept., 1926.
Andante patetico, pf, vc, op. 17, composed 1922, Mus. Sect. State Publ. Dept., 1926.

Alexandrov has written but little chamber music proper. At the very beginning of his career he wrote a string quartet, which was performed in 1917 and published considerably later—after the revolution. This quartet is very characteristic of its composer, whose manner has changed but little since those days. It is a harmonious and peaceful work, reflecting a certain inward purity and the mental tranquillity and equipoise natural to the composer. In the curve of the melodic line, in the harmony, which is full-blooded but free from any great complexity, the influence of Glazounov may sometimes be felt, but other composers—Medtner and Rachmaninov—have affected him more powerfully and characteristically. In the quartet, Medtner is recalled by a certain dryness of form, and Rachmaninov by the melody and the type of harmonic accompaniment. In general, one is agreeably surprised by the lucidity of the quartet and by the mastery displayed from the very outset of his creative work. At the same time it must be remarked that Alexandrov here shows himself to be lacking in broad lyricism and warm emotion. Still, he may be regarded as one of the significant composers on the contemporary Russian horizon.

Another chamber work, written considerably later, in the revolutionary period (1922–3), may be said to be even more characteristic—I refer to the *Andante patetico* for 'cello and piano. The form is big and broad, and the work far more independent, though Rachmaninov's influence makes itself felt in the curve and the characteristic turns of the melody. In spite of its title, there is not a great deal of pathos or emotion in the movement—such moods are on the whole foreign to Alexandrov. He displays fine taste, however, and manages to give interest and the appearance of novelty to a composition by employing very simple means of expression. In the andante there is no tendency towards the 'left'—rather the reverse—Alexandrov must be included amongst the reactionaries in music. *Inter alia*, this composition has an elusive suggestion of the salon, a quality inherent to a certain extent in Rachmaninov's creative work. L. SABANEIEV.

†ALEXANIAN, DIRAN, Armenian composer.

Little Armenian Suite, str. quartet, Mathot, 1919.

†ALFANO, FRANCO, b. 1877, Italian composer.

Quartet, str, D	Pizzi (Bologna), 1920.
Sonata, pf, v, D	Ricordi.
Suite, pf, vc	[MS.]

The distinguishing qualities of Alfano's music, particularly as exemplified in his chamber works, may be unhesitatingly set down as exuberance and restlessness. There is no mistaking the expansiveness and vitality of the composer's temperament. The warmth of his southern, or rather his Neapolitan nature was in no way modified by his lengthy sojourns in Germany, France, and elsewhere, and it emerges in his music as a torrential eloquence, an abundance of gesticulation, and an almost uncontrolled fantasy. A state of mind so restless and unstable inevitably results in an irregularity of outline and a distortion of the harmony; also sometimes in a superfluous elaboration of detail.

This meticulous virtuosity of technique, which is truly marvellous at times, is conspicuously evident in the string quartet in D. This composition was designed to strengthen the cause of the instrumental polyphony, which has now come into its own in Italy and other countries, and is therefore in strong contrast to the essentially picturesque and colouristic quartets of the impressionist school. Thus we find in Alfano's work an increased care for the structural framework, a constant and even passionate preoccupation with counterpoint, and an elaborate working-out of the thematic material which never fails to arouse admiration on a study of the score, but proves in the hearing not to possess the importance assigned to it by the eye.

In fact, the web-like intricacy of the crossing parts, instead of giving variety and mobility to the composition, ends by fatiguing the listener, and gives rise to a certain sense of oppression by, as it were, depriving the music of air to breathe, while it also conveys a feeling of weightiness not intended by the composer. This criticism does not, however, apply to the second movement, written more or less in the manner of a nocturne, which is a finely sincere and indubitably poetic piece of work, though not entirely free from mannerisms and Slavonic reminiscences.

The characteristic exuberance already referred to also shows itself in the dynamics of the composition; at certain points, of fairly frequent occurrence, the four instruments seem to be making spasmodic efforts to achieve noisy effects more appropriate to the orchestra than to the string quartet. Moreover, one is conscious almost all the while of a kind of tension and an anxiety to say something more, as if the composer feared he were not expressing himself adequately, or was not sufficiently stirring the souls and nerves of his audience. These defects are much less apparent in his works for orchestra, a medium which is evidently much more suited to his particular temperament. In the quartet, where the colours and contours are comparatively limited in range, and the proportions, therefore, need to be subtly balanced, the Neapolitan composer has to struggle continually with his temperament. If he gives free play to his fantasy the design becomes confused, and if he consents to be bound by the formal lines of the composition he appears somewhat chill and anaemic.

The same criticisms hold good, to some extent, of the more recent sonata in D for violin and piano (1922–3), although this is simpler and the general effect is of much more ease and agility. The emotional quality is well sustained throughout; the music is vibrant and passionate; violin and piano maintain the relative positions traditionally assigned to them, that is to say, the piano part, which is treated rhythmically with a wealth of detail and episodes entirely its own, is in general predominant. As a whole, the sonata is distinctly lyrical in style, a song-like quality making itself felt throughout.

In this respect it resembles the same composer's opera, *The Legend of Sakuntala*, the actual music of which it echoes here and there, although the opera is a more sober work, purer in line and colour. There are passages in the sonata, again, in which the piano appears to be emulating the orchestra. But, as has been said, this last work shows an advance on the quartet in the direction of a greater self-restraint, and it may be expected that the suite for 'cello and piano, as yet unpublished, will prove to be Alfano's best chamber work.

GUIDO M. GATTI.

[It should be mentioned that Alfano was entrusted with the task of completing Puccini's posthumous opera *Turandot*.]

†ALFVÉN, HUGO, b. 1872, Swedish violinist.

Sonata, pf, v, c mi	op. 1	Edn. Abraham Lûndqûist, Stockholm.

ALKAN, C. H. V. M., 1813–1888, French pianist (real name Morhange).

First trio, pf, v, vc, g mi	op. 30	Costallat (orig. Richault), 1847.
'Grand' duet, pf, v, f sharp mi	,, 21	Costallat, —.
'Grand' sonata, pf, vla (or vc), E	,, 47	,, 1858.

There are signs of a revival of interest in Alkan, but it is mainly directed to his piano music.

ALLEGRI, GREGORIO, 1582–1652, Italian composer.

Allegri is the composer of the first string quartet, and also of the famous *Miserere* for nine voices, so long used (and still sung) in the Sistine Chapel in Rome in Holy Week, and written down from memory in 1770 by the young Mozart. His printed works (which are chiefly in the archives of Santa Maria in Vallicella and the Sistine Chapel, with some copies in the library of the Gesellschaft der Musikfreunde in Vienna) include two books of motets (published 1621) for two to six voices, two books of concerti (1618–19) for two to four instruments, and this much-quoted string quartet, which is apparently in MS., but may be an extract from the printed (so-called) concerti, a term which was then very loosely used. The very large amount of MSS. in the Sistine Chapel Library will doubtless be a mine of wealth in the future for musical research. The large collection of Allegri's works in the library of Abbate Fortunato Santini (now housed in the University Library at Münster) may possibly reveal other pieces of Allegri for the string quartet combination.

The string quartet in question is one of the most frequently mentioned of all the old pieces, and yet the matter is not quite clear. Where is the original MS.? Prof. Edward Dent, in a letter, suggests that it may now be in either the Biblioteca Vittorio Emanuele or the Liceo di S. Cecilia Library at Rome. Eitner's *Quellen-Lexikon* mentions a string quartet by Allegri in the library of the Gesellschaft der Musikfreunde in Vienna; but he describes it as of doubtful authenticity, and 'probably an eighteenth-century work'. Ambros gives a long account of the piece, and compares it enthusiastically with the work of Handel. He says the manuscript came originally from the Altemps Library in Rome, and that it is now at the Collegio Romano. He calls it a *Sinfonia instrumentale a 4 voci per la Viola con Basso per Organo*. If this be accurate, clearly it cannot be regarded as a string quartet. But Allegri's sonata is printed in Kircher's *Musurgia Universalis* (page 487). Kircher's work may be seen in the British Museum (59. e. 19) or at the University Library, Cambridge. *Liber VI, De Musica Instrumentali* is the section which contains the Allegri information. The engravings represent different stringed instruments—a *Chelys*[1] *major*, a *Linterculus*, a *Chelys hexachordae*, a *Chelys minor*,[2] a *Lyra dodecachordae*,[3] a *Lyra mendicorum*, and a *Monochordon*.

He then adds,

> '*Apponemus concentum, sive symphoniam Chelyum iuxta omnes huic stylo proprias regulas summo ingenio compositam a celeberrimo Pontificij Chori musico D. Gregorio Allegri in quo symphoniacū artificium tam exacte exhibitum est, ut nihil ei addi, vel demi posse videatur.*
> *Paradig. I. Symphonia pro chèlybus omnibus numeris absolutissima.*
> *a 4. Duoi Violini, Alto & Basso di Viola.*'

Then follows quite a long piece (eighty bars in all), having all the appearance of an ordinary string quartet. The piece is written on four staves, with the upper two in the treble G clef and the lower with the C clef placed on different lines. The music is imitational in character; the tenor begins, the treble follows, then the bass, and finally the alto, all in close imitation. The tonality is not modern, but closely approximates to our scale of G major.

[1] Derivation, *Chelys*, literally tortoise; hence the lyre made from its shell.

[2] This seems to be the ordinary four-string violin.

[3] A twelve-stringed instrument.

Hullah, in his book, *The Transition Period of Musical History* (Longmans, 1876), refers to this piece as the earliest-known string quartet, and gives the following extract:

Andante from a Quartet of Allegri.

Rescored from Hullah by A. E. Hull.

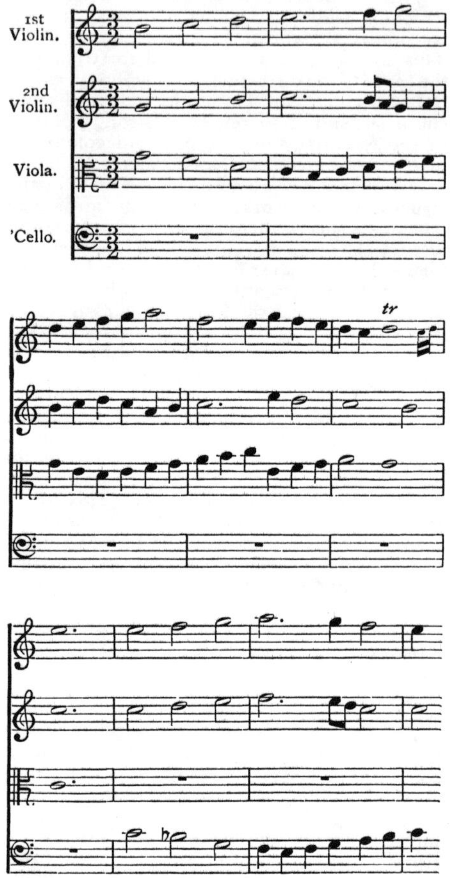

Ex. 2.

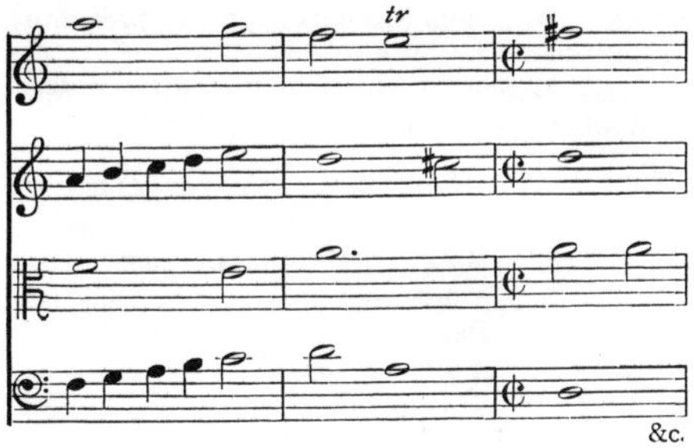

He continues, pp. 35–6:

'Few pieces of music have been honoured by more frequent mention than this quartet. It figures in almost every existing memoir and criticism having relation to the musical history of the seventeenth century. A copy of it has fortunately been preserved in a theoretical work now become rare, and certainly not likely ever to be reprinted, the *Musurgia* of Kircher, published in the year 1650. The obsolete notation and clumsy musical typography of this work must have rendered the performance of any of the examples it contains all but impossible for at least a hundred and fifty years past; and it is probable that the piece in question never found performers or audience, even during the last century; far less can it have done so in this. Thanks to the co-operation of four of my professional friends, you will in a few minutes be in a position to form an estimate of it. I need hardly warn you not to expect anything like any quartet you are likely to hear at the Musical Union or anywhere else. And you will forgive me for entreating you, once for all, to listen to this and other pieces of the same epoch, not with nineteenth, but with seventeenth-century ears.'

In an article on 'The Earliest String Quartets' in the *Monthly Musical Record* for November, 1903, Mr. (now Prof.) Edward Dent made out a case for Alessandro Scarlatti as the composer of the earliest-known string quartet. He could not then have known of the Allegri quartet, which, however, had been performed at Prof. Hullah's lecture in its entirety. It is useful to compare the dates of Allegri (*c.* 1580–1652) and Alessandro Scarlatti (1659–1725). In his article Prof. Edward Dent said, 'The first real string quartets were written within a few years of Corelli's death (certainly under his influence), by a composer who was traditionally his personal friend—Alessandro Scarlatti'.

In view of fresh Allegri discoveries, it seems worth while to give further details. I quote from Prof. Dent's article:

'In 1740 Dr. Benjamin Cooke, writing to his brother, sent him some pieces of music by Alessandro Scarlatti. The letter and the music are now in the British Museum (Add. MS. 32587), described in the catalogue as 'Twenty-one short pieces for the harpsichord'. They are, however, *not* harpsichord pieces, but a selection of movements from a series of compositions which were published by Cooke soon afterwards in London as 'VI. *Concertos* for Two Violins and Violoncello Obligato, with Two Violins more, a Tenor and Thoroughbass, Compos'd by Sig^r Alexander Scarlatti'. Only the single parts appear to have been published, and on looking through them with the idea of putting them into score, it became evident at once that the solo parts were identical throughout with those of the *ripieni*, except where the latter had rests and the solo played alone; in no case was there harmony in more than four parts. The labour of making a score from the parts was fortunately saved by the discovery that a set of six concertos for strings in the Fitzwilliam Museum at Cambridge, attributed by the copyist to 'Sig^r Scarlatti', and by the catalogue (though with some hesitation) to that very obscure composer Pietro Scarlatti, was in reality the score of these six concertos of Alessandro. The music is in English handwriting, and is on four staves only throughout; the words *solo* and *tutti* appear occasionally, but not more than nine times altogether in the whole of the six concertos.'

Prof. Dent pointed out that it was very rare to find Alessandro Scarlatti's compositions in the handwriting of contemporary Englishmen, and he therefore regarded the Cambridge score of the concertos with some suspicion, thinking it extremely probable that the arrangement of the composition in seven parts was more likely to be Cooke's than Scarlatti's. The combination of concerto grosso and concertino was common enough at the time, and it is obvious that a composer, writing for that combination, would not express his ideas in strict four-part harmony almost from beginning to end, with a preponderance of fugues and fugato movements in which the viola, usually much neglected by composers of that epoch, has as important a part as the other members of the quartet. And so it turned out. Research in the once famous collection made by Abbé Fortunato Santini in Rome revealed the separate parts of four out of the six so-called concertos, in the handwriting of a copyist frequently employed by Alessandro Scarlatti, bearing on the outside of the violoncello part, which served as a cover to the others, the title:

Sonata prima (seconda &c.) a Quattro
Due Violini, Violetta e Violoncello
Senza Cemb^o
Del Sig^r Caval^re Aless^o Scarlatti.

The violetta is, of course, the ordinary name for the viola in all Italian scores of the period. The viola, as late as Stradivari's time, was made in two sizes, alto and tenor, of which the larger, owing to its cumbrousness, eventually became obsolete; the diminutive term violetta was naturally applied to the smaller of the two varieties. From the title *Sonata a Quattro* we may reasonably infer that four solo instruments are implied, as in the sonatas of Corelli and Purcell; the use of the words solo, soli, and tutti is no proof of the contrary, the words being inserted merely to warn the player of a change to harmony in two, three, or four parts, as the case may be. And the direction *senza cembalo* makes it clear that the idea of a string quartet playing chamber music unsupported by the harpsichord was a novelty.

Prof. Dent does not consider the music of

these Scarlatti quartets very striking. Indeed, he admits that they are inferior to Corelli's chamber music. The material is good on the whole, he says; and the workmanship, as might be expected from Scarlatti, is always perfect. In the article quoted, Prof. Dent goes on to describe the Scarlatti quartet in detail, giving many musical extracts. He especially notes the fact that the Scarlatti minuets cannot be played with the stately step of the minuet in Mozart's *Don Giovanni*, and that they anticipate the scherzos of Beethoven. The one in the third quartet is marked vivace, and that in the fourth quartet comes very near being humorous. In this respect, the elder Scarlatti is before Haydn.

Purcell, and before him the Elizabethan lutenists, wrote quartets for the lute, but not of course for violins, viola, and 'cello.[1]

Joseph Haydn (1732–1809) is popularly called the 'father of the string quartet', but the epithet is used loosely, and is merely intended to give him the credit of firmly establishing the form. To sum up, until contradictory evidence is forthcoming, Allegri must be regarded as the composer of the first string quartet, as we now understand the term. A. EAGLEFIELD HULL.

[An erudite correspondent in Philadelphia, Mr. S. L. Lucian, writes me that he has in his extensive library, which includes 1,000 string quartets, a MS. work of Allegri, composed, so far as he knows, about 1630. The bass part never uses the lower octave of the modern instrument, and it is a matter of conjecture for which instrument the work was composed. The original, he says, is in the library of Santa Maria in Vallicella. EDITOR.]

†ALLEN, CHARLES N., English composer.

Suite (*Joys of Childhood*). pf, v — A. P. Schmidt, 1895.

Also pieces for two violins with piano, &c.

ALMEIDA, CARLOS FRANCISCO DE, Spanish violinist, court violinist in Madrid at the end of the eighteenth century.

Six quartets, str — Pleyel, 1798.

ALMEN, RUTH.

Sonata, pf, v, a mi — op. 3 — R. & E., 1923.

†ALNAES, EYVIND, b. 1872, Norwegian composer and organist.

Suite, pf, 2 v, D	Norsk. Musikförlag.	
„ pf, v, d mi	„	„

These works are technically rather exacting. The composer reveals mastery of counterpoint and powerful rhythms.

†ALOÏS (Aloiz), VLADISLAV (Ladislaus), b. 1860, Bohemian violoncellist.

Trio, pf, v, vc, F	op. 40	Jurgenson, 1898.
Suite, pf, v	„ 6	Steingräber, 1913.

Aloïs writes well for his instrument.

[1] But on this subject see article PURCELL.

ALONSO, LOPEZ FRANCISCO, b. 1887, Spanish composer.

Sonate libre, pf, v (sonata in free style) — Durdilly, c. 1900.

ALQUIER, MAURICE, b. 1867, French composer.

Sonata, pf, v, B flat — Eschig (Demets), 1902.

Alquier began his musical studies very late, going to the Paris Conservatoire in 1892. In 1900 he went on to the Schola Cantorum, where he completed his course in composition under Vincent d'Indy.

His only chamber work is the above-named sonata, performed several times at the Société Nationale.

This strongly temperamental and essentially dramatic work, which belongs to the Franckist school, is constructed in classical form and in very learned polyphonic style. The generous impulse of youth is evident throughout. The harmony, which is very rich, if often harsh, lends abundant colour to melody which is always expressive and has a strongly individual rhythm. ADOLPHE PIRIOU.

ALSAGER, THOMAS MASSA, 1779–1846. Part proprietor of, as well as writer on *The Times*, and an ardent lover of chamber music. He was associated with the so-called 'Queen's Square Select Society', whose members met at his house and with his co-operation founded the BEETHOVEN QUARTET SOCIETY (*q.v.*).

An interesting account of Alsager's activities is to be found in *Grove*. EDITOR.

ALTERNATIVO. Some time in the eighteenth century it became the fashion among composers to use the word 'trio' in place of 'alternativo' to describe the middle movement of a minuet or scherzo. Haydn, in his quartets, used it about eighty times, alternativo only once. Why a useful and explicit word should be replaced by one notoriously misleading belongs, like so many of the things of fashion, to the nature of mystery. The question is worth the attention of composers. It may be noted that Schumann revived the term. EDITOR.

ALTÈS, ERNEST EUGÈNE, 1830–1899, French violinist.

Trio, pf, v, vc, c mi	op. 29	Durand, 1887.
„ „ „ „ C	„ 37	Hamelle, 1908.
Sonata, pf, v, f mi	„ 31	Costallat, —.

†ALTMANN. *v.* BIBLIOGRAPHY.

AMANI, NIKOLAÏ, 1872–1904, Russian composer, pupil of Rimsky-Korsakov.

Trio, v, vla, vc, d mi — op. 1 — Belaiev, 1900.

The above is Amani's one chamber work (op. 1), slight, but pleasing, written in classical form, and presenting no characteristically vernacular features.

M. D. CALVOCORESSI.

[I wish to draw the attention of amateurs playing string quartets to this four-movement trio. How often it happens that the second violinist is late in arriving, or is absent altogether, when one has to fall back on string trios. One cannot always play Beethoven and Mozart, and the trios of Dohnányi and Reger are difficult. This one is very easy to play, full in tone, and, as Mr. Calvocoressi says, pleasing in effect.
EDITOR.]

AMATEUR. For centuries past the world's farceurs have indulged in satiric comments at the expense of the amateur in art, especially in music. They have been pleased to coin the most illogical adjective in the English language —'amateurish'. The result is that the intrinsic meaning of a word of noble derivation has been obscured.

The dictionary correctly describes the amateur as 'one who loves art without pursuing it with a view to gain', to which a corollary might be added, 'one who loves and serves art'. 'Ce titre d'amateur', writes Fétis, 'signifiait au XVIIIe siècle tout autre chose qu'il signifie aujourd'hui'. The amateur of that day was a supporter as well as a lover of the arts, a Maecenas like the dukes of Braganza, Esterházy, Lichnowsky, and many another of a tribe which no longer exists outside the realm of sport. Vincent d'Indy, in his article on CASTILLON (*q.v.*), describes the merging of the career of the amateur into that of the professional: a familiar phenomenon. It happened to Hubert Parry, to George Onslow, and to most of the Russian composers, of whom one, Borodin, stands apart from the rest as clinging to the amateur status to the last. His was a triple rôle, scientist, philanthropist, and musician. Borodin was the amateur *in excelsis*. EDITOR.

AMATEURS' EXCHANGE. Under this heading the *Musical Times*, with rare disinterestedness, inserts, free of charge, announcements by amateur musicians who wish to co-operate with others. I select a sample advertisement: 'Good amateurs wanted to join 'cellist to perform piano and string quartet for regular practice. Apply', &c. A scheme so wisely contrived cannot fail to produce the desired results. EDITOR.

AMBERG, JOHANN.

Suite (quartet), pf, fl, ob, cl, B flat	—	Hansen,	1905.
Trio, pf, cl, vc (or pf, v, vc), E flat	op. 11	,,	1912.
Fantasiestücke (trio), pf, v or cl, vc	,, 12	,,	1911.

AMBROS, AUGUST WILHELM, 1816–1876, musical historian. Worked on Schumann's paper under the pseudonym of 'Flamin'.

Trio, pf, v, vc, D	op. 6	Hoffmann (Prague), 1856.

AMBROSIO, ALFREDO D', 1871–1914, Italian violinist.

Suite (quintet), 2 v, vla, 2 vc, E flat	op. 8	Decourcelle,	1900.
Quartet, str, c mi	,, 42	,,	1908.

This composer is associated in the minds of most musicians with the production of elegant violin solos of the kind known as 'salon music', but those who are acquainted with his violin concerto and with the above quartet, know that he has the equipment of a technically accomplished musician. The themes, Italian in nature, contained in the quartet are pleasing, the counterpoint impeccable, and the writing for strings always upon the best part of the instrument. The scherzo, strange to say, is Irish in inspiration, and the finale very strongly rhythmical. Altogether a very attractive work. d'Ambrosio founded his own Quartet, led by himself, at Nice. EDITOR.

AMBROSIUS, HERMANN, b. 1897, German composer, pupil of Pfitzner.

Trio, pf, v, vc, a flat mi	op. 47	Kistner & Siegel.
Little suite, pf, fl, v	,, 14	Zimmermann.
Sonata pf, fl	,, 24	,,
Suite, pf, fl, F	,, 27	,,
Sonatina, pf, cl	,, 63*c*	C. F. Kahnt.

AMERICAN CHAMBER MUSIC. I.

The history of chamber music in America is recent—how recent may be estimated from the fact that in 1800, when Beethoven was the musical sensation of Vienna, and publishers were bidding against each other for his scores, the entire population of the United States numbered 5,300,000 or 2,000,000 less than the present population of Greater New York, of which one-sixth were slaves and 90 per cent. farmers, scattered at points along the Atlantic coast, protected inland by military posts, and concerned with matters far removed from chamber music.

Up to and including the first decade of the nineteenth century, the musical influences were English and French, and predominantly English. There is record of the activities of William Selby, the English organist, harpsichordist and teacher, who came to America in 1771, settled in Boston and became organist of King's Chapel in 1777, sold groceries and liquors, organized concerts at which 'advanced' programmes, including fragments of Handel's oratorios, were given, and composed in various forms. He produced music for organ and harpsichord, a sonata for two violins and two 'cellos, and other chamber music. He is mentioned as a matter of history and as illustration of what could be accomplished by an able musician in the early American environment.

Choral music and psalmody were the early forms of American composition. In instrumental music the English influence gradually gave way to the German. German musicians began to arrive in numbers about 1840, and became considerably more numerous after the revolutionary conditions in Germany of 1848–49. Prior to that date there had come to America, among others, Otto Dresel, pianist and composer, who arrived in New York in 1826, and later moved to Boston, where he died in 1890. He composed and performed a little chamber music of conventional German type, in which the piano consorted with the stringed instruments.

Similar figures were Theodore Eisfeld, who came to New York in 1848, and Julius Eichberg, who arrived the same year. Eisfeld organized an important series of local chamber concerts in 1851.

The first American chamber music organization to exert a nation-wide influence was the Mendelssohn Quintet Club, established in Boston in 1849, which accomplished much for the understanding and popularization of this form of art. The Mason-Thomas Quintet gave its first performance in New York in 1855, with Theodore Thomas (later famous as conductor of the Chicago Symphony Orchestra) as first violin. Up to this time the chamber music composed and performed had been almost entirely the product of foreign-born musicians.

An important step towards the development of a school of actual American composers was the founding of the first chair of music in an American University in 1862. The occupant was John Knowles Paine, b. 1839, an earnest and admirable musician, a pupil of Haupt, the organist (Berlin, 1858); at the same time a composition student of Wieprecht and Teschner, and a composer of substantial, though academic music. Paine left behind him a string quartet, a piano trio, a violin sonata, and chamber compositions in smaller forms. He left something else which perhaps counted for more in the succeeding years—a group of well grounded pupils, among whom are a number who have made significant contributions to American music.

We pass for the moment certain lesser figures, and find no material for this article in the compositions of Edward MacDowell and Horatio Parker,[1] two of the greatest American composers.

It is George Whitefield CHADWICK (*q.v.*), considered the doyen of the modern American school, who has made the most substantial contributions of any one now living to native composition, and whose chamber music has won deserved esteem. Chadwick, born in Lowell, Massachusetts, in 1854, studied first in Boston, then with Reinecke and Jadassohn at Leipzig in 1877, and with Rheinberger in Munich in 1879. This was the procedure followed by most young Americans of Chadwick's generation who planned a composer's career, and upon whom the German tradition exerted a strong influence.

Chadwick's first string quartet, in G minor (1878), was a student effort made in Germany. He returned to Boston in 1880, and produced four other works in this form: quartets in C major (1888), D major (1888), E minor (1896), D minor (1898). The quartet in E minor is evidence of the impression made upon young American composers by Antonin Dvořák, when, as teacher of composition from 1892 to 1895 at the National Conservatorium of Music of New York, he emphasized the availability of folk melody as material for the educated composer, and exemplified his teachings by his *New World* symphony, which utilized negro and Indian idioms, and his so-called 'American' quartet, which acknowledged similar sources of inspiration.[2]

These compositions of Dvořák preceded the composition of Edward MacDowell's *Indian Suite* for orchestra (1896), and had considerable effect upon other American composers. That Dvořák's quartet and symphony, despite their thematic bases, are unmistakably Bohemian in character, and that the *Indian Suite* of MacDowell, a native-born American of Celtic stock, is essentially Celtic in mood and accent, are among the illustrations of the confused sources of music in America; further, they are proofs, if such were needed, of the difference between the mere employment of folk music and music that actually arises from its period and environment.

Chadwick, in certain compositions, comes much nearer to what may be considered American (though American of a younger and less sophisticated day than the present) than many who have more loudly professed artistic allegiance to a national ideal. This is not the place to speak of Chadwick's miscellaneous productions, but, besides the quartets, his chamber works include two piano trios, a piano quartet, and a piano quintet (1887) which, though old-fashioned to-day, has enjoyed deserved popularity. Melodic invention, the hand of a sure craftsman, and an engaging and vigorous personality are shown in Chadwick's best music. It should be added that in later years the German influence which inevitably affected his early works is no longer in evidence, and he has become at once more individual and contemporaneous in his style.

Born a year earlier than Chadwick, Arthur FOOTE (*q.v.*) stands near him in his artistic attitude, if not in the number and range of his productions. He is one of the few American composers of significance to have gained his education entirely in his own country. Foote pursued his early studies in Boston, and was

[1] Parker wrote one published and three unpublished chamber works, MacDowell none. (Ed.)

[2] This question of the 'sources of inspiration' is fully discussed in Prof. Šourek's article on Dvořák, to which the reader is referred. (Ed.)

a pupil of Paine at Harvard. He has composed a considerable amount of chamber music. His writing is harmonically conservative, sincere, unpretentious, melodic in its style, distinguished always by feeling and good taste, and finished in its workmanship. No American has written with truer simplicity and absence of pose. Foote's chamber music has a place of its own which is not affected by later music of a more advanced description.

To the New England group represented by Chadwick and Foote belong also Mrs. H. H. Beach, Arthur Whiting, and the younger Henry Hadley and Frederick Shepherd Converse.

Mrs. BEACH (*q.v.*) (Amy Marcy Cheney) studied in Boston, and is the only American woman composer to have written effectively in the larger forms, including a violin sonata and a piano quintet. She is a composer of facile invention and excellent technical grounding, whose works, particularly her songs, have found a wide acceptance.

Arthur Whiting was a pupil of Chadwick, then of Rheinberger, in composition; is a teacher, lecturer, pianist, and composer of genial and scholarly cast, whose violin sonata did much to bring him to the attention of the public.

Henry HADLEY (*q.v.*) also studied with Chadwick, and later in Vienna with Mandyczevski. Following his early studies he was, and still is, active as a conductor. He was precociously musical, and produced his first string quartet before he was twenty-one. He has written in most of the accepted forms, great and small. His piano quintet is written with marked brilliance and swing. A certain youthful glow and exuberance, coupled with a ready technique of the post-Wagnerian order, is characteristic of many of Hadley's productions. But his facility is dangerous to him.

F. S. CONVERSE (*q.v.*), a pupil of Paine at Harvard, and of Rheinberger in Munich, does not find in chamber music his most sympathetic medium, but a violin sonata, op. 1, is excellently written, with freshness and continence of style. There is richness of resource and a deeper emotional quality in the string quartet, first performed in 1904. Converse is one of the most sincere and idealistic of American composers, who is best represented, however, by his orchestral compositions.

The generation of musicians represented by Chadwick and Foote includes other composers who laboured with similar sincerity and devotion to their art, in an environment far less propitious for musical development than America of to-day. One of these is Edgar STILLMAN-KELLEY (*q.v.*). It is not uncharacteristic of the career of an American musician that one of Kelley's earliest incentives to the pursuit of his art was hearing a performance by Blind Tom, a half-witted negro piano prodigy. Kelley's early study was in his native town; later he went to Chicago, then to Stuttgart, where he studied for four years. He became a musician of exceptional scholarship, a brilliant technician, and a composer highly respected in Germany—to which he often returned in later years—as well as in his own country. Stillman-Kelley is a man of wide culture and intellectual attainments, although he was not always fortunate in his artistic environment. The American pioneers in music, as in other fields, suffered the hardships, adventures, and deprivations of their calling. It may be for these reasons that Kelley's music shows a singular blend of the imaginative, fantastic, and original with the merely conventional or academic. His chamber music is, on the whole, conservative and somewhat Wagnerian in mould. His piano quintet heads the list in point of ideas, effective writing, and number of performances in America and Europe. A string quartet is also well spoken of.

A composer unique in the annals of American music is Charles Martin LOEFFLER (*q.v.*). He is American by residence and citizenship, and all of his important compositions have been composed since his arrival in America in the early 'eighties; his artistic background, however, is French. No other composer living in America has produced chamber music of a like exquisiteness of structure, poetic beauty, and, in the later works, grave and noble reticence. Loeffler's early productions showed traces of the influence of Wagner and Brahms, but he soon developed an inherent and temperamental sympathy with the French composers of the late nineteenth and early twentieth centuries, particularly Debussy and d'Indy. The impressionism of the one, and the form and ascetic passion of the other, were profoundly felt by Loeffler.

A movement from his first string quartet was performed in 1888. His sextet was introduced by the Kneisel Quartet in 1893, and a revised version of this work, *Le passeur d'eau*, was played in Boston by the same organization in 1909. Use is made in it of what is now the over-familiar Russian Song of the Volga Boatmen. The early works are distinguished by exceptional beauty of harmony and part writing, and by youthful glamour and romanticism. The later music becomes more mystical and austere, and plain chant is a persistent element. Following the sextet came the quintet for three violins, viola, and 'cello (1895); the octet for two violins, viola and 'cello, two clarinets, double bass and harp (1897); the *Two Rhapsodies*, which, like other of Loeffler's scores, sound the note of the fantastic and macabre, after the poems *L'Étang* and *La Cornemuse* of Maurice Rollinat, for piano, viola, and oboe (1901); the *Ballade carnavalesque* for piano, flute, oboe, saxophone, and bassoon (1904); the *Pagan Poem*, one of Loeffler's greatest works, originally scored in

1901 for chamber orchestra (with piano); later for two pianos and three trumpets, and finally for piano and full modern orchestra; and the *Music for Four Stringed Instruments*—those of the regulation string quartet.

In the last-named work the influence of the plain chant which has permeated much of Loeffler's music is particularly noticeable. Here, too, is the trend away from sensuous impressionism to a more formal and objective but not less intrinsically emotional utterance. Few, if any, American composers equal Loeffler in technical accomplishment, and none has surpassed him in choice of material and sensitiveness of taste.

It will be seen that New England was for years the headquarters in America of serious composition, including chamber music. In the meantime, through the 'fifties, 'sixties, and 'seventies, the stream was broadening. To go back chronologically for a moment: the compositions of William Wallace Gilchrist, educated entirely in America, are notable for copious, if not distinguished invention, and for craftsmanship highly creditable to his industry and enthusiasm. Gilchrist, who lived most of his life in Philadelphia, was active in many fields of musical organization. His works include a piano trio, a string quartet, a piano quintet, and a nonet for piano, strings, flute, clarinet, and horn. There is little originality in his music, and, despite the fact that it was a home-spun product, little that distinguishes it from conventional European models, but he was one of the most progressive and influential of the musical pioneers.

Adolph Martin FOERSTER (*q.v.*) is a prolific composer in many fields. He was a student at the Leipzig Conservatorium from 1872–1875, and became a teacher the following year at the Fort Wayne, Indiana Conservatorium, but in 1876 returned to his native town, Pittsburg. His chamber compositions include two piano quartets, two piano trios, a string quartet, suites, and a fantasia for violin and piano.

Henry Schoenfeld composed, among other works, a violin sonata which won the Henri Marteau prize in 1899, a 'cello sonata, and some pieces for ensemble groups of instruments in smaller forms. His sonata shows the effect of the folk-song theories of Dvořák.

Ernest Kroeger, one of the most active musicians in the development of the musical West, gained his early instruction from his father, and most of his musical education was received in his own city. He has written over 700 works, which include a violin sonata, a piano trio, quartet, and quintet, and a string quartet. His compositions follow German models, tinged with a certain exoticism and romantic feeling.

It is to be remembered that these composers grew up in the Wagner-Brahms period of composition in Germany, and inevitably followed its models. It was only after 1900 that other European influences, especially those of modern France and Russia, made themselves felt in America, and it is only since that date that the land may be said to be musically settled by American musicians cognizant as a class of the most recent developments in their art, and seeking self-expression with confidence and a wide horizon.

Among other American composers belonging to the 'seventies is Rubin GOLDMARK (*q.v.*), who has produced, among other works, a piano trio, a violin sonata, and a piano quintet. He is a nephew of the Viennese composer, Carl Goldmark. When he brought his piano trio to Dvořák, with whom he studied composition in New York in the 'nineties, the Bohemian exclaimed, 'Now there are two Goldmarks'. Rubin Goldmark is one of the most brilliantly equipped musicians of his generation in America, and has done most valuable work in many fields for the advancement of music.

Arne Oldberg, a pupil of Rheinberger, is now head of the music department of North-Western University. He has composed a great deal, including two popular piano quintets, a quintet for wood-wind and piano, and a string quartet in C minor.

A composer more French than American in his manner is Blair FAIRCHILD (*q.v.*), a pupil of Paine and Spalding at Harvard, later of Buonamici at Florence and Widor in Paris. Although he has been active in diplomatic and other non-musical ways, Fairchild has produced much music for string quartet, strings and piano, &c.

Among American composers of the more academic type is Daniel Gregory MASON (*q.v.*), author, lecturer, and composer. Among his teachers were Paine, Chadwick, Arthur Whiting; and d'Indy in Paris. His style is scholarly, of broad horizons, and owes much to Brahms and d'Indy on the formal side. His compositions for many combinations of instruments include a violin sonata; a piano quartet; a *Pastorale* for piano, violin, and clarinet; a clarinet sonata; a string quartet on negro themes; three pieces for string quartet, flute, and harp, and a second violin sonata, a prize work published by the S.P.A.M.

David Stanley SMITH (*q.v.*) studied composition with Horatio Parker at Yale. His first quartet, in E minor, was introduced by the Kneisel Quartet in 1912; the second, op. 37, was played by both the Kneisel and Flonzaley Quartets in 1915. Other works are a piano trio, op. 16 (1914), a violin sonata, a *Sonata pastorale* for oboe, and a string quartet, op. 46.

It is now possible to compare and appraise American composers who reached their creative prime at the turn of the century. Of those born in the 'nineties and after it is not easy to speak with very much perspective. Since the war, Europe is nearer America artistically than ever before, although there was a much more advanced state of musical development in the United States prior to that time than many Europeans realized. About 1900 the younger generation began to turn from Wagner and Brahms and to be aware of the import of the works of the modern Frenchmen and Russians. To-day the young men feel the influence of Stravinsky, Schönberg, and the contemporaneous Italians; and, in common with their European cousins, are cultivating the smaller forms of composition and the more intimate style of chamber music.

It is at the same time symbolic of the present state of affairs that the one American composer who takes a powerful and dominating position is Ernest BLOCH (*q.v.*), the Jewish composer, now an American citizen, but born in Switzerland. Bloch is, indeed, one of the significant figures of modern music, as he is perhaps the first great and uncompromising exponent of Judaism in the history of the tonal art. Before he came to America his compositions had attracted the attention and enthusiastic praise of Romain Rolland and other European critics.

Most of his important compositions, including his chamber music, have appeared since his arrival in America in 1916. In that year the Flonzaley played his B major quartet in a number of American towns. This has been followed by his viola suite, and his piano quintet (New York, 1923), which must rank as one of the finest of modern chamber works, because of its dramatic force and sensuous emotion, the power and unity of its cyclic form, and a harmonic audacity based, nevertheless, upon the most traditional relations of tonality.

Bloch, like Loeffler, is an American acquisition, not an American product. But whereas Loeffler has created no school or group of followers, Bloch has been fruitfully active as teacher as well as composer, and American music will be tinged with his ideas in the years immediately to come. Again, Loeffler's tendency is toward the rarefied or impressionistic, whereas Bloch is extremely virile, savagely rhythmical, and, with all his vivid colouring, direct and linear in his methods; and these qualities bring him the nearer to the American temperament.

The most promising of the young American composers of this period met an early and untimely end. This was Charles Tomlinson GRIFFES (*q.v.*). He studied with Humperdinck in Berlin, and in 1907 returned to America. He accepted a position of drudgery in a boys' school, where he taught, composing as he could, to the day of his death. Griffes had exceptional sensibility and harmonic and colouristic tendencies, which made him particularly sympathetic to the music of certain modern Frenchmen and Russians, but he had also a wealth of fantasy and impressionability. His *Two Pieces for String Quartet*, showing somewhat the Stravinsky influence, were played by the Flonzaley Quartet in 1918. There are also two *Sketches on Indian Themes* for string quartet, and an arrangement for wood-wind and harp of two *Piano Tone-Pictures*. Griffes died of lung disease in 1920, at a time when he showed every indication of producing new and important music.

Among Griffes's contemporaries may be named John POWELL (*q.v.*), a piano virtuoso and a student in composition of Navratil at Vienna. He has produced some weighty music of Teutonic hue, but has attained more spontaneous and fortunate expression in certain compositions which employ negro melody. In this vein is his *Sonata virginesque* for violin and piano, depicting scenes of Southern life. Powell has also produced a string quartet and a second violin sonata.

Younger men than Powell have had little opportunity as yet to prove themselves. There are composers of the extreme left, as Edgar Varèse, Carl RUGGLES (*q.v.*), Carlos Salzedo, who appear as yet to be experimentalists rather than men of unmistakable artistic achievements; composers of more conservative type, as Frederick JACOBI (*q.v.*), whose recent string quartet on Indian themes has been well received; pupils of Bloch, among them Roger Sessions, Bernard Rogers, W. Quincy Porter, Douglas Moore; four winners of the Prix de Rome offered by the American Academy in that city—Leo SOWERBY, Howard HANSON (*q.v.*) (now music director of the Eastman School of Music at Rochester, New York), Randolph Thompson, and G. Herbert Atwell; Leo ORNSTEIN (*q.v.*), of radical tendencies and unmistakable talent; Emerson WHITHORNE (*q.v.*), whose two quartets on Greek and Oriental motifs show his brilliant technique, facility, and ultra-modern way of thinking; Louis GRUENBERG (*q.v.*), born in Greater New York, partly educated there, but for some years resident in Europe, who has treated, rather from the European standpoint, the American 'jazz' style in *The Daniel Jazz* and *The Creation* for voice and chamber orchestra; and others, whose complete artistic personalities have yet to be disclosed.

One of the most independent, original, and vigorous of modern American composers, a man of singular clearness of aim and self-expression, though somewhat restricted technically, was Henry Gilbert (died in 1928), one of MacDowell's first pupils, and one of those who strove most earnestly to express racial temperament and ideals in his music. But he wrote little chamber music. There is in existence, however, a manuscript string quartet, and another work was commissioned by Mrs. Coolidge, patron of American chamber music, for performance at her annual festival held in the music-room of the Congressional Library at Washington, D.C.

For the rest, there is much activity and

experiment, and some solid achievement which is distinctive, but the day has yet to come when a native-born composer of ample technical resource and individual gifts will produce chamber music with the unmistakable stamp of its own land and era, and worthy to rank with the great masterpieces of this form of art. OLIN DOWNES.

[The above, which is a recapitulation of the splendid work already accomplished by American composers of chamber music, an earnest of things to come, would be incomplete without mention of the brilliant efforts of Leo Sowerby and Henry Eichheim, whose music is treated in another place. EDITOR.]

AMERICAN CHAMBER MUSIC. II.

During the past quarter of a century the rapid growth of interest in chamber music has afforded impressive evidence of the spread of musical culture throughout the United States. Two generations ago, American organizations maintained for the public performance of chamber music were few and comparatively unimportant. In 1855, William Mason, a distinguished American pianist, who had then taken up his residence in New York after several years spent with Liszt at Weimar, formed an association with Theodore Thomas, which he called the Mason-Thomas Quartet. Thomas, the first violin of the Quartet, was then becoming known as a conductor, and chose from his orchestra three associates to form the first string Quartet of artistic significance to appear in the United States.

The serious quality of its work will appear from a programme given in New York on November 27, 1855, which included the Schubert D minor quartet and the Brahms B major trio. This was one of the earliest performances outside Germany of the Brahms trio. In his *Memories of a Musical Life*, Dr. Mason states that he repeated it in Boston a few weeks later, with the assistance of two members of the Mendelssohn Quintet Club. This latter organization was composed of leading musicians (string and wind players of Boston), and for years the Club made extensive tours throughout the country, presenting programmes which included classical compositions as well as arrangements of a lighter character.

These organizations continued for several years, but the principal activities of their respective members were in orchestral and other work. At a somewhat later period, visiting European artists, notably Rubinstein and von Bülow, gave occasional ensemble programmes in the larger cities, assisted by local musicians. Still later, the Philharmonic Club in New York (not to be confused with the Philharmonic Society and Philharmonic Orchestra), which was composed of both string and wind players, presented programmes of chamber music until about 1890, and at about the same time the Dannreuther Quartet (of which Gustav Dannreuther, a well-known violinist and the brother of Edward Dannreuther of London, was the founder) held a leading position among local organizations in New York.

Not, however, until the Kneisel Quartet began its work in Boston in 1885 did America have a permanent Quartet of the first distinction and quality. Its original members, including Franz Kneisel and Louis Svecenski, were the leading string players of the then recently established Boston Symphony Orchestra. Upon its first appearance, the Quartet occupied a position of the highest distinction in Boston, and thereafter extended its activities to New York and the principal centres of the East. Still later, the Quartet made annual tours throughout the entire country, extending the love and appreciation of chamber music wherever it appeared. In 1905 the members of the Quartet accepted appointments in the faculty of the Institute of Musical Art in New York, and thereafter made their headquarters in New York. Until the close of the season of 1917, the Quartet, with some changes in personnel, but including Messrs. Kneisel and Svecenski, both of whom have passed away, continued its work on a national scale, and upon its dissolution left memories which have become one of the glorious traditions of American musical history.

In 1903, Edward J. de Coppet of New York, who was the most discerning and public-spirited American patron of chamber music of his generation, assembled four European artists, Messrs. Betti, Pochon, Ara, and d'Archambeau, to constitute the Flonzaley Quartet. The Quartet first appeared only in private, either in Mr. de Coppet's house in New York, or at Flonzaley, his country place in Switzerland. Guided, protected, and stimulated by the support and encouragement of its founder, the Quartet upon its first public appearance in 1905 achieved an artistic triumph, and before Mr. de Coppet's death in 1916 it had become known as one of the world's leading organizations.[1]

The work of both these Quartets in friendly rivalry has been of incalculable importance in stimulating and developing an appreciation of chamber music in every American music centre.

Their pioneer work has been recently followed by American tours of leading European Quartets, notably the London String Quartet; and the most eminent violinists, 'cellists, and pianists have joined from time to time in giving recitals of chamber music in the larger towns and cities of the country. The establishment of permanent orchestras in various cities has been followed by the formation of Quartets composed of leading artists from the respective orchestras, and these

[1] The present tour (1928) is announced as the last.

Quartets appear not only in their home cities, but also make tours of varying extent.

Another striking event in recent American musical annals bearing on the matter has been the foundation of the Berkshire Festival of Chamber Music. In 1917, Mrs. Elizabeth Sprague COOLIDGE (*q.v.*), now the leading patron of chamber music in America, built on one of the slopes of the Berkshire Hills, near Pittsfield in western Massachusetts, a festival hall surrounded by bungalows, the latter intended for summer occupation by herself and visiting artists. Beginning in September of that year, annual festivals have been held, at each of which five programmes of chamber compositions have been presented on three successive days. The artists have always been of the first distinction, and the audiences, who are all the guests of Mrs. Coolidge, include musicians and music-lovers from all parts of the world.

A prize of one thousand dollars is awarded each year for a work of prescribed form, and the first performance of the prize composition is given as a part of each final programme. The Berkshire String Quartet was at the same time established by Mrs. Coolidge, to provide a part of each festival programme, and this has now been succeeded by the Festival Quartet, of which Mr. Willem Willeke, who was the 'cellist of the Kneisel Quartet during its latest period, is the moving spirit.

The Festival Quartet collaborating with the Elshuco Trio, the latter of which has for several years held a leading position in America, and which was also established by Mr. Willeke with Mrs. Coolidge, was heard in a series of eight concerts in New York, at which were presented all of the chamber compositions of Brahms.

In addition, New York now has the Letz Quartet, of which Hans Letz, former second violin of the Kneisel Quartet, is the leader; the New York String Quartet, founded by Mr. and Mrs. Ralph Pulitzer; the Lenox String Quartet, also privately maintained; and several other Trios and Quartets of fine and distinguished quality, noticed elsewhere. Still other New York organizations are the Composers' Guild and the League of Composers, which aim to present the most modern compositions in the field of chamber music.

The foundation of the Society for the Publication of American Music, which was established chiefly through the energy of Mr. Burnet C. Tuthill, now of Cincinnati, and continued by the indefatigable efforts of his father, William B. Tuthill, a New York architect and music-lover, has brought about the publication during the past few years of chamber compositions by American composers. These works are chosen for publication by a jury which includes several eminent musicians, and upon publication these compositions are distributed annually among the members of the Association, who are widely scattered throughout the United States. The Society enables musicians and students of chamber music to keep in touch with the works of contemporary American composers, and it is believed to have a stimulating influence upon both composers and artists.

But perhaps the most important of all recent agencies for the extension of the appreciation of chamber music have been the clubs which are now maintained in many American towns and cities. These arrange for appearances before their members of leading Quartets and chamber music organizations. One of the largest is the Chamber Music Association of Philadelphia, which has now been in existence for about eight years and includes a membership slightly over one thousand. It arranges for eight concerts of chamber music in each year, given by the leading chamber music organizations of the country. For example, an announcement for 1924 included two appearances by the Flonzaley Quartet, one each by the Boyle-Gittelson-Penha Trio, the Rich Quartet and the New York String Quartet, and three by the Philadelphia Orchestra Ensemble. Another recently formed in Washington, D.C., is limited to two hundred members and proposes to give three concerts each winter, announcing only the works to be performed but not the names of the performers, who are screened from the audience and whose identity is not disclosed until the end of the evening.

These may be regarded as typical of the efforts which are now being made throughout the country to provide, through the members of the Associations, assured audiences for the Quartets, Trios, and other ensemble players touring the country. The maintenance of the different Quartets would in all probability be very burdensome but for the support so given, and, like the maintenance of the orchestras in the large music centres, they are at the same time evidence of a spontaneous desire on the part of the music-lovers of the country to hear and enjoy the presentation of the masterpieces of classical and modern chamber music.

Another organization recently formed in New York, mainly at the instance of Mr. Harold Bauer, is the Beethoven Association. Its original purpose was to present, through the voluntary co-operation of leading artists, some of the less known compositions of the great Viennese master at a series of concerts to be given during each musical season in New York. As the services of the musicians are given as a matter of artistic enthusiasm, the Association has been enabled to apply the proceeds of the concerts to musical purposes which otherwise might languish.

After the close of the first season, the Association voted to apply its resources to the first publication in English of Thayer's *Life of Beethoven*, which had been edited and revised by Henry E. Krehbiel. Later appropriations have been made for like purposes. The Association includes in its membership most of the distinguished American and European artists who have appeared during recent seasons in New York, and it now maintains club rooms in the city, which are intended to provide a social meeting-place for artists and music-lovers who constitute its membership. Concerts of the Association are always occasions of great distinction and interest, and these now present chamber works of composers other than Beethoven, but deemed worthy of association with his name.

The foregoing survey, which is necessarily incomplete, indicates that chamber music is no longer neglected in America. Creative effort has not yet kept pace with performance, but each city and music centre has a steadily increasing band of musicians and music-lovers, who help to extend the appreciation of the art in ways the significance of which can only be dimly foreseen. The field is enlarging constantly and steadily, and it may be confidently hoped that a most important chapter in the history of chamber music will be written by the present generation of American composers, artists, and music-lovers.

E. T. RICE.

AMERICAN PERFORMING ORGANIZATIONS.

(*a*) QUARTETS.[1]

BERKSHIRE QUARTET. Hugo Kortschak, Hermann Felber (jr.), Clarence Evans, Emmeran Stoeber.

CHAMBER MUSIC SOCIETY OF SAN FRANCISCO. *v.* PERSINGER STRING QUARTET.

CHICAGO STRING QUARTET. Hermann Felber, Carl Fasshauer, Robert Dolejsi, Theodore du Moulin. Originally known as the Great Lakes Quartet. Was founded during the Great War, when its members enlisted in the navy, and found themselves in the same regiment and company at the Great Lakes Naval Training Station. A first recital was arranged at North-Western University, Evanston, Ill. This was the beginning of a long list of appearances throughout the country, and ultimately led to the Quartet being chosen to accompany President Wilson to France, to attend the peace conference. After the war the Quartet made a trans-continental tour, and has since given regular series of concerts in Chicago.

Du Moulin was preceded successively by Walter Brauer, John Lingeman, and Naoum Benditzky.

Among the works presented is Haba's quartet in quarter tones.

CLEVELAND STRING QUARTET. Josef Fuchs, R. Ringwall, Carlton Cooley, Victor de Gomez.

[1] Names of performers are given in the following order: 1st violin, 2nd violin, viola, violoncello. Where a Quartet is named after the 1st violin, the name is not repeated.

This Quartet was organized by N. Sokolov, conductor of the Cleveland Orchestra, May 1919, at the close of the orchestra's first season. The Musical Arts Association, which supported the orchestra, undertook financial responsibility for the Quartet. The Quartet originally consisted of N. Sokolov, Louis Edlin, Herman Kolodkin, and Victor de Gomez, all principals of the respective sections in the orchestra. A winter season of concerts was followed by a summer season in California. In subsequent years the changes which took place in the personnel were too numerous to record. The Quartet was led in 1923–26 by Arthur Beckwith, and gave one concert at the Æolian Hall, London. Beckwith returned to England in May 1926, his place being taken by Josef Fuchs of New York.

The Quartet has an extensive repertory, both classical and modern, and has given first performances of some modern American works.

CURTIS QUARTET. Composed of eminent members of the faculty of the Curtis Institute of Music, Philadelphia. Its personnel consists of Carl Flesch, Emanuel Zetlin, Louis Bailly, and Felix Salmond. Owing to the teaching duties of the members of the Quartet, comparatively few public concerts are given.

GUSTAV DANNREUTHER QUARTET. E. Schenk, O. Schill, J. Kovarik.

DURRELL STRING QUARTET. A ladies' Quartet, formed in 1915, being an outgrowth of a quartet class under Joseph Adamowski at the New England Conservatory of Music. The personnel at the first public concert in 1916 consisted of Josephine Durrell, Hazel Clark, Anne Golden, and Mildred Ridely.

Since the début of the organization several changes have been made in the second violin: Jessie Hatch Symonds, Louise Sweet, Beatrice Griffin, Edith Roubound. For a short time Virginia Stickney played 'cello.

ELMAN STRING QUARTET. This Quartet, headed by Mischa Elman, the famous virtuoso, consisted originally of the following personnel: Mischa Elman, Edward Bachmann, Nicolas Moldavan, and Horace Britt. Moldavan was succeeded by Louis Bailly at the viola desk, and other changes are meditated at the time of writing. The organization was founded in 1924, and has appeared with great success in all the American music centres and in a number of smaller cities on tour.

[The performances of the Elman Quartet afford a fine opportunity, and one which seldom occurs, for the public to enjoy the stylistic and temperamental interpretations of a great solo violinist as applied to chamber music. EDITOR.]

FLONZALEY QUARTET. *v.* that article.

[FRENCH-AMERICAN QUARTET. Gustav Tinlot, Reber Johnson, Saul Sharrow, Paul Kefer. An

American Quartet composed of musicians resident in New York City. From Bachmann's *Encyclopedia of the Violin*.]

Jacques Gordon String Quartet. John Weicher, Clarence Evans, Richard Wagner, all members of the Chicago Symphony Orchestra, of which Jacques Gordon is the concert-master. The Quartet gives an annual series of three subscription concerts in Chicago, during which a large number of new works are played. The organization has given a complete cycle of the Beethoven quartets, under the patronage of the Elizabeth Sprague Coolidge foundation, as well as a series of six free concerts under the same auspices.

[Jacques Gordon was heard in London (1927) in sonatas by Medtner and Pizzetti, and proved himself an accomplished chamber music player. Editor.]

Hart House String Quartet. Geza de Kresz, Harry Adaskin, Milton Blackstone, Boris Hambourg. Hart House was built and presented to the University of Toronto by the Massey Foundation. The Hon. Vincent and Mrs. Massey, who are responsible for the permanent foundation of the Quartet, placed it under the management of Hart House Theatre, thus forming an alliance with a great educational institution. In one season, the Quartet gave seventy-four concerts and appeared in thirty-four cities, covering a territory extending from the Atlantic Coast as far west as the Rocky Mountains.

Kneisel Quartet. *v.* article Kneisel, Franz.

Lenox String Quartet. Founded by Emmeran Stoeber in 1922. The original members were Sandor Harmati, Wolfe Wolfinsohn, Nicholas Moldavan, and Emmeran Stoeber. In 1925 the personnel was changed to Wolfe Wolfinsohn, Edwin Ideler, Herbert Borodkin, and Emmeran Stoeber.

The Quartet has appeared at Mrs. Coolidge's Berkshire Festival, and under her auspices has given a series of Public Library concerts in New York and Boston and at the Congressional Library in Washington. Other important appearances have been made before the Beethoven Association of New York City, and at the Beethoven Festival in Boston, Mass.

Important compositions given first performance by the Lenox Quartet include Ernest Bloch's piano quintet, with Harold Bauer, Leopold Mannes's quartet, and Schönberg's quartet with voice, performed at the Berkshire Festival.

Letz Quartet. Founded in 1917 by Hans Letz, upon the dissolution of the Kneisel Quartet, of which Letz was a member. Its original personnel consisted of Hans Letz, Sandor Harmati, Edward Kreiner, and Gerald Maas. Several changes have since been made. Harmati was succeeded by Edward Bachman, Kreiner by William Schubert, and Maas by Lajos Shuk and Horace Britt, the latter being the 'cellist at present.

The Letz Quartet has given many New York recitals, has appeared before the Beethoven Association, and has made annual tours since its organization. Its repertory embraces practically all of the standard quartet literature. Among many first performances was that of Fritz Kreisler's string quartet in New York City, April 1919.

Minneapolis Symphony String Quartet. Joseph E. Shadwick, Eugene Kaltschmidt, Paul Lemay, Englebert Roentgen, the principal players of the Minneapolis Symphony Orchestra. An annual series of concerts is given in Minneapolis and St. Paul, and an annual tour is made of the North-Western States.

National String Quartet. Henri Sokolov, Max Pugatsky, Samuel Feldman, Richard Lorleberg. Organized in 1921 through the interest of Mrs. W. B. Howe, of Washington. Among important engagements the Quartet has filled was an appearance at the dedication of the Chamber Music Hall which Mrs. Coolidge presented to the Library of Congress, as well as in four concerts given in the Congressional Library.

New York String Quartet. Ottokar Cadek, Jaroslav Siskowsky, Ludvik Schwab, Bedrich Vaska. The first public appearance of this Quartet was made in 1922, following a three-year period devoted to daily rehearsals. Annual appearances have been made in all the larger music centres, as well as several extensive tours. The repertory includes the standard literature, and an attractive selection of novelties.

[Olive Mead String Quartet. Organized in 1904. Consists of Mrs. Olive Mead, Vera Foronof, Gladys North, and Lillian Littlehales. Editor.]

Persinger String Quartet (of Santa Barbara). The Persinger Quartet is an outcome of the Chamber Music Society of San Francisco, founded in 1916 by Elias M. Hecht, a chamber music patron and flautist of San Francisco. The Quartet of the Chamber Music Society consisted of Louis Persinger, Louis Ford, Nathan Firestone, and Horace Britt. Since then Walter Ferner has become the 'cellist of the organization.

When, in 1926, Hecht was obliged to discontinue his patronage of the group, its continuation was assured by the Community Arts Association of Santa Barbara, which engaged the Quartet to give a series of concerts in that city. Series of concerts are also given in Los Angeles and San Francisco. The Quartet was first heard in the Eastern part of the United States in 1923, when it played with considerable success at the Berkshire Music Festival. Several extensive tours followed, and among the important engagements was a programme given at the dedication of the new music auditorium of the Library of Congress, presented to the United States government by Mrs. Coolidge.

Many new works have had their first American performance by this organization. A feature of the Quartet has been its daily rehearsals from July 1 to October 1. A portion of the rehearsal period has always been set aside for the consideration of American works. This organization was disbanded in 1928.

SOUTH MOUNTAIN QUARTET. William Kroll, Karl Kraeuter, Conrad Held, Willem Willeke. Takes its name from the South Mountain Colony, Pittsfield, Mass., a summer colony of musicians sponsored by Mrs. Coolidge for the cultivation of chamber music. The original purpose was the preparation of the Berkshire Festivals of Chamber Music, which were held there in September for seven or eight consecutive seasons, until, in October 1925, the annual festival was transferred to Washington, where Mrs. Coolidge had built a chamber music auditorium and attached it to the Library of Congress.

In 1924 Mrs. Coolidge appointed Willem Willeke to be the musical director of the South Mountain Colony, and founded this Quartet. Its special function is to play weekly concerts of chamber music in the Temple originally built for the festivals. During the summer the South Mountain Quartet is Mrs. Coolidge's personal Quartet. In the winter, however, they have entire independence.

VERBRUGGHEN STRING QUARTET. Formed Oct. 1903, when Henri Verbrugghen was concert-master of the Glasgow Symphony Orchestra. Its original personnel consisted of Henri Verbrugghen, Guy McGrath, David E. Nichols, and James Messeas; Miss Jenny Cullen replaced McGrath in 1909.

After touring successfully in Great Britain, the members of the Quartet were engaged as instructors at the new State Conservatorium founded by the Australian Government, so that the ensemble remained intact.

Twenty-four concerts were given annually in Sydney alone, during the course of which they performed more than 250 works, both classical and modern. When, in 1923, Verbrugghen became permanent conductor of the Minneapolis Symphony Orchestra, the other members of the Quartet followed him and joined that organization. Since then, as far as their orchestral duties have permitted, the Quartet has been active in spreading a knowledge of chamber music in that district.

ZOELLNER QUARTET. Antoinette Zoellner, Amandus Zoellner, Joseph Zoellner (sen.), Joseph Zoellner (jun.). A notable feature of this Quartet is that its members are all of one family—father, daughter, and two sons. The personnel has remained unchanged since its first public appearance in Brooklyn, N.Y., in 1900, at which time the youthful Amandus fell asleep at the concert.

During a period in which the family resided in Brussels, the first European appearances were made at César Thomson's private soirées. Public appearances followed later in Belgium, and visits were made to Paris and Berlin. In 1912 the family returned to America, living in New York until 1917, when they removed to Los Angeles, where they founded a conservatorium in 1922. They tour extensively, and in their entire career have given over two thousand concerts. In their home city of Los Angeles, an annual series of six chamber concerts is given, where first performances of many new works are heard.

(*b*) TRIOS.[1]

BEETHOVEN TRIO. The Beethoven Trio of Chicago was organized in 1908 with a personnel consisting of Jeanette Loudon, Otto B. Roehrborn, and Carl Brueckner, the two latter being members of the Chicago Symphony Orchestra. The personnel remained the same for ten years, when Ralph Michaelis became the violinist and Theodore du Moulin the 'cellist. Michaelis died in 1923, and du Moulin resigned, their places being taken by Sidney V. James and Richard Beidel respectively. For several seasons the Beethoven Trio took part in a series of concerts at the Cordon Club, and filled as well many engagements throughout the Middle West.

CHERNIAVSKY TRIO. An international organization consisting of three brothers: Jan, Leo, and Mischel, who have toured extensively in all countries.

ELSHUCO TRIO. Founded in 1917 by the 'cellist Willem Willeke, the other members of the original personnel being Richard Epstein (pf.) and Samuel Gardner (v.). Epstein died after the close of the first season, and was replaced by Aurelio Giorni; Gardner was succeeded by Elias Breeskin and William Kroll, the latter being the violinist at present.

The Elshuco Trio gives an annual series of subscription concerts in New York City, and also makes extensive annual tours. In 1924–25 it gave a Brahms cycle of eight concerts, covering the entire twenty-four ensemble works of that composer. This was followed in the season of 1925–26 by a Schubert cycle of six concerts, comprising fourteen chamber compositions for various combinations of instruments, as well as two lengthy groups of the finest of the Lieder. The word Elshuco is a compound taken from the name of Mrs. Elizabeth Shurtleff Coolidge.

[1] Names of performers are given in the following order: piano, violin, 'cello.

HILGER TRIO. The Hilger Sisters were born in Czecho-Slovakia, and formed their Trio upon the advice of Prof. Ottakar Ševčík, while Maria, the violinist and eldest of the sisters, was studying with him in 1914. All three are graduates of the Imperial Conservatorium of Vienna, Elsa taking the 'cello and Greta the piano part in the Trio.

Their first concerts were given in Vienna in 1916. Other European engagements followed, and an American tour in 1921. They remained in America until 1926, when they toured Europe again, giving over one hundred concerts, returning to America for another tour in 1927.

NEW YORK TRIO. This Trio was organized in 1919, with a personnel that consisted of Clarence Adler, Scipione Guidi, and Cornelius Van Vliet. Guidi was with the Trio for four seasons, when his place was taken by Louis Edlin, former concert-master of the Cleveland Symphony Orchestra.

They make about twenty-five appearances in New York each season, in addition to tours in the United States and Canada, and have played at the Berkshire Festival, sponsored by Mrs. Coolidge. Each summer the organization appears at 'Ka-ren-i-o-ke', Clarence Adler's summer music camp at Lake Placid. The Trio has given first performances of many important works.

NORFLEET TRIO. Composed of two sisters and a brother: Helen, Catherine, and Leeper Norfleet. The Trio made its New York début at Æolian Hall, Jan. 22, 1923, followed by a trans-continental tour which included an appearance at the White House. They are the compilers of two volumes of trios published by Carl Fischer. Helen Norfleet is the composer of *Eight Little Trios* for young ensemble players, editor of the Chamber Music Department of *The Violinist* magazine, and author of the current official study course of the Junior Dept. of the National Federation of Music Clubs. The Trio has appeared in matinées for young people organized by the National Federation of Music Clubs. The 'Norfleet Trio Cup' is a silver trophy offered by the Trio for the best amateur ensemble in every state which conducts a chamber music contest. The Norfleet Trio was the first to record piano parts of trios for a reproducing piano. The Norfleets also direct a summer chamber music camp in the Ozark Mountains, where students and teachers are trained in ensemble playing.

[The exigences of space alone prevent a more detailed account of the manifold activities of the Norfleet Trio. EDITOR.]

SITTIG TRIO. Frederick V. Sittig, Margaret Sittig, Edgar H. Sittig (jr.)—father, daughter, and son. The Trio was organized and played its first concerts while the elder Sittig was a member of the piano faculty of the Eichelberg Conservatorium in Berlin. A number of appearances was made abroad, and concert work was continued after the family's return to America upon the outbreak of war in 1914.

TOLLEFSEN TRIO. Augusta Schnabel, Carl Tollefsen, and Paul Kefer organized in 1904 a Trio first known as the Schnabel Trio. It continued under this name until 1907, when the marriage of Miss Schnabel to Carl Tollefsen induced a change of name to the Tollefsen Trio. Paul Kefer has been succeeded by several other artists.

This Trio is one of the few permanent organizations that have been self-supporting, and has played in almost every state in the Union. The first performances of new works given by these enterprising artists are too numerous to mention.

(*c*) MISCELLANEOUS.

BARRÈRE ENSEMBLE OF WOOD INSTRUMENTS. Georges Barrère (fl.), Pierre Mathieu (oboe), Louis Letellier (bassoon), Fred van Amburgh (clar.), and Santiago Richart (horn).

GRISEZ WOOD-WIND QUARTET. Georges Grisez conceived the idea of this organization after long association with such bodies as the Longy Club of Boston, the New York Chamber Music Society, his own New York Art Chamber Music Society, and others. This experience convinced him that the most representative wood-wind ensemble was a Quartet composed of a flute, a clarinet, an oboe, and a bassoon. Accordingly, the present organization was founded, Oct. 1925, with a personnel consisting of Georges Grisez (clar.), Alexandre Duvoir (oboe), Ernest Liezl (fl.), and Henry Cunnington (bassoon).

Grisez has found that most string quartets are adaptable to the purposes of a wood-wind quartet, and has made a number of transcriptions for his own use.

[MASON AND THOMAS QUINTET. Theodore Thomas, Joseph Mosenthal, George Matzka, Carl Bergmann. Founded by William Mason, 1855, he himself playing the piano. Music soirées were given from 1855–68, when the chamber music of Brahms and Schumann was performed in America for the first time. (From Bachmann's *Encyclopedia of the Violin*.)]

NEW YORK CHAMBER MUSIC SOCIETY. This Society was organized in 1914 by Carolyn Beebe, pianist. The personnel, under the direction of Mme Beebe and Gustave Langenus, was as follows: Carolyn Beebe (pf.), Bonarius Grimson (v.), Herbert Corduan (2nd v.), Samuel Lifschkey (vla.), Jacques Renard (vc.), Ludwig Manoly (double bass), William Kincaid (fl.), Gustave Langenus (clar.), Henri de Busscher (oboe), Ugo Savolini (bassoon), and Josef Franzel (French horn).

The present (1927) personnel is : Carolyn Beebe (pf.), The New York String Quartet

(Ottakar Cadek, Jaroslav Siskovsky, Ludvik Schwab, Bedrich Vaska), Gustave Langenus (clar.), Lamar Stringfield (fl.), Bruno Labate (oboe), Benjamin Kohon (bassoon), Bruno Jaenicke (French horn), Anselm Fortier (double bass).

The Society has given approximately seventy-five first performances of important chamber works at New York concerts, as well as of music written especially for them.

STRINGWOOD ENSEMBLE. Arthur Loesser (pf.), Josef Stopak (1st v.), Samuel Kuskin (2nd v.), Michael Cores (vla.), Abram Borodkin (vc.), Simeon Bellinson (clar.). This ensemble of strings and wood-wind made its New York début in 1925, after 143 rehearsals.

It has won for itself a high place among the concert-giving organizations of America.

TRIO DE LUTECE. Salzedo (harp), Barrère (fl.), Kefer (vc.). Has made tours of the U.S. with trios and solos. A. L. GOLDBERG.

AMES, JOHN CARLOWITZ, 1860–1925, English composer, trained in Germany.

Sonata, pf, v, c sharp mi op. 8 André, 1921.

An excellent, but not very profound musician. He has written many chamber works which are still in manuscript.

Was recipient of a Cobbett prize for an orchestral suite for strings alone.

†AMON, JOHANN ANDREA, 1763–1825, German composer.

Modern republication:

3 quartets, fl, v, vla, vc op. 113 André, 1878.

A long list of original publications is to be found in *Fétis*.

ANALYTICAL PROGRAMMES. The credit for the introduction of annotations into programmes of chamber music belongs to John Ella, founder in 1845 of the Musical Union. They were sent round to his aristocratic patrons a few days before the concert, and, being aesthetically as well as technically interesting, and supplied with illustrations in music type, were universally approved. Arthur Chappell (1859) introduced annotations in his programmes of the 'Pops', and a similar course has been adopted by many concert-givers since. To-day the tendency is for them to fall into disuse, on account of the increased expense involved.

Their use is deprecated by many serious musicians, I do not know why. When well done, they are extremely helpful to the lay listener, especially when provided with musical examples. EDITOR.

ANDERS, ERICH, b. 1883, German composer.

Quartet, str, C op. 47 Simrock, 1925.

A work representative of modern 'linear counterpoint'. It is said, on the title-page, to be in the key of C, but as a matter of fact the key changes almost with each bar. According to Dr. Altmann, Anders is a gifted composer whose knowledge of the technique of stringed instruments leaves a good deal to be desired, but the *Signale* gives him credit for well preserving the balance of tone of the four instruments. *Expertis crede!* EDITOR.

†ANDERSEN, ANTON JÖRGEN, b. 1845, Norwegian violoncellist.

Sonata, pf, vc, d mi (prize work) Musik. Konstförlag. (Stockholm), 1876.

ANDRÉ, JOHANN, 1741–1799, German composer.

Founder of the well-known publishing house at Offenbach. Was himself a composer of chamber music. For works see *Fétis*.

ANDREAE, VOLKMAR, b. 1879, Swiss composer.

Quartet, str, B flat	op. 9	Hug,	1905.
,, ,,	,, 33	,,	1921.
Trio, v, vla, vc, d mi	,, 29	,,	1919.
,, pf, v, vc, f mi	,, 1	Schott,	1901.
,, pf, v, vc, E flat	,, 14	,,	1908.
Sonata, pf, v, D	,, 4	,,	1903.

Andreae plays an active and influential part in Swiss musical life. His trio, op. 1, at the time it was written, was regarded as revealing a personality whose modern leanings were balanced by clear judgement. It is a work of youthful sincerity, and not without romantic charm. Shortly after the trio appeared his violin sonata, which was much played in Switzerland and Germany, and a second trio in E flat, confirmed the favourable opinion formed of the composer. Of his two string quartets, the second, a recent work, is representative of Andreae's position in contemporary music, which is, so to speak, on the cross-benches, as a Conservative too liberal-minded to sit with his party. It is interesting to note that some Swiss musicians profess to trace in him the elements of a national movement. For instance, Jaques-Dalcroze writes:

> 'La musique d'Andreae, concentrée, mais énergique et ardente, est de caractère nettement suisse; après l'avoir entendue je ne crois pas qu'on puisse nier la possibilité chez nous d'une musique nationale, c'est-à-dire caractéristique de nos tempéraments.'

The string trio is a bright, melodious work, to be recommended to amateurs. It includes a short but charming allegretto accompanied by the 'cello, pizzicato, and a finale in the nature of a folk-dance. EDWIN EVANS.

†ANDRÉE, ELFRIDA, b. 1844, Swedish composer.

	Composed.	
Quintet, pf, str, e mi	1865	Musik. Konstförlag. (Stockholm).
Trio, pf, v, vc, g mi	1884	Musik. Konstförlag. (Stockholm), 1887.

ANDRICO, Michel Jean Georges, b. 1894, Roumanian composer, professor of chamber music at the Royal Conservatorium, Bucarest.

Four novelettes, pf, 2 v, vla, vc Hamelle, 1928.

Andrico was awarded the National Prize for composition in 1924. The above is his only published chamber work, but MS. works include a sextet and quartet for strings.

The novelettes consist of four short movements, the first, a lively allegretto in G major, a feature of which is the frequent use of the sharp fourth; this is followed by a lento, in B minor, in which the strings are mainly unaccompanied. The piano takes but little part, too, in the following andante (A major). The fourth movement (vivo, G major) is built on a variant of the subject of the first, and is a very lively piece. The piano here is kept busy throughout, but the writing is always very light, and it takes its part as one of five instruments; most of it, indeed, consists of rapid semiquaver passages in unison for the two hands.

M. Drake-Brockman.

ANGELET, Charles François, 1797–1832, Belgian composer.

Trio, pf, v, vc op. 3 Leduc.

Well spoken of by *Fétis*.

† ANSORGE, Conrad, b. 1862, Silesian pianist.

1st quartet, str, A flat op. 13 Dreililien, 1904.
2nd quartet, str, A „ 20 Hofmeister, 1911.
Sonata, pf, vc, d mi „ 24 Simrock, 1909.

The quartet, op. 13, is known in Teutonic musical circles as the ***Vigilien*** quartet, so called because it grows out of the motifs of Ansorge's vocal setting of three songs by Stanislaus Przybiszevski entitled *Vigils*, both music and words being full of the sad thoughts which haunt the watches of the night. The quartet is somewhat recondite in character, and inclines towards fugal form, but there is no lack of passionate feeling. The second quartet is conceived in a more amiable vein. At a meeting of the *Ansorge-Verein* in Vienna, the two quartets were performed in 1905 by the Holländische Quartett, but they have not yet been heard in London. A score of op. 13 may be seen at Chester's library.

Editor.

† ANTHIOME, Eugène Jean-Baptiste, b. 1836, French composer.

Trio, pf, v, vc, E flat Fromont.
2nd trio, pf, v, vc, F „ 1907.

Winner of the prize for composition given by the 'Institut', 1861.

ANTHOLOGY. An anthology of great interest to players of chamber music is the collection of difficult passages for the violin selected from the literature of the instrument by Ossip Schnirlin, published by Schott & Co., London, and entitled *Der neue Weg* (The New Way). It is planned to appear in five parts, of which two are already in print. No. 1 contains 172 passages extracted from violin concertos and chamber works, and no. 2, 112 passages selected from chamber compositions only (without piano). The as yet unpublished parts are announced to deal with chamber works with piano, and to include passages written for second violin and viola in various ensemble works.

There are subdivisions. No. 1 contains fifteen sections, each illustrating a particular technical difficulty, such as staccato, spiccato, double stops, trills, &c. No. 2, which is exclusively devoted to chamber music, is divided into seven sections devoted to the various combinations familiar to players of ensemble music, duos, trios, quartets, quintets, septets, and octets, the whole arranged in chronological order.

This is Mr. Schnirlin's scheme, and subject to certain reservations which an appendix can easily put right, it is admirably carried out. Every difficult passage included justifies itself, but of the passages omitted a few words need to be said. In the first part there are extracts from about forty concertos, but Elgar's concerto, incomparably the greatest since Brahms, is not included. It has been approved and played by Kreisler, Ysaÿe, Heifetz, Albert Sammons, and many other artists of high rank, and in these days when art is recognized by right-thinking musicians as international, it is unlikely that Mr. Schnirlin should have allowed bias of any kind to influence him. On the contrary, his book proves him to be a sincere worker in the cause of art, and I feel convinced that the appendix which inevitably follows in the wake of works of this kind will include passages from Elgar's concerto, a work which contains new problems of technique (as might be expected from one who has included in his many activities that of professor of the violin, and has himself published two important books of studies). Passages of the greatest interest to students are to be found in the Elgar concerto. Extracts from Glazounov's *Novelletten*, op. 15, appear, but there are passages of greater difficulty in his quartets, opp. 64 and 70, especially in the former, which I have myself had the privilege of playing in private, under the leadership of Heifetz and Zimbalist. Both those great artists considered the scherzo to be as interesting technically as it is brilliantly effective.

For Part I, I suggest two further sections: 'Enharmonics' and 'Metrical Changes'. Many instances of difficult enharmonic writing, useful as preparatory studies in intonation, are to be found in chamber music; to these an alternative part could be added in a corresponding simpler key in the stave below. (The publishers have done this in the slow movement of Dvořák's E flat string quintet.) There are enharmonic passages in Borodin's second quartet and Dohnányi's violin sonata which lend themselves to similar treatment. As to metrical changes, the finales to Ravel's quartet and to Dohnányi's D flat quartet suggest themselves, but Mr. Schnirlin himself will no doubt see to it that many additions are made when (and if) the appendix makes its appearance.

I compiled and published in 1910 a 'new way' on a very small scale, entitled *Passage Studies for the violin selected from the master works of chamber music with letterpress in three languages*. Part I was devoted to Haydn, Mozart, and Beethoven, forty studies in all, the reception by the press being favourable. Herr Andreas Moser, Joachim's collaborator in his violin *Method*, expressed the opinion that it would be a very handy book for chamber music players on tour to carry round in their travelling bags for practice purposes en route. I showed it also to Ševčík when he visited London, and he expressed approval. But—it did not sell, and I did not think it worth while to publish another series which I had compiled from the chamber works of divers composers. Mr. Schnirlin has followed up and elaborated the idea in a way I cannot pretend to have done, and he has my cordial good wishes for his success.

My *Passage Studies* were originally published by Stainer & Bell, but are now in the hands of Augener & Co., Ltd. EDITOR.

ANTOINE, GEORGES, 1892–1918, Belgian composer.

Quartet, pf, str, d mi	op. 6	Senart, 1916.	
Sonata, pf, v	„ 3	„ 1915.	

†ANZOLETTI, MARCO, b. 1866, Italian violinist.

Sonata, pf, v, c mi B. & H., 1896.

This composer writes well for his instrument.

APPLAUSE. An innovation is to be observed of late in our concert-rooms. Applause is deferred till the final bar of each sonata or quartet is reached; a proceeding in favour of which something is to be said. That it is done in a reverent spirit, none but a cynic can doubt. The contemplative mood of the devout listener and his sense of unity, as well as of the contrasts which exist between the movements, may be disturbed by applause; but, on the other hand, silence has a chilling effect upon both performer and listeners. It is an unnatural inhibition against a natural and generous impulse, and it encourages the racial reserve with which British audiences are only too plentifully endowed. Furthermore, the movements of a sonata are not seldom of unequal merit, and I am one of the many who hope that the public will reassert its right to applaud after each one, and even to re-demand a favourite number when deeply moved.

Incidentally, Pablo Casals shares this opinion. EDITOR.

APPONYI, COUNT, is said to have been the first to induce Beethoven to write string quartets. May the benison of all good chamber musicians attend his memory! EDITOR.

ARACIEL, ESTEBAN, Spanish composer, lived and worked in Milan, 1780.

Due quintetti per serenata, 2 v, 2 vla, vc	Ricordi.
Tre terzetti ad uso di serenata, v, vla, guitar	„

ARENSKY, ANTON, 1861–1906, Russian composer.

Quartet, str, G	op. 11	Jurgenson,	1889.
„ v, vla, 2 vc, a mi	„ 35	„	1894.
Quintet, pf, 2 v, vla, vc, D	„ 51	„	1900.
1st trio, pf, v, vc, d mi	„ 32 Bosworth	„	1894.
2nd trio, pf, v, vc, f mi	„ 73	„	1905.

Op. 35 is published also as an ordinary string quartet, op. 35a (Jurgenson).

Arensky studied under Karl Zikke at the Russian School in Petrograd, and under Johansen and Rimsky-Korsakov at the Petrograd Conservatorium. Later, he became a professor at the Moscow Conservatorium. From 1895–1901 he was director of the court chapel at Petrograd. He occupies a great place in the history of Russian music—far greater, indeed, than most people are aware, and the full significance of his contribution is not yet generally realized.

All Arensky's chamber music bears the impress of Tchaikovsky's influence, and is altogether free from the almost mechanical uniformity which characterizes the music of second-rate members of the so-called new Russian school, for Arensky, although belonging to this school by virtue of his period and education, carefully guarded himself against certain influences which were repellent to him, and especially avoided following the stereotyped tenets and practices that were in honour among many of his colleagues. His instinct and talent guided him surely, even if his inspiration never raised him to a level equal to that reached by the greater Russian masters.

In his quartets, Arensky avails himself of his instrumental resources far more sparingly and, so to speak, more diffidently than in the combinations with a piano, the latter being both more effective in sonority and more interesting from the point of view of working-out. These quartets are, however, unimpeachable as regards style.

Both quartets, and especially the first (Arensky's earliest chamber work), are somewhat limited in scope, and almost to be described as miniatures. The list comprises a diminutive slow movement, an unpretentious, altogether delightful minuet, and a finale written in the form of variations on a short and charming little motif taken from a Russian song. For all its merits, it is hardly to be described as a work in the grand style, to which the second quartet (inscribed to the memory of Tchaikovsky) aspires.

THE SECOND QUARTET. Tchaikovsky was the first Russian to introduce the practice of 'In Memoriam' quartets, which was followed not only by Arensky, but by Rachmaninov, and which, naturally enough, leads to the introduction of orthodox funeral chants in the music. This is done by Arensky in the first and the last movements of this quartet. In the last movement he also introduces the well-known theme of the folk-song *Slava!* (Glory!) used by Beethoven in one of his quartets, op. 59, and by many Russians in works of various descriptions. The variations in the second movement, on a theme taken from one of Tchaikovsky's *Children's Songs*, have rendered this quartet famous. They have been arranged for string orchestra, and are performed thus far more often than in their original form.

THE FIRST TRIO (inscribed to the memory of Karl Davidov) is better known than the second—indeed, most dictionaries do not mention the latter at all. The first subject of its finale foreshadows Rachmaninov's style and manner, and the coda contains a beautiful and most effective reminiscence of the second subject of Arensky's own *Elegy*.

THE SECOND TRIO is more characteristic of Arensky's maturity. But one feels that in the first movement there is a breath from the spirit of Schumann.

Lyrically, the second movement, *Romance*, is most characteristic of Arensky; it springs from the same origin as Schumann's piano *Romances*. The third movement is a scherzo, whose trio comes very near, in speed and style, to a waltz tune. Russian composers have often resorted to the use of idealized forms of waltz tunes in their music. Other cases in point occur in the finale of this trio, in which the waltz rhythm appears in the third variation (grotesque) and in the fifth (lyrical again). Let it be remembered, too, that the trio of the scherzo of op. 32 is also very near being a waltz.

THE QUINTET is a masterpiece of Arensky's maturity, for Arensky, a miniaturist by disposition, was far more at ease in chamber than in orchestral music—in which medium he did not always achieve adequate expression of his interesting and valuable ideas.

The quintet consists of the four usual movements, the first of which is in regular sonata form. Its first subject is a trifle formal; the second, less definite in contour and build, is most beautiful. The second movement consists of variations on the theme of the French folk-song *Sur le Pont d'Avignon*; and among these variations, the tempo di valse is particularly noteworthy for its shifting harmonies, which in a way seem to herald the harmonies of Scriabin (e.g. in the second prelude of op. 11). The scherzo is in sonata form, with two trios which mark the division between the main sections. The finale is a very free double fugue, whose subjects are the introductory phrase of the first movement and the theme of the second movement, the main subject of the first movement being introduced in the coda. This quintet is most effective, affords enjoyable playing, and comes off well in performance.

V. M. BELAIEV.

[If we exclude the accepted masterpieces, the first Arensky trio has been in its time the most popular of all works of the kind. Yet in recent days its tendencies have led to strictures from the anti-romantics. As an amateur, I can only say that I wish there were a prospect of more trios of the same type. It must be admitted that there are works which are unsuitable for one's musical daily bread, and this is one of them. Only the greater and, to some extent, sterner stuff of the masters can stand the strain of constant repetition, but music by such composers as Arensky, at chosen moments, will always prove attractive to those who think that sensuous beauty has its place in art. Features of his compositions are the brevity of his finales and the extreme brilliancy of his scherzos. That contained in the piano quintet is one of the brightest movements in the chamber music repertory. It sparkles like diamonds in the sun.

Arensky did well to rearrange the quartet, op. 35, for the usual setting. The original form, with two 'cellos, is unpractical, and, it seems to me, less effective. EDITOR.]

ARNE, DR. THOMAS AUGUSTINE, 1710–1778, famous English composer.

Modern republication:

Trio-sonata, pf, 2 v, vc, (ad lib.), e mi	op. 7 (no. 3)	Novello, 1907.

(A. Moffat, *Old Eng. V.-music.*)

Original publications, from *Riemann*:

Seven trio-sonatas, 2 v, fig.-bass	1750.

There is marked purity of style in Arne's string writing.

ARPEGGIO. When trying over new chamber music, I have found the presence of an accompaniment of broken chords or arpeggios in the piano part a frequent subject for unfavourable comment, nor is it a sign of fertility of invention, but it must not be forgotten that composers for the piano, when writing for strings, find arpeggios a better tonal contrast than chords sounded simultaneously, which bring into relief the percussiveness or shortness of sound which is a defect of the instrument. One can recall instances where arpeggios seem indicated so absolutely as to be almost inevitable. Of course, the more intellectual composer invents ornamentations in the way of passing notes—hence Chopin's superiority to Mendelssohn as a writer for the piano.

Arpeggios for string instruments are sparingly used in chamber music (magnificently by Beethoven in the ***Harp*** quartet). Rubinstein is an instance of a composer who uses them to excess. They belong rather to the technique of the composer for solo violin, who, before all, seeks brilliancy of effect. Played on the 'cello they are less attractive. EDITOR.

ARPEGGIONE. An obsolete instrument of guitar shape about the size of a small 'cello, and played with a bow. There were six strings and a fretted fingerboard. Invented in 1823. An instruction book was written the following year by Vinc. Schuster, for whom Franz Schubert wrote a sonata of considerable length, arranged in 1871 for 'cello and piano, and published by Doblinger, who have since (1928) issued arrangements for violin and viola as well. Another edition was issued in 1886 (edited by J. Mulder). It is in the nature of a concerto, and exhibits great affinity to Mozart.

E. W. ORGAN.

ARRANGEMENTS. These may be—the purist tells us they are—artistically of little worth, but their utilitarian value is beyond question. A few only of the thousands existing are catalogued in this book; but a tribute may well be paid to the vast army of nameless scribes who have done what is most unkindly called 'hack-work' for the benefit of performers who wish to enjoy in their own homes adaptations of works originally intended for the public platform.

It is interesting to note in this connexion that in England there is a vogue for two-hand piano arrangements, whilst on the Continent four hands are preferred. Why this should be I cannot say.

How valuable arrangements may be, if made by the composers themselves, is illustrated by a little experience of my own. When Brahms's clarinet quintet was first issued in 1892 by Simrock, a copy of it was sent to a friend of mine, Captain A. S. Beaumont, an ardent lover of chamber music, who at once organized a performance of it at his house in Norwood, engaging Clinton as clarinet and Harold Bauer (at that time a violinist and now, as everybody knows, a world-famous pianist) as first violin. Clinton, through illness, failed to put in an appearance, and Bauer, delegating the violin part to me, took the clarinet part on the viola (as arranged by Brahms himself). Thanks to his wonderful sight-reading, the performance went astonishingly well, and we all trooped, a few evenings later, to St. James's Hall, to hear the work in its original form played by Mühlfeld and the Joachim Quartet. It may be added that the clarinet quintet has also been arranged for violin and piano, and for clarinet and piano, in each case with the approval of the composer.

Another striking instance is also supplied by Brahms in his arrangement of the immortal horn trio. Horn players do not grow on every bush, so he wrote an alternative arrangement for either viola or 'cello. The authentic tone-colour is missing, but the strings have their own beauty, and the work is not one of the least prized in the trio repertory.

It is not necessary to multiply instances of the usefulness of arrangements, but I cannot resist mentioning the adaptation of Beethoven's septet as a string quintet, as it has often stood me in good stead. It is delightful to play, with (naturally) a very full part for all instruments concerned, and is, besides, of immense service to string players for rehearsal purposes when a performance of the septet is contemplated. Modern writers who score so often for instruments rarely available in the home circle, such as harp, oboe, bassoon, &c., will have to follow the adapter's example if they wish their compositions to become widely known.

The viola-player has a repertory so restricted that he cannot possibly dispense with arrangements. I shall not easily forget a performance I once heard of J. B. McEwen's introspective violin sonata in F minor, arranged and played by that great artist, Lionel Tertis, on the viola. The tone-colour of the instrument formed just the right background to the composer's musings. A more doubtful enterprise is that of Walter Damrosch, who has made an arrangement of the Kreutzer sonata, in which a small orchestra is used, notably in the tutti, to reinforce the violin solo and afford a greater contrast when that instrument enters with an important theme. Damrosch is, as every one knows, an accomplished musician, but here his judgement is, to my mind, at fault. If the piano lid is closed, a virile violinist can hold his own, even in the stormy first movement of the Kreutzer sonata, without the assistance of an orchestra. Those who lack tonal force should leave this mighty work severely alone.

Another error of judgement, and a more serious one, is the recent publication of an arrangement of Beethoven's *Cavatina* from the quartet, op. 130, as a solo for violin with piano accompaniment. In his book on the last quartets of Beethoven, the late Joseph de Marliave writes:

> 'Il a composé la Cavatine du quatuor en si bémol dans les larmes de la douleur, jamais encore sa musique n'avait atteint une pareille expression, et même le seul souvenir de ce morceau lui faisait venir les larmes aux yeux.'

When emotions so poignant are expressed, the composer's original setting is alone endurable, besides which, it is technically unsound to assign the throb of those moving triplets in the episode marked 'beklemmt' (oppressed) to a percussion instrument.

Reverting once more to Brahms, it comes to some as a shock to hear that he once played an arrangement of the finale of the third Rasoumovsky quartet at a concert as an encore piece; that he arranged Bach's *Chaconne* for the left hand at the piano; and that he gave to Henschel licence to alter the notes of his songs to suit his voice; but it only serves as a reminder that one of the greatest chamber music composers of his age never ranged himself on the side of the pedants. EDITOR.

(*v.* TRANSCRIPTIONS by W. Altmann.)

†ARRIAGA Y BALZOLA, J. C. D', 1806–1825, Spanish violinist and composer, pupil of Baillot and Fétis.

Three quartets, str, d mi, A, E flat	Dotesio (Bilbao), 1910.

These quartets were written at the age of 16. The influence of his contemporaries, especially of Haydn, is strongly felt in them, as might be expected in a youthful effort; but they were sufficiently promising to win the approval of his master, Fétis, who speaks of their elegance and purity of style. Musical Spain probably lost much by his premature death. The quartets were originally published by Ph. Petit, of Paris, in 1824. EDITOR.

†ARTCIBOUCHEV, NICOLAI VASSILIEVITCH, b. 1858, Russian composer, and contributor to *Les Vendredis*.

ARTÔT, J. D. M., 1803–1887, French horn-player.

12 quartets, 4 horns	Schott (Brussels), 1875.
12 quartets, 4 horns (or cornets-à-pistons)	,, ,,
12 trios, 3 horns (or cornets-à-pistons)	,, ,,

ASANTCHEVSKI, MICHAEL PAVLOVITCH VON, *c.* 1838–1881, Russian composer, pupil of Liszt.

Quartet, str, a mi	op. 3	C. F. Schmidt, 1863.
Trio, pf, v, vc, f sharp mi	,, 10	Kistner, 1866.
Sonata, pf, vc, b mi	,, 2	C. F. Schmidt, 1863.

Asantchevski studied music in Germany, and in 1870 was appointed director of the Petrograd Conservatorium. His works are praised by *Riemann*.

†ASHTON, ALGERNON BENNET LANGTON, b. 1859, English composer.

Quintet, pf, 2 v, vla, vc, C	op. 25	Peters, 1886.
Quintet, pf, 2 v, vla, vc, e mi	,, 100	Hofbauer, 1896.
Quartet, pf, v, vla, vc, f sharp mi	,, 34	Simrock, 1887.
Quartet, pf, v, vla, vc, c mi	op. 90	Hofbauer, 1896.
Trio, pf, v, vc, E flat	,, 77	R. & E., 1894.
Trio, pf, v, vc, A	,, 88	Hofbauer, 1895.
,, ,, ,, ,, b mi	,, 123	,, 1897.
Sonata, pf, v, D	,, 3	B. & H., 1881.
,, ,, ,, E	,, 38	Simrock, 1889.
,, ,, ,, c mi	,, 86	Hofbauer, 1888.
Sonata, ,, ,, A	,, 99	Simrock, 1889.
,, pf, vla, a mi	,, 44	Simrock, 1891.
Sonata, pf, vc, F	,, 6	Siegel, 1883.
,, ,, ,, G	,, 75	Simrock, 1893.
,, ,, ,, a mi	,, 115	Hofbauer, 1899.
Sonata, ,, ,, B flat	,, 128	,, 1899.

Ashton obtained his early training at Leipzig, proceeding later to Frankfort, where he studied under Raff. With something like 150 published works to his credit, he ranks as one of the most industrious composers of his generation.

It is not easy to explain the neglect which has befallen much of Algernon Ashton's chamber music. It may be that the composer's invention is too often cramped by the formalism of the period. Quite frequently, however, in the midst of his affected intricacies, there appears writing of such fine quality as to compel one's admiration. The violin sonata in E, op. 38, is a case in point. The very fact that most of this sonata attains so high a level provides but a further factor of difficulty in dealing with the bulk of his work. Why, for instance, should a composer possessing such exceptional technical equipment have gone on to write a companion work like the violin sonata, op. 86? For this sonata is totally lacking in the warmth and geniality which distinguished the earlier work. Such deficiencies are often partly attributable to the uncompromising and angular cast of the material, on which, even by the most prodigious exercise of ingenuity, he seems incapable of making any deep impression. A favourite device of his consists in breaking away from the ordinary rules of key-relationship in the recapitulation of a sonata movement, putting his first subject into the subdominant instead of the tonic, and thus reducing the whole section to a literal transposition of the exposition. The result, however, is frequently quite happy. Ashton is not a daring innovator, and he has certain limitations—reservations which, it may be conceded, might apply equally well to other and more widely acknowledged composers. But at the outset of his career, when British composers of artistic outlook were far fewer than now, he proclaimed himself the possessor of lofty ideals, even though a greater degree of clarity would be welcome in their presentation.

ADOLPH MANN.

ASIOLI, Bonifazio, 1769–1832, Italian composer.

Sonata, pf, vc, C — Simrock, 1868.

Played at the 'Pops', November 1869. *Fétis* mentions further compositions by Asioli.

†ASPLMAYR, Franz, 1721–1786, Viennese composer.

Modern republications:

Quartet (*Quatuor concertant*), str	op. 2, no. 2	(H. Riemann Collegium Mus. 40). B. & H., 1907.
Quartet, pf, 2 v, vc	op. 5, no. 1	(H. Riemann Collegium Mus. 39). B. & H., 1904.

For original publications *v. Fétis.*

Asplmayr was one of the first Viennese composers to follow the lead of the Mannheim school in chamber composition. The *Quatuor concertant* is a work of extreme simplicity, scored without cembalo. The opening movement is elementary, but its minuet (in D) is more striking, with a trio in the minor; the andante, again, is very simple, and the finale fresh and humorous.

ASSMAYR, Ignaz, 1790–1862, Viennese composer, friend of Schubert.

Quartet, str, E flat,	op. 60	Haslinger,	1854.
,, ,, D	,, 61	,,	1859.
,, ,, F	,, 63	,,	1860.

Grove says his music is 'correct and fluent, but wanting in invention and force'.

ASTORGA, Dom Oliver, eighteenth-century composer.

Modern republication:

Trio, 2 v, vc, C — Senart, 1922.

Jean Oliver Astorga was a Spanish composer, whose works were published at London. They include six trio sonatas, 2 fl (or v), bass.

For original publications *v. Riemann* and *Grove*.

†ATHERTON, Percy Lee, b. 1871, American composer.

Suite, pf, v, C — op. 4 — Schlesinger, 1897.

ATONALITY and POLYTONALITY.

N.B. In the articles dealing with composers who have adopted the methods here described will be found many examples quoted from their chamber-works. It has therefore not been considered necessary to draw the illustrations to this essay from the same source, especially as some suggested themselves that at once were clearer and required less space.

I. Introduction

In the early 'eighties the late Sir Hubert Parry, as a contributor to *Grove's Dictionary*, began his article on 'Tonality' by describing it as 'the element of key'. Clearly, then, atonality is the state of music from which this element of key is absent, and polytonality is the simultaneous employment of more than one key. He then proceeds to say of this element that in modern music it is of the very greatest importance; and his article was reprinted integrally in the 1910 edition. Even then the assertion was not unchallenged, for Schönberg's three pianoforte pieces and five orchestral pieces date from 1909. To-day it reads strangely, for the music which dispenses with tonality is one of many varieties of contemporary music to which, indiscriminately, the label 'modern' is popularly affixed. The article then proceeds to explain this importance of tonality: 'Upon the clearness of its definition the existence of instrumental music in harmonic forms of the Sonata order depends'. It should be noted that by qualifying such forms as 'harmonic' he tacitly admitted the possibility of forms other than harmonic arising in the future, just as they had unquestionably existed in the past. Parry was a man of deep convictions, but not a pedant. He proceeds:

'Chords which are derived from such roots as dominant, subdominant, and tonic define the tonality most obviously and certainly; and popular dance-tunes, of all times, have been generally based upon successions of such harmonies. In works which are developed upon a larger scale a much greater variety of chords is used, and even chords belonging to closely related keys are commonly interlaced without producing obscurity, or weakening the structural outlines of the work.'

Tonality is therefore a means of establishing both internal coherence and external cohesion, of making a page of music consistent in itself, and of so relating it to the pages before and after it as to endow the whole with an aspect of unity. This is established by means of root-functions, among which those of the tonic, dominant, and subdominant are so important that, even where other roots are transiently employed, it is generally possible to ascribe the entire passage in which they occur to one of these, and consider it as written over an imaginary pedal-note. They also indicate the nearest related tonalities, which are the simplest basis of connected forms in music. It is therefore not uncommon to find the most clearly defined tonality described as 'three-functional'.

These being the purposes of tonality, there are obviously two ways of envisaging its principles, for they are either the only means of achieving those aims, and therefore indispensable, or other means are conceivable, and their application is therefore optional. They may be regarded as an integral constituent in the laborious building up, through the centuries, of a consistent musical aesthetic. Or they may be regarded as offering an adventitious and temporary support to an art of music during its evolution towards a state in which it could afford to dispense with such aids—for tonality, like the so-called 'rules' of musical procedure, is an aid, not a hindrance. In all things it is easier to proceed by law than by unfettered judgement. Every circumscription of free choice helps the artist by eliminating a large proportion of the alternatives which offer themselves to him. Given the true artistic conscience, there is no more burdensome gift than freedom. Critics of modern music sometimes affirm that it is easy to write because nothing is forbidden. For those who possess the artistic conscience that is what constitutes its chief difficulty.

The divergence between the two views indicated above is not, as might be supposed, a conflict of conservatives and progressives. The true conservative in music regards the limits of tonality as having been reached, if not exceeded, and he is resentful of being shown further possibilities of extension. It is a divergence between different notions of progress, with protagonists equally 'advanced' on both sides. Nor is the difference between them as great in practice as it is in theory, for the field of tonality, constantly extended, appears to us as stretching almost to the horizon, so difficult is it for us to conceive of further extension. Therefore, except to the analyst, the present avenues of sound offer almost the same aspect, whether considered tonally or atonally. Even as far back as the prelude to *Tristan* the frontiers of tonality had become indistinct. This circumstance gives support to the faith of those who regard the reign of tonality as terminable, for frontiers which have become practically imperceptible seem destined in time to disappear altogether.

The emancipation of musical forms from dependence upon tonal functions is perhaps a more radical process. The antithesis between formal principles related respectively to the symmetry of architecture, and the asymmetry of painting, has not yet reached the point where those adhering to the latter can claim to have furnished a completely satisfying alternative, such as the painter's quantities, to the tonal functions on which symmetry, from the sixteenth century onwards, has been based. The most they can urge is that the option of endowing any note in the chromatic scale, incidentally or continuously, with the attributes of a dominant offers an unprecedented range of possibilities, but those attributes themselves are derived from the principles of tonality, and the tone-painter is still under reluctantly acknowledged obligations to the tone-architect. Where these tonal principles cease to find practical application there is generally a tendency to solve formal problems by dynamic means, by contrasts of intensity or of timbre, and it may be that some formal principles may eventually emerge from successful practice, but they are at present incapable of definition, failing which, form thus outlined remains a matter of taste upon which one may not adjudicate. The present discussion is therefore restricted to the texture, harmonic or contrapuntal, of a musical composition.

In that dual aspect of texture, whether described as harmonic or contrapuntal, vertical or horizontal, or by any other pair of complementary terms, lies the pattern of musical development; and nearly all controversy, whether critical or technical, arises from conflicting tendencies to ascribe paramount authority to one or the other, counterpoint being subjugated to harmony, and made dependent upon chord-formation, or harmony being subjugated to counterpoint, and made dependent upon a strict movement of parts. All recent developments show an undercurrent of revolt against either tendency or both. The impressionistic use of unresolved dissonances, the consecutive use of common chords and other parallel formations, the juxtaposition of unrelated chords, show a complete harmonic disregard of the laws governing the progression of parts, and the 'linear' counterpoint which finds so many advocates at present in Central Europe represents the corresponding determination to emancipate the horizontal line from the last bonds of chordal discipline. These two tendencies, flowing in opposite directions, have each their bearing upon the problem of tonality, and the new devices of atonality and polytonality are brought indiscriminately to the service of both, but the incentives are fundamentally different, and should not be confused, if their results are to be correctly understood.

Having accepted the extension and amplification of tonality to its remotest boundaries, music was for many decades—at least since *Tristan*, and probably longer—confronted with the problem of ultra-tonality, the beyond of tonality. This it proceeded to meet in two different ways, neither of them new, but tardy developments of principles latent in the music of the past. The first is the merging of all tonalities into one, which corresponds to the negation of tonality, or atonality. The second is the simultaneous use of two or more tonalities, or polytonality. If the principles of tonality were interpreted in the latter alternative with the same latitude as in the former, the practical effect would be identical with that of atonality, for the simultaneous tonalities would tend to merge upon their joint chromatic horizons. But the present practice in polytonality is to write in each of the superimposed keys with a diatonic strictness which, but for their conflict, would be regarded as reactionary by the more liberal traditionalists. Superficially considered, polytonality is far more conservative than atonality, and should logically demand first consideration. But it is precisely because it employs new procedures, the development of which is necessarily tentative, that polytonality presents this misleading appearance. At the present stage, to employ polytonality with the chromatic freedom of atonality would be to destroy its character from the outset, before its possibilities had been explored. If a conflict of two keys is to be accessible to our perception, each must be very sharply defined. A chromatic use of either would cause the other to prevail. A chromatic use of both would blend them beyond the possibility of aural extrication. There is, further, between the two principles the same opposition as between harmony and counterpoint. Harmony blends sounds. Counterpoint presents them as mutually independent. Atonality blends tonalities. Polytonality presents them as mutually independent.

Some theorists have construed this opposition in the sense that there is no such thing as atonality, that which is so termed being merely a process of modulation so rapid that each successive chord may be in a different key. In other words, atonality presents a number of tonalities consecutively, whereas polytonality presents them simultaneously, so that we are back again at the distinction between the horizontal and the vertical, their positions being, however, reversed. This does not vitiate the argument, for, as we have seen above, both are devices intended to stop a contrary process. In one case horizontal or 'linear' methods are adopted to escape from vertical fusion, in the other a vertical superimposition of keys is adopted to preserve horizontal independence. But though these are manifestly the respective 'long-felt wants' to which they owe their present emergence and recognition, their history begins long before the wants which they now purport to fill had begun to be felt at all. Traced to their respective sources, atonality is harmonic and chromatic, being ultimately a development of modulation, and polytonality is contrapuntal and diatonic, having its origin in the perfect canon (at any interval other than the octave) and in the real (not tonal) answer to the subject of a fugue. (A tonal answer is a curtailing of horizontal independence in deference to a single tonality.) But present-day usage applies both mainly—though not exclusively—to the service of contrapuntal polyphony, the one chromatic, the other diatonic.

A curious side-aspect of this distinction is worthy of mention because it affects the international situation in music. For a long time even superficial observers of musical developments have been conscious of a cleavage, originating unobtrusively about 1860, but clearly visible since the beginning of the present century, between the music of Central Europe and that of the Latins and Slavs. Whether the causes be fortuitous or not, it is of interest to note that whereas the Central European tendency has proceeded from the basis of the dominant seventh by means of chromaticism, the other tendency was to exploit the less-used triads of the diatonic scale, which, with or without intention, gave the appearance of reviving the Gregorian and Greek or Byzantine modes. There are, of course, local dissentients. Thus, among the Slavs, Scriabin is a convinced adherent of Tristanesque chromaticism. But then Scriabin has no kinship with the nationalist movement in Russia, and has never been counted a characteristically Russian composer. The typical Slavs, from Moussorgsky to Stravinsky, the typical Latins, from Fauré and Debussy to the young French composers of to-day, have shown what seems almost an atavistic repugnance for chromatic ambiguity, and reacted strongly towards unequivocal tonal clarity, even polytonality being based upon unambiguous, though superimposed, triads. Thus the cleavage is not only ethnic, or as some have even thought, politic. It is aesthetic as well, and reveals itself not only in idiomatic idiosyncrasies but actually in the choice of technical methods. England being musically hybrid, reveals both tendencies in full force, but it is at least interesting to note that those composers reputed to approach nearest to a national idiom are also restoring an Antaeus-like contact with the older tradition of the modes and their diatonic triads. Their affinities are thus across the Channel, and not across the North Sea. It is therefore without surprise that one seeks in vain for any suggestion of atonality in their music, whereas hints of polytonality abound in recent works of both Vaughan Williams and Holst, and the latter has lately written a terzetto for flute, oboe, and viola, each instrument playing in a different key.

II. Atonality

At present very few people appear to have a definite conception of what constitutes atonality. There are at least three different definitions in the field: (1) the negation, deliberate avoidance, or destruction of tonality; (2) the fusion of all tonalities into one, expressed in the twelve-note scale; and (3) a state of constant modulation, the horizontal equivalent of vertical polytonality. Each of these definitions is accurate in respect of some of the manifestations of atonality. None of them is wide enough to cover them all, or narrow enough not to have application to some phenomena which do not come under the heading of atonality. The deliberate avoidance of tonality is obviously based on an implication of its presence. Much music written in the twelve-note scale is nevertheless as redolent of tonality as any diatonic melody. Of the three definitions, the third is probably the best, for it appears to concede the point that, however vague, however undefined the relation of tonality may be that is created by the bringing together of two notes, it is nevertheless existent, and therefore material as accessible to constant and endless variation as any other ingredient of musical composition. But all three definitions are alike in being based upon harmonic conceptions. They ignore two of the strongest incentives to atonality, which are the allied reactions against harmonic fusion of the texture, and against the subjection of the horizontal or melodic line to harmonic rule. These incentives are deep rooted in musical history.

Music began as an art of line. Our present music was born when musicians learned to employ two or more lines simultaneously. But there developed immediately a tendency for these lines to fuse harmonically, and become once more a single line, harmonically coloured. The musicians, having tasted the sweets of polyphony, began to devise methods by which this tendency could be circumvented. There began a contest similar to that of the burglars and safe-makers. Towards the end of the nineteenth century some of the most elaborate scores, with a criss-cross of interwoven parts, sounded in reality homophonous, so complete was the harmonic fusion. Then, in the constant search for devices to maintain the polyphonic effect, musicians discovered that the fusion was indubitably aided and abetted by tonality. The more daring of them therefore essayed to overcome the fusion by offering opposition to tonality, and were rewarded by finding that parts moving in defiance of tonal principles were heard as separate parts, and not as a fusion of parts. That was one strong incentive to atonality.

The other incentive to atonality arose in part from the same cause, harmonic fusion, which had spread even to the melodic line. It would be easy to cite many examples where the alleged theme is nothing more than the uppermost notes of chordal progressions to which it owes its very existence. It was as if the lines of a picture, instead of being based upon draughtsmanship, were the mere outlines of the colour-masses, and the sometimes almost fortuitous lines of colour-fusion. Since the primary factor in music is line, this was putting the cart before the horse. Again, musicians have resorted to heroic remedies, one of which was to give their melodic line a character uncongenial to the harmonic system, into which it refused to be assimilated.

It is mainly from these two incentives that have grown the 'linear' methods which are now so prevalent in Central Europe, possibly because it was there that the harmonic Moloch had claimed the most victims. Clarity and precision are not the virtues most admired there, and the rhythmic sense which functions as the jealous guardian of lucid accentuation (and therefore frequently calls harmony to its aid) was not, congenitally, strong enough in them to preserve them from the gradual spread of a kind of harmonic ambiguity, until the more alert musicians, with Schönberg as their most commanding figure, awoke to the danger which lurked in the rich but flaccid texture which had become the staple product of their confreres.

Technically, atonality is the outcome of chromaticism, which softened the rigours of tonality, and of modulation, which weakened its frontiers. Its pre-history is the history of music, for it stretches far back into the polyphonic era. The false relations to which the Stravinskys of our Tudor period were addicted, which are so prominent in Gesualdo, and of which Casella quotes a significant example from Orazio Vecchi, were so many veiled attacks upon the then impregnable fortress of tonal integrity. The attacks were renewed in force with the advent of chromatic passing notes and appoggiaturas. When the latter began to overlap, the resolution of one being itself another chromatic appoggiatura, the position of the defence became desperate indeed. Long before that it had been persistently weakened by the encroachments of other forms of chromatic alteration, all of which ate into the very substance of tonality. Yet the structure remained. With justice Casella regards *Tristan* as the supreme triumph of classical 'chromaticized diatonism', where, in spite of all the chromatic devices from which it draws its sensual eroticism, allegiance is retained to the major and minor modes, and to the three great functions of tonic, dominant, and subdominant. Even in Scriabin, who represents the next *étape* along this road, these functions are still maintained. Here, however, the multiplying of appoggiaturas has brought its own nemesis, and a state of harmonic liquescence so advanced that the old sheet-anchors are insufficient, and others have to be manufactured in the shape of chords, originally resulting from chromatic alteration, but now pontifically endowed with dominant functions. The expedition had proceeded so far from its tonal base that an advanced camp had to be established before further progress could be attempted. That is the present state of chromaticism, one of the parents of atonality.

On the other side—that of modulation—its ancestry is at least equally ancient. In the following, which is quoted from an article by Philip Heseltine,

Ex. 1. Gesualdo, from 'Tu piangi.' Book VI.

the Prince of Venosa cannot accurately be said to have been a slave to rigid tonality. In any case the line reaches back at least to the moment when the adoption of the tempered scale made flowing modulation possible between non-related keys. Even before that it was a possibility to be considered theoretically, for in the transition between two related keys it is logical to imagine an intervening point at which they neutralize each other, and that point is harmonically atonal, though it may be, and often is, contrapuntally bitonal. But when a neutral chord was interposed in the progression from one tonality to another, atonality came into actual existence, and its expansion was only a matter of time, just as the first sanctioned use of an interrupted cadence opened the door to compositions which are in essence a cadence held up by an interruption which embraces their entire length. In that sense all modulation, and with it atonality, derives ultimately from the dominant seventh and its variants.

The next step towards atonality occurred when the pivotal note or notes of a modulation changed not only their functions, as when the dominant became the new tonic, but their very essence, as when a note approached as A flat was quitted as G sharp by an enharmonic modulation. However imperceptible the passage, there was clearly a moment of time at which it was neither, but a mere degree of the atonal twelve-note scale. In short, every step that facilitated modulation necessarily brought atonality nearer. But of all neutral interpolations and adjuncts, naturally those contributed most which were themselves negations of tonality. The basis of a tonality, to which it owes its recognizable characteristics, is a scale of tones and semitones unevenly distributed, and therefore representing an unequal division of the octave. Hence the most prominent of all neutral devices are those resulting from an equal division of the octave, for they are intrinsically devoid of tonality, and can acquire a precarious hold upon it only from their context. Of such devices there are four: the scale of semitones, or chromatic scale; the scale of whole tones, or hexatonic scale; the chord which results from the halving and quartering of the octave, that is to say, the diminished seventh under all its enharmonic descriptions; and the chord which results from a triple division of the octave, that is to say, the augmented triad.

Because of their contradiction of the diatonic scale, all these devices have a debilitating effect upon tonality, and therefore upon diatonic music, in which they constitute an element of ambiguity. Where clear, direct musical utterance is the aim, they are best used sparingly, as many composers past and present have discovered to their cost.

The disintegrating effect of the chromatic scale scarcely needs description. It was known to musicians even before John Danyel, in 1606, sang

> 'No, let chromatic tunes, harsh without ground,
> Be sullen music for a tuneless heart'

in a composition that is not without its atonal moments. It provides the subjects for numerous fugues and the thematic incentive for countless other compositions which, without departing from the principles of tonality, contrive to create a deceptive appearance of tonal freedom. The following—

Ex. 2. Klengel. Canon II. 17.

is not a representative example, for the procedure is often better concealed. It is given here because its very transparency adapts it to illustrate the device. The tonality is never in doubt. The first three bars are an ordinary downward progression to the dominant (E flat), after which the modulation proceeds by fifths through B flat, F, C, G, D, A to E minor (enharmonically). It is therefore no more atonal than any of the compositions—such as the two by Beethoven—which take you through all the keys. But there are compositions in which the procedure is sufficiently well concealed to produce the sense of 'perpetual motion' among tonalities which supplies one of the definitions of atonality. A. A. Klengel, who died in 1852, wrote forty-eight canons and fugues in which may be found, as in most compositions of the kind, many examples foreshadowing bitonality, but of atonality he stands acquitted.

Almost equally familiar nowadays are the effects of the hexatonic or tonal scale. It has its uses, harmonic and melodic, but where it gains the upper hand, tonality dissolves. Debussy succumbed to its exotic charm, which was obviously an evanescent quality, and will be difficult to recover after his excessive use of it. But as a contribution to atonality its influence has remained; and even in linear counterpoint progress by whole tones occasionally reminds one of the tonality that is thereby evaded. It is, moreover, noteworthy that most of the composers who have attained prominence in the practice of atonality have at some time or other felt the attraction of this neutral scale. For instance, in the following—

Ex. 3. SCHÖNBERG. 'Kammer-Symph.', Op. 9.

Schönberg has employed it for the first two bars, whilst in the last four notes of the fourth he uses the neutral chord to which we are to refer below. At least one of his best-known pupils has also used the tonal scale, and it further occurs in the earlier works of Paul Hindemith, not to speak of other young German composers now regarded as atonal.

The days are fortunately far behind us when the chord of the diminished seventh, with its enharmonic equivalents, was the most familiar device in all music. It then served a double purpose. It was one of the earliest romantic symbols, expressing dramatic surprise, just as later certain chromatic auxiliary notes were held to express pathos, and others, voluptuousness. In this capacity it has been variously superseded, the present tendency being to achieve the desired effect by polytonal means, as in Honegger's *Horace Victorieux*. But its use was even more widespread as a means of modulation. Because its symmetrical character in an asymmetrical scale makes it neutral, it is capable of serving as an atonal bridge, a *pons asinorum* from any tonality into any other. Students were taught that, being in a dozen keys at once, it was an ideal device, when they should have been told that therein lay its weakness. It is now discredited except for rare occasional purposes, but there is little doubt that, historically considered, it helped to soften the rigours of tonality, and, by accustoming the ear to tonal ambiguity, to prepare the way for atonality. In this connexion the following is not without interest:

Ex. 4. GOOSSENS. 'Kaleidoscope', Op. 18. No. 6.

Considered vertically, the chords themselves are of another type, but horizontally all the parts move by steps of a minor third or augmented second, and are therefore arpeggios of the diminished seventh. Moreover, there are only three such chords in the twelve-note scale, all others being inversions or enharmonic synonyms of these, and all three are simultaneously present. The passage is in six parts,

Ex. 5.

and it will be seen that parts 1, 3, and 6 represent one of those chords, part 2 another, and parts 4 and 5 the third. Thus all the 24 keys are simultaneously implied. Key-neutrality can surely go no farther. Goossens is not much attracted to atonality. Though he uses the twelve-note scale, and his music sometimes presents an appearance of riotous chromaticism, his tonality is usually well defined. But he makes much use of chromatic sequences, parallels, and convergences, the effect of which is to suspend tonality for the time being. There is no purpose in dwelling further upon the subject, but, as a curiosity of musical criticism, it is interesting to recall that when Debussy's *Pelléas et Mélisande* was given for the first time in London, in 1909, *The Times* said: 'That useful hack of the German composers, the diminished seventh, seems to have been banished from Debussy's studies altogether—which will endear him to many'; whilst another journal, the *Referee*, said: 'The diminished seventh has long been known as the "magician's chord" but it remained for Debussy to develop it and exploit its possibilities to their fullest extent.'

Just as the chord referred to above divides the octave symmetrically into four minor thirds, that of the augmented triad, consisting of alternate notes of the hexatonic scale, divides it into three major thirds, with the same effect of neutrality or atonality. Though latterly associated with the hexatonic, which it supplies with triads, it has also had its share of attention from the romantics in their search for 'neutral tints' of harmony. The following example might be matched a thousand times from the more sentimental music of the nineteenth century. It is chosen chiefly because it happens to begin the composition in question, the key of which is thus left indeterminate for several bars, which are, relatively speaking, atonal.

Ex. 6.

STCHERBATCHEV. Op. 15, No. 6.

These are by no means the only devices by which composers, whilst wooing the poetic charm which they persuaded themselves resided in ambiguity, assisted in the undermining of tonality. There are many other chromatic chords producing similar effects, and even the most diatonic passage can be made ambiguous by chromatic alteration. Moreover, nearly all modern sequential devices have a disturbing effect upon tonality.

Harmonically, atonality is the logical sequel to the ambiguity fostered by chromaticism and constant modulation. Contrapuntally it springs from the instinct of self-preservation. The composer who wished two or more parts to be heard polyphonically found that tonality and the harmonic processes based upon it were constantly frustrating him (especially in chromatic polyphony), and he proceeded to defy them. If two contrapuntal parts move in such a way that they offer no sequence of intervals suggestive of a definite tonality, they can be heard apart. It involves, of course, a more lavish use of dissonance, for consonant intervals are the most impregnated with tonal implications. The individual part is in a state of constant modulation, successive tonalities being implicit, just as successive harmonies are implicit in Bach's unaccompanied violin sonatas. Technically, the method is still at an empirical stage, though practical hints of it are scattered in many recent treatises, and a theoretical outline exists in Ernst Kurth's *Grundlagen*

Ex. 7. SCHÖNBERG. Op. 10.

des linearen Kontrapunkts (Berne, 1917). For the present it is best studied in the works themselves, and especially those of Schönberg, which are dealt with elsewhere. His gradual progress is particularly instructive. His Rubicon was crossed from op. 10 to op. 11. The former still retains a semblance of tonality, but the pending transition is visible in such passages as in Ex. 7.

Opus 11 consists of the famous three pieces for piano, which are definitely atonal throughout, as may be judged from Ex. 8. It will be seen that the distinction between one style and the other is, after all, not so very wide. Yet the step the composer took was decisive, and led to the composition of *Pierrot Lunaire*, unquestionably the outstanding masterpiece atonality has so far produced. The notation of such music involves an unprecedented use of accidentals, and, in their anxiety to be read correctly, composers constantly employ more than are required. Schönberg, who is lavish of them in the above examples, has even gone so far as to put naturals to the opening notes of a piece which has no key-signature.

Ex. 8. SCHÖNBERG. Op. 11, No. 1.

There are curious points about the last example. For instance, the fifth bar of 3/4 time consists of twelve semiquavers. If these are played in four triplets, making the time 2/4 or 12/16,

Ex. 9.

the effect is sequential and the tonality, though vague, can be established. Earlier in the same piece there occurs the following,

Ex. 10. SCHÖNBERG. Op. 11, No. 1.

which is merely five descending notes of a chromatic scale,

Ex. 11.

placed in different octaves. At this stage, and even later, the desire to characterize expressively the moving parts prompted a certain degree of distortion, behind which the crafty observer will unmask the tradition of Schumann or Mendelssohn. But that is no occasion for surprise, as Schönberg is in the direct line of that tradition. He has not broken with the past, but only with technical conventions.

During the interval which occurred in Schönberg's creative activities between op. 22 (1913–14) and op. 23 (1920–3), when, it has since transpired, his evolution was approaching another climacteric, Josef Matthias Hauer was studying the problem from an entirely different angle. He began in 1914 to work out the atonal system which is described in his pamphlet *Vom Wesen des Musikalischen* (1920), for which he appears to have found a starting-point and some suggestive analogies in Goethe's *Farbenlehre*. It would be inexpedient to attempt here a summary of a theory so elaborate and so subversive. Hauer preaches it with the ascetic fervour of a missionary, and a conviction which compels respect, but his converts are not yet numerous.

Schönberg, who had never liked the word 'atonal' and who expressly rejected it in his *Harmonielehre*, terms his newest manner (opp. 23–26) 'das Komponieren mit den 12 Tönen'. Its exegesis rightly belongs to the article in which his works are discussed. The same applies to other composers whose works are described elsewhere. It is, moreover, difficult to illustrate the more recent development of atonality with examples since, of the works concerned, the whole might just as usefully be quoted as any part.

Whether the terms 'atonal', 'linear', and so on have come to stay or not, the evolution of the music to which they are applied has caused an intense study of the mutual relations of the twelve notes, considered independently of all notions associated with tonality. From such studies will doubtless be evolved a new technique, to which all these varied experiences will have something to contribute. It must be clear to all that the possibilities of the twelve-note scale are still very far from exhaustion, and there is a wide field open to research. Even if it be disquieting to find composers so concerned with theory, which has usually been left to lag behind practice, it must not be forgotten that the Flemish contrapuntists had the same tendency, and that, under their guidance, polyphony came to no harm—far from it!—in the long run.

III. Polymodality

The writer considers some apology due for adding yet a third to the two cumbersome terms under consideration. His excuse is twofold. He has long considered the frequent occurrence of modal harmonies in modern music, from Debussy onwards, to be another avenue, similar in purpose to those offered by atonality and polytonality, of escape from the limitations of three-functional tonality as defined in the introduction. Meanwhile, Casella, who has devoted much study to the technical aspect of these problems, and has put this word into circulation, finds in the bimodal composition of the minor key the 'historic example of simultaneous scales and therefore of polytonality'. It is certainly true that the gradual subjection of Dorian and Aeolian to a somewhat adulterated 'harmonic' minor, and the divergent forms of the scale used in ascent and descent, were the most fruitful source of those 'false relations' in the older music which convey the impression that polytonality is no innovation, but merely an extension. Casella quotes several examples, notably the one from Orazio Vecchi which is mentioned above, but perhaps the most characteristic of them is this:

Ex. 12. Bach.

He incidentally suggests that this aspect of the minor scale has not been sufficiently studied, and it is not improbable that further investigation would throw light upon the obscure beginnings of polytonality.

Even the predominantly Aeolian character of the modern minor is not unchallenged. Regarding the intervals of the minor triad as the inversion of those of the major, the corresponding inversion of the major scale is not the Aeolian, but the Phrygian, which reproduces the same intervals downwards, in the same order.

Ex. 13.

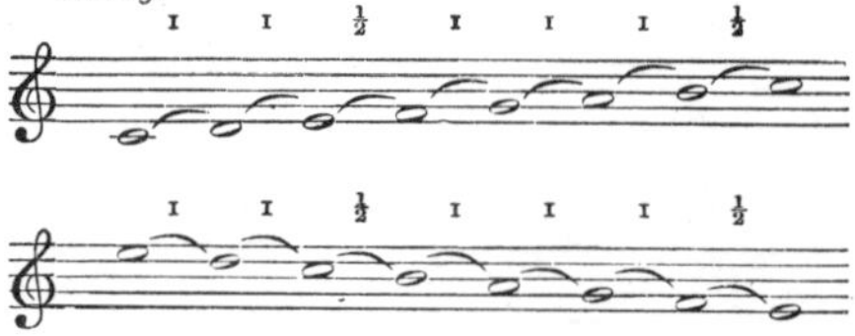

Early practice regarded this as the true minor. It is, for instance, the basis of the eight verses which constitute the first part of Josquin des Prés's wonderful *Miserere mei Deus*. More than one recent authority, notably Vincent d'Indy in the first volume of his *Cours de composition musicale*, and in his early pianoforte quartet, has shown an inclination to reinstate, as the true relative minor, this mode whose claim to be so regarded, in the face of modern practice, seems logically unassailable.

The major scale has also proved accessible to the introduction of notes previously regarded as chromatic. There are many composers—John Ireland, for example—who display a predilection for the sharpened, or Lydian, fourth not merely as a kind of leading note to the dominant, as in

Ex. 14. SIBELIUS. 4th Symphony, in E. Finale.

but as an essential note of the scale.

Meanwhile, there has taken place a gradual *rapprochement* between major and minor. Sometimes a mere harmonic note has the curious effect of suggesting the simultaneous presence of both modes. For instance,

Ex. 15. DARGOMIJSKY. 'Finnish Fantasy.'

admits of a very simple explanation which does not, however, remove the momentary impression of A minor. The growing prevalence of this tendency has led harmonically to an intermediate major-minor (cf. Kistler, *A System of Harmony*, 1899, and many other treatises), and horizontally to an ever-growing frequency of fluctuation between major and minor in the same composition. The latter is especially prevalent in French music of the last half-century. An imaginative investigator might be tempted to ascribe a widespread progeniture to the *tierce de Picardie*!

We are thus confronted with the situation that, since the fusion of major and minor gives us ten diatonic notes, the inclusion of the Lydian fourth in the former, and of the Phrygian second in the latter, has the effect of endowing every note of the chromatic scale with diatonic functions; that is to say, it will give us a twelve-note scale of which each degree is susceptible of being treated diatonically within the key.

In the above there is no question of 'modal' writing, but merely one of variants or additions to the orthodox major and minor, and their eventual fusion. But, concurrently with this progressive assimilation of major and minor, there has also been a parallel tendency to revive the old modes—not, however, in their authentic form, which in some of them would bring into conflict the harmonic and melodic dominants, but in a kind of approximation which is generally difficult to attribute to any particular mode, and which consists in the promotion to primary rank of triads hitherto regarded as secondary. Some of the earliest examples are furnished by that strange empiricist Erik Satie, who markedly influenced Debussy in the same direction. Satie's *Gymnopédies* (1889) entitle him to be regarded as a precursor. It is not given to many to be so hailed twice in a lifetime, as befell the *prophète d'Arcueil*. Ravel, Vaughan Williams, and many other modern composers have been drawn into this movement, with varying consequences. Whilst Ravel has modernized many archaisms, Vaughan Williams has medievalized as many modernisms. Debussy's method differed from that of either. His impressionistic use of chords prompted a degree of arbitrariness which would be foreign to both of the former, but which was justified by his singular, all but impeccable musical intuition. From modal progressions he passed on to the use of the common chord on any note as one of the colours of his brilliant harmonic palette, sometimes with vague and transient modal implications, but quite as often without a hint of them. The following Ex. 16, for instance, would, in spite of its notation, admit of explanation as a melodic phrase in E minor, between a chord in G sharp minor sustained as a pedal, and a harmonic figure which consists of a neutral chord of the diminished seventh, in

Ex. 16.

DEBUSSY. Preludes II, No. 2.

arpeggio, each note carrying with it a major triad.

Ex. 17.

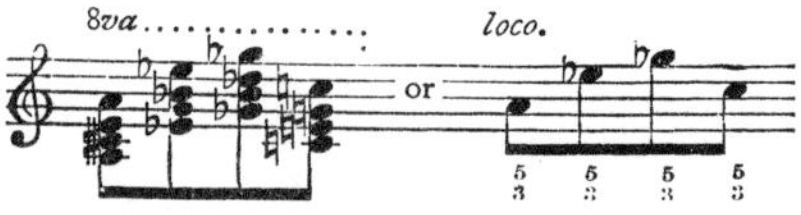

As neither the pedal nor the neutral chord affects tonality, this makes of it simply a passage in E minor, but it is not everybody who would have chosen this treatment for it. This, however, is wandering away from the subject. Debussy's music abounds in examples which, contrary to the above, can be definitely attributed to one or other of the old modes, though its prevalence may be of short duration. He, and many other composers after him, think little of passing with kaleidoscopic rapidity from one mode to another, from any of them to the orthodox major or minor, or vice versa.

We reach thus, by two widely different routes, an apparently similar goal, that of a system in which all the modes, major (Lydian, Ionian, and Mixolydian) and minor (Dorian, Aeolian, and Phrygian) can, at the composer's discretion, maintain a diatonic existence within the tonality; or, in other words, a bridge from the sixteenth century to the twentieth, over the intervening period during which the conventional major and minor held sway;—incidentally also a resumption of the classical Latin-Hellenic tradition. It is at this point that polymodality commences to impinge upon polytonality. Hitherto we have been concerned with horizontal fluctuation between mode and mode. It would probably not be difficult to find in the works of the composers named, or others of recent date, instances of a vertical impact of mode upon mode, corresponding more or less to the vertical impact of various accepted forms of the minor scale, but it will be sufficient for the present purpose to point to the vertical superimposition of major and minor as an accomplished fact. In its simplest form we have it in the following example, which is typical of many:

Ex. 18.

DE FALLA. 'Three-Cornered Hat.'

Six years earlier, however, it had already reached a far more complex stage in this:

Ex. 19.

STRAVINSKY. 'Sacre.'

Here the major-minor tonic triad is uncompromisingly stated at the outset, and as there is nothing in the sequel to contradict either mode, neither the D natural nor the D sharp can be explained away as an auxiliary chromatic note. A more definite example of polymodality it would be difficult to find, and, since the tonic major and minor are not theoretically regarded as immediately related, whereas all keys have become distantly so, it can also be cited as an example of polytonality. Such examples have become common in recent years, but they do not often take such a downright, wilful shape as:

Ex. 20.

POULENC. 'Les Biches.'

Glaring as this instance may be, it is no longer possible to condemn it as lacking precedent, and its intrinsic shrillness is condoned by the type of ballet in which it occurs.

With a glee that reads as if slightly acidulated, Casella points to the following as being apposite:

Ex. 21. MONTEVERDI. *Orfeo.*

and truly the father of modern music had much to answer for besides the unprepared seventh by which he is best remembered. Well may Artusi, the father of modern musical criticism, have written in 1608—*Orfeo* was first performed in 1607—'One hears a medley of sounds, a harmonic rumour intolerable to the senses. . . . How can the mind find itself amid such confusion?' Three centuries and more have elapsed since the battle was engaged, and its rigour is unabated.

IV. Polytonality

Like atonality and polymodality, polytonality also has a dual origin. In one aspect it reaches back to the polyphonic era, in the other it results from the reaction against the harmonic period, and especially its later chromatic stages. In spirit every canonic *comes* at an interval other than the octave, and every fugal answer, constituted tentatives towards bitonality; and the compromises effected in the intervals of a canon, or the transient modulations in its progress, and the substitution of a tonal answer for the real answer to a fugal subject, were so many concessions made by composers because the time was not yet ripe for contrapuntal *intransigeance*. The works of the more daring contrapuntists, especially those of Bach, abound in instances. One of them has become a kind of standard, having been quoted by several writers on the subject in turn. It is the following:

Ex. 22. BACH. Duetto, No. 2.

This is how Milhaud views it:

'Let us read the two parts separately: the upper part is clearly in D minor, despite the transient modulations in the third, fourth, and fifth bars; the lower part is exactly, with the same transient modulations, the upper part transposed a fifth below, into A minor. But the two parts are combined in such a manner that vertically each chord produced by this two-part counterpoint admits harmonization in one key. Nevertheless, the ninth and tenth bars contain a passage of incorrect writing which would vanish if the superposition of two tonalities were conceded. How explain the A of the second beat in the ninth bar, in the lower part, in relation to the F of the upper? Six-four? Two-part counterpoint does not allow it, especially approached thus. Chord of the sixth? Harmony does not allow the false relation which will arise between the C natural, the third of this chord of the sixth, and the C sharp on the first beat in the following bar.'

The whole passage shows that Bach, who anticipated so many things in modern music, was not far from including polytonality among them. Another interesting example is that quoted by Koechlin:

Ex. 23. MOZART. Fugue for two pianos.

but though the key of D major is indicated below, the interval of the diminished seventh above would be an element of vagueness were it not for the clearness with which the preceding bar gives G minor as the key. As a general rule minor composers have permitted themselves less freedom than the masters, but even in a scholastic writer such as Klengel one constantly finds passages like

Ex. 24. KLENGEL (1783–1852). Fugue I, 20.

the false relations in which clearly show bitonality.

Turning to the harmonic use of polytonality, that also has classical precedents, but these are neither so numerous nor so conclusive. For instance, the following, quoted by Koechlin,

Ex. 25. HAYDN. Quartet.

does not give a genuine impression of bitonality.

With regard to the next quotation,

Ex. 26. DVOŘÁK. 'Legend,' Op. 59, No. 2.

it cannot be more clearly described than in the words of Sir W. H. Hadow:

'I do not think that Dvořák had any idea of polytonality. But he belonged to a country which had virtually been left untouched by the diatonic period, he came at a time which was ripening for the chromatic scale, and he experimented in it without being hampered by any tradition. Polytonality is not a part of his work, but I think it is a consequence.'

This keen-sighted musical observer long ago wrote that Dvořák's music would probably revolutionize the whole system of harmony, and there can be little doubt that he was one of the forerunners of modern music. But because his works are less known beyond the periphery of the Central European musical world, his claims to be so regarded have been completely overshadowed by those of Moussorgsky, his Russian contemporaries, and his French successors.

Even in the horizontal line Dvořák occasionally drops a hint of polytonality. At the time it was written, the following—

Ex. 27. DVOŘÁK. Theme of Symph. Var., Op. 78.

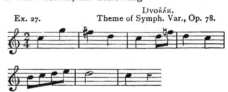

met with adverse criticism because the second bar suggested D major.

With the advent of the contemporary period the increasing amplitude given to various harmonic devices produced, in growing number, instances of what might be termed pseudo-polytonality. Every kind of parallel revealed them if one cared to consider the parallel parts as polyphonic, instead of treating the whole progression as one sweep of the harmonic brush. When Florent Schmitt wrote *Glas* in 1903, and slightly reinforced the harmonics in order to produce the effect of a bell,

Ex. 28. F. SCHMITT. 'Glas,' Op. 29, No. 6.

there was quite a stir about his writing in different keys! Similarly, converging processions of chords sometimes resulted in polytonal clashes. Sequences telescoped themselves like railway carriages in a collision, scattering polytonal splinters. Some of the simplest but not least interesting examples of this kind arise from the greater freedom in the use of pedals. For instance, in the following—

Ex. 29. CUI. 'Berceuse,' Op. 20, No. 8.

the superstructure temporarily relinquishes the key of E flat for that of E, whilst the former remains in the pedal. Of more striking effect is the second bar of the following—

Ex. 30. BIZET. 'Ghazal' from 'Djamileh'.

probably because of the downward trend of keys, and the presence of both dominants.

Even this quotation—

Ex. 31. RIMSKY-KORSAKOV. 'Scheherazade.'

could be brought into the pedal category, but the explanation given by George Dyson in *The New Music* is more plausible, though one suspects him of having reasoned backwards from Scriabin. He points out that 'two chords of the dominant seventh, an augmented fourth apart in pitch, have two notes in common, and it is possible to "switch" from one to the other and back indefinitely'.

The next example

Ex. 32. SIBELIUS. 4th Symphony, Finale.

probably admits of an explanation by enharmonics if one cared to delve for it, but it is simpler, and just as satisfactory, to regard it as a *point d'orgue*.

In Stravinsky's *Le Sacre du Printemps* there are several instances of a pedal continued with polytonal effects. Those occurring in his *Pulcinella* are even more striking because of the simple diatonic character of the thematic material.

Between a pedal bass and a repeated ostinato figure there is little difference in principle, though the transition may produce curious results, such as

Ex. 33.

MILHAUD.
'Le Bœuf sur le Toit.'

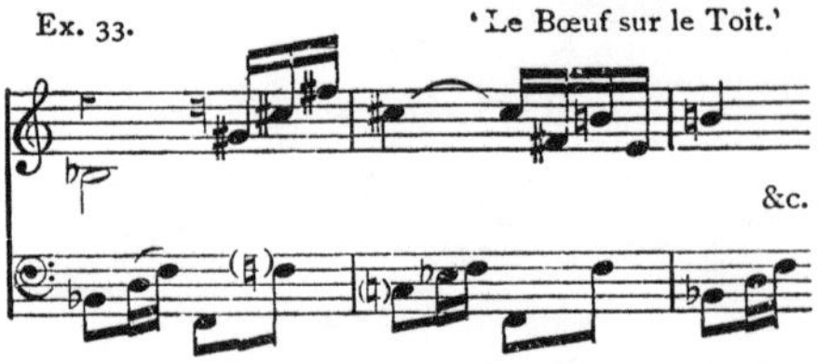

Ex. 34.

POULENC.
'Mouvements Perpétuels.'

either of which is transiently bitonal in exactly the same sense as the second bar of Ex. 30, as can be verified from their contexts.

Meanwhile, another development had been hastening the advent of true polytonality. At the commencement of the second section of this essay it was pointed out that musicians were driven to search for devices to maintain a polyphonic effect, one such device being atonality. Another was that of applying a different harmonic colouring to each of the polyphonic strands. These seldom exceeded two in number, and instead of embedding both in one comprehensive harmony, there grew a tendency to harmonize both individually. Here again it is Stravinsky who furnished the most illustrative examples, and those in *Pulcinella* are particularly striking. In its simplest form the device consists in rearing a second chord upon the uppermost note of the first, and it has been justified by urging that the major common chord itself is merely a minor third reared upon the upper note of a major third. One is reminded of Koechlin's demonstration that the same common chord is polytonal by virtue of its upper partials. Does not the C sound a B flat, the E a G sharp, and the G a B natural? Therefore the keys of G, E, and F are simultaneously present! But once it came to be realized that two individual parts could be simultaneously harmonized in different hues, the next step of giving them different tonalities became much less awe-inspiring.

Before that step was actually taken there had been instances of polytonality arising from dramatic, rather than musical, situations. It was suggested in the second section of this paper that polytonal devices had succeeded to the dramatic prerogatives which at one time fell to the chord of the diminished seventh. As far back as 1891 a French composer appears to have had a dim prophetic vision of the possibilities,

Ex. 35.

BRUNEAU.
'Le Rêve,' Intro. to 4th Tableau.

which has a curiously pathetic effect. Here is an instance which frequent quotation has made classic—

Ex. 36. STRAUSS. 'Salome.'

But, as was mentioned in the same connexion, a more conclusive instance will be found in Honegger's *Horace Victorieux*. Whether we should ascribe the following—

Ex. 37. STRAVINSKY. 'Petroushka.'

to similar motives is much more doubtful. It certainly has a unique dramatic poignancy, but *Petroushka* originated as a pianoforte concerto, and the clash of keys is most prominent in the second tableau of the ballet, where also the pianistic character is most pronounced.

Moreover, Stravinsky's instinct does not incline to programmatic illustration, so that, on the whole, one is justified in ascribing to a purely musical impulse this relatively early example of polytonality.

In 1904 M. Enrico Bossi published a set of *Satire Musicali*, harmless gibes at the 'moderns' of the beginning of the century. One of them took the form of a little piece in which the treble had the key-signature of A major and the bass, which was a mere tonic and dominant pedal, that of A flat major. Did he foresee how nearly his joke would correspond with realities to come? Probably not. But compositions employing simultaneously different key-signatures are by no means rare to-day. There is, for instance, a *Conceit* by Goossens which runs:

Ex. 38. GOOSSENS. 'Dance Memories,' Op. 20, No. 2.

Tempo di Valse.

Curiously enough, the more uncompromising practitioners of polytonality, such as Milhaud, seem to prefer to dispense with key-signatures altogether, and their presence is frequently associated, not so much with downright polytonality, as with ingenious handling of enharmonics. The polytonality is, so to speak, in the shop-window, whilst the music within follows more orthodox practice.

Ex. 39. HOLST. 'Terzetto,' Op. 44, No. 1.

Sometimes there is also a skilled use of the notes which triads of different keys have in common, as in Ex. 39, where each triplet ends with the chord of C major, which, need it be said? is presently to conclude the piece.

Ex. 40.

Vln. 1. SZYMANOVSKI. Op. 37.

 ATONALITY & POLYTONALITY

But in a fugue or a fugato the use of different key-signatures is a convenient aid to polytonality. In the same Holst piece from which the last quotation was taken there is fugal writing of this type, and Szymanowski's string quartet has for its last movement a fugue from which Ex. 40 is a typical quotation.

We have now reached the point where the method admits of being reduced to a system. Here Milhaud, one of its leading exponents and the most uncompromising of them all, comes to our aid with a tabular demonstration. Every bitonal combination being ultimately derived from two superimposed triads, he reviews the possibilities, assuming one of the two to be that of C:

Ex. 41.

But, since we are polymodal as well as polytonal, each of these combinations may take the following four different forms according as one or the other triad is major or minor:

Ex. 42.

Then there are the inversions to be considered. Obviously each of these compound chords allows of six dispositions. For example, the second chord of Ex. 41 in the first form indicated by Ex. 42 gives the following:

Ex. 43.

Inversions.

Example 41, II, in form of Example 42, A.

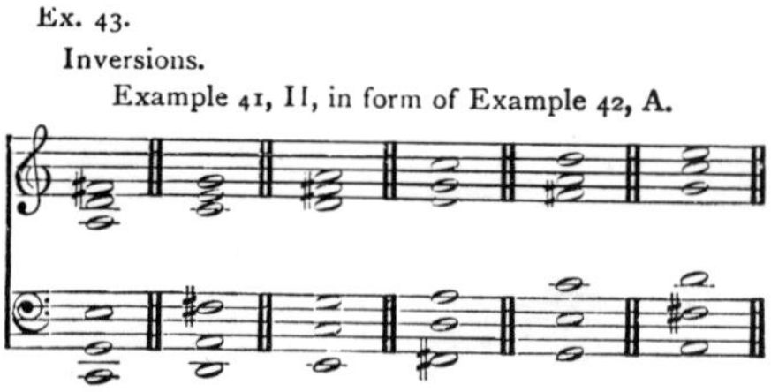

We are thus able to identify, for instance, the Stravinsky example (37) as being VI of Ex. 41, whilst the following—

Ex. 44. RAVEL, 'Sonate.'

must be attributed to XI of Ex. 41 in the form D of Ex. 42. In a like manner the Poulenc example (34) resolves itself as VIII A, whilst the following—

Ex. 45. MILHAUD. 'Saudades do Brazil.'

is clearly I B, and

Ex. 46. AURIC. 'Les Fâcheux.'

assez lent.

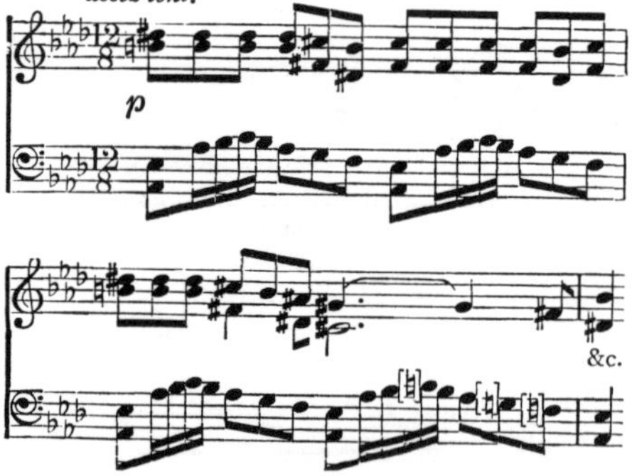

is III A. Another example from the same work is explicable as XI A, C major over the dominant harmony of D flat major. (Ex. 47.)

It is not suggested that this furnishes us with a method of procedure. It provides a kind of glossary or nomenclature, which is perhaps as much as can be expected at this stage of progress. But from such examples as these it

Ex. 47. AURIC. 'Les Fâcheux.'

can be seen how firmly the composers who follow this tendency are bound to diatonic writing in the individual parts. The first invasion of chromaticism, unless contrived with a degree of skill such as we can scarcely imagine at this stage, will make the two tonalities indistinguishable. Since this movement is in part a reaction against chromaticism, this may be counted a virtue. Certainly Milhaud, Poulenc, Auric, and others loudly proclaim their devotion to simple diatonic tunes.

The next stage of polytonality, that involving the simultaneity of three common chords in as many keys, gives an extraordinary array of potential combinations. The eleven chords of Ex. 41 become fifty-five; the four forms of Ex. 42 become eight; and the six inversions

Ex. 48. MILHAUD. Third Symphony (Serenade).

of Ex. 43 become nine. At the same time the superposition of these tonalities brings about the presence of others. Thus, in the chord composed of the major triads of C, D flat, and D there are also present the major of F and enharmonically of A, with the minor of both these, also of D, and enharmonically of F sharp and C sharp—a total of five major and five minor keys, representing polymodally six tonalities. Harmonically, this brings us very near to a chord comprising all the twelve notes of the chromatic scale, and therefore all tonalities, which, as Milhaud himself admits, establishes contact with atonality. But the route followed has been very different from that of chromaticism, and at every one of its stages there have been revealed numberless additions to the common fund of musical resource. Harmonically, the works of modern composers abound in examples of their use, and the experienced ear has little difficulty in distinguishing them from the results of chromatic alteration *à outrance*. Contrapuntally, progress is more cautious, doubtless because of the ever-present danger of chromatic ambiguity. Ex. 48, with which this section concludes, has few counterparts except in the works of the same composer.

V. Postscript

What is to be the outcome? That is the question which imposes itself after a survey of recent musical developments. There are many to whom the present appears as a period of unprecedented confusion. They are wrong, for it has precedents enough, though the perspective in which we see them reduces their significance for ourselves. It is convenient to divide musical history into periods. One can go even farther and adopt an oscillation period of one and a half centuries, the time that lapsed from the advent of the *New Music* (1600) to the death of Bach (1750). One can reckon backwards and assign, with good reason, the period 1150–1300 to the troubadours, and divide the three centuries 1300–1600 between the rise and the *Blütezeit* of the polyphonic masters. But whatever view one may take, there will always be such overlapping of periods as will create the appearance of confusion. The polyphonic era lasted long after 1600, and the sons of Bach were launching out in other ways before he died. Similarly, though another *volte-face* was due about 1900, it really began somewhere about 1860 and to-day, in 1925, there are still many for whom it has not yet occurred. Confusion there is, certainly, but no more than in 1625—except in one respect: Haydn and Mozart wrote for their patrons, whom they could not afford to displease. The composer of to-day is not salaried. No doubt he wishes he were, but he is wrong, for he is a free man. He has not to study a taste which, though of aristocratic culture, necessarily lagged behind the spirit of creative adventure. He can please himself. Of course, if he does so, he incurs the same penalties as would have befallen an eighteenth-century salaried composer in like circumstances, that is to say, he goes unrewarded. But in those days a man could live by writing for the cultured audience. It is not given to many to obtain a livelihood by doing so to-day. Therefore the composer who prefers art to a living feels to-day that he might as well be hung for a sheep as a lamb, and writes without compunction. Moreover, the profession has grown in proportion to the audience, and composers are more numerous to-day than they were in the eighteenth century, prolific as it was. Hence, with a larger number of composers, availing themselves of larger liberty, there is naturally a greater creative turmoil. But the issues are no more confused than they were in the seventeenth or eighteenth centuries.

The disappearance of so many rules and prohibitions is not to be regretted, for they belonged to the infancy or at most the adolescence of an art. It has come to be recognized that almost everything in music is permissible if you have enough skill to do it effectively, and enough taste to do it in the right place. But in the polyphonic period, music became, as Joannes de Tinctoris declared at the time, a new art, and in the youth of an art many things have to be done by rule which later can be left to the intuition meanwhile matured by generations of practitioners. The story of forbidden fifths is typical. First, all fifths were not only allowed but music consisted of little else. Then it was found that some of them were harmful, and taboos were set up for the protection of innocence. Now all fifths are once more allowed, but the musician intuitively knows better than to spoil good work with them.

Theoretically, the outcome of recent developments in tonality is simple and logical, however complex it may be in practice. In one way or another we are witnessing the installation of the twelve-note scale, which would probably have been effected earlier and with less ado but for the retarding influence of the seven-note notation in use. This does not, of course, imply either the abolition or even the desuetude of the tonalities as we know them, though possibly the growing laxity in respect of the notation of enharmonics may end in a revision of the present use of accidentals and agreement to employ one symbol for each of the twelve notes within the octave. Otherwise, all the resources that have grown from tonality will remain at the disposal of the musician, who is not likely to deprive himself of anything so useful except when it suits him to do so. Moreover, as we have seen under 'Polymodality', each of the twelve notes is susceptible of being endowed with diatonic rank within the key, which enables the composer to vary the character of atonality without abandoning it. Music is, however, an art not of notes but of intervals. Hitherto, intervals have been read as diatonic or chromatic in respect of the tonality in which they are employed. Henceforth these two readings will be increased to four. Intervals may be: (1) diatonic in respect of a determinable tonality; (2) chromatic in respect of a determinable tonality; (3) bitonal when their two component notes owe allegiance to different tonalities; and (4) omnitonal when both are employed in the atonal twelve-note scale. But this is scarcely likely to be of interest to other than theoretical students. Composers do not work like that.

It need not, therefore, be feared that the practical text-books of the future will be lumbered up with elaborate explanations of the procedure to be adopted in atonality or polytonality. It is far more likely that, as time proceeds, they will be relieved of much that encumbers them at present, and the student be invited to probe the mysteries of harmony as the aspiring painter probes those of colour.

Moreover, the present complications are a temporary exaggeration, similar to that stage of the polyphonic period when composers busied themselves with the most ingenious forms of canon, the outcome of which was not a permanent edifice of mathematical intricacies but the sometimes happy-go-lucky, plausibly effective canonic imitation which does duty to-day, save when the canon itself is the purpose of the composition. It is a healthy instinct to explore eagerly the possibilities of new devices, but when that is done they are added to those already available, and used as rationally as these. Compositions written specially to some polytonal recipe will soon become as obsolete as those written, for instance, by Rebikov, specially to parade the tonal scale. The richness which polytonality is capable of producing will remain with us, but who wants rich food all the time?

Already the vanguard is leaving this stage behind. Stravinsky is turning the experience he has gained to the service of classical ideals. Many years ago the present writer recorded the opinion that, just as a certain type of intellectual is predestined to end in the Roman Church, so Stravinsky was predestined to anchor in the haven of Bach, and some of his recent works confirm the prediction. Schönberg's *Pierrot Lunaire*, though an outstanding achievement, is aesthetically much more symptomatic of an expiring tradition than of one in the making, and his most gifted pupils are curiously sparing of new works. The more exuberant of 'Les Six' are becoming as sedate as their one-time colleagues, Erik Satie has gone to rest, God 's in His heaven, and all 's right with the world. EDWIN EVANS.

[It would border upon presumption for any amateur to pronounce, as yet, a definite opinion upon the ultimate value of the works known as atonal, which constitute practically a new art. Speaking of myself, after adventures of the soul spreading over a lifetime amongst the masterpieces of chamber music, I have to confess that I have experienced defeat when confronted with music which apparently sets consonance and normal rhythmic feeling at defiance, music compared to which the later quartets of Beethoven are crystal clear.

Composers would urge that I have not studied them sufficiently, and am not entitled to pronounce judgement. They would be perfectly right, but I would have them realize that a certain difficulty blocks the way to perfect enlightenment. Amateurs, and for that matter professional players too, those who, besides being of the *métier*, are ardent lovers of chamber music for its own sake, would be ready enough to study the masterpieces of modern music if they knew for certain which *were* the masterpieces.

I can imagine them taking up a work of the kind that cannot possibly be satisfactorily rendered until every player has memorized his part and his colleagues' into the bargain, and then taking up another requiring similar concentration and expenditure of valuable time. But I cannot imagine them taking up an endless series of such works, braving the possibility that they may prove a disappointment in the end. Life is too short. Time must reveal which are the few works destined to win universal acceptance, those which are richly inspired, not mere intellectual exercises leaving the heart cold. Then music-lovers will be heartened to devote their energies to preparing and rehearsing them, without fear that their labour will be wasted.

That appears to me to be the situation to-day. Meantime, music-lovers should give every encouragement to publishers and performers who specialize in the production of modern works, and to enterprising *entrepreneurs* like the International Society for Contemporary Music and its British filial the Contemporary Music Centre, who give the public a chance of hearing it. The truth will gradually leak out. The works of clever poseurs who strive at all costs to be original, who stigmatize the *cri de cœur* of the artist as sentimentality and excoriate our ears with dissonances of the most appalling kind, will be heard and after much painful travail rejected. Those which remain will take their rightful place in the repertory, the new art will blend with the old, and the muses, poor things, who must be very concerned at what is going on in the world of art here below, will rejoice once more.

Being an amateur advanced in years, I see no prospect of ever gaining an intimate knowledge of music of the atonal school, but at least I can retain an open mind. The following words, written in 1792 by a certain Marquis de Rangoni, whose critical observations are described by Heron Allen (*de Fidiculis Bibliographia*) as 'valuable and profound', may serve as a warning to those who dismiss all modern music as degenerate: '*La musique est considérablement déchue aujourd'hui.*' And those were the days of Haydn, Mozart, and Beethoven!

EDITOR.]

ATTWOOD, THOMAS, 1765–1838, English composer, pupil of Mozart.

He is little identified with chamber music. There is, however, an interesting facsimile of the MS. of a minuet for string quartet by him, re-written in the same page by Mozart, to be seen in T. F. Dunhill's excellent treatise on chamber music. EDITOR.

†AUBER, D. F. E., 1792–1871, opera composer.

Trio, pf, v, vc, D op. 1 Lavinée (Paris), 1858.

An example of the many operatic composers who have dabbled in chamber music. His trio is alluded to in de Sauzay's catalogue as follows:

'Ce trio est digne de sa plume spirituelle et habile, et fait regretter vivement que ce soit le seul ouvrage écrit par lui pour la chambre.'

And Pougin writes, 'In 1871 Auber composed [besides the trio] several string quartets in absolutely free form—to be considered rather as "pieces" for string quartet.' EDITOR.

†AUBERT, JACQUES ('le Vieux'), 1678–1753, French composer.
Modern republication:

Trio (suite) *Ma pinte et ma mie au gué*, pf, 2 v (2 v from fig. bass) Senart, *c.* 1917.

Aubert wrote several violin duets. His trio has at least a jolly title.

AUBERT, LOUIS FRANÇOIS MARIE, b. 1877, French composer.

Sonata, pf, v, d mi and D Durand, 1927.

Aubert, who is a prolific composer, did not take to concerted chamber music until after the death of Fauré (1924), who had been his teacher, and to whose memory he has dedicated his violin sonata. It is a finely finished work, with a reflectively lyrical slow movement which, in the light of the dedication, may be regarded as elegiac. The whole sonata has the refinement which is characteristic of Fauré, and of those who shared his cherished ideals.

EDWIN EVANS.

†AUER, LEOPOLD VON, b. 1845, Hungarian violinist and conductor.

This artist, now resident in America and known as a professor of the violin with more brilliant pupils to his credit than any teacher living, was once equally distinguished as soloist and chamber music player. In the 'seventies, I heard him lead many master works at Ella's Musical Union concerts, with unsurpassable purity of tone and perfection of style. When living in Petrograd, Auer founded a Quartet with Jean Pickel, Weickmann, and C. Davidov, the latter a superb 'cellist to whom he was much attached. After Davidov's death in 1890 he decided to relinquish quartet playing in public.

Auer was professor of the violin at the Petrograd Conservatorium up to 1917. He made his first appearance as conductor of the New York Philharmonic Orchestra in December 1927 at the age of 82! EDITOR.

AUGARTEN, a public garden in Vienna opened in 1775, of which an interesting account is to be found in *Grove*. A concert-room was built a few years later, in which music was heard at the curiously early hour of seven in the morning. Here Beethoven played the Kreutzer sonata with Bridgetower for the first time (in May 1803), 'the first two movements being read from autograph and the copy dashed down only just before the commencement of the concert'. EDITOR.

AULIN, TOR (BERNHARD VILHELM), 1866–1914, Swedish violinist and composer.

Little Suite, pf, v, E op. 15 Südd. Musik-V., 1903.

Sonata, pf, v, D „ 12 Zimmermann, 1924.

Aulin is an outstanding figure in Swedish chamber music. An extraordinarily talented violinist, he was held in high esteem by his master Sauret, of whom he was a pupil at Berlin (1884–6), and for a long time was looked upon as Sweden's most distinguished virtuoso. Through the medium of his Quartet ensemble, the Aulin Quartet, which quickly reached a high artistic standard, he made a permanent contribution to chamber music in Sweden (see SWEDISH CHAMBER MUSIC). His quartet party had often a thankless task to face; it was only gradually that Aulin's tireless energy, strong initiative, and profound love of his art was able to overcome the indifference of the public to serious chamber music. During the twenty-five years of its existence the Aulin Quartet gave concerts not only in Sweden but all over Scandinavia and in Germany, where it received wide recognition. By including the names of F. Berwald, L. Norman, E. Sjögren, and other new composers in the repertory of his chamber concerts and in other programmes, Aulin greatly encouraged native chamber music. He was also an admirable composer in the romantic-national style. His output was fairly extensive. It includes several compositions of merit, of which the majority, being written for solo violin, are outside the category of real chamber music. One string quartet (op. 1, unpublished), an extremely effective violin sonata (op. 12), and a suite for violin and piano (op. 15) constitute the whole of his actual chamber music. GUNNAR JEANSON.

*AURIC, GEORGES, b. 1899, French composer, was a member of the group 'Les Six'.

Auric has not hitherto composed chamber music in the ordinary sense, but his incidental music to Marcel Achard's play *Malbrouck s'en va-t-en guerre*, produced 1925 at the Comédie des Champs-Élysées, and afterwards performed at Brussels, Berlin, &c., is for a sextet of instruments of a type belonging to chamber music: clarinet, bassoon, trumpet, violin, 'cello, and piano. It has special interest in regard to the movements promoting 'Little Theatres' or 'Théâtres Intimes' in various countries, where chamber music of this type is preferable to reductions from orchestral scores. The music exists also in the form of a suite.

EDWIN EVANS.

†AUSTIN, ERNEST, b. 1874, English composer.

4th trio, pf, v, vc, D	op. 26	S. & B.
Trio, pf. v, vc		Larway.
Trio Pastorale (*In Field and Forest*) pf, fl, horn (or v, vc)		"
Lyric Sonata, pf, v, D		S. & B.

The pastoral trio carries out the promise of its title, and the fourth trio may be regarded as a favourable example of one-movement form. In the sonata we find a work effectively written for both instruments, conceived in a romantic vein and touched slightly by modern harmonic influences. EDITOR.

AUSTRIAN CHAMBER MUSIC. *v.* GERMAN.

†AVERKAMP, ANTON, b. 1861, Dutch composer.

Sonata, pf, v, D	op. 2	Rühle, 1890.

†AXMAN, EMIL, D.PH., b. 1887, Czech composer.

Sonata, pf, v	Hudební Matice.

One of his song-cycles (*Night*) has also an accompaniment for string quartet.

The violin sonata is probably the most effective of Axman's works, being rich in poetical and finely-modulated feeling. His music does not make an immediate appeal, for which its harshnesses are responsible; but it is convincing, and its serious emotional quality and rustic strength make a lasting impression.

Axman has written other chamber works as yet unpublished. VÁCLAV ŠTĚPÁN.

AYRES, FREDERIC, 1876–1926, American composer, pupil of Stillman Kelley and Arthur Foote.

1st trio, pf, v, vc, A flat	op. 13	Stahl, 1914.
2nd trio, pf, v, vc, d mi		S. P. A. M.
Sonata, pf, v, d mi	" 15	Stahl, 1914.

Few American composers of serious attainment can be named whose works are as free from academic thraldom as are those of this composer, whose enforced sojourn in the mountainous West may some day be accounted of permanent value. In 1902 he took up his residence at Colorado Springs, and in this rugged environment it was little to be wondered that he should have developed a highly individual idiom. There are more finished craftsmen than Ayres, but few among his American contemporaries possessed of equal lyrical intensity, such as is displayed, for instance, in the violin sonata, an intensity which is to be found in all his larger works. The sonata is a work of moderate proportions, in two movements; a lento espressivo in the manner of an intermezzo in idyllic mood, and a final presto con fuoco. The finale itself is a rollicking rondo, providing in turn an effective foil to the emotional intensity of the first movement.

The first piano trio, in three movements, is an earlier work, less dramatic than the sonata, but with many attractive features of its own, notably a fine unity in the structural design. The motto theme of the introduction (largo) serves admirably to establish a mood, the gravity of which is interrupted by a brief allegretto. The largo theme then becomes the chief burden of the second movement, which is developed in a spirit alternating between brooding profundity and lyrical aspiration. There is appropriate verve in the finale, a specially delightful feature of which is the final coda, a zephyr-like conclusion of infinite lightness and charm. In addition to various performances of the trio in America, it has also been played in England by the London Trio.

Stimulating as these two works undoubtedly are, the full stature of the composer is not revealed until the second trio. In the rhythmic vitality of the first movement there is something elemental; the harmonies have taken on a certain astringency, while there is a vaulting sweep in the melodic lines—notably in the second movement—heroically elegiac in mood. Throughout the three movements there is stark power tempered by inner heat, and forged into a whole that is at once eloquent and bracing. ARTHUR SHEPHERD.

AZEVEDO, F. D'.

Quintet, pf, 2v, vla, vc, G	Schott (Brussels), 1905.
Sonata, pf, vc, F	" "

B

BABELL, William, *c.* 1690–1723, violinist and harpsichord player, pupil of Dr. Pepusch.

Modern republication:

Sonata, v, fig. bass (pf), B flat (A. Moffat, *Old Engl. V.-Music* 3)	Novello, 1906.

Arrangements of sonatas with figured bass are not within the scope of this book, but Babell's excellent sonata is quoted exceptionally, in order to draw attention to a collection of old English violin music edited by Alfred Moffat and published by Novello, which contains a series of fine sonatas, testifying to the musical capacity of British musicians in Babell's day, accounted until lately obscure. Babell himself was organist at a little church in Bread St., Cheapside. One can only guess why composers so able did not accomplish very much more. They received, I imagine, little encouragement, and were overwhelmed by the towering personality of Handel. Editor.

BACH. Only the composers mentioned in this table are of J. S. Bach's family.

Members of Bach Family in this work.

Johann Sebastian
1685–1750

- Wilh. Friedemann (Halle) 1710–1784
- Carl Philipp Emanuel (Berlin and Hamburg) 1714–1788
- Johann Christoph Friedrich (Bückeburg) 1732–1795
  - Wilhelm Friedrich Ernst (Berlin) 1759–1845
- Johann Christian (Milan and London) 1735–1782

BACH, Johann Sebastian, 1685–1750.

[Note. In the hope that they will prove of use to players, the Editor has included, besides Bach's chamber music properly so called, a number of arrangements. Bach's music, woven commonly of independent parts, is unusually suitable for arrangement for solo instruments, and the small output and the great eminence of this composer render it desirable to include a type of music which is outside the present scheme. It may be noted that Mozart arranged five fugues—given in this list—for string quartet.]

List I. Original Works.

Trio, 2 v, fig. bass (pf), C	Peters; Durand.
Trio, fl, v (or 2 v), fig. bass (pf), G	Durand.
Trio, fl, v (or 2 v), fig. bass (pf), c mi	B. & H.
Six sonatas, clav, v,[1]—b mi, E, A, c mi, f mi, G	Augener, &c.
Those in E, and f mi, Nos. 2, 5, ed. Max Reger	No. 2.—Simrock. No. 5.—B. & H.
No. 4 — c mi — ed. F. David (*Hohe Schule*)	B. & H.
Sonata, clav, v, g mi	B. & H.
Suite, clav, v, A	Bach-Gesellschaft, 9th year.
Sonata, v, fig. bass (pf), e mi	(F. David, *Hohe Schule* 9), B. & H.; (F. Hermann), Peters, No. 236.
Three sonatas, clav, fl, b mi, E flat, A	B. & H., 1908.
Three sonatas, fl, fig. bass (pf), C, e mi, E	B. & H., 1908.
Three sonatas, clav, vla da gamba,[2] G, D, g mi	B. & H.

[1] Also arranged for fl, or vla—B. & H., 1908. See List II.

Note. The C minor sonata given in David's *Hohe Schule* for violin and unfigured bass is not known to be authentic. The work was found in the private library of the King of Saxony.

List II. Works arranged.

Brandenburg concerto No. 6, 2 vla, 2 vla da gamba, vc, cb, B flat	B. & H.
Overture (suite), str. quartet, g mi,	(Herm. Schröder), Vieweg, 1908.
Suite, from *Well-Tempered Clavier* and English and French Suites, str. quartet	(Al. Jiránek), M. Urbánek, 1909.
14 four-part fugues from *Well-Tempered Clavier*, str. quartet	(Rich. Hofmann), Siegel, 1885.
8 fugues and 4 preludes, from *Well-Tempered Clavier*, v, vla, vc	(K. von Bruyck), B. & H., 1867.
15 Three-part inventions, v, vla, vc	(Rich. Hofmann), Siegel, 1882.
15 Three-part inventions, 2 v, vla	(F. David), B. & H.

[2] For arrangements for vla, or vc, see List II.

15 Three-part inventions, 2 v, vc (Rich. Hofmann), Siegel, 1882.
14 Duets (from preludes, inventions, and suites) 2 v (L. Schubert), Peters, 1869.
Chaconne, 2 v (F. Hermann), Kistner, 1887.
Duets (after clavier duets), v, vla (F. David), B. & H., 1874.
Duets (after 2-part inventions), v, vla (F. David), B. & H., 1874.
20 preludes from *Well-Tempered Clavier*, v, vla (F. Hermann), Augener-Schott, 1905.
10 inventions (orig. clav.), v, vc (J. A. Findeisen), C. F. Schmidt, 1922.
15 Two-part inventions, 2 fl (W. Schönicke), Zimmermann, 1902.
Brandenburg concerto no. 6 { pf, v, vla, vc / pf, 2 v, vc } (arr. E. Naumann), B. & H., 1906.
Trio (or quartet), pf, 2 fl, vc ad lib (Max Seiffert), B. & H., 1920.
Six trios, pf, v, vc (*nach Vorlagen von Bach* [1]), (B. Todt), B. & H., 1905–6.
Trios (from organ sonatas, flute sonatas, &c.), pf, v, vla (B. Todt), B. & H.
Sonatas, pf, vla, arranged from v-sonatas, see List I. B. & H.
Arranged from vla da gamba sonatas, see List I. B. & H., U. E.
Three sonatas, pf, vc, arranged from vla da gamba:
No. 1. G (A. Piatti), Schott, 1894.
No. 2. d mi (M. Zweigelt), B. & H., 1899.
No. 3. C (Carl Schroeder,—*Klass. Vc.-Mus.*) Augener-Schott, 1911.
Four Pieces (from vc-solo works), pf, vc (F. von Liliencron), B. & H., 1887.
Suite (from vc-solo works), pf, vc (F. Grützmacher), Bosworth, 1903.
Partita (suite), pf, fl, a mi (M. Schedwer), Peters, 1917.
Suite (from suite fl, str), pf, fl, b mi (A. van Leeuwen), U. E., 1910.
Sonatas, pf, fl, arranged from v-sonatas—see List I. B. & H., 1908.

Special Arrangements.

I. Mozart.

Five fugues from the '48' (Book II),—str. quartet:—viz.

No. 2. c mi.
5. D.
7. E flat.
8. d sharp mi, transposed to *d mi*.
9. E.

II. R. Schumann.

Six sonatas, v solo—as sonatas, pf, v. B. & H., &c.

The editors of the authoritative *Bach-Gesellschaft* publications have included much else beyond what is included in the above list, under the general title of *Kammermusik*—the concertos (whether for instruments on equal terms, or for soli with ripieni), the suites and sonatas for unaccompanied violin or 'cello, and the secular vocal music, solo or choral. In regard to the music of this period, this is an arguable extension of the term; but in a volume like the present, it would obviously be out of place.

Clavier (or cembalo) is a general word including both the harpsichord and the very different clavichord; in all Bach's (as in Handel's) chamber music, the former instrument is no doubt exclusively meant.

In spite of the great varieties of moods, these twenty-one works (almost all of them dating, probably, from Bach's Cöthen period, 1717–23) have certain broad technical features in common: they are all, in the main, conceived as combinations of independent melodic strands. Those for clavier and one other instrument, whatever it may be, are often virtually trios (and one, indeed, sometimes so described); a great deal of their texture, especially in quick movements, is that of pure three-part counterpoint, either hand of the clavier-player being occupied with separate melodic lines, blending on completely equal terms with the melodic line of the other instrument. Occasionally, however (the third movement of the E major violin sonata is a good example), more vertical methods are employed, and, every now and then, exact texture is discarded, and a mere continuo with a figured bass supplied for a few bars at a time, usually so as to throw into special relief the first appearance of some important theme (e.g. the second movement in the B minor, and the second and fourth movements in the A major violin sonatas). The works which employ three instruments are, similarly, contrapuntal trios in essentials; in them there is only a continuo indicated, and the left-hand line of the clavier-part is the only one on equal terms with the individual lines of the two violins, or the violin and flute. These twenty-one works may, accordingly, speaking with exactness, be divided into four strict duos (the sonatas for one instrument and continuo), three strict trios (those for two instruments and continuo), and fourteen works describable—with occasional deviations of different kinds—as trios for two performers.

Six of the sonatas for violin and clavier—those in B minor, A major, E major, C minor, F minor, and G major—are connected together in all the four MSS. of them that are extant. The first three (the most frequently played, and on the whole the finest) are all designed on the same structural lines: slow and quick movements alternate in a four-movement scheme, all (however different in mood) being of approximately equal length and musical weight. The B minor sonata is in some respects the largest in scope; its opening adagio, with the uncommon and singularly expressive employment of double thirds and sixths to intensify

[1] Probably means from notes or sketches left by Bach.

the melodic outline, is not unjustly singled out by Parry as the most notable section of the whole set of sonatas. The A major is brighter in general tone, and, indeed, one of the most directly attractive of all Bach's instrumental works; the andante third movement in F sharp minor, a two-part canon over a free bass, is a famous example of the melodic possibilities of such writing, but there are none the less interesting (though shorter) examples in other movements—particularly near the end of the finale, where the clavier, having twice successfully achieved an imitation of the violin's

Ex. 1.

at half a bar's distance either way, attempts (in a delightfully humorous hurry at the last moment) to do the same at the distance of a crotchet, but has to renounce the idea. The E major stands between these two sonatas; its quick movements have a considerable measure of the cheerfulness of those of the A major, while the slow movements (particularly that in C sharp minor, on a ground bass) are, in their deeply emotional expressiveness, more akin to those of the B minor.

The other three sonatas are of somewhat different and, so to speak, more experimental types. In the C minor there is an expressive slow siciliano (in a 'repeat' structure elsewhere restricted to quick movements), with a very elaborate and somewhat austere allegro which rather overbalances the general scheme, followed by a slow and a quick movement of the same structural types as those in the earlier sonatas. In the F minor, the scheme is: (1) a lengthy largo of great emotional intensity, containing—a unique feature—a considerable quantity of pure four-part writing, (2) an allegro on the lines normally selected for a finale, (3) an adagio which is, like the first prelude in the 'Forty-eight', simply a study in the expressive possibilities of shifting harmonies as such,[1] (4) a vivace in mainly syncopated rhythms. The G major sonata is extant in three distinct forms. Bach's first scheme was: (1) a vigorous presto, with a great deal of bustling semiquaver motion in pure three-part counterpoint throughout; (2) a short largo in E minor, mainly in three but just occasionally in four parts, ending on the dominant chord; (3) an extended cantabile ma un poco adagio (a very uncommon indication) in G major, a duet for the violin and the right hand of the clavier player—a few notes every now and then in unison—with a supporting and always subordinate figured bass—a movement of exceptional melodic beauty, starting as follows:

[1] The clavier-part of this movement was, in the two earlier MSS., laid out in very bare semiquaver arpeggios of common chords, not, as afterwards, in demisemiquaver decoration with continual auxiliary notes in the right hand.

Ex. 2.

and continuing in a long flow of the same deeply expressive, curving figures, with a general mood of emotional intimacy strongly akin (as Spitta has pointed out) to much of the music written for weddings—notably the great alto air from the cantata *O ewiges Feuer* (a wedding cantata originally, though subsequently adapted for the ecclesiastical needs of Whitsuntide); then came (4) a short adagio in B minor (though written with only one sharp in the signature), in pure three-part counterpoint, and also very expressive in its quite different way:

Ex. 3.

(The right-hand clavier-part continues with the chromatic fall.) This movement ends on a D major chord, and for (5) Bach repeated the opening presto as it stood. In the second scheme we have: (1) a vivace that is the same as the original presto, (2) a variant of the largo, (3) a clavier solo in E minor which is a variant of the courante from the sixth partita in that key, (4) the B minor adagio as before, (5) a variant, arranged for violin and 'basso accompagnato', of another movement (the gavotte) from the E minor solo partita, transposed into G minor, (6) no. 1 da capo. In the third and last scheme Bach still retained nos. 1 (now called allegro) and 2, with slight modifications, and then supplied new material, inserting as (3) a different clavier solo, of some length, in E minor, followed by (4) a different adagio in B minor and (5) an extended finale, as lively as no. 1, but quite distinct. His hesitations are curious and interesting; presumably, he felt some lack of contrast in the first scheme, with its three adjoining slow movements, but (quite apart from the unsatisfactory effect of the silence of the violin for part of each of the later schemes) we cannot but deeply regret the disappearance of the cantabile ma un poco adagio, incomparably the finest of all the nine movements which, at one time or another, went to make up this sonata.

The remaining sonata for violin and clavier, in G minor, is a three-movement work of very thin texture and little interest; it is no doubt a quite early production. Its genuineness is vouched for by Bach's son Carl Philipp Emanuel—a fact which disposes of doubts otherwise natural enough. The work in A major ('Trio für's obligate Clavier und Violine'), generally known as a 'suite', is designed as a succession of seven movements (fantasia, courante, entrée, rondeau, sarabande, menuet, allegro), all comparatively slender in style, and with some occasional details of texture that seem to show a lack of their composer's revising hand. The rondeau, with its charming effects of alternately open and stopped strings, is perhaps the most attractive of these light-hearted, melodious little movements.

The single sonata for violin with mere continuo accompaniment throughout—four movements, all in E minor—is, on the other hand, a fine specimen of its composer's deeper moods. The opening moto perpetuo allegro is one of the most powerful movements of its type that he ever wrote, and the following adagio is full of singularly poignant expression, both melodic and harmonic; the sonata is completed by an allemande and a gigue, both masterly, but not rising to the heights of their predecessors.

Bach wrote nothing for the violoncello in collaboration with the clavier, but the three sonatas for viola da gamba and clavier are all—except for a few chords which are playable only on the five-stringed and differently tuned instrument—feasible enough for the 'cello (to which, indeed, they are better suited than is the well-known obbligato in *Mein gläubiges Herze*, written for the 'violoncello piccolo'). The sonata in G major was originally designed for two flutes with continuo; a comparison between the two versions is very interesting, but the later is the more mature in textural details, and is a work of much charm, particularly in its two slow movements, the latter of which (a short andante in E minor) is of singularly impressive beauty—though here, perhaps, the original wind version is the more attractive, so far as mere colour is concerned.

The D major sonata, also in four movements, is of much less distinctive quality (it is also extant in a probably unauthentic arrangement for violin); the G minor, however, ranks high in Bach's chamber music. It is, though considerably longer than the others, laid out in only three movements: first, a vivace of great power, at times almost passionate in expression (alike in the thematic material and in the general method of its development, there are marked resemblances to the opening movement of the G major Brandenburg concerto for stringed orchestra); then a tranquilly expressive adagio in the relative major key; and finally, another quick movement, less passionate but equally vigorous—with considerable contrast of subjects, one of them (specially marked 'cantabile') given out for the first time with plain arpeggio accompaniment over a steady pedal-point, and subsequently in quasi-canonic form with the arpeggios transferred to the bass.

For flute and clavier there are three sonatas. Of that in A major, only the expressive largo e dolce in A minor and the lively finale are printed in the ordinary editions; the *Bach-Gesellschaft*, however, supplies also what is left of the fine first movement, complete except for the loss of a portion (forty or fifty bars long) of the only manuscript. The E flat sonata is a comparatively slight work, no doubt of earlyish date; the charming siciliano in G minor, which forms its central section, has become familiar in a modernized (and spoilt) version for violin. The B minor sonata is laid out in four large movements (the third and fourth virtually forming a quick finale in two distinct sections), and is also musically much the most spacious and mature of the set, ranking, indeed, with the best of the sonatas already mentioned. Particularly noteworthy, perhaps, is the second movement (again a largo e dolce), an extended flow of floridly beautiful tune. The three sonatas for flute and continuo (C major, E minor, E major) are all slender works of no special value; the texture is mature and the material is graceful, but the composer was not, in any of them, taking himself otherwise than lightly. The last movement of the C major (a minuet and trio, a unique form in this position) has, however, one feature of much interest, as we possess in the composer's autograph his own filling up of sixteen bars of the continuo bass—these are the first eight of them:—

Ex. 4.

We see here that he rated flow and interest, as such, in the accompaniment far above pedantic rigidity of part-writing; a few bars later on, indeed, he frankly abandons any attempt to write in four, or even in three, real parts.

The trio in C major, for two violins and continuo, is an attractively cheerful four-movement work; the final presto gigue is the outstanding section, and is indeed, in its way, as perfect a thing as Bach ever wrote—it would not be easy to find anywhere eight bars that combine to such an extent supreme ease and polish of technique with infectious clean gaiety, as

Ex. 5.

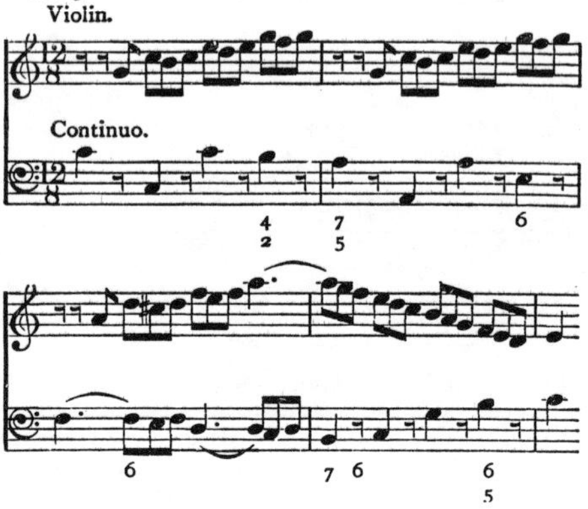

with the four succeeding bars in which, over the repetition of these four, the remaining violin throws in

Ex. 6.

The two trios for violin, flute, and continuo are both designed on the four-movement plan, but they differ in scope, that in G major being very pleasant, but quite short. That in C minor (forming part of the 'Musikalisches Opfer' presented to Frederick the Great in 1747, and most probably the latest of all Bach's chamber works) is much more elaborate, developing in alternately expressive and brilliant fashions various details of the king's own interesting theme; Dörffel has published the arrangement of the continuo of all four movements by Kirnberger, one of Bach's favourite pupils, which in all likelihood very fairly represents the composer's own methods.

Ernest Walker.

[Chaconne. Although written for a single instrument, Bach's magnificent *Chaconne* is so prominent a feature in the modern chamber music programme, that a brief allusion to it will not be out of place. As long as the interpreter is a violinist of distinction, it is a welcome feature, but, under any other circumstances, somewhat of an infliction to weary critics. Praise is due to young students of the violin who are able to affront the difficulties of the *Chaconne* in private, but public performance of a work so exacting should be reserved for days of ripe achievement. Piano accompaniments have been written by Schumann and Mendelssohn, and arrangements made for string quartet by Albert Maria Herz (Simrock) and Martinus Sieveking. These arrangements are, no doubt, useful to students of the work, but I should have thought that a transcription as made by Hermann for two violins would be of more practical service. It is said that Joachim was once taken in at the Hochschule by a pair of mischievous students, who played it as a duet in an adjoining room. The great man rushed in with the word 'splendid' on his lips, only to find that he had been hoaxed![1]

I suggest to the fiscal authorities that the entertainment tax, the tax upon ideals, should be abolished, its place taken by the adoption of Ernest Newman's humorous suggestion that a licence be imposed upon performances in public of the *Chaconne*—and other hackneyed masterpieces. EDITOR.]

BACH, WILHELM FRIEDEMANN.
CARL PHILIPP EMANUEL.
JOHANN CHRISTOPH FRIEDRICH.
JOHANN CHRISTIAN.
WILHELM FRIEDRICH ERNST.

Like their father, Bach's sons were prolific writers of chamber music, prefiguring the 'classic' school in the form, texture, and manner of their compositions. Carl Philipp Emanuel Bach's influence on Haydn is a familiar fact, and Mozart's attraction to Johann Christian Bach is also established. While a good deal of the brothers' chamber music is essentially orchestral, much of it shows them aloof from the heavier orchestral tradition which their father and Handel observed. Most of it remains in manuscript in scattered libraries, but enough has been published in recent years to indicate its character, and to suggest that a great deal of delicate and charming music of this genre has still to be brought to light. It is not the purpose of the *Cyclopedia* to analyse the music of the period preceding Haydn, and therefore this concise note merely indicates the compositions of Bach's sons that are now accessible in modern editions.

(1) WILHELM FRIEDEMANN (1710–1784). Of his trios, only one was positively written for strings. In B flat major, it is scored for two violins and violoncello, and is published in B. & H., *Collegium musicum*, nos. 1875 and 1876 (ed. Hugo Riemann). Piano arrangements of his concerti for clavier and strings are provided in the Steingräber edition, nos. 161, 162, 163, 164; they are in the keys E mi, D, A mi, and F. The concerto in E flat for two claviers, strings, horns, trumpets, and drums is in the same edition (no. 149). Two sonatas for two flutes, in G major and E minor, are published by Tischer and Jagenberg (Cologne). The same firm publishes the sonata in B major for piano and violin. A thematic index to Friedemann's compositions is appended to Martin Falck's *Wilhelm Friedemann Bach* (1919).

(2) CARL PHILIPP EMANUEL (1714–1788). Of his very numerous concerti for clavier and orchestra, one, in D minor, for cembalo, two violins, viola, and basso, is published in B. & H. *Partitur-Bibliothek* (no. 3086); a cembalo ripieno part is added. Senff (Leipzig) publishes a piano arrangement of the concerto in F minor for clavier and strings. The Steingräber edition (nos. 101, 102, 103, 104, 105) contains similar arrangements of the clavier concerti in C minor, G, D (two), E flat, and also (no. 2091) of the D minor (*supra*). In the same edition (nos. 2144, 2145), the concerti in E flat and F for two claviers and orchestra are arranged for two pianos. A sonatina in C for clavier, flutes, and strings is published by B. & H. (ed. Hjalmar von Dameck). Two string quartets, in A and G, edited by Hugo Riemann, are published by Hermann Beyer (Langensalza). Hugo Riemann also has edited the trio in G for two violins and 'cello (Breitkopf, *Collegium musicum*, nos. 1829, 1830). Two of Carl Philipp's three concerti for 'cello and strings are published, the one in A minor by B. & H. (no. 3836), the other in A major (Senart). Edition Peters (no. 2063) contains his sonata in G minor for clavier and viola da gamba ('cello), and also (nos. 3619a and 3619b) his sonatas in B minor and C minor for violin and clavier. Zimmermann publishes his sonata in C for flute and clavier. Alfred Wotquenne provides (B. & H., 1905) a thematic index to Carl Philipp's compositions.

(3) JOHANN CHRISTOPH FRIEDRICH (1732–1795). His compositions are in course of publication by the Bückeburg *Institut für musikwissenschaftliche Forschung*. Vol. vii contains a trio for violin, viola, and clavier in C, another, in C, for flute, violin, and clavier, and a septet, in C, for two horns, oboe, violin, viola, 'cello, and clavier. Zimmermann publishes six sonatas for flute and clavier, in D, G, C, A, F, B flat, which in their original form were quartets for flute, violin, viola, continuo. A sonata, in D, for 'cello and clavier, is in Collection Litolff (no. 2375). Senart publishes six quartets for two violins, viola, 'cello, in E flat, B flat, A, D, G, F. Georg Schünemann provides a thematic index of Christoph Friedrich's compositions in vol. 56 of the *Denkmäler deutscher Tonkunst* (1917).

[1] Moser tells a similar story of a performance of Tartini's *Devil's Trill* behind the scenes at some *tableaux vivants* given at Mendelssohn's house. Again Joachim was taken in by two students, one of whom played the trill while the other comfortably played the theme.

(4) JOHANN CHRISTIAN (1735–1782). A trio, in D, for violin, 'cello, and clavier, is in Breitkopf's *Collegium musicum* (nos. 1737, 1738). Hermann Beyer (Langensalza) publishes three quartets, in F, G, C, for two violins, viola, 'cello. Edition Peters (no. 3873) contains the concerto (op. VII, no. 5) in E flat for clavier and strings (two violins and 'cello). Piano arrangements of the clavier concerti in G (op. VII, no. 6), E, and D (op. VII, no. 3) are in Edition Steingräber (nos. 92, 106, 107). Two sonatas for pf. and violin (op. XVI, nos. 1 and 2) are in *Nagel's Musik-Archiv*. A thematic index is appended to the present writer's *Johann Christian Bach*.

C. SANFORD TERRY.

[Adolph Nagel of Hanover is publishing some interesting music in *Nagel's Musik-Archiv*, no. I of which contains sonatas nos. 1 and 2, for clavier and violin (or flute). Even now, Johann Christian's compositions are turning up in many European libraries.

(5) WILHELM FRIEDRICH ERNST, 1759–1845, son of Joh. Christoph ('Bückeburg' Bach), last descendant of J. S. Bach.

From *Fétis*:

Six sonatas, pf (clavier), v	op. 1	Berlin, 1788.
Three sonatas, pf (clavier), v	,, 2	,, 1790.]

BACH, LEONHARD EMIL, 1849–1902, pianist (b. Posen).

Sonata, pf, vc, a mi	op. 45	Schott, 1891.

BACH, OTTO, 1833–1893, Austrian composer.

Quartet, str, d mi	op. 6	Kistner, 1863.
Adagio and fugue, str. quartet, a mi	,, 8	R. & E., 1894.
Trio, pf, v, vc, c sharp mi	,, 7	J. Schuberth & Co., 1865.
Trio, pf, v, vc, E flat	,, 22	R. Forberg, 1872.
Duet, pf, v, G	,, 18	Kistner, 1870.
Duet, pf, horn, F	,, 10	Hofmeister, 1862.

BACHE, FRANCIS EDWARD, 1833–1858, English composer, brother of Walter Bache, the Liszt propagandist.

Trio, pf, v, vc, D	Kistner.

Bache's early death was a serious loss to British music. The trio showed considerable promise.

BACHE, J.

Sonata, pf, v, G	op. 7	F. Schuberth, jr., 1910.

†BACHMANN, ALBERTO, contemporary composer.

2nd Suite, pf, v, d mi	Schott, 1905.
Suite romantique, pf, v	Gallet, 1921.
Suite, pf, v, d mi	Fürstner, 1913.

Compiler of an Encyclopedia of the violin, which contains many features of interest to chamber musicians. Illustrations are included of various groups of quartet players, with an article on chamber music and a list of suggested metronome tempi for the Haydn and Beethoven quartets. Also a catalogue of solo and ensemble works, the latter including several little-known compositions for three and four violins, with and without piano accompaniment. But as the title indicates, the book is mainly concerned with the violin *qua* instrument. Published by D. Appleton & Co.

EDITOR.

†BACHMETEV, N., Russian composer.

Quartet, str, D	op. 16	Bessel, 1882.

BACHRICH, SIEGMUND, 1841–1913, Hungarian composer, violist in various Quartets.

Suite, pf, v	op. 7	Doblinger, 1872.

BACKER-LUNDE, JOHAN, b. 1874, Norwegian pianist, pupil of Busoni.

Suite, pf, v, d mi	op. 14	Norsk. Musikförl., 1897.
Sonata, pf, v, d mi	op. 15	,, ,, ,,

BAEKER, ERNST, b. 1866, German composer.

Sonata, pf, v, g mi	op. 8	Karl Köhler, *c.* 1903.

BAGGE, CARL ERNST, Baron von, d. 1791, chamberlain to the King of Prussia.

Fétis mentions:

Six quartets, str	op. 1	publ. 1773.

A clever amateur composer, known for his egregious conceit, of whom amusing stories are told. Rodolphe Kreutzer played a concerto of his at Paris with success. Further details will be found in *Fétis*.

BAGGE, SELMAR, 1823–1896, German composer and critic.

Two quartets, str, E flat, F	op. 1	Haslinger.
Quartet, str, C	,, 12	Weinberger, 1861.
Easy little suite, pf, v, e mi	,, 16	B. & H., 1884.
Easy sonata, pf, vc (also pf, v), F	,, 3	Haslinger, 1847.

BAILLOT, PIERRE MARIE FRANÇOIS DE SALES, 1771–1842, French violinist and a supremely gifted quartet leader.

Modern republications:

3 duets, 2v	op. 16	Schott, 1868.

[Six duets were originally published.]

For orig. publications see *Fétis*.

Baillot was a man of the highest culture, originally destined for a bureaucratic career. As late as 1791 he accepted a position in the

Paris Ministry of Finance, but continued practising the violin in his leisure hours. Considering that he was originally an amateur, his ardour for study must have been phenomenal, for he was in a position, a few years later, to secure a dual appointment as professor at the newly founded Paris Conservatoire, and solo violinist in the private chapel of the First Consul, Napoleon. In 1814 he set the seal upon his professional reputation by founding a series of quartet soirées, which stimulated the interest of musical Paris in the art of chamber music to a remarkable extent, and gave him a place in musical history as the most intellectual of the violinists of the French classical school. For him Cherubini composed his quartets, recognizing, no doubt, that he possessed all the qualities desirable in an interpreter of chamber music—nobility of thought, intense yet restrained emotional fervour, and adequate technique. As Fétis wrote, 'Dans le quatuor il était plus qu'un grand violiniste, il était poète'; and Mendelssohn's criticism of his playing was not less favourable. His own compositions are antiquated, and the violin method, in which he collaborated with Rode and Kreutzer, has long since been superseded, but his writings on musical subjects are still read. Among them are the following lines dedicated to the 'String Quartet':

LE QUATUOR

Sous un sceptre nouveau tenant république,
Se bornant à toucher pour toute politique,
Paraît le Violon: ce roi, ce soldat heureux,
Père de ses sujets, ami des malheureux,
Commande, obéissant aux passions qu'il exprime,
Sa voix, soumise ainsi, sa voix devient sublime;
S'il persuade et désarme ou subjugue en vainqueur,
C'est qu'il a su trouver le chemin du cœur!
Quand le modeste Alto joint sa voix à la sienne
Pour qu'en un quatuor l'intérêt se soutienne,
Le violoncelle Basse, à ce concert admis,
Devient régulateur de ce groupe d'amis,
Et mêlant ses accents à ceux qu'il favorise,
Sa grave mélodie avec eux fraternise.

EDITOR.

BAINES, WILLIAM, 1899–1922, English composer.

Baines revealed exceptional talents at an early age, but unfortunately he developed pneumonia in the army in 1918, and never fully recovered.

He left some songs, with violin and 'cello, and a string quartet which is still in MS.

A. EAGLEFIELD-HULL.

†BAINTON, EDGAR LESLIE, b. 1880, British composer.

Bainton's compositions are numerous, and mostly on a big scale. Unfortunately, none of his chamber music (which includes two string quartets, and sonatas for viola and piano, and 'cello and piano) has yet been published. He is well known as a performer of ensemble music, of which he is a refined and gifted exponent.

T. F. DUNHILL.

†BALAKIREV, MILY ALEXEIVICH, 1836–1910, Russian composer. Leader of the Nationalist school in Russia, associated in his work with Rimsky-Korsakov, Cui, Moussorgsky, and Borodin ('the Five').

He showed interest in chamber music by arranging a Beethoven quartet for two pianos, and there is a youthful piano octet in MS.

EDITOR.

BALFE, MICHAEL WILLIAM, 1808–1870, Irish operatic composer.

Trio, pf, v, vc, A	(Author's publication).
Sonata, pf, vc, A flat.	

Many writers of light opera have tried their hands at composing chamber music, and Balfe was one of the few who did so with success. Both the above works were selected for performance at the 'Pops', Joachim taking part in the trio (March, 1877). It is a melodious work, containing in the scherzo some reminders of his Irish nationality. It may be seen at the COBBETT FREE LIBRARY (*q.v.*). EDITOR.

BALORRE, CH. DE, French composer.

Quintet, cl, 2 v, vla, vc	Hamelle, 1906.
Quartet, str	Delauchy, 1891.
Trio, ob, vla, vc, c mi	Hamelle, 1899.
Trio, pf, v, vc	Legouix, 1900.

†BALUTET, M., contemporary French woman composer.

Sonata, pf, vc (also pf, v), g mi	Rouart, 1897.

BAMBERG, KARL.

Trio, 3 trombones	Merseburger.

Mention of this work is due to the singularity of the combination. The trombone is not an instrument likely to become popular in the drawing-room.

†BANTOCK, GRANVILLE, b. 1868, English composer.

	Composed	
Sonata (*Colleen*), pf, vla, F	1919	Chester.
Pibroch, vc, pf (or harp)	1918	,,

MS. WORKS:

Quartet, str, c mi	Composed 1899.
Serenade, 4 horns, F	,, 1903.

Bantock has written only one work which properly comes within the scope of this Cyclopedia, namely the viola sonata. The opening allegro is a powerful and stimulating movement. The first subject is announced at once by the viola, and the treatment follows traditional lines. It is succeeded by a restless, syncopated section, which in turn gives way to a joyous and passionate theme. The whole is full of the joy of life.

The slow movement, in 5/4, is in the nature of a nocturne, contemplative and tinged with melancholy. It is full of emotion, and rises to a fine climax before the quiet and wistful close.

The finale, vivace, has the lilt of a Scottish

jig. The first theme, which is in two sections, is given out by the piano before passing to the viola. The second episode is a rich melody on the viola, whilst later a slow passage for the same instrument heralds the entry of a theme similar to the first subject. The working-out displays much ingenuity. The sonata ends on a long coda based on the first subject, and the whole work forms a valuable addition to the repertory.

The *Pibroch* is a Highland Lament based on a Scottish folk-tune, which is utilized in various forms. The harp blends effectively with the 'cello, and introduces a definite Celtic atmosphere.

The remaining works—a *Fantastic Poem*, *Celtic Poem* (both for 'cello and piano), *Hamabdil*, a Hebrew melody for 'cello and harp (or piano)—being accompanied solos, are notable works, but not chamber music in the sense understood in this Cyclopedia.

W. S. MEADMORE.

BARBEDETTE, HIPPOLYTE LA ROCHELLE, 1827–1901, French composer.

Sextet, pf, 2 v, vla, vc, cb	op. 1	Heugel.
Trio sonata, pf, 2 v, A	„ 183	Hamelle.
Sonata no. 1, pf, v	„ 65	„
„ no. 6, „ „	„ 188	„
„ no. 1, pf, vc	„ 166	„
„ no. 2, „ „	„ 185	„

BARBIER, RENÉ AUGUSTE ERNEST, b. 1890, Belgian composer.

Pièce symphonique, pf, cornet (or trumpet) Evette & Schaeffer, 1921.

Other works in MS.

BARBIERI, M.

Sonata, pf, v, B flat Serra (Geneva), 1921.

BARBILLION, JEANNE, b. 1895, French violinist, pupil of d'Indy.

Sonata, pf, v, D Senart.

The Prix Marmontel has been awarded to her recently (1928) by the Société des Compositeurs de Musique, for a piano trio.

† BARBLAN, OTTO, b. 1860, Swiss composer.

Quartet, str, d mi op. 19 Hug.

BARGIEL, WOLDEMAR, 1828–1897, German composer.

Octet, str, c mi	op. 15a	B. & H., 1877.
1st quartet, str, a mi	„ 15b	(score & parts) B. & H., 1877.
4th quartet, str, d mi	„ 47	(score & parts) B. & H., 1877.
Trio, pf, v, vc, F	„ 6	Leuckart, 1856, 1876.
Trio, pf, v, vc, E flat	„ 20	„ 1860.
Trio, pf, v, vc, B flat	„ 37	B. & H., 1870.
Sonata, pf, v, f mi	op. 10	Fürstner, 1858, 1882.
Suite, pf, v, D	„ 17	Peters, 1859, 1879.

Bargiel was a step-brother of Clara Wieck, and it is evident from his works that he was an adherent of Robert Schumann. His compositions in general are distinguished by excellent and often highly artistic treatment of rather undistinguished themes, and his chamber music, though it sounds extremely well, has been undeservedly neglected of late.

FIRST STRING QUARTET. He wrote four string quartets, of which two only are published. The first, op. 15b, clear, transparent, and concise, will always win friends for the composer. The first theme of the opening allegro is melodious and pre-eminently adaptable, the second being more rhythmic in character. The second movement is an attractive combination of a vigorous Ländler and a mazurka; this is somewhat uncompromising, but the trio forms a very graceful contrast. The andante sostenuto is devotional in character, while the finale has a powerful, rhythmic main theme and pleasing subsidiary themes; there is, too, a frequently recurring, teasing motif, and the close is vigorous and effective.

PIANO TRIOS. Of these the exuberant op. 6 is deservedly the most popular in amateur circles; the third is, however, a riper work. In the opening allegro a graceful and rhythmically interesting theme is given to the strings alone, and then gives place to another, more emotional in character. The development section is effectively constructed, and cleverly worked out. There is a touch of folk-song in the expressive and slightly sentimental main theme of the andante, the middle section of which is forceful and energetic. The rather long-winded scherzo is in the main playful, resolving itself often into a lively dialogue between 'cello and violin, while the trio has the true Schumann fervour. The finale opens with a most effective flowing melody, the second theme being more rhythmic in character.

THE VIOLIN SONATA is worthy of notice, even at the present day. The first movement is a great effort, modelled to some extent upon the corresponding movement in Beethoven's op. 30, no. 2. The vigorous main theme is presented with weight and precision, and is followed by a second, which leads into the real second subject, in elegiac mood. The development is skilful, but rather difficult to play—indeed, the whole sonata is by no means easy. The andante consists of ingenious and tasteful variations on a simple, expressive theme, while the last movement is an original combination of a kind of scherzo, designed chiefly for rhythmical effect, with the actual finale, a flowing movement with a melodious first subject. The scherzo is introduced again after the second subject, and there is an extensive and brilliant coda.

THE SUITE is a skilful attempt to breathe new life into old dance forms. Its five movements are somewhat unequal in quality, the opening allemande being the least pleasing; the sicilienne, however, is absolutely typical in character, and has a charming melody, while there is wholesome humour in the burlesque (allegro). The similarity of the minuet with Verdi's *La Donna è mobile* is too evident, but the melodious trio has an original effect, obtained by the occasional insertion of a bar of common time. The finale is a most effective, exhilarating march, and is not without harmonic interest.

WILHELM ALTMANN.

[The repertory of piano trios being none too copious, Bargiel's contributions are most valuable to amateurs. Op. 6 was played at the 'Pops' in 1875, and it is doubtful if anything of Bargiel's has been heard since in London. In the writer's opinion, the third, op. 37, is the finest. The influence of Schumann is felt, but that composer's intensity and imaginative fervour are absent. EDITOR.]

BARIOLAGE BOWING. A word used by the French, and derived from the Latin *variolagium* = alternation. It describes what may be called parti-coloured bowing, the same note being sounded in alternation upon two adjacent strings as below.

Antonio Vivaldi is said to have invented this manner of crossing the strings, used to perfection in the much-played prelude to Bach's E major violin suite, and frequently to be found in chamber music, both ancient and modern. A familiar example is seen in the finale to Haydn's quartet in E minor, op. 50, no. 6, sometimes known as the *Frog*. EDITOR.

Ex. 1.

Ex. 2.

BARJANSKY, ADOLF, 1850–1915(?), Russian composer.

Quartet, str, E	op. 6	B. & H., 1893.
,, ,, A	,, 8	,, 1894.
Quartet, pf, v, vla, vc, c mi	,, 5	,, 1893.
Trio, pf, v, vc, G	,, 3	Cranz, 1892.
Sonata, pf, vc, a mi	,, 4	,, 1893.

Dr. Altmann (*Handbuch*) writes appreciatively of Barjansky's two string quartets.

† BARKWORTH, J. E., b. 1858, English composer.

Trio (*The Seasons*), pf, v, vc, a mi	Goodwin & Tabb.

BARLEY, ALFRED H.

Trio-Fantaisie, pf, v, vc, B	op. 11	Avison, 1907.

BÄRMANN, (1) HEINRICH JOSEPH, 1784–1847, famous clarinettist.

Modern republication:

Quartet, cl. v, vla, vc, B flat	op. 18	Schott, 1882.

For orig. publications *v. Fétis*.

Esteemed by Weber (who composed specially for him) as a 'truly great artist and a glorious man'. Also Mendelssohn wrote for him two duets for clarinet and basset horn, op. 113.

(2) KARL, 1811–1885, clarinettist, worthy successor to his father, Heinrich Joseph.

Sonata (duet), pf, cl, f mi	op. 4	Schott, 1843.

BARMOTIN, SIMON, b. 1877, Russian composer, pupil of Balakirev and Rimsky-Korsakov.

Serenade, pf, v, vc, c sharp mi	op. 13	Jurgenson, 1909.
Suite, pf, v, a mi	,, 11	,, 1909.
Sonata, pf, v, a mi	,, 14	,, 1910.

BARNEKOW, CHRISTIAN, 1837–1913, Danish composer.

Quintet, 2 v, vla, 2 vc, g mi	op. 20	B. & H., 1905.
Quartet, pf, v, vla, vc, D	,, 12	,,
Trio, pf, v, vc, f sharp mi	,, 1	Hansen, 1868.
Sonata, pf, v, F	,, 23	Norsk. Musikförlag, 1907.

BARNETT, JOHN FRANCIS, 1837–1916, English composer.

Quartet, str, d mi	op. 8	Augener-Schott.
Trio, pf, v, vc, c mi	,, 49	,, ,, 1889.
Sonata, pf, fl, g mi	,, 41	Rudall, 1883.

Other chamber works in MS. *v. British Musical Biography*.

J. F. Barnett was nephew of the operatic composer, John Barnett. Of his chamber music little need be said, except that it was more or less derivative. He is best remembered as composer of the cantata, *The Ancient Mariner*, and as having completed Schubert's E flat symphony from autograph sketches in the possession of Sir George Grove. EDITOR.

† BARNS, ETHEL, b. 1875, English violinist.

2nd sonata, pf, v, A	op. 9	Schott, 1909.
4th sonata, pf, v, g mi	,, 24	,, 1911.
Phantasy trio, pf, 2 v	,, 26	,,

The above works bear the stamp of the executant rather than the contemplative musician. The violin parts are the work of a skilled player who knows the legitimate capacities of the instrument, and conceives passages which lie well for fingers and bow. The piano, too, is in sympathy with its more brilliant qualities, the chief resource being resonant chords and wide-ranging arpeggios. The harmony is strong in six-fours and dominant sevenths, with frequent modulations, the composer's favourite device being to shift a passage by semitones from one key-plane to another.

The earlier sonata, although simple, has spontaneity and more variety than the more ambitious op. 24. In the trio, the writing for the two violins shows constructive care, and the two parts are of equal interest.

KATHARINE EGGAR.

[The sonata numbered second (the first being still unpublished) was played in Germany during Joachim's lifetime by the master himself (1903). The third is also still in MS. The fourth contains a slow movement which may be described as atmospheric, with a sensitively written, rippling variation for muted violin, and a finale which contains a double fugue and displays the composer's command of counterpoint. Other works by Miss Barns are in MS., including a violin sonata, which she introduced at one of her own concerts in 1927.

Her phantasy trio was frequently played by the composer with the late Émile Sauret, always with great success. It was among the works commissioned by W. W. Cobbett.

EDITOR.]

BARTH, KARL HEINRICH, 1847–1922, German pianist, pupil of Bülow.

Barth formed a Trio with de Ahna and Hausmann. He was also a composer, and wrote a violin sonata in D.

BARTH, RICHARD, 1850–1923, German violinist, pupil of Joachim.

Quartet, str, g mi	op. 15	Simrock, 1901.
Trio, pf, v, vc, a mi	,, 19	Peters, 1905.
Sonata, pf, v, D	,, 14	F. Schuberth, jr., 1899.
Sonata, pf, v, b mi	,, 20	Simrock, 1907.
Sonata, pf, v (*im alten Stil*), D	,, 23	Benjamin, 1915.

In his chamber music, Barth stands proudly confessed as a disciple of Schumann and Brahms, and his output is certainly worthy of notice. In his string quartet, op. 15, he proves himself a skilled contrapuntist; the work makes fairly stiff demands both on the technical and intellectual equipment of the performers. This is true particularly of the opening allegro, which has a decidedly complex development. It contains a cantabile theme of considerable attractiveness, which serves as second subject. The expressive adagio might well be called a counterpart to the corresponding movement in Schumann's op. 41, no. 3. The brief intermezzo is rightly designated 'vivo ed un poco strepitoso'; it has a trio, which is a charming little movement, very simply written, on Haydn-Mozartian lines. The finale is in the major mode; there is a real swing in this movement, to which a delicate singing theme lends a particular charm.

THE VIOLIN SONATAS. The first of these (op. 14) is distinguished by the same qualities as the string quartet, while the third is sufficiently described by its superscription: *Im alten Stil*. The second, which is the most important, has a somewhat uninspired first movement, but there is great delicacy in the second (un poco andante), which consists of variations on a simple, but very expressive theme. The scherzo, which has a fugato section, is interesting primarily by reason of its rhythm, while the trio is ingratiatingly tuneful. The rondo finale is, however, the most original, with its quasi-Hungarian first subject. This by no means easy sonata should come through the ordeal of the concert-room with honour.

WILHELM ALTMANN.

[Owing to an accident in his youth, Barth learned to bow with his left hand and finger with his right. His quartet has been played in London with success.]

BARTH, RUDOLF, German composer.

Sonata, pf, v (or vla, or vc), F	op. 7	Peters, 1883.
Sonata, pf, vc, d mi	,, 2	Cranz, 1869.
Sonata, pf, vc, C	,, 11	Kahnt, 1889.

*†BARTÓK, BÉLA, b. 1881, Hungarian composer.

		Composed	
1st quartet, str, a mi	op. 7	1908	Rószavölgyi; U.E., 1912.
2nd quartet, str, a mi	,, 17	1915–17	U.E., 1920.
Sonata, pf, v, atonal	,, 18	1921	U.E., 1923.
Sonata, pf, v, atonal	,, 21	1923	,, ,,

There is also a quintet for piano and strings, written in 1904.

Though he first studied with a grandson of the famous Hungarian composer, Erkel, Bartók owes most of his training to Hans KOESSLER (*q.v.*), a distinguished German teacher and composer, who succeeded Robert Volkmann at the Budapest National Academy. Apart from the marked individuality displayed in his original works, Bartók is noted for his enthusiasm for Hungarian folk-song, and is classed as a nationalist. He and Kodály are the acknowledged leaders of the national movement in Hungarian music. His first published chamber work, the string quartet, op. 7, was preceded by several compositions, notably a rhapsody for piano and orchestra, and a first orchestral suite, of which the latter was to carry his fame to Vienna and beyond. This might lead one to suppose that, like so many other composers, he had deferred approaching this branch of his art until he had won his spurs in the others. But he had already made two distinct beginnings in chamber music. Whilst still in his teens, and before studying with Koessler, he had written a piano quartet (1898) and a string quartet (1899). Then, when more serious study began, all tentative composition was temporarily suspended. Four years later, about the time (Feb. 1904) when Richter performed his early programme symphony (*Kossuth*) at Manchester, he made a fresh start with a violin sonata (1903) and a piano quintet (1904). Both works were performed with success at Vienna, but the young composer was not satisfied, and neither is available in print. That his decision was final is proved by his having published the violin sonata of 1921 as his 'first'.

THE FIRST STRING QUARTET comes at the end of his early stage of development. The works which preceded it were full of vitality, but somewhat unequal in constructive qualities. Here the form is concise. Kodály writes of it:

> 'The unity of the movements, preserved during the nineteenth century by devices which became more and more external, is established here in the manner of the old masters: by the homogeneity of the thematic material, with something more which I would call psychological unity—an intimate drama, a kind of 'Return to Life' of one who has reached the brink of the abyss. It is programme music, but does not need a programme, so clearly does it explain itself.'

It is in three movements, of which the first merges into the second, and the third is preceded by a declamatory introduction. The first movement (lento) opens with the four instruments entering in pairs imitatively:

Ex. 1.

Contrast to this polyphonic writing is provided by a central episode of more lyrical character. At the close of the movement the tempo gradually quickens to that of its successor (allegretto), a lengthy quotation from which is given in an article by Cecil Gray (*Sackbut*, November 1920). The finale, which is dominated by an energetic theme presaged in the introduction, is the most extended of the three movements. A fantastic fugato passage on the theme

Ex. 2.

furnishes an admirably contrasted middle section.

THE SECOND QUARTET. Before the second quartet came to be written, Bartók's style had undergone considerable development. His studies of the Hungarian peasant-songs—very different from the gipsy embroideries so long known to Western Europe as Hungarian—had exercised a marked influence upon his melodic line. As he has explained (*Anbruch*, March 1921), it revealed to him the possibility of complete emancipation from the tyranny of the major and minor system. The modal and pentatonic forms of the scale offered new melodic prospects, and, taken in conjunction, endowed the twelve degrees of the chromatic scale with a significance that conferred a wider freedom in their employment, both horizontally and vertically. Thus arose the more daring of Bartók's harmonies, of which there are many in the second quartet. Kodály ascribes Bartók's most 'execrated' dissonances to melodic origins, and applies to him what was formerly said of Bach, that with him there are not only passing-notes, but passing phrases; that a suspension may be, not merely a note, but an entire passage. As at the same time, and in the same process, Bartók also acquired a more elastic conception of rhythm, the effect was to make his later music somewhat difficult of approach. Yet the difficulty is largely due to the operation of conventions which are not his. The contact of the simple peasant idiom with the system of music-writing which centuries have painfully evolved causes the reproach of sophistication to be bandied to and fro. One side declares that the composer has self-consciously sophisticated the primitive material, and the other retorts that only the sophistication of its adversaries by tradition prevents them from seeing the glaring simplicity of both material and treatment. One is reminded of the aesthetic problem presented by Dvořák. There is, in fact, a perennial question involved in the confrontation of primitive material and the natural musician with the apparatus of musical procedure by precedent. Bartók's rhythmic sense was also developing at this period. He never discarded his affection for the quasi-brutal, insistent rhythms of the country-dance type, prevailing in all the south-eastern regions of Europe, but he acquired a strange and characteristic elasticity of rhythmic conception which sometimes gives an entire movement the aspect of a much magnified rubato.

The second quartet is in three movements. The first (moderato), which opens thus—

Ex. 3.
Second Quartet.
Opening of 1st Movement.

is concise in form and thematically developed, but in some respects the least easily accessible of the three. Its mood of dreamy unrest has moments of energy, but subsides towards the conclusion into a wistful calm. The scherzo is a ruggedly jovial piece of folk-dance type, recalling some earlier compositions, such as the *Allegro barbaro*. The apparent crudities in the harmony are made good rhythmically, that is to say, the strong pulsation makes them natural. In a quieter section occurs the following:

Ex. 4.
2nd Quartet. From 2nd Movement.

There is also to be noted the remarkably effective employment of unisons and octaves, in other music so frequently an element of weakness. The finale (lento) is a plaintive rhapsody, an extension of the mood that one encounters in the earlier dirges for piano. Writing of the quartet as a whole, Wellesz remarks that it is almost impossible to judge its effect from the score, but that in performance the clear-cut melodic outlines, pregnant rhythms, and lucid construction make it more easy to grasp than many another work of less daring conception.

We now reach the most controversial aspect of Bartók's chamber music, that revealed by the two violin sonatas composed for Miss Jelly d'Aranyi. Here, such explanation as could find place in a dictionary ceases to have value. The writing is mostly pure expressionism, and to apprehend it is a matter, not of understanding, but of sensibility. For that reason, all argument is futile. One hearer receives the impression, another does not, and therefore probably denies its presence, as is the usual practice. Neither can convince the other, and there the matter must rest. But those whose perceptions are receptive to this music find in it emotional depth alternating with elemental simplicity. It is, at the same time, near to nature, and expressed in a remote idiom, just as some forms of art among ancient races delight in an elaboration which does not in the least disguise the simplicity of the artistic impulse that initiates them.

The First Sonata is in three movements, of which the opening allegro appassionato, though rhapsodic in character, conforms in essentials to regular sonata form. The adagio opens with a recitative for the violin alone—

Ex. 5.

and maintains the character of lyrical declamation. The finale, allegro molto, reverts to the peasant idiom of which Bartók is such a master. (Ex. 6.)

THE SECOND SONATA, which is in two movements played without a break, is the more concentrated of the two, and therefore easier to the listener, if not to the performer, upon whom a heavier interpretative task is laid, quite

Ex. 6.
From Sonata I.
Violin and Piano. 3rd Movement.

apart from the executive difficulties. Though so short an interval separates the two sonatas, a distinct advance is felt. The writing is, however, more conscious, as if the composer had been on a voyage of discovery in the first sonata, and were examining his finds in the second. Passages such as that in Ex. 7 are frequent in the opening section, where the purely instrumental effects are most abundant, whilst in the allegretto the aspect of rustic simplicity is maintained in the face of some strange harmonic agglomerations.

As a contribution to the history of the violin sonata, these two compositions are unique. In

Ex. 7.
From Sonata II, Violin and Piano.

comparison, even the second quartet is more accessible to the unprepared listener. Bartók has travelled far on the road of expressionism. It remains to be seen whither that road will take him, or whether, like so many of his contemporaries, he will presently turn towards neo-classicism for a framework to his musical thought. EDWIN EVANS.

[Amateurs making a frontal attack upon these Hungarian fortresses of sound are warned that they are impregnable to any but virtuoso players. Nor are they fully equipped, unless they have ears attuned to Hungarian folk-song of the kind which owes nothing to the gipsies, but reeks of the soil.

One must respect the conviction arrived at by so many connoisseurs of the first rank, that Bartók's music is assured of a great future. EDITOR.]

BARTOLONI, JEAN.

Sonata, pf, v, c mi — Henn, 1919/21.

†BARTZ, JOH., b. 1848, German composer.

Sonata, pf, v, F — op. 22 — Reinecke, 1893.

BARYTON. An obsolete instrument of the viola da gamba tribe, with sympathetic strings passing under the finger-board. It was a favourite with German chamber music players in the eighteenth century. Numerous chamber works were written for the baryton by Haydn for his patron, Prince Esterhazy, a performer on the instrument (*v.* GERMAN CHAMBER MUSIC). For list of makers, performers, and composers *v. Grove*. EDITOR.

BASEVI, DR. ABRAMO, 1818–1885.

Instituted a yearly prize for composition of a string quartet in Italy, in which country he inaugurated by his efforts a new era for chamber music. He was one of the founders of the Società del Quartetto.

BASS, RODERICH.

Trio, pf, v, vc, c mi — op. 26 — Mozarthaus, 1908.

BASSOON. The bassoon is not a perfect instrument, nor are there two exactly alike, even when made by the same manufacturer. Its imperfections may, however, be overcome to a great extent by the skill of the performer. Beethoven and Mozart have both used the bassoon in chamber music, though in their time it was even more imperfect than now, having a very limited number of keys. It is, indeed, difficult to understand how these works were played at that period, though it is perhaps explained by the composer's avoidance, when writing, of the higher register.

An interesting sonata for bassoon and 'cello, by Mozart, recently played in London, shows the instrument to great advantage. With reference to modern works, Stravinsky has included the bassoon in his septet, *L'histoire d'un soldat*, for violin, clarinet, bassoon, trumpet, trombone, contra-basso, and side-drum. The bassoon part in this work is very difficult, the composer writing a great deal in the extreme upper register. EDWARD DUBRUCQ.

[The technique of the bassoon is rather a ticklish affair. Bordering as it occasionally does on the burlesque, it must be handled by a skilled performer, and then the tone is surprisingly beautiful, no less romantic in quality than that of the oboe (of which it may be said to be the bass). It has been used in chamber music largely as the bass of an ensemble of wind instruments. It is not suitable for combination alone with the strings, but is quite essential as one of the wind group in the Beethoven septet and Schubert octet. It has, in a few instances, been displaced as the foundation of the wind ensemble by the more solid but less facile bass clarinet.

An extended list of the works in which it is employed may be found in *Altmann*, among them sonatas by W. Y. Hurlstone, 1909, Saint-Saëns, 1921, and Gustav Schreck, 1887. There is an ineffective trio for clarinet, bassoon, and piano by Glinka. Of the three duets for clarinet and bassoon by Beethoven, arranged as a trio by Adolph MANN (*q.v.*), the third contains a remarkable theme and variations. Francis Poulenc has also written an effective sonata for this pair of instruments.

It is interesting to know that Sir Edward Elgar played the bassoon when a young man, for the purpose of a wind ensemble consisting of two flutes, oboe, clarinet, and bassoon.

EDITOR.]

†BASTARD, WILLIAM, English composer.

Trio, pf, v, vc, g mi	op. 3	Schott, 1908.

†BATON, RHENÉ (or Rhené-Baton, properly René), b. 1879, French composer.

Trio, pf, v, vc, c mi to E flat	op. 31	Composed 1923. Durand.
Sonata, pf, v, G	,, 24	Durand, 1921.

Much of Rhené Baton's chamber music is inspired by, though not directly borrowed from, Breton folk-lore. In each of the above works there are several interesting structural features. The trio is built on a curious plan, both as regards tonality and thematic structure. The former generally oscillates between C minor and E flat major. The first movement, preceded by a slow introduction, presents the tranquil mother-theme imbued with Breton melancholy—on muted violin and 'cello. This is then taken up and harmonized by the piano. The allegro (2/2) introduces a vigorous first theme, which belongs melodically to the key of C minor; but at the same time, by reason of the harmony of the piano, it partakes of the tonality of E flat—polytonality, of course. This interpenetration of the two relative keys is one of the features of this engaging work. The tranquil theme of the introduction, in E major, is used as a bridge to connect with the expressive second subject, which is in three sections in 6/4 and 9/4, with piquant harmony, in B major, G major, and then in different keys. The development begins in G minor, with an amplification of the second subject over the rhythm of the first, and offers the happiest combinations of the various materials. There is great variety of rhythm and continual insistence on the ambiguity subsisting between the two related keys of E flat major and C minor. The recapitulation (in 3/2 now) has the peculiar feature that the two themes are heard in combination, *ff*, the first rhythmically altered, in C minor, on the 'cello, the second much broader than before, in E flat, on the violin. The piano accompaniment has, in the treble, an augmentation of the opening C minor theme in notes of equal value, while the bass insists on the key of E flat. This grows gradually calmer; the violin and 'cello finally renounce their antagonism, and unite in the mother-theme, greatly augmented. The movement ends in absolute calm. The strings give the impression of C minor, while the piano has a chord of E flat, with the 'added sixth'.

The second movement, ***Divertissement sur un vieil air breton***,—the *Vin de Gaulois*, a rude barbaric tune—is a kind of scherzo with wild and strongly marked rhythm. Above this theme the strings soon bring in the mother-theme, which itself seems to be derived from it; they then announce a second element, full of animation. An andante in 4/2 follows, in which the theme of the introduction is heard in octaves on the strings, with the rhythm of the popular theme on the piano.

The third movement is preceded by a mournfully expressive introduction, leading to the final allegro, on a first subject in F minor, with an abrupt and broken rhythm, in alternate bars of 3 and 4 time. A bridge, formed of the opening theme of the work and the popular theme of the divertissement, connects this with the more tranquil second subject, in C major, derived from the mother-theme. The violin and 'cello, three octaves apart, present this melody very softly and faintly, with a suggestion of the wide-stretching *Landes* seen through a light veil of mist. The development starts in B minor, and is based on the abrupt opening figure, the popular theme of the bridge and that of the divertissement, ending, curiously enough, with a complete recapitulation of the second theme in C major. The first theme then reappears in F sharp minor, modulating back to the opening key of F minor to link up with the second subject, presented now as a larghetto, very calm, against undulating arpeggios on the piano, in E flat, while the strings sing the melody in C minor, and thus bring to a peaceful conclusion a work full of deep poetic feeling.

The attempts made by Rhené Baton to remodel constructional forms are extremely interesting, as is also his choice of themes. His work is full of harmonic colour and rhythmic invention.

ADOLPHE PIRIOU.

BATTANCHON, FÉLIX, 1814–1893, French violoncellist.

Trio, 3 vc, G	op. 38	Hofmeister, 1868.
Trio, 3 vc, c mi	,, 40	,, 1869.
3 duets, 2 vc (or vc, cb)	,, 15	,, 1858; Ricordi.
3 duets, 2 vc (or vc, cb)	,, 31	B. & H., 1863.
Sonata, pf, vc (orig. 3 vc), G	,, 36	Hofmeister, 1868.

In 1846–47 he attempted to introduce an instrument which he called the 'baryton', between 'cello and viola, but, though he played remarkably well, he failed to arouse much interest. It must not be confounded with the similarly named instrument for which Haydn wrote (*v.* BARYTON).

EDITOR.

BAUDIOT, CHARLES NICOLAS, 1773–1849, French violoncellist.

A very curious story is told by Fétis (who was present) of this artist. He was to play a solo of his own composition at a concert in Paris, in 1807. During the performance of the previous item (a work by Haydn) Baudiot had retired. When he appeared and began his solo, it was discovered that his piece began with the identical theme which Haydn had employed in the andante of his work. The audience laughed, and Baudiot became nervous and played out of tune; the laughter redoubled, and he found himself quite unable to continue and had to retire, when he fainted. Not till he recovered did he understand what had happened. He composed much chamber music, of which a list is given in *Fétis*. Some duets for two 'cellos have been republished. EDITOR.

†BAUER, MARION, b. 1887, composer, critic, and lecturer. Member of Faculty, New York University.

Fantasia, quasi una sonata, pf, v, f mi	op. 18	Schirmer, 1928.

†BAUSSNERN, WALDEMAR VON, b. 1866, composer of Transylvanian parentage.

Quintet, pf, v, cl, vc, horn, F	Simrock, 1905.
Serenade, pf, v, cl, E flat	,, 1905.

Baussnern's music has been well spoken of in the German press, and played with success in Vienna.

*†BAX, ARNOLD E. TREVOR, b. 1883, English composer, studied at the R.A.M.

	Composed	
Quintet (Lyrical Interlude), 2 v, vla, 2 vc	1907–8	Murdoch.
Quintet, harp, str. quartet	1919	,,
Quintet, ob, str. quartet	1923	,,
1st quartet, str, G	1918	,,
2nd quartet, str, e mi and G	1926	,,
Elegiac trio, fl, vla, harp, G	1916	Chester.
Quintet, pf, 2 v, vla, vc, g mi	1914–15	Murdoch.
Quartet (one movt.), pf, v, vla, vc	1922	,,
Trio (one movt.), pf, v, vla, E	1906	Chester.
1st sonata, pf, v, E	1910–15–20	Murdoch.
2nd sonata, pf, v, D	1915	,,
Sonata, pf, vla	1921–22	,,
Sonata, harp, vla	1927	,,
Sonata, pf, vc	1923	,,

Among the composers to whom is due the so-called British Renascence, Bax and Frank Bridge are the most copious contributors to chamber music. Already as a student Bax showed leanings in this direction. He was gifted with an extraordinary facility; the ease with which he read modern scores at the piano was only one instance of many, but it has become legendary. In composition this early proficiency led him to under-estimate difficulties of execution which did not exist for him, and at this early stage he did not always resist the resultant temptation to unnecessary complexity of texture, and general overburdening of the score.

It is the gradual emergence from this close-woven style that constitutes development in Bax's career. Its stages are: first, a period when the over-luxuriant growth of harmonic decoration constantly threatened to obscure the structure and present the appearance of diffuseness; then a phase when the harmonic decoration, whilst retaining and even increasing its complexity, was subordinated to the polyphonic interest, and the underlying clarity of conception became more apparent; and finally, a new tendency towards compression and directness.

The first turning-point may be placed about 1913. The second is a process too gradual to be dated. Moreover, any date one could name —and 1917 is the most feasible—would give the impression that the few intervening years were a period of transition. This they may have been, but only to the extent that a composer's progress is a continuous transition. At least one later work, the 'cello sonata of 1923, shows that the new tendency has not superseded the earlier style, but represents a new aspect of a complex personality.

Thus the only phase that admits of definition in point of time is the first, which opens, while Bax was still a student, with a string quartet composed in 1902–3, and so difficult that it was pronounced to be virtually unplayable and has remained in MS. It was followed in 1904 by a phantasy for viola and piano which also remains unpublished, and was one of the earliest of the many compositions to which the incentive was supplied by Lionel Tertis's superb viola playing. Two years later the list of Bax's published chamber music opens with a trio for piano, violin, viola (1906) which reflects his proficiency at that time, and also his predilections—mainly Strauss and Dvořák—but has ceased to be representative. Nevertheless, it has a certain attractiveness, and its unusual setting ensures it a welcome place among those works which players keep within reach for occasions when one of them—in this case the 'cellist—disappoints. It was followed by a string quintet, another composition of deterrent difficulty. This work has had a chequered history. At the outbreak of war the only MS. copy had been sent for performance to Germany, where it naturally remained. The composer regarded it as lost, but at the end of the war period it suddenly returned to him. Regarding it with an eye made critical by the intervening years, he restored to the shelf all but one movement, the least complex, which he revised and rearranged with two violas instead of two 'cellos. This piece, which is published as a *Lyrical Interlude* for string quintet, justifies its retention by the attractiveness of the mood expressed in it. Despite its charm, however, it is generally overlooked among the composer's works, probably because, when five players are gathered, a more substantial dish has to be put before them than an isolated movement.

The First Violin Sonata appeared at the close of this period. The original version was composed in 1910, before the date which we have suggested as a turning-point. Probably for reasons inherent to the subsequent change of style, it has undergone two very drastic revisions. As published, the third movement dates entirely from 1915 and the second from 1920. At the same time the first movement was abridged, so that not much of the pre-1913 music remains. Yet, despite this diversity in date, the sonata is a homogeneous work, even to the point of being in cyclic form. The opening theme, rhythmically modified, is the principal subject of the third movement (Exs. 1*a* and 1*b*), and is also quoted towards the end of the middle section. With this work we enter a new phase of Bax's style, during which the harmonic decoration reaches its greatest complexity, at the same time assuming its true function, that of supplying a constant stream of arabesques and harmonic variations subordinate to the thematic flow and the polyphonic interest. It has always been characteristic of the composer to avoid textual repetition. Even when retrospective, the ideas constantly generate new figuration. The appearance of the score then becomes deceptive, for it suggests extreme chromaticism, whereas the structure which bears this harmonic ornamentation is almost invariably diatonic. The following from the third movement

Ex. 1a.

Ex. 1b.

Ex. 2.

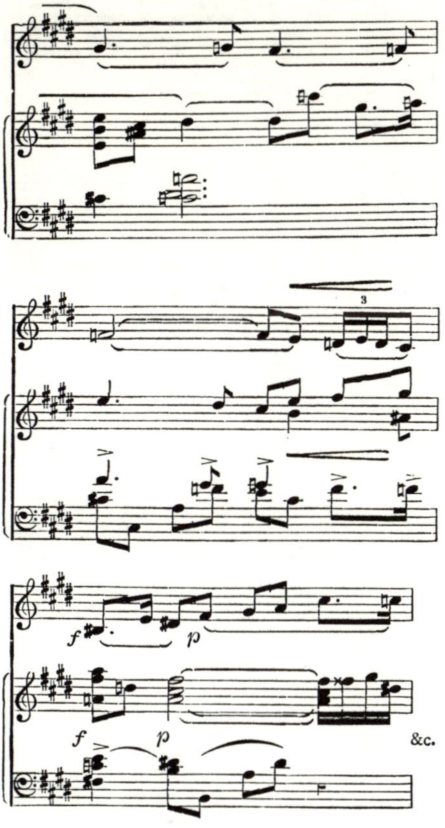

is a characteristic example of what might be called Bax's 1915 manner. It finds its fullest development in the symphonic variations for piano and orchestra, completed in 1916, probably the most richly elaborated of all his compositions.

The Piano Quintet. Meanwhile, however, he had engaged upon a work almost as complex, the vast quintet in G minor for piano and strings, which is dedicated to the present writer. Composed in 1914–15, this quintet has been the most assailed of Bax's works on the ground of excessive length, but in the first place its dimensions are in no sense due either to diffuseness or to redundant development, but to the uncommon richness and breadth of the material itself. Furthermore, the nature of the underlying thought is essentially dramatic. A spiritual state is expressed, and generates a profusion of impulses which are not to be denied if the work is to remain true to itself. Hence the interest is cumulative, and if the composition is long, it is without longueurs. Modern audiences, however, do not readily submit to the effort of prolonged attention except to music sanctioned by tradition, and this quintet, like that of Florent Schmitt, remains at the disadvantage of the time it occupies in performance. In form it is cyclic, at least as to its first and third movements, the latter being entirely derived from the material of the former, whilst even in the slow middle movement there are moments showing a rhythmic affinity with both.

Mention of this slow movement, with its song-like theme of distinctly Celtic character, brings us to another prominent feature of Bax's writing. He has always been strongly attracted by Irish folk-lore, and has close associations with the Dublin literary movement. Not only is the lyrical beauty that he so often achieves usually attributed to this

Ex. 3.
Piano Quintet.
Con sordini.

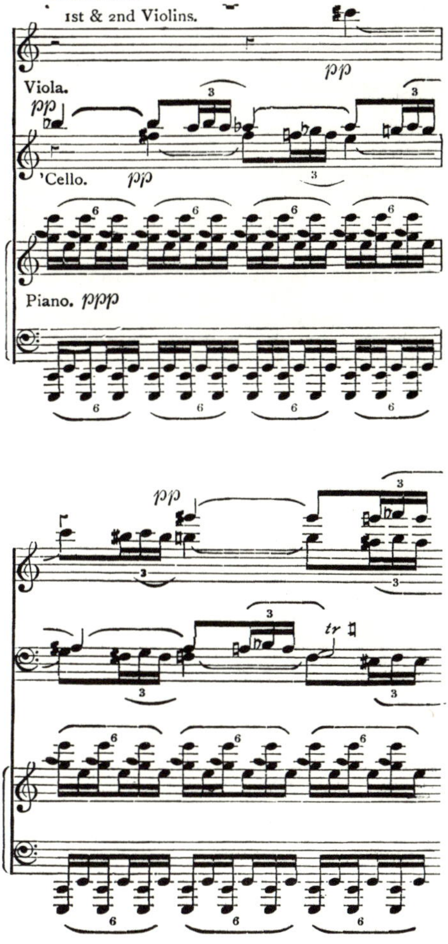

influence, but in some instances, one of which occurs in the string quartet in G, it has been rashly assumed that he was actually making use of Irish folk-song, but these Celtic-sounding melodies are original, and their characteristic inflexions, however they may have been originally assimilated, have become just as much an integral feature of his own melodic idiom as those of German folk-song became inherent to that of certain German classics.

From a host of striking passages in the quintet, the above (Ex. 3) from the first movement is quoted for its constructive interest, and Ex. 4 because of the liturgical associations evoked by its modal character.

Ex. 4.

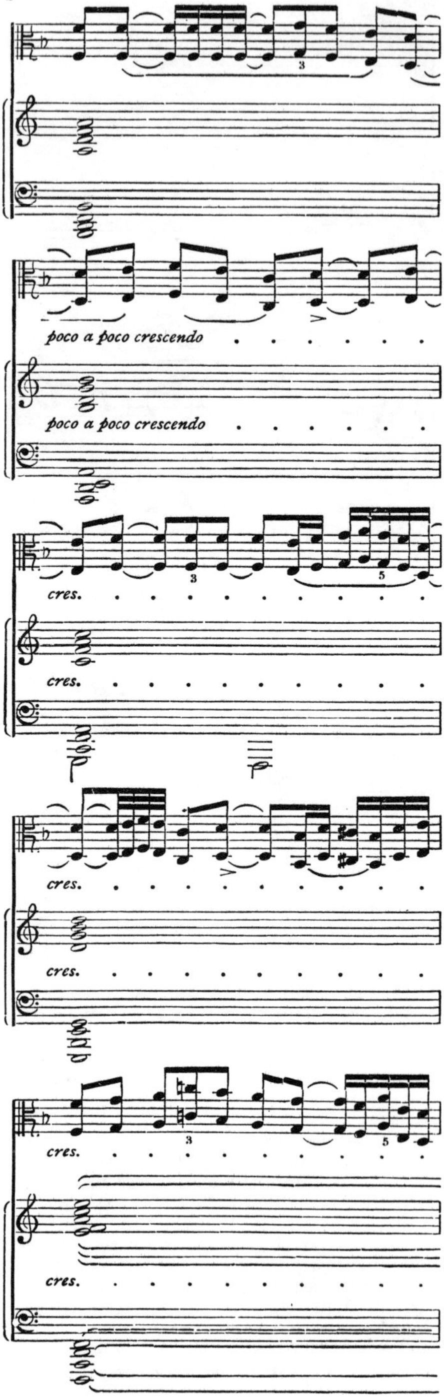

The following, from the slow movement,

Ex. 5 a.

Ex. 5 b.

deserves special mention for the passing hint it furnishes of the much discussed polytonality that has since arisen.

The Second Violin Sonata appeared in the same year, 1915, as well as a *Legend* in B minor. The sonata reflects the personal reactions of the war period, with its acid pathos. It is a cyclic work in four movements, played

Ex. 6.

Idée fixe. 2nd Violin Sonata.

Ex. 6.

Later development.

without a break. The subject which forms the *idée fixe* is common to the first and fourth sections, and intervenes between the second and third (Ex. 6).

Especially significant is the second section, described as *The Grey Dancer in the Twilight*, which conveys the effect of a *danse macabre*. It is in waltz time, and all its themes are based upon the same chord:

Ex. 7.

The three subjects from 'The grey dancer in the twilight'.
Tonic chord of the movement.

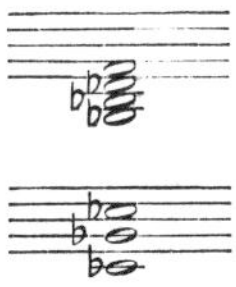

Ex. 7.
(b)

Ex. 7.
(c)

This characteristic, self-revealing work, performances of which have been relatively frequent, has a poignancy of meaning that leaves a deep impression. The idiom is also representative of its period; there is, for instance, a distinct thematic affinity between the opening of its last movement and that of the *Legend* composed the same year. The sonata, however, is best regarded as an elegy on a large scale, inspired by the tragic events which accompanied its composition. A less bitter, though also elegiac, feeling pervades the trio for flute, viola, and harp (1916), which is a gently flowing lyrical movement of much melodic charm in a Celtic vein. During 1917 Bax wrote *An Irish Elegy* for cor anglais, harp, and strings, inspired by events in the sister isle which had affected him very deeply, but this, like the *Ballade* for violin and piano of the same year, has remained unpublished, although it has been much appreciated at its few performances.

First String Quartet. We now reach the later phase of the composer's chamber music, characterized by compression and conciseness. In the first work of this period, the string quartet in G, this compression was conscious, though afterwards it became a congenial mode of expression. Not only is the quartet concise, but in texture more transparent than is the composer's wont; yet by then his reputation for complexity was so firmly established that even this ingratiatingly simple work is still sometimes loosely classed with his more exacting compositions. It is in three movements: an allegretto semplice, a lento of expressive lyrical quality of which the concluding bars deserve quotation:

Ex. 8.

and a brisk rondo. It is in the latter that occurs the theme referred to above, which has so often been mistaken for an Irish folk-song:

Ex. 9.

This relatively unpretentious work contains many moments of melodic beauty, and should become popular if opportunities of hearing it were more frequent.

The quintet for harp and strings, in one extended movement with two principal subjects, was his next work. This melodious composition conceals much textural ingenuity under a deceptively straightforward outline. Especially worthy of note are the passage ('veiled and mysterious') which leads to the recapitulation, and the characteristic harmonies of the conclusion.

Possibly the dedication of the preceding work foreshadowed the next phase, for we find Bax now once more in association with Lionel Tertis, for whom he wrote the phantasy for viola and orchestra (1920), also available with piano, in which form it is more like chamber music than can be said of most arrangements, though technically beyond the range of this review.

The Viola Sonata, which followed, is perhaps the most remarkable of his four string sonatas, and was played by Lionel Tertis and Harriet Cohen at the 1924 Salzburg Festival of the International Society for Contemporary Music, after several performances at home. It is in three movements, but although it ends with a return to the opening theme, it is not otherwise in cyclic form. The virile opening movement is in heroic vein, and in the composer's earlier period might have grown to epic dimensions, but has remained concise despite its weighty contents. An episode marked 'feroce' recalls the mood of the central portion of the scherzo in the first violin sonata, which bears the same indication. It also prepares the approach of the 'satanic' section which is the scherzo of this sonata. This striking movement, which a listener once christened 'Pandora's Box', is unique in Bax's music. The mood itself has sometimes put in a transient appearance, but it has never been given the same prominence, nor has it ever motived the use of the same musical means. The volcanic conclusion is of special interest. After it the quiet and almost wistful final section gives one a suggestion of an awakening from disturbing dreams.

Apparently there was some underlying psychological process at work during this phase, for the robust mood, at some times aggressive and all but brutal, at others gloomy, finds expression also in the symphony, which is contemporary with the viola sonata, and there are suggestions of it even in the first section of the later 'cello sonata. But for concentrated dramatic vigour Bax has written nothing like the quartet in one movement for piano and strings (1922), lasting only eight minutes. This, too, opens 'feroce', and has moments of almost martial ardour. Of relief in the lyrical sense there is little or none, probably because it would have seemed out of keeping with the dramatic trend, which is not relaxed even in cantabile moments. The following (Ex. 10) is a point of harmonic interest preceding the recapitulation.

THE 'CELLO SONATA. As if to compensate himself for this drastic compression, in the 'cello sonata, which was written for Beatrice Harrison, the composer once more allowed

Ex. 10.

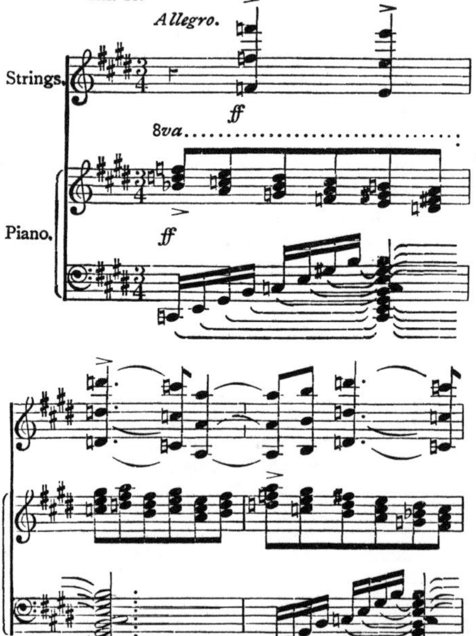

himself some of the elbow-room of his earlier works, though using it with more concentrated purpose. In mood it possesses some affinity with that spacious work, the piano quintet, and in the texture there is a more generous allowance of harmonic ornament, which, however, does not equal the luxuriant growth of earlier days, though its detail is richer in kind. The music is dramatic, and it suggests a poetic basis which might almost take a narrative form, especially in the first movement, where the transformation of the principal subject gives a hint of heroic adventure and conflict. The second might be entitled 'In an Italian Garden'. It has a rich sensuousness, of which the following (Ex. 11) gives a suggestion. The third movement opens in the satanic mood of the scherzo in the viola sonata, but becomes more lyrical and merges into an epilogue, in which the combative elements of the first movement return in peaceful suavity.

To the same year (1923) belongs a work of

radically different character, the blithesome quintet for oboe and strings dedicated to Leon

Ex. 11.

Goossens and doubtless suggested by that artist's mastery of his instrument and the beauty of his tone. It is in three movements, of transparent clarity, and in the main lyrical, with no more agitation than is required for contrast. In some respects one might compare it with the string quartet in G, but it has an even greater spontaneity. Whilst not unduly submissive to the pastoral suggestions which seem inseparable from the oboe, the composer has not resisted them, and the result is a mood which is not merely pastoral, but, in the larger sense, a nature-mood. The conclusion of the first movement (Ex. 12) has much of this feeling.

The Second String Quartet (written in 1926) differs markedly in character from his first work in this form, the two allegros being almost aggressive in the robustness of their expression, whilst the texture contains much more contrapuntal writing than is the composer's habit. At moments it seems as though he were consciously deserting the harmonic arabesque which has played so prominent a part in his evolution, in favour of a new and very personal mode of polyphony. The first movement (allegro, afterwards vivace) opens with a long declamatory passage for the 'cello alone, presently transferred to the viola, but not leading to the fugato one was tempted to expect, that device being reserved for the finale. Very characteristic is the insistence upon a rising fifth, at the opening, which is a prominent feature of the thematic material, not only of this work, but also of the viola and harp sonata which was to follow. The texture throughout is harsh in contrast with the gentler Bax of earlier days, but the manner of its utterance is justified by the contents. The second subject, however, relaxes the mood somewhat, and supplies the conclusion, the starker opening phrase being then again relegated to the 'cello. The slow movement, opening thus (Ex. 13) is one of those tone poems of which this composer has the secret. Though occasionally complex, ornate, or agitated, it is lyrical throughout. In the finale (allegro vivace) a mood returns corresponding to that of the opening, but with a clearer

Ex. 12.

vitality. Again the upward fifth presents itself, leading to a fugato. There is a chorale-like episode which suggests an unstated poetic basis, and the coda consists of two highly effective stretti.

THE SONATA FOR HARP AND VIOLA (composed in the following year, 1927), in four linked movements, is, apart from its musical qualities, a technical *tour de force*. Neither instrument commands a great variety of colouring, and only a composer confident of his resourcefulness would have attempted the feat of obtaining sufficient variety by other means to counteract the monochrome character of the sonority. Bax's confidence proved justified. The character of each movement stands out and is emphasized by structural means, sometimes by an original type of figuration, sometimes by a personal application of modal devices (the scherzo is in the Dorian), and by other processes too numerous to mention. The thematic material is closely related, and most of it recurrent, the rising fifth being again a

Ex. 13.

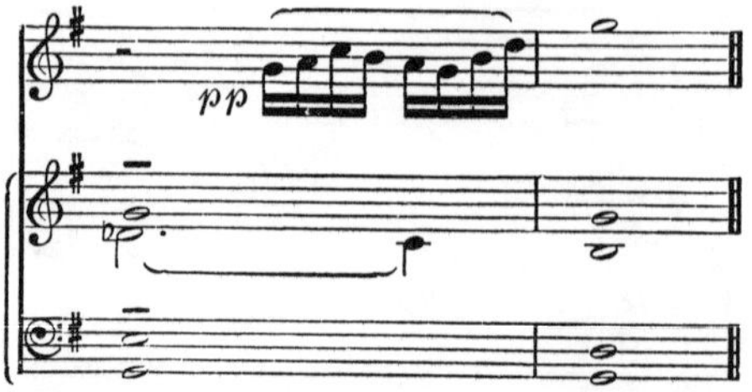

prominent feature as stated above. The content has the character of an epic. One could easily imagine that the composer had some Celtic or Northern saga in mind. The emotional climax is in the slow movement, which contains some extraordinarily ingenious writing for the harp. In the last section the upward fifth heralds a barbaric and warrior-like end of the story. In many ways this is one of Bax's most remarkable works.

This completes the output of one of the most remarkable British composers of to-day, and in a certain sense the most musical, for not only does music pour from him in a generous stream, but though its mood and flavour may vary, always there is evidence of a subtle sense of beauty which is second nature to him.

EDWIN EVANS.

[Bax has not laid himself out to please amateur performers who shirk technical difficulties. Those, however, who are genuine workers at their instruments will not find themselves overweighted by the quartet in G, the slow movement of which, a manner of Celtic lament, is one of the most beautiful I have met with in modern chamber music, and the Irish melody in the finale, of which Mr. Evans speaks, runs the Londonderry air very close for charm. It is assigned to the second violin, and was played, when first I tried it, by an Irish lady, who sang it on her fiddle as if it had been written for her. We were all thrilled, and called for it over and over again. Thus does melody come into its own. EDITOR.]

†BAZELAIRE, PAUL, b. 1886, virtuoso 'cellist.

Suite grecque, 2 fl, ob, v, vla, 2 vc, harp	Schneider (Paris), 1927.
Ballade, pf, 2 v, vla, 2 vc	Senart, 1924.

The Ballade, which has the sub-title, *The Trireme on the Nile—Dark Forebodings—Antony and Cleopatra—Death—The Bloody Imperator*, is after a poem by José Maria de Heredia. It is a kind of descriptive concerto in very free form, the impressions suggested by the various headings of the sub-title being condensed into a single movement. The means employed are very simple, the expression clear and straightforward.

The *Suite grecque*, in four movements, viz.:

eclogue — divertissement — epithalamium — dance—attests the composer's gift for the poetic and picturesque. ADOLPHE PIRIOU.

BAZZINI, ANTONIO, 1818–1897, Italian violin virtuoso.

Quintet, 2 v, vla, 2 vc, A	—	Ricordi, 1866.
Quartet No. 1, str, D	—	,,
Quartet No. 2, str, d mi	op. 75	Ricordi; Leuckart, 1874.
Quartet No. 3, str, E flat	,, 76	Ricordi.
Quartet No. 4, str, G	,, 79	Schott, 1892.
Quartet No. 5, str, c mi	,, 80	,,
Grand concert duet, pf, v, D	—	Ricordi, 1842.
Three pieces in form of a sonata, pf, v	—	,, 1866; Schott.
Sonata, pf, v	op. 55	Ricordi.

As a violinist, Bazzini was already playing in public at the age of 12, and subsequently toured the Continent as soloist with success. Schumann (*Gesamm. Schriften*) wrote of him with unqualified praise. But it is his connexion with chamber music with which we are concerned. He was a man of ideals, who gave up solo playing to devote himself to the introduction of classical quartet music into Italy. Bazzini's muse was Italian, but with a fascinating amalgam of German influence. His five quartets are violinistic in character, as might be expected from the composer of the famous *Ronde des lutins*, the D minor, owing to its charming gavotte, being the most popular.

No. 1, which was awarded a prize given in 1864 by the Società del Quartetto of Milan, exhibits a strange mixture of qualities. Bazzini's use of scale passages reminds one of the early symphonists, whilst his melodies are of Mozartian purity; but his harmonies smack of the Italian commonplace of the period. The scherzo should be specially mentioned as a captivating movement that might have been signed by Mendelssohn.

In 1879 Bazzini's G major quartet was played at the 'Pops'. It did not altogether please, the style being considered too theatrical.

EDITOR.

†BEACH, MRS. H. H. A. (*née* Amy Marcy Cheney), b. 1867, American pianist.

		Composed	
Variations, fl, str. quartet	op. 80	1916	Schirmer.
Quintet, pf, 2 v, vla, vc, f sharp mi	,, 67	1906	A. P. Schmidt, 1909.
Sonata, pf, v, a mi	,, 34	1896	A. P. Schmidt, 1899.

Mrs. Beach's compositions are a valuable addition to the repertory, and have played their part in the development of American music, though she has written but little chamber music.

THE VIOLIN SONATA was warmly received, not only on its native heath, but in Europe as well, having been played in various countries by distinguished artists, including Carreño and Halir, receiving in each case high approbation from public and press. The sonata comes from no pseudo-artistic impulse, but reveals genuine creative power and glowing fancy. The work is in four movements, and the form is at once concise and plastic. Warmly romantic in feeling throughout, it is also permeated with a verve and energy which bespeak remarkable vitality; the scherzo in particular is a little *tour de force*, with its banter and *élan*, and the trio is admirably contrasted, while the work as a whole is finely proportioned.

THE QUINTET is a brilliant work; here the composer is at her very best, and, if the harmonies verge at times upon the over-sweet, there is ample compensation in the emotional sincerity. The sonorities are finely adjusted—thanks to a piano part which is not overloaded.

THE VARIATIONS, op. 80, reveal the composer in a less romantic guise than do the foregoing works, but there is the same impress of a vigorous intellect, with the power to conceive and surmount intricate problems, while at the same time preserving sincerity of expression and beauty of detail. In this grateful instrumental combination the flute is treated with reticence, notwithstanding that it has its integral place in the ensemble. There are six variations in all, ranging from the serious to the jocose. This work of the composer's maturity should commend itself to chamber-music organizations in search of music affording an element of contrast. See also AMERICAN CHAMBER MUSIC. ARTHUR SHEPHERD.

†BEACH, JOHN, contemporary American composer.

Poem, str. quartet, f mi	Chester (Répertoire Flonzaley).

BEAU, LUISE ADOLPHA LE, German pianist, pupil of Rheinberger.

Quartet, pf, v, vla, vc, f mi	op. 28	B. & H., 1884.
Trio, pf, v, vc, d mi	,, 15	Küpper (Elberfeld).
Sonata, pf, v, c mi	,, 10	R. & E., 1882.
Sonata, pf, vc, D	,, 17	Cranz, 1883.

†BEAUMONT, ALEXANDER S., 1848–1913, was a generous patron of artists. He composed and published at his own expense (Woolhouse) several chamber works of ambitious design, amongst them two effective suites for piano and strings (one of them dedicated to myself)

which deserve more publicity than they are ever likely to get. It is one of the tragedies of musical life that so many composers, as in Beaumont's case, produce works which are good, but not *quite* good enough to gain entrance into the repertory. EDITOR.

†BECK, FRANZ, 1730–1809, German composer.

Early in life Beck went to France, where his works made a sensation about 1760. Although these, with the exception of a few short pieces, were mainly chamber symphonies, Beck deserves mention in this Cyclopedia, for it was he whose genius brought to its spiritual fulfilment the latest of the movements in music, on which he had been nurtured. The influence of Beck's genius extended far beyond the preclassical period. Not only was Boccherini directly influenced by Beck, but Beethoven also. Between Beck and Boccherini came a number of richly talented composers, of whom the following may be named as important representatives both of the new art and of chamber music:—Cannabich, Toeschi, Gossec, Rigel, J. C. Bach, and Eichner.

R. SONDHEIMER.

BECK, REINHOLD IMANUEL, b. 1881, German composer.

Quartet, 4 horns	op. 1	Gries & Sch., 1909.

Beck started life as a pharmaceutical chemist, but took up music professionally in 1906. A long list of his chamber works is given in *Riemann*.

BECKER, ALBERT ERNST ANTON, 1834–1899, German composer.

Quintet, pf, 2 v, vla, vc, E flat	op. 49	B. & H., 1887.
Quartet, pf, v, vla, vc, d mi	,, 19	Peters, 1881.

Grove speaks highly of the quintet, and mentions an effective work written for violin and organ (MS.).

He had a special fondness for adagio movements, of which he wrote several for violin with piano or organ accompaniment.

EDWIN EVANS.

BECKER, D. G., German composer.

Quartet, str, c mi	op. 4	Hofmeister, 1857.
,, str, g mi	,, 5	,, 1857.
,, str, E flat	,, 6	,, 1858.
Three duets, 2 vc (or vc, cb)	,, 16	,, 1862.
Sonata, pf, v, E flat	,, 15	,, 1861.
Sonata, pf, vc, c mi	,, 1	,, 1857.
Sonata, pf, vc, B flat	,, 40	Schott, 1888.

BECKER, (1) JEAN, 1833–1884, German violinist, pupil of V. Lachner and Alard. Leader of the famous Florentine Quartet, founded in 1865, the story of the early beginnings of which, under the auspices of Dr. Basevi, director of a society established in Florence for the furtherance of interest in Italian and German chamber music, is told by A. Ehrlich in his book *Famous Violinists*. Becker was a man of indomitable energy. His great difficulty was the finding of competent colleagues. For the second violin part he coached a youthful, inexperienced artist named Masi, lent him a Strad to play on, and then with Chiostri as violist and Hilpert as 'cellist, formed a Quartet which, after much assiduous practice, made its first début at Florence, and afterwards toured Europe with brilliant success. Becker's style was peculiarly sympathetic to the Viennese; but in London, when he appeared at the 'Pops', he was overshadowed by Joachim (then in his prime), and failed to make a very deep impression.

†(2) HUGO, b. 1864, violoncellist, son of Jean Becker.

Little Suite (*Liebesleben*), pf, vc	Brockhaus, 1894.

EDITOR.

†BECKER, REINHOLD, 1843–1924, Saxon composer.

Sonata, pf, v, g mi	op. 150	Leuckart.

This composer, for many years conductor of the Dresden Liedertafel (Glee-Club), is known chiefly by his vocal music. His one sonata is a by no means easy work. It shows not only mastery of technical form, but a high order of intellect and imagination. The first movement (maestoso) is impressive by reason of its plastic themes and its bold handling of classical form. The andante, however, is less inspired. The scherzo and its trio suggest elfin songs and revels, while the finale consists of variations on a theme of no great intrinsic significance, and forms a series of short, self-contained pieces.

WILHELM ALTMANN.

[In Becker's younger days he was a member, and afterwards leader, of the Eller Quartet, but in 1870 had to give up violin playing on account of muscular trouble. He subsequently devoted himself to composition. EDITOR.]

†BECKMAN, BROR, b. 1866, Swedish composer.

Sonata, pf, v, a mi	op. 1	Musik. Konstför. (Stockholm).

†BEDFORD, HERBERT, b. 1867, English composer.

Nocturne (*Summer Dream*), voice, str. quartet, harp	—	Boosey.
Song (*To a Water-Lily at Evening*), voice, str. quartet, harp	—	Chester.
Night-piece, no. 1 (*The Dancer*), voice, str. quartet, bass triangle	—	,,

Divertimento, pf, 2 v, vla, vc, cb	op. 44	Goodwin & Tabb.
Lyric Interlude (*Pathways of the Moon*), pf, fl, ob, v, vla	„ 50	„
Night-piece, no. 2 (*The Shepherd*), voice, pf, fl, ob (Carnegie Award, 1925)	—	S. & B.

Both Divertimento and Lyric Interlude are in one movement, taking about eleven minutes in performance, with many changes of tempo. Bedford has also written for voice with strings (*v.* VOICE).

The following is from the Carnegie Trust report on Bedford's Night-piece: 'A pastoral in the true sense of that much abused term. The writing is clear and transparent, with great delicacy and beauty of outline, and, despite the slender material, the interest is maintained unimpaired. It will be very effective in the concert-room.' EDITOR.

†BEER-WALBRUNN, ANTON, b. 1864, Bavarian composer and teacher of theory.

Third quartet, str, G	op. 14	Peters, 1897.
Quartet, pf, v, vla, vc, F	„ 8	„ „
Sonata, pf, v, d mi	„ 30	Wunderhorn-V, 1911.
Sonata, pf, vc, G	„ 15	A. Schmid Nachf. (Munich), 1897.

Beer-Walbrunn is a composer of sterling worth, sincerely devoted to the classical tradition, whose chamber music possesses both interest and charm.

The early quartet for piano and strings, signed 'Anton Beer', showed great talent, as instanced in the second subject of the opening allegro vivace, and the first appearance on the viola of the melodious main theme of the adagio molto, which in its turn is cut short by the largely fugal allegretto assai. Quite delightful is the conception of the spirited scherzo, whilst the finale, which ends in a triumphal march, is inspired by vigorous, wholesome humour.

Of Beer's three string quartets, op. 14 alone is published. This work is far more compact, and gains by its conciseness. The form of the first movement is masterly; the subject-matter is not on so high a level, though the second subject is very attractive. The variations on the folk-song, *Es waren zwei Königskinder, die hatten einander so lieb*, are excellent; they are written in changing moods, and their effect is one of real charm. Following immediately on the scherzo, a sort of uncouth peasants' dance, comes the finale, which is by turns graceful and rhythmically effective.

Beer-Walbrunn's best chamber work so far is the violin sonata, which breathes the spirit of Beethoven, particularly in the broadly constructed first movement (allegro passionato). This is a work of the first rank in respect of its structure alone. The subjects are extremely plastic in conception, chiselled, as it were, out of granite. The second part of this sonata consists of ingenious variations on a comparatively simple theme, and combines with great skill the variations and the slow movement, scherzo and finale. It is in these variations that the composer's contrapuntal skill is strikingly apparent. WILHELM ALTMANN.

BEETHOVEN, LUDWIG VAN, 1770–1827.

FOREWORD

A note may be necessary to English readers on the French terminology. I. The section of a movement here described as a 'terminal development' is usually known in England as a 'coda'. Monsieur Vincent d'Indy restricts the use of this latter term to the short conclusion of a movement. The larger coda, or terminal development, is, practically, an innovation of Beethoven's.

II. *The rondo.* In the description of a rondo, French writers employ a system of analysis which may require some explanation. The rondo is founded on the rondeau of poetry, a poem of 6–8 lines with two rhymes only; the opening and closing lines are identical, forming, thus, a circle or 'round'. These two rhymes are the basis of the terms 'refrain' and 'couplet'. In the simpler rondos, especially in rondos of the French school, this system of classification is quite satisfactory, the scheme then being:

1st refrain.
—1st couplet.
2nd refrain.
—2nd couplet.
3rd refrain and conclusion,

which may be extended at the composer's will. The couplets will be episodes founded either on the refrain (or first subject) or on new material. In cyclic works they commonly introduce themes of other movements, which may be combined in the conclusion.

In the highly developed Beethoven rondos the refrain may be taken as the first subject. The couplet contains bridge, second subject, and episodes, and the second couplet commonly contains a development as well. M. d'Indy's masterly analysis of the F major sonata, op. 24, and the trio, op. 97, will explain what the contents of a couplet may be. In some rondos the second couplet will introduce even a third subject, e.g. rondo of the *Pathetic* sonata for piano.

III. The term 'Lied' is more commonly described in England as 'aria' form. For origin of term 'Lied' see *Grove*, 2nd edn., vol. ii, p. 86, footnote. M. DRAKE-BROCKMAN.

N.B. Unless another publisher's name is given all works are published in B. & H.'s *Critical Edition*, 1862–5. *Supplementary volume*, 1904.

				Composed
Octet	2 ob, 2 cl, 2 horns, 2 fag	E flat	op. 103	*c.* 1792.
Octet, arrgd. as quintet	2 v, 2 vla, vc		„ 4	
Octet, arrgd. as trio	pf, v, vc		„ 63	
Rondino[1]	2 ob, 2 cl, 2 horns, 2 fag	E flat	„ '146'	Very early.
Septet ('septuor')	v, vla, cl, vc, fag, horn cb	E flat	„ 20	Before April 1800.
Septet ('septuor'), arrgd. as quintet.	2 v, 2 vla, vc			
Septet ('septuor'), arrgd. as trio.	pf, v (or cl), vc			
Sextet	2 cl, 2 horns, 2 fag	E flat	„ 71	'Early'.
Sextet, arrgd. as quintet, wind instr.				
Quintet	2 v, 2 vla, vc	C	„ 29	1801.
Quintet (arrgd. from op. 103)	2 v, 2 vla, vc	See above (Octet).		
Quintet (arrgd. from op. 146)	2 v, 2 vla, vc	See above (Rondino).		
Quintet (arrgd. from op. 1, no. 3).	2 v, 2 vla, vc	c mi	op. 104	
Fugue	2 v, 2 vla, vc	D	„ 137	
Quintet (arrgd. from op. 71)	fl, ob, cl, fag, horn	See above (Sextet).		

					Composed
Six Quartets	str	F, G, D, c mi, A, B flat.	Nos. 1 to 6	op. 18	1800.
Three quartets ('Rasoumovsky').	„	F, e mi, C	„ 7 to 9	„ 59	Before Feb. 1807.
Quartet ('Harp')	„	E flat	„ 10	„ 74	1809.
Quartet	„	f mi	„ 11	„ 95	1810.
Quartet	„	E flat	„ 12	„ 127	1824.
Quartet	„	B flat	„ 13	„ 130	1825.[2]
Quartet	„	c sharp mi	„ 14	„ 131	1826.
Quartet	„	a mi	„ 15	„ 132	1825.
Quartet	„	F	„ 16	„ 135	1826.
Quartet ('Grand Fugue').			„ 17	„ 133	(1825).

				Composed	
Three Funeral Equali	Sopr., Alto, Tenor, and Bass Trombones.		—	1812	
Trio	v, vla, vc	E flat	op. 3	—	
Trio	arrgd. pf, vc		„ 64	—	
Three trios	v, vla, vc	G, D, c mi	„ 9	—	
Trio	v, vla, vc	C (arrgd. from op. 87), see below.		—	
Serenade	v, vla, vc	D	op. 8	—	
Serenade	arrgd. pf, vla		„ 42	—	
Var^{ns}. on 'La ci darem'	2 v, vla		—	—	
Serenade	fl, v, vla	D	„ 25	—	
Serenade	arrgd. pf, fl (or v)		„ 41	—	
Trio	2 ob, cor angl.	C	„ 87	?1794	
Var^{ns}. on theme 'Reich mir die Hand'	2 ob, cor angl.		—	—	
Duet	vla, vc [with 2 *Augengläsern* obbl.]	E flat	—	—	Peters, 1912.
Three duets	cl, fag	C, F, B flat	„ '147'	—	
Quintet[3]	pf, ob, cl, fag, horn or pf, ob, v, vla, vc	E flat	„ 16	Before April, 1797.	
„	arrgd. as str. quartet		„ 75	Before April, 1797.	
[4]Andante maestoso	pf, str. quartet	C	„ '174'	1826	

1 The works thus numbered '146' have no opus numbers, but have been so numbered for convenience, as in *Grove's Dictionary*.

2 The finale was written in 1826, to replace the Grand Fugue—the original finale of this quartet. The present movement is Beethoven's last work.

3 According to Ries this was also arranged as a piano quartet.

4 Known as 'Beethoven's Last Musical Thought'.

Three quartets	pf, v, vla, vc	E flat, D, C	op. '152'	Composed 1785.
Bolero	voice solo, pf, v, vc		no opus no.	Publ. in 'Die Musik', 2nd year (recently).
Three trios	pf, v, vc (also vla)	E flat, G, c mi	op. 1	—
Trio	pf, cl (or v), vc	B flat	,, 11	—
Trio (Arrgd. from septet)	pf, cl (or v), vc	E flat	,, 38	—
Two trios	pf, v, vc	D, E flat	,, 70	—
Trio	pf, v, vc	B flat	,, 97	1811
Trio	pf, v, vc	E flat	,, '153'	1785?
Trio (1 movt.)	pf, v, vc	B flat	,, '154'	1812
Trio	pf, fl, fag		no number.	1786?
Fourteen var^ns^.	pf, v, vc	E flat	op. 44	—
Adagio, var^ns^. and rondo	pf, v, vc	G	,, 121*a*	—
Two trios	pf, cl, fag	C, F	—	—
Three sonatas	pf, v	D, A, E flat	,, 12	—
Sonata	pf, v	a mi	,, 23	*c.* 1800
Sonata	pf, v	F	,, 24	—
Three sonatas	pf, v	A, c mi, G	,, 30	1802
Sonata ('Kreutzer')	pf, v	a mi and A	,, 47	—
Adagio	pf, v		Discovered and published by Patrik Vretblad.	
Sonata	pf, v	G	op. 96	1812
Six allemandes	pf, v	F, D, E, A, D, G	,, '171'	1795
Two sonatas	pf, vc	F, g mi	,, 5	—
Sonata	pf, vc	A	,, 69	—
Two sonatas	pf, vc	C, D	,, 102	1815
Sonata	pf, horn (or vc)	F	,, 17	Before Apr. 18, 1800.
Twelve var^ns^. on 'Ein Mädchen' (Zauberflöte).	pf, vc	F	,, 66	—
Six very early themes varied	pf, fl (or v)		,, 105	1818–19

It is nowadays accounted an established fact that the life-work of all great creative artists who have fulfilled the normal term of years can be divided into three manners or styles, quite distinct one from another, which show the progressive development of the artist's work, and correspond to three successive stages in his career.

These three stages of artistic development of the creative genius may be thus defined:

1. Period of Imitation;
2. Period of 'Externalization' (French: 'Extériorisation'.)
3. Period of Reflection.

In the first period the young artist, already in full possession of his technique, acquired by long preliminary study, will apply himself simply to the task of continuing the art-production of his period, imitating, unashamed, the style of his predecessors or of his favourites among his contemporaries. He will be careful to avoid seeking originality at any price—resource of those who have it not, and barren of results—for he knows that the originality within him will show itself in due course and when the need arises.

None of the great pioneers of poetry, painting, or music has been exempt from this law. It was thus, to quote a few instances only, that Dante Alighieri, under the influence of Virgil and Brunetto Latini, wrote, in 1228, his *Vita Nuova*, of which Boccaccio said: 'And for having made this little book he felt great shame in his years of maturity.' It was thus that Rembrandt painted, in 1632, his 'Lesson in Anatomy' ('Leçon d'Anatomie'), an imitation of genius, yet none the less an imitation, of the corporation-pictures of Anthonizzen and of Mirevelt. It was thus that J. S. Bach, in his Weimar period, from 1703 to 1712, created his first cantatas and his magnificent chorales in the form of variations (partita), which, revealing his genius as they do, are none the less written in the manner of Pachelbel and Buxtehude.

The second period, the period of 'Externalization', is that in which the artist, freeing himself gradually from the leading-strings of past generations, begins to walk alone. Then, giving himself up more completely to his own inner emotions of sorrow or of joy, he comes, not without hesitation or groping, to self-expression in his art.

At this point he 'turns outwards', seeking to make his mark among his contemporaries by means of his discoveries and his innovations, yet continuing to follow closely the great highway of Art so clearly mapped out by his precursors and ancestors.

Thus, again, we see Dante, sixteen years after the *Vita Nuova*, writing in the vulgar tongue his curious *Convivio*, which, according to all authorities, is the reflection of his own life. So, too, Rembrandt, casting aside the reserve of his youth, will, in the *Nachtwacht*, throw high lights on the edges of the weapons and the curves of the armour, revealing his urgent spiritual need of sharp brilliance against the relative obscurity of that Dutch interior, and it will no longer be Tulp the physician, but Rembrandt himself that he will depict beneath the features of a Banning Cocq or a van Ruytenberg. As for Bach during his eleven years (1712–23) at Cöthen, who can fail to recognize the spirit of his life, the simple man, free from pride, full of robust gaiety, in his concertos for various instruments dedicated to the Margrave of Brandenburg? Who will not mark the depth of character of a man above the common herd, equipped with impeccable technique and chary of displaying his inner thoughts before others, in the preludes and fugues of the *Well-Tempered Clavier* as in the violin sonatas and the inexhaustible fount of melody of the partitas?

We have named the third phase the 'period of reflection', because it corresponds, ordinarily, to an epoch when the artist, freed from imitative tendencies, and wearied of pouring out his inner thoughts and feelings before a generally uncomprehending public, retires within himself, and, living a purely inward life, creates in pure joy or sorrow, with the single aim of exalting his soul and of materializing in works of art its entire creative power.

In this way was constructed the *Commedia*, wherein Dante brought together in one marvellous poem the whole of the knowledge acquired by humanity at the beginning of the fourteenth century. And could one imagine, were it not proved by Rembrandt's individual style, that the painter of the extraordinary lights of the *Nachtwacht* is the same painter who, nineteen years later, seeking neither after effect nor originality of colour, chose to concentrate, in the faces of the 'Staalmeesters' ('Syndics des Drapiers'), those qualities of orderliness and tenacity which characterize the Dutch race? In the same way J. S. Bach, in all the works of the Leipzig period—poems for organ, cantatas, Passions, and in the B minor Mass which perhaps marks the culminating point of his genius—shows to what sublime heights the will of the artist may aspire when concerned only to express in his art the emotions of a true believer.

Not only was Beethoven no exception to this natural law, but he was himself, with his three distinct creative periods, the most striking exemplar of the threefold expression of productive genius. The composer of the trios of 1793, written in imitation of the style of his master, Haydn, is as different from the composer of the seventh symphony as is the Beethoven of the so-called Appassionata sonata from the astonishing thinker who, eighteen years later, laid the foundations of the Missa Solennis in D, that incomparable masterpiece of musical art.

If the work of the composer of the ninth symphony be closely studied, one noteworthy and very strange peculiarity becomes evident, namely, the abruptness of the transformations which characterize the development of his art. Transitions from one epoch to another can hardly be said to exist, and very rare are the movements in which one can detect any foreshadowing, as it were, of the coming sudden change from one style to another.

Indeed, if the second manner—separated from the first by a whole world, the world of expression—is faintly suggested in the largo in D minor of opus 10, the transition from the second manner to the third is far sharper. There is no longer anything in common, as regards the spirit of the works, between the first of the quartets of the third period (the admirable twelfth, op. 127—written in 1824), and even the more 'advanced' works to be found towards the end of the preceding epoch—the tenth and eleventh. There is one single exception, an inspiration of pure and tender beauty—the *Elegischer Gesang* for four voices and strings, written on the death of the young Baroness Pasqualati (1814), which already foreshadows the religious outpourings of the Mass in D.

If, however, in the case of the above-mentioned artists—Dante, Rembrandt, Bach—it is difficult to find a satisfactory reason for these changes of style and inspiration, on the other hand, in Beethoven's case we can attribute them to causes as deeply rooted in the very life of the man as in the soul of the artist.

We reserve these causes for analysis later on, as we meet with their influence upon his work. For the moment we have only to examine the works of pure chamber music—sonatas for two instruments, trios, quartets and quintets with piano, and, finally, quartets for strings comprised in the three styles or manners which we have been discussing. In this examination we shall exclude the large number of short pieces with which the three manners are overlaid, pieces generally written to order, and considered by the composer as of no importance. A full list of the chamber works will be found in the general catalogue at the beginning of this article, but we shall consider here only those productions which really deserve to be regarded as masterpieces of Art.

First Period (Imitation)

During the first years of serious study under the guidance of excellent Viennese masters, Beethoven meditated, wrote little, and contented himself with preparing—with what tribulation!—for the production of his opus 1. But it must not therefore be concluded that the years spent at Bonn were barren. Like Dittersdorf, Mozart, and many other musicians of his time, he began to compose in his earliest years, knowing nothing of composition. From the sketches of three quartets for piano, violin, viola, and violoncello, dating from his fifteenth year, to the variations for piano and violin on a theme from Mozart's *Nozze di Figaro*—written shortly before op. 1—he had elaborated numerous compositions.

Does the reader wish to know how many chamber works were written during this sub-period of early student days? It reaches the respectable total of seventeen.

In this list we find the three above-mentioned quartets which date from 1785, two octets for wind instruments (the second re-written as a string quintet, 1796, under the title of op. 4); two sextets, one of which (two horns and strings) is a first version of op. 81 b, published in 1809, and the other a march for six wind instruments; a string quintet (unfinished); five trios—the first for piano, flute, and bassoon (1786), two others for piano, violin, and violoncello, a first version for violin, viola, and violoncello of op. 3, and some variations, for string trio, on an original theme in E flat; a sonata for piano and flute; and various pieces for flute and for piano and violin.

But, unlike so many young artists of to-day, who, enchanted with their first picture, novel, or symphony, cannot rest until these nebulous attempts have been exhibited, printed, or engraved, Beethoven attached no importance to the productions of these ten years. Except three piano sonatas, the first variations, and a Lied, he would allow none of these student works to be published, and determined to await technical mastery before consenting to hand over his works to a publisher.

Beethoven, then, had completed his additional studies under the guidance of Haydn and Albrechtsberger when he decided to put the inscription 'opus 1' on the manuscript of the three trios written to Prince Lichnowsky's order and perfected with such toil during 1793–94.

We may therefore consider his definitive entry on the career of a composer as dating from his twenty-third year.

The term 'period of imitation' for this first stage may be readily justified, for there is regularly visible the dominating influence—even the actual unconscious copying of the work of certain contemporaries or of artists of the preceding generation.

The musicians whose influence is evident at this time in Beethoven's work are three in number: C. P. E. Bach, Fr. Wilhelm Rust,[1] and, above all, Joseph Haydn.

Beethoven, a northerner, was in no way disposed to allow himself to be dominated by the purely sensuous charm of Italian music, as was Mozart, for instance, and there is nothing in his earliest pieces to remind one of foreign styles; the ornamental style of Fr. Couperin is no more to be discovered than the originality of Domenico Scarlatti. He is concerned only with the art of the German composers who were his immediate predecessors and almost his contemporaries.

The didactic works of John Sebastian's son supplied young Ludwig's clavier studies; and, together with the *Well-Tempered Clavier*, that excellent and clear-sighted teacher C. G. Neefe introduced to his pupil the Prussian and Württemberg sonatas, then very well known, by means of which Haydn himself had acquired his knowledge of modern music. Neefe, too, who had connexions with Dessau, must have known of the achievements of F. W. Rust, and there is every appearance of his having made his young virtuoso perform the first sonatas of the Prince of Anhalt's Capellmeister, which were engraved at Leipzig when Neefe was conductor of the orchestra in that town.

As to Haydn's influence, it is no matter for surprise, for, consciously or otherwise, every painstaking pupil always begins by imitating his master's methods, and we know what an admirable tutor the composer of the *Creation* was for the youth sent to him by the Elector-Archbishop of Cologne.

In a conversation with the flautist Drouet, Beethoven expressed himself as follows: 'My first three trios were not published in the form in which I originally wrote them. When I re-read the manuscripts I wondered at my folly in collecting into a single work materials enough for twenty. When a beginner, I should have perpetrated the most egregious follies in composition but for Papa Haydn's advice.'

It may be said, then, that the Beethoven of the *first manner* borrowed from C. P. E. Bach his style and his mode of writing, from W. Rust his creative thought, and from Haydn his faultless construction. The imitation of Emmanuel Bach's style is especially obvious in the early works, the largo of the second trio, op. 1, having a distribution of nuance and accent almost identical with the habitual style of Frederic II's chamber musician, and several sonatas remind one, even thematically, of the Prussian sonatas. Turning now to the works of Rust, do we not find the same modes of thought and expression as in many of Beethoven's pieces? For example, is not the final movement of Beethoven's sixth quartet (1799) dictated by the same poetic sentiment as the last movement of the Dessau master's eighth sonata (1792)? The sudden interruption of the *Malinconia* by the opening of a pastoral rondo, then its reappearance amid the rhythms of the countryside, is not this, so to speak, a tracing—in form at least—from Rust's melancholy (*Schwermuth*), softened by a thought of joy (*Frohsinn*), this

[1] It will be remembered that Dr. Wilhelm Rust, the composer's grandson, introduced extensive alterations in his grandfather's music, but we are concerned here only with the 12 sonatas for piano, the text of which is of undoubted accuracy, these sonatas having been exactly copied by Vincent d'Indy himself. (Ed. Rouart, Lerolle et Cie.)

last almost in Beethoven's own manner? As regards Haydn, the imitation is rather of form than of substance. It is as though the pupil, none too sure of his ability to walk alone, had borrowed his master's gold-headed cane to support him, without, however, going quite so far as to don the fine buckled shoes of the father of the symphony. Many indications of Haydn's peculiar methods of construction are to be found in the works of Beethoven's youth. It is from the sonatas and quartets of Haydn's last period that Beethoven has borrowed the idea of a second subject in three sections, in three distinct phrases which are yet inseparable one from another. Like his master, the youthful disciple is fond of piquant episodes and short excursions towards distant tonalities; among all the unusual rhythms and displacements of accent, so frequent with Beethoven, there is nothing that had not been employed in the same way by the musician of the Princes Esterhazy. If the scherzo of the first string quartet, op. 18, seems to us of so original a turn of thought, by reason of its bar-groupings of 3–3–2–2, is not an analogous case to be found in the curious minuet of Haydn's *Farewell* symphony, with its periodic rhythm of 4–2–3–3 bars?

We should, however, recognize, here and there, in this first period, certain pieces in the style of Mozart ('hommages à Mozart'), if only in the choice of several themes taken from *Figaro* and the *Magic Flute* to serve as themes for some interesting variations. We shall also find, curiously enough, the whole of the opening part of Zerlina's air, 'Batti, batti' from *Don Giovanni*, in the andante of the quintet, op. 16, for piano and wind instruments. It is true that here the rhythm differs from that adopted by the Salzburg master, but the melodic outline is nearly identical in the two versions.

This first epoch (Imitation) comprises nineteen chamber works, about a third of the total production of the period.

Among these we find: *Grand Septet* (Septuor), op. 20, for clarinet, horn, bassoon, violin, viola, violoncello, and double bass, written in 1799; two sextets (1796) for wind instruments, one of these being a second version of op. 81 b, the form of which was not definitely settled till 1809; twelve trios, of which seven are for piano, violin, and violoncello—among these latter the first is the work with which Beethoven decided to date the beginning of his career, three trios, op. 1 (in E flat major, G major, and C minor), dedicated to Prince Lichnowsky—the third of these already is evidence of a real effort on the part of the young man to raise himself above the level of his models. In 1796 appeared op. 3, a trio for violin, viola, and violoncello, a nearly complete sketch of which, dating from 1791, has been already mentioned; then op. 9, three trios in G, D, and C minor, dedicated to Count Browne. In 1798 we find a trio in B flat major for piano, clarinet, and violoncello, op. 11, and a certain number of works for various combinations of three instruments: the serenade, op. 8, for violin, viola, and violoncello; the trio for two oboes and cor anglais; and divers variations on themes of Handel and Mozart. Six sonatas, two being for piano and violoncello, op. 5 (1796), three for piano and violin, in D major, A minor, and E flat major, op. 12, dedicated to Salieri (1798), and one for piano and horn, op. 17 (1800); as well as three duets for clarinet and bassoon and a sonatina for piano and mandoline.

I have kept to the end of this list the first six quartets, op. 18, dedicated, in 1799, to Prince Lobkowitz, because it is here that we find the actual line of demarcation between the first and second periods of the musician under consideration, and also because they are evidence of the great artistic sincerity of that musician.

We are aware that the string quartet is incontestably the most difficult form of composition to handle, and that heedless composers, who, in their early efforts, venture upon this form, inevitably produce dull and lifeless results. The truth of this statement is easily verified, and the reasons are not far to seek. This, however, is not the place in which to treat of these reasons. It will suffice to say that the composition of a string quartet is not an achievement for one's youth, and that the development of the musician must have reached a certain stage of maturity in order to overcome the inherent difficulties of tonal architecture, if he is to produce a satisfactory result.

When, in 1795, Count Apponyi commissioned a string quartet from Beethoven with the promise of an excellent fee, the latter declined without hesitation both order and emoluments, judging himself to be as yet unfitted to succeed in so serious an undertaking. For his own edification, however, he made two attempts to write a work of this kind, but his efforts yielded results different from those intended. The first attempt ended, in 1796, by becoming the trio, op. 3, while the second, in which he made use of materials already employed at an earlier date, resolved itself into a quintet, op. 4, a third version of the above-mentioned op. 81 b.

Not until four years later, during his twenty-ninth year, did Beethoven, already under the influence of a change of style, allow himself a first incursion into the hitherto forbidden land. And this first essay, it must be owned, was anything but definitive. One realizes the abysmal depths which sunder the Lobkowitz quartets from the astonishing no. 12, conceived twenty-four years afterwards.

In order to give the reader an idea of Beethoven's first style, we shall confine ourselves to a brief analysis of two characteristic works of this epoch: firstly, the 'cello sonata, op. 5, in G minor—in which we observe, side by side with curious innovations, the tentative efforts of the well taught pupil, not yet quite sure of his technique; and, secondly, the third of the Lobkowitz quartets, which comes at the very end of the period of imitation.

We begin, therefore, with the sonata. It must first of all be noted that Beethoven's five violoncello sonatas all display a particular structure which is not to be met with in the violin sonatas, still less in those for piano. It would seem that the composer, attracted by the tenor voice of the instrument, has done his best to bring out this singing quality by means of broad, slow phrases, and to give it more importance than the element of virtuosity. This tendency explains why three of the sonatas open with a long and often pathetic introduction, and also why the second subjects of the quick movements—the expressive subjects—are treated at much greater length than in the other sonatas.

This is so in op. 5, no. 2, which opens with a broad adagio, developed at some length. In the allegro which follows, while twenty-six bars suffice for the statement of the first theme, the second, not content with spreading itself—at a length of ninety-five bars—over three phrases differing in character, sees fit to take to itself a further complementary coda, by way of ending to the expository section. We notice, in the transition passage between the two themes (the technical term for which is the 'bridge'), a rhythmic figure, employed by Beethoven eight years later, for the same reason, in the first movement of the third symphony (Eroica):

Ex. 1.

After the development, which calls for no particular notice, and the recapitulation, which is the usual repetition of the exposition, there appears, for the first time in the history of music, a modification introduced by Beethoven into the regular scheme of the sonata. The movement proper is concluded, but the composer is anxious to emphasize the several constituents, in order to drive them home, and he here introduces a fresh system of development which we call a 'terminal development', in the course of which the first theme reappears, hesitating and in broken rhythm, before he finally concludes:

Ex. 2.

Th. A.

Th. A (in broken rhythm).

This arrangement, unknown to Haydn and Mozart, is regularly employed by Beethoven in his remaining works.

The rondo, the second and final movement of the sonata, is much less perfect in structure than the first movement; the five refrains serve merely as a frame for the couplets—every one with a development, the effect being to overweight the couplet. Just as the construction of the first movement derives strength from the former innovation (the 'terminal development'), so the rondo form, already somewhat out of date, is rendered tedious by the latter device, which amounts to a grave fault in composition and compromises the unity of the sonata.

Turning to the quartet in D, op. 18, no. 3—the first of the set in order of composition—for the F major quartet only bears the number 1 because it was published before the others—we find it written in a much less daring style than the last-mentioned sonata, although it is three years later in date.

It seems as if Beethoven had wished to shelter himself behind a kind of permit given by his artistic forbears, by way of excuse for his audacity in daring to write a quartet at all, and had, in fact, merely sought to imitate his instructors.

The first movement, though charming in its musical content, shows no advance on similar works by Mozart, and the 'terminal development'—inferior to that of the sonata, op. 5—adds little to the interest of the movement.

The andante con moto in B flat has qualities of beauty and expressiveness which atone for the rather disproportionate length of the fourth section; the poetic peroration happily redresses the balance. As to the scherzo and the final presto they might very well have been taken from some quartet or symphony by Papa Haydn.

Nothing, then, in this, one of the latest works of the first period, tends to foreshadow the prodigious forward leap which Beethoven's art was to achieve, to which we owe certain of the piano sonatas and, above all, the quartets of 1806.

Rather should we seek premonitions of this sudden change in the last bars of the first movement of the second quartet, op. 18, and especially in the beautiful and mysterious *Malinconia* of the sixth, which, like a recurrent thought, interrupts so strangely the frolics of the joyous finale.

But, before proceeding to the study of this transformation, a brief summary of the causes of it seems to us to be indispensable.

Second Period (Externalization)

From 1801 onwards, Beethoven, who, until then, had composed in peace and security, solidly grounded on the principles laid down by his predecessors and scrupulously respecting those principles, seemed suddenly to abandon them and to turn abruptly into a new path. He writes sonatas in which not even a trace of sonata form remains. . . . Somewhat later, feeling the necessity in composition for a solid basis of construction, he returns almost with violence to this form, and seems to be proclaiming its excellence to the exclusion of all others; all the four movements, for instance, which constitute the seventh quartet, are written in this form. Further, in 1802, the rondo is proscribed, and henceforth appears but seldom in the works of his second manner; soon it is to disappear entirely from his sonatas and quartets. He does not, as yet, dare to lay hands on the form of the symphony, but he replaces the almost obsolete minuet by the scherzo, a type after his own heart, and one which he is later to raise to epic heights.

So far he has followed dutifully in the steps of his elders, but now we see him breaking with his models and tossed, as by a hurricane, from this side to that, unable, for some time at least, to proceed in any fixed direction.

So far he has written music only; now his writing is of life itself.

What, then, has happened to produce in Beethoven so great a change?

Simply this: in the course of his thirty-first year, passions which had, so to speak, but grazed his early manhood, have suddenly descended upon him and dragged him into their maelstrom.

He has felt, he has loved, he has suffered.

And perhaps, without being fully conscious of it, he has found himself in some way forced to reveal in his art his feelings, his emotions, and his sufferings. It is as though beneath some clear surface, his music allows our vision to penetrate to the depths of his soul.

In frenzy, he now reveals to us the three passionate desires with which, in this second period of his life, his soul is filled: love of woman, love of nature, love of country. Add to these impulses of the heart the anxiety with which he watched the progress of the malady, so soon to shut him off from all communion with his fellows, then do we understand the breadth and forcefulness of this second manner.

From 1801 onwards, Beethoven's life might be reconstituted almost step by step from his works. But such is by no means the object of the present study, and we must confine ourselves to tracing, in his chamber music, the effect of these three great passions.

It is known to every one that in April 1800—in the spring of his thirtieth year—'for the first time'—so he himself says—love, passionate love crushed, ravished, and tortured Beethoven's soul. He had met the young Countess Giulietta Guicciardi, he loves her, he proposes . . . His proposal is rejected, and then he reaches the climax of despair, manifested not only in the *Heiligenstadt Will*, but in the sonata, op. 27, no. 2, and in so many other works.

How many appeals to a loving and compassionate feminine heart, how many anguished laments, what wearied resignation may we not find in those compositions written between 1806 and 1815! To quote a few examples only, what is the adagio of the seventh quartet, what, too, the eighth quartet almost in its entirety, the mysterious largo of the second trio dedicated to Mme Erdödy, the first movement of the ninth quartet, but the lament of a suffering heart and the cry of one who still hopes for a woman to console him?

A woman to console him—for Beethoven what better consoler was there than Nature herself, his second love? And not only a consoler, but still more, a friend with whom he loved to hold familiar converse, the one comradeship left to him by his deafness.

But if Beethoven loved Nature ardently, it was in a way very different from the dry and theorizing manner of Jean-Jacques Rousseau. He is far from considering her 'immense, impenetrable and proud', as did Berlioz later, speaking through the mouth of Faust. No, a little spot in a valley, a meadow, a tree suffice to conjure up sublime inspirations in the soul of our musician; and in how many works of this period of his life do we not find some trace of the little path which climbs the slopes of the Kahlenberg, midway between the taverns of the Viennese suburbs and the rustic villages scattered through the forest?

So Beethoven, under the sway of these impressions, conceives and realizes not only the Pastoral symphony, op. 68, but ten, twelve, twenty pastoral symphonies; of those which concern us here we may note the violin sonata, op. 30, no. 3 (1802), three movements of the seventh quartet (1806), the whole of the superb tenth violin sonata, op. 96 (1812), and the finales of the trios, op. 70, no. 2, and op. 97, &c.

A third love, love for his 'German Fatherland', animated the spirit of our musician. Without disowning the plains of *Father Rhine*, he cherished an equal love for Austria, his adopted country, whose sorrows, distress, and eventual triumph he shared, morally and materially. But what share had his art in this feeling? How did the composer of the Eroica symphony regard his country, musically, and what means did he adopt for the expression of his patriotism in terms of music? His method was simply to cast his melody in a warlike rhythm. The well-known rhythm—

Ex. 3.

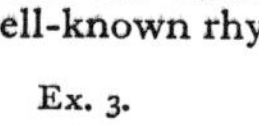

was current at that time for all military occasions in which music had a place: triumphal marches, funeral music, infantry charges, assaults, even for the retreat. And this rhythm retained its special military significance until Meyerbeer converted it to other uses by making indiscriminate use of it in his operas.

Why should we be surprised at this military expression of Beethoven's patriotism, seeing that his whole life, with the exception of the last ten years, was passed amid the sights and sounds of war—movements of troops, bombardments, invasions? Does it not seem natural that his conception of the Fatherland should be inseparable from the warlike display with which he was surrounded, and that a rather grandiloquent heroism, in the style of his favourite author, Plutarch, should materialize in a vision of gigantic plumes and glittering kurtkas, which he could only express musically by the rhythms of the drum and the gallop?

This, then, is the form in which heroism appears in the sonata for piano and violin, op. 30, no. 2, dedicated to the Emperor Alexander, the second subject of which is in the nature of a march to the attack by the Préobajenski grenadiers, and—to confine ourselves to chamber music—in the finale of the Kreutzer sonata, the third movement of the eleventh quartet, the scherzo of the twelfth, the march of the fifteenth, and also in the first movement of the sonata for piano and violin, op. 96.

It is in the growth of these three types of love, which Beethoven seems to wish to cry aloud before the whole world, and which he vociferously proclaims in works wherein passion and colour claim expression, to the point of encroaching, sometimes, upon form—it is in this growth that we discover the true reason for the sudden change of style which is evident from 1801, a change which was to dominate his production during nearly fifteen years.

To this second period (Externalization) we may assign thirty chamber works, distributed as follows:

Sextet, op. 81 b, for two horns and string quartet, completed in 1809, this being the final form of the attempts and sketches, already met with, of 1790 and 1796; a second quintet, for two violins, two violas, and violoncello, op. 29 (1801); five quartets for strings, the 7th, 8th, 9th, op. 59, dating from 1806, dedicated to Prince Rasoumovsky, the 10th, op. 74, to Prince Lobkowitz (1809), and the 11th, op. 95 (1810); then six trios, three of which are admirable masterpieces, namely the two, op. 70, dedicated, in 1808, to Countess Erdödy, and op. 97, to Archduke Rudolph. The other three are of much less importance; these are the little trio dedicated 'à ma petite amie' (Maximilienne Brentano), and two arrangements for piano, violin, and violoncello, one, of the first quintet, op. 4, and the other, of the string trio, op. 3. There are also various pieces in the form of trios, such as the serenade, op. 25 (1801), for flute, violin, and viola (arranged in 1802 with the title: sonata for flute and piano, op. 41), a theme and variations in E flat, op. 44, for piano, violin, and violoncello, and twenty-four ball-room and country dances, for two violins and violoncello; and further (the above-mentioned arrangement for flute not included), eight grand sonatas, seven of which are for piano and violin, opp. 23, 24, 30 (three sonatas dedicated to the Emperor Alexander), op. 47, known as the Kreutzer sonata (all of these compositions written between 1801 and 1803), and op. 96, of 1812, dedicated to Archduke Rudolph, and, finally, a sonata for piano and violoncello, op. 69, dating from 1808. To complete this list of chamber works of the second period, we may add a nocturne, op. 42, for piano and viola (after the serenade, op. 8), three duets for clarinet and bassoon (1814), and the pieces for four trombones, entitled *Equali*, written for the commemoration service for the dead of 1812.

In order to obtain a clear idea of this second manner, of which we have set out only the results, a close study of ten works or so, is necessary; we shall thus be able to realize the advance of Beethoven's art during these fifteen years. We shall select for a rapid survey five of the above-mentioned sonatas, giving them in chronological order, one trio, op. 97, and the five quartets of this period.

Sonata in F major, op. 24. The structure of the opening movement scarcely differs from that of the first period sonatas, with one reservation, namely that there is always a double exposition of the subjects, the melody being first given to the violin, and then repeated in the piano part, an arrangement employed by Beethoven exclusively in his sonatas for two instruments, and this almost without exception. The 'terminal development', anticipated in certain movements of the first period, can hardly be said to exist in this first movement and is suddenly curtailed by a somewhat commonplace coda.

The adagio molto espressivo, whose initial theme seems to have escaped from some opera by Mozart, is an aria (Lied) in five sections, the fourth of which is a finely expressive modulatory development, while the fifth is merely a conclusion with no definite return of the theme.

After a lively scherzo comes the finale, which is assuredly the most original movement in the work. Constructed according to the very distinctive Beethoven rondo form, it proceeds as follows:

1st refrain, in F.
 1st couplet: bridge and second theme, in C.
2nd refrain, in F.
 2nd couplet, founded on fresh material.
3rd refrain, in F.
 3rd couplet: bridge and second theme, in different keys.
4th refrain, which concludes.

Everything goes as usual until the third couplet, which, far from proceeding in the manner of its first period relatives, leads the second theme away into unexpected and distant tonalities (A flat, E flat minor, E flat major), from which the latter extricates itself with much difficulty in order to find its way back to the fourth refrain. This last, presented under the guise of an *ornamental variation*, soon gives place to one of those endings of which Beethoven possessed the secret. This secret consists in introducing an entirely new element, but one so near akin, in its very essence, to the movement itself, that it could not appear in any other sonata without doing violence to the work.

SONATA IN C MINOR, op. 30, no. 2. Although only one year later than the foregoing work, this sonata denotes an important change in the mind of the composer.

It seems as though Beethoven, deliberately repudiating the wise precepts laid down by Haydn and Ph. Emm. Bach, is seeking to numb his feelings, in order to fly the memory of the beloved Giulietta, who cannot be his, an end not to be attained till two years later, the accomplishment of which will be written in the pages of op. 53 and in the Eroica symphony.

At this moment, it is his two other loves that he so passionately invokes: firstly Nature, in the sonata, op. 30, no. 3, in G major, a true pastoral symphony which is full of rustic impressions and the bucolic spirit of the country dance; and secondly, patriotism, in this sonata in C minor, so essentially military in spirit.

What is the second subject of the first movement, allegro con brio, with its three distinct phrases, but a musical version of an attack by some regiment of the Emperor Alexander's guard?

In the first phrase:

Ex. 4.

we are present at a well alined march of the grenadiers with their pointed caps; the second:

Ex. 5.

is the charge against the enemy, and the third:

Ex. 6.

the song of victory. I do not think these forty-five bars can be interpreted in any other way.

In the development we find a new melody, a third subject—rather unusual this, and hardly to be met with elsewhere than in this sonata and the Eroica symphony; the theme is a plaintive one:

Ex. 7.

suggested, perhaps, by the groans of the wounded, and soon yields to the march which returns once more. After the recapitulation, which is quite normal, an important 'terminal development' recalls for a moment the plaintive theme, which vanishes at the shouts of victory of the concluding bars.

The adagio cantabile, an expressive aria (Lied) in five sections, seems like a rest between two battles, and even here, in the fourth section, the peaceful calm of the fine A flat theme is broken in upon, for an instant, by the sound of volleys. The curious canonic trio of the scherzo clearly shows, for that matter, that this peace is not to last.

With the rondo which ends the work, the turmoil of war begins again with renewed vigour; with beating of drums

Ex. 8.

and ringing trumpet calls:

Ex. 9.

Then, after the fourth refrain, all the themes of victory are mingled in a glowing final presto which forms a worthy conclusion to this fine work.

SONATA IN A MINOR, op. 47. We here find ourselves in the presence of a composition which, though not written exclusively in virtuoso style, is yet much nearer to the style of the concerto than that of the sonata as hitherto understood by Beethoven.

Of this he was fully aware, for, in the curious dedication which is an attempt to 'gild the pill' for the professor of the Paris Conservatoire, and to persuade him to accept the gift of a *modern* work, he specifically mentions this tendency.

The autograph dedication of op. 47 runs thus: '*Sonata per il pianoforte ed un violino, scritta in un stilo molto concertante* come d'un concerto, *dedicata al suo amigo Rodolfo Kreutzer*.'

The 'amigo Rodolfo' did not consider the work to be worthy of him, and never played it in public. Certain documents suggest that, when Beethoven realized this, he entrusted the sonata to one Bridgetower, an English violinist of mulatto origin, who had helped him with certain details, and that it was this violinist who gave the first performance of the work.[1]

After a short introduction comes a bold and vigorous allegro[2] with an important second subject in three sections, the third of which provides nearly the whole of the material for

[1] Full story in *Grove*.

[2] The movement is marked 'Presto'; M. d'Indy no doubt uses allegro in the general sense of a quick movement. (Ed.)

the development. The 'terminal development', after the recapitulation, has but slight interest.

The theme with variations in F major, which follows, is treated in purely classical style, and introduces no innovations into the art of music, though the violinist finds ample scope for the display of his skill.

The final presto, in A major, written in first-movement form, is full of energy and has the peculiarity that the two subjects are identical in rhythm, so that the entire movement turns on the same rhythmic figure:

Ex. 10.

1st Theme.

2nd Theme.

yet without any sense of monotony, thanks to the break made by a passage in 2/4 time which serves as conclusion to the second subject.

Development and 'terminal development' give us nothing in the way of fresh combinations, but the vivacity of the figures for both violin and piano compensates the hearer for their absence.

Sonata in G major, op. 96 (1812). (Dedicated to Archduke Rudolph.) This tenth sonata is assuredly the work which, together with the sixth symphony, arouses most strongly, in the minds of those gifted with understanding, the charm of the smiling Austrian country-side. The work is, in the highest degree, another pastoral symphony, and is also the latest in date.

From the start of the first movement one feels the caress of a soft breeze, and although the second subject twice brings to our ears the distant tramp of soldiers, the sounds of war are soon forgotten in the gentle charm of the country-side before us. The third section of the second subject consists of a singularly moving phrase, the emotional beauty of which is understood and rendered by very few violinists or pianists:

Ex. 11.

Most performers turn this eminently melodic phrase into a polka-tune, forgetting that in Beethoven's day a dot above a note in no way signified *detached* playing, but was, on the contrary, the equivalent of the stroke over a note which, for us, means playing 'à la corde' (with a flat bow):

Ex. 12.

The development of the movement, based almost entirely on this melodic figure, loses all meaning if performed contrary to the composer's intention.

In the recapitulation, this same third phrase of the second subject leads to a charming descent towards the subdominant, where Beethoven seems to have lost the principal key and to be anxiously seeking it among the figures of the bass; but the violin, which joins in this search, suddenly strikes the key of the opening pastoral section, and brings the first movement to an end with a gentle caress and a wild cry of joy in the happiness regained.

The adagio in E flat, in aria (Lied) form in four sections, is a masterpiece of touching melody—a reverie on a wooded slope which might form a pendant to the famous *By the Brook*. This adagio has no definite conclusion; the dream is suddenly interrupted by a peasant festivity which serves as a scherzo.

Nothing could be quainter than this scherzo. For the first time, perhaps, Beethoven becomes descriptive.

Lying in a meadow, or perhaps perched in the branches of a tree, the poet first takes note of a rustic dance with its clashing, almost savage rhythms, carried by the wind from the forests of the Kahlenberg—it is the scherzo:

Ex. 13.

Allegro.

Then, from another quarter, the quarter of the 'Wirtschaften' of the Viennese suburbs, taverns where, on Sundays, whole families of well-to-do burghers forgather, there came to him, as though carried hither and thither by the shifting breeze, the echoes of a ball-room waltz—'valse noble', Schumann would have said—which soon vanish, in order to make way, as a correct classical trio should do, for the scherzo *redivivus*:

Ex. 14.

This little descriptive picture, partly repeated, is no exception in Beethoven's works; it is found again in the finale of op. 53, in the minuet of the eighth symphony, and lastly in the trios, opp. 70 and 97.

The rondo, a paraphrase with variations—seven of them—of a popular Viennese song, still remains in the pastoral vein, though less strikingly so.

This fine sonata, the last written by Beethoven for the violin—very seldom performed by violin virtuosi as not being 'effective'—might be styled a *résumé* of the B flat trio, op. 97. Both works are dedicated to Archduke Rudolph, but the trio, despite its opus number, is a year earlier than the sonata, op. 96.

We shall now proceed to the analysis of this trio, composed in 1811.

TRIO IN B FLAT MAJOR, op. 97 (1811). (Dedicated to Archduke Rudolph of Austria.) The first movement opens with a nobly majestic phrase, composed of two elements; this gives rise to the bridge passage which leads to a second subject in G major, in three long phrases. After a development section in three distinct parts alternating between periods of activity and repose, the recapitulation takes place normally and is rounded off by a beautiful ending which serves as an emphatic commentary on the first subject.

The scherzo, a movement full of freedom and joy, contains, in the trio, a curious chromatic passage ending with an outburst in striking contrast; after which the movement dies away, almost motionless on the tonic at the close.

We now come to the two movements which are really *hors ligne*. Firstly, the andante with variations in D major, with a captivating melody, a model of the two-section theme, which, after four extended variations, seems about to end with a simple restatement of the theme, as is done by the composer in so many cases (adagio of op. 109, arietta of op. 111, &c.). But this time things turn out quite differently. The theme, after its second bar, seems as though distraught; with mournful change of key it hesitates, falters, and stops, as if tired out, on a cadence in E minor, a key absolutely foreign to the original one. But the concluding figure ('cellule')—

Ex. 15.

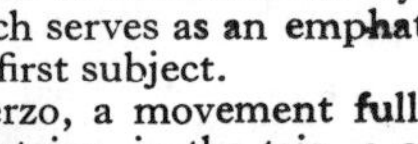

is there; it is watching over the healthful progression of the phrase entrusted to it, and in this way begins an admirable 'terminal development', which, bringing back the desired tonality, gives rise to a melodic amplification of the melody—a marvellous conclusion to the movement.

The finale (allegro moderato), which is linked up with the andante, is another pastoral symphony; not a landscape this time, but a joyous meeting of the rude peasantry, the themes of which should be interpreted almost brutally. As regards construction, it is a rondo in which the refrain appears five times, but on the last two occasions in a modified rhythm (6/8), bringing with it a curious simplification of the theme, and ends the work in most joyously brilliant fashion.

The schematic analysis may be stated as follows:

I. *Allegro*:

(1) A, B flat; complete phrase in two parts.
Bridge, founded on A.
B, in G, in three phrases.

(2) *Development* in three sections:
1. Rhythmic development, on A, E flat.
Period of repose on A, with fragmentary imitation.
2. Period of activity, then:
Period of repose—G—on A^2.
3. Period of activity; very animated; then:
Breaking off, towards:

(3) *Recapitulation*—A, with melodic alteration.
Bridge—short.
B—in B flat, with conclusion on A^1.

II. *Scherzo*: B flat; on the grand Beethoven model (scherzo repeated three times).
Conclusion with the trio.

III. *Andante*: in D:

(1) Theme in two periods, with repeats.

(2) Variation 1.—Rhythmic, founded on the concluding figure.
Variation 2.—Increased movement—in semiquavers ('agogic').
Variation 3.—Further increase of movement—triplet semiquavers.
Variation 4.—Peace once more, agitation confined to the bass.

(3) 'Terminal development', full of key changes; return to the tonic by means of the concluding figure and extending cadence, linking up with the finale.

IV. *Allegro moderato*—Rondo form:

A^1—in B flat (refrain).
Rhythmic *bridge*—B—in F.
A^2—in B flat.
Second couplet, containing new material.
A^3—in B flat.
Bridge—B—in E flat, then B flat, slackening towards:
A^4—in A, with change of rhythm and alteration to:
A^5—in B flat, simplified, and with greatly increased movement.

Only the quartets of the second period now remain to be discussed; these we have purposely kept to the last, although chronologically anterior to opp. 96 and 97, feeling, as we do, that the quartet is the culminating point of all musical forms—at least in Beethoven's case.

It is, in reality, in his quartets, far more even than in his orchestral works, that he displays his innovations in form, that he communicates to us the discoveries of his genius in the realm of composition, and that he reveals his own personality, his joys, and his bitter griefs.

With the first of the three quartets, op. 59, we find ourselves faced with a new music, which may bewilder those who are unacquainted with its genesis and consequently unable to follow exactly its application in these splendid monuments of art.

SEVENTH QUARTET IN F MAJOR, op. 59, no. 1. (Dedicated to Count Rasoumovsky.) The first subject, very much akin, both as regards feeling and rhythm, to that of the trio, op. 97, is stated simply and without preparation. Starting on the low C, in the middle of the bass stave,

Ex. 16.

it gradually rises until it reaches the extreme F of the treble clef:

Ex. 17.

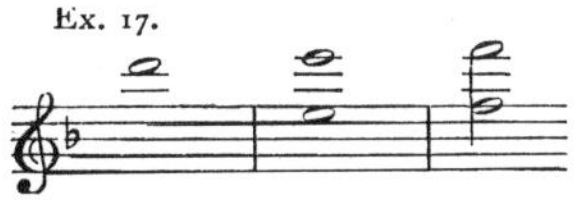

and of this ascent is born a second motif destined to play a part later.

Following on a somewhat agitated bridge passage, also constructed of two elements, there appears a second subject, the preparation of which, by a dominant G on the second violin, is of the strangest, coming as it does at a period when extreme dissonance was still shunned. This second subject, in three sections, is far inferior to the initial theme.

The development turns almost entirely on the first theme, and is divided into five episodes, the object being to make this theme known in its most intimate convolutions.

It is on account of this thorough working-out that Beethoven takes the liberty of beginning the recapitulation with the second element, so as not to exhaust interest in the first element, which, by this time, has been worked very hard. After the return of the bridge passage, now in D flat, and of the second subject, the opening phrase is repeated for the last time in full force, and then finds its completion in a majestic and definitive 'terminal development'.

The allegretto vivace, which serves as scherzo, is an exceedingly curious movement from the structural point of view. Contrary to the general usage in scherzi, this is in first-movement form, and has the peculiarity that, with the exception of the second subject, everything in the movement is duplicated. There are two first subjects, two bridge passages, and two distinct developments. It should be further noted that, for the first time, Beethoven adopts a procedure which he was later to employ with great effect, a procedure which consists in basing certain constituent elements of the movement on a *Variation* of a theme already heard. This system of composition was to lead, eventually, to the cyclic form, fathered by César Franck, and so frequently adopted in the nineteenth century.

Here are the first four constituent phrases of the movement, three of which are manifestly derived from the same melodic pattern:

1st subject, A¹,

Exx. 18, 19.

1st Theme.

(double)

Exx. 20, 21.

Bridge (double) variations of A¹.

These figures are connected by a persistent group ('cellule') which governs the whole rhythmic development:

Ex. 22.

Rhythmic figure.

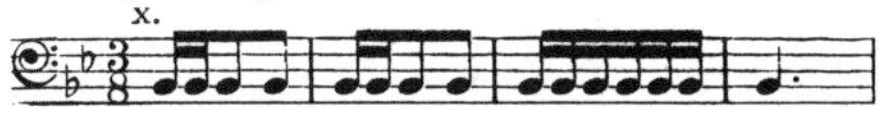

After the double bridge passage there enters a second subject, a beautiful and expressive phrase in F minor, in aria (Lied) form, but unique in character.

The first development, which precipitates us into the most sombre subdominant keys—D flat, G flat, C flat—introduces certain curious modifications of the original themes; thus, for instance, at a certain point, the above-mentioned rhythmic figure is adorned with melody, and becomes:

Ex. 23.

while, on the other hand, the melody of the second subject is simplified to such a degree that it retains only the harmonically essential notes (Ex. 24). Theme B becomes, in the fourth section of the first development (Ex. 24a):

Ex. 24.
Theme B.

Ex. 24 a.
Simplification.

The recapitulation once ended, a second development begins, more important than that which, up to now, we have designated 'terminal development', and after a final fragmentary exposition of the opening theme, the movement dies away, dissolving into a rhythmic mist.

The adagio molto e mesto, that mournful, sublime, and yet gentle lament, is also in first-movement form. The opening phrase, in F minor, is in binary form, and is linked by a very short bridge (seven bars) to a second subject, also binary, but more serene than the first; this is built on a single rhythm of mournful character. This rhythm is generally so ill understood by performers that it appears rather to be grotesque than to suggest a sob of grief. This faulty interpretation is again occasioned by the error which we noticed before, in the sonata, op. 96, an error which causes the dots of the expressive figure

Ex. 25.

to be interpreted by an elegant sautillé, whereas this rhythm was meant by the composer to convey all the anguish of a suffering heart; thus the notes, A (flat), G, require to be markedly 'pressed' out—very much 'à la corde':

Ex. 25 *a.*

The development, divided into four sections, reaches, near the end, a point of repose—remaining motionless in the key of D flat, in which this same phrase seems to acquire a wonderful power of alleviation; and here begins a short recapitulation of the three ideas, the movement being carried on without a break into the finale, by a very ornamental figure for solo violin.

Happy the artists who can understand and interpret such a masterpiece!

The fourth movement, in F major, though not lacking in interest, is far from equal to the earlier ones. It goes on its way through varied presentations of a Russian folk-song, interrupted later by a gently expressive second theme; and here, again, Beethoven adopts the first-movement type of structure, so that every movement of the work is written in this form, an example of construction rarely to be found in the history of music.

Subjoined is an analysis of the seventh quartet:

I. *Allegro*, in F:
- (1) A, in two elements.
  - *Bridge*, also in two elements.
  - B, in C, in three phrases.
- (2) *Development*, in five sections:
  1. Founded on A^1, F, B flat, G minor.
  2. On second bar of A^1, in imitations in changing keys, ending on point of repose on B^3.
  3. Amplifications of A^1 with changes of key.
  4. Fugal episode on coda of B, progressing from E flat minor to the dominant of C major.
  5. On A^1 and the rhythmic figure of B^2.
- (3) *Recapitulation*:
  - A^2 placed before A^1.
  - *Bridge*—D flat.
  - B, in F, leading to a complete expansion of A^1.
  - Peaceful terminal development, on A^1.

II. *Allegretto vivace e sempre scherzando*—B flat:
- (1) A^1, A^2, dominated by the rhythmic figure x.
  - *Double bridge*, formed from variants of A^1 and x—D minor and B flat.
  - B—*Lied-phrase*—F minor.
- (2) *First Development*—four sections:
  1. A^1—D flat; A^2—B flat.
  2. Melodic development of x—C flat, G flat.
  3. Rhythmic development of *bridge*^{2}—A minor.
  4. Harmonic simplification of B—G flat.
- (3) *Recapitulation*:
  - A^2—B flat.
  - *Bridge*^{1}—G minor, *bridge*^{2}—F, B flat.
  - B—B flat.
- (3)^{bis} *Second Development*—two sections:
  1. On rhythm of A^1.
  2. By simplification of B—B flat, A flat, C flat.
  - Fragmentary reappearance of A^2 and rhythmic coda.

III. *Adagio molto e mesto*—F minor:
- (1) A, binary phrase.
  - *Bridge*, short.
  - B, binary phrase—in C.
- (2) *Development*—four sections:
  1. On B—A flat, C sharp minor.

2. On fragments of A, with modulations.
3. On the second phrase of B—towards key of F minor.
4. Expansion of B—D flat.

(3) *Recapitulation*—more animated—A—*bridge*—B—F minor.
Terminal exposition of A; link with the finale.

IV. *Russian theme; allegro*, F major:
(1) A, proceeding by successive restatements, with alteration.—No *bridge*.
B, in C, three phrases, with interposition of A.
(2) *Development*, on A and rhythm of B^2.
(3) *Recapitulation*, A, B, in F.
'*Terminal development*', founded on rhythms of A and B^2, with slow episode.

EIGHTH QUARTET IN E MINOR, op. 59, no. 2 (1806). (Ded. to Count Rasoumovsky.) Again a quartet constructed almost entirely in first-movement form, with the exception of the scherzo. Though inferior to its predecessors, considered as a whole, the eighth quartet offers such interesting structural peculiarities, that we have no hesitation in giving a detailed analysis here.

A figure formed of two strongly accented chords, the sharp cry of an anxious soul, gives rise to a breathless, broken phrase directly derived from this germ; it pauses, breaks off, and ends in a kind of melodic 'suffix', deeply tinged with sorrow. This melody has no true conclusion, and, after a short transition passage, links up with the second subject (in three phrases), where its presence continues to be felt by means of its rhythms. The development turns entirely on the opening figure, and on fragments of the first subject, and the recapitulation, amplifying yet further the hesitations of the exposition, ends with a short 'terminal development', which seems unable to provide any answer to the unceasing queries of the first subject throughout the whole of the movement.

The second movement, molto adagio, opens with a theme in E major, filled with deep religious calm; one might have imagined it the prayer of an innocent and peaceful soul but for the fact that, after the repetition of the melody, there appears a vaguely uneasy rhythm, which, gaining the mastery, soon becomes a true second subject, a kind of call to arms, which has some analogy with the heroic themes of Wagner. Then this appearance of heroism dies away, to be succeeded by sobs of distress which the calm of the peroration is powerless to assuage. A very short development, in which the feeling of sorrow predominates, leads to the recapitulation; here, too, the restless rhythm persists unceasingly, and the movement ends in a tranquillity which is not that of joy.

The scherzo-allegro—three times repeated (one of the first examples of the great Beethoven scherzi)—does nothing to remove this impression of unrest; the continual syncopated rhythm and the indefiniteness of the melody cannot be counteracted by the five-bar Russian theme, which is rather monotonously treated in the trio.[1]

The final presto is, structurally, a combination of first-movement and rondo forms.

This latter seems to be established at the beginning by the exposition of two refrains which enclose a first couplet, with its bridge and second subject, but from the moment of the appearance of the second couplet—containing, as usual, new material—the form changes. Here begins a true development, preparing for a complete recapitulation, in which the second theme (in the tonic) precedes the first, and the bridge which follows serves only to lead up to a final exposition—positively the last—of the opening theme.

In spite of this attempt at an exceptional form, this finale cannot be classed among Beethoven's finer compositions.

NINTH QUARTET IN C MAJOR, op. 59, no. 3 (1806). (Dedicated to Count Rasoumovsky.) As in the two preceding quartets, first-movement form predominates in the ninth quartet, the minuet being the exception.

After an introduction of a few bars in which the key seems unable to assert itself, a rhythmic figure

Ex. 26.

suddenly appears, and opens the way to a first subject made up of two elements of very different rhythms. A melodic bridge and a short second subject complete the exposition, with the peculiarity that the initial figure repeatedly makes its impertinent comment during the exposition of the themes. It is again this initial figure which indiscreetly intrudes upon the three sections of the development, insinuating itself in place of the melodic elements, and even contriving to effect an expressive transformation in itself,

Ex. 27.

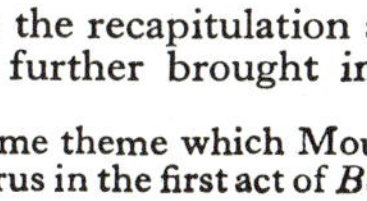

instead of

Ex. 28.

thus giving to the recapitulation a new aspect, which is still further brought into charming

[1] It is this same theme which Moussorgsky used in the great chorus in the first act of *Boris Godounov*.

relief by the decorations of the first violin. The rest of the movement is on the classical plan, without 'terminal development', but with a coda of fourteen bars, for which the initial figure, lively as ever, finds the whole material.

The andante con moto (A minor) which follows, although the opening theme is a regular song (Lied) phrase, none the less preserves unbroken the form of a first movement: first subject, melodic bridge with change of key, and short second subject in the dominant. Follows a development on the bridge theme, which steers first towards the more sombre keys, then, suddenly, by way of contrast, returns to the tonic major, bringing with it the second subject in its entirety. The movement, however, does not preserve this clarity throughout, and, after a search in many shadowy corners, it regains, in a greatly amplified recapitulation of the first subject, the original key of A minor, which it now leaves no more until the end, no attempt being made to recover even a glimpse of the luminous second subject. This movement, despite its intentional monotony (Beethoven might well have called this, too, 'Malinconia'), is a fine piece of music, in which may be found in substance, though on a different level, all that the art of a Mendelssohn, or even a Schumann, was later to achieve.

The last two movements are of an inferior order to the first two. The minuet is a return to the style of 1796, and the final fugue, despite its very curious adaptation to first-movement form, seems long-winded and devoid of real musical interest.

In this connexion, it is particularly noteworthy that Beethoven, with so assured a technique, did not venture to attempt to express his artist-soul in this splendid form—the fugue—until near the end of his career, after 1816, all his earlier essays in fugue-writing resembling rather a student's exercises than the compositions of a mature artist.

We feel that it will be of interest to give an analysis of this quartet:

I. *Introduction*: twenty-nine bars with no definite tonality.
Allegro vivace:
(1) A, in C, in two elements, dominated by the figure X.
Bridge, founded on X.
B, in G, in three short phrases.
(2) *Development* in three sections:
1. X and A¹—E flat.
2. *Bridge* and X—F.
3. Figure X, growing calmer by degrees.
(3) *Recapitulation*, much decorated and in soft colouring:
A and X.
Bridge—on X.
B and *coda*, on X.

II. *Andante con moto quasi Allegretto*:
(1) *Lied phrase*, with coda—A minor.
Bridge, same rhythm.
B, in a single phrase, rhythm unchanged.
(2) *Rhythmic development* (same rhythm):
1. Towards sombre keys, F minor, E flat minor, B flat minor, C minor, G minor, D minor.
2. B—in A major.
3. *Melodic development* of B, in E flat, with modulations.
(3) *Recapitulation* of A, theme amplified, A minor.

III. *Menuetto grazioso*—in C, with trio in F, and coda.

IV. *Allegro molto*:
(1) A, in C, fugal exposition.
Bridge.
B, in G.
(2) *Development* in four sections:
1. A, in direct and contrary motion, E flat, modulations.
2. *Bridge*, with modulations.
3. On fragments of A.
4. On beginning of A, G minor, with modulations.
(3) *Recapitulation* of A, with counter-subject, fugue exposition.
Bridge.
B, in C.
'*Terminal development*' on A—A flat—ending with
Dominant pedal, with C.S. and fragments of A—Conclusion.

The two quartets which we have yet to study, in order to complete the survey of Beethoven's second period works, are full of interest, as, together with opp. 96 and 97, they foreshadow, without actually accomplishing, a transformation in the creative idea, a transformation to be completely effected only in the sonatas of 1815 and the last quartets of 1825.

The troubled period, the influence of which has been discussed, is now over, and, from op. 74 onwards, we again find the regular disposition of the four movements of the sonata.

TENTH QUARTET IN E FLAT MAJOR, op. 74 (1809). (Dedicated to Prince Lobkowitz.) Out of a somewhat extended introduction, the idea of which is to create the right atmosphere for the following allegro, arises the thematic figure based on the notes of the common chord, which is to dominate the whole of this first movement, and to lead directly, without the aid of a transition passage, to a very short second subject in the dominant.

The development, in three sections, is entirely built on the first subject and the thematic figure. At the end of the third section, the recapitulation is approached by a series of pizzicato arpeggios, which account for the sobriquet 'Harp quartet', rather naïvely attributed to this work. After the classical recapitulation, a somewhat extended terminal development again affords amateurs the satisfaction of discovering the presence of harps, the whole ending with a melodic line in which first and second subjects unite to form an harmonious conclusion to the movement.

The adagio in A flat major which follows is a superb example of the lyric grandeur of Beethoven. The majestic calm, preserved unbroken throughout the movement, causes one to wonder what the slow movement will become with the Beethoven of the third epoch (sonata, op. 106, ninth symphony, &c.). A noble and melodious phrase asserts itself at the very outset; this is a binary phrase, provided with a final cadence of the kind employed so effectively by Mendelssohn thirty years later. This phrase, decorated and varied, is repeated in the third and fifth sections of the movement. The second section, in A flat minor, enunciates a fresh theme which reappears only in the sixth section, in order to prepare the conclusion of the movement, while the fourth section is built on a new phrase, in D flat major, an amplification of the opening theme, followed by a short development of this first theme. The whole ends with an evocation of the first movement, fading away into the most delicate colourings.

The third movement, presto, is an example of the great Beethoven scherzi, with trio repeated twice. It is important to be quite clear as to the speed of this trio (più presto quasi prestissimo) in which the crotchet has the exact value of a quaver of the preceding bars, in such a way that a single bar of the scherzo is equal to two bars of the trio.

This rhythmical division ('unwedging') often appears in Beethoven's last manner, and the example of this scherzo suffices to establish the correct speed in the case of the scherzo of the ninth symphony, which nearly all conductors take too slowly. The cases are absolutely identical in the two works.

An allegretto, followed by eight variations, ends this quartet, but adds no element of real novelty.

Eleventh Quartet in F minor, op. 95 (1810). (Dedicated to 'his friend' N. Zmeskall of Domanowetz.) The figure—

Ex. 29.

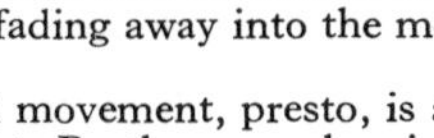

asserts itself straightway, even interrupting the exposition of the first subject, which, after a little while, inclines towards the key of D flat major, in order to give place to the second. This latter evinces the peculiarity, becoming more and more frequent in Beethoven's work, of being interpenetrated, in each of its periods, by rhythms and figures already presented in the first subject, in such a way that, far from forming a contrast, as in the former sonatas, the exposition is by this means pervaded by one single atmosphere. A short development (twenty-four bars) leads to the recapitulation, which is completed by a brief concluding passage hardly worthy of the title of 'terminal development'.

The key chosen for the second movement of this quartet may well astonish us. It is very rare with Beethoven, usually so respectful of natural musical law, to find, in a work in F minor, a movement in D major, an entirely unrelated key. We can explain this anomaly only by the frequency, in this work, of keys containing G flat, which, becoming F sharp, may excuse incursions into the sharp keys.

This second movement is an allegretto which conforms to aria (Lied) form, and is in five sections. First there is heard a gently caressing three-phrase melody, with here and there a melancholy touch, but the sadness lasts only for a few chords and soon vanishes. This melody reappears in the third and fifth sections; in the fifth, its actual reappearance is limited to the last two phrases, and it ceases, without a conclusion, in order to link up with the following movement, allegro vivace, in F minor, another of the grand scherzi; in this, however, the two trios are not identical, from the point of view of tonality, as with the preceding scherzi in this form. The first trio, in fact, oscillates between G flat major and D major, while the second, founded on the keys of D major and C major, leads through this latter back to the colouring of the flat keys. The hesitations of these trios have certainly some connexion with the rather adventurous tonal situation produced by the preceding allegretto.

A magnificent half-phrase in F minor—larghetto—which seems all too short, serves as preparation for the entry of the allegretto agitato, in rondo form.

At this point a comment is needed.

For a long time past Beethoven had been tending to enfranchise himself from the inevitable rondo as finale to a three- or four-movement work. Already, in the sonata, this form is becoming rare—from 1804 onwards—and even if he dared not take too many liberties with the rigid symphony, he had practically freed the quartet since op. 59, in 1806; and he was to continue in this path, for, if we except the rondo of the eleventh, and that of the fifteenth, op. 132, not a single rondo is to be found in all his last works written for strings.

This one is regularly constructed with three refrains and three couplets; after the third couplet, which seems to be the proper termination of the movement, there suddenly arises a kind of coda in F major, which hardly fits in with the style of the work. One might imagine it some light Rossinian operatic finale which had strayed into this atmosphere of sustained beauty, and we think that no interpretation could palliate this error of a genius.

THIRD PERIOD (REFLECTION), 1815–1826

The characteristics of the style of the second period, the chief chamber works of which have just been reviewed, may be summarized in a few words: deep trouble in the artist's soul produced by the first touch of the passions, resulting in a period musically almost disordered, between 1801 and 1805, and, following this, the need felt by the wounded soul to cry aloud its sufferings or to celebrate, in the sight of all men, the cult of Nature, the consoler. Then it is, for the first time, to the orchestra—to the instrument 'with a hundred voices'—that the artist especially entrusts the task of proclaiming his overflowing enthusiasm.

Thus, to these ten years alone, between 1804 and 1815, belong all Beethoven's purely orchestral works. The only work of this type before 1804 is the first symphony, a faint sketch of what was to follow, and, after 1815, the Choral symphony and the Mass in D, colossal works, but using the orchestra rather as a means of expression than as an end in itself. Thus, at the moment in our hero's career at which we have arrived, we have the right to say—paraphrasing the opening recitative of the finale of the ninth symphony: 'Friends, let us leave this mode, and let our song rise ever higher, even to the Kingdom of God!'

What, then, is so changed in Beethoven's state of mind that the moral and artistic quality of his works should suddenly, from 1815, become so different, both in form and inspiration, from what it was in 1814? With what event are we to connect this sudden change? We should seek in vain to attribute the birth of this new style to any external cause. No, the source of the evolution which we are discussing is only to be sought in the poet's very soul. From his heart, then, gushes the stream which is to refresh with its life-giving waters those other hearts athirst for the ideal.

This is not, as in the second period, a development outwards ('externalization') of feelings, but is, on the contrary, the purely inward workings of the thoughts of genius upon itself, in a soul henceforth closed to the tumults and agitations of the outer world.

This is why we have chosen the name, 'period of reflection', for these last twelve years of our hero's life.

Let us endeavour to state exactly, in a few words, the position in which Beethoven found himself at the beginning of this third period.

He has reached his forty-fifth year without meeting the woman who might have gladdened his lonely soul with the gentle influence of married love and family life. All the women whom he might have desired as companions are married; the unworthy Giulietta leads a miserable life, despite her title of Countess Gallenberg, Amelia Sebald is the wife of a Councillor of State, and Theresa Malfatti is betrothed to Baron Drosdick, whom she is to marry next year.

Beethoven has given up the fruitless search for that 'Gegenliebe' ('Love requited') that he has so often sung but which he now renounces.

After the year of the Congress of Vienna, a year so glorious for him, he remains, never theless, without official position. The income settled on him by the great Austrian nobles is considerably reduced, and barely suffices for his needs, still less for the foolish expenditure of his nephew Carl, whom he loves like a son, and who gives him so little satisfaction. For other matters, his deafness, now total, has taken from him not only all normal relations with his fellows, but also the most elementary functions of his art.

Alone, without wife, mistress, position, or resources, deprived even of the power of hearing the manifestations of his genius, his existence is, so to speak, a living death.

What, then, does Beethoven do?

Far from abandoning himself to despair, far from wishing to have done with a wretched life which no longer offers any external attractions, he turns inwards, to his own soul, which he has always done his best to guide towards God, the source of all good and of all beauty.

'Yes,' said he to Stumpff, in 1824, 'he who wishes to touch the heart must seek his inspiration from on high. Without this there will be naught but sounds and notes, a soulless body—is this not true?'

So he comes to lead a purely inward life, contemplative, almost monastic, but how intense and productive!

And he creates no longer with a view to passing success, as in his youth, nor to pour out his feelings and his passions, as in his second period; he creates in pure joy or sorrow, seeking only to elevate that soul in which he lives, alone.

This, then, is the cause of the change of style to which we owe the last six quartets. This, the true reason for that seeming break in his productivity between 1815 and 1818, a phenomenon noticed with astonishment by the rather ill-disposed critic of the *Allgemeine Musik-Zeitung*.

During these three years in which he finds himself, in a manner, forced henceforth to live an inward life, Beethoven reflects. So, too, Richard Wagner, at the dawn of his third period. And, as the result of this long reflection, the composer who had already written the sonata, op. 96, the trio dedicated to Archduke Rudolph, and the Rasoumovsky quartets, will then, and then only, acquire the full assurance that he '*knows how to compose!*'

He says this over and over again, notably of the sonata, op. 106: 'What I write now bears no resemblance to what I wrote formerly; *it is somewhat better* . . .' To the Englishman, Cipriani Potter, who complimented him, in

1817, at Nüssdorf, on the brilliant success obtained by the septet, op. 20, Beethoven replied: 'Oh! at that time I understood nothing of composition; now *I know how to compose*.'

How was this state of reflection, ending in the certitude of *knowing how to compose*, to be translated by Beethoven into music?

It was to be by a manifest and deliberate return to the old traditional forms.

Let us not, however, misunderstand the meaning of these words, 'return to tradition'. Far be it from us to suggest that Beethoven returned, in his full maturity, to a servile imitation of the types in use among his predecessors. But what we can affirm is that all the sense of beauty of the third manner is based on the ancient forms, till then untouched by him, forms whose noble and bountiful atavism endows the most daring compositions with a healthful and vigorous constitution.

These forms are: the fugue, the suite, and the variations on a chorale ('choral varié').

During the first two periods Beethoven, as we have mentioned already, had not ventured to attempt the fugue except on rare occasions, and then without making anything new of it; so far, this form is, for him, a meaningless exercise—a 'musical skeleton', in his own words. After 1815, a radical change is evident. He envisages the fugue as an end, and no longer as a technical means, and further, in his hands, this form—so often cold with the successors of Bach—becomes eminently expressive and, in the same way as the sonata, will bear witness to his inmost feelings of peace, suffering, or joy.

Thus, too, with the suite form, traces of which we shall find again in the last quartets.

But it is above all the old-time variations on a chorale which are to reappear in this third period. With the Beethoven of 1824 the form has the same spirit as with the Bach of 1720, who, by developing the attempts of Pachelbel on a larger scale, created the *amplified variation*.

This kind of variation, sometimes amplifying the theme to the point of causing a totally new melody to emerge from it (twelfth quartet), or, again, simplifying it to the point of melodic immobility (fourteenth quartet), will be met with only from 1820, more especially in the quartets of 1825–6. Thus it may be said that the renewal of a very old form was the last, and not the least sublime manifestation of Beethoven's genius.

It is thus by reliance on the traditional forms, and by identifying them with his own inner thought, and not by seeking to demolish everything in order to build anew at any cost, that this so-called revolutionary was able to contribute so powerfully to the true progress of his art, for, as he said himself, 'The new, the original arise spontaneously, without one's thinking about them.'

Leaving on one side the mighty masterpieces which lie outside the scope of this study, such as the *Missa Solennis*, the ninth symphony, and the last five sonatas for piano, we must confine ourselves to the chamber works, almost all of which are worthy of a detailed examination.

In this category we shall find only twelve examples, but nearly all of the first rank: two string quintets, one, op. 104 (1815), an original arrangement of the trio, op. 1, no. 3, for piano, violin, and violoncello, the other, a fugue for two violins, two violas, and violoncello, op. 137 (1817), besides an andante in G, taken from the sketches for an unfinished quintet; certain variations for trio (piano, violin, and violoncello) on an air from Müller's *Sisters of Prague*, op. 121 (1823); two sonatas, op. 102, for piano and violoncello, dedicated to Countess Erdödy (1815); and, finally, the last six quartets, each a colossus of music, the analysis of which we attempt only with trepidation, fearing our inability sufficiently to convey their unspeakable grandeur.

Appended is the chronological list of these masterpieces, in order of composition:

1824	—twelfth quartet,	op. 127.
1825	—fifteenth ,,	,, 132.
	thirteenth ,,	,, 130.
	Grand Fugue,	,, 133.
1826	—fourteenth quartet,	,, 131.
	sixteenth ,,	,, 135.

TWELFTH QUARTET IN E FLAT MAJOR, op. 127 (1824–5). (Dedicated to Prince Galitzin.) Commissioned by Prince Galitzin in 1822, this quartet was not sketched by Beethoven, then too much absorbed by work on the ninth symphony to think of anything else, until the spring of 1824, in the pine forests which surround the little spa of Baden; and this work is, in fact, the last of the pastoral symphonies written by the master. In it we find the crowning expression of that love of nature of which he gave such wonderful evidence in the course of his career.

At first sight, the opening movement may seem somewhat enigmatic, with its deliberate single rhythm, whose apparent monotony is broken only by the reappearance of the introductory theme. But, with closer study, one soon perceives that the first-movement form is perfectly clear, and that the introductory theme, contrary to usage, is something more than a fleeting preparation and serves two special objects in the scheme of the movement: firstly, it breaks the monotony of the rhythm, by supplying the contrast so indispensable in this form of composition; and secondly, it has the important function of determining the tonal architecture of the movement by means of its three appearances in E flat, G, and C.

One innovation, few examples of which have up to now been met with, but increasingly frequent in the last quartets, is introduced in the exposition of the second subject. This innovation consists in the interpolation of portions of the material already dealt with during the statement of the new theme. Thus, in the second subject of this movement, we find:

Ex. 30.

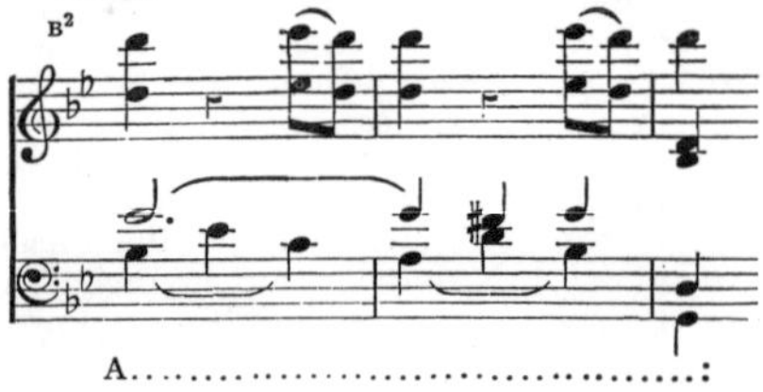

The development proceeds normally, according to the keys necessitated by the reappearances of the introductory theme. But, following on the recapitulation, a concluding phrase arises, founded on the third bar of the initial theme,

Ex. 31.

whose expressive insistence, in this final development, is a true manifestation of genius. After this gentle breath of air through the pine-trees, all dies away in the peace of the forest.

ADAGIO NON TROPPO E MOLTO CANTABILE. I see no possibility of finding a word of admiration strong enough to express the emotion that must be felt by a soul endowed with artistic feelings on hearing this adagio. Its grandeur is such that the human intellect is hardly capable of perceiving its outlines or appreciating the loftiness of its conception.

We must, therefore, confine ourselves here to a bare analysis.

A broad phrase in two sections, of incomparable beauty, gives rise to a series of variations, which amplify and exalt the theme to heights unexplored. But greater things are to come; not content with employing in these variations all the resources of music, Beethoven soars upwards to the conception of a *new musical state* of the given theme. In this evolution the spirit of the great musician seems to approach the manner of thought of the medieval mystics, whose works, at once grand and simple, remain incomprehensible to those who are not simple as themselves, so completely is this simplicity hidden under an exuberant wealth of detail. Such were the French master-architects of the thirteenth century.

The first two variations of this noble monument of art are in the tonic—A flat major. The theme, altered in rhythm, is at first given in outline by the violoncello; it then disappears and melts into a polyphony which seems to draw its life from the *soul* of the character-theme ('personnage-thème') which is still present, though its bodily form has vanished.

The second variation is a gentle twittering, a veritable dialogue of amorous birds, only interrupted by the appearance of the third variation, which is strange of form and altogether unusual: a new phrase arises, yet this phrase is in reality the theme itself, robbed of its decorations, but clothed with such majesty that it might be said to be transfigured in a divine ascension. And, in order the better to mark the change of state, Beethoven places his character-theme in a new environment, in the key of E major, giving by this means the effect of a mysterious, almost celestial radiance.

Ex. 32.

In the fourth variation the theme returns in the original key, and almost unaltered in rhythm.

Then comes a development of fourteen bars on the first and last notes of the theme.

In the fifth variation the theme is rarefied, so to speak, into diatonic figures of extreme delicacy (in the adagio of the ninth symphony there is a closely analogous transformation); then the movement ends with a peaceful conclusion of eight bars almost entirely derived from the last three notes of the great melodic phrase.

Need we point out that the splendid melody which forms the basis of this wonderful adagio seems to be an echo—almost a reminiscence—of the great phrase of the *Benedictus qui venit* of the Mass in D, an echo which, it must be admitted, has a much deeper intensity of feeling than its model? One might imagine that Beethoven, after the manner of the Fathers of the Church, had intended, in this theme with its five variations, to explain, in a sublime commentary, the nature of the 'Blessed One who cometh in the name of the Lord'. And the change of *place* and of *person* in the third variation, whilst retaining the inviolability of the *principle*, tends, in our opinion, to strengthen this hypothesis, and to become a perceptible musical emblem of the incarnation of that 'Blessed One'.

Whatever may be the intention, this adagio will remain the most sublime of prayers.

With the scherzo and the finale we descend to earth again and find once more the playfulness almost of the second-period Beethoven, wandering through a well loved country-side and delighted by the rude songs of the villagers.

The finale would suggest once again the pastoral impressions of 1808 and 1812, were it not for the concluding dream-like development, which raises the quasi-trivial phrase of the opening to heights beyond mortal ken, and comes as a reminder that all this no longer takes place between Döbling and the Kahlenberg, but solely within the poet's mind.

Appended is the analysis of op. 127:

I. *Introduction and Allegro:*

(1) { Maestoso—E flat.
Allegro^1—A.
Bridge founded on fragment of A. }
B^1—G.
B^2—'penetrated' by A.
B^3—cadence.

(2) *Development:*
{ Maestoso—G.
Allegro^2—G, C minor, then development of B^3. }
{ Maestoso—C.
Allegro^3—development by elimination. }

(3) *Recapitulation:*
A—E flat.
Bridge.
B—1–2–3, E flat.

'*Terminal development*'; concluding phrase on viola.

II. *Adagio ma non troppo e molto cantabile:*

THEME—A flat, two sections.

Var. I. TH. outlined by 'cello, then polyphonic amplification.

Var. II. *Dialogue* with amplification, by the two violins.

Var. III. *New phrase*, derived from TH. by simplification. Change of state. E.

Var. IV. TH., A flat, with altered rhythm. *Development* on first and last notes of TH., with modulation.

Var. V. TH. reduced to a decorative figure. Conclusion, on the last three notes of TH.

III. *Vivace*—E flat = scherzo with two rhythms —trio—E flat.

IV. *Finale*—E flat:

(1) A in two elements.
Bridge, on A.
B—B flat, short; enters into development.

(2) *Development*—three sections:
1. On A and B—C minor.
2. A and B in combination—C minor.
3. A—A flat (subdom.), long.

(3) *Recapitulation:*
A—E flat.
Bridge.
B—E flat.

'*Terminal development*' in rhythmic variations giving melodic phrase C, A flat, E. Conclusion—E flat.

FIFTEENTH QUARTET, A MINOR, op. 132 (1825–6). (Dedicated to Prince Galitzin.) Like the piano sonata in A flat major, op. 110, the whole of this quartet is a representation in music of the issue of a crisis, in this case probably a bodily one, since the date of the composition coincides with Beethoven's illness, lasting from April to August 1825, and serious enough to necessitate a month in bed.

But, unlike the sonata, this is not a description of a crisis at its height, ending in a song of triumph; it is, on the contrary, a remembrance of those terrible hours of pain, and a hymn of thanksgiving to Him in whose hands is the life of man.

The whole work, in fact, breathes a spirit of deep religious feeling and filial gratitude.

The introduction, a short phrase of four notes, given out at the start by the violoncello,

Ex. 33.

provides the master-key without which none can enter the superb edifice which forms the first movement.

This movement, in fact, is cast in a very remarkable form. It consists of three successive expositions, interrupted by developments of the introductory theme. It is this theme which throws open each chamber of the palace and gives rise to the appearance of the two constituent ideas, the first of which reflects the memory of the hours of suffering, while the second, in F major, bearing the impress of hopeful charm,

Ex. 34.
2nd violin.

combines, in its third phrase, the rhythm of the initial idea with the rather peculiar harmony of the key-phrase of the introduction.

The second entry of this key-phrase, blending with the development of the first idea, leads shortly to a second exposition of the two constituent themes, in the dominant; a third, and last, intervention of the key-phrase, blended with the development, opens a last door, through which rushes the hopeful theme (second subject) in A major, soon borne along by the theme of suffering, now transformed into a hymn of joy.

Indeed, one need only read through this first movement, so entirely new in form, to be perfectly convinced that Beethoven *knew how to compose!*

A scherzo, in A major, with a pastoral trio—a last echo of some wandering musician's bagpipe—suggests to us once more the still uncertain steps of the convalescent in his first outings.

Then we come to the 'Song of Thanksgiving, in the Lydian mode, offered to the Divinity by a convalescent'—a note written in French,[1] in Beethoven's hand, on the autograph manuscript, and translated, later, into Italian, at the instigation of some publisher.

At that time, as an aid to the composition of the great *Missa Solennis*, op. 123, Beethoven was closely studying the liturgical melodies of the Catholic faith which were to be found in the voluminous library of the Archduke Rudolph, paying special attention to the works of Palestrina.

There is no doubt that to his knowledge of the masters of vocal counterpoint is due that newly found understanding of polyphonic writing which enhances all his later works. We shall not, then, be astonished that the *Chant de reconnaissance* is written in the scale of the *Sixth Gregorian mode*, whence the indication: '*en style lydique*', *in modo lidico* in the Italian translation.

The movement is an example of an aria (Lied) in five sections. The hymn is set out at first in four sections, each prepared by a short instrumental prelude; then comes an episode (second section, in D major), treated at some length, wherein (as in op. 110) the sick man feels his strength returning. Second exposition of the hymn, line by line this time, and, around this line, the orchestral theme, which at first served as a formal prelude, now adds movement and emotion. After a fresh episode (fourth section) indicative of the renewed strength, very closely similar to that of the second section, there is a third strophe of the hymn, but this time it appears only in fragmentary form and leaves all the expressive interest to the instrumental theme, which the composer notes as to be played 'con intimissimo sentimento'. This theme then becomes the true song of gratitude of the human soul, while the melody of the hymn takes wing to celestial regions. And this indeed is pure Beauty!

A short march, almost military—a sharp contrast—brings us abruptly back to earth, after which a recitative, which lacks only words, comes to give wings to the finale—allegro appassionato, filled with radiant joy and constructed in the old rondo form, which Beethoven consents to revive for this one occasion.

[1] The French is: 'Chant de reconnaissance, en style lydique, offert à la Divinité, par un convalescent.'

It is worthy of note that this finale seems to be the source whence Mendelssohn appears to have drawn all his melodic ideas, but whereas the phrases of the Bonn master are touchingly expressive, the ideas of the amiable and faultless Berliner—derived, notwithstanding, from these phrases—appear cold and devoid of emotion.

Talent, however much encouraged, can never attain the heights of genius.

The analysis of the fifteenth quartet may be summarized as follows:

I. *Assai sostenuto* and *Allegro:*
First Exposition.
{ Theme (key-phrase) X, A minor.
{ Allegro.
  { A in A minor.
  { B in F, in three phrases. The third founded on rhythm of A and harmony of X.
Second Exposition.
Theme X—in G, mingled with development of A leading to
A—in E minor.
B—in C, complete exposition.
Third Exposition.
Theme X, in direct and contrary motion—A minor, mingled with development.
B—in A. First phrase only.
A—A minor, conclusion.

II. *Allegro ma non tanto*—Scherzo in A. Trio (on drone bass), in A.

III. *Molto adagio.*—Aria (Lied) in five sections in F (with B♮):
1. Chorale in five sections.
2. Episode—in D (sentendo nuova forza).
3. Chorale with variations.
4. Episode in D.
5. Chorale, expressive, concluding.

IV. *Allegro marcia, assai vivace*—in A, binary phrase, linking up with—

V. *Recitativo più allegro* and *Allegro appassionato.*—A minor:
Rondo with four refrains, ending with conclusion in A major.

THIRTEENTH QUARTET IN B FLAT MAJOR, op. 130 (1825—finished November 1826). (Dedicated to Prince Galitzin.) The first movement appears to be a struggle between two instincts in the same individual: the gently imploring instinct and that of inexorable violence. With the aid of an introductory theme which, as in the preceding quartet, is no mere prelude, but plays an important part in the movement (this theme appears seven times in the course of the movement), the gentler desires gradually permeate the substance of the violence-theme and accomplish its complete subdual.

It will be noticed that the introductory theme

contains the opening figure of the second subject, and that the whole of the development is founded on its rhythm:

Ex. 35.

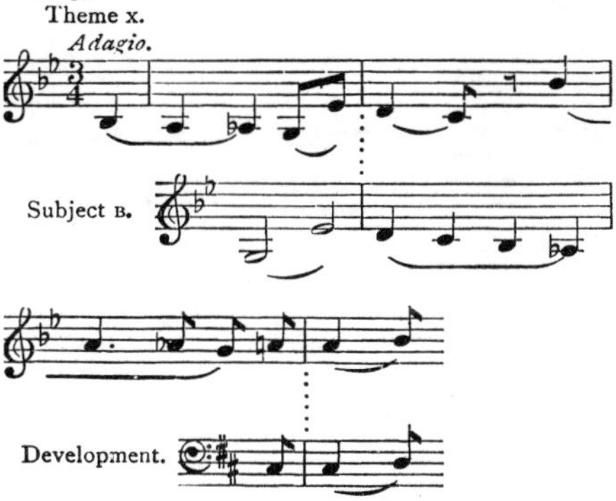

After a short scherzo in B flat minor, a charmingly fanciful movement, comes an andante con moto in D flat major, which is generally misunderstood, even by the best-intentioned performers. This andante is of a high order of beauty, with its intentional monotony, but how many artists are able to discern and to interpret satisfactorily the intimate and touching expression of the second subject?

Beethoven here recurs to a type of slow movement which he had frequently employed in the first two periods, and since discarded for more than twenty years: namely, the *sonata without development*, and, by the richness of his melody, he is able to endow this ancient form with renewed youth.

A fourth movement, the danza tedesca (German slow waltz), in G major, introduces the minuet-scherzo form for the second time in this quartet. Care must be taken not to exaggerate the nuance < > which is continual in the waltz, and to remember always that these dynamic signs indicate only a very slight inflexion within the range of 'piano'.

The cavatina in E flat major which follows is a marvel of melody. It is like a reminiscence, faint, yet full of restrained emotion, of two earlier masterpieces. In its general colouring it recalls the mournful poetic feeling of the *Elegischer Gesang*, op. 118, written on the death of the young Baroness Pasqualati, while the construction of its phrases and the echoes by which they are interrupted at once call to mind the great theme of the adagio of the Choral symphony. Its form is that of an aria (Lied) in three sections, the second of which (no more than eight bars) brings a fleeting sense of agitation into the calm and tranquillity of the melody which, however, soon gains the upper hand.

The original finale of this quartet was a great fugue of a length far exceeding that usual in this type of movement. Beethoven, yielding, not without regret, to the earnest solicitations of publishers and friends, consented to keep the fugue for separate publication, and, four months later, in November 1826, he substituted a new finale, which is, therefore, his last composition.

This allegro, the sixth movement of op. 130, affects the three-subject form, partaking both of first-movement form, in its general construction, and of rondo form, in the position of the third subject, which appears in the manner of the new material of a second couplet. There is an attempt at a similar form in the finale of the quartet, op. 59, no. 2.

Appended is the analysis of the thirteenth quartet:

I. *Adagio* and *Allegro* (first-movement form):
  (1) Introduction—adagio. Theme x^{1}—in B flat.
    Tentative exposition with A, in two elements.
      Theme x^{2}—in B flat.
    Allegro—exposition. A 1 and 2.
      Bridge.
      B—in G flat, in three phrases, penetrated by rhythm of A^{2}.
  (2) Theme x^{3}—G flat, A—F sharp minor.
      Th. x^{4}—D flat, A—in D.
    Development on Th. x, giving rise to new episodic figure—in G, and C.
  (3) *Recapitulation*—somewhat indeterminate.
      A, in the dominant of B flat.
      B, in D flat, then B flat.
      Th. x^{5}—in B flat—A^{2}.
      Th. x^{6}—in dominant of B flat—A^{2}.
      Th. x^{7}—in tonic of B flat—A 1 and 2, conclusion.

II. *Presto* . . . Scherzo form—B flat minor.

III. *Andante con moto, ma non troppo*—Sonata form without development—D flat.
  (1) A—in D flat, on viola—(Lied phrase, with modulation).
    B—in A flat, tending towards subdominant.
  (2) A—in D flat.
    B—in D flat, and '*terminal development*' on B.

IV. *Alla danza tedesca* . . . G. Scherzo form, with trio modulating into G, C, E minor.

V. *Cavatina—Adagio molto espressivo*—E flat—Aria (Lied) in three sections.
  A, Lied phrase in three periods—E flat.
  B, short episode, broken rhythm—C flat.
  A—E flat minor, then conclusion.

VI. *Finale*—Allegro.
  (1) *Exposition*: A—B flat.
      Bridge, founded on A.
      B—in F, short.
  (2) C, new complete subject—A flat.
      Development founded on A, fugato.

(3) *Recapitulation*: A—B flat.
Bridge.
B—B flat.
C—E flat, then B flat.
'*Terminal development*' on A, shortened, conclusion.

GRANDE FUGUE 'TANTÔT LIBRE, TANTÔT RECHERCHÉE', op. 133 (1825). (Dedicated to Archduke Rudolph of Austria.) The Grand Fugue in B flat major, entitled quartet no. 16 in some editions, was originally, as we have seen, intended as finale to the thirteenth quartet, Beethoven consenting to its excision only at the earnest solicitations of the publisher Artaria, who printed it separately.

In the original manuscript the twenty-nine bars which precede the fugue exposition were entitled: 'Ovvertura'. (*sic*).

This somewhat strange and rarely performed work is, nevertheless, of immense interest. It is worthy of deep and serious study, for the mysterious beauties with which it is filled are revealed only to those who can rise to the heights of the Beethoven spirit.

Is it not astonishing that chamber music societies never think of giving the Grand Fugue in its proper place, i.e. as peroration to the thirteenth quartet, where it would be the more fitting in that it is neither more nor less than the commentary on the first movement of this quartet? Thus we find in the fugue an opposition between two antagonistic views of Nature, one gently melancholy, near akin to the key-phrase of the fifteenth quartet:

Ex. 36.
Subject A.

the other, exuberant in its gaiety:

Ex. 37.
Subject B.

After the presentation of the two subjects, open war begins between careless merriment and serious thought, the latter gradually winning over its thoughtless and frivolous opponent.

To obtain this result, Beethoven adopts the following procedure:

The fugue is sharply divided into three parts, the twenty-nine bars' prelude not included.

The entire first part is devoted to the joyous idea (subject B) in a complete fugue with all its regular entries (seven entries separated by four episodes), and ends with an exposition in altered rhythm; in this the aspect of the subject, till then very decided, seems to be undergoing a change:

Ex. 38.
Subject B.

This last exposition guides the fugue towards the tonality of G flat major.

The second part presents the expressive idea (subject A) in this same key of G flat, in a short fugue (two entries and two episodes). This theme leads us back to the principal key (B flat major) by means of an exposition in altered rhythm, as in the first part:

Ex. 39.
Subject A.

after which the idea changes its ground, and moves away to the very distant key of A flat major,[1] where it settles down at some length through four entries *in augmentation*, followed by an episode which inclines towards the subdominant; and now it is that the battle begins.

The third part opens with a long episode in which the two subjects are brought face to face, subject A tending by its rough ejaculations—

Ex. 40.

to bridle the exuberant performances of its rival.

Failing to impose itself by force, subject A makes an attempt by a process of 'infiltration', if the term may be so employed; it enters in fragments and in all manner of ways, by direct or contrary motion, always accompanied by the capricious twists and turns of the other 'individual'; then, after twenty-two bars of uneasy hesitation, it comes to a decision, and, shedding its garb of gloom, it starts off cheerfully in the principal key, where it settles down in long, held notes. A last brief attempt on the part of subject B to gain the upper hand is soon repressed, and subject A takes charge of the conclusion in peace, subject B, now conquered, being reduced to the secondary rôle of a countersubject.

This will give an idea how intimate is the connexion of this movement with the first movement of the thirteenth quartet, of which it

[1] A situation which is quite analogous is to be met with in the final fugue of the piano sonata, op. 106, also in B flat.

is a magnificent image. But, for those who can understand, it far surpasses the other in its range of musical expression.

FOURTEENTH QUARTET IN C SHARP MINOR, op. 131 (1826). (Dedicated to Colonel Baron von Stütterheim.) This quartet is deserving of special attention, for its conception and the resulting form are absolutely new, and no composer since Beethoven has had the courage to make use of the inventions to be found in it.

Only one of the six movements of which it is composed is in sonata form, and the construction of these six movements—which should be played without break—is truly surprising in its marvellous balance, founded on the cadential formula of the key of C sharp minor.

The scheme of this curious structure may be shown as follows:

Tonic.	Subdom.	Rel. of Subdom.
No. 1. Adagio Fugue Form.	No. 2. Allegro vivace Suite Form.	No. 3. Recitative and Andante with Variations.
Rel.	Dom.	Tonic.
No. 4. Presto Scherzo Form.	No. 5. Adagio Aria (Lied) Form.	No. 6. Allegro. 1st Movt. Form.

Ex. 41.

A regularly constructed fugue forms the majestic entrance; its subject is almost classical, though the developments singularly enhance its significance.

Then, as though he wished to give in this quartet an historical survey of the ancient forms, Beethoven revives the suite form in charming fashion, in the sprightly vivace in D major.

After a short recitative the theme of the andante in A major is stated in dialogue, engendering seven extremely curious variations. These variations are laid out in such fashion that the theme, during the first half of the movement, seems gradually to 'congeal'—if the comparison may be permitted—to such an extent as to produce an impression of complete immobility. The fifth variation, in fact, contains nothing more than the harmony of the theme, and even this is simplified and in a state of absolute calm—it is almost complete silence. This simplification is of a very different kind from that employed in the third variation of the twelfth quartet, but it is no less touchingly beautiful. Recalled to life by another recitative, the theme seems to raise itself regretfully, wanders through various keys, and soon after sinks, sighing, to rest.

After a long and joyous presto (E major), another of the great scherzi in five sections, very pastoral in style, a superb Lied phrase in G sharp minor, profoundly moving, prepares the entry of the victorious finale, and here, at last, we reach first-movement form. The whole of this movement is very obviously dominated by the harmonic influence of the opening fugue subject; it ends with a lengthy terminal development which, *in extremis*, presents, as it were, a recapitulation of its various themes.

Appended is the analysis of the fourteenth quartet:

I. *Adagio ma non troppo e molto espressivo*: Fugue, C sharp minor, regular.

II. *Allegro molto vivace*: Movement in suite form—in D. Ascent towards A major, descent towards D.

III. *Andante ma non troppo e molto cantabile*: Theme and variations—in A, in dialogue, preceded by short recitative.
- Var. I. Simply decorative.
- Var. II. Melodic amplification.
- Var. III. Imitation of theme altered in rhythm.
- Var. IV. Melodic phrases derived from harmony of theme.
- Var. V. Harmony of theme almost without movement and reduced to its simplest expression.
- Var. VI. Decorative and animated.
- Var. VII. Recitative, formed by periods of the theme extended.

Conclusion by return and development of theme.

IV. *Presto*: Grand scherzo form—in E, five sections.

V. *Adagio*: Lied phrase in two sections—G sharp minor—linking up with *quasi un poco andante*.

VI. *Allegro*: First-movement form—C sharp minor.

(1) *Exposition*, A, inflexion towards B, in E, single phrase.

(2) *Development* on A fugato, with C.S. in long notes.

(3) *Recapitulation*—A—C sharp minor. B—D then C sharp major.

Extended '*Terminal development*', with recapitulation of themes.

SIXTEENTH QUARTET IN F MAJOR, op. 135 (1826). (Dedicated to his friend J. Wolfmeier.)

Despite its very great beauties, the sixteenth quartet (numbered seventeen in some editions) will hardly bear comparison with the four preceding.

The opening allegretto, with its first subject constructed of two elements, is full of charm, but shows no modification of the classical first-movement form.

The lento assai e cantante tranquillo, in D flat, may be compared, as regards structure, with the cavatina of the thirteenth quartet. It, too, is a Lied phrase of simple and peaceful beauty; sections 1 and 3 are separated by a hesitating and irregular episode of nine bars. After a second exposition the theme is veiled by a cloud of nimble, decorative figures which hide its contours, and at length it ends very softly.

Beethoven himself wrote at the beginning of the finale of this quartet: 'Der schwergefasste Entschluss'.[1] What is the exact meaning of the question:

Ex. 42.

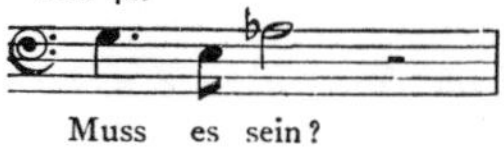

—Muss es sein?[2]—which opens the slow introduction, and the answer:

Ex. 43.

—Es muss sein![3]—the first active element of the final allegro?

A satisfactory answer can hardly be found to this question; and it must remain as one of the frequent musical jokes to be found in Beethoven's work, from the tic-tac of the metronome in the eighth symphony to the *Verlorene Kreutzer*[4] rondo and the canons: *Hoffmann* and *Kühl nicht lau*. However it may be, this finale is in no way representative of the sublime third manner of Beethoven. In the whole quartet, the lento alone shines like a precious jewel in the midst of the common materials of the structure.

The reader must not expect any conclusions to be drawn from this study. We have used enough laudatory terms to absolve us from the need of again proclaiming our admiration for the work of the composer of the *Missa Solennis*, an admiration which, even at this distance, remains as keen as ever. But we feel it necessary to add these few concluding words:

Beethoven raised the significance of chamber music to artistic heights till then unexplored. If the musical elements of certain of the solo sonatas for piano are equal in beauty to those of the last quartets, yet we cannot find any work so completely a *unified whole* as are, for example, the twelfth and fifteenth quartets.

[1] The resolution taken with difficulty.
[2] Must it be? [3] It must be.
[4] The lost kreutzer.

The theory may then be advanced that the incomparable art of the last three years of Beethoven's creative life opened up the way to the whole of our polyphonic and cyclic art of the end of the nineteenth century, the foremost representative of which was César Franck; and we should concede to chamber music the honour of having enormously contributed to this progress, in that it was the intimate confidant and expressive medium of the soul of a Ludwig van Beethoven. VINCENT D'INDY.

[Further reference to Beethoven's chamber music will be found in Professor Donald Tovey's article on Chamber Music; and in that of Dr. Hugo Leichtentritt on German Chamber Music.]

The quartets of Beethoven have constituted for a century past the favourite musical pabulum of innumerable chamber music lovers, the bulk of them amateurs. A publisher assures me that amateur string players have been purchasers, during that time, of 90 per cent. of the copies printed. It may then be conceded that a brief comment from myself, one of their number who has been taking part in those immortal works during sixty years of musical life, is not out of place as a modest corollary to the masterly exposition with which an expert of European fame has graced these pages.

The paramount sentiment to which I desire to give expression is one of amazement that after so many years of iteration and reiteration of the same phrases and the same harmonies, they retain their hold upon players and listeners alike. If I may speak for myself, after a lifelong experience, it is *far stronger*, the freshness and the beauty of it, and its essential greatness *far more apparent* than ever. Surely there is something godlike in music of which this can be said. Not godlike in the remote sense of the word, but blending, as Shakespeare did, the human and the divine.

For Beethoven was very human, after all, with a streak in his nature, which is unmistakable, of the practical, for which musicians have reason to be eternally grateful, as I shall try to show. A certain fretful remark to Schuppanzigh notwithstanding, it was his constant care that his writing should be tonally effective, full, rich, always radiating the brightness which belongs to strings at their best. Even during the dark days when he heard only with the mind's ear, this preoccupation was equally noticeable. The string tone, for instance, in the C sharp minor and A minor quartet is at times dazzlingly bright and a noble medium in which to express noble thoughts.

Another evidence of Beethoven's striving for perfection is to be seen in his selection of themes. The opening phrases of the first quartet, for example, played unisono, to impress it upon the listener's attention, underwent many mutations (seen in his note-books) before it assumed a form suitable for musical treatment. It is perhaps less inspired melodically than most of his themes. I have known a profane student endow it with a frivolous jingle of words,[1] not an unusual proceeding even among mature musicians possessed of a sense of humour. It is said of Ebenezer Prout, a devout Bach enthusiast, that he endowed every one of the '48' with burlesque words of his invention, by way of expressing the rudeness which Britons associate with affectionate intimacy, a feature of our social life not always *goûté* by our Latin brethren. In the 313 bars of the allegro the theme is used, according to de Marliave, whether as melody, imitation, or counterpoint, not less than 102 times, and with infinite variety of effect.

The scale passages, though not difficult, find out the weak spots in the technique of amateur players who have neglected their scale-practice. Possibly it was the violinistic element in this quartet which attracted the attention of that prince of fiddler-composers Spohr, who pronounced it the 'finest of its *genre*'. One can imagine the exquisite smoothness of his playing of the trio to the scherzo, which has given to generations of fiddlers (myself included) many an anxious moment. Its technical difficulties gave me the idea of publishing the 'passage studies' of which I have spoken above (*v.* ANTHOLOGY).

The adagio, on Beethoven's own admission, which must not be taken too literally, was inspired by the tomb scene in Shakespeare's *Romeo and Juliet*. That it bears traces of Italian influence (reaching him possibly through Mozart) the following incident tends to confirm.

It is not generally known that Paganini was an enthusiastic admirer of Beethoven's quartets. My old friend Thomas Lintott, most refined of amateur quartet players, who died about twenty-five years ago, related to me that one afternoon at a reception given by ALSAGER (*q.v.*), a patron of music who rallied round him all the musicians of distinction who passed through London, the artist who was to have played second violin to Paganini in Beethoven's first quartet failed to appear. He (Lintott) was asked to take his place, and, nothing loath, for he knew the work backwards, boldly stepped into the breach, enjoying in the sequel the most thrilling experience of his musical life. Not that Paganini's qualities were those of a chamber music player. On the contrary, he violated all the accepted canons of the art, took startling liberties with the tempo, played octaves and double stops where single notes were indicated, and introduced supplementary trills and grace notes of his own. But his emotional intensity was such, that after his playing of the adagio, a movement congenial to his Italian nature, there was a suspicion of moisture in the eyelids of those present, most of them hard-shelled critical listeners supposed to be immune from such weakness. The rather complicated finale of this quartet is much praised for its rhythmical charm, and for the series of modulations bringing back the subject at the end, but I remember it chiefly as having an especially delightful viola part, which I have occasionally been called upon to play when violas were scarce. The key, F major, is an open one and a favourite one with Beethoven, but it has one trifling drawback. The final chord usually assigned to the violin—

Ex. *a.*

Ex. *b.*

jars a little, still more so if, as in the sixteenth quartet, the upper F is used.

It gives me a thrill of pleasure merely to write of the second quartet in G, which, if not one of the greatest, is one of the most ingratiating of the series. I confess I do not take kindly to the sobriquet given to it in Germany of 'Complimentir' or 'compliments' quartet. The initial four bars and the replique are supposed to convey the idea of bowing and scraping, but I find it distasteful. This spontaneous, or, as Monsieur d'Indy would say, pastoral music is surely not a thing of powder and patches, or of ceremonial. If it suggests anything but itself it suggests the sounds of nature and the song of birds. In the final bars the theme soars heavenwards on the chanterelle, and then swoops to earth in the lower strings. I once heard Wieniawski sing this passage on his Guarnerius at one of the famous Popular Concerts, and his tone rings now in my head as I write, though more than fifty years have elapsed. More wonderful still are the three chords (sevenths rising to a minor ninth) which occur before *points d'orgue* quite near the close. For me, then but a tyro, they made history. Beethoven the metaphysician, subtle thinker as well as musician, appeared for the first time upon the scene, and in a flash I recognized, as doubtless countless other players had done before me, that here was a composer who transcended the limitations of ordinary musical speech, even the speech of Haydn and Mozart, and that a greater than either had arisen, one who had extended the field of beauty to regions hitherto unexplored. The 'period of imitation' and the 'period of externalization' overlap in those three fateful bars, as well as in the *Malinconia* of the sixth quartet, every strain of which awakens in the hearer the sense of mystery. The melancholy foretold in the title is there, but, the composer being still a young man, it is quickly dispelled. Joyous thoughts appear in the bars which follow. The dance strain resumes its sway with leaps of joy in the coda, and rushes madly on to the final note of this drama of sound. The truth of W. H. Hadow's observation that 'Beethoven's quartets are as dramatic as a play of Shakespeare' is brought

[1] Oh! what a whopping bee!

home to the listener and, with still greater force, to the player.

Returning to the G major, no. 2, the theme, in C major, of the adagio recalls a similar movement in Mozart's superb quartet in G, in the same key, but it is even more beautiful (shade of Oulibicheff forgive me!) and still more original, for it is interrupted by a piquant little intermezzo in F, which was new at the time, but which established a precedent which other chamber music writers, notably Brahms, have not been slow to follow. As to the finale, it is the jolliest, most rollicking piece of music I know, though even in this joyous movement the introspective Beethoven is momentarily heard (*v.* twenty-eight bars before the end, where the effect of the sudden F natural is magical).

The D major, no. 3 (first in order of composition and treated as the first in Helm's analyses) is less provocative of comment. I am moved, however, to give Hadow's so admirably written *aperçu* of the finale. 'It is Beethoven's idea of a gigue, a breathless whirl of scattering triplets and streaming melodies which Tam o' Shanter might well have envied. There is no other piece of music which flies so fast or with so complete and triumphant a sense of escape.' (*Vide Beethoven Quartets, op. 18*, by W. H. Hadow, Oxford Univ. Press.)

When Schuppanzigh recommended that this quartet should not be published as the first of the series, he was conscious, perhaps, of the slight inferiority of the slow movement, beautiful as it is, to the rest. The scherzo, however, is typical Beethoven—to be improved, perhaps, by a slight stress on the up-beat.

No. 4, in C minor, is beloved of amateurs, for whom it provides many glorious opportunities without too much technical strain. It opens with a sonorous theme played on the G string, the use of which by Beethoven responded to a temperamental need. I have, wondering, played in my time an incredible number of violin movements in which no use is made of the fourth string. The music might have been scored for the flute. What would be thought of a writer for voice who ignored the vocalist's lower register? Beethoven made no such mistake, and assigned to the second violin a theme similar in character, so much so that writers take exception to it. I confess that I find in this similarity the added charm of homogeneity. Also, I take delight in Beethoven's (mainly antiphonal) use of double stops in this quartet. The chords roll out under the bow with rich sonority achieved with a minimum of effort, and I have sometimes wondered that he has not employed double stops more frequently, both in his quartets and his string trios, though 'not permitted' by every teacher of composition. But what mattered such inhibitions to Beethoven, to him who asked permission from no one when the spirit moved him to rebel?

The andante scherzoso is a gem containing clever contrapuntal writing that passes unnoticed by the average audience. It is a question, perhaps a disputed one, which I leave to lecturers on musical appreciation to decide, whether lay listeners should impose upon themselves the strain of tracing to its lair every canon, fugue, or imitational passage in the score, or merely surrender themselves to the joy of listening. In this particular instance the music trips along in such dainty fashion that learned and unlearned alike are charmed.

The minuet is grave in character, a reminder that Beethoven neither envisaged a minuet always as a dance, nor a scherzo always as a joke. But the trio which follows is lighthearted enough, and an opportunity for the leader to show off his spiccato bowing in sparkling triplet passages, which form an accompaniment to the theme played by the second violin. The minuet harbours consecutive fifths between the violin and 'cello, anent which Hadow tells an excellent story in the above-mentioned book, which every chamber music lover should acquire.

The finale is very exciting—a passionate rush of notes followed by a number of fascinating episodes built upon the initial theme, achieving variety without change either of metre or tonality. When, after sonorous violin arpeggios, a refreshing change to the major is reached, the second violin plays a lively phrase which is taken up by the leader, who ascends the higher regions of the violin to a delicious running accompaniment. This is built on the simplest lines, yet one feels the presence of genius in every bar.

The no. 5, in A major, irresistibly reminds me of Lady Hallé, and of the charm with which she invested this music, so suited to her style. Beethoven, the virile, the tempestuous, is rarely as naïve—or, it may be said, as feminine—as in this quartet. The minuet and trio are fairy dances, the whirl of the latter accentuated by the sforzando on the weak part of the bar. But the delicacy of the writing reaches a climax in the hushed whisper of the fourth variation (andante cantabile). Such *sotto voce* passages as these need the most consummate art of the quartet player if they are to be played really pianissimo, yet so firmly as to be heard in every part of the auditorium. It is not sufficiently understood that strength is required no less for pianissimo than for fortissimo playing.

A year after the op. 18 quartet came the great quintet in C, op. 29, composed in 1801, which may be grouped with the same series. I am grieved that this master work, enriched by the addition of an extra viola part, is so rarely heard in London concert halls. In the days of the 'Pops' it was given forty-six times, and was one of the numbers best beloved of audiences which included the *élite* of London's musical amateurs, held spellbound by the calm dignity of the opening, the exquisite lyricism of the adagio (a favourite movement of Schumann), and the melodrama of the presto, to which it owes the sobriquet of 'Storm Quintet'. The two little scherzoso episodes which follow the tumult of the elements like a glint of sunshine between clouds, formed originally part of a little song of which the manuscript was found long after Beethoven's death. Listen to the chords at the close of each episode. They are of the stuff that dreams are made of.

Helm, with justification, considers this quintet to be spiritually affined to the first quartet in F. The slow movements are, it is true, different in character, but both contain the bars of pregnant silence of which Beethoven, among the great, has a monopoly (the long silences in the adagio of Schubert's C major quintet excepted). Lesser composers have shown good judgement in avoiding them. The tensity of attention required from the audience is not always sustained, and the silences are liable to be occasionally filled up by disconcerting snatches of conversation.

The op. 59 quartets followed the op. 18 after a lapse of five years only. Five years, however, of a great master's ripest period are full of possibilities. During that time the Kreutzer sonata, the Eroica, and *Fidelio* were composed, but the gap in style which sunders the two periods is not to be accounted for by musical experiences alone, for, as Monsieur d'Indy points out, Beethoven had been affected by agonizing life experiences, whilst the marvellous newness of it all is only to a very small extent to be accounted for by the influence brought to bear upon him by the Russian Ambassador, Count Rasoumovsky, who desired that the folk-songs of his nation should be incorporated into the three quartets he commissioned him to write, influence strongly felt in nos. 7 and 8, but absent from no. 9. Monsieur d'Indy's articles should attract readers to a study of the psychology of the 'period of *Externalization*' which here and there reflects with almost painful fidelity the tragedy of the composer's inner life. With relief, one notices in the adagio of no. 8 a certain serenity of outlook, to be disturbed later by the composer's distressing experiences during the siege of Vienna. In the slow movement of no. 10, the air is again heavy with tragedy.

Reverting to no. 8, Henry Webb, violinist in the quartet led by Joachim at St. James's Hall, induced his colleagues to play the adagio to him in his last days, and one can imagine what comfort the dying artist derived from its consolatory strains, and how strictly in accordance with Beethoven's indication was their interpretation on an occasion so moving—*si trattò questo pezzo con molto di sentimento*.[1]

[1] One of the performers was the late Louis Ries, who, I have been told, also asked that a Beethoven quartet should be played to him in his last days—prompted, it may be, by recollection of the above incident.

Of all Beethoven's themes, the most impressive and the most haunting is that found in the opening bars of no. 7, assigned to the 'cello. It is an example of the simplicity of great classical art, consisting of little else than a succession of ascending scales, commenced and recommenced like the graded stairs of a hilly city. In this theme I have on very rare occasions known the 'cellist replace the B flat by a B natural in the third bar, a slip due, I have always thought, to absence of mind, but de Marliave (p. 70) records that certain violoncellists, Franchomme and Delsart among the number, made this alteration deliberately—and he adds justly that the B natural is *plein de fadeur*.

The summit of the *scala* once reached, musical developments ensued which startled our forefathers. The criticism they evoked is a lesson for all who judge of modern music too rashly. It is curious to note that Rossini, written down as the most frivolous of men, was one of the first to appreciate these works, heard by him in Vienna in 1833.

Ten years previously the no. 7 was played in St. Petersburg, through the influence of Rasoumovsky, on a famous occasion often alluded to, when Romberg, one of the greatest virtuosi of his time, is reported to have flung the 'cello part down after playing the scherzo, and trampled it under foot as unplayable! A ridiculous story, but the structure of this strikingly original movement was strange to the players, and it may well have been a bad ensemble that provoked this ebullition of temper.

The three Rasoumovsky quartets were played by the Bohrer Quartet in Paris in 1831. The following year Habeneck produced the adagio of no. 7 and the fugue of no. 9 at a Conservatoire concert, played by all the strings of the orchestra, the first named receiving a cold, the latter an enthusiastic reception. I understand that the Vienna Philharmonic sometimes plays it thus arranged, and it is no doubt prodigiously effective, being essentially an orchestral conception.

Monsieur d'Indy's criticisms invariably rest on a solid foundation of musicianship, but as a distinguished composer writes me apropos of this book, to which authors of all shades of opinion have contributed, 'it would be unnatural and undesirable if all thought alike'. I have no scruple in saying that this applies to the fugal writing in no. 9, which on paper may seem ordinary to the eye of an expert contrapuntist, but which has driving power behind it which cannot be expressed in terms of musical science. After the unisonal passage in the dominant, the fugue recommences in a tense atmosphere of suppressed excitement, culminating in an onward rush of battling quavers to the triumphant termination, which gives a semblance of justification to the sobriquet, given to the ninth quartet by the Austrians (Helm, page 102), the 'Heroic'. It may be admitted that it is bravura writing, but surely it is the bravura of genius.

The allegretto of no. 8 (in lieu of scherzo) smacks more of national influence than the music of Russian composers of to-day, whose tendency is cosmopolitan. The major, with its strange rhythm, has the swing of a Russian dance (some one has spoken of it as the precursor of the Chopin mazurka), and the minor a theme which is altogether *paysan*. One can hear the stamp of the moujik's feet. But, that so many composers, with a wonderful series of folk-tunes to choose from, should have seized upon this particular theme as if it were the only pebble on the beach, is a mystery. Rimsky-Korsakov and Moussorgsky in opera, Arensky, Borchmann, and other Russian composers of chamber music, have used this tune as thematic material, always, be it added, with fine effect.

The double repeat indicated in the allegretto is seldom observed by chamber music players. I hazard the suggestion that it reflects the tendency of the Russian peasant of the melancholy steppes to glory in the monotony of endless repetitions. The presto of no. 10 (also in lieu of scherzo) has a similar feature, the repeats and da capos being unusually numerous. This movement provokes invariably the comment that it recalls the C minor symphony, in which players notoriously find it difficult to avoid giving the impression of triplets in the opening bars, except by slightly stressing the second quaver of each group—

Ex. *c*.

a proceeding not altogether orthodox. The movement is full of dynamic contrasts, and includes an exceptionally strenuous episode in C major.

Music more ethereal, more other-worldly than that contained in the brief introduction to no. 10 cannot be conceived (the like may be said of the introduction to no. 9). The so-called 'harp' quartet, op. 74, is considered by some to be Beethoven's finest quartet—but then so are several others of the series. The last one plays is always the best. The first movement of no. 11, styled by Beethoven himself quartetto serioso, is the most typical of what we recognize to be the Beethoven spirit. The passion, the impetuosity of it, are overwhelming. The canvas of this musical picture is crowded with struggling figures, sforzandos striking hard like the hacking of battle-axe upon shield. The allegretto which follows is full of the artistic contrasts in which Beethoven delighted—a serene movement interrupted by an emphatic allegro assai. The chord of the diminished seventh which precedes it, and another which precedes a subsequent resumption of the allegretto, are strangely moving; with almost cruel emphasis one is torn from dreams of infinity back to reality. How peremptory Beethoven can be one hears in the final bars, reminiscent of the *Fidelio* overture:

Ex. *d*.

The five posthumous quartets form a sanctuary of superlative musicianship which it would ill become a simple amateur to invade, the more so that they have been treated already by a writer who brings special gifts to the task. My remarks, then, will be of the briefest.

Fortunately, these marvellous works appear to all of us who have come lately face to face with the harrowing complexities of modern composition, less recondite than of old, which is all to the good. Even the formidable C sharp minor, austere though it be in the opening fugato, furnishes afterwards a constant flow of engaging melody. The great A minor contains some of the most ethereal as well as some of the most dramatic music ever written for string quartet, whilst the F major, last of these miracles of musicianship, after symbolizing in a few sinister bars the inexorability of fate, fitly finishes by 'babbling of green fields' in the mood of the 'period of imitation'.

Thus falls the curtain upon a series of works which, taken collectively, form an artistic whole which entitle Beethoven, though he had written nothing else, to a place among the Immortals.

The string trios, op. 9, have more modest qualities, though no less perfect of their kind. The C minor is so full and satisfying that it has been spoken of as a quartet without a second violin part. In the opening movement, a succession of intervals excites interest as a link with the C sharp minor quartet, though thirty years divide the two works.

In the trio there occurs the following:

Ex. *e*.

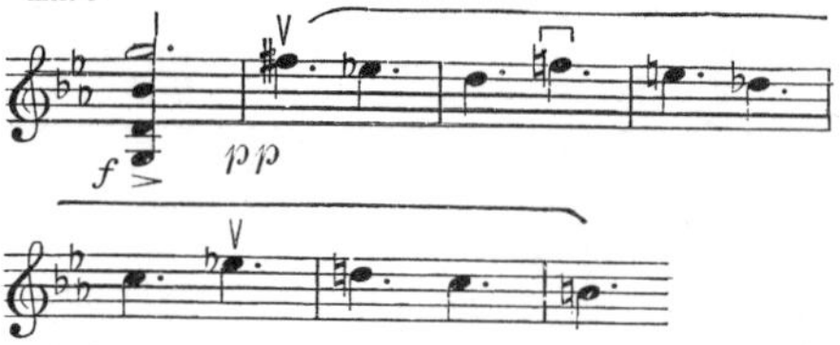

and, in the concluding bars of the C sharp minor quartet, a phrase which may be said to grow out of, or reply to, the theme of its opening movement also recalls the C minor trio:

Ex. *f*.

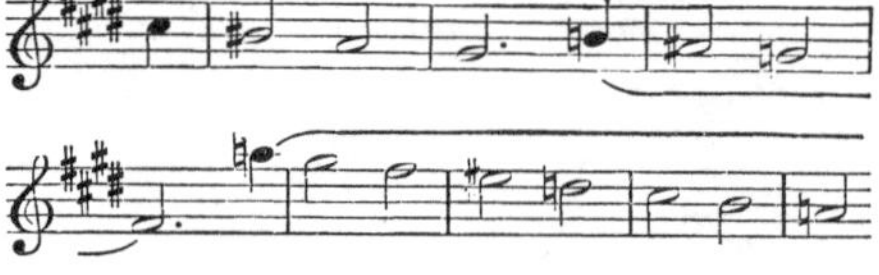

The similarity is striking and no mere coincidence. These intervals appear also in the sketch books, and they may be said to form a melos in the nature of an attendant spirit ever whispering the same message into Beethoven's ear. A similar phenomenon is to be observed in the music of many another composer, haunted to the verge of obsession by certain melodies, harmonies, and progressions.

The 'Grosse Fuge', which passes as the seventeenth quartet, was, as everybody knows, intended for the finale of no. 13, but it is not so well known that the danza tedesca in G was an importation from the fifteenth quartet, for which it was originally written in A major. Odds and ends of rare magnificence! It remains for some enterprising Quartet party to give these two quartets, for the edification of scholars, in their original form.

Monsieur d'Indy informs us that he frequently assigns the 'great fugue', so difficult both of comprehension and execution, so rugged yet so noble, to the strings of his students' orchestra at the Schola Cantorum, and that the effect is astounding. In 1826 it was universally condemned, and even now, after the passing of a century, it cannot be said to have secured universal acceptance; but it is cheering to know that it has found its way lately into the programmes of the artists who give cyclic performances of the seventeen quartets, and it is only a matter of time for complete appreciation to follow.

The subject of Beethoven's chamber music is inexhaustible. Each writer in turn can only hope to draw attention to points which may have escaped observation. Here is one which I commend to the attention of those who favour enterprise in concert giving. In London (I cannot speak of the Continent) no public performance has yet been given of Beethoven's masterly arrangement of his own pianoforte trio from op. 1, no. 3, for 2 violins, 2 violas and violoncello. Inasmuch as the trio was published by Artaria in 1795, and the quintet by the same house in 1819, one expects and finds in the latter the fruit of the master's intervening experiences.

This is the work referred to in a letter addressed by Beethoven writing from Vienna to Ferdinand Ries, London, in the spring of 1819. 'I should like you to see the two enclosed works—a solo sonata for pianoforte, and a pianoforte sonata[1] adapted by myself as a quintet for 2 violins, 2 violas, and violoncello. Taken to a publisher in London, they would sell easily for perhaps 50 ducats in gold.' The letter is in the possession of Messrs. Chappell & Co., Bond St. EDITOR.

BEETHOVEN ASSOCIATION, New York, founded 1919, under the presidency of Harold Bauer. The activities of the professional artists, of which this society is composed, are purely disinterested. Besides encouraging the performance of the later chamber music of Beethoven, they aim at the promotion of interest in the art generally. EDITOR.

[1] Dates prove that the trio is here alluded to. Such works were often known as sonatas.

BEETHOVEN QUARTET SOCIETY. This was founded by T. M. Alsager of *The Times* in 1845, and a short account written by Henry Hill, the accomplished viola player of the Society, was prefixed to a reprint of its first five programmes. Its purpose was, he wrote, 'to make known some of the most perfect of musical compositions which have long been left comparatively unnoticed, and to assist in removing some unhappy prejudices relative to the later works of Beethoven'.

In the first season, entirely devoted to the works of the Bonn master, the artists engaged were Sivori, Vieuxtemps, Sainton, Hill, and Rousselot, and, on a single occasion, Teresa Milanollo, who is reported to have held her own with her colleagues of the sterner sex. In the second season, two additional concerts were given, confined to the quartets of Haydn and Mozart, the venue being at the old Beethoven rooms in Harley Street. A pleasing feature of these concerts was the alternation of the famous violinists engaged in the parts of first and second violin. Even Joachim, then a young man, was heard in second violin parts, and in the third violin part of Mendelssohn's octet (Vieuxtemps leading). Andreas Moser describes his generous enthusiasm for Ernst's magnificent interpretations of the later Beethoven quartets. Although I am not old enough to have been present, these concerts were so often the subject of tea-table talk at the musical parties to which I was invited, that my youthful mind was filled with pictures of wonderful musical happenings. In particular, I remember that my old friend Alfred Pawle, a distinguished amateur Quartet leader in his day, was a subscriber, and never tired of telling of the quartet playing he had heard by teams all of whose members were virtuosi of the first rank, and especially of their wonderful tone production. Such music may never be heard again. The virtuosi of the present day are intent upon making fortunes as soloists, and do not appear anxious to emulate the achievements of the members of the old Beethoven Quartet Society.

A large framed document, with the signatures of most of the musicians who belonged to the Society, is in possession of a descendant of the founder, T. M. Alsager. EDITOR.

†BEHM, EDUARD, b. 1862, German composer.

Trio, pf, v, vc, e mi	op. 14	R. & E.,	1899.
Sonata, pf, v, A	,, 15	,, ,,	1899.

The trio was played at South Place—a work the interest of which is chiefly intellectual. Among unpublished works is a string sextet with violotta.

The violotta is a kind of tenor viola with strings tuned:

†BELAIEV, Mitrophan Petrovitch, 1836–1903, Russian publisher.

This book affords me the opportunity of placing on record the debt of gratitude which every lover of Russian chamber music owes to a Maecenas among publishers. Of him Rimsky-Korsakov wrote:

> 'He organized [in 1885] his concerts and publishing business without the smallest consideration for personal profit; he sacrificed large sums of money while concealing himself from the public eye, . . . his wealth, being the means to an end, was applied to lofty and irreproachable aims.'

Details of his numerous endowments are to be found in a *History of Russian Music*, written by M. Montagu-Nathan, who contributed in 1915 to the Chamber Music Supplement (*q.v.*) an interesting article on the *Vendredis* and how they came to be written. They grew out of the desire of certain composers, who periodically enjoyed Belaïev's generous hospitality, to pay homage to their host in the way they knew would please him best. They wrote quartets of album dimensions on the theme B-la-f:

also a series of variations on a popular Russian theme, three Belaïev birthday numbers, and two volumes of the *Vendredis*. Like other gatherings of a kindred nature, the Belaïev Fridays—following the example of Schumann's Sundays, Sainte-Beuve's and Daudet's Mondays, the *Punch* Wednesdays, and the days and nights of the Parnassian and North British Ambrosian groups, respectively — got unto themselves a 'literature'. Editor.

BELGIAN CHAMBER MUSIC.—It is only some fifty years since chamber music really began to flourish in Belgium. After the period of musical splendour of the Belgian provinces in the sixteenth century—the epoch of the great polyphonists whose influence was felt throughout Europe—music in Belgium underwent an almost total eclipse. The disturbed state of political affairs caused by the succession of foreign dominations and internal tumults created an atmosphere unfavourable to works which need quiet, reflective thought, and the whole artistic powers of the country were concentrated on painting. It is only after the beginning of the seventeenth century that the names of any Belgian musicians begin to attract attention, and these still continued to settle abroad and develop in foreign lands. They are—to confine ourselves to those who have contributed to chamber music—Lœillet, Gossec, and Grétry.

Jean-Baptiste Lœillet, b. Ghent, 1653, emigrated to London, where he died in 1728, after winning for himself a brilliant position. He arrived in 1705, and became a flautist in the Haymarket Theatre orchestra. In 1710 he started a series of concerts, at which the works of Corelli, in particular, were made known. In the domain of the sonata da camera, Lœillet bequeathed works for flute or violin with basso continuo, and some trio-sonatas (for two violins and bass, for two flutes and bass, and for flute, oboe, and bass) of which a dozen are published. But, from the fact of his living in England, Lœillet exerted no influence on the evolution of Belgian music.

Somewhat earlier than Gossec, van Malden (1727–1768), a composer of Brussels, and *musicien de la chambre* to Charles of Lorraine, must be included among the earliest composers of string quartets.

Gossec (whose correct name was François-Joseph Gossé), born a century later than Lœillet, is, like the latter, an isolated instance. Gossec, like Lœillet, lived abroad from youth upwards. Born in 1734 at Vergnies, he eventually settled in Paris, where he spent a very productive life. Founder of the Concerts des Amateurs and director of the Concert Spirituel, Gossec showed in his chamber music (trio-sonatas, six quartets for flute, violin, viola, and bass, and six string quartets) the qualities of a sound and skilful composer, but was lacking in personality and the 'divine spark' of genius. He died in 1829.

Grétry, 1742–1813, the delightful writer for the theatre, appears here only as the composer of two quartets with piano, and six string quartets, works of merely subsidiary importance among his large number of operas.

And thus, at the approach of the political upheaval of 1830, Belgian music was still slumbering. But with the winning of independence, the newly established kingdom entered upon a period of tranquillity and prosperity in which musical art was at last free to develop. At first it was in the field of mere technical display that Belgian artists found their development, and it was in this that they won their fame, for these great virtuosi turned their thoughts but little towards composition. The most famous, and the greatest artist among them, was Henri Vieuxtemps (b. 1820), who had been deeply impressed by becoming acquainted at Vienna with Beethoven's last quartets. He left only three chamber works, and these almost entirely forgotten—the three quartets, opp. 44, 51, and 52.

A passing mention suffices for various ensemble works written by famous Belgian virtuosi on themes from well-known operas, in order to please the public taste of the period. Bad taste and mere technical display were then in fashion, and the first trios of César Franck did nothing to dethrone them from favour.

It is not until the last quarter of the nineteenth century that the influence of the great master of Liége came to the rescue of 'absolute' music in Belgium, as it had already done in France.

These trios of César Franck's, published in 1841 as op. 1 ('Three trios for piano, violin, and 'cello, dedicated to H.M. Leopold I, by César Auguste Franck')—of which one at least forms the foundation of the modern revival of chamber music—remained unnoticed in Belgium; and Liszt was almost the only person to appreciate their value and their far-reaching importance.

The first of them, in F sharp major, is nevertheless the real prototype of cyclic form, which had been foreshadowed by Beethoven, and which was to find its full development through the genius of César Franck, and to form the starting-point of modern developments, animated by an inspiration both original and forcible; the trio in F sharp is far superior to the other two, which their composer himself considered as mere *morceaux de salon*.

After this significant beginning, Franck had to pass through a critical period of inactivity in composition, which lasted till the end of the war of 1870. And if then French music began to develop after the revelation of *Rédemption*, the *Éolides*, and, in our own field, of the quintet, several years were needed before the effect of the movement was felt in Belgium.

Two men then played a part which it is important to notice here, for it is they who were, in truth, the authors of that connecting link, thanks to which it was possible to form a centre from which chamber music could develop in our country: Eugène Ysaÿe and Octave Maus. Ysaÿe, the admirable interpreter of the works of César Franck, gathered round him his brother Théo the pianist, the violist van Hout, and the 'cellist Jacob, in order to give the first performances of the sonata and the quartet. Octave Maus, a dilettante barrister interested in every expression of new ideas in art, was the founder of the salons of painting of the XX, and of the Libre Esthétique, where each year performances devoted to new musical works brought the younger Belgian musicians into contact with the productions of the 'Franckist' school, and gave them the chance to become aware of their own capacity, and to realize that at last a literature of chamber music could live and flourish on Belgian soil.

It is unnecessary to dwell here on the works and the influence of César Franck. Vincent d'Indy will have shown in his article how, in the quintet, the A major sonata, and the D major quartet, his illustrious master had liberated the music of the Latin peoples from the domination of Wagner, giving it a direction towards the basic forms which Beethoven had already enlarged in his latest works, pouring into these forms a radiating life which was destined to bring them to blossom in fullest perfection.

From the Belgian point of view, the important fact to notice is the fertilizing influence of Franck—either directly on his few immediate disciples, Lekeu and Théo Ysaÿe, or through the medium of Vincent d'Indy, a faithful executor of the teachings of the master, and transmitter of them to our younger musicians.

Guillaume Lekeu, 1870–94, appears in our musical history as a flaming meteor, who in his brief period of productivity (barely three years) wrote some of the most moving and impassioned pages in the whole range of instrumental music. His was a soul romantic to the core, and he tells us in his music of his gusts of passion, of his anguish, his fierce joy, or his poignant melancholy.

He had a strongly marked individuality, shown from the outset in a highly characteristic style of melodic invention, in the overflowing lyricism of his development, and in the aspirations which govern and hold in check the volcanic outbursts of the imagination. 'Is not the artist's mission', he wrote, 'to toil all his life in order to bring to perfection one single ideal which each individual work is but an attempt to realize?' The realization of this ideal was sought by Guillaume Lekeu in his sonata in G (1892), and in the first two movements of his piano quartet, which death prevented him from completing. The sonata, although conceived in cyclic form, follows rather the scheme of a free fantasy; it has been discussed both from the point of view of formal construction and of development. But in its broad and clear themes, its richness of harmony, its powerful and masterful inspiration, it constitutes a new type of romanticism in chamber music, the charm of which will strongly influence younger composers.

The unfinished quartet appears, in its overflowing and mournful beauty, as the 'last will and testament' of an anguished soul, as though haunted by the foreboding of death. Guillaume Lekeu was at work on it from the beginning of 1893, and all the correspondence of his last year reflects the anguish and the joy in the conception of this work, the pride which he feels in having found a first theme—'wild, impetuous, with a burst of melody of 47 bars'—his aspiration to produce 'a thing of beauty, of audacity, beside which the sonata will seem a child's plaything'. 'Perhaps', he writes, 'my quartet will be accused of extravagance. What matter, *I shall continue on my way without other idea than to write down the thoughts that arise in me*.' These words illumine the whole artistic ideals of Guillaume Lekeu, taken away at the very crisis of his romanticism.

Belgian music was thus robbed of a personality equalled in its exceptional vitality by none of our composers.

On the other hand, at the moment of Lekeu's death, Joseph Jongen, b. 1873, began to show an individuality whose development is the most important landmark in the history of chamber music in Belgium during the first quarter of the twentieth century. It is interesting to note here, that in this field Walloon composers have far outdistanced their Flemish contemporaries. The racial temperament of the latter has directed their energies towards the opera and the symphony, forms which are in accordance with their sense of vivid colour and of the picturesque, and with their strong impressionism.

The Walloons, inclined to dreamy meditation, would rather find their path in the realms of 'absolute music', in the expression of the response of the mind to sensations apart from objective realities. This is precisely the case with Joseph Jongen, whose nature is one of a subtle and delicate sensitiveness. From his twentieth year he shows these qualities in a series of chamber works equally engaging in the quality and the variety of melodic and harmonic invention, and in the profound skill in construction and development, which follow the course of contemporary evolution without sacrificing to it anything of his personality or independence.

Jongen's entire work gives proof of the most perfect taste and the utmost sobriety of style, together with perfect self-control in ideas and in the manner of writing. His first string quartet (1894) and his first trio (1897) won prizes from the Académie Royale of Brussels. Of chamber works he then published a piano quartet (op. 23), two violin sonatas (opp. 27, 34), the trio (op. 30) for piano, violin, and viola (1906)—which will remain in the freshness and plasticity of its themes among the most perfect works of contemporary chamber music, a sonata (op. 39), and two *Poems* for violoncello and piano. During the war Jongen lived in England, where he continued to compose; since then he has published two string quartets, two serenades for string quartet, an important sonata for flute and piano, and the *Concert à Cinq* (concerto for five instruments) for violin, viola, 'cello, flute, and harp.

By his works and by his teachings (he is professor of fugue at the Conservatoire Royal of Brussels and has numerous private pupils), Joseph Jongen is undoubtedly the musician who exercises the most profound and healthy influence in Belgium at the present time.

Victor Vreuls, b. 1875, at present principal of the Grand-Ducal Conservatoire of Luxembourg, was trained at the Conservatoire of Liége, and then received further advice from Vincent d'Indy at the Schola Cantorum. This education under an exact and strict discipline has not prevented the expansion of his artistic temperament, which is impetuous and fiery and somewhat rugged. The music of Vreuls, with its intense rhythmic life, retains, even in moments of gaiety, a certain harshness and waywardness which endow it with a very personal quality. In the realm of the symphony and of lyric opera, Vreuls shows a lyric power, the traces of which are to be found even in his chamber works—a piano quartet, two violin sonatas, a trio, and a string quartet.

Lastly, of the Franckist school, comes a composer of extremely refined musical temperament: Théo Ysaÿe, the younger brother of the great violinist. Born in 1865, he died at Nice during the European war. In his youth an eminent pianist, he began to develop as a composer when about thirty. Among the works published at this time is a quintet for piano and strings (1913), in which an ardent and concentrated temperament asserts itself, a spirit completely saturated with the poetry of nature, together with ingenuity and vigour in construction. One might say that the personal style of Théo Ysaÿe results from a combination of the influences of Liszt and César Franck, with an evident spiritual relationship with Ernest Chausson, with whom he shares a keen sensibility and a profound melancholy. And it is the quintet that best serves to bring out together these distinctive features of his work.

Among the Walloon composers of the generation of 1870 or thereabouts, in whose works chamber music occupies an important place, there is Désiré Paque, b. 1867, to-day living in Paris, who in his numerous compositions, of which a few only are published (sonatas, a quartet, and a quintet), practises independence, contrapuntal and tonal; and François Rasse, b. 1873, a facile composer endowed with a charming nature, but whose great facility in composition leads him at times to produce works which assume somewhat the form of improvisations, with a certain lack of restraint in the writing and in the choice of themes. He has published, besides violin and 'cello sonatas, two string quartets, two trios, and a piano quartet and quintet.

Among the Flemings, Joseph Ryelandt, b. 1870, stands almost alone in his resolute cultivation of music of the abstract kind. A pupil of Edgar Tinel, he acquired from his master the science of choral polyphony and mysticism of conception, but with a more contemplative and intimate note, which is shown in his chamber works. With Ryelandt, again, one would wish to find a severer and more strictly disciplined technique, an attribute rarely possessed by over-fertile composers. But some of his sonatas, trios, and quartets show great poetic charm.

The greater number of our lyric and dramatic composers have brought only a casual contribution to chamber music. Mention will, therefore, be made only of those of M. Philippe Rüfer, b. Liége, 1844, but lived at Berlin; of Henri Waelput of Ghent, 1845–1885, both of the German Romantic school; the two principals of the Conservatoire of Antwerp, Jan Blockx, 1851–1912, and Émile Wambach, 1857–1924; Fernand Leborne, b. 1861, educated and domiciled in Paris; General Baron Victor Buffin, b. 1867; Adolphe Biarent, a native of Hainault,

1871–1916; Louis Delune, b. 1876, pupil of Tinel and to-day settled in Paris; and Albert Dupuis, b. 1877, a pupil of the Schola Cantorum, composer of several lyrical dramas, amongst which we find quartet, quintet, trio, and sonatas showing an extreme facility of inspiration and of technique.

Since 1918 the younger generation, in Belgium to a greater extent than elsewhere, has been deeply impressed by the rapid evolution of music in the last ten years, which, by force of circumstances, remained unknown to them till after the end of the war. Belgian musicians, suddenly put within reach of the temptations to formlessness and atonality, were troubled with hesitation and restlessness. It seems that the more vigorous among them have begun now to assert themselves, and it is precisely in the realm of chamber music—including wind instruments—that their most interesting attempts are to be found. Some of the veterans have been attracted towards the new formulae, such as Léon Delcroix, b. 1880, pupil of Vincent d'Indy and Théo Ysaÿe, a dexterous and distinguished composer, whose first string quartet was awarded a prize (1903) by the Académie Royale de Belgique; his style towards the end broadened, and his manner of writing grew more modern in his quintet and his violin and 'cello sonatas; and Henry Sarly, b. 1884, whose first compositions bear the impress of a leaning towards the style of Debussy (violin sonata), and who in his quintet shows also the desire to give renewed expression to Belgian national music.

Some of the new-comers go boldly to extremes: heading the list comes Fernand Quinet, b. 1898, who won the Grand Prix de Rome in 1921, of fiery temperament and with a wealth of invention in harmony and in the use of instrumental timbres. His violin sonata (written during the war) is instinct with the divine fire, and, although deriving directly from Lekeu's sonata, appeals to the hearer by its breadth and spirit. Of recent works, Fernand Quinet has completed only a *Rhapsody* for three clarinets, and a viola sonata; his preferences lie wholly in the direction of the objectivism of Stravinsky.

Georges Antoine, b. 1892, fell a victim to the war at Bruges in 1918. His early works betoken an exuberant character which has been likened to that of Lekeu, but evidently his two completed works (violin sonata, op. 3, and piano quartet, op. 6) are no more than a promise of future achievement.

René Barbier, b. 1890, also a pupil of Sylvain Dupuis at the Liége Conservatoire, has written a trio and a quintet, in which he shows himself a faithful follower of the ideas of the younger French school, while Jules Strens, b. 1892, shows a tendency to react against the pessimism of the years of war and trouble, with music full of joy, concise and vigorous in its expression, the symbol of which he strives to realize in a *Suite brève* for string quartet, and a quintet for wind instruments.

We should further notice the contribution to chamber music (sonata and serenade for 'cello) of Paul de Malingreau (born in France of Belgian parents in 1887), a vigorous spirit who, especially in the realm of organ music, has succeeded in combining modern harmony with the great classical forms.

It is clear, from this sketch, that 'individualism' reigns among our musicians, and that in consequence there exists in Belgium no chamber music which can be called 'national'. In order that such a movement should become clearly defined with specific and original characteristics, beginners will have to rid themselves of foreign influences (notably those of France, Russia, and Austria) by which they are bewitched at present, in order to develop their racial characteristics and to seek in forms and expressions fashioned anew, the path opened by César Franck and Joseph Jongen.

GEORGES SYSTERMANS.

BELGIAN PERFORMING ORGANIZATIONS.

Fifty years ago Louis Brassin, professor at the Conservatoire of Brussels, founded (together with Vieuxtemps and Servais) a Trio whose repertory consisted of the great classical and romantic works, their mission being continued by Jules de Zarembski, Jenö Hubay, and Joseph Servais. For the String Quartet, after the first association had been formed by other professors of the Conservatoire (notably MM. Colyns and Alexandre Cornélis), there came the YSAŸE STRING QUARTET (with the younger Crickboom, the violist Van Hout, and the 'cellist Joseph Jacob), whose activities ceased when Ysaÿe resigned his position as professor at the Conservatoire. There were several successive attempts to form String Quartets, but none of them achieved permanency. The following are the principal Belgian chamber music organizations:

AD ARTEM (PIANO) QUARTET (Liége). Mlle Jeanne Maison, Jules Robert, Jean Rogister, Marcel Dorssers. Founded in 1897 by Charles Radoux (piano), Jules Robert, Oscar Englebert (viola), and René Cuddell ('cello). The 'cello was taken successively by René Dechesne (1899) and Dorssers (1926), Englebert was replaced by Rogister (1910), in 1918 Radoux retired and made way for Mlle Maison. Their repertory is extensive.

BRUSSELS STRING QUARTET, founded by M. Schoerg, consisted, before 1914, of H. Daucher, P. Miry, and J. Gaillard (later Doehaerd). The two violinists being of German nationality, the events of 1914 necessarily led to the dissolution of this association, which had acquired lasting reputation in Europe and America. This Quartet has, happily, been re-established by Désiré Defauw, Pecker, Jeremy, and Doehaerd.

CHARLIER QUARTET.[1] Léopold Charlier, Georges Lequarré, Jean Rogister, Mme Lydie Rogister-Schor. Founded in 1904 by Léopold Charlier with three virtuosi from the Liége Conservatoire—Jules Harzé, Herremans (viola), and Jean Falla ('cello). The second violin was taken successively by Oscar Lemal, Tummers, and Hody; the viola by Croufer and L. Lhoest; the 'cello by Albert Dechenne and Marcel Dorssers.

LEJEUNE QUARTET (Liége). Marcel Lejeune, Léon Wollseifen, Nicolas Dehareng, Hubert Rogister.

PRO ARTE QUARTET. Alphonse Onnou and Laurent Halleux (leading alternately), Germain Prévost, Robert Maas. This Quartet really dates from the end of 1918. Before the war a Quartet of young men (including Onnou and Halleux) had been formed in Brussels. After the armistice, General Buffin, a good composer, undertook to reconstruct the combination with musicians doing military service in the 1st regiment of Guides, viz. Onnou, Halleux, Prévost (viola), and Fernand Quinet ('cello).

They devoted themselves from the first to modern music. In 1923 Quinet was replaced by Maas.

The Pro Arte, while remaining the chief protagonist of advanced music, does not neglect the great classics. It takes part in the festivals of the S.I.M.C., and has played several works there for the first time. At Brussels it has widened its scope, including, for certain ensemble works, the pianist Paul Collaer and a group of wind instrumentalists led by Arthur Prévost, the bandmaster of the first regiment of Guides.

QUATUOR PHILHARMONIQUE. Delvenne and Desclin (leading alternately), Van Schepdael, Rassart. This Quartet, formed by four newly fledged students of the Brussels Conservatoire, has given several concerts at Brussels, performing Beethoven and contemporary composers.

REDELÉ QUARTET (Women). Mlle Gilberte Redelé, Mme Godelieve Mathys, Mlle Yvonne Redelé, Mlle Gabrielle Redelé. Founded in Brussels in 1922 by the three sisters Redelé and Mlle Callewaert (now Madame Mathys).

They have already made a reputation by numerous performances at home and abroad.

ZIMMER QUARTET. Albert Zimmer, Frédéric Ghigo, Édouard Piel, Émile Doehaerd. Founded at Brussels, in 1896, by a group of young musicians of Liége. The only member of the original Quartet is Zimmer, who has been leader throughout, the others, in order, being: Georges Jamar, Nestor Lejeune, Édouard Brahy, the brilliant conductor, who died in 1919.

[1] There have been further changes in the personnel since this information was received.

From 1896 to 1899 the new Quartet appeared only in Belgium. Then, Jamar and Brahy being called away, the combination broke up. But it was re-formed in 1900, Franz Doehaerd being second violin and Émile Doehaerd 'cello. In 1902 their European tours started with a performance at the Paris Philharmonic Society. After some time Lejeune gave up the viola to Barsen, Gaillard took the 'cello, and Franz Doehaerd was replaced by the young violinist Ghigo.

The activities and the reputation of the Zimmer Quartet are yearly increasing. During their continental tours, as well as in their annual series at Brussels, they introduce or give first performances of modern works by various composers.

Among the classics, they specialize in the interpretation of Beethoven's quartets, the whole series having been repeatedly given in Belgium and abroad.

In 1924 they gave twenty-eight concerts in Mexico, Gaillard (the 'cellist), who was ill, being replaced for the tour by Émile Doehaerd.

TRIO DE LA COUR DE BELGIQUE (Brussels). Émile Bosquet, Alfred Dubois, Maurice Dambois. This group, previously in existence for some years with Émile Chaumont as violin, was broken up, and eventually reconstituted in 1924, with Hector Clokers, as the *Trio Belge*. In 1925 H.M. the Queen authorized the adoption of the title TRIO DE LA COUR.

GEORGES SYSTERMANS.

BELICZAY, JULIUS VON, 1835–1893, Hungarian composer.

Quartet, str, g mi	op. 21	B. & H.,	1878.
Trio, pf, v, vc, E flat	„ 30	„	1883.

The quartet is a pleasing work, without marked national characteristics. Beliczay was the author of a Method of Composition.

†**BELL, WILLIAM HENRY, b. 1873, British composer.**

Trained at the R.A.M.; now principal of the South African College of Music, where he is making the practice of chamber music a prominent feature. He has composed a brilliant sonata for violin and piano, not yet published, and other chamber works (MS.).

EDITOR.

BELLIO, GINO.

Sonata, pf, vc	Pizzi, 1919.

BELLON, J., French composer.

Trio, pf, v, vc, A	op. 32	Costallat.
Sonata, pf, vla (or v)	„ 33	„

BENDA, FRANZ, 1709–1786, German violinist and founder of a school of violin-playing.

Benda was one of four distinguished brothers, and Capellmeister to the Crown Prince of

Prussia, afterwards Frederick II, whose accompanist he was during forty years' service. His violin solos and ensemble music are excellent, but not of the type which interests modern musicians.

The only works of his that have been republished are three violin sonatas, with figured bass, in Alfred Moffat's *Meisterschule* 22; G. Jensen's *Klass. V-Musik* 33; A. Schering's *Alte Meister des Violinspiels* 13. EDITOR.

BENDEL, FRANZ, 1832–1874, Bohemian pianist, pupil of Liszt.

Trio, pf, v, vc, g mi — Challier, 1876.
Sonata, pf, v, e mi — ,, ,,

†BENDIX, VICTOR EMANUEL, b. 1851, Danish pianist, pupil of N. W. Gade.

Trio, pf, v, vc, A — op. 12 — Hansen, 1888.

BENDL, KAREL, 1838–1897, Czech composer.

Quartet, str, F — op. 119 — Simrock, 1895.

A once popular composer, who touched many branches of composition, but is now almost forgotten. An exception, however, is the above quartet, which is distinguished by its melodic freshness, strongly marked rhythms, and ingenious developments. A serious work, written in true chamber music style.

VÁCLAV ŠTĚPÁN.

[Bendl's one quartet appears frequently in the repertory of the Bohemian Quartet. Alternately elegiac and vivacious, in folk-song and dance style, with occasional recitative and canonic writing, it is well calculated by its variety to interest an audience. EDITOR.]

BENEDICT, (SIR) JULIUS, 1804–1885, settled in England, 1835.

Quartet, str, c mi — op. 87 — Schlesinger, 1875.
Sonata, pf, v, E — ,, 88 — Kistner, 1870.

I took part in the above quartet at a concert at the Beethoven Rooms in Harley Street about 1876, and found the music agreeable in quality, but mediocre. EDITOR.

†BENESCH, JOSEPH, b. 1795, Moravian violinist.

Two quartets, str, G, F — opp. 20, 30 — Haslinger, 1865, 1871.

*†BENJAMIN, ARTHUR L., b. 1893, Australian pianist and composer, pupil of Stanford.

Three Impressions, voice, str. quartet — Curwen, 1926.
Pastoral Fantasy, str. quartet, a mi (Carnegie Award, 1924) — S. & B.
Sonatina, pf, v, G — O.U.P.

1. PASTORAL FANTASY. The characteristics of this quartet are (1) its melodic relationship with the sources from which a prevailing 'English' idiom has been derived; (2) remarkably clean workmanship; (3) unconventional form. It cannot readily be compared with other English quartets. Its movements are (roughly) four, its controlling themes no more than four. By a curious recurrence of certain sections, the general build is sevenfold. The pastoral element is most apparent in the first section, or wherever this section is drawn upon. There is no 'first-movement' feeling anywhere. The slow movement comes second. It is delicately transformed into a sort of slow dance by a novel device of independent rhythm in the second violin part. The scherzo is followed by a musette, obviously pastoral, which delights in a union of very elastic melody with a rigid rhythmical background. It is dovetailed into the scherzo section. Its return, as a moment of poise just before the end of the work, is an exceedingly happy stroke.

2. SONATINA is an unassuming title for a three-movement work that can rise—as this does—to considerable heights of technique and expression. It fits, however, the scherzo ('in modo antico' as to form, but very much of to-day), which is made up of brief, happy objective tunes, and is singularly well designed to contrast with the neighbouring movements. To some, the form of the first movement will always seem loose; it has the moods of an April day, and the rhythmic line is often broken up. Little sections appear and disappear with surprisingly episodic effect. The final rondo, on the other hand, is compact and closely reasoned; it has liveliness of rhythm and charm of melody, and is free from the redundancy that has ruined so many examples of its kind.

This sonatina is more representative of its composer than either the quartet or the *Three Impressions* for voice and string quartet.

HERBERT HOWELLS.

BENNETT, (SIR) WILLIAM STERNDALE, 1816–1875, English composer.

Sextet, pf, 2 v, vla, vc, cb (or vc), f sharp mi — op. 8 — Kistner, 1846.
Trio, pf, v, vc, A — ,, 26 — ,, ,,
Sonata, pf, vc, A — ,, 32 — ,, 1853.

Of the above works, the trio, in three movements, is a slender but graceful work, too delicate in texture to make its intended effect, except in a very small concert-room. The first movement is on the model of early Haydn, the first and second subjects having the same initial phrase. The middle movement (a canzonetta) has the melody on the piano, the violin and 'cello affording a light accompaniment pizzicato throughout. With a modern piano, a whole orchestra of strings would be needed to afford a proper balance of tone, but the intention is charming.

THE SEXTET is a more ambitious work. According to the custom of the period, no score was printed, and the piano part contains only the most indispensable cues, but the string parts are rather slight. An arrangement of the double-bass part for a second 'cello is given, regardless of the fact that the substitution would entirely alter the character of the work. As the work is written, the double-bass gives due firmness and solidity to a first movement that without it would sound decidedly thin. The opening subject is very mild:

Ex. 1.

The second subject, according to the custom of the day, consists merely of a tuneful two-bar phrase,

Ex. 2.

immediately repeated and made into a half-sentence, *secundum artem*, but the scherzo has a capital broken rhythm, and a good feminine phrase:

Ex. 3.

The trio, nearly all in dotted minims,

Ex. 4.

presents an excellent contrast. The andante is the best movement, with a picturesque subject with more varied note values, though harmonized in the manner of Spohr (ever Bennett's adoration),

Ex. 5.

but the finale, though lively, is sadly conventional, and ambles along in even quavers, like so much of the piano music of the period, and after the first page a machine could have done the remaining nine. Indeed, there is no discernible reason for its being a sextet at all; yet it is all very pretty music.

It is singular that 'cellists, who are always deploring the poverty of the repertory for their instrument, at the same time neglect so many beautiful works. Sterndale Bennett's sonata affords a case in point. It is true that all its movements are in the same key, but the first, which is the best part of the work—engaging, brilliant, and effective—would make an excellent piece by itself. It has an introduction which returns to make a coda, with a satisfactory effect of completeness. The other movements suffer from the drawback that—as in the case of most of the music of this period—the harmonic progressions go too frequently over the same ground, a weakness emphasized by the composer's persistence in the tonality of A. Had the middle movement been in F sharp—a key too alarming for the period, but by no means impossible nowadays[1]—the charming finale would have gained. Would it be a crime to transpose it? F. CORDER.

[Mr. Corder has avoided the obvious by ignoring the Mendelssohnian influence which was common to all the music of Bennett's period. The viola has an exceptionally attractive part in the andante grazioso of the sextet. All that can be said of the alternative 'cello part is that it is useful as a *pis aller*. The double bass is not a drawing-room instrument. EDITOR.]

*†BENTZON, JORGEN, contemporary Danish composer.

Quartet, str	op. 3	Borups Musikförlag. (Copenhagen).
Divertimento, v, vla, vc, G	,, 2	Skandinavisk Musikförl.
Sonatina, fl, cl, fag	,, 7	Borups Musikförlag.

†BENVENUTI, GIACOMO, young contemporary Italian composer, pupil of Bossi.

His quartet, in one movement and in variation form, introduced to London by the Poltronieri Quartet in 1928, will, it is expected, be shortly published. 'It is Latin in the lyric quality which dominates it, in the spirit which seems to model its outlines in a precise form, in the polyphony that relates it to the works of the Italian madrigal masters of the sixteenth and seventeenth centuries, but it reveals a certain spiritual affinity with the last quartets of Beethoven.' I quote this from *Modern Music*, a quarterly published in New York by the League of Composers. EDITOR.

BÉON, A.

Suite, pf, vla, D — Costallat, 1922.

BERBIGUIER, TRANQUILLE BENOÎT, 1782–1838, French flautist, and composer for his instrument.

Famous in his day (he played left-handed), Berbiguier was a voluminous composer for his instrument, and many of his works, being of a popular nature, still survive. The total

[1] It should not be forgotten that the largo of Haydn's quartet in D, op. 76, no. 5, is in F sharp major.

number of his works exceeds 200, and includes *c.* 150 duets for two flutes, 32 trios for three flutes, and several chamber pieces for various combinations of instruments. In the latter, many passages are well calculated to show off the flute, but owing to the absence of double-tonguing passages, they are sometimes a trifle monotonous. His duets are his most appreciated works, though not so concertante as those of Kuhlau. The best sets (each of three duets) are op. 15 (Schlesinger), op. 38 (B. & H.), op. 47 (Schott), op. 61 (Simrock)—the composer's favourite, op. 71 (Ashdown), op. 99 (Ricordi), op. 2 (Schott), op. 28 (B. & H.).

The best trios are opp. 13 and 110 (Ashdown), op. 40—also arranged for flute, and violin and viola (B. & H.), and op. 51 (Schlesinger). Berbiguier's other chamber works include, amongst others, a quintet for flute and string quartet, a quartet for flute and strings, op. 86, &c.

His compositions are much simpler in style and less interesting than those of Kuhlau, Kummer, Walckiers, and Gabrielsky, to whose works they are, on the whole, inferior.

For other works of Berbiguier *v. Altmann*, *Fétis*, and the *Q.-L.* H. M. FITZGIBBON.

BERENS, HERMANN, 1826–1880, son of Carl Berens, pupil of Reissiger, German composer.

Quartet, str, E	op. 78	Leuckart, 1864.
Three trios, v, vla, vc, D, c mi, F	,, 85	Haake, 1873.
Quartet, pf, v, vla, vc, c mi	,, 1	Haslinger, 1848.
Quartet, pf (4 hands), v, vc	,, 23	Cranz, 1852.
Quartet, pf (4 hands), v, vc, D	,, 48	,, 1856.
Quartet, pf (4 hands), v, vc, a mi	,, 72	,, 1863.
Quartet, pf (4 hands), v, vc, f mi	,, 80	,, 1869.
Trio, pf, v, vc, E	,, 6	J. Schuberth & Co., 1847.
Trio, pf, v, vc, E flat	,, 20	B. & H., 1852.
Three trios, pf, v, vc, F, g mi, D	,, 95	O. Forberg, 1911; Peters, 1876.
Sonata, pf, v, G	,, 5	Cranz, 1848.

Berens's works do not appear to have gained an established position in the repertory, but two of his three trios, op. 85, are mentioned in Bachmann's *Encyclopedia of the Violin*.

*†BERG, ALBAN, b. 1885, Austrian composer, pupil of Schönberg.

Quartet, str	op. 3	1909–10, Schlesinger, 1920.
Lyrische Suite, str. quartet	—	U.E., 1927.
Four Pieces, pf, cl	op. 5	Schlesinger, 1913.

Berg and Webern are commonly regarded as the most faithful and thorough disciples of Schönberg, and certainly, in Berg's music, his influence is very pronounced. The string quartets and the pieces for clarinet are all atonal. The quartet, op. 3, is in two movements of exceedingly complex construction, abounding in Schönbergian polyphony, with the characteristic leaps in the melodic line, and frequent recourse to all manner of instrumental devices, such as flageolet tones, &c. There is, however, an undercurrent which links it, both thematically and technically (cumulative sequential passages, *Steigerung*, &c), with the Wagnerian past, of which more traces remain than are discernible in Schönberg, except, of course, in the latter's first manner. The following, which occurs at the climax of the first movement, is a characteristic example of the idiom (Ex. 1). Writing of Berg in general, and incidentally of this particular work, in the *Chesterian* of

Ex. 1.

October 1922, Erwin Stein expresses himself as follows:

'The works of Alban Berg are symphonic in character. They consist generally of extended movements, where the thematic material is developed polyphonically and in very free variation. This explains, at the same time, their form, which is created by uniformity of the themes and clarity of cohesion. Thus, in his Orchestral Prelude, op. 6, nearly all the manifold musical occurrences are evolved from a motive of three notes. In other cases, a number of themes are placed next to or over each other from the very beginning. Contrasts, which in older music create a sense of symmetry of expression and form in large spaces, are here given a new function: the fact that they appear simultaneously—that is to say polyphonically—or nearly so, imparts a variety and an extent to the expression, within which, as in the human soul, there is room for contradictory notions. The relation between the themes is, at the same time, of so intimate a nature, and they are so compellingly summarized in the working-out, that the whole, although rich in contrasting colours, makes an impression of the greatest unity. In Berg's string quartet, op. 3, for instance, three motives of entirely different character are opposed to each other in the first three bars, yet they are related to each other through some formal device or other, such as inversion, augmentation, or rhythmic completion, and the development unfolds their affinity: the common experiences of dissimilar relatives. "Music describes the adventures of themes," as Schönberg says.'

The clarinet pieces are, perhaps, even more representative, not so much of Schönberg as of the Schönberg school. The following phrase is a sample of their thematic aspect, but the elaborations, especially in the timbre employed, are many and varied:

Ex. 2.

The *Lyrische Suite* for string quartet, which had its first performance at the Baden-Baden chamber music festival of July 1927, is Berg's most important chamber work. It is in six movements, and conforms, for the most part strictly, to the technical precepts laid down by Schönberg for composition in the scale of twelve equal degrees. He has adopted the description 'suite', to indicate that the character of the work is not symphonic, as in the case of most string quartets, but that does not exclude certain analogies with sonata form. The connexion between the movements is loose, except in two aspects: the alternative and progressive intensification of the tempi, and the recurrence of thematic passages. The former is best illustrated by enumerating the movements: I. allegretto gioviale; II. andante amoroso; III. allegro misterioso—trio estatico; IV. adagio appassionato; V. presto delirando—tenebroso; VI. largo desolato. Thus allegretto—allegro—presto forms one sequence, and andante—adagio—largo another, and the divergence between them widens with each step. The thematic associations derived from the textural use of the same note sequences is slight, but there are more direct marks of thematic affinity. For instance, bars 13–15 of the second movement are recalled at bars 77–78 of the third; the trio of the latter, in which these bars occur, furnishes material for the exposition of the fourth, and at the very end of the work reference is made to a phrase that presented itself early in the first movement. In form, the allegretto corresponds to a sonata movement without development, the andante to a rondo with two episodes, the allegro to a scherzo with its trio, the scherzo-mood being continued in the presto, with a corresponding alternation. The adagio forms the lyrical climax of the work, and is structurally the most complex movement. The stretto with which it opens gives a foretaste of its intensely polyphonic quality. The concluding largo is declamatory and rhapsodical. It is curious to find in it a reference to *Tristan*:

Ex. 3.

As an example of the consistently atonal mode of writing, the following may serve, being taken almost at random from the main portion of the third movement, just before the intervention of the trio:

Ex. 4.

The effect of the misterioso is astonishing, and well merits the superscription. At the end of the composition the music dies away, the instruments leaving off one by one.

Berg took an active part in the Verein für Musikalische Privataufführungen, which was the means of introducing Viennese audiences to much modern music. EDWIN EVANS.

[For the comprehension and appreciation of works like those of Alban Berg a special mentality is needed, but that he has many admirers (among them the well-known critic, Rudolf Kastner) there is no doubt.

EDITOR.]

BERG, CONRAD MATHIAS, 1785–1852.

French pianist and composer (Alsatian). His music is somewhat out of date. For list of quartets and trios see *Fétis*.

†BERG, NATANAEL, b. 1879, Swedish composer.

Quintet, pf, str, b mi   Musik-Konstförlag, 1917.

Berg is best known as a composer of symphonic poems. His works include a string quartet (MS.).

BERGER, WILHELM, 1861–1911, German composer.

Quintet, 2 v, vla, 2 vc, e mi. (Prize work—Beethovenhaus-Verein.)	op.	75	B. & B., 1899.
Trio, v, vla, vc, g mi	op.	69	Simon, 1898.
Quintet, pf, 2 v, vla, vc, f mi	,,	95	Kahnt, 1905.
Quartet, pf, v, vla, vc, A	,,	21	Rühle, 1887.
Trio, pf, cl, vc, g mi	,,	94	Kahnt, 1905.
Sonata, pf, v, A	op.	7	Rühle, 1882.
,, ,, ,, F	,,	29	Peters, 1888.
,, ,, ,, g mi	,,	70	Simon, 1898.

This highly gifted composer, whose death prevented the fulfilment of the great expectations he had aroused, received a most thorough training in counterpoint under Friedrich Kiel, and was particularly drawn to Brahms. He was an earnest, level-headed artist, very self-critical, no sworn follower of the classics, but modern in his outlook and full of noble ideals. His chamber music has permanent value, though it will be fully appreciated only by people of refined judgement who turn to music for enlightenment and edification. If it is less often performed than it deserves, it is mainly because the youthful enthusiasts of the atonal school have latterly been so prominent in concert programmes. The present writer has found Berger's works greatly appreciated whenever performances of them are given.

THE PIANO QUINTET, op. 95, is distinguished by breadth of conception and power, and also by excellent treatment of the thematic material. In this work, Berger strives after delicate sound-effects, and from time to time opposes the strings, employed most effectively and skilfully as a separate mass, to the splendidly written piano part. The first movement, allegro non troppo, opens with unusual vigour and importance; it is wonderful to see what has been made of this main subject, and also of the elegant and appealing cantabile theme. The music is healthy, and full of life and emotion. On far simpler lines is the expressive and melodious poco adagio, with a very energetic principal section in the short middle part. The scherzo has an unusual rhythm, and overflows with vigour and animation; it is not, however, without its moments of attractive melody. The finale, allegro moderato e con brio, F minor, is in the form of a mighty passacaglia, not indeed in the customary 3/4 time, but in 2/4; here the composer has full scope for his ingenuity in exhausting the possibilities of so rugged a theme.

THE STRING QUINTET, op. 75, forms a valuable addition to the restricted number of good string quintets with two 'cellos. In this work (which gained a prize from the Beethoven House Society at Bonn) the two 'cellos are very skilfully exploited with regard to beauty of tone; and, indeed, the work as a whole is remarkable for the correct and beautiful treatment of the strings by a composer to whom the piano was more familiar. But, though the results are admirable, the music is none too easy. There is, further, an extraordinary mastery of forms, and, above all, on the intellectual side, the work is not merely praiseworthy, but of striking value. The first movement, allegro con passione, opens straightway with the well marked and rhythmically pleasing principal subject. This soon presses forward to a powerful subsidiary theme, which in its turn makes room for a graceful singing theme, with a subsidiary, of pregnant rhythm. A somewhat archaic note is struck by the following theme:

the leading idea of the vivace scherzando, which is developed in fugal form with delightful humour and skill. Another idea, of passionate character, becomes allied with it, and a tone-picture full of life and colour is displayed, sinking to a fine close in the brief and particularly charming coda. The broad principal melody of the adagio has nobility and distinction, and is varied and embellished with the utmost delicacy. The finale leads off with an introductory molto vivace in 4/4 with a strongly-marked rhythm, out of which the main section, resembling a tarantella, is evolved. The capricious second subject returns to 4/4 time, but the tarantella supplies the effective ending, though not until the introduction, with its incisive 4/4 rhythm, has once more intervened.

Only a brief reference can be made to the pleasing piano quartet, an early work (1887); it is, however, a matter for regret that another piano quartet, op. 100, a fine and mature work, should still remain unpublished.

The trio for piano, clarinet, and 'cello is chiefly notable for the adagio, in which there is an exquisite duet between clarinet and 'cello.

THE TRIO FOR VIOLIN, VIOLA, AND 'CELLO, op. 69, is admirably suited for performance either at home or in the concert-room, for it is both extremely effective from the players' standpoint, and full of melodious fancies charmingly presented. In the first movement, ***lebhaft***, there is an enchanting idyll, noteworthy for its transparency. The second, ***etwas belebt***, consists of very charming variations on a march-like theme. The variation in the minor key and the fine scherzo are in fugal form. The finale, in G major, is preceded by a longish introduction in the style of a recitative, and the cheery naïveté of the movement is reminiscent of Haydn.

THE FIRST VIOLIN SONATA is most successful for so youthful a work. In the first movement, allegro vivace, the natural freshness of the main subject and the expressive singing character of the second at once delight the hearer. Both instruments are effectively treated, and the form is very skilful. In the adagio Berger's rich temperament finds its best medium, the somewhat quicker middle part in the minor mode being melodically most attractive. The main section of the scherzo, vivace e giocoso, is reminiscent of Mendelssohn's fairy music. The trio is quieter in character. With respect to melodic invention, the finale is not equal to the earlier movements; it has, however, a certain breadth, and is superficially attractive enough.

THE SECOND SONATA is long, although there is no scherzo, and makes rather heavy demands on the players. Stamped everywhere with the taste and judgement of a composer versed in all the intricacies of form and counterpoint, the work yet suffers from an attempted preciosity and a corresponding lack of spontaneity; this refers to the first two movements only, the allegro and andantino grazioso, and may possibly explain their failure to grip. The finale, however, is a fascinating movement, broadly planned and with fine thematic material. One motif has a Hungarian touch, and slightly recalls the first movement of Beethoven's Kreutzer sonata.

THE THIRD SONATA has much originality, and is one of the best of its kind. Even experienced players will find it a test of their powers, both musically and technically. The two outer movements are big and impressive. The first subject of the opening movement suggests the trio of Chopin's funeral march. The second movement, ***sehr langsam***, is deeply emotional; the scherzo breathes real humour; in fine, the whole work is well calculated to show Berger's importance in the clearest light.

WILHELM ALTMANN.

[Chamber works by Wilhelm Berger were performed in Jan. 1904 at a Popular Concert, when the composer was in London.]

BERGH, RUDOLPH, 1859–1924, Danish composer.

Quartet, str, d mi	op. 10	Nord. Musikförl., 1903.
Sonata, pf, v, e mi	„ 20	Dreililien, 1905.

Bergh was originally a university professor, but eventually devoted himself to music. His compositions show few signs of national tendencies.

BERGHOUT, JOHANN, pianist and composer.

Quartet, pf, v, vla, vc	op. 42	Steingräber,	
Quartet, pf, v, vla, vc, G	„ 46	„	1908.
Trio, pf, v, vc, E flat	„ 45	„	1909.
Sonata, pf, v, c mi	„ 47	„	1910.
Sonatina, pf, vc (or v), G	„ 34	Augener, 1905; Schott, 1911.	

BERGT, ADOLF, 1822–1862, German organist.

Trio (4 movts.), 3 fag	Merseburger, 1880.

This work is included on account of the unusual combination, and in the hope that it may be of service to bassoon players.

BÉRIOT, CHARLES AUGUSTE DE, 1802–1870, famous Belgian violinist, husband of Malibran.

Works include:

Three *Duos concertants*, 2 v, g mi, e mi, D	op. 57	Schott, 1847; Bosworth, 1906; U.E., 1901.
Six *Duos caractéristiques*, 2 v	„ 113	Schott, 1863.
Two quartets, pf, v, vla, vc, a mi, d mi	opp. 50, 55	Hamelle.
Two trios, pf, v, vc, D, c mi	„ 59, 64	Schott.
Four *Duos concertants*, pf, v, D, g mi, c mi, e mi	„ 63, 68, 69, 71	Schott.
1st sonata concertante, pf, v	op. 67	Brandus, Paris.

De Bériot's tuneful duets for two violins are his only compositions of any real interest to chamber music lovers. His ensemble works consist largely either of operatic arrangements or of pieces of the kind once known as 'brilliant', and which, though useful in their day, need not be considered here. Yet he was a writer deservedly held in great affection by every violinist of a past generation and by not a few of the present. His 'airs variés', concertos, and other solos for the violin are attractively written, and form good stepping-stones to better things. He was a man of amazing versatility, with whom fate dealt hardly, for his last years were spent in total blindness. EDITOR.

BERLIJN (or BERLYN), ANTON, 1817–1870, a prolific Dutch composer.

Works include:

Quartet, str, E flat	op. 112	Peters, 1859.
Trio, pf, v, vc	„ 88 (posthumous),	André, 1872.

BERLIOZ, HECTOR, 1803–1869, French composer and littérateur.

Although Berlioz's fame, as every one knows, reposes upon his vocal and instrumental compositions, it is interesting to learn that he was, like Wagner, by no means insensible to the beauties of chamber music. Between 1848 and 1855 he visited London on four different occasions, and in his *Soirées de l'Orchestre* recounts his various experiences in that city. He was aroused to enthusiasm by the concerts of the BEETHOVEN QUARTET SOCIETY (*q.v.*), and though he indulges in a sly dig at the amateur who brings along scores of the latest quartets of Beethoven, and fixes his eyes upon page 4 whilst the executants are discussing page 6, he is full of admiration for the four virtuosi (two of whom were English-born), interpreters of 'ces œuvres extraordinaires'. He writes:

'Le premier violon est l'Allemand Ernst, rien que cela! Ernst! plus entraînant, plus dramatique qu'il ne le fut jamais. La partie de second violon est confiée à M. Cooper, violiniste anglais, dont le jeu est constamment irréprochable et d'une netteté parfaite, même dans l'exécution des traits les plus compliqués. Il ne cherche pas à briller hors de propos, néanmoins, comme le font beaucoup de ses émules, il ne donne jamais à sa partie que l'importance relative qui lui fut dévolue par l'auteur. L'alto est joué par M. Hill, Anglais comme M. Cooper, l'un des premiers altos de l'Europe et qui possède en outre un incomparable instrument. Le violoncello, enfin, est aux mains sûres de M. Rousselot. Ces quatre virtuoses ont déjà exécuté une vingtaine de fois l'œuvre entière des quatuors de Beethoven; ils n'en font pas moins ensemble de longues et minutieuses répétitions, avant chacune des exécutions publiques. Vous concevez alors que ce quatuor soit un des plus parfaits que l'on puisse entendre.'

So that the cycles of Beethoven quartets, beloved of the modern concert-goer, had their counterparts as long ago as the 'fifties.

I have not yet done with Berlioz. He wrote so admirably about music that I am tempted to quote once more from the *Soirées*. He is listening at his London lodgings to a Trio of artists playing Beethoven's C minor trio in an adjacent chamber, and writes:

'Un soir, j'entends retentir le trio en ut mineur de Beethoven . . j'ouvre toute grande ma porte . . . Entre, entre, sois la bienvenue, fière mélodie . . . Dieu! qu'elle est noble et belle! . . . Où donc Beethoven a-t-il trouvé ces milliers de phrases, toutes plus poétiquement caractérisées les unes que les autres, et toutes différentes, et toutes originales, et sans avoir même entre elles cet air de famille qu'on reconnaît dans celles des grands maîtres renommés pour leur fécondité? Et quels développements ingénieux! Quels mouvements imprévùs! . . Comme il vole à tire-d'aile, cet aigle infatigable! comme il plane et se balance dans son ciel harmonieux! Il s'y plonge, il s'y perd, il monte, il redescend, il disparaît . . . puis il revient à son point de départ, l'œil plus brillant, l'aile plus forte, impatient du repos, frémissant, altéré de l'infini.'

EDITOR.

†BERNARD, ANTHONY, contemporary English composer.

Suite (*Aucassin et Nicolette*), pf, v	Winthrop Rogers.

†BERNARD, ÉMILE, 1845–1902.

Divertissement, 2 fl, 2 ob, 2 cl, 2 horns, 2 fag	op. 36	Durand.
Quartet, str		Janin (Lyons), 1903.
„ pf, v, vla, vc, c mi	„ 50	Durand, 1899.

Trio, pf, v, vc, a mi	op. 30	R. & E., 1885.
Sonata, pf, v, e flat mi	„ 48	Durand, 1897.
Suite, pf, v	„ 34	Hamelle, 1910.
Sonata, pf, vc G	„ 46	Durand, 1896.

Bernard's most important chamber works are the 'cello sonata and the piano quartet. The latter is powerfully inspired, and displays rich melodic invention, coupled with great variety of rhythmic combinations. The divertissement for wind instruments is, as the title indicates, conceived in lighter vein.

Contemporary with Gabriel Fauré and Widor, and, like them, an organist, at a time when César Franck's star was already rising, Bernard retained an individuality free from all influences. He was awarded the Prix Chartier (for chamber music). ADOLPHE PIRIOU.

[The violin suite was in Sarasate's repertory.]

†BERNARD, ROBERT, French composer.

Sonata, pf, v, D — Durand, 1927.

BERTELIN, ALBERT, b. 1872, French composer, pupil of Widor and Th. Dubois.

Quintet, pf, 2 v, vla, vc	Max Eschig.	
Trio, pf, v, vc, a mi	„ „	
Sonata, pf, v, E flat	„ „	1907.
„ pf, vc, d mi	„ „	1910.

(The last two orig. publ. by Demets.)

The violin sonata is in four movements; the first, allegro energico, is constructed on two themes, one full of energy and decision, the other tenderly expressive. Both are developed at first in an atmosphere of calm and mystery, then with growing assurance; they combine forcefully, and the vigour of the opening is resumed. The adagio opens with a 'preamble' in form of a poignant recitative. This recurs between the appearances of the Lied-phrase,[1] which is derived from the principal theme of the first movement. This Lied-phrase, grave at first, later grows more serene, and sings to an accompaniment upon the higher register of the piano; then, in the last section, it becomes dramatic, closing softly with a reminiscence of the opening recitative. The intermezzo is preceded by an introduction in which the principal themes of the previous movements reappear. This leads, *pp*, to an allegretto scherzando, built on a transformation of the principal theme of the first movement, and passes without break into the finale, the spirited theme of which lends itself to the most varied combinations.

The 'cello sonata is in three movements, of dramatic character and classical structure. The trio is also in three movements, the first written in the form of certain of Bach's organ preludes and based on two themes. The second is an andante in Lied-form. In the rondo finale the whole development is built on an amplification of the opening theme; the second theme reappears at the end of the development and leads to the recapitulation, with a coda in stretto as conclusion.

The quintet, a solidly constructed work, has four movements, all in classical form, but two cyclic themes recur in each. They form the first and second subjects of the first movement, the trio of the second movement (scherzo), the middle section of the Lied (third movement), and intervene actively in the finale.

Bertelin employs the cyclic methods of the Franckist school; he belongs to a school little interested in modern innovations, and his harmonic scheme always shows great restraint.

ADOLPHE PIRIOU.

BERTELMAN, JAN GEORG, 1782–1854, Dutch composer, and skilful contrapuntist.

Quartet, str — Richault.

BERTINI, HENRI, 1798–1876, French composer, born in London.

Nonet, pf, fl, ob, vla, vc, horn, fag, trpt, D		Lemoine.
5th sextet, pf, 2 v, vla, vc, cb, E flat	op. 124	Schott, 1845.
6th sextet, pf, 2 v, vla, vc, cb, E flat	„ 172	Lemoine.
Two trios, pf, v, vc	„ 21, 22	Simrock, 1851.
Three sonatas, pf, v, E, a mi, d mi	„ 152, 153, 156	Schott, 1844–46.

Bertini's name is well known to pianists by his studies, some of which are still in use at the present day. Of one of his piano trios, Schumann (*Gesammelte Schriften*) concedes to the composer that he writes easily flowing harmony, but considers that all the movements are too long, and makes the following comment: 'With the best will in the world, we find it difficult to be angry with Bertini, yet he drives us distracted with his perfumed Parisian phrases; all his music is as smooth as silk and satin. The trio may fulfil its destiny, to be worn out and then laid aside.' His music is highly spoken of in *Grove* and *Fétis*, however. EDITOR.

BERTONI, FERDINANDO GIUSEPPE, 1725–1813, Italian composer.

Modern republication:

Quartet, str — op. 2 (no. 1) — (A. Toni), Ricordi, 1922.

For original publications *v. Fétis*.

†BERTRAND, MARCEL, French composer.

Sonata, pf, v, e mi — Rouart, 1921.

[1] See Foreword, art. BEETHOVEN.

BERWALD, FRANZ ADOLF, 1796-1868, Swedish composer.

Septet, v, vla, vc, cl, fag, horn, cb, B flat		Musik. Konstför. (Stockholm).
Quartet, str, a mi, posth.		Elkan & Schildknecht, 1905.
Quartet, str, E flat, posth.		Bagge (Stockholm), 1887.
Two quintets, pf, 2 v, vla, vc, c mi, A	opp. 5, 6	J. Schuberth & Co., 1856–58.
Three trios, pf, v, vc, E flat, f mi, d mi		„ 1852–54.
4th trio, pf, v, vc, C, posth.		Musik.Konstför.
Sonata, pf, v, E flat		„ ; B. & H.
Sonata, pf, vc, B flat	op. 7	J. Schuberth & Co., 1859.

Berwald, the greatest of Sweden's older instrumental writers, only became really known as a chamber composer after 1850. His early works are a piano quartet (MS.), a string quartet (MS.), and a septet for wind and strings. In the septet Berwald shows a tendency towards romanticism, but in general keeps to Beethoven as his model. Later, he made his mark with the three piano trios (E flat, F minor, D minor) and two piano quintets, as well as the 'cello sonata. After his death, other chamber works were published: the quartets in E flat and A minor; the piano trio in C, and the violin sonata. His most noteworthy works are the piano trio in D minor and the two piano quintets, which called forth Liszt's admiration and were also appreciated by Wagner and Bülow.

The outside influences which were obvious in his early works are hardly noticeable in the later compositions. He very soon developed an individual romantic style, which is pervaded with the originality and personality of genius. There are national traits in his music, but his art is, on the whole, not predominantly national. (Berwald was of German origin, and spent much of his life in Germany.) A particular feature of his chamber music is his transparent clarity of form, which is always unhampered by traditional principles; indeed, they are often remarkably free in construction. He loves to weave his parts into a fine contrapuntal web; his rhythm is ingenious and often humorous; his harmonies are sufficiently audacious at times, producing harsh and bizarre effects. There is much charm in his fine enthusiasm, which is always restrained and noble, never sentimental. It was only in the latter years of Berwald's life that his work met with appreciation, but towards the end of the century his genius became universally acknowledged, and from that time onward his compositions have received increasing recognition.

GUNNAR JEANSON.

BESTÄNDIG, OTTO, 1835–1917, German composer.

Quartet (Sonata), pf, harmonium, v, vc, E flat	op. 27	Simon, 1873 & 1888.

The above is a combination for which few works have been written.

BEYER, GEO., German composer.

1st suite, pf, cl (also v), D		Tonger, 1920.

†BEZECNY, EMIL, b. 1868, Bohemian composer.

Sonata, pf, v, c mi	op. 3	B. & H., 1890.

BIAGI, ALAMANNO, 1806–1861.

Of this Italian composer Pougin writes that in 1861 he won a prize offered by Dr. A. Basevi, in a quartet competition. The composer did not live to receive his prize, nor, so far as I know, was the quartet published.

EDITOR.

BIBER, HEINRICH JOHANN FRANZ VON, 1644–1704, famous German violinist.

Virtuoso violinist, and composer for his instrument. Biber's work has importance both in the development of sonata form and in the rapid advance of violin technique. His writing for the violin is difficult and elaborate, the double stops and contrapuntal passages showing that his skill must have been considerable. He appears to have been the first to employ unusual tunings (scordatura), of which much use is made in his suites and partitas. His music is too austere in character to please the musician of to-day, yet many of his violin sonatas have been republished in Austria (U.E., &c.) from patriotic motives and as homage to his fine musicianship. (See *Grove*, articles *Biber* and *Sonata*.) EDITOR.

BIBL, RUDOLF, 1832–1902, Viennese composer.

Sonata, pf, v, B flat	op. 42	Brockhaus, 1880.

BIELFELD, A., German composer.

Sonata, pf, fag		A. E. Fischer, 1889.

BINDER, ADOLF, German composer.

Trio, v, vla, vc, C	op. 1	Simon, 1900.

BINDER, FRITZ, German composer.

Trio (in form of a suite), v, vla, vc, G	op. 1	Leuckart, *c.* 1900.

A useful work for practice purposes, but rather banal.

BINENBAUM, IANKO, b. 1880 at Adrianople.

Binenbaum spent his childhood in Sofia, and studied music at Munich under Victor Gluth and Rheinberger. It was in Munich that his first works were performed. Later, he went to Paris, where he produced the following chamber works: first string quartet (1910), second string quartet (1911), piano quintet (1912). Since then he has written a *Poème lyrique* for double string quartet, and a trio entitled *Poème intime* (performed 1921 and 1923).

The *Poème lyrique* is in four movements, and bears by way of epigraph the following axiom of Spinoza: 'Knowledge of nature is the greatest boon to the human mind.' An introductory note says: 'Here the composer has attempted never to transform, develop, or work out a theme. Each musical idea appears only once, and in this one statement fulfils its whole expressive function.' Hence, in the first movement, as many as seven themes are introduced in succession. The scherzo has eight short themes, the slow movement nine, and the energetic, seething finale has ten, all closely related to one another. The unity of purpose and style remain unquestionable, despite the great variety of the materials used.

M. D. CALVOCORESSI.

[These works, being all in MS., do not come within the scope of this Cyclopedia, but Mr. Calvocoressi tells me that they are full of interest and stamp the composer as one of the strongest and most striking personalities of his time.

An example of his originality of thought is afforded by the above-mentioned *Poème lyrique*. EDITOR.]

BISCHOFF, KASPAR JACOB, 1823–1893, German composer.

Trio, v, vla, vc, c mi	op. 5	Heckel, 1854.
Suite (*Aus dem Nachlasse des tollen Geigers*),[1] pf, v	opp. 36, 38	André, 1872.

†BITTNER, JULIUS, b. 1874, Viennese composer.

1st quartet, str, A	U.E., 1913.
2nd „ „ E flat	„ 1916.

Bittner, though predominantly a dramatic composer, is by no means averse to chamber music, a fact which has been but little realized, for his 'cello sonata is still unpublished, his first string quartet was not at first circulated, and his second was only published in 1916—and even then was not engraved, but only reproduced from a rather bad manuscript. Nevertheless, the last-named work can be warmly recommended to quartet lovers, though some may consider that it is not written in conventional quartet style.

The first movement (*leicht bewegt*) opens in captivating style, and the first subject has a true Austrian appeal, and contrasts well with the second, which is of a rhythmic character. The two main themes, accompanied by shorter subsidiary ones, are then played off one against the other in a most charming manner. The slow movement is expressive and nobly lyrical, with occasional dramatic moments. The scherzo (or intermezzo) opens with a theme which is purely rhythmic, but afterwards the violin introduces so exquisite a melody, with a charming accompaniment, that one can never tire of it. There follows yet another melody, then comes the trio, which is a deliberate, grandfatherly minuet. The finale is full of genuine Austrian feeling; it opens with a delicious Ländler, against which the second, more humorously conceived theme can make but little headway. As in the first movement, everything in this finale sings and sounds well, and the whole quartet affords an example of a work suited both for the home and the concert-room. The same praise cannot, however, be awarded to the first quartet, which is at times rather dry and uninspired.

WILHELM ALTMANN.

[1] *From the mad fiddler's legacy.*

BLAGROVE, H. G., 1811–1872.

This violinist gave an historically interesting series of quartet concerts at the Hanover Square Rooms in 1838–42, with Gattie, Dando, and Lucas as colleagues. I have seen the programmes, which are more lengthy than those of present-day concert-givers. They announce first performances of Mendelssohn's A major quintet and E major quartet (then in MS.), and of Sterndale Bennett's sextet, with the composer at the piano. A side-light is thrown upon the respect paid to rank in those days by the announcement of prospective visits of certain of the 'nobility and gentry', and by the elaborate dedications published in the programmes. For instance, the B flat trio of Beethoven is announced as dedicated to 'His Imperial Highness the Archduke Rudolph of Austria', and the Ries trio to 'son altesse royale le prince Radziwill', the audience being expected to listen, as a consequence, with reverential awe to the music. EDITOR.

BLANC, ADOLPHE, 1828–1885, French composer.

Blanc was an amazingly prolific chamber composer. In 1862 he obtained the Prix Chartier for chamber compositions. Full list of works in Pougin's *Supplément* to *Fétis*. A great many are given in Altmann's *Catalogue*, including many string quintets. All his works were originally published by Richault, and latterly by Costallat. EDITOR.

Almost all Blanc's works are written in ancient style, and reveal the composer's acquaintance with archaic modes. Blanc was one of the last representatives of the purely classical school. ADOLPHE PIRIOU.

BLAVET, MICHEL, 1700–1768, one of the earliest French flautists of note.

Blavet was self-taught. He played first flute at the Paris Opéra, and Voltaire speaks enthusiastically of his performance, which also attracted the attention of Frederick the Great. Half a dozen of Blavet's eighteen sonatas for flute and figured bass, written in 1732, have been republished, edited by L. Fleury (Rudall & Carte, London). They each consist of several short, simple movements, chiefly in dance measures, somewhat in the style of Handel. No. 1 contains a capital presto, and no. 4 is excellent throughout. He also wrote some sonatas for two flutes. H. M. FITZGIBBON.

BLEICHMANN, JULIUS IVANOVITCH, 1868–1909, Russian composer, pupil of Rimsky-Korsakov.

Quintet, pf, 2 v, vla, vc, D	op. 16	B. & H., 1892.
Sonata, pf, v	„ 15	Jurgenson, 1904.

*BLISS, ARTHUR, b. 1891, English composer.

Rout, soprano voice, chamber orch.	composed 1919, Curwen.
Rhapsody (nonet), soprano and tenor voices, fl, cor angl, 2 v, vla, vc, cb (Carnegie Award, 1921)	S. & B.
Conversations, fl (bass fl), ob (cor angl), v, vla, vc	composed 1920, Curwen.
Madame Noy, soprano voice, fl, cl, vla, cb, fag, harp	Chester.
Quintet, ob, str. quartet	O.U.P., 1927.
Quartet, str, A	Out of print.
Rhapsody, str. quartet	Chester, 1922.
Quartet, pf, v, vla, vc, a mi, op. 5	Out of print.

Two of the above works, a string quartet in A major and a piano quartet in A minor, were performed while Arthur Bliss was on active service, one of them being awarded a prize at the War Emergency concerts. They were also published, but on his return to musical life he destroyed the plates and the unsold copies, being convinced that neither work corresponded in any sense with his musical aims. The works are, however, still procurable from circulating libraries, and a copy is occasionally quoted in second-hand catalogues. In 1919 he paid a musical visit to Paris, the sequel to which was a piano quintet, performed at the Aeolian Hall in April, 1920. This was so truly Parisian in character that it may be regarded as the effect of an inoculation resulting in immunity after the immediate effects had passed. The composer must have felt this, for the work was immediately withdrawn, and a contemporary rhapsody for two pianos and wood-wind has not even had a public performance. This was the last of Bliss's early ventures in chamber music.

It was in the course of 1920 that his more characteristic works came before the public. The first of these, *Madame Noy*, is a 'witchery' song, the poem being anonymous. The setting makes a piquant background to the gruesome story, with its wealth of opportunities for musical illustration. Compared with what had gone before, it established the direction which Bliss was to take.

The second chamber *Rhapsody* (nonet) was the next work to reach the public, in October, 1920, two performances taking place within a few days; it had thus a better chance of carrying conviction. It is idyllic in character, the two voices vocalizing on 'Ah' throughout, and being placed as instruments in the ensemble:

Ex. 1.

In many ways, this rhapsody is more definitely personal than the preceding composition. It is one of Bliss's most poetical works, and, owing to the poetry being in gentler vein, the improved sense of definition and of responsibility to the instruments employed attracted less notice than the more salient characteristics of his other works, in which the colouring was in brighter hues. Here, at least, one could absolve the composer completely from any attempt to amuse the ear with jugglery. The work was accepted for publication by the CARNEGIE TRUST (*q.v.*), and, when the score in due course made its appearance, there were many who were surprised to find how straightforward was a work which, like its predecessor, had aroused sharp differences of opinion.

Rout, one of Bliss's best-known compositions, goes beyond the scope of this Cyclopedia, the spirit of the work being rather orchestral than intimate.

The *Conversations*, which followed, were performed for the first time in January 1921. They consist of five pieces for violin, viola, 'cello, flute (alternating with bass flute), and oboe (alternating with cor anglais). The subtitles are: *The Committee Meeting*, *In the Wood*, *In the Ball-room*, *Soliloquy*, and *In the Tube at Oxford Circus*. Although their instrumental ingenuity is conspicuous, much of their interest is polyphonic, especially in the first and last numbers. The 'Committee' seems to have had a chairman of more than usual obstinacy,

Ex. 2.

who contrived to have his own way by persevering in spite of interruptions. If realism had been intended, Bliss would doubtless have infused more hatred into the other parts. But he is not a realist in the sense in which Moussorgsky was. He is preoccupied solely with musical effects, and finds music even in the rumble that drowns conversation in the Tube—

Ex. 3.

—where, by the way, he appears to have come upon a sentimental idyll.

Even more idyllic is the scene in the wood, in which occurs the following:

Ex. 4.

In comparison, the ball-room episode is more conventional, but the *Soliloquy* for cor anglais is an attractive and original piece of unaccompanied cantilena.

The *Two Nursery Rhymes* of 1921 properly belong to the sphere of chamber music, and are among Bliss's most popular compositions. One, *The Ragwort*, is for soprano, clarinet, and piano; the other, *The Dandelion*, for soprano and clarinet unaccompanied.

A string quartet composed in 1923–4 is provisionally held back for further consideration. When it eventually appears, it will probably be one of a pair.

Bliss's style is remarkable for its energy and for a certain quality of exhilaration. This is not to say that he cannot express the gentler emotions. He has expressed them, for instance, in the *Rhapsody*, which is in the vein of lyrical poetry, and in the second of the *Conversations*—

In the Wood. His treatment of sound is more objective than is the case of the majority of English composers. He has an instinctive delight in the reactions of timbre, from which he unfailingly derives an effect of buoyancy. It is mainly by such means that he is able to express in music the breeziness of his own personality.

His most recent chamber work is a quintet for oboe and strings dedicated to Mrs. Coolidge, and first performed under her auspices at an invitation concert given at Venice, Sept. 11, 1927. The players were Léon Goossens and the Venetian Quartet. It is in three movements: allegro, andante, and finale. The composer has succeeded in avoiding associations which tradition had made almost obligatory for the oboe: there is neither eclogue, bucolic, nor pastoral. In addition, he has transposed some traditional qualities of his first two movements, the allegro being essentially lyrical and the andante at one point almost dramatic. Throughout, the music has a good 'line'—original without aggressiveness. The finale, a brisk 6/8 movement, makes incidental, but considerable use of *Connolly's Jig*, an old Irish fiddle-tune to which the composer's attention was drawn by the present writer:

Ex. 5.

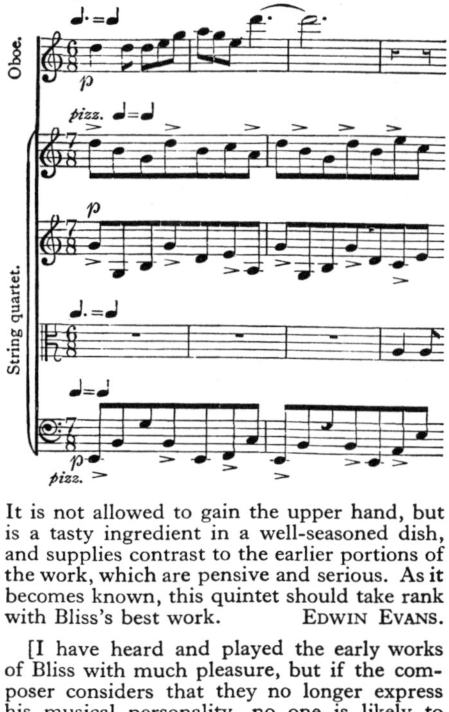

It is not allowed to gain the upper hand, but is a tasty ingredient in a well-seasoned dish, and supplies contrast to the earlier portions of the work, which are pensive and serious. As it becomes known, this quintet should take rank with Bliss's best work. EDWIN EVANS.

[I have heard and played the early works of Bliss with much pleasure, but if the composer considers that they no longer express his musical personality, no one is likely to cavil at his decision to withdraw them. The lovely cor anglais solo in his *Conversations* is, I believe, the first solo appearance in chamber music of this instrument, so eminently fitted by its delicate charm for the purpose.

EDITOR.]

*†BLOCH, ERNEST, b. 1880, Swiss-American composer, pupil of Ysaÿe (violin) and Jaques-Dalcroze. Is now a naturalized citizen of the U.S.A., and musical director of the Institute of Music in Cleveland, Ohio.

	Composed	
1st quartet, str, G	1916	Schirmer, 1919; U.E., 1921.
Night (four pieces), str. quartet	1924	Carl Fischer, 1925.
Three Landscapes (*North, Alpestre, Tongataboo*), str. quartet	1924	„ „ 1925.
Quintet, pf, 2 v, vla, vc	1923	U.E.; Schirmer, 1924.
Sonata, pf, v	1920	U.E., 1921; Schirmer.
Baal Shem (Three Pictures of Chassidic Life), pf, v	—	U.E.; Carl Fischer, 1925.
Suite, pf (or chamber orch.), vla	1919	U.E., 1921.

(Coolidge Prize, 1920.)

Much of Bloch's finest work is in the form of chamber music, which constitutes a large proportion of his total output. Its place among the music of the day is of great significance, his originality being such that his style seems to have sprung into being with little relationship to what has gone immediately before, or to that of other contemporary composers. It is characterized by a declared and conscious Hebraic quality—the natural language of his race, and very different from the assumed Orientalism so often found in modern music—allied to a rugged and almost brutal directness and a passion at times bitter, at times idealistic.

In these last, as in several other characteristics, can be distinctly traced the influence of his intimate study of Beethoven, for whose music he feels an especial understanding and affinity, and whose tradition he in a sense carries on. Indeed, as Beethoven's strong individuality and often harshly intense feeling repelled some of his listeners, so to-day does the challenging quality of Bloch's music have an alienating effect at first, on certain natures, which are, however, usually stirred out of themselves eventually by finding that they cannot remain indifferent to it.

THE STRING QUARTET, the first three movements of which were written in Geneva in the spring of 1916, and the last in the autumn of the same year, is conspicuous among works of its class in virtue of these qualities. It is a work of great power, imagination, and beauty, using to the full the resources of the instruments, and abounding in melodic and contrapuntal interest. The first performance took place in New York, when it was played by the Flonzaley Quartet, and it is worth mentioning that not one note had to be altered during rehearsal, the many complicated and daring effects 'coming off' exactly as intended by the composer.

As regards its material, one subject is of chief importance, appearing in different moods at intervals throughout. This phrase, like so much of Bloch's music, is based on a scale of markedly Oriental character, and is announced in dramatic and declamatory fashion soon after the opening of the quartet:

Ex. 1.

The first movement is written in clear and easily followed sonata form, even to the orthodox keys in which the second subject appears in exposition and recapitulation. This subject is little used, however, in the development, interest being chiefly centred upon the rhapsodical treatment of the first subject. A particularly beautiful and expressive coda (tempo dell' andante moderato) brings the movement to a close.

The second movement (allegro frenetico)—in many ways the most interesting of the four—is very characteristic of Bloch in its exhilarating rhythms and audacious yet simple harmonic texture. It opens by fairly hurling its subject at the listener's head.

Ex. 2.

In some parts of this movement the time-signatures vary almost from bar to bar, 5/8, 11/8, and an unusual grouping of 8/8 constantly alternating with 6/8 and 9/8. These changes are so logical, however, in their cumulative effect, that they are absorbed in the general strong rhythm without any feeling of effort. A secondary subject, during which the second violin plays the phrase at Ex. 2, contains a startling but entirely convincing dissonance, in which the 'cello has a deliberate B natural against the C of the viola in a passage otherwise an octave apart.

Ex. 3.

A curiously pungent quality marks the middle section of this movement.

Ex. 4.

This is pursued to some length, after which a return is made to the allegro frenetico, and the movement ends with an upward rushing passage, followed by an emphatic unison motif of Beethoven-like abruptness.

The slow movement, a pastorale of great beauty and simplicity, is opened by the viola with a dreamy phrase, which is echoed by the second violin and then taken up by the other instruments:

Ex. 5.

Andante molto moderato (Pastorale).

A mood of mystical sadness lies over the continuation of this melody, through which the 'cello produces a darkly shimmering effect by a rocking unison in semiquavers between the open and the stopped A. A second theme is also introduced by the viola, after which the chief subject of the work reappears. From this point onwards the movement becomes more and more animated, bringing in several new phrases, until it reaches a section which suggests far-away horn-calls:

Ex. 6.

(*Animato.*)

This is worked up to a vivid climax, and is echoed in the distance, after which the melancholy mood of the opening is resumed, finally fading away to the accompaniment of a rocking unison on the second violin.

The finale begins with an introduction, in which fragments of the previous movements are passed in review one by one and lead to the principal subject of the last movement (allegro con fuoco), which has some resemblance to that of the second movement.

Ex. 7.

Allegro con fuoco.

This is pursued with much energy, and is soon reinforced by a strongly rhythmic new subject, in which the three upper instruments move together in parallel lines, a device much favoured by Bloch.

Ex. 8.

Ben ritmato (*ma senza ruvidezza*).

His rhythms are sometimes very closely calculated, as in the following:

Ex. 9.

Tempo I.

(*agitato, ma un poco più moderato*).

A section marked 'molto espressivo (come un lamento)' continues on this pattern with a monotonous phrase, which is presently complemented by a dolce espressivo melody, of which some use is made later. In the working-out of these passages, two and even three subjects are sometimes combined simultaneously, the parts occasionally having conflicting time-signatures. The motto theme of the work reappears dramatically in a cadenza-like passage, which leads back to the original last-movement subject, after which the feeling becomes increasingly frenzied, leading through a presto to the final section, marked 'lento, grave' (funèbre). Here the 'cello is given a drum-like, articulated pedal note on the open C string, while the upper instruments play subdued harmonies, which herald the last statement of the chief subject, and this, after brief reminiscences of the other movements, ends the work in a mood of quiet resignation.

The Suite for Viola and Piano (Coolidge prize, 1919) is a most valuable addition to the literature of the viola, being written with rare understanding of that much-neglected instrument. Bloch had the orchestra continually in mind while writing this work, and intended to score the piano part for orchestra (which was done in 1920); he felt that he could thus best convey the peculiar effects and strongly marked rhythms of the work, which is meant to suggest the atmosphere of different Oriental countries.

There are four movements, all connected thematically: the first opens with a mysterious introduction leading to an allegro which teems with life and fantastic imagination; the second (allegro ironico) has a grim and caustic humour; the third (lento) is strange and beautiful; the fourth has a very Chinese character, and here much material from the other movements is employed.

THE FIRST VIOLIN SONATA is even more barbaric than the viola suite, the first movement opening with a three-note subject of wonderful vitality. The writing, which is more or less rhapsodical throughout, is brilliant in the extreme for both violin and piano, and the three movements contain some of Bloch's finest and most personal work.

THE QUINTET FOR PIANO AND STRINGS, considered by Bloch to be one of his finest works, is simpler and more direct than some of his other writing, though his demand for quarter-tones may appear alarming. These are, however, only occasional, and when present are always above or below the next note of the ordinary scale, never standing alone as separate entities. In writing them he uses the signs / and \, placed before a note to indicate the quarter-tone above or below. In the opening of the quintet he thus obtains the following rhythmical figure, played in unison by the strings:

Ex. 10.

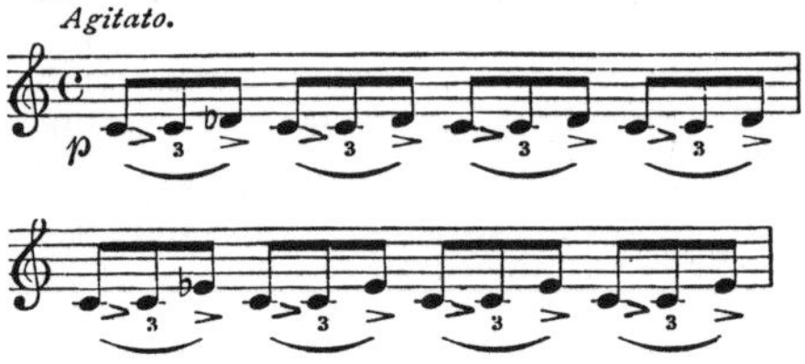

Against this, the piano announces the chief subject, which appears in varying forms throughout the work.

Ex. 11.

This subject is divided into two distinct sections, here marked subject A and subject B. These differ in character, and often appear separately, subject A generally being in the bass or one of the lower parts. A mysterious second subject is introduced by the viola,

Ex. 12.

after which subject A appears on the 'cello, first in its original form, then in an alternative version in which it is also frequently employed.

Ex. 13.

A continuation-theme of the second subject is again given to the viola,

Ex. 14.

and is answered by its own inversion on the 'cello:

Ex. 15.

Upon this material the movement is built in sonata form, with a rich and interesting development and a spirited recapitulation and coda.

The slow movement (andante mistico) is based chiefly upon subject B in a quieter form already foreshadowed in the first movement, the interval of a seventh becoming that of an octave.

Ex. 16.

This is continued in a very different mood from that of the preceding movement, and leads to passages of great beauty and calm, during which a new theme is introduced by the 'cello.

Ex. 17.

Subject A also reappears in the bass, and presently a new and characteristically simple motif makes its appearance, played in unison by viola and 'cello, the viola pizzicato, the 'cello arco.

Ex. 18.

These subjects are worked up and woven together, and the movement finally dies away in the mood of mystical contemplation in which it began.

The last movement (allegro energico), of great vitality and barbaric rhythm, opens with subject A in a new aspect; there is also a striking tune of supposedly Swiss character.

Ex. 19.

Another vigorous subject which is much used proves to be an inversion of subject A.

Ex. 20.

The writing throughout this movement abounds in unusual effects, such as the grace notes and accents alternating between first and second violins in the following unison passage:

Ex. 21.

during which the lower strings play pizzicato chords as primitive and exciting as strokes of a tam-tam. Another section, bearing some resemblance to it, has an almost overpowering impetus.

Ex. 22.

Subject B also makes a reappearance in new guise on the piano.

Ex. 23.

String passages in harmonics, pizzicato, ponticello, glissando, tremolo, sulla tastiera, or col legno all add to the colour and rhythm of this remarkable movement, which, after gathering itself into a mighty climax, leads to a beautiful melody for the viola, gradually producing calm after the preceding turmoil.

Ex. 24.

A succeeding phrase is also important, as it is used again towards the end of the movement,

Ex. 25.

and between these two comes a curious motif on the piano, marked 'like an exotic bird'. A return of some length to the tempo I is followed by a 'vivo' on a long quasi-pedal passage based on subject B. The movement then gradually slows down to a final section marked 'calmo', in which the viola again plays the melody given in Ex. 24; this has a sense of peace and fulfilment which suggests it as the inevitable conclusion towards which the whole work has been leading. The phrase at Ex. 25 also reappears, its slow triplet urging on to the culmination, and there is a fleeting reminiscence of Ex. 16, after which subject B—now reduced to the starkest simplicity—leads in a passage for strings alone to a surprisingly Strauss-like but most convincing dominant-to-tonic cadence, from which the movement draws calmly to an end.

In January and February 1924 Bloch composed four short pieces for string quartet called *Night* and *Three Landscapes* (*North*, *Alpestre*, and *Tongataboo*). These are highly descriptive and picturesque, as well as most effectively written for the instruments. During the same months he also wrote three nocturnes for piano, violin, and 'cello. Among his latest chamber works is a second sonata for violin and piano, which is the antipodes of the first, and is designed to be performed after it as a kind of continuation.

In reviewing Bloch's chamber music as a whole, perhaps the strongest impression it makes (apart from its immense power) is one of sincerity, supported by a masterly technique. His effects, though dramatic and full of originality, never give the impression of having been made for their own sake, but are always essential to the deeply-felt meaning of his ideas. His music is in essence simple and straightforward in spite of its seeming complexity, and it is this that makes it stand out among the work of present-day composers. At a time when music too often aims at a somewhat passionless perfection, sacrificing sincerity to technique and vitality to polish, his glowing works, almost elemental in their directness, bring the breath of a new and powerful life. REBECCA CLARKE.

BLOCH, JOSEPH, 1862–1922, Hungarian violinist.

Quartet, str, A	op. 32	Rosznyai,	1904.
Trios faciles, 3 v	,, 34	,,	1905.

Joseph Bloch was a teacher of the violin at the Budapest Conservatorium, and for six years member of the Hubay-Popper Quartet. He was one of the first to investigate by personal tours the music of Hungarian localities.

The adagio of the quartet in A is typically Hungarian, without any direct Tzigane affinities, the most striking of the movements being the *Scherzo fantastique*. The fantastic element is here produced by a combination of double stops and trills, with effective chromatic runs for all instruments. EDITOR.

BLOCKX, JAN, 1851–1912, Belgian composer, educated at Leipzig.

Quintet, pf, 2 v, vla, vc, G	Heugel,	1899.
Printemps Suite, pf, v	,,	1914.

Blockx is a composer with modern, but not ultra-modern tendencies.

†BLUMENFELD, Felix Michailovitch, 1863, Russian composer.

Quartet, str, F	op. 26	Belaiev, 1898.

Won a prize offered by the Petrograd Chamber Music Society.

Blumenfeld is one of the numerous composers who owe their training to Rimsky-Korsakov. He studied, and afterwards taught, at the Petrograd Conservatorium. He is a pianist, and most of his work is for his instrument. His one quartet is an unpretentious, straightforward work, displaying the same technical elegance as his piano works, but less resourcefulness, probably because of his relatively less extensive experience. He writes too frequently in octaves (violin and 'cello at opening, viola and 'cello in the scherzo, &c.), but otherwise the quartet is a favourable example of a somewhat large category, that of Petrograd composers of the second rank under the Rimsky-Korsakov régime. If it opens no new vistas, it is certainly pleasant to play and to hear. Edwin Evans.

[The words 'pleasant to play and to hear' are surely a recommendation to those who do not regard chamber music as a 'self-imposed martyrdom', and may be taken to refer not only to Blumenfeld's quartet, but also to that notable group of works by the second-rate Russian composers of which Mr. Evans speaks. I have myself taken part in at least a score of such quartets, and found them almost invariably melodious and ingratiating, not always avoiding banality, yet obviously the work of artists who have not neglected their studies in counterpoint. The scherzos are especially piquant in almost every instance. For each instrument an attractive part is written; the difficulties are not of the virtuoso kind, and so it happens that they are 'pleasant to play'.

'Pleasant to hear?' Yes, in private, but there is room for doubt if they carry sufficient weight for public performance.

The style of Blumenfeld's quartet is not independent, and recalls that of Glazounov, and to a small extent that of Rubinstein. Editor.]

BLUMENTHAL, Joseph von, 1782–1850, violinist.

Composer of a vast number of duets for two violins, issued by various publishers—Haslinger, Hofmeister, Peters, Cranz; and other chamber works (*v. Fétis*). Editor.

BLUMENTHAL, Sandro.

Quintet, pf, 2 v, vla, vc, D	op. 2	Eulenburg, 1900.
Quintet, pf, 2 v, vla, vc, G	,, 4	,, ,,

BLUMER, Theodor, b. 1882, German composer.

Suite (serenade and theme with var^{ns}.), wind quintet	op. 34	Simrock, 1918.
Tanzsuite, fl, ob, cl, fag	,, 53	,,
Sextet (theme and var^{ns}.), pf, fl, ob, cl, fag, horn, F	,, 45	,, 1922.
Quartet, str, g mi	,, 51	,, 1925.
Trio, v, vla (or cl), vc, d mi	,, 55	,,
Quintet, pf, 2 v, vla, vc, b mi	,, 21	Kistner, 1906.
Quartet, pf, v, vla, vc, c mi	,, 50	Simrock.
Two sonatas, pf, v, d mi, c mi	opp. 33, 43	Simrock, 1920.
Capriccio, pf, v	op. 42	,,
Sonata, pf, vc, b flat mi	,, 23	Kistner, 1908.
Two suites, pf, fl, F, A flat	opp. 40, 46	Simrock, 1919–1922.

Blumer is a composer of whom *Riemann* speaks favourably. His quartet is in four sections, played through without a break, and contains much strong, rhythmical writing. Another notice describes the piano quartet, op. 50, as 'straightforward and heartfelt'. A characteristic and excellent quality in Blumer's work is the absence of diffuseness. Editor.

BOCCHERINI, Luigi, 1743–1805, Italian 'cellist and composer.

Note. Boccherini's system of opus numbers involves a separate set of numbers for each type of work. It is therefore very difficult to give an accurate list. Authorities differ.

2 octets, various instr.
16 sextets, various instr.
12 quintets, 2 v, 2 vla, vc.
[113] quintets, 2 v, vla, 2 vc. Twenty-four of these belong to op. 37.
18 quintets, fl (or ob), 2 v, vla, vc.
[102] quartets, str (*Riemann* says 91).
12 trios, v, vla, vc.
48 trios, 2 v, vc (*Riemann* says 42).
Many duets, 2 v.
6 sonatas, v, bass.
6 sonatas, vc, bass.
12 quintets, pf, 2 v, vla, vc.
21 sonatas, pf, v.

Six 'cello sonatas, A, C, G, E flat, F (?), A, were republished with piano arrangement.

(1) Ed. A. Piatti. Ricordi, 1864–65.

(2) F. Grützmacher (very free transcription). Simrock, 1881.

Several of these sonatas have been issued by other houses, e.g. Augener, Schott, &c., with various editors.

For details of above works see *Altmann*,

where the publishers of a large number are given. Ninety of the string quintets were published by Janet & Cotelle, of Paris, in 16 books. A few of the other works have been republished, notably the string quartets and trios.

As in Mozart's case, it was Boccherini's fate to lead a wretched outward existence while his inner life was rich and full of creative experience. From 1769 he lived in Madrid, where he held a court appointment. He and his numerous family had only a back room, with a loft in which the composer worked, and he died in absolute poverty, though blissful in his inexhaustible store of fervent melody. Gerber (*Lexicon*, 1791–2) calls him the greatest of Italian instrumental composers, whose only rival among the Germans was Haydn. In spite of this, little is known to-day of his works, which include no fewer than 125 string quintets and 91 string quartets. Recently, however, new editions of Boccherini's compositions have begun to multiply, among them being Sondheimer's edition of the E flat quintet, op. 12, no. 2.

Boccherini is the first great perfecter in modern music. Everything for which his predecessors worked, singly and laboriously, was garnered and absorbed by him. Sammartini's beginning, Stamitz's radicalism, Pugnani's tentative efforts, and Beck's inspirations—all these had their experimental value for Boccherini, and the achievements of all these hot-bloods of the new art are at last justified and brought to fulfilment in his music. In his hands, the new style yields up its most secret properties and possibilities.

Just as the theme, which constitutes the backbone of the modern sonata, is made up of many constituent parts, varying in their subject-matter, rhythm, harmony, and dynamics, so does the new style abound in new methods. The wide choice of means offered to the composer is adequate to express his multiform inventive qualities. This does not mean that his style is based on a medley of principles, but rather that the varying forms of expression were an integral part of the new 'free' treatment out of which our modern musical language evolved.

Objection may no doubt be taken to the barren framework and often insignificant detail of the new style in its beginnings, and even BECK (*q.v.*), for one, was unable to sustain the fire kindled by his own heated imagination. But in Boccherini's case a sensitive and exuberant spirit is seen inhabiting, as it were, a tropical world. Of this spirit, subtle melodies are first conceived. Boccherini then concentrates on the independent leading of the parts (based on a plurality of motifs), achieving at times truly plastic effects, which belong rather to the romantic epoch than to the severe linear art of the classics.

No longer is the structure filled with coarse substances and dynamic contrasts. A technique of the utmost flexibility and virtuosity now informs the material, and it is in this connexion that Boccherini may be considered the first to have definitely fixed the style of modern chamber music. His native Italian lyricism obliterates the hard boundary lines which are apt to obtrude themselves when thematic periods are divided into precise sections. By dint of continuous singing, he bridges over the whole, combining his motifs intuitively, with results that are in no wise inferior to the more formal 'working' of the classics, while they escape the effect of deliberation.

What constitutes an epoch-making characteristic of Boccherini's work is the skilful manner in which he contrives to vary his forms of expression within the smallest framework, as, for instance, in the tempo di menuetto of op. 16, no. 3 (1775). Here is a finished style, diametrically opposed to that of the suite in the great preceding epoch. In this respect, none of Boccherini's contemporaries can compare with him; not even Gluck—whose work, though contemporary, is antiquated as regards style—and not even the classics, the value of whose work is qualified by the strong formal contrast of exposition and working-out.

Pre-classical music aims, as its compressed style suggests, at presenting the instantaneous impression—the intensity of the moment—and it is to this characteristic that Boccherini so firmly clings, rejecting the long working-out of the development section. Once the idioms employed had lost their freshness, however, the habit arose of regarding Boccherini's music—and, indeed, all music immediately preceding the classical—from a mistaken angle, and denouncing it as shallow. Whereas Junker, in 1776 (*Twenty Composers*), described Boccherini as 'dark and indistinct', as 'indulging in unnecessary complications', and as 'on the whole evoking horror', despite his poetical ideas and divine lyricism, the nineteenth century frequently quoted the judgement of the *Allg. Mus. Z.* (Leipzig, 1779, p. 54), which declares that Boccherini never achieved the 'complete fulfilment of a bold genius', but was 'superficial, monotonous, and unimpressive'.

To-day one is able to admire the happy proportion of invention and ingenuity, naïve intelligibility and artistry, which is peculiar to pre-classical music in particular and to Italian music in general. Boccherini, for all his technical versatility, never deviated in the direction of classical thoroughness of detail or German profundity. The following example, taken from the second movement of the quintet, op. 12, no. 2 (see mus. ex. no. 4 later), is a good illustration of Boccherini's vehement climaxes, and may help to explain how even a Beethoven could adopt not only his methods but also many of his idioms.

In his early work Boccherini still follows Sammartini. His actual point of departure as regards style is, however, Pugnani. Beck, Rigel, and Gossec, all living in France, next claimed his attention, and he reached his height, rising by a steep curve, in 1775. He then settled down to a blissful, contemplative existence, while Haydn proceeded to take the world by storm. The *Zeitgeist* intimidated him, and several of his later works are rendered conventional by the persistence of his idioms, but from time to time he still sent forth poetical outpourings of tender sadness and love, which rang true from his heart.

A few examples may be quoted. The tempo di menuetto of op. 16, no. 3, may serve as a general example of his style, as it illustrates the great variety achieved within the smallest space, the multiplicity of motifs and plasticity of form, the freedom and spontaneity of the ideas which invariably present themselves as intuitive and inevitable, and finally the soft, flexible manner of writing which dominates his style and subdues all harshness of contrast or transition.

It should be obvious to every one capable of understanding and appreciating an artistic musical composition that a piece such as this calls for a correspondingly sensitive interpretation, one which brings out its rhythmic, dynamic, and polyphonic features—in a word, the individual expression. It must not be played in the glib, undiscriminating manner so often considered suitable for old music. Although Boccherini attempted nothing on a large scale—and the scale is never a fair test of so mobile an art as music—he was by no means one of those artists who lose themselves in perfecting elegant trifles. An example (from quintet op. 13, no. 5, 1774) (Ex. 1) will serve to show how, while his mind was engaged in working out his ideas, his powerful flow of melodic inspiration blended the individual sections into one unbroken melos.

The opening subject in G major (which

Ex. 1. Op. 13, no. 5.

Nine bars later.

occurs earlier, note for note, in Cannabich) is here, in the working-out, an adaptation in contrary motion and in inverse order of the main theme,

Ex. 2.

which has already undergone the following transformation:

Ex. 3.

In the fourth bar of ex. 1, Boccherini evolves from the existing subject material a cantilena which grows in intensity, repeating, nine bars later, the descending notes of the opening in double tempo, and reaching its climax two bars before the end of the extract given, in a movement a quarter the speed of the original. In spite of its fine detail work and minute elaboration of motifs, this movement has a notable breadth of line.

In the second movement of the quintet, op. 12, no. 2 (1773) (Ex. 4), the thematic development is more confined and closely connected, but the effect is only the more inexorable—one might say heroic. It should be observed how naturally the theme in bar 5 springs out of the opening subject, how a part of this theme is foreshadowed in the first bar (viola and 1st 'cello) in contrary motion, how depth is secured by polyphonic treatment, and how the whole is rounded off into the new unity of a 12-bar period.

Then, in the working-out, the boldness and vigour displayed in keeping the motifs in play and turning about the original polyphonic

Ex. 4.

From the working-out.

Fourteen bars later.

structure not only justifies the position we have claimed for Boccherini as the first to embrace the new music in all its aspects, but also shows him to have been a pioneer of the classical and romantic music of the future. There is further proof of this in the character of the false relations which occur in the harmony. They are not merely incidental to the independent leading of individual parts, but are born of a new, instinctive feeling for the effect of simultaneous sounds which required chromatics as an enriching element.

The following example from the largo, op. 12, no. 1 (second movement), written in 1773, will serve both to illustrate this, and as a further instance of Boccherini's clear, finished handling of the melody within the thematic period, and the new aspect of the same melody in the period that follows :

Ex. 5.

Molto espress. Op. 12, no. 1.

The technique of stringed instruments, which, in conformity with the demands of the development in style, progressed during the eighteenth century from almost primitive simplicity to all-embracing brilliance, was led on to its final stage by Boccherini. At the present day, it may seem that the permanent artistic value of Boccherini's work is but small. His personality was, indeed, soon to be overshadowed by the classical masters, but, in the history of musical development at least, he deserves a place among the principal composers of all time. R. SONDHEIMER.

[Spohr, writing of Baillot, says, 'He plays Boccherini's quintets frequently and with pleasure. It is curious . . . to note how his interpretation makes one forget the mediocrity of the works.' Spohr goes on to say that he is 'surprised that Baillot could play such childish stuff, and that Paris must have been fifty years behind the times to listen to it'.

Vidal, writing fifty years later, says that his works are still heard with pleasure, and quotes the obituary notice in the *Allg. Mus. Z.* of Leipzig as saying that Boccherini was too little known in Germany. EDITOR.]

BOCHSA (junior), ROBERT NICHOLAS CHARLES, 1789–1856, distinguished harpist.

Fétis, who gives a list of Bochsa's ensemble works with harp (without publishers' names), writes that negligence and haste are found in his most inspired works, and fine talents wasted. His harp septet, however, had the distinction of a performance at the London Philharmonic Society on 28 May, 1821. EDITOR.

BÖDECKER, LOUIS, 1845–1889, German composer.

Trio-Phantasie, pf, v, vc, f sharp mi	op. 18	Peters, 1883.
Phantasie-Sonata, pf, v, e mi	„ 15	„ 1880.
Sonata, pf, v, f mi	„ 22	Kistner, 1884.
Serenade, pf, horn	„ 20	Peters, „

BOEHM, Joseph, 1795–1876, distinguished violin teacher.

Varns. pf, v, on a theme of Beethoven (entitled *Clement*, *Hellmesberger*, *St. Lupin*, *Mayseder*, *Schuppanzigh*, all famous violinists of Boehm's time). Mechetti (Vienna).

Hellmesberger, Ernst, and Joachim were his pupils. He resided for fifty years in Vienna, and was the first to lead the quartet in E flat, op. 127, of Beethoven, whose directions at rehearsal for its interpretation he well remembered. When Schuppanzigh was absent from Vienna, Boehm took his place in the famous quartet concerts given in the Prater (with Holz, Weiss, and Lincke). Andreas Moser was present, and preferred his leading to that of the brothers Müller and F. David. In his *Geschichte des Violinspiels* (p. 515), Moser speaks of him as being in private a deep and earnest student of chamber music, whose ideals must have coloured the artistic life of his pupil Joachim. His addiction to private playing was owing to the attacks of nervousness from which he suffered in public, and which were the cause of his withdrawal from the concert platform in 1827. Editor.

BOËLLMANN, Léon, 1862–1897, Alsatian organist.

Quartet, pf, v, vla, vc (Prize), f mi	op. 10	Hamelle.
Trio, pf, v, vc (Prize), G	,, 19	,,
Suite, pf, vc	,, 6	,,
Sonata, pf, vc	,, 49	Durand.

Essentially an artist and a scholar, Boëllmann has left a collection of works full of colour, and admirable for the science which has known how to blend the peculiarities of the ancient modes with the discoveries of modern harmony.

The piano quartet is in four movements: a spirited allegro, a scherzo full of delicacy and originality, a sombre andante, and a breezy and joyous finale.

The trio marks a stage in Boëllmann's evolution. The form is new: the first section comprises the introduction, allegro, and andante; the second combines the scherzo and finale. This strong and original work, like the quartet, was awarded a prize by the Société des Compositeurs.

Boëllmann, who was, above all, an organist, was somewhat under the influence of Franck's genius. The early death of so thorough a musician is to be deplored. Adolphe Piriou.

BOËLY, Alexandre Pierre François, 1785–1858, French composer.

Quartet, str, a mi	op. 27,	Costallat, 1861.
,, ,, e mi	,, 28	,, ,,
,, ,, G	,, 29	,, ,,
,, ,, E	,, 30	,, ,,
3 trios, v, vla, vc, D, C, g mi	op. 5	Costallat, —
Trio, v, vla, vc, f mi	,, 23	,, 1861.

A disciple of Bach and an interesting personality (*v. Grove*).

†**BOGHEN, Felice**, b. 1875, Italian composer.

Four toccatas, v, vla, vc, a mi, A, d mi, F — J. & W. Chester, 1926.

BOHEMIAN STRING QUARTET. *v.* Czechoslovakian Performing Organizations.

BOHLIN, Karl.

Sonata, pf, v, e mi — F. Schuberth (jun.), 1907.

BÖHME, Ferdinand, 1815–1883, German violinist.

1st quartet, str, g mi — Peters, 1857.

Böhme was a pupil of Spohr and Hauptmann. His second quartet was not published. A fourth quartet was withdrawn from circulation, and the fifth published as op. 10. A German critic writes as follows of the third: 'The harmonic and melodic structure of the work is clear and well defined; the themes used are for the most part of an appealing nature, but not always characteristic or individual.' Editor.

BÖHME, Oskar.

Trumpet-sextet, corn. à pist, 2 trpt, bass trpt (or althorn), tromb (or tenor horn), bass tuba (or baritone), e flat mi, op. 30. Eug. Böhme.

BÖHNER, Johann Ludwig, 1787–1860, German organist and composer.

An amusing account of his eccentricities is to be found in *Grove*. For list of works see *Fétis*.

†**BOHNKE, Emil**, b. 1888, Polish composer.

Quartet, str, c mi	op. 1	Simrock, 1923.
Trio, pf, v, vc	,, 5	,, 1920.
Sonata, pf, vc, f mi	,, 7	,,

Bohnke was viola in the Bandler Quartet and Adolf Busch Quartet (1919–20). His music, which is exceedingly clever, and shows modern tendencies, is inclined to be derivative.

BOHRER. A family of Mannheim musicians. The chief members were Anton (1783–1852), violinist, and his brother Maximilian (1785–1867), 'cellist. The brothers toured together. Fétis gives an interesting account of their adventures in Russia. In 1827 they visited Paris, where they gave chamber concerts, playing, with Urhan (viola) and Tilmant, the late Beethoven quartets. The performances were notable for the introduction of these quartets to the Parisian public. Both brothers were composers, and sometimes collaborated, Anton being the abler of the two, though less accomplished as executant. *Fétis* says that in his compositions for 'cello, Max was helped by Anton, and that they played together duets for violin and 'cello.

ANTON's works include:

Trio, pf, v, vc, E	op. 39	Schott.
,, ,, ,, ,,	,, 47	Alisty (extinct) (Darmstadt).

For other works see *Fétis*.

Schumann (*Gesammelte Schriften*) writes upon Bohrer's trio, op. 47, one of his characteristic recensions. He thinks it would be 'certainly effective played by a Bohrer Trio party, the string parts being treated in a practical, instrumental style, but the piano, what a hodge-podge! enough to spoil any fingers brave enough to tackle it'; and of the harmonies, Schumann writes, 'they make one's very ears tingle'. One does not wonder, then, that since the demise of the publishing firm, Alisty, no more has been heard of the trio, op. 47.

Fétis mentions other chamber works by Bohrer. EDITOR.

BOIELDIEU, ADRIEN LOUIS VICTOR, 1815–1883, French composer.

Trio, pf, v, vc, D	op. 5	Senart.

Son of François Adrien Boieldieu, the opera composer (1775–1834).

BOISDEFFRE, CHARLES HENRI RENÉ DE, 1838–1906, French composer.

Sextet, pf, fl, ob, cl, fag, horn, cb	op. 49	Hamelle.	
Quintet, pf, 2 v, vla, vc, d mi	,, 11	,,	1883.
Quintet (sextet), pf, str, wind, cb ad lib. (or pf, 2 v, vla, vc), B flat	,, 43	,,	
Quintet (sextet), pf, str, wind, cb ad lib. (or pf, 2 v, vla, vc), a mi	,, 81	,,	1900.
Quintet, pf, v, vla, vc, cb, D	,, 25	,,	1890.
Quartet, pf, v, vla, vc, g mi	,, 13	,,	
Trio, pf, v, vc, E flat	,, 10	Heugel,	1882.
Trio, pf, v, vc, g mi	,, 32	,,	,,
Trio-suite, pf, v, vc, D	,, 83	Hamelle.	
Trio-serenade, pf, fl, v	,, 85	,,	
Sonata, pf, v, e mi	,, 50	,,	
Sonata, pf, v, G	,, 67	,,	
Suite poètique, pf, v	,, 19	,,	
Suite romantique, pf, v	,, 24	,,	
Suite orientale, pf, v (also pf, vc)	,, 42	,,	1904.
Suite, pf, vc	,, 56	,,	
Suite, pf, vc, F	,, 63	,,	
Sonata, pf, cl (also pf, v), A	,, 13	,,	1875.

Boisdeffre was especially attracted towards chamber music, which forms the most important part of his total output.

The 2nd trio, which won the prize of the Société des Compositeurs de Musique in 1884, is in four movements: (*a*) prelude, andante maestoso, the first theme of which is not unlike that of the andante of Saint-Saëns's trio in F; (*b*) scherzo, vivace e leggiero, which recalls the G minor quartet of Castillon; (*c*) andante, grandiloquent in style, especially in its conclusion; (*d*) finale, allegro energico, in rondo form. The principal subject ('refrain')[1] in triplets is abrupt and full of energy, the second ('le thème du couplet')[1] being characterized by its simple charm and easy grace. It does not appear that Boisdeffre shows any further development in works later than this trio. His second sextet (op. 81), very loosely written, shows a great poverty of ideas. The same observation applies to the second quartet (op. 91), with the exception of the andante, which has more inspiration.

Boisdeffre's music, taken as a whole, is well written for the instruments, and easy to play, but he has broken no fresh ground.

ADOLPHE PIRIOU.

[Boisdeffre's piano quartet (op. 13) was played at South Place, when traces of the influence of Gounod in the opening movement, and some clever cyclic treatment of leading themes in the finale, were noticed. EDITOR.]

†BÖLSCHE, FRANZ, b. 1869, German composer and teacher of theory.

2nd quartet, str, c mi	op. 27	Simrock, 1904.
Trio, pf, v, vc, D	,, 12	Buselmeier, 1895.

Bölsche's first quartet is unpublished. The second, which comes under Brahms's influence, may be recommended for home playing.

†BONAVIA, FERRUCCIO, b. Trieste, 1877, musical critic.

Originally a violinist by profession, he is now a writer on musical subjects on the staff of the *Daily Telegraph*, and is especially competent to write upon chamber music, having himself composed a quartet and octet (MS.), played under Brodsky at Manchester and elsewhere.

EDITOR.

†BONAWITZ, JOHANN HEINRICH, b. 1839, German pianist.

Quintet, pf, 2v, vla, vc, g mi	op. 42	Simrock, 1886.
Trio, pf, v, vc, c mi	,, 37	J. Schuberth & Co., 1872.
Sonata, pf, v, a mi	,, 40	B. & H., 1868.

Bonawitz's chamber works have been played frequently in London, chiefly at his own concerts, but are unknown to the present generation of concert-goers.

[1] See Foreword, art. BEETHOVEN.

BONN: ITS BEETHOVEN HOUSE AND CHAMBER MUSIC FESTIVALS.

That the birthplaces of great artists and the scenes of their labours are preserved to posterity is due partly to an instinct of veneration and partly to professorial shrewdness. These dumb traces of their lives and strivings are conducive to meditation, and not only have places connected with the masters of poetry and art been saved, but, in some cases, also those associated with great musicians. In Eisenach the house where Bach was born is still standing; in Salzburg the city's musical life centres in Mozart's birthplace; and Bonn has its Beethoven House.

Those who are now able to visit Beethoven's house in Bonn, and conjure up visions of electoral court life in a bygone age and of the artistic activities of the eighteenth century, owe this privilege mainly to the self-sacrificing devotion and enthusiasm of certain music-loving circles, who, in the late 'eighties of the last century, gained possession of this notable house, and gradually made it what it is. It was felt, quite rightly, that it must neither be left to fall into ruins, nor be converted into a music hall of dubious character. It was no easy matter to clear away the structural additions and alterations of a later date, prop up the tumble-down portions, and restore the building in its original form. Passing through the front into the garden to-day, we find ourselves before the little house at the back, in the garret of which was born the great son of Johann van Beethoven, a musician of the electoral court. To modern eyes these rooms—and equally those of other small court officials of the time—appear incredibly cramped and primitive. The museum is installed both in this interior and in the front house connected with it, and can hold its own in some respects with the rich Berlin and Vienna collections, thanks to a succession of gifts and purchases.

The collections in the museum consist chiefly of objects used by Beethoven and his family, numerous pictures, the Graff grand piano and the four old stringed instruments, given to Beethoven by Prince Lichnowsky, which are occasionally played upon even now on festive occasions. Among the most valuable exhibits is the fine array of manuscripts; these include a number of sketch-books with notes for the *Missa Solennis*, the Seventh Symphony, some chamber works, and the originals of several important compositions. In addition to the musical manuscripts, there is a quantity of notes and letters in Beethoven's handwriting, among them some of the greatest importance. The large number of manuscripts available presents a clear idea of the composer's penmanship and mode of expression, even to those who are not Beethoven experts.

The Beethoven House Society set itself wider aims than the securing and rebuilding of the birthplace and the founding and developing of the collections; honour was to be done to Beethoven's memory by offering prizes for chamber music, assisting talented young musicians by grants and allowances, and aiding artistic enterprise. A particular point was made of establishing chamber music festivals from time to time, which should preserve the perfect tradition of Beethoven's art, and, in general, infuse new life into our musical undertakings; these festivals—extending from 1890 to the present day—have, in fact, fulfilled an artistic mission, and have played a considerable part in establishing chamber music as an important feature in the modern concert world. For a long time Joseph Joachim was the driving power and the soul of these festivals. To the music lover and—still less—to the professional musician, the arrangement of the programmes, the kind of music offered, and particularly the strangely selected historical concert programmes, could not be always acceptable; apart from this, however, all devotees of instrumental music must have been filled with gratitude by the performance at these festivals of such an array of the finest and most outstanding creations of our eighteenth and nineteenth-century masters. Beethoven's music rightly filled the central place, while that of Brahms received special consideration. The works of Mozart, Haydn, Schubert, and Schumann were of course not left out, but modern composers were also given their opportunity. Between the chamber music items, piano solos and songs were occasionally heard. The *élite* of quartet and other musical societies were pressed into service. In the arrangement of future chamber music festivals the committee have anything but easy tasks to face.

The idea of these festivals at Bonn originated with responsible members of the Beethoven House Society, and did not at first meet with the response expected. It was only gradually that it became known and won the approval now universally bestowed upon it, at home and abroad. All chamber music festivals in German cities are really formed on the Bonn model; and the wide popularity which they enjoy is undoubtedly inspired and fostered by the Bonn chamber music propaganda. From the first of the festivals, in May 1890, to the present time, it has been a standing principle to arrange a series of chamber concerts on several days in succession. Thus the first festival had this programme:

First Day.

1. Quintet C major, op. 29.
2. Violin sonata, G major, op. 96.
3. Quartet E flat major, op. 74.
4. Piano trio, B flat, op. 97.

Second Day.

1. Quartet C minor, op. 18, no. 4.
2. Fifteen variations with a fugue, E flat major, op. 35.

3. Piano trio, D major, op. 70.
4. Quartet C sharp minor, op. 131.

Third Day.

1. Quintet for piano and wind, op. 16.
2. *Adelaide*, by Matthisson, B flat major, op. 46.
3. Violin sonata (Kreutzer), op. 47.
4. Three songs with piano accompaniment.

Fourth Day.

1. Quartet F major, op. 59, no. 1.
2. Quartet F minor, op. 95.
3. Quartet B flat major, op. 130.

Fifth Day.

1. Sonata for piano, B flat, op. 106.
2. *To the absent loved one* (*An die ferne Geliebte*), op. 98.
3. 'Cello sonata, A major, op. 69.
4. Scottish songs with accompaniment for piano, violin, and 'cello (from op. 108).
5. Septet, op. 20.

The artists were: the Joachim Quartet, Heinrich Barth (Berlin), J. Buths (Düsseldorf), Anna Falk-Mehlig (Antwerp), Traugott Gentzsch (Leipzig), Adolf Gütter (Leipzig), F. Gumbert (Leipzig), R. Heckmann (Cologne), H. Heermann (Frankfort o/M.), G. Kinke (Leipzig), G. Holländer (Cologne), Jensen (Cologne), J. Kwast (Frankfort o/M.), Litzinger (Düsseldorf), C. Mayer (Cologne), H. Petri (Dresden), A. Piatti (London), C. Reinecke (Leipzig), A Schröder (Leipzig), I. Seiss (Cologne), Hermine Spies (Wiesbaden), F. Wolschke (Cologne).

Both here and at the second chamber music festival (May 1893) the programme was devoted exclusively to Beethoven, but at the third (May 1897) room was made for Brahms, who had recently died. At the fourth festival (May 1899) Sebastian Bach and Schubert shared the honours with Beethoven; at the fifth (May 1901), Mozart, Haydn, and Schumann. And so the cult of Beethoven's chamber music and of the classical, romantic, and modern masters has been continued till the present day, the old-established quartet societies of recognized repute being reinforced by others, younger and of rising fame, such as the Klingler, Rosé, Leipzig, and Busch Quartets.

In connexion with the festivals, special programme books containing literary contributions and facsimiles were issued, and—more recently—scientific musical publications which aimed at assisting Beethoven research. The audience, which invariably fills the Beethoven Hall to overflowing, arrives in festive and exalted mood, and, after being thrilled by the works of the great masters, is able to find joy and harmony in the lovely German Rhineland country around. LUDWIG SCHIEDERMAIR.

†BONNER, EUGENE, contemporary American composer.

Flutes.—Four songs, med. voice, fl, cl, fag, harp (or pf), op. 10		Chester.
Quartet, str		Senart.
Suite sicilienne, pf, v		,,

The four numbers of *Flutes* are entitled: 1. *La Chanson du Porc-épic*. 2. *La Complainte de Monsieur Benoît*. 3. *Chameaux*. 4. *Paysage de Neige*. In this work Eugene Bonner reveals himself as a humorist who has caught to perfection the note of the peculiarly dry quality of Franc-Nohan's amusing nonsense verses. The songs have a certain mock-solemnity that imparts to them the character of parodistic satire.

†BONPORTI, FRANCESCO ANTONIO, *c.* 1660–after 1721.

Interesting, as being one of the earliest instrumental composers of importance. He was an amateur.

For modern republications see *Altmann*.
For orig. publications see *Fétis*.

BOOM, JOHANNES VAN, 1807–1872, Dutch composer.

Quartet, pf, v, vla, vc, E	op. 6	B. & H., 1843.
Trio, pf, v, vc, E	,, 14	J. Schuberth & Co., 1847.

Boom was one of the most prolific writers of chamber music in the Netherlands during the nineteenth century. His compositions were above the average of his own countrymen at that time, and several MS. quartets and trios retained their place in the repertory until after his death. HERBERT ANTCLIFFE.

†BOORN-COCLET, HENRIETTE VAN DEN, b. 1866, Belgian composer.

Sonata, pf, v, d mi	B. & H. (Brussels).

This sonata, an interesting example of woman's work, won a prize in Paris in 1907.

BORCHMAN, ALEXANDER ADOLPHOVITCH, b. 1872, Russian composer.

Quartet, str, C	op. 3	J. H. Zimmermann.

Borchman, who was originally trained for the medical profession, studied between 1904 and 1907 under Glière and Gretchaninov. His quartet, which shows traces of the influence of the first-named of his teachers, Reinhold Glière, is a captivating work, and has but one drawback, its extreme length. However, the tema con variazioni is complete in itself, and may be recommended for performance separately. Many concessions are made in this, as in most Russian music, to popular taste, especially in the case of the variation in waltz rhythm; but only a fine musician could have written the fugal variation (molto sostenuto). Fugues are an accepted form of scholastic objective art, but neither adjective applies to this fugue, in which Borchman conserves the spirit of romanticism so characteristic of the whole work. His flair for effect may be sneered at by some, but I, for one, feel grateful to a composer so accomplished technically, who deliberately sets out to please, and succeeds so admirably. EDITOR.

BORDES, CHARLES, 1863–1909, French composer.

Suite Basque, fl, 2 v, vla, vc, D — op. 6 — Borneman (Paris), 1901.

Although Charles Bordes wrote but a single chamber work—the *Suite Basque* for flute, two violins, viola, and 'cello—it is so original, both in its thematic material and in the variety and unusual nature of its rhythms, that some notice of it is necessary in any history of chamber music.

Even before he had had the chance of hearing Basque music, Bordes had been greatly struck with its peculiar characteristics, and from 1885 onwards he gave himself eagerly to the study of the folk-songs of the country, in the books of Francisque Michel, Vinson, and, above all, in Salaberry's collection of song. The delightful song *Charinoak Koislan* (The Caged Bird) was continually on his lips, and later provided him with one of the principal themes of the *Suite Basque*. This, in its original form, was written for flute, violin, two violas, and 'cello, during 1886 and 1887, at the same time as his *Rhapsodie Basque* for piano and orchestra.

In 1889 Bordes was sent by the Ministry of Public Instruction to the Basque country, in order to study its music and its popular songs. Now, for the first time, he was to make the acquaintance both of the beautiful scenery of this corner of France and of the high-spirited race which lives there.

As on many other occasions in his life—for instance, when he formed the Association des Chanteurs de Saint-Gervais, or again, when he founded the Schola Cantorum—Bordes saw intuitively the right thing to do at the exact moment when it needed to be done. He had already divined and penetrated the Basque spirit before he had studied it on the spot, and had seen in imagination, so to speak, the natural 'atmosphere' peculiar to this race apart—and this merely from the study of a few themes and popular rhymes—and he was not mistaken.

When his mission was ended, in 1890, he rearranged his *Suite Basque*, and re-wrote it completely, this time for the usual quartet of strings, with flute. In this final version the poetic feeling and the musical ideas combine with the peculiar rhythms of the *Zortzico* and the *Pordon-dantza* to produce a work entirely original and full of suggestiveness; the whole of the Euskaleria is revealed to us in these four movements, one of which especially, the *Paysage* (Landscape), is a little masterpiece of sentiment and expression.

Following a prelude, in which two folk-song themes (the second of which—

Ex. 1.

is to be used as a cyclic theme) appear alternately, an intermezzo starts off, in scherzo form. The first part of this affects the 5/4 rhythm beloved of the Basques, which is very frequent in the dances named *Zortzico*. A second theme—an original one this time—serves as a trio to the scherzo.

The third movement is the *Paysage* already mentioned. This reverie, with its deep poetic feeling, conjures up visions of the vast solitudes of the Pyrenees, solitudes broken in upon now and again by the call of a shepherd, afar off—this call being represented by the cyclic theme of the prelude.

In order, so to speak, to isolate this movement—so different from the dances of which the rest of the work is composed—Bordes chose a key somewhat remote—B major, whose relationship to the principal key is confined to a single note—F sharp. The construction of this *Paysage* is also quite unusual. It is a Lied of considerable length, and is in five sections, the even-numbered sections being formed—the second from the cyclic theme of the prelude, the fourth from a song of the sweeping wind, which enters boldly in the midst of the development of the first two themes of the movement.

The finale is, again, a characteristic dance—*pordon-dantza*—which has a 5/8 rhythm, thus: 𝅘𝅥𝅮 𝅘𝅥 𝅘𝅥. It is in rondo form,[1] the 'refrains' becoming more and more rapid. In the last 'couplet' the two themes of the prelude reappear as a reminiscence, in B major, the key of the vast mountain spaces; they are then caught up as in a whirlwind by the final refrain.

An analysis of the work is appended:

I. Prelude (andante), in D, introducing two main themes, the second being the cyclic theme.

II. Intermezzo—founded on the national dance the *Zortzico*. Scherzo with trio. In D.

III. *Paysage*. Three original themes are introduced, and combined with the cyclic theme of the prelude. In B. In Lied form, and in five sections.

Ex. 2.

IV. Movement in rondo form (5/8); the cyclic theme takes an important part in

[1] The French rondo. See Foreword to art. BEETHOVEN.

the development, and reference is made to the key and the mood of the *Paysage*. The movement constantly quickens to a conclusion, molto vivace 2/4.

The *Suite Basque*, which Bordes himself numbers op. 6, was performed for the first time, and in its original form, at the concert of the Société Nationale de Musique on 21 January, 1888, the performers being: MM. Lafleurance (flute), Rémy, van Waefelghem, A. Parent, and Delsart. The first performance in its final form took place at the Société Nationale's concert of 10 January 1891, with MM. Hennebains (flute), Heymann, Gibier, Balbreck, and Liégeois.

This composition, the work of a highly gifted artist, is unique in the literature of chamber music, and deserves to be known for its musical charm; and it is for this reason that we are anxious that it should be noticed in the present work.

VINCENT D'INDY.

BORGORAN, (1) ANDREI V., (2) ION V., *vide* ROUMANIAN COMPOSERS.

BORGSTRÖM, HJALMAR, 1864–1925, Norwegian violinist, pupil of Svendsen.

Quintet, pf, 2 v, vla, vc, F	op. 31	Norsk. Musikförlag, 1922.

Other works are in MS.

Borgström's quintet is in three movements. The opening allegro moderato contains a well-marked theme with an effective development and splendid crescendo effects. The theme of the adagio is tuneful, and shows an interesting development. The finale, allegro, is in kinship with Norwegian musical feeling; here the themes of the other movements are re-introduced, whilst the whole development bears witness to great mastery of counterpoint.

M. M. ULFRSTAD.

†BORNE, FERNAND LE, b. 1862, Belgian composer, pupil of Franck and Saint-Saëns.

Quartet, str, c mi	op. 23	Rouart (Gregh), *c.* 1896.
Trio, pf, v, vc, d mi	,, 32	Rouart, *c.* 1900.
Sonata, pf, v	,, 28	Rouart (Gregh).
,, ,, ,, E	,, 29	Hamelle, 1911.
,, pf, vc, A	,, 41	,, 1899.

Le Borne, who settled in France, won the Prix Chartier in 1901.

†BORODIN, ALEXANDER PORPHYRIEVITCH, 1834–1887, Russian composer.

Quartet (on a theme of Beethoven), str, A	Belaiev, 1884	N.Ed., 1894.
Quartet, str, D	,, 1888	,, ,,
Quartet, str (on name B-la-f) (with Rimsky-Korsakov, Liadov, and Glazounov)	,, 1895	

See also *Les Vendredis*.

Borodin, despite the small number of his works, occupies a place of honour among nineteenth-century Russian masters of the national school. As Sir Henry Hadow wrote (*Edinburgh Review*, Oct. 1906): 'No musician has ever claimed immortality with so slender an offering—yet if there be, indeed, immortalities in music, his claim is incontestable.'

This sentence may well be recorded by way of introduction to a survey of his chamber music, which consists of no more than two string quartets, a couple of pieces in the collective works, and a very few early, unpublished works of various descriptions. But these two quartets are among the very finest things in Russian music, and, indeed, in all modern music.

Borodin was always greatly attracted by chamber music. In his childhood he learnt to play the flute and the piano. He and a friend of his (named Shtchiglev) started teaching themselves to play the violin and 'cello. The first fruits of these early studies were a concerto for flute and piano, and a trio for two violins and 'cello, the latter founded on motifs from Meyerbeer's opera *Robert le Diable*. Both these works were written in 1847, when the boy was only thirteen years of age, at a time when he had received no instruction whatever in the technique of composition. They have not been preserved.

Three years later, Shtchiglev, Borodin (who had become a tolerably proficient 'cellist), and an amateur violinist friend of theirs clubbed together to secure the services of a professional viola player, and thus constituted a String Quartet. In order to attend practice meetings, Borodin had to trudge ten miles with his 'cello, not being able to afford cab-fares. Neither fatigue nor bad weather ever discouraged him. And it is recorded in Braudo's biography (Petrograd, 1922) that on one occasion the players, in their enthusiasm, kept on practising 'for twenty-four hours on end'.

Another of Borodin's friends used to give chamber concerts at his home. It was there that Borodin became acquainted with works by Spohr, Gade, Boccherini, Onslow, and Goebel. In 1855 he wrote a trio for two violins and 'cello on the motif of an old Russian song. This is the earliest extant example of his chamber music. The MS. of it was found, together with that of a piano quintet composed in 1862—at the time when he started work on his beautiful first symphony—among the papers left by the publisher Belaiev. This trio is said to have been written very much under the influence of Glinka.

Of the quintet Braudo writes:

'It is significant enough for its time, considering that in 1862 Borodin was unacquainted with Schumann's music and with the works of his own Russian contemporaries (the members of Balakirev's circle). It shows imagination and boldness, coupled with an obvious lack of technical proficiency.

Here and there, Borodin's true individuality comes to light; the germs of *Igor* are unmistakably to be found lurking within the Glinka-Mendelssohn amalgam which predominates in this early attempt.'

In 1860, during a stay at Heidelberg, Borodin wrote a string sextet which was publicly performed there. The MS., which he presented to one of the Heidelberg musicians, is lost. Later, he described the work as 'very Mendelssohnian in character, and written to please the Germans'.

The first string quartet was composed in 1877–78; but he had started sketching it as early as 1875—'to the great dismay of Moussorgsky and Stassov', he wrote at the time to one of his friends. The second was composed in 1880.

The First String Quartet bears the inscription 'angeregt durch ein Thema von Beethoven', which means either 'called up' or 'animated' (but not exactly 'inspired') by a theme of Beethoven. The theme in question occurs in the finale of the B flat quartet, op. 130:

Ex. 1.

it gave birth to the first subject of the first movement of Borodin's quartet (Ex. 3 below), and by a further derivation to one of the motifs used in the andante (Ex. 9), and again as part of the first subject of the finale (Ex. 13). To investigate how far the actual plan and spiritual content of Borodin's quartet were really influenced by Beethoven's op. 130 would greatly overstep the bounds of this article. Let it be pointed out, however, that the work is very different in spirit and quality from any instrumental music produced in Russia during the early 'eighties; it shows a closer affinity with classical tradition, and a rare introspective power. Its glowing eloquence, entirely free from sentimentality and mere formalism, is as remarkable as the sense of beauty and fitness revealed by the quality of the instrumental writing. Thomas Dunhill, dealing with this work in his *Chamber Music, a Treatise for Students*, rightly quotes certain passages of it as signal examples 'of the great sonority and passionate sweep of sound that a fine craftsman can obtain from slender means ... pure quartet music, obviously conceived for the medium in which it is written, resourceful and fanciful, and repaying careful analysis'. Essentially original, essentially 'Russian' in character, this masterpiece of Borodin is in the direct line of the best and purest tradition.

The first movement (moderato-allegro) has an introduction founded on the following motif:

Ex. 2.

The first subject of the allegro is:

Ex. 3.

The treatment is contrapuntal, and this is the case almost throughout the work.

The bridge passage introduced at [A], and perhaps derived from the second bar of the first subject, is:

Ex. 4.

The second subject [B] is:

Ex. 5.

The working-out of these various materials is carried out with remarkable ingenuity and thoroughness. After a reappearance of the bridge, heralding the modulation, we have, in A flat major, both subjects and the bridge in close contact (first subject lines 1 and 2 in first violin, bridge l. 3 in second violin, first subject modified in the 'cello, second subject l. 4 in first violin and viola). At [D] a modified form of the first subject is given out fugato, in anticipation of a similar fine effect in the andante. This leads up to a climax, after which, at [F], the theme of the introduction is brought back over the bridge (Ex. 6). This affords a typical illustration of a quality peculiar to Borodin—the almost incredible simplicity, ease, and sense of fitness with which he combines motifs that do not seem, rhythmically or

Ex. 6.

harmonically, conceived with a view to association, nor even particularly suited for it.

With the reappearance of the second subject, the style changes temporarily to a pure accompanied cantabile—one might say, by way of an anticipation of a similar effect in the lovely fairy-like trio of the scherzo. But soon Borodin reverts to the polyphonic method. The bridge passage plays an important part in the recapitulation, in the course of which an entirely new motif appears in conjunction with the second theme,

Ex. 7.

constituting the first intrusion in this quartet of a tune directly suggestive of pure Russian musical lore (and, be it noted, reminiscent of a dance tune in Glinka's opera *Russlan and Liudmila*).

The first subject of the andante con moto is:

Ex. 8.

—lovely music, in which Borodin is seen at his very best, and which, compared with the music written by Debussy and Ravel in their most dreamy, meditative moods (e.g. with the slow movements in their string quartets), clearly shows how strong was Borodin's influence on both of them.

An impassioned phrase in triplets on the first violin heralds the second (or rather, the incidental) subject (Ex. 9). Among the accompanying patterns, the figure used in the following fugato occurs for the first time in the second

Ex. 9.

violin part (p. 23 of the miniature score, line 4, last two bars).

Immediately afterwards, the subject of the central fugato—

Ex. 10.

is introduced. At the close of the fugato, the first violin again gives out the impassioned phrase in triplets, which plays a comparatively important part in the final section—where the figure

Ex. 11.

shows the relation between that phrase and the first subject. The incidental subject is hardly alluded to in this final section.

In the scherzo, the rhythm and speed established with the appearance of the main subject

Ex. 12.

persist throughout the movement, producing a sense of pure exhilaration. The tissue is of the utmost delicacy, and Borodin's ingenuity in varying it without swerving from the rhythmic scheme is surprising. The trio, with its poetic combinations of undulating figuration and harmonics, can be described only as a dream of fairyland, as contemplative as the scherzo is elfin and whimsical.

The finale (andante; allegro risoluto) has a short introduction built on a theme (derived from the first subject of the first movement, and encountered in the second movement) which is part of the first subject of the following allegro risoluto, in which it is announced by the viola.

Ex. 13.

The motif in the first violin is strongly suggestive of a Russian dance tune.

A short bridge, which seems to be a mere slackening echo of this dance-rhythm,

Ex. 14.

introduces the second subject,

Ex. 15.

whose affinities with the second subject in the first movement are obvious. This movement, in sonata form, is as substantial and original as the foregoing three, and its contrapuntal treatment is equally admirable.

SECOND QUARTET. As pointed out by Braudo, this quartet is more accessible than the first, and therefore more popular, although the first gives a deeper insight into Borodin's musical mind. It is simple in structure, intimate in tone, and accordingly requires less comment than its predecessor.

The first subject of the first movement, allegro moderato,

Ex. 16.

Allegro moderato. 𝅗𝅥 = 84.

is started on the 'cello and continued by the first violin. One of its motifs—

Ex. 17.

contains in germ the short bridge.

Ex. 18.

The second subject is:

Ex. 19.

The working-out is free from complications. One noteworthy point is that in the recapitulation this second subject finally reappears, not in the principal key, but in D minor, before the principal key is definitely re-established.

The scherzo has two subjects: the first breezy and full of bustle (Ex. 20), the second sensuous and lyrical (Ex. 21), recalling a theme in the *Polovtsian Dances* (and also the Flower Maidens in *Parsifal*—with which Borodin was certainly not acquainted at the time of writing this quartet). There is no trio.

Ex. 20.

Allegro. 𝅗𝅥 = 80.

Ex. 21.

Ex. 22.

The third movement (notturno) is a tuneful, expressive cantilena, lyrical in mood throughout, and very delightful.

The finale (andante, vivace) is in rondo form. The main subject (or refrain) is Ex. 22. The same materials are used at the beginning of the vivace, and there is a sufficient variety of interest in the episodes. As a whole, however, this movement does not altogether maintain the exceptionally high standard of invention and execution which characterizes the remainder of Borodin's chamber works.

M. D. Calvocoressi.

[Borodin's was an absorbingly interesting personality. He was a crowning example of the successful merging of contrasting forces, at once amateur and artist, the composer of chamber music pleasing alike to layman and musician, and of the kind that the world sighs for and seldom gets. Unfortunately, he wrote all too little. Deeply versed in the technique of his art, a practised 'cellist, with a passionate love for chamber music, and a really accomplished contrapuntist, his writing was as spontaneous as Schubert's, and informed with a charm so magical that, on the strength of two quartets conceived in purest lyrical vein, he was able, as Sir Henry Hadow puts it, to 'claim immortality' in the world of chamber music.

How to account for this? The learned musician who tries to do so will certainly fail. I who am not learned find that the source of his power lies mainly in the lovely harmonic idiom which was natural to him, and which has haunted Russian music ever since, and has not been without influence on French music. There is nothing for it but to surrender oneself to the sheer enjoyment of music written by a composer of whom Mr. Abraham, in his excellent book (*v.* Bibliography), speaks as the 'supreme justification of the amateur in music'.

Although it is outside the province of this Cyclopedia to deal with biography, I cannot refrain from pointing out that the same writer, dealing with Borodin's medical and sociological work, shows incidentally that his nature as man was no less idealistic than his nature as artist, and that the music which streamed so spontaneously from his pen was absolutely the expression of himself. He was one of the rare instances of a man equally celebrated in two very different spheres. He was an eminent scientist, held the post of professor of chemistry at the Academy of Medicine in Petrograd, and served both art and science with equal devotion.

On his monument at Moscow his achievements are recorded; those of the musician on one side, and those of the scientist on the other.

EDITOR.]

BÖRRESEN, Hakon, b. 1876, Danish composer, pupil of Svendsen.

Sextet, str, G	op. 5	B. & H., 1903.
Quartet, str, e mi	,, 20	Hansen, 1915.

Börresen's sextet has been performed at South Place.

†BOSSI, (1) Marco Enrico, b. 1861, Italian composer and organist.

Trio, pf, v, vc, d mi	op. 107	Peters, 1896 & 1918.
Trio sinfonico, pf, v, vc, D	,, 123	Rieter-Biedermann; Peters, 1901 & 1918.
Sonata, pf, v, e mi	,, 82	Composed 1892. B. & H., 1893.
Sonata, pf, v, C	,, 117	Kistner, 1899.
Four pieces in form of a suite, pf, v	,, 99	B. & H., 1895.

Bossi's piano works, with their Schumannesque poetic titles, belong to the neo-romantic school; his violin sonatas, however, follow classical models, though not too rigidly.

His temperament and the somewhat eclectic nature of his musical figurations impelled him towards dramatic or lyrical types of theme, which accounts for the freedom in his treatment of pre-established forms.

The Sonata in E minor shows from the exposition of the first subject, allegro con energia,

Ex. 1.

an intensely dramatic feeling, emphasized by the rhythm of the piano part. The second subject, obscure in harmonic colour, is in C minor instead of the more usual G major (Ex. 2).

Here the following lines, written by Verdi to Bossi, may well be quoted:

'I have admired your work with Boïto (who was here), especially the beginning of the first movement, a most beautiful and powerful phrase; and if I said that the composition in general appears to me to be too much based on dissonance, you might answer: "Why not? dissonance and consonance are both essential elements in music; I give the preference to the former." And you would be right. On the other hand, why should I be wrong?'

Ex. 2.

The second movement, andante sostenuto con vaghezza, combines the andante and the scherzo into one movement, which is entitled a *canzone*. The simplicity of the melodic opening in thirds somehow gives this movement a popular character, well in keeping with the central section.

Ex. 3.

The construction of the third and final movement diverges from the traditional binary form. It is based on a single theme,

Ex. 4.

from which Bossi develops contrasting periods as well as ingenious and brilliant accompaniment figures for the piano, over which the violin unfolds rapid bravura passages. Thus the sonata towards the close deviates somewhat from its general austerity.

THE SECOND SONATA, written soon after the first despite its opus number 117, shows a noteworthy progress in plasticity of ideas and harmonic simplification. The influence of Brahms is traceable here and there (especially in the opening of the first movement), and the desire for simplicity and conciseness is obvious. This, however, does not prevent the use of certain graceful but rather superficial devices, of which the second subject (in G major) may serve as typical.

Ex. 5.

The second movement (a scherzo and trio) is rich in harmonic episodes, elaborated upon the rhythmic pattern of the opening.

Ex. 6.

In spite of its excessive length, this scherzo must be counted among Bossi's most ingenious and engaging contributions to chamber music. The predominant feature in the following adagio is a broad and elegiac phrase. The fourth movement, allegro con fuoco, is rather dry, but there is an interesting fugal development at the end.

THE FIRST TRIO, in D minor, op. 107, is classical in structure; in style, however, it conforms rather to the neo-romantic school, but the spirit of the composition appears to be imbued with a greater sense of colour and lyric sentiment. The first movement (allegro moderato) is almost wholly constructed on its initial theme.

Ex. 7.

The adoption of melodic repetition, as well as the similarity of figuration, recalls the first movement of Goldmark's suite for violin and piano. The second subject, a sort of cantabile, is similarly treated, variety being secured in both cases by harmonic changes. The title of the second movement, *Dialogo*, is fully justified by the treatment of the string parts, in which the respective melodic phrases answer each other, increasing the interest of the musical discussion, and giving free play to the composer's fancy without regard to academic formulae. After the entry of the 'cello,

Ex. 8.

the violin answers in F major:

Ex. 9.

the dialogue then becomes more concise, and the melodic line takes an almost melodramatic turn. A few bars of adagio quasi recitativo lead to the return of the initial phrase, which dies softly away. The scherzo is linked to the finale, though it might stand by itself, having its own development and a central section corresponding to the trio of a minuet. The brilliant staccato figuration of the scherzo contrasts with the festive entry of the finale in D major, built solely on the opening theme, and more lively than original.

THE SECOND TRIO, op. 123, bears the title of *Sinfonico*. The term is fully justified by the general character of the composition, the nature of the thematic material, an evident tendency towards dramatic expression, and the abandonment of the restraints of chamber music. The piano part is far more important than in the previous works, and the movements are longer than is usual with Bossi. If the disposition of the parts clearly shows the composer's intention to follow pre-established forms, it must also be noted how certain external embellishments of the musical ideas illustrate the orchestral tendencies of his music. The trio is elegiac in character, and its themes run the whole gamut, from the lyrical to the dramatic—at times even the melodramatic. The general character of the work is established at the opening of the first movement (moderato).

Ex. 10.

The second movement, adagio, funereal in character, with the sub-title *In Memoriam*, discloses no particular strength of invention. It is followed by a graceful *novelletta*, leading to a somewhat uninspired finale constructed on the same lines as most of Bossi's other finales.

In conclusion, it may be said that Bossi's chamber music should be regarded mainly as the outcome of a period when he was content to proceed on traditional lines, and as merely the harbinger of his later and more venturesome achievements, for his chamber music represents but a fraction of his total activities as a composer. GAETANO CESARI.

[Reverting to the letter addressed to Bossi by Verdi, I have recently taken part in the sonata to which he refers. It appears to me to be particularly smooth and free from harmonic eccentricities, typically Italian, in fact; but then the point of view in such matters has changed materially since 1893. EDITOR.]

His son (2) RENZO, b. 1883, is also a composer, and wrote a piano trio which he dedicated to his parents on the occasion of their silver wedding.

†BOTTESINI, GIOVANNI, 1822–1889, famous contrabassist.

Quintet, 2 v, vla, 2 vc	Ricordi.	
Quintet, 2 v, vla, vc, cb	,,	
Quartet, str, D	,,	1862.
(Basevi Prize, 1862.)		

Bottesini made a sensation in 1849 at Ella's Musical Union by playing the 'cello part in an Onslow quintet on his instrument, which was a small, three-stringed bass by Testore, of the type called basso da camera. The bow he used was made and held somewhat like that of the 'cello. His success was a 'succès de curiosité', and his example is not likely to be followed.

Although he gained the 'Basevi' prize in 1862 for his quartet, it cannot be said that his music soars above mediocrity. EDITOR.

BOUCHER, ALEX. JEAN, 1778–1861, French virtuoso violinist, associated in his youth with Boccherini as a quartet player.

An executant of remarkable talent and still greater eccentricity. Spohr, after hearing him play a Haydn quartet, wrote that 'he added so many ornaments that it was impossible to take any pleasure in his performances'.

Boucher was something of a charlatan. He had a noticeable facial likeness to the great Napoleon, on which he sometimes traded. Spohr remarked on this in his Autobiography. *Grove* gives an account of how he pretended that he was persecuted by certain Governments of the day on account of this resemblance, and quotes one of his concert advertisements to this effect. EDITOR.

†BOUCHER, M. LE.

Sonata, pf, v, b mi	Costallat, 1910.

†BOUGHTON, RUTLAND, b. 1878, English composer.

Trio (1 movt) (*Celtic Prelude*), pf, v, vc		Augener.
Sonata, pf, v, D	op. 49	Curwen, 1921.

Rutland Boughton has, in a sense, been singularly fortunate in the measure of speculation aroused by his two chamber works, owing to the well-deserved popularity of his work for the stage. It is to be feared, however, that he does not emerge wholly satisfactorily from the test. The *Celtic Prelude* is undoubtedly the better, although it would seem, with its one solitary movement, to be a less ambitious work than the sonata. The modal writing well reflects the title, while the structural scheme resolves itself mainly into a species of 'divisions on a ground' as viewed in two aspects, to which a bright little coda imparts a jovial finish.

In the violin sonata the composer finds the inspiration for its three movements in so many quotations from Nietzsche's *Also Sprach Zarathustra*. Though it is difficult to say how far the music reflects those portions of the philosophy which the composer has elected to illustrate, it is not beyond the power of a competent listener to discern a certain lack of musical distinction in the hearty optimism of the opening subject of the first movement.

In the face of a scheme so adventurous, one is surprised to encounter phrases of a Handelian character. Nor is the composer proof against rhythmical irregularities, for all his advocacy of the Nietzschean ideal of 'the perfect and rectangular', the complete quotation affixed to this movement being, in fact, 'Most honestly and purely the healthy body speaketh, the perfect and rectangular; it speaketh of the significance of Earth'.

The second subject of this movement provides a foil to the bustle of the first subject. The quotation to the ensuing movement is taken from that section of Nietzsche's book which treats 'Of Delights and Passions', and how these become transformed from evil into good. Here the composer's sympathies seem to find a more secure expression. From a beautiful yet grave melody, marked 'slow and severe', and modelled on the Æolian mode, there develop two episodes which, fragmentarily, are afterwards used in combination. In the course of this device the good eventually prevails over the evil, until, finally, the scheme is rounded off in dance fashion by a measure of quite Arcadian simplicity. It is at this point that the composer's ingenuity asserts itself to excellent purpose. By what would appear to be the simple expedient of a change of key and rhythm, both episodes are eventually shown divested of the last touch of malignity and reflecting only innocence and virtue.

The finale is based upon the following cryptic observation: 'I am the advocate of God in the presence of the devil. But he is the spirit of gravity. How could I, ye light ones, be an enemy unto divine dances? or unto the feet of girls with beautiful ankles?' Luckily, the musical equivalent gains in lucidity. 'Gravity' is well characterized in a fugato opening, and its counterpoise by a second subject given to the violin alone, and curiously reminiscent of the opening bars of the Kreutzer sonata. Thereupon follow some effective passages, bringing with them a convincing picture of the latter portion of Nietzsche's above-quoted protest. Structurally, the movement follows accepted lines, and as a whole the sonata shows a stronger feeling for colour than for texture, inasmuch as Boughton seems inclined at times to overlook the all-important factor of adjustment of balance between the instruments employed. ADOLPH MANN.

†BOULNOIS, JOSEPH, 1880–1918, French composer, killed in the war.

Trio, pf, v, vc, B	Senart, 1922.
Sonata, pf, vc, g mi	,, ,,

I gather from the *Gazette musicale et théâtrale* (Henri Collet) that this sonata was written at the front in 1917, and that it treats, curiously enough, in the initial movement, of the 'awakening of amorous sentiment'. To quote his words, 'à travers le scherzo (fuga) c'est l'évocation quelque peu dantesque d'un enfer grimaçant et railleur—il n'y a point d'amour sans souffrance. Enfin, l'allegro chante le triomphe du sentiment.' EDITOR.

BOUMANN, a family of musicians in Holland living chiefly in 's Hertogenbosch, four of whom formed a string Quartet which achieved a good reputation. The best known, who was also the one who as a composer was most devoted to chamber music, is LEONARDUS †CAROLUS, b. 1852. He has spent most of his life as a church organist and conductor of choirs; but besides works arising from these activities, he has found time to write a trio for piano, violin, and 'cello, three *Fantasiestukken* for violin and piano (crowned by the Nederlandsch Toonkunst Vereeniging), and a set of variations for string quartet (MS.). HERBERT ANTCLIFFE.

BOURGAULT-DUCOUDRAY, LOUIS ALBERT, 1840–1910, distinguished French musicologist.

Quartet, fl, v, vla, vc	Lemoine.

Made important researches in music which he put into practice in his works. *Dent* says his works deserve to be better known, and that he was a composer of high originality and genuine feeling.

BOURGES, MAURICE (JEAN MAURICE), 1812–1881, French composer and critic.

1st trio, pf, v, vc, a mi	Hamelle.
2nd trio, pf, v, vc, B flat	Durand, 1862.
1st sonata, pf, v, d mi	,, ,,
2nd sonata, pf, v, E flat	Hamelle.

BOUSQUET, FRANCIS, b. 1890, French composer, pupil of Gédalge and Widor, director of the Roubaix Conservatoire.

Quintet, pf, 2 v, vla, vc, d mi	Senart.

BOUSQUET, GEORGES, 1818–1854, French composer.

Quartet, str, G	Composed 1852	Durand.

Much praised by Fétis, who mentions unpublished works.

†BOWEN, York, b. 1884, English pianist.

Quartet (Carnegie Award), str, d mi	op. 41	S. & B.
Trio (Phantasie), pf, v, vc (or vla)	„ 24	Ascherberg.
Suite, pf, v, d mi	—	Schott, 1909.
1st sonata, pf, vla, c mi	—	„
2nd sonata, pf, vla, F	—	„
Sonata, pf, vc, A	„ 64	composed 1921, Schott.
Miniature suite, pf, fl	—	Chappell, 1907.

Widely known as a brilliant pianist and a composer with a rare aptitude for piano writing, York Bowen has contributed works of importance to the chamber music repertory. He has earned his chief distinction as a composer in connexion with music for the viola, his two sonatas being amongst the most striking works ever composed for that instrument. Like his friend Dale, Bowen was inspired to explore the possibilities of the viola by the magnificent playing of Lionel Tertis, with whom he has frequently been associated on the concert platform.

The First Viola Sonata opens in a reflective manner, but gradually gains in brilliance as it proceeds. The slow movement is noteworthy for grace and charm rather than emotional feeling, and the finale, which begins with a forcible introduction, has an almost rampageous main theme, and contains passages of considerable dramatic emphasis.

The Second Sonata boasts a slow movement which deals with deeper issues than any attempted in the first. The sombre main theme is finely conceived for the viola; there is passionate beauty, also, in the middle section. The finale, consisting for the most part of dance rhythms, is in light-hearted vein.

The String Quartet is another extremely well-wrought piece of music, planned on broad and classic lines. The first movement, which has a dignified main theme and a Schumannesque second section in good contrast, keeps all the instruments continuously active. The style is chordal rather than contrapuntal. The lay-out of the instrumentation is perhaps suggestive of a string orchestra rather than four solo strings, for there is considerable employment of the two violins in octaves with forcible chords for viola and 'cello. In the poco lento movement, which follows, there is a superior sense of texture, and much expressive solo writing for each instrument in turn. The finale is of a bustling character as regards its main material, and shows a sense of exuberant humour. There are touches of wistfulness here and there, and a poco sostenuto episode (which brings relief from the energy of the principal ideas) shows a ready skill in the use of unusual harmonic relationships, and yet contrives to retain a definite sense of tonality. As a whole, this is bright, optimistic quartet music, not soul-stirring nor strongly emotional, but within its limits one of the most clearly effective contributions to British string music of recent years.

The 'Cello Sonata was composed for Miss Beatrice Harrison, and is rhapsodical in character, though faithful to tradition in form. The finale has the sustained rhythmical impetus which Bowen always contrives to impart to his finales. The piano writing is massive, and bristles with difficulties of a modern pianistic kind. It is one of Bowen's most advanced chamber compositions, if not one of the most immediately attractive.

The two suites, for flute and piano and violin and piano respectively, are in a different genre from the works reviewed above. They are frankly 'salon music', and do not call for serious criticism as chamber works. The latter is undoubtedly the better of the two—since the days of Bach how few works of real distinction has the flute inspired!—but there is a tendency to 'sugary' harmonization here which places the music on a lower level, particularly in the *Barcarolle*, which is rather in the vein of Rubinstein, and, despite the modernity of the harmony, a little out of tune with present-day musical feeling.

York Bowen's chamber music is predominantly brilliant in style. He may be described as a romanticist with sympathies in the direction of impressionism. His themes are in the main direct and diatonic, but he succeeds in clothing his subject-matter in harmonies which give to the music the attributes of novelty and surprise. If these attributes are inclined to emphasize the mellifluous character of some of his ideas, which approach at times a somewhat sentimental type of expressiveness, his healthy, rhythmical vitality is a strong counterbalancing factor. Music so full of boyish high spirits can never be accounted dull, and Bowen has succeeded in retaining his youthful outlook in a very remarkable way. He is not unduly shy of obviousness. He is happily not afraid to be natural. But in all he has written he has shown a great respect for the dignity of clear outlines. Though fond of playful experiment in harmony, his very strong constructive sense has kept him from indulging in what is merely nebulous and meandering. In his flair for effect, and in his ability to juggle with his themes, he takes his place as a facile exponent of an essentially healthy and breezy phase in modern art. T. F. Dunhill.

[York Bowen performs *en amateur* on the horn, and has written a quintet (MS.) in which that instrument joins the string quartet. The combination is from the tonal point of view most satisfactory. Editor.]

BOYCE, William, 1710–1779.
Modern republications:

Trio-sonata, no. 3, pf, 2 v, vc (ad lib.), A (G. Jensen, *Klass. V-Musik* 32), Augener; Schott, 1911.

Trio-sonata, no. 7, pf, 2 v, vc (ad lib.), d mi (A. Moffat, *Old Engl. V-Music* 8), Novello, 1909.

Trio-sonata, no. 11, pf, 2v, vc (ad lib.), c mi (A. Moffat, *Trio-Sonaten* 24), Simrock, 1913.

The above works are taken from *Twelve Sonatas for Two Violins with a Bass for the Violoncello or Harpsicord* [sic], *by William Boyce, Composer to His Majesty, London: Printed for the Author and sold by I. Walsh.* MDCCXLVII. The movements of the three republished works are:

No. 3. Largo, fuga, adagio, minuetto.
No. 7. Andante, fuga, adagio, allegro.
No. 11. Adagio, fuga, affettuoso, allegro.

The most interesting of the twelve is the last, in G major, which has not yet been republished. The gavotte, however, is arranged for organ (vol. xi of Novello's *Village Organist*).

Taking the sonatas as a whole, the first thing that strikes the hearer is their variety of form. No two are exactly alike; sometimes there are four movements, sometimes only three. Six include a fugue; no. 4 has a march, no. 8 a siciliana, no. 9 a canon.

Then again, there is the utmost freedom in the order of the movements. The position of the slow movement alone is quite sufficient to show how little Boyce was tied to any prearranged scheme. A slow movement appears in every position, except as a finale, or is even omitted altogether, as in the case of the twelfth sonata.

Another point deserves consideration, namely, the total lack of contrast in the key system. Nos. 1 and 7 keep to the same key throughout; the rest vary only between relative major and minor, or between tonic major and minor, with the exception of no. 4—G minor, E flat, G minor.

Some years ago a most successful experiment was made at one of the Leeds Bohemian chamber concerts. No. 12 was put down to follow Novák's string quartet in G, op. 22. Not only did it serve as an excellent foil to the modern work, but—to judge from the applause—its simple English idiom made a direct appeal to ears which had, perhaps, been rather taxed by the less familiar Bohemian dialect.

G. SURTEES TALBOT from Cobbett's *Musical Supplement* (revised).

[The republished trios are extremely beautiful, especially No. 7 in D minor. All were played about the time of their publication, in every London theatre, in company with the trios of Corelli, and even at the present day are occasionally heard in private and public.

EDITOR.]

BRADFORD FESTIVAL OF CHAMBER MUSIC. On the afternoon and evening of 5th and 6th October, 1926, a series of master works was performed by artists of the first rank in the Queen's Hall, Bradford. The festival was initiated by Mr. Keith Douglas, a Yorkshire patron of the art, through whose efforts chamber music lovers in the north of England have been, and will be able in years to come, to enjoy concerts of music of the nobler kind without the fatigue and expense of a journey to the metropolis. It remains to add that the programmes are annotated and illustrated by quotations in music type.

In 1927 the festival was continued on the same lines.

EDITOR.

BRAHMS, JOHANNES, b. Hamburg 1833, d. Vienna 1897. German composer.

Sextet, str, B flat	op. 18,	Simrock,	1861.
,, str, G	36,	,,	1866.
Quintet, 2 v, 2 vla, vc, F	88,	,,	1882.
,, 2 v, 2 vla, vc, G	111,	,,	1891.
,, cl, 2 v, vla, vc b mi (also arranged 2 v, 2 vla, vc)	115,	,,	1892.
Two quartets, str, c, a mi	51,	,,	1873.
Quartet, str, B flat	67,	,,	1876.
Quintet, pf, 2 v, vla, vc, f mi	34,	Peters,	1866.
Quartet, pf, v, vla, vc, g mi	25,	comp. *c.* 1860, Simrock,	1863.
,, pf, v, vla, vc, A	26,	comp. *c.* 1860, Simrock,	1863.
,, pf, v, vla, vc, c mi	60,	Simrock,	1876.
Trio, pf, v, vc (or vla), B and b mi	{ 8, rev. ver.	,, ,,	1854. 1891.
,, pf, v, vc (or vla), C	87,	,,	1882.
,, pf, v, vc (or vla), c mi	101,	,,	1887.
,, pf, v, horn (or vla, or vc), E flat	40,	,,	1868.
,, pf, cl (or vla, or v), vc, a mi	114,	,,	1892.
{ Sonata, pf, v, G Arranged in D for vla, or vc	78,	,,	1880.
Sonata, pf, v, A	100,	,,	1887.
,, pf, v, d mi	108,	,,	1889.
,, pf, vc (or vla), e mi	38,	,,	1866.
,, pf, vc (or vla), F	99,	,,	1887.
Two sonatas, pf, cl (or vla, or vc), f mi, E flat	120,	,,	1895.
Sonata, pf, cl, arranged from cl. quintet	115,	,,	

The chamber-music of Brahms is comprised in twenty-four works, which probably represent scarcely a quarter of the bulk of composition which he devoted to that branch of his art. Works of art are like icebergs; what is allowed to see daylight is but a fifth of the whole. Great artists differ externally in their way of disposing of the underlying bulk; but its proportion probably remains much the same. Some, like Handel, combine an enormous physical industry with a Johnsonian indolence, and, writing as easily as Johnson talked, give it all to the public in the forms occasion demands.

Others, like Bach and Mozart, are not less adroit in using the daily occasion, but are always exploring in organization and technique; so that, as Brahms said of Schubert's six hundred songs, there is something special to be learnt from each work. Inspiration is a wind which 'bloweth where it listeth'; but it prefers to visit artists who are constantly practising their art. 'Genius', said Beethoven, 'is always prolific'; and Beethoven, of all men of genius, practised his art with a technique that changed with the nature of each work. This made it impossible for his art to thrive on methodical mass-production; his innumerable sketches for each individual work are the substitute for the enormous productivity of those masters whose technique was more reducible to routine. The habit of sketching saved him at all events from the necessity of writing half a dozen completely scored symphonies in order that one might survive. It is not known how far Brahms sketched in Beethoven's way; that is to say, by dashing down, on one stave to a line, the whole course of a composition, leaving harmony, texture, and instrumentation for consideration at final stages, and committing oneself to nothing that cannot be as easily altered as improvised, if need be, in a dozen such sketches, all of which will then retain the spontaneity of improvisation enhanced by every gain of insight. The method is admirably convenient for a style in which the texture does not determine any important features, and it is a necessary method in all branches of vocal music where words are to be declaimed with dramatic continuity. But where the texture determines the course of the music, outline-sketching becomes less efficient, and the composer must rely on carrying the flow of the music in his head through all the labour of detail. A fugue is composed from the texture outwards; and in the many bad fugues that have been published the failure is more often in the general composition, which has never been successfully taught, than in the counterpoint, where decent craftsmanship is not unusual. A set of variations cannot be sketched at all, for it presents nothing to write but full detail.

Hence Brahms, whose style was from the outset almost evenly balanced between the most dramatic sonata-form and the highest polyphony, can have effected comparatively little by the practice of outline-sketching. As he took extraordinary pains throughout his life, and especially during his last illness, to destroy all unfinished and unpublished manuscripts, we are almost reduced to guess-work as to his methods of composition. A few sketches are preserved in the library of the *Gesellschaft der Musikfreunde* in Vienna; these comprise some beginnings of small pianoforte pieces and sketches of a projected orchestral overture in E flat minor, but no sketches of extant works are known. On the other hand, it appears from Brahms's correspondence that many important finished works were suppressed; and it is by no means certain that the art of music has not lost more than it has gained through Brahms's exceptionally scrupulous judgement as to what was fit to represent him. For instance, there were two pianoforte trios, in D and E flat, written about the time of that in C major, op. 87; and at least one of these was preferred to the C major by Clara Schumann, a most candid friend and fastidious critic. Again, Professor Jenner of Marburg, in an account of his experiences as a student of composition under Brahms, tells us that what we know as the first violin sonata, op. 78, was really the fifth. The actual first violin sonata was in D minor and was written in the period comprised between the pianoforte sonata, op. 1, and the original version of the B major trio, op. 8. Brahms had arranged for its publication, but the manuscript went astray. The loss is undoubtedly to be regretted; if only as a document in the history of the art the work must have been as important as the B major trio. But had the manuscript been found some ten years later, it is extremely unlikely that Brahms would then have published it. His recomposition of the B major trio after twenty odd years will show us, as will nothing else in the history of music, how ruthlessly he treated anything that seemed defective to his mature sense of movement. Of the other three unpublished violin sonatas there is no individual record. We may, then, assume that Brahms attained the mastery shown in all his published work by means of a much larger bulk, not of sketches, not even of exercises (though these he also carried on in a correspondence of exchange and mutual criticism with Joachim), but of actually completed works, most of which would have passed as masterpieces to anybody but their composer. The fact that the extant works have by no means passed without dispute as masterpieces, and that controversy is maintained about them to the present day, may indicate that opinions can differ as to what constitutes good technique in music; but if the critic lives who has thought more deeply than Brahms on the matter, that critic's opinions will meet with even more opposition than Brahms's work, in proportion as they are more above the comprehension of the aesthetic official mind.

The most convenient way to enter into Brahms's aesthetic system is to begin with his first extant piece of chamber-music, the B major trio, op. 8, and to compare it with the new version published between twenty and thirty years later. To call the later version a revision is absurd; and to talk of passages in the original as being excised in the later version is like saying that incidents in Schiller's *Jungfrau von Orleans* have been excised in Shaw's *Saint Joan*. What Brahms has done in his later version is to take the broad openings of the first movement and finale (about sixty-four bars each, down to the transition-passage to a contrasted key) and to use them as the openings of movements otherwise entirely new; different in sentiment, in theme, in form, and, above all, in sense of movement.

In music, as in life, this sense may be either active or passive; there is the movement of the athlete and the movement of the passenger in the motor-car. In neither case does the measurement in miles an hour determine the aesthetic value of the motion. Even in the most passive movement it is only by jolts, vibrations, and the apparent contrary movement of the surroundings that the motion is realized; and when the roads are good, the car well made, and the driver capable, the faint and rhythmic remaining traces of motion suffice to lull the passenger to sleep. Such is the much-praised Rossinian 'sense of pace', in virtue of which Figaro stands singing *Largo al factotum* at ten syllables a second, pointing symmetrically to right and left as the music swings from tonic to dominant; and thus the Rossinians gibe at Mozart's slowness with the solemn insolence of a *nouveau riche* giving the dust of his limousine to the riders who brought the good news from Ghent to Aix.

Now it is one of the first principles of sonata-style that it is dominated by an active rather than by a passive sense of movement. All kinds of movement may, indeed, must be there, but sonata-style is neither architectural nor cosmically epic, but thoroughly dramatic. The sublime motion by which the dead and living are 'Roll'd round in earth's diurnal course With stocks and stones and trees' is present in the form of a tempo which, in spite of the violence often done to it by sentimental and arbitrary virtuoso players, does not undergo abrupt or capricious change any more than the paces of a horse; a quick tempo, or changes in tempo can, merely as such, produce no sense of active movement unless the composer exerts his invention by varying the proportions of his phrases.

Mozart, in the finale of his *Musikalischer Spass*, held up the mirror to the nature of all road-hog composers in the following cadence-theme:

Ex. 1.

It must be heard in its context for the full fun to be revealed; but, *a priori*, a movement in which that is the nearest approach to a terse procedure will be a slow business however fast it is played; indeed, the quicker the tempo the more open the confession that actual progress is disappointing.

Now the period of Brahms's early works was singularly disturbing to the cultivation of a sonata-like sense of movement. The music-drama of Wagner, though only just about to ripen to the undreamt-of technique and scale of the *Ring*, had already fired the imagination of young composers (not, at first, excluding Brahms and Joachim) with the possibilities of a kind of movement which, instead of exhausting itself within each of the four usual divisions of a sonata (say, in ten minutes) should be capable of carrying on dramatic action for hours *pari passu* with a poetic stage-drama. Had the Wagnerian propaganda ever been precisely formulated as concerned with a generalized and positive problem of movement, it is conceivable that controversy might have taken less mutually repressive lines; and certainly the issues would have been far less confused had it been possible for Wagner to produce the *Ring* before asserting his aims, instead of using for their illustration works like *Tannhäuser* and *Lohengrin*, which every honest musician has now long since admitted to be almost evenly balanced between the true but immature Wagner and a composer more of the order of the pompous Spontini if not rather of the pariah Meyerbeer.

Even if Mendelssohn, then so obviously the great master for whom nothing seemed difficult or obscure, had not died most inopportunely in 1847, before he had time to realize that the new tendencies in music were more important in their essence than in any crudeness of their first expression, the controversy would still have wasted much energy as between 'classicists' who reduced all instrumental art-forms to pre-established jelly-moulds and 'romanticists' to whom all music existed for purposes of illustration. As a matter of fact few composers have written more 'programme-music' than those 'classicists' Mendelssohn and Spohr; and the real issues of musical development have never been divided into such obvious oppositions. But it was true that Mendelssohn's musical forms, though immediately effective, were too loose to serve as a foundation for the art of any future master who had attained enough insight to admire them intelligently; while Spohr's forms, to say nothing of his mannerisms, had in his ripe old age settled down to a mastery like that of the 'spot stroke' in billiards which became a nuisance calling for the institution of 'spot-barred' matches. Meanwhile Schumann had raised an attractive side-issue, not at first recognized as such, by his symphonies and chamber-music in which everything is started in rigidly square antithetic epigrams, and a distant effect of development is produced by long slabs of cumulative sequence; in short, a kind of musical mosaic which has its own merit and the merits of its precious material just so long as it does not pretend to be a painting. Nothing shows more glaringly how the musical propagandists of all parties in the 'fifties failed to grasp the essentials of their art than the fact that Brahms was from the outset criticized, admired, and persecuted as a follower of Schumann. It was natural to assume that the subject of Schumann's famous article entitled *Neue Bahnen* would be an artist in sympathy with Schumann's art; but it showed scanty appreciation of Schumann to suppose that, while he had health and strength to write that article, he would have devoted it to an imitator of his own style, to say nothing of entitling it 'New Paths'.

Brahms's art was from the outset so manifestly beyond the scope of all parties that partisans of opposite tenets eagerly proved their intelligence by claiming him as among their leaders. The genuine freedom of his art-forms made his pianoforte sonatas acceptable to the romantic extremists grouped around Liszt; while it was evident to any one whose interest in the classics was not merely conventional that, with inequalities conspicuous by their rarity, this music showed a mastery of classical technique unknown since Beethoven. Brahms never accepted the position of leader of a party, and neither journalists nor friends could have forced that position upon him but for two things: his own horror of artistic bureaucracy and *claques*, and the catastrophic revulsion which took place in Joachim's feelings towards Liszt when, after his friendship had ripened to intimacy, he made the acquaintance of Liszt's more serious compositions and found in them every quality of style and emotion that most repelled him. This and the indisputable fact that Liszt, if not himself responsible for the position, was the centre of a press-bureau almost as well organized as Meyerbeer's, brought about an explicit declaration of estrangement between the masters of the two main musical forces of nineteenth-century music—forces that perhaps might never have been sundered if German and Hungarian musical party-politics could have been as separable from aesthetic-moral judgements as English parliamentarianism. Both these forces lost incalculably by the separation, for Joachim's own profoundly original fountain of composition finally dried up, Liszt was deprived of all the interchange of ideas by which Joachim exercised so stimulating an influence upon Brahms, and Brahms himself did not escape from a somewhat ascetic attitude towards artistic resources which he would have had no difficulty in developing to legitimate purpose had not the word 'lisztisch' become current in his correspondence with Joachim as a synonym for 'damnable'.

As to Wagner, in whom the real issues of the *Zukunfts-Musik* were finding their goal, Brahms's attitude was never satisfactory to his partisan friends; and in his later years persons who tried to curry favour with him by talking against Wagner met with fierce rebukes for their pains.

Let us now see what light is shed upon the problems of musical movement in the 'fifties by comparing certain themes in the two versions of Brahms's B major trio, showing his views of the problem before and after he had formed his style.

The first theme, extended for over sixty bars, is common to both.

Ex. 2.

These twelve bars, the mere first phrase of a long lyric melody, already suffice to raise a problem in sonata style. Such melodies are rare as opening themes of sonatas, and from such an opening it is a *tour de force* to swing naturally into dramatic action.

Brahms was from the outset quite aware of the difficulty; and two solutions were possible to an artist of his calibre. Either this melody must be a normal item in a scheme that is breaking away from sonata style, or it must be an exceptionally big item in a normal sonata scheme. There is, of course, a *via media*, the cheerful ambling along in the king-can-do-no-wrong convention that pervades all bourgeois music from Mendelssohn's D minor trio, onwards through Rubinstein, till a highly experimental government intervenes and, innocently enacting that composers shall be paid by the crotchet, causes a temporary return to a sixteenth-century notation in which the standard note is worth four times as much. Brahms's instinct went to the root of the matter no less in the first version of his B major trio than in the last. I place, one below the other, the first phrase of the main 'Second Subject' in each.

Ex. 3.

1st version.

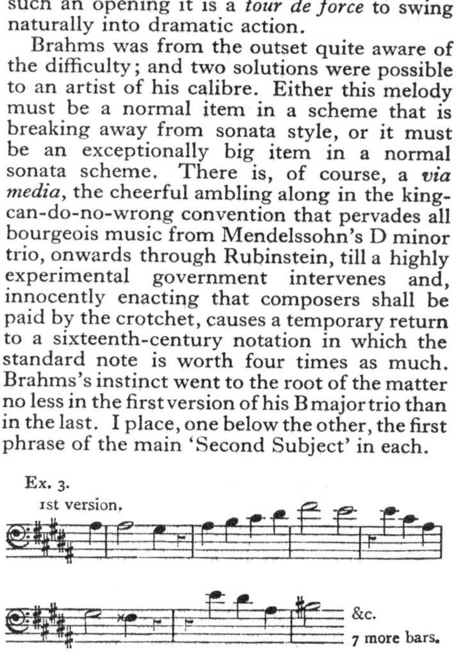

2nd version.

The early theme, as far as quoted, is only half the sentence, and it cannot be followed up except by shorter phrases. Its movement is, intentionally and effectively, slower than that of the opening theme, which will contrast with it as sunshine after gloom, but which will never again sound so big as it did at the outset. The young Brahms's instincts were right when he broke away from the idea of a formal recapitulation of such material when it is due to return after the development. The fugato digression which he is inaccurately said to have 'excised' in his later version is no fault in the earlier scheme, which does not break down until the ambitious young composer is confronted with the impossible task of ending with a grand climax on his main theme; whereupon he anticipates the recent policy of the composers whose government paid them by the crotchet, and winds up with an imitation of a chorus and organ, in semibreves and minims presto. To get thus excited over a naïvely beautiful melody is what inexperienced composers might call taking it seriously, and what conventional critics would call taking it too seriously. The first time Brahms really took this theme seriously was when in the light of full experience he became inspired with the possibilities of a scheme in which it should be the largest item instead of a mere indication of the average flow. From that moment the first movement and finale became new compositions having literally nothing in common with the old but their first sixty bars. Some years ago an eminent violoncellist had a misadventure in a public performance of this work. He knew only the final version, and knew it as nearly by heart as first-rate chamber-music players are in the habit of knowing well-rehearsed works. But he had not even realized the existence of the old version, a copy of which had been mistakenly put on his desk, and it was only on turning the page that he found himself confronted, in full career of performance *coram publico* with a totally unknown continuation. This nightmare shock could happen with no other printed piece of chamber music, and even here could not have happened to the violinist. For Joachim, who had a strong dislike to a long rest for the violin at the beginning of a chamber work, complained that it made the opening sound as if the violin was to enter after the tutti of a concerto, and made Brahms interpolate a little arpeggio figure three times during the first twenty bars of the early version. A violinist would therefore notice at once if he had the wrong version, for Brahms afterwards overruled Joachim's objection, and decided that if that opening was to inspire him to a new composition it needed no such tinkering.

The 'Second Subject' themes of the two versions of the finale show up still more obviously against each other.

Ex. 4.

1st version.

2nd version.

It will be seen that the young Brahms has good reason to write 'Più presto' over his pretty F sharp major melody, and that the quickest possible tempo will never make these twelve bars anything more lively than four bars of a leisurely 9/4 rhythm covering only half of his first sentence. Then this twenty-four bar sentence, having closed in the tonic, must be followed by a second part with wider range of key and higher lyric pathos, culminating in a return to the first strain more fully scored. After lyric inaction on such a scale, whatever else might be right, orthodox sonata procedures must be at least partially wrong, and it is not surprising that of the many interesting and some abstruse features of subsequent developments only one, a quiet passage leading to a crescendo at the beginning of the coda, could be used in the later version where it sounds ten times bigger and more romantic than in its original context.

The new work is not an unmixed gain upon the old, especially in the finale where the experienced Brahms grips the young Brahms so roughly by the shoulder as to make us doubt whether a composer so angry with the sentimentalities of his own youth would not be over-ready to tease and bully, or, still worse, to ignore young composers anxious to learn but less sure of their ground. But his attitude to the scherzo shows that his impatience had nothing in common with the timid fretfulness of the Superior Person, who will never get over the climax of the glorious tune of the trio, in which the three instruments, finding themselves able to blaze away in the grandest style of a Viennese waltz-band, do so without the smallest scruple. Brahms, finding that the resulting quality of tone happens to be excellent in spite of its resemblance on paper to the most commonplace failures of its kind, not only retains this passage in his later version but puts its most impertinent final gesture an octave higher. *Pecca fortiter* is his motto. The original end of the first movement fails because the three instruments cannot imitate a chorus and organ; the trio of the scherzo succeeds because if an orchestra can sound like that it will sound very well indeed. From the genteel fear of vulgarity Brahms was as free as the most Norman of duchesses.

With his early treatment of lyric or episodic forms Brahms later found little matter for regret; and it was only at the end of the scherzo that he found his mysterious early coda too clever and, as usual, too slow. With the adagio the case is more complex. In its original form it consists of a mysterious dialogue between the pianoforte and the strings, followed by a lyric episode in the subdominant, after which the dialogue returns, with a wonderful new modulation. Just before the close it breaks into an abstruse discussion of one of its figures, allegro doppio movimento (i. e. at exactly double the pace, so that the change is more in notation than in tempo). This rises to a climax with many abrupt dramatic gestures, after which the last clause of the adagio dialogue closes the movement in its original mysterious calm. In the new version the probability is that, as in the first movement and finale, Brahms was inspired by new material to set the old opening in a more sublime light. Nothing can be less likely than the commonly accepted view that he rejected the E major episode because of its resemblance to Schubert's *Am Meer*: the resemblance is of the kind which amateurs discover with infantile ease but which to persons experienced in composition are like 'puns partially intelligible with the aid of italics and a laryngoscope'. Brahms's own views of such 'reminiscences' may be conveniently cited here. To a composer friend who apologized for borrowing a theme from one of his symphonies he wrote to the effect that 'plagiarism is one of the stupidest topics of stupid people; you have made into one of your freshest themes what was only an accessory detail in my work'. And when somebody pointed out a resemblance between certain points in the finale of his C minor pianoforte quartet and Mendelssohn's C minor trio, his now famous comment was, 'Any fool can see that'. The main objections to the original E major episode are that the pizzicato accompaniment, which looks picturesque on paper, is disappointing in sound, even with the finest playing, and that Brahms has failed to make its irregular phrasing and broken conclusion express that freedom of form which is already so conspicuous in his earliest work, e. g. in the wonderfully placed extra half-bars, expressed by 3/2 time at the beginning of the first movement in both versions. In the new version of the adagio we are confronted with a totally new middle part, a passionate stream of subtle melody in G sharp minor (the same key as that of the second subject in the first movement) worked out on a very large scale. The concentrated gloom of this contrasts with the mysterious brightness of the opening, which returns with all the greater mystery and simplicity. The strange allegro doppio movimento coda is no longer needed and disappears without leaving a scar. One extra bar in the penultimate cadence is all that is required to bring in the last line.

Between these two different works with the same openings and the same opus number lie most of Brahms's remaining chamber music and the development of nearly his whole range of style. After thus sketching the nature of the changes Brahms made in the B major trio, we shall find it easy to follow the course of the other extant works.

The next published piece of chamber music is the first sextet, in B flat, op. 18. Here we find in a mature form the expression of a deliberate reaction towards classical sonata style and procedure—a reaction which Brahms had achieved wittily and violently in his first orchestral serenade, op. 11, originally written as a divertimento for solo instruments. In the B flat sextet Brahms is no longer constrained to unite new and old elements under cover of jokes to justify his masquerading, like Beethoven in his sonata, op. 31, no. 1, and other transitional works. Humour the sextet displays in Haydnesque measure and Beethovenish breadth at the end of the luxurious rondo-finale, and the tiny scherzo is circumscribed within limits that might have sufficed for the earliest Beethoven. But these points are not irreconcilable with a pervading Olympian calm, asserted in the opening and maintained throughout at a height which annihilates the distinction between 'classical' and 'romantic', and which is as far above formality as it is above more tempting foolishnesses. Joachim, to whom Brahms at this time sent all his compositions to be criticized movement by movement, found that the opening theme moved in its twelfth bar too abruptly to the rather remote key of D flat, and suggested to Brahms that instead of beginning at once with all six instruments it would be better to announce the first nine bars (already a significantly irregular phrase) in the violoncellos and viola, letting the violins sail in with the connecting tenth bar so as to take up the theme in their own octave by way of repetition; after which the modulation to D flat would sound as welcome as it is rich. This is the scheme followed in the opening of the B flat sextet, as we know it, and the effort of imagining it otherwise shows us the difference between Joachim's suggestions and the question-begging generalities of critics to whom everything is a matter of taste and inspiration, an indefinable and incommunicable essence of just what the critics happen to like at the moment. The finale likewise opens with a statement of its theme by the violoncello, repeated in the upper octave by the violin; and Brahms pointed this out to Joachim as a further result of his advice: a statement, however, to be taken playfully, as such treatment of a strophic rondo-theme is a matter of no technical subtlety.

The slow movement is a magnificent set of variations of which Brahms made a pianoforte version which he used to play many years afterwards. Though this was only a case of unwritten score-playing, we may be glad that the arrangement has now (1928) been published; for every contribution of Brahms to the aesthetics of the pianoforte as a vehicle for the expression of general musical ideas is a contribution valuable to the special character of the instrument in proportion as the ideas are remote from what would occur to the hand of an extempore player. As the next three works we have now to consider, besides thirteen of the remaining nineteen, are works with pianoforte, this is a convenient opportunity for dealing with his general treatment of such combinations. The statement that the piano does not blend with other instruments either indicates a fact of positive aesthetic importance or, in its more common question-begging form 'does not blend satisfactorily', is a testimony to a type of professional incapacity manifested by pianists who have no experience of chamber music. Nothing blends with anything unless you know the measure of the contrasts involved. The bass-tuba does not blend imperceptibly with the trombones: hence Wagner invented a special family of tubas and developed for them a characteristic life of their own in his *Ring*, also inventing a double-bass trombone in order that the trombones might have their own deep bass. But in *Tristan*, *Meistersinger*, and *Parsifal*, that is to say, in two works written after the first two *Ring* operas, and in a final work written exclusively for Bayreuth and with the fullest experience of Bayreuth conditions, Wagner was as satisfied as Brahms with the earlier use of the tuba as a bass to the trombones, leaving it to correction at rehearsals if the player fails to blend where contrast is not intended. Orchestral players expect to be instructed by conductors, and it is, if anything, more usual for great conductors to understand something of composition than for great composers to know how to conduct. From this it may be inferred that after every allowance has been made for superior opportunities and education, chamber-music players, especially pianists, would have much better current ideas as to their business if it were their habit to perform under the bâton of composers or conductors versed in chamber music—an important qualification, for no amount of purely orchestral experience will give either composer or conductor the remotest idea of the totally different values which single instruments assume when the orchestral environment is removed. As to the pianoforte in chamber music, it is nowadays high time frankly to admit that the Schumann tradition itself is not faultless even in regard to Brahms. It naturally accepts Schumann's pianoforte quartet and quintet as normal, if simple, solutions of the problem; and this is as hopeless a basis for tackling Brahms's trios and quartets as to use Haydn's trios as a basis for the study of Beethoven's, or even of Mozart's. Chamber music, in the sense understood by Mozart, Beethoven, Brahms, and the Haydn of the string quartets, begins to exist when every note essential to euphony is assigned to the instrument which is in a position to play it, when no instrument is so constructed that in playing one written note it produces artificial overtones by combinations of organ-stops or harpsichord octave-strings, and, lastly, when the whole organization rejects unnecessary or colourless doublings in the unison. When the pianoforte is combined with groups of other instruments this last criterion has to be reconciled with another, known to all the classics since the days when Palestrina wrote double and triple choruses; viz. that when voices or instruments are divided into antiphonal groups, the harmony of each group must be complete in itself, even when the groups are sounding together. Schumann satisfies the antiphonal criterion, but, like Haydn in his trios, at the ruinous cost of making it constantly impossible to decide which of two players in unison is the more unnecessary.

One of Brahms's most often quoted maxims was, 'If we cannot write as beautifully as Mozart and Haydn, let us at least write as purely'. The notion of purity was primarily applied by him to part-writing in the generalized grammatical sense of harmony and counterpoint; but the matters usually classed under the head of instrumentation are the more extensive consequences and cases of the same grammatical laws, even where they seem to work out in opposite ways, like a balloon rising 'in defiance of the law of gravitation'. On purity, in the sense of economy in instrumentation, Brahms acquired the severest views, stimulated by the criticism and advice of Joachim, whose ear in such matters was probably the most sensitive since Mozart's time.

The questions here involved must not be confused with matters of what is commonly called 'colour' in music. Brahms is supposed to be an indifferent 'colourist', and many official Brahmsians defend him as 'more concerned with what he has to say than how he says it'. Our notions of pure instrumental colour, however, will never do justice to Brahms—or indeed to any symphonic or chamber music—so long as we think that Wagnerian instrumentation sets the normal standard. Wagner writes habitually for the stage, and his instrumentation stands, with all its marvellous refinements, to the general problems of sonata style as the language of a drama stands to the question of what styles are good in novels and narrative poems. Yet, in spite of the incredible *naïvetés* which Wagner-bred critics and conductors (or even composers) commit when they discover chamber music late in life, it would be an excellent thing for pianists who think Brahms's chamber music incorrectly balanced in tone to learn the trumpet or tuba and experience the rough side of the tongue of a respectable conductor when they show a deficient sense of the weight of their instrument. Two quotations from one of the tersest works in Brahms's ripest and most powerful style will define the issue completely. The 'second subject' of the first movement is scored thus:

Ex. 5.

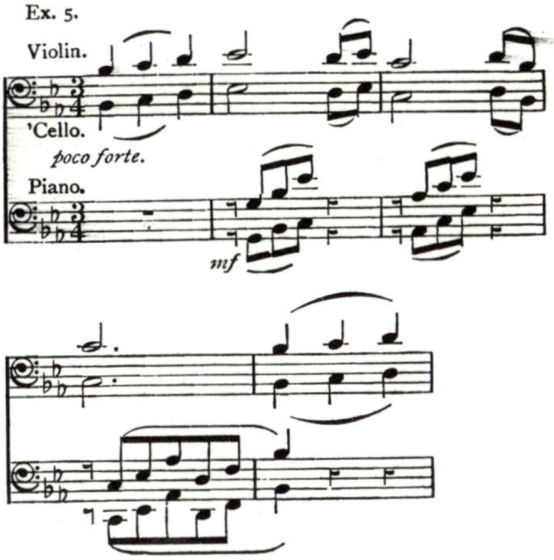

and, after ten more bars, is taken up by the pianoforte with the following scoring:

Ex. 6.

The crudest of pianists cannot make a mistake as to the effortless sonority and transparence of the few notes in which the piano richly harmonizes the powerful melody of the low strings in octaves; but even a good pianist whose classical experience of his instrument is based mainly on Chopin and Liszt, with an occasional condescension to the Schumann quintet, is apt to feel insulted and ridiculed in every professional fibre when he has to learn that beyond a ringing cantabile in the little finger of his right hand he must use no more energy in his counter-statement than in his accompaniment of the strings, and that, instead of getting excited by the enormous 'pianistic' possibilities of his part conceived as a Chopin ballade, he must put all his pianistic inspiration into blending his left hand with the pizzicato of the strings, which then becomes one of the most exciting sounds ever imagined in chamber music. At least, it will if the string-players have not been so permanently discouraged by the theory of pianistic incompatibility as to have forgotten that, like harpists, and unlike pianists, they can produce twice as much tone by spreading their chords instead of cutting them short. Brahms took this for granted, and accordingly does not give the violin the arpeggio signs which are necessary for the left hand of the pianoforte. Not until Reger discovered that string-players had forgotten their own instincts and required an arpeggio sign to every three-part and four-part chord to prevent them from choking it, did it ever occur to an experienced composer to provide such signs.

The violoncello part of these pizzicato chords reveals another point, inasmuch as there is not one composer in a hundred, especially among 'great colourists', who could be trusted not to make chords of them instead of single notes. But the bass of such chords vanishes before the top, unless the player puts all his accent below, a precaution which is impossible in any tone above mezzo-forte. Single notes, which look so humble on paper, provide the only sonorous bass, and, blended with the playing of a pianist who has a Bayreuth contrabass-tubist's knowledge of the weight of his instrument, give all their weight to the chords of the violin.

Another pizzicato passage that has caused much disappointment and censure is the quiet beginning of the development of the violin sonata in G major, op. 78:

Ex. 7.

Brahms must have suffered much from the conventions of 'pianistic' pianists (their average standard of intelligence has, in fact, greatly improved since mechanical and phonographic records have enabled them to hear themselves as others hear them); but he did not anticipate a time when violinists who would harp this passage like angels if they thought it part of a popular piece of musical cookery, could think that classical chastity compelled them to tighten these chords into dry clicks while the pianist, in a burst of 'noble manliness without sentiment', uses six times the tone that Brahms requires for his ethereal melody over its distant bass.

But the most crucial case of a pizzicato passage is in the third movement (or scherzo) of the last violin sonata (in D minor, op. 108). This, in the light of the published correspondence between Brahms and Frau von Herzogenberg, proves that he was always willing to act upon good advice that condescended to concrete facts instead of moving in an aristocratic atmosphere of the *je-ne-sais-quoi*; and in its own light it exemplifies one of the most important relations between form and instrumentation, viz. that a version of a theme that would seem impossibly crude or artificial for a first statement may be the one acceptable and admirable thing by way of counter-statement. Thus, the passage just quoted from the G major sonata is a return, not a first statement. Again, no reasonable person has ever objected to the orchestral version of the theme of the rondo of Beethoven's E flat concerto, first announced in magnificent solo style by the pianoforte; and in the finale of the G major concerto everybody is delighted with the variation in which the pianoforte repeats the theme which would have been unplayable in a literal transcription of the original orchestral announcement. But both these counter-statements would be out of the question as original themes. In stage-music, where everything has to fit the action of the movement, and musical form as such has no power to pick up lost threads, this relation between form and texture is either almost undeveloped, or developed in ways which would require another special essay to identify. But in all the opposition to Brahms nothing has been commoner than the two tricks, first, of criticizing his counter-statements as if they were initial statements, and, secondly, when a pianoforte statement and a string statement prove to be equally brilliant, of saying that Brahms is a follower of Schumann and never gets away from the pianoforte.

The pizzicato passage in the D minor sonata is the recapitulation of the main theme of the scherzo (Ex. 8).

In the opening statement the pianoforte gives the theme in cold octaves instead of two-part contrary motion and the violin chords are half-sustained with the bow. But Brahms originally made them pizzicato, and changed them into arco chords when Frau von Herzogenberg persuaded him that it was otherwise impossible to get a convincing colour into the opening. The pizzicato becomes rich and delightful as a new colour in the recapitulation when added to the contrary-motion two-part

Ex. 8.

harmony. That two-part harmony itself would have wasted its opportunity if it had been used at the opening instead of cold octaves.

We are now in a position to resume and conclude the chronological survey of Brahms's extant chamber music in the light of the principles here illustrated.

The two huge pianoforte quartets in G minor, op. 25, and A major, op. 26, were for Hanslick (the first journalist to support Brahms since Schumann) the centre of Brahms's art from which he was to deviate at his peril. Useful as Hanslick's support was to Brahms, it came from an unfortunate quarter as regards its effect on musical history; for Hanslick was the original of Wagner's Beckmesser—in the first draft of the *Meistersinger* text that character's name is actually Hans Lich. He found in these quartets the direct result of the last works of Beethoven; an appreciation based mainly on the correct conviction that such abstruse works were the sort of thing a high-minded young composer would study. Brahms, who made and kept friendship with Hanslick as a gentleman of culture and benevolent intentions, cannot be supposed to have had much respect for the judgement of a critic to whom Beethoven was acceptable only in his middle works, as being puerile in his first period and decadent in his third; to whom Haydn and Mozart are court composers, an aria of Bach a piece of running clockwork, and Palestrina as incomprehensible a hocus-pocus as Newman was to Kingsley. If this is not a fair account of the light Hanslick was able to shed upon the classics, it is a quite adequate statement of what the general reader will get from a perusal of his writings in so far as they are not devoted, much more amusingly, to violent abuse of Wagner, Berlioz, and Liszt. The loneliness of Brahms was intensified by the accession of such a partisan.

In these two piano quartets the forms are peculiar to Brahms, and in some respects to the works themselves. The themes, especially in the A major quartet, have a way of grouping themselves in pairs, the members of each pair alternating in an actual binary form which narrowly escapes self-completion by breaking out at the last moment into the wider field of dramatic action. This is quite a different state of things from the problem raised by the opening of the B major trio; Brahms has already in the B flat sextet thoroughly acquired the swing of classical sonata movement and is now enlarging his scale. To deal successfully with the enormous spaces these pairs of themes and counter-statements fill to repletion, Brahms, for all the resulting length, summons up an energy which is really identical with terseness. For obviously, as regards the use of materials, a monument made of twenty Stonehenge blocks is a terser product than one of the same size made of a million bricks. The difference between such masonry as that of these quartets and that of the proverbially 'lapidarisch' Bruckner is that Brahms takes his risk in forms of lyric melody, whereas Bruckner's materials are huge Wagnerian Nibelungen-Ring processes. On the very rare occasions when Brahms writes an introduction he shows as much mastery of such processes as Wagner himself; see the introduction to the finale of the very next work, the quintet, op. 34. But it is one of the points on which, perhaps, he felt himself driven into opposition to the tendencies of the day, and he nearly always begins plumb on the tonic with his main theme. The exceptions show that he had plenty of invention in other directions, and that his view of fine imaginative introductory flights was rather that they were too easy to be often true.

The connexion between form and instrumentation becomes more and more intimate as the composer's mastery grows. Brahms had already shown an astonishing maturity in the scoring of the first version of his B major trio, which becomes crude only where the composer's material has made the task of a climax impossible. From the outset Brahms showed an immense talent for counterpoint, and Joachim, whose delicate ear could not tolerate the slightest harshness, saw to it that Brahms should never allow a contrapuntal device to attract attention by even a Beethovenish collision. Hence, from first to last, Brahms had unlimited means of making his themes do duty as humble but not lifeless accompaniments; and this is one of the resources which make the forms of these two quartets possible. For pages together Brahms's texture at all periods invites analysis as close as that of a

Bach fugue, while the form is as dramatic as instrumental music can be without attenuating itself to the drastic simplicities of the operatic stage. An error, very mischievous in the teaching of composition, is that which, fascinated by this thematic analysis, mistakes its 'logic' for that of the composition as a whole. An example from the quintet, op. 34, will show where the logic really lies.

Ex. 9.

The fact that the semiquaver figure is a 'diminution' of the previous theme is an item of high aesthetic value, but does not constitute the 'logic' of Brahms's exposition. Any other semiquavers that fitted the harmony and kept within the rhythm might be substituted without destruction to the real scheme. But close up those gaps in the rhythm (e.g. by fitting the semiquavers of bar 6 into the last crotchet of bar 5) and mis-handle the process to the close on the dominant, or drift in some other direction, and all the thematic connexions in the world will not put sense or life into the drama you have stultified. Later on, when the semiquaver figure has become a quiet accompaniment to long lyric stretches in the 'second subject', Brahms makes the pianoforte preserve it accurately, but simplifies it into

Ex. 10.

because an exact version would be a little more difficult, and therefore a little heavier in a pianissimo for the strings.

Before returning to finish the account of the first two pianoforte quartets, it will be convenient to quote another transformation of this theme, in order to deal with the general topic of metamorphosis of themes as practised by Brahms. His anti-Wagnerian friends got into difficulties when they tried to distinguish his classical ways of development from the damnable heresies of Wagner and Liszt, for their analysis never got beyond the identification of themes, and was not up to ordinary police methods at that. But when Brahms turns the first eight notes of his opening theme by a simple rhythmic displacement into the lilt of an ancient ballad, thus,

Ex. 11.

the stroke of genius is of the same order as those by which Wagner develops the thought of world-power from the Rhine-maidens' golden toy through the darkness of the Nibelung's mind to the fore-doomed splendours of Walhalla. In point of form it differs from this and similar miracles in Beethoven's B flat trio, op. 97, in that Brahms's transformation is immediate. But, immediate or gradual, such transformations are governed by a very different law from that which permits or even encourages the counter-statement of a whole theme to take a form that would be unconvincing as a first statement. A metamorphosis or a fusion of two originally separate figures into a new unity has either the value of an independent inspiration or it has none. It cannot be accomplished mechanically. Brahms would have jumped at the sprightly combination of the boy Siegfried's horn-theme with that of his sword; but the attempt, in *Götterdämmerung*, to turn that horn-tune into an expression of matured virility by sophisticating its rhythm would no more have satisfied him than the text of *Götterdämmerung* satisfies that perfect Wagnerite Bernard Shaw.

This art of thematic metamorphosis was completely mastered by Brahms with inexhaustible fullness and no vestige of artificiality in his very first works, and pervades every opus, vocal and instrumental, from the sonata, op. 1, to the *Vier Ernste Gesänge*, op. 121, and the small posthumous collection of figured chorales, op. 122. It is the musical essence of Wagnerian *leitmotiv*, and as such its function is not architectural, but illustrative and decorative. It cannot create noble proportions in composition, but it can and must enhance them or condemn itself. Thematic organization can no more build Wagnerian music-drama or Brahmsian symphonies than tracery, mouldings, and stained glass can build cathedrals.

We may now return to opp. 25 and 26 and finish with a brief history of each remaining work.

The G minor Quartet, op. 25. The first movement is one of the most original and impressive tragic compositions since the first movement of Beethoven's ninth symphony. The association of two themes (characteristic of these quartets), one in G minor, the other in B flat, produces an astonishing dramatic result when, after the development section, the recapitulation begins, not with the first of the pair, but with the second in the sunniest G major. Still more astonishing is the transformation of the whole latter half of the enormous procession of triumphant and tender 'second-subject' themes in D major into tragic pathos in G minor; an operation on a scale unprecedented in classical music, and surpassed only by Liszt's transformation of the bulk of the first movement of his Faust symphony into the Mephistophelian scherzo; a comparison by which perhaps Brahms would not feel flattered. How much the work owes to Joachim is not known, but the austerely diatonic transition to the 'second subject' must, as we know it, be very different from the passage which Joachim found 'positively painful'. The second movement, entitled 'Intermezzo' is, in outline, a gigantic scherzo and trio, each highly organized and independent in the details of their form. In style it is a mysteriously tender and pathetic romance, and, with its strange 9/8 rhythms and its muted violin, is one of Brahms's most typical movements. The following andante is another enormous design in dramatic ABA form, the broad main theme (a lyric melody in E flat) leading in a spaciously developed transition-passage to an exciting military episode in C major. At the climax of this, where Brahms has no more scruple in writing orchestrally than he had in the scherzo of the B major trio, the solo pianist who incautiously lets himself go will find himself playing wrong notes; and, if asked to correct these, will complain that the passage is badly written for accurate playing with full tone. This is true, but it seems a roundabout approach to the discovery that Brahms knows how to balance the pianoforte against the strings in his most violent climax. The main theme resurrects itself out of a ruinous crash in C major, and swings round to its original E flat by a change of harmony which delays its course for only a few bars.

The finale, a Hungarian rondo inspired to terrific energy by that in Haydn's 'Gipsy' trio, came as a great shock to the Superior Person. Its sectional, dance-like structure is a bold addition to the high organic resources of the whole work, and is brought into complete harmony with them by the wonderful cadenza in which all its themes are combined in a polyphony as accurate as Bach's and a rhythm as fantastic as Liszt's. The fact that this movement is, from beginning to end, without precedent or parallel in Brahms's other works, is in itself a fact with plenty of precedents and parallels in Brahms and the classics.

THE A MAJOR QUARTET, op. 26, gave those who could understand it at all much less trouble to digest than the G minor. Its serenity is Olympian and the high spirits of its finale are, in spite of Hungarian traits, athletic rather than Bacchanalian. Indeed, the C major theme in the 'second subject' region of the finale stretches to the utmost limit the possibility of arching a slow theme over a quick tempo without collapsing from sonata style into Wagnerian operatic obliteration of tempo. Brahms, however, knows what he is doing in thus testing the matter. Terser and more aphoristic methods are for older men; an unaffected young composer is wise in learning to tell his story in full before his experience has enabled him to judge which half to omit in order that the half may be greater than the whole. Critics who have no respect for youthfulness of this calibre are preparing for an old age that will be merely unpleasant for themselves and others. There is abundant economy and halves greater than wholes in other musical dimensions and categories throughout Brahms's early works; and the all-pervading problem of movement is eminently one where the broadest solutions must precede the terser ones.

The first movement is of statuesque beauty, but any one who imagines on that ground that it is cold will be lucky if he has the experience of happening to hear or recall the climax where its recapitulation breaks into the coda, and to mistake it for a crescendo in a Wagner opera. The mistake is quite possible, and the effort to place the passage will be amusingly confined to the highest climaxes of *Tristan* or *Die Walküre*. No insight into the emotional values of the purely instrumental is possible until we abandon the popular delusion that because good stage-music is, in its own surroundings, more exciting, it is made of more passionate stuff. With the exception of Mozart the great masters of sonata form are inhibited from operatic writing not by lack of passion but by excess of concentration in their passion.

The slow movement of the A major quartet, another masterpiece of romantic colour with use of mutes, is in a fully developed rondo form, a fact that, with the size of its themes, involves a length which it is a triumph of economy to keep within bounds. The first theme may be usefully quoted as an example of the kind of phrase that can occur to no composer who is not constantly in the practice of setting words to music.

Ex. 12.

We have no evidence that this ever was associated with words; but, besides its five-bar rhythm, those triplets with their manifold drift of connexion are unmistakably the invention of a composer to whom all the shapes that verbal sentences can take are objects of musical interest, to be interpreted, not by Wagnerian declamation fitted into an orchestral scheme, but by musical sentences equally intelligible in themselves. We must learn to understand Brahms's mastery of absolute musical form in the light of the fact that fully two-thirds of his work, from first to last, was vocal, and that this prince of 'absolute' musicians was the most circumstantial of verbal illustrators where words were involved. That is why there is no composer with whom it is more futile to impute unauthorized 'programmes' to his instrumental works.

The scherzo and trio of the A major quartet are a pair of binary movements developed far beyond the limits of mere melodic form, and constitute in their alternation a movement fully on the scale of the others.

A hundred and twenty years earlier Bach had impudently plagiarized Brahms's main theme in the overture to his Fourth Partita in the *Clavierübung*; no doubt with Brahms's full pardon.

QUINTET IN F MINOR FOR PIANOFORTE AND STRINGS, op. 34 a. Here we come to the climax of Brahms's first maturity. The work was originally written as a string quintet with two violoncellos (like Schubert's) instead of the more usual two violas. To us, who are accustomed to its terrific power as a pianoforte quintet, it is not surprising that Joachim, after thorough practical proof with his colleagues, persuaded Brahms that no mortal strings could cope with its climaxes. Brahms then arranged it as a sonata for two pianofortes, published as op. 34 b. The result was magnificent as to power and clearness, but the total loss of string tone is regrettable in the quiet passage at the beginning of the coda of the first movement, and a real difficulty to the understanding of the mysterious introduction to the finale. Finally, the work took its shape as a pianoforte quintet, the most sonorous of all extant works for pianoforte and strings, and yet the most lightly scored. The first movement has already been quoted; it is powerfully tragic. The slow movement is a broad lyric in ABA form. The thunderous scherzo, in its main body follows the form and modulations of that in Beethoven's C minor symphony more closely than Brahms ever elsewhere followed a single example. The resemblance disturbs nobody, and the trio, a big, triumphant binary melody in the major, goes its own Brahmsian way. The finale is, like that of the A major quartet, a big binary movement with the development section omitted, or rather replaced by a considerable discussion between the recapitulation of the 'first subject' and that of the second. This form was amplified from Mozart by Schubert, whose spirit pervades this quintet more than any other work of Brahms, though from first to last it is by far the most conspicuous influence in the origins of his style. Beethoven is the founder of his art-forms, and Bach the founder of his polyphony; but their influence on his style is as impersonally general as the influence of the sum of classical literature upon Milton. Brahms was bound to Schumann by every tie of personal affection, sympathy, gratitude (with him no irksome feeling) and sorrow, but Schumann's music had no more influence on his style than Spohr's, for whose *Jessonda* he confessed to an auld-lang-syne affection of the kind which he personally could never lose. Schubert, however, is always looking over his shoulder, and in this quintet might have been guiding his pen for pages, in the second subject of the first movement, the main theme of the slow movement and the whole body of the finale. The savage flat supertonic acciaccatura (D♭ C) at the end of the scherzo comes straight from the end of Schubert's quintet, and from nowhere else in the whole history of final chords. And the art-forms of this quintet are the nearest conceivable approach to what Schubert would have achieved if he had lived to bring his instrumental unorthodoxies to mature consistency, not through those amputations by which a cocksure teacher can so easily implant in his pupil a profound scepticism as to any part of a work being more necessary than any other part, but by accumulated experience of what his ideas really imply.

From the opening onwards, the F minor quintet abandons the device of alternating couples of themes, and thus sets itself free to expand its material more rapidly. This freedom henceforth extends over every type of Brahms's forms.

Brahms would have acted more kindly to posterity, and not less prudently for his own reputation if, instead of destroying all his unpublished works and sketches, he had made legal provision that ghouls should not be allowed access to his grave until fifty years after his death. No doubt the best string-players of 1947 would come to the same conclusion as Joachim and Brahms himself about the original version of the F minor quintet, if it could be called up from the flames; but they would learn incalculably more than that conclusion from the experience which led to it. As things are, however, the only four notes which indicate that the pianoforte quintet is not an intact original are at the beginning of the introduction to the finale, where the pianoforte has to do duty for the original second violoncello. This, however, need cause no distress if the pianist can be shaken out of his professional etiquette to the extent of realizing that the lack of pianistic character in his faintest audible touch is here a merit instead of a defect. The violoncello is here equally deficient in 'cellistic tone. It is the character of all whispers to have no character.

SECOND SEXTET IN G MAJOR, op. 36. From the symphonic massiveness which annihilated op. 34 as a string quintet, this sextet shows a delightful reaction. The first sextet was sonorous like an organ, or better, like Mozart's serenade for thirteen wind instruments. The G major sextet is the most ethereal of all Brahms's larger works, and is penetrated by sunshine which the shadow of the unearthly pathos of the slow movement eclipses only to reveal the corona and the stars. The first movement swings along in rhythms which are now subtle as well as broad; its development, like that of the A major quartet and many of Brahms's later first movements, concentrates itself around a single remote new key instead of rapidly modulating. Here it does not go to this distant key (C♯ minor) until it has opened in D minor with one of the most brilliant contrapuntal *tours de force* extant, which, like all the counterpoint Brahms admitted into his mature works, presents not a note that does not strike the ear as the best possible melodic step in the best possible harmony. The *marche-ou-je-t'assomme* ingenuity of similar canonic devices in, e.g., the tenth of the variations, op. 9, on a theme of Schumann, was in after-years marked by Brahms with a huge '?' in the copy of a friend.

The scherzo of this sextet is of a new kind and tempo, its main poco allegretto (2/4 time) portion being a highly organized binary movement with two well-defined themes and considerable development, aerial in scoring (like the whole work) and quietly plaintive in an elfin way. The key is G minor. The trio is a rousing dance (presto 3/4), returning to the main movement in a picturesque diminuendo. Brahms's scherzos generally have a simple da capo with no coda, and, unlike Beethoven, he does not usually alter the dynamics or scoring of his da capo so as to necessitate writing it out in full. But here he does so because the original quiet end, without change of a bar in the plan, breaks away in a lively rush of triplets. Altogether a study of childhood worthy of Haydn, Wordsworth, or even of life itself. Still more profound is the slow movement, a set of variations in E minor on a theme more subtle than has ever been so treated elsewhere. The theme is binary, but its sections are not repeated until after two quiet variations; it arises in wrath in the third and fourth variation, where the repeats reveal its firm solidity. The fifth variation is separated from the others by a few bars of quiet introduction, upon which it unfolds itself in the major, in a tempo half as fast and therefore twice as big (the semiquavers continuing the original quaver motion, so that no change of pace is felt). And so, sustained by an adequate coda, this last variation arches itself over the whole like a sky in which all clouds are resting on the horizon and dazzlingly white. This movement is the quintessence of Brahms, in a form which neither puzzled his admirers nor offered to his opponents a region of art in which they could imagine that their writs were current. Not so the finale, which presented far too wide a range of style for the growing band of 'Brahmins' to feel comfortable. The movement is not less brilliant than subtle, one of the very few which Brahms opens by preluding in harmonies that lie obliquely across the key, and misleading rather from the fearless simplicity of its first cantabile theme (another sublime study in childhood) than from the abstruse intellectuality that was imputed to it by Deiters and other friends of Brahms.

First Sonata for Pianoforte and Violoncello in E minor, op. 38. This first extant duet of Brahms is a work of dark colour, in which full advantage is taken of the superb bass that a violoncello can give to the pianoforte, even in massive pianoforte chords, provided that all meaningless doubling is avoided. In this work the violoncello hardly rises beyond its tenor region. The first movement marches like 'solemn tragedy in sceptred pall' until the quiet major end of its indignant 'second subject' is, in the recapitulation, expanded into a pathetic coda in which the movement expires in peace.

The development is very broad and is remarkable in form for using very large unbroken passages of the exposition, instead of following the orthodox habit of breaking the material up. There is no slow movement; the middle movement is a graceful minuet in A minor, with an exquisitely coloured trio in F sharp minor, requiring a rather slower tempo for its proper expression (though Brahms gives no indication). The finale is unique in chamber-music in being a strict fugue with a free middle section and a da capo. The most official of 'Brahmins' used to call this 'the crabbed and canonic finale'. It would have done their souls good to have it proved by experiment that their musical schooling had made them really hate all fugues as Byron hated Horace, and that they would have automatically talked of the 'sublime poetry in which the severest art is used but to conceal art' if this fugue had been introduced to them as by Bach. With later composers the noses of such critics are in the air and their fingers in their ears the moment the composer answers a one-part melody by another part a fifth higher; no further evidence is required that he is guilty of writing a crabbed fugue. With performers (not excluding some orchestral conductors), a more particular obstacle to the enjoyment of this finale is the widespread doctrine that the only element of a fugue that is fit for publication is its subject. This is a mistake, for the virtue of classical counter-subjects is that, even when there are two or three of them in combination, they are so contrasted in rhythm, type of melodic movement and phrasing (e.g. staccato leaps against smooth conjunct runs), and harmonic function (as, for instance, a chain of suspended discords) that they are all transparent to each other. And as most of the middle section of this finale consists of a most graceful dialogue in which the counter-subjects are turned into melodic schemes in binary form, it is folly to ignore them in the exposition. Further trouble is caused by the fact that the look of the page is exciting enough to tempt the pianist to far too quick a tempo. Players who have reverently treated the fugue in Beethoven's D major violoncello sonata as a proposition by no means unnegotiable, come to this fugue-finale of Brahms with something like the feelings of the pianist whose fingers sink into the cushions of Chopin's most powerful polonaise after he has been struggling with the end of Schubert's Wanderer-Phantasie or the still more wild-cat score-playing of Brahms's first pianoforte works.

TRIO FOR PIANOFORTE, VIOLIN, AND NATURAL HORN, IN E FLAT, op. 40. The invention of the ventil horn had by the middle of the nineteenth century turned one of the most primitive of instruments, which possessed no scale but the harmonic series (ratios $\frac{1}{2}$, $\frac{1}{3}$, $\frac{1}{4}$, &c.) as 'open' notes with the addition of such muffled adjacent lower semitones or (with extreme muffling) tones as could be obtained by partially closing the bell with the hand, into an instrument with a complete chromatic scale and a capacity for blending imperceptibly with all other orchestral tones throughout its compass, except when forced to extreme height, when it becomes nervous. This capacity for blending depends, however, upon the horn-player's retaining one of the classical methods in use with the primitive instrument, by which the tone of the 'open' notes was softened so as to allow the 'closed' notes to be used, where melody required them, without obvious patchiness. In the 'first fine careless rapture' of the ventil horn this habit was abolished, like aristocratic manners in a reign of terror, and the ventil horn threatened to become no better than that 'chromatic bullock' the ophicleide. Stronger language could not be used than that of Wagner in the preface to *Tristan*, the very work which first fully explored the possibilities of the ventil horns, and not a page of which could be re-scored without them. Yet Wagner says that he would have made up his mind to do without the new instrument, had not he found that by careful practice under proper instruction the player could acquire *nearly* the qualities of the old horn style.

Brahms was doing nothing more reactionary than illustrating Wagner's preface to *Tristan* when he laid special stress upon using a valveless horn with an E flat crook for this trio. He explained to his friends that, if the player were not compelled to blend his open notes with his closed ones, he would never learn to blend his tone in chamber music at all. Nowadays, when every horn-player accepts the demands of *Tristan* as classical, it is not necessary to risk a public performance of Brahms's horn trio on the natural instrument, on which many unavoidable difficulties are merely vexatious. But every horn-player should, before resting satisfied with his easy mastery of this work on the modern instrument, find out, by practising it on the E flat crook without using the valves, what a wonderful variety of tone-colours it presents when he is compelled to blend closed notes with open ones. On the modern instrument he is in no danger of playing brassily as in the days of Wagner's preface to *Tristan*; the trouble nowadays is that the soft legato technique is distributed uniformly, one may not unfairly say artlessly, over the whole scale, and that the player has no longer the slightest idea of what his instrument could do if he played Brahms, to say nothing of Mozart and Beethoven, on the intended *Waldhorn* method. When he has explored that possibility to its limits, then let him use the ventils to remove merely vexatious difficulties and minimize the risks of aesthetically expressive difficulties. But the attitude of a chauffeur to an obsolete make of motor-car does not lead to distinction in the fine arts. All wind-instrument players must live by orchestral work in default of scope in chamber music, and most orchestral wind-players must imperil even their orchestral technique by scavenger-work in revues and cinemas. In these conditions, financial endowment is required if a horn-player is to have leisure to discover what Brahms's trio really means.

The first movement is in a form which Brahms may have remembered to have seen in a little-known violin sonata of Mozart in C, where an andante theme alternates with a lively allegro in the complementary key, the two sections then recurring both in the tonic so as to balance in a binary form without development. Brahms's balance of keys is new and delicate (andante 2/4 in E flat; più mosso 9/8 in C minor and G minor; andante again in E flat; più mosso in E flat minor and B flat minor, so as to lead to andante in G flat, with a dramatic crescendo leading to a climax in the tonic followed by a solemn dying away).

The scherzo is exceedingly lively, and gives the horn plenty of scope for energy. A personal reminiscence may be pardoned here and may serve to indicate that many statements in this article have been left in the form of unsupported dogma merely from lack of space. When I played this trio with Joachim and Rüdel in Berlin in 1902, I was ferociously attacked by a critic for 'not feeling the impertinence of bolting like that in the presence of Joachim'. But during rehearsal Joachim had found neither my first nor my second starting of the scherzo fast enough, and he was exactly satisfied with my tempo at the concert. In the quiet B major passage where the violin and horn pull the theme out by holding every third note for an extra bar while the pianoforte interpolates pianissimo arpeggios, a custom has long arisen of taking a slower tempo. This I can testify, from the above experience, to be a mistake. Though this way of 'augmenting' a theme (here devised for the first time) became a characteristic of Brahms's later style, he had not yet come to the point when his action was so rapid and his texture so concentrated as to compel him to slacken his tempo. The time when marks like più sostenuto are required for stormy and exciting developments is not reached until the G major violin sonata, op. 78; in the horn trio Brahms is still solving his problems on the broadest lines. This B major episode is no ruminating profundity or concentrated development, but the lightest and most playful episode in the work.

The dramatic mystery and gloom of the powerful slow movement is lightened by one gleam of grey dawn before it closes in darkness. This gleam foreshadows the theme of the finale, which, in full sonata form, closes the work in a glorious hunting-scene; appropriately, for to what other purpose is the natural horn called *Waldhorn* and *cor-de-chasse*?

Two String Quartets, in C minor and A minor, op. 51. The history of Brahms's pianoforte quintet, and the fact that up till now his two other works for strings alone were sextets, may incline us to believe that Brahms had extraordinary difficulty in reducing his massive harmony and polyphony to the limits of four solo strings. We know that he destroyed an unascertainable number of string quartets before the appearance of op. 51, and it is very unlikely that this pair of works was fashioned with ease. Their criterion is of impeccable economy and purity of quartet style, if we do not inculcate a disciplinarian idea that it is a crime to *succeed* in making four solo strings sound like an orchestra. On that disciplinarian view we shall, without any need to use our ears, not only condemn the agitated middle episode of the andante of the A minor quartet, with its tremolo accompaniment to a canonic recitative between violin and violoncello, but shall deliver to the common hangman the development of the first movement and the main bulk of the scherzo of the very quartet of Beethoven from which the author of the article *Quartet* in *Grove's Dictionary* cites, as the criterion of quartet style, a passage 'for which the most perfect earthly orchestra would be intolerably coarse'. Brahms's string quartets, especially the A minor, have plenty of such ethereal passages, and to expect a big string quartet to consist of nothing else is like expecting a cosmic epic, which provides the only environment in which the lines Matthew Arnold cites as 'touchstones of poetry' can grow, to provide lines of no other type.

Another difference between Brahms's string quartets and those of Beethoven and Mozart is that there is far more double-stopping. This might be expected in any case from the fullness of harmony necessary for even the most ascetic statement of Brahms's ideas; but his double-stopping has no tendency to destroy his quartet style; the four instruments retain their individuality even though, as at the end of the romanze in the C minor quartet, the viola sounds like a pair of deep-sea horns and the violoncello like all the harps of the sirens. How the purity of chamber-music style may be affected by double stops will appear from a glance at the opening of Schumann's pianoforte quartet, which shows pressing practical reasons why it should have been a quintet; while, perversely enough, the Schumann quintet might, from first to last, be arranged as a quartet, or even as a trio, such loss as might exist being compensated by the disappearance of characterless doublings. Double-stopping will spoil a quartet style in two ways, first by succeeding in making it into quintet or sextet style, and, contrariwise, by interpolating casual notes needed for the harmony but coming from nowhere. The following detail from the unscrupulously brilliant wind-up of Brahms's F major quintet, op. 88, neatly defines the issue:

Ex. 13.
Viola.

It is amusing to hear a good player practising this nasty corner and swearing at it for its 'ineffectiveness'. Its business is to supply necessary notes which would, even if accessible, be a nuisance to the instruments who have to make themselves 'effective'. At the cost of a trivial difficulty Brahms gets these notes into an intelligible pattern. The necessities of the case might have led to the following arrangement—

Ex. 14.

which would have been easier to play, but which Brahms would have certainly rejected as a clumsy and unrhythmic makeshift.

The first movement of the C minor quartet is a dark and stormy tragedy, the 'second subject' being not less agitated than the first. The lines of the exposition are broad and flowing, while the development is, as in the following A minor, compressed.

The romanze is the first slow movement in which Brahms puts his full resources into a simple ABA form, both sections being regular binary melodies, and all necessary development being supplied by the subtlety of the few bars which contrive the return to the main theme. So original are the rhythms and so gorgeous the scoring and the variation of the main theme on its return, that the movement has often been supposed to be far more complex than it really is.

The scherzo is in its main body like a querulous brother or sister of that of the G major sextet, in darker colour throughout.

The trio (also analogous to that in the sextet as regards major mode and the contrast between duple and triple time) is highly picturesque in scoring.

From the F minor key of the scherzo the opening figure of the short finale arises in wrath. Brahms never indicates that two independent movements are to follow on without break; but not only does he in all cases calculate the effect of the last chord of one movement on the first of the next (Haydn and Beethoven are very particular in this matter), but he here for the first time contrives to make a short finale gain in weight by its effect as a kind of epilogue to the previous movement and to the whole work. Such is the sense of the finales of the C major trio, op. 87, the violoncello sonata, op. 99, and the clarinet trio, op. 114. Their wonderful completeness of form and climax is disguised by their extreme terseness, but produces an effect of the noblest proportions and final emotional aptness if the listener regards these movements as codas to the preceding scherzos.

This impression of finality is enforced in the C minor quartet by the fact that the opening figure of the finale is a compound of those of the romanze and the first movement. This might have happened without intention, but the allusion is made quite explicit in the last bars. As a single movement this finale is not one to convert the sceptical or to flatter the 'Brahmins', but players who have outgrown mad-bull methods of attack find it excitingly sonorous, and listeners find it a convincing and impressive end to a work full of tragic passion.

The A minor quartet, though also full of tragedy and often dark in colour, has abundance of relief, the 'second subject' of the first movement being one of the most attractive and graceful passages Brahms ever wrote. Polyphony of Bach-like thoroughness and Mozart-like euphony is the normal texture except for the tremolos above described, and these occur in passages of close canon. In the first movement the pathetic first theme (placed obliquely across the key) is foredoomed to a tragic end. The slow movement is a broad and elaborate ABA design with considerable expansion in development and coda; its ruminating first theme is of a kind that many 'Brahmins' have eagerly imitated under the mistaken impression that such things can be achieved by 'logical development'.

In the place of scherzo the third movement is a slow minuet with pathetically drooping cadences, alternating with a polyphonic trio in duple time and running rhythm, twice interrupted by the minuet-tempo with a combination of the two themes, wonderfully transforming that of the trio.

The finale is a lively rondo, not tragic, but master of its fate and in high spirits of a kind which exhilarate the listeners without suggesting that their temper is to be trifled with.

Third Pianoforte Quartet, op. 60, in C minor. This work had been drafted, how far finished we do not know, at the same time as the other two pianoforte quartets. It was then in C sharp minor, but we do not know whether the key relation of the other movements was the same as now, nor indeed whether the draft proceeded beyond the first movement. The scherzo was long believed to be of a still earlier period and to have been expanded from that of a violin sonata written on the musical letters of the name of Joachim's friend Gisela von Arnim (Gis, e, la) by Schumann, Brahms, and Dietrich, each writing a movement. Joachim himself was under this impression until he saw this sonata again some years after Brahms's death, and found that the scherzo (which it was then decided to publish as a posthumous work) had no resemblance to that of op. 60 beyond being in 6/8 time, free in form and of a fiery temper.

The first movement of op. 60 seems in its original form to have got into difficulties, the nature of which it is useless to guess. All we know is that at the time of the first draft Brahms told a friend to think of the opening as of a man resigned to utter despair; a description which still holds good in its present form. For the rest, it has been a misfortune to critics, especially to the 'Brahmins' themselves, that the work was ever known to have had a history. Hanslick dropped expressions about 'the technique of a beginner' which showed how unlikely it is that Beckmesser ever will attain the status of a beginner even in the knowledge of the art which he most sincerely admires. The only passage in the whole work which might have been achieved with an earlier technique than that of the B flat sextet is the grandiose transformation of the first theme in the development, with its Schubert-like twofold appearance in B major and G major. If, as is likely, this belonged to the first draft, its retention with its drastically simple scoring only shows that a great artist's view of the range of styles that can be united in one work of art is that of a 'spectator of all time and existence'. It gives rise to a far more drastically simple passage by which the recapitulation (which is in an unexpected new key) leads to the abrupt tragic coda. From beginning to end the first movement is written with a technique as far beyond that of the two other piano quartets as Beethoven's fifth symphony is beyond the possibilities of his second. We have no record of the changes Brahms had to make in this work, but they must have been enormous; for Joachim told me in private conversation that in its first version this C minor (then C sharp minor) quartet was 'very diffuse'. And, as we have seen, its two predecessors, though not diffuse for their own purposes, strain to the utmost permissible limits the length of their themes and the completeness of their statements and counter-statements. A work that can have seemed to Joachim diffuse in comparison with the G minor and A major quartets cannot have proceeded for more than two or three successive staves upon the lines of op. 60 as we now know it. Diffuseness is the last quality to impute to a work in which the Schubertian process already cited and the leisurely handling of the 'second subject' of the slow movement give an effect of exceptional breadth. A comparison of that Schubertian process with typical examples by Schubert himself will show that Brahms has made and repeated his point in the time it takes Schubert to show the pattern of his sequence. No other works of Brahms, not even the first and fourth symphonies, show so wide a range of forms. The most astonishing novelty is the casting of the 'second subject' of the first movement into the form of an eight-bar melody ending on a half-close and followed by a set of five variations. In the recapitulation, which is very unexpectedly in the bright dominant key of G major, Brahms begins with two new variations marking the return to the old ones by an expansion, the original third and fourth variation being expanded into the tragic coda. The key of G major had been arrived at as a revelation of the predestined result of a mysterious incident in the opening of the movement, when over the first pause on the dominant a pizzicato E natural asked an unexpected question, to which an immediate fortissimo replied with what was evidently an angry refusal to consider it. Thus Brahms is now developing his forms entirely from their dramatic import outwards, as in the maturest works of Beethoven. He was always too great an artist to set up forms *a priori* and shovel his music into them; but he has now reached a level of organization at which *a priori* notions of form not only fail to illustrate his work, but often simply mislead.

The short and powerful scherzo is best understood as both a reaction from and a coda to the audaciously abrupt tragic end of the first movement. Some of its themes are near enough to the style of the sonata, op. 1, to have deceived Joachim (as we have seen) into a mistaken 'recollection' of it as a draft of that early period, but the form and technique is of Brahms's ripest. Bull-headed attacks will get nothing out of this movement, which demands (and rewards) perfect tone-production and the most articulate phrasing, especially the Schubert-like but compact G minor theme, with its solemn ritardando cadence in the major.

The slow movement begins with what has always been acknowledged to be one of Brahms's greatest and most original melodies. It is in the remote key of E major; this key-relation first occurred in Beethoven's C minor concerto, and soon afterwards Brahms used it again in his first symphony.

This andante comes as near to full sonata-form as Brahms permits in his extant slow movements, the only exception being that in his classical exercise-work the serenade in D, where it is significant that the tempo-mark adagio is almost impracticable for the long, trailing lines of its form. In the C minor quartet nothing can be grander and more natural than the flow of the whole. The development is represented by two steps of a glorious modulating sequence, and the recapitulation of the very leisurely 'second subject' is represented by a coda-like summary.

In the finale certain obvious but superficial resemblances to features in the first movement and finale of Mendelssohn's C minor trio caused comments which provoked Brahms to his oft-quoted remark about the habit of 'mutton-heads' who notice such things. Apart from this, no movement of Brahms has been more misunderstood; it is usually taken far too fast, and the tranquillo directions in the mysterious development (the first and most elaborate development of a kind peculiar to the composer) seem often to escape notice. Little help can be given to uncomprehending players and listeners by pointing out the incredible molecular combinations of its thematic organization; it is easy to dismiss such things as pedantries, though it is demonstrable that in great music they are worked out to atomic accuracy without attracting attention, whereas in pedantic music they are a bluff which breaks down if you 'call' it. The only clue to this finale, with its childlike pathos and power, is in a clear understanding of the nature of tragedy, as distinguished from the merely pathetic or melodramatic. Those to whom Brahms's third pianoforte quartet is not one of the greatest pieces of all purely tragic music may go and keep company with Hanslick in a heaven consisting of the A major quartet and such passages from the middle works of Beethoven as can be seen to be in good taste without any reference to such tiresome things as contexts.

THIRD STRING QUARTET IN B FLAT, op. 67. The tragic work that proved indigestible to the orthodox 'Brahmins' was promptly followed by a Haydnesque comedy that gave far more offence. Solemn people do not like being teased, and in real life Brahms never quite got over the teasing habit. But he did not take the trouble to tease people whom he disliked; and that is where the humour of the alternately teasing and coaxing first movement of this quartet resembles Haydn's and differs radically from that of Wagner, who certainly did not like either Beckmesser or the original Hans Lich.

The slow movement is, in form, like a popular version of that in the A minor quartet. It does not deserve disparagement, but it does suggest the probability that Brahms had in his rejected works many written like it, on the border-lines of easy conception and laboured execution, and that here we have the only example that did not overstep those lines. Undoubtedly he would have become far more popular if most of his slow movements had been replicas of this.

The third movement, a scherzo in form and a passionate lyric in style, has always made a profound impression. It is, both in its freely expansive main section and in its trio, a viola solo, the other strings being muted. It requires a moderate tempo and great natural freedom of rhythm in the viola part.

Throughout the first movement, scherzo, and finale of this quartet the prominence of the viola has rather scandalized the orthodox, but there is nothing in it antagonistic to quartet style. The criterion of absolute equality of the four parts is impracticable and allows for nothing but the most complex styles. The effect of giving special prominence to the viola, or (as in Mozart's last three quartets) to the violoncello, is, as here, a special effect of colour; and obviously to give special prominence to the second violin would be either to produce an accompanied violin duet or, in excess, to exchange the terms 'first' and 'second'.

The finale is a set of variations on one of the most kittenish themes since Haydn. Brahms nowhere shows a profounder insight into sonata style than in his clear preservation of the melody throughout a set of variations when it is a movement in a sonata. In the sonata style we feel our way by identifying the themes as melodies; hence a set of variations as part of a sonata should not, in Brahms's opinion, treat the mere harmonic and rhythmic scheme as equivalent to the melody in the ways which are so interesting and desirable in independent variations.

Nothing could have been easier than to drag in the ghost of previous movements in free variations towards the end of the finale; in this way a popular idea of musical evolution is readily jerry built when invention fails. But Brahms does something very different. Towards the end of these Mozart-Haydn melodic variations the main themes of the first and second subjects of the first movement are combined not contrapuntally but with the melodic lines of the variation theme. And so the work expands in grand proportions and childlike happiness to its close.

First Sonata for Pianoforte and Violin, in G major, op. 78. This fifth of Brahms's efforts in the most difficult of all problems in chamber music solves its problem in terms of an extraordinary predominance of cantabile, in which the violin is leading almost the whole time. In the first movement the development is the only stormy passage in the whole work, and room is made for its crowded incidents by slackening the tempo (più sostenuto)—so that the 'poco a poco tempo Imo' which leads to the return is a slight accelerando, a point not always understood by good players without special experience in Brahms.

The adagio is a solemn, dramatic, and highly developed ABA movement with themes of great rhythmic freedom and a coda in which those of the agitated middle section are 'augmented' in a passage of tremendous depth. The influence of the adagio of Beethoven's G major sonata, op. 96, may be suspected here. Disaster awaits performers who attack the middle section without understanding that Brahms uses the words 'più andante' in their correct Italian sense of 'going on', i. e. faster.

There is no scherzo, and the finale is a gently flowing rondo in G minor, ending in the major only in the coda. The theme, though its rhythmic initial figure suggests that of the first movement, comes from a couple of songs (*Regenlied* and *Nachklänge*) written some years earlier; but a flood of light is thrown on the nature of musical form and rhetoric by carrying the comparison beyond the first two bars. It will be found that not only is the continuation different in each of the songs, but that within the sonata there are several fresh continuations, rising in proper order to their climax. An equally significant point is the use of the theme of the slow movement for the second episode and coda of this rondo. It is no mere ghost, such as can be easily evoked by writing out the old theme in the notation of the new tempo in disregard of the resulting stagnation of movement; but it consists of the first six notes of the adagio with a new continuation that makes it not only the warmest but the most urgent theme in the finale. In the coda its new iambic rhythmic figure gives rise to a series of modulations anticipating on a small scale the solemn end of the third symphony.

Trio in C major, op. 87, for Pianoforte, Violin, and Violoncello. Three movements of this work are on the largest possible scale, while the short finale is, as has been suggested above, best understood as if the scherzo had led to it. The first movement is as broad as those of the first two pianoforte quartets, with the difference that its numerous themes, instead of being immediately of the utmost permissible breadth, are terse statements with unlimited powers of expansion. The style is grandly energetic with deep shadows of mystery, the mystery of nature rather than romance. The development is remarkably Schubertian and transforms the first theme into an 'augmentation' for which Brahms requires a quicker tempo, an unexpected phenomenon for him, especially in so late a work.

The slow movement is a glorious set of variations on a theme of heroic pathos, akin to that of the first sextet, but on a higher plane. At first one might think that the quiet fourth variation in the major mode was an exception to Brahms's rule that in sonata works variations should preserve the melody, but in this movement there are two simultaneous melodies, one for the strings and the other for the pianoforte; and here the pianoforte theme is carried straight through with ornamentation which combines the harmonic luxuriousness of Brahms with the schematic accuracy of Mozart.

The dark pianissimo scherzo, with its huge white cloud-bank trio, is extremely difficult for the pianist to execute with the necessary lightness of touch, but never fails to make an impression. The finale, on the other hand, is usually ruined by being played far too fast, when nothing results but an admirably terse exercise in form. In real life it is full of humour and mystery, and leads to a magnificently sonorous end. Brahms's notation goes too far in prescribing common instead of alla breve time, but at all events it conveys a hint.

STRING QUINTET IN F MAJOR, op. 88. This comparatively neglected work is one of Brahms's most unconventional compositions. It has all the sonorousness of the first sextet, and one is tempted to think that Brahms enjoyed in it a feeling of relief after the restraint which string quartet writing imposed on his love of full harmony. The first movement begins with a melody so tuneful and square that only by comparison with earlier works can we realize how terse Brahms's form has now become. The slow movement is one of Brahms's very greatest inspirations. A tragically impassioned declamatory theme in C sharp minor (3/4 time, grave)[1] is worked out into a movement that might almost stand alone as a complete cavatina. Then a quiet little binary scherzo in A major 6/8 appears and completes itself. The grave returns, quickly at first, but rising later to more than its former passion. When it has died away again, the A major scherzo appears in an alla breve presto variation. Then the grave returns for the last time, beginning now in A major, but working round to its utterly tragic conclusion in C sharp minor. But now comes the miracle, predestined from the outset. The final chords hover between C sharp, as a resigned major chord, and A major as a dark submediant, the more despairing from its having been the tonic chord of the scherzo interludes. At last the A major chord gives way to an unexpected D minor chord, which, as subdominant, brings about a final plagal close to the whole movement in A major. Nothing else like this is to be found in music; and it shows what Brahms could achieve by his abstention from all such chromatic resources as could distract attention from the function of simple tonality in sonata form. It is as certain as any 'if' outside the world of winged pigs, that if Brahms had thought fit to develop a modulating style like Reger's, he would have abandoned sonata forms altogether.

[1] It first occurred to Brahms in 1855 as a Sarabande for pianoforte.

The finale of op. 88 is not a movement whereby to convert the Anti-Brahmins; and least of all Brahms's movements does it yield up any secrets to wild-cat or mad-bull attacks in performance. It is in the highest of spirits which one cannot but imagine enhanced by the hilarious reaction which high-spirited creatures often experience at the sight of shocked solemn faces whom their levity has surprised. Yet it is not humorous, and has no more leisure for jokes than an athlete in mid-play. In form and texture it combines the tersest sonata form with the closest fugal polyphony; and it hardly takes six minutes in performance.

SECOND VIOLONCELLO SONATA IN F MAJOR, op. 99; SECOND VIOLIN SONATA IN A MAJOR, op. 100; TRIO IN C MINOR. These three works were all produced in the same year, and (like Mozart's last three symphonies produced within six weeks) make an excellent concert programme, their contrasts being, in the nature of the case, exactly what represented the happiest reactions of the composer himself.

They are the tersest of all Brahms's works, the only passage which takes up any room on paper being the 'cloud-capped tower' opening of the coda of the first movement of the A major violin sonata. Their forms, though presenting few abnormalities, show all the more clearly in their extraordinary compression that Brahms never constructed on an *a priori* scheme and never exactly repeated a form.

The F major 'cello sonata gives this instrument far more range than it had in op. 38. This is splendidly illustrated by the transition from first subject to second.

Ex. 15.

The broken rhythm of the main theme and the ways in which it is transformed into sustained figures in the course of development constitute a notable addition to the resources of sonata style. The whispering chromatic episode in F sharp minor at the beginning of the development is another peculiar feature, and in its choice of key prepares the ear for the remote key of the slow movement. The tremolos for the pianoforte and (legato across the strings) the 'cello shocked the orthodox at the time this work appeared, but Brahms knows no aesthetic criteria but those of the ear and of the individual work as a whole, and does not hesitate to add two magnificent new colours to the resources of chamber music. The 'cellist should keep the bow evenly on the two strings involved, with a movement hardly distinguishable from a sustained double note; and the pianist should observe that Brahms follows Beethoven (in the D major trio) and Liszt *passim* in regarding the best tremolo as not indefinitely fast but consisting of an exact even number of notes. The marks of damping down the sound (*sf p; f* > *mp;* &c.) should be carefully acted upon. Brahms, however, once found himself playing this sonata with a 'cellist of no great promise or accomplishment, and accordingly opened the throttle of the pianoforte and let her rip and roar. The 'cellist's voice penetrated the din with the complaint, 'Master, I can't hear myself at all'—and Brahms barked back at him, 'Lucky for you'. But this is not the way classical traditions should be formed.

The slow movement in F sharp major, the key a semitone above the tonic, might have been written in G flat, had not its important modulation (after the return of the main theme) to D major been a troublesome affair to read in E double-flat. The unusual key-relationship is thought out with the profoundest thoroughness and accuracy. There are three important earlier classical examples which neatly show the stages of progress in the handling of such ideas. First there is Carl Philipp Emanuel Bach, who in a symphony in D major has a short middle movement in E flat. To justify this he introduces it by a dramatic passage tacked on to the end of the first. Translated into English prose this means, 'grotesque and foolish as it may seem to the sober listener, it is absolutely true that the slow movement is in E flat'. Very different is the procedure of Haydn, to whom such a key-relation is a paradox true enough to be worth stating violently. In his last pianoforte sonata, which is in E flat, the slow movement is in E natural (=F flat). Haydn begins the slow movement straightforwardly on its tonic, and pointedly begins his finale with the one note which, unharmonized, most flatly contradicts the key of the slow movement without reasserting the key of E flat until the bass explains it. The third stage is represented by Beethoven in his C sharp minor quartet and (in a more extreme form) by Brahms here. To Beethoven and Brahms this remote key is simply that of the flat supertonic, as used ever since mid-classical tonality of major and minor modes in scales of all pitches communicating with each other by chords in common. The founder of classical tonality, Alessandro Scarlatti, already used this flat supertonic so constantly in ultra-minor cadences that the form of chord in which it conveniently occurs is called, after his *scuola*, the 'Neapolitan sixth'.

This F sharp major slow movement compresses a great amount of design into a small space, which nevertheless seems able to expand without limit. The pizzicato of the 'cello here makes a splendid and novel bass to the full harmony of the pianoforte and is worked to a tremendous climax when the strain is brought back after the dark remote depths of the F minor middle episode. Hausmann, with Brahms's approval, made a great accelerando at this crescendo, thus providing a natural means of carrying the resonance of the pizzicato over the notes before they dry up.

The impassioned and highly developed movement which takes the form and place of scherzo and trio requires free rhythm and more legato and cantabile in both instruments than the look of the page suggests. The opening pianoforte theme, though difficult, should not be conceived as a brilliant *tour de force*. Other contrasted themes must press forward, but as a whole the movement is not to be hustled. The great melody of the trio is also in no hurry, and in the B major passage beginning seventeen bars after the double bar, the pianist must realize that his light figures are no mere accompaniment but are outlining the continuation of the melody. The rondo which ends the sonata with the smallest and most childlike of Brahms's finales is one of those cases where the small finale has the effect of an epilogue to the previous movement. Brahms liked a lively tempo for it. In any tempo it is difficult to achieve the necessary lightness of touch and accent in both instruments.

The A major violin sonata, op. 100, is throughout one of Brahms's most melodious works. It is sometimes known by the 'mutton-head' title of Meistersinger sonata, because of its first three notes, but Wagner's own text tells us that the Meistersinger rules enact that a song counts as original when it does not trespass upon 'more than four syllables' of another master-song.

The first movement, with its impressive coda, does not strike one as very terse until its proportions are actually measured against those of, say, the A major quartet, op. 26. The slow movement is an alternation of andante and scherzo, a counterpart in pastoral comedy to the sublime mystery of the slow movement of the F major string quintet. Here, if ever, we must judge by ear and not by eye; the dangerous little learning in form leads to a state of mind which refuses to be convinced that two lines and a half of andante can be correctly balanced against two pages and a half of vivace; yet in point of time such is the result, and not one master in a hundred (on the plane in which there are hundreds) could have guessed it. As in the rondo of the G major sonata, the andante theme here has a different continuation every time it recurs. It is more often played too slow than too fast; for, though broad, it should not be adagio. The direction 'vivace di più', on the second appearance of the scherzo theme, does not, as it might, mean only 'vivace again', but 'faster than before'. In any convincing tempo it is very difficult to play with a sufficiently light and accurate pianoforte touch, and, in the second version, the pianoforte should be light enough for the violinist to risk playing his pizzicatos without effort. At the juncture of the two tempi there should be no perceptible ritardando or pause, and where the last 3/4 cadences are 'augmented', the rhythm should be felt not as a syncopation but as a change to 3/2 time, thus,

123 | 123 | 123456 |

The finale is a rondo, deeply thoughtful in tone, and so terse that a description of its form would convey the impression of a movement three times as long. It is often played too fast, but suffers still more from being played with too small a tone and too timid a style in its opening theme, which should be taken as one of the outstanding cantabiles for the fourth string. The tempo should be measured by reconciling the alla breve time-signature with the compression of four bars of this cantabile into two bars in double-stopping towards the end of the movement.

The C minor trio concludes this group of works with one of Brahms's most powerful creations. The first movement is tragic in the heroic manner of Coriolanus, not of Hamlet, Othello, or King Lear. For all its pride, however, it has its tender moments, especially in the beginning of the C sharp minor passage in the development. After the passionate close of the first movement, the presto non assai, which takes the place of a scherzo, hurries by like a frightened child. It is one of Brahms's most impressive pieces of tone-colour, and has something in common with the intermezzo in the G minor quartet, op. 25, though with its shuddering trio and its coda on an entirely new theme combined with the opening phrase in a strange augmentation, it is all over in about the time the earlier work takes for a couple of statements and counter-statements.

Another child of the gods, free from terror, greets us in the exquisite andante with its mixture of 3/4 and 2/4 bars (which do not always make the same 7-beat or 5-beat phrases), and its quite simple ABA form with eight regular bars of playful coda. Then, in full sonata form, comes the grimly energetic finale, which in the latter part of the 'second subject' requires a slower tempo for its crowding, tempestuous incidents. Everything is in dark minor keys until the moment arrives for the coda, which transfigures the main themes in solemn triumph in the major.

SONATA IN D MINOR, op. 108. Here Brahms achieves a violin sonata on a symphonic scale, and obviously as full of effortless power as any conceivable quartet or sextet. The first movement is unique in that its entire development portion is on a dominant pedal, which is reproduced as a tonic pedal in the coda. From Joachim I learnt that at the first *forte* Brahms made a decided animato which he might as well have marked in the score; this, of course, implies that the tempo of the outset must be broad, though, of course, flowing. The cross accents of the impassioned 'second subject' require not less emphasis and tone in the single notes of the violin than in the big chords of the pianoforte. The most difficult passage is, of course, the intensely quiet development on the long dominant pedal. The violin, which begins it by distributing the opening melody with its counterpoint across two strings, must keep the bow over both strings in the manner of double-stopping instead of letting the passage sound dry; the pianist must let all his melodic figures quietly penetrate the whole texture, and the moment where the violin holds a high E for a bar, before climbing down the scale of D major, must assert itself like a long sunray through the clouds.

The slow movement is a cavatina, that is to say, a single melody achieving the spaciousness of an entire movement by expanding without allowing a middle section to partition itself off. This idea was first achieved by Haydn in his wonderful little D minor quartet, op. 42; and even the cavatina of Beethoven's quartet, op. 130, has more of a separate middle episode. Such simplicity comes of the concentration of a life's experience; it cannot be imitated by merely writing a tune and refusing to develop it. The third movement puts far more than the contents of a scherzo into four minutes of plaintively elvish music in a design which, without an enclosed middle section, ranges from F sharp minor to the immense distance of F major. The history of its scoring has already been described.

With the finale we return to symphonic dimensions in a powerful sonata rondo with a grandly tragic climax. The only passage which is liable to be misunderstood is that in its middle development where the violin, after stating a cantabile transformation of the opening figure (in G minor), accompanies the answers of the pianoforte with a syncopated counter-subject. Here it is important not to let the tone of the violin become dry or husky against too full a pianoforte; the well-meant practice of letting the violin murmur indistinctly against a leading pianoforte passage is (*pace* César Franck in the second movement of his violin sonata) always thoroughly unsatisfactory in its result. With an even balance of tone we appreciate the depth of the harmony and the dramatic force of its modulations.

STRING QUINTET IN G MAJOR, op. 111. At its first London performance, before printed parts were available, I distinctly remember that there was no difficulty in hearing the violoncello with its theme in the lowest bass under the Niagara of sound in the other four high-lying instruments, who seemed to me to be 'letting themselves go' without scruple. This shows the importance of properly balanced marks of expression to the composer, and of exact observance of them, for we know that at first there was great difficulty in getting the opening theme through; and Brahms went so far as to draft a scoring (the draft has been preserved) in which the upper strings divided their movement with alternating rests, so as to halve the mass of tone while still keeping the movement going. This, however, was abandoned as patchy in colour, and, as the experience of a listener with no score to guide him shows, by the time Joachim brought the work to London, the difficulty was triumphantly settled by damping the violins and violas to a mezzo-forte as soon as the violoncello enters. If nowadays the opening still fails, that is because the players get too excited to act according to directions. The whole work is an immensely powerful outburst of high spirits. The first movement seems unlimited in its capacity for expansion, and actually has a leisurely tonic-and-dominant peroration in its coda such as had not been heard since Beethoven's Eroica and ninth symphonies; yet the movement is by no means long. The adagio is another cavatina, if its form admits of codification at all, and is one of the most impressive of all Brahms's tragic utterances. Its proper tempo is slower than that of any other movement in classical music since the largo of Beethoven's C minor concerto.

Then comes an exquisite plaintive little scherzo and trio, with a simplicity of effect which conceals a microscopic complexity of polyphonic detail; no figured chorale of Bach is more closely knit.

The finale, beginning in a foreign key, is a sonata movement of such range and vigour that the listener will never realize how short it really is. At the end its coda breaks away into a completely new dance tune, the phrases of which reel down in bacchanalian irregularity to explain themselves with impudent assurance as connected with the main theme by ties as intimate as a borrowed visiting-card.

Brahms was beginning to talk of regarding this work as representing the end of his career, when the wonderful clarinet playing of Mühlfeld inspired him to four more works which made another definite extension to the range of his own style and restored wind instruments to the place in chamber music appointed for them by Mozart.

The trio for pianoforte, clarinet, and violoncello, in A minor, op. 114, is overshadowed by its great neighbour the clarinet quintet; but it is by no means the small and unimportant work it is often supposed to be. From Steinbach I learnt that Brahms at first intended its opening theme for that of a fifth symphony; and if the first movement and slow movement had been followed up on a larger instead of a smaller scale, or had the finale been pathetic instead of alternately defiant, reflective, and humorous, the work would not have been easily eclipsed. The first movement is broad and full of romance, with a development which, as usual in Brahms's later works, is compressed and thoughtful, and must not be dryly delivered. The colour of the coda, especially the last line, is very romantic, and in the slow movement, which is in a broad arioso-sonata form, no more gorgeous colouring has been achieved in chamber music. Not less charming in colour is the following andantino which is in the form of a minuet in A major with two trios (F sharp minor and D major). Its themes have been severely censured, but are inseparable from their ingenious scoring.

The finale is over in five minutes, and contains everything that a full-sized sonata movement has room for. Its development, like some in Beethoven's last works, is a single process of a sequence of falling thirds, and should, if properly interpreted, be as full of a sense of the silent workings of gods, fates, and nature, as any similar monumental simplicities in Greek tragedy.

THE QUINTET IN B MINOR FOR CLARINET AND STRINGS, op. 115, made an immediate impression which eclipsed the trio, and would have eclipsed the clarinet sonatas had they not appeared after another year's interval and been from the outset regarded as smaller works. The quintet is one of the most original and also one of the most pathetic of all Brahms's works. Its ambiguous opening in a key that seems to be D major instead of B minor is another interesting development of an idea suggested by Philipp Emanuel Bach in a sonata beginning

Ex. 16.

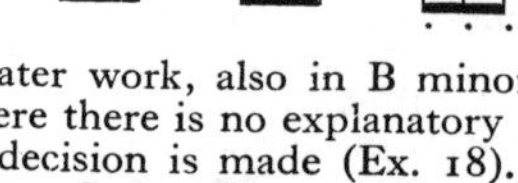

and carried out by Haydn in two of his most subtle quartets, that in B minor, op. 33, no. 1,

Ex. 17.

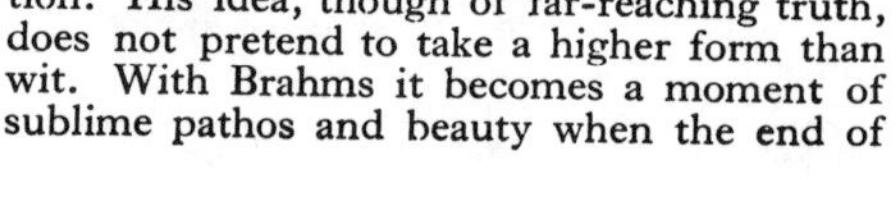

and the later work, also in B minor, op. 64, no. 2, where there is no explanatory harmony until the decision is made (Ex. 18). Haydn is thinking of the effect of these openings on repetition after the close of his exposition. His idea, though of far-reaching truth, does not pretend to take a higher form than wit. With Brahms it becomes a moment of sublime pathos and beauty when the end of

Ex. 18.

the exposition leads back, not to the first bars (though these have the necessary ambiguity for Haydn's point) but to the entry of the clarinet on the full chord of D.

Ex. 19.

The abrupt catastrophe of the first movement, leaving barely time to re-establish B minor after having recapitulated the 'second subject' in another key, is, like the similar case in the first movement of the C minor pianoforte quartet, op. 60, balanced by the effect of the next movement following on with the same tonic. Here, however, it is the slow movement that follows, in a seraphic B major melody with muted strings. A wildly romantic middle section in the minor, with extraordinary arabesques for the clarinet, works itself out on still broader lines of melodic binary form. In spite of its strict form, it is unlike anything else in classical music; but if one has the good fortune to hear a genuine Hungarian band whose leader happens to be a clarinettist, one will be thrilled on recognizing exactly Brahms's treatment of the instrument here. The passage leading back to the main section is exceptionally dramatic, and no subtler stroke has ever been achieved than that by which the last bar of the common time does duty for the first bar of the 3/4 opening theme,

Ex. 20.

The third movement is unique in form. It begins with a pair of themes in D major, common time, andante, which, after a climax, come to a quiet close. Then a transformation of these themes in contrapuntal combination, 2/4 time, presto non assai (the beats hardly faster than those of the andante), is worked out in B minor into a terse binary movement with a contrasted 'second subject' in syncopated rhythm in F sharp minor. The whole exposition of this is pianissimo. After some development a complete recapitulation follows, with a coda that bursts out vigorously and leads without change of tempo to the theme which appeared at the climax of the andante, and so, in a few lines, to its quiet close in D. The abruptness is not more astonishing than the fact that the effect is more and more convincing on every hearing.

The finale is a set of variations, Mozartian in their strictly melodic principles, with all Brahms's Bach-like logic of polyphony, and unique in the subtlety of their theme which, for all its apparent simplicity, cannot be expressed by a single voice. After the fifth variation, which is in 3/8 time in contrast with the previous 2/4, the 3/8 bars are merged into the 6/8 bars of the first movement, the opening theme of which appears and combines with the cadence of the 3/8 variation. And so the work closes in sorrow.

THE TWO CLARINET SONATAS, op. 120, no. 1, in F minor, and no. 2, in E flat, end Brahms's chamber music. It is noteworthy that they are described as for clarinet and piano, not vice versa as with all classical violin and violoncello sonatas from Mozart onwards. Yet the piano is, if anything, less subordinate to the other instrument than in the G major violin sonata. As the forms are extremely terse the range they cover is very large. In the F minor sonata the first movement is full of passionate melancholy, the coda, with its strange canonic development of an ornamental figure arising out of the main themes, being specially impressive. The two middle movements are both in the same key, A flat major, a thing unprecedented in four-movement sonatas, and of delicious effect here where both are so short, the slow movement being an ABA design highly organized in detail, and the scherzo the most deliciously Viennese of all Brahms's works. The finale, in rondo form with very whimsical themes, is high comedy of the wittiest kind.

The E flat clarinet sonata begins with a quiet first movement in a mood not unlike that of the first movement of the A major violin sonata (also headed allegro amabile). The mysterious triplet episode in the development is one of those profundities which players inexperienced in Brahms are apt to reduce to the aesthetic level of the multiplication table. Players who cannot make of this movement one of the most mellow products of all chamber music should leave Brahms alone.

There are only three movements, the second being an impassioned scherzo in E flat minor with a sonorous trio in B major (=C flat). The finale is a set of variations on an andante theme in 6/8 time. The fifth variation breaks into vivace 2/4 time in E flat minor, and then settles down in a peaceful coda which finally arouses itself to a spirited end.

Students of chamber music should not neglect Brahms's two arrangements of these clarinet sonatas for violin and for viola. These are on quite a different plane from the use of a viola as substitute for the clarinet in the quintet and trio, though Brahms authorized the issue of parts so transcribed. But in the trio and quintet the relation of the clarinet to the string parts makes it impossible to alter the position of anything, and transcription accordingly reveals all the points where the viola fails to represent a clarinet. But with these sonatas Brahms could use a free hand. In the violin version he sometimes alters the piano part. Joachim, who would have nothing to do with transcriptions as a rule, took great pleasure in playing the violin version of both sonatas. The viola version is better, besides being a welcome opportunity for viola players. In it the piano part is unaltered, but the viola part is a fine demonstration of the different characters of the instruments. The viola is querulous and strained just where the cantabile of the clarinet is warmest. The lowest octave of the clarinet is of a dramatic blue-grotto hollowness and coldness, where the fourth string of the viola is of a rich and pungent warmth. A comparison of Brahms's viola part with his original clarinet part makes every difference of this kind vividly real, and these viola versions deserve frequent performance in public.

If every one of Brahms's works in sonata form rewards the effort of a reasoned defence on all points on which attack has been directed, this is not because Brahms is either himself infallible, or acceptable only to those who are ready to take him as gospel. It is, on the contrary, because Brahms was so far from thinking himself infallible that he consented to the publication of nothing to which he had not devoted more severe criticism, long after the work was finished, than could be collected from all the sensible remarks that have ever been made on his works since they appeared. In his early days, what his own criticism might have let slip was subjected to the sensitive ear and practical experience of Joachim, and Brahms's docility was strictly reasonable, never revolting against the authority of proved fact, and therefore never imputing unsympathetic motives to so disinterested a friend. The result is that the defence of his works is an infinitely more fruitful line of criticism than that of attack; for attacks are easy on superficial grounds, while the defence rests on bedrock.

DONALD F. TOVEY.

SOME PERSONAL RECOLLECTIONS OF BRAHMS AS PIANIST AND INTERPRETER.

After Professor Tovey's splendid article on Brahms's chamber music it would seem almost superfluous for me to add anything on this subject; and it is only because I have enjoyed the inestimable privilege of hearing several of these works played by Brahms himself, that I feel I may accept the Editor's invitation to write a few words about Brahms as interpreter and pianist.

To attempt to put on paper a description of his playing is difficult. One is dealing with a towering creative genius recreating his own creations. Brahms's manner of interpretation was free, very elastic and expansive; but the balance was always there—one felt the fundamental rhythms underlying the surface rhythms. His phrasing was notable in lyric passages. In these a strictly metronomic Brahms is as unthinkable as a fussy or hurried Brahms in passages which must be presented with adamantine rhythm. Behind his often rugged, and almost sketchy playing, there never failed to appear that routined and definite school of technique without which he might sometimes have become almost a caricature of himself. When Brahms played, one knew exactly what he intended to convey to his listeners: aspiration, wild fantastic flights, majestic calm, deep tenderness without sentimentality, delicate, wayward humour, sincerity, noble passion. In his playing, as in his music and in his character, there was never a trace of sensuality.

His touch could be warm, deep, full, and broad in the *fortes*, and not hard even in the *fortissimos*; and his *pianos*, always of carrying power, could be as round and transparent as a dewdrop. He had a wonderful legato. He belonged to that racial school of playing which begins its phrases well, ends them well, leaves plenty of space between the end of one and the beginning of another, and yet joins them without any hiatus. One could hear that he listened very intently to the inner harmonies, and of course he laid great stress on good basses.

Like Beethoven, he was most particular that his marks of expression (always as few as possible) should be the means of conveying the inner musical meaning. The sign <>, as used by Brahms, often occurs when he wishes to express great sincerity and warmth, applied not only to tone but to rhythm also. He would linger not on one note alone, but on a whole idea, as if unable to tear himself away from its beauty. He would prefer to lengthen a bar or phrase rather than spoil it by making up the time into a metronomic bar.

That Brahms in his earlier years must have been a pianist of remarkable technique is clearly shown by the well-known story of his transposing the Kreutzer sonata at a public concert on the spur of the moment, because

Reményi could not alter the pitch of his violin for fear of breaking the strings. The achievement was not the transposition, but his ability to produce at a moment's notice such a different readiness of finger as is required for a Kreutzer in A flat instead of a Kreutzer in A. This shows how complete a master of technique he was, especially considering the brilliance of the first and last movements. Again, in the Paganini studies, in the Chopin F minor study arranged in thirds and sixths, in his arrangement for left hand alone of Bach's chaconne, as well as the two books of finger studies published much later, we have ample proof that Brahms knew all about virtuosity and that he wrote pianistically. He very soon left off the habit of many young composers of writing for an abnormally large hand.

In the years during which I heard him (1884–96), Brahms had long ceased to practise regularly, and when one has reached the age of fifty, one's fingers are not apt to improve, unless used constantly. Brahms had a way of apportioning his work to different periods of the year. Thus, for instance, in the early autumn he usually corrected the proofs of any new works about to be published; then he would begin to practise for the public performances to come. It was his custom to introduce his new compositions personally in several important towns: if for the piano, playing them himself; if orchestral or choral, conducting them himself. He had made it a rule never to publish a new work until he had heard it performed, and so it came about that he made a rendezvous in Baden-Baden with the orchestra and Joachim and Hausmann, in order to go through the manuscript of the then new double concerto for violin and 'cello. The same afternoon the master wanted to play his C minor trio, op. 101, then almost new. I was in Baden-Baden, and Madame Schumann asked me whether by chance I had a copy with me, for nowhere in Baden was there one to be found. The only work I had brought with me to study was just this C minor trio, and gladly and proudly I laid it at the feet of Brahms. Then Madame Schumann asked the master to allow me to listen. He growled and grunted his approval, and I sat in a corner of the little private sitting-room in a small hotel, drinking in every note, and marking my copy afterwards with the impressions I had received while Brahms had played from it.

A simple room, a small upright pianino, the three giants, and Clara Schumann turning over the leaves. What a picture! and what sounds! I can see him now, looking eagerly, with those penetrating clear grey-blue eyes, at Joachim and Hausmann, for the start; then lifting both of his energetic little arms high up and descending 'plump' on to the first C minor chord—somewhat in the manner of the incomparable Rubinstein—as much as to say: '*I* mean *THAT*'. And I can see him visibly expanding over a diamond-shaped phrase, when he would resemble the well-known picture of himself seated at the piano with crossed hands (no doubt the B minor *Rhapsodie*) which is supposed to be a caricature, but which is very true to life.

In my copy I wrote the word 'wild', to remind me of the way he played the tempestuous arpeggios, cutting them off exactly as he has marked them, without clipping their vibrations. And I can hear those fundamental G's for the strings, upon which he laid great importance, so that from the moment the G chord enters, the idea of the pedal-point comes to light. It was all so wonderfully poised. Seven bars before the change of key-signature to C sharp minor I wrote the words, 'mysterious, always more and more until the *pp*, but without ritardando'. In those bars Brahms, like Beethoven, takes us suddenly on to another plane. And at the beginning of the coda I wrote the word 'tremendous', for it is overwhelming, and Brahms, his colleagues, and his listeners were completely carried away with the magnitude of the idea.

The second movement was notable—presto non assai. What one usually hears is 'presto'. What one heard from Brahms was 'non assai', and that tempo gave the movement the impression of mystery—I can only call it shadowy flitting! Notwithstanding the 'non assai' of the tempo, the signature of alla breve was made apparent by the rhythmical flow from the first beat of the bar to the third beat. (I marked my copy 'not the least idea of presto'.) At the second part Brahms stopped the trio to discuss the effect of these delicate phrases; the two distinct pizzicato broken chords, each with its own diminuendo, one for the 'cello, one for the violin, which form the bass of the D flat chord. These led melodically and gently into the three short chords for the piano. Brahms intentionally delayed his entry with these chords, allowing the strings plenty of time to round off exquisitely in the diminuendo of each pizzicato group. It is a wonderful little moment, and worth deep thought, in order that the emotional value as well as the beautiful design may come fully to light. The rest of the F minor section was passionate, as the music demands, and played vibrato in contrast with what had gone before; and plenty of time was given to the rests, so that the undercurrent of breathless agitation which these phrases contain should not be choked by notes coming before their time. The three discussed all this very fully. Later, when Brahms restates his opening theme with the first note greatly lengthened, it suggests a requiem, particularly when the piano chords are played with very full though soft tone, and the nuances from piano to pianissimo so well controlled that the line, though broken, moves on in continuity of idea, until the short return of mysterious flitting which forms the end. All this was played without any suggestion of ritardando, and the effect was deeply impressive.

The third movement—andante grazioso—Brahms played with unbelievable transparency of touch, elegance, simplicity and ease of phrasing. He gave out the melodic line very beautifully with the thumb or little finger—not declaiming it, but putting it very clearly and elegantly. At the beginning, he was very particular that the 'cello should hold on well to the foundation note C, starting with a very full tone before the phrase 'walks up', as it were. It was the same with the E of the violin, and Brahms wished the little phrasings inside the musical line, in the violin solo, to be gently detached, just as marked. This was one of the occasions when Brahms would lengthen infinitesimally a whole bar, or even a whole phrase, rather than spoil its quietude by making it up into a strictly metronomic bar. This expansive elasticity—in contradistinction to a real rubato (of course depending upon the musical idea)—was one of the chief characteristics of Brahms's interpretation. This is a small example, but quite a useful one.

Last movement—allegro molto—but a 6/8, and not a two in a bar allegro. It was most illuminating to hear how Brahms differentiated the two trumpet-calls in the piano part almost at the beginning. The first one, starting on G, was made to be strictly the outcome of the violin phrase which precedes and overlaps it. But the same trumpet-call, before the phrase modulates into F minor, was almost delayed in the start (intentionally) by Brahms, and therefore given an emphasized energy as compared with the first. With such phrasing and interspersing it seems that the tempo cannot ramp! Now comes something very important. The much discussed meno allegro was started a little slower, but not very much at first; then it broadened, until at the 'sostenuto sempre' the tempo became very much slower, leaving plenty of scope for the wonderful melody for the strings, and of course this continued until tempo I. The second time this comes, Joachim, by his amazing elasticity, did indeed solve the problem of agitato ma sempre sostenuto. At the beginning of the wonderful coda, that majestic variant of the original theme (now the song in C major) soared freely in the same slower tempo until the poco stringendo. Never could one forget either the playing of the strings, nor of Brahms with his glorious basses, until the movement reaches its triumphant conclusion. That melody gave Joachim the opportunity of bringing out that golden tone, when his violin would sound like a horn or a clarinet.

Though metronome marks, as everybody knows, are not satisfying, they are, all the same, useful sometimes. Therefore it may be interesting if I try to give some idea of the tempi by quoting those I put into my copy after verifying them with Joachim while the impression was fresh, as well as in many performances with him during the following years.

Brahms took the first movement on that day in Baden-Baden at about ♩ = 104, as a main tempo. The second movement about 𝅗𝅥 = 84 to 92. The third I marked '♩ = 72 and roundabout', and the quasi animato 'a little forward'—about ♩ = 96, 'drängend', i.e. an eager going-on, but not clipping. The last movement about ♩. = 120; at the much discussed meno allegro about ♩. = 88. Then the tempo broadened gradually, until at the violin solo with semiquaver accompaniment it had become about ♩. = 72. The violin solo I marked 'very much brought out', the 'cello the same—a real solo. Then came a very fine shading to *pp*, a 'taking off', but hardly to be called a ritardando. Tempo I, then, of course (♩. = 120). The song in C major and the first four bars of the poco stringendo started at about ♩ = 76—at first quietly, then going on in musical phrases and becoming rather 'wild', as marked in my copy—through 100 and 108 to 120, as in the beginning. Then, at the piano chords and octaves, the rhythm continued to be adamantine to the end. I marked, 'Not hurried', down the last page of the trio. And how often has Joachim said 'Don't budge on that last page'!

There is very much more to speak about, but what I have described is thoroughly typical of the style in which Brahms both conceived and performed his works. There remains for me only to emphasize perhaps the most important essential in starting to reproduce a work of Brahms—and that is the tempo. The tendency is usually to play the andantes too slowly, and the quick movements, scherzos, &c., too quickly. All Brahms's passages, if one can call them passages, are strings of gems, and that tempo which can best reveal these gems and help to characterize the detail at the same time as the outlines of a great work must be considered to be the right tempo. There is no doubt that the same artist will take a different tempo at a different time of life. The balance of dignity with detail comes with experience, but in gaining the one, the artist must not lose the other. Artists are, of course, not only of different temperaments but of different schools of craft. Therefore, one must not uphold one single and only way of arriving at a great goal, the aim being surely to arrive at conveying the highest message in any great work. I heard Brahms say once, 'Machen Sie es wie Sie wollen, machen Sie es nur schön' ('Do it how you like, but make it beautiful'). After such words from the master himself, is there anything more for me to say? FANNY DAVIES.

[Shortly after Brahms's death an article from the pen of Frau Horowitz-Barnay appeared in the Vienna *Neue Freie Presse* entitled 'An hour with Joachim' of which I have retained a note. It was the record of a visit paid by the lady to the maestro, in the course of which he spoke of Brahms in a way which both interested and surprised me. It goes without saying that Joachim expressed unstinted admiration for the genius of his life-long friend, but when he is represented as comparing Brahms to Beethoven to the latter's detriment I am inclined to doubt the strict accuracy of the report. It is so easy to misinterpret the spoken word. In other respects Joachim's remarks were so full of wisdom and warm appreciation of the glorious gifts of his dead friend that I do not hesitate to quote them in full.

Joachim said, 'In the domain of musical form Beethoven appears to me to rank third among the masters. On the topmost peak stands Bach, the all-powerful, the incomparable, the creator, the great beginning. Mozart follows as originator of new forms of beauty, and then comes—Brahms.' 'And Beethoven?' interpolated the interviewer.

'In respect of invention, progressive development, in independence, and conciseness of form, Brahms appears to me to stand higher than Beethoven or Schubert. Beethoven studied to his life's end with unwearying efforts; Schubert, too, in spite of his wondrous melodic gifts, worked on to the last. Brahms, on the other hand, neither studied nor searched, but invented. He was no Epigone (descendant), no scion of a noble house. Contained within himself were root, branch, and blossom; for his whole kingdom he had only himself to thank. He is the quintessence of a whole musical period, and Schumann spoke prophetically when he wrote, "With Brahms has come to us the experience of wonderful things." Schumann was right. Brahms has brought us a new beauty, nor is he only wonderful in respect of depth, invention and concentration; he astonishes by his many-sidedness. He is lyrist and symphonist in one, and has written big choral works, including the splendid Deutsche Requiem; chamber music, with its quartet of voices, is the deeper for his influence, and he has enriched it by the re-introduction of half-forgotten wind instruments. His music has been slow in its entry into the repertory. The New, and especially the Super New (*das übergrosse Neue*), is always rejected by the conservative members of the community, whereas the old familiar things are anxiously defended against all new-comers. But is Brahms destructive? On the contrary, he is an up-builder among those who bring to the old the beauty of the new. His is the element of enrichment and progress.

'As a man, too, Brahms was often misunderstood, and yet, though externally rough (*schroff*), he was of noble nature without vanity or arrogance.'

What Joachim said of the man is true of his music. Its outer shell is hard enough at times, but underneath there is an intrinsic nobility which shines through all. If comparison between Brahms and Beethoven must be made—for my part, to quote the famous phrase of Talleyrand, *je ne vois pas la nécessité*—it may be said that whilst these two great men had in common the quality of stark masculinity, yet both confirmed the truth maintained by the ancient Greeks that the element of femininity is never entirely absent from the artist nature. It would seem as if Nature, having imposed limits to the creative activity of Woman, gives the mandate to the masculine artist to be her interpreter. The response of Brahms to the challenge is found most often in his songs, and not seldom in his chamber music. Many examples occur to me. Following on the tremendous force of the opening movement of the F minor quintet is the purely lyric andante. The lovely second subject of the A minor quartet, the andante of the B flat, and especially the allegretto of the same quartet, with its viola solo accompanied by muted strings (surely one of the most passionate rhapsodies ever penned by mortal man!), are all tone-poems with Woman as theme. In spite of the efforts of some modern musicians to brand this blending of strength with tenderness as 'sentimentality', his victory is assured. Brahms's symphonies are heard more often every year, and, as to his chamber works, they enter into the scheme of every concert-giver and every private player, the world over, and will continue to do so as long as the art of chamber music endures. EDITOR.]

BRAILOI, CONSTANTIN. *v.* ROUMANIAN COMPOSERS.

BRAMBACH, KASPAR JOSEPH, 1833–1902, German composer.

Sextet, pf, 2 v, 2 vla, vc, c mi	op. 5	B. & H., 1862.
Quartet, pf, v, vla, vc, E flat	,, 14	Kistner, 1868.
Quartet, pf, v, vla, vc, a mi	,, 43	Wernthal, 1880.
Quartet, pf, v, vla, vc, g mi	,, 110	Kistner, 1899.
Sonata, pf, v, d mi	,, 55	Wernthal, 1884.
,, ,, ,, a mi	,, 74	Kistner, 1890.

†BRANCOUR, RENÉ, b. 1862, French composer and critic.

Sonata, pf, v	Rouhier, 1900.
Suite, pf, v	Evette & Schaeffer, 1922.

Dent describes his chamber music as 'unpretentious'.

BRANDL, JOHANN, 1760–1837, German composer.

Originally destined for monastic life, Brandl displayed in early life great talent for the violin, and was dissuaded from burying himself in a cloister. His subsequent musical career was a chequered one, his activities including service under many aristocratic patrons, and the composition of much chamber music. *Fétis* gives a long list of his compositions, and speaks highly of his talents. EDITOR.

BRANDT, Fritz, German composer.

1st quartet, str, a mi	op. 14	Bisping, 1922.
2nd ,, ,, d mi	,, 15	,, —
Sonata, pf, vc, c mi	,, 6	,, —

The sonata is clear in form, and melodious, though not without temperamental features.

Though the quartet, op. 14, is strictly formal, the composer's personality is expressed strongly in the music, which is worked up to an impressive climax.

The quartet, op. 15, has received warm eulogy from a number of German critics, who accord to the composer all the virtues of a competent quartet-writer. Editor.

BRANDTS BUYS, (1) Cornelis Alyander, 1812–1890, Dutch organist and carillonneur.

This composer wrote a piano quintet, crowned by the Maatschappij tot Bevordering der Toonkunst, a string quartet, and some smaller chamber works. His music is clear and melodious, without modern experiments in harmony or rhythm. Herbert Antcliffe.

†(2) Jan, b. 1868, nephew of the above, composer of Dutch extraction.

Sextet, 3 v, 2 vla, vc, D	op. 40	Weinberger, 1917.
Quintet, fl (v), str. quartet, D	,, 6	Doblinger, 1903.
Quartet, str, c mi	,, 19	Weinberger, 1911.
Suite in old style, str. quartet (also pf, v), D	,, 23	Doblinger, 1908.
Romantic Serenade, str. quartet, d mi	,, 25	Weinberger, 1910.
Sicilian Serenade, str. quartet	,, 28	,, 1917.
Trio, pf, v, vc, G	,, 1	Hofmeister, 1890.
Sonata, pf, v, a mi	,, 26	Drei Masken V., 1910.
Suite, pf, v, D	,, 43	Doblinger.

Jan Brandts Buys has lived for many years in Vienna. His quartet, op. 19, is an excellent work, to be recommended for private or public performance. The *Romantic Serenade* opens and closes with a nocturne, instead of the march usually associated with the instrumental serenade. In the andante which follows, the viola has a prominent part, effectively accompanied by the other instruments in triplets. The adagio, inscribed 'Alla Marcia', is, in Dr. Altmann's opinion (*Handbuch*), intended as a parody of a funeral march. This serenade is as a whole light in texture, and requires poetical treatment to bring out its intrinsic worth, whilst the *Sicilian Serenade*, in five movements, is touched with humour. It has a quaint sub-title, 'Cheerful music for morose musicians'.

The style of his first suite in D may be inferred from the old-world titles of the movements—preludium, gavotte, arioso, minuet, fughetta.

Brandts Buys belongs to the third generation of a family of musicians. His chamber music was first made known by the Fitzner Quartet. Editor.

BRAUER, Max, 1855–1918, German composer, pupil of V. Lachner.

Quartet, str, F	—	B. & H., 1920.
Sextet, pf, fl, ob, cl, fag, horn, g mi	—	,, ,,
Suite, pf, v, D	—	,, 1919.
Sonata (*Idyllische*), pf, v, G	op. 3	Wernthal, 1880.

BRAUN. A family of musicians of Scandinavian birth. Carl Anton Philipp, 1788–1835, and his brother Wilhelm, b. 1791, were oboists, both writing ensemble music for their instrument (*v. Fétis*).

BRAUN, Rudolf, b. 1869, blind Viennese composer.

Quintet, 2 v, vla, 2 vc, e mi	op. 38	U.E., 1912.

BREE, Jan Bernard van, 1801–1857, Dutch composer.

1st quartet, str, a mi	Simrock.
2nd ,, ,,	Theune (Amsterdam).
3rd ,, ,, d mi	,, (,,); Alsbach, 1851.

Though little above mediocrity, van Bree's music is agreeable to play. I remember that in younger days, when the repertory was more restricted than now, his quartets were very welcome. Editor.

BREITENBACH, Clemens.

Sonata, pf, v, a mi	op. 24	Coppenrath, 1913.

BRETAGNE, Pierre, b. 1881, French composer, pupil of Guy Ropartz.

Quartet, str, B flat	Rouart, 1900.
Sonata, pf, vc, g mi	Dupont, 1914.

BRETÓN, Tomás, 1850–1923, Spanish composer.

Trio, pf, v, vc	Unión Musical Española.

BRÉVAL, Jean-Baptiste, 1756–1825, 'cellist at Paris Conservatoire.

He wrote thirty string quartets, opp. 1, 5, 6, 7, 18, and a large number of string trios for various combinations. For list of his works and original publishers *vide Riemann*, *Fétis*, and *Vidal*. Some duets for violin and 'cello and for two 'cellos have been republished (*v. Altmann*).

There are six quartets, op. 1 (Lachevardière [=Leduc]), which are all good, no. 4, in G minor, especially so. The presto of this quartet which will be republished by S. & B. (ed. Jas. Brown), contains a foreshadowing of Mendelssohn's fairy music. EDITOR.

†**BRÉVILLE,** PIERRE ONFROY DE, b. 1861, French composer, pupil of César Franck.

	Composed	
Sonata, pf, v, c sharp mi	1918–19	Rouart, 1920.
2nd sonata, pf, v, C	1927	,, 1927.
Poème dramatique, pf, vc	1924	,, 1925.
Une Flûte dans les Vergers, pf, fl	1920	,, 1920.
Sonatina, pf, ob	1924	,, 1925.

[First performances of *Une Flûte dans les Vergers* and oboe sonatina both at the Société Nationale, 15 January 1921 and 28 February 1925. The first was played by M. Fleury, the second by M. Bleuzet and Mlle Smets.]

Although the chamber-music sense is a late development with Pierre de Bréville, and although, up till now, he has confined himself to the combination of two instruments, yet one cannot but admire the perfection with which he treats the instruments employed.

He has no objection to modern harmonic developments, but has always kept to those that are purely musical, realizing that the first duty of a musician is to write music.

Bréville is a craftsman, of the family of those fifteenth-century painters, sculptors, and workers in precious metals who left nothing to chance and wrought with equal perfection the minutest details of a costume or the remotest corners of a landscape. This is the way in which all artists worthy the name have laboured, feeling the obligation to present the subject chosen to the best of their ability, clearly, and as a whole.

The use of the term *subject* with regard to Bréville's chamber works is deliberate, for he admits that he intended to express, in terms of music, ideas of essentially dramatic nature, the influence of which is frequently felt and sometimes affects the musical structure.

POÈME DRAMATIQUE FOR VIOLONCELLO AND PIANO. Curiously enough, the dramatic element is least noticeable in the violoncello work, though this is specifically named *Poème dramatique*. There is a contest, an antagonism between two opposed themes, but the dramatic character is purely general, and reminds us of the two Beethoven influences, *das Bittende* (the beseeching), *das Widerstrebende* (the resisting).

In this poem, which is finely conceived musically, the composer has endeavoured to express the feeling of revolt against injustice, a feeling to be affected neither by pleading nor by supplication, be it never so charming, and the work ends with the inexorable refusal of forgiveness. First performance, Société Nationale, 24 January 1925, by MM. Gérard Hekking and J. Gentil.

SONATA FOR VIOLIN AND PIANO IN C SHARP MINOR. We shall treat rather more fully of the sonata for violin and piano, one of the finest works of the kind written since the war of 1914.

The sonata is, in fact, a result of the Great War; it is an expression of personal sorrow for the loss of a loved one. It is dedicated to the memory of Lieut. Gervais Cazes.

The first movement, in C sharp minor—mouvement modéré, mais sentiment énergique et impétueux (moderato, ma energico e con fuoco)—presents, in classical form, ideas of deep significance, ideas so exuberant that they seem about to burst the bonds of form, and this might indeed happen were not the structure designed with so marvellous a sense of proportion and of musical dynamics.

The second movement, in scherzo form—gai, mais pas trop vite (scherzando non troppo)—opens with a short motif, a military call or a shout of enthusiasm, which is, as it were, the key to the whole movement. Notice here the peculiar and uncommon rhythm of the trio in C major—4½/8,  —a rhythm essentially oriental. The scherzo theme then resumes, but shortly dies away in the depths of the bass, to give place to the Lamento, which follows without break, a memorial to grief.

Lamento—extrêmement lent (molto adagio). On hearing this movement one cannot help investing it with a concrete dramatic meaning. The death is announced by a passing bell, a quotation from a vocal work of the composer, *Héros, je vous salue*, poem by Henri Régnier. Then comes the catastrophe, Death himself blindly striking at the beloved friend.

But the bitter despair is gradually softened, and a melody—which has already been announced—now appears, bringing consolation, as if called into being by a voice from beyond the grave, and the Lamento ends on a note of serene hopefulness.

This movement is of a high order of beauty, and arouses the deepest emotion in those who know how to listen.

The fourth and last movement—assez animé et martial (animato e marziale)—seems a kind of march to victory; this, after a development which is perhaps rather too long, bursts into a song of triumph, in the key of C sharp major, and ends with a kind of funeral march, sadly recalling the price paid for victory. The first performance in Paris was at the Société Nationale, 20 March 1920, by M. Enesco and Mlle Blanche Selva. VINCENT D'INDY.

BRICCIALDI, GIULIO, 1818–1881, Italian flute virtuoso.

Quintet, fl, ob, cl, horn, fag	op. 124	Schott, 1875.
Trio, pf, 2 fl, D	,, 67	,, 1853.
,, ,, ,, A	,, 130	,, 1881.

Also some flute duets (Schott).

*† BRIDGE, Frank, b. 1879, English composer.

	Composed	
Sextet, 2 v, 2 vla, 2 vc	1912	Augener.
1st quartet (*Bologna*), str, e mi	1906	,,
2nd quartet, str, g mi	1915	Winthrop Rogers.
3rd quartet, str		Augener.
Phantasy, str. quartet, f mi	1905	,,
Sir Roger de Coverley, str. quartet, A	1922	,,
Three idylls, str. quartet	1906	,,
Three novelletten, str. quartet	1904	,,
Two old English songs (*Sally in our Alley; Cherry Ripe*), str. quartet	1916	Winthrop Rogers.
Irish melody (*The Londonderry Air*), str. quartet	1908	Augener.
Quintet, pf, 2 v, vla, vc, d mi	1905–12	,,
Phantasy quartet, pf, v, vla, vc, f sharp mi	1910	,,
Phantasy trio, pf, v, vc, c mi	1908	,,
Nine miniatures, pf, v, vc	1906 et seq.	,,
Sonata, pf, vc, d mi and D	1917	Winthrop Rogers.

Frank Bridge entered the R.C.M. as a violin student, but won a composition scholarship in 1899, and became for four years a pupil of Sir Charles Stanford. On leaving the College he joined the Grimson Quartet as second violin, but was soon in greater demand as a viola player. When Wirth, the viola of the Joachim Quartet, was taken ill in 1906, it was Frank Bridge who temporarily replaced him. Later on he joined the English String Quartet, of which he remained a member until 1915. He has also had considerable experience as a conductor, but is best known as a composer, and chiefly of chamber music. One cannot help recalling the number of composers whose role as performers has been that of the viola-player in various ensembles. Among them are Waldo Warner (London S.Q.), Paul Hindemith (Amar S.Q.), Oskar Nedbal (Bohemian S.Q.), and Conrado del Campo (Cuarteto Francés). Frank Bridge's compositions range through many branches of music, but his chamber music may be taken as representative, especially of his earlier style. From about 1920 onwards he has inclined to a chromaticism which shows some points of affinity with that of Scriabin. At the outset, however, it is the more conservative Frank Bridge with whom we are concerned, and the essential features of his style are first and foremost consummate craftsmanship, as regards both the technique of composition and the executive practicability for the instruments employed. This craftsmanship is so thorough that it has sometimes been converted into the reproach of being 'too professional', but it unquestionably increases the comfort of the players, who are confronted with few problems either of performance or of understanding. This may be the reason why his hold is much stronger on the private circles where chamber music is cultivated than upon the concert world, though he has not lacked attention from the latter. In his chamber music Bridge avows himself an eclectic of the post-romantic era. He does not seek to startle or to gain credit (or the reverse) for revolutionary innovations, but has assimilated from tradition all that suited his purpose, and has developed therefrom a personal mode of expression. At present, as hinted above, he appears to be moving towards new horizons, partially revealed in the string quartet which is his latest chamber work. We may eventually be compelled to readjust our perspective, but meanwhile he stands as one of the foremost representatives of the 'right wing' in British chamber music, and one of those who have done most to enrich its literature. Especially noteworthy are his contributions to the smaller forms, in the first place the phantasy revived by W. W. Cobbett, as well as minor pieces (novelletten, idylls, folk-song transcriptions, &c.).

Of this latter class is Frank Bridge's first chamber work, the Novelletten for string quartet, 1904, consisting of three short and eminently playable movements. Of these the most attractive is the first, a tranquil, meditative piece, characterized by a B flat in the upper register which persists for twenty-two bars at the beginning and returns at the close. The second is a kind of scherzo, with a four-bar ritornello which also serves as introduction. There are two sections, allegretto and moderato, the first of which becomes a presto on its return, with the time-signature altered from 2/4 to 6/8. The third piece opens with a march-like theme, and has as central episode a viola solo, afterwards treated in canonic imitation by the two violins. The following year (1905) brought the first of the Cobbett competitions, the subject being a phantasy for string quartet. There were sixty-seven competitors, of whom six received awards. The first prize went to W. J. Hurlstone, who died only a few weeks later; the second to Haydn Wood; the third to Bridge, for his phantasy in F minor, which eventually became the most popular of the series among habitual players of chamber music, in which it was perhaps aided by its relatively moderate technical difficulty. Unfortunately the score is not available for analysis, only the parts being published, but according to W. W. Cobbett 'it has a stirring rhythmical opening, the first subject being announced in unison, and completed with accompaniment of detached chords. The second subject is one of singular charm—it may be described as a delicious sort of crooning, accompanied by simple arpeggios on the 'cello. The andante section contains some splendid violin writing and enharmonic modulations of singular beauty. The finale does not attain quite the same high level, but finishes brilliantly.'

Piano Quintet. During the same two years (1904–5) the composer was engaged upon the first version of his quintet in D minor for piano and strings. He had not then travelled far along the road his development was to take, but though he soon left this stage behind, the work was too good to suffer the usual fate of early efforts, and he returned to it in 1912. One objection being its excessive length, he telescoped the two middle movements into one, and subjected the whole to a drastic revision. He discovered, for instance, that in one seemingly dull passage of the finale, the harmonies actually implied the presence of the principal subject, which, when added in the revision, placed the whole in a new light. As it now stands, the work has three movements: a dramatic allegro with a charming lyrical melody for its second subject; an adagio which is still commonly regarded as one of Bridge's inspirations, contrasted in the middle by a brief but fascinating scherzo; and a finale, concluding with a reminiscence of the first movement.

First String Quartet. In 1906 the composer obtained a 'mention d'honneur' in an international competition at Bologna for a string quartet. Hence the work he submitted, the string quartet in E minor, is familiarly known among players as his Bologna quartet. By a curious coincidence he was again one of sixty-seven competitors. Except perhaps for a tendency to length in the first movement, this is one of Bridge's best works, and though it is excelled by the more mature quartet in G minor, it is the first of his compositions that, with these reservations, may be regarded as representative. The slow movement, in particular, which opens as follows:

Ex. 1.

has a harmonic flavour which was characteristic of Frank Bridge's music prior to the recent development to which reference is made above, and the viola solo, afterwards passed to the 'cello with some interesting polyphonic figuration for the other instruments, is very typical of his method at this stage. The scherzo is on an old model, with a D.C., and the finale should follow with no more than a pause between. For those who are sensitive to key idiosyncrasies, another quality of this quartet is the fidelity with which it exhibits those of E minor. To the same year belong also the *Three Idylls* for string quartet, written before the *Bologna* and somewhat in the earlier manner of the *Novelletten* but more mature, with a deeper sentiment and a richer sonority. Arnold Rosé, whose Quartet played them at the Wigmore Hall, evinced much admiration for them. The first, adagio with a middle section allegretto, has a suggestion of tragedy. The second is almost too brief for the wistful charm it exhales, though perhaps the composer was wise not to give it time to evaporate. The third is sparkling and buoyant. It was also in 1906 that Frank Bridge wrote his first set of *Miniatures* for piano, violin, and 'cello, to which he has since added two more. This one consists of a minuet, gavotte, and allegretto of unpretentious character, but well suited to players of moderate attainments.

Phantasy Trio. In 1907 W. W. Cobbett announced his second competition, this time inviting composers to submit phantasy trios for piano, violin, and 'cello. It seems almost incredible, but for the third time Bridge found himself one of sixty-seven competitors. His phantasy trio in C minor, which was awarded the first prize, is a very good example of the form, which corresponds to a sonata-allegro with an andante displacing to a large extent the usual development, and again a scherzo furnishing a contrasted middle section to the andante. Of this work Dr. Ernest Walker has written:

'Structurally the scheme is very successful except that, even after close acquaintance, I still feel that the end is over-abrupt—a more spacious coda would, it seems to me, have been a better balance to the varied and complex central portion of the trio. But, however this may be, there is undeniable power about the main ideas, which are treated in very broad and dignified fashion. On paper it looks as if the forty-six consecutive bars of exactly the same rhythmical accompaniment figure in both hands of the piano part would prove monotonous;

Ex. 2.

but at neither of the two recurrences of the principal subject is this really the case, so well designed are the curves of the string melodies and the broad lines of the harmonies.'

It was in this year also (1908) that the Hambourg family commissioned a number of composers to collaborate in a quartet on the *Londonderry Air*. From this incentive grew an allegro movement by Frank Bridge, scherzo by Hamilton Harty, variations by J. D. Davis, minuet by Eric Coates, and finale by York Bowen. Of these the first, third, and fourth have appeared, not however as portions of a composite work, but as separate pieces issued by different publishers. This places Frank Bridge's contribution at some disadvantage, for, although there are hints of the theme from the very first bar, so much 'leading-up' intervenes before it is stated in complete form that one is tempted to urge him to 'get on with it'. But viewing this movement as part of a much larger work, the introduction is by no means disproportionate, and in method it follows the best classical tradition. Of the many compositions that have been based upon this beautiful melody, this is one that goes farthest in probing the character of its constituent phrases and particles. Whether such dissection serves a high aesthetic ideal is perhaps more debatable, but here the aim was concerned more with craftsmanship than with aesthetics, and the result is certainly a successful example of the former.

PHANTASY QUARTET. After his second competition Cobbett varied his practice by commissioning twelve British composers to write as many phantasies, each for a different combination of instruments. The quartet for piano and strings fell to Frank Bridge, who was given a free hand as regards both method and time of composition. Possibly as a result of this greater freedom, the work in F sharp minor is not only his finest phantasy, but also one of the most striking of the many works which have been the result of Cobbett's initiative. For his form the composer chose that of an extended andante con moto enclosing a central allegro vivace and followed by a concluding tranquillo having the character of a retrospect. The general tone is sombre, reflective, and emotionally significant. The opening andante is somewhat brief, so that, although the composer allows ample development to the vivace section, he still has time to proceed with some leisure to his conclusion, avoiding the breathlessness apparent in some phantasies whose begetters have taken their patron's injunctions too literally. Of this conclusion Dr. Ernest Walker writes:

'I know few things in British chamber music more satisfying than the last five and a half pages, from the *ff* return of the first subject (the long unheard F sharp minor chord, especially with the F sharp in the bass, instead of the expected C sharp, is curiously powerful here), through the long succeeding diminuendo to the frail tranquillo in the major key—twenty-eight bars of really fine music, with a serene largeness and dignity about them which are none too common anywhere nowadays. The colouring of this last passage is also first-rate and very original. But, after all, many of our moderns can use their paint-boxes excellently. It is the other things, the individuality and the imaginativeness of the ideas, that really matter.'

Ex. 3.

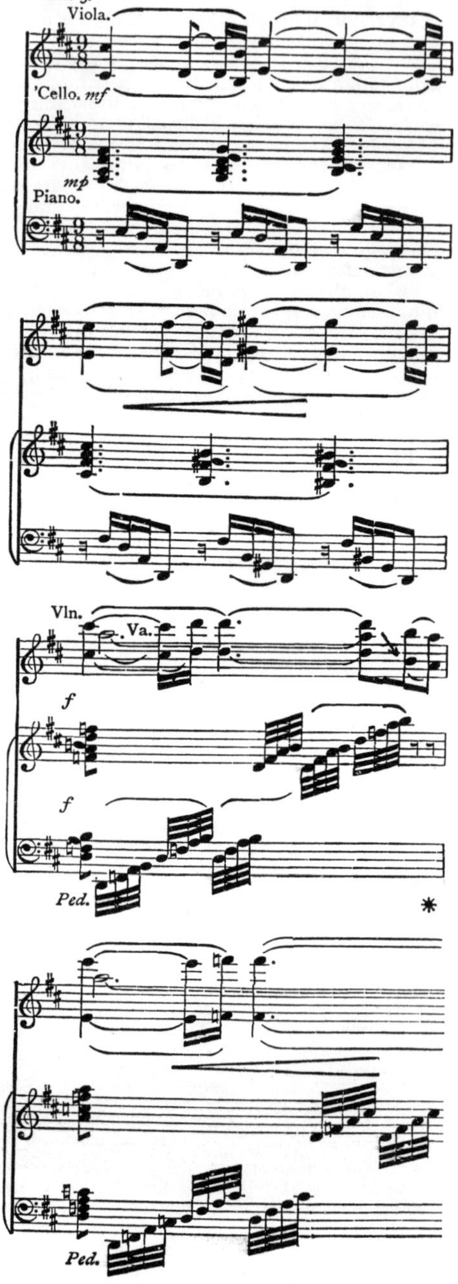

This work was out of print for six years, owing to the plates being at Leipzig at the outbreak of war, but it has since been re-issued.

String Sextet. Though the composer's progress towards a more complete individuality has been continuous, the preceding work denoted a quickening of the pace. This quickening became still more apparent in the string sextet which had been growing for some time; it was begun in 1906 and finished on April 8, 1912. This, by the way, was the year in which the piano quintet came under revision. A programme annotator thus describes the texture of the sextet:

'As in the string sextets and quintets of Brahms, which seem in some ways, naturally enough, to have served as technical models, the texture of the music is notably clear throughout. There is very little strict six-part writing: there is abundance of very rich colour, but it is usually secured by some reinforcement (in unison or octave) of special detail. Not, on the other hand, that the writing is ever orchestral, for the line drawing, so to speak, is invariably that of definite chamber music, and in certain respects Bridge secures attractive contrasts of timbre about which Brahms does not seem to have cared. In the first movement, for instance, he keeps both violins in reserve for long stretches at a time, and thereby gives additional brightness and vigour to their re-entry.'

The work is in three movements, of which the opening allegro moderato is the most extended. The second movement takes a form to which the composer probably became addicted through the writing of phantasies—that of an andante con moto in which is enclosed a scherzo-like allegro giusto. In the concise finale, allegro ben moderato, attention is concentrated upon the first subject (Ex. 4). In the coda the opening theme of the entire work is quoted in association with material from the finale, which involves an effective interpolation of four bars of triple time.

Second String Quartet. In 1914 Cobbett offered a prize for a string quartet, which was awarded the following year to Bridge for his string quartet in G minor. This fine work was first performed by the London String Quartet in November 1915, and first published under

Ex. 4.

the auspices of the R.C.M. Patron's Fund founded by Sir S. Ernest Palmer. It found immediate favour. Of the first movement a contributor to *The Times* wrote:

'It is not the actual invention of themes which impresses one at once. Rather it is the power of suggesting many ideas by different uses of the same theme which makes the first movement grow up into a remarkably eloquent whole. For instance, the principal theme in G minor,

Ex. 5.

with which the movement starts, has a certain force and nervous energy, but it is not until the recapitulation, when it appears on the violoncello in a wholly different mood (tranquillo),

Ex. 6.

that one realizes its complete power of expression. The capacity to use sonata form without being ruled by it is the surest sign of maturity in a composer, and Bridge's treatment of the recapitulation shows that he has gained that capacity. The movement grows until the end, for he never falls back upon the formula of "As I said before". The gradually slackening energy is charged with a heightened emotion by its reflective use, especially when it is accompanied by a figure of wavering triplets which first appeared as a delicate point of colour in connecting with the second subject.'

Ex. 7.

Resuming his usual practice, the composer has made of his second movement a scherzo enclosing a brief andante, of which the writer quoted above says that in an indefinable way it reminds one a little of Elgar. The finale is preceded by a short adagio founded on the second subject of the first movement.

Ex. 8.

Presently the tempo changes to allegro vivace, and the movement proper proceeds in a bright and exuberant mood until, just before the climax, its two subjects are heard in association:

Ex. 9.

This leads to a *fff* chord of E major, followed by the briefest possible coda.

The following year (1916) produced the two old English songs (*Sally in our Alley* and *Cherry Ripe*), with an ad libitum double-bass part to make them available for stringed orchestra. These bear to each other somewhat the relation of andante and scherzo—the latter a very sprightly version of the old song. Both are concisely treated, and differ markedly from the earlier setting of the *Londonderry Air*.

'CELLO SONATA. Meanwhile another composition, begun in 1913, the year following the completion of the sextet, was occupying the composer's attention. This was the sonata for 'cello and piano, which he finished in 1917. It is a broadly conceived, spacious work, which marks a new point of departure, in the sense that it contains many textural features that one cannot imagine as being written by Bridge only a few years previously. They are mostly points of detail, such as a use of fifths, fourths, and in one place

Ex. 10.

of common chords, which is common enough in modern music, but was not characteristic of the tendency to which Bridge had previously subscribed. Some of the transient modulations presage the chromaticism of those more recent works to which reference was made at the outset. But all this is subordinate to the contents of the sonata. The sweeping, somewhat rhetorical phrasing which permeates most of his music holds complete sway here. Most of the themes are broad enough to convey a rhapsodic, not to say dithyrambic impression, and they are generously treated. In the first of its two movements their grip upon the listener's attention is complete. The second is, almost of necessity, episodical, and the frequent breaks create an effect of over-punctuation which one is inclined to resent, until the form is so familiar that one realizes at once the sequence of moods and the need of 'paragraphing' them. As always in the case of works whose foremost quality is breadth, the remedy lies in the interpretation, which, if not sufficiently sympathetic or intelligent, might easily leave an impression of loosely knit fragments. There are many modern works of which the same might be said, and it is one of the many risks which a composer has to take. Happy are those whose position is so assured that they are never blamed for the shortcomings of their interpreters!

Another work which calls for mention is the setting for string quartet of the old Christmas dance *Sir Roger de Coverley*. There is much argument concerning the origin of this tune, which has been disputed by Lancashire, Yorkshire, and Cheshire in England, and claimed in Scotland as *The Maltman comes on Monday*, but of all versions the least trustworthy is that given by Addison in *The Spectator* (1711), where he refers to Sir Roger as a Worcester gentleman whose great-grandfather was the inventor of the dance. As every one knows, it is a tripping measure in 9/8, with a cadence which permits of D.C. ad lib. Bridge has shown much ingenuity in breaking the rhythmic obsession, and the piece is a welcome pendant to his earlier adaptations of traditional tunes.

THE THIRD QUARTET is one of the numerous works due to the direct incentive of Mrs. F. S. Coolidge, to whom it is dedicated and under whose auspices the first performance was given, Sept. 17, 1927, by the Kolisch Quartet at Vienna. The interval of twelve years which had elapsed since its predecessor, had seen a marked transformation in its composer's outlook. Of the intervening works, the one that affords the most insight into this development is the piano sonata composed 1921–4, but, possibly because the quartet medium compels a greater discipline than the keyboard, the latter work is the more convincing of the two. It comprises two allegro movements, one moderato, the other energico, enclosing between them an andante, the quasi-elegiac wistfulness of which is greatly enhanced by the forceful downrightness of the music which precedes and follows it. One consequence of this is that, whilst the two allegros are probably in the constructive sense the best movements, as they are musically the most important, the andante, human nature being what it is, wins the most sympathy in performance. At Vienna, for instance, an audience which a conservative observer would probably have described as of 'modernist' tendencies, and therefore *a priori* little disposed to romance, was won by this movement and applauded it more warmly than the sections which were 'absolute music'. These, whilst acknowledging no direct indebtedness to Scriabin, parallel that composer's prolongation of Tristanesque yearning by chromatic evasion of diatonic resolutions, whilst at the same time counteracting, by means of a display of robust energy, whatever debilitating effect may result from such chromatic methods. The outcome is

Ex. 11.

extremely characteristic. One feels that only Frank Bridge would have thought out those two movements in that particular way. The Russian epigoni of the Scriabin harmonic evolution would have made them much more feminine and more sensuous. The Germans would have made them more cerebral. Bridge has worked out a personal equation between harmonic hyperbole and plain-speaking.

The slow movement, which recruits friends for this work from those not ready to bestow approval upon the allegros, is a miniature tone-poem of great charm, in which the composer makes an extremely skilful—not to say artful—use of a recurring musical idea which alternates the functions of ostinato and ritornello. The main theme being of quiet, wistful character, scarcely troubled by a momentary influx of a more passionate element, the always impressive and generally pathetic effect of the recurrence makes the whole so touchingly persuasive that only the composer's healthy musical outlook preserves it from overstepping the bounds of sentiment.

An example is given on p. 194 (Ex. 11).

EDWIN EVANS.

[When Frank Bridge's chamber music first appeared, it was a revelation to amateurs as well as to professional players, and a valuable addition to the repertory. With the exception of the *Miniature Trios*, written for students in the elementary stages, they are not very easy to play, but amply repay intensive study. The earlier works, especially the piano quintet, display an exquisite gift of melody and some exceptionally effective writing for his own instrument, the viola. The later works excite the admiration of the expert musician to a far greater extent, but amateurs will always have a soft corner in their hearts for music which expresses the aspirations and enthusiasms of youth. The trio phantasy is the most important work (in trio form) of the British repertory. EDITOR.]

BRIGHT, DORA, contemporary English composer.

Suite, pf, v	Ashdown.
Suite, pf, fl	Rudall & Carte.

There is delicacy of touch in Miss Bright's compositions which fits her for the writing of chamber music. A piano quartet of hers is still in MS. EDITOR.

BRISTOL MUSIC CLUB, formed in 1903. Present president, Sir Henry Hadow; former president, Dr. Joachim. Meetings have averaged thirty-six annually. There have been 832 evenings of chamber music, at which 1,200 different works for various combinations of instruments have been given.

A few years after the club was formed, a Ladies' Musical Club was started, and affiliated to the above. Before these clubs sprang into being, there were meetings in private houses for chamber music, and some private clubs still carry on.

Hubert W. Hunt, who is a leading spirit in chamber music organization in Bristol and Clifton, besides being a competent performer, is a writer of scholarly annotations to many of the programmes given. EDITOR.

BRITISH CHAMBER MUSIC.

To any one associated with chamber music, the revival of activity in this branch of musical art is at once a most healthy and a most hopeful sign. As English men and women it is additionally gratifying for us to find that our own native composers are in the forefront of this activity.

Perhaps, when one comes to think about it, it is natural that English musical talent should manifest itself in intimate art of this kind. We are always being told that we are a reticent and undemonstrative race, and that our music is lacking in excitement and heated emotional impulse. No one (not even those foreigners who profess themselves convinced that an Englishman cannot compose music) will accuse us of either a lack of feeling or a lack of sensitiveness. It is for a certain absence of warmth in expressing ourselves that we are criticized. Certainly an Englishman does not generally wear his heart upon his sleeve. He thinks before he speaks—and when he speaks he does not feel the need of extravagant gestures to enforce his remarks. For such a national temperament chamber music is truly the most fitting musical outlet, since, at its best, such art is thoughtful—not dryly intellectual or wanting in feeling or exuberance, by any means, but always governed and controlled by the intellect.

There is yet another reason why the present activity of our composers is a hopeful sign. Chamber music is essentially uncommercial, and a musician who spends his time in producing or performing it can have no other motive than the expression of his inmost and sincerest musical thoughts. It is not for the crowd—it cannot, indeed, be enjoyed to the full in the presence of crowds. It is essentially delicate, intimate, quietly sociable in character. The English have been dubbed 'a nation of shopkeepers', but our most characteristic expression in serious music has, happily, stood far aloof from our commerce.

It is the purpose of this article to present a brief historical survey. British chamber music may be conveniently divided into three periods —periods which are very definitely separated from each other by wide tracts of musical barrenness. We can therefore claim no continuity of national development in music, such as was manifested by Germany or even by France.

The first period (of which we are only just becoming fully aware) came at the tail-end of the flourishing epoch which is generally conveniently described as the Elizabethan era. Indeed, it is probable that the first instrumental ensemble music of importance was produced by the English madrigal writers towards the close of the sixteenth century. For many years music had been greatly cultivated as a private intellectual diversion, but this music had been solely vocal. After a time, many wealthy amateurs became the proud possessors of 'chests of viols' (see art. CONSORT OF VIOLS), and composers began to issue their madrigals with a note on the title-page to the effect that the music was 'apt for voices or viols'. It very soon became evident, however, that the writing of concerted music for strings was a distinct art by itself. And so a few of the composers of the time began writing what they called 'fantasies' or 'fancies', which were intended to be purely instrumental in style, and these were the first ensemble works which had a separate existence—

the forerunners of the chamber music of the present day. We must never forget, however, that there were two essentials which make our modern chamber music what it really is, which did not exist in Elizabethan days. These two essentials are our instruments and our instrumental musical forms. Few people realize, perhaps, that when they hear performances of Elizabethan instrumental music at the present day they are, in reality, only listening to arrangements, and that the sounds which they hear are very unlike those imagined and intended by the composer. The stringed instruments then in use—the lute and the viols—were quite unlike anything employed in the music of later times. The lute was a twelve-stringed instrument plucked like a guitar—the tone of the viols was sombre, and lacked the brightness which we now associate with bowed instruments. The wind instruments are even more difficult for us to imagine —most of them are known to us only in name. That their tones were strong and harsh we may conjecture from the fact that few of them were ever used except in the open air.

The other essential which was not then in existence, a developed musical form, makes the dividing line between past and present even more marked. Nevertheless, instrumental music of a restricted scope was undoubtedly much cultivated and enjoyed, and, within very narrow limitations, a few composers succeeded in expressing beautiful ideas with skill and assurance. The most noteworthy of these composers was William BYRD (*q.v.*), 1543–1623, who wrote a large number of concerted works for the viols. Next in importance was his contemporary, Orlando GIBBONS (*q.v.*), 1583–1625, whose instrumental music was so remarkable for elaboration of texture and freedom in rhythm. Other madrigal writers of the period who distinguished themselves in work of this class, and deserve to be remembered as pioneers, were Tomkins, Ward, Dering, and Martin Peerson, all of whom wrote 'fancies' for viols in concert.

It is generally supposed that the civil wars and the Puritan rule acted as checks upon the continuance of England's musical growth. However that may be, it is certain that music in this country suddenly dropped to insignificance during the early years of the seventeenth century.

The torch of chamber music, however, was rekindled by Henry PURCELL (*q.v.*), 1658–1695, who was the central figure of the second period. In the department of pure instrumental music, Purcell produced works that had a very strong influence on the trend of musical development all over Europe. It is customary to speak of the influence of the Italian musicians upon Purcell's style—an influence which undoubtedly existed and was proudly acknowledged by the composer himself—but it is interesting to note that Purcell's first set of sonatas for stringed instruments and harpsichord or organ were published in the very same year as Corelli's first works, so that Corelli (the supreme Italian master of this time) could not have been his model. Purcell's utterance in these works, and more especially in a later set of ten sonatas published after his death, was indeed that of an entirely original thinker. He showed none of Corelli's easy grace. His music was rougher, bolder, and more decisive. He indulged in strong contrasts (unknown either to the Elizabethans or to the contemporary Italians), and imparted to his grave movements a solemnity which amounted almost to austerity. His gay movements, which had a kind of English rustic jollity about them, were thus thrown into strong relief. As Sir Hubert Parry has pointed out, 'the movements are worked out on an imposing scale, and no pretence is made of being light and familiar'. He aimed in these sonatas at 'methods of art which had the dignity of tradition about them. . . . Thus the works represent Purcell's purest ideals of art, just as quartets would represent the highest ideals of a modern composer . . . they have singular strength and spaciousness, and move with perfect ease even in the most complicated situations'.

It should be noted that Purcell had advantages for the presentation of his chamber music denied to the Elizabethans. During the interim makers of instruments had been busy, especially in Italy, and the viols had been superseded by instruments of the violin type, which were played upon with lighter bows, and these were far better adapted both for brilliance of execution and the control of tonal variety.

As has already been hinted, Purcell towered in eminence above his contemporaries, but two or three minor composers who succeeded him, and to some extent carried on the traditions, should be mentioned in connexion with British chamber music. Henry Eccles (16– – 1742) wrote some sonatas for violin and harpsichord which are worthy of remembrance. William BOYCE (*q.v.*), 1770–1779, produced a limited number of string works in the forms then in vogue. William Shield (1750–1829), although chiefly occupied in writing theatre music, forms an interesting if not a very important link with the chamber music composers of the next period. He published six trios for two violins and bass, and six duos for two violins. It is interesting to note that Shield came under the influence of Haydn during that master's visit to England in 1791, and his work shows signs of progressive sympathies (especially in the matter of rhythmic freedom) which were unusual at that date. Three other writers of the period who deserve mention for their able instrumental work in the earlier sonata forms are William Babell, 1690–1723, Charles John Stanley, 1713–1786, and Joseph Gibbs, 1699–1788.

On the whole, however, it must be confessed

that British chamber music was once more practically extinguished after the death of Purcell, and British musicians took no part whatever in the real development of the art, which made such astonishing strides on the Continent during the whole of the eighteenth century. For this, to some extent, Handel, the Saxon, was responsible. He came to these shores in 1710 from Hanover on a visit, but remained as a conqueror, holding English musicians in thrall, and taking not only our English gold, but the musical taste and education of the country into his own hands. This was a real tragedy from the national point of view, for the tremendous musical force of Handel was undoubtedly responsible for deadening the creative genius of England for at least a century and a half.

When English composers at last began to hold up their heads once more, it was natural enough that the dominant influences should come from lands other than their own. The scope of music had entirely changed. All the advanced thinkers and real creators were in Germany and Austria. Our would-be composers, in choosing to be educated in the best school, were impelled to such a course because they realized that it was the only means by which they could train their talents, broaden their minds, and come into touch with modern methods.

We find the third period of British chamber music beginning, therefore, rather timidly and imitatively in the early years of the nineteenth century. The developed forms of the new chamber music had already been made classic by Haydn, Mozart, and Beethoven, and Continental music was coming under the sway of the masters of the so-called romantic school of Weber, Mendelssohn, and Schumann.

The first British composer who made a serious attempt to write chamber music after this prolonged lapse was Sterndale Bennett, 1816–1875. Like other English musicians of the same period, he did not escape the all-powerful influence of Mendelssohn. But it is a mistake to regard him as merely a pale reflection of his great German friend. Strong kinship there was, but there dwells in Bennett's music a kind of Wordsworthian gentleness which, as Stanford wrote, 'reflected the quiet atmosphere of the English countryside'.

Bennett, who was a fine pianist, did great work for chamber music in this country during a very difficult and apathetic time. One can believe that he was peculiarly fitted as a performer in ensemble works, for his was not an assertive personality. It is strange, however, that with all his sympathy and constant association with chamber music, he wrote only three important works of this kind, each with strings in association with the piano. (*v.* article Sterndale Bennett.)

If he did not wholly escape the German influences of his day, neither did his immediate followers quite succeed in doing so. At the same time the chamber work of the three chief musicians of the next group, A. C. Mackenzie (b. 1847), C. H. H. Parry (1848–1918), and C. V. Stanford (1852–1924), was of infinitely greater resourcefulness. Their works are fully commented upon in another place, and I need only say that the bulk of their chamber music was composed when they were still young men, and before they had definitely formulated their distinctive styles. Of living composers this is to be said. The musical production of this country is vastly greater than it was thirty or even twenty years ago, and there is infinitely more variety of thought and style in the work which is now being produced than can be observed in that of any previous period of our musical history. There are various causes for these two self-evident facts. One of them is the increased thoroughness of musical education in England, which is primarily due to the fine training afforded by the schools and colleges of music. When Mackenzie, Parry, and Stanford were young men, the Royal Academy of Music (founded 1822) stood alone without competitors. This monopoly did not make for progress. However excellent may have been the work which it accomplished in early days, there is no doubt that the advent of such institutions as—writing chronologically—the Trinity College of Music (1872), the Guildhall School (1880), and the Royal College of Music (1883) made a vast difference to our musical opportunities.

More composers were taught their business, more executants were trained, and more music of all kinds was heard, especially chamber music. In course of time we formed our own English quartet parties, and, instead of being entirely dependent upon the visits of foreign players for our chamber concerts, we were able to organize them ourselves. The recognition of British players came first. The recognition of British composers followed a little later.

The public for chamber music in this country, however, is still a limited one, and it is not always easy to find publishers willing to print music for which there is only a slow sale. At the same time a good deal of encouragement has latterly been forthcoming for those composers who have desired to express themselves in chamber music forms.

The most noteworthy patron of chamber music in England is W. W. Cobbett, whose tireless services to this special cause have certainly acted as a great stimulus to British composers for a good many years past. Through his enthusiasm in organizing and financing a long series of prize competitions, and giving special commissions to individual composers, there has been a valuable increase in the number of modern British works of this class, and a large proportion of them is now published.

One of Mr. Cobbett's happiest ideas was his revival of the old English title of 'Phantasy' or

'Fancy' (*v.* Cobbett Competitions). He set British composers to work, with modern methods, in a form which was essentially their own particular inheritance. There were no prescribed structural limitations, but the works were required to be tersely designed in one continuous movement. Some composers chose to compress three or four brief movements into one; others evolved schemes of construction for themselves, avoiding formality on the one hand and rhapsodical treatment on the other. There is no doubt that Mr. Cobbett's encouragement brought forth a great many admirable works, and did much to call public attention both to the art of chamber music and to the skill of native composers.

That British chamber music of to-day has entirely shaken itself free from foreign influences, however, cannot truthfully be affirmed. Alongside of our amazing abundance of production, we find, as has already been hinted, an equally amazing diversity of character. Sometimes this diversity is disquieting. It has been said that we have escaped from the German domination only to be tossed hither and thither by every wind that blows. Whilst the public is, perhaps, no longer so apathetic as it used to be towards British music, the native composer of to-day must be prepared for the assumption that, however clever or striking his work may be, it is 'not really his own, but a skilful imitation of something much better from abroad'. This assumption, which is not altogether unfounded, has led, curiously enough, to the still greater multiplication of styles, for we now have an anti-foreign brigade, or folk-song cult, in chamber music, the leader of which is Ralph Vaughan Williams (b. 1872), a composer of real distinction in many departments of music.

To enumerate the native writers who have added compositions of indisputable value to the chamber music repertory during the past few years would be merely to present the reader with a catalogue of names already included in the Cyclopedia. To these creative artists English musicians, full of hope for the future, are able to point with some pride in the present. Thomas F. Dunhill.

[Among Englishmen who have earned much distinction in the composition of chamber music must be reckoned Mr. Dunhill himself, who has also contributed three books (*vide* Bibliography) to the scanty literature on the subject. His music receives treatment in the Cyclopedia. Editor.]

BRITISH PERFORMING ORGANIZATIONS.[1]

(1) Historical Survey.

Chamber music under ideal conditions may, perhaps, be described as the intimate speech of musicians. It is not designed to attract large masses of unthinking people; it does not seek to electrify the crowd; it rejects entirely the idea of virtuosity or display. It is the music of friends sitting together in a room, friends sharing a quiet, intellectual enjoyment with each other, and with those who are performing.

Nowadays, however, the ideal conditions are rarely possible. Chamber works are performed in large concert halls, and one is apt to forget that this type of music had its origin in a desire to provide art of a domestic nature. When such music became more fully developed, it made greater demands upon the skill of the performers, and its adequate presentation became a specialized professional accomplishment. This led to the establishment of chamber concerts, so that people unskilled in music, but alive to its charms, might at least gather together and enjoy listening to the playing of those whose powers of interpretation were sufficient to present the music in a favourable light.

It is the aim of this article to give a brief historical sketch of the various systematized concerts and musical entertainments in England which have been devoted to such performances, from the early days of chamber music to the present time.

The task of the writer is an exacting one, for the records of the first English chamber concerts are scanty and not always reliable, whilst the activities of recent times are so numerous and so important that it is impossible to summarize them adequately in a small space. It is, moreover, difficult to know where to begin, for it is not always possible to draw a definite distinction between a private musical gathering and a public performance, nor is it entirely easy to differentiate between real chamber music and music which cannot justly be so described.

Almost the earliest records of regular public meetings in England for the performances of chamber music appear to be concerned with the musical life of Oxford. In 1665 a music school was established in that city, and furnished 'with a number of instruments, including an organ of four stopps, and seven desks to lay the books on, at two shillings each'. Here, according to Hawkins, subscription concerts were given which were, for a time, the only regular gatherings of the kind in the kingdom.

Setting aside certain 'concerts in unison', as they were called, which were part of the regular attractions at booths and fairs in or near the metropolis during the reign of Charles II, the first actual concerts in London at which chamber music was performed before a public audience paying for admission are said to have been those organized by John Banister, an English violinist of distinction, between 1672 and 1678. These concerts were first held at Banister's house, known as the Music School, 'over and against the George Taverne in White

[1] Many of the names referred to in this article are dealt with under their own headings in the body of the book.

Fryers', Fleet Street. According to advertisements in the *London Gazette* of the period, these musical performances took place daily during the season, 'beginning precisely at four of the clock in the afternoon'. In North's *Memories of Music* we read that Banister 'erected an elevated box or gallery for the musicians, whose modesty required curtains', and 'the rest of the room was fitted with seats and small tables, alehouse fashion'. One shilling was apparently the uniform price of admission, and members of the audience were entitled to have some say in the music performed. 'There was very good music, for Banister found means to procure the best hands in London, and some voices, to assist him, and there wanted no variety, for Banister, besides playing on the violin, did wonders on the flageolet to a thro' base, and several other masters likewise played solos'.

In the year 1678, which was probably the date of the cessation of John Banister's musical activities in London, a kind of concert club for the practice of chamber music was formed by a certain Thomas Britton, who was called 'the musical small-coal man'. This remarkable character was born in Northamptonshire in 1651. In his youth he was apprenticed to a coal-dealer in London, and afterwards he established a business of his own as a dealer in small-coal (probably charcoal), which he was in the habit of carrying through the streets on his back. Of his musical achievements we have but scanty records, but he was evidently a cultivated and progressive literary man, whose talents were recognized by the great book-collectors of his day.

The concert club meetings were held in a modest little room situated over Britton's shop (in a corner of Jerusalem Passage, Aylesbury Street, Clerkenwell), and attracted many musical and artistic enthusiasts. To begin with, no charge for admission was made; but when the performances became better known, subscribers (who paid ten shillings a year) were obtained, and the concerts became established in fashionable favour. Amongst the performers were Handel (who, it is believed, occasionally presided at the harpsichord), Pepusch (of *Beggar's Opera* fame), John Banister (probably the son of the previously mentioned violinist), Henry Needler, John Hughes, Philip Hart, Henry Symonds, Abel Whichello (a notable song-writer and harpsichordist), Obadiah Shuttleworth (a skilled violinist), and many others, both professional and amateur. Britton, we are told, provided the guests with coffee 'at a penny a dish'. Of the music presented at these gatherings no details have survived, but, from the reputations of the performers, it is evident that the programmes were of a serious order, and as the concerts appear to have flourished for something like thirty-six years they are of great historic importance, and the influence which they exercised upon the tastes of several successive generations of music-lovers must have been considerable. It is interesting to note that a contemporary portrait of Britton, painted by Wollaston, has found a place in the National Portrait Gallery.

The success of Britton's efforts no doubt led to the formation of similar organizations in London. At all events, we know that in or about 1680 a small concert hall was erected 'by the principal music masters of London' in York Buildings, and here many of the best performers were heard at regular music meetings.

During the eighteenth century, concerts in London became more frequent and more firmly established in popular estimation. Mention should first be made of an association called the ACADEMY OF ANCIENT MUSIC, which came into being somewhere about 1710. The concerts of the Academy were held at the Crown and Anchor Tavern in the Strand. The programmes were not entirely confined to chamber music, but included orchestral and choral works. Many of the performers who had contributed to the success of Thomas Britton's concerts were requisitioned, Dr. Pepusch, Dr. Maurice Greene, and afterwards Dr. Arnold being amongst the chief directors of its activities. The famous Italian violinist and composer, Francesco Geminiani, made frequent appearances at these concerts, at which no doubt he produced many of his numerous concerted compositions for strings. The Academy of Ancient Music continued its performances until 1792, when it was dissolved.

Similar musical meetings, under the auspices of the ANACREONTIC SOCIETY, founded about 1770, were also held at the Crown and Anchor Tavern, though here the chief feature was the rendering of vocal ensemble music such as madrigals, glees, and catches. Membership was accounted a valued privilege, and the supporters were chiefly members of the aristocracy and wealthy musical amateurs. It is recorded that Haydn was present at one of these concerts. It appears that the Anacreontic Society came to an abrupt end in 1786, owing to the performance of some comic songs which were considered unfit for the ears of the Duchess of Devonshire, who was present. In great disgust the members resigned one after another, and it was impossible for the Society to save its face after such a sad debasement of its former high aims and unimpeachable good taste.

The CONCERTS OF ANTIENT MUSIC or KING'S CONCERTS, founded in 1776 by an influential committee, were on a more imposing scale, and had a long and distinguished history. They were, in fact, the first really important concerts given in London. Orchestral music was the main attraction, but instrumental works of smaller dimensions found a place in the programmes. These concerts were held till 1795 in Tottenham Street, at rooms which were afterwards known as the Queen's or West

London Theatre. In 1795 a move was made to a concert-room in the Opera House, and 1804 saw a further change of locale, the more commodious Hanover Square Rooms (which had been opened in 1775) being now available, and far more suitable for musical performances on a large scale. Here the concerts continued their excellent work until 1848. For the first few years of their existence the policy of the King's Concerts was avowedly conservative, the works of Handel occupying the chief place on the programmes, but later on the music of Haydn and Mozart, and even Beethoven, was admitted, and during the penultimate season, in 1847, at a concert directed by Prince Albert, Mendelssohn played organ solos.

While dealing with concerts at which orchestral music constituted the main fare, it must not be forgotten that at those given in early days by our venerable and still-existing PHILHARMONIC SOCIETY (which started operations in 1813) chamber music was frequently included in the programmes, and that many concerted chamber works by Mozart, Beethoven, Ries, Spohr and others, were performed for the first time in England under this Society's auspices.

To turn to concerts which consisted solely of chamber music, pride of place, for pioneer work, must be accorded to those given by Joseph Dando, a London-born violinist, who, after a successful experiment at the Horns Tavern, Doctors' Commons, in 1835, was encouraged to institute, in the following year, a regular series of quartet performances at the Hanover Square Rooms. These are of capital importance in the history of the art, as they were actually the first concerts in England to be devoted exclusively to instrumental chamber music, and principally to string quartets. The original party of performers consisted of Henry Blagrove (1st v.), Henry Gattie, Charles Lucas (vc.), and the concert-giver himself. When Blagrove seceded from the group in 1842, Dando promoted himself to the position of 1st violin, and engaged John Loder as viola. In the same year the party removed their concerts to Crosby Hall, where they continued to flourish until the deaths of Gattie and Loder, in 1853, broke up the party. It is interesting to record that, so far from ceasing his energies, Dando continued his work as an orchestral player for many years, and ultimately, in 1875, became music-master at Charterhouse School, teaching there until within a short period of his death, which occurred as recently as 1894, at Godalming. As an old man of eighty-seven he must have been able to review with great interest a period of active progress in chamber music such as few men can have witnessed in a lifetime, with the added satisfaction of having been the first to kindle public enthusiasm for the highest form of intimate musical art in this country.

Soon after Dando's fame as an exponent of chamber music had been established, an important project of a similar nature was initiated by John Ella, a Yorkshire lawyer who became a violinist and settled in London. The chamber concerts, which bore the title of the MUSICAL UNION, were started in 1844, and under Ella's immediate supervision they flourished for something like thirty-five years in the heart of the metropolis. The concerts were given in the afternoons, and a large number of notable chamber classics were presented under excellent conditions by the most distinguished players of the time, both British and foreign. Two features of special interest may be recalled in connexion with Ella's enterprise. One was the erection of a platform for the performers in the centre of the hall, the seats for the audience being ranged round this raised daïs—a system which was revived with success many years later at St. James's Hall for the concerts of the Joachim Quartet. The other feature, an innovation of even greater moment, was the publication for the first time of analytical programme books, the object of which was to assist listeners to a fuller understanding of the works performed. These programme books were issued to subscribers a few days before each concert, a plan which might with advantage be adopted at the present time.

The concerts of the Musical Union continued until 1880, eight years before the death of their founder, who certainly deserved the gratitude of those interested in serious music, by his devoted efforts to present the best chamber works in the best manner possible.

Two further contemporary ventures of a like character must be mentioned—the chamber concerts given by Sir William Sterndale Bennett from 1843 to 1856 (noteworthy for the concert-giver's charming participation as pianist in the works performed), and the concerts of the QUARTET ASSOCIATION, organized in 1852 by a strong combination of eminent string players:—Sainton, Cooper, Hill, and Piatti. The latter institution survived for three seasons only, but the performers were of the highest class, and many works not then generally recognized were introduced, such as Beethoven's posthumous quartets and the chamber music of Schumann, as well as some by British composers, including Bennett, Loder, and G. A. Macfarren.

It was not, however, until January 1859, when the famous POPULAR CONCERTS at St. James's Hall, familiarly known as the Monday 'Pops', came into being, that chamber music received adequate and consistent support from a really large and appreciative section of the public. Organized by Chappell & Co., the music publishers, with the primary object of benefiting the shareholders of the hall, these concerts started somewhat inauspiciously from both the financial and artistic aspects. The programmes, to begin with, were of a miscellaneous description, comprising old ballads and familiar instrumental pieces, and public interest at the outset fluctuated rather seriously. But, on the wise suggestion of J. W. Davison, the music critic of *The Times*, the experiment was tried of devoting concerts to special classical composers. A Mendelssohn night was followed by a Mozart night, a Haydn and Weber night, a Beethoven night, and so on. With this policy Mr. Arthur Chappell, the manager of the venture, persevered in spite of temporary discouragement, and in the course of a short time the concerts began to pay their way, and ultimately became firmly established in public favour.

As was said at the time, however, the appellation 'Popular' was a misnomer. 'The music given was of the most consistently un-popular character. Most speculators would either have altered the name of the entertainment or modified the selection of the compositions performed; Mr. Chappell took a bolder course—he changed the public taste.'

In 1865 the Saturday afternoon 'Pops' were added to the scheme. Originally these Saturday performances were of the nature of semi-private rehearsals for the Monday concerts, but in course of time separate programmes were presented, and by 1876 these additional concerts were regularly established and met with equal public favour and support. The greatest players of chamber music in Europe were engaged season by season, and the noblest works in the classical repertory were given memorable performances throughout the winter months for nearly forty successive years. It was a great achievement. Amongst the celebrated artists whose English reputations were established at these concerts were Joachim, Popper, Piatti, Mühlfeld, Clara Schumann, Sir Charles and Lady Hallé, Rubinstein, von Bülow, Fanny Davies, Mathilde Verne, Leonard Borwick, Dohnányi, the Henschels, Marie Fillunger, Liza Lehmann, Plunket Greene, and hosts of others of almost equal distinction. Captious critics have often complained that the programmes of the 'Pops' were almost always of a conservative type, and there is some truth in the impeachment, but they were none the less noteworthy on that account. It must not be forgotten, moreover, that the promoters were not devoid of enterprise in certain directions, for practically the whole of the chamber music of Brahms was made known to English audiences through the medium of these concerts, despite the apathy with which it was at first regarded. An occasional production of a composition by Parry or Stanford represented a mild concession to patriotic sentiment, which was sometimes even apologized for in the programmes! As a general rule, however, British composers were ignored, a fact which certainly delayed the recognition of native chamber music by the concert-going public.

On the other hand, British string players, such as Alfred Gibson, W. E. Whitehouse, and Haydn Inwards were, in course of time, allowed to mount the platform and take part in quartets and quintets with their distinguished foreign colleagues, and thus the way was prepared for the more general acknowledgement of British musicians in chamber music, which came about in the early years of the twentieth century.

In April 1887, when the thousandth concert took place, a notable landmark was reached, and the 'Pops' continued to prosper until 1898, when they appeared to have lost their unique hold upon the public, partly owing to the numerous other chamber concerts which claimed the attention of music-lovers, and partly, perhaps, from the ultra-conservative nature of the programmes. At all events they were not resumed in 1899, to the great regret of thousands of regular patrons.

An attempt by Johann Kruse to revive their glories in 1903–4 was not very successful, nor did the rather severe programmes provided by Donald Francis Tovey, or the enterprising Broadwood Concerts (which endeavoured to pursue a more liberal policy in chamber music in the same hall at about the same time) meet with the support they deserved. Eventually, in 1905, the old St. James's Hall was demolished to make room for the erection of the Piccadilly Hotel.

Despite numerous disadvantages—its hideous mock-Moorish decorations, its draughty corners, the smells of cooking from an adjacent restaurant, the insistent disturbances from the bell of a muffin-man in the street, who always contrived to spoil at least one work on the Saturday afternoon, not to speak of the tinkling of banjos, bones, and tambourines which frequently emerged from the lower hall, where the Moore and Burgess Minstrels entertained the bourgeoisie—despite these nerve-racking distractions, St. James's Hall had come to be regarded with a peculiar affection by concert-goers. It is as the home of the 'Pops', perhaps, that the old building will be best remembered, for at these wonderful concerts, notwithstanding a certain element of hero-worship, which could not fail occasionally to detract from the enjoyment of those who came for the music alone, the art of chamber music came to fruition in England, and a really willing and appreciative public was educated to take an intelligent interest in intimate music of the highest type.

To attempt to summarize the principal concerts of chamber music which came into existence during the latter years of the nineteenth century, and especially after the Popular Concerts ceased their regular ministrations, is an almost hopeless task. Amongst the foreign Quartet and Trio parties which have frequently visited this country and maintained a fine interpretative standard may be mentioned the Joachim Quartet, the Bohemian, Kneisel, Flonzaley, Rosé, Budapest, and Lener Quartets, the Moscow and Cherniavsky

TRIOS, and many others. The CLASSICAL CONCERT SOCIETY, which was the means of introducing several of these players to London, for a good many years maintained a clientèle of music-lovers similar to those who supported the old 'Pops'.

It is even more interesting and encouraging to speak of the Quartet and Trio combinations which have been formed everywhere in our own country, some wholly British in constitution, some containing a proportion of British players. We have had such organizations as the GOMPERTZ, LUDWIG, WESSELY, BRODSKY, and CATTERALL QUARTETS, the LONDON TRIO, the NEW TRIO, and others, with English players included. We have had also the SHINNER, MOTTO, NORAH CLENCH, the GRIMSON, LONDON STRING, PHILHARMONIC, SPENCER DYKE, SNOW, and KINSEY QUARTETS, the ALBION TRIO, the EYRE TRIO, and many more besides, formed entirely of native artists. All these organizations have given concerts on their own account, and accomplished excellent work throughout the country in the cause of chamber music. In another direction, the concerts run for several seasons by the late George Clinton, the clarinettist, did something to call attention to the beauty and value of the almost unknown repertory of wind ensemble-music.

Praise is also due for the fine work on behalf of chamber music which has been accomplished by the PEOPLE'S CONCERT SOCIETY (*q.v.*), founded as far back as 1878, and for many years active in promoting enterprising chamber concerts at very low prices, not only in London, but in other centres in the home counties.

Of even greater importance, musically, if more restricted in their quiet and unobtrusive influence, the chamber concerts held regularly at SOUTH PLACE INSTITUTE (*q.v.*), Finsbury, on Sunday evenings, have earned for themselves a special niche of distinction in the history of a good cause. They were started in 1887. Under the management of an enthusiastic amateur musician, A. J. Clements, and heartily supported by such devoted artists as Richard H. Walthew and the late John Saunders (a most refined and gifted violinist who was an ideal ensemble player), these concerts have consistently pursued a comprehensive and progressive course, and have appealed especially to Londoners unable to afford the luxury of expensive subscriptions. The most distinguished artists have ever been generously ready to give their services for nominal fees at South Place, and nowhere in England can better performances of chamber music be heard, although no charge is made for admission.

Chamber music has naturally been cultivated assiduously at the ROYAL ACADEMY OF MUSIC and the ROYAL COLLEGE OF MUSIC, and both these institutions make a strong feature of their chamber concerts. The R.C.M., in particular, long ago established a high reputation for the quality of its performances, which, under the guidance of such masters as Gompertz, Arbos, Rivarde, Sons and others, have often equalled the efforts of mature and experienced players. More recently Lionel Tertis's classes at the R.A.M. have produced even more wonderful results.

The long neglect of British music at the Popular Concerts was an injustice which was not allowed to pass without effective comment, in the shape of chamber concerts devoted mainly or entirely to native compositions. In this connexion, the name of Ernest Fowles must be given pride of place. Mr. Fowles, who incidentally was the first to give a concert in London entirely devoted to the works of Brahms, launched a series of CONCERTS OF BRITISH CHAMBER MUSIC at the small Queen's Hall in 1894, and continued fearlessly to practise what he preached until 1899. It may be of interest to record the names of some of the composers who figured on his programmes. S. Wesley, Macfarren, Mackenzie, Parry, Stanford, Algernon Ashton, Ernest Walker, W. H. Speer, and J. C. Ames were amongst those with already established reputations who were accorded a hearing, whilst Coleridge-Taylor, Hurlstone, Alfred Wall, Walford Davies, Joseph Speaight, and R. H. Walthew formed a strong group of representatives of what was, at that time, the young musical blood. The executants engaged included some of the most competent players of the day, and the scheme was supported by an imposing list of subscribers.

The frequent and persistent efforts of Joseph Holbrooke to familiarize Londoners with the chamber music written by himself and his English contemporaries must not be passed by without a special word of recognition. Holbrooke was ever a fighter, and if his somewhat truculent methods alienated the sympathies of certain musicians, his strong driving force has not been without its influence upon the progress of the gentlest and most intellectual phase of musical art.

[The concerts given by the writer of this article, known as the THOMAS DUNHILL CONCERTS, which were begun in 1907 and continued for ten seasons, had similar aims, and, in addition, special efforts were here made to rescue and revive British chamber works which had been neglected or had received only one performance previously. Among other native composers, now universally recognized, to whom attention was directed in this way, may be mentioned particularly John Ireland, whose works were repeatedly performed. ED.]

It should be remembered, also, that the R.C.M. PATRON'S FUND (endowed by Sir Ernest Palmer for the encouragement of British composers) gave several concerts of chamber music in the early years of its ministrations; nor should one forget the work of Isidore de Lara, who kept the flag flying in difficult times with his so-called War-Emergency Concerts, devoted solely to British music. The chamber concerts given by Eugene Goossens, himself an accomplished ensemble player, have been devoted to the most modern manifestations of this form of art, and deserve special mention, if on that account alone.

Of the numerous regular concerts of chamber music promoted in London suburbs and in important provincial centres there is not space to give details. But the pioneer work at Hampstead in the 'eighties and 'nineties (where 'Pops' were given on the lines of those at St. James's Hall), of Brodsky, Catterall, and Edith Robinson in Manchester, of Samuel Midgley in Bradford, of Isobel McCullagh in Liverpool, of Edgar Haddock in Leeds, of Donald Tovey and R. F. McEwen in Edinburgh, of Stella Fife in Reading, of Alfred Wall and others in Newcastle should not pass unacknowledged. Most of the chief towns and cities of the British Isles now possess more or less flourishing societies which exist for the encouragement of chamber music, and even in some quite small centres, such as Haslemere and Sevenoaks, the great masterpieces of the art may now be heard under favourable conditions at well supported subscription concerts. Nor is private enterprise alone responsible for such a happy state of affairs. The British Music Society, at its various branches throughout the country, has done vigorous work in the same direction, by helping to finance and provide lecturers and performers to encourage a widespread interest in the art; and the Faculty of Arts shows the promise of similar good work to come.

That the love of chamber music is spreading is proved conclusively by the fact that classes for its performance have at last found their way into the programmes of most of the Competitive Festivals throughout the kingdom. It is now no rarity to find an excellent level of efficiency reached, and considerable public interest manifested in local amateur performances of this kind. W. W. Cobbett has somewhere declared that 'the amateur is the backbone of a nation's music', and from this one may infer that his place is no longer merely that of a patron or listener. Indeed, the amateur is often a most skilful performer of chamber music. This has been recognized from very early times, for we have already seen that many of the players who assisted at Britton's concerts in the seventeenth century were amateurs.

At the present day, one may point with satisfaction to many amateur organizations long devoted to the practice of chamber music. The great educational centres of Oxford and Cambridge have each their prosperous chamber music clubs, and many of the members, on leaving the University, join the Oxford and Cambridge Musical Club in London, where the periodical performances are on similar lines. Both here and at the more informal meetings of the King Cole Chamber Music Club, amateur members and their friends enjoy and participate in programmes of ensemble music amongst more or less Bohemian surroundings. In such quarters, chamber music amongst the amateurs certainly 'lives, moves, and has its being' under ideal conditions, even if the performances do not always reach the highest professional standard.

A final line or two of this long dissertation must be reserved for the subject of Broadcasting. Many people who were never, in former days, quite enthusiastic enough to go to chamber concerts to 'listen' have, nevertheless, found great delight in sitting in their own arm-chairs at home and 'listening-in'. The gratitude of all believers in the influence of good music is due to the British Broadcasting Company for the many opportunities they have given their patrons of becoming acquainted with the great literature of chamber music.

It is a matter for intense satisfaction, too, that the transmission of chamber music, especially string quartets, is more faithful than that of any other kind of music.

Wireless chamber concerts have certainly come to stay, and it is even reasonable to anticipate that, when the methods of carrying the sound to our ears become more perfectly controlled, we shall find in such performances an approach to the true realization of the intimacy of chamber music, and the conditions under which it may be most completely enjoyed.

Thomas F. Dunhill.

(2) Present-day Organizations.

A few of the most important of these are dealt with under separate headings.

(*a*) String Quartets.[1]

Allied Quartet. Desiré Defauw, Charles Woodhouse, Lionel Tertis, Émile Doehaerd. An exceptionally strong combination, which, unfortunately, was only a war-time organization. Gave several performances at the Oxford and Cambridge Musical Club. Defauw has transferred his main activities to Belgium, where he holds a very distinguished position, both as conductor and chamber music player; whilst Doehaerd is now 'cellist in the Zimmer Quartet in Brussels.

Rhoda Backhouse Quartet. Jean le Févre, Rowena Franklin, Lilly Phillips. Founded by Rhoda Backhouse in 1919, the viola parts being played by Margaret Savory until 1926.

Bath Quartet Society. The excellent work done in the West of England during a number of years by this organization, which has ceased to exist, deserves to be chronicled. The personnel consisted of Josef Ludwig, Collins, Blagrove, and Whitehouse.

[1] The names of the performers are given in the following order:—1st v, 2nd v, vla, vc. Where a Quartet is named after the 1st violin, the name is not repeated.

ARTHUR BECKWITH QUARTET. Pierre Tas, Arthur Blakemore, Anthony Pini. The Quartet first played for the B.B.C. in Nov. 1926. The ensemble and string tone is excellent. Arthur Beckwith spent three years in America (Cleveland, Ohio), where he founded the Cleveland String Quartet. (*v.* AMERICAN PERFORMING ORGANIZATIONS.)

BIRMINGHAM STRING QUARTET. Percival Hodgson, Grace Burrows, Frederick Mountney, Joan Willis. Founded in 1918. Charles W. Bye was the original 2nd violin and was succeeded by Frank Venton, whilst Paul Beard was the original viola. There has been no change since 1922. Joan Willis is the wife of the leader. The Quartet has toured the British Isles, and played at almost every music club and society of importance.

[RAWDON BRIGGS QUARTET. John Bridge, Mrs. Rawdon Briggs, W. Hutton. Rawdon Briggs (b. 1870) was a pupil of Joachim at the Hochschule, and, after much experience as second violin in the Brodsky Quartet, formed his own party, which has played in most of the large towns in the North of England. EDITOR.]

ADOLPH BRODSKY, b. Russia, 1851. Whilst studying at Vienna (1860–62) was 2nd violin of the famous Hellmesberger (his teacher's) Quartet. In 1883 he became the chief professor at the Leipzig Conservatorium, where, with Hans Becker, Novaček, and Julius Klengel, he formed his first Quartet, which achieved a world-wide reputation. In these years Brodsky was the close friend of Brahms, Tchaikovsky, and Grieg, whose chamber music he interprets with special authority. In 1895 he came to Manchester as the Principal of the Manchester Royal College of Music, and immediately formed a Quartet which, after thirty-two years, is still in existence and regularly playing in public. The original personnel consisted of Brodsky, Mrs. Helen Rawdon Briggs, Simon Speelman, Carl Fuchs. Naturally, during the leader's long career there have been many changes, which, summarized, are as follows: 2nd violin: John Bridge, 1920–1922, since Alfred Barker. Viola: Frank Park, 1920–1922, since Mrs. Helen Rawdon Briggs. 'Cello: Walter Hatton, 1915–1925, since Carl Fuchs. It will be noticed that the members of the original Quartet played together for twenty years, and that three of them are now together again. The Quartet has played through the whole gamut of the classical repertory, and has introduced many modern and contemporary works to Manchester audiences. It has rendered incalculable services in fostering the love of chamber music in the Midlands, and, indeed, its far-reaching influences can never be properly estimated. Brodsky himself, with his deep and penetrating knowledge of chamber music, and his capacity to merge his own individuality into the music, is an ideal leader, and a violinist whose playing is distinguished for its insight and nobility of tone.

ANTONIO BROSA QUARTET. J. H. Greenbaum, Leonard Rubens, Anthony Pini. Formed in June 1926, and, after playing at South Place, gave its first London recital under the auspices of the Nonesuch Press Series of Period Concerts at the Wigmore Hall on Nov. 17th. Although its members have only played together for two years, the ensemble has already made a very high reputation for itself. Gave the first English performance of Honegger's quartet in C minor at the London Contemporary Music Centre on Oct. 20, 1927.

CATHIE QUARTET. Formed in 1904, originally consisting of Philip Cathie, Tom Morrison, George Cathie, and Herbert Withers. Subsequently, Orry Korjak became 2nd violin, and Arthur Trew 'cello. Played at most of the well-known chamber concerts throughout the country, and gave, on an average, six recitals every year in London. For many seasons appeared at the old Broadwood concerts and at South Place. Was disbanded in 1914.

ARTHUR CATTERALL. This Quartet was formed at a chance meeting of Catterall, Hock, and Reggel, at a concert in Birmingham in 1909, these three players together with Ernest O'Malley constituting the original personnel. In 1915 Reggel became the principal viola of the Damrosch Orchestra in New York, O'Malley taking his place, and John Bridge became the new 2nd violin. In 1916 O'Malley retired, Frank Park, the principal viola of the Hallé Orchestra, then joining the Quartet. This personnel continued until 1925, when Bridge retired, and his place was taken by Leonard Hirsch. Shortly afterwards the party assumed its present personnel: Arthur Catterall, Maurice Ward, Frank S. Park, Johan C. Hock. The Quartet has produced many new works, and occupies a distinguished place among native performing organizations. Its many European tours have included a visit to Berlin, where it played with much success. It records for both the H.M.V. and Columbia companies.

NORAH CLENCH QUARTET. Lucy Stone, Cecilia Gates, May Mukle. Founded about 1907. Gave many successful concerts, but is now disbanded.

EDGAR DRAKE QUARTET. Arthur Boothroyd, Harry Thornton, Herbert Drake. Gave its first concert in 1913 in Bradford. In 1919 Reginald Boothroyd took 2nd violin, and George S. Drake became 'cello. The 2nd violinist is now Albert Hepton, and the 'cellist Edward Wright. Except during the war, Harry Thornton has been the permanent viola. The Quartet was intimately associated with the well-known Bradford Free Chamber Concerts for the last ten years of their existence.

SPENCER DYKE QUARTET. Edwin Quaife, Ernest Tomlinson, B. Patterson Parker. With the exception of Edwin Quaife, all the players were originally members of the Wessely Quartet. The ensemble was formed in 1918, and its personnel was unchanged until August 1927, when Bernard Shore became viola and Tate Gilder the 2nd violin. It has given first performances of a whole series of new works by composers British and continental. Besides recording many interesting works for the Vocalion Co., the Quartet has also recorded copiously for the N.G.S.

It specializes in no particular school of composition, although a point is always made of including an English work in each programme. The ensemble, besides frequent London concerts, has toured extensively in England, but has had to refuse repeated offers of outside tours, owing to the stress of individual members' engagements. It has a great reputation for the soundness of its interpretations, its restraint and innate refinement.

EDINBURGH QUARTET. Watt Jupp, J. M. Begbie, J. Fairbairn, Bernard Beers. These artists form an admirable ensemble.

HELEN EGERTON QUARTET. Helen Gough, Dorothy Jones, Gwendolen Griffiths. The Egerton Quartet assisted W. W. Cobbett in the Competition—1914–1915—by playing a series of string quartets to the judges assembled at his house in St. John's Wood. The first and second prizes were awarded on this occasion to Frank Bridge and W. H. Reed.

ENGLISH QUARTET. Formed in 1902, the original personnel being the late Thomas F. Morris, Herbert H. Kinsey, Frank Bridge, Ivor James. It was the outcome of the association of the players whilst they were together studying ensemble playing at the R.C.M. Thomas Morris joined the R.A.F. in 1915, and Marjorie Hayward has since been the leader. In 1918 Edwin Virgo became 2nd violin. The Quartet came to an end in 1925, and in the latter years of its existence played mostly in private. For many years it performed at all London and provincial chamber music societies, and had an extremely high reputation.

ENTENTE QUARTET. Originally known as the Boris Pecker String Quartet, which was formed in 1924, consisting of Boris Pecker, Dorothy Churton, Mary Stewart, and Edith Churton. When in 1927 Boris Pecker associated himself with the International Quartet, his place was taken by Cecil Bonvalot, and the ensemble renamed. James Lockyer has since replaced Mary Stewart.

FACULTY OF ARTS QUARTET. Edgar R. Wilby, H. Greenbaum, James Lockyer, Arthur Maney. Only plays at the Faculty of Arts Concerts in Upper John Street. Has given the first performances of many works by English composers.

HORACE FELLOWES QUARTET. John McArthur, Spencer Malcolm, John Dickson. These young players (2nd v, vla, and vc) are Scottish born and bred, and are all leading players in Glasgow. Horace Fellowes led the Scottish Orchestra until the winter of 1926.

JOHN FRY QUARTET. In 1920 the players forming the Quartet at the chamber music class under Ludwig Lebell at Trinity College of Music consisted of John Fry, Henri Peros, Vera Henkel, and George Roth. Roth soon resigned, and was succeeded by Alec Compinsky. This combination appeared at several concerts as the 'Trinity College Chamber Music Players', but eventually called itself the 'Mandeville'. Elsa Martin joined the ensemble as 'cello in 1922, the players still studying with Ludwig Lebell. After several tentative but successful appearances, the Quartet gave its first recital at Wigmore Hall in 1922. In 1925 Walter Price became the 2nd violin, and when, in 1926, Gastone Marinari joined as 'cello, the Quartet took its present title, the personnel now comprising John Fry, Walter Price, Vera Henkel, and Gastone Marinari. The Quartet has given many first performances.

JESSIE GRIMSON QUARTET. Original personnel: Jessie Grimson, Frank Bridge, Ernest Tomlinson, Edward Mason. Formed about 1902, and re-formed after the war with Charles Woodhouse, Raymond Jeremy, and B. Patterson Parker. One of the Quartet's first appearances was at the old St. James's Hall 'Pops', where it also gave the last performance of the famous series. The Quartet also played at the Broadwood concerts, and frequently, in early days, toured the provinces. In 1907 it gave the first performance in Brussels of Frank Bridge's *Three Idylls*. It has been closely identified with the South Place concerts for the last twenty years, and there has done splendid work in the performance of classical works, of which it can always be relied upon to give a sound and straightforward interpretation. Following an illness in 1927, Jessie Grimson decided to retire from public playing, and the Quartet was then disbanded.

ARTHUR HYTCH QUARTET. A Birmingham ensemble founded *c.* 1914. Original personnel: Arthur Hytch, T. Smith, David Reggel, Percy Dyche; by 1919 the 2nd vn., va., and vc. were Harold Mills, Frank Cantell, Frederick Bye. Subsequently, Leslie Smerdon became 2nd vn., and Ernest Element va. From 1919 to 1921 the Quartet played for the Coventry Chamber Music Society, and gave concerts in the Midlands generally. The Quartet also plays at the Tea-Time Concerts at the Midland Institute, Birmingham, organized under the direction of Arthur Hytch in 1926.

INTERNATIONAL QUARTET. André Mangeot, Boris Pecker, Frank Howard, Herbert Withers. Originally known as the Music Society String Quartet, and founded in connexion with the

Society of that name in order to perform works not normally played by other ensembles. The formation of the Quartet was then André Mangeot, Dorothy Christison, Rebecca Clarke, and May Mukle. On the departure of May Mukle for America, the 'cellist was Ambrose Gauntlett, the 2nd violin Kenneth Skeaping, and the viola Raymond Jeremy. In 1923 the personnel was again changed, Mangeot still leading, but the other instrumentalists were Boris Pecker, Cecil Bonvalot, John Barbirolli. These players continued until the spring of 1926 (except that Harry Berly had replaced Cecil Bonvalot), when the retirement of John Barbirolli was the occasion for further changes, and the Quartet at last attained its present formation, with Mangeot and Pecker leading alternately. The name was then changed, in consequence of the confusion caused to continental critics by the original title. An agreement was further made between the players that they would not identify themselves with any other ensemble.

The Quartet has introduced to continental audiences many works by native composers, both classic and modern. In 1925 it was specially engaged to give a three days' festival of English music in Hamburg. Amongst other compositions, the Purcell fantasias have been performed for the first time in various countries, as well as being revived in England, where the ensemble has given first performances of many modern works.

The Quartet has also done valuable work in recording chamber music for the N.G.S. Its recording of Ravel's string quartet has a special interest, as, after hearing the test records, the composer said that if certain alterations were made, the interpretation was just in the spirit and mood in which he had conceived the music. The re-recording of these parts completely satisfied the composer.

Constance Izard Quartet. Dorothy Churton, Mary Stewart, Margaret Izard. Formed and gave its first recital in 1926.

Kendall Quartet. Founded in 1920, the original personnel being Katherine Kendall, Marjorie Clemens, Dorothy Jones, and Edith Hanson. In 1922 Miss Clemens resigned, her place being taken by Dorothy Brook, since when the personnel has remained unchanged. The ensemble began by giving small concerts in country villages. Miss Kendall on these occasions always gave short explanations of the music to be played, being of the opinion that it is of immense value to focus the interest of the audience on one or two special points, and that many listeners with a prejudice against chamber music have ultimately become interested by this method. It was the second ensemble to broadcast from 2 LO—this, of course, in the very early days of broadcasting in this country. Later, it gave the first concert at the Victoria and Albert Museum under the auspices of the League of Arts, and it still plays regularly every season at these now widely reputed concerts. The Quartet has given concerts for many of the principal English schools, and has twice played in Lincoln Cathedral. In 1925 it left England for an extended Empire tour, first playing in Ceylon and then touring the Malay States, performing chiefly in clubs, and concluding with a concert in the Victoria Hall, Singapore, and a reception at Government House. In Java, the Quartet was engaged by the Dutch clubs, and toured the country, playing chiefly classical compositions. Whilst in Melbourne, Australia, the Quartet played in the cathedral to an audience of 2,000 people. South Africa concluded the tour, which finished with a command performance at Government House, Pretoria. This organization was not only the first women's Quartet to undertake such an extensive tour, but also the first ensemble from England to visit the places mentioned. In all, 110 concerts were given, the tour lasting for ten months, and over 40,000 miles were covered.

Herbert Kinsey Quartet. John Fry, Frank Howard, Anthony Pini. Original personnel: Herbert Kinsey, Frank Howard, Ernest Tomlinson, B. Patterson Parker. Founded in 1919. An excellent and popular combination.

Johann Kruse Quartet. G. Whitaker, L. Rubens, D. Sisserman. J. Kruse, who was a pupil of Joachim, first formed a Quartet in Berlin in 1882, and from 1892–1897 played 2nd violin in the Joachim Quartet. In the latter year he settled in London and formed another Quartet, and gave chamber music concerts at Leighton House and Wigmore Hall. He is chiefly remembered in London for his valiant though fruitless efforts to save the 'Pops' from final extinction. He died in 1928.

Samuel Kutcher Quartet. Kenneth Skeaping, Cecil Bonvalot, Edward Robinson. Formed first in 1922, and re-formed in 1924, in which year it gave its first recital at the Wigmore Hall. Has frequently given first performances of modern works. The repertory consists of many unhackneyed compositions by contemporary composers. The performers are artists of the first rank, and noted for the brilliancy of their ensemble.

This Quartet was disbanded in Oct. 1927.

Leeds String Quartet. Founded by Alexander Cohen in 1910, with the object of enabling West Riding music-lovers to hear something of contemporary work in chamber music, as well as the less frequently performed classics. These remarks also apply to the Trio which was formed in the same year. The original personnel of the Quartet included A. Cohen, J. Thorpe, Lily Simms, George Schott, but there were many subsequent changes. The second violin passed in succession to F. Kitchen, B. Ghent, S. Nagley, L. Buenle,

A. Boothroyd, and Elsa Stamford. When G. Schott seceded, his place was taken by A. Hemingway and later by Kathleen Moorhouse. The Quartet and Trio were responsible (1912–1919) for the first public performances in England of many modern works, and furnished the programmes for the well-known Leeds Bohemian Chamber Concerts. (*v.* MISCELLANEOUS, below.) It is now disbanded.

ISABEL MCCULLAGH QUARTET. Gertrude Newsham, Helen Rawdon Briggs, Mary McCullagh. Formed in 1920, and is the only string Quartet in Liverpool. In 1923 it was engaged by the Contemporary Music Centre to play at the festival of the International Music Society at Salzburg, being the only British Quartet which has performed at these annual festivals. In 1927 all of Beethoven's string quartets were performed at six concerts in Liverpool. Every year the ensemble gives a unique performance on Good Friday in Liverpool Cathedral of Haydn's *Words from the Cross*, playing it as it was originally written. It has achieved a very high standard of ensemble and interpretation.

[MAGI STRING QUARTET, a party now disbanded, composed of competent amateurs, all undergraduates of Oxford University, assisted by Mrs. H. W. B. Joseph, who took the viola part. It gave a successful concert at Wigmore Hall. EDITOR.]

MANDEVILLE. *See* John FRY.

MARIE MOTTO QUARTET. Gave its first concert at Wigmore Hall in 1903, when the personnel consisted of Marie Motto, the late Thomas Morris, Frank Bridge, R. Purcell-Jones. This ensemble played together with very great success for ten years. After the war, it began again with George Whitaker as 2nd violin and Charles Woodhouse as viola. It is well known in private circles.

NEW PHILHARMONIC QUARTET. Bessie Rawlins, Winifred Stiles, Christopher Southward, Brenda Sichel. Formed in 1926. Specializes in the performance of modern works.

PENNINGTON QUARTET. Originally formed in 1919, it then consisted of John Pennington, M. O'Donnell, C. Bonvalot, and E. J. Robinson, the players all being students at the R.C.M., and coached in ensemble work by A. Rivarde. This personnel continued for three years, when Kenneth Skeaping became 2nd violin and Bernard Shore the viola. Among the new works performed was the van Dieren quartet, which took nearly two months to prepare. It had been written in two full scores, two instruments to each score. John Pennington now leads the London String Quartet.

PHILHARMONIC QUARTET. Founded in 1915. The original personnel was A. Beckwith, E. Goossens, R. Jeremy, C. Sharpe. Subsequent changes: 1918, F. Holding (v.), T. Peatfield (2nd v.). 1920, S. Kutcher (2nd v.). 1922, C. Bonvalot (2nd v.). This excellent Quartet unfortunately came to an end in 1924. During the nine years of its life it gave over fifty concerts in London and several in Paris. It is to be deplored, for obvious reasons, that so many organizations have taken the word 'Philharmonic' as title.

PHILHARMONIC STRING QUARTET. Paul Beard, Harold Mills, Frank Venton, Herbert Stephen. Formed in 1925 principally for the Philharmonic Mid-day Concerts under the direction of Johan C. Hock in Birmingham. Its programmes are usually strictly classical.

QUEEN'S HALL LADIES' QUARTET. Doris Houghton, Gay Handcock, Patience Lucas, Doris Griffiths. One of the best of the ladies' Quartets.

W. H. REED QUARTET. Charles Woodhouse, Ernest Tomlinson, B. Patterson Parker. Founded at the suggestion of Alfred Hobday, and originally known as the British Quartet, having Hobday as viola and C. Crabbe as 'cello. Played for many years in London.

WYNN REEVES QUARTET. George Whitaker, Ernest Yonge, Charles Crabbe. Original personnel: Wynne Reeves, Henry Gibson, Herbert Goone, Joseph T. Field. Formed in 1903, it gave its first concert in 1904. In 1907 the personnel underwent changes, and in this year the Quartet gave its first recital at the Steinway Hall. In 1922 it was engaged for the I.S.M. conference at the Queen's Hall. It frequently performs at South Place, and has also broadcast.

EDITH ROBINSON studied principally at Leipzig, where she founded a series of trio concerts in conjunction with von Bose and Julius Klengel. She is now a teacher of ensemble at the Royal Manchester College. The Quartet was formed in 1905, and originally consisted of Edith Robinson, Isabel McCullagh, Edith Craven, and Mary McCullagh. I. McCullagh played until 1915, when her place was taken by Gertrude Barker. Lily Simms succeeded E. Craven as viola until 1915, when Hilda Lindsay came into the Quartet. In 1921 Kathleen Moorhouse became the 'cello. It will be seen that the Quartet has always been composed exclusively of women, and has been the means of introducing to Manchester audiences an interesting series of chamber works by modern composers, besides doing propaganda work for the music of Max Reger, of whose quartets and piano quintet repeated performances have been given. The Quartet has also specialized in Brahms, of whom Edith Robinson was a contemporary. She was often present when he took a part in his own music in Leipzig. This ensemble has frequently played in London, the last time (1927) at the Aeolian Hall, introducing Eric Fogg's quartet in A flat. The Quartet performed in Manchester the whole cycle of the

Beethoven quartets, and has also performed on the following special occasions: Brahms Festival (Leeds University, 1912), Schumann Centenary concerts (Liverpool, 1910), César Franck Centenary concert (Sheffield University), the first Brahms Festival in Manchester (1926), when nine of the bigger chamber works were played in the course of one week; two Civic Week performances in Manchester, and the Beethoven Centenary celebration at Repton (1927).

JOHN SAUNDERS QUARTET. John Saunders was one of the most remarkable figures in the musical life of London from 1890 until his untimely death in 1919. Born in 1867, his early training was in a hard school. He studied at the G.S.M. under Carrodus and Hollander. It was Hollander who first filled him with that love of chamber music which remained his chief interest throughout his life, and of which at the height of his powers he was acknowledged to be a leading exponent in this country. He was an ideal Quartet leader, dominating the situation when required, and merging into the ensemble with rare understanding. Saunders early came under the influence of Sarasate, whose beauty of tone and ease of execution he successfully emulated, but later, the more serious playing of Joachim gave him a fresh direction. He has been well described as a violinist's violinist. He founded his Quartet in 1892, but it was not until two years later that it became known by its more familiar title, at first being called the South Place Quartet. The original personnel, in addition to himself, comprised A. G. Kentleton, Thomas Batty, and F. Casano. In 1900 Charles Woodhouse became the 2nd violin; in 1903 Ernest Yonge became the permanent viola; and in 1894 J. Preuveneers joined the Quartet and continued until his death in 1911, when C. Crabbe took his place. In the early days of the Quartet there was no other permanent ensemble in London, and except for occasional recitals by Ludwig and Whitehouse at the Prince's Hall, the only chamber music to be heard was furnished by Quartets of a very scratch nature. The Saunders Quartet (in addition, of course, to their South Place work) began by playing at the various music societies then existing in London. In those days the public taste was such, that rarely more than a movement from a quartet was performed. About 1894 chamber music became more popular, and concerts wholly devoted to chamber music were given at the Westminster Town Hall and other centres in London. At South Place the Quartet continued to appear regularly, and indeed John Saunders played at no less than 239 of these concerts, taking part in every important work in the chamber music repertory. It would be difficult to estimate the services and the influence of the Quartet in promoting a love and better understanding of chamber music; it is certain that they did much to make the South Place concerts the most famous series of chamber music concerts in England since the days of the old St. James's 'Pops'. One of the most remarkable characteristics of the Quartet was the willingness with which John Saunders assisted young composers. No matter how crude were their efforts, he was always ready to give a new work a chance. It made no difference how difficult the music was, or how often extra rehearsing was required to make it 'sound'. No young composer ever lacked encouragement from John Saunders, and a list of the works given under these conditions would fill much space. Nearly all the chamber music of Walthew, Holbrooke, and Speaight owes its first performance to him. Indeed, Joseph Speaight has often remarked that it was solely through the efforts of John Saunders that his early chamber music was ever produced.

In addition, the Quartet produced the clarinet quintet of Coleridge-Taylor, the sextet of Cyril Scott, and all the six prize quartets in the Cobbett competitions of 1905, played first at a special 'Phantasy Concert' given at Bechstein Hall, and afterwards at South Place. His death in 1919, at the early age of fifty-two, was an irreparable loss to English chamber music. His memory is kept green by the John Saunders Scholarship for the violin at the Guildhall School of Music, which was subscribed to by his many friends and admirers on his death, to show their appreciation of the passing of a great man and musician. Upon his tomb in Norwood Cemetery are inscribed a few bars from Schubert's C major quintet, his favourite work.

SCHWILLER QUARTET. The original personnel was Isidore Schwiller, E. Simpson, A. Fossati, and Jean Schwiller. Formed in 1910, it gave the first performance of the Vaughan Williams Quartet in G minor and the same composer's song-cycle, *On Wenlock Edge*, the singer in the last-named work being the late Gervase Elwes. The Quartet is at present being reconstructed.

[EMILY SHINNER QUARTET: Lucy Stone, Cecilia Gates, Florence Hemmings. Founded in 1888. The Shinner Quartet was one of the most successful of those founded by ladies in London, and deserves special mention. ED.]

WINIFRED SMALL QUARTET. Louis d'Oliveira, Susan Spain-Dunk, Marie Dare. Formed in 1926. The 2nd violin and the viola interchange. At Mr. Cobbett's suggestion this Quartet has rehearsed so-called 'Anthology' programmes, intended to attract the attention of semi-musical laymen to the beauties of chamber music. One concert of this kind was given on the occasion of the Beethoven Centenary, at a dinner of the Musicians' Company, selected movements from quartets of each of the composer's three periods being included in the programme. The reception by the audience was enthusiastic. A trio programme on the same lines, including movements by Mendelssohn, Goldmark, and Schütt, was given on another evening, with the co-operation of the pianist, Adolph Mann, and received with equal favour.

JESSIE SNOW QUARTET. Kenneth Skeaping, Ernest Tomlinson, Edward J. Robinson. This Quartet was formed in 1922, Frank Howard then being the 2nd violin, but in 1923 the ensemble was constituted as at present. It has given first English performances of chamber music by Dunhill, Reed, and Prokoviev; also of a quintet by Sir Walford Davies at the Hereford Festival, Sept. 1927, with the composer at the piano. A native work is always included in its programme at London recitals. The Quartet has also been one of the few ensembles to tour in Ireland. Gave first broadcast of Vaughan Williams's quartet, on the composer's special recommendation.

GEORGE STRATTON QUARTET. William Manuel, Lawrence Leonard, John Moore. Formed by Stratton in 1926. A young organization, displaying great energy, with a promising future.

TRINITY COLLEGE CHAMBER MUSIC PLAYERS. *See* John FRY.

WALENN QUARTET. Founded in 1905. Personnel: Gerald Walenn, Herbert Kinsey, James Lockyer, Herbert Walenn. Gave a series of annual concerts in London, and, in addition to the usual classical repertory, consistently performed native music. From time to time new works were produced under the direction of their respective composers, and in such a manner the Quartet gave the first performances in this country of H. Walford Davies's *Peter Pan* suite. It was well known in the provinces, and fulfilled engagements at the principal music centres throughout the country, but was disbanded in 1919, when Gerald Walenn went to Australia to an appointment at Sydney.

WAYFARING QUARTET. Formed in 1920. Original personnel: Dorothea Christison, Rhoda Legge, Dorothy Jones, Valentine Orde. In 1923 Emily Nicholas became the viola, and the Quartet was disbanded the following year on the marriage of Miss Christison. Did much useful work during its existence, tours being made in various counties, and concerts given in the villages as well as the towns. The programmes were always strictly classical, and were preceded by explanatory remarks. It was the experience of the Quartet that village people appreciated Beethoven, Mozart, and Haydn at the first time of hearing far more than music which they heard at the ordinary village concert. The Quartet also gave a large number of school concerts.

WESSELY QUARTET. Founded in 1900, and in that year had over 100 rehearsals before giving its first concert at Bechstein Hall. The original personnel was Hans Wessely, Spencer Dyke, Lionel Tertis, and B. Patterson Parker. The only subsequent change was that in 1903 Ernest Tomlinson became the viola. Spencer Dyke and Lionel Tertis were pupils of Hans Wessely, who had been a professor at the R.A.M. since 1889. The Quartet very rapidly established a great reputation for beautiful string tone and perfect ensemble, and gave first performances of many quartets by contemporary British composers. It continued until a year or so before Hans Wessely's death in 1926, and just after the war toured in Ireland.

WESTMINSTER QUARTET. Dorothy Ewens, Phyllis Newton, Ada Stuart, Dorothy Dening. Formed in the autumn of 1923 as the result of an invitation to take a Quartet to Christ Church, Westminster, to perform chamber music on Tuesdays during the lunch hour. Gave first recital there in December 1923, and has since played regularly on the Tuesday of each week, except at holiday times. Specializes in the giving of concerts at schools such as Charterhouse and Mercers, and has also performed in several provincial towns.

WOOD SMITH QUARTET. George Stratton, Jessie Stewart, Alice Grassie, John Moore. The Quartet receives its name from its founder, R. F. Wood Smith, who, although taking no active part in its performances, organized the Quartet in 1922 in 'that spirit of enthusiasm for music whereby the patrons of older days did so much for its advancement'. The 2nd violin and 'cello parts were originally played by Stella Pattenden and John Francis. The ensemble playing of this Quartet is particularly noteworthy, probably owing to the immense amount of rehearsing which is zealously performed. The Quartet has frequently played at the South Place concerts, at which it is extremely popular.

MARIE WILSON QUARTET. Gwendolen Higham, Anne Wolfe, Phyllis Hasluck. Formed in 1927. An excellent ensemble, with a promising future. The leader is a gifted violinist.

CHARLES WOODHOUSE QUARTET. Herbert Kinsey, Ernest Yonge, Charles Crabbe. Well known as sound classical players in every chamber music centre in London, the leader being one of the best known and most versatile among British artists. He is a familiar figure at South Place.

YORKSHIRE QUARTET. Founded in 1919 under the name of the Sheffield String Quartet. Original personnel: John Collins, J. E. Bingham, Allan Smith, Colin Smith. In 1922 F. Mountney became leader and N. Rouse 2nd violin. In 1923 the Quartet's present title was adopted, Bentley Ghent becoming the leader. He was succeeded in 1925 by Laurence Turner, since when the personnel has remained unchanged, the remaining members being Norman Rouse, Allan Smith, and Colin Smith. They have given first performances of many works new to the North of England, where they are well known and highly reputed.

(*b*) PIANO QUARTETS.[1]

AEOLIAN PLAYERS. Gordon Bryan (pf.), Joseph Slater (fl.), Antonio Brosa (v.), Rebecca Clarke (vla.). Formed in 1925 with the object of playing unusual chamber works, mainly those which included the flute as part of the ensemble. Constance Izard was the violinist in 1926. Several works have been specially written for the Aeolian players, who have also given first performances in England of works by Friedrich Bach, Marteau, and Honegger, in which the flute has a leading part.

CHAMBER MUSIC PLAYERS. William Murdoch, Albert Sammons, Lionel Tertis, Cedric Sharpe. The original personnel included Felix Salmond ('cello), but when he settled in New York his place was taken by Cedric Sharpe. After a private series of subscription concerts, a first public appearance was made at Wigmore Hall on 6 Jan., 1921. At one of their concerts the players, with the assistance of W. H. Reed as 2nd violin, gave the first performance of the Elgar piano quintet, the string quartet being also introduced at the same concert. Heavy engagements as soloists have prevented these artists from undertaking tours, but they have played a great deal in the British Isles. They do not specialize in any particular school, but have played nearly all the works of the rather limited piano quartet repertory. Murdoch, Sammons, and Sharpe also play together as a Trio under the title of the Chamber Music Trio. The members of this organization are all very distinguished solo performers.

ELZY PIANO QUARTET. Had its genesis during the war, when Lena Ashwell asked Mrs. Herbert Withers to form a piano Quartet to play daily for the soldiers at Ciro's, which had been taken over by the Y.M.C.A. Mrs. Withers thereupon organized regular fortnightly concerts of serious chamber music, apart from the playing of more popular music. So widely appreciated, however, were the concerts of chamber music, that at the conclusion of the war many of the men requested that they should be continued. This was done by the formation of a committee, and later by the inauguration of the Chamber Music Club at Lindsey Hall, Notting Hill Gate (still in existence). The original personnel of the Quartet was: Mrs. Withers, Evelyn Cooke, Gertrude Bower, and Phyllis Hasluck. When the concerts started at Lindsey Hall, Jessie Grimson became the violinist and Mary Stewart the viola. The Quartet, during their existence, played practically the whole of the piano quartet repertory, as well as other chamber works. Many concerts were also given for other music clubs. Owing to unforeseen circumstances and the illness of Mrs. Withers, the Quartet was disbanded at the end of the 1926 concert season, but not until it had rendered very valuable propaganda work among audiences (particularly the soldier audiences at Ciro's, a large proportion of which followed the Quartet to Lindsey Hall) who had doubtless, hitherto, been unfamiliar with the charm of chamber music.

ENGLISH ENSEMBLE. Kathleen Long, Marjorie Hayward, Rebecca Clarke, May Mukle. This association is primarily a piano Quartet, but its concerts include on occasion piano and string trios and sonatas, in short programmes of a varied nature. It has, among other things, given the first performance in England of Ernest Bloch's piano quintet.

HENKEL PIANO QUARTET. The first English ensemble definitely formed to play piano quartets. This was in January 1911. The original personnel consisted of Lily Henkel, F. Hirt, Alfred Hobday, and Ivor James. Owing to various reasons, the strings were subsequently replaced by A. Beckwith, R. Jeremy, and J. Mundy. At the inaugural concert, the first performance was given of Frank Bridge's *Phantasy Quartet*, which had recently been awarded a prize in the Cobbett Competitions. Other first performances in England included the piano quartets of Amédée Reuchsel and Chausson. Besides these works, the ensemble frequently played seldom-heard quartets by d'Indy, Taneiev, P. Juon, J. Jongen, &c., and established its reputation in London and the provinces. In 1915 it was engaged for three concerts by the Madrid Philharmonic Society, and was among the first combinations of British artists to visit Spain. The reputation of the Quartet was so quickly established that it fulfilled engagements all over Spain, the tour concluding with a command performance at the palace of H.R.H. the Infanta Isabella. It introduced into Spain many works which had never before been heard there. In 1918 both Beckwith and Mundy accepted appointments in America, and in their absence the Quartet had to be disbanded.

HERBERT KINSEY QUARTET. Olive Bloom, Herbert Kinsey, Frank Howard, Anthony Pini. Formed by Herbert Kinsey in 1925, and for their first recital had upwards of twenty rehearsals. A well-known London ensemble.

MARGUÉRITE MEREDYLL QUARTET. Desiré Defauw, Raymond Jeremy, Émile Doehaerd. Formed in 1919, the original violin being Bessie Rawlins, who played until 1925. The Quartet has toured in various continental countries. Produced Arnold Bax's piano quartet in London, and introduced piano quartets by

[1] The names of the performers are given in the following order:—pf, v, vla, vc.

Frank Bridge and Herbert Howells in Scandinavia. Marguérite Meredyll (Madame Doehaerd) went, with her husband, to live in Brussels in 1927, but the ensemble still occasionally plays together.

PHILHARMONIC QUARTET. Charles Kelly, Paul Beard, Frank Venton, Johan C. Hock. Came into existence in Birmingham in 1922, when the Beatrice Hewitt Piano Quartet ceased to function owing to the illness of the founder. The string players thereupon invited Charles Kelly to join them, and the Quartet received its present (much too often used) title. The performers in this ensemble are identified with chamber music in the Midlands.

QUARTET PLAYERS. In January 1921, Mrs. G. B. Bullin, Miss E. Bunny, Major R. Bullin, and F. Cranmore started a series of chamber music concerts in Portsmouth under this name. Admission was free (with a collection). The concerts met with an enthusiastic reception from the public. At the first there was an attendance of over 1,100, and at the second the audience exceeded 1,350. The concerts have been continued regularly up to the present time, with no abatement of public interest. The personnel of the Quartet subsequently changed; the violin is now Stanley Blagrove and the 'cello Ernest Zeffertt.

[SCOTTISH CHAMBER MUSIC PLAYERS. Mary Grierson, Gladys Clark, Theo Hunter, Ruth Waddell. Of these artists Professor Donald Tovey speaks with much approval. ED.]

(*c*) PIANO TRIOS.

BLAGROVE TRIO. Ida Blagrove, Stanley Blagrove, Arthur Blagrove. Founded 1897. The two string players are brothers, and come of a family which has been connected with music and court concerts since the reign of Charles I. Henry Gamble Blagrove, an uncle, first appeared as a prodigy in 1817, and from 1836 until 1872 led a Quartet of which the other members were H. Gattie, J. H. B. Dando, and C. Lucas, all artists associated with the earliest performances of ensemble playing in England. The pianist is the wife of Arthur Blagrove.

CHAPLIN TRIO. Founded by Nellie Chaplin in 1904, to revive old music and dances, and to play them on the instruments for which they were written. The personnel has always consisted of three sisters: Nellie (pf and harpsichord), Kate (v and vla d'amore), and Mabel (vc and vla da gamba). The Trio revived the folk dances from Playford's *Dancing Master* after a lapse of 200 years. Their performances do not come strictly within the scope of this book, but they are instinct with the true chamber music spirit and are therefore mentioned.

CHERNIAVSKY. A notable Russian Trio of three brothers, naturalized British in 1922: Jan (b. 1892), Leo (b. 1890), Michael (b. 1893). The Trio was formed in 1900 in Russia, where it met with immediate success, and since 1904 has toured practically all over the world.

[CORTOT-THIBAUD-CASALS. Though the nationality of this superb Trio of artists is obviously not British, they are grouped here on account of their regular appearances on English concert platforms. Their performances form one of the chief attractions of the London season. The gramophone recordings of this Trio are of singular perfection.

DORIAN. Kathleen Washbourne, Pauline Taylor, and Enid Lewis; an organization largely engaged in the educational work carried on in Wales by Sir Walford Davies. EDITOR.]

ENGLISH TRIO. Wilfred Ridgway, Charles Bye, Frederick Bye. Founded in 1921. Under the name of the New Concerts Society it gave in 1922 a series of twelve concerts in Birmingham. Has broadcast, and is well known locally.

HARMONIC TRIO. Olive Byrne, Dorothea Walenn, Edith Vance. Formed in 1918, and rehearsed for over a year preparatory to giving first concert. Recitals in London 1920, '21 and '22. The Trio was disbanded in 1924, owing to lack of time for adequate rehearsal.

INTERNATIONAL TRIO. Formed in 1918 under the name of the Modern Trio, the personnel originally consisting of Serge Krish, A. Melzak, Livio Manucci. Subsequently, William Primrose became the violinist. Has given many first performances in London. In 1923 toured the U.S.A. with success.

LEEDS TRIO. Herbert Johnson, Alexander Cohen, G. Schott. A. Hemingway subsequently became the 'cello, except during 1916–17, when Kathleen Moorhouse took his place. F. A. Tyrer was the pianist during 1918–19. See also the LEEDS STRING QUARTET, much of whose history is also relevant to the Trio.

PHILHARMONIC TRIO. F. Ticciati, Albert Fransella (fl), Leon Goossens (ob).

MAX PIRANI TRIO. Leila Doubleday, Charles Hambourg. Founded in 1923. Gave first London performances of trios by Pizzetti (1925) and Turina (1926). A Trio of extremely capable players.

(*d*) MISCELLANEOUS.

GRIMSON OCTET. This combination is probably unique in the history of chamber music ensembles, consisting as it did solely of the members of one family:—Jessie, Sam, Harold, and Nellie (vns), S. Dean (paterfamilias) and Annie (vlas), and Amy and Robert (vcs).

HARP ENSEMBLE. Marie Korchinska (harp), Constantin Kony (fl), Sybil Eaton (1st v), E. Virgo (2nd v), R. Jeremy (vla), Cedric Sharpe (vc). Formed in 1925. V. Orde was the original 'cello of the ensemble, whose repertory, as the title indicates, mainly consists of compositions in which different ensemble combinations are employed in conjunction with the harp. Many modern works of outstanding interest have been included in its programmes.

LEEDS. A series of Bohemian Chamber Concerts was given in Leeds in 1899, Messrs. E. Elliott, H. Fawcett, W. Haigh, and A. Boulton taking part in the first concert. Many changes have since taken place in the personnel of the Quartet. E. Elliott, the leader, was succeeded by Alexander Cohen, who not only played admirably, but proved to be a programme annotator with original, well-expressed views. In the final season of 1926, the party included the YORKSHIRE STRING QUARTET (*q.v.*).

Among the leading spirits in the organization of chamber concerts in Leeds may be mentioned F. E. Fulford, an enthusiastic local patron, Johann Rasch, a Dutch artist from the Hague, and the Misses Ford, three sisters belonging to a well-known musical and philanthropic Leeds family, who have carried on a series of free chamber concerts for the last thirty years. These concerts were founded by the late Bessie Ford, and continued after her death by Emily and Isabella Ford. The latter died in 1924, and the concerts are now run by the surviving sister. Alfred Giessing, the well-known 'cellist, has been mainly responsible for the programmes and for other necessary arrangements. W. S. MEADMORE.

BROADCASTING.

GENERAL.

Of all instrumental music, chamber music is most suitable for the broadcasting medium. The small number of instruments taking part and the correspondingly small number of individual essential parts result in a less complex wave to modulate and reproduce. A string quartet, for instance, can be reproduced almost perfectly through all the broadcasting process of emission and reception; similarly, a chamber orchestra is more perfectly broadcast than a full symphonic combination.

For broadcasting, classics are as a rule most satisfactory from the programme point of view, not only because of the vast number of listeners new to this kind of music, to whom the less complex work naturally appeals more, but because the simple melodic curves and comparatively straightforward harmonic structure of the piece are more ideal for mechanical reproduction.

Modern chamber music, however, is quite feasible, for it can be broadcast and received on a reasonably good set in such a way as to give the intelligent listener a fair suggestion of its qualities.

PROGRAMME POLICY.

(a) *Public Reaction.* From the outset, chamber music has formed an important ingredient of British broadcasting programmes. But, at the beginning, programme builders had to contend with a peculiar difficulty. A vast majority of the listening public had never heard chamber music. It was necessary, therefore, to proceed warily, giving them the most tuneful and simple of classical music—easily understood movements, and seldom complete quartets. In this way people gradually became interested in chamber music. On the other hand, the serious music-loving public were so far not interested in broadcasting from the musical standpoint, and programmes likely to attract them had to be included.

The general proportion of programmes of a modern tendency (e.g. Debussy, César Franck, Bridge, &c.) to classical was as 1 to 4.

The mail-bag, the only real contact with the audience, has given a rough indication of the gradual growth of appreciation of unaccustomed types of music. A chamber concert of, say, Mozart and Tchaikovsky quartets early in 1923 usually produced half a dozen disapproving, even abusive, postcards, and perhaps one solitary encouragement. It was obvious, however, that a steadily increasing number of listeners enjoyed the concerts, and in this, as in other lines of life, an average person is as a rule inclined to write to the B.B.C. or to a newspaper on any subject.

(b) *Present Service.* Now there is a broadcast service of a steady stream of chamber music programmes averaging one per week per station all the year round. The Daventry Experimental Station (5 GB), which is designed as a definite alternative programme to London (2 LO), Daventry (5 XX), and other stations, usually has two or even three such programmes.

Many classical and modern works generally accepted as of outstanding value (e.g. Beethoven's septet and his quartets, op. 18, and the Debussy and Ravel quartets, say, of these days) recur every few months, and other accepted works at greater and varying intervals, although it is impracticable to work to any arbitrary rule in this matter.

No preference is given to any particular school or nationality, but English music, both old music and outstanding contemporary works, have their fair share of the programme—roughly 25 per cent. of the total time devoted to chamber music. Various works of the Carnegie collection have been given, some of them often; young composers are always encouraged; and first performances of worthy works are often given.

SPECIAL CONCERT SERIES.

(a) *Composer Programmes.* An early attempt to bring the work of contemporary native composers into the home via broadcasting was the series in 1925 of fortnightly broadcast hours devoted to works by McEwen, Bax, Ireland, Scott, Bridge, Dale, and Gerrard Williams. Similar programmes of Delius, Vaughan

Williams, Warlock, Moeran, van Dieren, and others followed at wider intervals.

(b) *Public Concerts*. In line with the general policy of affording the public opportunity for hearing chamber music in its original form, two series of chamber concerts were given by the B.B.C. in London. It was obvious from the audiences at the concerts that a large number of people, hitherto unaccustomed to attending concerts of this nature, had by broadcasting been interested to the point of doing so for the first time.

1. Spring Series of chamber concerts, 1926. These were six concerts given in the Chenil Galleries, Chelsea. Programmes (which included two by chamber orchestra) contained the first performance in England—in some cases the actual first performance—of the following works: *The Daniel Jazz* (Louis Gruenberg); scene from *The Woodlanders* (Patrick Hadley); rhapsody for flute, violin, viola, and piano (Honegger); sonata in C for flute, violin, and piano (Friedrich Bach); *Ode to a Nightingale* for baritone, strings, and harp (Eric Fogg); trio for oboe, violin, and viola (Randerson).

2. International Chamber Concerts, 1926–7. Six monthly concerts were given in the Grotrian Hall, and broadcast from various stations. They were a definitely new and somewhat daring departure in policy, and were intended to afford English hearers interested in the progress of musical thought abroad an opportunity of keeping abreast of the times. The artists taking part were all of international reputation, and included the Zika Quartet (Czechoslovakia), the Amar Quartet (Germany), the Vienna Quartet (Italy), the Hungarian Quartet (Hungary), and others, for some of whom it was the first appearance in England.

First performances in this country included quartets by Molnar, Dohnányi, Guarnieri (second), Labroca, Hindemith (op. 22), Jarnach (op. 16), Krenek (op. 12), Schulhoff and Vycpálek; oboe sonata by Koechlin; flute sonata by Dresden; 'cello sonata by Pijper.

The reaction of the public to these concerts was interesting; they proved definitely stimulating, and the performances were the equivalent of important events in contemporary international festivals abroad.

3. Concerts of Contemporary Music, 1927–8. These are eight monthly concerts given in the London B.B.C. studios. It was felt that chamber music, essentially an intimate thing, was heard by listeners to best advantage through the wireless medium, and this was a reason for returning to the policy of studio concerts. Further, the programmes are arranged, not in international groups, a policy found by previous experience to be undesirable, but in mixed and varied programmes. The foreign artists include some of the foremost European musicians, e.g. The Vienna, Pro Arte, Roth, and Hungarian Quartets; and Marcelle Meyer, Sarah Fischer, Prokoviev, Schulhoff, &c.

Two features are included which are very characteristic of present-day musical activities abroad, namely, one concert with chamber orchestra, and one with chamber opera and ballet. The series is designed to give a picture of what is generally regarded as most valuable in the chamber music of all countries. Schönberg and Stravinsky, whose influence is paramount in the modern movement, are represented by 'key' works little known in England. Among the younger composers are included only those who have reached a certain celebrity; no work that is simply experimental is included.

The series should be regarded as an essential part of the season's activities, which covers a wide field and includes the previously stated proportion of roughly 25 per cent. of British music, old and new.

The list of composers includes—Great Britain: Bridge, Warlock, Moeran, van Dieren, Walton. Austria: Schönberg, Webern, Berg. Germany: Hindemith, Jarnach. France: Delius, Ravel, Milhaud, Poulenc, Auric, Honegger, Koechlin. Hungary: Bartók, Kodály. Czechoslovakia: Schulhoff. Russia: Stravinsky, Prokoviev.

The B.B.C. feels that Great Britain has always lagged behind the rest of the world in musical development, refusing to recognize new paths opened up by pioneers in other countries, and its present endeavours to remove that centuries-old reproach are beginning to meet with some measure of recognition abroad, a fact which it is hoped may afford a certain gratification to listeners as a whole.

L. Stanton Jefferies.

[The fundamental scientific limitation to the transmission of music by broadcasting is the fact that the air vibrations which constitute sound must first be translated into electric waves, and these must be translated back into sound. The former process is the task of the transmitting apparatus, and this begins at the London microphone and ends at the aerial in Oxford Street or at Daventry. Between the microphone and the aerial there is a complicated chain of electrical apparatus comprising low frequency amplifiers, telephone lines, high frequency generators, modulating valves, and high frequency amplifiers. It is not to be expected that all the nuances of tone and timbre should survive these transformations, but nowadays, it may be asserted, the loss between the studio and the ether is relatively slight in many of the well-equipped broadcasting stations of the world. The second process—the translation of the electric waves back into sound—is accomplished by the listeners' receiving apparatus and loud speaker. Here there is great opportunity for the introduction of imperfections. The set purchased by the listener may range from very good to very bad, according to the skill of the designer and manufacturer; and the loud speaker may be suited or not suited to the set. Moreover, the adjustments made by the listener may be skilful or maladroit. The result is that more distortion and more suppression occurs at the receiving end than at the transmitting station.

The chief of the faults introduced by these electrical transformations is unevenness of reproduction of the notes of a chord and of the harmonics of a tone. This fault can be described briefly by saying that, as a rule, only the vibrations between, say, 200 per second and 2,000 per second are reproduced in the same proportional strength as they occur in the original sound. A great deal of the apparatus sold loses practically all the vibrations below 150 per second or above 2,500 per second; that is to say, the notes and the harmonics higher than the third octave above middle C disappear, as well as the tones lower than the first octave below middle C. A similar fault, also due to unevenness of reproduction, may occur in the middle register, namely, resonances of particular tones. Nearly every loud speaker has its favourite tones, and emphasizes them undesirably. This is one reason why many people with musical feeiings prefer the head phones to the best of loud speakers.

Another fault that haunts broadcasting as it haunts the gramophone is the failure to reproduce percussion instruments properly. The piano and the drums, and pizzicato passages on the strings, suffer severely. The trouble has been studied and partly alleviated at some of the transmitting stations, but continues to affect most samples of receiving apparatus. Unfortunately, the complete cure of this defect still seems rather remote. W. ECCLES.]

BROCA, MARIO LA. *v.* LABROCA.

†BROCKWAY, HOWARD A., b. 1870, American composer.

Sonata, pf, v, g mi	op. 9	Schlesinger, 1894.

'Excellent workmanship and refined musical taste mark his works' (*Dent*).

BROD, HENRI, 1801–1839.

Modern republications:

1st quintet, fl, ob, cl, horn, fag	op. 2	Lemoine.
2nd quintet, fl, ob, cl, horn, fag		,, 1921.

Celebrated oboist and composer for his instru ment. Made improvements in the oboe and cor anglais. For earlier publications *v. Fétis*.

BRODERSEN, VIGGO, b. 1879, Danish composer.

Quartet, str, G	op. 16	Steingräber.
Sonata, pf, vc, g sharp mi	,, 18	,,

There is spontaneous writing in Brodersen's string quartet, the animated scherzo and finale of which are worthy of especial mention.

BROGI, RENATO, 1873–1924, Italian composer.

Quartet, str, b mi	Carisch, 1904.
Trio, pf, v, vc, d mi	,, 1909.

Brogi is best known as an operatic composer. An effective feature of his quartet is the slow minuet.

BRONSART, HANS VON, 1830–1913, German pianist, known professionally as Bronsart von Schellendorf.

Trio, pf, v, vc, g mi	op. 1	U.E., 1877.
Fantaisie, pf, v	,, 21	Kahnt.

It is chiefly through his piano trio that Bronsart made his name known, and this work is still considered his best. It is, in truth, a masterpiece which most skilfully combines clear, well defined form with noble contents. Both as a whole and in detail it makes a favourable impression, and reveals original thought.

A vigorous introduction leads to the first movement, which, beginning *pp*, gradually increases in force, hastens to a powerful climax, then calms down again, whereupon the second subject appears, the soft, elegiac mood of which forms an effective contrast to the defiant first subject. The second movement begins with a piquant measure in quavers, as a contrast to which a cantilena of considerable harmonic interest follows, scored for the strings. The adagio is particularly beautiful. After the three instruments are heard in turn, the mood becomes more and more animated, until a powerful climax is reached, whereupon the excitement subsides and the movement comes dreamily to an end. A *grave* of two bars leads to the gay, cheerful finale. The left hand starts some lively passage work on the piano, the strings joining in with long, sustained notes; then they take up the lively measure again, accompanied by the piano in rich, syncopated chords. The development contains some original traits, and numerous fascinating contrapuntal combinations which bear witness to Bronsart's technical mastery.

It is to be regretted that the composer was not more productive, as he had it in his power further to enrich chamber music literature.

RUDOLF FELBER.

[Bronsart's trio was introduced at the 'Pops' by Hans von Bülow, who played it with Lady Hallé and Piatti. It was of this trio that Liszt wrote, in a letter to Joachim (1857): 'I think it may rank with the best music which has been written during the last few years.'

EDITOR.]

BROUSTET, ÉDOUARD, b. 1836, French composer.

Sonata, pf, v		Durdilly, *c.* 1905.
,,	pf, vc	,, *c.* 1906.

According to Pougin, a composer of talent and imagination. Broustet had a special interest in the music of the Béarn.

BRUCH, MAX, 1838–1920, German composer.

	Composed	
Quartet, str, c mi, op. 9	1856	B. & H., 1859.
Quartet, str, E, op. 10	1860	„ 1860.
Trio, pf, v, vc, c mi	1857	„ 1858, 1910.
Eight pieces, pf, cl, vla (or vc), op. 83		Simrock, 1910.

Two string quintets and a string octet are still in MS.

Bruch's name is known principally by his big choral works and the violin concertos, but, as only the earlier portion of his chamber music is published, the idea has spread that he felt himself to be spiritually estranged from this—surely the most distinguished—branch of creative music. It was not so, however. In 1876 he wrote a piano quintet for a friend in Liverpool; this indeed remains unprinted, but the original manuscript was bought at an auction by the Prussian State Library, and has, since the summer of 1924, been preserved in the music department there.

The present writer, though in frequent association with Bruch, had never heard of this quintet, and was greatly surprised when told by the composer a few months before his death that he had completed two quintets (A minor and E flat) for two violins, two violas, and 'cello, as well as an octet for four violins, two violas, 'cello, and double-bass, his inclusion of the last-named instrument being the subject of a rather full and detailed defence. These three compositions were tried over by Willy Hess and his pupils, who also gave a performance of the A minor quintet as a sort of memorial funeral celebration; but in spite of the great success which attended the performance, the work remains unprinted like the other two.

His published chamber works are one and all distinguished by beauty of tone and musical architecture. They are naturally modelled on classical lines, and are not especially prominent among the mass of similar productions.

The first quartet begins with an introduction, andante, tinged with pathos, followed by a powerful and energetic allegro ma non troppo, the best points of which are the delicate transitions and a beautiful cantabile theme. The richly melodious adagio is a sort of song without words, relieved by a quicker interlude. The rhythmical scherzo is sufficiently described by its superscription, allegro molto energico; but there is grace in the melodious middle section. The last movement, in the major, is a really jolly rondo, in which the chief melody resembles a tarantella, the second has a rocking movement, and the third is lyrical in character.

THE SECOND STRING QUARTET is a more effective work. If the first movement, allegro maestoso, has touches of Mendelssohn, it atones by its almost orchestral breadth and vigour. The slow movement opens simply like a song, but is treated later with a wealth of elaboration, particularly in the repeated portion, while a fine contrast is provided by the middle section, with its important entry and its broad melodic design. The third, scherzo-like movement, vivace ma non troppo, has a fascinating rhythm; it has two trios, one smooth and flowing, the other again remarkable for its rhythm; here the influence of Schumann was probably at work. The movement, which is in E, ends with a coda in G sharp minor. The lively finale is distinguished by its elaborate figure work and incisive rhythm.

THE PIANO TRIO begins with a broadly laid out and highly attractive andante molto cantabile, followed by an allegro assai, in which the pathetic element is still present. The finale, by contrast, appears the more fiery; in this movement the fine opening melody of the first movement returns once more before the end is reached in a noisy prestissimo.

The eight pieces, op. 83, may also be counted as chamber music; Bruch might very well have published them as two suites. How nobly inspired are the melodies that he produced thus late in life; how masterly his development of them, and how effective his handling of each individual instrument! Special praise must be given to nos. 3, 5 (Roumanian air), and 6 (*Night-song*). Nos. 2 and 7, both in fairly quick time, are distinguished by unusual vitality of invention, whilst each piece has its characteristic mood. Although all these pieces are, in the best sense, music for the home, they deserve the greatest consideration at the hands of trio concert-givers, more especially as they sound equally well whatever combination of instruments be selected.

WILHELM ALTMANN.

BRUCHETTINI, MARIO.

Suite, pf, v	Pizzi, 1922.

BRUCKNER, ANTON, 1824–1896, Austrian composer.

	Composed	
Quintet, 2 v, 2 vla, vc, F	1879	Gutmann, 1884; U.E., 1913, New Ed. (J. V. v. Woss), 1922.
Intermezzo (quintet-movt.), 2 v, 2 vla, vc, posthumous		U.E., 1913.

Bruckner's string quintet was first produced by the Hellmesberger Quartet in 1885. The first movement is one of those melodious Bruckner allegros which are not allegro in the accepted sense, but have rather the character of an animated slow movement, corresponding to the composer's own inner rhythm. Other distinctive characteristics are Bruckner's fondness for shifting harmonies, his charm of modulation, and that broad sense of tonality possessed by Schubert. Thus the main theme of the first movement modulates to the submediant on the last crotchet; the second subject does not begin in C (the dominant), but in F sharp, and finds its way into C by a happy inspiration. Equally expressive of Bruckner's personality is the spiritual side of this movement, with its initial uncertainty and depression, and its bold upward sweep into the joy of deliverance. The scherzo, in D minor, is somewhat reminiscent of the scherzo of the fifth symphony—at least as regards its opening leap of a fourth and its cheerless D minor mood. It is interrupted by a graceful trio in E flat with a soaring semiquaver figure; here there is the same key-shifting (D to E flat) as in the first movement (F to F sharp). The leader, Josef Hellmesberger, who had suggested the writing of this quintet, declared the scherzo to be unplayable at rehearsal, whereupon Bruckner substituted an intermezzo. This movement, written in Ländler style, is easier to play, and was once performed (in 1904) by the Fitzner Quartet; it did not, however, supplant the original scherzo. The adagio is described by Theodore Helm, who is a Bruckner enthusiast, as 'the musical heart' of the whole work. It is in G flat—once more characteristically a semitone above the original key—and is an example of that combination of variations and adagio which is typical of Bruckner's deeply religious temperament. A characteristic finale forms the close (F minor), in which the orchestral conception obtrudes itself; in fact, it might be called an orchestral piece for five instruments. Its wealth of themes, peaceful, bold, traditional, and redolent of Austro-Hungarian soil, afford scope for a masterly display of combined effects. In this movement is discerned the ingenious contrapuntist as well as the architect capable of shaping the great vaulted dome that crowns the structure. The quintet, which aims at carrying the Beethoven tradition in chamber music into the sphere of religion, is, unfortunately, the only chamber work of Anton Bruckner. ERNST DECSEY.

†BRÜGGEMANN, ALFRED.

Quartet, str, A		Ricordi.	
Quintet, pf, 2 v, vla, vc (cb ad. lib.)	op. 16	,,	1920.
Sonata, pf, vc, C	,, 14	,,	1914.

†BRÜLL, IGNAZ, 1847–1907, Moravian pianist and composer.

Trio, pf, v, vc, E flat	op. 14	Leuckart, 1876.
Suite, pf, v, a mi	,, 42	Gutmann, 1882.
Sonata, pf, v, b mi	,, 48	Doblinger, 1884.
,, ,, a mi	,, 60	Siegel, 1890.
Sonata, pf, v, e mi	op. 81	Simrock, 1899.
,, ,, C	,, 97	U.E., 1906.
,, pf, vc (or v), d mi	,, 9	Doblinger, 1871.

Brüll was a talented composer who became known chiefly by his opera, *Das goldene Kreuz*, but is already almost forgotten. Of the round hundred of his compositions, not one-tenth belong to chamber music. The suite for violin with piano accompaniment, op. 42, which contains much fine writing, may be included, though it is rather a solo work. There are, however, six chamber works, properly so called, not one of which is really striking, though the trio was played at the 'Pops' in Feb. 1881.

The second violin sonata, op. 60, for instance, is pleasing and easy to play, but by no means profound, though the opening allegro has an expressive second subject. In the cavatina the middle section falls below the level of the first part; in the scherzo, on the contrary, the trio is more impressive than the main section, while the lively finale is at its best in the second, cantabile theme.

The fourth violin sonata, op. 97, is another pleasing work, and is well suited for the home circle, though the finale contains some rather difficult double-stopping. The subjects of the first movement are pleasing and melodious, but not sufficiently contrasted; both of them reappear shortly before the coda of the last movement. Very simple is the melody of the andante con moto, the middle section of which forms a kind of scherzo. The final rondo is very playful, and the first bar of the principal subject recalls the huntsmen's song from *Der Freischütz*. WILHELM ALTMANN.

[The trio, op. 14, is an extremely well written and effective work. The same may be said of the violin suite, which is in four sections (prelude—scherzo—Reigen—air varié) and is brilliant and violinistic. The sonatas are not known to me, but they seem to have won acceptance in the sonata-playing community. EDITOR.]

†BRUN, FRITZ, b. 1878, Swiss composer.

2nd quartet, str, G	Hug, 1923.
Sonata, pf, v, d mi	Hüni (Zürich), 1920.

Brun in his chamber music has a style entirely his own, and although his music may sometimes be wanting in spontaneity, it is marked by high artistic purpose. The string quartet is more difficult to understand than the violin sonata, by reason of the excessive polyphony employed and the length of the individual movements, and makes heavy demands, both technical and musical, on its interpreters if all its qualities are to be fully revealed. FREDERICK HAY.

†BRUNE, ADOLF GERHARD, b. 1870, German composer.

Sonata, pf, v, d mi	op. 33	Schott, 1912.

BRUNEAU, E., French composer.

Quartet, pf, fl, ob, horn — Pérégally (Paris), 1902.

BRUNETTI, GAETANO, *c.* 1740–1808, violinist and composer.

Brunetti's music is forgotten, but being in his time a rival of Boccherini at the court of Madrid, some interest attaches to the lists of his chamber works to be found in *Fétis* and *Eitner*.

EDITOR.

†BRUNI, ANTONIO BARTOLOMMEO, 1759–1823, Italian violinist.

Bruni's numerous duets for two violins and violin and viola are still esteemed by teachers. They are not, however, of sufficient importance to catalogue in full, but mention may be made of the publishers who have from time to time issued them: B. & H., Litolff, Rozsnyai, Peters, André, and Schlesinger. He also wrote sixty string quartets (*v. Vidal*). EDITOR.

BRUSSELMANS, MICHEL, b. 1886, Belgian composer of the Flemish school.

	Composed	
Sonata, pf, v, b mi	1915	Senart, 1921.
Sonata, pf, vc, D	1916	,, ,,

†BRZESZINSKI, FRANCISZEK (FRANZ XAVER), b. 1867, Polish composer, pupil of Max Reger.

Sonata, pf, v, D — op. 6 — Peters, 1910, 1918.

The distinguishing feature of his style is polyphony. Fugal writing is to be found in nearly all his works.

BULLERIAN, HANS, b. 1885, German composer.

Sextet, wind instr.	op. 38	Simrock.
2nd trio, pf, v, vc, B	,, 27	,,
Sonata, pf, v, e mi	,, 29	,, 1923.
,, pf, vc, b mi	,, 18	,, 1922.

Bullerian's trio in three movements is manifestly the work of a thoroughly competent composer who puts forth poetic ideas without stint. But his consistent orthodoxy in the manipulation of abundant material prompts one to question whether a less lavish imagination and a proportionately fuller concentration of purpose might not have resulted in greater homogeneity.

The finale is over-rhetorical, even for a composer whose methods derive a good deal from the Richard Strauss of the piano quartet and violin sonata days, but the middle movement (*langsam*) is noteworthy for some extremely well planned and sonorous writing, the claims of melody being nowhere obscured.

ADOLPH MANN.

BÜLOW, HANS GUIDO, FREIHERR VON, 1830–1894, famous pianist, pupil of Moritz Hauptmann.

Bülow, between 1855 and 1864, gave a series of chamber concerts in Berlin, and played frequently at the London 'Pops'. He was a man of many talents and eclectic taste. Of his compositions in general, Fétis speaks highly, but his only chamber works appear to be two concert duets for piano and violin. EDITOR.

BUMCKE, GUSTAV, b. 1876, German composer, pupil of Max Bruch.

Tone poem, *Der Spaziergang* (The Stroll), harp, 8 wind instr.	op. 22	R. & E., 1906.
Tone poem, *Von Liebe und Leid* (Love and Grief), harp, 6 wind instr.	,, 24	Saturn-V., 1913. (G.B.)
Sextet, cl, cor angl, saxophone, hunting horn (Waldhorn), bass cl, fag, A flat	,, 19	,, ,, 1908.
Two quartets, 4 saxophones	,, 23	,, ,, 1908.
Sonata, pf, cl, f sharp mi	,, 9	Simon, 1905.

Bumcke has written exclusively for wind instrument combinations. He was the founder of a Society (1906) for the performance of chamber music with wind.

BUNGERT, AUGUST, 1845–1915, German composer.

Quartet, pf, v, vla, vc (Prize) — E flat — op. 18 — Peters, 1877.

This composer, whose reputation rests chiefly on his songs, was already a mature artist when he went to study counterpoint with Friedrich Kiel. His only chamber work is the above, which was awarded the Florentine Quartet prize in 1877, on the recommendation of Brahms and Robert Volkmann. It will, for many years to come, be a source of enjoyment —to amateurs especially—on account of the prevailing folk-song character of its melody. The first movement (con brio) is distinguished by the skilful development of the two themes, the vigorous second subject being the finer of the two, though the first is undeniably captivating. The adagio con moto has an expressive main theme, very rightly labelled '*Im Volkston*'; the gloomy middle section (cleverly introduced into the coda later) provides a good contrast, but there is a sense of relief when the main section re-enters—this time with a figure reminiscent of the recapitulation in the corresponding movement of Schumann's piano quartet. A disturbing, thunder-charged atmosphere pervades the main section of the third movement (un poco agitato); whilst the middle section has a heroic ring, which disappears in the coda, however, where the two leading ideas are combined in a most expressive manner. The melodious and broadly executed finale is full of gaiety, and runs its course like a merry hunting scene.

The lines which the composer has written in the front of this work—*Und dein Streben sei's in Liebe, und dein Leben sei die Tat!*—are an excellent commentary on its general character. It is by no means difficult to play, and is effectively written for all four performers. Vigorous and refreshing as it is, this piano quartet is, nevertheless, inspired by the true German spirit of romanticism.

WILHELM ALTMANN.

[In 1911 a Bungert-Union was formed to make the composer's works known.]

BUONAMICI, GIUSEPPE, 1846–1914, Italian pianist, pupil of Rheinberger.

Quartet, str, G		Carisch, 1902.

This quartet, which is dedicated to Joachim, is recommended to amateurs, both for its clarity and comparative simplicity.

BÜRGEL, KONSTANTIN, 1837–1909, German composer.

Sonata, pf, v, a mi	op. 14	R. & E., 1869.

Riemann writes in laudatory terms of this sonata.

BURGMÜLLER, NORBERT, 1810–1836, German composer, pupil of Spohr and Moritz Hauptmann.

4th quartet, str, a mi	op. 14	Hofmeister, 1844.
Sonata, pf, cl, E flat	,, 15	Kistner, 1865.

In his memorial of this young composer, Schumann begins by saying that since the early death of Schubert nothing more deplorable had happened (*Gesammelte Schriften*, iii, 145). Burgmüller would have taken a high place as a composer but for his early death. Fétis says that this was due to his own excesses, and goes on to say that his music shows the same refusal to be bound by rule and convention as he displayed in his life. This was Fétis's usual reproach to all the Romantics, from Schumann downwards, but it is clear that Burgmüller showed very great ability, and even Fétis allows him originality. Most of his music was unpublished at his death, the last of his four string quartets (op. 14) appearing eight years after that event. Dr. Altmann analyses this quartet sympathetically, though he does not recommend it for public performance. EDITOR.

BURLEIGH, CECIL, b. 1885, American violinist.

Sonata (*The Ascension*), pf, v	op. 22	Schirmer.

†BUSCH, ADOLF, b. 1891, German violinist.

Quartet (one movt.), str, b mi	op. 29	B. & H.
Serenade, str. quartet, G	,, 14	Simrock, 1919.
Five preludes and fugues, str. quartet	op. 36	B. & H.
Trio, v, vla, vc, a mi	,, 24	,, ,,
Introd., theme with var^{ns} and rondo, cl, v	,, 26b	,, ,,
Quintet, pf, 2 v, vla, vc	,, 35	,, ,,
Trio, pf, v, vc, a mi	,, 15	Simrock, 1920.
Passacaglia, pf, 2 v	,, 4	,,
Sonata, pf, v, G	,, 21	B. & H., 1925.
Suite, organ, v	,, 33	,, ,,
,, pf, vc, a mi	,, 18	,, ,,

Adolf Busch was founder of the much esteemed Busch Quartet, and one feels, when studying his chamber works, that he has profited as a composer by his intimate knowledge of ensemble music. He is slightly, and favourably, influenced by Max Reger. His dynamic changes are violent, with a certain heaviness of motion, but he contrives to be harmonious even in the most complex polyphony. As a performer of chamber music, Adolf Busch is in the first rank, and made a very favourable impression on London concert-goers in 1927. EDITOR.

*BUSH, ALAN, b. 1900, English composer.

Quartet, str, a mi	op. 4	S. & B. Carnegie Award, 1926.
Phantasy, pf, v	,, 3	Cobbett Commission, R.A.M. (MS.)

In the report of the Carnegie Trust, Alan Bush's quartet is spoken of as 'a work of very striking beauty, original without effort, well constructed and well written for strings. It contains some first-rate melodic phrases, and shows a firm and mature sense of texture and design. The style is terse and close-fitting, adequately expressing the thoughts without a superfluous bar or phrase. It certainly is one of the best chamber works that have been submitted to the Trust.'

BUSONI, FERRUCCIO BENVENUTO, 1866–1924, Italian composer and pianist.

	Composed	
Quartet, str, c mi, op. 19	1886	Kistner, 1886.
Quartet, str, d mi, op. 26	1889	B. & H., 1889.
Sonata, pf, v, e mi, op. 29	1891	B. & H., 1891, 1919.
Sonata, pf, v, e mi, op. 36A	1901	,, 1901.
Little suite, pf, vc, op. 23	1886	,, 1887.
Serenata, pf, vc, op. 34	1883	Ricordi.

and some smaller works.

Busoni's father and mother were excellent musicians, the latter, a gifted pianist, becoming naturally the first teacher of the young prodigy, who early acquired an astounding technical facility, not only as a performer, but also as a composer. The popular notion that his creative efforts were simply the outcome of a virtuoso's ultimate ambition, when no further laurels remained to be conquered in his own sphere, is wholly erroneous. There can be little doubt that if he had been a less brilliant executant, his music would have received a greater meed of attention. This is the great tragedy of Busoni's career.

After a brief period of study at Leipzig (1886), Busoni accepted a post as professor at Helsingfors, in Finland (1888); this he gave up after a year in favour of a post in Moscow, which he probably owed in large part to his having obtained the Rubinstein prize. He then went to America, but after a short stay in Boston, he returned in 1893 to Europe. Since then his only official appointments were one at the Vienna Academy, abandoned after a year, and the directorship of the Conservatorium at Bologna, which lasted no longer. None of these appointments provided him with the opportunities which he desired, and he remained equally dissatisfied with his experiences as conductor of the Bologna orchestra, and with those of a similar post at Zürich during the last years of the war. His almost unparalleled successes as a pianist, so far from giving him satisfaction, tended more and more to make him impatient of popular applause, and consequently he appeared less and less often in public. Only after the change of régime in Germany did Busoni, hitherto regarded as a futurist and iconoclast, receive such official recognition as granted him the desired opportunities. He threw himself with great fervour into his task as director of the 'master classes' for composition at the State Academy in Berlin. The results of his activities in post-war Germany were making themselves ever more felt, and quite a school of young composers, inspired and guided by him, had spread gradually over the Continent, when his health, gravely undermined by the ruthless demands made upon it, gave way entirely. He died in 1924, after a year's illness.

Busoni's significance as a composer has often been grievously under-estimated. In natural talents he was richly endowed, and in technical command and versatility of achievement possessed phenomenal powers. One need only point to such a work as the *Fantasia contrappuntistica* in support of this contention. Yet he was never able to devote himself exclusively to composition, or even to achieve more than one or two works with which he could feel really satisfied.

Busoni's early musical education was severely academic, and in his youth he remained practically ignorant of modern music. This is very evident in his early work, of which a fair amount was published from 1879 onwards. He had always been attracted to chamber music, and a number of representative compositions in that genre appeared throughout the two clearly separate stages of his artistic career. In his later years a pronounced tendency becomes apparent to employ chamber music combinations for experimental compositions, with the result that there is a striking contrast between these late works and the early ones. His strong innate predilection for linear composition, together with more abstract theoretical considerations, inevitably induced him to turn to a medium which, in the first place, suggests a style founded on polyphonic construction, and in the second place demands a more predominantly intellectual mentality than any other.

The earlier works are purely derivative, their most remarkable qualities being their technical polish, absolute command of form and complete mastery of academic devices. No aged academician could, after the study of a lifetime, have attained to a greater ease and precision in stylistic imitation than did Busoni at an age in which the mind would generally be incapable of grasping the intricacies of fugato or canonic stretto. But a composer's career started under these conditions would presume the genius and tenacity of a Busoni, if it were to escape the danger of for ever remaining that of a mere disciple. After the production of a series of works, mostly for piano, derived from Bach and Mozart, came those written under the influence of Brahms and the later Beethoven, with occasional hints of Liszt and Wagner.

To this period belong a smoothly written but not very important string quartet (no. 1, in C); a more virile and interesting quartet in D minor, in which occasional bars suggest something of the searching Faustian ponderousness that characterizes much of Busoni's later work; and two violin sonatas. It was the first of these sonatas which was awarded the Rubinstein prize, and is very much what one would expect of a composition chosen by a jury of professional musicians. The second, though distinctly reminiscent of Brahms in its thematic material, is most brilliantly written for both instruments, and concludes with a number of variations on a Bach chorale which, more than anything else in his early work, foreshadows the great change about to take place in the composer. In the second of the two quotations which follow, something more than a mere presage of his later style is distinctly discernible (Ex. 1a, 1b).

But hardly anywhere in these works does Busoni attain to the personal expression that is so powerfully developed in the works of his second period. After a long period of introspection and almost Trappist silence, during which he re-classed his materials and distilled the most personal elements from amongst the vast accumulation of derivative acquisitions which characterize his earlier productions, Busoni ruthlessly broke with the dominance of old traditions, and succeeded in divesting his

Ex. 1 a.

Ex. 1 b.

mind of all the preconceived notions and postulates which had hitherto directed his efforts, without, however, at once definitely evolving an individual idiom. Recognizing the necessity of an inchoate period preceding an ultimate discipline, he started to lead his mind into the revolutionary purgatory through which most artists pass unconsciously at a very much earlier stage. But it is evident that after such a rigorous schooling as that through which he had gone previously, he was unable altogether to abandon the habit of ordered thinking, and even his boldest experiments are moulded in forms which reveal methodical workmanship. At the same time, they rather lack the enthusiasm and spontaneity which most experimental work possesses, a fact which reminds one of Arnold Schönberg, whose transition period presents similar features.

These experiments are mostly to be found in works for piano; there is, however, one chamber composition in which the change is visible, and this work incidentally constitutes a return to a greater simplicity of texture. For Busoni's previous tendency had been rather in the direction of increased complexity, and this was to some extent deliberate. 'Music must become so complex and intricate as to kill automatically all dilettantism', he once opined, in somewhat truculent mood. The work referred to is the *Berceuse élégiaque* (the man's lullaby at his mother's grave), op. 42 (B. & H.), written for a quartet of muted strings, flutes, one oboe, clarinets, horns, harp, celesta, and gong. In spite of the considerable number of instruments employed, it is nevertheless a real chamber work, not merely because of the intimate nature of its appeal, but also for its delicacy and tenuity of sound. Particularly noteworthy is the painstaking subtlety with which every instrumental voice is balanced in a chord in such a way that, without any violent contrast of timbre or dynamic intensity, the most important tone stands out from the fragile web of sound. In this work, all the more poignant for its deliberate reticence, there is from the technical point of view an economy of means which achieves that much discussed but rarely encountered phenomenon of 'every note producing its effect'. The mystic weaving of its harmonies deserves attention, because here, in an impressionist form, appear chord formations which, in Busoni's latest works, are handled as mastered material possessing no emotional implications—such as:

Ex. 2 a.

Ex. 2 b.

Of his latest works, the only one which can be considered chamber music is the *Gesang vom Reigen der Geister*, without opus number (B. & H.), for a few strings and six wind instruments. It is consistently kept in half tones and soft shades. Though in many ways similar to the *Berceuse*, it abandons the intangible relations of texture which characterize the latter, and the lines are finely and carefully drawn. The reverse of impressionistic, it indicates a return to tonality on the part of the composer, and, so far as melody is concerned, to diatonic structures which contrast with the extreme chromaticism of his middle period.

To conclude, the earlier chamber music, written in a period when he had never attempted to find the personal note which his abstract speculations on music had convinced him was necessary, does not show his most significant qualities; while in his last years he virtually abandoned the medium in its stricter sense. Nevertheless, his influence and example have played a very important part in the present revival of interest in the medium, by converting many minds to artistic principles which are commonly and justly considered essential to chamber music. First and foremost, he taught and practised the virtues of a linear organism, and led the reaction which is beginning to manifest itself against the tendency to rely on effects of abnormal tone-production (pizzicato, col legno, &c.) and continual double stopping—methods which are wholly opposed to the principles of chamber music. His influence in this direction cannot be over-estimated, and is without doubt destined to increase in the near future. Busoni's aim and ideal was the creation of a *Junge Klassizität*, or neo-classicism, and in no department of music are the qualities denoted by the word more fruitful, more desirable, than in chamber music.

CECIL GRAY.

[London concert-goers had the advantage several times of hearing certain of the classic sonatas for piano and violin superbly rendered by Busoni and Ysaÿe. 'The little suite for 'cello and piano is charming, and gives a graphic picture of the quaint character and graceful spirit of the rococo times with the use of modern harmonies'.—*Strad* magazine.

EDITOR.]

BUSTINI, ALESSANDRO, b. 1876, Italian pianist, pupil of Sgambati.

Quartet, str, g mi	op. 13	Jurgenson, 1911.
Sonata, pf, vla, g mi		Ricordi, 1919.

Bustini has not been brilliantly successful as a writer of chamber music, but the scherzo of his quartet, in the Mendelssohn manner, is a movement of great piquancy.

BUTTERWORTH, GEORGE SAINTON KAYE, 1885–1916 (killed in action), English composer.

Song-Cycle (4 songs) *Love Blows as the Wind Blows*, barit. voice, str. quartet	Novello, 1912.

George Butterworth, who was identified with folk-song, was a young musician of whom much was expected. There is little to write of Butterworth except to deplore the tragic end to the career of a promising young musician.

BUTTING, MAX, b. 1888, German composer, pupil of Courvoisier and Klose.

1st quartet, str, A	op. 8	Tischer & Jagenberg, 1919.
2nd quartet, str, a mi	,, 16	,, ,, 1920.
[1]3rd quartet, str, f mi	,, 18	,, ,, 1919.
4th quartet, str, c sharp mi	,, 20	Simrock.
Ten short pieces, str. quartet	,, 26	Schott, 1924.
Duet, pf, v	,, 32	U.E.

Max Butting is a native of Berlin, but more closely associated with Munich during the formative years of his career. He regards himself as too modern for the old, and not modern enough for the young. In date he is old enough to have inherited a share in the academicism which his juniors so lightly discard—in some instances to resume it later—and to have come under the influence of Strauss and Reger. He remains until op. 20 well within the limits of the Munich tradition, but consistently avoids the trammels of strict sonata form, as can be seen already in the first movement of the quartet in A major, op. 8. Of Brahms there is no reminder, except, perhaps, when a simple lullaby occurs in the third movement of the same quartet.

[1] This work is shortly to be revised.

THE SECOND QUARTET denotes a new point of departure in the constructive sense, but here also the legacy of the past seems to hamper him. Melodically it is nervous, excited, and it progresses non-symmetrically in a constant tension. Taking a hint from Reger, he seeks to tighten rhythmically the melodic line. The conflict between traditional, retrospective elements and the individual onward impulse makes these early works intensely interesting.

A few points are to be noted. The finale affords a glimpse of the characteristic method of construction which runs through all Butting's work. Formal unity is sought by continuous melodic and metric metamorphosis of the thematic material, in the course of which much use is made of inversions. This movement brings together the material of the whole work, and subjects it to a constant transformation. This determination to find a new solution of the problem of form brings him nearer to Schönberg than would otherwise appear, and is so strong in him that he sometimes sacrifices to it the actual flow of the music. A striking characteristic of the style is the vacillation between the free melodic writing (to which he strives without completely attaining it) and a docile allegiance.

THE THIRD QUARTET shows this same characteristic, but here the musical force is greater. It ordains the elements of construction in broad lines of tension which now determine the lay-out of the entire work. The old quartet-form in four movements no longer suffices. The sequence allegro—scherzo—adagio—finale is still recognizable, but it is modified by inner pressure into a two-movement sequence. Free counterpoint is here more prominent than in any other work of this period. Even in the fourth quartet, with its tendency to look backward, it plays no such important part as it does here, particularly in the outer movements. The scherzo section, on the other hand, harks back once more to the Munich mode of writing, and the harmony betrays the influence of Reger. Nevertheless, op. 18, in its original form, denotes a distinct forward step in the composer's evolution. The work is now undergoing a complete revision, amounting almost to re-writing. It will be interesting later to compare the two versions and observe the reaction of the mature mind to a work of the formative period.

The task now was, on the one hand, to develop these newly acquired formal principles beyond the harmonic ties, and to attain greater concentration and mobility in the melodic line; and, on the other, to eliminate from the melodic line the moments of late-romantic excitation, in order to set the constructive elements free to follow their organic course—in other words, to discover a melodic language that should be personal and rhythmically more alive, and correspond more with the stylistic tendencies of the time.

This second phase of the composer's development is represented by seven or eight works, and is brought to a close by the *Pieces for String Quartet*, op. 26. The chamber music comprised in it consists of the fourth quartet and two important works which remain as yet unpublished: a quintet, op. 22, for piano, oboe, violin, viola, and 'cello, which was performed at Donaueschingen in 1922, and a string quintet, op. 24, for two violins, viola, 'cello, and bass.

THE FOURTH QUARTET is essentially modern in its restlessly changing rhythms and tempi, the significance of its thematic material, and its aversion from sentimentality and romanticism. But the composer's style is not determined by any demands of the times, and still less by externally applied musical doctrines. His modernity is not intentional, or an end in itself, but inevitable and of secondary importance. The entire work is dominated by one musical idea, and comprises three movements, of which the second forms an animated interlude between two which are slow and earnest. There is no suggestion of filling a predetermined framework. The music grows from the germinating idea, and develops its own form. As Dr. Richard H. Stein points out, the music grows like a tree, ignoring subject-groups, development sections, recapitulations, and the like. The skill displayed in the part-writing is remarkable for the degree of interest sustained in those parts which do not for the moment hold the chief thematic thread. On its appearance it was held in Germany as one of the best of recent quartets.

The visit to Donaueschingen brought Butting into personal contact with a number of young musicians whose aims were more or less analogous, and probably had some influence in shaping his immediate outlook. Whether that be the reason or not, he successfully steered past the dangers of this phase. The ten pieces for string quartet, which mark its conclusion, reveal absolute emancipation of the melodic line, complete release from key relation, and the strictest concentration of musical thought. Butting himself is inclined to regard them as the first work representative of his maturity. No. 2 is typical of this style, in which a sensitive feeling for the inner balance determines the play of the motifs. It should be noted how the principal theme emerges from the four introductory bars which have anticipated its constituent parts, and how the first climax, reached by the entrance for the four parts in imitation, passes through a viola cantilena to a broader treatment of the main theme in the upper parts, and how the coda lets the dotted triplets subside. This piece belongs to the scherzo type, the most expressive type being represented by nos. 1, 4, and 7. Nos. 3 and 8 are in march form, with an attack which undisguisedly recalls Hindemith. Within the small frame Butting realizes his formal principles with precision and clarity. The fullness of the form, which embraces improvisation (no. 4), loose contrapuntal articulation (nos. 3 and 6), imitation (no. 8), and strict fugal writing (no. 10), corresponds with the richness of the contents. The pieces do not admit of any classification. The most varied elements of style come together in them. The melodic line ranges from late romantic in no. 5 to a new objectivity in nos. 8 and 10.

In the Duet for violin and piano, op. 32, Butting seems to suggest a further development. The writing is extraordinarily clear, and rarely in more than three parts. The slow movement shrinks to the role of an episode, the march, though hailing from Hindemith, is given a more personal shape. The principal movements are the toccata-like introduction and the rhythmically joyous finale, both of which prove how much Butting has benefited by that contact with his juniors which began at Donaueschingen.

[Adapted by Edwin Evans from an article by Heinrich Strobel and a review by Richard H. Stein.]

†BÜTTNER, Paul, b. 1870, Saxon composer.

Quartet, str, g mi	Leuckart, 1918.
Sonata, pf, v, c mi	,, 1919.

The string quartet, which is in five movements, is interesting and personal, and easier to understand than most modern works. The andante and allegretto are the most successful movements.

The sonata contains a warmly felt slow movement and brilliant finale.

†BUTTYKAY, Akos von, b. 1871, Hungarian, composer.

Sonata, pf, v, a mi	op. 10	Zimmermann, 1908.

BYRD, William, 1543–1623, English polyphonist.

Modern republications:

Two fantasias, str. sextet, c mi, e mi	S. & B., 1922.
Fantasia, v, vla, 2 vc	,,

It is as a composer of vocal music that Byrd occupies a conspicuous position in musical history, for in the polyphonic school he stands beside Palestrina, Orlando di Lasso, and Luca Marenzio. This type of music reached its full development in the sixteenth century. The closing years of that century may be said to have seen the birth of chamber music; a century or more was still to elapse before this branch of composition was to come to maturity; indeed, the string quartet did not begin to reach a satisfactory degree of development as an art-form until the days of Haydn and Mozart. Yet it is not generally realized that in England several composers were exploring new possibilities in writing concerted music for strings before the year 1600. The 'consort of viols' normally consisted of six instruments, and this was the most popular combination with the early English composers, but works were also produced for quintet, quartet, and trio. Among these English pioneers of chamber music Byrd stands out as the most important. A list of some twenty works of this class by Byrd are given by the present writer in his *William Byrd, a short account of his life and work* (Clarendon Press). Many of these have not yet been scored, and their value cannot therefore be estimated, but the two fantasies for sextet are works of remarkable interest, considering their date; they may be said to consist of three short movements, which follow each other without a break and are well contrasted except in the matter of key, the conditions as well as the convention of that date greatly limiting the scope for modulation. They have been published in score and parts (S. & B.) under the writer's editorship. Byrd is certainly to be regarded as one of the greatest of those who laid the foundations of chamber music.

Byrd also did work of great value in writing for the key-instruments of his day. He is in many ways to be regarded as the father of secular key-board music; he was certainly one of the first composers, if not the actual first, to develop variation-form, and some of his original themes and variations are of no little beauty. Considerably more than a hundred of Byrd's pieces for the virginals have survived, and a list is given in the writer's *William Byrd* already mentioned.

E. H. Fellowes.

C

CABALT DE ATAIDE, ENRIQUE, Spanish composer. Lived in the second half of the eighteenth century.

Six string quartets 1790. Dr. Strahe Library, Geissen.

†CADMAN, CHARLES WAKEFIELD, b. 1881, American composer.

Quartet (*To a Vanishing Race*), str, John Church Co., 1917.

Trio, pf, v, vc, D, op. 56, White-Smith Music Publishing Co., Boston.

Cadman's trio in D was first performed from manuscript in Denver, Colorado, by the Denver Trio. The finale, which he calls 'idealized rag-time', is one of the first examples of the use of American popular rhythms in chamber music.

Cadman's music in general is fundamentally lyrical, and though not without touches of modern harmony, remains within conservative limits. A. L. GOLDBERG.

CAETANI, ROFFREDO, b. 1871, pupil of Sgambati.

1st quartet, str, D	op. 1	Schott,	1888.
2nd ,, ,, f mi	,, 11	,,	1907.
Quintet, pf, 2 v, vla, vc, F sharp	,, 4	,,	1897.
Trio, pf, v, vc, D	,, 5	,,	1897.

Dr. Altmann (*Handbuch*) speaks of Caetani's first quartet as written in the manner of Liszt's symphonic poems, in one long, diffuse movement, showing intimate knowledge of fugal form. In his second quartet, dramatic and lyrical themes are effectively contrasted. There is no scherzo, and the finale is slightly coloured by Slav influence. Dr. Altmann, without recommending these works for public performance, considers them useful for dilettante players. EDITOR.

CAJA, ALFONSO, b. 1889, Italian composer, pupil of Malipiero.

Quartet, str, d mi Senart.

Among unpublished works are a piano quintet and a *Poem* for chamber orchestra. The quartet is an interesting work.

CAMBINI, GIOVANNI GIUSEPPE, 1746–1825, Italian composer.

Modern republication:

Sonata, v, fig. bass (pf), F, (Cesare Barison), Schmidl, 1912.

Earlier publications (*Fétis*, &c.), include 144 string quartets and other chamber works.

Cambini was a pupil of Padre Martini. If readers are interested in the romantic stories told of musicians, they are recommended to consult Fétis's lengthy article on Cambini. With regard to his chamber music, it will suffice to point out that although the 144 quartets attributed to him, 133 of which were published in his life-time, are said to be his best work, it must be admitted that if played to-day they would be pronounced, in the language of one of his critics, weak and puerile. Some were faked in the style of Boccherini, and published by Pleyel as his work. It is said of Cambini, however, that he was much sought after by quartet players of distinction, and that he interpreted chamber music, especially the viola parts, with elegance and purity of taste. His somewhat dissipated career ended at the Bicêtre Hospital in Paris. EDITOR.

CAMBRIDGE UNIVERSITY MUSICAL CLUB.

Founded in 1890, this club has many points of affinity with the OXFORD MUSICAL UNION (*q.v.*). Its members are chiefly (though not entirely) undergraduates. An annual interchange of visits is made both with the Oxford Union and the Oxford and Cambridge Musical Club, London.

Keen interest is shown in chamber music in private circles in Cambridge. EDITOR.

†CAMONDO, I. DE, amateur composer.

Quartet, str, *Le Kief*, g mi	Astruc.
,, ,, *Pifferarina*, A	,,
,, ,, *Poussières de valses*, Nos. 1, 2, and 3	,,

CAMPAGNOLI, BARTOLOMMEO, 1751–1827, Italian violinist.

Campagnoli was a prolific writer for the violin, and some of his work (which consists mainly of violin duets) has recently been republished by Ricordi and Haake. These are easy duets for teaching purposes.

His three duos, op. 9 (*c.* 1795), are more brilliant, with use of higher positions and much double stopping. In no. 2 the last movement is strangely entitled 'Potpourri quasi presto'. There are also three duos, op. 19, of less difficulty, but lacking in strength and individuality. These two sets were published by B. & H. E. VAN DER STRAETEN.

†CAMPO Y ZABALETA, CONRADO DEL, b. 1879, Spanish composer, violist, and writer on music.

Quartet (*Caprichos Románticos*), str, f mi, Unión Musical Española, 1924.

Campo has been a member since their foundation of the Cuarteto Francés and Quinteto de Madrid (now dissolved).

Though once a pupil at the Madrid conservatoire, del Campo as a composer is a self-taught modern progressive artist. His works, free from experimental audacity and the limitations imposed by musical nationalism, are not of the type that makes an immediate appeal to the uninitiated, but always exhibit his own fundamental qualities: absolute sincerity and consummate musicianship. At times his writing becomes unduly intricate through an exuberance of polyphonic devices, while the sustained intellectuality of his conceptions puts the listener's attention to a severe test. However, considering the quality and quantity of his works, as well as his position as a performer, del Campo must be acknowledged as the leading figure in the otherwise rather uneventful history of Spanish chamber music. The fact that only one of his quartets is available in print nowadays should be regretted by all having the cause of chamber music at heart. *Caprichos Románticos*, the work alluded to, is inspired by four of the 'Rimas' (unconnected stanzas without title) by the Spanish Heine, Adolfo Gustavo Becquer, corresponding in mood and atmosphere to the contrasting characters of the usual movements of the classical quartet. These short poems are freely translated, together with a summary analysis of the musical composition as follows:

I. Prelude.

'I know a hymn, a strange and swelling hymn, that announces to the darkened soul the break of day . . . My songs are but the echoes of that hymn, strange, distorted, like shadows, by the wind.'

Ex. 1.

The unfolding of the previous phrase in imitative responses, in obvious allusion to the line 'my songs are but the echoes', leads to a second subject, dolce con melancolia, allotted to the viola:

Ex. 2.

The movement contains many passages of arresting beauty.

II. Scherzo.

'Nameless spirit, imponderable essence, I live the formless life of the idea . . . In the lute I am sound, in the flower perfume; among the ruins, a creeper, among the graves, flame . . . In the silvery brook I chase the playful nymphs, unseen.'

This movement must be singled out, not only as the best in the quartet, but as a model scherzo. The musical quality of its texture is adequately emphasized by the elusive use of 'pizzicati', 'sordini', and harmonic effects that colour the rhythmical and melodic restlessness of the following motifs:

Ex. 3.

III. Andante.

Ex. 4.

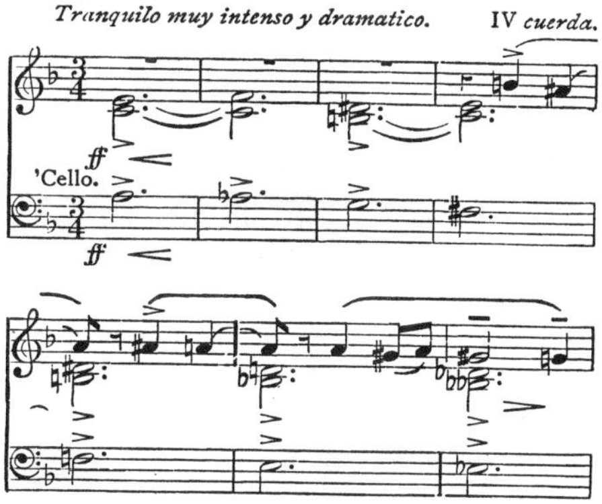

'I put the light away and sat by the bed, my gaze fixed on the wall . . . How long did I remain alone and silent? I know not . . . When the spasm of grief released my mind, the candle flickered and the sun smiled in at my window.'

IV. Presto.

First it is a trembling clearness, a silver thread across the sea. Then it quivers and grows and breaks into a glowing flood of light . . . The blinding brightness is joy; the monstrous shadow, sorrow . . . Alas! when will day break in the dark night of my soul?'

A particular feature of the finale, which opens with a long preamble 'rather slow and very severe', leading to the main section marked 'vivo', is the quotation of phrases from the first and second movements before the recapitulation and coda. *Caprichos Románticos* was written in 1908, when it was performed for the first time by the Cuarteto Francés.

A version in use in 1915 contained an intermezzo interposed between the last two movements of the actual edition as published.

PEDRO G. MORALES.

[Besides the work described, del Campo has written the following string quartets, all in MS., and all previous to the published work: E major (no. 1); E major (no. 2); C minor; *Cuarteto Asturiano*; *El Cristo de la Vega* (with recitation of José Zonilla's legend similarly entitled); *Cuarteto Oriental*; *Las Horas de Nietsche*. EDITOR.]

CANNABICH, (1) CHRISTIAN, 1731–1798, German violinist and conductor.

Modern republication:

Quartet, str, e mi	op. 5 (no. 2)	(*Riemann*) Published in *D.T.B.*

Early publications, see *Fétis*.

Cannabich won the praise of Mozart for his conducting of the orchestral performances at Mannheim; and his compositions enjoyed, in his time, a limited degree of popularity.

(2) CARL, 1764–1806, son of Christian, violinist and conductor.

Fétis gives six trios, 2 v, vc, op. 3, and six duets, fl, v, op. 4.

†CANTELOUBE DE MALARET, JEAN, b. *c.* 1879, French composer.

Suite, *Dans la Montagne*, pf, v	Rouart, 1906.

Canteloube's chief characteristics are attachment to his native soil and a deep love of nature. His work may be said to be a continuation of that of his friend, Déodat de Sévérac.

His one chamber work is in four movements, based on a broad and tranquil principal theme, and is redolent of his native soil. The theme of the prelude (*En Plein Vent*) is developed in the second movement (*Le Soir*); it is at first lento, 6/8, in G minor, and tenderly melancholy in character; then 'assez animé', 9/8, in D major. Here it gives rise to a popular dance tune, but growing calmer by degrees, the lento is resumed and the dance dies away in the distance.

The third movement (*Jour de Fête*) is a sort of lively scherzo, wherein the opening theme is varied by means of fantastic rhythms of great diversity. The finale (*Dans les Bois au Printemps—Vers l'Absente*) is highly descriptive; we have here the dream as yet unrealized. Then, gently, appears the principal theme, in D flat, amid the murmuring of the rills in their mossy beds. With its entry the music grows ever more impassioned, leading to the second section, in D major.

Now the poet in his dream rejoins 'Her who is absent'. Passion returns, in the splendour of the opening theme (*En Plein Vent*), which is here restated broadly in powerful chords. Then the calm of evening descends, and the work closes with a song of love.

A work of youth, no doubt, but one which strikes a note as unexpected as it is rare in violin and piano literature. ADOLPHE PIRIOU.

[In view of the 'regional' tendency in recent French music, which associates composers with provinces, as, for instance, Sévérac (mentioned above) with the Languedoc, it is of interest to note that Canteloube de Malaret is intimately associated with the music of the Auvergne, and has collected Auvergnat folk-songs. EDWIN EVANS.]

CAPET, LUCIEN, 1873–1928, French violinist.

1st quartet, str, C		Mathot.
2nd „ „		Senart, 1922.
Trio (aria), pf, v, vla		Mathot.
Sonata, pf, v, a mi	op. 7	Mathot, 1908.

The second of the compositions by the leader of the famous Capet Quartet (*vide* FRENCH PERFORMING ORGANIZATIONS) is inspired by verses taken from Dante's *Inferno*.

†CAPLET, ANDRÉ, 1879–1925, French composer.

Miroir de Jésus, 4 voices, str. quartet, harp	Durand.
Conte Fantastique, harp, str. quartet	„
Sonata, pf, voice, vc	„
Épiphanie, pf, vc	„
Sonata da Chiesa, organ, v	„

A septet for three voices and string quartet has frequently been performed, but is not yet published.

It was chiefly under the influence of Debussy that Caplet's attractive, refined, and highly imaginative personality developed. Indeed, he is one of the few composers who really benefited by Debussy's influence.

This is clearly felt in two of his most significant chamber works: a septet for three female voices (used instrumentally, yet with a great sense of fitness, very much as they are in Debussy's nocturne *Sirènes*), and a sonata for one voice, 'cello and piano. The septet, written in 1909, is probably the first modern instance of the introduction of voices in chamber music.

Two other chamber works, the *Conte Fantastique* for harp and string quartet, inspired by Poe's *Masque of the Red Death*, and the *Épiphanie* for 'cello and piano, are music of the picturesque, poetically descriptive order, but entirely self-supporting and enjoyable without the help of any reference to the allusions or descriptions they may contain. Both make excellent playing, and the *Épiphanie* is instinct with feeling.

Caplet has also written a few smaller pieces for 'cello and piano, for flute and piano, a *Sonata da Chiesa* for violin and organ, a quintet and a *Suite Persane* for wind instruments—the last two are early works and remain unpublished. His beautiful mystical *Miroir de Jésus* was originally written for four singers, harp, and string quartet. It is therefore justifiable to include it in the list of his chamber music.

M. D. CALVOCORESSI.

CARNEGIE TRUST, THE.

This is amongst musicians the familiar name of the Carnegie United Kingdom Trust, founded by Royal Charter in 1917 under the will of Andrew Carnegie, the Scottish-American multi-millionaire and philanthropist (1837–1919).

The expenditure of the fund upon musical objects is varied from time to time. From 1917 it has included the bearing of the cost of publication of the works of contemporary British composers. It is understood that this particular activity ends in 1928, but, whilst it has lasted, it has been very helpful to a number of composers in enabling them to bring before the public compositions that might otherwise have remained unknown. The method of award has been the appointment of anonymous adjudicators, who have examined and reported upon works submitted.

The chamber works published are as follows:

Bedford, H. Night Piece: *The Shepherd*, for contralto solo, wood-wind, and piano (1925).
Benjamin, Arthur. Pastoral Fantasia for string quartet (1924).
Bliss, Arthur. Rhapsody for flute, cor anglais, string quartet, bass, and two voices (1921).
Bowen, York. String quartet in D minor (1922).
Bush, Alan. String quartet in A minor (1925).
Dyson, George. Three Rhapsodies for string quartet (1919).
Finzi, Gerald. *A Severn Rhapsody* for chamber orchestra (1924).
Gurney, Ivor. (*a*) *Ludlow and Teme*: Song-cycle for voice, with accompaniment for string quartet and piano (1921).
(*b*) *The Western Playland*: Song-cycle with string quartet (1924).
Hay, Edward Norman. String quartet in A major (1918).
Howells, Herbert. (*a*) Rhapsodic quintet for clarinet, two violins, viola, and 'cello (1920).
(*b*) Quartet in A minor for piano, violin, viola, and 'cello (1917).
Mark, Jeffrey. *Scottish Suite*, for four violins and piano (1927).
Miles, Percy Hilder. Sextet in G minor for two violins, two violas, 'cello, and bass (1919).
Morris, R. O. Fantasy for string quartet (1922).
Scott, Cyril. Quintet for piano and strings (1924).
Wall, Alfred M. Piano quartet in C minor (1918).
Walton, W. T. Quartet for piano and strings (1924).
Warlock, Peter. *The Curlew*, for tenor voice, flute, cor anglais, and string quartet (1923).
White, Felix. (*a*) *The Nymph's Complaint for the Death of her Fawn*: Poem for oboe (or violin), viola, and piano (1922).
(*b*) *Four Proverbs* for flute, oboe, and strings (1925).
Whittaker, W. G. *Among the Northumbrian Hills*, for piano, two violins, viola, and 'cello (1921).

In addition to the above publication awards, the Trustees, in order to facilitate performance of certain works commended by the adjudicators, agreed to provide manuscript copies of the following works:

Erlebach, Rupert. Rhapsody quintet for flute, cor anglais (or oboe), violin, viola, and 'cello.
Gibbs, C. Armstrong. String quartet in G.
Walker, Ernest. Quartet in C minor for piano and strings.

P. A. SCHOLES.

†CARO, PAUL, b. 1859, amateur composer.

Four quartets, str. B, b flat mi, d mi, f sharp mi	opp. 6, 7, 19, 20	Robitschek, 1881–1897.
Trio, pf, v, vc, E	op. 8	Robitschek, 1886.
Sonata, pf, v, F	,, 2	Cranz, 1883.
,, pf, vc, d mi	,, 42	Robitschek, 1911.

Paul Caro's chamber music is spoken of in the German press as suited for amateur performers.

†CARPENTER, JOHN ALDEN, b. 1876, American composer.

Sonata, pf, v, G — Schirmer, *c.* 1917.

Carpenter's sonata is less original or personal than are his other and later compositions. It is, however, well written for both instruments, without excessive difficulties. The opening larghetto establishes a mood of idyllic repose, broken only once or twice by flashes of greater intensity, while the following allegro offers a happy contrast. After a vigorous opening, a second theme of minuet-like cast and feeling leads to a free development and brilliant climax. The third movement is a largo mistico, and somewhat reminiscent of Grieg and Franck. As regards thematic material, the last movement is the most felicitous.

CARL ENGEL.

CARREÑO, TERESA, 1853–1917, famous Venezuelan pianist.

Quartet, str, b mi — Siegel, 1896.

It has been almost forgotten that this eminent piano virtuoso wrote a string quartet; a thoroughly sound piece of work, written with a knowledge of the classical quartet style, in which only certain passages in the finale betray the fact that the composer was first and foremost a pianist. Great demands are made on the performers at times. The concise form of all four movements is praiseworthy. The first (allegro) opens with a well-characterized melody, but the second subject, appearing first on the viola, is more expressive; most effective of all is the subsidiary theme marked 'con dolore'. The main theme of the slow movement recalls the andante in the corresponding movement of Haydn's op. 77, no. 2, but the scherzo is more original, despite its Mendelssohnian flavour. It is a provocative, restless little piece, with a trio which introduces a lovely melody by way of contrast. Vigour is the outstanding characteristic of the finale, the last section of which takes the form of a fugue with a well marked subject.

The work will chiefly interest those who were admirers of Carreño during her lifetime.

WILHELM ALTMANN.

CARRI, HERMANN.

Romantic suite, pf, v, G op. 35 André, 1906.

†CARSE, ADAM, b. 1878, English composer.

Sonata, pf, v, c mi	Augener, 1922.
Suite in old style, pf, v	,, ,,

Adam Carse has distinguished himself by writing many string works of considerable educational value. His violin sonata shows him in the light of an individual thinker, touched, but only slightly, with modern influences.

EDITOR.

†CASADESUS, (1) FRANÇOIS LOUIS (Francis), b. 1870, French composer.

Sonata, pf, vc Deiss & Crépin, 1922.

(1) François Casadesus is one of a family of five French musicians who formed themselves into a society known as 'La Société des Concerts des Instruments Anciens', reviving the cult of the old viols and the music written for them; † (2) The actual founder, in 1901, was HENRI GUSTAVE (b. 1879), an accomplished performer † on the viola and viola d'amore; (3) MARCEL LOUIS LUCIEN (b. 1882), 'cellist and gambist, was killed in the war; (4) MARIUS ROBERT MAX (b. 1892) is a violinist and composer; and (5) ROBERT MARCEL (b. 1899) an excellent pianist. These artists found able coadjutors in M. Malkin, performer on the quinton, M. Devillers, a 'cellist who also presides over the bass viol, and M. Alfredo Casella (clavecin).

The society performed in London some interesting old chamber works, including a quartet by an English composer named Nicoley, of whom no record has been found, up to the present, in any dictionary. (v. *Strad.* Aug. 1908.)

EDITOR.

CASALS, PABLO, b. 1876, Spanish violoncellist and conductor.

Holds the leading place among the world's 'cellists. Studied chamber music at the Royal Conservatoire at Madrid and played with MONASTERIO (*q.v.*). Has made many appearances as an ensemble player, but is identified chiefly with solo playing, excelling by his masterly interpretations of the Bach suites. Some wonderful gramophone records exist of the Thibaud-Cortot-Casals Trio organization (H.M.V.).

EDITOR.

CASALS QUARTET: Enric Casals (leader of the Symphony Orchestra of Barcelona—on staff of Casals Institute), Manuel Gimenez, Joan Ribas, Bernardi Galvez.

Enric Casals is brother of the famous 'cellist.

*†CASELLA, ALFREDO, b. 1883, Italian pianist, pupil of Fauré.

		Composed	
Concerto, str. quartet		1923–4	U.E., 1924.
Five pieces, str. quartet		1920	Mathot, 1904; U.E. 1921.
Siciliana and burlesca, pf, v, vc		1914–17	Ricordi.
Sonata, pf, v, c mi	op. 6	1907	Mathot, 1907.
Sonata, pf, vc			U.E., *c.* 1927.

While still a child Casella went to Paris and entered the Conservatoire, where high opinions of his ability as a pianist were formed. He took up concert work, in the course of which he visited the chief European countries, and made the acquaintance of musicians of all nationalities. When the European war broke out he returned to Italy, and with his arrival an element of restlessness entered into the musical life of the country. He evoked many loud protests, but also produced some notable results, especially in the improvement of musical taste.

Casella himself distinguishes three successive manners in his work, and at a first glance one is disposed to agree with him; but on further consideration it appears doubtful if the differences are more than superficial. For the musical substance of his work can, strictly speaking, be reduced to a few well-defined and isolated nuclei, which reappear in his successive phases, variously disguised and elaborated, bent into new schemes of construction, or filled out with new harmonies. Even his warmest admirers must admit that his vein of composition is neither rich nor spontaneous. His earliest works afford sufficient proof of this, for it is in the production of a man's first youth, when the impulses are warm and untrammelled by theory, that the wealth of his nature is bound to reveal itself.

An instance is afforded by the 'cello sonata, op. 6, finished in Russia in February, 1907, when he was twenty-four. It is not altogether academic in style, though it follows traditional sonata form; it shows the influence of the last stage of German romanticism, and also, to some extent, that of the Russian nationalists, while possessing some individual features. But, as a whole, the sonata lacks the characteristic spring or vitality of youthful work, and there is no sign of the grandiloquence which is essentially the fault of youth.

The truth is that at twenty-four Casella was already master of his material and methods, with absolute control over his imagination—though possibly this may not have been inordinately hard to restrain. There is no exuberance, no bubbling over, but a correctness which is nothing short of icy. The composer seems to be too skilful for his years, and too prudent to allow any outpouring of the imagination.

Seven years later he wrote a *Siciliana and Burlesca* for flute and piano, for the 1914 competition of the Paris Conservatoire, and dedicated it to a well-known flautist. This work would not require special consideration but for the fact that, three years later, Casella wrote another version of it in the form of a piano trio. In the opening bars one is immediately struck by the theme of the *Siciliana*, which is characteristic of Casella, not because it is overwhelmingly original, but because it recurs, with some degree of variation, in several later works. (It may be remarked that Casella is especially fond of a slow, languid tempo like that of a siciliano or a berceuse; he has introduced examples of the latter into several of his compositions.) The harmony does not lack savour, and already gives clear indications of the transformation in style which was effected in his later work. The diatonic sense of tonality is still untouched, but there is abundance of harmonic and rhythmical experiment.

The *Burlesca* is very lively and full of movement; but, judging from this early sample of his musical humour, it is safe to prophesy that Casella's mirth will never be of a frank and jovial kind. His comic spirit always inclines toward caricature, and suggests the forced smile of a mountebank, which has to be assumed even if his heart is breaking.

Undoubtedly, the composer's skill in this type of music is remarkable. He understands the art of carrying his ideas onward, varying the effects, regulating the proportions and balancing the different elements in the design, with the result that, instrumentally, the trio sounds very fine indeed. Casella has succeeded in blending the sound effects of the piano with those of the strings as few composers have contrived to do in this far from happy instrumental combination, which, in the writer's opinion, usually produces so unbalanced and heterogeneous an effect.

Casella's second manner was first shown in the *Nove pezzi* (Nine Pieces) for piano, and subsequently further developed in various works, vocal, orchestral, &c., which do not belong to the scheme of this Cyclopedia. Italian music was then still in the phase of harmonic impressionism, when the tendency was to create an atmosphere, and then leave it to stagnate. Casella alone believed that it was possible to renew the art by extending the range of chord formation even to the point of absurdity, and when he perceived that the system had led him into an impasse, he stopped short and kept silence for two or three years.

During this interval he prepared the ground for what he designated his 'third manner', first manifested in the five pieces (*Cinque pezzi*) for string quartet. Whether this is the third or the fourth manner, it is certain that a change is perceptible, not only in the technical treatment, but still more in the whole conception of the work. From the standpoint of harmony, an advance has been made towards the complete abandonment of chromaticism, that is to say, in the direction of polytonality; moreover, the whole composition seems to be constructed with much greater ease, and to have much more vitality of line. The *Cinque pezzi* comprise: (1) Preludio, (2) Ninna-Nanna, (3) Valse ridicule, (4) Nocturne, (5) Foxtrot. There is no connexion between them; the different pieces follow one another with merely a change from allegro to lento, or whatever it may be.

The Preludio (allegro vivace e barbaro) unmistakably shows the influence of Stravinsky in the spirit of the conception, though not in its harmonic treatment, which is very different from that of the Russian composer; the movement makes a considerable stir, runs its course rapidly, and leaves the hearer in a state bordering on stupefaction. Its merit does not consist in particular details of sound effects, and even less in any beauty or originality of the melodic line, but in its impetuosity, which is thrown into higher relief by an episode marked 'dolce e grazioso'. Everything is here subordinated to the ensemble effect; yet, in asserting that such and such an effect has been achieved, it is well not to look too closely into the details. It may be observed, however, that there is hardly anywhere more than one real part, and there is no sign of polyphonic counterpoint. The linearity is reduced to something which may be described as decomposition; chords are reiterated and dismembered until they engender a false atmosphere of dynamism in which the melodic parts move—in fine, it may be said that the dynamism of the music is essentially mechanical, partly because of the feeble propulsive powers of the atonality.

In the Ninna-Nanna or lullaby, which follows, the chief interest lies in the particular sound effects; Casella is very skilful in clothing extremely simple little tunes with very suggestive instrumental colouring. This piece contains much-admired mysterious effects, obtained by *frôlements* of the accompanying instruments in the vibrating atmosphere created by the quick tremolando of the second violin above the bass C major of the 'cello.

The Valse ridicule contains some bizarre contrasts of sound, and is written with much spirit, yet there is a certain far-off suggestion of melancholy, rather like the sound of a hurdy-gurdy in a deserted street on a Sunday afternoon.

The Nocturne (marked lento, grave, funèbre) is more ambitious, and its continuation, like the opening, seems to warn us of dread things to come; this appears to the writer the least successful portion of the whole work. Though pianissimo almost throughout, it is too heavy, and is broken into bits by the continual repetition of the opening motif, which has little connexion with the interpolated episodes. These do not fail to exhibit striking effects of sonority, in which the composer has truly realized the ethereal effect at which he aimed, by making the four strings play *sul tasto* (the 'cello in the higher octave), and by giving the second violin double harmonics to play. The last movement, Foxtrot, displays the same virtues and defects as the Preludio; it makes use of the rhythms, less exploited in 1920 than at present, of negro dances, with their traditional glissandi and pizzicati.

Between the *Cinque pezzi* and the concerto for string quartet intervened the whole of the neo-classic phase, which had representatives in every country. The vogue for linear counterpoint, which originated in Germany, soon spread to other countries, in which it not only initiated a musical renaissance, but revived in each the prototype of the true and authentic national style reinforced by the 'great tradition'. Something of the same kind happened in Italy, where Casella, always in the van of any new movement, was indefatigable in his efforts to impart an Italian colouring to the new ideas. The concerto was the fruit of these endeavours, and, considered by itself, it must be acknowledged that it affords yet another confirmation of the composer's marvellous ability, for in it he has succeeded in inducing opposites to live together, if not in complete unity, at all events in neighbourly relations.

This work shows the composer to be preoccupied with form as much as or more than with style. Casella evidently desired to create something which should state and solve problems, not of design and colour alone, but also the real problem of composition, in the painter's sense of the word. He went back, in some ways, to the early instrumental concertos of the eighteenth century, particularly to those in which the Italian genius was most brilliantly manifested, and, starting from a prescribed scheme, has sought to modify this in such a way as to admit of its use as a vehicle for his very modern idiom.

This intention is particularly evident in the first movement, sinfonia, the architecture of which is extremely simple and clearly defined. The movement is built on two themes (or is it the same theme in two guises?), one vigorous, of which the treatment is confined within such narrow limits that it is slightly suggestive of a piano exercise, the other not very different in its melodic configuration, but more melancholy and more lyrical in feeling. The two themes appear alternately in a series of episodes, which are skilfully linked up and give homogeneity to the movement.

The part-writing, which is nervous and full of sound effects, gives this section of the work an importance in the whole design analogous to that of the first movement of a sonata. The two middle movements are superficially rather attractive (especially the second), but though they are more pleasing to the ear than the sinfonia, they possess distinctly less significance. The Siciliana is a graceful piece of writing, which at once recalls the Casella of the earlier works, by reason of thematic affinities as well as certain colour effects which were a feature of the *Cinque pezzi*.

The first subject, announced by the viola alone, is of great delicacy and breathes a tender melancholy; it is not directly derived from the lovely inheritance of Sicilian folk-song, so far as the writer knows, but it partakes of its spirit and poetic feeling; and the parts allotted to the other instruments which harmonize and accompany the theme are just as exquisite in their own way. The entry of the episode marked 'allegro vivace e gaio' is contrived with great skill and sureness; its motion is that of a dance (possibly the Sicilian Tarantella, which is less unrestrained and bacchanalian than the Neapolitan variety), and most of the recapitulation is masterly. Here Casella displays consummate technical virtuosity, and maintains the interest by unceasingly varying the effects until the movement arrives at its far-away, dreamlike ending. But when all possible praise has been given to the Siciliana, considered on its own merits, it has most certainly not been fitted successfully into the concerto, for it has no sort of connexion, either of form or spirit, with the first movement. The same may be said of the third movement, a minuet, recitative, and aria, in which the technical preoccupation of the craftsman is much in evidence and the artist's imagination seems impoverished to the verge of baldness. The minuet is insignificant, the recitative merely an ugly display of cleverness in the shape of a cadenza of doubtful effectiveness (even in the matter of sonority), and put there, apparently, for no special reason. Nor can the aria really be said to justify its existence; the theme vaguely echoes that of the sinfonia, but is less worthy. The interest, however, is reawakened by the last movement, the canzone, which, technically speaking, is perfectly bound to the first, though it would make an equally satisfactory close to the concerto without the repetition at the end of the first theme of the sinfonia—a wearisome device.

In this last composition Casella has abandoned the sterile lexicographic labours which weighed down his previous works, in order to tackle vaster problems. His speculative mind is no longer occupied with what may be called linguistic research, but attempts to solve the problem of modern musical form, which, however, is not yet apprehended as the problem of producing a work of art which shall be an aesthetic entity. There are as yet no signs of that profound and sincere spiritual revolution without which no amount of formalistic ingenuity can achieve anything of value, but already the atmosphere of abstraction in which most of his preceding works were immersed is beginning to disappear. Above all, the concerto is important as contributing to the development of chamber music, for it shows no disposition to go beyond the precise limits set by the nature of the instruments employed and the environment for which it is intended. And this is undoubtedly a great merit, especially in view of the considerable influence which it is likely to have on the activities of the youthful composers in whose hands lies the immediate future of Italian music. GUIDO M. GATTI.

† CASSADÓ, GASPAR, b. 1898, Spanish virtuoso 'cellist.

Sonata	pf, v	U.E.
,,	pf, vc	,,
Sonata in old Spanish style	,, ,,	,,

† CASTÉRA, RENÉ D'AVEZAC DE, b. 1873, French composer, pupil of the Schola Cantorum.

	Composed	
Concerto, pf, vc, fl, cl (or v), A	1911–22	Rouart.
Trio, pf, v, vc, d mi	1904, 1908	,,
Sonata, pf, v, e mi	1910	,,

Castéra's trio, op. 5, composed in 1904, was remodelled in 1908. It consists of four movements: the first, in sonata form, abounds with bold ideas. It is preceded by an introduction announcing the 'mother theme', which appears again in the slow conclusion. The second (divertissement), in rondo form (G minor), is popular in style, and presents a fresh rhythmic idea—a Basque dance in 5/8—in the second couplet.[1] The third (assez lent) is a Lied[1] in three sections, in D major, finely conceived and carried out. The finale (très-animé, very lively)—in D minor, ending in D major—is in sonata form, and is full of fire and colour.

The trio is not strictly cyclic, though the kinship of the themes is evident, but it is chiefly in the works described below that René de Castéra has sought unity in complete affinity of thematic material.

THE VIOLIN SONATA, op. 13, is quite typical in this respect. It has three movements preceded by a short introduction, in which the elegant and flexible mother-theme is announced in the manner of a recitative. From this springs the principal subject, 'animé et énergique', proud and care-free in its youth. A transition leads to the second subject, calm and gentle, derived from a fragment of the first. In the development, impulsive and full of life, in which all these constituents react in contact with each other, the first subject reappears, this time in the brighter key of E major, to dominate at first in its strength, and end in peace.

The second movement (lent) is a Lied[1] in five sections. It begins in G minor, in the style of a folk-song of touching melancholy, then modulates, evolving a transformation of the principal subject of the first movement, and leads to a triptych in F sharp major. This suggests a forest-scene in the Landes, and presently, above the faint murmur of the piano, there emerges a pastoral theme; on this again the violin superposes a broad and tranquil phrase derived from the second subject. The whole of this charming triptych is instinct with poetic feeling. After a development of the modulatory section, in which a variation of the principal theme appears in triumph in G major, the first section, grave and sombre, is repeated in G minor, the gloom lifting a little to allow a peaceful conclusion in G major. In the finale, a sonata-rondo, with a brief introduction, the elastic and varied rhythms of Basque folk-song and dance are utilized in the happiest fashion.

THE CONCERTO is in three movements which display the same characteristics as the foregoing sonata. The first movement, *Paysage*, is preceded by a poetic 'preamble' (très-modéré) suggesting the Landes country with its pine forests dotted with pools. From this there gradually emerges the first theme, in clearer outlines and in '*mouvement trimé*'. This is in the major key, and is full of freshness and sunshine. The second theme, in E major, is all tenderness and charm. Then, after a bright development, both themes appear in the major: the first is condensed in clear and joyous polyphony; the second, beneath a very delicate embroidery high up on the piano, grows louder and more animated in the middle section, calming down at the return of the preamble, with its suggestion of the gentle poetic charm of the Landes.

The second movement, 'Interlude—lent et grave', begins with a scherzo which is thoroughly Basque in character, on a Zortzico theme in F. This is interrupted by the trio in A flat (très-modéré), a flexible and pastoral melody. Then comes the scherzo again, linking up with a Lied, in D minor (lent et grave), mournful and sombre in character, which is brightened but momentarily by a tender reminiscence of the second subject of the first movement, and ends in an atmosphere of deeply moving melancholy.

The third movement of the concerto is a rondo with variations in sonata-form. The first refrain,[1] in A minor, sets forth a martial theme, with a first couplet[1] in F sharp minor,

[1] See Foreword, art. BEETHOVEN.

which is a veritable interplay of rhythms. The second refrain (with variations), in A minor, is developed with a second couplet, the first part of which is derived from the pastoral theme of the trio of the interlude, and the second part from the Lied theme, here given by flute and clarinet over delicious triplet harmonies on the 'cello, while the piano repeats fragments of the principal theme of the first movement. Then comes a reminiscence of the preamble, with its suggestion of the Landes country. The refrain appears for the third time, in A minor, in an expressive form. It is combined with the theme of the preamble, and has a third couplet which modulates and is increasingly varied. This leads to a bright conclusion on the fourth refrain, this time in A major, the theme of which bursts out *ff*, then dies slowly away to end with a memory of the 'paysage landais' as through a faintly iridescent veil of mist.

All these works, flexible in style and solidly constructed, full as they are of freshness, gaiety, and ardent enthusiasm, breathe also deep and heartfelt emotion. They are the outcome of the temperament of an artist steeped in the poetry of his homeland, and, as in the case of the Breton composers, his themes, even those of popular type, are all truly born within him, not merely borrowed from the folk-songs whose flavour they preserve.

ADOLPHE PIRIOU.

CASTILLON, ALEXIS DE, 1838–1873, French composer.

		Composed	
1st quartet, str, a mi	op. 3	1871	Durand, 1900.
Quintet, pf, 2 v, vla, vc, E flat	„ 1	1870	Durand, 1890.
Quartet, pf, v, vla, vc, g mi	„ 7	1871–2	Hamelle.
1st trio, pf, v, vc, B flat	„ 4	1871	Durand.
2nd trio, pf, v, vc, d mi	„ 17	1872	Heugel.
Sonata, pf, v, C	„ 6	1871–2	„

Of all the musicians who contributed, during the last quarter of the nineteenth century, to the foundation in France of a symphonic school —till then lacking in that country—Alexis de Castillon was undeniably the most highly gifted, especially in chamber music.

It is well known that this brilliant cavalry officer of the Imperial Guard gave up a military career in order to devote himself entirely to the music which he had always so passionately loved. But, grievously misled by the nature of the teaching received from his professor of composition—Victor Massé—uninspired and utterly lacking in artistic feeling, he had finally lost all faith in his aptitude for music. He was even on the point of completely abandoning his studies, when, in the early days of 1870, he became acquainted with Henri Duparc, who was to become the dearest of his friends. The latter, struck by the young officer's musical gifts, advised him to see César Franck, who alone, he thought, could enlighten him and teach him the art of composition.

This interview was for Castillon the beginning of a veritable resurrection. With the help of the composer of the *Béatitudes*, he set to work bravely, and, in a few months, the quintet in E flat was finished.

Then it was that he destroyed all his early works written under Victor Massé's guidance, including the symphony, op. 1, dedicated to his former master, this same opus number being allotted to the new quintet.

One curious fact should be noted; in the whole history of music we find no composer who has written so many really fine works during so brief a career.

When one reflects that Castillon's productive period is limited to the last three years of his life, one is amazed at the activity of the artist's genius and the amount of work produced by a musician of unfailing loftiness of inspiration, whose style was as painstaking as it was individual.

In fact, from 1870 to the end of 1872, when he was attacked by the disease which was to prove fatal, Castillon wrote no less than seven chamber works, besides a considerable list of compositions that lie outside our province.

If we now pass to an examination of Castillon's chamber music we cannot fail to observe the perfect suitability, both of subject matter and of style, to the essential character of this class of music.

No man was ever more thoroughly a chamber composer than Castillon, and it is especially in this kind of music that his personality is most fully revealed.

It must not be inferred that its construction was entirely free from faults. Movements are to be met with in his works in which the sense of constructive balance is distinctly at fault, a fact which should cause no surprise, in view of the haste of his studies. He may also be accused of a tendency to follow some of Schumann's forms and to reproduce certain of his harmonic schemes; nevertheless, his work as a whole, by reason of its musical worth, may be allowed a high place among the manifestations of the Beautiful created by the masters, both predecessors and contemporaries.

We shall confine ourselves to a brief analysis of three of Castillon's works; and first the

PIANO QUINTET IN E FLAT MAJOR, OP. 1.

I. The opening allegro ben moderato, is quite in the classical style. A first theme (A), very melodic, and in the purest symphonic manner, is stated repeatedly, and leads to a transition ('bridge') of no great length, the rhythm of which grows slowly weaker and dies away in the bass.

Ex. 1.
Th. (A).

&c.

Then, suddenly, a loud trumpet call rings out,

Ex. 2.
(B^{1}).

given to the second violin, and repeated again on all the instruments; this is the opening figure of the second theme (B^{1}), which is linked to a gentler melodic passage somewhat after the manner of Beethoven (B^{2}), and ends with a purely rhythmic reminiscence of theme (A). This exposition is entirely in the key of the dominant, B flat, first minor, then major.

In the development which follows he has made the mistake of repeating the same passage, first in D flat major, then in G flat major, the second being merely a repetition of the thirty-eight preceding bars transposed a fourth higher.

Such a method of development by repetition, too frequently employed by Schumann, is always to be condemned, for, since nothing fresh is added, one's interest must needs decrease.

This is, however, the only occasion on which Castillon has committed such a fault. The remainder of the movement is devoted to the recapitulation of both themes, and is adorned by a charming and expressive ending.

II. The scherzo, allegro molto, A flat major, is a charming movement which reminds one of Saint-Saëns's scherzos. The trio, developed at some length, by combining the two main themes, returns, perhaps rather tardily, to the principal key.

III. Adagio molto maestoso, A flat minor. Here we meet with a movement in cyclic form, for the two themes, the primary elements of the adagio, will be used again and fully treated in the following movement which brings the work to a conclusion.

Our attention is at first occupied by a kind of ecclesiastical chant,

Ex. 3.
Th. (C^{2}).

preceded or announced by a figure of four semibreves.

Ex. 4.
Th. (C^{1}).

This chant, after several slight modulations, returns to the key of A flat, the major, this time leading to a broad ascending melody, quite characteristic of Castillon's genius. In the third section of the adagio we are plunged once more into the gloom of A flat minor, but soon the expressive melody rises anew, and, ending on the dominant of E flat, leads into the finale.

IV. At the beginning of the allegro molto, the theme (C^{2}), already heard in the adagio, bursts forth in agitated rhythm, and forms a lengthy preparation for the principal subject, derived from the 'announcing' figure (C^{1}). This new theme, which enters in E flat major, runs its course entirely in this key, and, shortly afterwards, appears again, after a development, which, it must be admitted, offers but little interest.

At length the two themes of the adagio unite with the principal subject and bring the work to a masterly end.

Sonata in C major, op. 6, for Piano and Violin. Very curious is the structure of this sonata, in which the composer seems to have tried to invent new forms, in three, at least, of its movements, but, having not yet acquired complete mastery of the art of tone-building, Castillon was unable to avoid the dangers arising from his temerity, and fell into some of the traps which this very audacity had laid for him. Nevertheless, one cannot help admiring the proportions of the structure, as well as the materials of which it is built.

I. Allegro moderato, C major. After an introduction of thirty-six bars, the scarce articulate utterance of an idea in the course of formation, there springs forth a theme full of freedom and beauty, which provides in itself almost the whole basis for the movement (Ex. 5). Given out by the piano, the theme is repeated in its entirety by the violin; it is then broken into short figures in changing keys, which thus form the transition to the second subject in E flat major—too brief to contend with the opening theme, which then reappears, with an unexpected return to C major, a mistake which seriously compromises the balance of the movement.

The development is founded almost entirely

Ex. 5.

Th. (A).

on the first theme, and, on a long dominant pedal—already employed earlier—leads to the recapitulation of the same theme, now rather too familiar.

However, in order to avoid the monotony which would result from a complete recapitulation, Castillon had the idea of replacing the 'bridge' passage by a fugal development which presents the theme disguised by a fresh rhythm, and in A flåt major,

Ex. 6.

Th. (A) (with change of rhythm).

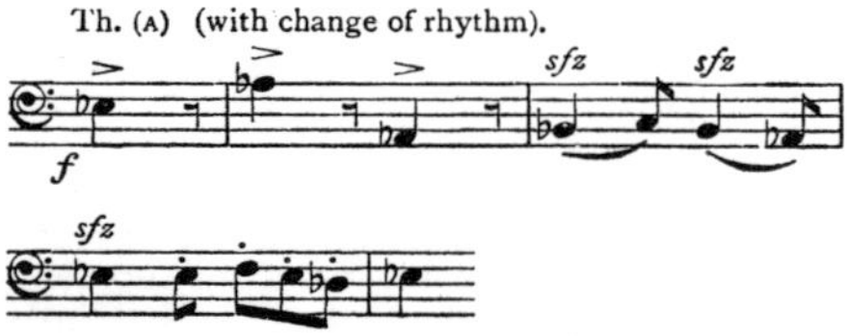

a very happy modification of the ancient sonata form; this slowly dying down, gives place to a fragmentary reminiscence of the second theme in the dominant key (G major). Here the movement, properly so called, ends, for the last two pages (thirty-six bars, on the dominant of A) are merely a kind of preparation for the appearance of the scherzo, thus balancing the thirty-six bars of the introduction.

II. The allegro scherzando is charmingly fanciful, but presents no particular structural features.

III. An andante in A minor, in Lied form, in three sections, the beautiful first theme of which is a prolonged and melancholy air, echo of some deep inner sorrow. A theme which requires no practising, and yet is extremely difficult to play, for it is not merely a question of the performer's bow, but of his heart and of all his emotional faculties in their highest degree.

The air, with harmonies based on the third Gregorian mode, endeavours to arise and cry aloud its sorrow . . . but, three times, an anguished and inexorable figure

Ex. 7.

bars the way, and forces it back once more. Yet it manages to escape this instrument of torture, and, in a burst of enthusiasm, flees to the latitudes of F major (beginning of the third section); but soon, as though exhausted by an effort beyond its strength, it sinks back, endeavouring to clutch at the tonality of A major, and, at last, ends its career in the prison whence it has vainly attempted to fly (third section).

This movement is of great beauty, and should, undoubtedly, arouse the admiration of all true lovers of art, and especially so if one reflects that Castillon's sonata was written six years before Gabriel Fauré's, and fourteen years before Franck's, the only violin sonatas with which it can be compared.

IV. The finale, allegro molto, opens with a theme which might be described as 'chivalric', glowing with noble pride, and with quite an individual rhythm.

Ex. 8.

This fine theme has only one fault, that of appearing too often. The second theme, much more tranquil, is, unfortunately, given out in a key (D major) too remote from the principal key. A development, very well treated, thanks to the striking rhythm of the opening, leads—perhaps at rather undue length—to a complete recapitulation of both themes, followed by a dazzling coda. The originality of this movement is mainly due to the persistence of the opening rhythm, which, combined in most interesting ways with the diverse elements of the movement, becomes thus its real and principal subject.

PIANO QUARTET IN G MINOR, OP. 7. In this work, which followed immediately on the foregoing sonata, Castillon is evidently seeking a renovation of symphonic forms, at least in the first and last movements, but his skill was insufficient to extricate him from certain hazardous situations in which his fancy had run away with him.

I. Larghetto and allegro deciso, G minor. As in certain quartets of Beethoven's last period, the introduction plays an important part in the first movement of the work. A motto phrase, which is to be treated later in the allegro—

Ex. 9.

opens the way to a broad and noble melodic theme on the dominant of G, which connects with the allegro by means of the passage already mentioned.

The exposition of the first theme, interrupted by a partial reminiscence of the introduction, in the relative major, seems to hesitate awhile before leading into a second theme, in three sections, the melodic style of which is, perhaps, rather too closely akin to that of Schumann. With this theme, which begins in E flat major, he commits the grave fault of slipping back, after the second section, into the original key (G minor) and concluding in it—which brings us back to where we were at the beginning of the exposition.

After a third appearance (four bars) of the introduction, the development—in two sections of no great length—leads to the recapitulation, in which the motto phrase, introduced in augmentation, leads swiftly to the second theme (G major), the third section of which is here replaced by a brief final development. This latter serves merely to bring in, for the fourth time, the great introductory phrase, which reappears in its entirety, with the addition of a melodic conclusion in which we discern both the opening phrase of the second theme and the motto phrase, which brings the movement to a close.

II. Scherzando (D major). A dainty minuet, full of curious rhythmic effects, but in the purest classical form. After the repeat of the scherzando, the trio returns once more, but a fragment only, in the key of C sharp major, and ends with a sudden return to the tonic key.

III. Larghetto, quasi marcia religiosa, in B flat major. Lied in three sections, the second of which (G minor) is very engaging. At the end of this second section the themes on which the finale is to be founded already make their appearance. The third section is short, the melodic phrase dies slowly away, and we pass, without a break, into the finale.

IV. This movement (allegro, G major) is oddly conceived. It is in the nature of a dance—in rondo form—the animation of which grows with each successive reiteration, so that the latter part has a speed about double that of the opening. The movement is in two distinct divisions. The first phrase, (A), is twice stated in the tonic key, then disappears almost entirely, and is replaced by the second theme, (B), in E minor. This theme consists of three phrases, the third of which is none other than theme (A), now in augmentation.

Now we come to an episode derived from this same theme, in B flat major; then the second theme is repeated once more, in G minor, and continues with a third and final statement in G major, leading to a short and brilliant conclusion.

From these examples one may gather that it is not too much to state that Alexis de Castillon was one of the most interesting figures among the originators of the movement which revived the cult of chamber music in France.

VINCENT D'INDY.

CASTRO, FRANCISCO JOSÉ DE, Spanish composer.

Lived in Italy in the second half of the seventeenth century. Composer of *Trattenimenti armonici da camera a tre, per due violini, violoncello e cembalo* (1695). (Liceo di Bologna.)

PEDRO G. MORALES.

CATALANI, ALFREDO, 1854–1893, Italian composer.

Suite (*A Sera Serenatella*), str. quartet. Ricordi.

CATHEDRALS AND CHURCHES, CHAMBER MUSIC IN.

I had the opportunity many years ago of taking part in chamber music in various churches in and near London. I can only remember the name of one of them, St. Stephen's, Lewisham (where Dr. Warwick Jordan, an excellent and enterprising musician, was organist); and only the name of one piece, performed in a church at Highgate, I think, viz. Rheinberger's trio for organ, violin, and 'cello; but I do remember that the acoustics were in every case so good that it was a joy to draw the bow across the strings.

In the 'seventies I travelled on more than one occasion in Sweden, where there was a dearth of concert halls. Chamber concerts in that country were then held almost exclusively in churches, and the same phenomenon of good acoustics was to be observed.

Now, in this new century, there is an interesting movement for the promotion of chamber music performances in our cathedrals, and what, indeed, could be more appropriate for such surroundings than music of the devotional character to be found in the slow movements of the great masters, especially those of Haydn and Beethoven? Dr. G. J. Bennett, of Lincoln Cathedral, is one of the pioneers of this movement, and has favoured me with two programmes of quartet recitals given by the Kendal Quartet in November 1923 and December 1925. These programmes include Beethoven in D, op. 18, and C, op. 59; Brahms's C minor, op. 51; and Dohnányi in D flat, op. 15.

Dr. Bennett tells me that he took care to have a raised wooden platform with plenty of room for the players, and the effect was very fine. The players were situated in the centre of the nave, which is very extensive, but it was never felt that the music was lost in the large space. All the parts came out wonderfully well, and the atmosphere of the building seemed to impart an added beauty to the music.

Another pioneer was Mr. Henry Coleman, who, in Oct. 1923, as an experiment, brought the McCullough Quartet to the Cathedral at Peterborough (of which he is the organist), to play Beethoven's op. 59, in C, Schubert's *Death and the Maiden* variations, and Tchaikovsky's andante from op. 19. I was much interested to hear from Mr. Coleman that during the preceding days he visited about eight of the elementary schools, with gramophone records of the pieces, and talked to the children about them, teaching them to sing the tunes. As a result, about 500 children came to the recital of their own free will, and listened with deep attention.

Musical history tells us that chamber music (musica da camera) began in the church, and should, or would, find its place in the church to-day but for the financial question. The truth is that either the clergy or private individuals will have to grant subsidies if these recitals are to be continued, for I understand that the collections taken do not suffice for the engagement of a professional Quartet. Another alternative is to give the proceeds to a charity, and so secure the suffrages of a public whom the music alone fails to attract.

I do not pretend that the above exhausts the list of chamber recitals given in churches; on the contrary, I believe that the custom prevails in many parts of the world of giving this 'offering of music', as it has been fitly called, in consecrated buildings. .Mr. Hubert Hunt tells me of chamber music played in Bristol churches, and Miss Fanny Davies related to me a thrilling experience she had as listener at the Koppelkerk in Amsterdam, a very fine round church in which the Bohemian String Quartet gave a special concert in 1920. It was the twenty-fifth anniversary (silver jubilee) of their first concert tour in Holland, and they selected the Schubert D minor and the great A minor of Beethoven for performance. 'They had', Miss Davies writes, 'tried the acoustics of the church late the night before on their way from the station to the hotel, after a concert and a long train journey. They chose the centre of the large gallery. A platform was put there, the seats being removed for a moment. When they started it was broad daylight (in November), but a friend of theirs and myself had matches ready to light up the candles[1] on each side of their desks as soon as the light failed, the church being otherwise unlighted. During the first quartet there was enough daylight for the beginning of the Beethoven. Then it began to darken and we lighted the candles. They grew brighter as the church dimmed, and the effect of these four devoted artists offering up such music in such surroundings was indescribable.

'When they left, after going very carefully down the dark staircase from the gallery and getting safely into the street, there had congregated several hundreds of people who shouted "Thank you, thank you (*Dank*). Come back, come back"; and they cheered so loudly that one might have heard them all over Amsterdam. Then they drove off in the prosaic hotel omnibus.'

That these artists play in other churches from time to time, and that this is but one of their many adventures of the kind I doubt not.

I could also write much more about piano recitals in churches, but that is not within the province of this book. However, I may mention that Miss Fanny Davies, in July 1921, played successively in Westminster Abbey, in York Minster, and in the splendid Cathedral of Winchester; on charitable as well as artistic aims intent. Her very first piano recital, and probably the first in England given in a church, was at Bloxham, on 27 June, 1921. EDITOR.

[1] The mention of candles reminds me of an amusing incident which happened to me a few years ago. I was playing Bridge's phantasy trio with Septimus Webb and Felix Salmond at a concert of the Tonal Art Club. The electric light temporarily vanished, and there was nothing for it but to ask listeners to hold candles to each part—a device which enabled us to finish the work, the audience remaining in darkness. [ED.]

CATOIRE, GEORGES LVOVITCH, 1861–1926, Russian composer, pupil of Liadov.

Quintet, 2 v, vla, 2 vc, e mi	op. 16	Russ. Musik-V., 1909.
Quartet, str, f sharp mi	„ 23	„ „
Quintet, pf, 2 v, vla, vc	„ 28	Russ. State Ed., 1920.
Quartet, pf, v, vla, vc	„ 31	„ „ „
Trio, pf, v, vc, f mi	„ 14	Jurgenson, 1902.
Sonata, pf, v, b mi	„ 15	„ 1924.
Poème, pf, v	„ 20	Russ. Musik-V., 1909.

Catoire is now a professor at the Moscow Conservatoire. His music attracted the notice of Tchaikovsky, whose influence is very noticeable in Catoire's early works. But the composer soon began to display an individuality whose main features are harmonic refinement and a keen sense of tone quality and rhythm, by virtue of which he occupies a place of his own among contemporary composers. To-day he is one of the oldest Russian composers, and may be considered as the father of Russian modernism, for in his work are asserted the very principles which guide the composers who most fully represent the newer tendencies in Russia. For instance, Catoire evinces a great fondness for syncopated rhythms, and deals with them in masterly fashion.

His output in chamber music is considerable and attractive. It may be divided into three groups: the violin sonatas, the music for bowed instruments, and the music for combinations including the piano. Of the two violin sonatas, the more significant is the second, which bears the title *Poème*, and is remarkable not only for its technical mastery, but for the quality of its substance, which is powerfully eloquent and deeply emotional.

The string quartet and string quintet are simpler and more perspicuous in style than the works for bowed instruments with piano, in which the composer often resorts to ample figured patterns, whose texture, from the harmonic point of view, is far from simple.

This last group comprises a piano trio, a piano quartet, and a piano quintet. The trio is an early work, but the others belong to the period of the composer's maturity. Yet all have a good deal in common from the point of view both of style and of instrumental technique. V. M. Belaiev.

CELLIER, Alexandre, b. 1883, French organist, pupil of Widor.

Quartet	str	a mi	Leduc, 1919.
Second quintet	pf, 2 v, vla, vc	b mi	Senart, 1922.
Sonata	pf, vla	G flat	,,
Sonata	pf, vc	G	Rouart, ,,

The quartet is a work of restricted length, written mainly in classical form, with a recapitulation in the finale of the themes of the preceding movements. The 'cello sonata is sincerely felt, personal work, classical in construction, and effective.

CENTOLA, Ernesto, b. 1862, Italian violinist.

Petite Suite napolitaine, pf, v	op. 12	Augener-Schott, 1905.
Petite Suite italienne, pf, v	,, 14	Decourcelle, 1904.
Petite Suite orientale, pf, v	,, 15	Augener-Schott, 1904.
Petite Suite militaire, pf, v	,, 31	Augener-Schott, 1906.
Petite Suite napolitaine, pf, v	,, 32	Kistner, 1907.
Petite Suite romantique, pf, v	,, 33	Rahter, 1906.

Music of a not very serious kind which seems to have attracted the attention of many publishers.

CETTIER, Pierre, b. 1874, French composer.

1st quartet	str.	D	Hayet.
2nd quartet	,,	F	Senart.
Quintet, pf, fl, ob, cl, fag		G	,,

† CHADWICK, George Whitefield, b. 1854, American composer, pupil of Jadassohn, Reinecke, and Rheinberger. Director of the New England Conservatorium (Boston).

	Composed	
4th quartet, str, e mi	1895	Schirmer, 1902.
5th quartet, str, d mi	1898	,, 1900.
Quintet, pf, 2 v, vla, vc, E flat	1887	A. P. Schmidt, 1890.

Chadwick's chamber compositions occupy an important and distinguished place in American music, on account of the presence of traits peculiar to American folk music, or what has been accepted as such. He has written five string quartets and one piano quintet, of which only the quintet and the last two quartets have been published. The period during which these six works were produced stretches over two decades, from 1878 until 1898, since when he has ceased to write chamber music. They do not, therefore, represent the composer in his later and ripened phase; but they make up in youthful vigour and spontaneous melody for what they may lack in depth of feeling. Their chief merit is the adroit handling of the instruments and the scholarly treatment of the musical fabric, to which may be added the quality, alluded to, of being more recognizably native, in certain ways, than any music written previously; indeed, Chadwick deserves to rank as a pioneer in the musical development of America.

The Fourth String Quartet is in four movements: (1) andante moderato, (2) andantino semplice, (3) giocoso, un poco moderato, (4) allegro molto risoluto.

The second and third movements especially are distinctly idiomatic; many of the themes are pentatonic in character. While some of the melodies suggest either the plaintive chants of the old negro slaves or their more exuberant mood of gaiety, there is no absolute borrowing of either 'spirituals' or syncopated dance tunes of the coloured race. It is rather a free imitation of and a refinement upon the idiom of negro music. The result of that process is not a foreign substance, an exotic ingredient, for the composer, in assimilating these characteristics, has made them his own—perhaps a little bleached—but for that matter all the more native, all the more representative of the white man of North America, of the Anglo-Saxon become Yankee, as he was at the end of the nineteenth century. The ultimate product is a melody of unmistakably folk-song cast and clearly national feeling. The following themes, (*a*) from the second movement, and (*b*) from the third, may serve as instances:

(*a*) *Andantino semplice.*

(*b*) *Giocoso.*

THE FIFTH STRING QUARTET is in four movements: (1) allegro moderato, (2) andantino, (3) leggiero e presto, (4) allegro.

The quartet begins in a rather sombre mood, suggestive of a ballad or weird tale such as tradition has preserved many in the New England states. The music, again, reeks of the soil, and the same impression prevails in the quiet and contemplative second movement. The third movement is, to all intents and purposes, a scherzo, and shows the composer in the happiest possible light. Chadwick's humour is marked, but never heavy or grotesque; the music is sparkling and fluid in spite of its designedly jerky rhythm, and is a bravura piece in the best sense of the word. The concluding movement takes up the thread, and spins it on with touches of frank and almost rustic gaiety.

THE QUINTET is in four movements: (1) allegro sostenuto, (2) andante cantabile, (3) intermezzo (allegro un poco risoluto), (4) finale (allegro energico).

It is the earliest of Chadwick's published chamber works, and the least personal. It is strongly diatonic in harmony and severely classical in form, but abounds in felicitous moments, betrays throughout the hand of experience, and in the second movement proves the composer capable of writing a broad and poignant cantilena. It begins on the first violin, accompanied by the other strings. A short transitory passage leads into a more animated section, which calms down, and is finally interrupted by a mysterious horn call. Then the piano takes up the cantilena, and after another interruption by the imaginary horn, this time a fourth higher, the song comes to a fervent but subdued close. The third movement might be termed a quasi-minuet. It is graceful and has an old-world touch, though it successfully avoids being laboriously archaic. The final movement begins *pp* with an accompanying figure on the piano that savours of the pentatonic jingles, over which the strings enter with the horn-like main theme. Material and development follow classical lines, even to the fugal section, and the use of the fugue subject in the manner of a chorale in an antiphonal discourse between piano and strings, which culminates in a brilliant peroration.

CARL ENGEL.

[My own first acquaintance with Chadwick's compositions was in 1890, when his piano quintet was sent to me from Germany. At that time there was not the plethora of new music which exists at present; perhaps we were not as critical then as now. Certain it is that this new writer, versed in the best German traditions, both surprised and pleased us by his themes of exceptionally long breath, his harmony, pure and diatonic (it was not then unfashionable to write diatonic harmony), and by the chamber musical physiognomy of the whole quintet. Quite different and distinctively American is his string quartet in E, which, like Dvořák in F, appeals to musicians and laymen alike. I, for one, am very grateful to Mr. Chadwick for the pleasure his chamber music, as much as I know of it, has given me.

EDITOR.]

CHAMBER MUSIC.

(*a*) BEGINNINGS.

The expression 'chamber music' (Italian 'camera', German 'Kammer') signified originally the music belonging to the household of a prince, as opposed to the music of the church or the theatre. The modern meaning of the term has become both enlarged and restricted: chamber music is no longer the prerogative of princes, but its range is generally limited to music suitable for private rooms, performed by not more than one instrument to a part. Before the middle of the eighteenth century it is difficult to distinguish separate categories of secular music apart from the theatre. Up to the end of the sixteenth century it is often impossible to distinguish vocal from instrumental music; during the seventeenth and even part of the eighteenth it is equally hard to draw a line between the instrumental music intended for solo players and that intended for massed instruments. It is towards the beginning of the seventeenth century that the term 'chamber music' comes to be applied to music for domestic performance, but it was not necessarily limited to instrumental music. Probably its first appearance in English is in the title of Martin Peerson's *Mottects or Grave Chamber Musique* (1630), which is a collection of 'songs of five parts'. Peerson had in 1620 published another collection of 'songs of four, five and six parts' under the title of *Private Musicke.*

It is erroneous to suppose that the sixteenth century was an age of pure vocal music unaccompanied by any instrument. The standard musical form at the beginning of the century was the *chanson* or *canzone*, sometimes a folk-song, sometimes an original melody, given generally to the tenor in its simple form, and accompanied by the other voices in imitative counterpoint, with the result that the individual strains of the tenor melody are separated by rests of varying duration. This form may have been originally intended for voices, but it was at once adapted to all sorts of instruments. The parts (generally four) could be played by viols, either as accompaniments to a solo voice or without voice at all; they were also arranged for the organ, for stringed instruments with keyboards, and for the lute. Later in the century, when the madrigal had begun to take shape, it was often accompanied by instruments, especially when performed on ceremonial occasions, and it was nothing unusual for the melody to be sung by a voice with instrumental accompaniment. Byrd in the preface to his

Psalmes, Sonets, and Songs of Sadnes and pietie (1588), tells us that most of these were originally composed as solo songs with accompaniment of four viols, afterwards arranged for five voices. Music of this type may certainly be classed as chamber music, especially in England, where there was considerable musical ability among amateurs both in town and country. Later sets of madrigals are often described by their composers as 'apt for voices or viols'. The history of this early English school of chamber music has been discussed in another article. (See Consorts of Viols.)

In Italy, the real home of the madrigal, music seems (as far as we can ascertain) to have been practised more in the numerous small princely courts than in the middle-class circles which pursued music with so much assiduity in England and Germany. The madrigal in time became practically obsolete, though its name was sometimes applied to a vocal form which is to some extent descended from it: namely, the duet for two voices accompanied by a figured bass, in which the voices are treated with great elaboration of counterpoint. They were studies, or possibly show-pieces, for singers, and are often of very great beauty. This form survived up to the middle of the eighteenth century, Handel being one of its greatest exponents. The vocal chamber music of Italy in the later seventeenth and early eighteenth centuries, though hardly coming under the category of chamber music as we understand the term to-day, is of considerable importance in the history of musical form, and also on account of the influence which it had on the instrumental music of the time. It will be discussed later in this article.

Towards the end of the sixteenth century the word 'sonata' makes its appearance, denoting a piece of music composed for instruments and not for voices. It seems to have been applied originally to music composed for the church, not for the chamber, and its home is Venice. In character it bears more affinity to orchestral than to chamber music, such instruments as trumpets and trombones being employed in addition to strings in considerable number. But the most obvious function of instruments is to play dance music, and as a natural consequence the forms of classical instrumental music are derived chiefly from dance forms. A collection of canzoni by Florenzio Maschera, published at Brescia in 1584, shows that the term canzone, as applied to instrumental music, included straight-forward dance tunes as well as those treated in imitations. There is nothing specifically instrumental about the style of these pieces; they might just as well be sung as played. Canzoni for instruments were published about the same time by Floriano Canali and Costanzo Porta for double quartet of eight instruments. It must be remembered that, in practice, music of this kind was played with variations of considerable elaboration, according to the inclination of the performers. Giovanni Bassano's *Ricercate, Passaggi e Cadentie* (1585) gives examples of the style. Impromptu variation of this type, reasonable enough when a dance tune had to be played over and over again for dancing, soon led to the practice of composing really artistic variations on a tune, such as are found in great quantities in the English composers for the virginal.

A definitely instrumental style appears in the ricercari and canzoni of Antonio Cifra (1619), and soon after this time it becomes customary to indicate the instruments by their own names, instead of calling the parts simply by the names of voices (canto, alto, &c.). A nearer indication of the modern style appears in the compositions of Biagio Marini (1600?–1655?). His works cover a period of nearly forty years, and his output was considerable. He is the most important early composer of chamber music in the modern sense, if indeed he is not its creator, and he seems to have been the first travelling virtuoso violinist. He paid several visits to Germany, and exercised a notable influence on German composers. His favourite combination appears to have been that of two violins and bass, in preference to larger groupings, and although to modern ears chamber music in three parts may sound thin, the step was in those days a very important one to take, for it allowed the two violins much more freedom of range than was possible in strict four-part harmony. It established the system of the basso continuo or thoroughbass for bass viol, lute, organ, harpsichord, or whatever instrument might be convenient, as the foundation of instrumental music, whether for chamber, church, or theatre. The reader will gather from Professor Donald Tovey's article on Haydn how modern chamber music could not come into being until the continuo system was abandoned altogether, but from the beginning of the seventeenth to the middle of the eighteenth century it was regarded as indispensable. During that period the classical sense of harmony and tonality was gradually growing, and the continuo, improvised at the harpsichord, represented the general background of harmonic feeling. But in playing seventeenth-century chamber music to-day, whether the accompanist plays a piano part worked out for him by some modern editor, or whether (as is far more desirable) he follows the practice of the seventeenth century and extemporizes from the figured bass, it is necessary never to lose sight of the fact that the bass part, intended originally for a bass viol or violoncello, is conceived by the composer *as a melody*, as well as a support for harmony; and if, as often happens, it has to be played on the piano, the player must treat it with a careful sense of melodic phrasing and in an expressive cantabile style. Indeed, it often happens that Italian sonatas for two violins and bass will sound far better played by two violins and 'cello (without piano) than by two violins and piano (without 'cello), even though this entails the sacrifice of the harmonic background; the contrapuntal gain more than compensates for it. The right combination, of course, is 'cello with piano or harpsichord as well.

How far Marini was himself responsible for the new style it is impossible to say, but it is noticeable that other composers came under a new influence about this time. Thus Tarquinio Merula's first book of four-part canzoni (1615) belongs definitely to the earlier period, while his second book, containing canzoni for two violins and bass (1639), belongs equally definitely to the new generation, and shows leaping figures clearly characteristic of the violin. These works of Merula are further important as showing the germs of the true sonata style, in which a series of contrasted movements is linked together in an organic whole. The practice of linking pavan and galliard with a common theme, as practised by the English composers (*vide* CONSORTS OF VIOLS), had to some extent foreshadowed this, but the tendency of composers who based their style on the contrapuntal forms—fantasias, ricercari, &c.—was to treat single movements at sometimes wearisome length. Dance forms were treated with great skill and vivacity by Andrea Falconieri, whose *Canzoni, sinfonie e fantasie*, mostly for two violins and bass, were published at Naples in 1650. Biagio Marini's *Sonate da chiesa e da camera* of 1655, for two violins, viola, and bass, show a definite grouping of movements, generally three in number, and the employment of a slow introduction to an allegro. Marini, it may be mentioned, was the first composer of sonatas for solo violin, but such works are outside the scope of this Cyclopedia.

Another interesting composer of this period is Maurizio Cazzati, whose sonate a tre show the alternation of slow and quick passages. He also wrote some very effective dances for five instruments, in which we can see that the new style of writing for strings could be made useful even with massed instruments. But perhaps these works are hardly to be classed as chamber music. Cazzati's music was well known in England in his time, and had some influence on English composers. To the same period belongs Giovanni Battista Vitali—not to be confused with Filippo Vitali, a composer of the early seventeenth century, or with his own son Tommaso Antonio Vitali, who also wrote for the violin. His works cover the period from 1666 to 1692, so that he brings us to the age of Corelli. Vitali was a very accomplished contrapuntist, but this did not prevent him from producing dances which in their freshness and vigour of melody are worthy of Purcell. French music, as shown in the operas of Lully (who, after all, was an Italian by birth), had at this time a strong influence on all other nations of musical Europe. It is shown in the sonatas of Vitali by the appearance of such new dance forms as the sarabande, gavotte, and bourrée. Vitali shows clearly that he realized how a sonata might be unified by using variants of the same theme for each movement. This does not prevent the movements from being thoroughly well contrasted, for the thematic unity is merely suggested and not pedantically insisted upon.

Following these writers comes a large group of Italian composers of chamber music who lead up to the historic figure of Corelli. The sonata was by this time more or less standardized in form, whether for church or chamber. In our day it may seem strange that a sonata for two violins and organ should form an habitual part of a church service, but the custom of performing them in connexion with religious ceremonies prevailed for a very long time. Tartini played regularly at the church of St. Anthony in Padua, and the form survived even as late as Mozart's early Salzburg days—his sonatas for two violins and organ, composed for the cathedral of Salzburg, are still worthy of performance, though known to very few Mozart lovers.

Early instrumental music was derived, as we have seen, from vocal music, and this dependence on the vocal style for some time hampered the development of instrumental freedom. As the violin gradually ousted the viols, a more vigorously rhythmical style came into music, not into instrumental music alone, but into that for voices as well. The classical style which arose in the early seventeenth century, to reach its culmination in Bach and Handel, depended ultimately on a strongly stressed sense of rhythm, such as only instruments could properly express. As Parry says, 'the pre-eminent characteristic of instrumental music was rhythm, whereas the pre-eminent characteristic of vocal music was melody'. The Italians fortunately had far too strong a vocal and melodic sense ever to lose sight of melody in writing for the voice, but, towards the middle of the seventeenth century, it becomes evident that the violin style had given a new brilliance and energy to vocal music, and this new style was naturally turned to the fullest advantage in the music of the opera. Vocal music for a long time took the lead in Italy. In spite of all the absurdities of Italian opera, in spite of all that we read about the vanity and stupidity of singers, it is abundantly evident that Italy had singers who were musically and intellectually a good deal in advance of the instrumentalists. The chief proof of this lies in the extensive cultivation throughout the seventeenth century of the chamber cantata.

The popularity of the chamber cantata may be estimated from the fact that Alessandro Scarlatti alone composed over 500. It was in his days a stereotyped form, just as the violin sonata was, but it was actually a more advanced form in some ways. It generally consisted of an introductory recitative, an aria, another recitative, and a second aria in a contrasting style. It was in fact a sort of sonata for a voice and bass, if the contradiction in terms may be permitted. Italian chamber cantatas must in fact generally be criticized more as abstract music, like violin sonatas, than as direct expressions of a poet's emotions. To compare them with scenes from operas is to miss their intention entirely. The best of them invariably show a contrapuntal interplay of voice and 'cello which is quite unsuited to the stage and is conceived in the purest spirit of chamber music. Sometimes cantatas were accompanied by additional instruments—a solo violin, two violins, or the whole quartet, or in other cases wind instruments, always treated with careful regard for their separate individualities. One of the most interesting features of the arias is the elaboration of their form. Italian poetry, even of that quite conventional type which was inevitable when cantatas were produced in such immense quantity, always had a certain deliberately unsymmetrical arrangement of lines, and this, coupled with the practice of repeating words and phrases, led to a most ingenious elaboration of musical motifs within a form that was perfectly balanced as regards tonality. Scarlatti, and some other composers, evidently regarded the chamber cantata as a field for experiment, and we frequently come across cantatas in which, within a single aria, are to be found the most astonishing modulations and the most subtle designs of phrase and motif. As studies in musical form these cantatas are far in advance of anything written for violins. But the cantatas were not without their influence on the instrumental sonatas. Some composers, such as Legrenzi, distinguished themselves in both fields, and those who confined themselves to instrumental music, like Corelli, undoubtedly felt the influence of the delicately expressive vocal aria. Later on, in the following century, the influence of operatic music on symphonic music is very apparent; even vocal recitative finds its instrumental counterpart. Definitely dramatic expression, e.g. the repetition of some single passionate word, intensified by the operatic composer with imitative treatment in the bass or other parts, was taken over by instrumental composers, and gradually led on to what in the days of Beethoven we call thematic development.

A natural result of this vocal influence was the gradual disappearance of the sonata for two violins, and the emergence of the sonata for violin solo with a bass, but the two-violin sonata held its ground to the end of the seventeenth century and for some little time beyond. The chief fault of the sonata for two violins was that composers, in their anxiety to make both violin parts equally interesting, often spoiled the beauty of their melodies by too frequent crossing of the parts. In a quick movement, where the instruments take each other up with short bustling figures in semiquavers treated in imitation, this crossing of parts is very effective, but in long sustained melodies—and as vocal influences became more powerful the instrumental melodies naturally became longer and more personally expressive—one instrument must either become frankly subordinate to the other or it must insist on its equality at the cost of mutual interference.

The chief composers of this period are Andrea Grossi (fl. 1679–1685), Tommaso Motta (1681), whose only claim to interest is that he seems to have been the first composer to employ in two-violin sonatas the quasi-extemporary rhapsodical prelude beloved of the harpsichord and organ composers; Giovanni Battista Bassani (1657?–1716), whose works were the chief model for Purcell's sonatas; Giuseppe Torelli (d. 1708), the first writer of concertos for solo violin, but also a composer of sonatas for two violins (1686); Domenico Gabrielli, Giovanni Battista Gigli, Giovanni Legrenzi (1682) and Giovanni Battista Mazzaferrata (1674). Mazzaferrata's sonatas, though they are all in the contrapuntal style of the church sonatas, without dance movements, show an extraordinary vivacity and brilliance; in this quality they surpass Corelli.

Arcangelo Corelli (1653–1713) published his first set of twelve sonate da chiesa for two violins in 1681. They have no dance movements, but consist of an introductory grave, an allegro of serious character, generally in common time, an adagio, generally in triple time, and a final allegro which is often in 6/8. The allegros are always contrapuntal, but not strictly fugued. The subjects of the serious quick movement at times closely resemble those of vocal arias of the same period, which lend themselves well to contrapuntal treatment, not unlike that pursued by the vocal writers in their chamber duets. The final movement, though contrapuntal, is generally based on a strongly rhythmic theme which falls naturally into regular periods of two or four bars; it is, in fact, not very far removed from a gigue. In the ninth sonata the introduction is enlivened by rhapsodical arpeggios on one chord, rather suggesting trumpet passages, and leads to the allegro by a solemn strain of four bars which reappears with slight modifications after the final allegro in 3/4, as a conclusion to the whole sonata. The final allegro is based on an arpeggio figure obviously akin to those of the introduction.

The second set of sonatas is for the chamber, and exhibits a totally different style. The movements are short and (except for the introductory grave, which does not always make its appearance) in the form of dances, whether so called or not—that is, they are not contrapuntal and derived from the old canzona, but divided into two halves by a double bar with repeats. Contrapuntal writing appears now and then, but it is discreetly kept in the background. The place of the slow movement in triple time is taken usually by a corrente, which sometimes suggests that the slow movement of the church sonatas is not far removed from a corrente played at a more sober pace. These chamber sonatas show a far greater variety of forms than the church sonatas, for Corelli will sometimes treat a dance movement in imitation, and will sometimes open his sonata with a grave or adagio which has the regular binary form of a corrente or allemande. His gigues, too, are by no means squarely conventional; they obtain delightful rhythmic freedom by the unexpected mixture of three-bar and four-bar phrases. The twelfth sonata is in one movement only; it is a chaconne on a ground bass which starts with sixteen bars of largo and then breaks into an allegro. The ground is treated with great freedom, sometimes transferred to the violins, and sometimes modulating into different keys; the theme of the ground itself is considerably varied even when kept in the bass. These sonatas were published in 1685.

In the third set (1689) Corelli returns to the church style, but we note at once that this set is much more vigorous, and indeed vivacious, than the first. In the very first sonata the place of the slow movement is taken by a movement in 3/4 time, marked vivace and divided into two repeated sections like a corrente. It is, as a matter of fact, more lively than most of his corrente movements, though it conforms in some way to the ecclesiastical style by a certain breaking of the square rhythm and the employment of contrapuntal passages. The twelfth sonata is peculiarly interesting for its greater freedom of style; it begins with an extended rhapsodical introduction consisting of arpeggios for the two violins on the chord of A, while the bass holds a tonic pedal. This is followed by an allegro in 3/4, consisting of a still longer pedal on E above which the violins execute more fantastic arpeggios and scales, arriving finally at seven bars of simultaneous arpeggios in gigue rhythm, dropping suddenly to a solemn adagio of linked suspensions. The next movement is an energetic vivace in which the violins play in square cut rhythm above a bustling bass in semiquavers, ending with a few bars of adagio; after this comes an allegro in the manner of a fugue, and the sonata ends with another allegro in 6/8. This third set of sonatas represents Corelli in his mature style. All the movements have striking melodic themes treated in a broad and masterly manner; the first allegro is generally based on a subject of vigorous character which clearly foreshadows the typical fugues of Bach and Handel.

In the fourth set (*Sonate da camera*)—1694—we are struck by the vigour and energy of the style, but at the same time we cannot fail to notice a sign that points to the coming decadence of the sonata for two violins:—the first fiddle is plainly master of the situation, and the second is gradually receding into the background. In the few contrapuntal movements, which now appear obviously conventional in character—though their convention survived, growing more and more archaic, for another hundred years or more, traceable in the quartets of Haydn, Mozart, and even Beethoven, where it seems like an echo of the old ecclesiastical style—the second violin has certain pretensions to equality, but he is rarely allowed to cross above his partner; the first violin may occasionally condescend to meet him on equal terms, but he will permit no familiarities from one who is definitely his inferior. Corelli's fifth set of sonatas (1700) was for one violin only; the seventeenth century is at an end.

On the testimony of Georg Muffat (1701) Corelli was the creator of the concerto grosso for two solo violins and 'cello accompanied by string orchestra in four parts. According to Muffat these had excited admiration in Rome as early as 1680, although Corelli did not publish his concertos until 1712. Corelli in that case supplied the model for the concerti grossi of Torelli, but Torchi (*Rivista Musicale Italiana*, 1898) says that concerti grossi had been written still earlier by Stradella. The concerto grosso, although it may have been considered chamber music in Corelli's days, lies outside the scope of this work.

The early chamber music of other countries now requires consideration. French chamber music is dealt with in another article; Mr. Dolmetsch has treated English chamber music up to the disappearance of the viols. Before continuing the history of English chamber music in the latter half of the seventeenth century, it is more convenient to turn to that of Germany, which is closely connected with both English and Italian chamber music.

In the days of Shakespeare several English actors, acrobats, and musicians visited Germany, where their performances excited much admiration. The visit of the Shakespearian actors is a landmark in the history of the German theatre, and the English musicians had a still greater influence on the course of German music, for many of them accepted posts at German courts and in the Hanseatic cities. A great deal of English instrumental music was printed in Germany in the early years of the seventeenth century, some of which is hardly known in England at all. The most noteworthy of these English musicians were John Dowland, Walter Rowe, John Price, Thomas Simpson, and William Brade. Price held posts at Stuttgart and Dresden; Rowe settled at Berlin, where he founded a school of players on the viola da gamba. Even later in the century Germans went to England to learn the art of playing this favourite instrument. Simpson published various collections of English music in Germany, and so did Brade. The latter, whose works hardly exist outside the libraries of Wolfenbüttel and Liegnitz, was a strikingly original composer. He published four collections of pavans and galliards for six instruments before his death in 1630. Brade is also considered to be the founder of the Hanseatic school of violin playing, and a chorale with variations for violin solo (MS. in the library of Upsala) shows him to be one of the first composers of solo virtuoso music for the violin.

It is difficult to say how far these English works should be considered as chamber music. In Simpson's miscellaneous collection there are several pieces which we can identify as belonging to masques which had been performed at the English court, but it is probable that in Germany, if not in England as well, such music served the purpose of domestic entertainment too. The Thirty Years' War was a severe hindrance to all branches of German art, but gradually in the course of the seventeenth century there sprang up in Germany numberless small musical societies, very largely consisting of amateurs, who met to play together in what was called a Collegium Musicum. Towards the beginning of the eighteenth century these meetings were called by the name of Akademie, from the Italian *accademia*, which was the regular word for a concert in Italy; it has not yet entirely died out there, and is still the habitual word for analogous performances, such as an assault-at-arms. The Collegium Musicum drew little distinction between chamber and orchestral music; such differences depended mainly on the number of members that the society possessed. Music was much cultivated at the universities, as it was in England, where Oxford was a leading musical centre. It was customary for students to make up a band, and serenade their professors and other distinguished persons at night. Rosenmüller's suites of 1654 were composed for this purpose. The influence of the English composers is clearly apparent in the German suites for several instruments, but the chief use made of these suites seems to have been at banquets or on other ceremonial occasions. But as early as 1617 mention is made (Schein's *Banchetto Musicale*) of the amateur, and as late as 1704 J. P. Krieger expected his *Lustige Feldmusik* (i.e. military band music) to be played in the same way as Schein's wind-music—by amateurs in private with strings.

Travelling Italian virtuosi came to Germany, beginning with Biagio Marini (1623), and stirred up the German players to the development of high technical skill. The travelling virtuosi were not altogether free of charlatanism; Farina of Mantua, who was in Germany from about 1627 to 1637, published compositions which are partly studies in extravagant effects of technique, and partly farm-yard imitations. The Germans seem to have been deeply interested in technical devices such as SCORDATURA (*q.v.*) and elaborate double-stopping. One of the most famous executants was Thomas Baltzar of Lübeck (1630–1663), who came to England, where he published solos which are full of four-part chords. Sonatas for two violins in the Italian style are comparatively rare in Germany; the Germans seem to have preferred either suites which must be regarded as orchestral music, or solo sonatas for a single violin. A curious and characteristic example is that of Nicholas Bruhns, a distinguished organist and pupil of Buxtehude, who according to Mattheson's account played elaborate polyphonic music on the violin, and himself played the bass for it on the organ pedals at the same time. Rosenmüller published some church sonatas after the manner of Legrenzi in 1682; the best works of this class produced in Germany are the sonatas of Evaristo Felice dall' Abaco, a Veronese who settled at Munich in 1704. He was a pupil of Torelli and Vitali, and his work shows great dignity. The most daring and original of the German violinists, H. F. von Biber (1644–1704), seems to have confined himself to solo sonatas and suites for string orchestra.

In England after the Restoration French influences were naturally strong, but Purcell, in spite of owing a good deal to French methods, was a fervent admirer of the Italians, whose music he considered to be much more serious. He was in much the same position as a young English composer of early Victorian days might have been if he had despised the predominant Italian school and professed admiration for Beethoven and Schumann. In 1683 he published his first set of twelve 'sonatas of three parts' for two violins, bass, and harpsichord, stating in his preface that they are a deliberate imitation of the Italian style. It has generally been supposed that Bassani provided his model, but Mr. Fuller Maitland thinks it more probable that the style was based on the sonatas of G. B. Vitali (1677). The question is of small moment, for Purcell's individual English character is very apparent in these works, and, in spite of his professed admiration for the Italians, it is clear that the English tradition of Matthew Locke was an equally powerful influence in the formation of his style.

These sonatas are in the style of the sonata da chiesa, without dance movements. They are often longer than the Italian sonatas, having sometimes six or seven movements, and the single movements are all developed at some length. Purcell's contrapuntal mastery is of the first rank, and his fugue subjects have singular originality. Even where he adopts a conventional Italian type of theme, he soon betrays himself by some peculiarity of counterpoint, or by some strange harmony resulting from his characteristic use of the melodic minor scale, descending as well as ascending. The slow movements in triple time have much more affinity to English songs than to Italian arias or dances; the English hornpipe rhythm peeps out in his allegros, and in the slow introductions the rhythms are often those of the old English masque music familiar in the work of Lawes and Locke.

The second collection—ten 'sonatas of four parts'—is for the same instruments, in spite of the misleading title. These were not published until 1697, two years after the composer's death. They are also sonate da chiesa in type, and show a greater mastery of the form than the previous set. The harmonies are often astonishing, and the whole style shows Purcell's individuality in a very marked manner. Indeed, they have far more originality than any of Corelli's works, even those of later date, though they have not that Italian charm which has won Corelli the affection of all generations and all countries. The fifth sonata is noteworthy as being one long chaconne on a ground bass repeated without variation on the bass forty-four times. The ninth is the so-called *Golden Sonata*.

Purcell's sonatas unfortunately founded no school of chamber music in England. The only English works of any merit in that form after Purcell's are those of William Boyce (1710–1779), which show the curious English habit of keeping up traditions which other countries have long cast aside.

Chamber music on seventeenth-century models gradually died out in the first half of the eighteenth century. It gave place to the solo sonata and the concerto. Alessandro Scarlatti wrote a few unimportant chamber works; a sonata for flute and two violins, which is of very little interest, and four sonatas for string quartet, expressly marked senza cembalo. They are agreeable works in the style of Corelli, though they must have been written after 1715. Except for the fact that they are probably the earliest string quartets apart[1] from the music of the Elizabethan period, they contribute nothing new to the history of chamber music. They found their way to England and were printed by an English publisher as concerti grossi, along with two other concertos which are probably not by Scarlatti, added in to make up the conventional set of six. Bach, prolific as he was in every branch of music, left only two sonatas for two violins and one for violin and flute, all three of them works of great beauty and charm. Handel's output is larger. In his early days at Halle he composed a set of six sonatas for two hautboys and bass, which he revised later and published in London. They are of great originality and beauty. A second set of six sonatas was printed by Walsh in 1733 for two violins, hautboys or flutes. Chrysander printed three trios found in MS. at Dresden along with these in the German Handel Society's complete edition. A third set of seven was printed by Walsh in 1739. All of these works show Handel's distinct individuality, and many of them are interesting as showing the influence of native English music. There is a very attractive set of sonatas for two violins by Pergolesi, and trio sonatas of interest were also published (many in London) by the brothers Giuseppe and Giovanni Battista Sammartini. The younger brother, who is the more important of the two, was the teacher of Gluck. The music of Sammartini clearly foreshadows the style of Haydn, and he is in fact one of the chief creators of that symphonic style which led to the symphonies of the classical school of Vienna.

[1] See art. ALLEGRI.

There is a complete break between the chamber music described above and the classical chamber music which begins with the string quartets of Haydn. The ancestry of Haydn's quartets is not to be sought in such works as the quartets of Alessandro Scarlatti, but in the symphonies of Sammartini[2] and the South German composers at Vienna and Mannheim who followed in his footsteps. The classical string quartet is a reduction and refinement of the symphony for string orchestra, which accounts immediately for the entire want of connexion between the style of Corelli or Handel and that of Haydn and Mozart. String quartets in the classical manner do not appear in Italy until about 1770, and it is obvious that these works derive more from the model of the Viennese school than from their own Italian forerunners.

EDWARD J. DENT.

(*b*) GENERAL SURVEY.

The purpose of this Cyclopedia is to deal with chamber music in the main sense in which the term has become classical. But, like most classical terms, chamber music has meant different things at different periods, and has developed by evolution. It is a mistake to try to reduce early and late products of an evolutionary process to a common definition, but even a cyclopedia of chamber music must set practical limits to its scope. There are theoretical objections to any limit that can be proposed. These may be removed by a statement which clearly shows the relation of what is excluded from the main scope of the work to what is included.

The great change which came over the whole art of music after the middle of the eighteenth century affected chamber music no less profoundly than it affected opera. Nobody would quarrel with a history of opera for beginning with Gluck, so long as it did not wholly ignore his antecedents, archaic, prophetic, and decadent. But the kind of operatic art from which Gluck revolted rested on principles so radically

[2] Haydn strenuously denied that he was influenced by Sammartini. [ED.]

and, to our notions, so obviously wrong, that all attempts to revive it must savour of antiquarianism. This is not the case with the chamber music of the earlier eighteenth century; its principles, though now obsolete, were consistent and true to the nature of the instruments, and its masterpieces can never become antiquated. And their quantity is enormous. The whole mass of the chamber music of Bach, Handel, the Italian violin masters and the French clavecinists, must be far more voluminous than the sum-total of important chamber music from Haydn onwards, even if vocal music be excluded. And to review it, or even to read a review of it, is a task at which librarians might quail.

Fortunately for the reader, though it cannot be ruled out on artistic grounds, it is all based on two principles which are radically opposed to those of the later classical chamber music with which this Cyclopedia is mainly concerned. Accordingly, the first part of the following article is devoted to illustrating the theory and practice of the continuo in the earlier chamber music, with occasional remarks on the other archaic principle, the mechanical use of 4-foot and 16-foot stops on the harpsichord and organ, the instruments to which the continuo was entrusted.

Though much has been written about the continuo, no writer has hitherto shown its relation to the aesthetics of later chamber music. But unless this relation is clearly understood, we cannot properly understand the revolution effected by Haydn and Mozart, nor fully appreciate the qualities of purity and euphony in chamber music style. The continuo and the use of 4-foot and 16-foot doublings represent important musical instincts. To ignore or misunderstand them is to deprive the earlier chamber music of its euphony.

In the later chamber music the continuo instinct sometimes reasserts itself (often without the composer's realizing its origin) as an impurity of style; especially when he is in the habit of composing at the piano.

The first part of the following article is therefore essential to the scheme of this Cyclopedia. Though it seems, *ex hypothesi*, to fall outside the main scope of the book, that scope cannot be defined without it, and its topics are too often and too fundamentally misunderstood for any less detailed explanation to suffice.

The Continuo Period.

For the general purposes of a dictionary, chamber music may be defined as instrumental music written for a group of individual performers, and intended to be heard for its own sake in such rooms as are to be found in private houses. Dance music, and music intended 'to accompany the clatter of dishes at a princely table' exclude themselves from the category of music intended to be heard for its own sake.

The size of the room is not a matter for rigid definition; the hundred and fifty years during which the classics of chamber music were composed were a period of royal and aristocratic patronage, and the rooms for which the music was designed were the rooms of palaces. And it is not an unmixed evil that chamber music should be heard in halls that are too large for it. The necessity can arise only because of a remarkable public demand for the highest and most spiritual form of music, and the acoustic disadvantages have a distinct value as a stimulus to the imagination. The listener naïve enough to expect the *ff* of Schubert's D minor quartet to sound loud in a concert-room holding an audience of 2,000, learns in five minutes to prefer spiritual to material values in music, if he can learn anything. Nevertheless, the classical idea of chamber music implies bigness as well as intimacy, and the listener is not enjoying the normal effect of a trio or quartet unless the sound is filling the room. This classical notion of bigness determines the art-forms; no classical chamber music is merely lyric. Beethoven's fugue in D major, op. 137, for string quintet takes less than four minutes to play, and begins and ends softly; but fugues are not lyrics, and Beethoven's sketches for this opusculum are entangled with ideas of a fugal opening which afterwards took shape in the scherzo of the ninth symphony. Other short pieces of chamber music are either large sets of variations or fragments of projected complete sonata schemes. Schumann's *Märchenerzählungen* and Dvořák's *Dumky* trio are exceptional groups of lyrics by composers who otherwise accept the classical view that a chamber work must contain at least one movement in developed sonata form. This rule is a natural result of the feeling that when two or more people are gathered together to play music, they may as well take the opportunity of doing more than can be done by one person. In Germany it is even considered a solecism to call a duet concert a chamber concert; chamber music is held to begin with trios. An upper limit has not been assigned. Mozart's serenade in B flat for thirteen wind instruments is, for reasons which will appear in the course of this essay, within the limits of classical chamber music, though even the most experienced wind players will feel in its performance that a conductor adds much to the comfort of a group that is twice the size of the wind band of any symphony before Beethoven.

Mozart's group of thirteen, however, does not include trumpets and drums, that is to say, it includes nothing which is either enormously stronger in tone or enormously inferior in musical resource to the rest of the ensemble. The trumpet in Saint-Saëns's little septet is almost the only instance[1] of the introduction of such powerful orchestral artillery into

[1] See art. Trumpet.

chamber music in a classical style, and here the classical style is jocosely archaic.

The double-bass (or as in Mozart's serenade, the contra-bassoon) does undoubtedly bring into chamber music the question of inferiority in musical resource. This will be discussed later, but here we may conveniently note that inferiority in musical resource is not to be measured by the amount of conspicuous display, whether in melody or flourishes, but by the necessity for the use of the instrument. And the double-bass may obviously be very necessary for the support of so large a group as eight or more instruments.

The criteria thus far indicated for classical chamber music seem simple and not formidably exacting. Every part is to be necessary, and the ensemble is to be complete in itself. Therefore an instrumental group must be capable of making a coherent ensemble, so that, whatever the art employed in combining sounds on different planes of tone, the chamber music style does not encourage the use either of an instrument which cannot be allowed to use its normal strength, or of one which cannot make itself heard without constant strain on its own part and constant repression of the other instruments.

Obvious as this all seems, there is a whole classical period in which none of these criteria can be taken literally. In the article on HAYDN it is shown that the main life-work of that composer may be regarded as devoted to organizing the art of making groups of instruments cohere as effectively as groups of voices. Instruments do not normally so cohere, and the commonest form of bad instrumentation is that of the composer whose orchestral and quartet writing is choral and organ music distributed among combinations of instruments. The worst feature of such a style is that it does not sound obviously bad, except to a highly experienced and discriminating ear, which resents the feeling of wasted opportunity as immediately as an insulting cacophony, for the grammar of the chorus and the organ has a universal validity in virtue of which its use as a basis for instrumentation may best be vindicated and condemned by the term 'fool-proof'. But during the period of supreme mastery of the chorus and the organ which culminated in Bach and Handel, nothing is more significant than the absolute and instinctive renunciation of all attempt to make groups of instruments cohere in the same way as groups of voices. Haydn showed how to make them do so as effectively, but on principles fundamentally different; this he could never have done if the masters before him had not cultivated their sense of the different planes of instrumental sounds with minds untroubled by the problem of focusing the planes together. Nor were they wrong in neglecting this problem. Difference of plane gives rise to an enormous number of the highest aesthetic qualities in all arts; and there is no imperfection in a scheme of instrumental music in which the main parts are left completely free to execute polyphonic designs, while the task of supporting these designs with a coherent mass of harmony is relegated to a continuo player extemporizing on a suitable keyboard instrument from a figured bass.

In modern performances of such music grave errors may arise from ignorance of two matters which were common knowledge to all Bach's musical contemporaries: first, the art of filling out a figured continuo part, and, second, the general characteristics of early eighteenth-century musical forms. Without a careful explanation of these matters it is impossible to appreciate the immensity of the task achieved by Haydn and Mozart, an immensity hardly understood by any of their contemporaries, in obtaining the harmonic background from the principal instruments themselves without the aid of any permanently subordinate part. Until this was achieved, chamber music could not be defined as an ensemble to which each player contributes an individual part. For not only did the individual parts themselves not claim to be complete without the impersonal continuo, but the very notion of an individual part was purely musical, and independent of the number of performers. Bach's organ trios are trios for two manuals and a pedal-board, to be played by one organist. But his trio in *Das Musikalische Opfer*, for flute, violin, and continuo, realizes its intended effect only when four instruments play it, viz. the flute, the violin, a 'cello to play the bass of the continuo, and a keyboard instrument to fill out the harmonies according to the figures. Without the 'cello to lift the bass of the continuo on to its proper plane as one of the three trio parts, the mere filling out on the keyed instrument fails to complete a trio in Bach's sense.

In modern times four great errors arise in the treatment of the continuo. First, there is the total omission to fill it out—an error which so little impairs Bach's gorgeous polyphony that most listeners devoutly admire the resulting coldness of tone as a mysterious classical virtue. Secondly, there is the filling out with a tone on the same plane as the real parts—an error impossible to a harpsichord player, who had but to draw the right stops for an accompaniment instead of playing on solo or tutti registers. The third error is the attempt to work out the figuring in a kind of polyphony that competes with the real parts. The fourth and worst error is the filling out with parts that avoid doubling or otherwise colliding with the main lines. This error is assiduously inculcated by theorists who also fiercely denounce the substitution of the piano for the harpsichord. But the piano is, as Philipp Emanuel Bach pointed out, even better than the harpsichord for continuo work, only it must be remembered that the contemporaries of Bach's sons knew both instruments, and could make no mistakes as to the kind of piano touch required. A piano filling-out can be made into an ideally soft background, but the instincts of the average modern pianist do not incline that way, and nothing can be more banal than the intrusion of an ordinary pianistic mezzo-forte into the background tone of an eighteenth-century polyphonic design. The error of a too elaborate polyphony in continuo work rests upon records of Bach's own marvellous freedom therein, but a little practical experience shows that ordinary skill in handling harmonic progressions will, with the aid of an occasional imitation of four notes of a scale in thirds or in contrary motion, cause the naïve listener to gasp with astonishment, and spread abroad the legend that everything has been decorated in six-part canonic counterpart. As a fact in practice and aesthetics, nothing is more miserable than the attempt to fill out Bach's polyphony with additional individual counterpoints. The efforts of Robert Franz were thought, in their own day in the middle of the nineteenth century, to be indistinguishable from Bach's own real parts. At the present day it is hard to understand how anybody could have thought such bundles of dropped stitches and loose ends acceptable on any theory, though worse things have been perpetrated in more recent editions of Bach. The fourth error is all the worse for the erudition that is still spent on its cultivation. Franz, in his edition (B. & H.'s *Kammermusik-Bibliothek*) of Bach's trio (from *Das Musikalische Opfer*), condemns the continuo realization by Bach's masterly pupil Kirnberger as a setting that 'tramples on all the fine flower of Bach's polyphony'. Unfortunately it is Franz's own setting that tramples on the fine flower, systematically, and exactly as he differs from Kirnberger. Franz thinks of the filling-out as on the same plane of tone as the main parts, or, to conceive the matter conversely, he thinks of the ensemble as it would sound if the flute and violin were played on one piano and the continuo on another. In such conditions a collision between a plain chord and the same chord plus a long appoggiatura would be hideous, as any one may satisfy himself by playing the D major cantabile theme in Beethoven's G major concerto on two pianos instead of one piano with orchestra. But when the sounds are on different planes, the chords on the lower plane must always be complete in themselves, and should seldom double even the weightier ornamental discords of the main parts. No harshness whatever can result from collisions between ornamental notes in the main planes and essential chords in the background, nor between two distinct main planes. Bach, in this very sonata, rejoices in collisions between the violin and the flute which he would not have allowed between two violins. Kirnberger's continuo is right in two important matters: first, that it gives Bach's essential chords completely without doubling his ornamental discords, and second, that it is in strict four-part harmony. But it gives no countenance to the impossible theory that such four-part writing must avoid moving in unison with the main parts. Such asceticism can never have been attempted in real life, for the continuo-player never had anything but his figured bass to play from, and so could not have dodged unisons with the main part however much he might wish to do so. And to succeed therein is only to violate one of the first principles of instrumentation, viz. that when two or more bodies of sound are on different planes, each must be intelligible by itself whatever the others may add to its meaning. The idea that the continuo-filling could ever have attempted to avoid doubling the main parts cannot survive one intelligent perusal of the relation between voices and orchestra in any chorus of Bach or Handel where the orchestra has florid independent parts.

But though Kirnberger is true to his art and technique in setting his continuo in four real parts, the intention of his setting is not adequately represented merely by playing it softly on the modern piano. Bach's harpsichord had 16-foot as well as 4-foot stops, and we know from his first biographer Forkel that he was so impatient of gaps in the middle of the continuo harmony that he would often put in 'three new parts' (i.e. a handful of inner notes) over the continuo-player's shoulder. It so happens that the only practical normal position for continuo harmonies is for the right hand to play three notes to a chord at a safe distance from the bass. The drift of the suspensions and other discords is sure to go downwards, and the bass is sure to rise frequently, until the harmony is forced into close quarters and will have to spring apart again. But the 16-foot register of the harpsichord, or the Lieblich Gedackt stop of the choir-organ, fills up the gap exquisitely softly, and the piano can reproduce the effect either by filling out the chords extremely fully, or by taking almost everything an octave lower, in either case with the smoothest pianissimo and no sense of percussion at all. A 'cello should always be used to play the bass throughout in as cantabile a style as the upper instruments, and the pianist should refrain from doubling its ornaments and rapid details.

The following example from the beginning of the trio in *Das Musikalische Opfer* will show the principles involved. Here (Ex. 1) is the ensemble of flute, violin, and continuo, the main part of this last being played by a 'cello. (Note the collision Bach allows between violin and flute in bar 6.) And here (Ex. 2) is a schematic filling-out of the figuring on Kirnberger's lines, but with the assumption that a 'cellist is

Ex. 1.

playing from his own part so that its throbbing rhythm and expressive details (e. g. the theme in bar 5) need not be doubled by the modern piano.

Ex. 2.

And this is the sort of way in which the piano can compensate for the loss of the 16-foot register of Bach's harpsichord; the quaver rest in the fifth bar being designed to let light upon the 'cello with its theme (Ex. 3).

Ex. 3.

Kirnberger, whose copy of the continuo evidently differed from the original score in detail, as all Bach's various copies differ from each other, often takes account of the long appoggiaturas in bars 1 and 3, which are neglected on principle here. Sometimes such points are in the figuring. But it would be a fundamental error to fill out the first bar thus—

Ex. 4.

taking its final anticipation as seriously as the complete triad at the end of bar 5. And the attempt to avoid unisons between the continuo and the main parts could only lead to such miseries as

Ex. 5.

which no human touch could render a tolerable filling-up of Bach's harmony.

From all this it is clear that it was a mighty task to bridge the gulf between chamber music on the continuo-hypothesis and the dramatic sonata style of Haydn and Mozart with its substitution of pure instrumental self-sufficiency for depersonalized melodic polyphony. Perhaps the most important fact which separates the earlier from the later chamber music is the power of harpsichord registers to multiply the written sounds in different octaves. This power, which the organ develops on an incomparably larger scale, utterly obliterates the qualities on which chamber music from Haydn onwards is based, and it is this, rather than the accident of ecclesiastical associations, that has debarred even a small domestic organ or (*pace* Dvořák) the best of harmoniums from sharing in anything that we now call chamber music.

The art forms of early instrumental music are embodied with such crystalline clearness and solidity by Bach, and the conceptions underlying them are so essential to a correct understanding of how to perform not only his works, but those of Purcell and Handel, that a mention of the main elements is essential. The dance forms used in Corelli's sonate da camera are obviously in line with those of the suite, partita, or ordre. Corelli's type of sonata da chiesa, with its introductory or intermediary adagios and its fugal allegros, is an equally obvious origin of Lully's French overture; and the French overture, again, stimulated by the importance of the ballet in French opera from the earliest times, after beginning like a sonata da chiesa, naturally develops the forms of the sonata da camera in a series of dance tunes.

Another early art form to which Purcell and Biber clung as if to save themselves from drowning in the pathless ocean of early instrumental music was the ground-bass, a form which by its constant repetition of a single sentence in the bass provided a rigid principle, immediately intelligible and capable of indefinite extension and fine cumulative effect. Bach's examples of it in its rigorous form are so famous that we forget that they are very few. In chamber music he developed a modified form in which the ground-bass now and then turns into a new key, so that in about four groups of variations the movement has accomplished a circle of keys without either abandoning or interrupting its ground-bass. The typical example of such a modulating ground is the third movement of Bach's A major sonata for cembalo and violin.

But the paramount art form of early eighteenth-century chamber music is derived from the concerto. The origins of concerto form are vocal, and so slight are the barriers between vocal and instrumental art forms in the early eighteenth century, that Bach, the most accurate exemplar of all forms, is the master who achieved the most astonishing translations from one medium to the other, transcribing concerto movements and overtures into great choruses, and, conversely, turning arias into slow movements of concertos. This explains and almost justifies the policy of the Bach-Gesellschaft editors in classifying all his secular vocal works as chamber music.

Indeed, the continuo period might just as well be called the aria period, and the whole of its chamber music be regarded as primarily vocal; the only objection would be that no definite notion of chamber music would be left. For it makes no great aesthetic difference whether two or three arias are grouped, with interspersed recitatives, into a chamber cantata, or thirty arias into an opera, and presented amid gorgeous stage trappings to a large public. At least three-quarters of Handel's numerous vocal cantatas are to be found dispersed in his forty-two operas, and it is a matter of indifference whether the operatic or domestic environment came first. The essential point is that the principal art form of the period was neither the fugue nor the binary dance form, but the aria And the form of the aria is precisely that of the concerto. It depends on the fact that the voice inevitably thrusts all instrumental sounds into the background. Hence the most effective way to expand a vocal melody into a big movement is to let instruments play the gist of it in a single musical paragraph, so that it becomes lifted to a higher plane when the voice takes it up and expands it with other themes and brilliant passages. The instrumental ritornello will then intervene, entire or in part, wherever closes are made in foreign keys, and it will complete the whole by its final delivery in the tonic.

Now with proper treatment a solo instrument throws an orchestral tutti into the background as naturally (though not so forcibly) as the human voice does with all instruments. Hence the aria form became the foundation of the concerto style as soon as composers began to value the contrast between solos and orchestral groups. And this contrast was closely imitated by the various registers of the organ and the harpsichord, the composite tones of the octave registers giving a clear representation of tutti ritornellos, while a solo stop on one manual and a soft accompaniment on the other cannot fail to produce the effect of the entry of a solo instrument. When we have learnt to recognize this concerto form wherever it occurs in early chamber music, our notions of interpretation will be delivered from many an arbitrary and misleading tradition, and our imagination will have a better stimulus than guess-work. Of course Bach's Italian concerto, for harpsichord alone, is as nearly schematic in its illustration of the method as a work of genius can be, but it does not stand alone. In his chamber music almost any large allegro not in binary form will become clear as soon as we mark out three types of passage, viz. the tuttis, the solos, and the ensemble passages which imitate the blending of solo work with independent orchestral detail. Each type of passage should be kept on its own plane of tone, and, while no artificial restraint should be imposed on the capacity of modern instruments for expressive nuances, the players should regard it as nonsensical to drift from one plane of tone to another in such a way as to blur the lines of concerto form. No such mistake was possible to the players of Bach's age; and the composer seldom gave explicit directions, for he could not foresee that doubt would ever arise.

The present work cannot attempt to deal with any but the outstanding composers of genius, whose works shine against the background of a period in which the art of continuo music was almost a gentlemanly accomplishment. To catalogue even the names of these gentlemen of the background is as hopeless as to represent the common run of pamphlets and sermons in a review of eighteenth-century literature. More to the purpose is it to indicate what instruments are represented by numerous and important works, and this part of the subject is in the hands of Mr. Dolmetsch.

THE CENTRAL CLASSICS OF THE SONATA STYLE.

Every peculiarity of the piano is in keeping with the new and dramatic spirit which entered into all kinds of music from the operas of Gluck to the symphonies and string quartets of Haydn. To those who have in modern times been thrilled by the rediscovery of the organ-like richness of plain two-part writing on a harpsichord with 4-foot and 16-foot registers in play, nothing in the history of the sonata style is more surprising than the cheerfulness with which Mozart and Haydn accepted the renunciation of all attempts to apply such registers to the piano. Henceforth no written note was to represent more sounds than that of its own name and octave. The enrichment of harmony by doubling in octaves must be achieved by individual human fingers or players, and not by mechanical couplers. On the other hand, the sustaining of harmony was no longer exclusively the work of individual fingers; a pedal could prevent the dampers from stopping the sound when the fingers left the key, and so an arpeggio of single notes might leave behind a chord vibrating throughout four or five octaves with a rich and slowly evanescent sound transparent to all other instrumental tones. Thus the sonata ideals of chamber music and the style of the piano stimulated each other, and speedily determined the criteria which are valid from the time of Haydn to the present day. These classical criteria may be formulated under two headings, as follows.

I. Chamber music is music in large forms for a group of solo instruments on equivalent planes of tone and of equivalent musical capacity. The planes of tone need not be the same; on the contrary, the value of the piano in chamber music depends largely on its being inevitably on a different plane from all other instruments, but it has no difficulty in refraining from shattering the ensemble like a trumpet or a trombone, and the ear takes pleasure in low notes on a 'cello as a bass to full chords on the piano, the difference of plane being essential to the special effect. The introduction of the singing voice into the scheme, as in Schönberg's second string quartet and sextet, introduces a non-equivalent plane of tone, and accordingly goes beyond the classical criteria. A further step, both as to planes of tone and non-equivalence of musical resource, is shown in Schönberg's *Pierrot Lunaire*, where the singer is required to follow a prescribed rise and fall of pitch in a speaking voice, carefully avoiding definite musical notes. In the opposite direction, Cyril Scott and Arthur Bliss use the singing voice without words in an instrumental ensemble.

The question of equivalent musical capacity was frequently raised in classical masterpieces by the use of the double-bass. In a mature style of chamber music this instrument, which, with the best of playing, cannot compete effectively with other stringed instruments in cantabile passages, justifies its existence as a support to large groups, especially such as contain wind instruments, as in Beethoven's septet and Schubert's octet. Even so, it associates itself naturally with the lighter and looser style of art typified by the serenades and divertimenti of Mozart. Early in the nineteenth century, Onslow, a prolific writer of chamber music, having occasion to use a double-bass as a makeshift for a 'cello, found the effect so satisfactory that he wrote numerous quintets for two violins, viola, 'cello, and double-bass. It is not clear from his notation in what octave he means the double-bass to play. Even in Dvořák's far more highly organized quintet in G, the double-bass does not seem quite at ease in the drawing-room, and its one shy cantabile remark in the minuet of Goetz's piano quintet is a pathetic triumph of unconscious humour.

Stravinsky's introduction of drums, trombones, and similar artillery into chamber music marks another new epoch with new criteria. What these criteria may be, we shall know when a propagandist arises who can convince us that a totally unprepared extemporization by a dozen players will not pass muster with him as a masterpiece of modern music. Stravinsky knows what he is doing; and experimental art is more important than experimental propaganda.

II. Chamber music requires no more than the number of players for whom individual parts are written; and every note written is intended to be heard. We have seen that chamber music before 1760 did not aim at this criterion; it was created with infinite labour by Haydn. The masters who may be taken as realizing it instinctively and imaginatively from first to last are Mozart, Beethoven, and Brahms. All who have attempted to write chamber music approximate to it at their best moments. But we may here profitably glance at some typical cases where music, otherwise beautiful and important, shows a defective sense of this criterion. It is interesting to note, by the way, that the criterion is never more severely maintained than in the most experimental works of the present day. Indeed, the desire to experiment with non-equivalent planes of tone and non-equivalent musical capacities goes naturally with the utmost sensitiveness to the individuality of each instrument. It is rather to the immediate successors of Beethoven that we must turn for examples of the confusion of thought natural to men who feel secure in a classical tradition not of their own making.

Certain tremolo passages in the string quartets of Mendelssohn are often, and not unfairly, quoted as bad examples of orchestral writing in chamber music. But here we must beware of a worse confusion of thought than Mendelssohn's. There is no harm whatever in one kind of good music sounding like another kind, if it has the virtues of both kinds.

If any good orchestral sounds can be realized by a string quartet, so much the better for the quartet. What is wrong with Mendelssohn's tremolos is that they are conceived mechanically on the analogy of orchestral passages, and carried to lengths which only an orchestra could make acceptable. On paper the storm in the development of the first movement of Beethoven's quartet, op. 74, looks quite as coarse, but it would at the outset be far too thick for orchestral writing, and its wonderful diminuendo is all drawn exactly to scale in a quartet which, as a whole, is one of the most ethereal compositions ever written. The same praise is due to such apparently crude simplicities as the stiff minims with which the violins and 'cello accompany the viola solo in the second variation of the finale. Dante or Milton never surpassed that calm—

'They also serve who only stand and wait.'

We are on less slippery ground in dealing with the integrity of the parts in classical chamber music. The immaturity of Haydn's piano trios in this respect is discussed, together with traces of piano ideas in one or two of his string quartets, in the article on HAYDN, due warning being given there against neglecting to view the value of the parts in relation to the degree of polyphony suited to the style. An honest violinist will be compelled to say that the second violin part of a Mendelssohn quartet is more interesting than that of one by Mozart. But this does not make Mendelssohn a better quartet-writer than Mozart. His work is on such a much larger scale that it often droops and fails, like the full-sized machine of an inventor who does not realize that its powers do not increase in the ratio of its bulk to that of the working model. The sympathetic but critical study of Schumann's chamber music will show more clearly where the criterion applies. With a full and sonorous piano style, he has even more than Haydn's curious inability to refrain from putting into the piano part all that the other parts have to say. Indeed, he has altogether lost the power of sorting out his material into its proper planes, and the exquisite first trio of the scherzo of the piano quartet is in such a tangle of useless and arbitrary doublings that it is impossible to discover the persons of the dialogue. Mozart, Beethoven, and Brahms would have delighted in making it stand out as a beautiful dialogue between five singing parts, the three strings and the pianist's right and left hand, with no confusion between these parts and the supporting chords to which each instrument would contribute between its own distinct entries with the themes. It is impossible to argue that there is aesthetic value in Schumann's unclarified scoring of this passage. The piano quartet is more highly organized than its delightful and popular brother the quintet. But the perversity of inattention to the integrity of parts can hardly be more clearly demonstrated than by the fact that, while the string parts of the quintet are such a primitive mass of harmony that there is no reason why they should not be arranged for quartet, sextet, or string orchestra, the opening of the piano quartet shows serious practical reasons why it should have been a quintet!

We must not confuse the criteria of mere part-writing with those of the treatment of an instrument as a whole. There is no reason why a string quartet should not, by means of double stops, produce a passage that effectively imitates an octet. But there is no excuse for making a string quartet play for pages together in such masses of double stops that there is no more evidence of four individual players than in a piano four-hand duet. It is no defence that such writing (as in Grieg's G minor quartet) is 'effective'; to prolong it is to do a ridiculously easy thing at the expense of all higher possibilities. César Franck's string quartet is in this way a disappointment to every one who can appreciate the essential, if sometimes harmlessly orchestral, quintuplicity of his great piano quintet. The string quartet is full of excellent organ music, and it imitates the organ very skilfully. But, except for the scherzo, which is full of anybody's brilliance, there is strangely little evidence that it is a quartet at all.

These criteria are unquestionably correct, whatever disputes may arise as to their application. In conclusion, it may be as well to enumerate, and occasionally comment on, some of the principal combinations used in chamber music, beginning with Haydn.

I. *Duets.*

(*a*) Two violins: magnificently exploited by Spohr, whom the severe discipline of this problem stimulated to his best work.

(*b*) Violin and viola, represented by two masterpieces of Mozart written to help Michael Haydn to complete the execution of a commission for six. The extra low fifth of the viola greatly eases the pressure on an imagination confined by the violin to a bass no lower than its open G.

(*c*) Two 'cellos: a magnificent medium, very sonorous in spite of its severe restrictions, and very little explored.

(*d*) Piano and violin. The most frequently attempted form of chamber music, and by far the most treacherous. The progress, from the use of the violin as a hardly necessary accompaniment to its perfect partnership in the ensemble, is beautifully shown in the works of Mozart's childhood, from his seventh year to his twelfth. There is a gap between these and his adult sonatas. With occasional lapses, his later sonatas, like Beethoven's, make severe but legitimate demands on the players' and listeners' capacity to focus the two planes of tone into one picture. For this reason duets for

(*e*) Piano and 'cello are much easier to write when it occurs to a composer to attempt them. There are far fewer 'cello sonatas of all kinds than violin sonatas in existence; but a much larger proportion of the former is good.

(*f*) Piano and a wind instrument. Here, as with other combinations, the horn and the clarinet have had the best chances, the flute being inconveniently weak for the piano, the oboe being apt to pall when not frequently relieved by other tones, and the bassoon being insufficiently appreciated except as a comedian, though Mozart wrote a sonata for 'cello and bassoon. Technical limitations, even when so severe as those of the natural horn, do not hamper the composer's imagination once it has been stirred, but he is absolutely inhibited by the suspicion of an incompatibility of tone.

II. *Trios.*

(*a*) String trios for violin, viola, and 'cello are a rare tour de force not necessarily less valuable than string quartets. Mozart's divertimento—trio in E flat—is a marvel of euphony, and proceeds for pages together without a double stop. Beethoven's string trios are among the very greatest works of his first period.

(*b*) Trios for two violins and 'cello are mostly the aftermath of the continuo period.

(*c*) Trios for piano, violin, and 'cello. Of all combinations with piano this is the one that has stimulated composers to the finest results. Haydn's trios, imperfect as they are in point of integrity of parts, are full of his grandest forms and most pregnant ideas. Mozart sets the standard with his inevitable schematic accuracy. The autographs of his trios are written in a way that shows to the eye one of the important normal criteria of the style. He writes the violin above and the 'cello below the piano. And with all their rich subsequent developments of piano style, both Beethoven and Brahms retained the idea of the 'cello as an independent bass below the piano, but, like Mozart, giving it freedom to mount to its highest regions, and neglecting none of its possibilities.

The ordinary notation which puts the violin and 'cello together above the piano expresses another fact about the combination: viz. that when the piano is combined with two or more instruments, these tend to form a single antiphonal body of tone. This is equally the case when a wind instrument enters the combination; the three distinct planes of tone separate easily and naturally into two groups, namely the piano and the other two instruments. Some of the combinations represented by important works are:

(*d*) Piano, clarinet, and viola (Mozart);

(*e*) Piano, clarinet, and violoncello (Brahms, Beethoven);

(*f*) Piano, violin, and horn (Brahms).

The piano and two wind instruments have also been successfully combined, the softest combination being with clarinet and horn. Publishers are reluctant to undertake the sale of such works unless alternative arrangements for more usual instruments are provided. When the composer executes these with freedom, the results are extremely instructive, both where they succeed and where they fail to give an adequate translation of the original.

(*g*) Among curious trio combinations mention should be made of Beethoven's tour de force for two oboes and cor anglais, a full-sized four-movement work within the compass of less than three octaves and with no possibility of a chord in more than three parts. His jocular serenade for flute, violin, and viola has inspired Reger to two essays in this slender combination.

III. *Quartets.*

(*a*) In the string quartet for two violins, viola, and 'cello we have the purest and highest revelation of chamber music and perhaps of all music. Its criteria need no further discussion here.

(*b*) The flute and the oboe have each been deliciously combined with strings in short works by Mozart.

(*c*) Quartets for piano and strings are surprisingly rare considering the popularity of the existing classical examples. Mozart's two masterpieces should have belonged to a set of six (*vide* article MOZART). They show with the utmost clearness the principle of setting the strings in antiphonal mass against the piano, and are at the same time exquisitely polyphonic. Later publishers tried to atone for former errors by arranging Mozart's clarinet quintet, D major string quintet, and quintet for piano and wind, as piano quartets. Nothing can be learnt from these.

Apart from three juvenile essays, Beethoven's only piano quartet is an arrangement of his quintet for piano and wind, op. 16. The piano part is unchanged, but the string parts are full of excellent new detail inserted during the long rests of the wind instruments, these rests being unnecessary for string players.

Mendelssohn's three juvenile quartets are wonderful for a boy of thirteen, and the third, in B minor, has many intrinsic merits. After this there is nothing important, except the beautiful Schumann quartet, before the masterpieces of Brahms.

IV. *Quintets.*

(*a*) String quintets differ little from quartets. The favourite extra instrument is a second viola, but, apart from the merely decorative works of the 'cellist Boccherini, the combination with a second 'cello is revealed as a majestic art form by Schubert in his great C major quintet. See the article on BRAHMS for the history of his own effort for this combination.

(*b*) The clarinet makes a glorious combination with a string quartet, as has been shown by Mozart and Brahms. Mozart also wrote a charming little quintet for the curious combination of one violin, two violas, 'cello, and horn. His most unclassifiable quintet is the adagio and rondo for flute, oboe, viola, 'cello, and glass harmonica, evidently a most skilfully planned combination.

(*c*) Quintets for wind instruments present a peculiar problem, especially centred in the group of the five different members, flute, oboe, clarinet, horn, and bassoon. Even under the stimulus of a prize competition, nothing great has been achieved, though an extraordinary amount has been written for this combination. Towards the middle of the nineteenth century that ingenious calculating machine, Reicha, turned out an incredible number of such quintets. He was too sure of his ground either to fail in securing euphony or to show why he took all this trouble. The great composers have not been attracted by the problem of making coherent chords out of five utterly different timbres, and the only time Mozart combined the flute with another wind instrument in chamber music was when he also employed the glass harmonica. The term 'wind quintet' suggests to lovers of classical music a work of very different calibre, namely, Mozart's glorious quintet for piano, oboe, clarinet, horn, and bassoon. Beethoven's early and easy-going imitation of this is also well known, especially in his above-mentioned arrangement as a quartet for piano and strings. With Mozart the oboe leads, and with Beethoven the clarinet.

(*d*) Piano quintets, i. e. quintets for piano and string quartet, differ in no important aesthetic point from piano quartets. It is surprising how few have been written, and how abnormal is the position of those that are known as classics. Schubert's comparatively early *Forellen* quintet is a voluminous and loose-knit serenade in five movements. Schumann's, the most popular of all, has, as already noted, no inner necessity to be written for a quintet rather than for a quartet or sextet or any larger combination. The masterpiece of Brahms, which sets a pure standard for the style, attained its final form only after a chequered existence, first as a quintet for strings with two 'cellos, and then as a sonata for two pianos.

V. *Sextets, &c.*

(*a*) The two glorious masterpieces of Brahms for two violins, two violas, and two 'cellos are unmistakably inspired by the example of Schubert's great string quintet.

(*b*) Octets for strings, i. e. four violins, two violas, and two 'cellos have tendencies to top-heaviness and internal congestion. Spohr accordingly hit upon the device of double quartets, for two string quartet groups treated antiphonally. The genius of the boy Mendelssohn had, however, already discovered at the age of fifteen that two hundred and fifty odd antiphonal combinations are more interesting than Spohr's pair, and so he enjoyed himself without scruple in his octet, and communicated his enjoyment to others.

(*c*) Most of the larger combinations of chamber music result from the grouping of strings with more than one wind instrument. The effect is often said to be semi-orchestral, but this is a mere illusion arising from the fact that wind instruments are seldom heard outside the orchestra, which they therefore suggest to the hearer. As a criterion, it is on a level with that of the backwoods critic who regretted that so superior a composition as Beethoven's op. 59, no. 1, had not been played by a larger band. The character of works like Beethoven's septet and Schubert's glorification of the same scheme and combination as an octet (with the addition of a second violin) is neither orchestral nor hybrid, and in the one point where they differ from the purest chamber music, the introduction of the double-bass, the effect is essentially different from that of an orchestral bass. The style was perfectly understood by Mozart and Haydn, the serenades and divertimenti of Mozart being on every sort of scale, and sometimes for the queerest combinations. Such works are often voluminous, Beethoven's and Schubert's schemes of six movements with grand introductions to first movement and finale being typical, but the style is festive and the texture loose. In fact, the brilliant fixed contrasts of tone between the various instruments of these combinations go best with as light a style as the grand sonata forms will allow. The very terms serenade and divertimento suggest as much, and if the notion of chamber music is widened to tolerate the heavy-footed double bass, it may as well also allow the first violin to behave more like the solo instrument in a concerto than would be seemly in a string quartet.

(*d*) Compositions for wind instruments alone are most successful when pairs of each kind are taken, otherwise the balance of every chord is a tour de force. The greatest works in this line are Mozart's two octets for two oboes, two clarinets, two horns, and two bassoons. Both are entitled serenades (like all Mozart's works for wind instruments alone), but the one in C minor is a grand and pathetic work, full of wonderful counterpoint and a most un-serenade-like seriousness. It is led throughout by the oboes, the tone of which becomes very fatiguing to the ear even with the finest playing. Perhaps this is why Mozart afterwards arranged it as a string quintet, in which form it is well known. The other octet is led by the clarinets, and, though far slighter, can thus be far more easily produced. But the fact that Mozart is said to have first expanded it from a sextet by adding the oboes, and afterwards to have added two cors anglais, shows that we are leaving the region of a chamber music that tolerates no vagueness as to the number of players. The limit is reached in the same composer's glorious serenade for two oboes, two clarinets, two basset horns (alto clarinets), four horns, two bassoons, and contra-fagotto or double-bass.

Beethoven's works for wind instruments tell us only what he could learn from Mozart, and to pursue the subject into later times would be to lose our thread in a mass of detail.

After the Sonata Style.

Wagner's revolution in the whole category of musical movement has had curiously little effect upon the forms of chamber music. One can only ascribe to pure formalism the way in which composers with atonal styles (like Ravel's) and perpetually modulating styles (like Reger's) cling to a set of forms and a group of four movements of which the sole meaning lies in propositions of classical key-relation and classical rapidity of action. There is a singular dearth of chamber music counterparts to the symphonic poem. The only general remark that is feasible here is that W. W. Cobbett's Phantasy prize-competitions have induced many of the best English composers of the twentieth century to relieve this dearth with a series of remarkable works in one continuous movement (with changes of tempo on original lines). For the rest, the tendencies of modern music are best discoverable by sympathetic accounts of the works of modern composers. In this Cyclopedia such accounts will be found under their proper headings. Donald F. Tovey.

CHAMBER MUSIC LIFE, THE.

The limitless enthusiasm which has reigned in my heart during the greater part of my life for the study of chamber music did not exist in early youth. I believe it sprang into existence the first time I heard Joachim lead a Beethoven Quartet at St. James's Hall, for then I realized that here was an art for which I had a definite affinity. It is not an exaggeration to say that there opened out before me an enchanted world into which I longed to gain an entrance. I had previously heard and attempted to play a little chamber music, and my interest had been further stimulated by occasional visits to Crosby Hall, where I heard my violin master, J. H. B. Dando, lead string quartets. His neat performances of the Haydn, Mozart, and early Beethoven quartets were full of charm, and I looked forward to playing such music myself as a pleasant recreation in which to indulge at odd moments; but my conception of its possibilities altered completely when I heard Joachim play. It was a revelation. I became a regular attendant at the 'Popular' concerts, and the true inwardness of chamber music became so well known to me that had I continued to regard it as a mere pastime or hobby I should have been untrue to myself. From that moment onward I became a very humble devotee of this infinitely beautiful art, and so began for me the chamber music life.

This article will deal frankly and unreservedly with my own personal experiences in the belief that they may be of some service to those who come after me. There are lessons to be learned from the most modestly endowed man, and in these days, when modern hygiene has done so much to add to the normal span of human existence, one such lesson resides in the mere fact that at the age of 80 I am still continuing[1] the regular practice of ensemble music with far more zest than in very early days. Many when they are nearing the sixties lay down the bow and take to the arm-chair and silk-cushion life, missing by so doing the crowning reward given to those who have worked at an art in youth—the power of enjoying its delights in later years.

Since I first began to play chamber music with serious intent I have regarded this branch of the art with a crescendo of interest which has to my amazement gathered in intensity with the flight of time, and even yet may not have reached its culminating point, although I am well aware that, like the typical Beethoven crescendo, it must eventually end in a piano subito, in the rush of life followed by —sleep. But if my activities cease to-morrow I have lived long enough to be able to testify, in my own not particularly robust person, that the will to live is strengthened, and mental juvenescence to some extent retained in advanced age, by a steady continuance of the practice of chamber music. There are those among my own countrymen who look upon my enthusiasm as exaggerated. It is certainly not an English trait, and unless associated with some form of sport, not considered 'good form' in society. But who would not be enthusiastic, who would not be profoundly grateful, if he felt as I do that the happiness which I have enjoyed for so many years, this 'vision of fulfilled desire', has its source in my addiction to this particular activity of mind and body? Yes, body, for the chamber music life is not sedentary like that of the artist who dreams

[1] Since writing the above I have been compelled in the interest of this book to lay down the bow temporarily—no longer does my *Himmel* hang '*voller Geigen*'. [Ed.]

before his easel while the light lasts, or that of the man of letters who broods motionless over the problems of existence before his writing desk. The movements of brush and pen are imperceptible, but to play a violin means constant vibration in every nerve and fibre of the body, and it is this vibration which gives to chamber music practice the therapeutic value of which, I may add, my medical friends are all convinced. Furthermore, the incessant throb and flow of melody, harmony, and polyphony, which constitute the sounds known as chamber music, must react favourably, in a musical sense, upon the sensory apparatus.

THE TITLE.

The title of this article is not designed to apply to a life devoted exclusively to chamber music; I doubt, indeed, if such a life is led by any musician, certainly not by any group of musicians, unless one erroneously places music (originally composed for performance in private but played in public by the gifted artists who travel the world, giving quartet concerts in various cities) in the same category as that defined by that lover of homely expressions, Mr. Percy Grainger, as 'Room music'. They devote themselves to the public performance of what is known as 'solo' chamber music, but that is an art apart, with a technique and psychology of its own, and unknown, it may be added, to early eighteenth-century music-lovers, when scarcely a concert-room, properly so called, existed in all Europe. Chamber music was then purely a domestic affair.

Nor does the title apply to the life led by the cultured dilettante dabbler in all the arts, whose activities are of a desultory nature, who plays a little, listens a little, and regards chamber music as one of an interesting series of pleasant hobbies. I have already made it clear that to me it has been more than a hobby; it has filled my life as it has filled that of many another amateur, and made it worth living. It is *continuous* from year to year, from decade to decade, and is lived by men who do their share, as becomes good citizens, of the work of the world, but religiously reserve all that can be spared of the leisure which remains to the serious study and practice of chamber music. I myself during the last sixty years have been able to devote on an average about two hours daily to the playing of concerted music, to practising the violin or viola parts in advance, to studying scores and, as far as possible, keeping up my technique. I sometimes think of this as a poor allowance; just 14 hours snatched from the weekly 168 hours of prose which make up a normal man's existence, transmuted into poetry; but then it is good to rise from the table of life unsated. With satiety comes boredom, a condition of mind unknown to those who are deeply interested in any form of art. Even the Russians, at whose elbow, according to Maxim Gorki and other Muscovite writers, the demon Ennui is always lurking, reveal in their string quartets an unexpectedly sunny spirit, attributable, I suggest, to the beneficent influence of the medium in which they work. There are, no doubt, pessimistic moments in the otherwise suave chamber music of Tchaikovsky, and sombre thoughts are not entirely absent from the music of Taneiev, Medtner, and the younger composers whose works are published in Moscow by the Soviet Government; but the sentiments of Russian composers in general would appear to have been entirely different from those which inform their more gloomy literary brethren. To read Russian poems and novels, even to listen to some of their folk-songs, is to court the pessimistic mood, but to listen to, or better still to play, Russian chamber music is to breathe an atmosphere of rejoicing. It is this conviction which has induced me to devote so considerable a space to notices of the numerous composers, not all of the very first rank, to whom the above remarks apply.

With regard to the therapeutic value of chamber music practice, the following seems worthy of relation. I am not exceptionally robust, but the considerable strain involved in three hours' strenuous playing of quartets and sonatas not only leaves me unfatigued, but with a greater sense of buoyancy when the last note is heard than when the first note was sounded. Even when the music has chanced to be heavy and complex, with slow movements that weigh on the soul, a corrective is always at hand. A familiar and beloved work by one of the masters can be sought out and placed on the stands, refreshing the players by its Olympian strains and restoring them to equanimity.

ETHICS.

Chamber music has an ethical as well as an aesthetic basis. The exercise of altruism in quartet playing is, however, not so much a virtue as a necessity. There *must* be team work, without which chamber music degenerates into an inferior order of solo music. I once heard some quartets led in a drawing-room by a famous violinist, who brought his party with him from abroad. His playing was magnificent from the purely violinistic point of view, but his colleagues, sternly repressed, were hushed down to a painful extent, and I have rarely heard a more disappointing performance. How different this to the principle laid down by Beethoven, who, when he sent to the Schuppanzigh Quartet the manuscript of one of his later quartets, wrote to each member adjuring him to 'outshine his fellows in the way he played the solo sections'. A solo piece, *qua* solo, is acceptable to all of us. We understand that the accompanist surrenders himself and his artistry for the moment to the service of the soloist. But ensemble music, a manner of conversation amongst musicians in which all have the parole in turn, belongs to another order of things, and if I had my way all four parts of a quartet would be equal in importance. I championed the principle of equal rights for all instruments in one of my competitions, in which the stipulation was made that there should be two violin parts but no *second* part. Although several composers expressed approval of the scheme, it has not as yet made much headway. The voice of the first fiddle is still heard in the land, though less insistently.

Editors have occasionally honoured me with a commission to write on chamber music, and before taking up the pen I have naturally passed in review my own experiences, with this unvarying result: on each occasion I have been impelled to state and re-state to the verge of monotony the homely truth, realized by all whose experiences are similar to my own, that the playing of chamber music *makes for happiness*. Readers will be tolerant of repetition if they reflect upon its implications in this vale of tears, in which dull misery has been more prominent of late than ever before in the world's history, and if they stop to think of what it means to enjoy happiness without penalty, of which Schopenhauer has denied the very existence, they will forgive my persistence.

The word happiness has not the splendour of such words as love, honour, courage, patriotism; those, in short, in which the underlying element of sacrifice is present. It is a manner of egoism if you will, yet it must not be forgotten that if chamber music is to be practised with success, there must also be the subordination of self which belongs to all team work, and it is therefore happiness free from all epicurean taint. The following lines of which I have a note, but the source of which I cannot trace, may aptly conclude this section of my article:

'Music is a moral law. It gives soul to the universe, wings to the mind, flight to the imagination, a charm to sadness, gaiety and life to everything. It is the essence of order, and leads to all that is good, just, and beautiful, of which it is the visible, but nevertheless dazzling, passionate and eternal form.'

INDIVIDUALITY.

On the other hand, let us be frank and admit that Whistler's theories were not altogether wrong, that *over* insistence on the ethical and literary basis of art may tend to insipidity and sentimentality, that independence of thought and action are the forces that count; in short, that self-expression is the constant aim of the true artist. It is certainly the aim of the modest amateur executant. Be his technical resources ever so slight, his admiration for the greatest exponents of the art and his desire to hear their superb performances on concert platforms ever so great, his main desire is to *play himself* as competently as his limitations will allow. It is playing which has the first hold and the first possession of his mind. Whilst listening is a glorious feature of the chamber music life, especially in early days when acquaintance is first made with master works, playing is the main preoccupation of the executant, and this may help to explain why chamber concerts are not so well attended by amateurs as they deserve to be. Spending as they do so much of their leisure time instrument in hand, little remains for concert-going. I will indulge in a frank expression of opinion on this subject. It is destructive to the musical sense to attend too many concerts. One becomes blasé and that is the end of all things.

ECLECTICISM.

Eclecticism is the vice of the derivative composer, and is not accounted a virtue wherever found. Yet I have to admit, in my own person, the possession of an eclectic taste. To me, the best in all the genres from grave to gay are in their turn acceptable, and though this tendency banishes me from the worshipful company of highbrows, it is useful to the compiler of a cyclopedia; furthermore, it adds to the variety, and therefore to the joys of the chamber music life, so that, though I have no pride, I have much gladness in its possession.

I once played to a dear old lady, nourished on the classics, a delightful Russian quartet containing a waltz, a mazurka, and an orientale subtly suggesting the movements of a snake-charmer. Sensuous music if you will, but light and witty, of the kind which proceeds only from the pen of a great craftsman. She was horrified. 'How can you,' she said, 'who are a lover of the finest music, descend to play mere dance stuff?' I replied, 'I play it because I love it and because, by way of interlude, I find it refreshing.' She was not placated, and no doubt continues to deplore my bad taste to the present day.

A love of dance rhythms has been, as every student of music knows, a characteristic of nearly every great composer. Mozart is reported by his own wife to have said that he 'preferred dancing to music'. It is significant that some of the greatest of the masters passed their lives in Vienna, once the gayest of all cities, filled with echoes of light music at all hours of the day and night. The influence upon their mentality has obviously not been unfavourable, nor am I sure that their music has not been the better for it. It certainly quickened their sense of rhythm, and has it not given us Schubert's idealizations of the lovely Austrian Ländler?

Vienna is less gay to-day for reasons to which I need not refer, and its chamber music composers are more 'cerebral' than in the old carefree days. Deep thought furrows the brows of Arnold Schönberg, his pupils and disciples, to whom the true eclectic must, however, also turn, only to find that the divine insouciance which informed the music of a Schubert has gone, to return, we all hope, in happier days to come. That the love of great music is still a Viennese quality was shown by the city's finely organized celebration of the Beethoven centenary in 1927, but the Austrian composers of to-day have not yet come into their rightful inheritance of Viennese gaiety.

Little incitement, I imagine, is necessary to induce musicians to take interest either in light music which is really artistic, or in music which belongs to the classical or romantic schools, but the case of modern music is different. A Viennese critic and composer, Mr. Otto Siegl, in a number of the *Musikbote* (of which he is editor), made an appeal to the chamber music dilettanti of the present day.

> 'You', he writes, 'who are the only ones who play chamber music from disinterested motives, should court intimacy with the moderns . . . for once put aside your Haydn, Mozart, Beethoven, Schubert, Brahms, and Dvořák and delve deeply into some modern work. Try Pfitzner, Schönberg, Stravinsky, Hindemith, or, if you like, one of the younger of the moderns, but be sure you give to the works chosen close and sympathetic attention. Above all, do not fall into the apathetic sleep that is satisfied with what comes easiest to brain and fingers, nor wave off with pompous gesture everything that is not readily understood.'

I have done my best—*Ich Armer*—to follow Herr Siegl's excellent counsel, but for me the task is a heavy one. When listening to Arnold Schönberg's very lengthy quartets, for instance, I have become conscious of occasional apocalyptic moments, with which I have been profoundly impressed, but his music as a whole, probably for want of complete knowledge, wears a recondite air. The trouble is that, being advanced in years, I am never likely to find time to study his music as it needs to be studied, nor to arrive at a complete understanding of his idioms, with the exception of the *Verklärte Nacht*, which through its affinity with Wagner is easily assimilated. And although my efforts to cope with modern modes of thought will, I hope, continue a little while longer, the limitations from which I, in common with all amateurs, suffer as a player in the matter of technique, will always stand in the way. Some of the moderns are guilty of writing passages for strings that are only suited to piano, wind, or orchestra, not even always to these, whereas the older masters almost invariably wrote music which lies within the tracks of the fingers. Modern composers seem to forget that professional players are not all virtuosi, and as to amateurs, they will never take to their hearts music that is alien to the genius of their instrument.

Nevertheless, Herr Siegl is justified in appealing to them not to be satisfied with playing exclusively the music in which by God's grace they have rejoiced in the past. 'Your duty', he writes, 'is to go with the new' ('*mit allen Neuen mitzugehen*'). To this let me add a rider prompted by my own experience. The study of contemporary chamber music has had with me an unexpected sequel. It has in some mysterious way greatly quickened my capacity for appreciation of the old. This explains the crescendo of interest of which I have already spoken, and which astonishes no one so much as myself. It is due to the chamber music life that I have held the consciousness of age so far at arm's length; and I am able to say that, if I finish to-morrow, life will have retained its savour till the end.

The *Musikbote* printed in March 1925 a response to Mr. Siegl's appeal from a Dr. Kielhauser, schoolmaster and amateur 'cellist, in which he gives an interesting glimpse of musical life in an Austrian provincial town. His letter is so full of excellent matter that I am sorry I cannot spare space for printing it in full. The gist of it is that he is unwilling to live exclusively with the classics as within a Chinese wall, but, his means being limited, he sighs at the cost of new music, to buy which is a gamble, for it may not in the end prove attractive. He touches also upon the expense of concert-going, and from his remarks one gathers that the tax upon ideals, known as the 'entertainment tax', lifts up its ugly head in Austria as well as in Britain, and that even if he were able to attend concerts, the make-up of the programmes is a bar to the gratification of his wide and evidently enlightened taste. In a provincial town the old works are found to be the only safe draw, and Dr. Kielhauser's thirst for novelty remains unquenched as far as listening goes, but his selection of works for home consumption is eclectic enough to satisfy Herr Siegl himself. He is all for the '*neue Bahnen*' in German and Austrian chamber music; but I am sorry to see that up to the present no British or French chamber music has reached (or touched?) him, and that he singles out Rachmaninov's trio, which is practically a piano solo with strings obbligato! as the only Russian work worthy of mention, But that is a detail. I take off my hat to one whom I regard as a brother enthusiast, and a descendant, in a musical sense, of the brave schoolmaster whom Wagner has immortalized in his autobiography. The passage is worth quoting:

> 'Go and listen one winter's night in that little cabin; there sit a father and his three sons; at a small round table; two play the violin, a third the viola, the father the 'cello; what you hear so lovingly and deeply played is a quartet composed by that little man who is beating time. He is the schoolmaster from the neighbouring hamlet, and the quartet he has composed is a lovely work of art and feeling. Again I say, go to that spot, and hear that author's music played, and you will be dissolved in tears; for it will search your heart, and you will know what German music is, will feel what is the German spirit.'

I rejoice to hear from friends who know, that the German spirit extolled by Wagner has survived the direful happenings of recent years, and that the people's love for domestic music of the nobler sort shows no signs of flagging. Societies exist in every German and Austrian town, great or small, for the practice of chamber music. Marx writes somewhere of the German tendency (*Neigung*) for quartet players to gather together in a modest room, '*gleichsam in heimlichem lauschigem Winkel*'. 'There they await each other, find each other, and take joy together in a lifelong musical friendship.'

SIGHT-READING.

In my experience there are three stages in the study of difficult modern music. First the preliminary reading, then the period of slogging hard work, and finally the performance to which an audience may be invited. It is best not to disturb this sequence of events. Woe to the listeners who (sometimes, it is only fair to say by their own desire) are present at the earlier stages, when the players, poor dears, are struggling in a maze of musical intricacies, adding to the clashes of dissonance for which the composer is responsible clashes of their own making. There are inevitably discordant moments on such occasions, and it is surely best that the performers should be left to fight their way alone through a welter of sounds. I am all for the good repute of chamber music, jeopardized as it so often is by imperfect, unrehearsed performances played to puzzled listeners. Chamber music, of all arts most misunderstood of the general, can never become popular unless heard under the most favourable circumstances.

Nevertheless, sight-reading is one of the most delightful experiences of the chamber music life. There exist, fortunately, many works, even modern ones, those of them that are free from embarrassing metrical devices and counterpoints of tonalities, which can be played at sight quite easily. To alternate sight-reading with the careful and painstaking study of works by the great masters has been the routine I have adopted and from which I have derived permanent satisfaction. The attainment of facility in sight-reading is simply a matter of practical experience (with a little audacity added); and I am free to confess that without this facility my own interest in the art could never have been sustained. Most musicians, like myself, are keenly desirous of exploring new paths; but I have met occasionally with performers who, from conscientious motives, or perhaps for reputation's sake, refuse to play any music not carefully studied in advance, not even a second violin part. They know not what they lose. As to the narrow and intolerant, the neophobists, the downright haters of everything new, they have a good conceit of themselves, but are in reality the dullest of dull dogs.

Apropos of sight-reading, a word may be said on the homely subject of *counting time*. I side with the experienced player who expects his colleagues to abstain rigidly from loudly counting time in familiar works. He rightly construes it as an intrusion, almost an impertinence. But in unfamiliar works the conditions are very different. Modern composers indulge in constant changes of tempo and metre. They do not 'keep step' as the older masters did. The mental process which suffices for works of simpler facture, breaks down when the necessity arises for reading complex works at sight, and choice has to be made between counting time and—chaos. Beating time with the foot is undesirable. It is noisy and unsafe. Players are carried away by the excitement of the moment and are apt to put down the foot in the middle of a bar, or upon a cross accent—in short irregularly. Only the counting of time by the leader is endurable, and those to whom it is distasteful should bear in mind that it is the sole way of avoiding cacophony when complex contemporary music is attempted.

To the possible objection that the voice is an irritating interruption, I would suggest that it is, or should be, the voice of a friend, for if ensemble music is to give perfect enjoyment, those who participate in it must be, in all senses of the word, friends.

FRIENDSHIP.

Richard Walthew was happily inspired when he wrote that chamber music was the 'music of friends'. In my younger days the amateurs with whom I forgathered showed me much kindness. My earliest recollection is of a visit in company with my old friend Thomas (better known as Tom) Lintott to the house occupied by his two brothers, both 'cellists, in the late 'sixties. They gave me much encouragement (I was horribly nervous) and allowed me, to my great delight, to take part in some Boccherini quintets, which I am ashamed to say I have not played since, though I have tried without success to interest myself in that composer's quartets, which appear to me to lack tonal fullness. Boccherini has been called 'the wife of Haydn', with whom, however, he had little affinity. Indeed, de Sauzay records of him that, to retain his own individuality, he deliberately ignored the compositions of his contemporaries. Reverting to the quintets, I remember that the two 'old' gentlemen (I should not call them 'old' to-day) pointed out to me the thumb passages and difficult arpeggios written by Boccherini for the 'cello, the many clefs used in the old editions, and if I remember aright, signs indicating where the performer was licensed to add decorative twiddles of his own. I was filled with wonderment at their prowess, though I remember that the 'twiddles' made me laugh.

In the days which followed, I played almost exclusively with amateurs, and have very vivid memories of snug evenings passed in the rooms of suburban villas making acquaintance for the first time with the thirty '*berühmte*' of Haydn, the great ten of Mozart, and the six op. 18 of Beethoven. There was much stamping of feet, much going back to the beginning (rehearsal letterings were unknown in those days), and many were the shouts of protest from the leader that everybody was playing too loud; but there were moments, too, when the glory of the music was dimly apparent even in our poor interpretations, and at any rate it was for me an initiation into joys destined to last a lifetime.

I could fill pages with recollections of weeks spent at country houses where chamber music was played on rainy days, morning, noon, and night; sometimes, also, in village concert-rooms for the benefit of rustic listeners and local charities; of the cordial welcome I received in bachelor days from friends who were at once musically and hospitably inclined, and of the families with whom in married days I exchanged visits from week to week, from year to year, for the definite purpose of joining forces in the playing of ensemble music both with piano and strings. But Time has ended always in severing the threads which bound us together, either by change of residence, or by the great inevitable change which ends everything. The happenings of such a musical life are symbolized in Haydn's *Farewell Symphony*. One after another the players blow out the candles and put their instruments away for the last time, and then comes the haunting fear that one may be left solitary behind. Fate has dealt kindly with me in this respect. New friends have made their appearance, instrument in hand, to replace the never-to-be-forgotten old ones. The lights have been turned up again, and the last candle flickers on. Many of these friends are artists of high rank in their profession, with whom I have passed some of the happiest moments of my life, the playing of chamber music being a bond between artist and amateur of the most intimate kind. In short, it is a promoter of friendship, and on that score alone is worthy of consideration by those who are concerned with mapping out a scheme of life for young people in whom they discern musical proclivities. My best hope for this book is that it may fall into the hands of youthful students and prove suggestive.

THE INSTRUMENTS.

Every violinist in love with his art is possessed with an ardent desire to acquire an instrument which responds to his tone ideals. His objective is a well-fitted, not too expensive, violin, pleasing in timbre and quickly responsive to the touch of the bow. The actual quality of the tone he produces is mainly the expression of his own ego. Nevertheless, the timbre of the instrument chosen is his ally in tone production, and of such importance to a violinist that it is both natural and desirable that the quest for a fine instrument should be incessant till the right one is found. Some never find it. It is, of course, largely a 'question d'argent'. To some, sad to say, the opportunity of acquiring a fine old violin at a price corresponding with their means never presents itself, and they are condemned to play on a mediocre instrument for the period of their musical life.

Personally, I have been exceptionally lucky. My father, when I began my studies, purchased for me a Guadagnini violin for £28, the cost of which to-day would be at least six or seven hundred pounds. It was an exquisite instrument upon which I should probably be playing still, but for an accident which had a prejudicial effect on the tone. I looked out for another violin, and had a most wonderful stroke of luck. I acquired at a low price a Guarneri del Gesù of supreme beauty, both of tone and appearance, upon which I have played ever since, but was advised some years ago by an expert not to overplay it, violins, like human beings, being subject to fatigue. The advice was sound, and I immediately started in search of what sporting people would call a 'stable companion'. After trying, by way of experiment, innumerable violins, including twelve Strads, of which I was the temporary possessor, I found at last one which responded to my needs. It is neither the most powerful nor the most valuable in a commercial sense, but it is perfect for chamber music playing, and I am happy in its possession. I presume the Guarneri is not jealous, for it never sulks, if allowed an occasional rest, and sounds better than ever.

The possession of such attractive violins has been, it will readily be understood, a bar to an exhaustive, personal study on my part of the tonal characteristics of new violins. But though I have not played much myself upon the instruments produced by modern makers, I have frequently heard them played by very competent artists, and am convinced that there is a good time coming for violinists of the future. Several quartet parties perform habitually upon new instruments exclusively, among them the Capet Quartet in France and the Vienna Quartet in Austria; and our own Albert Sammons has on many occasions used a modern violin for concert purposes; whilst numerous public competitions (two of them organized by myself) have gone far to prove that it is difficult for listeners to distinguish between the new and the old. I have dealt with this subject in another place (*v.* VIOLIN).

PRACTICE.

The cherubs that sit up aloft and watch over the fate of the struggling chamber music player have been more than kind to me. Beside frequently practising ensemble music with expert quartet players of admitted eminence, I have had many opportunities of playing with virtuoso violinists who have gratified me by expressing their personal pleasure at taking part in my home music-making, and proved their sincerity by repeated visits; and, as already hinted, Cremona instruments of exceptionally beautiful tone quality have been my constant companions during a long life; and further (Oh, bathos!), I have been spared the mental discomfort which attends those who dwell in flats and hotels. I am not insensitive to the feelings of the unwilling listener, and have been glad to be able to practise my violin without fear of disturbing neighbours, thanks to the fortunate circumstance that my life has been exclusively spent in detached houses. Would that all my brother musicians could share my good fortune in this respect, but I look around and see with regret that London is gradually becoming a city of flats.

Immunity from the so-called 'drudgery' of practice is, I suppose, the chief argument in favour of mechanical music. Every musical instrument is in a way a tyrant, but a reasonable tyrant whose smiles one can secure by submission to his will. He does not demand the impossible, but he does demand that such time as can be spared for practice shall be given regularly, with concentration and with self-observation. In short, practice must not degenerate into mere amusement. A witty Frenchman has said: 'Si vous laissez l'art pour un jour, il vous laissera pour trois jours'; and an Englishman (Dr. Johnson) has written: 'The lapse to indolence is soft and imperceptible, but the return to diligence is difficult.' It follows that only the constant player has constant enjoyment. The inconstant find their enjoyment marred by an ever-present sense of painful effort. One hears of virtuosi who tell interviewers that they practise very seldom; of exceptional artists who worked so strenuously in early youth that technique became second nature. This may perhaps be said of Paganini, Sarasate, and Kreisler, but Joachim, Sivori, and many others needed to practise constantly to keep in form, and it must be remembered that solo artists spend a part of their lives on the public platform with programmes of long, difficult pieces to play, which forms the best practice it is possible to conceive.

Personally, I have always found pleasure in practising passages previous to trying an unfamiliar work of chamber music, and have known the pleasures of anticipation to exceed those of realization. This, at least, is not 'drudgery'.

To young amateur players a certain experience of my own may be useful. Many years ago, it dawned upon me that passages in the dark keys—E flat, A flat, D flat, &c.—were less easy to master than those written in the more open keys, and I remembered that in the violin studies most familiar to me flat keys were very much in the minority (Rode excepted). Thus, when I first studied the leading part in the 'Harp' quartet, op. 74, the brilliant arpeggio passage at the end of the opening movement failed to yield to practice as I expected, and I felt that something must be done to familiarize my fingers with similar intervals. This was accomplished by the frequent transposition of studies from bright to dark keys. Kreutzer's second I played in A flat, his eighth in E flat, and so with the studies and concertos of other writers. Soon it became indifferent to me whether I played in dark or bright keys; in fact, in all I found myself playing equally—badly. Every key represents a mood, but I will make a confession of weakness. It sometimes happens that when I am trying a modern quartet for the first time and see stretching before me a grim-looking adagio in five, six, or seven flats, I do sigh for the chirp of an open string, with its attendant harmonics, for a gleam of light amid the darkness of the stopped strings.

I venture to suggest that in these days increasing attention should be given to the practice in the studio of ponticello bowing, artificial harmonics, and rapid pizzicati. The use of these effects by composers of chamber music is no longer a departure from the normal; it is an everyday occurrence, and should not come upon the amateur—as I am afraid it does—as a surprise, for want of practice.

I will conclude my remarks upon practice by quoting what many famous players have said on the subject of 'sons filés' (long sustained notes in a single bow). They all consider that of all forms of practice it is the most helpful for the acquisition of a satisfactory tone production. It must be admitted that all of us have not the superhuman patience required for compliance with this counsel of perfection. I have heard of long, slow bows containing three distinct transitions from crescendo to diminuendo before a change is made. Such patience deserves and receives its reward.

NERVOUSNESS.

The word *nervous* was originally, I suppose, a colloquialism, but not a very logical one, for in the dictionary it stands both for strength and weakness. It is, in fact, a word, or condition, of pathological interest, as I know from personal experience. In youthful days I was entirely free from it, but after two serious illnesses it permanently invaded my constitution. To this day, after fifty years of uniformly good health, I am unable to fight successfully against it, but being an amateur, whose place is not on the public platform, it matters little. Indeed it has thrown me back upon the playing of music for its own sake, and contributed to my realization[1] of the happiness which, as I have already pointed out, fills the chamber music life to overflowing.

[1] 'Happy the man of the fields if only he realized his happiness.' (Virgil.)

But to public performers, or would-be public performers, the subject is one of overwhelming importance. The finer the sensibilities of the artist the more likely he is to be attacked by stage fright, and, if nature has not endowed him with adequate powers of resistance, his public career quickly comes to an end. Professor Auer tells us, in his book on the violin, that Joachim and Rubinstein were 'extremely nervous on the stage'. Both were strong men and able, nevertheless, to make a brave show before the world, yet Rubinstein 'only displayed the full grandeur of his conceptions in private', and even Joachim, whose life as a quartet leader was largely spent before the public, is reported to have said, 'one really ought to play for oneself and a few friends'. His master Joseph Böhm (*q.v.*) was a sufferer from nervousness, and confined himself in his latter days to private playing.

I have heard nervousness described as the scourge of the self-conscious, but I would rather think of it as one of the infirmities of noble minds, the result of excessive anxiety to please.

COMPETITIONS.

The chamber music life brought me twenty-five years ago into frequent contact with youthful instrumentalists and students of composition at the colleges. With the abilities of the latter I was deeply impressed; there was an evident renaissance of interest in an art which had shown a tendency to droop since the passing of the 'Pops'. My conversations with these clever young people influenced me, to some extent, in my decision to organize the chamber music competitions of which I have written an account in another place. Compared with the dazzling rewards offered to-day to successful competitors on the other side of the Atlantic, mine were modest enough—the single prizes in no instance exceeded fifty guineas—but they sufficed in pre-war days to attract attention, and endowment ensures their continuance. I wish to believe that Professor Stanford, whose success as a teacher of composition in those days was phenomenal, voiced the feeling of students at that moment when he spoke of these prizes as the 'blue riband of chamber music'.

In this article my chief preoccupation is with the part they played in my musical life. The International Competition, of which the subject was a sonata for piano and violin, took heavy toll of my leisure hours. No less than 134 MSS. arrived from all parts of the world, and for six months I was kept busy with the initial weeding-out process. Some were obviously 'duds'; others were clever, but bore the fatal stamp of mediocrity. It was considered, I suppose, *infra dig.* for composers of established position to compete, and indeed the object most prominent in my mind was the discovery of new talent. I dreamed of a masterpiece coming from some country as yet little known to the world of chamber music. I thought, for instance, that I might possibly receive from Spain something national and distinctive; but, in the event, not one of the brilliant names which have come to the front since—de Falla, Turina, Chapi, Manén, Del Campo, Granados—was represented in the dozen so-called 'sonatas' sent in. Some were national enough—far too national in fact, just *pots pourris* of Spanish dance tunes with echoes of castanet, tambourine, and guitar; others were strangely reminiscent of early Italian opera, especially of Rossini, and were suspiciously yellow of aspect. I can picture a clairvoyant, holding one in his hand and evolving the pathetic vision of a grizzled professor who had built unfulfilled hopes in his younger days based upon this very manuscript, and decided to give it one last chance. In more downright language, these yellow parchments were hopelessly 'dated'.

New talent eventually made its appearance from another quarter, and, to the surprise of many, the jury, which included Baron d'Erlanger, William Shakespeare, and Paul Stoeving, pronounced in favour of a young English composer named John Ireland. His sonata in D minor is now an accepted number in the repertory, and has been played abroad (recently in Vienna) as well as at home. A striking confirmation of Ireland's merit was supplied by his success in a fresh competition for a violin sonata, organized in private circles, in which he was again awarded the first prize. This work, the sonata in A minor, no. 2, was played several times at Aeolian Hall by Albert Sammons and William Murdoch to crowded audiences—an almost unprecedented incident in chamber concert life.

In the early phantasy competitions the most interesting personality was William Hurlstone. He was an intimate friend of mine, and I knew—or thought I knew—his style and idiom well. But the winning phantasy was totally different from anything he had written before, and great was my surprise when, breaking open the seal of the envelope containing the name of the composer, I found that it was he who had won the first prize. He died shortly afterwards, at the age of 30, and at the beginning of what promised to be a new period of creative activity. The phantasy is a mosaic of themes, beginning with one of the four-crotchet order beloved of the greatest of all the masters. It was full of promise, but less effective for public performance than Frank Bridge's phantasy, which on this occasion came in second. On the next occasion Bridge came in first, his trio phantasy being the best thing written as yet for piano and two strings by any British composer. I had hopes, from a correspondence I had with Sir Edward Elgar, that he would add to his laurels by writing me a piano trio in full sonata form, but it was not to be.

Friskin's quartet phantasy is a piece of light music opening with a burst of rollicking fun. It has been played with success in New York, where the composer now lives and works, but here it is never heard. Yet in the opinion of Sir Charles Stanford it was deserving of the first prize. The tradition that chamber music must be, throughout, a serious piece of business dies hard.

Holbrooke's phantasy is practically a suite, and one of the best things he has done. Haydn Wood, in the same competition, made what was practically his début as a chamber music writer. His phantasy is so full of charm that one regrets that he afterwards deserted a field of activity in which he seemed destined to win distinction. Without denying the attractiveness of the path which the composer of *Roses in Picardy* has chosen, he might surely have turned for a moment from his lucrative career as a song-writer to the art of chamber music, and given us a little graceful music of the kind which reflects his particular mentality.

Although the folk-song and dance phantasy prizes did not respond exactly to my conceptions, they were by no means disappointing. In fact, Waldo Warner's folk-song phantasy, *Dance to your Daddy*, which is more brilliant than 'folk-songish', was played in nearly every American State with the greatest success by the London String Quartet, and Armstrong Gibbs's romantically conceived *Enchanted Wood* contains music with which I am much in sympathy; but it has not, as I hoped, the imperious urge to the dance to be found in such works as Glazounov's *Noveletten*; and *Suite*, op. 53.

A piece of music which represents so exactly the phantasy as I conceived it that it may well serve as prototype to those who care to write in this form in the future, is the string quintet which Dr. Ralph Vaughan Williams wrote to my commission. It was played at the dinner offered me on the occasion of my eightieth birthday (July 11, 1927) and was coupled with Frank Bridge's splendid phantasy for piano quartet, also a commission. This article sets out to be autobiographical so that I may speak of the gratitude I feel to the 219 friends who, presided over by Sir Hugh Allen, assembled at Prince's Hotel on that to me delightful occasion. Before attending this function I played at home with my colleagues the thanksgiving movement from the great A minor quartet of Beethoven, the noble and austere strains of which I thought might well serve as Grace—not after meat but after the enjoyments received, during a long life, from the playing of music of a type upon which Beethoven set the seal of perfection, carrying it beyond even the horizon of the beautiful, away to the very brink of the Infinite.

EDITOR.

CHAMBER MUSIC SOCIETY OF WASHINGTON.

This Society, which has elected as honorary members Mrs. Coolidge, Mr. de Coppet, and myself, presents many features of interest. Concerts of chamber music of various periods are held, under ideal conditions, in private salons. The performers' names are not mentioned in the programme, but at the conclusion of the concert they are introduced to the audience, the original intention being that they should play behind a screen, though that was abandoned.

The list of about forty works performed during 1924–6 includes British works by Bax, Goossens, and Vaughan Williams. Mention should be made of the programme notes, which are admirably written. EDITOR.

CHAMBER MUSIC SUPPLEMENT.

This publication ran its monthly course from June 1913 to November 1916, being the gift of its editor, W. W. Cobbett, to *The Music Student* (now become *The Music Teacher*), with every issue of which it was presented to the reader. So far as is known, it was a complete innovation to devote a journal exclusively to chamber music, and since its discontinuance no journal has occupied its place.

The plan of the *Chamber Music Supplement* was novel. It pursued a course systematically laid down. Its first number was devoted largely to a consideration of duos, its next to trios, the following three to quartets, the next two to quintets, and another to sextets, septets, and octets. There was a number devoted to wind chamber music, and nine or ten successive numbers carried out a methodical study of the repertory of British chamber music. Certain numbers were of a more general character, and, naturally, every number contained some general matter, including news, or reviews of new chamber works.

The contributors to the *Chamber Music Supplement* included, in addition to the editor (who was responsible for a monthly 'Chamber Music Causerie'), Richard H. Walthew, Misses K. E. Eggar and Marion Scott (who contributed jointly a page devoted to 'Women's Doings in Chamber Music'), Gilbert Webb, J. Wharton Sharp, Alex. Cohen, T. L. Southgate, Thos. Dunhill, Ernest Walker, Nicholas C. Gatty, J. A. Fuller Maitland, M. Montagu-Nathan, E. Douglas Taylor, R. Vaughan Williams, G. Jean-Aubry, Oscar W. Street, Felix Salmond, Rev. G. Surtees Talbot, Adam Carse, Harold Samuel, Douglas Donaldson, James A. Findlay, Walter Wearenear-Yeomans, W. H. Harris, Wells-Harrison, Peter Warlock, and Percy A. Scholes.

This record of the three and a half years' course of a paper devoted to a journalistically neglected branch of the musical art may be of some particular interest to readers of the present Cyclopedia, since the idea of compiling the latter undoubtedly took rise in the mind of Mr. Cobbett as a result of the wide appreciation and evident usefulness of his earlier editorial labours. P. A. SCHOLES.

CHAMBER ORCHESTRA.

The term 'chamber orchestra' is a recent importation into the musical vocabulary. It does not appear to us to have been used before the war of 1914, and though current in the idiom of to-day, no one would care to define it exactly. The term is employed in the sense of a combination for the purpose of performing orchestral works with a small number of players. But, when one realizes that the most effective items in their repertory are classical symphonies which need no more than twenty to thirty performers (the correct number for the symphonies of Haydn and Mozart, when played in their original form), one cannot help feeling that this new label has been affixed to a bottle of very ancient wine. In fact, every orchestra before Berlioz was more or less a chamber orchestra, in respect both of its numbers, and the size of the halls in which its performances were given.

A simpler explanation of this new nomenclature has occurred to the writer, the chamber orchestra being thus defined: a body of instruments sufficiently numerous to have no word to describe it in our existing vocabulary (I think, so far, we have not gone beyond the 'Dixtet'), and few enough not to need the conductor's bâton. Thus Bach's cantatas might pass for a model of works suitable for such a combination. But this definition is negatived by recent performances of works which required only a very limited number of performers, yet of such difficulty that it was out of the question to attempt them without a conductor.

A typical work of the kind just described is Schönberg's curious *Pierrot Lunaire*, recent performances of which have raised so many controversies. It is impossible to mistake this work for any kind of abstract music, the use of the instrumental combination is entirely orchestral, and has neither more nor less importance and significance than the orchestra in Wagner's operas. Although the orchestra often takes the lead, it is intended solely to illustrate, or to provide a commentary on, the text of Albert Giraud. The instrumentation is for only five musicians, who play eight instruments: piano; flute and piccolo played alternatively by the same player; violin and viola; clarinet and flute; and violoncello. The incredible difficulty of this strange work puts out of the question any idea of performing it without a conductor, and this music is entirely orchestral. Yet the orchestra consists of five musicians! It is evident that the number has nothing to do with the name.

It is thus impossible to draw a hard and fast line according to the number of instruments employed. It would be very tempting to consider a chamber orchestra as one which has no more than one of each kind of wind instrument, together with a string quartet. But this would lead to absurd conclusions; if two horns were employed in a small combination, to the exclusion of other wind instruments, we should be obliged to class an orchestral suite with such instrumentation among ordinary orchestral works, while certain symphonies would have to be included in the chamber orchestra repertory. It would be better, once for all, not to seek too exact a definition, and to use the expression in its literal sense; thus, a chamber orchestra is to be considered as an orchestra small enough to be heard in a drawing-room, or a very small concert hall, without any inconvenience due to the limited space.

The whole of the orchestral music of the eighteenth century, as well as part of the early nineteenth century music, is included at once, therefore, in its repertory: this statement will avoid the necessity of giving a list of suitable works, which, in fact, would be nothing but a lengthy catalogue of classical music. But it is quite another matter when we come to modern music. In this case the chamber orchestra is certainly a novelty, and, like other novelties, supplies a need.

For those who are inclined to look at the ideal aspect of things, this need might be a purely artistic one. It would then be explained as an inevitable reaction against the monstrous overgrowth of the modern orchestra. In order to describe his little domestic troubles in terms of music, Richard Strauss must have a colossal orchestra—from a hundred to a hundred and twenty musicians at least. Any artist with a care for, and a sense of proportion would be only too strongly tempted to react against such non-sense, and one who loves to deal in paradox would hasten to treat some vast subject with the minimum of means. It is quite possible that some composer has had this idea, but, so far as we know, there has been no noteworthy manifestation of the kind. A more prosaic explanation may be risked.

The chamber orchestra, or orchestra with few performers, is a war-substitute. The absence of the majority of orchestra players (who were called to the colours), and further, the continual rise in salaries, threatened to give the death-blow to most orchestral performances. Having only limited means at their disposal, young composers, anxious to have their works played, adapted themselves to the changed conditions, and sought a means of expressing their ideas without having recourse to combinations that were now unattainable.

There were, no doubt, in the orchestral repertory some works which needed but few performers: a very characteristic example of these is to be found in Lalo's two *Aubades*. But, in every case, when a composer of the last generation employed a greatly reduced orchestra, he did so only when he wished to express sentiments of grace or delicacy. The masterpiece of the kind is the *Siegfried-Idyll*, and it is not one of the least of Wagner's merits that he was able, amid the most passionate scenes in all his operas, to find inspiration for a movement so full of grace, and that he was able also, with means intentionally reduced, to express the feelings aroused in him by the birth of an ardently desired son. But here again, the sentiments to be expressed were of a particular kind. Wagner wrote but one such piece in a lifetime. Accustomed, as he was, to find to his hand whatever materials he required, he never knew the restrictions under which composers of the present day have been, and still are, obliged to labour.

By a singular paradox the present generation is not at all inclined to limit its art to the delineation of graceful and delicate subjects. Never has there been a more 'brutal' period, and even in the case of those musicians who did not fight in the war (one might say, with these especially), violence, the striving after physical effect, and exaggerative caricature seem to occupy a far more important place in their thoughts than the desire to give musical expression to exalted sentiments. Now the sudden invasion of European life by a musical element hitherto confined to quite special circles of the American upper class, has overturned the aesthetic standards of a whole generation. The allusion is to 'Jazz', and to its influence on serious music, an influence which it would be childish to deny. Whether one likes jazz or not, one is obliged to recognize its immense influence on contemporary creative art.

Now the essence of jazz is to make much noise with few instruments, and, more particularly, with few performers, for each one of them is a little orchestra in himself. This has not escaped the notice of composers in search of executants for their works, men who would have had to give up all idea of ever hearing their works played, if they made the same demands as a Strauss or a Mahler. The greatest of all, and, from the practical point of view, the most skilful (the writer feels no diffidence in crediting him with the last-named quality, for he does not consider it as a stigma), Stravinsky, perceived at once the advantage of utilizing jazz as a model, and whereas he had formerly written for full orchestra, with the management of great masses which this implies, he now suddenly restricted himself to a very small number of instruments. The most characteristic example of his new manner is the wonderful *Histoire d'un Soldat*, in which, for forty minutes, the composer holds his audience spellbound by music overflowing with life and full of contrast; and for this he employs no more than seven musicians. He does not even make use of the piano, the usual stopgap in conceptions such as these, as would assuredly have been the case with a musician of less masterly technique. Evidently his subject lent itself to this kind of treatment, and the whimsical collection of violin, double-bass, clarinet, bassoon, trumpet, trombone, and complete jazz percussion would not have suited every kind of subject. But, in his works since the war, Stravinsky has remained faithful to the reduced orchestra. In *Mavra* the quartet is reduced to the absolute minimum: one player for each instrument. In the *Noces* we find the same restraint. For the orchestration of his *Rag-time* he is content with eleven musicians. For that of the *Berceuse du Chat* he employs nothing but three clarinets. In each new work he shows the fixed determination to employ the absolute minimum of performers, and his mastery is so incontestable as to remove all regret that he shows no sign of a return to his earlier manner. Every one of these combinations sounds well, and in none of them is there any feeling that a greater number of parts would add to the effect.

This style is not peculiar to Stravinsky alone. Darius Milhaud, who has written no less than ten symphonies (very short ones, however), never employs more than ten to twelve instruments, and most of these works are anything but gentle drawing-room pieces. They are, for the most part, thoroughly orchestral in style, of tremendous force, reaching at times even a kind of savage harshness, which is deliberately sought by the composer, and is an aspect of his creative talent which he esteems most highly. So, if this technique becomes general, we may expect to have entire concerts of modern music originally written for chamber orchestra.

That this style of orchestration will have an influence on the very essence of music is not to be doubted. As 'cubism', with its precise and fixed lines, followed on the softness and hazy contours of impressionism, so polyphony, with its intensive use of the horizontal lines of counterpoint, succeeds the over-refinement, and lack of definite outline, which reached their zenith in Debussy, whose imitators have exaggerated the 'vagueness and morbidity' of this pioneer of genius. This style of writing has already reached its limits, and a fresh reaction is bound to follow in the direction of the full orchestra.

But it can be foreseen that the impulse which has been given, and above all, the lack of improvement in material conditions, will, on the other hand, keep the music of the present and the near future to the paths which it is now pursuing.

Does this mean that we are to see the disappearance of our full orchestras? Evidently not, for the masterpieces of the past still exist, and hold their place in popular favour. And further, there is nothing easier than to form a small orchestra out of the members of a larger one. But it is possible that we may see the growth of special orchestras, under the name of 'chamber orchestras'. London already has one of its own, under the conductorship of Anthony Bernard, and Georges Barrère founded a similar organization in New York some years ago, under the name of the 'Barrère Ensemble'. The little Spanish combination, which made its first appearance in London in 1925 under the name of the 'Orquestra Bética', would seem to belong to the same category. When these combinations have a sufficiently important repertory of their own, they will be able to do excellent work, for they will find it easy to obtain a first-class personnel. Such a combination, where every artist is a soloist, requires, from each of its members, a talent of the highest order. LOUIS FLEURY.

†CHAMINADE, CÉCILE, b. 1861, French composer, pupil of Benjamin Godard.

1st trio, pf, v, vc, g mi	op. 11	Durand.
2nd trio, pf, v, vc, a mi	,, 34	Enoch.

The above trios represent Madame Chaminade's contribution to chamber music. No. 1 opens with an allegro in clear, logical form, fluently and agreeably written. The andante which follows is a serene movement, based chiefly on melodic passages for the strings, with harmonies sustained on the piano by reiterated chords.

In the scherzo, presto leggiero, the piano has a Mendelssohnian brilliance and copiousness, but the string writing suffers from lack of rhythmical variety.

The finale, as so often happens in works of four movements, just lacks that dash of freshness which is needed after the scherzo. Its square vivacity does not animate the rather tame subject-matter, although the music is eminently playable.

The more ambitious plan and more virile style of the second trio is, perhaps, not so attractive as the delightfully feminine grace of the earlier work. The prevalence of scale progression in the melodies and some lack of character in the rhythmical construction prevent the first movement from being quite interesting enough for its length (twelve minutes). In the next movement (lento, E major) there is much doubling of parts, with some sacrifice of interest, although clarity of sound and shapeliness of form are apparent. In the finale (allegro energico, A minor) the piano is kept very busy, but the string parts are lacking in interest.

Taking the works as a whole, the composition shows affinity with the music of Benjamin Godard, and the influence of Le Couppey and Marsick, her other teachers, has borne fruit in the elegance and sureness of her writing for piano and strings. The soundness of the workmanship should command appreciation for the grace of the music, when a taste for that particular quality, at present somewhat obscured by interest in crudity, is revived.

KATHARINE EGGAR.

CHAPI Y LORENTE, RUPERTO, 1851–1909, Spanish composer.

	Composed	
1st quartet, str, G	1903	Sociedad de Autores Españoles (Madrid).
2nd quartet, str, F	—	
3rd quartet, str, D	1905	
4th quartet, str, b mi	—	

The best known of these long-neglected works is no. 1. It represents the first attempt of any consequence among Spanish composers to adapt national music to the string quartet medium. Chapi was chiefly a composer of light operas. PEDRO G. MORALES.

[A further short note by J. B. Trend gives some idea of the character of Chapi's work. EDITOR.]

The first quartet was described by the late Padre Villalba as bringing a breeze from the back streets of Madrid, which results in an expressive and catchy andante on a popular air employed also by de Falla in his ballet *The Three-Cornered Hat*. There is also a *Zapateado* (Spanish clog dance) in a dissolute gipsy style, and a *Zortzico* (Basque dance in 5/4) alternating with slum dances of unknown origin.

†CHAPUIS, AUGUSTE PAUL JEAN-BAPTISTE, b. 1858, French organist.

Serenade, 4 v	Durand	—
Trio, pf, v, vc, G	,,	1912.
Sonata, pf, v, g mi	,,	1921.
Suite, pf, vc (*Impressions Sylvestres*)	,,	—
Sonata, pf, vc, a mi and A	,,	1919.

Chapuis's chamber works are solidly constructed, skilfully written, and full of ideas. The most important of these is the trio, in four movements, the first of which (G minor), 'animé, pas trop, et très expressif', is full of vigour. It is developed fugally at first, then melodically, with a powerful conclusion in G major. The second, 'assez vif, spirituel et chantant', is a scherzo, light and lively, with an extremely flexible trio in G major. The third (B major), 'calme sans lenteur, contemplatif avec un grand sentiment', is a Lied,[1] with a slow march rhythm of quasi-religious character, a finely expressive theme, which is broadly developed, and is both calm and strong.

The finale (G major), 'gaîment, dans l'allure d'une ronde populaire', is full of life, and after a middle section, 'modéré, dans le sentiment d'une vieille ballade', ends with frank and healthy merriment.

A pupil of César Franck, Chapuis brings to his art the integrity which was the noble tradition of his great master.

ADOLPHE PIRIOU.

†CHARPENTIER, RAYMOND, b. 1880, French composer, pupil of Gédalge.

[1] See Foreword, art. BEETHOVEN.

Two poems by Baudelaire, pf, voice, str. quartet	Senart.

Charpentier has written a considerable number of chamber works as yet in MS.

CHARTIER, Charles-Jean, French musical amateur and donor of the Prix Chartier, annual prize of 700 francs for 100 years for chamber compositions. First awarded, 1861, to Mme Farrenc and Charles Dancla. The story of the legacy is in *Pougin*.

M. Drake-Brockman.

CHAUSSON, Ernest, 1855–1899, French composer.

	Composed	
Quartet (unfinished), str, c mi, op. 35	1899	Durand.
Concerto, pf, v, str. quartet, D, op. 21	1891	Rouart Lerolle.
Chanson perpétuelle, pf, voice, str. quartet	—	Durand.
Quartet, pf, v, vla, vc, A, op. 30	1897	Rouart, 1908.
Trio, pf, v, vc, g mi, op. 3	1882	Rouart, 1919.
[Trio, pf, v, vc		MS. composed 1882.]

If the well-known adage, 'The style is the man', expresses a truth, no artist's career could offer a better illustration of it than that of Ernest Chausson. Sincerity, good-heartedness, modesty—sometimes exaggerated to the point of a lack of faith in himself—such were the characteristic qualities of this fine musician, whose early death—the result of a wretched accident—was universally deplored, for he was loved by all who knew him. And these qualities are seen clearly throughout his works, written with a care and a talent, which was assured and ripened by ten years of study under the skilful teaching of the master, César Franck.

Chausson was, in fact, a member of that splendid brotherhood of musicians of the last generation who were ranged under the banner of the Société Nationale de Musique, and who did so much for the formation of a productive school of symphony and chamber music—types of composition till then unknown, or very rarely, and very ill cultivated in France.

It is especially in chamber music that Chausson's art is revealed, more completely even than in his dramatic or symphonic works. It is in this branch especially that his ascent towards the highest becomes assured, and it is here that the transformation is seen in continuous—one might almost say in gradual—fashion, of the richly endowed scholar into the master called to tread the loftiest summits of music.

From 1881 onwards, when he had only just ceased to take lessons with Massenet (who did not altogether satisfy him), in order to work with Franck, he was writing a trio in G minor for piano, violin, and 'cello. This is in four movements: introduction and allegro, intermezzo, andante, and finale. In this work, amidst its beauties and its weaknesses, one already feels the aspirations, as yet unrealized, of an artist-soul, whose loftiness of thought foreshadows works in which he will come to his own. The trio, op. 3, was performed for the first time at the concert of the Société Nationale of 8 April 1882, the artists being MM. André Messager, Rémy, and Delsart.

Maturer works were not long in making their appearance. On 8 July, 1891, Chausson signed the last page of the concerto in D major for piano and violin with string quartet—op. 21. This work, upon which he had been engaged since 1889, was the fruit of his studies with Franck.

The Concerto in D major, op. 21, shows themes which are all of high artistic merit, for Chausson had nothing in common with the mere scribblers of haphazard notes or chords, so frequently to be met with to-day. He was very meticulous in his choice of subjects for treatment, and did not begin to write until his musical ideas were completely settled in his head. But, in order to bring this work to the point, through what crises of doubt, through what periods of suffering must his spirit have passed, ever troubled, as he was, with the fear of 'not doing well enough', and of falling too far short of the ideal of which he had caught a glimpse! And again, with what affectionate gratitude he received the least sign of appreciation on the part of a friend whom he knew he could trust! Thus it was that after the first performance at Brussels of the concerto of which we speak, he wrote to Eugène Ysaÿe: 'I feel sure that this week spent with you will give me spirit and self-confidence. I scarcely know myself since my return from Brussels; I have never been so light-hearted and happy, and I cannot think of you all without emotion. I feel that I am going to do far better work than before, and it is to you that I shall owe this.'

The concerto (sometimes known as the sextet), which, according to the title, is in D major, is, in reality, as little as possible in this key. The first movement alone is constructed in major keys, which are recalled only in the very last pages of the finale, while the other three movements (the middle one especially) are impregnated with that rather wistful melancholy which is rarely absent from the work of the composer of *Le Roi Arthus*.

After thirty-four bars of preparation, there bursts forth a melody full of noble sincerity, which is to be the principal subject of the first movement. A second theme, in B major, also carefully prepared, but of a more dreamy character than the first, brings with it a somewhat fleeting element of charm, for this theme is scarcely developed at all, and appears only at the customary points required according to sonata form.

If the charming *Sicilienne* in A minor, which follows, leads us at times towards the gardens where bloom the charming fancies of a Gabriel Fauré, on the other hand, in the 'grave' it is Chausson himself who speaks to us—the Chausson of the farewells of Arthus and of the largo of the symphony. This is unmistakable, and the composer's strong individuality is evident throughout, especially, it may be added, in the statement of the second subject, with such anguish in its melody and rhythm, which brings back with a happy inspiration the key of D minor for a moment; then, despite its efforts, subsides into its original key of F minor, mastered by the fateful theme, appearing here not quite in its original form but in a formidable paraphrase which sinks little by little into the rigidity of death.

In this connexion it is perhaps interesting to observe how far those of the musicians of this period who died young seem, in the more emotional parts of their work, to have been haunted by a foreboding, as it were, of this premature journey to another world.

We have already met with this tendency in the case of Alexis de Castillon; we shall meet it again in the works of Guillaume Lekeu; and the mournful resignation of Ernest Chausson has nothing in common with the sufferings of a Beethoven, often terrible, yet ever full of hope.

The finale (très-animé) of the concerto is somewhat oddly conceived, and partakes rather of the nature of variation form than of one of the forms regularly employed in the sonata. In the finale there is, strictly speaking, but a single theme, which is treated in many different ways—by simple development, by amplification or abbreviation; it is, however, the method of rhythmic variation that is chiefly employed.

It is set out at considerable length in the key of D minor, nor is there any diversion made by the introduction of a fresh subject; the key then returns, like a restatement by means of a vigorous call, which is none other than the second theme of the preceding movement (the grave). At length, after adventures of various kinds, a new variation of the first theme recalls perhaps too briefly the key of D major, which, since the first movement, has been wellnigh forgotten; its appearance here justifies, at last, the title of the work.

This concerto is and remains, all things considered, a fine work. Those who were present at the first performance will certainly not have forgotten the enthusiasm with which it was received. This performance took place on 4 March, 1892, at Brussels, in the Salon des XX, where Octave Maus, that great pioneer, defended with such ardour the art of the 'younger generations' of those days. The performers were: Auguste Pierret (piano), Eugène Ysaÿe (solo violin), supported by the Quartet Crickboom, Biermasz, Van Hout, and Joseph Jacob.

THE PIANO QUARTET. Chausson could not remain idle. An indefatigable worker—after writing a piece for 'cello and piano (which was not published or played till 1925)—he began work on a quartet for piano, violin, viola, and violoncello. This composition was to mark a culminating point of his work, and here it is evident that he had made an immense stride forward, quite as much in the merit and charm of the ideas as in the novelty of the form, in which cyclic constituents, rhythmically modified, end by acquiring a double nature, which enriches and greatly strengthens the architecture of the work.

It is a curious thing, especially when one reflects that the quartet was written only two years before the composer's death, that, in this work, sadness seems to have given place to confidence. In fact, although the second cyclic theme (which appears first in the opening of the slow movement, and reappears in the finale) is always in the major key—yet retaining an undoubted melancholic character—one might say that Chausson, free at last from his doubts and his distress, thinks only of a flight to new and loftier regions of art, into which a way—hitherto unexplored—will open for him, a way so soon afterwards debarred to him by an unforeseen catastrophe.

If one studies the composer's very interesting sketch-books for the *Chanson perpétuelle*, one discovers traces—from the year 1896 onwards—of the quartet in a piece written for oboe and viola soli with an accompaniment of piano and string quartet, a tribute intended for his Belgian friends Guidé and Van Hout—from the composer of the concerto; but which was never finished. In this sketch, almost from the beginning, there is found, in the piano part, a statement of the second theme of the first movement of the A major quartet, in this form:

Ex. 1.

Then, there is a complete cessation of work till 20 July 1897, the date of the finishing of the intermezzo, soon followed by the first movement (17 September), and by the finale (23 October). The magnificent adagio is not to be found in the sketch-book which contains the other movements, but it is to be presumed that it was composed in the month of August of the same year.

This quartet merits a detailed analysis.

First movement. The first section (animé) opens with a strongly marked theme, which will appear again in the development of the finale.

Ex. 2.

A 'link', or 'bridge subject', based on two component parts, one rhythmic, the other melodic, leads, through varied modulations, to the second theme, which is in C major with flattened seventh, a cyclic theme which will appear again later.

Ex. 3.

The development, which is in three sections, begins, in C, with a rhythmic 'explanation' of the first theme, in order to bring out, in the other two sections, the second theme from the shadows, and to lead it, little by little, into the clear and luminous tonality of E major. After this effort, a subsidence both of rhythm and melody prepares the way for the recapitulation. This takes place normally, the second theme being this time presented in a more extended form than in the exposition, and in the key of F major. A 'final development' or coda deals anew with the first theme, at the beginning by augmentation, then by change of rhythm (to 6/4) in the principal key, and the movement dies away with a reminiscence (much fainter) of the second theme.

Second movement. The Lied (très calme), which forms the second movement of the quartet, is one of the loftiest melodic inspirations to be found in Chausson's works, an inspiration haunting and infinitely sorrowful, although it is in the major mode, in D flat.

Ex. 4.

The second section of the Lied presents a new phrase in F major, and leads, through modulations ever changing and growing more restless, to a true development of the first theme. This starts in A major and is built up in successive stages, ending at the third section, where the full phrase bursts forth, triumphant at last, in D flat, only to sink finally, soon after, into the dim obscurity of the key of C sharp minor.

This movement, written with consummate skill, will ever retain a poignant effect for all who have artistic sensibility.

Third movement. The third movement (simple et sans hâte), in D minor with flattened second, which takes the place of a scherzo, seems to be constructed, thematically, on some folk-song,

Ex. 5.

and keeps steadily to the same mood, even during the second section, which itself seems to be, as it were, an echo of the first. At length, the first melody reappears, more restless than at first, and ends in the key of D major.

Fourth movement. The first subject of the finale, which may be derived from the foregoing scherzo, is agitated, and characterized by a rhythm of somewhat individual nature; it begins in A minor, then, growing gradually calmer, it gently modulates towards the tonality of D flat major, in which key the second subject is at first outlined in the piano part, and then is transferred to the strings in a long and beautiful ascending phrase. It will be noticed that the beginning of this second theme is nothing more than a slightly varied reminiscence of the cyclic motif which commences the statement of the second subject of the first movement.

Ex. 6.

1st Movement.

From the start of the middle section of the finale the development is mainly concerned with the first theme, which is developed, and is treated—perhaps at rather too great length—in various guises and rhythmic forms, before leading to a double entry of the superb melody of the Lied (second movement); the solemn appearance of the saviour-prophet who comes to restore order among the revolted tribes. The melody appears first on the viola, in A flat major (Ex. 7); then, the voice mounts a tone higher—to the key of B flat major—and is intensified by the warmth of tone of violin and 'cello. After a short time we come to the recapitulation, where the first theme returns with certain modifications, followed, very quickly,

Ex. 7.

by the second, in C major. Then follows a final development, in which the forceful intervention of the cyclic theme—

Ex. 8.

is made use of to mark the definite return to the key of A major. Then, all this forceful display dies down, to be succeeded by a final serene statement of the Lied, completed by the brilliant escort of most of the cyclic themes employed in the course of the work.

Here is a detailed analysis of this fine quartet:

First Movt. (Animé):

I. EXPOSITION, (A^1) Key of A.—Link, with two constituents.—(B^1) Key of C.

II. DEVELOPMENT:
- 1. Derived from (A^1) and the Link.
- 2. Derived from (B^1). Key of D, with modulation.
- 3. Derived from (B^1) E.

III. RECAPITULATION:
(A^1) A, Link, (B^1) F.
Final development (coda):
(A^1) in augmentation E.
(A^1) by change of rhythm A.
Reminiscence of (B^1).

Second Movt. (Très calme):
(A^2) Lied-theme in three sections—D flat.
(B^2) F, agogic development of (A^2)—A.
(A^2) D flat; conclusion in C sharp.

Third Movt. (Simple et sans hâte):
(A^3) D.
(B^3) by development of (A^3).
(B^3) by change of rhythm—D.

Finale (Animé):

I. EXPOSITION.
(A^4) derived from (B^3)—A—Modulatory Link—(B^4)—D flat.

II. DEVELOPMENT:
- 1. Derived from (A^4) by change of rhythm.
- 2. ,, ,, (A^2) in notes of double length—A flat.
  ,, ,, (A^2) idem—B flat.
- 3. ,, ,, (A^2) by change of rhythm.

III. RECAPITULATION:
(A^4)—A—(B^4)—C.
Coda, derived from (A^1) then:
(A^2)—A, with (A^4) and (A^1).

The quartet in A, op. 30, dedicated to Auguste Pierret, was performed for the first time at the concert of the Société Nationale of 2 April 1898, by MM. A. Pierret, Armand Parent, Denayer, and Baretti.

Chausson's last work, which his sudden death prevented him from completing, is again a chamber work: a quartet for strings, in C minor. We shall not spend further time on a detailed analysis of this fine composition, as we consider that we have given the reader a sufficient insight into the artistic workings of Chausson's mind in the foregoing analysis. We feel, however, that a note is needed on the splendid style of the first movement (grave, puis modéré) in which a noble introductory theme serves as subject for the whole development of the movement.

The second movement (très calme), in simple Lied form, is built upon two very lovely songs, in A flat major and A flat minor, which give proof of the ever more strongly marked evolution of the composer of the concerto in D towards pure melody, springing directly from the artist's heart to be elaborated afterwards in orderly harmonious progress—the mark of a talent which has arrived at full maturity.

I may, perhaps, be excused for bringing myself forward personally in connexion with the third movement of this quartet (gaîment et pas trop vite). The movement begins in classic fashion, with the statement of a theme in F minor, followed, almost at once, by a second theme, which can be resolved into two component parts, in the key of E major (the A flat = G sharp serving as pivot-note). After a short development, this same theme appears in the recapitulation in C major (dominant of the principal key), and leads into a coda, or 'final development', in which this second theme is presented under a new rhythmic aspect—in 5/8 time. Here Chausson's manuscript breaks off (page 48 of the printed score). It is probable, since this movement takes the place of a scherzo (though not in scherzo form), that the composer had intended to write a finale which should restore the tonic harmony of the work.

Having undertaken to complete the unfinished quartet, so as to make its performance practicable, I thought that it would not violate the ideas of my dead friend if I were to end this movement, begun in the subdominant, by a return to the principal key of the work. Making use, therefore, of a few indications very shortly sketched by the composer, I reconstructed in the key of C major what Chausson would probably have written in F major, intending to write a finale. If this can be considered as a fault, I alone must bear the responsibility.

The quartet in C minor, op. 35, dedicated to Mathieu Crickboom, was composed in 1899, in the course of the very year in which Ernest Chausson died. It was performed at the concert of the Société Nationale of 27 January, 1900, the executants being MM. Armand Parent, Lammers, Denayer, and Baretti. This, then, was the last conception of a lofty spirit, a sincere lover of the beautiful, the development of whose very original style in chamber music seemed to be leading towards new paths in the realm of our Art. VINCENT D'INDY.

*†CHAVEZ, CARLOS, contemporary Mexican composer.

Henry Cowell writes of him that 'he has developed a method of writing polyphonic music of freshness and virility, in which there is almost absolute independence of the parts, so that each one has a charming melody of its own, but in which there is nevertheless a certain harmonic co-ordination which prevents meandering and unifies the whole fabric of the work. He does this by confining himself for certain periods to the diatonic scale. It has recently been shown that all the tones of any major or minor scale are related and can appear together as a harmony, if the spacing is arranged in such wise as to relate the various tones according to their position in the overtone system of the fundamental tones of the scale. Chavez has taken advantage of this for his counterpoint. He gives himself absolute freedom, within the limits of certain scale notes; but all of these notes are harmonically related in such a way that no matter in which direction the melodies turn, their harmonic balance is assured.'

Though he is an authority on Mexican folktunes, he does not base compositions upon them. On the other hand, it is not improbable that his music is influenced to some extent by his nationality. EDWIN EVANS.

†CHELIUS, OSKAR VON, b. 1859, German composer.

Sonata, pf, v, G op. 11 Junne, 1891.

A soldier, 'Flügeladjutant' to the Kaiser, trained as a musician.

CHERUBINI, MARIA LUIGI CARLO ZENOBIO SALVATORE, 1760–1842, famous composer.

	Comp.	
Quintet, 2 v, vla, 2 vc, e mi	1837	B. & H.
1st quartet, str, E flat	1814	Peters.
2nd quartet, str, C	1815–29	Peters.
3rd quartet, str, d mi		Peters.
4th quartet, str, E	1835	Payne.
5th quartet, str, F	1835	Payne.
6th quartet, str, a mi		Payne.

Cherubini also wrote two piano trios and a piece for string quartet for Baillot's music album. These have apparently not been published.

It is interesting to note that Cherubini's last quartets were composed at the age of seventy-five, when he wrote 'only for himself and his friends'.

Cherubini was one of the last great contrapuntists of the old school. His quartets may be divided into two sets of three each. The first set, dedicated 'to his friend Baillot', was published during his life; the second is posthumous.

THE FIRST QUARTET opens with a slow introduction of symphonic character. The following allegro agitato retains this symphonic style; it is built on three clearly distinguishable themes, which are splendidly vehement. At the beginning of the development the first subject reappears, with much modulation. This shortly leads to a return (in unison, *ff*) of the final episode of the first section of the movement. Then the second subject reappears, in counterpoint, with frequent changes of key; this is given out *ff*, in F minor, is slightly prolonged, then followed by a transition, working up with a steady crescendo to the reprise.

The recapitulation is normal, and a brilliant and vigorous stretto brings the movement to a conclusion.

The theme of the larghetto sans lenteur is in the nature of a prayer, and the writing is somewhat polyphonic. This theme gives rise to four variations. One of these, *pp*, in peaceful quavers, with its chromatic modulations, is reminiscent of Beethoven. The last (energico), which is of vehement character, ends with a peaceful coda.

The scherzo (in G minor) is in a style almost Spanish, with a trio in the major, which is nothing but a 'perpetuum mobile', written in striking fashion.

The finale is in sonata form and opens with seven bars in unison. Broad themes, scales in contrary motion, strong, regular, and powerful rhythm, give to this movement rather a symphonic character, and one is inclined to wonder if this first attempt of Cherubini in string quartet writing was not a transcription of an early symphony, as is the case with the next quartet.

THE SECOND QUARTET is, it appears, a transcription of the symphony written in 1815 for the London Philharmonic Society. It appears in the catalogue of his works drawn up by the composer, with the date 1829. The absence of appreciable change of style in the fourteen years between these two quartets seems less remarkable when one realizes that it was written only a year after the first quartet. The adagio was re-written in 1829, when the symphony was transcribed.

The question arises whether this work is the same as the one mentioned by Dr. Nef[1] as having been written by Cherubini for the London Orchestra; in fact, the author quotes a symphony in D major 'finished on April 24, 1815', the autograph of which is in the Berlin library.[2] The slow movement of the original symphony was a larghetto. But it is possible that Cherubini may have transposed into the key of C this symphony in D major, which is placed by Dr. Nef among the French works.

The work opens with a romantic introduction, of ethereal, gentle, and mysterious character. The charming echoes seem to have been intended for wind instruments. The allegro which follows is in the style of an overture (without repeat). The materials are as follows:—(1) a first subject, the continuation of which after the first few bars is considerably prolonged, and which, on passing to the second violin, is decorated with figures woven by the first violin; (2) a second subject in the minor mode—this is in canon (at first between treble and bass); (3) a continuation, or rather, a third, and very graceful subject, decorated with trills, which is given out by the first violin, and passes later to the bass. The whole section is prolonged by a weighty and powerful final episode, quite in the symphonic style. The transition leading to the development is curious and unusual. In the development itself, founded on the first subject, all the composer's contrapuntal resources are brought into play; the recapitulation follows: second subject, third subject, and final episode, leading to a return, *f*, of the first bar of the allegro, in the principal key, followed immediately by a coda, presto, as brief as it is powerful.

The movement which replaces the larghetto of the symphony begins with a recitative of dramatic character, which colours the whole of the movement. The emotion of this movement is too intense to be expressed in a continuous song; a cantilena on the first violin, with broken utterance, ends suddenly in a kind of variation in the major mode, quite in the Italian manner, *alla* Rossini; this is heard again in the continuation, in the course of which there reappears, in the major, the passage which followed the first variation. The cantilena ends with a mysterious coda, and two *ff* chords bring this profoundly dramatic movement to a close.

The scherzo, short, and full of energy, reminds one of Beethoven, and not less so the trio in the minor mode, with its warring rhythms and its breathless speed.

The finale is also inspired by Beethoven, both in the character of the themes and in the manner of their treatment. This virile and powerful movement in sonata form, with its double exposition, first in the tonic, then in the dominant, and its fugato in the middle section, seems to be influenced by Beethoven's ninth quartet; the opening theme, which is gathered together and concentrated to serve as a conclusion, preserves the symphonic style. The whole work is really a symphony, strong, brilliant, and concise.

THE THIRD QUARTET in D minor is a very fine and powerful conception.

The first allegro opens with a sort of prelude on the first violin in the style of a recitative, which gives rise to an ascending triplet figure in high notes, the bass answering with the same phrase, but with the triplets inverted. Then the first violin announces a noble and very violinistic theme, boldly rhythmic, soon to be interrupted by the appearance of the opening recitative with change of key. After this the second subject, a true Italian song, is given out by the first violin, to a strongly marked accompaniment, with a quasi-Spanish rhythm. The development, after the repeat, brings into play the figures used in the first section, and particularly the opening recitative. In the recapitulation it appears again in a shortened form; the first subject with its continuation also reappears, but leads at once to a return of the second, this time in D major. This is not the end; after a pedal point, the minor returns with a new and expressive treatment of the recitative, interrupted from time to time by the opening bars of the first subject; it is then linked to a coda in the major by the recitative, also in the major, the movement ending with a semiquaver passage, the four parts at first in unison, then in contrary motion.

The larghetto scherzando is a song for the first violin, and has a vocal quality akin to Bellini, or, taking into account that the singer is a violin, to Viotti. This song soars above a most expressive accompaniment:

Ex. 1.

[1] Dr. Oskar Nef, *Histoire de la Symphonie*, p. 170.
[2] See Hanslick, *Aus dem Konzertsaal*, 1870, p. 352.

The great scherzo which follows also shows the influence of Beethoven; the syncopated theme, presented first by the 'cello, then by the viola,

Ex. 2.

has a stern, rude energy. By contrast, after the repeat, a new subject bursts forth, *ff*, which leads into wild imitations, ending in a rugged unison passage. Then, with a polonaise-rhythm, comes the section in the major, which is announced by the first violin over an accompaniment of the other parts in quavers, ending on a tonic chord, pizzicato, played *ff* by all four performers. This major section again leads into a kind of fugato by way of trio, in which little triplet figures seem to dance over descending scales, the whole being closely woven together. Then comes a return of the major section in its entirety. Now the minor section reappears in shortened form, and, after the rugged unison passage, the major comes back once more on the first violin, but without accompaniment. The movement ends with a coda far more in symphonic than in quartet style, as, indeed, is the case throughout this scherzo.

The same fiery energy glows in the finale, which, although wholly in the major mode, and with a more kindly touch, retains the same dramatic and forceful note, and suggests the idea of unceasing strife.

The other three quartets were also, doubtless, intended for some violin 'star', probably Baillot.

THE FOURTH QUARTET opens with a telling bravura phrase, given out by the first violin, upon whom in all three quartets high demands are made; yet this in no way prevents the quartet from being as solidly written as if there were no question of instrumental virtuosity. Cherubini had evidently made a profound study of Beethoven's quartets; further, he had in mind the playing of Baillot. He had to sacrifice to the *manes* of the great master and to satisfy the desires of the virtuoso; hence the rhythmic variety, the interplay of the parts, the unyielding severity of the technique of composition, and also the very remarkable, very Italian way in which he suits his musical idiom to his instruments. To these qualities we may add almost always a strong feeling for the dramatic. For example, take the larghetto which succeeds the first movement of this quartet:

Ex. 3.

The ascending figure quoted above gives rise to all sorts of echoes, passing from key to key before leading into a song, in which every resource of the purest classical art is commingled with the dramatic, at times tragic, feeling of the Italian cantilena, even when the latter seems calm and reposeful. This larghetto, as a whole, is one of the most haunting instrumental movements ever penned by the great Florentine master. The final effect of the little figure followed by the pizzicato quaver, then dying away into silence, gives to the movement a poetic conclusion.

The scherzo consists merely of a few introductory bars, which lead up to an andantino con moto (muted),

Ex. 4.

which is a fantasy *alla* Beethoven, with varied interludes, now pastoral, now contrapuntal, then carried away by fury (all the parts in unison, *ff*, for more than a page), and finally a brilliant stretto, with use of the very highest harmonics.

In the finale (allegro assai) the Beethovenish vigour persists, but is tempered by the intervention of a broad singing theme of Italian style, which passes from the bass to the two upper parts.

THE FIFTH QUARTET is a model of style; in the first movement with its quiet prelude, and its first allegro where a theme is unfolded to sweep later in melodic curves through a series of quasi-Wagnerian chromatics, the composer displays daring harmony. The development is very short, but admirably carried out. The adagio is very simple and flowing, and the scherzo again breathes the spirit of Beethoven. The trio, in the major, is a kind of solo-capriccio for first violin, where one feels that the composer is seeking new paths. And one is again somewhat forcibly reminded of the famous fugato in Beethoven's ninth quartet as one listens to the finale of the work under consideration, in which the composer also employs the fugato now and then, a method which he manages with the most perfect freedom.

THE LAST QUARTET has a rather simpler first movement than its predecessors, with a double exposition of the first subject—a proceeding of frequent occurrence with Cherubini. One should note, in each section of the movement, the appearances of passages in the major, the frequent imitations, and the brilliant coda. The form of the andante grazioso answers more or less to that of the romance with two expositions, the second with variations; a middle section, also in two parts, the second again with variations. This andantino is something after Haydn's manner; it ends with a cadenza in the highest register of the violin.

The scherzo has a very romantic second section (or trio). But it is in the finale that the greatest surprise is in store—for this provides a most perfect example of cyclic form! At page 28 (of Payne's edition) the movement is interrupted by a series of short scales for first violin, followed by a pedal-point; soon the moderato theme of the first movement reappears, with the addition of a cadenza leading into the key of F major, in which key follow five bars of the andante grazioso; then comes the 3/4 of the scherzo; and then the finale continues once more on its way, ending brilliantly in the major. The present writer believes this to be one of the first examples, since Beethoven, of a method constantly employed by modern writers.

Cherubini's knowledge was wide and profound. He was ignorant of nothing concerning the later manner of the Bonn master; he had sounded its depths, and sought to reproduce even its passion, with the addition of a theatrical and dramatic element. In these six quartets the influence of Beethoven is clearly perceptible; a man of the intellectual stature of the Florentine could hardly have escaped it. But it must be said that Beethoven himself was not free from the influence of Cherubini, for whom he openly professed the warmest admiration.

One of the principal biographers of Cherubini, Denne-Baron,[1] states that, after a performance of these quartets and of the quintet (Cherubini's last chamber work) before an audience of connoisseurs, Cherubini was placed by them in the same rank as his predecessors, Haydn, Mozart, and Beethoven. Perhaps, one may add, the reason why he has not won fame in this branch of music is precisely because he was too skilful—had seen too much, and studied too deeply; his individuality, despite all his science, is not clearly stamped on his themes, marking them indelibly as his own, as is that of a Schubert or a Schumann. He was certainly no stranger to the romanticism then reigning; his quartets teem with effects which are directly derived from this source. But the grandeur, often tragic, of the Florentine master's art, the depth of his thought, his harmonic discoveries, leave no place for the woe so characteristic of the romantic school. He seems to have known neither tenderness nor agitation of spirit. These alone were lacking to him, and these cannot be acquired.

He was one of Beethoven's predecessors, and, in his quartets, one of his successors. That his place among these, as among the predecessors of Richard Wagner, should have been forgotten, is a grave injustice. For his quartets were written, for the most part, between 1829 and 1837, and he was one of the last to speak a language which is dead since his time. Had he written none but these six quartets, Cherubini would still have remained one of the heirs of the loftiest musical traditions of the past. He is among those who never compromised, a man of noble character and a great artist. GEORGES DE ST. FOIX.

[Four of Cherubini's quartets were played at the 'Pops', and I well remember Joachim's delightful playing of the trio to the scherzo of no. 1 (there are no opus numbers). It might have been signed Mendelssohn, yet neither knew the other's music. Truly *les beaux esprits se rencontrent*. An equally delightful trio is contained in the third quartet, and this also is a favourite with violinists, especially those who command a good spiccato bow. It has a roguish character, unlike any conception one may have formed of the tendencies of the austere academician whom Schumann compared to Dante. These quartets, indeed, are somewhat heavy in type, and have lost their hold on modern chamber music players.
EDITOR.]

CHEST OF VIOLS. *v.* CONSORT OF VIOLS.

[1] Denne-Baron, *Cherubini*, p. 53.

CHESTER'S LIBRARY, 11 Great Marlborough St., London, W. 1.

Founded 1860. Contains 3,000 chamber works, classical and modern. Proprietors, J. and W. Chester, Ltd., publishers of the *Chesterian* magazine, in which the references to chamber music are numerous and interesting. EDITOR.

†**CHEVAILLER**, LUCIEN, French composer.

1st sonata (*L'Enfant*)	pf, v	Senart.
2nd ,, (*L'Éveil*)	,, ,,	,,
3rd ,, (*Les Souvenirs*)	,, ,,	,,

All three sonatas were written especially for amateurs.

CHEVILLARD, CAMILLE, 1859–1923, French composer and conductor, son of Pierre Alexandre of the Chevillard Quartet.

Quartet, str, D flat	op. 16	Durand,	1901.
Quintet, pf, 2 v, vla, vc, E flat	,, 1	,,	1903.
Trio, pf, v, vc, F	,, 3	,,	1884.
Sonata, pf, v, g mi	,, 8	,,	1894.
Sonata, pf, vc, B flat	,, 15	,,	1897.

Though the influence of César Franck is felt to some extent in Chevillard's chamber works, he has plenty of originality and a first-rate sense of form.

THE QUINTET is an agreeable work to play, in spite of an occasional crudity, the scherzo, coming as it does after a somewhat funereal slow movement, being particularly exhilarating.

THE TRIO shows a decided advance in technique, but is a little more difficult to play. A notable feature is a cadenza given to the piano just before the coda of the finale, dealing not only with the subjects of this movement, but also with the main subject of the first movement. The finale is extremely brilliant, and full of *joie de vivre*.

THE VIOLIN SONATA is a work of very different character, and repays careful study, though at first sight it is somewhat forbidding. The rhythmic figure for the violin in the first bar will be found to be the germ from which spring many of the ideas which follow. The slow movement is practically a long recitative on the subjects of the first movement, and makes some demand on the musicianship of the performers. It leads without a break into a finale which partakes of the character of a polonaise. The violinist has here some opportunities for display unusual in a work of this kind.

THE 'CELLO SONATA is much less difficult. The themes and their treatment are more obviously attractive and there is nothing remarkable in the form of the work, except that the slow movement takes the rather unusual form of a barcarolle.

THE STRING QUARTET, though in the key of D flat, is not a work of any great difficulty. The manner of using the themes is modern, some of them appearing in each movement. The slow movement, like that of the quintet, is somewhat tragic in nature, ending with a well written viola solo.

It should be added that Chevillard was awarded the Prix Chartier in 1903.

W. J. MITSON.

CHILDREN AND CHAMBER MUSIC.

(*a*) AS PERFORMERS.

It is strange to think that individualized effort for communal ends is upheld as an ideal of our education in every school activity, that of music alone excepted. At school you play games; not for yourself, but for your side. At school you learn lessons; not by yourself, but with your fellows. At school you learn music, if you want to (or rather if you are wanted to). And what does that mean? A piano lesson all to yourself, and perhaps a class singing lesson in which you do exactly the same thing as everybody else at exactly the same time—synchronized duplication; and neither of these musical endeavours is individualized effort for communal ends; neither teaches you to be yourself for the common good.

Now this playing your game for the side is actually the essence of chamber music, and therefore it were well for it to find its place in the curriculum. Once the time is granted, the means for this exercise are more easily found than might appear, for it is not at first necessary to unearth full-blown quartets for practice. There are, unfortunately, few of these within the compass of juvenile capability. The budding Mozart may take his place among his elders, and partake of the same fare, but there is not much in the repertory that four ordinarily musical children can tackle. It is this that keeps back endeavour. But there need not be four; there may be two violins alone, or a piano and two violins; or these combinations and a 'cello. And what shall they play?

Here is the opportunity for initiative and power of adaptation in the teacher—or, even better, the parent—for it is chamber music performances by two or three in the home that will take the deepest root. Let music written for other purposes be used for these ends. Vocal duets can be played on two violins, with or without piano accompaniment. If the ear-training and harmony classes are producing simultaneous melodic lines—i.e. counterpoint—let these be tried on separate instruments. Even two children at the piano, each playing one of the tunes, will give the right idea and perhaps the necessary spurt. It is just the feeling for each individual part that it is necessary to cultivate, with the power to detect it, to make it stand out, to subordinate it, as required.

If four instruments should really be available, let them try the slower-moving Bach fugues from the *Forty-eight*; for instance, the superb

E major in Book II. Violin and 'cello can essay the two-part inventions. The point is briefly this: not to wait till numbers or capacity are equal to the achievement of a set work. There is always something to be done, however few there may be to do it and however limited their powers. And by such steps can be approached the playing of real quartets. HARRY FARJEON.

[Mr. Farjeon was one of the founders of a children's chamber music club, an organization which aimed at bringing the music to the notice of the children by performance and commentary. The first performance was held at the Francis Holland School, Belgravia. EDITOR.]

(*b*) AS LISTENERS.

Fifteen lecture concerts of chamber music have been given by me in the last few years under the auspices of the Schools Musical and Dramatic Association of London Elementary Teachers. The children are brought in hundreds to large halls in the various districts, paying from one penny to ninepence according to the class of district.

Any audience, whatever its age or stage of musical culture, will listen to an orchestra. It interests by its bustle, its many activities, and can storm the inattentive into listening. But chamber music cannot dominate: its realm is quietness. Where, then, audiences of a thousand and more children of the poor, of ages from eight to fourteen, are collected together for chamber music concerts in the town halls of East and South-East London, it is obvious that real listening is not to be expected at once but must be *induced*. Their lively interest in the music must be awakened before it is performed.

To show how this has been done it will be best to quote from the programme of one of the lecture recitals. In four respects it is typical. It contains (*a*) the first movement from Schubert's piano trio in B flat, (*b*) a piece of chamber music with a title such as a trio, *Impressions of a Holiday*, by Eugene Goossens, (*c*) short picturesquely named solos for piano interspersed between the concerted items, (*d*) a choral interlude half-way through the programme for the children to sing in unison (this gives welcome physical release to their young energies).

The talk to the children before the Schubert trio is directed to show how just two tunes can make long and delightful music. The themes are spoken of as if they were two chief characters in a story. They are played first, and sometimes sung by the young audience. Excerpts from the whole movement are played by myself at the piano and colleagues, accompanied by a running fire of comments of the kind likely to enlist the active interest of a child, e.g. the 'development' is treated as the adventures happening to the tunes—one becomes sad; another storms; the two meet and are heard together—till they come back in their original form to be heard clearly again, like the happy ending of a story.

During the subsequent performance the real enjoyment of the children is evident in their faces and in the hushed listening to pianissimo passages; even where the musical sensibility is low there is interest in following, in recognizing the themes, in noting the interplay of the instruments. But some faces may remain vague and listless, their owners quiet only because of the prevailing atmosphere of attention. These quicken at the other concerted items, always chosen to catch the attention of the less musical by some extraneous interest.

For instance in Goossens' trio there are numbers headed *The Water Wheel*, *The Village Church*, and *At the Fair*. As the reader may imagine, the opportunities are many of amusing children with reference to the splash of water, the sound of bells, the whirr of roundabouts, &c., and at the same time of *exercising* them in listening to the individual voices of each instrument, to the intimate interplay and to the ensemble. Thus one tries to gain continuous and complete listening—not confined to the top line and to catchy bits of the music; to awaken interest in the development of much music from short themes; and to train the power to recognize and to enjoy their manifold manifestations.

The response is unmistakable and surprising. CLARISSE SPEED.

CHOPIN, FRÉDÉRIC FRANÇOIS, 1810–1849, Polish composer.

Trio, pf, v, vc, g mi	op. 8	1828	Costallat critical edn.	B. & H., &c.
Sonata, pf, vc (or v), g mi	,, 65	—		B. & H.
Introduction and Polonaise, pf, vc, C	,, 3	1828		Peters, Litolff, &c.

In Chopin the romantic school found its highest expression; but it was through one instrument, the piano, that he chiefly expressed himself.

THE POLONAISE BRILLANTE, op. 3, for piano and 'cello, is of the order of a brilliant drawing-room piece. It was written at the age of nineteen, when the composer had not yet formed any style worth talking about. Though an excellent piece in its own way, it cannot be said to be the Chopin known to all of us. The opening of the polonaise is somewhat commonplace; there is more individuality in the introduction. Niecks observes, 'What subdued the composer's individuality was, no doubt, the 'cello, which, however, is well provided with grateful cantilene'. This criticism does not take into account Chopin's age, and the superficial life which he led up to the age of twenty. It was not until he left Poland for good (in 1820), and had encountered the patriotic Polish colony in Paris, two years later, that his romantic patriotism blossomed forth. Without this stimulus he might have died a 'mute inglorious Milton'; so that we see this first chamber piece stands outside the real body of his music. Nevertheless it contains some prophetic touches, especially the counter-subject in F major for the 'cello. In the piano part the leaning towards Hummel is evident. Some of the passage-work gives a hint of Weber's *Moto Perpetuo*, a piece which Chopin almost certainly knew, but the 'cello has the best of the bargain. Chopin himself under-estimated the work, but he recognized its true character. Writing to his friend, Titus Woyciechowski, he says:

'I wrote an *Alla Polacca* with 'cello accompaniment during my visit to Prince Radziwill. It is nothing more than a brilliant drawing-room piece suitable for the ladies. I should like Princess Wanda to practise it. I am supposed to have given her lessons. She is a beautiful girl of seventeen, and it was charming to guide her delicate fingers.'

Joseph Merk (1795–1852), to whom the piece is dedicated, was a highly polished Viennese 'cellist at the court opera, Vienna.

THE TRIO is the only instance of Chopin's writing for the violin at all. It is a youthful work, for it dates from his eighteenth year. In August 1830 he wrote:

'Last Saturday I tried the trio, and, perhaps because I had not heard it for so long, was satisfied with myself. "Happy man," you will say, won't you? It then struck me that it would be better to use the viola instead of the violin, as the first string predominates in the violin, and in my trio it is hardly used at all. The viola would, I think, accord better with the 'cello.'

Schumann praised it on its publication in 1828, but reminded his readers that it had been written some years before. There is too much of the tonic key in the first movement. The scherzo is lively and flowing, the adagio charming, and the finale cheerful and vivacious. 'Its classicism may be disputed,' wrote Huneker, 'nevertheless it contains lovely music.'

THE 'CELLO SONATA was the last composition published during Chopin's life-time. Sir Charles Hallé gave an interesting account of his hearing Chopin and Franchomme play this sonata soon after it was written:

'Chopin grew weaker and weaker to such a degree that when we dined together at Leo's or other friends' houses, he had to be carried upstairs, even to the first floor. His spirits and his mental energy remained nevertheless unimpaired. . . . On our arrival we found him hardly able to move, bent like a half-opened penknife, and evidently in great pain. We entreated him to postpone the performance, but he would not hear of it; soon he sat down to the piano, and as he warmed to his work, his body gradually resumed its normal position, the spirit having mastered the flesh.'

Judged by the standards of the 'cello sonatas by Beethoven, Mendelssohn, and Brahms, Chopin's is naturally found wanting. The first movement is weak in construction, and is too crowded with ideas, &c. Chopin himself, when playing it in public, omitted the first movement, and played the scherzo, adagio, and finale. The logical development which is so often expected in the longer forms is not there, but there are many beauties which atone for its absence. The sonata certainly deserves to be more frequently heard.

A. EAGLEFIELD HULL.

[It is generally conceded that Chopin's piano trio is vastly inferior to his compositions for piano alone, which gave to the world new conceptions of romantic beauty; but Schumann, always indulgent, wrote of it (*Gesammelte Schriften*) as follows:

'What can I say of this trio that every one who understands it has not already said to himself? Is it not as noble as possible, more enthusiastic than the song of any poet, original in detail as in the whole, every note life and music?'

I am glad that Dr. Hull has drawn attention to the beauties of the 'cello sonata, in which there are traces of the real Chopin we all love.

EDITOR.]

CHOREGRAPHY: ITS ALLIANCE WITH CHAMBER MUSIC.

In my time—I scarcely know why—I have fought against realization of the truth that in all music, including the most serious, there is a subconscious suggestion of bodily movements, of miming and the dance. I was jealous, perhaps, of the intrusion of any conception of music other than the spiritual, but in the end capitulated, and now am reconciled to the conviction that music and the dance are indivisible. The point is illustrated by a little experience of my own, which I think is worth relating.

Some years ago I was favoured with a visit from Ruth St. Denis, the famous danseuse, who, after listening several times to my home Quartet, which then included Efrem Zimbalist (already well known as a violin virtuoso), said: 'This splendid music surely lends itself to illustration by dancing and miming; it is "asking" for it.' Miss St. Denis, a woman of strong character, proceeded to deeds; at her instance we had the carpet up in my drawing-room, and she improvized a little scene which gives me much reminiscent joy. She asked us to play the andante from the F major quartet of Dvořák, and this is the story which she illustrated in her own inimitable way: 'A geisha who had lost her lover visits the shrine erected over his burial-place, and honours his memory in the only way she knows how —by dancing before it; first of all with quiet dignity, and then, as the excitement of the music grows in intensity, with frenzied animation. During the final melodramatic bars she falls to the ground unconscious.' This little drama was illustrated by Miss St. Denis in a manner so arresting that we quartettists had difficulty in keeping our eyes from wandering in the direction of the danseuse. From that day I have held the conviction that here were the germs of a new adventure in concert-giving, promising success if only artists of the calibre of Miss St. Denis were available. Russian chamber music, which draws inspiration in almost every page from the ballet, appears to be indicated for further experiment. It is of interest to record that Madam Karsavina made a great success by dancing in the open-air theatre (Naturtheater) at Salzburg, and afterwards in several continental cities, to the strains of Mozart's *Eine kleine Nachtmusik*, which, as every one knows, is of the nature of chamber music; and that at Leicester, under the direction of Lady Cholmondeley, a ballet has been danced (and mimed) to the music of Haydn's string quartet, op. 76, in G major, played by the Kutcher Quartet. A similar performance is being arranged by students of the R.C.M. (1929).

Since writing the above I have received the following article from Mr. Leigh Henry, who pursues the subject farther. EDITOR.

To suggest union between dancing and chamber music is almost offensive to some. This is largely the result of stiff nineteenth-century conventions, by which the intimate original significance of chamber music has been forgotten. Yet there is a close and essential relationship between the origins and forms of chamber music and the art of the dance. It is a matter of history that, from the earliest, pre-instrumental, vocal forms of social music, —carols, rounds, and the later sarabandes and 'ballets to voices'—it was customary to accompany the singing with dancing. When dealing with the formal evolution of chamber music—with those suites whence evolved successively the sonata da camera, concerto da camera, and, finally, the classical sonata form—the original relationship becomes undeniable. A succession of dance airs formed the movements of the earliest suites, such as those of Sweelinck, and this continued through the works of the Jacobeans and of Lully, Purcell, Vitali, Corelli, the Couperins, Rameau, and the Scarlattis, to the culminating suites of Johann Sebastian Bach, with their dance forms—coranto, allemand, gigue, &c. These masters, supplemented by Haydn and Mozart, developed the conception of sonata form, which originated in an extension of the earlier, looser suite form. Indeed, with composers such as Domenico Scarlatti, for example, the sonata was itself a succession of dance movements, specifically so designated. Further proof is found in the conventional employment of the 'minuet and trio' in the earlier phases of sonata form. That the minuet should have kept its ground until well over a century after the appearance of the first suites goes far to prove that this association between dancing and chamber music forms existed in the minds of musicians and public alike.

While the hyper-aesthetical dislike to such an association is thus seen to be historically unsound, it must be admitted that the progress of social usage in dancing has gone far to create a rift between that art and any true type of chamber music. On the other hand, almost any phase of the development of chamber music provides movements—rhythms and themes—which irresistibly suggest dancing, and which may even create a keen desire to behold dance rhythm visualized.

The immediate question, however, is—what form shall such visualization take? Shall it be an impulsive emanation from the music, carried out instinctively and *à l'improviste*, in movements entirely subordinated to the music itself? Or shall it, itself, reconstitute the old art of dancing with chamber music, along lines of combined formal development? Shall the dancing itself follow a clear formal scheme corresponding to, but not merely dominated by, the music? In other words, since the rhythm of the music itself is founded on dance movement, shall not the dance in turn owe something quite explicit to the formal design of the music, with its thematic balance, its reprises, its alternations, not merely of mood, but of phrase and movement? Does not the dancer to chamber music require to be essentially musical in the understanding of musical form, i.e. a choregraphist proper?

An example may point the question. In May, 1922, the writer and fellow members of the Council of the Faculty of Arts held a meeting at which the speakers included so eminent a musician as Sir Landon Ronald, and it was felt that adequate representation of music should be made in the evening's entertainment. The Hungarian Quartet were asked to play, and one of their contributions was the Ravel quartet. Ruth St. Denis, another of the associates and guests present, was greatly moved by this music, and expressed the feeling already alluded to by Mr. Cobbett that it seemed to demand actual dancing associated with it—a feeling natural in a dancer. After discussion, so much interest was evinced that the Council agreed to arrange what may be termed a test event. Mr. Finn, the well-known artist, offered his Chelsea studio for this purpose, and here, some evenings later, the attempt was made, the Hungarians playing Ravel's quartet again. Their playing was inspired by the unusual occasion, and Miss St. Denis's dancing was full of poetic imagination. Nevertheless, for the writer at least, though the incidental moments were charming, it still remained unsatisfactory. Music and dancing were coincident, but not correspondent, scarcely even complementary. This was probably because Ruth St. Denis lacked insight into the actual musical design, and was improvizing (always a dangerous thing, especially when actuated by poetic sentiment) rather than interpreting or counterbalancing the music in choregraphic design. One noted this particularly when the recurrence of identical phrases brought movements diametrically opposed in mood and design. One noted it again in the 'take-off' of movements and their rhythmic flow, which neither corresponded to the musical rhythm nor fulfilled that asymmetrical principle which would have given it a counter-significance. Ultimately, indeed, the artists themselves (more honest than many of their audience) declared the experiment aesthetically a failure. It had, however, its very positive interest. It represented, so to speak, a rhetorical conception of dancing-out music, rather than a reading, such as a conductor gives of an orchestral score.

To this a counter-impression. Some time ago the writer worked considerably with pupils of Annea Spong. Their teacher's principles were admirable, but when it came to the interpretation of a Bach suite as compared with the Debussy quartet, a plain difference appeared. The formal outline of the Bach suite permitted of an architectonic plan fitting the dancing to the music; in the Debussy, the dance-architectonic subordinated the musical one. The movements reached a formal design which took away the character of the musical rhythm.

Lastly, the preliminary essays with Adolph Bolm may be considered. These took place before he returned to America to launch his *ballet intime*, explicitly designed to interpret in terms of chamber ballet the varied types of musique de chambre and chamber orchestra. Here was a consummate dance artist who was also possessed of a keen knowledge of music. It was remarkable to note how he chiselled at his conceptions until his initial movements became in all essentials the equivalents of subject enunciation in sonata form; and how, no matter how impulsive became the evolution of his dance plan, the initial motif form of the dance figures was maintained recognizably through all mutations. This refers, of course, to his solo designs; in ensemble dancing (probably, to give the true characteristics of chamber music, an ensemble of dancers as well as of players is needed), his dancers became true 'dance voices', coinciding with the part-playing of the instrumentalists, without one medium being dependent on the other.

Since that time, happy circumstances have brought the writer into contact with Mr. Cobbett, and from conversation it has emerged that he, ever eager to further anything that tended towards a virile and human conception of the art of chamber music, had also made experiments on the association of dancing with chamber music. While these experiments appear to belong rather to the improvisatory type, the dancer had the advantage of hearing the music first, and thus was able to establish a clearer plan of its rhythmic scheme and general mobile design.

Mr. Cobbett has recently inaugurated what one might term household 'eisteddfodau'—social gatherings of string players competitively reading from scores at sight. Research would be greatly benefited by the establishment of many similar home eisteddfodau for this purpose. For the rhythmic sense developed amongst children by action-songs would supply the required data; and, further, groups of amateur or professional dancers could be invited to co-operate, with the idea of discovering how far it is possible to invent 'real part' dance forms to correspond with chamber music. Probably then, as with his revival of the phantasy form, Mr. Cobbett would once more resuscitate tradition and bring to life again the age of the 'Ballet of voices', of chamber art origins and associations.

LEIGH HENRY.

CHOVAN, KOLOMAN, b. 1852, Hungarian composer.

Trio, pf, v, vc, f mi	op. 10	Rózsavölgyi, 1891.

†**CHRÉTIEN**, MADAME HEDWIGE, contemporary French composer.

Scène Rustique, pf, ob	Evette & Schaeffer, 1921.

CHVALA, EMMANUEL, 1851–1924, Bohemian composer.

1st quartet, str, d mi	Fr. A. Urbánek, 1886.
2nd quartet, str, c mi	Simrock, 1898.
Volkstänze in Kammerstil, str. quartet	Fr. A. Urbánek, 1894.
Trio, pf, v, vc, g mi	,, ,, 1902.

Chvala's first quartet may be recommended to amateurs who are not possessors of an advanced technique. No. 2 in C minor is a more important work, in which the contrast in feeling between the dramatic opening movements and the light and attractive final rondo is very marked. It is impregnated with the Czech spirit.

EDITOR.

†**CIMADOR**, GIAMBATTISTA, *c.* 1761–*c.* 1808, Italian violinist and pianist, settled in London.

It was Cimador who made Mozart's symphonies known in London. The orchestra of the King's Theatre refused to play them on account of their difficulty; he therefore arranged six as sextets (2 v, 2 vla, 2 vc; cb and fl, ad lib.) and got them performed. He also wrote duets for two violins and violin and viola.

M. DRAKE-BROCKMAN.

CIUNTA, PAUL. *v.* ROUMANIAN COMPOSERS.

CLAFLIN, Avery, b. 1898, American composer, pupil of Erik Satie.

Trio, pf, v, vc, b mi — Senart.

CLAPISSON, Antonin Louis, 1808–1866, French violinist.

1st quartet, str, c mi — Costallat.

CLARINET IN CHAMBER MUSIC.

The clarinet is the wind instrument most used in chamber music by reason of its beautiful and flexible tone, wide range of dynamics, and large compass. Unfortunately few laymen, and too few among amateur musicians, realize the tenderness and richness of its timbre, judging from the sounds heard from the clarinet section of the ordinary military or jazz band. The brilliance and power of its tone in the symphony orchestra give an insufficient impression of its power of diminuendo, for the clarinet can play softer or louder than any of the stringed instruments, throughout its entire range of three and a half octaves.

The clarinet is at once an instrument of melody and accompaniment. Its tone, the antithesis of that of the thin and penetrating oboe, is yet able to give pathos and poignance to a phrase (*v.* Brahms's quintet, op. 115). Limpid as the flute, and as agile, it is at the same time more graceful and has more body. Reducible to a vanishing point in nuance, it will blend with any combination of strings or wind, adding richness, but never being intrusive.

Early Works. The clarinet was not technically developed at the time of Bach and Handel, and thus does not share in the fine legacy of sonatas left by these masters to the flute and oboe. Its first appearance is in a quartet with strings by Karl von Stamitz.

Mozart. It was Mozart who first appreciated the unusually beautiful tone and expressive quality of the clarinet, and gave it its rightful place in the family of classical instruments. His quintet with strings and his trio with viola and piano (not to mention the concerto) utilize the instrument to the full, and are more played than any other works for the instrument.

Weber. Next to Mozart comes Weber in point of time and technical development. His works are more florid and brilliant than those of his forerunner, and the characteristic sudden contrasts in dynamics and wide skips in pitch are used with much dramatic effect. The duo concertant with piano, and the quintet with strings are the show pieces of the repertory.

Brahms. Chronologically, Brahms comes third on the list, but he stands close by Mozart in the heart of the clarinet devotee. Inspired by his friend the great clarinettist Mühlfeld, he composed some of his masterpieces for this instrument, and brought out to the full its expressive and romantic qualities. Now it yearns and strives, now it cries in grief; its formality is humanized; it rejoices and is gay; it is graceful and piquant; it is strong and masculine; it is elegiac and pastoral; it is roughly defiant. Brahms's four works—the trio with 'cello and piano, the superlative quintet with strings, and the two sonatas with piano—are among his very best, and reveal a perfect understanding of the artistic resources of the instrument.

Reger wrote three excellent clarinet sonatas, and what is perhaps his finest chamber work, the quintet in A with strings, op. 146, in which the possibilities of its tone-colour are abundantly demonstrated.

Modern Composers. Among more modern composers who have developed still farther the artistic resources of the timbre and technique of the clarinet may be mentioned, first, Stravinsky with his suite of three pieces for clarinet alone, his songs, *Berceuses du Chat*, with three clarinets (note the marvellous purring in No. 1), and the trio for violin, clarinet, and piano based on the music of *The Soldier's Tale*, though the last-named is perhaps not chamber music in the strict sense, since it needs the stage picture to make its meaning entirely clear. Another is Alban Berg, disciple of Schönberg, who, in his suite of four very short movements, has introduced the flutter-tongue effect and the unbeautiful roughness possible to the chalumeau (low) register, which is, however, sometimes capable of producing great dramatic effect, as in Weber and Elgar. And a third is Arthur Honegger, in the last movement of whose sonata with piano the slide of the jazz player is playfully introduced.

Clarinet with Voice. Now that the singer (when provided with more background than that of the piano alone) has been received into the exclusive realm of chamber music, mention must be made of the great beauty of clarinet tone in combination with the voice. Operatic obbligati were earlier examples of this juxtaposition, but the effect is much heightened in the more intimate song forms. Spohr has given us six beautiful songs with clarinet and piano; Schubert the well-known *Shepherd on the Rock*, which is not, however, one of his masterpieces; and Arthur Bliss his delightful *Nursery Rhymes*, one of which is for voice and clarinet alone. Also there are the Stravinsky songs above mentioned. Composers should dream more in these tone-colours.

Appended is a list of all the chamber music known to be published, in which the clarinet is combined with piano and strings. Works in which the clarinet is one of a group of wind instruments are reserved for another article. Beside each listing is a brief comment on the character and 'playability' of the work, this being handier for reference than in the body of the text.

The Various Types of Clarinet. Of clarinets of other sizes than the usual instruments in B flat and A in chamber music, no use is made of the shrill E-flat clarinet except in the Stravinsky songs. The bass clarinet finds a part in these same songs and in the Schönberg song-cycle, *Pierrot Lunaire*, where it is used interchangeably with the B-flat clarinet. But the now unfortunately disused basset horn, an alto clarinet in F with additional low tones, with its soft mellow timbre of rich beauty and phenomenal range of four full octaves,

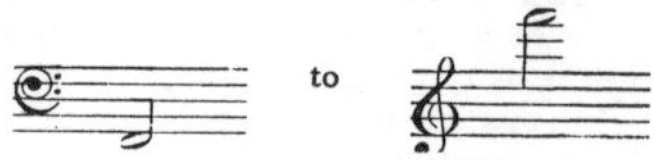

deserves more literature than the two effective phantasy pieces for clarinet, basset horn, and piano by Mendelssohn. These are but seldom heard because of the rarity of the instrument, which is generally possessed only by first-class opera orchestras for performances of Mozart's opera *Titus*, and Beethoven's seldom-heard ballet, *Prometheus*.

Sonatas for clarinet and piano.

1. Adaievsky, Ella: Greek sonata. Tischer & Jagenberg, 1913. Good as Greek atmosphere, and musically effective if shortened by judicious cuts.

2–4. Bach, J. S.: Three sonatas transcribed by E. Stievenard. Evette & Schaeffer, Paris. Not originally written for clarinet, but such great music that attention is called to their availability for study by clarinettists.

5. Boisdeffre, René de: op. 13. Hamelle, 1875. Not of great value.

6, 7. Brahms, J.: op. 120, no. 1, F mi.; no. 2, E flat maj. Simrock, Berlin. The greatest sonatas for the instrument.

8. Bumcke, G.: op. 9, F sharp mi. Simon, 1905. Not vitally interesting.

9. Draeseke, F.: op. 38. Kistner, 1888. Playable, but little more; good for early study.

10. Gouvy, Théodore: op. 67, G mi. Richault, Paris, 1882. Well written for the instrument in rather melodramatic but brilliant style.

11. Heap, C. S.: B flat maj. B. & H., 1880. Enjoyable, but antiquated.

12. Hill, Edward Burlingame: sonatina. S.P.A.M., 1927. Very attractive and melodious.

13, 14. Hofmann, Richard: op. 48, no. 1 in G sharp; no. 2 in F. Siegel, 1885. Useful as studies.

15. Honegger, A.: Atonal. Rouart, Lerolle, 1924. Modern, but playable. Last movement *à la* jazz.

16. Ingenhoven, Jan. Tischer & Jagenberg, 1916–17. Modern, purposeless, and ineffectual.

17. Jenner, Gustave: op. 5. B. & H., 1900. Very much after Brahms, and very good music.

18. Juon, Paul: op. 82. Schlesinger, Berlin, 1924. Very interesting; in one extended movement.

19. Karg-Elert, S.: op. 139 b. Zimmermann, 1924. Modern, difficult, but very piquant and effective.

20. Karren, L.: *Sonate d'église* (also for organ instead of piano). Millerau, Paris, 1890.

21. Kornauth, E.: op. 5, F mi. Zimmermann, 1922. A striving after something that does not seem to come off.

22. Mason, Daniel Gregory: op. 14. S.P.A.M., 1920. A very interesting work, effectively written for both instruments. The scherzo based on the whole-tone scale.

23. Pogge, Hans: op. 14 in F. Eulenburg, 1912. Well made German music, but says nothing much.

24. Prout, E.: op. 26 in D. Augener, *c.* 1886. In late classical style, grateful and brilliant, if stiff and schoolmasterish.

25. Rheinberger, Jos.: op. 105, E flat mi. Kistner, 1893. Good to play at home. In a difficult key for clarinet.

26, 27. Reger, Max: op. 49, no. 1 in A flat; no. 2 in F sharp mi. Aibl, 1903. Two very fine sonatas requiring very intelligent performance.

28. Reger, Max: op. 107, B flat. B. & B., 1909. Finer than the earlier works, using to the full the possibilities of the clarinet for delicate nuances. Needs very careful performance for its full effectiveness. Next to the Brahms examples the greatest clarinet sonata.

29. Saint-Saëns, C.: op. 167 in E flat. Durand, 1924. A very effective though rather light work. Very good for concert performances.

30. Setaccioli, G.: op. 31 in E flat. Ricordi, 1921. Well written, and full of rather novel effects.

31. Stanford, Chas. V.: op. 129 in F. S. & B., 1919. The best of the English sonatas. The 'lament' (slow movement) is very fine indeed.

32. Tovey, Donald F.: op. 16 in B flat. Schott & Co., 1912. Not very interesting.

33. Weber, C. M. von: op. 47. Grand duo concertante. Several editions. Very brilliant. Best show piece in the literature, using the whole compass of the clarinet. Wears well in performance.

Suites or extended movements for clarinet and piano.

1. Baermann, Carl: opp. 84–87. Phantasy pieces. André. Twelve pieces in four suites by a famous clarinettist. Good for study, but not of much musical value.

2. Baussnern, W. von: Suite no. 3. Velweg, Berlin, 1924. Fairly interesting, using well the capabilities of the clarinet.

2a. Berg, Alban, op. 5. Four pieces. Very *outré*; interesting as studies in effects. U.E., 1920.

3. Clifton, Chalmers: Intermezzo and Humoresque. H. L. Le Roy, Paris, 1926. Very fine indeed. Good for public performance.

4. Fairchild, Blair: Suite, three numbers. Pitault, Paris. Pleasing; the first andantino the best of the group.

5. Frugatta, Giuseppe: op. 44. Suite in six numbers. Ricordi. Pleasing, light and brilliant.

6. Gade, N. W.: op. 43. Phantasy pieces. Kistner. Very melodious and effective.

7. Hurlstone, Wm. Y.: Suite of four pieces. Cary & Co., London. Imaginative, dramatic, and bright. Very well-written and effective concert numbers.

8. Laurischkus, Max: op. 4. Eight miniatures. Simon, Berlin. Delightful pieces in vivid colours.

9. Laurischkus, Max: op. 30. Three pieces. Simrock. Very brilliant and effective.

10. Longo, A.: op. 2. Suite in two movements. Ricordi. Not important.

11. Reinecke, Carl: op. 256. Introduction and allegro. Bosworth & Co., London. Well written and quite interesting.

12. Schumann, R.: op. 73. Three phantasy pieces. Pohle, Hamburg. In Schumann's best vein; difficult for clarinet.

13. Stanford, Chas. V.: op. 13. Three intermezzi. Novello. Good music, well written.

14. Walthew, Richard H.: suite. F. Boosey & Co. Pleasant, but not deep.
15. Weiner, Leo: op. 8. Ballade. Rózsavölgyi. Flowing, melodic, effective, difficult.

For two clarinets.

1. Mozart, W. A.: Twelve duos for two basset horns.
2. Poulenc, F.: Sonata. Chester. Interesting, very modern, very difficult.
3. Stark, Robert: op. 49. Studies in sonata form. Schmidt.

Trios: clarinet, violin, and piano.

1. Baussnern, W. von. Simrock, 1905. Not very interesting.
2. Mason, Daniel Gregory: Pastorale. Mathot. A very beautiful work which bears repetition.
3. Stravinsky, I.: *The Soldier's Tale*. Chester. (Setting for trio by composer.) Very modern and difficult, but vivid.
4. Walthew, Richard: trio. Boosey, 1897. Fluent, but unimportant.

Trios: clarinet, viola, and piano.

1. Amberg, J.: op. 12. Phantasy pieces. Hansen, 1911. Weak.
2. Bruch, Max: op. 83: Nine pieces. Simrock, 1910. Well made but of varying interest.
3. Hollander, A.: op. 53. Six character pieces in canon form. Schlesinger, 1898. Very good.
4. Mozart, W. A.: K. 498. Trio. B. & H. Mozart's finest trio for any combination. Pure delight from beginning to end.
5. Reinecke, Carl: op. 264. Trio. Simrock, 1903. Well made.
6. Schumann, R.: *Fairy Tales*. 1854. Not Schumann at his best.

Trios: clarinet, basset horn, and piano.

1. Mendelssohn, F.: Concertstück, no. 1. B. & H.
2. ,, Concertstück, no. 2. B. & H. Most effective writing, in Mendelssohn's best style.

Trios: clarinet, 'cello, and piano.

1. Amberg, J.: op. 11. E flat. Hansen, 1912.
2. Beethoven, L. van: op. 11. Not Beethoven at his greatest, but very enjoyable.
3. Berger, Wilhelm: op. 94. Kahnt, 1905. Makes full and effective use of all the colour of the combination. A very good work.
4. Brahms, J.: op. 114. Simrock, 1892. The finest trio extant for the combination.
5. Farrenc, Louise: op. 46. Leduc. In late classic style, a pleasing salon trio.
6. Hartmann, Emil: op. 24. Serenade in three movements. Simon, 1890. Effectively written but too saccharine.
7. Hünten, Franz: op. 175. Terzetto. Schott, 1851. Old-fashioned in style.
8. Indy, Vincent d': op. 29. Hamelle. A long work of intellectual beauty. Splendid slow movement. A big work by a master.
9. Kahn, Robert: op. 45. Schlesinger, 1906. Fluent though not vital.
10. Ries, Ferd.: op. 28. Old-fashioned.
11. Skraup, Franz: op. 2. Hoffmann, Prague, 1846. Old-fashioned.
12. Zemlinsky, Alex.: op. 3. Simrock, 1897. Full of ideas, vital and well worth playing.

Trios without piano.

1. Heidrich, Maximilian: clarinet, viola, and 'cello. Schmidt. An unsuccessful struggle.
2. Juon, Paul: divertimento for clarinet and two violas. Schlesinger. Strange, but rather amusing.
3. Stark, Robert: sonata for two clarinets and basset horn. Schmidt. Not interesting.
4. Mozart, W. A.: adagio in canon form. B. & H. For two basset horns and bassoon.
5. Mozart, W. A.: Four small pieces, for same. B. & H.

Quartets with piano.

Rabl, Walter: op. 1, pf, v, cl, vc. Simrock, 1897. Tuneful and playable, with a particularly ingratiating intermezzo.

Quintets with piano.

1. Baussnern, W.: v, cl, horn, vc, pf. Simrock, 1905. Mediocre.
2. Fibich, Zdenko: op. 42. For same. Ubra, 1896. With good use of the colour of this combination.
3. Hauer, J. M.: op. 26. Cl, v, vla, vc, pf. Schlesinger, 1924. Not interesting.
4. Kahn, Robert: op. 54. V, cl, horn or vla, vc, and pf. B. & B., 1910. Effective, energetic, enjoyable.
5. Labor, J.: op. 11. Cl, v, vla, vc, and pf. U.E., 1912. An excellent work.
6. Weingartner, Felix: op. 50. For same. B. & H., 1911. Made music with many dry spots, though interesting at times.

Sextets with piano.

1. Berezovsky, N.: op. 7. Theme and fantastic variations. Cl, pf, and str. quartet. MS.
2. Petyrek, Felix: pf, cl, and str. quartet. U.E., 1924. Very modern and difficult.
3. Prokoviev, S.: overture on Yiddish themes. B. & H., 1922. Modern and difficult, but playable and enjoyable.

Septets with piano.

Moscheles, Ignaz: op. 88. Pf, v, vla, vc, bass, cl, and horn. Kistner. Rather out of style.

Quartets: clarinet and strings.

1. Bärmann, Heinr.: op. 18. Cl, v, vla, vc. Schott, 1882.
2. Kinzi: Cl, v, vla, and vc. Schott, 1882.
3. Müller, Friedr.: op. 80. Cl, v, vla, vc. Hofmeister, 1860.
4. Pugni, C.: Three quartets. Cl, v, vla, vc. Ricordi.
5. Stamitz, Karl: op. 8. Cl, v, vla, vc. Raabe & Plothow, 1919. Good.

Quintets: clarinet and strings.

1. Balorre, C. de: Hamelle, 1906. Very poor.
2. Blatt, F. T.: Theme and variations. Simrock (old). Old-fashioned and amusing. Each player does his stunt.
3. Brahms, J.: op. 115. Simrock, 1892. Great.
4. Coleridge-Taylor, S.: B. & H., 1906 (no score). Very fine indeed.
5. Fuchs, Robert: op. 102. Robitschek, 1919. Playable and interesting.
6. Hoesslin, F. von. Simrock, 1924. Written by a well-trained composer. Difficult ensemble.
7. Holbrooke, Jos.: op. 27, no. 1. Novello.
8. Holbrooke, Jos.: op. 27, no. 2. Chester. Not very good.

9. Howells, Herbert: op. 31. Rhapsody quintet. S. & B. (Carnegie Trust). Very good and interesting.
10. Krehl, S.: op. 19. Simrock, 1902. Tuneful, but not inspired.
11. Krein, Alex.: op. 12. Hebrew Sketch. Jurgenson.
12. Krein, Alex.: op. 13. Hebrew Sketch. Jurgenson. Both characteristic and effective.
13. Marteau, Henri: op. 13. Südd. Musik. Verlag, 1909. Difficult, and hardly repays necessary study.
14. Mozart, W. A.: K. 581. B. & H.; also Peters. Perfect.
15. Pape, L.: Adagio. Cranz, 1863.
16. Raphael, G.: op. 4. Simrock, 1925. Clever and playable.
17. Reger, Max: op. 146. Simrock, 1916. Great.
18. Reicha, A.: op. 107.
19. Spohr, L.: op. 34, Andante with variations. C.F.S.; op. 81, Fantasie with variations. C.F.S. Florid, melodious, with clarinet employed largely as a solo instrument.
20. Stieber, Hans. Klemm, 1920. Not easy, and not inspired.
21. Straesser, Ewald: op. 34. Simrock, 1920. Well written, but difficult.
22. Täglichsbeck, Th.: op. 44. Heinrichs, 1863. Old-fashioned.
23. Weber, Karl M.: op. 34. Schlesinger. Florid and effective.

Sextet.

Hermann, Ed.: op. 33. Oboe, clarinet, and quartet. Raabe & Plothow. Effective.

Quartets and quintets for clarinets.

1. Crosse: suite for four clarinets. Hawkes, 1906. Good practice.
2. Mozart, W. A.: adagio for two clarinets and three basset horns. B. & H. Beautiful.
3. Waterson, James: grand quartet (*sic*). Mahillon & Co.

BURNET C. TUTHILL.

CLARKE, REBECCA, b. 1886, English composer and violist, pupil of Stanford.

Trio, pf, v, vc — Winthrop Rogers, 1927.
Sonata, pf, vla, atonal — Chester, 1921.

Rebecca Clarke comes of a musical family, and was familiar from childhood with the intimacy of chamber music. Whilst at the R.C.M. she decided upon the viola as the instrument with which she should make her concert career, and her mastery of it soon brought her into prominence, both as a soloist and as a member successively of several important chamber music organizations. But from the beginning she was even more attracted to composition.

As a composer her fame dates from the 1919 Berkshire (U.S.A.) festival. In the previous year she was taking part in a series of chamber concerts at Honolulu, and it was there that she began the composition of her viola sonata, which was completed at Detroit, and sent in for the Coolidge International Prize. The judges found themselves evenly divided between Ernest Bloch's suite and Rebecca Clarke's sonata, and Mrs. Coolidge had to give her casting vote, which she did in favour of Bloch. Both works were performed at the festival by Harold Bauer and Louis Bailly, and both have become welcome additions to the none too rich literature of the viola, Miss Clarke's work, in particular, having had very numerous performances in proportion to the infrequent opportunities of viola music in general.

THE SONATA is a brilliant work in three movements, imaginative rather than profound, steeped in a fantastic atmosphere. Though written with some freedom, its formal outline is sufficiently definite to counterbalance both the rhapsodical character of some of its thematic material, and the fanciful impressionism suggested by its harmonic texture, which has some affinities with French music of its period. All this finds ample justification in a quotation from Alfred de Musset's *La Nuit de Mai* which serves as motto to the work:

'Poète, prends ton luth; le vin de la jeunesse
Fermente cette nuit dans les veines de Dieu.

That is the spirit of the declamatory passage, marked 'impetuoso', with which the first movement opens, and which also links its first and second subjects, and serves as a bridge to the recapitulation, besides contributing subsidiary figures, so that it has really greater importance than the themes given formal prominence. The scherzo is a fascinating movement, slight of texture, but ingenious and personal in conception, and very effective in performance. A brief introduction precedes the finale. It opens with a theme which, as first stated, derives its melodic flavour from the pentatonic scale, which elsewhere also appears to have influenced the composer's melodic invention. The finale itself employs as its principal theme that of the introduction to the whole work, whilst the pentatonic theme recurs with fine effect before the coda, where both are combined. As a whole the sonata is an admirable instance of well-used freedom in writing. The formal outline which binds the whole nowhere becomes an irksome discipline. One feels that it grew with the music instead of being imposed upon it.

THE TRIO. In 1921 Miss Clarke again entered for a Coolidge competition, and again secured the second place with her trio, the most important work she has yet written. Its three movements are constructed round a central idea, which is used in different forms throughout the work. The first movement, appassionato, opens with the chief subject in rhapsodic form *ff* on the piano with a chord sustained on the strings:

Ex. 1.

It is then taken up by the strings and brought to a climax, after which a trumpet-like phrase, played *pp* on the piano, ushers in the second subject, on a pedal bass, marked misterioso, and also announced by the piano. A quiet codetta, in which the second subject appears in imitation on the strings, leads to the development section, which is based chiefly on the first subject. A coda, in which a slow version of the first subject is played by the 'cello, makes a sombre and somewhat elegiac ending. In the second movement, poco lento e molto semplice, the strings are muted throughout, and the violin opens with the following subject, accompanied by a single G on the piano:

Ex. 2.

The same passage, played at half the speed on the piano, presently makes an ostinato, above which the strings carry on a dialogue. Later, by means of double-stopping, they play in four-part harmony below arpeggios on the piano. A very quiet melody of quasi folk-song character then appears on the piano, with a rocking accompaniment in harmonics on the strings. The movement dies away with a passage on the violin similar to that with which it started. The last movement, allegro vigoroso, opens with the subject hammered out on the piano, with pizzicato chords on the strings:

Ex. 3.

This appears in many different guises, including a rhythmical figure in 7/8 time, and becomes more and more wild until it reaches a quieter second part, the theme of which is the same as the second subject of the first movement, but in close canon and with different harmonies. There is here also a reminiscence of the slow movement. The trumpet-like passage from the first movement now reappears on the piano, and leads to the elegiac passage which concluded that section, the violin now joining the 'cello. A short and animated last section makes a 'happy ending' to the work.

In 1923 Mrs. Coolidge, following her custom, commissioned Miss Clarke to write a composition for 'cello and piano, which took the form of a rhapsody and was duly performed at the Berkshire Festival of that year.

EDWIN EVANS.

†CLAUSETTI, P., Italian composer.

Sonata, pf, v, A — Pizzi, 1923.

†CLAUSSMANN, A.

Sonata, pf, v, e mi — op. 43 — Lemoine, 1906.

CLEMENTI, MUZIO, 1752–1832, famous composer.

Modern republication

Six sonatinas, pf, v (Max Reger), Augener, 1895.

These sonatinas have been repeatedly republished; there are five modern editions besides the above.

Clementi settled in England (*v. Grove*).

CLINTON, JOHN, 1810–1864, was professor of the flute at the R.A.M.

His chamber works are fairly numerous, and some possess considerable merit. The following, all published by Ashdown, are the most noteworthy:—trios for two flutes and piano, op. 2, B flat; op. 3, A; op. 10, F; op. 33, G; op. 34, G minor; op. 35, E flat; two *trios ongarese* in G for the same, opp. 11 and 12; trios for three flutes, op. 7, A; op. 9, G; op. 30, F; a quartet for four flutes, op. 32, G; grand duo for flute and B flat clarinet with piano, op. 43; and some duets for flute and harp.

H. M. FITZGIBBON.

†CLOUGH-LEIGHTER, H., b. 1874, American organist.

Lyric suite (*The Day of Beauty*), pf, high voice, str. quartet, op. 48, The Boston Music Co., 1910.

COBB, GERARD, 1838–1904, English composer.

Quintet, pf, str, C	op. 22	Charles Woolhouse.
Quartet, pf, v, vla, vc, E	,, 34	B. & H., 1898.
Suite, pf, v, D		Ashdown.

Gerard Cobb was an accomplished musician and a popular man at Cambridge, where he took a double first in 1863. His quintet, an early work, is an effective piece of monophonic salon music, but the quartet, which was played at South Place, is a much more ambitious work. Unfortunately it is much too long (thirty-five minutes), and the interest flags before the close is reached. The violin suite is admirably written for the instrument.

EDITOR.

†COBBETT, WALTER WILLSON.

Some friendly souls have surprised me by suggesting that I should give, in addition to the account of my activities contained in the articles 'The Chamber Music Life', 'Phantasy', and 'Violin' (*q.v.*), a few further details of my own uneventful career. I do so with some reluctance, being well aware that they contain no element of public interest.

I was born near Blackheath on 11 July 1847, my father being a man of business with literary and musical tastes. As a supplement to my home education he sent me to France and Germany, where I received private tuition. To this happy circumstance I owe the cosmopolitan trend of thought which clings to me to this day. In Caen (Normandy) I associated daily with students of the University, and acquired considerable knowledge of French literature. The literary culture of the French always was, and is still, the wonder of the world. In Frankfort-on-the-Main I stayed with a German pastor who, though not a musician, was proud to be a compatriot of the world's greatest composers—an attitude characteristic of the layman in Germany. He taught me to *respect* as well as love the art of music. This was not the matter of course it is now supposed to be in England. In any case, it was very far from representing the attitude of the English gentleman of that period, who was all for sport; and the lesson was the more valuable.

I have touched elsewhere upon my youthful experiences as a musical amateur, but of my practical experiences of life there remains a little to say. I was in the 'City' for a time, working under an underwriter at Lloyd's, later fulfilling the duties of a foreign correspondent, and finally entering the lists as an exploiter of certain patents, one of which turned up trumps. I found collaborators who worked splendidly with and for me; a company was formed with branches in many parts of the world, and a measure of success attained. This enabled me to retire at the age of sixty, and devote myself to what I consider to be my life's work, though it only really belongs to the last twenty years of my existence. I made propaganda for an art, chamber music, highly considered by every true musician, yet, strange to say, somewhat neglected. This Cyclopedia represents my final effort in this direction.

In it my own activities have been subjects of comment, and it would seem that I have been of some little service to young composers. These activities have been a source, to me, of constant pleasure, though I have to admit that the actual compilation of the cyclopedic part of this book has been wearisome and laborious. I expected it to last for two years, but it has occupied more than double that time. However, to complain of trouble which I have deliberately courted would be indeed unphilosophical, and at the moment of writing—on my eighty-first birthday—an 'exceeding great reward' has come my way. Monsieur Vincent d'Indy, one of the master musicians of our time, writes me as follows:

> 'Croyez bien que j'apprécie hautement votre rôle de Mécène de la musique de chambre, estimant qu'il n'existe guère de gens *de notre âge* (je viens d'entendre sonner mes 77 ans) qui auraient eu l'audace de se charger—pour l'amour de l'art—d'une pareille entreprise . . . Aussi je crois que tous les musiciens doivent vous en être reconnaissants.
>
> Et croyez qu'en tout ceci, l'une des choses qui m'a fait le plus de plaisir a été d'être mis en rapport avec un homme qui aime *sincèrement* la musique—ce qui devient de plus en plus rare en notre siècle de spéculation avant tout!'

In this letter I have the joy of reading fulfilment of my desire—the desire of an amateur to win the approval of musicians, and I may add that the principals of the leading English colleges of music have shown themselves no less sympathetic, in two instances awarding me a Fellowship.

I have been most fortunate in my experiences as a player. I have made much music with the leading pupils of Professor Auer, with the members of the Flonzaley and London String Quartets, with Albert Sammons, Émile Sauret, and many other artists. The frontispiece[1] is taken from a picture by Frank Salisbury exhibited in the Royal Academy, Burlington House, representing the members of my home quartet engaged on the Chausson Concerto for piano and violin with string quartet. The words within the scroll are not very legible. They run thus: 'Music of the nobler kind is the soul of things expressed in sound.'

EDITOR.

COBBETT COMPETITIONS AND COMMISSIONS.

In 1905 I instituted a series of chamber music competitions, mainly designed to bring to light the talents of young British composers and to encourage the occasional adoption of a short form of ensemble music. The prizes were in the first instance supplemented by generous donations from liverymen of the Worshipful Company of Musicians, an ancient but not very wealthy City Guild, whose members showed great interest in the scheme. The subject of the first competition (1905) was the composition of a 'Phantasy' in the form of a string quartet, the piece to be of short duration and performed without a break, but, if the composer desired, to consist of different sections varying in tempo and metre. It was recognized that this so-called 'new' form was a modern analogue of the old English Fancy or Fancie, which was cultivated as a short instrumental form of chamber music down to the Stuart period. Sir Frederick Bridge, in one of his Gresham Lectures, said that it was made clear that the Fancies played an important part in the evolution of chamber music, and that they were worthy of more attention than they had yet received. There are, he said, examples of them on record by nearly every composer of note during about eighty years previous to 1670, the Fancy being the counterpart in petto of the chamber quartet and trio of the present day.

So came into being the so-called Phantasies; a circular was issued, sixty-seven MS. quartets were received in 1905, and with the co-operation of eminent musicians as jury, six prizes were awarded, the first (£50) to W. HURLSTONE (*q.v.*), who died a few weeks after receiving it. In 1907 a similar competition was held, the subject this time being a piano trio, and once more sixty-seven MSS. were submitted. Frank Bridge, John Ireland, and James Friskin gained the three prizes awarded on

[1] Omitted from the 1963 edition.

this occasion, when the Musicians' Company again generously co-operated; after which I continued the series off my own bat.

In November 1915 Dr. Ernest Walker contributed an article on the Modern British Phantasy to the *Music Student Supplement*, from which I select a few passages. These, besides being descriptive, include a useful table of results:

'Mr. W. W. Cobbett is, in Shakespearian phrase, the "onlie begetter" of the Modern British Phantasy —a fortunate reincarnation, in exact musical parallel, of men like Rasoumowsky and Galitzin, who not only commissioned string quartets from Beethoven, to the composer's own personal advanage and to the still greater advantage of posterity, but took themselves an enthusiastic part in performing the music they had called into being. It is now ten years since Mr. Cobbett started these beneficent activities; and since then twenty-four British chamber works, in this form alone, have been produced, the composition or the publication (or both) of which is in one way or another due directly to him. Sometimes they have been prizewinners in competitions instituted by him . . . and sometimes they have been directly commissioned from the composer. . . .'

These are the twenty-four works alluded to:

Phantasy Quintets.

(*a*) J. Friskin, for pf and str. quartet.
(*b*) *J. B. McEwen, for str (2 vc).†
(*c*) R. Vaughan Williams, for str (2 vla).†
(*d*) R. Walthew, for pf, v, vla, vc, and double-bass.†

Phantasy Quartets.

(*a*) Frank Bridge, J. Friskin, J. Holbrooke, W. Y. Hurlstone, A. Sammons, H. Waldo Warner (2), Haydn Wood, for strings.
(*b*) Frank Bridge, for pf and str.

Phantasy Trios.

(*a*) Frank Bridge, J. Friskin, J. Ireland, Alice Verne-Bredt, *Susan Spain Dunk, for pf, v, and vc.†
(*b*) T. F. Dunhill, for pf, v, and vla.†
(*c*) Ethel Barns, for pf and 2 v.†
(*d*) *Adam Carse, for v, vla, and vc.

Phantasy Duos.

(*a*) *York Bowen, for pf and v.
(*b*) B. J. Dale, for pf and vla.†
(*c*) *B. W. O'Donnell, for pf and vc.†

'The English language is notoriously difficult to spell; and the composers of these works present their titles in no less than five different ways. "Phantasy," "Phantasie", "Fantasie," "Fantaisie," all appear in print, and "Fantasy" . . . It is a wonder that "Fantasia", the only other apparent alternative, is not also found; but as the first of these is that which Mr. Cobbett personally chooses to write, it will be exclusively used in this article.

THE "FANCY"

The one other possible form, "Fancy", is now out of date, but it has a considerable British history, which has been outlined by Mr. Cobbett himself. "Fancy" or "Fantasia" (English composers very often used the Italian term) denoted simply an instrumental piece founded on original material, and not, like the "In Nomine", on fragments of plain chant. Later on, it developed into a form of concerted chamber music, particularly popular in England during the period between the death of Elizabeth and the early years of Charles II. It was practised here by men of very diverse powers and diverse habits of mind. In the hands of Orlando Gibbons, an essentially serious composer in madrigals as elsewhere, the Fancy was grave and dignified, wellnigh ecclesiastical; in those of John Ward, one of the pioneers of the "new music" in the church as well as outside, it became rhythmical, pointed, vigorous. Not that instrumental chamber music was by any means confined to originally instrumental pieces. Madrigals were continually played on viols, and, in general, music-lovers troubled themselves about the music very much more than about the medium of its performance—they wanted the sounds, but did not care how. And when they had not at hand the Madrigals of Wilbye or Bateson, or the Fancies of Gibbons or Ward or other composers who could write instrumental music possessing harmonic richness or rhythmical vivacity, they fell back on anything they could get; and so, side by side with Fancies that have real musical worth, we find what Sir Hubert Parry (*Music of the Seventeenth Century*, p. 326) aptly calls "drouthy aberrations"—pages of mere aimless meandering, sometimes vaguely instrumental in texture, sometimes polyphonic and more or less vocally designed. The demand seems to have been very great, and it was supplied in careless profusion by composers, native and Italian-born, good, mediocre, and bad, writers of counterpoint, of dance-measures, and of nothing in particular.

It is usually said that the English Fancy was killed by the spread of French taste under the influence of the court; but, true as this is, we must discriminate. It had, no doubt, its special native features, which showed, in some respects, an artistic advance, but it was not isolated from foreign influences. Italian instrumental music was developing rapidly, and never really lost its hold here. The contrapuntal Fancy of the older type came, indeed, to an end, largely because Charles II could not count his way through it; but there was certainly no break in the progress of English chamber music. In the great instrumental works of Purcell we find all the threads that are worth anything firmly held together, the harmonic subtlety, the contrapuntal richness, the rhythmical swing. And if, after Purcell, the stream of such music ran as a rule rather shallow for many a long year, still it never ran completely dry. But names changed, of course. We talked not of Fancies, but of Sonatas, Trios, Quartets. And so the word Phantasy comes to us, under Mr. Cobbett's auspices, with a pleasant old-world flavour about it that, perhaps, rather obscures its essential features; it is not musically a resurrection of something in the past, it is a modification of something in the present.

THE MODERN PHANTASY

What then is the modern British Phantasy? Let us, to start with, examine two *loci classici* on the subject. Firstly, Mr. Fuller-Maitland's article in the appendix to the second edition of *Grove*.

A piece for concerted instruments in a continuous movement (with occasional changes of tempo and measure), occupying a shorter time than the usual classical works, and free from the structural laws of the "classical" form. In place of these it is enjoined, or at least recommended, that the development section of the sonata form is to be replaced by a movement in slow tempo,

* In MS. † Commissioned.

which may include also a scherzando movement. In any case a logical connexion with the thematic material of the first part is maintained. A return to the characteristics of the first part of the movement is made, but not necessarily a definite repetition; and a developed coda is added as finale. Thus the fundamental outlines are retained, but there is not a hard and fast line. It will be seen that the revival of an old form takes proper cognizance of the tendencies of modern music since Liszt, with his "transformation of themes".

Secondly, Sir Charles Stanford's account in his book (1911) on *Musical Composition* (pp. 162–3):

> The reason for their (i.e. the Phantasies') existence may not improbably be a natural rebellion against the excessive length (and disproportionate interest) of many modern works. . . . The form which the remedy has taken is to condense all the movements of a work in sonata form into one. . . . This tabloid preparation of the three or four movements of a sonata must contain all the ingredients of the prescription, and yet not exceed the proportions of any one of them.

To which may be added the fact that neither in his first competition nor, so far as I am aware, on any other occasion has Mr. Cobbett ever laid down any definite rules, except (1) the moderate length, (2) the continuity of flow throughout the varying moods.

Mr. Fuller-Maitland, it will be noticed, enters into some structural details; Sir Charles Stanford generalizes rather more, though by mentioning (after the words "into one" quoted above) precedents in Schumann's D minor Symphony and Mendelssohn's Violin Concerto—to which, of course, he might, on these lines, have added several other classical works—he seems to have in his mind a rather different design. But an examination of the Phantasies themselves brings to light the fact that many of their composers since 1910 and 1911 have not attended at all to these instructions, which have, moreover, only a partial foundation in the Phantasies written before those dates. The duo of York Bowen, the string quartets of Holbrooke, Bridge, Friskin, and Haydn Wood, and the quintets of Friskin and Vaughan Williams are the only Phantasies that fulfil, more or less, what seem to be Sir Charles Stanford's conditions: while Mr. Fuller-Maitland's are fulfilled in exactness only by Ireland's and Susan Spain-Dunk's trios, and—with somewhat less exactness—by Bridge's trio and piano quartet, Dunhill's trio, and the quintet of McEwen. Consequently, some half of these twenty-four Phantasies decline to be included under these particular definitions; and so we are thrown back on Mr. Cobbett's two simple rules, to which, by universal practice, may be added a third, namely, the necessity for one or more palpable changes of tempo. In Sammons' string Phantasy, however, this last feature is reduced to a bare minimum; and I dare say Mr. Cobbett would have accepted works in which it was absent altogether, provided, of course, that they were, to a sufficient extent, examples of unity in diversity.

The Phantasy as a Type of Chamber Music

Let us take, then, the Phantasy in this very broad and general sense. What may be said for and against it as a type of chamber music? Let us start by considering one point on which Mr. Cobbett has never insisted, but on which Mr. Fuller-Maitland seems to lay stress—"in any case a logical connexion of thematic material is maintained," . . ."proper cognizance of the tendencies of modern music since Liszt with his 'transformation of themes'." A good many (not all) of these composers do, indeed, pay attention to this point; some more, some less. But Mr. Fuller-Maitland's words seem rather open to misconstruction. Elgar's first symphony is not, for example, a more "logically" homogeneous work of art than his second merely because, in the former, the theme of the adagio consists of the same string of notes as that of the scherzo. The E minor symphonies of Dvořák and Tchaikovsky are not more "logical" in construction because of their motto-phrases. Nor do pompous and circumstantial references to the opening movement help "logically" any of the dozens of finales of modern orchestral and chamber works in which this feature occurs. As (in another connexion) Mr. P. Robinson has well said in his witty book on *Handel and his Orbit*, "such things put, in truth, no terrific strain on the intellect": the music depends for its merits, or demerits, on much deeper and subtler points of artistry. The snippets that form the groundwork of Liszt's *Tasso* or *Les Préludes* are not made any the more appetizing by being served up, without any variety, in a sort of continuous hash; rather do we become still more sick of them. There are two pieces of advice often given to a young composer which are very dangerous: to "transfer" his themes instead of inventing others that will fit, and to take his themes from folk-music without inventing any at all. Of course, in either case the thing can be done, and done very well; but there is surely no virtue in the methods as such.

By the conditions of its existence, the form of the Phantasy cannot be that of a single-centred lyric; it must be a composite whole, made up of more or less diverse parts. Sir Charles Stanford writes somewhat pessimistically about the various snares which beset the path of a Phantasy-composer; but the "tabloid" idea of the structure, in the very rigidly miniature form that he pictures, has no real existence in the works under consideration. He imagines, I think, that they should be shorter than (when designed on the lines he lays down) they usually are. Nevertheless, the length has, of course, to be moderate, and he, no doubt, puts his finger on a crucial point when he refers to the difficulties of construction which, under the circumstances, this requirement involves. I feel, indeed, that some of these composers have not quite overcome these difficulties; they seem to be trying to get rather too much into the space, and to be hampered in consequence. We cannot institute parallels with the variation-form, in which sharp and short contrasts are perfectly feasible, because we are able to consider all the variations as, so to speak, separate beads strung on a single thread. The Phantasy-composer need not economize in invention, but he is bound to economize in the conditions necessary for the presentation of his ideas; and excellent practice, too, it is for him. Conciseness without breathlessness, that is the ideal. The supreme writers of string music can afford at times to write for two or even three instruments in octaves, because they have all the degrees of richness at their command: similarly, the best exponents of a comparatively compressed form like the Phantasy can afford occasionally to take things in an extremely leisurely fashion, merely because they know how to be terse elsewhere. There are several examples of this up and down these Phantasies. One of the best, to my mind, is to be found in the closing pages of Bridge's piano quartet.

I do not altogether agree with what Sir Charles Stanford, in a continuation of the passage I have quoted, says about the "value of moments of silence in music, those gaps which rest the hearers in the intervals". Apart from the fact that in practice these gaps are apt to be filled by the distractingly non-musical sounds of applause, there is, I feel, a great deal to be said in favour of continuity of flow —of course, up to a reasonable length. It secures a certain type of organic unity, which is, otherwise, never quite feasible; it secures concentration of idea and expression, and of the listener's attention also. Moreover, many composers, like many painters, do their best in work that they can envisage at a single look, which need not in the least mean that there is only a single thing to look at. I feel convinced that the chamber-music Phantasy—whether under this or under any other name or names—has a distinct future before it, and its forms are capable of well-nigh unlimited variety, without in any way transgressing the spirit of Mr. Cobbett's own rules. And there is also a purely practical consideration. A composer can easily find a place on a programme with a short work, while he will not so easily find a concert-giver ready to allot him three-quarters of an hour or perhaps more.

Is the Modern Phantasy British?

Can we say that the modern Phantasy is a purely British art-form? I may as well frankly confess that I am myself a musical anti-chauvinist of the deepest dye. The geographical and racial origins of the things of the spirit seem to me very secondary concerns, and I see no reason for not now enjoying my Strauss and Reger (not to mention my Wagner and Brahms) just as much as ever. And so it does not seem to me in the very least derogatory to say that the British Phantasy happens to be British only because Mr. Cobbett happens to be a Briton: no more than the old Fancy is a national art-form—if there is, indeed, any such thing. What, apart from personal help to composers, Mr. Cobbett has done, has been to afford a chamber-music outlet to activities that have hitherto been mainly exercised in orchestral channels. Long ago, symphony and overture and concerto began to throw out new and various shoots; their new shapes have never (in the hands of any composer worth the name) been formless any more than the old; they have been different, but they have not lost touch with their ancestry. And, almost always, they have been faithful to Mr. Cobbett's two canons. But in chamber music the movement has been less marked. We can think of such old classical examples as Schubert's two C major Fantasias, and of the many modern sonatas, from Liszt to Scriabin, which are Phantasies in everything but the name. Nevertheless, it remains true (perhaps, partially, because "programme-music" is, as a rule, unsuitable for a string quartet) that the bulk of concerted chamber works have been written in the more extended, divisible forms. Still, the non-realistic chamber-music version of the latter-day orchestral piece was very obviously bound to come into its own sooner or later: Mr. Cobbett's very valuable work has been to give the stimulating impetus in this country. No doubt Mr. Cobbett's "Phantasy" will before very long become, under that or another name, as "academic" as Liszt's "Symphonische Dichtung" is, under that or another name, nowadays. But in music, while the children grow up, the parents—if their children prove to be worth anything—do not themselves die. Composers still write symphonies, often long ones; and they still write string quartets in four movements: as a matter of fact, Mr. Cobbett himself has just been giving prizes for such things. And the first prize seems to have been won by a composer who is represented three times over in the list of these Phantasies. There are many sides to modern music, and it is the most broad-minded musician who gets the most out of it for himself, and gives the most to others.'

Since 1915 many more Phantasies have gained prizes, among them the following:

Phantasy Quartets (str).

(*a*) H. Waldo Warner. Folk-Song Quartet.
(*b*) Herbert Howells. Folk-Song Quartet.

Phantasy Trios (pf and str).

(*a*) *J. Cliffe Forrester. Folk-Song Trio.
(*b*) Arnold Trowell. Folk-Song Trio.

Phantasy for pf, solo v, and str.

(*a*) *C. Armstrong Gibbs. Dance Phantasy, *The Enchanted Wood.*
(*b*) *Dr. Cecil Hazelhurst. Dance Phantasy, *The Red Plague.*

Phantasy Duos.

(*a*) York Bowen, for vla and pf.
(*b*) Dorothy Howell, for v and pf (R.A.M. Commission).
(*c*) *Alan Bush, for v and pf (R.A.M. Commission).

Other Phantasies were awarded at the annual competitions held at the R.C.M. (*v.* art. Cobbett Prizes at the R.C.M.). Notices appear in the Cyclopedia of the above Phantasies, excepting those marked with an asterisk, which are unpublished at present.

The following are winners of Cobbett prizes for works in full sonata form:

Duo.

(*a*) John Ireland. Sonata. Pf and v. (International, with 134 competitors.)
(*b*) *C. Villiers Stanford. Sonata. V solo with pf acc.† Not a Phantasy, but a modern analogue of the old-time sonata with figured bass.

String Quartet.

(*a*) Frank Bridge. Quartet. Two v, vla, vc.† (Published by the Patron's Fund.)

Commissions to compose string suites for chamber orchestra were executed by Percy Fletcher, Cunningham Woods, and J. C. Ames, forming additions to the repertory which have been greatly appreciated. They are published by Hawkes, and have proved useful to cinema orchestras.

In addition to the above, commissions to chamber music composers, as yet unexecuted, have been given; also a large number of small prizes, some of them supplementing those awarded in the course of the competitions mentioned. One of these is perhaps of interest as it was a *ballon d'essai*, antedating the prizes of 1905. It was awarded by Dr. Cummings at

* In MS. † Commissioned.

the Guildhall School of Music for a piano trio, to H. Waldo Warner, then a youth, and since then a frequent prize-winner in competitions. Another was one of several prizes given in war-time during the season of Isidor de Lara's Emergency concerts at Steinway Hall. A newly published sonata for piano and violin was the subject of what may be described as a posthumous prize which was handed to the widow of the composer, COLERIDGE TAYLOR (*q.v.*).

VIOLIN COMPETITIONS. Of these there were two, both of them bearing direct relation to chamber music. The competitors were luthiers of British birth, and the awards related to the suitability of the violins submitted for quartet playing. Concerts were given at Æolian Hall in 1918 and 1923, the audience assisting by their votes in the adjudication of the prizes. The leading prize-winners were: in 1918 A. Richardson and W. Glenister, in 1923 A. Vincent and W. Robinson; since when violins from the workshops of the successful competitors have been much in demand. (See also VIOLIN.)

In my article on the CHAMBER MUSIC LIFE (*q.v.*) I have written on the subject from a personal point of view, so that I need add nothing to this brief survey of the various Cobbett Competitions. EDITOR.

COBBETT FREE LIBRARIES. The most important of these is the free library of British chamber music administered by the Society of Women Musicians at their headquarters, 74 Grosvenor St., W. It contains every chamber work of importance published by British composers, and is open to the general public. Libraries of chamber music intended for the use of students of the G.S.M. and for members of the Faculty of Arts are found at the respective institutions. EDITOR.

COBBETT LECTURES ON CHAMBER MUSIC.

Besides lecturing on various occasions on chamber music himself, Mr. Cobbett commissioned T. F. Dunhill and Sam Midgley to give lectures on the subject at Trinity College of Music by way of propaganda.

COBBETT MEDAL, for services to chamber music, awarded annually under a Cobbett endowment by the Worshipful Company of Musicians, to workers in this field.

The present adjudicator is Sir Hugh Allen, principal of the R.C.M., the first recipient being T. F. Dunhill (1924), composer, pianist, and author. Then followed Mrs. E. S. Coolidge (1925), American patron of music; A. J. Clements (1926), organizer of chamber concerts for the people; H. Waldo Warner (1927), violist and composer; Sir Edward Elgar (1928), who, in later years, turned his attention to chamber music; and Frank Bridge (1929).

The original was a silver medal. In 1928 it was decided by the Court of the Musicians' Company that the medal should in future be struck in gold, with corresponding endowment.

COBBETT PRIZES at the Royal College of Music.

These were instituted in 1920, at the instance of W. W. Cobbett, F.R.C.M., who gave the sum of fifty guineas annually for the study of chamber music at the College, from that year to 1927; in 1928 Mr. Cobbett, by means of a generous endowment, established the prizes on a permanent basis.

This benefaction is unique of its kind, for it fosters both the composition and the performance of chamber works, and, further, lays particular stress on the encouragement of groups of players who form their own Quartets or Quintets, and rehearse without professional aid.

This happy combination is brought about by varying the conditions of the competition from year to year. In 1920, for instance, the prizes were awarded for the performance of (1) standard works of the chamber music repertory and (2) chamber music by British composers, a special prize being given for groups of players who chose and studied their works without professional aid. In 1921 prizes were offered for the performance of chamber works by British composers, the competitors' choice being works by, amongst others, Eugene Goossens, Vaughan Williams, Hurlstone, Friskin, and Walford Davies. In 1922 the prizes were awarded for the performance of standard chamber music, preference being expressed for works by British composers. In 1923 prizes were offered, firstly for the composition of chamber works by College students, and secondly for the performance of the prize works: these prize works were *Celtic Phantasy* for string quartet by A. Davies Adams, and a *Phantasy* for string quartet by H. M. Strickland-Constable. In 1924 the prizes were given for the best performances of chamber music, certain prizes being reserved specially for British works, and special encouragement being given to the performance of British works rehearsed without aid and performed at the College informal concerts. In 1925 and 1926 the prizes were given for the composition of a phantasy quartet or quintet for strings, not exceeding fifteen minutes in performance, and for performances of the prize works and of standard chamber music. In 1927 the prizes were awarded for performances of standard trios and quartets at the chamber and informal concerts.

That these prizes have proved highly valuable and extremely popular goes without saying. Composers have been encouraged to experiment in the difficult art of phantasy writing, and performers have been encouraged to make up their own quartet of players, and delve into the hidden store of chamber music in order to discover lesser known works to rehearse and offer for performance. Further, groups of players, stimulated by the prospect of prizes for unaided work, have formed themselves into regular Quartets, and in many cases laid the foundation of a permanent combination, which has led to subsequent engagements as an established Quartet. Thus the Cobbett Prizes may be regarded as one more illustration of the debt which British chamber music and British chamber music players owe to the founder. CLAUDE AVELING.

COENEN, JOHANNES MEINARDUS, 1824–1899, Dutch bassoon player.

Sonata, pf, fag Weygand (The Hague), 1864.

†COERNE, LOUIS ADOLPHE, b. 1870, American violinist, organist, and conductor.

Three little trios in canon-form, pf, v, vc, C, a mi, G	op. 62	Bosworth.
Petite Suite, pf, v, vc	,, 64	André.
Swedish sonata, pf, v	,, 60	Hofmeister.

†COINDREAU, PIERRE, contemporary French composer, pupil of the Schola Cantorum.

Trio, pf, v, vc Rouart, *c.* 1900.

COLBERG, PAUL.

Sonata, pf, v, d mi Forlivesi (Florence), 1893.

COLERIDGE-TAYLOR. *v.* TAYLOR.

COLING, G., French composer.

Quintet, 2 v, vla, vc, cb Grus (Paris), 1897.

COL LEGNO. An effect produced by tapping the strings with the wood of the bow. Frequently used in modern orchestral music, never in chamber music by a composer of taste. EDITOR.

†COLLET, HENRI, b. 1885, French writer on music.

Spanish Suite, *Castellanas*, pf, 2 v, vla, vc	op. 32	Mathot.
Trio, pf, v, vc	—	Eschig.
Sonata, pf, v, A	,, 60	Mathot.

COLOUR IN CHAMBER MUSIC.

Of all the elements of music, colour is the most difficult to isolate for purposes of discussion. To define tone colour, one must start by eliminating all irrelevant metaphors that occur in current talk. The next step is a comparison with the art of painting, which will help to eliminate further elements of ambiguity. In painting, colour is not pigment; a medley of the strongest and brightest pigments may produce less colour than a few touches judiciously applied. The same is true of music; too lavish a use of diverse tone colours may result in dullness. Again, colour is not only value (relation in respect of light and shade); colour in music depends primarily upon both tone colour and value—that is, upon elements which are not in the least recondite or elusive. More technically speaking, it is the result of one or several of the following three agents: (1) timbre, or tone-quality; (2) contrast of key; (3) harmonic writing—including both the selection of harmonies and the spacing or duplication of the notes of which they consist.

Let a last source of ambiguity be disposed of by the remark that colour is not character. Often, when one speaks of the colour of a melody, its character is meant. Melody (that is, a single line), apart from timbre, can only possess colour so far as it contains contrasts of keys or forcibly suggests definite harmonies. It may, of course, by resorting to figures consisting of harmonic notes, become particularly rich in actual colour as distinct from character or value, and apart from considerations of timbre. Bach's chamber works for solo instruments teem with admirable instances of this order of colour:

Ex. 1.

Violin.

The whole question of colour in chamber music is particularly subtle and interesting. In the string quartet especially, the resources are strictly limited and yet practically boundless. From Haydn and Mozart and Beethoven to Borodin and Franck and Debussy, the infinite variety of colours obtainable from four bowed instruments is displayed in its fullness: the most obvious element of pure colour, instrumental timbre, is restricted to the essentials and really includes all essentials. Thus composers are compelled to obey the chief law of colour in music, namely, that colour must be part of the warp and woof of music, not a coating applied on the surface or to mask crevices. Each instrument, each string, each method of attack, gives a tone colour of its own, which for depth and definition is all that can be desired. Definition of pitch is so accurate that contrasts of keys acquire their maximum significance apart from the fact that a good deal of all such contrasts is due to differences between the tone of open and stopped strings.

As regards colour resulting from harmonic

contrasts, in the andante con moto of Beethoven's op. 130, one may call attention to the modulations from B flat minor to D flat major, A flat major, and thence gradually to C major and back. Another equally splendid example is to be found in the modulatory order and harmonic contrasts of the finale of the quartet, op. 131.

With the use in chamber music of the piano, harp, and wind instruments—not to mention percussion, which occasionally appears (*see* article PERCUSSION IN CHAMBER MUSIC)—other, though not necessarily greater, possibilities offer.

The piano often tends to introduce something of orchestral colour—or at least of a substitute for this. There can be no hard and fast distinction between orchestral colour and colour in chamber music. Even in the string quartet, it is occasionally felt that the whole colour scheme tends towards orchestral polychrome and intensity—this has often been said of Beethoven's op. 59, and especially of no. 3; there are characteristic instances, too, in Glazounov's works. But the piano acts quite differently. It is an instrument often used for transcription from the orchestra, and many composers of chamber music use it—often unconsciously—to obtain colour effects thought out in terms of the orchestra. No example is given here, in order to avoid inviting controversy; but Ravel's trio may be quoted as a characteristic example of the use of the piano free from any such tendency.

The piano is an instrument with which many fine colours may be achieved by duplicating notes and by spacing. Koechlin's sonatas for violin and piano, viola and piano, 'cello and piano, flute and piano (*v.* KOECHLIN), contain admirable examples. One characteristic instance may be quoted here (Ex. 2).

Ex. 2.

With wind instruments, alone or in combination with strings, the question of colour becomes mainly one of timbre, although, of course, the other elements of colour stand firm in their rights and power. The tone colour of the various registers of each wind instrument naturally stands out very definitely in chamber combinations—especially when one wind instrument is associated with strings (Mozart's quartet for oboe, violin, viola, and 'cello; clarinet quintet; Reger's serenade, op. 77 *a*, for flute, violin, and viola; Arthur Bliss's oboe quintet, are cases in point). Combinations of wind only or of wind and piano (e.g. Mozart's and Beethoven's quintets for wind and piano; Roussel's serenade for wind instruments) include a great diversity of timbres, but there is, as a rule, no corresponding increase in the intensity and variety of colour.

Nowadays, the range of tone colours admitted in chamber music is unrestricted, and includes much that must be regarded as purely experimental, even if one is not inclined to abide by the old-fashioned distinction between what is allowable in chamber music and what is 'illicit'—a distinction dating from the time when it was alleged in all earnestness that the harp or the cor anglais should not be used in a symphony. Curiously enough, the harp is one of the instruments whose introduction into chamber ensembles is quite recent, if music by writers for harp, such as Bochsa, be disregarded. As examples, may be quoted Bax, sonata for viola and harp; Caplet, quintet for harp and strings, *The Masque of the Red Death.* Yet the harp provides colours that are both soft and brilliant.

Even if one grants unreservedly that chamber music should preserve its fundamental idiosyncrasies of character and style—as indeed all orders of music should—one cannot help feeling that the ban of certain instrumental colours from chamber music is largely a matter of mere convention. Even the trombone (here mentioned because it has been introduced of late in chamber music—Poulenc's sonata for trumpet, horn, and trombone) can be made to play a fitting part in utterly restrained and simple colour schemes. It is a question not of colour, but of style. A sense of the style that appertains to chamber music will naturally exclude all effects which from the point of view of tone, volume, or colour would be out of keeping. But the restraint that is an essential feature of good chamber music excludes neither variety nor boldness of colour.

Another tone colour recently introduced, with excellent results, in chamber music is the human voice used as pure timbre (Caplet, sonata for voice, 'cello, and piano; septet for female voices and strings; in both of which the voice parts are vocalization, no words being used). M. D. CALVOCORESSI.

[I am favoured by Messrs. Breitkopf & Härtel with the following notes (translated from their circular) on Coloured Light Music (*Farblichtmusik*).

One of the most interesting but most difficult problems of art that has engaged for centuries the attention of painters, musicians, physicists and mathematicians of rank, such as Goethe, Newton, Schopenhauer, Wilhelm Ostwald, and Scriabin, is in our times approaching its solution. The attempt is made to weld colour and music into a new species of art. The basis of feeling and thought of the problem is clear, without any further explanation. When we contemplate a painting with glowing contrasts of colour, we often get an impression conceivable in terms of music; and, on the other hand, when we hear a musical work there is aroused in us a conception of movement and colour, of light and darkness. After many vain attempts at a solution, which in the first place failed because what was desired was artistically impossible, the Hungarian pianist and composer Alexander László has now found one which aims at the artistically possible; that is, to set a sequence of tones against a colour. After many years of painful labour, he succeeded in constructing the Colour Piano, i.e. an apparatus that reproduces colour-light compositions by means of projection.

At the German Musical Art festival at Kiel in 1925, the first compositions for colour-light and piano, the creator of which is Alexander László himself, were first produced. Of these works the following are printed and published for the present:

(1) Alexander László: Eleven Preludes for coloured light and piano: 1. Blue; 2. Yellow; 3. Violet; 4. Foliage green; 5. Grey; 6. Red; 7. Ice Blue; 8. White; 9. Sea Green; 10. Cress; 11. Black.

In preparation: László, op. 9, Dreams; Five pieces for piano and coloured light. Op. 11, sonatina for piano and coloured light.

The coloured light part, for which László has invented his own notation, is printed above the piano score, and several illustrated supplements illustrate his colour-light-musical conception of especially interesting passages of the preludes. In a voluminous theoretical work, László develops the problems of colour-light music.

(2) Alexander László: *Colour light music*, with seven coloured plates and five black and white illustrations, and many illustrations in the text, as well as a movable colour scale.

László precedes a demonstration of his own views with a detailed survey regarding the previous history of colour and tone parallels. The theoretical researches and practical experiments of Johann Leonhard Hoffmann, A. W. Rimington, Hermann Schröder, Alexander Scriabin, and of other predecessors are critically examined in order to obtain the basis on which the author builds up his own system. Valuable explanations regarding the standpoint that the painter, as well as the musician, is to take up towards colour-light music (or not to take up, as the case may be) is followed by a detailed demonstration of his theories of composition. A detailed description of the colour-light piano, as well as of colour-light notation, conclude this epoch-making work. Another work which may be mentioned in this connexion is Vladimir Stcherbacher's Nonet for piano solo, harp, string quartet, solo violin, solo dance and light.

An interesting article on 'Colour and Sound' appeared in *Musical News*, Oct. 15, 1927, from the pen of Christina Walshe. EDITOR.]

COMMERCIALISM AND CHAMBER MUSIC have hitherto not been on speaking terms. Joachim could have quadrupled his income if, instead of leading quartets in European concert-rooms, he had toured the world as a soloist, and played at fashionable receptions. Concert-giving with programmes devoted to chamber music alone is the least paying of all such ventures; and as to compositions, the shelves of publishers are witness that purchasers for music of this type are few and far between. In short, chamber music is the art of the idealist, and, until recently, has been of the smallest possible interest to the commercial man. There has, however, been a tendency lately in London on the part of concert-givers to sacrifice the welfare of art to the interests of the box office. The few quartet players who have had the luck and ability to capture public attention are deserting the smaller halls, with their atmosphere of intimacy, for halls accommodating much larger audiences. Chamber music played in Queen's Hall or Albert Hall is still delicately beautiful, of course, but there is less warmth, less magnetism, less penetrating power. Berlioz, who was a master of the *mot juste*, described what was wanting 'when music was heard at a distance'. It was like, he said, 'gazing at a fire from afar. The flames are seen but the heat is not felt!'

The following remarks from the pen of

W. H. Pierce, taken from an article in the New York *Musical Quarterly*, are to the point:

'It was my good fortune to be present at a quartet concert given by an excellent, but at that time not yet famous Quartet, in a dingy little hall seating scarcely two hundred, in one of the smaller cities of New York State. The acoustic properties of the hall were excellent, and the audience, in spite of the fact that it was composed largely of persons whose musical culture was rudimentary, was appreciative of every note. A few years later I heard the same Quartet in New York City, in the old Mendelssohn Hall—not a tremendously large hall, either, and commonly regarded as a poor place for chamber music—and although the technical excellence of the players was, if anything, improved, I failed to experience anything like the same sensuous delight of the ear that I did on the former occasion. Even Mendelssohn Hall was really too large; what then should we say of so-called chamber music in a place that seats several thousand?'

EDITOR.

COMPETITION FESTIVALS AND CHAMBER MUSIC.

The history of concerted instrumental playing during the eighteenth century—which was the second culminating period, the first being the English movement which produced a thousand fantasies for viols—is extremely imposing. Planted in the rich soil of a living musical tradition, and smiled upon by aristocratic patronage, the noble art of chamber music grew and flourished. The rich and the aristocracy, in those days, took a great pride in music (as in other arts), and in the most practical and effective way possible they gave to musical artists exactly what they most needed to produce the best that was in them, namely, freedom from financial worry, congenial surroundings, and a sympathetic atmosphere. Many nobles went even farther, themselves practising the art which they so much admired, and having their children instructed in music by eminent artists of their choice. Lucky children, who, if they really loved music and showed some executive aptitude, could fulfil every musical desire up to the limit of their natural talent! Taught by musicians of genius, who not only showed them how to play, but who also composed music for them as required; playing upon beautiful new instruments made by Italian luthiers; with boundless leisure for practising and playing in spacious music-rooms; these youngsters had at least their fair share of musical advantages. As for the musicians who took part in this arrangement, it is true that they accepted their whole subsistence from the nobles, but they gave in return at least as much as they took. It is the fashion to speak of the age of patronage as in some way degrading to the artist, and no doubt the economic existence of musicians was—as it also had been in monastic times, and as it is to some extent even in the present industrial era—essentially parasitic. But, in return for material support, professional musicians gave good value out of their own natural store of riches, and were rewarded, not merely in terms of board and lodging, but also by the gratitude and homage of those who accepted their bounty. The special gift which the musicians carried in their hands was a tradition of musical order and musical fine manners, equal to, and indeed the counterpart of, that other tradition of social order and courtesy which was the heritage of the gentry during their best period. It is therefore in a double sense that one may speak of the aristocratic origin of instrumental ensemble. Out of the alliance between the aristocracy of rank and riches and the aristocracy of musical genius sprang the essentially aristocratic art of chamber music.

In this reflection, as to the origin and character of early chamber music, lies a notable significance. Chamber music is for the elect. It presupposes a long and noble musical ancestry, or, in other words, a tradition of technique and training, handed down by a royal line of instrumental masters through many generations. It also involves an intensive culture in courtly manners, musically speaking. There is no hearty, uneducated 'joining in' with a jolly, well-meaning mob or majority, for each player is individually responsible for his own part. Finally, he must always chime in sweetly and in just harmony with his fellows and equals, and he must be at every moment sensitive to what they are doing, thinking, and feeling. This is the very height of musical courtesy or good manners. All these considerations are paramount in chamber music, and, in common practice, almost peculiar to it. It must be admitted that a great deal of modern chamber music lacks these qualities. Doubtless the same principles could be, and occasionally are, applied to other forms of musical art. Singers, for instance, like Plunket Greene and Chaliapin, a certain number of orchestral players (who have been brought up on chamber music), and a few conductors thoroughly understand this aspect of music. But, on the whole, our ideals of performance are democratic. The early training of choral amateurs in time-reading and pitch-reading, in pronunciation, breathing, phrasing, &c., and the academic training of our professional string players in bowing style, phrasing, and general musical quality is, on the whole, insufficient, and the consequence is a sort of cunningly disguised crowd music, in which the individual singer or player, however good in himself—and even the conductor—is helplessly carried along on a flood of crowd-feeling, the resultant effect, such as it is, depending on the average pulsation, intensity, tone-quality, &c., of the majority.

Much is said in recommendation of team work, and there is much to be said for it in social and other matters. But there is something to be said, too, on the other side. Oneness and all-together-ness are vital to the race, but so also is the free expression of the single human soul. In music, a distinction ought really to be made between crowd-work (e.g. community singing, &c.) on the one hand, and, on the other, that wholly different true musical ensemble, in which each performer retains the possession of his own creative soul and will, and the power of expressing himself as a master man, not merely as a slave to the group-impulse of the untrained. Those who wish to express themselves musically on these (less popular) lines will turn naturally to chamber music.

Elsewhere in this work the course of the history cf chamber music throughout the nineteenth century has been fully told, and a slight sketch will therefore suffice to bring the narrative down to present-day doings. The Golden Age of chamber music came to an end after about sixty years, through the operation of the social and economic causes which brought about the French Revolution and modern industrialism. New means of locomotion tended to break up the repose and stability of eighteenth-century life; the nobility were no longer able to afford expensive establishments; musicians, deprived of their liveries and pensions, became, and still remain, dependent on fees in return for public performance and private teaching. All professional players of instruments grew incredibly more skilful, and turned in the direction of solo exhibitions at public concerts and away from the more intimate ensemble demanded by the string quartet, &c.

During the second half of the nineteenth century there was indeed a remarkable revival not only of quartet playing, but also of chamber music composition, but the art was now no longer solely domestic, neither was it, in the old sense, dilettante or amateur in character. The new 'chamber' concerts were given in great public halls by groups of eminent professional artists. In the case of England, the players nearly all came from abroad, and remained for a part of the year only. Meanwhile amateur playing was just kept alive by a few well-to-do enthusiasts, mostly elderly, few of whom possessed more than a slight acquaintance with the technique of ensemble playing. The chamber music repertory, too, had become greatly restricted. Nine or ten quartets by Mozart, the finest of Haydn's, all Beethoven's except the latest (generally considered incomprehensible), and perhaps a short series by Schumann and Schubert—these were about all that were left of the two or three thousand works produced during the period 1750–1850.

It is worth while to interrupt the story for a moment, in order to consider this curious neglect by players of all that mass of fine work which, taken together, forms the main relic of eighteenth-century chamber music. To those who study an art form of any kind whatever, it is a necessary part of culture to know a great deal about the subject, and especially to possess examples in multitude. The finest pictures and musical works are indeed fine in themselves, apart from comparisons. But it is only when they are reviewed in a setting of a mass of similar and contemporaneous work, that their true greatness can be appreciated. Take, for example, the string quartets of the eighteenth century. Each quartet, whether composed by Stamitz, Haydn, Van Hal, or Mozart, is first and foremost a standard eighteenth-century work, constructed mainly out of musical material which was common property, and expressed in the current musical idiom. Secondly, it is an expression of personality. Before the work can be duly appreciated under the second (and more important) of these two aspects, it is necessary to know how to separate the personal from the more ordinary matter, and, in order to be able to do this, it is further necessary to be acquainted with a large number of compositions by artists who worked during the same period and on the same material. Again, it would be a capital error, in these days of fresh musical research, to accept without question the curious estimates which the critics of the late nineteenth century used to make of the so-called 'lesser' chamber music of the eighteenth. It is not the case that the works of the minor writers were imitations, either of Haydn or of anybody else, or that their works perished because they were imitations. To take one example only, Van Hal (or Wanhal) was born only seven years after Haydn and he died only four years later. He composed a hundred string quartets, as compared with Haydn's eighty-three, and his later works are certainly immeasurably inferior to the latest and best of Haydn's. But Van Hal's earlier work is, in the writer's opinion, better than Haydn's earliest; it shows a finer feeling for strings, for equal part-writing, and for effect. The significance of these and other little-known facts concerning the minor composers of the great age of chamber music will appear later in the present article; meanwhile, this hint will serve to put a finishing touch to the picture of stagnation in which chamber music (considered as a *domestic* art) found itself at the close of the nineteenth century.

The dawn of the twentieth century brought a striking renewal of interest in chamber music. Encouraged by the great schools of music, the younger players began to play 'in consort', and now (1927) there are hundreds of String Quartets and other chamber music teams throughout the world, performing the concerted masterpieces, and, what is more, actually earning their living by doing so, either in public performances or by means of gramophone recording and broadcasting. All this is to the good, and a lawful cause for rejoicing. Nevertheless, it is a departure from the original idea of chamber music as a domestic art for people who love music and want to play it together. Fortunately it is possible, while duly praising these professional chamber musicians and while thoroughly appreciating their public exhibitions, to point to another and entirely independent revival, more in line with the fundamental conception of chamber music as an art in which the devotee is the actual producer, and not merely an appreciator of the doings of others. It is quite possible that many who read this are unaware that the art is being taken up and carried on into the future by the young men and women in the modern industrial world, and that this form of musical activity, already considerable, is notably increasing year by year. Not long ago this remarkable Competition Festival movement, copied from the Welsh, started in a small way, and soon grew to enormous proportions. The first objects were mainly social: group singing, folk dancing, &c., and there was, and still is, a great deal of solo singing and playing. But, thanks to the wisdom and foresight of the musical councils at the competition festivals, there have always been classes for ensemble or chamber music of some sort, however simple. The result, to date, is that there are some thousands of junior, amateur and embryo teams of chamber music players at work throughout the country. In the mass, this amounts to saying that, with certain qualifications, the genuine art of chamber music as a domestic recreation has been quietly revived, and promises gradually to transform the quality of the musico-social life of the nation. There is no need to expect that chamber music will ever exceed the dance or choral or solo music in general popularity. Chamber music always has been, and always will be, a musical occupation for the elect. It is the birthright of the gifted few who passionately love order and delicacy; who have the power to understand the intricacies of musical design, and who are willing to spend what leisure they have in acquiring, first an impeccable technique in the delivery of notes and time-values, and secondly, a fine conception of musical style and quality.

The interest of this revival can best be brought out by a short comparison between the chamber music-making of a hundred and fifty years ago (described above) and that of to-day. Most of the details, as to outward splendour, size and convenience of music rooms, margin of leisure, opportunities for good tuition, repertory, quality of instruments, &c., show a deficit on the modern side of the account. With regard to the question of relative brain power and musical intelligence, there are records to prove that the old nobility, educated in the traditions of the Renaissance, produced many examples of brilliant and sensitive youth, but it is quite possible that a musical modern mechanic who can design an efficient automatic lift, or a girl graduate school teacher or secretary, might be able to play a part in a string quartet as well as any grand duke of the Golden Age. In fact, the present movement, taken altogether, is quite as important as the earlier one, and in mere numbers it is far ahead.

The present (1927) is too early a date for a statement of results. Optimistic forecasts and amiable tolerance of poor work would be a great mistake. Chamber music is, and remains, an aristocratic occupation. It still implies an ancestry, not of social position but of musical tradition, and, above all, it still requires, and always will require, intensive training in the finest (musical) manners. Judging from a considerable number of recent festivals, the work, at the lowest, is sometimes very bad, and the best is often mistaken in all sorts of ways, but it nearly always shows signs, however dim, of promise for the future. The main fact is that, to the surprising extent above indicated, modern work-a-day youth has, of its own accord, taken up chamber music, and apparently means to go on with it.

It remains to indicate, for the information of those who wish to forward the interests of chamber music, the few ways in which assistance can be given. Two handicaps hamper the junior and amateur aspirant, viz. (1) lack of instrumental (string) tradition, and (2) poverty of repertory. If all good string teachers would join the musical councils of the local competition festivals, and if they would then see to it that suitable tests—not forgetting violin duets and other works leading up to the string quartets—are included in the instrumental classes, there would soon be an improvement under the first heading. With regard to the question of repertory, it is nearly true that, as an eminent authority (Mr. Dunhill) recently said to the writer, 'There are no easy string quartets' in print to-day. This requirement is now being attended to, but there is room in this department for valuable voluntary work which could be done by chamber music enthusiasts acquainted with the subject and possessed of means and leisure. It is only by means of some such plan as here foreshadowed for the provision of a repertory of string quartets, &c., by older and living masters, that the undoubted promise shown by the present generation of junior and amateur chamber music players can be fulfilled. JAMES BROWN.

[My own knowledge of the working of the competition festival movement in Britain is limited, and I am both surprised and impressed by what Mr. Brown writes on the subject. I have always thought of chamber music as an aristo-democratic art, and in Mr. Brown's article I see further confirmation of this view, my conception of the word 'aristocratic' having no reference to heredity, riches, or social position. One may learn from musical history that the world's aristocratic (i.e. most distinguished) music and the 'finest musical manners' have proceeded almost invariably from composers and executants of proletarian descent.

Be that as it may, the particulars given of competition festivals are full of good cheer for those who believe in the future of British chamber music, which, at least, is going to have a chance of development among the younger members of the community.

EDITOR.]

CONAS, F., French composer.

Sonata, pf, v Hachette, 1901.

CONCERTINA.

The attitude of string players towards the concertina is so well known that it will offend none if I remark that stress is habitually laid by them upon its limitations. This is not quite fair, for when the history of chamber music comes to be written, it will be recorded that such musicians as Molique, Macfarren, and Silas did not disdain to write ensemble music in which the concertina takes a prominent part, that enthusiastic performers upon treble, tenor, and bass concertinas give quite a respectable version of a string quartet, and that no less an authority than Mr. Fuller Maitland (in *Grove*) writes that Richard Blagrove, a violist in great request as a quartet player, was also a performer on the concertina, and obtained from it effects that were unexpectedly artistic.

EDITOR.

CONDUCTING.

The use of a conductor's bâton in chamber music is almost unknown, for the obvious reason that it would mean death to all individuality in interpretation; yet I remember an exceptional instance when it served the purpose of a composer who, wishing to hear his MS. quartet played before submitting it publicly to a continental audience a few days later, asked me to run it through with my Quartet. This I agreed to do, and as the work contained many metrical changes and a bare two hours were available for rehearsal, I suggested that he should beat time for us. This he did, and professed himself satisfied with the result. Having obtained a rough idea of how it sounded, he was able to make a few desirable corrections. But the conditions were exceptional, and the experiment is not likely to be repeated.

EDITOR.

CONSORTS OF VIOLS.

During the period 1550–1660 there flourished in England a kind of chamber music which has not been surpassed. It was written for viols of various sizes in various combinations, the number of instruments ranging from two to six. The tone of the viols, though not as powerful as that of the violins, is more easily produced, distinct, pure, and even in all the parts. It was a perfect medium for the realization of this intimate music, in which the enjoyment of the performers was the chief consideration. Moreover, it is much easier to play the viol than the violin; anybody can in a short time learn to play the viol well enough to enjoy taking part in a consort, for not only is the viol easy to play, but the parts in themselves are simple and never make any demand on virtuosity, an important consideration at a time when music had its proper place in everybody's life. It was the composer's task, and a very difficult one, to create by simple means music of the highest order and often of infinite complexity.

It was accomplished in many different ways by the English masters of the sixteenth and seventeenth centuries. Of these compositions, Thomas Mace, in his *Musick's Monument*, published in 1676, says:

> 'They were so many *Pathetical Stories*, Rhetorical and *Sublime Discourses; Subtil and Acute Argumentations; so Suitable and Agreeing to the Inward, Secret, and Intellectual Faculties of the Soul and Mind*; that to set Them forth according to their True Praise, *there are no Words Sufficient* in Language; yet what I can best speak of Them, shall be only to say, *That they have been to my self* (*and many others*) *as Divine Raptures, Powerfully captivating all our unruly Faculties, and Affections* (*for the Time*), *and disposing us to solidity, Gravity, and a Good Temper, making us capable of Heavenly and Divine Influences.*
>
> *'Tis Great Pity that Few Believe Thus Much*; but *Far Greater*, that so *Few Know it.*'

The writer and others who have had the privilege of playing a part in a consort of viols are unanimous in saying that it is the most satisfying experience that music can afford.

The fancy or fantasie is chief amongst viol music. Thomas Morley, in his *Plaine and Easie Introduction to Practicall Musicke*, published in 1597, says:

> 'A musician taketh a point at his pleasure, and wresteth and turneth it as he list, making either much or little of it according as shall seeme best in his own conceit. In this may more art be showne than in any other musicke, because the composer is tide to nothing else but that he may adde, diminish, and alter at his pleasure. And this kind will bear any allowances whatsoever tolerable in other Musicke, except changing the ayre and leaving the Key, which in fantasie may never bee suffered. Other thinges you may use at your pleasure, as bindings with discordes, quick motions, slow motions, proportions, and what you list.'

In practice, these fantasies are written in the most profound and elaborate counterpoint, but with such mastery that no effort is apparent, and the complexity is not even noticed by the untrained auditor. He is merely conscious of a flow of extraordinarily rich and beautiful decorative music.

The composer, being free to do whatever his fancy dictates, sometimes abandons the 'concerted' style and takes to vertical harmony, the parts moving simultaneously; but never for long. The piece always concludes with something that has art and excellency in it. The end of these fantasies is not the least admirable part of them; the musicians of that time could always find a beautiful close, something never heard before, which brought the piece to a natural and perfectly satisfying conclusion.

The freedom and logic of the parts often leads to extraordinary combinations of notes, producing the effect of daring modern harmonies, but always in a logical and unavoidable way. Obviously, these harmonies are not introduced for their own sake, but are a result, a by-product, and the effect is all the more surprising and beautiful on that account.

A striking example of such discords is found in Coperario's fantasie for five viols *Chi può mirarvi*, in which a descending passage in the first treble ends in a stressed C sharp, whilst the tenor, ascending, culminates on a C natural at the same time, both phrases being logical, beautiful, and unalterable.

These consorts were practised in all the countries of western Europe, but in England they attained a freedom and intensity of expression greater than anywhere else. Many English consorts have been lost, for few were printed, and they were misunderstood and often derided for three hundred years.

Yet we possess a large number of them, for an immense amount was written, probably exceeding the sum of those of all other countries. The pre-eminence of the English consorts was recognized everywhere. They are found in most of the libraries of Europe. Mersenne, in his great book, published in 1637 under the title of *L'Harmonie universelle*, selected an English fantasy for six viols as an example of that kind of music.

In England, under James II, fashion turned against fantasies, and English music generally, just at the time when that music had reached its greatest perfection. Good people protested, however—John Playford, *Philo-Musicae*, wrote in the preface of *Musick's Delight on the Cithren*, 1666:

'It is observed that of late years all *Solemn* and *Grave Musick* is much laid aside, being esteemed too heavy and dull for the light Heels and Brains of this Nimble and wanton age: Nor is any Musick rendered acceptable, or esteemed by many, but what is presented by Forreigners; Not a City Dame though a Tap-wife, but is ambitious to have her Daughters Taught by Mounsieur La Novo Kickshawibus on the Gittar.'

Thomas Mace, page 236 of *Musick's Monument*, says:

'Very little of *This Eminent Musick* do we hear of in *These Times* (the Less the greater Pity).

'Then again, we had all *those choice Consorts* to *Equally-Sciz'd Instruments*, (*Rare Chests of Viols*) and as *Equally Performed*: For we would never allow *Any Performer to Over-top or Out-cry* another by *Loud Play*; but our Great Care was to have *All the Parts Equally Heard*; by which means (though sometimes we had but indifferent or mean *Hands to Perform* with; yet This Caution made the *Musick Lovely* and *very Contentive*.

'But now the *Modes* and *Fashions* have cry'd *These Things* down, and set up a Great Idol in their Room; observe with what a *Wonderful Swiftness* They now run over their *Brave New Ayres*; and with what High-Priz'd Noise, viz. 10 or 20 Violins, &c. as I said before, to Some-Single-Soul'd Ayre; it may be of 2 or 3 Parts, or some *Coranto, Serabrand*, or *Brawle*, (as the New-Fashioned Word is) and such-like *Stuff*, seldom any other; which is rather fit to make a Mans *Ears Glow*, and fill his Brains full of Frisks, &c. than to *Season and Sober his Mind, or Elevate his Affection to Goodness*.

Christopher Simpson in his *Compendium of Music*, published 1665, says:

'We must now speak a little more of Musick made for Instruments; in which, Points, Fuges, and all other Figures of Descant are in no less (if not in more) use than in Vocal Musick.

Of this kind, the chief and most excellent, for Art and Contrivance, are Fancies of 6, 5, 4, and 3 parts, intended commonly for Viols. In this sort of Musick the Composer (being not limited to words) doth employ all his Art and Invention solely about the bringing in and carrying on of these Fuges, according to the Order and Method formerly shewed.

When he has tryed all the several ways which he thinks fit to be used therein; he takes some other Point, and does the like with it: or else, for variety, introduces some *Chromatick* Notes, with Bindings and Intermixtures and Discords: or, falls into some lighter Humour like a Madrigal, or what else his own fancy shall lead him to: but still concluding with something which hath Art and Excellency in it.

Of this sort you may see many Compositions made heretofore in *England* by *Alfonso Ferabosco, Coperario, Lupo, White, Mico, Dr. Colman*, and many more now deceased. Also by Mr. *Jenkins*, Mr. *Lock*, and divers other excellent men, Doctors and Batchelors in Musick, yet living.

This kind of Musick (the more is the pity) is now much neglected, by reason of the scarcity of Auditors that understand it: their Ears being better acquainted and more delighted with light and airy Musick . . . .

'You need not seek outlandish Authors, especially for Instrumental Musick; no Nation (in my opinion) being equal to the *English* in that way; as well for their excellent, as for their various and numerous Consorts, of 3, 4, 5, and 6 parts, made properly for Instruments; of all which (as I said) *Fancies* are the Chief.'

Thomas Mace gives another list of the best composers of fancies. He says (p. 234):

'The *Authors* of such like *Compositions* have been divers *Famous English Men*, and *Italians*; some of which, for Their very *Great Eminency* and *Worth* in that *Particular Faculty*, I will here name, viz. Mr. Alfonso Ferabosco, Mr. John Ward, Mr. Lupo, Mr. White, Mr. Richard Deering, Mr. William Lawes, Mr. John Jenkins, Mr. Christopher Simpson, Mr. Coperario, and one Monteverde, a Famous Italian Author; besides divers, and very many others, who in their *Late Time*, were *Substantial, Able* and *Profound Composing Masters* in *This Art*, and have left *Their Works* behind them, as fit Monuments and Patterns for Sober and Wise Posterity, worthy to be *Imitated* and *Practised: 'Tis Great Pity* they are so soon forgot and *Neglected*, as I perceive they are amongst many.'

These lists are valuable. They are a sure guide for those who are in search of fantasies. Some of the composers best known at present are not mentioned, for example, Wm. Byrd, Wilbye, Th. Morley, John Bull, Gibbons; but they have been wisely omitted, for whatever they may have achieved in other ways, they did not distinguish themselves in that line. The few fantasies we know of W. Byrd's are not very good. Thomas Morley published in 1595 nine fantasies for two viols, delightful little pieces, but of no great importance by themselves. Orlando Gibbons published nine fantasies in three parts which are extraordinarily dull, but which, unfortunately, were the only things known to musical historians for a long time; and upon them were formed the absurd opinions which our 'authorities' have given of this music.

Several foreign names appear in the lists given above, but they do not always indicate foreign composers; Coperario's real name was John Cooper, which he Italianized after a journey to Italy.

Thomas Lupo and Alfonso Ferrabosco, although of Italian parentage, were born in England, and are thoroughly English in their style and methods.

As to Monteverde, it would be interesting to know his fantasies, but the author, to his great regret, never succeeded in finding them.

Pieces called *In Nomine* are often found amongst collections of fantasies. They are based on a canto fermo, generally the plainsong of the *In Nomine Dei*, which being played very slowly by one of the viols, the other two, three, four, or five weave round it a fantasy as free and beautiful as if the presence of the C. F. produced no additional difficulty.

Sometimes another tune served as canto fermo, for example, ut, re, mi, fa, or 'La My', or even one single note, as in that wonderful 'Fantasy upon one note' of Henry Purcell, perhaps the last fantasy ever written, in which, whilst the tenor keeps playing middle C, the other parts from this centre evolve a series of complex themes with chromatic passages, modulations to remote keys, striking rhythms, forming a succession of pictures of marvellous variety and beauty.

Next in dignity after a fantasy is a pavan. It is simpler than a fantasy, being a tune more or less richly accompanied. The pavan is in duple time, in three sections of eight breves or multiples of four breves, always conforming to the rhythm of the dance from which it originated, but often developing counterpoint too rich and complex for dancing purposes, and becoming a purely instrumental piece.

Some pavans even partook of the nature of the *In Nomine*, as, for example, the exquisite *Four Note Pavan* of Alfonso Ferrabosco, the treble part of which entirely consists of the famous 'Divinity' Theme 'Do, re, fa, mi' transformed in rhythm and tonality like a Wagner 'Leit-motif' and adorned with the richest counterpoint imaginable.

The galliard is the complement of the pavan, being generally based on the same tune, transformed in rhythm from duple to triple time, and, like the pavan, based on the dance bearing its name.

Galliards are not very common in viol music.

Allmaines sometimes follow fantasies, as in the six fantasies for six viols of Martin Pierson, simple, effective tunes, but with little depth, even in the fantasies.

The composers of the middle of the seventeenth century, especially Will. Lawes, often follow their fantasies by an *ayre* abounding in rich harmonies, imitations, dramatic passages matching the fantasy.

Jenkins, and especially Matthew Locke, made regular suites for viols, as constant in form as the quartets of Haydn.

There are six consorts in four parts by Matthew Locke, which invariably consist of a slow introduction, followed by a fantasy, which is the most dignified part of the work, like the first movement of the string quartet; then follows a coranto, an *ayre*, and a very lively saraband which sometimes concludes with a slow movement, the whole forming a complete, satisfying work of art, with all the variety and unity to be found in the very best chamber music.

Let musicians study this music, and, above all, play it; for its beauty cannot be realized by mere study of the scores. They will find in it the lost secret of creating beauty by simple means, of bringing music of the highest order within reach of everybody.

They can no more afford to ignore Old English chamber music than painters could ignore the so-called Primitives.

THE CHEST OF VIOLS.

The name 'Chest of Viols' meant a set of six viols: two trebles, two tenors, and two basses. The music played upon a set of instruments of the same kind was called a 'Whole Consort'. When instruments of various kinds, as lutes, viols, recorders, &c., were combined, it was called a 'Broken Consort', or 'Broken Music'.

Now let us refer to Mace again on this point. He says, p. 245:

> '*Your Best Provision*, (and *most Compleat*) will be, a *Good Chest of Viols*; Six in *Number*; viz. 2 *Bases*, 2 *Tenors*, and 2 *Trebles*: All *truly*, and *Proportionably suited*.
>
> Of such, there are no Better in the World, than Those of *Aldred*, *Jay Smith* (yet the Highest in Esteme are) *Bolles*, and *Ross*, (one Bass of Bolles's, I have known Valued at £100). These were old; but We have Now very Excellent Good Workmen, who (no doubt) can Work as well as Those, if They be so well Paid for Their Work, as They were; yet we chiefly Value Old Instruments, before New; for by Experience, they are found to be far the Best.'

There is one point which Mace had no need to explain, but which is important at the present time, namely: what is the difference between viols and violins, which have so many points in common?

1st. The form: In the viol, the shoulders join the neck at a tangent, while in the violins they meet it at right angles.

2nd. In the viols, the back is flat, not round, as in the violins.

3rd. The sides of the viols are wider in proportion than those of the violins, making the instrument thicker.

4th. The back and belly of the viols are flush with the sides; they do not project, as in the violins.

5th. The corners of the viols turn inwards, they are not curled out, as in the violins, the outline being therefore much simpler.

6th. The sound holes are in the form of C's, with their backs turned against one another, instead of *f*'s.

7th. The neck of the viol is broad, to accommodate six strings, with plenty of space between them.

8th. The head is longer than in the violin on account of the six pegs; it ends in a human, a lion, or some fantastic shape, or an open decorated scroll.

The viols are almost always decorated with purfling, interwoven in more or less intricate patterns, often forming very interesting and beautiful designs.

But some of these points may be missing; viols exist with round backs, *f* holes, projecting sound boards, plain scrolls, &c.

What then is the fundamental difference between a viol and a violin?

1st. The number of strings, which in the viol is generally six, sometimes seven, but never less than five.

2nd. The tuning, which is in fourths, with a third between the two middle strings.

3rd. The kind of strings, which in the viols are thinner and less tight than in the violin.

4th. The seven frets, which are formed of a piece of gut string, tied round the neck with a peculiar knot, which keeps them firmly in their places but yet allows of their being shifted to obtain accurate intonation.

The frets are indispensable; without them the accuracy of intonation and clearness of tone upon which the proper performance of consorts depends could not be obtained, or, at best, only by experienced players, which must ever be rare.

The English excelled all others in viol making, just as they did in their viol music.

English viols of great beauty of workmanship and exquisite tone can still be found in comparatively great numbers. The trebles and tenors are rarer than the basses, for they proved of little use after the viols had become obsolete, while the basses were turned into indifferent violoncellos. Needless to say, these, when found nowadays, are promptly turned back to their original form.

TUNING.

The tuning of consort viols is as follows: *Treble*, starting from the treble, D A E C G D, the A and the G being in unison with the second and fourth strings of the violin.

Tenor: G D A F C G, the D and the C being in unison with the second and fourth strings of the viola.

Bass: D A E C G D, the A and the G being in unison with the first and third strings of the violoncello.

The lowest string D is tuned down to C whenever the music requires it. It will be seen that the bass stands one octave, and the tenor one fifth below the treble.

An alto or counter-tenor viol is also used, in size between the treble and the tenor. Its tuning is C G D A F C one tone below the treble in all its strings, except the fourth, which is a minor third below the C of the treble.

All the viols, even the smallest, are held downwards in playing; the treble and tenor between the knees, the bass resting on the calves of the legs, as some violoncello players still do at the present time and many more will in future. It is difficult to understand why violoncello players adopt the peg to support their instrument, for, except in special cases, it has few advantages and many inconveniences.

It was François Servais, the great Belgian virtuoso, who rendered the peg fashionable. In his old age he had become too fat to hold his 'cello comfortably between his knees, and the peg relieved his fatigue. Thereupon his imitators adopted the peg, in the hope that it would help them to play like him.

The position of the left hand on the viol is that used by good violoncello players; the extremity of the thumb rests on the back of the neck, opposite the second finger, the fingers being perpendicular to the strings. The neck is never grasped as is done by violin players.

The art of viol bowing is so well described by Th. Mace in *Musick's Monument*, and so much of the precepts are applicable to all stringed instruments, that we may be pardoned the rather long quotation.

'Then take *your Bow* betwixt *your Right Thumb* and 2 Forefingers, near the Nut; the *Thumb* and *1st Finger* fastening *upon the Stalk*, and the 2d Fingers's End turned in Shorter *against the Hairs*; by which you may *Poyze*, and *keep up the end of your Bow*; but if that Finger be not Strong enough, joyn the 3d *Finger in Assistance* to It; but in Playing *Swift Divisions, 2 Fingers, and the Thumb is Best*.

This is according to Mr. *Simpson's Directions*.

Yet I must confess, that for *my own Part*, I could never *Use It so well* as when I held *It* 2 or 3 *Inches off the Nut* (more or less) according to the *Length or Weight of the Bow*, for *Good Poyzing of it*; But it is possible, that by *Use* I might have made it *as familiar to Myself* as it was to *Him*.

So likewise, for the *Exact Straitness of the Bow-Arm*, which some do *contend for, I could never do so well* as with my *Arm*, (Straight enough, yet) something Plying, or Yielding to an Agile Bending; and which I do conceive most *Familiarly Natural*.

For I would have no *Posture, Urg'd, disputed*, or *contended* for; that should *Cross*, or *Force Nature*.

Now being Thus far *ready for Exercise*, attempt the *Striking of your Strings*; but before you do That, Arm yourself with Preparative *Resolutions to gain a Handsome-Smooth-Sweet-Smart-Clear-Stroak*; or else Play not at all; For if your Viol be never so Good, if you have an *Unhandsom-Harsh-Rugged-Scratching, Scraping-Stroak*, (as too many have) your Viol will seem *Bad* and your Play *Worse*.

Now the way to gain *This Right Stroak*, is from your Intent *Care* (at first) in the *Order* and *Right Motion* of the *Bow*; And although, as concerning the *Holding of the Viol*, the Bow, Order of the Arm, and Use of the Wrist, several Very Excellent Masters do something *Differ*, yet *All Perform Rarely Well*, because they agree in the *Main and Principal Thing*, viz. the *Care in Gaining the Good Stroak* (as aforesaid), which is done after *This Manner*, viz.

Only to draw your Bow just Cross the Strings in a Direct Line, endeavouring to Sound One Single String, with a Long Bow, wellnigh from Hand to Point, and from Point to Hand smoothly, and not Dripping or Elevating the Point in the least.

This is the First and Best Piece of Practice you can follow, and till you have gain'd This, think of Nothing Else.

And as to the *Place* where your *Bow must move*, you are to regard 4 Things, viz. *The Scize; The Stringing; The Pitch*; and also the *Various Uses of the Viol*.

1st. If it be a *Large Consort Viol*, your *Bow must Move* about 2 *Inches and an Half from the Bridge*; if a Treble-Viol, about *an Inch and a Half*; and so upon all others, according to *this Suitable Proportion*.

2dly. According to Its Stringing, Viz., if It be *Stiff Strung, or Stand at a High Pitch*; (which is both as one), then Play a little *Further from the Bridge*.

3rdly. According to *Its Use*, viz. If for *Consort Use*, Play *nearer the Bridge* than when you Play *alone*; which although It be not so *Sweet*, yet is more *Lusty*, and that little *Ruffness* is *Lost* in the *Crowd*; so likewise you may do, if you be to Play at a *Great Distance* from the *Auditors*, for the same Reason; for the *Roughness* will be *lost* before it come to *Them*. But if you be to Play very near your Auditors, especially unto *Curious Ears*, Play a *little too far off*, rather than *too near*, for by that means your Play will be the more *Sweet*, &c.

Your next Thing is to gain the *Motion of the Wrist*, (which with the Former is the *Accomplishment* of the *Right Arm*), and is *Thus* gained, viz. only by causing the *Hand at the very turning of the Bow* (either way) to incline to a *Contra-Motion*; the Arm (as it were) leaving the *Wrist behind It, Explained* otherwise thus, viz.

Let your *Stroak* be at what *length* it will; before you would leave the *Motion of your Bow* (If it be a Long Stroak) *Stop the Motion of your Arm Suddenly*: yet *Jet your Wrist still onwards*, 3 or 4 Inches, and it is done: But if It be a Shorter Stroak; then according to *Discretion, a shorter* Jet of the Wrist Performs It.'

This manner of holding the bow is the best for all instruments held downwards. It is the easiest, gives the greatest freedom to the wrist, permits the use of a longer bow, facilitates the reach of the extreme strings, gives greater power and at the same time greater delicacy, and is very graceful to see.

The bass instruments of the violin family were all bowed in that way until, in the second half of the eighteenth century, when violoncello players, having discovered that their instrument, hitherto used only to play basses, could also play solos, soon tried to apply to it all the technique and tricks, good and bad, of the violinists; and they imagined that it would help them if they imitated the bowing of the violinists. It did not help them, but the fashion was established all the same. Now we see double-bass players whose ambition is to emulate violoncello players, also adapting the violinist bowing! But the viol method of bowing is now used by many players; they see its advantages, and there is no doubt that it will be practised more and more in future, even on the violoncello.

THE REVERSED BOWING.

In viol bowing the movements are the reverse of those of the violin. The 'forward movement', the 'poussé' of the French, that is, when the bowing begins at *the point* of the bow, is given to the accented notes, whilst the backward stroke, 'tiré' in French, is used for unaccented notes.

This is the natural way of bowing viol-way; it has the advantage of equalizing the tone, for one cannot press the bow on the string as hard at the point as at the nut. Therefore the 'bite', the powerful stress of the down bow on the violin, is not available on the viol. But these strong accents are not used in viol music. As says Jean Rousseau in his *Traité de la viole* (1687):

> 'One must take care in gay movements not to accentuate too much, so as to preserve the character of the instrument, which will not be treated in the manner of the violin, the property of which is to animate, whilst the property of the viol is to flatter.'

But in the eighteenth century, when orchestras began to assert themselves; when the upper parts played by violins made a point of strong accents, the bass instruments, violoncelli and violone, had to stress their accents likewise. As this can only be done near the nut of the bow, viol bowing became reversed in many cases, and the 'tiré', misnamed 'down-bow' (for there can be no 'down-stroke' where the bowing is horizontal) was used on strongly accented notes.

THE VIOLONE.

There is one member of the viol family, the violone, which has not been mentioned yet, because it was not used in consorts of viols. It became very important later as the deepest-toned instrument of the violin family. It is a large viol with six strings in its complete form, tuned one octave below the bass viol and played standing, being too large to hold between the knees. In size it approaches the ordinary double-bass; but its strings are much thinner, and it has frets. Its tone in consequence is much more clear and musical than that of the double-bass, and it can execute runs with the same rapidity and precision as the smaller instruments. It is indispensable for the performance of florid bass parts such as are found in the music of Purcell, Handel, Bach, and other composers of that period. Everybody knows the horrible confusion, the heavy rumbling noises with which the ordinary double-bass spoils such music.

The violone was well known in Italy and in Germany in the sixteenth century. Praetorius in *Syntagma Musicum* (1618) gives a full description of it, in its various sizes, number of strings, and tunings. We know from Dominicino's *St. Cecilia* that it was used in Italy to accompany the voice, and there is a story of a Frenchman named Granier who used one that must have been very large, for he put a boy inside to sing the treble part, whilst he sang the tenor and played the bass on the instrument, and his performances were much liked by 'La reyne Marguerite'.

Now that the music of Bach is so frequently played, it becomes imperative that the violone should be revived, or at least that double-basses with thin strings *and frets* should be used; for this music demands just the same clearness in the bass as in the upper parts. Its whole conception depends on that point.

SEVENTEENTH-CENTURY CHAMBER MUSIC FOR VIOLINS.

The sonatas of Corelli are generally considered the earliest examples of chamber music for violins worthy of attention. It is true that one of the twenty-four sonatas in three and four parts of Henry Purcell is fairly well known, and they are anterior to Corelli's. But Purcell, in the preface to his first book of sonatas, declares, most probably to appease the English enemies of English music, that he has endeavoured to imitate the Italian sonatas. He did not do it, probably could not have done it if he would; he remained his great self for the benefit of humanity. But still, to what Italian sonatas was he alluding? It can only be the sonatas of Legrenzi, in two, three, four, five, and six parts, published in 1653.

The sonatas are exceedingly beautiful, expressive, lyrical, and effective on the instruments for which they were written. There is some resemblance between them and Purcell's, and they ought to be better known than they are. But, before Legrenzi's sonatas, there had been many English compositions for violins by Jenkins, Lawes, &c., quite as good as any, though never published; and above all, perhaps, there were the sonatas of William Young, published in London in 1653, of which one copy only has survived, now preserved at the Library of Upsala in Sweden. A manuscript copy of these is now in the British Museum. These also deserve to be known, for no better music has been written since for the violin. They prove that in this line the English were at least equal to any other nation, and were probably the first in that field also.

Then what becomes of this continual progress of music, still the shibboleth of so many modern composers? They believe that the music written before them was a mere beginning, a series of experiments in tone combinations and form of little value but as a preparation to their own achievements. This comfortable state of mind is the result of ignorance. William Morris once showed the writer of this article a copy of the Bible printed by Gutenberg, one of the very first products of the printing press, and told him it was the most perfect example of a printed book he had ever seen!

Music is an art, like literature, painting, and printing, the ideals of which are continually changing. The latest acquisition is easily seen, but few can appreciate the corresponding loss. For those who know and are sensitive to the various aspects of beauty, there is as much satisfaction in playing a fantasy of William Lawes or a sonata of Legrenzi as in playing a quartet of Beethoven. Each one is a perfect work of art, and no one can demonstrate the superiority of one over the other.

ARNOLD DOLMETSCH.

CONTEMPORARY MUSIC CENTRE.

Towards the end of 1920 a meeting was held under the auspices of the British Music Society, with the object of starting a new Centre of that Society which should be distinguished by a special function, viz. that of 'hearing little known or unknown chamber compositions, published and in MS., by contemporary British composers, and for papers, lectures, and discussions on subjects closely related thereto'. The Centre was founded there and then with those present as the nucleus of a committee. Four of their number—Dr. Eaglefield Hull, Mr. York Bowen, Mr. H. Kling, and Mr. Philip Wilson—continued to be associated with the Centre in subsequent years, as were a number of members co-opted later, notably Professor E. J. Dent, Mr. W. W. Cobbett, Mr. Edwin Evans (permanent Chairman from 1922 on), Mr. Gerald Cooper, Mr. Arthur Bliss, Mr. Dunton Green, and Mrs. Lee Mathews.

The objects for which the Centre was ostensibly founded were somewhat modified within the first eighteen months. It concentrated its efforts on the performance of chamber music, and abandoned its exclusive preoccupation with British composers, admitting to its programmes foreign music in the proportion of one-third; a regulation treated, however, with considerable latitude, the desire to give the British composer prominence being tempered by the consideration that no country can produce two works of merit to every one that is contributed by the remainder of the world.

This change in policy was appropriately followed, at the end of 1922, by the most important event in the Centre's history, viz. its appointment as British Section of the newly founded International Society for Contemporary Music, and furthermore as the headquarters of the International Society itself. This function was bestowed on the Centre as much on account of the prestige of the International's president, Edward J. Dent, as on account of the supposed ability of the British in matters of organization.

As a body devoted to the performance of chamber music, the Contemporary Music Centre has been increasingly successful. In 1921 it gave two concerts only, at which the audiences scarcely outnumbered the performers; but by 1924 its membership had reached nearly three hundred. The first programme of all, given on March 4, 1921, consisted of a string quartet by William Albon, sonata no. 2 for piano by L. Collingwood, and a string quartet by W. T. Walton. The Walton quartet, in a revised form, was subsequently chosen by the International Society's jury for their festival at Salzburg in 1923.

The first foreign work admitted to the Centre's programmes was Malipiero's quartet *Rispetti e Strambotti*, given in March 1922, and followed in July by the first performance in England of Ravel's sonata for violin and 'cello.

From the autumn of 1922 till the end of 1925 the Centre held its concerts at the Art Workers' Guild Hall, Bloomsbury. Among the works which there received early performances were Bax's piano quartet, string quartets by Vaughan Williams (revised), Moeran, Hindemith, Jarnach, van Dieren (no. 4), and Casella; violin sonatas by Howells, Moeran, Bartók (nos. 1 and 2), and Pijper; and 'cello sonatas by Pizzetti, Ireland, Kodály, and Hindemith.

In 1925 the Centre gave its first concert for chamber orchestra, and performed van Dieren's serenata, and a prelude and *Severn Rhapsody* by Gerald Finzi.

Public concerts were given in 1923 and 1924, the first with a programme of contemporary French music, with Fleury, Milhaud, Wiener, and Mme Freund, and the second with the Roth Quartet, who played Stravinsky's concertino and Jarnach's quartet, op. 16.

Distinguished composers who have played at the Centre include John Ireland, Josef Holbrooke, Cyril Scott, Béla Bartók, Ildebrando Pizzetti, and Willem Pijper.

Contemporary Music Centres were opened in Manchester in 1923 and Liverpool in 1924, each being in touch with, but entirely independent of, the London organization.

The London concerts at present (1928) take place at the Court House, Marylebone.

D. Wadham.

[This admirable society, with which I have the honour to be associated as committee-man, suffers from the drawback that with the funds at disposal it is not able to organize for its concerts an adequate number of rehearsals. New works that would be the better for twenty rehearsals receive perhaps three. Nevertheless, the results achieved have been remarkable.

Editor.]

†CONVERSE, Frederic Shepherd, b. 1871, American composer, pupil of Rheinberger and G. W. Chadwick.

Quartet, str, a mi	op. 18	Schirmer, 1903.
Sonata, pf, v, A	,, 1	Boston Mus. Co., *c.* 1900.
Sonata, pf, vc	without opus	New Eng. Conserv. Mus. Store (Boston), 1922.

Converse is a man of abundant energy, and the possessor of an ample and dexterous technique. His work is permeated by a robust romanticism, touched here and there by a gentler mysticism.

The Violin Sonata can hardly be taken as indicative of the composer's true powers, but it is a creditable opus 1. Already there is mastery of sonata form, together with an unaffected simplicity which gives throughout a feeling of spontaneity.

The Quartet, though published so long ago, bears none the less the stamp of maturity. It is in three movements, of which the first is notable for its rhythmic diversity, while the ensuing adagio forms an appropriate contrast. In this movement, with its finely sustained cantabile, the outstanding features are simplicity and clarity, together with an ever-present resourcefulness which serves to maintain the interest so often lacking in slow movements. The third movement abounds with a vivacious energy quite in keeping with the spirit of the first, and again the composer's resourcefulness is manifest in a graceful middle section affording a dexterous foil to the almost boisterous vigour pervading the rest of the finale.

The 'Cello Sonata is in two movements, an adagio and an allegro, and may be described as the typical product of an adept in every medium of musical expression. The romantic fervour that characterizes all Converse's works is here abundantly in evidence. He has seized upon the poetic warmth of the tone of the 'cello as the medium for his rhapsodic lyricism, and achieves a notable brilliance of effect without excessive demands on the technique of the performers. Arthur Shepherd.

†COOLIDGE, ELIZABETH SPRAGUE (Mrs. Frederick Shurtleff Coolidge) is the Lady Bountiful of chamber music. Her benefactions are on a scale so generous as to transcend the bounds of what any lover of the art could in his most sanguine moments have expected from a single individual. The theme is one which, for obvious reasons, requires some delicacy of treatment, and I must be satisfied with offering her the homage of every musician the world over, whose interest is centred in this branch of music. In the interests of the future as well as the present, Mrs. Coolidge has lately elected to work under the aegis of the American Senate, but is nevertheless cosmopolitan in her sympathies. Her competitions are international in scope; it is interesting to note that the prize-winners have so far been from different nations. Mrs. Coolidge gives support to artists of all nationalities, and has organized concerts in many European cities as well as in America, whilst her invitations to attend the festivals she organizes annually are extended to prominent musicians in every country where chamber music flourishes.

It would fill a volume to give particulars of all that Mrs. Coolidge has done for chamber music. Indeed, I hope that in the fullness of time such a work will appear. Meantime, the attention of readers is invited to the following condensed account of her activities.

1. THE BERKSHIRE FESTIVAL. Instituted in 1918 for concert-giving in what came to be known as a Temple of music, built on South Mountain, Pittsfield, Mass., and capable of holding an audience of 500, and therefore of ideal size for chamber music. This audience consisted of invited guests, most of them receiving hospitality at a pleasant hotel of the old English type. Each year up to 1924, three days in the autumn were devoted to concerts of chamber music—three in the evening and two in the afternoon—in which various concert organizations took part, some of the executants being of British nationality.

2. PRIZE COMPETITIONS. Instituted in connexion with the Berkshire Festival, composers of all nations being asked to submit MS. to a jury of experts. Held each year with the exception of 1923 and 1925.

3. COMMISSIONS given to composers to write chamber works; given in 1923, 1925, and 1928.

4. The offer, made in 1925 (as an outcome of the Berkshire Festivals which terminated in 1924), to the Congress of the U.S., through their Librarian in Washington, to donate the sum of $94,000 for the construction of an AUDITORIUM dedicated to the performance of chamber music, and to make a further provision in the nature of endowment of $25,000 annually for giving FESTIVAL CONCERTS specially designed for the encouragement of chamber music composition. This offer was accepted by the Treasurer of the U.S. in the name of the nation; the auditorium was built, and since then two series of concerts have been given in 1925 and 1926, the programmes including, as in Pittsfield, certain of the older masterpieces, coupled with examples of the advanced modern school.

5. The continuation of the series of so-called Berkshire Prizes, in future to be known as the ELIZABETH SPRAGUE COOLIDGE PRIZES.

6. The giving of FREE CONCERTS in the public libraries or museums of large American cities.

Various minor activities of Mrs. Coolidge—minor only from a comparative point of view—need to be mentioned. She has given support to the so-called OJAI VALLEY FESTIVAL in California. Certain chamber organizations have received from her the initial impetus, including the ELSHUCO TRIO (the title of which is a combination of syllables in her own name), which was sent by her to give performances at various universities. Finally, she has been lavish in hospitality to her European friends, to whom she has offered musical entertainment in many of the cities of Europe.

Of such munificence it is, in the words of the Librarian of Congress, 'difficult to write with moderation. One can only say that it speaks for itself to us who are living, and who are able to see the results of the moment. It will continue to speak for itself to posterity.'

In 1926 the Cobbett medal 'for services to chamber music' was awarded to Mrs. Coolidge by the Worshipful Company of Musicians, London. EDITOR.

†COOLS, EUGÈNE, b. 1877, French composer, pupil of Gedalge.

Sonata, pf, v, a mi	op. 79	Max Eschig.
Sonata, pf, fl, F	,, 64	,, ,,
Concertstück, pf, fag		Evette.

Cools's sonata for flute and piano is rather unusual both in form and tonality. It opens with a slow introduction, in which the main themes are announced, leading to an andante which takes the place of the customary first movement in sonata form. This is built on an elegant first subject, followed by a second of tranquil character; in place of the development there is a reappearance of the slow introduction, then the andante returns, to connect with the final allegro. This is in breezy rhythm, and is entirely constructed on the two themes already employed, with rhythmic transformations. The whole is full of life and freshness.

The violin sonata opens with a dramatic allegro in A minor, classical in form.

The second movement is a Lied[1] in C major, in three sections, and shows the influence of Franck.

The finale, in A major, is in rondo form, with four refrains[1]—the couplets being constructed on the principal themes of the preceding movements.

[1] See Foreword, art. BEETHOVEN.

Sincerity of emotion, elegance, and clarity of style are the essential qualities of the work of Eugène Cools. ADOLPHE PIRIOU.

COPPET, E. J. DE. *v.* FLONZALEY QUARTET.

COPPET, L. C. DE.

Quartet, str, a mi Decourcelle, *c.* 1900.

COPPOLA, PIERO, b. 1888, Italian composer.

Poema appassionato, pf, v Senart.

COR ANGLAIS.

What has been said elsewhere regarding the oboe in chamber music applies also to the English horn, except that this instrument, which is even more an instrument of special colour, is still further limited in use. Apart from the Beethoven trio for two oboes and English horn (mentioned under OBOE), the writer only knows of a trio for oboe, clarinet, and English horn by Karg-Elert (scholarly but somewhat dry), and the trio by Donald Tovey for violin, English horn, and piano. A trio for flute, English horn, and piano by Vinée is an interesting experiment. The most effective chamber work in which prominence is given to the cor anglais is Arthur Bliss's *Conversations* for violin, viola, 'cello, flute (alternating with bass flute), and oboe (alternating with cor anglais). BURNET C. TUTHILL.

CORBETT, WILLIAM, *c.* 1669–1748, British violinist.

Burney says that Corbett travelled in Italy on behalf of the English Government, who paid him to watch the movements of the Pretender. His many chamber works, now obsolete, included six sonatas for two oboes or trumpets, two violins, and bass. EDITOR.

CORELLI, ARCANGELO, 1653–1713, famous Italian composer.

		First published
12 sonatas a tre, 2 v, vc, bass	op. 1	1683.
12 sonatas da camera a tre, 2 v, vc, cb (or cembalo)	,, 2	1685.
12 sonatas a tre, 2 v, archlute, bass	,, 3	1689.
12 sonatas da camera a tre (and sonatas, v, bass), 2 v, cb (or cembalo)	,, 4	1694.

There are many spurious works in existence also. Although Corelli was founder of the classical school of violin playing and violin writing, he belongs to the pre-Haydn figured bass period, and his work is dealt with in other articles on early chamber music. His sonatas have found innumerable publishers in their original form and in various arrangements, and it may be sufficient to mention here that an edition of his complete works was published in one volume of the *D.D.T.* and afterwards by Augener in two volumes (Edition Joachim and Chrysander), op. 1–4 containing *sonatas a tre*.

The sonatas and trios of Corelli were much played at the concerts of the old PHILHARMONIC SOCIETY (*q.v.*). A further note on this composer's work will be found in the articles, PIANOFORTE AND STRINGS and CHAMBER MUSIC, BEGINNINGS OF. EDITOR.

CORTICELLI, G., Italian composer.

Quartet ('brillant'), pf, v, vla, vc			Ricordi.
Three trios (*The Three Styles*)			
1. *Genere romantico*	pf, cl, vc	op. 56	,,
2. *Genere fantastico*	pf, cl, vc	,, 60	,,
3. *Genere religioso*	pf, cl, vc	,, 63	,,
Divertimento pastorale, pf, fl, v		,, 64	,,
Terzetto, pf, ob, fag		—	,,

COSSART, LELAND A., b. 1877, composer of mixed nationality.

Suite, harp, 2 fl, 2 ob, 2 cl, 2 fag, 2 horns, F	op. 19	Heinrichshofen.
Sonata, pf, v, D	,, 27	Heinrichshofen.
Sonata, pf, vc, C	,, 18	Kistner.

According to *Riemann*, Cossart was born in Madeira of an English father and a German mother. His violin sonata is a work of some distinction and originality.

COUPERIN, (1) FRANÇOIS ('Le Grand'), 1668–1733.

Modern republications:

Pièces de Concert (Prelude, Sicilienne, LaTromba, Plainte, Air de Diable), vc solo, str. quartet	Leduc, 1925.
Concerts royaux, pf, v, vc	Durand, 1903.
Trio sonata, *Les Nations* (no. 3 L'Impériale), pf, 2 v (vc ad lib.)	Durand, 1916.
Trio sonata *Le Parnasse ou l'apothéose de Corelli*, pf, 2 v (vc ad lib.)	Durand, 1903.
Trio sonata, *L'apothéose de l'incomparable Lulli*, pf, 2 v (vc ad lib.)	Durand.
Sonatas (Trios, 2 v, bass), pf, 2 v, C mi, d mi, g mi, B flat	Senart, 1917.

A well-known family of musicians, of whom this, the younger François, is the most celebrated, chiefly as a writer for the harpsichord. Nephew of Louis. He was organist of St. Gervais, as were several of the family.

FRANÇOIS COUPERIN may be considered as the inspirer of many musicians of the modern school. His writing is of the very first order; he created new musical architecture, and made his influence felt all over Europe, his works being so much admired by J. S. Bach that the latter was known to copy out Couperin's music in order to grasp its peculiarities of structure. All the productions of this musician, as great in some respects as Bach or Mozart, are worthy of intensive study.

Of his chamber works, special mention should be made of the *Concerts Royaux* (1722), *Grande Sonate en Trio* (1724), *Concerto Instrumental* (1725), the *Nations* sonatas (1726), and *Suite de Symphonies en Trio* (1728). Among his MS. works must be cited four sonatas for two violins, bass-viol, and figured bass, and a collection of so-called *Brunettes* (duets and trios).

Couperin's music reveals quite modern harmonic tendencies, flexibility of the sonorous lines, and distinctive characteristics of accent and syncopation, with clarity and order directing their development. His lyricism he does not fear to state precisely by means of verbal indications. The embroideries—different from German and Italian embellishments, which are only augmentations of the sonorous intensity of the principal note—are, with Couperin, expressive 'melismata'. They must, therefore, never be played monotonously or even in strict time.

In the fourteen *Concerts Royaux*, all composed at the end of his life, Couperin attained to the complete expression of his genius. He knew that music must consist of sonorities made to be heard and not read, for which reason his material is beautiful, pliant, full, and iridescent. Though he wrote no large-scale compositions, François Couperin takes his place among the great creators of music.

GEORGES MIGOT.

(2) LOUIS, 1626–1661, uncle of François 'le Grand'.

Modern republication:

Two so-called *Symphonies*, pf, v, vc	Eschig (Demets), *c.* 1913.

†COURVOISIER, K., b. 1864, Swiss violinist, pupil of David.

Trio, pf, v, vc, D	op. 40	Wernthal, 1885.

Written for amateurs in the elementary stage. Has the merit, not always observed in easy works, of being equally divided among the instruments.

Courvoisier has written a violin School (Augener).

CRAMER, (1) WILHELM, 1745–1799, German violinist, pupil of Stamitz.

Modern republication:

Trio, 2 v, vc, B flat	op. 3 (no. 2)	(Riemann) D.T.B. (Bavaria) vol. 28.

For orig. publications see *Fétis*.

Wilhelm Cramer left Mannheim for London in 1772. Was leader of the Handel Festivals at Westminster Abbey in 1784 and 1787. *Riemann* speaks of his music as 'respectable'. He was the father of J. B. Cramer and of the less famous Franz Cramer, violinist, who played in the orchestra of the old Philharmonic Society on sixty-eight different occasions.

(2) JOHANN BAPTIST, 1771–1858, famous pianist, son of the above.

Once much played, his works are now out of date, except the pianoforte School. A list of his numerous trios, violin and flute sonatas, &c., is to be found in *Fétis* and *Riemann*. Some works also in Altmann's *Catalogue*.

J. B. Cramer, a pianist of whom Beethoven had a high opinion, was resident in London for the greater part of his life. He was a leading spirit at the concerts of the old Philharmonic Society, where, in the chamber works performed, one reads of him as being 'at the piano'. Amongst these works were the following of his own composition: Concertante for pf, wood-wind, and horns, and two quintets for pf and strings.

EDITOR.

CRANE, HELEN C., German composer.

Trio, v, vla, vc, g mi	op. 21	Vetter (Leipzig), 1908.
Trio, pf, v, vc, E	„ 20	„ „ 1907.

†CRAS, JEAN, b. 1879, French composer.

	Composed	
Quartet, str	1909	Rouart, 1921.
Trio, v, vla, vc		Senart, 1927.
Quintet, pf, 2 v, vla, vc, C	1922	„ 1924.
Trio, pf, v, vc, c mi	1907	Durand, 1916.
Suite, pf, v		Senart, 1927.
Sonata, pf, vc, E	1901	Durand, 1920.

Jean Cras, who is a naval officer, grew up in a thoroughly musical family. His naval career seems to have had some influence on his characteristics as a composer. This does not apply to the trio, of which the distinguishing features are clarity and elegance. An interesting point occurs in the second movement of this work, where the key-signature of the violin part is B flat and A flat only, with a note 'Attention: le mi n'est pas bémolisé!' an uncommon signature, and an even more uncommon direction. The two lower parts have the signature of C major, but an F sharp occurs not infrequently for the viola.

His very individual quartet is much influenced by Beethoven; it is full of variety, as well as deep poetic feeling, and is overflowing with life.

THE QUINTET has a robust and straightforward first movement. The second, lent, is a Lied[1] (calme et paisible); here a theme full of engaging sentiment is opposed to a very picturesque second subject which has a most curious nasal effect. The scherzo (assez animé, alerte et décidé) is very lively, with an incisive rhythm. The finale (modéré, ardent et fier) has an imperious and fiery principal subject, which detaches itself from a stormy background and has in it something of the surge of the angry sea; this is developed in opposition to, or in combination with, various very characteristic

[1] See Foreword, art. BEETHOVEN.

themes in a series of highly original and varied episodes.

Cras was a private pupil of a musician of genius, Henri Duparc, who called him 'le fils de son âme'. His life in 'the open, with its boundless horizons', has led to breadth and simplicity in his works, which have a wealth of rhythm and the breath of inspiration.

ADOLPHE PIRIOU.

CRÉMONT, PIERRE, 1784–1846, French violinist and clarinettist.

Modern republications:

Three trios, 2 v, vla (also arrgd. vc) F, D, G	op. 13	B. & H.; Litolff, 1892; Merseburger, 1891.

He also wrote an easy quartet suitable for amateurs (B. & H., 1819).

†CRICKBOOM, MATHIEU, b. 1871, Belgian violinist.

Sonata, pf, v, d mi	op. 11	Schott (Brussels), 1911.

Crickboom specializes in the playing of chamber music. He and Casals founded a string quartet at Barcelona.

†CRISTIANI, GIUSEPPE, b. 1865, Italian pianist, pupil of Sgambati.

Sonata, pf, v, g mi	Jurgenson, 1907.

Founder of the Roman Quintet.

CROFF, GIOVANNI BATTISTA, b. beginning of nineteenth century; d. 1868, Italian composer.

Quartet, str, G	Ricordi, 1863.

He gained first prize in a competition organized by Dr. Basevi at Florence.

†CROME, FRITZ, b. 1879, Danish composer.

Sonata, pf, v, g mi	op. 3	Hansen, 1905.

CROWNDALE ROAD, WORKING MEN'S COLLEGE, LONDON, N.W.

A Sunday evening concert society, on the lines of the SOUTH PLACE SOCIETY (*q.v.*), was founded in 1920 for the purpose of giving to the people, during the winter season of each year, free concerts of chamber music of the highest class, performed by artists of eminence resident in London. The 185th concert, being the last of the eighth season, was given on April 1, 1928, and there is every prospect of their successful continuance.

EDITOR.

CRUSELL, BERNARD HENRIK, 1775–1838, Swedish clarinet virtuoso.

Divertimento, ob, str. quartet	op. 9	Peters.
Quartets, cl, v, vla, vc	opp. 2, 4, 7, 8	Peters.

A trio by this composer for cl, horn, and bassoon (MS.) appears in the programme of a Philharmonic concert (1826).

CUCLIN, DIMITRI. *v.* ROUMANIAN COMPOSERS.

CUES. *v.* PUBLISHING OF CHAMBER MUSIC.

CUI, CÉSAR ANTONOVITCH, 1835–1918, Russian composer.

Quartet, str, c mi	op. 45	Simrock, 1893.
Quartet, str, D	,, 68	Jurgenson, 1907.
Quartet, str, E flat	,, 91	Jurgenson.
Five little duets, fl, v (with pf)	,, 56	Belaiev, 1897.
Petite Suite, pf, v	,, 14	Rahter.
Sonata, pf, v, D	,, 84	Jurgenson, 1911
Twelve miniatures, pf, v	,, 20	Russ. Mus. Agency.

To the profession of a composer and musical critic, Cui allied that of a military engineer. He was one of the principal promoters of the so-called 'New Russian School' and a member of the 'potent little crowd'—the group of five Russian composers whose banner bore the device 'Russian National Art'. Cui expressed himself in every style of musical creation, including opera, and is considered one of the most eminent Russian song-writers. His chamber works are not distinguished by any special merit.

V. M. BELAIEV.

[Cui's somewhat colourless violin sonata was introduced by M. Gregoriwitsch, leader of the Petersburg String Quartet, to a London audience. His quartets are more ambitious works, in which there is a blend of Russian and cosmopolitan influence; but they are lacking in inspiration. EDITOR.]

CULWICK, JAMES C., 1845–1907, English organist.

Quartet, pf, v, vla, vc	E flat	op. 7	B. & H., 1884.

Other works in MS.

CUNDELL, EDRIC, b. 1893, English composer and conductor.

Quartet, str, g mi	op. 18	Curwen.
Rhapsody, pf, vla (or vc)		Paxton.

The opening allegro of this quartet, an interesting work of moderate difficulty, is based on a rhythmic first subject and episodes of a less important character. In the development section, fresh material, as an outcome of them, is introduced. A tranquil coda closes the movement. The second movement is a combination of adagio and scherzo. The adagio opens with a plaintive theme for the viola, the subsequent harmonies being characterized by considerable warmth of feeling until a vivace section is reached. Here the writing is rugged and vigorous. A return of the adagio section follows.

The finale consists of a theme with variations and an extensive coda, a noteworthy feature of this movement being the flowing nature of a seven-beat rhythm. The variations are free in style, and possess much contrast. There is reference in some of them to the earlier movements of the quartet.

EDITOR.

†CUTTER, BENJAMIN, American composer.

Trio, pf, v, vc, a mi op. 24 A. P. Schmidt, 1894.

CZECHOSLOVAKIAN CHAMBER MUSIC.

THE OLD BOHEMIAN MASTERS. Since the middle of the eighteenth century the cultivation of chamber music in Bohemia has kept pace with that in other countries, although for nearly a hundred years it moved along the beaten tracks of classical tradition without a star of the first magnitude rising to throw new light upon its progress. But although in the eighteenth century Bohemia could not point to a Haydn, she possessed several secondary composers who were greatly appreciated by their own generation. Such were Mysliviček (1737–1781), most brilliant of the Bohemian emigrants, the favourite of the Neapolitans, who, baulked by his Slavonic name, re-christened him 'Il Boëmo divino'; Gasman, or Gaszmann (1729–1774), the teacher of Salieri; and Jan Zach (1699–1773), pupil of the monk Černohorsky ('il Padre Boëmo'), who settled for a time at Assisi and taught Tartini and Gluck.

Mozart knew Mysliviček and liked his sonatas for piano, which he recommended to his sister Anna as 'easy and effective'. Among his works he left a trio for two violins and 'cello, and twelve quartets. Florian Leopold Gasman, court composer to the Emperor Joseph II, was very popular in Vienna. He wrote six quartets for flute, violin, viola, and bass, and sonatas for string quartet. Jan Zach is particularly interesting, because his chamber music actually reflects something of Czech nationalism.

In 1910, Nestor Lejeune, violinist and professor at the Schola Cantorum, Paris, gave a concert in the Salle Pleyel devoted to the music of forgotten Bohemian composers. The result was illuminating. Lejeune selected two MS. sonatas for string quartet by Gasman, which he had discovered in the library of the Paris Conservatoire. At the same time he unearthed a quintet by Mysliviček, and a sonata for harp by Jan Krumpholz (1745–1790), a famous virtuoso on this instrument. But his most attractive finds were copies of some of Jan Zach's quartets, procured from the Grand Ducal library at Darmstadt. The critic of *Le Monde Musical* spoke of these embryonic quartets as 'precursors of Haydn's chamber music, agreeable to hear and by no means despicable in their admirable simplicity'. Zach, by his masses in the Bohemian style, had acquired a reputation for mysticism coupled with an eccentric disposition (he died in an asylum near Baden). In his chamber music, however, the distinguished Czech critic, Dr. Veselý, finds nothing fantastic or mystical. The quartets, he says, are conceived in 'a lively and robust style, expressive of smiles and sunshine, freshness and joy. The writing for strings is brilliant and sonorous. The slow movements are distinguished by a sincere and fervent lyricism, with the added virtue of terseness. The minuets and quick movements charm by their playfulness.' They display, in fact, many of the temperamental qualities and turns of style rediscovered a century later in the chamber music of Smetana and Dvořák.

Gasman's works are more advanced in form than those of Zach, and, emotionally, there is greater depth and seriousness. Veselý considers that the 'sonata a 4' revived in Paris is probably intended to be played by more than four executants, as it contains indications of solo and tutti. It is in three movements: an adagio, distinguished for sudden dynamic changes from *f* to *p*, is followed by an allegro with a fugal introduction, while the third movement —in three sections with a coda—is remarkably incisive and pungent as regards rhythm. 'If Zach's work', says Veselý, 'might bear the signature of Haydn, Gasman's might be signed by Mozart.' A concert of Mozart's (Czech) predecessors and contemporaries was given at the Prague Conservatorium in the autumn of 1926. Works by Dussek, Brixi, Pichl, and Vranický were borrowed from the archives of the Lobkowitz library at Roudnice, which is rich in forgotten eighteenth-century music. The examples by Dussek and Brixi, which include works for wind instruments, proved forerunners of Mozart's sextet in imitation of village musicians, and Beethoven's sextet in E flat. But the best discovery appears to have been a fine 'cello concerto by Vranický.

Not long since, the writer saw a number of works by Vanhal advertised in a catalogue with a reference to him as a Dutch composer. Jan Vanhal, whose music was known in England earlier than Haydn's, was born in Bohemia in 1739, and at the age of twenty-one was taken to Vienna by a wealthy patroness, a member of the Schafgotz family. Here he studied under Dittersdorf, from whom he seems to have acquired the quality of assiduous industry, for Dlabač, in his biographical dictionary of Czech musicians, tells us he left a hundred symphonies and a hundred string quartets, not to mention operas, masses and other church music. Burney sought him out in Vienna in 1772, having heard some of this century of symphonies, which pleased him so much that he confesses himself prepared 'to rank them among the most complete and perfect compositions, for many instruments, which the art of music can boast'. But Burney's praise of another Bohemian, Jan Wenceslaus Stamitz (b. 1717), warns us that his judgements are apt to be over enthusiastic.

Jan Vitásek (Wittassek) (1770–1842) was one of the best pianists of the school of Dussek. It was at Dussek's house, in the suburbs of

Prague, that he first met Mozart, to whose service he gratefully devoted his great talents as a pianist. Vitásek's music, which was deeply coloured by his admiration for Mozart, was forgotten when the enthusiasm for that master waned with the rise of Beethoven, but his six string quartets—if indeed they still exist—might resuscitate the faded fragrance of an interesting period in the musical history of Bohemia.

Paul Vranický or Wranitzky (1756–1808) was one of the leading spirits of the Bohemian circle in Vienna, consisting of his brother Anton, Gasman, Koželuh, Josef Štěpan, and Vanhal.[1] Vanický's chief period of composition was between 1790 and 1800, and though best known by his operas, he wrote many trios, quartets, quintets, and sextets. The chamber works were much in vogue at court, for Francis I played them with his household Quartet, consisting of Count Wrbna, General Kučer, and Capellmeister Eyblen.

In Bohemia the work of collecting and reissuing the compositions of the old classical masters has proceeded slowly. Only since the establishment of Czech independence in 1918 has there been a definite movement in this direction. The works are not always to be found in their own country; they are scattered as widely as the activities of the Bohemian emigrants themselves in the eighteenth and early nineteenth centuries. Perhaps no ruby of great price will ever be unearthed, but works of charm and musicianship—such as can be compared with fine Bohemian garnets—well adapted to intimate performance, may undoubtedly be discovered at any time.

MODERN CHAMBER MUSIC. With the awakening of the national spirit, about the middle of the nineteenth century, a new life-giving breath stirred the stagnating depths of Czech music, but the firstfruits of this revival were seen in the collecting and harmonizing of the folk-songs, and in the composition of choruses suitable for the use of the male voice choral societies springing up in every direction. The tide of national feeling touched the fringe of chamber music in Smetana's trio for piano, violin, and 'cello, op. 15, and his two string quartets ('From out my life'). As in his operas and symphonic poems he threw into relief special phases of Czech scenery and history, so in these works he illuminates for us the soul of a typical Czech individual—himself.

Dvořák approached chamber music from a different standpoint. He began life filled with memories of folk rhythm and melody. Whatever he afterwards poured into the chalice of his musical temperament—and we know that he was always susceptible to outside influences—the aroma of that first ingredient clung to almost all his creations. He gave style and artistic value to many simple Slavonic dance forms, and used them perhaps more effectively in his chamber music than anywhere else. But the works of Smetana and Dvořák are treated in full detail in this book.

Dvořák's contemporary, Karel Bendl (1838–1897), who earned his reputation chiefly as an operatic composer, left one admirable string quartet (op. 119, in F) which is permanently in the repertory of the Bohemian Quartet, and combines, as frequently found with Dvořák, an interesting blend of classical and romantic feeling.

Zdeněk (or Zdenko) Fibich (1850–1900), the third of the classical triumvirate of the nineteenth century, wrote most of his chamber music before he was thirty. The fresh, romantic charm of his youthful string quartet in E minor popularized it all over Europe. A later work is the quintet in D major, for piano, violin, 'cello, clarinet, and horn, op. 42. Brahms, who made the horn and clarinet speak with such tenderness and eloquence in his chamber music, never attempted to combine them in the same work. Fibich's quintet is an interesting experiment in tone colour; the quality of the music cannot be compared with that of the Brahms clarinet quintet, but there are beautiful moments, and the work might be heard more often with advantage.

With the example of such leaders before them, it was a foregone conclusion that the next generation of Czech musicians should show an aptitude for this branch of art. Josef SUK (*q.v.*), the most devout of Dvořák's disciples, took to chamber music as a duck to water, and wrote his first string quartet at fourteen. The first opus of Vítězslav NOVÁK (*q.v.*), also a pupil of Dvořák at the Prague Conservatorium, was a piano trio in G minor. Both these composers have remained faithful to chamber music, and Suk has spent thirty-five years of his life as a member of the Bohemian (Czech) Quartet.

Josef B. FOERSTER (*q.v.*) (b. 1859) is regarded as a master of chamber music. If it is necessary to trace his musical descent, his ancestry is to be found rather in Fibich than in Smetana or Dvořák. He has many devoted disciples among younger musicians.

Leoš JANÁČEK (*q.v.*) produced his chamber music late in life, but it has wonderful vigour, freshness, and originality. His sextet for wind instruments reflects the joy and spirit of springtide, and is well named *Youth*.

The serial concerts of the Czech Chamber Music Society in Prague (about sixteen concerts during the season) engage the various quartets alluded to in my article on CZECHOSLOVAKIAN PERFORMING ORGANIZATIONS, and thus open the way for the production of new works, and the Society for Modern Music also encourages chamber music.

[1] It is interesting to note that there has almost always been a succession of Czech-born musicians active in the Austrian capital—J. B. Foerster, Gustav Mahler, Josef Mraczek, and others.

A glance at the *Musical Almanac for the Czechoslovak Republic*, edited by Dr. Jan Branberger, reveals the fact that nearly all the younger Bohemian musicians have made essays in chamber music. Many of these contemporary composers have written only one or two works, but most of them are well worth a place in the repertory of modern chamber music. The following is a list which is by no means complete, but contains the names of many of the rising composers of the present day:

Emil Axman, Emil Chvála, Oswald Chlubna, Robert Haas, Otakar Jeremiaš, K. B. Jirák, Václav Kálik, Rudolf Karel, Egon Kornauth, Josef Kouba, Miroslav Krejči, Arnošt Křenek, Jaroslav Křička, Jan Kunc, Jaroslav Kvapil, B. Martinu, Jaroslav Novotný, František Ondřiček, Otokar Ostričil, Vilem Petrželka, Nicolas Schneider-Trnavský, Václav Štěpán, Jaroslav Tomašek, Ladislav Vycpálek, Jan Zelinka.

The works of some of these composers are not yet printed, because for various reasons the publication of new works is necessarily slow in Czechoslovakia, which has not, as yet, produced a Mitrofan Belaiev, or a Carnegie.

ROSA NEWMARCH.

CZECHOSLOVAKIAN PERFORMING ORGANIZATIONS.

The following are the chief chamber music organizations in Czechoslovakia:

CZECH STRING QUARTET, well known in this country before 1913 as the BOHEMIAN QUARTET. In 1892, four pupils of Professor Hanuš Wihan at the Prague Conservatorium formed a permanent association for the practice of chamber music: Karel Hoffmann, Josef Suk, Oskar Nedbal, Otto Berger. On Wihan's recommendation, the Quartet was engaged by the Chamber Music Society of Prague within a few months of its foundation. The name of the Bohemian (Czech) String Quartet was not adopted until after its first independent concert in Prague, October 22, 1892. Although associating themselves with the national movement, they did not restrict their repertory, which gradually included all that is best in classical and modern chamber music, although, with characteristic modesty, they did not come before the public with the entire cycle of Beethoven's quartets until 1911.

Some changes of personnel have taken place in the Quartet during the thirty-five years of its activity. In 1893, the 'cellist, Otto Berger, resigned on account of ill-health. Professor Wihan took his place, and remained until 1918, when he was succeeded by Ladislav Zeleuka. Nedbal left in 1906, his place being occupied by Jiři Herold.

From 1895 the Quartet began to make extensive tours: Russia (1895–6); Finland, the Baltic Provinces, and S. Russia (1899–1900); Italy (1895), at the invitation of the Società del Quartetto of Milan and the Società Benedetto Marcello, Venice; Holland and England (1898); the Balkans and Constantinople (1901 and 1902); in the latter year the association celebrated its tenth birthday and thousandth public appearance. During the second decade of its existence the history of the Quartet repeats itself, until its activities abroad were checked in 1914 by the European War. In May and June 1919 it took part in the Czechoslovak musical festival in London.

In the season 1922–3 the Quartet commemorated the thirtieth year of its existence by a series of fifteen concerts devoted to classical and modern music, both national and international. The Beethoven festival of 1927 was celebrated by a special series of concerts including all the master's string quartets.

All who have heard the Czech Quartet know the peculiar qualities of its interpretations: a fervency which precludes the least shadow of negligence in the performance of the most oft-repeated works; unflagging rhythmic vigour; an ensemble acquired by an unusually long period of association and temperamental reciprocity. The depth and authority of its readings are owing in great measure to the inspiration of the second violin, Josef Suk.

THE NOVÁK-FRANK QUARTET made its first public début at a concert of the Society for Modern Music, Prague, in 1925. It consists of the following members: Stanislav Novák, Josef Stika, Bohamil Klabík, a pupil of Herold (*v.* CZECH QUARTET), Maurits Frank, formerly a member of the Rebner Quartet, who co-operated in 1921 with Paul Hindemith in founding the Amar Quartet, and afterwards occupied the position of first 'cellist at the Vienna Opera. The Novák-Frank combination is, therefore, partly the outgrowth of the famous Czech (Bohemian) Quartet.

THE ONDŘIČEK QUARTET started its career in 1921 as the ARTISTS' STRING QUARTET, but its close association with the famous virtuoso, František Ondřiček, during the time in which it was working at his quartet in A flat major, led to its adopting his name shortly before the master's death at Milan, April 12, 1922. The Quartet gave its first independent concert in Prague in 1922, and followed it up by a tour through Czechoslovakia. This organization is often heard in Prague at the concerts of the Society for Modern Music and the Czech Chamber Music Society. It has an extensive repertory, classical and modern. Its members are: Jaroslav Pekelský, Kamil Vyskočil, Vincenc Zahradník, Bedřich Jaroš.

THE ŠEVČÍK-LHOTSKY QUARTET, founded at Warsaw in 1903, was first known as the Ševčík Quartet, and only added the name of the leader, Bohuslav Lhotsky, at a later date. The second violin, Karel Procházka, and the viola, Karel Moravec, are, like the founders of the organization, pupils of the great teacher Ševčík. The original 'cellist, Bohuslav Vaška, was succeeded in 1911 by Ladislav Zeleuka (*see* CZECH QUARTET), who in turn gave place to Antonio Fingerland. The Quartet toured Russia in 1904, and, since the war, has visited England, Italy, and most of the chief Continental musical centres.

THE ZIKA QUARTET was established in 1920 at Laibach, where the members were engaged as teachers in the music school, and in the orchestra of the State Opera. The organization is also known as the CZECHOSLOVAK QUARTET. The personnel is: Richard Zika, Herbert Berger, Ladislav Czerny, Ladislav Zika, brother of the first violin.

The Quartet made its first appearance in Jugoslavia, and was invited shortly afterwards by Prince Alexander of Thurn and Taxis to visit Vienna, where it played at a concert of the Gesellschaft der Musikfreunde. It took part in the International musical festivals at Salzburg (1924) and Venice (1925).

ROSA NEWMARCH.

CZERNY, CARL, 1791–1857, piano teacher, pupil of Beethoven.

The compositions of Czerny are without interest to modern players of chamber music. He was among the most productive composers of his time, his published works amounting to nearly a thousand. As author of the *Complete theoretical and practical pianoforte school*, he has won enduring reputation.

D

†DAFFNER, HUGO, b. 1882, German composer, pupil of Reger.

Trio, pf, v, vc, F	op. 10	Junne, 1910.

Daffner has composed numerous other chamber works (quartets, &c.) still in MS.

DAHMEN.

A family of Dutch musicians which for three generations in the eighteenth and nineteenth centuries had a great influence on music in Holland.

PIETER, 1757–1835, was a composer of several trios and quartets which were played first in London and later on the Continent.

† JOHAN ARNOLD, 1760–1840. A fine 'cellist, playing chiefly in London, and the composer of three string quartets, three string trios, and several duets for two 'cellos.

† HUBERT, 1813–1837, the second and best known son of Arnold, like most of his family, was an excellent flautist, and wrote a number of works for wind instruments and strings.

† In the third generation WILLEM HENDRIK, † 1797–1847, and HERMAN JOHAN, 1807–1875, were violinists esteemed both as soloists and quartet players.

HERBERT ANTCLIFFE.

DALAYRAC (or D'ALAYRAC), NICOLAS, 1753–1809, violinist.

Modern republications:

Quartet (no. 5), str, E flat		(L. de la Laurencie), Senart, 1921.
Quartet, str, D	op. 7, no. 3	,, ,,

The vicissitudes in the career of this composer are set out in *Grove*, and add to the interest awakened by a musician whose gifts brought him considerable fame. *Vidal* gives a list of eighteen string quartets and six string trios.

EDITOR.

†DALBERG, JOHANN FRIEDRICH HUGO, FREIHERR VON, 1752–1812, German pianist, composer, and author.

Dalberg appears to have been a musician of remarkable attainment considering that he was technically an amateur. *Fétis* gives particulars of his instrumental works.

†DALBERG, NANCY, b. 1881, Danish composer.

Quartet, str, g mi	op. 14	Tischer & Jagenberg, 1926.

Dr. Altmann (*Handbuch*) writes on the above quartet: 'Nancy Dalberg published this work without giving her front name, and, had I not learned by accident that it was composed by a woman, considering also the austerity and native strength of her music, it would never have occurred to me that the author was of the feminine sex. Her mastery of the technique of composition is remarkable, and she has something definite to say.'

D'ALBERT. *v.* ALBERT.

†DALCROZE, ÉMILE JAQUES-, b. (Vienna) 1865.

Paysage sentimental, sopr. voice, str. quartet, A	op. 31	Jobin (Lausanne).
Quartet, str, E	no number	Enoch (Paris), 1904.
Serenade (six movts.) str. quartet, C	op. 61	Jobin, 1905.
Seven dances, str. quartet	no number	Jos. Williams, 1926.
Échos du Dancing (Six impromptus) pf, v, vc	no number	Senart, 1924.
Little suite, pf, v	op. 6	Weiller.
Suite, pf, vc, D	,, 9	Siegel, 1891.

and some smaller works.

In all Dalcroze's work a marked feature is his fondness for irregular or unusual rhythms. He seldom employs a complex rhythmic texture, with several simultaneous conflicting rhythmic patterns, but inclines to bars and beats of irregular length. Like many of his contemporaries, he often prefers to take a unit of measurement smaller than the classical bar, so that while the beat is constant throughout, the accentual grouping varies elastically. Developing from this, he frequently takes a still smaller value as constant, such as the quaver or semiquaver, and forms unequal beats by increasing or lessening the number of these forming the beat. This tendency is carried almost to excess in certain of the *Novelettes and Caprices* (1920), arranged for piano trio from piano solo, but is seen to be productive of vivid and effective rhythm in many of the *Dances*.

His harmony in the later works occasionally betrays the influence of the whole-tone scale, but the bulk of his music is more or less diatonic. He writes effectively if simply for strings, and, though not precisely easy, none of his chamber works presents great difficulties of execution.

The E major quartet and the serenade are both in his earlier style. The quartet opens with a lyrical moderato assai, followed by an intermezzo (tempo di marcia) in A. A larghetto in F sharp minor corresponds with the usual slow movement, and is followed by a lively intermezzo in 6/8 time (G major), the first subject of which is written over a tonic and dominant pedal. The final allegro scherzando, in C major, makes no allusion to the key or subject-matter of the first. It is in 4/8, 3/8, and, unlike the rest of the work, full of irregular rhythm.

In *Paysage Sentimental* the strings do not merely accompany the voice, but are of equal importance. The work, though largely rhapsodic, opens with a theme of folk-song character, which is later developed instrumentally, and finally taken up by the voice towards the conclusion.

The three suites of *Dance-Rhythms* (1922), another arrangement of a piano work, and the *Seven Dances* are full of effective rhythmic devices, and contain many charming little numbers, such as No. VIII in Suite 2, in which the occasional suppression of a quaver is used very happily.

The *Échos du Dancing* are longer and more intense emotionally than these, but, like them, are full of rhythmic vitality.

CYNTHIA COX.

[It is presumably known to readers that Jaques-Dalcroze is the distinguished founder of the 'Eurhythmic' system. Its relation to chamber music chiefly regards the conflicting rhythms which are among the commonplaces of the modern composer, and which, in some of his lectures, Dalcroze illustrates with the co-operation of dancers, time patterns being executed by feet and hands working independently. For children and students generally such manœuvres are a valuable exercise in time-keeping, and in developing the sense of rhythm.

Dalcroze is generally regarded as a Swiss composer. EDITOR.]

†DALE, BENJAMIN JAMES, b. 1885, English composer.

Sonata, pf, v	E	op. 11	Augener.
Phantasy, pf, vla	D	,, 4	Schott, 1912.
Suite, ,, ,,	d mi	,, 2	Novello.

MS. Introduction and andante, 6 vlas.

Dale studied at the R.A.M., where he was a pupil of Frederick Corder for composition. His earliest works date from 1900, and the first of them to attract attention was the piano sonata in D minor, completed in 1902, and still regarded as one of the outstanding works of the English neo-romantics.

His first venture in chamber music was prompted by Lionel Tertis, and took the form of a suite in three movements for viola and piano, which that great artist produced at the Æolian Hall in 1906. Subsequently, its second and third movements were orchestrated, and were played by him in their new dress at a Philharmonic Concert in 1911. Though begun soon after the completion of the sonata, the suite shows greater originality of invention, and, in the first and third movements, a more developed sense of humour. Despite lavishness of material and a certain freedom from formal restrictions, the first movement retains a thematic coherence which gives an effect of conciseness. This is accomplished in part by thematic transformations such as that by which the principal subject

Ex. 1.
Piano (dble. 8ves.).
Maestoso.

becomes

Ex. 2. *Tranquillo.*
Viola. *p espress.*

and later

But the gem of this attractive work is its middle section, the Romance, which is often performed by viola players as a separate piece. It is constructed on strictly classical lines round a central, extended melody composed of two sentences and a ritornello. It opens thus:

Ex. 3.

Viola. *p espress. molto.*

At the first statement the ritornello is accompanied by a portion of the second sentence, but, at the close of the movement, the two sentences, which were previously joined 'end on', are heard in association, thus:

Ex. 4.

Piano (omitting harmony).

The title of the movement is sufficient palliation, if any be needed, for its overflow of sentiment. It breathes the very spirit of romantic poetry, and is one of the most polished examples of pure lyric form in chamber music since the classics. In the finale the composer gives free play to his more lavish and exuberant mood, and the movement is no less remarkable for its buoyant humour than for its brilliance.

Technically, the viola part was edited by Tertis, and is an early example of the marked influence he has had upon the exploitation of the executive resources of his instrument. Without such authority, Dale might have hesitated to take the viola up to such a height as

Ex. 5.

which occurs in the finale.

His next chamber work was again for the viola, being a phantasy for viola and piano commissioned by W. W. Cobbett, one of twelve for various combinations of instruments. Owing perhaps to the condensation incidental to this form (which Dale adopted more in the spirit than in the letter, for it is one of the longest of the Cobbett phantasies), the music has an aspect of greater maturity, but it is otherwise conceived in the same vein of romantic feeling. Its principal subject is a simple tune somewhat resembling folk-song, and the central andante espressivo from which we quote (Ex. 6) is a remarkable example of the composer's ability to sustain the interest in an extended melodic line. Dr. Ernest Walker describes the form as follows:

'It consists, in its main outline, of a lento introduction, repeated in varied form as a coda; two allegro movements (the first, perhaps, rather too short for balance); and an andante between them. Themes are, to some extent, transferred from one section to another, but no stress is laid on such methods, the homogeneity of the work being emotional rather than formal. The slow movements (especially the two lentos) contain a great deal of finely grave and sombre beauty, and the close of the whole is singularly spacious and dignified. . . . The main subject of the first allegro . . . is harmonically distinctly unusual, especially in its cadence, but everything comes off. On the other hand, there is something about the long and elaborate second allegro which is, somehow or other, less satisfying; the glittering cleverness of certain portions of it seems a little hard and unsympathetic, and the transition from it to the final lento is, I have always felt, the weak point of the phantasy. . . . But these pages do not really detract from the value of a very individual work, full of warm, finely felt colour and melody, which is also amazingly effective for both instruments.'

Ex. 6.

Dale's next contribution to chamber music remains in manuscript, but is of such interest as to warrant an exception to the rule which confines this Cyclopedia to published works. Again Lionel Tertis furnished the incentive. Appointed professor of the viola at the R.A.M., he had in a very short time trained five first-class players. To celebrate this achievement he invited Dale to write a special piece for performance at a lecture-recital which he gave on 19 June, 1911. Thus originated the introduction and andante for six violas, which, despite its unusual setting, has had quite a number of public performances. Describing it as a work of 'remarkable beauty, power, and originality', Corder writes:

> 'The six instruments have all highly independent parts, they imitate the sounds of other instruments, they do things that one would have thought impossible for any viola-player, and the effect of the whole is of an almost Beethovenish majesty and grandeur and a melodic sweep such as none other of the present generation of string-writers seems able to approach.'

In short, it is a striking display of musicianship of the highest order.

The next three years were occupied with professional activities which impeded composition. In 1914 the outbreak of war overtook Dale in Germany. He was interned at Ruhleben until March 1918, when he was exchanged and removed to a camp in Holland, whence he returned shortly before the armistice. These four years taken from a young composer's life are an irreparable loss to music. He brought back with him two short pieces, but they are of small importance, and it was plain that his internment had had a deep effect upon his constitution and his artistic outlook. It was not easy to resume creative work. A quartet in three movements for piano and strings was planned in 1919, but the sketches were never completed. That autumn he went to Australia and New Zealand on an examining mission, which involved a tour round the world. Returning much refreshed in the spring of 1920, he resumed the round of professional tasks, and the following year found him engaged upon a violin sonata in E, which was completed in 1922, and performed for the first time by Rowsby Woof and York Bowen at the Wigmore Hall on 27 October of that year.

In this composition he reverts to the form of his opus 1, the piano sonata: an opening movement in sonata form, followed by a theme with variations, the earlier of these being combined into a movement corresponding to a slow movement and scherzo, while the last is extended to the dimensions of a finale. The theme is in A minor. Towards the end occurs the following,

Ex. 7.

which acquires much importance later. The order of the variations is as follows:

1. Pastorale (allegretto con moto);
2. Rêverie (molto adagio);
3. Intermezzo (allegretto amabile);
4. Dance (allegro energico);
5. Caprice (allegretto, con alcuna licenza).

The intermezzo contains a reminiscence (probably unconscious) of the Romance for viola.

Ex. 8.

The third movement (molto allegro) is preceded by an extended introduction developed from Ex. 7. It constitutes at the same time the final variation and the finale to the whole work. At its conclusion it returns to the opening theme of the first movement (lento espressivo) with modified harmonies.

In the polished beauty of the craftsmanship the work fulfils the promise of earlier days, but its romantic atmosphere is given a despondent tinge by the fact that the main tempo of the first movement is lento (though there is a vivace episode), and it is followed by an andante theme, the second variation on which is a Rêverie marked molto adagio. This prevalence of slow tempi creates an impression too pronounced to be easily dispelled by the subsequent allegro vigoroso, and leaves the listener with mixed feelings, charmed by the writing, much of which is exquisite, but disappointed of the flavour which the piano sonata and viola suite led him to expect. Nevertheless, it is encouraging, for Dale's musical organism was ever sensitive, and the fact that it should have so far recovered from such experiences as he had to face warrants the belief that the next work will prove a more complete recovery.

EDWIN EVANS.

[Dale's violin sonata needs, and amply repays, a long and intensive study of both parts, for it does not yield its secrets to casual performers. A few more cues in the violin part would be helpful. EDITOR.]

DALL' ABACO. *v.* ABACO.

†DALLIER, HENRI, b. 1849, French composer pupil of Franck.

Trio, no. 1, pf, v, vc, c mi	Fromont, 1898.
Duo, pf, cb, G	Evette & Schaeffer, 1915.
Allegro de Sonate, pf, fag, b flat mi	,, ,, 1903.

Dallier's trio was awarded a prize by the Paris *Institut*.

†DAMROSCH, WALTER JOHANNES, b. (Breslau) 1862, a celebrated conductor in New York.

Sonata, pf, v op. 6 J. Church Co. 1899.

DANCE. *v.* CHOREGRAPHY.

†DANCLA, J. B. CHARLES, 1818–1907, violinist, pupil of Baillot.

He wrote some 150 chamber works, but although he won the Prix Chartier (1861)[1] and the prize of the Société Ste. Cécile, Bordeaux (1857), both for chamber compositions, it cannot be said that they are of sufficient interest to modern players to make it worth while to cumber this book with particulars of the quartets, trios, and duets issued by various publishers. The days are over when purely violinistic salon music, however melodious, interests the musical world. The violin duets, however, are still of use as teaching material.

He gave quartet soirées (1820–62) in conjunction with his brothers Leopold and Armand, but they are not reported to have risen to a very high level of excellence. Some of his works are given in *Altmann*. EDITOR.

DANDO, J. H. B., 1806–1894, violinist and violist.

Dando was one of the pioneers of public quartet playing in London. In 1842 he started what proved to be a long series of chamber concerts in the Throne Room at Crosby Hall, Bishopsgate, the programme including most of the classic masterpieces, with a sprinkling of works then considered modern, by Spohr, Onslow, Mendelssohn, and others. Among his colleagues of the strings were Henry Hill, a violist of great distinction, Chas. Lucas the 'cellist, and Alfred Mellon. At the piano he was on more than one occasion assisted by 'Dr. Felix Mendelssohn', who was announced to take part in a 'new' trio on June 3, 1844.

I have good reason to remember Dando, from whom I had a few lessons, for I was taken as a youth to hear him at Crosby Hall by my father in 1861, and there heard my first string quartet. EDITOR.

†DANDRIEU [D'ANDRIEU], JEAN-FRANÇOIS, 1684–1740, French organist.

Modern republication:

Trio sonata, pf, 2 v, e mi Senart, *c.* 1917

Set published originally 1705.

He wrote a suite of pieces for strings called *Caractères de la Guerre*, an early example of programme music.

[1] This was the first year in which the prize was awarded, and it was shared with Madame FARRENC (*q.v.*).

†DANEAU, Nicolas Adolphe Gustave, b. 1866, Belgian composer.

Works include:

Quartet, 2 v, vla, vc, D		Cranz, 1921.
Suite in sonata form, pf, v, d mi	,,	1912.

DANISH PERFORMING ORGANIZATIONS. *v.* Scandinavian.

DANZI, Franz, 1763–1826, German 'cellist, Capellmeister to the court of Baden.

Modern republication:

Quintet, fl, ob, cl, fag, horn, g mi, op. 56, no. 2 (*Riemann*), D.T.B. (Bavaria), B. & H., 1914.

Numerous original publications are given in *Fétis*.

DAUPRAT, Louis François, 1781–1868, famous French horn player.

Altmann gives:

Three quintets	horn, str. quartet	op. 6	Lemoine.

Dauprat was chamber musician to Napoleon and Louis XVIII, and professor of the horn at the Paris Conservatoire. He wrote a large number of chamber works, all of which included the horn. For details of his works, *vide Fétis*.

DAUVERGNE, or d'AUVERGNE, Antoine, 1713–1797, French violinist.

Recent publications include two violin sonatas (Schott & Senart).

Original publications include a number of trio sonatas.

Dauvergne was the first Frenchman to win success in light opera, and to this success the origin of the Opéra Comique is due.

DAVICO, Vincenzo, b. 1889, Italian composer, pupil of Max Reger.

Trio, pf, v, vc, f mi	Sirène edn., 1911.

All Davico's music shows the influence of French impressionism; that is, it is vague and indeterminate in expression, the melodic ideas are fragmentary and sterile, and the harmony consists merely of bands of colour, the chords creating an impression of ambiguousness and immobility. The rhythm only makes itself felt in the fragments of melody. Davico's works are, however, invariably graceful and sincere.

A. Casella.

DAVID, Félicien César, 1810–1876, French composer.

24 quintets, *Les Quatre Saisons*	Set. I. *Soirées de Printemps*	2 v, vla, vc, cb	Schott, 1845
	II. ,, *d'Été*		1846
	III. ,, *d'Automne*	or 2 v, vla, 2 vc	,,
	IV. ,, *d'Hiver*		,,

Also publ. in Paris by Escudier frères.

David lived for some time in the East, and brought into his music an oriental touch. He is best known by his Ode-Symphonie, *The Desert*.

He was a great friend of Onslow, to whom he dedicated one of the above sets of quintets. Between them they wrote about sixty quintets in which the double-bass has a part.

Editor.

DAVID, Ferdinand, 1810–1873, famous violinist and quartet leader.

Sextet, 3 v, vla, 2 vc, G	op. 38	B. & H., 1861.
Quartet, str, a mi	,, 32	,, 1862.

David, one of Joachim's teachers, is at present better known by his editions of famous old masterpieces for the violin (*Die hohe Schule des Violinspiels*) than by his compositions, which are interesting from a violinistic point of view, but in their musical substance somewhat antiquated, though well written. Early romantic traits, principally from Spohr and Mendelssohn, are re-echoed here.

Hugo Leichtentritt.

[At the age of nineteen, David had experience of quartet leading at the house of an amateur, whose daughter he subsequently married. A very fine artist and a pupil of Spohr, one is surprised to learn that he was given to 'decorating' chamber music with trills and grace notes, a fashion of the time which has fortunately disappeared. His chief claim to fame is based on the helpful suggestions he is known to have given to Mendelssohn when composing his violin concerto. He played on a superb Guarneri violin, now in the possession of Jascha Heifetz. Editor.]

†DAVID, Karl Heinrich, b. St. Gallen, 1884, lives in Switzerland.

Trio, pf, v, vc, g mi	op. 7	Hug, 1911.

DAVIDOV, (1) Carl Juliewitch, 1838–1889, Russian 'cellist.

Sextet	str	E	op. 35	Rahter, 1880.
Quartet	,,	A	,, 38	,, 1882.
Quintet	pf, str	g mi	,, 40	,, 1884.

Davidov's chamber works contain much good writing for strings. The quintet is a conventional work of the German romantic school, with a finale conceived in humorous vein, and has enjoyed, in its time, much popularity.

Davidov made his début as executant on a viola da gamba. When studying the 'cello in youthful days at the Leipzig Conservatorium, Ferd. David said, after hearing him take part at a moment's notice in a trio by Jadassohn, that 'he had never met with a greater talent for the instrument'. Amongst his later activities was that of 'cellist in the Quartet founded at St. Petersburg by Leopold Auer, whose opinion of him was so high that after his death he no longer cared to continue playing quartets (I had this from Auer's own lips).

(2) Alexis Davidov (nephew of Carl), b.

1867, composed a sextet in E flat for strings, op. 12 (Jurgenson), and a string quartet which gained the Belaiev prize. EDITOR.

† DAVIES, FANNY, b. 1861, English pianist.

Holds a leading place in the London musical world as a performer of chamber music, and is also well known on the Continent both as soloist and ensemble player. She was a personal friend of Brahms and Joachim, as well as of her teacher, Clara Schumann. Scarcely any pianist living possesses to the same extent the traditions of the school to which those famous protagonists of the musical world belonged; thus her interpretations of chamber music repertory may be considered authoritative. She was constantly heard at the 'Pops', and took part in the first performance of several important choral works. Miss Davies is an esteemed contributor to this book. EDITOR.

† DAVIES, SIR HENRY WALFORD, b. 1869, English composer.

Quartet (*Peter Pan*), str		Curwen (on hire).
Six pastorals, pf, 4 voices, 4 strings	op. 15	Curwen, 1897.
Sonata, pf, v, e mi	,, 5	Novello, 1894.
Sonata, pf, v, d mi	,, 7	,, 1896.

Walford Davies has produced a large amount of chamber music, the greater part of which remains in MS. Some, however, is published, and reference is possible, accordingly, to a portion of it. Beginning with the early sonata in E minor for violin and piano, it will be sufficient to say that the slow movement is the best, and that the whole sonata is severely restrained in the writing for both instruments.

THE VIOLIN SONATA in D minor shows a great advance on its predecessor, and it is difficult to realize that only two years separate the two works. The first movement, allegro energico, starts with a rhythmic figure given out by the violin and instantly answered and elaborated by the piano. This theme marks the first appearance (in his chamber music) of that particular development of the composer's thought which later was to lead him to his finest work, and foreshadows the songs of 'Death' and 'Riches' in the cantata *Everyman* (1904). That same stern forcefulness which marks Walford Davies's handling of certain grave aspects of the morality play is felt in the impulsive opening bars of this sonata.

Ex. 1.

The second movement, allegro semplice, begins lightly and joyously, but becomes unaccountably laboured as it advances. The *Burden*, andantino espressivo, which follows, leads into the finale, allegro tranquillo, whose main subject is parent of the suave pastoral tunes that the composer was to produce in later years.

Ex. 2.

THE SIX PASTORALS may be regarded as the composer's first significant chamber work; the thought here runs clearly and consecutively and finds adequate expression. The words are by sixteenth and seventeenth-century poets, and a shapely formality is observed alike in the choice of the poems and in their disposition. At the beginning and end stand Fletcher's *Morning Song* and *Evening Song*, connected by thematic allusions in the music. The second is the *Shepherd's Wife's Song* (somewhat inappropriately set for vocal quartet), which describes the simple existence of a careless shepherd, who sings his songs all the evening and thereafter lies snoring in bed. In the fifth song, the *Dialogue of Dorinda and Thyrsis*, the maid speaks her fear of what shall come after this sweet earthly life, and the man replies that in Elysium they will meet again and listen to 'the music of the spheres'. The middle pair of songs make the climax, the one of sense, the other of beauty. *Sweet Content* recounts the excellence of honest labour which 'bears a lovely face', a sentiment in which may be discerned a declaration of the composer's personal faith. The other song, the *Dialogue of Clorinda and Damon*, is the most perfect in form and interpretation. A serene feeling, almost the joyous philosophy of pastoral Greece, penetrates the music. Its pace (andante tranquillo, ma non troppo) is unbroken during the first long span. The thought of Pan's presence causes the pulse to slacken for a few bars; then the time changes from triple to duple, and a più mosso leads into a più allegro which carries the song to its ecstatic ending. Throughout all the songs of this cycle, the string writing is free and effective. In the first duet-dialogue, violin and 'cello comment upon the discourse of the contralto and bass voices, supporting and elaborating their utterances. In the fuller numbers the viola especially is used with much distinction.

Eleven years lie between the last-named work and the *Songs of a Day* for 'voices and other instruments'. During that time Walford Davies was composing in other media, and the influence of these labours is to be seen in the later chamber music. Already in the *Six Pastorals* he had shown himself the possessor of well-developed technical powers. But the difference between the early and the later chamber music is not one of technique. It is to be perceived rather in the strengthening of the composer's ideals and the amplification of his mental outlook, which brought with it a corresponding assurance and breadth of style. The choral and orchestral *Everyman*, a large amount of choral music and many charming songs, had all left their traces of mysticism and, again, of childlike gaiety of spirit. He was now definitely fixed in the way from which he was only to be turned by the war of 1914. It was an ideal of simplicity, an unaffected delight in Nature and a Wordsworthian appreciation of her differing aspects. Neither deep nor intense, it yet had delicacies and inspirations none the less strong for being hidden. Always easy of approach, his chamber music was to hold messages for those who were unable or unwilling to give themselves up to more vehement expressions of faith.

THE PETER PAN miniature suite for string quartet is founded on his own idea of Barrie's child-hero, and mirrors the composer's feelings with regard to the boy's life as portrayed by Barrie; the suite, therefore, is predominantly programme-music. Each of the five movements is headed with a quotation which gives the key to what follows, and directs the attention of the hearer into definite paths. The definition is very close; the hint given is slight, but so is the movement that comes after. In so confined a space, these literary associations have the effect of binding the music down to a main idea in a manner that admits of no variation, but this was probably intended by the composer. The suite would serve perfectly for a ballet or a puppet-play.

After a short introduction comes the first movement, presto leggiero, descriptive of Peter's flight 'over the houses to the gardens'. At the return of the principal theme, there is much passage-work portraying the flight. The second movement, *The Serpentine* ('It is a lovely lake and there is a drowned forest in it'), is a slow measure, very placid and even, with a graceful melodic outline. *Peter and the Fairies* is the title of the third movement, a lively scherzo. Here the theme of the opening movement, which seems to denote Peter Pan, is ingeniously employed. (This theme appears, in part or unbroken, in each of the five movements of the suite.) The fourth movement, *Peter's glad heart* (allegro felice), is delicate, and somewhat *schwärmerisch*, true Barrie, true Walford Davies. *Peter's Lullaby to his Mother*, the fifth movement (andante tranquillo), with its frequent references to what has gone before, ends in the same pleasant mood. The suite is not technically difficult; the writing is fluent, and it presents no unwonted angularities. The expressive effects, always supported by sound, constructive skill, are fortified by the composer's knowledge of the capacity of the instruments. The simple end is reached by the smoothest possible means, and the general effect is one of grace and gaiety. It is Walford Davies's most masterly chamber work.

SCOTT GODDARD.

[Since the above was written, a performance has been given, at the Hereford Festival, of a new quintet, in two movements, for piano and strings, at present in MS.

EDITOR.]

†DAVIS, JOHN DAVID, b. 1870 English composer.

Song of Evening, str. quartet, cb ad lib.	Novello.
Var^{ns}. on an Irish Theme, str. quartet	Bosworth, 1911.
Quartet, str, g mi	Hawkes.
Idyll, *Last Summer's Eve at Cookham Lock*, str. quartet	,,

A commission from Mark Hambourg executed by five composers to write variations on the *Londonderry Air* produced the above from the pen of J. D. Davis. It is one of the most musicianly of the series.

The *Songs of Evening* is a piece of programme music, being an impression of the peace of a late summer's evening.

Summer's Eve at Cookham Lock would appear to be similarly inspired. It is in abbreviated sonata form, and, as the title indicates, contemplative in character.

EDITOR.

DAYAS, WILLIAM HUMPHREY, 1863–1903, American composer and pianist, pupil of Busoni.

Quartet, str, C	op. 9	Kistner.
Sonata, pf, v, D	,, 11	,,
,, pf, vc, F	,, 12	,,

Albert Tottmann (in his *Führer*) speaks of Dayas as a thoughtful, careful, and conscientious composer.

DEBUSSY, CLAUDE ACHILLE, 1862–1918, French composer.

Quartet, str, g mi	op. 10	Durand.
Sonata, fl (or v), vla, harp, g mi		,, 1916.
Sonata, pf, v, g mi and G		,, 1917.
Sonata, pf, vc, d mi		,, 1915.

Apart from the *Danse Sacrée et Danse Profane* (1904) for harp and stringed orchestra (which are in no sense chamber music, though sometimes played in a reduced setting) and a relatively unimportant rhapsody for clarinet and piano (1910), Debussy's chamber music consists of the string quartet (1893) and the three sonatas 'pour divers instruments' (1915–17) which are all that he completed of a set of six, upon which he was engaged at the end of his life. It is thus placed at the beginning and end of his career as a composer, for his works prior to the *Prélude à l'Après-midi d'un Faune* (1892) comprise, among much that is exquisite, little that is of corresponding development or importance. There is an interval approaching a quarter of a century between the two periods which makes of them two definite and self-contained chapters.

At the time when the quartet was written Debussy was already engaged upon *Pelléas et Mélisande,* which was to occupy him intermittently from 1892 to 1902. He was then at the height of the enthusiasms which had their rallying point in the rooms of Stéphane Mallarmé, and had so determining an influence upon the ideas from which is derived that subtle quality in his music, vaguely described as 'impressionism'. In point of fact it had always more in common with the Pre-Raphaelitism of this side of the Channel than with the literary currents flowing on the other. But there were other influences at work. Debussy, who had visited Russia as far back as 1879, without, however, coming into very close contact with Russian music, had renewed acquaintance with it ten years later, when these slight and latent memories had not only been recalled to life, but acquired greater importance. Though he was inclined to wax ironical whenever a parallel was drawn between the methods of Moussorgsky and those employed in *Pelléas*, there can be little doubt that there is a reflection of the former in much of Debussy's vocal music. In instrumental music, as with most young Frenchmen of the period, it was Borodin, among the Russians, who impressed him most, though there is also a suggestion of Rimsky-Korsakov in *L'Après-midi.* Both Debussy's quartet and Ravel's of ten years later show distinct traces of their admiration for Borodin. It was the Russians who saved Debussy from the dangers of Wagnerism. At Bayreuth in 1889 he had been moved to tears by *Parsifal*, the only one of the music-dramas which has left permanent traces in his work. Before returning there the following year, he had come under the spell of *Boris Godounov*, and was less susceptible. However, the Leitmotif had long since had its repercussion in France, for although César Franck derived his 'cyclic form' from the Beethoven sonata, he regarded Wagner's metamorphosis of themes as similarly derived from the Beethoven variation. Except for a very brief attendance at his organ class, Debussy never came into the Franck entourage, which would certainly not have been a sympathetic environment for him, but in the last few years preceding the master's death in 1890, his principles, constantly propounded by a group of devoted and brilliant pupils, were much in evidence, and the influence of his composition class was not limited to them, as may be seen in the works of many who never belonged to it, notably Paul Dukas. There is in this case another link. César Franck's violin sonata is dedicated to Ysaÿe, and Debussy's quartet to Ysaÿe, Crickboom, Van Hout, and Joseph Jacob, who formed the Ysaÿe Quartet.

THE STRING QUARTET. Debussy's quartet blends the various influences enumerated above. It owns a qualified allegiance to cyclic form in three of its four movements, and even in the andante, if one concedes a certain latitude to metamorphosis of themes. In that movement, and less markedly in the scherzo, it testifies to the fascination of Borodin, not by thematic reference but by inner qualities. And the whole work is pervaded by that indefinable atmospheric beauty which has caused Debussy to be regarded as the greatest, if not the only, musical impressionist. Technically the novelty of its idiom is more apparent than real, being derived from procedures which were already existent though not familiar. Three of these procedures play a prominent part. The first is the very frequent employment of unusual concatenations of common chords, of which perhaps the simplest examples occur in Erik Satie's *Gymnopédies.* The second consists in dalliance with the church modes. For this it is not necessary to look beyond the first bar—

Ex. 1.

to which the flattened second degree of the minor scale imparts the distinct flavour of the Phrygian mode. The third is the use of the Hexatonic or tonal scale, with its complement, the augmented triad, which in some of Debussy's later works was to become more frequent even than the diminished seventh in Weber. Of this,

Ex. 2.

which precedes the central climax of the slow movement, is a striking instance, with its accompaniment of consecutive major thirds. To what extent this element in Debussy's idiom is due to Russian influences is impossible to determine. It furnishes the leading theme of Dargomijsky's last opera, *The Stone Guest* (1868), and occurs far more frequently in the works of his successors than in those of any contemporary composers of other countries, but the present writer prefers to assume that, though Russian examples may have stimulated him, it must be ascribed in the main to Debussy's natural inclination to explore unfrequented harmonic territory—the same predilection that caused him, when a student in Guiraud's harmony class, invariably to introduce into his home lessons progressions which the professor was bound to exclude as unorthodox, however attractive. If these three technical features are taken for granted, the idiom of the quartet offers, even in the light of its own day, only such minor audacities as must be conceded to any composer of original outlook. In short, the quartet is classical in feeling, and has already come to be so regarded.

The generating theme, Ex. 1, is the first subject of the opening movement (animé et très décidé). At the thirteenth bar the first violin has a more flowing melody, afterwards taken up by the 'cello, to a running accompaniment of semiquavers. The treatment of the first subject is then resumed until the first violin announces the second:

Ex. 3.

This is continued with a remarkable sequence, until a pause is reached, followed by the development, an early feature of which consists in the restatement of the main themes with double-stopping on all four instruments. The recapitulation is curtailed by the omission of the second subject.

In the scherzo (assez vif et bien rythmé), the generating theme, first entrusted to the viola, takes the form,

Ex. 4.

whilst the other instruments comment in pizzicato. In the middle section the first violin extends it to

Ex. 5.

and in the resumption it is again modified to

Ex. 6.

In fact, one might say that the whole of this movement is derived from the main theme, for the subsidiaries are given little prominence.

In contrast the andantino (doucement expressif) appears to ignore the generating theme, though some commentators claim to trace remote affinities with it. It is this movement more than any other that recalls Borodin (notably the lovely slow movement of his first symphony), not that there is any thematic or harmonic resemblance, but only a similar lyrical feeling in the suave melody that enters, in each case, at the fifth bar. This beautiful line scarcely needs quotation, but in the sequel there is a point that may be cited for its characteristic harmonic flavour.

Ex. 7.

It would surely need no more than this one bar to identify the composer! The middle section of this movement opens almost like a two-part invention, but from the entrance of the viola, presently relieved by the 'cello, the other instruments have only an accompaniment until second violin and 'cello in octaves work up to the climax referred to above (Ex. 2), followed by the entry of the first violin. The music then subsides, and the opening melody reappears. The last movement is preceded by an introduction in which the generating theme can be traced through

Ex. 8.

to Ex. 9.

and finally to

Ex. 10.

on which a fugato is worked from the 'cello upwards. Then the finale begins (très mouvementé), with a subject more conventional than most of those figuring in this work, and continued by the simple process of first treating its second bar sequentially, and then using it as the first bar of a new subject. For the second subject proper we have a final elongation of the generating theme:

Ex. 11.

and for coda, the generating theme itself.

Debussy has been taken to task for presenting his *Sonates pour divers instruments* attired in a title-page from another era and signed 'par Claude Debussy, musicien français'. It is making mountains out of molehills to do so, but if any defence is needed it suggests itself. He obviously desired to symbolize his allegiance to a conception of music that became eclipsed in the nineteenth century, partly by the intrusion of ethical and didactic, or, at the best, literary ideas into music, and partly by the overwhelming influence of the German classics. He therefore adopted the fashion of an earlier century and added his nationality. Had he called himself a Latin he would have avoided the suggestion of jingoism, and would have made himself clearer, but it did not occur to him that he might be misunderstood. In these works, as in most others, he serves the ideals of Rameau in preference to those of Beethoven, but the former were not exclusively those of any country. Had Debussy lived a few years longer he would probably have considered the inscription superfluous, for every year seems to take us all farther away from those things from which he desired to dissociate himself. However, the point is immaterial. The three sonatas explain themselves. They are to be judged not by the profundity of their significance but by their deftness and charm, as one judges the music of the eighteenth century.

Whilst under the spell of the earlier Debussy it is difficult to appraise what followed. At what particular point a personal expression becomes a mannerism is always a knotty problem to determine, and there clings to us so much of the nineteenth century that we instinctively accord a greater latitude to Brahms than to Debussy, whilst admitting that each became addicted to mannerisms. It is probable that Debussy himself was as conscious of his own Debussyisms as he was of those of the Debussyites. From 1910 onwards he began to show signs of that slackening of impulse which comes sooner or later to all men. How, then, do these sonatas of later date stand in relation to his memory? A categorical answer would be premature. The present writer takes the view that, amid the slackening to be discerned in them, there may be traced also the quickening of a new impulse, and especially in the second of them, the sonata for flute, viola, and harp. There is in this work a freshness of allure which might have heralded a new vein of inspiration had the composer lived to develop it. But such impressions cannot be defined, and still less can they be illustrated by quotation, so that a brief summary of the three sonatas must suffice.

THE SONATA FOR 'CELLO AND PIANO comprises three movements: prologue, serenade, and final, the last two being linked. The prologue corresponds to its title as to length, and is mostly declamatory. There is little of sonata treatment even in the final, the normal progress of which is so soon abandoned that it appears fragmentary. It is the least satisfactory of the three sonatas.

THE SECOND SONATA FOR FLUTE, VIOLA, AND HARP consists of a pastorale, interlude, and final, and it is the first of these that indicates the character of the whole, governed, no doubt, by the timbres of the combination of instruments, which somehow convey a Trianon suggestion. Debussy was always at his happiest in music of this description, which may be taken to include the minuet which follows the pastorale. The final is the most original of the three, but the whole work wears an aspect of spontaneity which was rare in the Debussy of the last phase.

THE THIRD SONATA FOR VIOLIN AND PIANO, being constructed of materials that could be accommodated to orthodox sonata form, is the most formal of the three, though not to any degree approaching orthodoxy. In quality it is superior to the 'cello sonata . It consists of allegro vivo, intermède (fantasque et léger), and final. There are attractive ideas in all three, but they leave an impression of insufficient expansion.

The fact is that these three sonatas, which might have been warmly welcomed had they come from a lesser man, are the lesser works of a great man, and must therefore face comparison with his greater works. This they can scarcely do, and therefore they arouse a feeling of disappointment. But they are far from being the hopeless failures, the senile meanderings, that some critics would make of them. So far as they appear to meander, to fumble, as it were, it is in their search for new forms of expression, and that impulse is in itself the best evidence for the defence, since decaying powers would always rather brood than search.

EDWIN EVANS.

[Debussy once declared to an interviewer that in his one quartet he had said all he had to say in that form, but a composer, as every musician knows, is not always the best judge of his own powers. The apparent eccentricity of his later sonatas must not blind us to the proofs they afford of his sensitiveness in his last days to the possibilities of string effect, exploited to the full in his violin sonata, one of the not too numerous modern works that is able to stand the acid test of frequent repetition. My experience is that at each hearing more of the special beauties of colour quality which distinguish Debussy among writers for strings are revealed, yet being combined with the piano, an instrument with a tempered scale, they leave something to be desired in regard to intonation. Upon this ground I base the opinion that if he had written a second quartet in the days of his maturity, it would have proved a unique example of what a poetically inspired composer could achieve in the idealization of string tone.

It is perhaps significant that Debussy edited and fingered the sonatas of Bach. EDITOR.]

DECKER, KONSTANTIN, 1810–1878, German pianist.

Two quartets, str, d mi, a mi	op. 32	Heinrichshofen, 1853.
Quartet, str, c mi	,, 14	Hofmeister.
Sonata, pf, v, b mi	,, 33	Heinrichshofen, 1853.

Schumann writes amusingly (*Gesammelte Schriften*) of the quartet, op. 14, after hearing it played in private. The performers 'prepared with their usual enthusiasm to plunge into a newly arrived quartet from Berlin and found it just the thing for an enthusiastic mood, i.e. of a very cooling nature!'

Decker's music is not entirely devoid of merit, but laborious and dry. EDITOR.

DEDIEU-PETERS, MADELEINE, b. 1889, French composer.

	Composed		
Three pieces, str. quar.	1920	Senart,	1922.
2nd quartet, str	1925	,,	1927.

The second quartet (the three pieces counting as No. 1) made a favourable impression on the Parisian critics. The work is in three movements, the first of which is in E minor; the other two follow no definite key scheme.

The quartet is described by the Parisian press as 'full of life and warmth, with almost a superabundance of ideas. It seems to be conceived in successive stages rather than as a whole, by means of which it gains in variety.' The second movement, molto expressivo, was particularly remarked. 'The themes show good contrast and the writing is well balanced.'

The composer's works have been repeatedly awarded prizes, two of these being for her chamber works, viz. Prix Marmontel, 1925, for the second quartet, awarded by the Société des Compositeurs, and the Prix Halphen for a piano quintet. Unpublished works include a septet for the unusual combination of piano, flute, trumpet, and strings.

M. DRAKE-BROCKMAN.

†DEFESCH, WILLIAM, d. *c.* 1758, Flemish composer, settled in London.

A violin sonata (Ricordi) has been republished, and three 'cello sonatas (Schott; Simrock; Ricordi). He wrote a good deal of chamber music, mostly published by Roger of Amsterdam. List in *Fétis* and the *Q.-L.* The name s given in *Altmann* as Fesch.

†DELAFOSSE, L., French composer.

Sonata, pf, v — Heugel, 1900.

†DELCROIX, LÉON, b. 1880, Belgian composer.

Trio, pf, v, vc, b mi	op. 4	Schott (Brussels), 1917.
Sonata, pf, v	,, 34	Evette & Schaeffer.

Delcroix's early piano quartet, op. 1, was crowned by the Belgian Academy. His trio is quite a remarkable work of considerable length and rather difficult. The first movement (modérément animé) is rhapsodical in style; the second (pas trop lent), interrupted by scherzo-like sections (assez vite), returns to the original tempo and terminates peacefully. No. 3 (très animé) is a very dramatic movement, which ends jubilantly, as though reminiscent of a fête. There must be some personal reason for his use of a trivial theme of the chansonette type, which ill assorts with the otherwise dignified tone of an extremely fine work, which I cordially recommend to the notice of trio players. EDITOR.

*†DELIUS, FREDERICK, b. Bradford, 1863.

2nd quartet, str	Augener, 1917.
2nd sonata, pf, v	Forsyth, 1915.
3rd ,, ,, ,,	Hawkes, 1924.
1st sonata, pf, vc	U.E., 1922.

Delius's father was a naturalized Englishman of Dutch extraction, who, though exceedingly fond of music, was resolutely opposed to it as a profession for his son. The young Delius started to learn the violin at the early age of seven, and, although it had been decided that he should eventually enter the family business, he was allowed to go to Leipzig, where he continued to study the violin with Hans Sitt. Then, after a few years spent mostly in travelling for the family firm, he came to the conclusion that he was unfitted for a business career, and the usual unavoidable family conflict ensued. A compromise was arrived at, however, in the shape of a career which was neither artistic nor entirely commercial, namely orange planting in Florida. He seems to have spent most of his time there, however, in teaching and being taught music. Eventually he was allowed to return to Europe and to take up seriously the study of the art at the Leipzig Conservatorium. There he was at last initiated into the mysteries of harmony and counterpoint, and incidentally made the acquaintance of many musicians, one of whom, Edvard Grieg, was destined to exercise a considerable influence upon him. It is, in fact, the only clearly discernible influence in his mature work.

Since then Delius has been living practically uninterruptedly in France, first in Paris, then at the little village of Grèz-sur-Loing, without ever taking an active part in musical life. This aloofness and detachment are everywhere reflected in his work, and constitute an important element of its irresistible appeal and fascination.

Delius is not primarily a composer of chamber music. In early years he conceived a marked distaste for the medium, and it is only in later years that this disinclination has been overcome. This is not in itself an unusual course of development. A young composer is nearly always first attracted to the orchestra, and only comes later to the realization of the subtler possibilities of the more restricted medium. But there is a special reason also for it in Delius's case. His manner is to a very great extent that of chordal mood-suggestion, and though he has a subtle appreciation of instrumental individuality, the linear structure of his music does not play an essential or primary rôle in his style. He is essentially a romantic, and like all the romantics he does not excel in the treatment of the smaller instrumental combinations. The interplay of thematic developments which, in imitation and fugato, plays such an important part in the shaping of chamber music, is not a procedure which comes naturally to Delius. In practically every one of his sonatas and string quartets it is the slow movement that is the most successful, because it does not traditionally demand this kind of texture. In these slow movements he finds an opportunity for displaying his greatest qualities in writing a simple and haunting cantilena, occasionally interrupted by brief interjections and intimate exchanges of arabesque which compellingly present the poetic atmosphere which Delius, more successfully than any one else, conveys through a musical medium.

In the violin sonatas, for example, it is often evident that out of respect for the exigencies of conventional form, Delius felt constrained to violate, to a certain extent at least, his personal sense of musical logic; and while there are many musical beauties to fascinate the hearer, they are not always knit together by a convincing inner necessity, with the result that the entire movement does not present that unmistakable unity which his works reveal when he speaks with perfect freedom. Formal claims often lead him, in his chamber music, to restatements which are apt to make the listener impatient and to overlook the charm and polish of those parts which are handled without any submission to preconceived notions.

It is not, generally speaking, easy to grasp on a first hearing or scrutiny the formal structure of Delius's chamber compositions. The clearly contrasted themes, which in the classic tradition generate dramatic juxtapositions, are not exactly abandoned altogether, but instead are made definitely subservient to a manner of expression in which the dramatic implications are to be found in the underlying mood rather than in the actual structure of the music itself. The abstract musical ideal of the older composers as revealed in their chamber music might be broadly defined as the attempt to establish organic unity in the diversity of parts by the distribution of the thematic material. One way of attaining this object is the employment of fugal forms, in which each part acquires equal importance by its presentment of the integral subject. In such a medium as a sonata for piano and a single string instrument this procedure is clearly unsatisfactory. Instead of employing as many thematic 'characters' as there were parts, it became customary to restrict their number to that of the instruments employed, and in consequence of this arrangement the musical themes themselves assumed the rôles which formerly the parts (or voices) played. Consequently, we find that in this way two well-contrasted themes, each of which is specially suited to the technique and character of one or other of the instruments, usually constitute the material out of which the movement is constructed.

The idea of dramatic contrast which thus came into existence ultimately determined the composers' conception of the form. The first and second themes of a sonata movement came to represent two strongly contrasted moods, and the development (especially since Beethoven, whose elemental dramatic conceptions, of a predominantly ethical character, pointed the way) presented the victory, after a breathless struggle, of one mood, one faith, one desire, over another. In the chamber works of Delius this convention is to a great extent retained, but the spirit underlying it is profoundly modified. The elasticity of his musical periods and the smooth gradual manner in which the themes alternate or replace one another by subtle metamorphosis, lead us so gently from one mood to the other, that we are more struck by the emotional range through which the movement has conducted us than by any sudden conflict or unexpected transition.

This seeming lack of contrast is inevitably apt to create a certain impression of placidity, and the fascination which the work exercises tends to be of a somewhat vague and dream-like quality. In order to discover the dramatic interest which these works undeniably possess, it is necessary to be familiar with their entire construction. One then discovers, spread over long distances and separated by transitions which remind one strikingly of the harmonic modulations of Schumann and Spohr—which equally efface violent contrasts—a far greater emotional diversity and an infinitely greater degree of light and shade than one would at first sight be inclined to suspect.

These general remarks apply equally to the structure of the works as a whole. The original contrast in the traditional form between the three or four movements has been to a great extent lost in the process of welding the whole work into a single movement. It is not always easy, at a superficial glance, to decide which section of his sonata takes the place of the slow middle movement, or where the rudimentary remains of the original exposition and developments of the first and last movements give place to a subsequent new sentence.

Moreover, there is often a distinct family likeness between the various themes which, while it secures an impression of organic unity, makes it exceedingly difficult to decide whether a fresh theme is being introduced or merely a variant of a preceding one. Take, for example, the two fragments from the second violin sonata (Exx. 1–2).

In both of these quotations it will be observed that the string part is more definitely melodic than that of the piano. It is undoubtedly characteristic of all the sonatas that the thematic invention has been stimulated primarily by a feeling for the individuality of the stringed instrument, which is practically throughout the bearer of the idea and the chief actor in the drama. Even when the piano assumes a certain amount of independence and interest, it is generally either announcing a pending utterance, or lingering over a phrase that has already been announced with more convincing eloquence by the other instrument. One might almost say that in his chamber music Delius employs the piano in much the same way that he often employs the massed body of the strings in his orchestral works, i.e. as a kind of harmonic background or setting for the display of a melodic line. When the piano, in these sections where both instruments are in the full heat of action, temporarily abandons the many toned chords which sustain the melody, it is mostly in order to increase the volume of sound and the rhythmic vitality by breaking up the chord progressions into wide-spread arpeggios. It must be admitted that this constant reliance on a single method is apt to become monotonous in the long run. On the other hand, the writing for the string instrument, whether violin or 'cello, is in marked

Ex. 1.

Ex. 2.

contrast to the somewhat unresourceful treatment of the piano, and reveals a considerable amount of serious study and reflection as well as an uncommon understanding of the demands and possibilities of each instrument. The composer's early training as a violinist is undoubtedly largely responsible for this.

The incessant flow of the music is perhaps the most noteworthy characteristic of Delius's chamber music. He hardly allows either of the players to take breath, metaphorically speaking, from beginning to end of the respective works, and the moments of repose, in a mental as well as in a physical sense, are few and far between. In this sense they present a remarkable contrast to the orchestral and choral works. The stormy eloquence and restless preoccupation of the sonatas are at the very opposite pole from the serenity and delicate restraint of the larger works. It is not easy to explain the causes of this striking difference. It is of course largely to be sought in the fact that his means of expression consist rather of timbre and colour than of line, symmetry, or polyphonic construction; but the fact remains that Delius has not chosen, like so many modern composers, to extend the principles and methods of the modern symphonic style to the domain of chamber music. On the contrary, when he writes for the smaller combinations, he almost entirely abandons the stylistic possibilities afforded by impressionism, even where their exploitation might be reconciled with the due observance of the claims of line and pattern. The string quartet is to a certain extent an exception to this general rule, the second movement in particular being more characteristic of the Delius of the larger forms.

If we have chosen to treat all these works

together rather than to examine each separately and in detail, it is because there is very little to differentiate the one from the other. They all present much the same qualities and defects, except, of course, the early unpublished violin sonata and string quartet which are immature and lacking in individuality, and consequently deserve only a passing mention. But on the whole, if one had to make a choice, it is the 'cello sonata to which one would give the first place, and the string quartet the last, for of all possible mediums it is the one which is least suited to the expression of the qualities which have won for Delius his high position among contemporary musicians. CECIL GRAY.

†DELMAS, MARC, b. 1885, French composer.

Trio, pf, v, vc, c mi Leduc, 1920.

The first three sections of this trio are composed in classical style, the finale being in cyclic form. The opening movement is fiery in character, and contains some clever writing in double counterpoint. The brilliant scherzo in E major with trio in A major is original in rhythm.

This work is dedicated to the Belgian composer, Paul Gilson.

In 1919 Delmas was awarded the Prix Chartier for his chamber works, namely the above trio and a *Légende et Danse* for string quartet. EDITOR.

†DELUNE, LOUIS, b. 1876, Belgian pianist and conductor.

Sonata	pf, v	d mi	B. & H., 1896.
1st sonata	pf, vc	b mi	B. & H., 1902.
Suite Galante (7 pieces)	pf, vc		Hérelle.

Louis Delune studied at the Conservatoire Royal, Brussels, where he gained the Prix de Rome. A prolific all-round composer, his first chamber work was the violin sonata in D minor. This lively and youthful work is of the nature of a fantasy-sonata in three movements, traditional in form, with modern harmonic tendencies, especially in the finale.

His first 'cello sonata is classical in form, and consists of three movements: (1) allegro; (2) adagio in Lied form, the melody of which is periodically interrupted by a theme serving as interlude; (3) finale in rondo form, lively and brilliant.

Two string quartets are still in MS. In MS., too, are the second sonata for 'cello and piano (1908) and a *Fantaisie en Trio*, for piano, violin, and 'cello, completed in 1917. In these works the harmony is seen to become more and more modern.

In 1910 were published six old sonatas for 'cello, on the figured bass of which Delune has constructed an independent piano part, the origin of this idea being the fact that the eighteenth-century accompanists, who were excellent clavecinists, did not confine themselves to a mere series of chords on the given bass, but used to improvise a contrapuntal accompaniment in keeping with the style of each composer.

Lastly, Schneider of Paris published, in 1925, twelve 'cello sonatas of Cervetto, with piano part arranged by Delune.

During the last two years Delune has devoted himself mainly to composition and is at work on more important chamber compositions which he hopes shortly to finish.

GEORGES SYSTERMANS.

†DELVINCOURT, CLAUDE, b. 1888, French composer, pupil of Widor.

Sonata, pf, v, d mi Senart, 1922.

Delvincourt's music is the expression of a soul deeply affected by the sufferings and horrors of war. His nature is fiery and imaginative.

The sonata, in free form, has three movements: the first (très large), dramatic and sorrowful, is like a plaint gradually intensified into the revolt of a spirit goaded by bitter suffering, yet with flashes of humour and unrestrained joy. The second (vif et gai, in C sharp) is in the nature of a scherzo of very independent form with piquant rhythm. The opening of the finale (calme, mystérieux et lointain) is of strange charm, the melody shrouded in a perplexing polytonality; it leads suddenly into the animé avec impétuosité joyeuse, which concludes the work in a curious mixture of whimsical rhythms with highly coloured polyphony. After a piquant and fantastic cadenza on the violin, the work ends with a return of the opening slow movement of the sonata, leaving an impression of calm and plaintive resignation, into which the final chord allows a ray of hope to penetrate.

It is a powerful and original work, and very difficult to play. The writing is very bold, and the rich harmonic texture with free employment of ultra-modern audacities, as well as the nature of the ideas themselves, seem to designate Delvincourt as the successor to the genius of Gabriel Dupont, and his work follows the same lines as that of Florent Schmitt and Arthur Honegger. ADOLPHE PIRIOU.

DEMANET, ÉMILE, Belgian composer.

Fantasie-trio, pf, v, vc op. 14 Schott (Brussels).

†DENÉRÉAZ, ALEXANDRE, b. 1875, Swiss organist.

2nd quartet, str, D Foetisch, 1908 (Lausanne).

†DEPAS, ERNEST, French composer.

Wrote ten seldom-played piano trios (Legouix & Leduc).

DÉRÉ, JEAN, b. 1886, French composer.

1st sonata, pf, v, d mi	Senart, 1922.
2nd „ „ „	„ —

The first sonata is short and concise; it includes the elements of sonata form, but eliminates all development.

DERFFEL, JOSEF, Austrian composer.

Sonata, pf, vc, D	Doblinger, 1887.

D'ERLANGER. *v.* ERLANGER.

DEROSIERS, NICOLAS, French musician living in Holland in the later seventeenth century.

Published a number of chamber works (Roger, Amsterdam), including one in 1689 for two violins (or flutes) and bass, entitled *La Fuite du Roi d'Angleterre.*

† DESHEVOV, VLADIMIR, b. 1902, Russian composer.

Ballade, pf, vc	Mus. Sect. State Publ. Dept., 1925.

Deshevov belongs to the later generation of Russian composers who have come forward since the Revolution. His only contribution to chamber music up to the present is the *Ballade* for 'cello and piano. In this work he sets out to simplify the musical tissue, and to endow it with the elements of clarity, incisiveness, and even something of harshness, whereby the composer expresses a certain contempt for purely tonal beauty. He is altogether a son of the new revolutionary Russia, and his music reflects the psychology of his generation, a psychology which has little in common with the previous Russian temperament. On the technical side Deshevov's music is still half amateurish, and the skilled and experienced hand is not always perceptible in his musical innovations. L. SABANEIEV.

DESMARAIS, CYPRIEN. An eccentric series of essays by this author upon the quartets of Beethoven is to be seen in the British Museum Library. The work is entitled *Les 18* (sic) *poëmes de Beethoven,* and to each quartet is allotted a floridly written essay, in which the relation between the text and the music is undiscoverable. He writes that the eighteenth quartet is not found in the ordinary editions! It is curious that Berlioz also makes mention of 'the eighteen quartets of Beethoven'.

The eighteenth quartet is probably the piano sonata in E major, op. 14, arranged as a quartet in F, and found in the lists of some publishing houses; or the arrangement of op. 16, sometimes described as op. 75. EDITOR.

† DESREZ, MAURICE, French composer.

Trio, pf, v, vc, D	Senart, —
Sonata (musical poem in four movts. entitled *Spring*), pf, v	Leduc, 1921.

DESSAU, BERNHARD, 1861–1923, German violinist.

Suite, pf, v, G	op. 40	Simrock, 1908.
Suite, pf, v, d mi	„ 51	„ 1911.
Suite in dance-form, pf, v, G	„ 54	„ 1913.

DESSOV, FELIX OTTO, 1835–1892, German composer and conductor.

Quintet, 2 v, vla, 2 vc, G	op. 10	Kistner, 1880.
Quartet, str, F	„ 7	„ 1878.

Dr. Altmann prints a very interesting correspondence between Dessov and Brahms (his intimate friend). Dessov wished to have Brahms's candid opinion as to the merit of his quartet in F, and wrote him to that effect on March 16, 1878. The reply came quickly on March 22, pronouncing that he found in it 'the creative urge (Schaffenslust) from beginning to end'. EDITOR.

† DESTENAY, E., French composer.

Quintet, harp (or pf), 2 v, vla, vc, E flat	op. 12	Hamelle, 1905.
Quintet, pf, 2 v, vla, vc, E flat	„ 11	„ 1899.
Quartet, pf, v, vla, vc, g mi	„ 38	„ 1911.
Trio, pf, v, vc, a mi	„ 34	„ 1910.
Trio, pf, ob, cl, b mi	„ 27	„ 1906.
Sonata, pf, v, a mi		„ 1907.
Sonata, pf, vc		„ 1920.

DESZCZYNSKI, JOSEPH, 1781–1844, Polish composer.

Quartet, pf, v, vla, vc	Hofmeister.

† DEVANCHY, P.

Sonata, pf, vc, e mi	Mathot, 1913.

DEVIENNE, FRANÇOIS, 1759–1803, French flautist and bassoon player.

His compositions for the flute, once celebrated, are now antiquated. He wrote over eighty duets for two flutes. The following have been republished in recent times: opp. 1, 10, 80 (Richault, Paris) and op. 82 (André, Offenbach). He also wrote trios for three flutes, for flute, clarinet, and bassoon (or 'cello), op. 61; three quartets for flute, violin, viola, and 'cello, op. 62; sonatas for two flutes and bassoon (or 'cello), op. 77, and for flute and 'cello, op. 58. H. M. FITZGIBBON.

[*Fétis* gives 36 quartets with flute, 66 trios, and very many sonatas for various combinations.]

DÉVREESE, GODEFROID, b. 1893, Belgian composer, pupil of César Thomson.

Sonata, pf, v, E	Senart.
Sonata, pf, vc, F	„

Dévreese is the violist of the Concertgebouw-quartett of Amsterdam. He has written a number of important works in other branches of music, some of which have obtained wide recognition in Holland and Belgium.

DIABELLI, Antonio, 1781–1858.
Modern republication:

Sonata, pf, v, F	Augener-Schott, 1902.

The founder of the great publishing house of Diabelli. Chiefly remembered for his relations with Beethoven and Schubert. Riemann describes his chamber music as 'ephemeral'

DIÉMER, Louis, 1843–1919, French pianist.

2nd trio, pf, v, vc, A	op. 23	Durand.
Sonata, pf, v		,,
Sonata, pf, vc, D	,, 22	,,

Diémer was Alard's favourite pianist for his chamber music performances. Diémer, Alard, and Franchomme gave a complete edition fingered and marked of the works of Haydn, Mozart, and Beethoven for piano, violin, and 'cello.

*† DIEREN, Bernard van, b. 1884.

	Composed	
Sonnet of Spenser, baritone voice, octet	1923	O.U.P.
2nd quartet, str	1917	,,
3rd quartet, str	1918	,,
5th quartet, str	1927	,,
Sonatina Tyroica, pf, v	1913	,,

There are three string quartets, and some songs and recitations with string quartet still in MS.

Bernard van Dieren is generally, but inaccurately, referred to as a Dutch composer. Although born at Rotterdam, his father was half French, his mother entirely so, and, like Joseph Conrad, he has deliberately chosen England as his country of adoption since 1911. The prevailing spirit of his work is clearly and unmistakably Latin, and, apart from his predilection for elaborate contrapuntal forms, there is nothing specifically northern in his music.

Van Dieren is first and foremost a composer of chamber music, for most of his works for large combinations of instruments, such as the *Diaphony* and the *Serenade*, are, like the *Kammersymphonie* of Arnold Schönberg, expressly designated by the composer as works for chamber orchestra.

The most striking feature of his music is that each work is the outcome of an entirely separate line of thought, and, since performances of his music are rare and hitherto for the most part unsatisfactory, this characteristic renders it difficult for the listener to penetrate into the spirit of the music. But although one work does not to any great extent throw light on any other, they all possess in common a strictly logical structure and an integrally polyphonic texture. His polyphony, however, is neither of the arbitrary kind that necessarily involves harmonic brutalities and crudities, nor, since the harmony is originally generated by the part writing, of the type that adapts the melodic line without reference to chord formations. Although his harmonic idiom is highly individual, it is neither really complex like that of Schönberg, consciously iconoclastic like that of Stravinsky, nor simply idiosyncratic like that of Debussy or Scriabin. If it disregards to a certain extent the conventions of consonance and dissonance, it is not perverse in methodically rejecting the former, or in deliberately avoiding the latter. Chords which are generally regarded as complex are often treated by him as primitive, while some which older theoretical assumptions found to be simple are reserved for rarer occasions, or handled with precautions similar to those which marked the tentative introduction of discords in ancient music. Other characteristics of van Dieren's chamber music which recall the methods of early composers are his economy of means and thematic material; the strictness of his forms, which are derived from old contrapuntal devices; and the sobriety of his part writing. It is of the rarest occurrence to find in his chamber music any doubling of parts, double stopping for the strings, or similar devices. A work for four instruments is written throughout in four real parts, and even when, as in the Spenser sonnet, he writes for voice and eight instruments, each separate part possesses a logic and interest of its own similar to that found in the music of Palestrina and other masters of the old polyphonic period.

The bewildering complexity of much of the first string quartet militates considerably against both immediate appreciation and adequate performance. It makes the utmost demands on both performer and listener, and it must be admitted that this objection applies to a good deal of van Dieren's earlier work. The second and third quartets, on the other hand, though still difficult to perform, are, with the exception of their first movements, readily intelligible even at a single hearing; while the fourth, with double-bass instead of 'cello, is comparatively simple from the point of view of both listener and performer. It was one of the works chosen to represent the English section at the festival of the International Society for Contemporary Music, held at Frankfort in the summer of 1927. Both the fifth and sixth string quartets bear witness to their composer's increasing preoccupation with simplicity and lucidity of thought and expression.

This progression from complexity to simplicity, presenting such a striking and welcome contrast to the development of most modern composers, is also to be noted in the works for voice and string quartet, and even in the abovementioned sonnet, despite the larger number of parts. They are all excellent examples of van Dieren's refined and subtle art; the sonatina for violin and piano, on the other hand, is not a particularly characteristic production, and should probably be regarded as a highly sophisticated kind of parody of classical sonata form, although, like all good parodies, it has an intrinsic value and interest apart from the object caricatured. CECIL GRAY.

DIETRICH, ALBERT HERMANN, 1829–1908, German composer.

Trio, pf, v, vc, C	op. 9	B. & H., 1855.
Trio, pf, v, vc, A	„ 14	Cranz, 1863.
Sonata, pf, vc, C	„ 15	„ 1870.

This composer, a pupil of Robert Schumann and a friend of Brahms, is to-day almost forgotten, but the unprejudiced amateur will find much that is worth attention in his chamber music, in which the influence of Schumann is undeniable. For true Schumann lovers, his piano trio, op. 14, for instance, improves on acquaintance. The opening allegro is splendidly melodious, and the hearer is carried along by a flow of tone, and bathed in its warmth and vitality. The elegiac main theme of the adagio has the appeal of a northern folk-song; in the sequel, however, the composer's inspiration weakens somewhat. The dashing scherzo has a charming second subject, and two trios. The first of these has one theme that is fascinating by reason of its rhythm, and another that is very melodious. The second, which, starting from C major, modulates very happily, has a broad and noble melody. There is movement and youthful vigour in the finale—and this not merely in the march-like section. The stringed instruments are provided with effective tasks, and the piano part is splendidly written.

WILHELM ALTMANN.

[Dietrich collaborated with Schumann (of whom he was a devoted friend) and Johannes Brahms in a joint violin and piano sonata written with humorous intent as a greeting to Joachim on his arrival at Düsseldorf in 1853. Dietrich wrote the opening movement (A minor), Schumann an intermezzo (F major) and finale (F minor), and Brahms a scherzo (C minor), the latter published by the Deutsche Brahms-Gesellschaft in Berlin. Joachim, when playing the sonata through for the first time with Clara Schumann, recognized, of course, the respective composers. EDITOR.]

†DIETRICH, OSKAR, Austrian composer.

Suite, pf, fl (or v), g mi — Doblinger, *c.* 1925.

DIETZ, FRIEDRICH WILHELM, 1833–1897, violinist, pupil of Spohr.

Sextet, 4 v, vla, vc, d mi	op. 15	Henkel (Frankfort), 1865.
Quartet, str, D	„ 17	André, 1869.

†DIMITRESCO, CONSTANTIN, contemporary Roumanian composer.

Quartet, str, F — op. 42 — F. Schuberth, 1890.

D'INDY. *v.* INDY, V. D'.

DISTLER, JOHANN GEORG, 1760–*c.* 1798, German violinist.

Fétis states that Pleyel, Neukomm, and Distler were the only three pupils (Beethoven excepted) formed by Haydn, Distler, according to Wasilevski, being his favourite.

Vidal gives a list of fifteen quartets published by Gombart of Augsburg; they were also published in Paris by Louis and Pleyel.

DITTERSDORF, KARL DITTERS VON, 1739–1799, German violinist.

Modern republications:

Six quartets, str, D, B flat, G, C, E flat, A — (Müller) Fürstner, 1866.

For earlier publications see *Riemann*, also *Fétis*.

This contemporary, and in a certain sense rival, of Haydn wrote a considerable amount of chamber music. His string quartets are still occasionally played; and six of them have been made easily accessible by a cheap reprint in Eulenburg's collection of miniature scores. Dittersdorf was one of the earliest advocates of the new Mannheim style (*v.* MANNHEIM SCHOOL), continuing very happily on the lines of Stamitz's innovations, though surpassed by Haydn in variety and inventiveness.

The six quartets in the Eulenburg collection (in E flat, D, B flat, G, A, C) are identical with the quartets in the same keys published in 1866 by the famous String Quartet, the Brothers Müller with Arnold (Elberfeld) and Fürstner (Berlin). The quartet in E flat has also been edited by Johann Lauterbach (Peters, 1887), with the addition of an andante, taken from the quartet in B flat and transposed from F to G major. The statement frequently made that twelve Dittersdorf quartets were published in 1866 is erroneous. Though all of the six quartets are distinguished by fine details, a quaint humour, and charming melody, the one in D major stands out as his masterpiece. HUGO LEICHTENTRITT.

[Dittersdorf's intimacy with Haydn no doubt influenced his development as a composer. One regards his quartets as a pendant to those of the greater master.

There is a gramophone record (Elman Quartet) of part of one of his quartets (H.M.V.).

EDITOR.]

†DOBROWEN (DOBROVEIN), ISSAYE ALEXANDROVITCH, b. 1893, Russian pianist.

Sonata, pf, v, f sharp mi	op. 15	U.E.; Jurgenson, 1914.
Ballade, pf, v	„ 17	„

Dobrowen is a talented composer of the younger generation of Russian impressionists. He made his début in the musical world as a pianist and conductor, and everywhere showed himself to be an extremely gifted personality. His creative work, with which he began to occupy himself in 1909, is moderate in its tendency, and largely influenced by three men —Scriabin (of the early period), Rachmaninov, and (to a certain extent) Medtner—who in those years (1908–1916) pre-eminently dominated the musical moods of young Russian composers. Later, the style of Dobrowen's creative work was brought to maturity and its orientation altered; nevertheless its direction was not too far to the left, and he did not subscribe to any of the new tendencies in the musical art of the day.

The violin sonata, composed before the Revolution, reflects mainly the pathetic style of Rachmaninov and the early Scriabin, and at one time was in great favour with Russian violinists. L. SABANEIEV.

[Dobrowen's music is not up to the usual bright level of the composers of the Russian school.]

DOBRZYNSKI, IGNAZ FELIX, 1807–1867, Polish pianist.

Sextet, 2 v, vla, 2 vc, cb, E flat	op. 39	Hofmeister,	1848.
Quintet, 2 v, vla, 2 vc *or* 2 v, 2 vla, vc, F	,, 20	,,	
Quintet, 2 v, vla, 2 vc	,, 38	Hofmeister,	—
Quintet, 2 v, vla, 2 vc, a mi	,, 40	,,	1846.
Trio, pf, v, vc, a mi	,, 17	B. & H.	—

Dobrzynski was friend and fellow pupil of Chopin. Fétis speaks of his work as distinguished.

*† DOHNÁNYI, ERNST VON, b. 1877, Hungarian composer.

Quartet, str, A	op. 7	U.E. 1908; Doblinger, 1903.
Quartet, str, D flat	,, 15	Simrock, 1907.
Quartet, str, a mi		Rószavölgyi.
Serenade, v, vla, vc, C	,, 10 U.E	Doblinger, 1904.
Quintet, pf, 2 v, vla, vc, c mi	,, 1 ,,	Doblinger, 1902.
Quintet, pf, 2 v, vla, vc, e flat mi	,, 26	Simrock, 1919.
Sonata, pf, v, c sharp mi	,, 21	Simrock, 1913.
Sonata, pf, vc, b flat mi	,, 8	Schott, 1903.

Dohnányi showed proclivities for the writing of chamber music in his earliest days (*v. Grove*). In his compositions we have art in which the form arises organically from the matter. We also have mastery, describable in academic terms and traceable beyond anything that academies have codified. Fortunately, there is no need for Dohnányi to justify himself to the critics of the future by writing feeble passages to show his modernity, for he is a musical administrator as well as a composer, and the contemporary composer, whatever his tendencies, has no grievance against either the programmes or the performances of the Philharmonic Orchestra of Budapest as directed by Dohnányi.

Meanwhile, Dohnányi's own work shapes itself without interference or inhibition from external pressures. The things that have influenced it are such as make for the freedom that comes from mastery, though this does not mean that Dohnányi has been influenced only by perfect works of art. Mastery in the sonata forms and style is nowadays attributed automatically to the influence of Brahms, and Dohnányi unquestionably owes much to his intimate knowledge of Brahms's works and also to some considerable acquaintance with Brahms himself. Passages in Dohnányi's ripest works can still be traced to an origin in Brahms. For instance, it is impossible to know the 'augmented' return of the theme in the first movement of Brahms's fourth symphony and fail to recognize it in principle and dramatic effect when we meet the device in Dohnányi's violin sonata, op. 21. It is the influence of a master on a later master, and such influences operate with complete disregard for common notions as to the nature and obligations of originality.

But the influence of Brahms is neither in form nor in style the dominating feature in Dohnányi's work. The preface to the *Philharmonia* miniature score of his first string quartet in A major, op. 7, describes the first movement as of classical perfection in form, and the whole as modelled on Brahms in themes and part-writing. This is an acceptable criticism, but it needs adjusting to the fact that when Brahms's way of moving was anything like as easy-going as that of the first movement of Dohnányi's A major quartet, it was also more reckless of consequences. Dohnányi's music, even in his early works, shuns boredom absolutely; and the easy fluency of the first movement of this quartet owes more to this instinct than to any classical models. In later works this fluency is developed into a distinct type of movement more akin to the music-drama or symphonic poem than to the older sonata styles, but here, with all its mastery, it is little more than typical youthful ease within limits approved by orthodoxy.

Dohnányi's eight published chamber works may be conveniently discussed in chronological order without classification. The quintet for piano and strings, op. 1, need not detain us long. Noble though it is in themes, it probably owes much of the impression it first made to the fact of the composer's taking the piano part at the first performances on, or shortly after, his début as one of the greatest of pianists. In itself the work is not much more than a conservatorium prize-winner of its period; and its scoring is less enterprising than its forms. An experienced listener, unbiased by the playing of the composer, might perhaps suspect that there was something unusual in the freedom from bathos in the otherwise youthful style. And so we may be wise after the event, but the detached judgement is more likely to be that the first quintet, op. 1, is what the Germans would call 'eine brave Musik'; a well-behaved composition, perhaps not better than the sextet produced at the same time (mentioned in some works of reference but never published).

THE SONATA IN B FLAT MINOR, op. 8, for piano and violoncello, is an important work. The first movement is the most weighty and majestic, and its themes are well able to support their Brahmsian treatment. A lively scherzo in G minor, with a quiet trio in E flat, shows that the intention of the work is not tragic, and in the variation theme of the finale we already encounter the wit which becomes one of the prominent characteristics of Dohnányi's developed style. The notion of using the themes of the other movements, neither as apparitions breaking in upon the finale nor as rhetorical allusions at its climax, but as integral figures in a regular set of variations, is adopted by Dohnányi from Brahms's string quartet in B flat, and is here enthusiastically developed with more ease and less cogency than similar devices in later works.

THE QUARTET IN A MAJOR, op. 7, the first movement of which has already been mentioned, has many interesting features of form. Its second movement applies the variation form to the purposes of a scherzo (in this case with a well defined trio) in a way which Dohnányi develops in two later works. Details remind one superficially of the second movement of Brahms's C minor trio, but the form, with its burden in the tonic major, is quite new. The only other external influence on the style is the Haydnesque breaking up of the burden by measured pauses at the end, a joke rather too elementary for the style of the whole work, and certainly not traceable to Brahms. The sombre slow movement is the ripest, though not perhaps the most attractive, part of the work. No page of the quartet could have been written by anybody but a consummate contrapuntist; in the first movement the inversion of the first theme forms the bass of two of the most striking passages, and the principal return of the main theme of the slow movement is given to the bass with powerful effect.

The finale is amusing, but is one of those youthful diversions in which no liveliness of tempo can avail to bring the pace above an imperturbable amble. At first this seems humorous and intentional, especially when the first episode (C sharp minor, the finale being in A minor) enters as a quite separate section drawling canonically over drone-chords and frankly rejoicing in its laziness. Apart from the question whether the humour, like the Haydnesque joke at the end of the second movement, is on the same plane as the general style, doubts arise as to the composer's intentions when the main theme (a Hungarian minor scale descending from E to E with an augmented second in both tetrachords) is later on developed in a fugato with a four-bar rhythm as rigid as any dance-music. Interest and surprise are present to the last, but the art of movement is lacking. Much may be learnt by comparing this finale with that of Dohnányi's latest published chamber work, the quartet in A minor (written in 1926), where we seem to have the mature and energetic expression of the high spirits which fail to find an outlet in the earlier work.

THE SERENADE IN C MAJOR for string trio, op. 10, while apparently a much slighter work, makes a great advance towards the attainment of Dohnányi's later style. Dvořák's little terzetto for two violins and viola may or may not have been in Dohnányi's mind, but the comparison between the two works is instructive. In both cases the composer might have sat down to write the first movement with nothing particular in his head, getting inspiration in due course from the pleasure of handling the delicate instrumental medium. The important movement in Dvořák's terzetto is the finale, where inspiration arrives in a set of variations on a single epigrammatic musical sentence with unsymmetrical rhythm and recondite harmonies. Here, and nowhere else, we may find a prototype of Dohnányi's variation themes as exemplified in the beautiful fourth movement of this serenade. But Dohnányi's wit and technique are too resourceful to keep him waiting for inspiration until a fourth movement. The opening march soon proves dramatic as well as witty, and provides the first example of the kind of short cut which becomes so important a characteristic of Dohnányi's later forms, and which enables him to weld whole sonatas into a unity like that of a symphonic poem without loss of the terseness of true sonata style, and without any feeling that material is lacking for the later movements when they draw upon themes already employed. Nobody would believe *a priori* that a march could adequately represent a da capo after a trio by three meditative murmurs of its first bar followed by a figure like a sneeze; but such is the end of the first movement of this serenade; and the finale, after a vigorous career as a fully developed rondo, ends by bursting into the trio of the march. This dies away, and the work ends with the same figure as the march, but without alluding to the first theme. To the learned musician the humour is accentuated by the fact that Dohnányi is here following the precedent of the classical serenades and cassations which began and ended with a march (*vide* Beethoven's string trio, op. 8). Each movement of this serenade has some point of form or style peculiar to Dohnányi's mature works. The second movement, entitled *Romanza*, ends on the dominant with an effect akin to that of the

Mixolydian mode and also to the tendencies of much recent Spanish music (*vide* Granados the *Goyescas passim*; Mixolydian for major keys, and Phrygian for minor). The third movement is a scherzo in fugue style, in which a trio-like theme is eventually combined with the first theme in double fugue. The key is D minor, which follows dramatically upon the Mixolydian close of the F major Romance and, ending in D major, makes the only deviation in all Dohnányi's works from the key-system of classical models. This deviation arises quite naturally and is in artistic harmony with the ostensibly irresponsible style of the whole. From D major the G minor of the beautiful theme and variations follows inevitably. This movement is the most serious and romantic part of the work. Ending in G major, it is an admirable antecedent to the prosaically witty rondo-finale, with its theme plunging into C via D minor, its mocking vein, and its indignant end with the trio of the opening march.

A student of the relation between musical form and dramatic expression could hardly fail to see in this serenade clear signs that Dohnányi was not only an inveterate comedian but an artist with a genuine gift for operatic writing; he has, in fact, composed three operas and a pantomime. It is not altogether agreeable to the orthodoxies of criticism to note the dramatic vein in his instrumental works; for the usual way to recognize a composer's ability to write operas is by discovering his inability to do anything else. And Dohnányi's chamber music is without flaw in the purity of its style and the complete freedom from anything dependent on stage-conditions for its effect. But, just as the theme of the slow movement of Brahms's A major quartet shows rhythms that could only have been invented by masters of the musical treatment of words, so the forms and devices of Dohnányi's chamber music, from the serenade onwards, have a Mozart-like perception of what is and what is not adequate to produce intelligible form with rapid movement, a perception which betokens a composer who can handle stage-drama with a fastidious perfection of musical form. This is not necessarily connected with staginess of style, as Mozart demonstrated once for all. The power to move at any and every pace from point to point of the plot is essential to both drama and pure music. Sonata forms themselves arose from those of music-drama, and a sonata style that is not essentially dramatic is nothing. On the other hand, the sonata has its own rate of movement, which is not that of the drama. Its forms are based on two principles: first, its rate of movement, and secondly, its exposition of key-relations in sharp contrasts on a large scale. Why Bruckner and Reger should have encumbered themselves with these forms is a mystery which must remain unsolved, seeing that they were really suited to neither composer. His rhetorical power, and his mastery of texture on certain schematic but elaborate lines, make it indifferent what forms he uses, so long as he keeps himself and us interested; but the interest is neither dramatic nor formal. Dohnányi, with far greater variety of form, is incomparably nearer to classical foundations. In his mature work there is no stroke of form without its dramatic value, and no stroke of drama that does not serve to complete the form. The question of tonality is intimately connected with that of movement, and from the outset Dohnányi's sense of tonality is classical on other than conventional grounds. A mere list of the key-relations in the first string quartet shows that his power of modulation is not likely to be frittered away in the facile exercise of musical wit. The first movement, in A major, has F sharp (minor and major) for the complementary key. The second movement has C sharp minor plus major (D flat) for its main theme, and A major plus F sharp minor-major for its trio. After the close in D flat the slow movement follows in F minor, alias E sharp. These three movements transposed a semitone higher would give the series of rising major thirds (B flat, D, F sharp) to be completed in an enharmonic circle by the finale. After the chord of F minor, try the effect of the Hungarian-Phrygian descending scale E, D sharp, C, B, A, G sharp, F, E; and it will be seen how vigorously Dohnányi takes up the line of thought marked by Haydn, Beethoven, and Brahms when they place in juxtaposition movements in widely distant keys. The episodes in C sharp minor (afterwards recapitulated in F sharp minor) and F major complete the symmetry of the whole previous set of key-relations.

THE SECOND STRING QUARTET in D flat, op. 18, reveals the full power of Dohnányi's art, and, amongst other things, the attainment of an artistic fusion of what may be called Wagnerian or symphonic-poem movement with the essentials of sonata style. The first movement combines a slow introductory phrase with a quick tempo. This is not more than has been done by Beethoven (sonata, op. 31, no. 2, quartets in E flat, op. 127 and in B flat, op. 130, to say nothing of the first movement of the sonata, op. 109), but what is new, as well as brilliantly successful, is the organization of vast spaces of development at full speed with the slow theme running through them. Many composers have tried this and have simply failed to notice that the tempo has merely become a matter of notation, and that what is heard is merely the original slow tempo accompanied by vibration, which achieves fussiness without movement, whereas, instead of this nightmare paralysis, Dohnányi achieves Wagnerian movement together with the swift dramatic action of sonata style. As we listen to these mature works we are aware from the outset that large processes are developing at leisure, and it is difficult to believe that the whole scheme is completed in less than half an hour. The Bruckner-Wagner qualities are there, though Bruckner could hardly express himself in less than an hour; the sonata qualities are there also, except for some sacrifice of the old swiftness of movement. The scherzo of the D flat quartet moves only as does the storm in *Die Walküre*, driving rain beating incessantly on the same spot. Yet the sacrifice of classical movement has positive results and differs widely from the stagnation of our modern Rossinians. The real movement is latent, as in Greek choruses; and it is only necessary to note the effect of the Phrygian end of that scherzo (on the dominant of F minor) followed by the chord of C sharp minor on the beginning of a molto adagio, to see that the action of this music has that intensely and maturely dramatic quality by which a situation prepared for generations explodes in a moment into an inevitable catastrophe.

The finale is the adagio in C sharp minor, which gathers up the themes of the scherzo and first movement, working them first into its own tempo, which finally approaches that of the introduction to the first movement. Thereupon it settles on the chord of D flat major, and builds up a climax and decline for over forty bars all on the opening theme with which the first violin dies away (on the unresolved sixth).

THE VIOLIN SONATA in C sharp minor, op. 21, is a work in a similar vein of romantic pathos, with a quiet first movement more nearly on the lines of Brahms, as has already been shown in regard to the 'augmented' return of the main theme. Yet this very detail is worked out in such a connexion with the end of the development as to produce the Bruckner-Wagner movement typical of Dohnányi's maturer works. The second movement, which follows without break, is one of Dohnányi's variation-scherzos, and it works in a longish episode on the 'second subject' of the first movement, which is made to behave partly like a variation and partly like a trio. The finale bursts out as soon as the scherzo has died away. Beginning with the motto figure of the first movement (C sharp, D sharp, E) in shrill chords, it transforms the rest of that theme into an agitated strain, somewhat as Liszt turned the whole first movement of his Faust symphony into a Mephistophelian scherzo, but this is not rigorously carried out. On the contrary, this finale develops on its own lines, not unlike a free scherzo with a quiet trio (A major) and a return in a foreign key with modulations. As soon as the tonic (C sharp minor) is reached the music settles on a long dominant pedal and, after a great climax, returns to the tempo and opening of the first movement, bringing the work to a romantically pathetic close.

THE SECOND QUINTET in E flat minor. With mature masterpieces a class-list in order of merit is the most futile impertinence, but this is certainly the most immediately impressive of Dohnányi's works, even if we include his orchestral music.

Here we have, even more unmistakably than in the D flat quartet, the perfect fusion of sonata style with Bruckner-Wagner movement, and a finale that gathers up the threads of the first movement with an effect of normality not before attained. For this normality is quite different from that achievable by a style which is a mosaic of short epigrams, as in Schumann's fourth symphony; and an impassable gulf separates it from the worldly wisdom of Saint-Saëns.

Dohnányi's mastery of the severest forms of counterpoint has an intimate connexion with the art which rounds off the whole design in little over twenty minutes, while seeming to go through vast cosmic processes from the outset. The enemy would blaspheme at a list of the contrapuntal devices in this work, and would say *a priori* that such a tissue of inversions and diminutions and augmentations and combinations was as incompatible with poetic inspiration as the construction of a triple acrostic in palindromes. He would also say the same of Bach's B minor Mass. And Metastasio 'expiring in a canzona' is not a greater 'formalist' than Bach, blind and on his death-bed, dictating *Vor Deinem Throne tret' ich* in four-part chorale-fugue by inversion.

Elaborate contrapuntal devices are to music as argumentative dialogue is to drama. The writer who still thinks such things clever will dissipate his action in his proud pursuit of them. The writer whose command of them is supreme will find in them a powerful means of concentrating his action, as Beethoven came to do, though his mastery of counterpoint was by no means supreme. He did not, however, think these things clever, but he grasped their purport and found them necessary. Dohnányi, who could at any time have amused himself with the most outrageous contrapuntal talks, produces in his second quintet a counterpoint in which every combination is a masterpiece of tone-colour, and every masterpiece of tone-colour is the result of fine counterpoint. This is the relation between form and drama in another category.

The tone of the whole work is very sombre, only the delicious scherzo variations affording relief to the prevailing solemnity. The finale is almost entirely in fugue, beginning slowly with the strings alone until the piano enters with a chorale-tune which must have brought the spirit of Bruckner from his communings with Wagner in Walhalla to bless Dohnányi for bringing his grandest ideas into relation with human time as well as Wotanesque eternity.

As in all Dohnányi's works, the scoring is rich and yet economical. It conveys the ideas in the fewest notes with the finest sounds and the most practical technique. So long as it conveys ideas, no scoring will be popularly regarded as brilliant. A great Russian composer has classified orchestration as (*a*) that which sounds well with competent sight-reading, and wonderful after proper practice; (*b*) that which does not sound well until it has been adequately practised; and (*c*) that which does not sound well under any circumstances. This classification makes no allowance for ideas, and provides for nothing more than the culinary department of musical art. Certainly Dohnányi's scoring is not fool-proof enough for that Russian first class, unless competent sight-reading is held to include an instantaneous grasp of the composer's idea on the part of every player. Very few great ensemble works will sound well throughout with even the best of sight-reading. The highest type of great instrumentation is that which requires much practice, but which sounds wonderful as soon as it begins to sound well.

THE THIRD STRING QUARTET in three movements, in A minor, is a large work, but less serious than the D flat quartet. The impassioned first movement has a temper that averts tragedy by letting off steam in a long, runaway coda. The middle movement is a lovely set of variations, and the direction andante religioso is rather a warning not to play too fast than a claim to any such solemnity as that of the E flat minor quintet. The finale is in high if satiric spirits. In the first movement some notable concessions are made to recent tendencies in harmony, chiefly by way of obstinate clinging to one key by some voices after the others have gone the opposite way.

Three operas and a pantomime are what it is hardly slang to say 'a good alibi' for having produced no more than eight pieces of chamber music. Nothing is more necessary in an age of artistic experiment than that composers should test the objective reality of their ideas by writing operas. Verdi produced *Falstaff* when he was over eighty. If Dohnányi will continue to that age producing chamber music and operas in the present ratio of eight to three, there will be no excuse for complaining of the exhaustion of the higher artistic resources in modern music, 'absolute' or illustrative. DONALD F. TOVEY.

[I have but a few words to write upon Dohnányi's very beautiful chamber music, and those must be to express my sincere admiration firstly that Mr. Tovey, a pianist, should write with so much sympathy and understanding upon string music, and secondly that Dohnányi, also a pianist, should compose so effectively for strings. This applies to the string quartets, but especially to the one in D flat, the scherzo of which, with its sinister recurring notes, expresses a sense of fatefulness in grim Beethovenish fashion, though in Dohnányi's own idiom. It is a companion movement to the Bonn master's scherzo to op. 135. The figuration for the two violins in the finale is brilliantly designed, though technically difficult to play, and this glorious quartet may be summed up as one of the best written by any living composer. The romantically conceived sonata for piano and violin, op. 21, requires very finished playing and exceptionally perfect intonation in the enharmonic passages, which do not lie altogether comfortably for the fingers of an amateur. Our own Albert Sammons plays the lovely coda (muted strings) with enchanting effect.

EDITOR.]

†DOIRE, RENÉ, French composer.

Sonata, pf, v, f sharp mi Durand, 1922.

The sonata is in three movements—conceived in classic mould, but sounding a modern note, and cyclic in form.

†DOLMETSCH, ARNOLD, b. France, 1858, violinist, pupil of Vieuxtemps; performer upon and builder of old instruments.

Space is not available in this book for giving a full acount of the part played by this remarkable man and his not less gifted family in the revival of interest in the music and instruments of past centuries. It must suffice to quote the felicitous sentence in which H. C. Colles sums up his career (in *Grove*): 'Dolmetsch re-created the domestic consort of the seventeenth century.' See art. CONSORT OF VIOLS, by A. Dolmetsch. EDITOR.

DONATO, V. DI, Italian composer.

Sonata, pf, vc op. 4 Ricordi, 1920.

DONAUESCHINGEN CHAMBER MUSIC FESTIVALS (1921–1927).

List of chamber works performed:

FIRST CHAMBER MUSIC FESTIVAL, 1921: Alois Hába, string quartet, op. 4; Ernst Krenek, serenade for string trio and clarinet; Franz Philipp, piano quartet; Philipp Jarnach, string quintet; Rudolph Peters, violin sonata; Paul Hindemith, string quartet, op. 16.

SECOND FESTIVAL, 1922: Ernst Krenek, symphonic music for nine solo instruments, op. 9; Richard Zollner, string quartet; Max Butting, quintet; Hermann Grabner, trio-sonata; Fidelio Finke, string quartet; Rudolf Dinkel, grotesque fugue for string quartet; Bernard van Dieren, string quartet; Reinhold Laquai, clarinet sonata; Felix Petyrek, sextet; Paul Hindemith, *The Young Maiden*, and chamber music, no. 1.

THIRD FESTIVAL, 1923: Frank Wohlfahrt, string quartet; Robert Oboussier, string quartet and voice; Alois Hába, 2nd string quartet in the quarter-tone scale; Bruno Stürmer, *Erlösungen* (*Deliverances*), for voice and string quartet; Hermann Reutter, piano trio; J. F. Hoff, string quintet; Fidelio Finke, string trio; Philipp Jarnach, string quartet.

FOURTH FESTIVAL, 1924: Erwin Schulhoff,

sextet; Josef Matthias Hauer, five pieces for string quartet, op. 30; Alex. Jemnitz, string trio, op. 22; Ernest Toch, string quartet, op. 34; Max Butting, little pieces for string quartet, op. 26; Anton Webern, six bagatelles for string quartet, op. 9; Yosip Stolcer, string quartet, op. 3; Georg Winkler, sonata for viola and piano, op. 5; Arnold Schönberg, serenade, op. 24.

At no period in recent years has such systematic encouragement of contemporary music been seen as at the present time. It is well to look back and see the methods by which musical products of the nineteenth and early twentieth centuries found their way into the concert-room and so achieved publicity. New chamber works of that period were usually included in a chamber concert programme in which, beside the new works, some important classical work of long standing also figured. It appears to be a natural instinct to bring into close association works which present a contrast. A programme which is so constructed that the new art is placed in direct juxtaposition to that of established tradition suggests that the new represents a more or less graduated advance upon the old, whereas the same work, offered with more or less courage, as the case may be, for public criticism, may well appear too daring, if isolated, and remain incomprehensible on that account. The whole of the musical development of the nineteenth century, from Beethoven to Strauss, will in fact appear in future surveys of musical history as one continuous growth which, though it assumed vast dimensions, did not develop any essentially new impulses.

But with the beginning of the twentieth century these essentially new impulses sprang up, having their foundation indeed in the late nineteenth century—as we see from Arnold Schönberg's works—but yet having elements directly opposed to the principles of nineteenth-century music derived from Beethoven's classicism.

Performances of these novelties, which took place, according to custom, in combination with older works, had now an alienating effect, for whereas in former times comprehension of the new work (by Brahms or Strauss, let us say) was assisted by the proximity of a classical piece on the same programme, the tremendous gulf which separated the new from the old only became more apparent under such conditions. The listener was forced to undergo a fundamental transformation in his attitude within a short space of time, and this was all the more difficult in that the basis for understanding the new work had still to be sought. It is in recognition of these difficulties that organizations have recently sprung up for the purpose of the exclusive encouragement of contemporary music.

It was as a direct result of the most recent musical development that contemporary chamber music obtained the chief consideration in such performances. There had been a marked return to chamber music as a vehicle of expression. This arose out of a sharp reaction against the exaggerated use of orchestral and choral forms—for every little piano piece, every modest song-accompaniment, had been orchestral in character towards the end of the nineteenth century—and the step was taken from tone-value to line, from tonality, chromatic and enharmonic though it might be, to atonal linearity which finds its characteristic expression in the means and formulae of chamber music style, but not in orchestral technique.

There had been individual concerts here and there in which this new development had received due consideration. But it was not until the first Donaueschingen chamber music festival in 1921 that any important organization was found to devote itself exclusively to the new development in music. That the undertaking was fully justified is evident from the later organizations which followed this first festival, and, above all, from the adoption of the Donaueschingen idea by the chamber music festivals at Salzburg and in various other German and Austrian towns.

The festivals owe their inception to Fürst zu Fürstenberg, who resides at Donaueschingen, and the 'Friends of Music' Society in that town. They lent a willing ear to the suggestions of the young musical director of Donaueschingen, Heinrich Burkard, who, with a sure instinct for the particular need in contemporary musical life, and with the help of a few kindred spirits, was untiring in his efforts to bring the festivals into being.

The following words of introduction, written for the first festival in 1921 (by Burkard, the composer Eduard Erdmann, and Joseph Haas, professor of composition at the Munich academy), give a clear description of the meaning, aim, and object of the Donaueschingen movement:

> 'In every branch of art and literature to-day the appearance of a new work arouses lively controversy; but in the case of a composer there are obstacles to overcome before his work is brought before the public for discussion at all. The creative musician is dependent on performers and publishers, who act as intermediaries between himself and the world around him, but their own position is so precarious at the present time that they are in most cases unable to assist an unknown composer. The Friends of Music Society has therefore conceived the idea of doing what it can for the encouragement of the rising generation of musicians by organizing a special society for the benefit exclusively of unknown talent or of such talent as arouses controversy. If these chamber music performances should take root in the little town of Donaueschingen, it will be not as exotics on foreign soil but as the natural product of the local musical culture which for 150 years has been encouraged by the princely dynasty and is now a tradition.'

In his introductory remarks on the interesting combinations in the modern works performed at the fourth Donaueschingen festival, Burkard was able to write as follows:

'When, three years ago, we were permitted to translate our ideas into action, the new art was for the first time offered systematic encouragement and a spacious setting. Some of the talent to which we drew attention is recognized to-day as representative of the new tendency.'

The surroundings amid which the Donaueschingen concerts took place were in every respect particularly favourable. The little town lies remote from the noise of the capital. Here the fever of competition is unknown, and both the productive and the critical faculties of the listeners are able to function without spasmodic effort. The hospitality of the Prince and of the Society of the Friends of Music surrounds the artists with an atmosphere of intimacy and social intercourse, for the practice as well as for the performance of their works. If prejudice exists it is only of the positive order, being directed against the art of clichés, stale and cheap forms of expression, and comfortable bourgeois art. Many a composition of this order, which had by some means found its way into the programme list, was coolly received, while others, which struck out in new directions, aroused animated discussion.

The greatest difficulty confronting the organizers of an undertaking such as this—which sets out definitely to act as a pioneer and to assist the coming development, both in respect of the artist and of the audience—is that of selecting from among the almost overwhelming number of compositions sent for approval those which show the strongest signs of future promise. The examiners are in constant danger of overlooking works of definite importance. It must be admitted, however, that the Selection Committee—of which Heinrich Burkard, Eduard Erdmann, Joseph Haas, and, in 1924, Paul Hindemith were members—have on the whole shown very sound judgement. At the first festival, in 1921, the names of Hába, Krenek, Jarnach, Berg, and Hindemith appeared, and the intellectuals assembled on that occasion at once found themselves at the parting of the ways. Representative masters of the older generation, such as Richard Strauss, Hans Pfitzner, Franz Schrecker, and Siegmund von Hausegger, who were on the honorary committee, took a more or less active interest in the first festival, but afterwards quickly withdrew on realizing their total lack of sympathy with the latest productions. Only the late Ferruccio Busoni and Arnold Schönberg were in full accord with the intention and scheme of Donaueschingen.

Next in importance to the first festival in 1921, at which the fundamental lines of the latest musical development were clearly perceptible, came the 1922 and 1924 meetings, when important works, first heard there, afterwards found their way into a number of concert programmes. Krenek's symphonic music for seven solo instruments, Hindemith's chamber songs (*The Young Maiden*) and his *Kammermusik* no. 1, which rapidly became known as Donaueschingen Chamber Music, all date from the 1922 performances, and the serenade for chamber orchestra and one voice by Schönberg may be singled out from the yield of 1924.

In summing up the results achieved by the Donaueschingen organization, it becomes evident that only a comparatively small number of the great mass of compositions produced during the four years have received complete recognition. On the other hand, it is to the credit of the festival organization that such works as have been safely launched by it have proved to be the standard works of Young-German music; for Hindemith's, Krenek's, Hába's, and Jarnach's compositions have all arrived by way of Donaueschingen, and Schönberg has come to be known as the patriarch of the moderns. Among the works of the remaining composers (see the complete list of those performed at Donaueschingen up till now) there were many valuable and interesting pieces; but they are of secondary importance as compared with the productions of the above-mentioned personalities, being all more or less manufactured articles—in the best sense. They prove, however, that the modern movement flows in a broad current, and that within a brief period a series of individual technical forms have developed out of a permanent musical foundation. The responsible organizers have indeed gladly and consistently admitted experimental work of every kind. Opportunity was repeatedly afforded of hearing music cast in a traditional mould, so that a decision might be taken as to the possibility of musical development on the basis insisted upon by academic and cautious musicians. On the other hand, the doors were flung wide to such utterly radical departures as Wense's or Erpf's compositions, which aimed at a complete simplification of the medium of expression, or those of Joseph Matthias Hauer—a theoretician of some standing—who experimented with a new scale-system based on the 'twelve tones'.

What, then, has actually been achieved? Positive results, undoubtedly, in many directions. The general course of musical development may be traced in the programmes given above. The first festival, in 1921, showed linearity to be the element which present-day music sought mainly to embody; atonality followed as a logical result, since all the earlier laws of harmony had to yield to the supremacy of the melodic line. This decisive step had no parallel in the domain of rhythm or dynamics. Only in the realm of musical form did Schönberg's serenade (performed in 1924) strike out in a new direction; here the free-flowing abstract form of expression is exchanged for one that is strictly formal and concise. Can it be that the father and leader of the moderns has again hung out a sign? Is it that a new age of formal restraint is to succeed the age of unfettered musical expression? Some such development would be in keeping with the latest well-defined tendencies in the sister-arts—architecture and painting—where abstraction and unrestraint have been followed by a tendency to austerity and constraint, and ecstatic individualism by a tendency to positive objectivity.

THE 1926 FESTIVAL. The festivals described above aimed at giving a general survey of the chamber works of the New Music. As a direct result the new chamber music began to establish itself in the concert-room. A still more important result was the discovery of certain outstanding personalities among the composers, who have since proved their worth as leaders and typical representatives of the present-day movement in music at home and abroad.

These things achieved, the artistic directors of the festivals—in particular Heinrich Burkard and Paul Hindemith—proceeded to lay down some leading principles for the organization. It was felt that interest should be focused on such categories and expression-forms as had been pushed into the background or lain fallow in the immediate past, or on those which seemed most representative of the present and promising for the future.

At the 1925 festival the effect of this policy was already shown in the production of works for chamber chorus in which Hindemith, Krenek, and other leaders of the new music demonstrated the possibility of reviving this neglected category.

In 1926 chamber chorus works were again represented, while, as a new category, compositions for wind instruments in the combinations usually found in open-air bands were introduced. Finally, as the most important of the new expression-forms, compositions for mechanical instruments were given a hearing, for it was thought that, particularly just then and in the near future, this form would assume considerable importance.

The choral works and wind music performed, much appreciated though they were by the assembled audience, are not subject-matter suited to this book. Nor does mechanical music belong to the category of chamber compositions; but it excites so much public interest at the moment that readers may like to hear of the happenings in what is practically a new province of the musical art.

It is essential to understand the nature of this mechanical music. The highly-finished modern mechanical instruments have up till now been employed exclusively for the purpose of reproduction. They consist chiefly of mechanical pianos or organs designed to play works written for ordinary pianos and organs, works that can be played by the human hand. The Donaueschingen compositions, on the contrary, are written expressly for the mechanical instruments, and cannot be played by the human hand unaided.

The point of the experiment was to prove the necessity of writing essentially for the particular instrument, exploiting the peculiarities possessed by it and no other. That is, not only does the restriction imposed by manual execution cease to exist, and a keyboard without limits become possible, but there appear as new formative factors the machine-like precision and the relentless forward drive of the mechanism. It is obvious that these things must exercise a decisive influence on the musical idea and general form of a composition for a mechanical instrument. Equally obvious is the assumption that mechanical music is bound to dispense with fine shades of expression and will instinctively do so, since delicate nuance and clockwork are diametrically opposed. Another factor that will strongly influence the musical idiom of such compositions—though the composer may be unconscious of it—is the probability, inherent in the possibility of mechanical reproduction, of frequent repetition and, above all, of wide circulation. On that score alone it will be necessary to avoid complicated music, intelligible to the initiated, but unintelligible to the eventual consumers of this type of composition—restaurant and cinema audiences, &c.—for this would rightly be rejected as unsuitable.

Even more than in the case of wind music did the works for mechanical instruments betoken a beginning, an experiment. Here, too, Toch led the way, with his clear grasp of the new possibilities, in *Three Original Compositions for Welte-Mignon* (mechanical piano) and his *Juggler* for the same instrument. Hindemith's *Toccata for Welte-Mignon*, which was also performed, likewise does justice in a convincing manner to the mechanical instrument's natural qualities. It was instructive to hear, in juxtaposition to these genuine original works, the reproduction of a pure piano piece, the rondo from Hindemith's *Piano Music*, op. 37, for it at once became clear that music for a mechanical instrument must be conceived with due regard for its special qualities. In the adaptation, the charm and alluring naturalness of the works expressly composed were totally lacking. Far too abstract, and at the same time midway towards a solution, seemed Hindemith's long drawn-out music for a small mechanical organ with built-in percussion (also a Welte-Mignon invention), written as accompaniment to the no less mechanically conceived *Triadische Ballet* by Oskar Schlemmer of the Dessauer *Bauhaus*. Here was an immediate example of the practical utility of mechanical music.

Beside the above-mentioned works, a little pure chamber music was heard, including a particularly good concertino for flute, viola, and double-bass by Erwin Schulhoff and a string quartet by Hans Krasa. The remaining works were without intrinsic value. The truth is, personalities are at the moment less in the foreground than basic problems concerning the interpretation of the new music.

HANS CURJEL.

[The 1927 FESTIVAL. In 1927 the festival was transferred from Donaueschingen to Baden-Baden, when the following chamber works were performed:

Berg, Alban, *Lyrische Suite* for string quartet.
Butting, Max, duo for piano and violin.
Krsto, Odak, string quartet.
Reutter, Hermann, 'cello sonata.

The 1928 FESTIVAL. The programmes for this year contain no chamber music.]

DONIZETTI, GAETANO, 1797–1848, Italian operatic composer.

At Bergamo there is to be seen a collection of MS. quartets by Donizetti, written at a period of his life when he devoted himself to serious studies in counterpoint and composition under Pilotti and Mattei; interesting, though only to be regarded as student's work. Quartet No. 4 in D was played at the 'Pops' in March 1860.

EDITOR.

DONNER, MAX.

Sonata, pf, v, B flat op. 40 Carl Fischer, 1909.

DONT, JAKOB, 1815–1888, Austrian composer and violin teacher.

Dont wrote ensemble works useful for teaching in class. He was the author of an admirable book of violin studies, which still retains its popularity.

DOST, RUDOLF.

Septet, pf, fl, ob, cl, fag, horn and timp [triang and tamb], G	op. 55	Zimmermann, 1923.

DOTZAUER, JUSTUS JOHANN FRIEDRICH, 1783–1860, famous German 'cellist, pupil of B. Romberg.

The following works are obtainable to-day:

Quintet, 2 v, 2 vla, vc, d mi	op. 134	Hofmeister.
Two quartets, str, E flat, g mi	,, 12	,,
Three quartets, str, a mi, F, G	,, 45	,,
Trio, pf, v, vc, e mi	,, 180	Leuckart, 1851.

He wrote twenty-two string quartets in all (*Vidal*).

DOUBLE-BASS.

As far as technique is concerned there is not much to be said about the double-bass in chamber music earlier than the present century. Although so essential in providing foundation for a number of instruments, in the quartets and quintets written by the older masters it is obvious that the more mobile violoncello served quite adequately as foundation, and as soloist on exceptional occasions.

GEORGE ONSLOW (*q.v.*) wrote thirty-four quintets for strings. These were originally composed for two violins, one viola, and two 'cellos, but as a 'cellist was missing on one occasion, Dragonetti, the famous contrabassist offered to play the part on his instrument. The innovation pleased Onslow so much that he rescored most of the works referred to, arranging them for violins, viola, 'cello, and bass. They have seldom been performed, however, in latter years.

The best-known chamber music in which the double-bass part is as important as the others, comprises Beethoven's septet and Schubert's octet and his Trout quintet. In these classic compositions, and it may be added in the piano sextet by Weingärtner, the double-bass is treated in the same manner as in the orchestra with regard to the range and type of musical passages.

When, however, we come to consider the ultra-modern composers such as Stravinsky, Schönberg, and van Dieren, it is evident, from what is expected by them, how immensely the standard of double-bass playing has advanced during the last twenty-five years. The technically difficult passages, involving the use of higher notes than were ever included in older compositions, the chords, and the harmonics, could never have been achieved with the old style of bowing and fingering. The following examples indicate the very marked differences between the requirements of modern music and those of the older works.

The following passage is from the *Trout* quintet:

Ex. 1.

In contrast we have this passage from Stravinsky's *Histoire du Soldat*, written for violin, double-bass, clarinet, bassoon, trumpet, trombone, and drum:

Ex. 2.

This pizzicato note and short chord at the opening of the work represent a toy side-drum.

Later we get this chord of excellent effect on the bass:

Ex. 3.

The following are examples of some of the harmonics met with in this work:

Ex. 4.

The quartet by van Dieren, for two violins, one viola, and double-bass, in which the last named takes the place of the usual 'cello, is an exceptionally difficult work, since it makes use of the tenor and treble clefs (which double-bass executants do not meet with very often), harmonics, and double stops.

Another recent composition by van Dieren is written for tenor voice, viola, and contrabass. Here we find great difficulties again for all concerned. A passage from the double-bass part follows:

Ex. 5.

In conclusion, it should be recalled that Bottesini, the famous double-bass virtuoso, wrote an excellent duet for violin and bass with piano accompaniment, and a duet for two double-basses, which is interesting as an experiment, if for no other reason.

For these and other solo work, Bottesini used a smaller instrument than is employed in the orchestra to-day, known as a basso da camera, with three strings only, all very thin, and with a different tuning of one tone higher, viz. 1st string A, 2nd and 3rd strings E and B, instead of the usual G, D, and A; this was done in order to achieve a brighter tone for solo work.

Mention must also be made of the living virtuoso on the double-bass, Kussevitzky, well known as a conductor. He has written several compositions of some value, but no chamber music.

For the rapid progress which has taken place in the technique of this instrument during comparatively recent times, we have, undoubtedly, to thank Bottesini, who first introduced the straight bow for the bass, and made it apparent by his own solo performances what a totally different type of execution was possible on this grandfather of the stringed family.

VICTOR WATSON.

[Although, for obvious reasons, the double-bass is little employed in chamber music, a few works may be added to those mentioned by Mr. Watson. Among the most important are Spohr's nonet, Hummel's two septets, sextets by Sterndale Bennett (pf) and Dvořák (str), and Goetz's piano quintet. The last is (as regards combination) a companion work to Schubert's *Trout* quintet, and much to be recommended for home performance.

Lighter works are the twenty-four quintets of FÉLICIEN DAVID (*q.v.*) and three serenades by GOUVY (*q.v.*). As of antiquarian interest the quintet of P. L. HUS-DESFORGES (*q.v.*) may be added to the list.

F. A. Hadland (in the *Strad*) speaks of the playing of Mori, Lindley, and Dragonetti in the sonatas of Corelli, in which the double-bass was heard at its best. This was in the early days of the old Philharmonic Society.

EDITOR.]

DOWLAND, JOHN, 1563–1626, English composer.

An old English composer of considerable note in his day. A quintet has been performed in public, taken from the *Lachrymae, or Seven Tears, figured in seven passionate Pavans, with divers other Pavans, Galiards and Almands.* The work was written *c.* 1603 for viols, and the whole has been transcribed for 2 v, vla, 2 vc, by Peter Warlock (O.U.P.).

† DOYEN, ALBERT, French composer.

Quartet, str		comp. 1921	Leduc.
Trio, pf, v, vc, D	op. 15	1907	,,
Sonata, pf, v		1905	,,

The quartet represents this composer at his best. It is in four movements, and varies in character from the pastoral, in the early stages of the work, to the dramatic in the finale. The 'cello plays an important rôle in each movement.

EDITOR.

DRAESEKE, FELIX AUGUST BERNHARD, 1835–1913, German composer.

Quintet, 2 v, vla, 2 vc, F	op. 77	Simrock, 1903.
Quartet, str, c mi	,, 27	Kistner, 1885.
Quartet, str, e mi	,, 35	,, 1887.
Quartet, str, c sharp mi	,, 66	R. Forberg, 1899.
Suite, 2 v, A	,, 87	Steingräber, 1912.
Quintet, pf, v, vla, vc, horn, B flat	,, 48	Kistner, 1889.
Sonata, pf, vc, D	,, 51	R. Forberg, 1892.
Sonata, pf, cl (or v), B flat	,, 38	Kistner, 1888.

Draeseke was a musician of an unusual type, whose works, even in his lifetime, received far fewer performances than they deserved in view of their high artistic value. His chamber works are fairly numerous, and he was at pains to include at least the clarinet and horn among the wind instruments employed. He even went so far as to write, in 1897, a quintet (still unpublished) in which he used Dr. Alfred Stelzner's invention, the violotta (something between viola and 'cello), an instrument which enjoyed no longer a life than some of its predecessors. (It is only necessary to recall the fate of Bach's invention, the viola pomposa.) It is a pity that Draeseke's two sonatas for viola alta and piano, written in 1892 and 1901–2 respectively, should have found no publisher.

THE STRING QUINTET may be considered his most important chamber work. Truly, Beethoven's later quartets are easy to understand, compared with this. In view of its masterly thematic and contrapuntal treatment the quintet arouses some admiration, but not much intellectual satisfaction, nor the affection that is born of understanding. The composer would have done well to supply a programme with each movement—for here it is clearly a question of programme music. Did he, one wonders, intend to describe his own artistic career, or the dissatisfaction that he was bound to feel at the little interest shown in his creative work outside Dresden? Or was this quintet designed as a musical expression of gloomy pessimism? Be that as it may, the music gives the idea of the fierce struggles of a sullen Titan. It makes great demands on the performers, particularly in regard to intonation. The gloomy introduction (langsam und düster) is brought into the finale—and that twice over. In the same finale (rasch und feurig) there also appears a theme from the first movement (twice as quick as the introduction). Both the outer movements are stamped with undeniable dramatic power; cheerfulness and lightheartedness venture but timidly to raise their heads. The scherzo seems to represent a kind of witches' sabbath. The hero is caught up in a wild orgy; then, in the slower trio, he is approached by pure love, but is past saving. This trio is a really charming inspiration. The slow movement is rhythmically interesting, but is, above all, imbued with the gloomy character of the whole work, which should be frequently played, though it is true that it calls for great mental efforts on the listeners' part.

THE FIRST STRING QUARTET, again, is a Sleeping Beauty which deserves a more speedy awakening. There is much vigour in the opening of the first movement, though it soon makes way for a more cantabile secondary theme. The graceful second subject is presently succeeded by a delicate passage of dialogue, in which 'cello and violin are chiefly concerned. The development is complex, and consequently not so well balanced in tone as the rest of the movement. There is a fine flow of melody in the principal section of the largo, to which the quicker middle portion presents a good contrast, with its note of unrest, produced mainly by figure-work. The minuet, in which, as in the first movement, this rhythm

is much favoured, has a powerful principal theme; the second is attractive, and full of tenderness and charm. The usual trio is replaced by an intermezzo, an exceptionally delicate and transparent piece of writing, in which the melody is given chiefly to the 'cello. Quite charming is the cleverly devised coda, after the repeat of the minuet. The last movement, C minor and major, is particularly effective, with its contrast between an element of passionate unrest and a broad, soothing melody—almost a chorale—which is jubilantly triumphant when it comes in the major. There is more in this finale than the scattered bits of fugue to attest the composer's mastery of form.

THE THIRD STRING QUARTET has serious claims to be considered the most important. It begins with an andantino elegiaco, which does actually express a peculiar sadness, though there are intervals of storm. In spite of the complexity of the part-writing, the movement sounds beautiful. The scherzo lives up to its title, allegro spumante, the slower trio forming a soothing contrast with its easy tunefulness. The adagio non tanto, which opens in G minor and ends in B flat, is a very expressive movement with a touch of melancholy. This is followed by a graceful intermezzo, with a rather quicker Ländler-like middle section, while the finale, allegro risoluto, is capricious, but has an attractive cantabile theme.

THE SUITE FOR TWO VIOLINS, op. 87, also deserves mention. The smaller works of acknowledged masters of composition are always interesting, but unfortunately it is not easy to feel enthusiastic about this one. Although the composer's intellectual skill is to be admired, it suffers from poverty of invention. The most approachable is the middle movement, a slow minuet in A, with a vigorous trio. The first movement, grave, has a beautiful secondary theme; the finale is mainly concerned with contrapuntal devices, but the opening of the grave reappears near the end. The suite presents some peculiar experiments in harmony. WILHELM ALTMANN.

DRAGOI, SABIN. *v.* ROUMANIAN COMPOSERS.

DRAGONETTI, DOMENICO, 1763–1846, famous contrabassist, resident in London for over half a century.

Although an orchestral player (he was said to have played for fifty-two years at the same desk with Lindley) Dragonetti was a great lover of chamber music, taking the 'cello part on his double-bass in quartets. His playing in the Onslow quintets convinced the composer that the second 'cello part could be played on the larger instrument with much better effect (*v.* ONSLOW).

Of his playing, a contemporary critic wrote: 'Although his instrument is a giant among violins, he has so conquered its unwieldiness, and destroyed its roughness, that in the middle of the thunder he creates, he can charm you by the exquisite softness of his bow.'

A touching episode of his last days is recorded. His comrades of the orchestra, knowing his love for chamber music, came to his rooms in his last days, and played to him the consolatory strains of some of his favourite quartets. EDITOR.

DRAKE-BROCKMAN, MAURICE, b. 1880, English composer.

	Composed	
Suite, str. quartet, E	1921	Senart, 1928.
Suite, pf, vc, D	1922	,, 1928.

The suite opens with a prelude (lento) in mixed 5/4 and 3/4 time, an atmospheric misty movement, the recapitulation being entirely in 3/4. This is followed by a rapid scherzo (D major), polyphonic in style, which requires very light handling; a slow movement follows, this is mournful and impassioned with a strenuous allegro middle section; the slow time is then restored, and the themes of the two sections are woven together, the theme of the allegro section appearing on the viola. The finale has a suggestion of the countryside, and is more 'in old style'. The greater part of it consists of a fugue on the main subject, led off by the viola.

The 'cello suite is in five short movements, the first four based on the same short phrase in various guises, with an independent theme which is used only as a coda to each. In the finale this coda becomes the main theme, and is treated fugally, with the first theme as counter-subject. The work, which is within the powers of competent amateurs, was played at a concert of the Society for Contemporary Music in 1922. EDITOR.

†DRESDEN, SEM, b. 1881, Dutch composer, director of the Amsterdam Conservatoire.

	Composed	
Quartet, str	1924	Senart.
Sonata, pf, vc		,,
Sonata, harp (or pf), fl	1918	,,

THE 'CELLO SONATA, the first of Dresden's published works, asserts his fondness for freedom in matters of rhythm by the direction 'avec une grande liberté de rythme et de mouvement'. The first two movements are both of a quiet, tranquil character, built up with the utmost economy of thematic material, some of which suggests the influence of folk-song. The 'cello part ranges over the whole gamut of the instrument, many of the effects being produced by the contrast of tone between the different registers. The finale (there are only three movements) is 'vif et impétueux', in accordance with the composer's own marking, but with a number of quiet passages interspersed. Broken chords in irregular grouping, with rapidly repeated single notes, add much to the agitation.

THE SONATA FOR FLUTE AND HARP (or piano) has somewhat the same tranquillity of character, but owes more to the influence of Debussy, in spite of some undeniably original thoughts. It was introduced to the public at the first festival of the Contemporary Music Centre at Salzburg, and shortly afterwards played at a concert given before the London section by Willem Pijper and Johan Feltkamp. The harp part, though thoroughly characteristic of the instrument, generally supplies little more than a light accompaniment to the tuneful flute part. The work is in three movements, in the second of which (très vif et léger) the folk-song influence again appears.

THE STRING QUARTET is in the classical four-movement form. The whole of the themes are based on fragments of two Dutch folk-songs, *Er was een sneeuwwit vogeltje* (There was a snow-white bird) and *Het daghet uyt den Oosten* (The dawn comes up in the east); and the composer states that the poetic basis of the entire work is based on the words of these songs. The first movement has an ostinato figure of four notes E, A, G, A:

in various positions and generally in quintuple rhythm, running right through it. Apart from its considerable artistic value, the work is an interesting study of harmonic, rhythmic, and instrumental methods.

HERBERT ANTCLIFFE.

DRESSLER, FRIEDRICH AUGUST, German composer.

Trio, pf, v, vc, A	op. 18	B. & B., *c.* 1890.
Sonata, pf, v, g mi	,, 10	,, 1877.

DRESSLER, RAPHAEL, 1784–1835, flautist to the Hanoverian court.

In 1820 he visited England and became bandmaster to the 10th Hussars. He composed over a hundred works, some of considerable merit: over sixty duets for two flutes, including opp. 3, 17, 36, and 42, all B. & H.; three quartets for fl, v, vla, and vc, opp. 10 (A), 30 (D), and 37 (C), all B. & H.; and trio concertante for three fl, op. 64 in D (Simrock).

H. M. FITZGIBBON.

DREYSCHOCK, (1) ALEXANDER, 1818–1869, Bohemian pianist.

Quartet, str, A	op. 105	Cranz, 1855.

Dreyschock was a great pianist and a composer of some note, though his work is somewhat dry.

(2) FELIX, 1860–1906, nephew of above.

Sonata, pf, v, d mi	B. & B., 1888.

†DROZDOV, A., contemporary Russian composer.

Sextet, pf, str — Mus. Sect. State Publ. Dept., 1922.

Drozdov began his career with the glittering group of composers of the new generation—Stravinsky, Gniessin, Miaskovsky, Prokoviev. His first works reveal the influence of the French impressionists in a somewhat coarsened and simplified form. Later he succumbed to the rather superficial influence of Scriabin. Drozdov has no very strong individuality, but is a very intellectual and mature composer, and his creative work is by no means wanting in taste. The majority of his compositions are for the piano (he himself is a fine pianist), one of the best being the piano sextet, written in the year of the Revolution, and to some extent reflecting the vague searchings of the Russian musical world of that period. In this distinguished example of contemporary Russian chamber style many pre-eminently German influences are perceptible, but they are skilfully transformed. It is almost the first instance in which a Russian composer has reacted to the music of Reger. In any case we have here a respite from Scriabin and the impressionists. This work is a masterly achievement and sounds splendidly on the instruments.

L. Sabaneiev.

†DSÉGUÉLÉNOK, Al., contemporary Russian composer.

Poème, pf, v, vc — op. 9 — Mus. Sect. State Publ. Dept., 1926.

DUBOIS, Théodore [Clément François Théodore], 1837–1924, French composer.

Dixtet (*Dixtuor*), 2 v, vla, vc, cb, fl, ob, cl, horn, fag, d mi	Heugel,	1909.
1st suite, 2 fl, ob, 2 cl, horn, 2 fag	,,	1898.
2nd suite, 2 fl, ob, 2 cl, horn, 2 fag	Leduc,	—
Quartet, str, E flat	Heugel,	1909.
Quintet, pf, v, ob (or cl or 2nd v), vla, vc, F	,,	1905.
Quartet, pf, v, vla, vc, a mi	,,	1907.
Trio, pf, v, vc, c mi	,,	1903.
Trio, pf, v, vc, E	,,	1911.
Sonata, pf, v, A	,,	1900.
Sonata, pf, vc	,,	1905.

Pougin, writing in 1878, speaks of him as 'one of the rising masters who seem destined to be the honour and mainstay of the younger French school', a promise which was hardly fulfilled.

The violin sonata was played by Ysaÿe and Pugno, and was a favourite of the former, though not a very serious work. It is, however, so effectively written for the violin, especially the andante quasi adagio, that it enjoys a greater measure of popularity among performers upon that instrument than is accounted for by its slender intrinsic merit.

Editor.

†DUCASSE, Roger [the name is sometimes written Roger-Ducasse], b. 1873, French composer, pupil of Fauré.

Quartet, str, d mi	Durand,	1909.
Quartet, pf, v, vla, vc, g mi	,,	1910.
2nd sonata, pf, v, E	,,	1918.
Allegro appassionato, pf, v	,,	1917.

Ducasse is a man of culture with solid musical gifts. Nurtured on Bach, the contours of his flexible contrapuntal writing are often very daring, the clashing of dissonant parts being carried to great lengths with much ingenuity. His melodies have a kind of natural tenderness with youthful touches, like a distant reflection from the eighteenth century. He is very sincere, and greatly concerned with the integrity of his art.

The string quartet is free in form, thick in texture, and difficult to play, but there is abundance of subtle and elegant invention.

The first movement of the piano quartet has an impetuously developed alternating ternary and binary rhythm of the sort beloved of the composer, while a second theme is reminiscent of Fauré. A coda follows, and the movement comes to an abrupt and powerful conclusion. The second movement, andantino ma scherzando, is a kind of fantasia on a single theme, with variations. The third is sombre and mysterious, and linked, by means of a prolonged low pedal with an impressive decrescendo, to the finale, in G major. Here the leading themes are combined with those of the preceding movements. This powerful movement, with its architectural strength and high musicianship, admirably balances the rest of the work.

Fauré's pupil, and, as it were, his spiritual son, Roger Ducasse has also a happy touch of Debussy's influence, though he is mainly a traditionalist and of strong and healthy nature.

His place is in the line of the French classics, but without relationship to the Franckist school.

Adolphe Piriou.

[There are many composers, Roger Ducasse among the number, whose inner significance his compatriots alone are able to grasp. I have tried to appreciate and understand his music, but without, I fear, much success.

Dr. Altmann, however, who writes in Berlin (*Handbuch*), gives a sympathetic recension of his quartet, and mentions that Ducasse pays homage to his teacher Fauré by using a motto-subject FAGRÉ. The U in the name appears, somewhat cryptically, to be replaced by G.

Editor.]

†DUCOUREAU, Madame M., contemporary French composer.

Trio, pf, v, vc, G — Rouart Lerolle.

The above is the only published chamber work by this composer, who directs at St.-Jean-de-Luz (Pyrenees) the Société Charles Bordes, and is a disciple of the Schola Cantorum. It is conceived in the cyclic form adopted by the pupils of César Franck, reference being made in each of the three movements to the initial themes. It is clearly written, without much complexity, well developed, and warm in expression. Prominence is given to the violin part.

Among her unpublished works is a *Rapsodie Basque* for piano and violin. H. WOOLLETT.

DUETS FOR STRINGS.

The following article treats sparingly of duets of a type which have not been considered of sufficient chamber musical importance for inclusion in the body of the Cyclopedia. They are mostly to be described as teaching material, especially the innumerable duets written for two violins unaccompanied, my own experience of which, since the early days of elementary practice, is very limited. Indeed, during the last fifty years I believe that with one exception I have not taken part in any duets but those of Spohr. To nothing that this great master has written do violinists owe such a deep debt of gratitude as for his contributions to duet literature. His opp. 39 and 67, selections from which were introduced at the 'Pops' by Joachim and his colleagues, are examples of Spohr at his best. The opening andante to the second duetto, op. 39, is one of the most remarkable known pieces of writing for two violins. It is written throughout in double stops, and the effect is that of a complete quartet of strings.

The 'exception' to which I alluded above refers to the duets published by Glière, a modern Russian composer, to which I have referred elsewhere.

Böhm, the teacher of Joachim, gave much attention to the study of duets for two violins, and Professor Grünwald, a fellow-student of Joachim's, relates that they were played incessantly until the pupils became 'thoroughly tired of them'.

Van der Straeten in his article writes on duets for two violins, with supplementary notes by W. Henley, the well-known violin expert, who is engaged on an encyclopaedia of the violin.

The remaining duets for two instruments neither of which is strictly harmonic are of far less importance, and are dealt with in a short addition to W. Henley's article.

This Cyclopedia does not set out to deal comprehensively with the vast mass of duets that have been published. A glance at *Fétis* will show how enormous was the number of duets for two flutes (to quote one type only) published during the eighteenth and early nineteenth centuries, when the flute was 'the gentleman's instrument'. A large number of duets for all combinations is given in *Altmann's Catalogue*, to which the reader is referred.

EDITOR.

The evolution of the instrumental duet is closely bound up with the history of the violin. Soon after the appearance of the latter, instrumental music began to break the fetters of vocal music, which imposed its forms and limitations upon it until the beginning of the seventeenth century, when the canzona, a term applied interchangeably with that of sonata, for instrumental compositions, generally of three movements, began to acquire a more instrumental physiognomy. As long as the polyphonic, contrapuntal style of the preceding centuries still predominated, these canzone were generally written in from two to six parts for violins and bass with an accompaniment for organ, harpsichord, or archlute. Towards the middle of the seventeenth century, when the sonata form began gradually to develop, sonatas were mostly written for two violins with a bass for the 'cello, sometimes with alternative or additional harpsichord or organ, and this combination remained in favour down to the beginning of the nineteenth century, and supplied an important part of the literature of instrumental music. Such sonatas were generally accompanied duets, the bass supplying the harmonic foundation. When the 'cello, however, took its share in the thematic material and figuration, the composition became a trio-sonata, and an additional bass for the organ or harpsichord was always added in that case.

Giuseppe Torelli (b. Verona middle of seventeenth cent.; d. 1708), who played an important part in the evolution of instrumental music, must apparently also be credited with having written the first unaccompanied duets for two concertante stringed instruments, viz. concertino per camera, op. 4, for violin and 'cello. This work, published *c.* 1690, is remarkable for the introduction of abstract movements into the chamber sonata style, the first of the twelve duets beginning with a preludio, the rest with a solemn introduction. His example was soon followed by Jacchini, Michelletti, Aldovrandini, Manfredini, and others who wrote concertini or concerti, as they called their chamber sonatas for the same combination, in which both musical expression and instrumental technique were considerably advanced. It was reserved, however, for Dr. Chr. PEPUSCH (*q.v.*) to write the first unaccompanied duets for two violins. Neither Corelli nor his pupils wrote unaccompanied duets, with the exception of Pietro Locatelli, who wrote six sonatas for two German flutes or two violins, op. 4, which rank with his best work.

The unaccompanied duet was further developed not only by violinist composers but also by masters of the classical school. As music was at that time chiefly cultivated in the homes of the people, where the violin and the flute were practised to a far greater extent than the 'cello, the unaccompanied duet became very popular, as it supplied a complete form of concerted music, even in the absence of any bass or keyboard instrument. Duets began consequently to appear in large numbers, but the majority of these merely reflected the general atmosphere of their time, without showing any new and distinctive features, and, although they pleased their contemporaries, they are of little interest to the present generation.

For those who feel inclined to explore this field, it may be useful to remember that the eighteenth century offers the spectacle of a gradual decadence of all arts into shallow conventionalism and artificiality, from the midst of which there arose the great and shining lights in the firmament of arts and literature, surrounded by stars of lesser magnitude. The rest was darkness. The duet for two violins was moulded for the most part in sonata form, in which the evolution of instrumental music found its principal means of outward expression. Its chief importance coincides, therefore, with that period which was concerned with the development of instrumental figuration and the freer movement of individual parts. When form and figuration had reached a certain stage of perfection, and harmony had entered upon its evolutionary career, the interest in the duet began to decline, and lessened still more when the intensive system of instrumental training began during the latter part of the nineteenth century, for the teacher who had to give his undivided attention to technical detail no longer found leisure to take up another instrument and play duets with his pupil, however instructive they might be. These reasons account for the fact that very few duets are written now by composers for the violin.

In order to arrive at a correct appreciation of existing duet literature we have to classify it under three periods:

First period: from the end of the seventeenth century to *c.* 1735. The style of this period is noble and dignified, and shows the influence of the church sonata. It found its expression rather in the concerto grosso and in the solo sonata than in the unaccompanied duet, which had only just made its appearance.

Second period: from about 1735 to the latter part of the eighteenth century, often erroneously referred to as the rococo period, which is strongly reflected in its music, elegant and full of homely humour, though at its best by no means devoid of deeper thought and feeling. For its graceful mood the duet supplied the means of adequate expression, and we see it appearing in rapidly increasing numbers towards the middle of the century. During the later decades of the eighteenth century the style degenerated into shallow formalism.

Third period: later eighteenth century and most of the nineteenth, including the height of the classical as well as the romantic period, which produced some of the rarest gems of duet literature. Parallel to the romantic school ran that of the Victorians. The works of this school are often pleasing and refined, even excellent in their way, but uninspired. These periods were, of course, not divided by rigid limits, and each survived well into the following period.

Duets for Two Violins (unaccompanied).

First Period, 1700–1750.

Pepusch; Locatelli; Leclair; Tessarini. *Vide* special articles.

The Delightfull Musical Companion, select duets for two German flutes or violins, by Hasse, &c. (John Walsh, *c.* 1750). The work is of importance, as it preserves some early eighteenth-century compositions which would otherwise have been entirely lost. Unfortunately it gives the composers' names only for a comparatively small number of pieces. Two sonatas, however, nos. 8 and 9, bear the name of Valentini, op. 14. This is no doubt the English flautist, Robert Valentine, who called himself 'Valentini of Rome'. The existence of these two sonatas seems to have been overlooked by modern biographers; they do not appear in the lists of his works given by Fétis and Eitner. Samuel Howard figures in the book with a number of airs in folk-tune character, and there are also airs by Dr. Maurice Green, Dr. Boyce, Lampe, Leonardo Vinci, and Handel, the latter as well as Hasse being represented by a number of pieces, but no sonatas.

Defesch, Willem. Six duets, op. 9 (*c.* 1735). Very pleasing compositions, showing still the influence of Corelli.

Bach, J. S. Wrote no original violin duets, all those that have appeared being arrangements from other works, such as: five duets from inventions (Artaria); fourteen duets from preludes, inventions, suites (ed. L. Schubert, Peters, 1869); Chaconne from fourth solo sonata (ed. F. Hermann, Kistner, 1887).

Second Period, 1750–1800.

Apollo's Collection (James Oswald, London, 1750), book I, twelve duet-sonatas by various masters. The composers' names appear only on the title-pages of the two books, but the great Rameau reveals himself unmistakably in the seventh duet, beginning with a movement, in G minor, entitled *Sommeil—Tendrement*, an exquisite impressionistic conception which stands out from all the rest. A second book of six sonatas appeared in 1755, mostly by the same authors. The second sonata, in II, apparently by Jomelli, begins with a fine 'Scocese' (Scottish melody), marked 'Largo cantabile', followed by an allegro ma comodo, likewise in the Scottish character. A delightful *Peasant's Dance*, *Musette—amoroso*, and *Hornpipe* in sonata 4 point to Rameau's work.

L'Abbé Le Fils (Joseph Barnabé de St. Sevin). *Premier Recueil d'Airs François et Italiens avec des Variations pour 2 Violons, 2 Pardessus, &c.* (*c.* 1750); *Deuxième Recueil* etc. for do. do. (1755). They are among the last works written for the pardessus de viole, and contain a large collection, partly the only record, of many delightful airs, very skilfully arranged for the instruments, a careful selection of which should justify republication.

Giardini, Felice, *vide* special article.

Taillart l'aîné. *Recueil d'airs de Pièces Françaises et Italiennes*, for flutes, violins, pardessus de viole, &c. A work similar to that by L'Abbé

Fils, by which many interesting and fine old tunes have been preserved.

Gerard, James. *6 sonatas or duets for two German flutes or violins* (John Johnstone, *c.* 1765). They are simple and pleasing, no. 6 revealing something of the folk-song element.

Pugnani, Gaëtano, *vide* special article.

N., Steffano, called Spadino, a Dalmatian nobleman. Six sonatas for two violins, op. 6 (Amsterdam, Hummel, *c.* 1770). Excellent short sonatas in which the folk-song element prevails. A Polacca, a form which had become very popular at that time, appears as last movement in no. 3.

San Raffaelle, Benevento Count di. Six duets (Bremner, 1770); melodious two-movement sonatas of medium difficulty, mostly ending with a minuet.

Barthélemon, François Hippolyte. Six duets, op. 4 (1770), contain some good canonical and fugal writing as well as attractive melody.

Shield, William. Six duettos, five for two violins and one for two flutes, op. 1 (W. Napier, *c.* 1775); melodious two-movement sonatas for amateurs of moderate ability; six duets, op. 2 (*c.* 1780), evidently intended for young pupils.

Vachon, Pierre, *vide* special article.

Bach, John Christian. Two sets of six duets each (Longman, Luckey & Co., *c.* 1775); tuneful, but in a style which had already become obsolete. The second set is the more important, both technically and musically.

Boccherini, Luigi. Three duets, op. 5 (Edition Peters, ed. by H. Sitt); four duets, op. 10 (1775). They show more life, variety, and individuality than J. Chr. Bach's duets, but the conventional element of the time is here also much in evidence. The second violin part is often a mere accompaniment.

Lorenziti, Antonio l'aîné. Six duos, op. 8 E (Md. Heina, *c.* 1775), of medium difficulty, well and effectively written, although somewhat lacking in variety of figuration and bowing; six easy duets for beginners (Bellmann & Th., 1883).

Noferi, Giov. Battista. Six sonatas or duets, op. 4 (Welcker; Longman & Co.; B. Hummel, The Hague, *c.* 1775); six sonatas, op. 14, three for two violins, three for violin and 'cello (The Hague, B. Hummel, *c.* 1775). Melodious and very effective, concerted violin writing of medium difficulty.

Gaviniés, Pierre. *Six sonates à deux violons* (1780); excellent part-writing; they contain some fine spirited movements, worthy of republication.

Stamitz, Carl. Six duos (Amsterdam, J. Schmidt, *c.* 1780); six easy duets for two flutes or two violins (London, G. Gardom); these works, showing the influence of Haydn, are interesting, and deserve the attention of modern players.

Campagnoli; Pleyel, *vide* special articles.

Borghi, Luigi. Six divertimenti, op. III^{a} (1780); melodious, and fairly easy to moderate.

Vanhal, Johann. Six duets, op. 28 (London, S. Babb, *c.* 1780); eight duos, op. 56 (Schott); three duos faciles, op. 57; three do., op. 60 (Simrock); six progressive duos (Schott). They are the works of an excellent composer, who was overshadowed by the giants of his time. Most of these duets are easy, some fairly easy to moderate.

Fiorillo, Federigo, *vide* special article.

Kennis, Guillaume G., a Belgian musician; six duos, op. 12 (*c.* 1785), creditable works of medium difficulty.

Fodor, Joseph. Six duos, *VIIe œuvre de duos* (Imbault, *c.* 1790); six duos, op. 21; four duets, op. 30. Good concerted writing; he uses higher positions freely, and the passages offer much variety in bowing. His easy, flowing melody is naïve, fresh and joyful, and sometimes betrays his Hungarian origin.

Viotti, Giovanni Battista, *vide* special article.

Nicholls, George. Twenty-five easy divertimentos for two German flutes or violins.

Fabbri, S. Andrù. Six duets, op. 2 (author, *c.* 1793). They are well written, melodious, and of moderate difficulty.

Haydn, Joseph. Nine sets of violin duets, but apparently only the following, viz. op. 58, six duos (publ. without opus number by Witting, 1868, and Hug, 1891); op. 99, three duets (Litolff, 1891; Peters, 1913); op. 102, six duos after the quartets, op. 17 (Litolff, 1884; Bellm. & T., 1885), have been republished, the others being six concertante duets, op. 46 (Hamilton, *c.* 1810); duetto I in F maj., op. 52 (on margin: 'Hummel, éd. de l'œuvre 92'), evidently the first of a set of duets, with a charming *Romanza* in B flat, and an arrangement of the familiar gipsy rondo; three *grands duos dialogués*, op. 88 (F, G, B flat; Vienna, Witzendorf); three duos, op. 91 (André); three duos each, opp. 102, 103, 105 (Bonn, Simrock). Many of the duets are Haydn's own arrangements from other works of his.

Bruni, Antonio Bartolommeo, *vide* special article.

Cartier, Jean-Baptiste. Three *grands duos dialogués et concertans*, op. 14, fourth book of duos (*c.* 1800), moderately difficult, with use of higher positions; some nice subjects, quite French in character, but figuration lacks variety.

Hoffmeister, Franz Anton. Six *duos concertants* (new ed. André, 1870); apparently not republished: three duos, op. 9 (Hofmeister), three duos, op. 10 (Simrock), three duos, op. 11 (Hofmeister), three duos, op. 17 (Amsterdam, Steup). All were published between 1795 and 1805.

Mozart, Wolfgang Amadeus. Has written only one original violin duet in C major, K. 487. It consists of an andante, allegro, minuet and trio, short and very simple movements, which appear as separate movements also in the twelve pieces for two basset horns (Paris, Imbault). It has been argued that they might have been written originally for the latter instruments, as the last three bars of the second violin part of the minuet are in the bass clef. But second violin parts in the eighteenth century were often written an octave below the actual pitch. The parallel passage in the first part of the minuet, moreover, appears in the G clef, and it is evident that the sudden downward jump of two octaves which the actual pitch of the bass clef would imply in the latter part could not be intended. The two parts of the whole sonata are, moreover, thoroughly violinistic.

Krommer, Franz, *vide* special article.

Romberg, Andreas. Three duos, op. 4, three duos, op. 18 (both works ed. by K. Nowotny, Litolff, 1910); three duos, op. 56, have apparently not been republished. All are well written and melodious.

Third Period: (a) From 1800 *to c.* 1850.

Haensel, Peter. Three duos, op. 23 (Simrock, *c.* 1800); three duos, op. 24 (Simrock; Schott); three duos, op. 38 (Artaria). They are fully developed sonatas of medium difficulty. The work of this gifted pupil of Haydn is virile and masterly.

Lacroix. Three duos each, opp. 15, 16, 18, 20 (B. & H., *c.* 1800); three duos, op. 21 (Hanover, Bachmann). Good concerted part-writing of medium difficulty.

Ries, Ferdinand. Op. 5, three *duos concertants* (see *Altmann*). Nine books of progressive duets, edited by Ernst Heim, have been republished by Augener. Easy to medium difficult, masterly part-writing, very melodious.

Dussek, J. L. Six *duos faciles et agréables*, op. 58 (Hanover, Bachmann, *c.* 1800).

Schwindl, Frederic. Twelve duets, op. 3 (*c.* 1800); twelve easy duets, op. 4. Well written, melodious; they rank among the best of their class and time.

Jarnovick (Giornovichi), G. M. Six duos each, opp. 16, 24 (André); three duos, liv. 3 (Hamburg, Böhme). Not without merit, but the second violin often has mere accompaniment.

Baillot, Pierre. Three duos, op. 8 (André, Peters); three duos, op. 16 (Schott, republ. 1868). Melodious and variety of bowings, but often poor part-writing.

Rolla, Alessandro. Three *duos concertants*, op. 3 (ed. A. Schulz, Litolff, 1880); three easy duets (Ricordi, 1841); five duettini, op. posth. (Ricordi, 1843). He is a brilliant writer in conventional style, and a favourite with some amateurs.

Rode, Pierre. Three sets of violin duets, of which only one apparently survived, viz. six duos, op. 18, books 1 & 2, republished between 1876 and 1891 by Fr. Scharnack, Litolff, and Hug; book 1 was published 1859 by André as three duos, op. 1.

Kreutzer, Rodolphe. Six duos, op. 11, liv. 1, 2; *duos concertants*, publ. by André; three op. A (1858); three op. B (1861); three op. C (?); six, seven cah. (1858); three *grands duos concertants* (Hug, 1861). Kreutzer shows greater variety of figuration than Rode. The duets are mostly of medium difficulty.

Maurer, Ludwig Wm. Three *duos concertants*, op. 61 (Peters, *c.* 1820). He is best known by the famous *concertante* for four violins.

Mayseder, Joseph. Three *duos concertants*, opp. 30, 31, 32 (ed. Nowotny; Cranz, 1901); duo in G, published by Ricordi with a German title (early nineteenth century). They exhibit some excellent and effective violin writing of a kind once immensely popular.

Reicha, Anton. Three duos, op. 45; three grand duos, op. 53 (B. & H., *c.* 1830).

Präger, Heinrich Aloys. Three duos each, opp. 16, 25 (B. & H., ed. Nowotny, Schlesinger, 1888); three *duos concertants* (Peters).

Jansa, Leopold. Ten books of duets, from easy to medium (see *Altmann*); they are refined and attractive, and of instructive value.

Spohr, Louis. Three *duos concertants*, op. 3; two do., op. 9; three *grands duos*, op. 39; three *duos concertants*, op. 67, and three grand duos, opp. 148, 150, 153, dedicated to the brothers Alfred and Henry Holmes, the two celebrated English violinists who toured as duet players in Germany in 1856–7. For particulars about editions of the above duets see *Altmann*.

The duets by Spohr belong to the greatest classics in violin literature, especially the last three. For loftiness of thought and wealth of technical and harmonic devices they stand unapproached, even to this day, among all works of their kind.

Holmes, Henry. Two *grands duos concertants*. The second duo, op. 9 (Peters, 1858), abounds in brilliant passages of the virtuoso type.

Dancla, Jean-Bapt. Charles. Wrote twenty sets of duets from easy to medium difficult. They are generally pleasing and useful for teaching purposes. For particulars see *Altmann*.

Hering, Carl. Nine sets of duets, well written and useful for teaching. See *Altmann*.

Molique, Bernard. *Duos concertants* (ed. H. Dessauer; Schott, 1906); three *grands duos*, op. 3 (*c.* 1860). The form and writing is masterly, and frequent use of double stopping produces a very full effect. They show nobility of thought but lack originality.

Beriot, Charles de. Six duos arranged from his op. 17 by A. Schulz, liv. 1, 2, 3 (Berlin, Schlesinger); three *duos concertants*, op. 57; twelve elementary duets, op. 87; six *duos caractéristiques*, op. 113, on themes from Prince Youssoupoff's Spanish ballet (Schott, 1863). This is really a brilliant solo, of medium difficulty, with accompaniment of a second violin. The numerous editions of opp. 57 and 87 are given by *Altmann*.

Kalliwoda, Johann Wenceslaus. Particulars of eleven books of his duos are given by *Altmann*. A collection of twelve selected duets has been published by Boosey & Co. They are melodious, fairly easy, and excellent for beginners.

Mazas, Jacques Féréol. Sixteen sets of duets. For particulars *vide Altmann*.

Hauptmann, Moritz. Op. 2, *deux duos concertants* (Peters, 1887–90); op. 16, *trois duos* (Cranz, 1847); op. 17, three *grands duos* (André, 1848). Masterly in style, and pleasing but uninspired.

Alard, Delphin. Op. 22, four elementary duets; op. 23, four *duos faciles*; op. 27, three *duos brillants* (ed. E. Heim, Augener). Well written and melodious; excellent for teaching.

Schön, Moritz. Nine sets of duets, with particulars in *Altmann*. Excellent violin writing, mostly for teaching purposes.

Ries, Hubert. Three duos, op. 5 (B. & H.); two *duos concertants*, op. 8 (Peters). Three do., op. 8 (Berlin, Trautwein); three duos, op. 17 (B. & B.); three duets, op. 21 (André, 1852); duets from violin tutor (ed. Sitt, Hofmeister, 1915).

Gebauer, Mich. Jos. Twelve easy duets, op. 10 (ed. H. Dessauer, Schott, 1912); standard works for teaching on account of their technical and melodious interest.

(*b*) *From c.* 1850 *to c.* 1925.

Ahn Carse, A. von. Easy duets (Augener-Schott); belong to the best works for young students.

Bastl, K. Op. 26, *trois duos concertants* (Urbánek, 1908).

Barnbeck, Fr. Duos no. 1 (C) (Stuttgart, Allgemeine Musikhandlung, 1842).

Bernards, Jos. Op. 38, instructive and progressive duets (Aix-la-Chapelle, Jacobi, 1889); op. 54, sonata, first pos. (Jacobi, 1891).

Bloch, Jos. Op. 33, *duos faciles* (Rozsnyai, 1905).

Blumenthal, Jos. v. Thirteen books of duets for beginners; particulars in *Altmann*.

David, Ferdinand. Sixty duos (B. & H.). *Vide* Haydn.

Decker, Wm. Op. 164, thirty little duets (Ruckmich, 1911).

Dont, Jakob. Op. 26, easy duets (Leuckart, 1883); duos, opp. 43 and 48 (Brockhaus, 1881). Dont's work is justly esteemed for its musical as well as its educational value.

Dorn, Ignaz. Op. 3, duet (Cranz, 1860).

Draeseke, Felix. Op. 86, suite (Steingräber, 1909); op. 87, suite (Steingräber, 1912). Excellent writing but uninspired.

Fuchs, Robert. Op. 55, twenty duets (U. E., 1908).

Glière, R. Op. 49, twelve duos (Jürgenson, 1911). Original and melodious writer of the Young Russian School.

Gurlitt, Cornelius. Op. 150, three easy progressive duets (Schott, 1911). Attractive, and well adapted for teaching purposes.

Halven, Ernst. Op. 11, three suites in canon form (Litolff, 1889).

Hellmesberger, Geo., junr. Op. 4, duets (Cranz, 1849).

Henley, William. Op. 8, twelve easy duets. (B. & H., 1893).

Henning, Karl. Op. 36, three duets (Merseburger, 1864).

Hering, Karl. Nine sets of duets, mostly elementary; *vide Altmann.*

Hermann, Friedrich. Two grand duets, op. 14 (André, 1860).

Hoffmeister, E. Collection of favourite duets (Ruckmich, 1911).

Hofmann, Rich. Duets from the works of old masters for beginners (Kistner, 1895); duets for pupils, op. 109 (Zimmermann, 1900); thirty short pieces, op. 113, first pos. (Augener); fourteen instructive pieces, op. 114 (Augener).

Köhler, Henry. Three duos, opp. 148, 156; three *duos très faciles* (B. & H.).

Köhler, Pius. Four sets of duets, chiefly for teaching; *vide Altmann.*

Meerts, L. J. Four sonatinas (Leuckart).

Moór, Emanuel. Suite (Schirmer, 1922).

Norman, Ludwig. Suite in canon form, op. 27 (Stockholm, Bagge, 1877).

Patha, Jan. Easy duets (Urbánek, 1883–5).

Pirlinger, Jos. Eighteen easy duets (Haslinger).

Prume, François. Op. 18, *duo concertant*; op. 19, *2e duo de concert à la champêtre* (both Schott, 1874).

Reger, Max. Op. 131^b, three duos; canons and fugues in the olden style (Simrock, 1914).

Schoen, Maurice. Ten books of duets, chiefly for teaching; *vide Altmann.* Eighteen short duets; six easy duets, all first pos. (Augener).

Schröder, Hermann. Op. 25, five easy duets in form of a suite, first pos. (Rühle, 1898).

Schubert, Ferd. Fifty easy duets (J. Schuberth & Co., 1871).

Sechter, Simon. Fugues and canons (ed. Nowotny, Cranz, 1890). One of the greatest contrapuntists of the nineteenth century, and master of many famous musicians.

Sherwood, Percy. Suite, op. 23 (Leukart, 1913).

Sitt, Hans. Five books of easy and instructive duets; *vide Altmann.*

Speier, W. Three duets, op. 4; two duets, op. 15 (both André, 1863); duo, op. 73 (Henkel, 1864).

Wichtl, Georg. Seven books of duets; *vide Altmann.*

Willner, Artur. Two sonatas, op. 23 (Madrigal-V., 1920).

Wohlfart, Franz. Five books of easy and instructive duets; *vide Altmann.*

E. VAN DER STRAETEN.

SUPPLEMENTARY NOTES.

André, Anton. Op. 27, two duets. Very good—Mozart-Romberg style.

Aubert, Jacques. Suites and sonatas. These new editions are worth consideration—probably the finest of the old French.

Baillot, Pierre. Op. 16. Rather dry, and after the style of Viotti, slightly advanced.

Bériot, de. Brilliant in every way, but the passage-work is trivial, and there is a lamentable absence of established form.

Blumenthal, Jos. Large collection of duets, all of the instructive order, musically of slight value.

Bruni. Excellent classic type. Easy and instructive.

Dancla, Charles. These are all exceedingly pretty—and rather serviceable for teachers, but cannot be termed of the first order, owing to indifferent adherence to form. Op. 108 contains the most advanced, and the only ones worth the attention of the cultivated amateur.

Draeseke, F. Rather interesting musically, but not ideal two-part writing for violins.

Ehrhardt. All easy and instructive.

Eichberg, J. Very good; brilliant and effective.

Fiorillo, F. Here is something for the amateur to take delight in. The form is splendid, there is no triviality, it has no difficulties, it is sheer good writing, and is well-sounding.

Fontaine. Very brilliant for period. As good as any of the better-known Germans.

Fuchs, Robert. Also very interesting and well worth playing.

Halwen, E. Op. 11. Amateurs will appreciate these.

Hauptmann, M. These are all excellent, though not ideal. They reveal occasional emptiness (possibly in the attempt to avoid technical difficulties).

Hellmesberger, Geo. Op. 4 (Cranz). Another excellent work allowed to 'drop out'.

Henley, William. Op. 8 (B. & H.). Easy, and brief movements containing some interesting imitative work.

Hermann, Fr. Op. 14. Very fine indeed.

Hoffmeister. Interesting up to a certain point, but decidedly out of date.

Holmes, H. Op. 9. These are really magnificent. They are, unfortunately, out of print. They are fit to rank with Spohr, by whose style he was impressed, though he did not copy, like Molique.

Kalliwoda. These are generally brilliant, but the form is not really very good; there is no depth or inspiration, and the accompaniment is always very sketchy; there is never any contrapuntal writing, though he was a sound musician. These may be termed 'orchestral duets'.

Kayser. These are all instructive. The best is op. 52.

Kreutzer. The resuscitation of these duets has been worth while.

Krommer. Krommer's duets are more brilliant than any others of his period, but he indulges too freely in continuous semiquaver passages in the accompaniment. The slow movements are always lacking in depth, and the second violin never has an equal chance with the first.

Küffner, J. These duets are of the French overture type.

Leonard. The duo de concert is rather difficult, but decidedly effective. The style resembles that of de Bériot, but they are rather more musical.

Maurer. Op. 61. These are real duets, and are splendid. The final rondos are particularly exhilarating, as they are always based on Russian dances.

Loder, J. D. Three duets (Ashdown). These are pleasant, but made their reputation by using popular melodies for the rondos.

Mayseder. Opp. 30-2. These are violin solo-sonatas (very brilliant) with a poor second violin part. They seem rather trivial to the modern mind, though excellent in form.

Mazas. All these are good in their way, but again

the form is frequently defective, and upsets the musician. Not one is in true sonata form; they are really a series of pieces for two violins. However, they sound well, and please the uncritical.

Molique. These are perfect in every way, and next to Spohr's are technically the most advanced of any. The only criticism to be made is their absolute plagiarism of Spohr. The writer thinks that this was due rather to an idea of homage to that composer than to lack of creative power. The parts are beautifully distributed, and each movement has a rhythmic variety which is captivating.

Moór, E. His suite certainly shows musicianship but no inspiration, and not much idea of effect.

Pleyel. Though easy, these contain delightful imitative work, and equally delightful is their adherence to perfect form. On this account advanced players can enjoy playing them when they indulge in an easy-going half-hour.

Praeger, H. Op. 16. These, too, are excellent. They are fairly advanced technically.

Prume. His duets are very brilliant and full-sounding. They are rather in the style of de Bériot. Musically they are not very satisfying.

Reger. These are very clever, of course, but there is no emotional appeal in them. The combination is too small for his genius.

Ries, Hubert. All these (Augener) are used extensively by teachers.

Rode. These duets are perfect examples of that period.

Rolla. Technically Rolla goes a little higher than his contemporaries, but musically a little lower. The duets are not in sonata form, but merely movements, alternately slow and in rondo style.

Romberg, A. Next to Spohr's these may be considered the most musical duets. They are not difficult, but perfect in every way. The thematic material is always attractive, and there is never anything commonplace.

Sauret. Adagio and rondo. Magnificent.

Spohr. The composer's favourites (which he most frequently played in public with his pupils) were op. 39, E♭ and E major, and op. 67, D and G minor. In these he reached his zenith. They are the most advanced.

Viotti. Viotti's duets have furnished splendid models for later and better composers. In their day they were greatly and deservedly appreciated, but to the present-day violinist there is a lack of real melodic beauty and perfect part-writing; there is, too, a certain monotony in the rhythmic ideas.

W. Henley.

Duets for other Combinations.

(1) *Violin and Viola*. These are not very numerous, many of those which do exist being arrangements. Among the more important are works by Haensel, the two Haydns, Fiorillo, and Pleyel. There are also two by Mozart, K 423, K 424.

(2) *Violin and 'Cello*. The same may be said of this combination, but in our own times several works of greater interest have been written, notably Ravel's sonata, suite by Em. Moór, works by Glière, Hans Eisler, and Fr. Hermann. Some have also been written by Haydn, Pleyel, Viotti, and Boccherini.

(3) *Violin and Double-Bass*. Of this grotesque combination there is at least one example, a *Sonata fantastica* by C. San Pietro.

(4) Duets for *Two Violas* are few and offer little interest, but those for:

(5) *Two 'Cellos or 'Cello and Double-Bass* have more importance. Among these may be noted a suite for two 'cellos by J. R. Horton, and one by Em. Moór, both modern; also works by Glière, Jul. Klengel, M. Boukinik, and A. Romberg.

(6) *Duets for a string and a wind instrument* are few, but there is a sonata by Mozart, K 292, for bassoon and 'cello.

(7) *Duets for wind instruments* are many, but are mostly for two flutes, two clarinets, two oboes, &c. These, which consist mainly of teaching music or popular music of the type already described, offer little real interest as a rule. There is, however, an allegro and minuet for two flutes by Beethoven, who also wrote three duets for clarinet and bassoon.

In recent times a few works of interest have been written, notably two sonatas by Francis Poulenc for two clarinets, and clarinet and bassoon; also two sonatas by Ch. Kœchlin for two flutes.

†DUKAS, Paul, b. 1865, French composer.

Dukas has published no chamber music as yet, but is engaged on the composition of a violin sonata.

†DULAURENS, A., French composer.

Suite (*Pastoral*), pf, v, b mi	op. 7	Eschig (Demets), *c.* 1903.

†DUMAS, Louis, b. 1877, French composer.

1st quartet, str.		Poulalion, 1907.
Sonata, pf, v, d mi	op. 8	Leduc, 1906.

†DUNHILL, Thomas Frederick, b. 1877, English composer.

	op.	Composed	
Phantasy, str. quartet	47	1906	J. B. Cramer & Co., 1923.
Pleasantries, 2 v, vla	63	1923	J. B. Cramer & Co., 1925.
Quintet, pf, v, vc, cl, horn, E flat	3	1898	Rudall Carte, 1913.
Quartet, pf, v, vla, vc, b mi	16	1903	Novello, 1908.
Phantasy-trio, pf, v, vla, E flat	36	1911	S. & B., 1912.
Sonata, pf, v, d mi	27	1908	,, 1911.
Sonata, pf, v, F	50	1916–17	Augener, 1920.
Variations on an original theme, pf, vc, G	18	*c.* 1905	Curwen (Goodwin & Tabb).

Throughout his career, Dunhill's services to chamber music have been manifold, and of so much value that he holds a unique position among British composers in relation to it. Not only has he written a number of chamber works distinguished by their pure style, attractively fresh ideas, and admirable suitability for their purpose, but he has also brought to performance a great number of new works by other composers. The Dunhill chamber concerts, initiated by him in 1907, were carried on for twelve years in London. and had as their principal object the production or second performance of new works by contemporary British composers. Furthermore, Dunhill has written a book on chamber music for students (Macmillan & Co., 1913), which has become a standard work on the subject. In his ensemble classes and composition lessons at the R.C.M., in his lectures, in his adjudication at competitions, and in his own performances as an ensemble player, he has consistently inculcated the best and highest principles of the art. It is therefore appropriate that he should have been the first recipient of the Cobbett Chamber Music Medal (1924).

Though a chamber music expert, Dunhill is not exclusively a chamber musician. His all-round abilities enable him to write with success in almost every form of composition. His chamber works have come at intervals among compositions of other kinds. As those which are published constitute a good proportion of his output, they may be considered typical of the whole.

THE QUINTET, op. 3, was composed while Dunhill was still a student at the R.C.M. It opens with a theme and variations; the second movement is a graceful and rather formal allegretto, combining the functions of a lyrical movement with a minuet and trio, whilst the finale cleverly unites the characteristics of a scherzo with glimpses of a gigue. The quintet shows certain traces of immature workmanship:—e.g. an occasional loose knitting of the instrumental parts and an over-carefulness to demonstrate harmonic progressions that are already perfectly understandable. In the main, however, the music goes through with melodious good sense, simple but very effective devices, and an easy command of charming tone effects.

THE QUARTET, op. 16, won the Lesley Alexander Prize. Here the music is still tinged with Brahmsian influence, but otherwise shows its composer as mature. The craftsmanship is clear and firm, the material equally grateful to play or hear.

In the opening allegro, pensively emotional in character, the charming themes are continuously to the fore, and unfold themselves naturally. The second movement (adagio non troppo) touches deeper springs of emotion, engaging sympathetic interest throughout. It is a real cantabile movement, where the instruments sing forth in their sweetest tones. The scherzo and trio are full of good tunes. The finale, with an introduction (molto lento e serioso) and a broadly treated allegro, is the most closely packed, intellectual section of the work, and solves with mellow wisdom the philosophic doubts postulated in the first movement.

THE VARIATIONS, op. 18, are in genuine concertante style; yet they are almost as useful for solo purposes as the later set of *Capricious Variations* for 'cello and orchestra (alternatively available in an arrangement with piano), since both are written with scrupulous regard for the true nature of the 'cello and its tonal balance with the piano part.

THE PHANTASY TRIO, op. 36, forming one of the series of Cobbett commissions, has proved itself most useful and welcome. Designed as a short continuous work, it nevertheless passes through phrases that imply the larger scope of cyclic form. Here, as in kindred examples, Dunhill shows the British gift for effecting a happy compromise between differing administrative systems. Other points to note in the phantasy are the admirable adaptation of the material to the medium employed, the delicacy of the colouring, and the great discretion with which the piano part is written.

Both the phantasy string quartet, op. 47, and the *Pleasantries*, op. 63, are short works of moderate difficulty. The phantasy is pleasant and unaffected, tinged with the idiom of folk-song, and modal in colour. The *Pleasantries* are neatly described by their name, and certainly constitute very useful additions to the limited repertory for two violins and viola.

Of the two sonatas for violin and piano it may be said that they stand a little apart from the rest of Dunhill's chamber music, since he seems to have found in this flexible, sensitive medium, the freest expression for his most intimate ideas.

THE FIRST SONATA, in D minor, starts with dramatic energy. The slow movement, a finely designed romanza, is practically in aria form, but with a central episode that represents the scherzo of the sonata. The finale (allegro, vivace assai) is an extended movement, in which the tunes go with a good swinging lilt. To any one acquainted with the music of Arne or the hornpipe tunes of the eighteenth century, it will be interesting to see how their typically English spirit shines again in the work of this modern composer.

THE SECOND SONATA in F, op. 50, is the most mature of all Dunhill's chamber works. Here the opening allegro swings along as easily as ever, but the links are tightened, the harmonic scheme is fuller. Beyond the direction 'adagio lamentoso' no clue is given to the poetic idea of the second movement in B flat minor;—yet the strong though controlled intensity of utterance, the hint of funeral drums in the accompanying figure, and the heroic qualities of the movement as a whole, link it with the Great War. A paean-like finale makes a brilliant close.

Dunhill's chamber music is English through and through. It has, however, more affinity with the English national songs of the seventeenth and eighteenth centuries than with the folk-song idiom. Every work shows his marked instinct towards orderly and complete mental processes, and lucidity in exposition distinguishes both his musical and literary styles. His melodic invention, felicity in statement, and logic in design are notable. From the academic point of view it may be objected that the main substance of almost every movement is carried forward on predominantly melodic lines, but from the performer's and listener's point of view, the fresh abundance of his melodies is a constant source of delight.

For harmonic texture Dunhill keeps generally to the diatonic style, enriched by normal discords and chromaticisms. This comparative simplicity is united, however, to a gift for getting the fullest value out of every progression, and a happy knack for dovetailed rhythms and unexpected twists of melody. He has also a fondness for setting the simple and compound counterparts of a time value against each other for the first and second subjects of a work, and he usually develops his closest intellectual efforts in his finales. Above all, he is considerate and equitable towards his instruments, scores for their best natural tone qualities, and writes for their actual combinations of sound. In string-players' parlance, his effects all 'come off'. His chamber music is as companionable, healthy, and English as the South Downs on a sunny day.

MARION M. SCOTT.

† DUPÉRIER, JEAN, b. 1896, Swiss composer.

Sonate poétique, pf, v, a mi — op. 7 — Rouart, 1909.

An ambitious effort of the composer to sing the story of his poetic longings in sonata form. It is French in sentiment.

† DUPIN, PAUL, b. 1865, French composer.

1st suite (*Poèmes*) str. quartet — Senart, 1922.
Trio, pf, v, vc, C — Durand, 1916.
Sonata, pf, v, a mi — ,, 1912.

and some smaller works including *Pièces dialoguées, Esquisses instrumentales d'après six peintres français. I. Watteau* . . . fl, vc, harp (Durand), and a *Pastorale* for piano and string quartet.

Paul Dupin is a self-taught musician who left his situation in a factory, at the age of 21, in order to devote himself to the study of composition.

His is an original and somewhat antique spirit. If his writing sometimes lacks clarity, it is individual and interesting by reason of its sincerity and a polyphony which is all his own. Dupin has no objection to harmonic audacities, but he does not employ them of set purpose. With him expression is the main consideration, and form is subservient to it.

The *Pastorale* is one of a series of works inspired by Romain Rolland's *Jean Christophe*. It has the sub-title of *Sabine, No. 1 (Dans le Jardinet)*. In this work one recognizes the composer's tendencies towards the description of states of feeling. It is full of freshness, with, as it were, bells sounding through it, and with free dissonances à la Debussy. The form is that of a simple Lied.

The *Poèmes* spring from the same fount of inspiration:—the first number is the *Tale of Uncle Gottfried*. In the episodes which follow we have *La Mort, Lamentation, Révolte*, and *Apaisement*. The second number is entitled *Bienvenue au Petit*.

THE VIOLIN SONATA is an essay in 'absolute' music. But Dupin is always carried away by the needs of expression, and, whatever may be the musical value of the work, one cannot help regretting that the abundance of his ideas is not always in accordance with purity of form. One seems always to be listening to a prolonged improvization. But there are bursts of emotion, and the strength of its appeal is undoubted.

The plan of the work is but distantly related to the traditional sonata form, the violin having short phrases against persistent figures on the piano. The third movement is a canon in free contrapuntal style, and the key of C dominates it almost throughout (Ex. 1). The preceding themes appear in new guise in the finale, the work being in cyclic form. The introduction,

Ex. 1.

Ronde gaiamente e presto alquanto.

largo religioso, opens with the first theme of the sonata in 6/4. This is then taken up in the allegro in 6/8, and ingeniously developed (Ex. 2*a*, 2*b*).

THE TRIO is more heavily scored, the construction is less clear, and the counterpoint is wayward and lacking in elegance. There is also abuse of contorted and somewhat unnatural figures, in thirds and in contrary motion. Nevertheless, as a whole, the work has force and life.

In the first movement the tempo alternates frequently between animato and lento. One passage, 'lent et religieux', in chords on the strings, has originality, and brings a sense of clarity and calm into the midst of the agitation. The melody of the violin, in the second movement, is very fine, but the very free counterpoints by which it is surrounded and sub-

Ex. 2 a.

Ex. 2 b.

merged produce a sense of restlessness. And the finale, vigorous, agitated, and very heavily scored, plunges us once more into incessant strife. H. WOOLLETT.

[Dupin's unconventionalism is perhaps explained by the fact that he only took up the study of theory in ripe manhood.]

DUPONT, AUGUSTE, 1827–1890, Belgian pianist.

Quartet, str, E flat	op. 38	Costallat.
Trio, pf, v, vc, g mi	„ 33	B. & H., 1860.
Sonata, pf, v, E	„ 14	„ 1852.

Articles on Dupont are to be found in *Riemann*, *Grove*, *Fétis*, and *Pougin*.

DUPONT, GABRIEL, 1878–1914, French composer.

Poème, pf, 2 v, vla, vc, c mi Heugel, 1911.

Gabriel Dupont studied at the Paris Conservatoire and at the age of twenty won the second Grand Prix de Rome. A doughty worker throughout the vicissitudes of a long continued disease of the lungs, his music was considerably affected by his long and tragical fight with death.

The remarkable *Poème*, dedicated to his teacher, Widor, is a masterly work, in which all the composer's individual characteristics are to be found. It is in three movements.

The first, in C minor (sombre et douleureux), begins first with a kind of tragic exclamation. This to play an important part in the evolution of the work, and leads at once to the exposition (animé), in which we meet the dramatic first subject, in C minor (in the recapitulation this is in E flat minor, these being the two essential keys of the work), and the introductory theme, which here assumes an appealing character. The second subject (un peu plus lent) is in three sections, the first, much overlaid, is in the nature of a touching prayer. This appears at first in D minor, and is founded on a melodic variant of the first theme. The second section comes with an outburst in full chords on the piano; then, calming down, it leads, by means of a short cadence on the second violin, to the third phrase, which is more agitated, and ends, with a great crescendo, on a cadence in A minor, the starting-point of the development. This last, extremely complex, falls into two main divisions, in which the different themes are varied and combined with ever new resources, now dramatic, now impassioned in feeling. At the reprise the first theme bursts forth, at full power, in C minor. The recapitulation then proceeds, at first, much as did the exposition. The last phrase of the second subject is here a melodic transformation of the tragic exclamation of the introduction, and leads to a terminal development[1] founded on the beginning of the second subject, sung by the muted first violin to arpeggios on the piano, in A. This passes in turn to the other instruments, and modulates to a point of repose in B flat. Here the animato returns, the strings come in gradually, and the first theme reappears on the violins above the second part of the same theme on viola and 'cello, with clean-cut chords ('comme des rafales') on the piano. Then, after an altered version of the beginning of the second subject, modulating and growing ever more agitated, the second part of the first subject (together with the tragic exclamation of the introduction) bursts forth, very broad, and with sorrowful expression. This is thrice interrupted by the short incisive introductory figure of the first theme, in close canon on the strings. This imposing movement ends with a peroration in C minor delivered at full power, and swift and breathless in its course; it is founded on the last phrase of the second subject and the opening tragic exclamation.

The second movement (clair et calme) is a simple Lied[1] in three sections. The first, in C major, very pure and peaceful in character, is announced by the quartet, over a long pedal C on the piano. A transition to the gloomy and mournful key of E flat minor leads to the second section; here another theme (doux et expressif) is announced by piano and viola, followed by a second more animated element, in A minor. The theme in E flat minor reappears on piano and viola, then the second element on first violin, but this time in C minor. The Lied-phrase is re-stated, as at the beginning by the quartet, but here on a dominant pedal (G) on the piano, with a quicker-moving accompaniment, and, after a glimpse of the key of E flat minor, it ends in C. A movement of the highest beauty.

The finale (joyeux et ensoleillé) is in C major. It expresses the 'fullness of joy', and is, in turn, joyous, warmly expressive, breathless and impassioned, gentle and dreamy, or animated and incisive, concluding with a most impressive terminal development, which at first suggests the 'melancholy of happiness, ineffably sweet and dreamy'. Then the music quickens and takes on a 'gloomy and mournful' tinge. Beneath the popular theme of the refrain[1] in diminution, which forms the basis of a tremolando accompaniment on the strings, the piano gives out, as a series of answers in close canon, the principal subject of the first movement. The answers become more frequent, the figure of the strings more agitated, while on the piano is heard the principal subject of the first movement in the bass, combined with the second constituent of the refrain in augmentation in the treble. The writing becomes closer and closer; finally there comes an outburst on the strings of this same second constituent, much broader and delivered with great power. It is again the 'fullness of joy'. Meanwhile the piano gives out the principal subject of the first movement, still at full power, with the tragic exclamation of the introduction inverted in the treble. The movement quickens, and the light breaks through with the return of the second element of the refrain, in melodic form, supported by arpeggios and full chords on the piano. The ending is truly 'joyous and sunny', and after a reminiscence of the first couplet[1] the work concludes.

This *Poème* shows daring originality in the superposition of parts, suggesting already the effects of the 'polytonality' so much in fashion to-day, and often so ill-employed. The work has great dramatic force, and an inspiration and passion which are always pure and wholesome. It shows care for solid architecture, yet is free and unfettered.

By Dupont's premature death the French school lost a star of the first magnitude.

ADOLPHE PIRIOU.

DUPORT, JEAN LOUIS, 1749–1819, famous French 'cellist.

Modern republication:

Sonata, vc, fig. bass (pf), C (K. Schroeder) Kistner, 1877.

For other works see *Fétis*.

Considered as the originator of modern 'cello technique. He was taught by his brother J. P., 'Duport aîné', J. L. being generally known as 'the younger Duport'. His instrument was his father's fine Stradivarius, which Franchomme bought later for 25,000 fr. (£1000), an enormous sum for those days.

It was either with J. L. Duport or his brother that Beethoven played the two sonatas, op. 5, at the Prussian court in 1796.

[1] See Foreword, art. BEETHOVEN.

DUPRÉ, Marcel, b. 1886, French composer, pianist, and organist.

Sonata, pf, v, G   op. 5   Leduc, 1920.

Dupré gained the Premier Prix du Conservatoire in 1905, and, like our own Harold Samuel, has since devoted himself largely to the study of Bach. At the conclusion of one of his Bach recitals he was addressed as follows by Widor: 'Nous regrettons tous, mon cher Dupré, l'absence parmi nous du principal intéressé, le grand Jean-Sébastien Bach lui-même. Soyez assuré que, s'il était ici, il vous serrerait dans les bras et vous presserait sur son cœur!'

Editor.

DUPUIS, Albert, b. 1877, Belgian composer, pupil of Vincent d'Indy.

Quartet, pf, v, vla, vc, D   Senart.
Sonata, pf, v, d mi   ,, 1922.

Dupuis, who is director of the Verviers Conservatoire, is an accomplished musician. His chamber music shows technical mastery coupled with inspiration. Has written other chamber music.

DUREY, Louis Edmond, b. 1888, French composer, professor at the Schola Cantorum.

Images à Crusoé, med. voice, str. quartet, fl, cl, celesta   op. 11   Chester.
Two quartets, str   Édition de la Sirène (Paris).

Durey was the senior member of the long since dissolved group of 'Les Six'. Though the disparity in age was to some extent offset by the circumstance that he did not begin to study music until he was twenty-two, there can be little doubt that, as in the case of Honegger, a more mature outlook was the main incentive to secession. Another was furnished by his more retiring disposition, which was ill suited to the flamboyant tactics of the group, and has since led to his abandoning Parisian musico-politics to live quietly in the South of France. The first of his quartets belongs to the days of 1917, when he was with, but scarcely of, the group; the second to 1922, after he had not only left it in the spirit, but officially terminated his association with it. The first, despite an aggressively bitonal opening and other modernisms, suggests in its melodic outline that, like Debussy and Ravel before him—composers by whom he was then influenced—he was fired with the ambition to write quartets comparable with those of Borodin. The harmonic audacities do not conceal the essential suavity of the musical thought, to which they sometimes appear extraneous and always secondary. In the second quartet the advance made towards maturity is shown by a greater preoccupation with true, if dissonant, polyphony, as in the following:

which is taken from the third and final movement. The middle section is a scherzo based upon the finale of Haydn's well-known piano sonata in D major. There is about the whole work a faint suggestion of 'neo-classicism', but the respective dates scarcely justify the suggestion that this is related to the movement in the same direction of Stravinsky, for whom, however, the composer professes a deep admiration. It was Durey who declared that *Le Sacre du Printemps* would come to stand for this generation as the B minor Mass stands for that of Bach. But this admiration nowhere expresses itself in a predilection for dynamic effect. Durey's own tendency is manifestly towards a more gentle and reticent mode of utterance in the idiom of to-day.

Edwin Evans.

DUSCH, Alex. v., German composer.

Quintet, 2 v, vla, 2 vc, a mi   op. 3   Heckel, 1903.
Trio, pf, v, vc, d mi   ,, 6   ,, 1910.
Sonata, pf, v, E flat   ,, 7   R. &. E, 1913.

†**DUSSEK**, Jan Ladislav, 1761–1812, Bohemian pianist and composer.

The following list is taken from B. & H.'s catalogue for 1900:

Three quartets, str, G, B flat, E flat   op. 60.
Quintet, pf, v, vla, vc, cb (ad lib.), f mi   ,, 41.
Quartet, pf, v, vla, vc, E flat   ,, 56.

Three trios, pf, v, vc, C, B flat, e mi	op. 2.
Three trios, pf, v, vc, F, B flat, D	„ 24.
Three trios, pf, v, vc, B flat, C, D	„ 31.
Two trios, pf, v, vc, E flat, B flat	„ 34.
Trio, pf, v, vc, E flat	„ 37.
Trio, pf, fl, vc, C	„ 21.
Trio, pf, fl, vc, F	„ 65.

Riemann mentions eighty violin sonatas. Op. 20 contains six sonatinas, and opp. 28, 46, each six sonatas (not difficult). The remainder in B. & H.'s list are:

Opp. 4, 8, 12, 13, 14, 17, 18, 25 (v or fl), 51 (v or fl), three sonatas each for violin and piano.

Opp. 5, 69, two sonatas each. Op. 69 contains the most famous sonatas, those in B flat and G.

Grand sonata, op. 36.

Op. 7 contains three, op. 19 six sonatas for flute and piano.

Posthumous works are:

Two trios, pf, v, vc, E flat, B flat.
Three „ „ „ „

The above list is not complete. French, English, and German publishers have adopted different systems of opus-numbering. The reader is referred to *Grove* for further information.

Dussek was originally a student of theology, music being a later study. He was a great virtuoso on the piano as well as a composer. His chamber music, like his other work, is very unequal. Side by side with compositions of artistic worth and noble character there are many of a very trivial nature, and in juxtaposition with excellently finished and original periods one finds superficial meaningless phrases and shallow melodic passages, in which the composer's virtuosity, bent only on effect, breaks out and gains the upper hand at the expense of artistic value.

The Form of Dussek's Chamber Works. These mostly consist of an introduction, an allegro, a slow movement, and an animated finale. The first and last are usually in the same key, the middle movement in a related key, though sometimes in one more remote—an unusual departure in his time.

The first movements always show the same structure: exposition, development, and recapitulation in the principal key. Dussek's first and second subjects are very sharply contrasted, which was not the case with his predecessors; furthermore, the second subject is prepared for in a striking manner. His developments likewise show a decided advance, for, unlike most of his contemporaries, he was not satisfied merely to repeat the first part with modulatory modifications, but elaborated both subjects. Contrary to contemporary usage, his developments do not begin in the dominant, but in other keys; these are sometimes related to the tonic, sometimes remote. Dussek's daring harmonic innovations are to be ascribed to his highly romantic nature, revealed in his harmonic and dynamic differentiation, and frequent employment of chromatics and dramatic climaxes. He has a penchant for modulation to the key a semitone above or below. Often he does not develop the whole theme, but only parts of it; this may be traced to the influence of Clementi, who, in his turn, followed Haydn and Beethoven; at all times, however, Dussek is at pains to exhaust all developmental possibilities.

The finales are mostly very effective, and are usually in rondo or sonata form. In the rondo form the repetitions of the themes are generally in variation, while the intermediate sections (or couplets) either contain brilliant passage work or are founded on fragments of the theme; daring harmonic treatment is often to be found in them. Dussek endeavoured to express manifold moods within the limits of this form, and to give them new and interesting features by constant differentiation. The finales are not very profound, and obviously only aim at mere effectiveness, but they are always carefully worked out and rich in interesting details.

The Trio, op. 65, may be singled out as one of Dussek's best chamber works; it is a peculiar and very intellectual composition. The attention is at once arrested by the first movement with its lovely melodious first subject, and the colourful and varied harmonic scheme of the development is noticed with pleasure. The second movement, a larghetto, also has fine melody, but is less satisfactory with regard to rhythm. The final rondo is worthy of high praise; the first four bars are based on the harmony of the dominant seventh, an interesting feature which had not in his time become hackneyed. Flute and 'cello are mostly obbligato, and are sometimes entrusted with difficult passages.

The two Violin Sonatas, op. 69, are also very characteristic of Dussek's manner of composition. In the first, monotony of rhythm is frequent; further, the composer is frequently tempted to enlarge too much on one idea, artistic quality being thus subordinated to outward effect. Yet there are many interesting and fascinating artistic details which reconcile the hearer to his occasional superficialities.

The second sonata is worthy of greater appreciation. It is far more spirited, and ranks higher both technically and artistically. Interesting turns of harmony are continually to be met with, and the entire work is so fresh and natural, and so full of youthful fire and adventurous spirit, as speedily to captivate the hearer.

Here, as in his other works, is reflected the dual personality of Dussek, at once the true artist and the mere virtuoso; at times both combine with good results, but the virtuoso often overshadows the artist. Dussek's manner of composition and his feeling are decidedly romantic, and this is especially shown in his proclivity for daring harmonic turns, modulations into keys remote from one another, frequent use of chromatic passing notes and sudden, surprising changes of key. With regard to rhythm he is less inventive, but he was one of the first to make frequent use of syncopation. He sought to perfect sonata form by means of sharply contrasted principal subjects and by increasing the developmental possibilities. In spite of some weaknesses, Dussek is to be regarded as an important link in the development of chamber music.

RUDOLF FELBER.

[Dussek's music was frequently played at the old Philharmonic Society's concerts. His piano quintet was included in one of the programmes of the first season (1813).

The sonatas, op. 69, referred to by Dr. Felber, are interesting examples of the divergence of opinion which may exist among musicians with regard to the merits of a piece of music. In the days of the 'Pops' the audience loved and applauded the first, in B flat, so much that it was repeated in fourteen subsequent concerts. The last news I had of it from the publishers (Augener & Co.) was that it was 'out of print'! Yet the romantic side of Dussek's nature, of which Dr. Felber speaks, is eloquently represented in this sonata—not only in the adagio, which has for sub-title *Les soupirs*, but also in the impassioned lament which forms the minor section of the finale. The latter begins and ends in a mood of jollity which recalls Haydn in his most humorous mood. This sonata is a small work, but a most charming one, and well worth reviving by concert-givers. Haydn, by the way, spoke of Dussek, in a letter to his father, as an 'eminent musician' with 'remarkable talents'.

EDITOR.]

DUTCH CHAMBER MUSIC.

From the time when the great Netherlands school of composers declined at the end of the sixteenth century, Holland was for a couple of centuries concerned so largely with the struggle for existence, that little time or energy was available for the serious study of music. For this reason, musicians have been chiefly concerned with church music or the music of the home. Those who desired a wider scope sought and found it abroad, in England, Germany, France, and Italy. Thus, much of the best music written by Hollanders during the last three centuries has been for small combinations, for string and wind quartets, trios, and duos. Until Holland's new era, beginning in 1813, nearly the whole of this music was either of an ephemeral character, or was written by men who preferred to be known as Germans, Englishmen, or Frenchmen. With the second generation of the DAHMEN family (*q.v.*) and their contemporaries, however, came new life and almost the beginnings of a new national feeling in music. For another century it was still struggling with foreign (especially German) influences, and although much meritorious music was written, there was little that differed sufficiently from the general run of German capellmeister music to be worth repeating to-day. Even now the number of chamber works of high standing is but small, for, with the emancipation from German influence, the broadening of interest and the apparent beginnings of a really national school, the tendency has been towards works on a larger scale. And, even more than in other lands, most of the chamber music written has remained unpublished.

Allowing for strong individualities and for all the experiments that are being made, there are two quite distinct divisions among Dutch chamber composers: those who follow the German classical masters, and those who look to France for a lead. The latter are generally, but not always, the younger men, and also the more eclectic. The best chamber works of Dirk Schäfer on the one side, and those of Sigtenhorst Meyer, Ruyneman, Dresden, Pijper, Zagwijn, and Voormolen on the other, are such as may be included in any repertory with honour to the composers as well as to the performers. In both groups there has been a real reversion to and emulation of the glories of the Old Netherlands School, particularly in choral and chamber music, accompanied, in the latter case, by a ready and careful experimentalism that has resulted in such works as Sigtenhorst Meyer's programmatic string quartet, and Ruyneman's *Hieroglyphics* for two flutes, two mandolines, guitar, piano, harp, celesta, and cup-bells.

If in the matter of composition not much is to be said as regards performance and cultivation, it is easy to speak with certainty of the strength and utility of many and varied activities. In proportion to its population, Holland has been well in advance of most other countries in its devotion to the performance of chamber music. This refers less to the type of performance which seeks publicity than to the more intimate and distinctive music-making of the home. The Dutch people, though essentially musical, are also extremely conservative. Consequently the study of chamber music has been chiefly confined to the classics, and in the libraries and in the programmes of both public and private performers the names of Haydn, Mozart, and Beethoven are the most frequent. It is this spirit that has kept alive the fine musical feeling which constantly surprises those who first come into touch with the social life of the Dutch middle classes, particularly the trading classes. Yet it is almost entirely spontaneous, for, apart from the concerts, which only a few of them attend, and which are often given in unsuitable halls, there is little help or encouragement. The schools attended by the children of these classes are, in fact, somewhat backward in teaching both the practice and the appreciation of music.

Chamber music is not, however, neglected in the music schools, and there is a number of excellent professional Quartets, Sextets, &c., which give concerts and recitals in such central places as the Concertgebouw in Amsterdam, Diligentia in The Hague, the various halls in Utrecht, Haarlem, 's Hertogenbosch, and even sometimes in the great Kursaal at Scheveningen. Like the private performances, these are largely classical and almost entirely foreign in the choice of works, though from time to time a modern native work creeps in. Much is done by private enterprise, in too many cases on the initiative of the composers themselves. Yet a tribute must be paid to the work, particularly (but by no means entirely) in the presentation of works of standing and popularity, of such combinations as the Dutch String Quartet, the Hague String Quartet and Sextet, and others of less note all over the country. They wisely combine much that is written in a familiar style with a little of the less easily comprehended modern work, for the latter often entails a sacrifice both of personal popularity and pecuniary gain. The Dutch people are very critical, but, as they are mostly self-educated in the appreciation of chamber music, their lack of understanding often leads them to condemn works which do not conform to the older methods and standards. That they are beginning to appreciate music for the smaller combinations, not specifically written as chamber music, is perhaps the best omen for the future. The country has now both composers and executants of the highest order, and is slowly rising to its opportunities of supporting and encouraging its leaders in artistic matters. And all this activity seems to be but the beginning of an era of fine music of all kinds, in which chamber music will not take the lowest place. HERBERT ANTCLIFFE.

DUTCH PERFORMING ORGANIZATIONS.

(*a*) QUARTETS.

AMSTERDAM STRING QUARTET. Formed (1912) from members of the Concertgebouw Orchestra in Amsterdam. Original members: Louis Zimmerman, Johan Herbschleb, Herman Meerloo, Gerrard Hekking. Hekking was later replaced by Fritz Gaillard, and he in turn by Marix Loevensohn. Meerloo was succeeded first by Ferd. Hellman, who in turn was replaced by De Vreese, who is also a gifted composer. Present personnel:—Louis Zimmerman, Johan Herbschleb, Godefroy de Vreese, Marix Loevensohn.

DUTCH STRING QUARTET. Originally formed in 1911. War-time conditions disturbed its work for several years, and in 1922 it was reconstructed with the original members—Herman Leydensdorff, Julius Röntgen, jr., Bram Mendes, and Thomas Canivez. Since then it has visited various countries in Europe, and, besides giving very fine interpretations of the classics, has introduced many new works. The Quartet, it is claimed, is the only one in Holland the members of which devote themselves entirely to the playing of chamber music.

HAAGSCH (*or* THE HAGUE) STRING QUARTET. Founded in 1917, the members being Sam Swaap, Adolphe Poth, Jan Devert, and Ch. van Isterdael, all of whom are leading members of the Residentie Orchestra.

The Quartet has given concerts in all the principal European centres, and its members have received distinctions from the French, Belgian, and Roumanian governments for their work on behalf of the music of those countries. Educational concerts are given, alone and in conjunction with the Hollandsch Sextet, in connexion with the Volks Universiteit at The Hague. On Nov. 5, 1924, the Quartet gave its 250th concert.

HAAGSCHE TOONKUNST QUARTET. Formed at The Hague in 1901, and continued until 1913. Henry Hack, H. Voerman, Bart Verhallen, Ch. van Isterdael.

HOLLANDSCHE STRIJKKWARTET (*v.* Dutch String Quartet).

ROBERT QUARTET. Willem Robert, senr., Jan Tak, Willem Robert, junr., Th. C. de Maaré.

This quartet existed from 1896 to 1903, and gave the first performance in Holland of César Franck's Quartet.

(*b*) TRIOS.

FRENKEL TRIO. Formed in 1925. Paul Frenkel, Sam Swaap, Ch. van Isterdael. Gives subscription concerts in The Hague, and has travelled to various European countries. Has also done much recording for the gramophone.

ROTTERDAM TRIO (*v.* Wolff-Verhey).

WOLFF-VERHEY (*or* ROTTERDAM) TRIO, 1900–1914 (dissolved).

(*c*) MISCELLANEOUS.

HOLLANDSCH SEXTET. Founded in 1917, by Dirk Fock, the well-known conductor and pianist, and D. van Emmerik, principal oboist in the Residentie Orchestra. With them were associated Bram Best (fl), Anton Witt (cl), C. van den Berg (horn), and C. J. van Heyst (fag). There have been several changes of personnel, the present members being: Jan Poolman (fl), Jaap Stotyn (ob), Anton Witt (cl), Piet Veenstra (horn), Jaques Poons (fag), and Paul Frenkel (piano). All the wind players are principals in the Residentie Orchestra.

The performances are of the highest standard, and the programmes eclectic.

Thanks to a subsidy from the municipality of The Hague, the Sextet is able, alone and in association with the Haagsch String Quartet, to give educational concerts in the Volks-Universiteit and other institutions. These concerts are followed with close attention and keen appreciation by the crowded working-class audiences for which they are intended.

CONCERTGEBOUW SEXTET. Founded in Amsterdam, in 1909, by members of the Concertgebouw Orchestra: Joh. de Veer (pf), N. Klasen (fl), G. Blanchard (ob), P. Swager (cl), J. S. de Groen (fag), Hans Tak (horn). De Veer was succeeded in 1910 by Evert Cornelis, who continued till 1923, when Jaap Spaanderman took his place, while in 1922 Willem Brohm became the clarinettist. Concerts have been given by the Sextet in all the towns of Holland, but not abroad. The repertory is a very wide one, including new works by Dutch and foreign composers.

HOLLANDSCHE VEREENIGING VAN OUDE INSTRUMENTEN (*v.* Société Hollandaise d'Instruments de Musique Anciens).

ISTERDAEL, Charles van (b. in Belgium, 1878), has for many years been principal 'cellist in the Residentie Orchestra at The Hague, and a leader in all that pertains to chamber music in that city. From 1914 to 1918 he organized a long series of chamber concerts, at which works of all kinds from duets to sextets, gathered from all periods from the sixteenth to the twentieth centuries, were presented. To his example and initiative many of the very large number of excellent chamber music organizations in Holland owe their existence.

MAATSCHAPPIJ TOT BEVOORDERING DER TOONKUNST (*v.* Chamber Music Soirées; Hollandsch Sextet; Conservatoire Quartet, &c.).

SOCIÉTÉ HOLLANDAISE D'INSTRUMENTS DE MUSIQUE ANCIENS, LA. Formed in The Hague (1918) with the special purpose of studying ancient music and playing it on the original instruments. The instruments used were the property of the late Dr. D. F. Scheerleur, and are lent by the Scheerleur Museum for this purpose. A number of concerts have been given, and many lectures on old music supplied with illustrations. Hans Goemans (clavecin), Sam Swaap (quinton), Adolphe Poth (viola da braccio), Jean Devert (viola d'amore), Ch. van Isterdael (viola da gamba).

DÜTSCHKE, HANS, German composer.

Sonata, pf, v, F	op. 22	E. Hecht, 1898.

DUVERNOY, ALPHONSE, 1842–1907, French pianist.

Quartet, str, c mi	op. 46	Durand, 1899.
Serenade, pf, 2 v, vla, vc, cb, trpt		Heugel, —
Trio, pf, v, vc, e mi		Leduc, —
Sonata, pf, v, G	„ 23	Fromont (*c.* 1870).
Sonata, pf, v,	„ 51	Heugel, 1905.
Duet, pf, vc	„ 30	Hamelle.

Duvernoy won the Prix Chartier for services rendered to chamber music. In 1869 he founded a chamber music society with a professional string Quartet.

DVOŘÁK, ANTONIN, 1841–1904, Bohemian composer.

				Composed	
Sextet	str	A	op. 48	1878	Simrock, 1879.
Quintet	2 v, vla, vc, cb	G	„ 77 (orig. 18)	1875	„ 1888.
Quintet	2 v, 2 vla, vc	E flat	op. 97	1893	Simrock, 1894.
Quartet	str	a mi	„ 16	1874	B. & B., 1894.
Quartet	str	d mi	„ 34	1877	Schlesinger, 1880.
Quartet	str	E flat	„ 51	1878	Simrock & U.E., 1910.
Quartet	str	C	„ 61	1881	„ „ 1912.
Quartet	str	E	„ 80	1876	Simrock, 1888.
Quartet	str	F	„ 96	1893	„ 1909.
Quartet	str	A flat	„ 105	1895	„ 1896.
Quartet	str	G	„ 106	„	„ „
Ten Love Songs (*The Cypresses*).	str. quartet		„ 8	1865	Hudební Matice, 1888.
Terzetto	2 v, vla	C	„ 74	—	Simrock, 1887.
Quintet	pf, 2 v, vla, vc	A	„ 81	1887	Simrock & U.E., 1909.
Quartet	pf, v, vla, vc	D	„ 23	1875	Schlesinger, 1880.
Quartet	pf, v, vla, vc	E flat	„ 87	1889	Simrock, 1890.
Bagatelles	pf (or harm), 2 v, vc		„ 47		„ 1880.
Trio	pf, v, vc	B flat	„ 21	1875	Schlesinger, 1880.
Trio	pf, v, vc	g mi	„ 26	1876	B. & B., 1879.
Trio	pf, v, vc	f mi	„ 65	1883	Simrock & U.E., 1913.
Trio (*Dumky*)	pf, v, vc		„ 90	1890–91	„ „ 1911.
Sonata	pf, v	F	„ 57		„ „ 1912.
Sonatina	pf, v (or vc)	G	„ 100		„ „ 1908.

Besides the above, Dvořák wrote a rondo for 'cello and piano, op. 94 (U.E.), and seven early works, including five string quartets, a string and a piano quintet, which have remained unpublished.

Antonin Dvořák, together with Bedřich Smetana, was one of the joint creators of the modern, and consciously national, school of Czech music, also one of the most gifted and individual composers of the nineteenth century.

He began to compose directly he had finished his studies at the Organ School in Prague (1859), but until 1873 he was very little known, even in his own country. It was in this year, while Dvořák was still employed as a viola player in the orchestra of the National Theatre at Prague, that the public first showed some interest in him, and by the end of the 'seventies he began to be heard of abroad, largely by the help of Brahms, who, recognizing his rare talent, recommended his works to the firm of Simrock, and remained his friend to the last. In 1884 Dvořák first went to England in order to conduct some of his works at the chief musical festivals there, and became famous in a day. He returned to Great Britain on several occasions, and several of his masterpieces were composed expressly for the English musical festivals. From 1892 to 1895 he was director of the National Conservatorium of Music in New York, where he won fresh laurels. On his return to Bohemia he became professor of composition at the Prague Conservatorium, and director of this institution from 1901.

Dvořák was one of those great creative artists who live, feel, and think in music. Music was his life-blood, his whole inner existence; and only in music could he fully express himself. Thus he created spontaneously, without profound and systematic reflection. His inspiration sprang direct from intuitive sources, and although on occasion he could be the highly cultivated musician, he rarely permitted the dominance of intellect to guide him. In his admirable versatility Dvořák succeeded in handling every branch of musical art, and in each department he left works of permanent value. Nevertheless, his innately musical nature—as genial, spontaneous, and direct as that of Haydn or Schubert—displayed itself most completely where he was able to reveal it in freedom, through the medium of legitimate and logical musical form, to which he was highly sensitive. In short, he was at his best in absolute music, unburdened by any programme, and, above all, in chamber music. This branch yielded some of the finest blossoms of his art, flowering in beauty and characteristic fragrance. In absolute music Dvořák's fancy broke out in fresh melodic ideas, in wonderfully coloured harmony and elemental rhythms. Here was the most suitable soil for the cultivation of the quality in which he had few rivals in his day: his gift of purely instrumental ideas, from which issued his feeling for beautiful instrumental effects, produced with the greatest simplicity and most natural use of his resources. His chamber music differs from his symphonic style as widely as a modest, deeply intimate utterance differs from a vehement and sweeping gesture. It has won him innumerable friends, perhaps because it is quickly assimilated and has been perseveringly propagated, but more especially because it directly reflects the lofty simplicity of his inmost feelings and ideas, expressed in some of the most charming musical imagery known to the world's chamber music lovers.

Dvořák's chamber works, including those in MS., amount to exactly thirty. They extend throughout the whole of his artistic career, from his first opus, in 1861, to op. 106, in 1896. The largest group consists of works for combinations of strings only, the majority of these being string quartets, in which Dvořák—himself a violinist—delighted to reveal his most intimate soul-experiences. He composed thirteen string quartets, a terzetto, three quintets, and one sextet. Equally important is the group of compositions for strings and piano, including two quintets, two quartets, four trios, and two sonatas. Finally, in the category of chamber music must be placed the second serenade, for wind instruments. This method of dividing Dvořák's chamber music into three main groups affords the best possible survey of his whole development.

I. Works for Strings only.

When Dvořák began to make his name known as a composer, first in his own country and shortly afterwards abroad, he had already long years of eventful development behind him. Starting from classical tradition as the germ of his whole creative existence, his talent, his nature, and his artistic methods were all rooted in classic soil. In youth he came almost immediately into close touch with the German romantics, especially Beethoven and Schubert, who both strongly influenced him, and in many respects guided the whole of his further artistic evolution. His first compositions obviously originated under the influence of these two great models, as may be seen from his two earliest chamber works: the string quintet (with two violas) in A minor, op. 1 (1861), and the string quartet in A major, op. 2 (1862). These are the works of an invention not as yet wholly independent, and evidently still struggling with the plastic sonata form. But with all their romantic, youthful freshness there is also the promise of a serious talent, both as regards ideas and workmanship. The love of (classical) romanticism suddenly gave place, however, to a strong admiration for the great neo-romantics, Wagner and Liszt. Dvořák now experienced a violent mental crisis. The dominance of these two masters, both as regards expression and form, altered his outlook and made his work less natural and more obscure. Two of his chamber works seem like offerings to this passing agitation: the two string quartets dating from 1870. Of these, the one in D major, in four movements, is interesting because the melody of the Slovak national hymn *Hej Slovane* is used in the scherzo. The quartet in E minor is in one movement only, and Dvořák afterwards arranged the slow middle section as the *Nocturne* for the string quintet published by Bote & Bock as op. 40. An immeasurable advance, both in freedom of expression and clarity of form, is noticeable in the two quartets belonging to the year 1873. Here again, the one in F minor is in four movements, and the other in A minor in one only. Both have remained unpublished and unperformed, except for the extended slow movement from the former, of which Dvořák made use in the romance for violin with orchestral accompaniment, op. 11.

By this time Dvořák had left his neo-romantic fervour behind him. It had not been altogether unprofitable, for it strengthened his powers of expression both in harmony and sonority. Nevertheless it was a wrong road, in which a Czech artist of Dvořák's disposition was unlikely to go permanently astray. This was the time at which Bedřich Smetana—himself an enthusiastic but highly critical admirer of Liszt and Wagner—had begun to build up a new school of Czech music—Czech in spirit, subject-matter, and expression. Dvořák realized the necessity of following in his steps in order to find his own personality.

Simultaneously with the return to the legitimate paths of cyclic classical form, a further logical change took place in his principles. This is first shown in the string quartet, op. 16 (1874), which was also the first of Dvořák's chamber works to be published. The sudden change was not effected without some sacrifice. The quartet is fresh in conception, and its ideas are expressed in a noble lyricism; but the anxious endeavour to adhere both in form and matter to a severe classical design obviously cramps the composer's inspiration, and hinders the free flow of his individual utterance. Incomparably more glowing and independent is the quintet in G, for two violins, viola, 'cello, and double-bass, which, dating at the earliest from the first half of 1875, was originally numbered op. 18, and afterwards altered by the Berlin publisher Simrock, in 1888, wrongly and against Dvořák's wish, to op. 77. The style of the first and last of the four movements which make up this work is light, and resembles that of an operatic overture, but the scherzo captivates the hearer with its characteristic rhythm and the originality of its ideas; while the poco andante already shows the depth of spirit to be found in the more beautiful of Dvořák's slow movements.

THE STRING QUARTET IN E, op. 80, written in 1876, heads a series of particularly important string quartets; this work was also chronologically misplaced when, years later, Simrock brought it out as op. 80. This quartet, by the weight of its subject-matter, the beauty of its harmony, its polished form, and the clarity of its thematic working, shows how docile and accomplished a disciple of Beethoven Dvořák had already become. The maturity of the quartet in E is of course more intelligible when we reflect that it was begun just before the fine *Stabat Mater*. The work also seems to hint at the time when the happiness of Dvořák's home life was clouded over by the loss of his child. Its prevailing mood is one of gentle melancholy, not a little due to the fact that, although ostensibly in the major, it moves for the most part in the minor. For instance, the second subject of the first movement, though it is enlivened by the intermittent pizzicato quavers of the viola and 'cello (a distinctive mannerism of Dvořák's instrumentation), betrays a purely Slavonic tender sadness; again, in the same movement the true Dvořák oscillates in parallel major keys, by which he succeeds in colouring the mood of the whole. The slow movement is written in the tender tonality of A minor, a key so often impregnated with melancholy yearning. Though this is not one of his most profound utterances, but rather a miniature form, it is very noble in sentiment. It has two themes, both of which are sombre and touching South Slavonic songs, the second being passionately emotional. (In the mood and character which are one in this movement, and in the artistic treatment of a Slavonic song, the melancholy fundamental theme of which alternates with typical shifting elements of joy, Dvořák's later *dumky*[1] (elegies) are already discernible. The contrast of these two elements of joy and grief was, however, first developed in his own *dumky* at a later period, and introduced into several of his chamber works, but especially in the series of *dumky* used in the piano trio, op. 90.) In the scherzo, too, with its waltz theme, unmistakably romantic and Schumannesque in colour, the basic key of E major serves only to mask the tonality of C sharp minor; and in the finale, which is remarkably agitated, there is a long conflict with various related minor keys before E major triumphs in the end.

QUARTET IN D MINOR. Fresh sorrows in Dvořák's family in 1877 may perhaps explain why this quartet is plunged in plaintive melancholy and gloomy meditation, and why this work is again so unusually intimate and introspective. In comparison with the preceding quartet it is more serious in thought, more original in workmanship, and as regards the structure of its movements, far from mature. It must always be remembered that in Dvořák there is a reconciliation of two elements. One

[1] Singular, *dumka*; plural, *dumky*.

of these derives from Schubert, and concerns the method of exposition and the figuration of the theme as well as certain details of harmony and rhythm; the other from Brahms, who began at this time to have considerable influence upon Dvořák, particularly in the plastic structure of the movements, and on his musical culture in general. But in this quartet Dvořák is already acquiring his own highly characteristic colouring. This is seen, for instance, in the second subject of the first movement—so obviously Czech in its tender, sensitive, and fervent lines—which calms the agitation and gloom that sometimes weigh upon the beautiful chief theme. Again, the first and last sections of the scherzo show an idealized polka form, while the trio section maintains the smooth motion of a *sousedska* (a slow Czech folk-dance, in 3/4 time, related to the German *Ländler*) with a tender and tuneful theme, its bass part in places taking the leading melody. The climax of the quartet is the adagio, in which rare nobility of expression and warmth of feeling blossom into one of the broadest, most beautifully conceived and profound of all Dvořák's slow movements. Its subject is a long-drawn and tranquil meditation, sometimes rising to heavenly heights, sometimes expressing painful yearning, according as the fundamental key of D major alternates with the parallel key of B minor. The mood and expressive tenderness of the whole movement is effectively brought out by the muted strings. A wonderful effect occurs at the close of the adagio, resulting from the sudden recurrence of the second theme of the first movement, which now emerges unexpectedly like a painful reminiscence of long past sorrow. The sense of suffering which pervades the quartet is not obliterated by the finale, for though it is full of rhythmic agitation—the principal theme especially—the sense of grief is never absent. The movement is firmly constructed, and worked out with much skilful imitation.

The national character in Dvořák's music became strongly marked when he began to make his appeal outside his own country, and felt impelled to emphasize his racial origin and characteristics. This was about the beginning of 1878. It was then that he took to designating some of his compositions as 'Slavonic': the *Slavonic Rhapsodies* and the famous *Slavonic Dances*, a cycle of works in which he took pleasure in idealizing the characteristic melodies or dances of Czech and South-Slavonic type, especially the *dumka* and *furiant*. But besides these he treated also the *polka*, the *sousedska*, and the *skočna*. These, and similar forms, brought him into close touch with the rich sources of Slavonic folk-dance, particularly the Czech and Moravian dances. He had no intention of employing the national tunes as they stood; he sought rather by means of his own ideas to embody their pure and delicate fragrance, their deep, though naïve, emotions, and also some of their typical melodic and harmonic features. For instance, he made use of the fact that many melodic periods in the major flow in the end into a parallel minor key, and vice versa, or there is a characteristic modulation into the key of the minor second.

Among the chamber music for strings only, one of the first works of this period is the sextet, op. 48. It is the most suggestive composition written at this time; each theme pulses with strong Slavonic life-blood; each thought is coloured by national feeling and national ornamentation; each folk mood is of the simplest and most sincere type; not perhaps very profound, but full of a fascinating and fervent lyricism, moving in joyous and fiery rhythms. An outstanding feature, too, of the sextet is the fullness and brilliance of its melody, harmony, and sonority, to which the use of two violas and two 'cellos contributes substantially. The first movement has the normal form of a sonata with three main themes which balance each other admirably. In contrast to the main theme, which is of a delicate and placid character, the subsidiary theme introduces into the movement an agogic and rhythmic agitation. Meanwhile the third theme returns to the mood of the chief subject, joining it as in a tender epilogue. The second movement is a *dumka*, in D minor, in which in the first and last sections a melancholy and dreamy polka (very characteristic in its periodicity of five bars) alternates with a song, rather gipsy in colouring; the middle section is a lovely lullaby, slumbrous, poetic, and expressive. The third movement, entitled a *furiant* in A, does not, however, quite justify its name, for by this word is understood a Czech folk-dance, fiery in movement, in alternate duple and triple time, obtained by means of syncopated accents on the weak beat of the bar, and always in pairs:

Ex. 1.

Now the *furiant* in the sextet has not the true rhythm, for it maintains a regular 3/4. Nevertheless, it is an eloquent example of Dvořák's rhythmic and melodic freshness, and in the trio section a few reminiscences of the Slavonic Dances are interwoven with astonishingly delicate effect. The finale of the sextet consists of variations on a mournful and dreamy theme, the harmony of which fluctuates between B minor and A major, only growing brighter in its middle section where it modulates into D major. The variations, of which there are six, keep to the harmonic character of the theme, but modify its melodic line, extending it by the use of delicate figuration and witty imitations. The last variation is a spirited stretto which frees the movement from its original melancholy mood, and brings it to a brilliant conclusion.

The sextet was the first of Dvořák's chamber works to be performed outside his own country; it was heard in Germany as early as 1879, played by Joachim's Quartet. It was first performed in England at the Popular Concerts on Feb. 23, 1880, under the same leader.

QUARTET IN E FLAT. The success of the sextet contributed greatly to the composer's fame. Jean Becker, then leader of the well-known Florentine Quartet, approached him immediately afterwards with a request for a new work, making it a condition that it should again be in the 'Slavonic' style. Dvořák complied, and in 1879 started upon his E flat quartet (op. 51), which is one of the most attractive and individual of his chamber works. It reflects the very nature of Dvořák himself, his lofty sensibility and wealth of ever-changing inner emotions. Its structure is perfectly plastic, and, with all its simplicity, it shows remarkable polyphonic invention, while the melodic ensemble of the parts is as natural as the fascinating colouring and ethereal quality of tone. Unlike the melancholy quartet in D minor, the prevailing mood of this quartet is one of charming and frank humour. At the outset, the chief theme of the introductory allegro con moto is heard, and, although it is rather subdued in its development over a long-drawn tonic triad, a smile shines through at the end when the rhythm is enlivened by figure *a*:

Ex. 2.

And the smile broadens still more as the rhythmic element, shown above, is further employed in the figuration which decorates the melody. The polka which forms the second subject sounds very merry when interwoven with this figure *a*, being already quite humorous in itself.

Ex. 3.

The second movement of the quartet, as fascinating as it is original, is again a *dumka*, in G minor. There is a remarkable contrast between the moods of its two sections, although both grow out of the same thematic germ. The theme of the introductory division has a melancholy sound in the dialogue between violin and viola over harp-like pizzicato chords for the 'cello.

Ex. 4.

It acquires, however, a totally different aspect in the second section, when it appears in G major, as a wild dance, Czech in sound and rhythm (*furiant*).

Ex. 5.

The first of these two alternating sections, which is a continuous song over a rocking accompaniment, deserves attention; while the rapid section, on repetition, returns to the tonic (G minor), whereby it loses much of its joyous character.

The next movement, in B flat, entitled 'Romance', is a tender and poetical nocturne, comparatively simple in structure, but a beautiful and serene utterance, built on noble lines. Humour, silenced in the slow movement, revives in the finale, which may be described as an artistic treatment of a Czech dance —the *skočna*. Its fundamental theme has a wanton and sportive character, and bounds along in joyous semiquavers, while in the second there are found leaping and capricious syncopations, ending finally in a *furiant*:

Ex. 6.

There is humour, too, in the theme of the episode, which succeeds in driving away the melancholy of the second subject; as this becomes brighter—either on account of the major key, or because of firmer and more decided accentuations—it finally rises to a climax, and the close is wildly joyous. The *dumka* is here and there enlivened by the figure *a* from the first movement, which also reappears as a contrapuntal element in the finale, thereby appreciably strengthening the unity of idea in this fine work.

THE QUARTET IN C MAJOR, which followed on as op. 61, has not the direct connexion with the folk-spirit of Bohemia which distinguishes the preceding work. The specifically national now made way for Dvořák's own conception, which was necessarily divided into two ideals, which are difficult to define clearly, since both spring from almost the same source: the nationally limited basis of the composer. Nevertheless the C major quartet, judged from this point of view, is not specially characteristic of Dvořák. It contains a something which is remote from his entire nature. In the order of the ideas, he shows here a controlled exaltation and a wonderful translucence which spreads over the work, both in its harmony and quality of tone, and seems like the morning sun, illuminating the pure and immovable summits of the mountains. In its expressive power the quartet recalls the classic spirit, and particularly Beethoven, of whose influence one is forcibly reminded. It is a distinguished and charming work, poetical in thought and wonderfully strong in form and expression.

Beethoven's classicism exhales immediately from the beautiful opening theme of the first movement. Broadly laid out in three extended groups, it is the vital nerve of the whole movement, as bold as it is interesting in its plan of modulation. This theme overmasters the significance of the quiet and, on the whole, rather inexpressive second subject, and also that of the closing theme, in which alone there is an echo of Dvořák's native land.

The slow movement (poco adagio e molto cantabile, in F major) breathes an atmosphere of romanticism. A tender, intimate dialogue between the two violins alternates with a dreamy and mournful melody, with a characteristic fluctuation between major and minor. It is significant of the nature of this work that the scherzo, which, as we know, is usually very individual, keeps to purely classical lines in form and expression. Its first and last sections, in A minor, have the clear-cut Beethoven style, while the trio (A major), delightful both in melody and quality of tone, sounds distinctly Schubertian, especially in the softness of its modulations, although the theme itself, with its close in the parallel major, is typical of its composer.

Ex. 7.

The absence in this quartet of national and racial characteristics, which has already been noted, is not complete. They appear in the finale, in that elastic but persistent rhythm at the close of the first theme, and in its indefinite harmony, hovering between C major and E minor:

Ex. 8.

and again in the melancholy Slavonic colouring and characteristically wide intervals in the second subject:

Ex. 9.

The joyousness and brightness of this movement is particularly effective at the close, and forms a sharp contrast with the deeply-felt cadenza of the first violin. The proportion between the character of the themes and the fine, bold, and extended form of this finale recalls Beethoven's *Rasoumovsky* quartet in F.

During the six years following this period, Dvořák was engaged in writing new works of considerable dimensions, commissioned by his English admirers. He now found himself without time, or the needful quiet, in which to compose intimate works of chamber music. He returned, however, to this branch of music as soon as the rush and activity of this period ceased.

THE TERZETTO. Among the chamber music for strings written at this time, one stands out as particularly intimate in form and idiom: the terzetto, op. 74, written early in 1887, for three friends—amateurs who met to play together. From this happy accident originated a little work in which the charm of the ideas, the treatment of the themes, and the expressive form bear witness to the hand of a master. The first of the four miniature movements is in three sections, the quiet principal theme contrasting with a lively second subject of a purely rhythmic character. The third section ends suddenly, merging after a few modulatory chords into a larghetto in E major having the same form and same relation between its two themes, which expands into a tender song breathing a sweet and romantic atmosphere.

The rapid scherzo in A minor again suggests a Schubertian descent. It is interesting to note that the animated and rhythmically expressive first subject and the quiet, yearning theme of the trio both grow out of the same melodic elements. The finale consists of fascinating miniature variations on a short theme of archaic stamp, resembling a grave dramatic recitative in the classical manner.

Other examples of string music were the outcome of Dvořák's sojourn in America, and a series of new characteristics is evident in these compositions. A few words of explanation are needed here. Dvořák went to America in 1892 to take up the direction of the National Conservatorium of Music in New York, and was received there with remarkable enthusiasm as one of the foremost composers of the day. Many American papers published interviews, in which certain statements attributed to Dvořák provoked a whole host of criticisms. One of these statements concerned the possibility of developing a school of American national music based on Indian and negro folk-tunes. Much enthusiasm was shown in support of this notion,—opponents of the idea deprecated the direct use by composers of negro songs in their works. It is probable, however, that Dvořák was drawn by journalists into these newspaper discussions, and that some of his words were incompletely understood and erroneously commented upon. With his simplicity of nature and imperfect knowledge of English, this was, perhaps, unavoidable.

The mistaken idea of his intention to evolve an American national music arose from his first American compositions, in which certain themes recall the folk-songs of the primitive inhabitants. Happily Dvořák was too serious an artist and too exclusively individual to be led astray by such delusions. It is a great mistake to assert that he made direct use of Indian or Negro tunes. He himself protested strongly against this idea immediately after the first production of the *New World* symphony:

'I have not actually used any of the melodies. I have simply written original themes embodying the peculiarities of the Indian music, and, using these themes as subjects, have developed them with all the resources of modern rhythm, harmony, counterpoint, and orchestral colour.'

Dvořák therefore created his *own themes* in the spirit of these songs, which had for him the charm of a new, hitherto quite unfamiliar, flavour. They are nevertheless often pure Dvořák, and happen to amalgamate very well with the composer's non-American themes. The reason why Dvořák employed these elements is not far to seek. Like all artists, he was tempted to refresh the sources of his inspiration by new nuances; but, above all, while in America he wished to emphasize in his works the special features of the new impressions gathered across the Atlantic, and so to give a distinctive character to his idiom. The fact speaks for itself that these peculiarities are most striking only in the first three works which originated in America, i.e. in the symphony *From the New World*, the quartet in F (op. 96), and the quintet in E flat (op. 97); and that they recede into the background until quite lost to view in the later compositions, in proportion as the longing for his native land began to dominate his first strong impressions of the New World.

Both the quartet and the quintet are typically 'American' works, and have much in common with the symphony which preceded them. The majority of their themes show just those characteristics in harmony, melody, and rhythm which Dvořák recognized in the folk-songs of America, which, of course, are also indicated occasionally in the music of other races—the Chinese, Japanese, &c. Essentially these characteristics are: firstly, the use of melodies in the pentatonic scale—the major key with the omission of the fourth and seventh (in the minor keys, the flattened, or mixolydian, seventh frequently appears, and beside this the sixth is often omitted); secondly, the custom of returning to the fixed (appointed) key, probably the tonic or the dominant, which increases the melancholy expression of the theme. Typical of the harmony is the frequent pause on the tonic, or dominant, or on the drone of their combination. A prominent feature of the rhythm is the extremely frequent use of punctuation and syncopation, especially when used in alternation. But these two chamber works also have structural analogies with the symphony. The movements often keep to a purely classical design; the themes are mostly short, rhythmic, and pregnant, and generally freely arrange themselves in simple alternation, instead of growing out of each other organically and interweaving polyphonically. Bewitching quality of tone predominates over structural ingenuity. Further, there are no traces here of that great breadth and span which is as typical of Dvořák as of Schubert.

Where, however, the symphony expresses the first strong impressions which flooded Dvořák's spirit in the noisy and motley atmosphere of New York, in the quartet and quintet Dvořák had in mind the intimate experiences of his visit to the Czech emigrant settlement at Spillville (Iowa), where he spent the summer holidays of 1893.

The Quartet in F. It is thus the nature and content of both these works should be elucidated, beginning with the quartet in F. Dvořák spent eight months in the chaos of metropolitan life in a society and nation quite strange to him, in a journalistic world both sensational and polemical, amid vociferous praise and celebrations given in his honour; then suddenly found himself in the strangely quiet beauty of the heart of America, surrounded by a circle of Czech agriculturists, worthy farmers, lusty peasants, cheery priests, and kindly old wives, who listened with tears in their eyes to the old church music of their native Bohemian villages which the musician played for them on the organ at Mass. Here, then, is the origin of the fundamental mood which inspired this charming, quickly written (in three days) but detailed work, touched in places with painful yearning, yet with a smiling, idyllic sentiment prevailing throughout. Here, too, is the reason why so many of the ideas in the quartet are simple in substance, and why the themes are frequently exposed in a kaleidoscopic fashion, without profound and systematic elaboration and with a preponderance of homophonic structure. The quartet is interesting harmonically on account of its swift and unexpected modulations through related and remote keys, in which there is a surprising charm of artifice that only serves to strengthen the fundamental —as it were improvised—style of the whole work. A twilight calm colours the opening, which suddenly leads into a rippling movement, only to subside again into a quiet dreaminess. It suffices to show the three principal themes:

Ex. 10.

Allegro ma non troppo.

Ex. 11.

Ex. 12.

The deeply felt lento (D minor) consists of a long-drawn, melancholy song, culminating in a sense of yearning in the beautiful, extended middle section. The fundamental melodic line floats throughout the entire movement above a monotonous rocking accompaniment and figure, in an eight-bar period, presented alternately by violin and 'cello:

Ex. 13.

Lento, mp molto espressivo.

It is a genuine pearl among Dvořák's lyrical movements, captivating in its lovely, singing melodic line, its depth of sentiment, and the special charm of its pure harmony. It reveals to us the composer dreaming in solitude in some silent forest in America, and letting his thoughts fly back to his own far-away land.

The third movement, consisting of delightful miniature variations, is very ingeniously constructed on a single theme which starts somewhat abruptly, and comes to a quiet undulating close.

Ex. 14.

Molto vivace.

The movement is constructed in two sections, which appear three times in alternation. The second of these divisions is in F minor, with the theme systematically augmented. The entire movement has a strongly exotic flavour, due to the feeling and structural nature of the theme, the brusque rhythms, and the violent ejaculation of the bare fifths alternating between F major and D minor, and also to certain special tonal combinations which vary with each fresh exposition of the theme.

The finale is a very gay rondo, in which purely American humour alternates with the simple emotionalism of the folk-songs of Dvořák's own country. The cheerful style of the movement is shown in the leading theme, which, until the middle section is reached, runs persistently through the music.

Ex. 15.

Vivace ma non troppo.

A second theme, tacked on to the first without transition, with a genuine Dvořák waywardness, is lyrical in style, and sometimes a little trivial in colouring. In the middle of the section suddenly comes a general hushing of the music, and there appears a short imitation of a chorale, such as might be improvised softly on the organ. This is undoubtedly a reminiscence of the church at Spillville. But soon the lively mood returns, and reaches a wild climax in a brief coda.

THE QUINTET, op. 97, differs from the quartet alike in sentiment and construction. The atmosphere is more exotic, the form broader, the working of the themes more complex, and the dexterity of its polyphonic structure greater.

The sentiment of the first movement is revealed in the nature of the three leading themes, of which the first and second have a purely American flavour. The subject is a pentatonic melody with a dominant suspension (*a*) and a secondary phrase with the mixolydian seventh in the minor key; there is, too, a drum-like spiccato figure (*b*), noticeable in other parts of the quintet also, which is taken over by the closing theme.

Ex. 16.

Allegro ma non tanto.

G minor.

The entrance of the principal theme (inverted and augmented) as a violin solo awakens a sense of disquiet. The sadness increases when the theme is repeated by the 'cello in the minor, but the spirit grows gradually accustomed to its surroundings, and finds peace, as it were, in the quietness of solitude.

In the scherzo, one of the most exotic of Dvořák's American inspirations, it would seem that the composer depicts the Red Indians in their dances and songs. The thematic material has all the characteristic peculiarities of a race undeveloped in musical culture, yet fundamentally musical in feeling. As an example may be quoted the theme of the first and third sections of the scherzo, with its dry, staccato crotchet rhythm, the monotony of which is only occasionally broken by minims. An original feature is a curious little drum-like figure in the viola:

Ex. 17.

Allegro vivo.

Exotic, too, is the long drawn-out theme of the middle *minore*, a melancholy song-like viola solo. But nowhere in his creative work does Dvořák describe his purely objective experiences with accuracy. In the dreamy melodies contrapuntally woven around the basic themes sounds the voice of his own soul; it is heard, too, in the song of the Indian dancers, in which he rejoices to recall the Czech folk of his own land. The larghetto is written in the form of variations on a lovely melody of devotional character.

The introductory theme expresses suffering (*a*), the change to the major suggests reawakening confidence (*b*):

Ex. 18.

Larghetto.

the variations, five in number, are for the most part formal, maintaining the fundamental moods and tonalities of the theme; here there is a sincere manifestation of that pure religious feeling so noticeable in Dvořák's nature.

The finale brings with it a prevailing sense of high spirits. The chief theme, which sounds a little frivolous, is developed in rondo form, in a movement of five alternating sections. Two accessory motifs are used, both typically American in style. Where, however, the first is characterized by a primitive ruggedness, the second winds its way along on charming song-like lines. If this finale is not in the purest chamber style, it is amply atoned for by the fine tone-colour and the spirited craftsmanship with which the movement pursues its onward rush.

Dvořák stayed only three years in America; he could not resist the longing for his native land, though he was pressed to stay. How boundless was his joy when, in the summer of 1895, he found himself once again in his beloved home, among the Czech folk and scenery! His creative soul could not fail to express this intoxication of gladness. It resounds in the two string quartets written soon after his home-coming. These quartets, in A flat major, op. 105, and G major, op. 106, are, as it were, the swan songs of Dvořák's chamber music, which reaches its zenith in these two compositions. They are strong and beautiful in their complex musical idiom, and Dvořák's artistic nature is manifest here in all its purity and individuality. He not only seeks to identify himself once more with the art of the great classicists and romanticists, but he strives for still further progress, and for fresh extension of his creative forces. And his ends are here attained.

THE QUARTET IN G MAJOR is actually the earlier of the two, except for a portion of the first movement of the A flat quartet. Here there is just one flash of an involuntary reminiscence of the far-away country; otherwise the mood is one of fervent thanksgiving on his return to his native soil. The significance of this quartet lies in the first two movements, both of which in their way belong to the greatest things which ever came from Dvořák's pen. Whilst the opening allegro is filled with warmth of feeling and original thought, the structure is bold and on a large scale. The chief theme, apparently so slightly built, is certainly surprising in itself,

Ex. 19.

Allegro moderato.

but still more surprising is the art with which Dvořák elaborates and discusses this simple and joyous theme. The cantabile second subject,

Ex. 20.

which breathes the fragrance of Bohemia's fields, is really the more important, for it is again significantly employed in the finale. The adagio which follows all grows out of one theme, but a theme of such melodic beauty and intimate expression that it was not difficult to build upon it a movement of rare breadth, a splendid example of musical architecture. In the original key of E flat major it sounds like a grave and fervent prayer; but the change to E flat minor colours it with a feeling of painful agitation, which increases later on with a fresh exposition of the subject in F sharp minor, in order that it may pass suddenly in the middle section into a strong, lyrical hymn in C major. Then peace returns once more, and the movement ends in an enchanting coda.

The scherzo that follows is interesting rather on account of its ingenious construction than by any power to transport or move the listener. This power is still more completely lacking in the gay finale, for even the principal subject has no basis on which to build efficiently. But it boasts one surprising device, for the second subject of the opening movement (Ex. 20) several times interrupts the rapid flow of the leading theme with a sorrowful, meditative episode in the minor, as though the approach of old age cast involuntarily a dark shadow on this utterance of careless joy; the leading theme, however, proves sufficiently strong to carry everything defiantly before it at the close of the movement.

THE QUARTET IN A FLAT is the last of Dvořák's chamber works. It has, perhaps, no movement on so great a scale as the first two of the G major quartet, nevertheless it surpasses it because of the more perfect balance in all its parts, each of which bears eloquent testimony to Dvořák's freshness and inventive power. In the slow introduction, in A flat minor, there is no hint of the idyllic and sunny spirit which prevails throughout the allegro in the major. The principal theme is immediately irradiated with a feeling of warmth and brightness, and this mood is maintained in the melodies derived from it (Ex. 21).

The movement is captivating, and although in principle it deviates little from sonata form, it is never commonplace in structure.

The scherzo (F minor) is one of the best Dvořák has written. Its first and last sections are in a lively dance measure derived from an expressive theme in the nature of a *furiant*, the

Ex. 21.

Allegro appassionato.

four closing bars of which are used farther on as an independent counter-theme.

Ex. 22.

Molto vivace.

The middle section of the scherzo is in D flat major, and sings its course along the lines of an enchanting melody; later, when it joins in two-part canon in the violins, it gives the impression of a choir of skylarks in full song.

Ex. 23.

The romantic lento e molto cantabile (F major) starts off very simply with a theme of folk-song character, but develops into a broad melody, richly extended and full of warmth and emotion. The charm of this theme is enhanced when, after an agitated middle section, it returns surrounded by a series of delightful figures played by the two violins. The radiant feeling cast over the introductory section increases in the finale to an expression of pure joy. It speeds along accompanied by many devices in the working of the motifs, one after another, always in readiness for some capricious sally, until the movement grows under the composer's hand to rather greater length than perhaps was originally intended. But he does not, therefore, lose his capacity to rise to a final climax in a paean of wild joy.

II. Works for Piano and Strings.

From this group we must leave out of account the piano quintet in three movements (A major, 1872), still in MS. But the published works which immediately followed it show Dvořák's creative powers remarkably on the up-grade, and structurally they were already as vital a part of his work as the string quartets.

Dvořák was never a piano virtuoso, but he succeeded in becoming a sound pianist, virile in tone and sincere in emotional expression. These qualities are clearly reflected in his piano works. There is none of the acquired brilliancy of a Chopin, or a Liszt; but there is in them something which is on a level with the classical standard of piano technique—the Beethoven standard. With Dvořák, the piano is used to great advantage in combination with other instruments; indeed, it is occasionally the piano which decides the intimate expression in his chamber music.

The first trio (in B flat major) lacks as yet the true personal touch of Dvořák, but it is not without distinction, and delightful in form.

The same may be said of the trio in G minor, which differs from the preceding work only in these respects—that the thematic material employed is greatly curtailed (not more than two themes to each movement), and that the prevailing feeling is stressful and touched with painful yearning.

The Piano Quartet in D, which was begun between the two trios, is a work of similar value, distinguished, however, by greater intimacy of feeling. The first movement, in sonata form, is somewhat self-conscious at first; not indeed in its chief theme, which consists of two bars only, but in the scope and energy of the extended middle section, and the firm start made by the closing motif. But soon the broadly-woven second subject, with its tender melodic line and touch of national colour, checks the promised extension and does not permit of its elaboration, even in the working-out; the recapitulation, also, dies softly away after two agitated outbursts.

The andantino (B minor) consists of variations on a simple theme in the form of a song in two sections. The subject begins with an eight-bar period (in B minor); the second period passes into the parallel D major; and the third period returns to the tonic key—in the variations, frequently with a characteristically gloomy Dorian final cadence (through A major). The variations, five in number, keep to the key of the theme until the fourth is reached, which diverges into E flat major. It ends with a coda, which in its powerful melodic beauty is the climax of the work. On the whole this movement is most attractive, even if it is not the most logical and interesting of Dvořák's variations from the point of view of its form. The last movement of the quartet is interesting because it combines the functions of scherzo and finale. It is planned in two sections, each with its own independent theme; the motif of the allegro scherzando moving in a quiet dance measure, while the allegro agitato has the character of an undeveloped finale. Both sections, however, flow naturally into each other while preserving their relationship as principal and accessory.

THE BAGATELLES, op. 47. The period during which Dvořák expressed his racial and national origin most markedly in his music can scarcely show a more typical work than this, in which the instrumental parts are distributed as unpretentiously as in the terzetto, op. 74—the *Bagatelles* for two violins, 'cello, and harmonium (or piano), a little composition which is the outcome of simple and tender intimate feelings. In this modest composition is hidden—as in the terzetto—a serious work of art in which the parts are used in ingenious imitations, and which shows charming tone-quality. Even this simple group of pieces is not lacking in a unifying idea. The first number consists of the exposition of a theme for which the second half of the humorous folk-song *Hraly dudy* (The Pipes were playing) is used; this accounts for the characteristic instrumental colour. The minuet in G major, which follows, may be compared to the second section of a sonata, just as the third piece, which returns to the theme and sentiment of the first, is a kind of working-out section. The andante (E major), a delightful two-part canon, is followed by a joyous poco allegro in G major, which grows out of a humorous and rhythmic theme. In their markedly Czech feeling, the *Bagatelles* show some relationship with the *Slavonic Dances*, which have the same distinguishing quality of humour.

THE VIOLIN SONATA, op. 57, is another work of deep intimacy. It is most simple, delicate, and idyllic throughout. Dvořák's individuality is most perceptible in the first and last movements, whereas the influence of Brahms is evident in the poco sostenuto. Noble as it is in form and idea, this sonata is not strongly characteristic of Dvořák.

THE TRIO IN F MINOR, a magnificent work, is unusually grave in character; the music unfolds itself in a kind of gloomy, passionate defiance. It is as though the composer confronted Fate with a stubborn and persistent—Why? Not until the very end of the work does the prevailing sense of gloom make way for a feeling of peace and resignation. Hence the passion and power which permeate the work in thought, structure, and formal development; hence the tendency to a symphonic grandeur which can only be realized in chamber music by the sonority and expressive co-operation of the piano.

The first movement is not only the most impassioned, but its thematic material is the richest and most articulate. The principal subject consists of two independent members, the first of which springs out of darkness on the firm lines of the violin and 'cello, and ends suddenly on a note of interrogation which is taken up by the piano, and closes with a vehement final gesture.

Ex. 24.

As though waiting to answer, the composer follows on at once with the second period of the theme, a defiant and extended idea:

Ex. 25.

The second subject, for which the two preceding have prepared the way, is played first by the 'cello and then by the violin in strongly emotional, long-drawn lines, full of passionate restlesssness.

Ex. 26.

The third theme, ruggedly rhythmic, is again impregnated with defiance and resolution.

Ex. 27.

The chief material on which the movement is constructed consists of the two sections of the main subject, already fully developed in the exposition. They are treated with a wealth of modulation in the bold, clear-cut structure, and finally in the agitated coda. The entire movement has an air of conflict and pathos, with a powerful and extended climax.

The second movement, which, though marked allegro grazioso, is essentially a scherzo, is connected by its content with the preceding movement. Over a monotonous staccato figure a dreamy song is persistently repeated, and the alternating rhythm of a crotchet and two quavers has again an air of defiance and caprice. This mood pervades the first and last sections, in C sharp minor, the theme shown below alternating between the piano and the strings in varied harmonies:

Ex. 28.

The middle section, in D flat major, provides a beautiful sense of contrast. The aggressive spirit vanishes and gives place to dreamy meditation; over an undulating figure flows a quiet cantilena, which sometimes becomes strongly emotional.

The poco adagio in A flat which follows is a very broad and deeply felt movement. The gloomy, yearning principal theme, in which all the sorrow in the musician's heart seems to be welling up, is announced by the 'cello over heavy chords from the piano (Ex. 29).

The second subject, which is in canon between violin and 'cello, enters with a note of quiet resignation. Somewhat plaintive at first, it grows more fervent in the course of its development. Suddenly the defiant mood returns with a stubborn theme in G minor, but not for long, and it finally vanishes in the warm, long-drawn melody of the opening, which leads into the finale.

In this allegro con brio the combative mood of the first movement returns with even greater vehemence. Defiance stamps it from the first bar, and the rebellious spirit is further carried

Ex. 29.

on into the *furiant* with its alternating triple and duple measures. But, like the subject of the first movement, this also has the character of a sudden interrogation:

Ex. 30.

On this theme the first half of the movement is broadly constructed, in an agitated and sharply accentuated mood. It continues in the same vein after a brief interval of quiet with the second subject (in C sharp minor), which speaks of doubt and anxiety. In the working-out section the music grows dark and stormy, but this exhausts itself, and in the coda the chief theme is heard again in tranquil warmth.

THE PIANO QUINTET, on the whole, expresses a spirit which is the opposite of this. It is an absolute revelation of the personality of Dvořák, a man apparently locked within himself, moving only in the sphere of divine beauty, now plunged in gloomy meditation, his vision lost in eternity, now smiling brightly, bubbling over with happiness and breaking forth in outbursts of the frankest joy. Such a spirit was Dvořák, and thus he appears in this quintet—one of the freshest and most characteristic creations of his genius. So far, only Schubert has produced a work of such lovely and varied tone-colour, so profuse in contrapuntal melismata. And none but Dvořák could give us all this in such a full and expressive Slavonic spirit.

The highly changeful nature of the work is at once revealed in the exposition of the first movement. The leading theme has a dreamy and melancholy air:

Ex. 31.

Suddenly, however, there springs up a modification of the theme over a firm progression on the piano; the motif grows brighter, its lively rhythm being derived from a fragment of the first subject. And now joy breaks forth suddenly, subsides, and gives place to a new metamorphosis of the leading theme—a luminous and ascending version. Then there is another burst of gladness in the theme of the middle section, when triplets of the piano are entwined with staccato quavers on the viola, the rest of the strings having an ostinato rhythm, until another sudden transition leads to the second subject, which begins at once in a vein of melancholy.

Ex. 32.

In the course of its development, however, it warms up and bursts forth tempestuously at the end of the exposition. In this way the movement continues in alternating moods to a broad and delicately worked development, which reaches a climax at the forceful repetition of the principal theme, and is followed by a recapitulation extended by a spirited coda.

This work, in which Dvořák so freely displays his Slavonic tenderness of emotion, must inevitably contain a movement entirely characteristic of the composer and his swiftly alternating moods. The second movement is therefore a *dumka* (andante con moto, F sharp minor). Within the frame of the four-bar motif (like a refrain) that gives the movement something of the tone and colour of a ballad

Ex. 33.

is the germ of a broad theme in three parts, with a dreamy, contrapuntal motif embroidering it:

Ex. 34.

Then sorrow vanishes slowly from the music, while the melody of the second subject is unfolded in a dialogue between the violins.

Ex. 35.

This subject is very widely extended, and a sense of sombre rêverie often alternates with its smiling mood. Then comes an abrupt change; in the middle section there starts off a rapid vivace, with a lively motif directly derived from the ballad-like theme which encompasses the gloomy chief subject. The closing section corresponds to the opening part, with this difference, that here the second subject is in F sharp major and is full of new and varied tone colour.

The scherzo of the quintet is described as a *furiant*, a description not in strict conformity with its content, but it is a vigorous dançe which reveals its Slavonic origin. It is again in three symmetrical sections. The gay opening portion in A major grows out of three themes which afford lively contrasts of mood and measure. The first, which recalls Schubert, has an incisive rhythm and joyous, extended melody; the second, in slower time, in a rocking rhythm, sings of longing; while the third is characteristically Slavonic. The slighter, more amorous lines of the trio (F major) are enlivened by the joyous elements of the first theme.

The quintet ends with a stirring finale, very lively and varied in rhythm, and freshly worked out with contrapuntal devices. Throughout the movement, its themes keep up a gay chatter which is typical of Dvořák (Ex. 36). The gaiety is in the handling of the themes, which is at once elastic and delicate, until the fugato is reached; the climax comes later, and the end is tremendously jubilant.

Ex. 36. *Allegro.*

The Piano Quartet in E flat is of nearly equal value with the quintet. It is distinguished by similar ideas, beauty, and expressiveness, and is equally admirable in its structure, workmanship, and fine tone colour. It differs, however, in its subject-matter. The quartet has not the elasticity and Protean changefulness of the quintet; but it has a greater emotional intensity. It is dominated by sane virility, depth of feeling, and serious purpose.

The striking and energetic theme with which the work opens, played by the strings in unison, is the vital element from which the movement is constructed, and defines at once the sense of manly joy:

Ex. 37. *Allegro con fuoco.*

Its energy is still further increased by the rapidity of the rhythmic element which is directly linked to the theme, and from which it takes growth. The second subject brings the customary contrast of mood.

Ex. 38.

In the exposition and repetition this same theme is skilfully used. An effective episode occurs when it reappears in the recapitulation, where suddenly its delicate line in B major is introduced by the plaintive tone of the diminished seventh (G sharp) on the 'cello, and again when the unexpected modulation reverts to the tonic key, E flat major. The working-out is effected chiefly with portions of the principal theme, and is very direct and impassioned.

The lento, in G flat minor, is one of Dvořák's loveliest gems of lyricism. The structure grows out of a grave emotional theme for the 'cello, followed by a peaceful idea allotted to the violin; and here also the middle section (in C sharp minor) is worked up in pathetic but virile accents.

The first and last sections of the scherzo—which are alike—are melodious, and in a somewhat pensive vein, as befits its two themes, the first of which is in minuet time.

Ex. 39. *Allegro moderato, grazioso.*

The second motif, monotonously harmonized—it is based entirely on the chord of G minor—has an unmistakably oriental character.

Ex. 40.

The middle section is enlivened by restless triplets in the accompaniment and the hopping rhythm of the theme. This section is pleasing, and skilfully rounded off.

The finale (allegro ma non troppo) is full of energy, and the form is more clearly cut than that of the first movement. The theme is simple, with no lengthy discussions, but with a wonderfully free scheme of modulation. It is certainly curious that the finale only goes into the basic key of the quartet when the recapitulation is reached. At first the chief subject is given out with energy, in E flat minor, in expressive, plastic lines; the middle section is in G flat major, so that the enharmonic change through F sharp major may introduce the second subject in B major (*a*), the close again being in F sharp major (*b*). Both themes soar on wings of an expressive and sensitive lyricism (Ex. 41 *a*, *b*). The development winds its way through a series of modulations, returning in the recapitulation to E flat minor, in which it started. Here this varied modulatory design comes to an end, and the music passes into the tonic, E flat major, in which it continues till the close.

Ex. 41.

The Dumky Trio is a work which is remarkably characteristic of Dvořák's chamber music. In the form of the *dumka*, the principal characteristic of which is the alternation of yearning melancholy with wild gaiety, there is vent for Dvořák's emotionally complex and fiery temperament, which plunged him at times into rêverie and showed itself at other moments in outbursts of gladness. If, earlier in his career, Dvořák interpolated into some of his chamber music an idealized *dumka* doing duty either for slow movement or scherzo, in the trio he created a work made up exclusively of *dumka* movements of his own. There are six in all, each thematically independent and separate from each other.

This free arrangement of movements, remarkably alike in character, might give the impression that the *Dumky* trio is not a chamber work in the strict sense of the words, but this is not the case. Even if it has not the unity of thought that marks the cyclic sonata form, the subject-matter is linked organically, and conforms to the required standard of variety in form and expression. It is significant that the first three *dumky* are connected by the indication 'attacca subito' into a coherent whole, and are reconciled by their tonalities, because the first *dumka* in E minor ends in C sharp minor, in which key the second one is continued, while the third is in A major. Then they are also connected formally by the thoughtful sections alternating with the strongly contrasting dance variants, which are linked by their content, passing on from quiet exclamations of sorrow to emotional conclusions. In the first *dumka*, associated with the recitative of the 'cello and the sorrowful melody of the violin, there is a delightful allegro on the same theme, embroidered with gay figuration. In the second the slow section grows out of a plaintive melody for the 'cello, and a warm, soothing cantilena for the piano, and with the vivace there enters a new theme of folk-song type. In the third only one theme is prominent, but with many modifications.

The independence of the next two *dumky* is signified by the direction—'after a short pause'; for they represent the cyclic whole, the slow movement and scherzo. Of these, the fourth *dumka*, in D minor, springs from a melancholy theme heard in the 'cello over a weighty ostinato progression in the piano part, and below the monotonous quavers of the violin, bringing with it an exquisite sense of eventide calm. It briefly tells its tale, and goes on in the spirit of a lively Russian folk-song. This quiet vein prevails in the *dumky*, which are interrupted in the middle only by a short burst of joy. The fifth *dumka* contrasts with the preceding one, being in E flat major, and in a restless rhythmic measure. The theme, which is at first energetic, alternates later with one more playful and tender, and its harsh rhythm and sombre harmony have in themselves something almost brutal.

The last *dumka*, in C minor, completes and clinches the whole work, returning to the form and sentiment of the opening one. A grave lento with a pathetic theme contrasts with a quick section, and the music is alternately wild and quietly expressive. It ends in a broad, plaintive, and effective coda.

The *Dumky*, even if not distinguished by the unity of thought and structure expected in a serious chamber work, is full of charm, with a touch of the simplicity of folk-song. The tone colour, which varies with each *dumka*, reveals everywhere the great master of instrumental technique. The 'cello is very prominent throughout, its full rich tones according remarkably well with the mood of the work.

The Sonatina, Dvořák's only essay in this form, is the last of the group of works belonging to his American visit, and was written for his children in New York, 1893. It is a modest work, clear in outline and intimate in its subject-matter. The themes of the first half of the work have an echo of America in their tonal and harmonic peculiarities; the rest of the sonatina is concerned rather with the idiom of the composer's own country. It is interesting that in almost all the themes there appears this connecting motif:

Ex. 42.

The sonatina is in four movements. The first is a new advance in sonata form, with three themes. The larghetto, in G minor, is a tender and symmetrically constructed cradle song, with a touching, rather mournful melody in the outer sections and a bright and agreeable intermezzo as a middle section.[1] The third

[1] This has been separately popularized in various arrangements and under different names, such as *Indian Canzonetta*, *Indian Lament*, &c.

movement is a gay and fascinating scherzo, classical in form. The same applies also on the whole to the finale, in sonata form, with remarkably broad themes; the exposition of the third of these is one of the most charming pages in the sonatina. The whole character of the little work gives the clue to Dvořák's own words: 'It is intended for the young, but the grown-ups, too, may not be unwilling to amuse themselves with it, as in truth they have done.'

If it is desired to assign to Dvořák his place in the history of chamber music, the statement that, next to Brahms, he is the greatest composer of the later nineteenth century should not be disputed. There are, moreover, distinct links with Brahms, for they were friends, and mutually supplemented each other's genius. If Brahms was the more cultivated, more distinguished in utterance and workmanship, more concentrated, disciplined, and logical in construction, Dvořák had greater resilience; and if he was less serious-minded, he was amazingly lusty and productive. If Brahms was a spiritual aristocrat, reserved and fundamentally pessimistic, Dvořák was a true son of the people, with a joyous perspective of life and a clear and confident outlook. Moreover, he was certainly a musician of strong personality. Czech art may take pride in him as the inspired founder of our national chamber music, Czech in spirit and in idiom.

OTTOKAR ŠOUREK.

[Professor Šourek's appreciations of Dvořák's chamber works are so exhaustive that little remains for me to say. For us amateurs they are priceless treasures, and I hope that the above article will help to open the eyes of the many whose knowledge is confined to a few selected works, such as the piano quintet, the E flat, and the 'Nigger' quartets, &c., to the beauties diffused over all the chamber compositions of Dvořák, to which complete justice, as far as I know, has not been done in the past. He was not one of the many composers who overwrote themselves. Everything he published is worthy of attention, even his transcriptions for string quartet of ten love songs, under the title of *The Cypresses*, of which Dr. Šourek makes no mention. They are tender and intimate, and were played with success in Prague, but in this arrangement they are just a little monotonous. EDITOR.]

DYSON, GEORGE, b. 1883, English composer and author.

Three rhapsodies, str. quartet op. 7 S. & B.

Dr. Dyson won the Mendelssohn scholarship, travelling in Italy and Germany (1900–4).

The three rhapsodies obtained the Carnegie Award in 1920. Each movement is headed by a quotation from Dante which may be assumed to provide some clue to the composer's intentions. They are light in texture, modern in treatment, and deeply imaginative.

EDITOR.

E

EASTMAN SCHOOL OF MUSIC, Rochester, New York.

The teaching of chamber music in this school may be classified under three heads:

1. The training of students in the art of chamber music playing.
2. The giving of chamber music concerts for the general public and for the students.
3. The encouragement of the writing of chamber music by American composers.

1. There are classes in all types of chamber music ensemble, where the students get actual training in string quartet playing, piano ensemble with other instruments, and the like.

2. The school possesses an excellent chamber music hall, which is probably the most perfect of its kind in America, where series of chamber concerts are given by the best Quartets, Trios, &c., and also programmes by the Little Symphony, which is picked from the players of the Rochester Philharmonic.

3. The third division is a part of a general programme which is being undertaken for the development of the American composer. Each year a number of concerts is given, including little symphony and chamber music concerts, the programme being composed entirely of works by American composers. These works are carefully selected, and the best of those which are still in MS. are published by the Eastman School of Music through the agency of C. C. Birchard Publishing Co., Boston. The last phase of the work is in its infancy. What is being done is in reality a combination of the Patron's Fund programme of the R.C.M. in London and the work of the Carnegie Foundation, in publishing good works which as yet have no commercial value.

The director is Mr. Howard Hanson, whose personal work has been confined more to orchestral compositions than to the other forms. He has, however, written two quintets and one quartet, the last being the subject of a Coolidge commission in 1925, and since published. EDITOR.

†EBERL, ANTON, 1766–1807, Viennese pianist.

A distinguished musician, and friend of Mozart. Some of his compositions were published (and popular) under Mozart's name. His symphony in E flat was played at a concert with the *Eroica*, and was contrasted favourably with it by the reviewer. His numerous chamber works include three string quartets (Mollo, Vienna), a piano sextet with strings and horn, piano quintet and quartets, &c. List in *Grove* and *Fétis*.

EBERWEIN, Traugott Maximilian, 1775–1831, German violinist.

Works include:

Three quartets, str	op. 1	B. & H.
Three quartets, str, G, C, G.	opp. 71, 74, 79	Hofmeister.

The quartets published by Hofmeister were originally for flute and strings. Eberwein was acquainted with Beethoven and Salieri at Vienna, and was friendly with Zelter and Hummel. His brother Carl was also a composer of chamber music.

†ECCLES, Henry, English violinist.

Sonata, v, fig. bass (pf), d mi	(A. Moffat, *Old Eng. V-music* 2)	Novello, 1906.
Sonata, v, fig. bass (pf), g mi	(J. Salmon)	Ricordi, 1914.
Sonata, vc, fig. bass (pf), g mi	(A. Moffat, *Meisterschule* 7)	Simrock, 1905.
	(E. Cahnbley)	Schott, 1919.

Henry Eccles was one of a family of musicians. Though his republished music consists only of sonatas with figured bass, yet they are so much played to-day that a list is given here. These works were published about 1720. Eccles was a member of the king's band from 1674 to 1710; he then went to France, where he became a member of the French king's band. His birth and death dates are not known authoritatively.

ECKERT, Karl, 1820–1879, German violinist and pianist.

Trio, pf, v, vc, b mi	op. 18	B. & H., 1845.

Eckert was a pupil and friend of Mendelssohn, who spoke of him as a 'sound practical musician'. He was a child prodigy, but hardly bore out his early promise.

EDELMANN, Johann Friedrich, 1749–1794, French composer (b. Strasbourg) and doctor juris.

Modern republications:

Sonata, pf, v, c mi	op. 2, no. 1	D.T.B. (H. Riemann), vol. 28, 1915.
Sonata, pf, v, f mi	,, 4, no. 3	

Edelmann, besides being a musician, was a revolutionary who was eventually guillotined. *Fétis* has given interesting biographical details of this composer.

†EDMONDS, Paul, contemporary English composer.

Two miniature suites, str. quartet	S. & B.

EECKHAUTTE, Edm., double-bass player.

3rd suite, pf, cb, B flat	Maison Beethoven, 1908.

EGGAR, Katharine, b. 1874, English pianist and composer.

Was the first Englishwoman to give a public London concert of her own chamber works, which include a piano quintet and a 'cello sonata, both as yet unpublished.

†EGGERT, Joachim, 1780–1813, Swedish violinist.

Quartet, pf, v, vla, vc	B. & H.

For other publications see *Riemann*.

EHRENBERG, Carl E. Th., b. 1878, German composer and conductor.

Quartet, str, e mi	op. 20	Simrock; R. & E., 1923.

Also early chamber music, two string quartets and pf trio (*Riemann*).

The E minor quartet is a well written and noble chamber work, characterized by purity of form and style. A slow movement of fine spiritual elevation shows Ehrenberg as a disciple of the later Beethoven. Ultra-modern tendencies are absent in this score, which appears as a synthesis of Beethoven and Brahms, with occasional Wagnerian traits.

Hugo Leichtentritt.

EHRMANN, Rosette, b. 1887, French composer, pupil of d'Indy.

Fantaisie, pf, 2 v, D	Senart.
Sonata, pf, v, E	,,
,, pf, vc, g mi	,,

EICHBORN, Hermann Ludwig, 1847–1918, German composer.

Sonata, pf, horn (or vc), E flat	op. 7	B. & H., 1889.
Suite, pf, horn (or vc)	,, 12	,, 1893.

Eichborn was a skilled horn and trumpet-player, and inventor of a new type of horn of increased compass.

†EICHHEIM, Henry, b. Chicago, 1870.

Has written but not published a string quartet and a violin sonata. He is known to fame as the composer of a series of *Oriental Impressions* for pf, harp, violins, flute, oboe, cor anglais, bells, and percussion, sketches based on music heard by him in China and Japan. They are not, strictly speaking, chamber music, but rather the echoes of oriental music heard in Buddhist temples, theatres, tea houses, &c., &c.; but they are delicately and chamber musically transcribed. When listening to them at the Berkshire festival in 1921 it occurred to me that Henry Eichheim had succeeded in tracking some of the modern impressionistic music of the French school to its source.

Editor.

EICHNER, Ernst, 1740–1777, German bassoon player.

Modern republications:

Quartet, fl, v, vla, vc, D	op. 4, no. 4	D.T.B. (H. Riemann), vol. 27, 1914.
Trio, pf, v, vc, c mi	,, 1, ,, 3	D.T.B. (H. Riemann), vol. 28, 1915.
Trio, pf, v, vc, A	,, 2, ,, 1	D.T.B. (H. Riemann), vol. 28, 1915.
Sonata, pf, v, F		Hofmeister, —

†EIMERT, Herbert, contemporary German composer.

Five pieces, str. quartet	B. & H.

This work is written on the 12-tone system.

EISLER, Hanns, b. 1898, German composer, pupil of Schönberg.

Palmström, voice declaiming, fl, cl, v, vla, vc	op. 5	U.E., 1926.
Duo, v, vc	,, 7	,, 1925.

Eisler's aesthetic ideas, harmonic system, and speculations on musical form have been profoundly influenced by Schönberg. Thus *Palmström* reflects not only Schönberg's *Pierrot lunaire*, but also the same master's later speculations on the twelve-tone series. His *Tagebuch* is a little cantata for two sopranos and alto, with piano and violin accompaniment, mixing together little vocal pieces with instrumental pieces, in a parodistic manner. The duo for violin and 'cello, in two movements, employs dance rhythms in the parodistic, grotesque modern style, offering unusual and interesting technical problems to the players.

Hugo Leichtentritt.

EITNER, Robert, 1832–1905, German musical historian.

Author of the *Quellen-Lexikon*, completed 1904. A new edition, with additions and corrections, is being brought out by B. & H. since 1912 and published in parts. It purports to give a complete list of works of all composers. Readers are referred to this compilation for works which do not fall within the scope of this book.

†ELGAR, Sir Edward, b. 1857, English composer.

Quartet, str, e mi	op. 83	Novello, 1920.
Quintet, pf, 2 v, vla, vc, a mi	,, 84	,, 1920.
Sonata, pf, v, e mi	,, 82	,, 1919.

In the future Edward Elgar will probably be regarded as the father of the modern school of British composers, much as César Franck is regarded in France and Belgium. Elgar's music appeared as something new, both harmonically and melodically—something entirely different from any of the music produced by his contemporaries. Each work, as it came from him, created something of a sensation, and set all the tongues of the theorists wagging; the sheer beauty of his themes, and the daring originality of his ideas (notably the Demons' chorus in *Gerontius*, the unusual juxtaposition of keys in the first symphony, and the theme describing the thirty pieces of silver in the *Apostles*), all show his versatility, and masterly handling of the various musical forms.

These attributes were bound to react upon the minds of the younger British composers. In Elgar they found realism, mysticism, new and remarkable orchestration, and a breaking with many of the old traditions. This undoubtedly encouraged many of them to explore new fields, to gain wider visions, and to free themselves from the fetters of the past. Small wonder that some of them have already wandered very far afield; so far, in fact, that it is not every musician of to-day (1927) who can follow them, perceive what exactly is their intention, or gauge the ultimate value of their production. In any case Elgar has supplied the yeast needed to set up the fermentation now taking place in modern music, the final outcome of which it is impossible to foretell. Apart from his influence upon the modern school of British composers, he has enriched the literature of English music with a large number of works—works which most musicians are convinced will live for all time; works worthy to hold their own, and rank with the great masterpieces of the past.

When, in the spring of 1918, Elgar took a country cottage at Fittleworth, Sussex, his decision had important artistic results, for then he suddenly began to write chamber music, and, in his usual tempestuous fashion, when once seized by the creative spirit, did not cease from his labours until he had produced three fine examples of this form of art.

One is almost tempted to include the concerto for 'cello and orchestra, which was written under the same influence as the three chamber works above mentioned, and possesses many of their salient characteristics; but, in spite of the intimate style of the work, the fact that it is orchestral rules it out of the domain of pure chamber music.

The surroundings in which the three chamber works were written may be briefly described, as their effect on the composer's music is clearly discernible. Imagine, then, an old oak-beamed cottage set on a wooded hill, and across an old-world garden another building resembling an artist's studio. From this studio there is a view of a hill sloping down to more thickly wooded country; beyond this the river Arun and, in the distance, the heights of the South Downs are visible. Here there is a very good piano, and here the sonata, quartet, and quintet received tentative trials.

Near the cottage rises a strange plateau, on which there are a number of trees with gnarled and twisted branches, bare of bark or leaves—a ghastly sight in the evening, when the branches seem to be beckoning and holding up gaunt arms in derision.

In the first movement of the quintet the composer's subjective impressions produce a very eerie effect upon the hearer. Their influence is also apparent in the sonata (second movement), and the finale of the quartet, in which there is a striking ponticello effect.

THE SONATA, while conforming to accepted sonata form, has, in common with all Elgar's works, several unusual characteristics. The first bar is apparently in A minor, but in the succeeding bars comes the D sharp which establishes the key of E minor. The opening theme (risoluto) is of a rugged and forceful character, and contains some unusually wide skips, notably in the second and fourth bars.

Ex. 1.

At the ninth bar is a descending passage, marked *ff* con forza, which is unmistakably Elgarian, the rhythm consisting as it does of an accented crotchet, a rest, and a long quaver, this figure being repeated for several bars.

Ex. 2.

One can almost hear him say: 'Don't starve the quavers'—one of his favourite expressions. The same figuration occurs at (2) at the bar marked *a tempo*.

At (3) there is a kind of inversion of the opening, but now broadly laid out, and legato; this serves as a bridge passage leading to a highly original new subject at (5),

Ex. 3.

and this new subject betrays the fact that Elgar is himself a violinist—the arpeggio passages in the violin part being truly violinistic. The effect might almost have been suggested to him by the breeze blowing through the surrounding trees.

The rest of the first movement is constructed from these themes, which are very freely treated and full of fire and vitality. It ends, as it begins, in a rugged manner.

The second movement is quite extraordinary. It is entitled *Romance*, though it might almost have been *Meditation*, with its note of underlying mysticism. In this strange movement the scene appears peopled with romantic beings. There is even a thought of the baleful wood, and its dead trees and beckoning branches.

Ex. 4.

The actual construction of the movement is very simple. The broad second section, where the key-signature changes to two flats, makes a perfect contrast to the opening,

Ex. 5.

and, after a passionate climax, the music subsides, and there is a recapitulation of the first part, the theme being now played *con sordino*.

The finale begins with a feeling of complete tranquillity,

Ex. 6.

and, although marked *allegro non troppo*, must move along with a certain swing and feeling of movement. At (40) there occurs another of those themes to which it is unnecessary for Elgar to sign his name, but it is here the semiquaver that must not be 'starved'.

Ex. 7.

A new light breaks upon the scene after the 2/4 bar (41), and we are introduced to a wistful theme:

Ex. 8.

this is treated very plaintively, notably at (43), and until the return of the first subject at the double-bar. The extensive development of these themes leads, after a recapitulation (in which, however, there is no exact repetition), to a reminiscence of the *Romance*, but now in 3/2 time. The coda (55) is quite short but sums up the whole movement, and at (56) becomes very strenuous, and the sonata closes in a spirited and virile manner.

THE QUARTET bears, like the sonata and quintet, the impress of the composer's personality. It shows, perhaps more than any other of his works, his love of the country-side, of simple things, cottages, hedgerows, and open-air life. In all its three movements it breathes calm and contentment, and the contemplation of nature in summer mood. It opens somewhat restlessly, with short, broken fragments of the main theme.

Ex. 9.

These gradually unite, and at figure (4) appears the smoothly flowing second subject,

Ex. 10.

a broad swinging tune of much warmth. The opening theme and this second subject contain the material for the whole movement, the form of which, though more or less on orthodox lines, is highly ingenious. The composer's skill in presenting his themes with new treatment, the constant change of light and colour, and the individual interest of the four string parts make the music a constant joy for each player, and a fruitful field of study for the student. The second movement opens with a very simple melody suggestive of a warm, sunny afternoon in the open. It is played first of all in its entirety by the second violin, accompanied by viola and 'cello, a most happy and delightful example of three-part writing.

Ex. 11.

The first violin does not enter until the twenty-third bar, when there is an amplified repetition of this soothing melody with richer harmony, producing a feeling of warmth and contentment. This is followed by a characteristic section with a pulsating phrase, which suggests the languor of a hot summer afternoon, and the myriad life that throbs in the warmth of the sunlight.

Just as this movement suggests peace and the sheer joy of idleness, so is the last movement alive with restless and abounding energy. It opens vigorously, for liveliness and vivacity are the key-notes of the music.

Ex. 12.

The passage work for the strings is brilliant in the extreme, the swirl of the semiquavers and their onward rush and sweep breathe gaiety and the joy of life.

The key of the second subject at (43) (Ex. 13) is difficult to determine, for its tonality constantly changes. In this movement, as in the others, Elgar is very economical with his thematic material, relying upon his genius for presenting his ideas in new lights, and his mastery of all the means of development for his architectural effects.

A characteristic figure at (45) contains an

Ex. 13.

ingenious treatment of three repeated notes in groups of four, the accent falling in turn upon a different note.

Ex. 14.

This figure, however, merely serves as background for a fragment of the second subject, both rambling far afield through numerous keys. In the midst of all the warmth and vivacity of this movement, there is a sudden warning (just before (49), where the lower strings are directed to play ponticello) that there are other and harsher moods of nature. But it is only a fleeting one, and the hearer basks in summer warmth until the end of the work.

The Quintet is a greater conception, and planned upon a larger scale than Elgar's other chamber works. Like the sonata, it is in three movements, the first movement in each case being in a minor key, and the finale in the tonic major. The finale of the quartet, however, is in E minor, and only *ends* in E major.

The quintet begins with the main theme (marked *serioso*), pregnant with mysterious significance.

Ex. 15.

The piano theme, simple as it looks, is destined to play an important part throughout the work (see the treatment at figure (55) in the finale). The strings, with their broken semiquaver figure, appear to hesitate, but are pulled up suddenly at the pause bar (4).

Then comes a modulation to A major, and with it a slow and swaying dance measure, which is Spanish, Moorish, or possibly Oriental in character,

Ex. 16.

and again the sinister influence of the wood is felt.

At figure (6) the music again changes key and becomes more animated, and though it still has the lilt of the dance measure, it is more definite and human. This subtle change is short-lived, however, for soon after (7) there is again the sense of foreboding as at (1), though now (8) the position is reversed, the strings playing the theme, and the piano the broken semiquaver figure.

With alternations and elaborations of these moods, this remarkable movement proceeds through the development and recapitulation sections, until it ends in rather a gloomy manner, leaving the listener with an uncanny feeling of awe.

The beautiful slow movement which follows opens with a sublime melody entrusted to the viola.

Ex. 17.

It abounds in finely shaped and polished phrases, and, with its warmth of expression and inspired moments, it appears to have grown like some work of nature, without the help of human hands. It seems supererogatory to attempt technical analysis of such a piece of music, which expresses all the higher emotions of which humanity is capable. It expresses them so truly and sincerely, and goes so much farther into the hidden meaning of things than can any mere words, that it seems to be a message from another world.

The finale opens with the questioning phrase which appears frequently in the first movement.

Ex. 18.

Almost at once it reaches a fierce climax, then, after a pause, as if to take breath, it breaks forth into a dignified and ringing melody, played by the strings in unison, against a few fragmentary chords in the piano part.

Ex. 19.

This theme is treated at considerable length, and reappears at (46), *sostenuto*, expanded and more fully harmonized.

At (49) a new theme appears, of an Eastern character, reminiscent of the haunting dance measure heard at (5) in the first movement.

Ex. 20.

At (51) and (52) the movement becomes more animated and almost violent in character, with its rushing triplet figures and wild descending passages in semiquavers, first on one instrument and then on another. After (53) the excitement gradually subsides, and the mood becomes more tranquil and sombre, as it leads back to the idea of the first movement. This is now treated differently, and transformed, as if the mystery had been removed. The staccato crotchets with which the strings now accompany the principal theme no longer hesitate, but trip along lightly and fearlessly, until they, too, join in the mystical spirit that pervades this section of the movement.

The remainder consists of further development of the themes, and a gradual drawing together of all the threads. The sonority seems to grow towards the end of the work, until at (72) (grandioso) the supreme climax is reached, and with a further quickening of the tempo and a brilliant peroration, the whole work ends in triumph. W. H. REED.

[I am glad to add a few words to the above article, if only to place on record the enthusiasm with which the news was greeted in 1919 by every ensemble player in the United Kingdom, that Elgar had added three master works to the repertory. He had so long been engaged upon the composition of works conceived on a large scale that his entry into the chamber music world was as unexpected as it was welcome.

The first time I heard the sonata I was surprised at the knowledge displayed by Sir Edward of the inner life of the violin. I have learned since that he is the author of a book of studies written for virtuoso players, so that of all modern composers he is the best qualified technically to write for that instrument. The arpeggios in the first movement, of which Mr. Reed speaks, are worthy of Bach, and they are followed at intervals by sustained semibreves which appeal heavenwards in a strain of impassioned idealism. The remaining movements needed several hearings before I was able to appreciate them at their full value. Later, the tender romanticism of the middle movement made a great impression, though the fantastic element which predominates seemed at first a little strained. A brilliant violinistic effect is heard in the concluding bars of the finale. One is dazzled by the final chord as by a flash of light.

I first heard the quartet led by Albert Sammons, an ideal interpreter of Elgar's music, especially of the violin concerto of which fragmentary reminiscences are heard in the two outer movements. He took the opening bars a shade slower than the metronome tempo (dotted crotchet = 80), with, I thought, fine effect. The developments later on are less spontaneous than the rest of the quartet. In any case this section needs, to make it interesting, the co-operation of artists of high rank at all the desks.

Every single bar seems to be carefully thought out, the close once more providing a thrill. The viola intones a sonorous octave C in the lower strings; then, after a catch of the breath, the major is reached and a pianissimo chord brings the movement to a restful conclusion.

In the pastoral, essentially English middle movement, the summer breeze sets leaves stirring and branches swaying, and sweeps over the strings of an Aeolian harp. Mingling with these sounds of nature is heard the murmur of a human voice, sad yet without a trace of bitterness. It was a favourite movement with Lady Elgar, and was played in the chapel on the occasion of her funeral.

Of the slow movement of the piano quintet, which gives the viola so grand an opportunity, Mr. Reed has written fully. The outer movements recall Brahms as far as the strings are concerned, but the piano part is written in a style quite new to chamber music, not in the concerto style usually adopted by composers for piano and strings, but as one part in five; a highly artistic, if not a pianistic conception.

EDITOR.]

†ELLERTON, JOHN LODGE, 1807–1873, amateur English composer.

Ellerton's fertility of production, but unfortunately not of invention, resulted in a large output of string quartets and other chamber music. *Grove* mentions fifty-four quartets, of which I have particulars of twenty-one, published by Augener and Schott between 1849 and 1874, and of other works, with details of which I do not propose to encumber this book.

He wrote at a time when British composition was at a low ebb, and consequently his very mediocre work received some attention from amateurs. It is only fair to add that I received a letter from an American musician (Mr. H. D. Hewitt) in which he says, 'Our Quartet Club has often played a quartet by Ellerton in F major, and a good quartet it is too, with a beautiful andante'.

Ellerton was a good friend to Wagner when the latter was in England. EDITOR.

†EMBORG, JENS LAURSON, Swedish composer,

4th quartet (*Oktober*), str op. 42 Leuckart, 1922.

†EMMANUEL, MAURICE, b. 1862, French composer.

	Composed	
2nd quartet, str, B flat	1903	Durand, 1912.
Trio-sonata, pf, fl, cl	1907	,,
Sonata, pf, v, d mi	1902	,, 1910.
Suite on Greek folk-tunes, pf, v	1907	,, 1918.
Sonata, pf, vc, b mi	1887–90	Senart, 1922.

At the present time (1927) professor of history at the Paris Conservatoire, whence he was expelled in his youth for using the modal scales of his native Burgundy in his earliest works, Maurice Emmanuel is now considered to be a learned musician.

A declared partisan for extending the use of ancient, popular, or oriental tonalities to music in general, he found himself in disgrace, and, in his despondency, decided to write works in a more academic style—works which he later destroyed.

It was only in 1905 that he clearly perceived the path which he must follow. Henceforth all his works bear the impress of a strong personality, and are systematically written in those tonalities which are most completely opposed to the classical sense of key.

THE 'CELLO SONATA is akin to the classical form, but with certain variations. The first theme of the allegro is in B minor with C natural—the second in B minor with the C sharp and A natural. The largo is in Lied form: A—B—A. The finale, in the form of a gigue, is lively and rhythmic, and is developed at some length, the work being in cyclic form.

THE VIOLIN SONATA is developed at great length; it is somewhat influenced by the great sonatas of Franck and d'Indy. The style is, however, very individual, and the harmonies are bold, with a free use of dissonances.

The first theme of the opening allegro is given out in the bass, then taken up by the violin in augmentation. The second theme (in F) is short, and the repeat follows immediately. In the development the opening theme is transformed; it is inverted; it appears in canon. After the recapitulation of the two themes they are developed afresh in a lengthy coda.

The adagio is in the form of a recitative, in which the theme A reappears. The finale opens with an introduction; then the rondo, bold and lively, is set forth. The theme is derived from the first theme of the first movement. Beginning in quavers, it returns later, in crotchets, to form the first couplet[1]; the refrain[1] is now in B flat minor. The second couplet brings back the theme in crotchets, interrupted by a brief reminiscence of the adagio, then the refrain returns again, leading to a coda in which the same theme appears once more, this time in minims (A).

Ex. 1.

1st Movement.

and farther on:

[1] See Foreword, art. BEETHOVEN.

STRING QUARTET. Emmanuel's first quartet (in MS.) belongs to an epoch when he hesitated before breaking with the forms of the past; the second quartet, on the other hand, is the full manifestation of his present tendencies. The work is of a high order, and is the utterance of a fine musician who knows what he wants, and who formulates his ideas entirely in his own fashion.

The first movement reminds one somewhat of Beethoven's last quartets in its continual alternation of quick and slow tempi, and in the violent contrast of ideas which are diametrically opposed to one another. The second movement, after a few bars of andante, contains a charming allegro vivace (6/8), beautifully clear both in ideas and in style.

Ex. 2.

Allegro vivace.

and farther on :

This motif, interrupted by a scrap of adagio, is further developed before the expressive ending.

The finale, *alla Zingarese*, is full of life. With chords from viola and 'cello to mark the rhythm, the theme is developed on the violins before passing to all the instruments. Fierce semiquaver passages continually sweep through it, and give to the whole movement a character of wild fury.

Ex. 3.

Allegro con fuoco alla zingarese.

H. WOOLLETT.

ENACOVICI, GEORGES. *v.* ROUMANIAN COMPOSERS.

*†**ENESCO**, GEORGES, b. 1881, Roumanian composer and violinist.

Octet, str, C	op. 7	Enoch (Paris)	1905.
1st sonata, pf, v, D	,, 2	,, ,,	1898.
2nd sonata, pf, v, f mi	,, 6	,, ,,	1901.
3rd sonata, pf, v		In the press.	

From 1888 to 1894 Enesco studied at the Conservatorium of Vienna, violin under Hellmesberger, and composition under Rob. Fuchs. From 1895 to 1900 he was at the Paris Conservatoire, studying violin with Marsick, composition with Massenet, Fauré, and Gédalge. He took a first prize for violin in 1899.

Enesco is a man of genius whose influence on the younger generation of Roumanian musicians has been decisive. F. LAZAR.

[The third sonata for pf and v, dedicated to Franz Kneisel, is in course of publication. The octet is a wild, impassioned work, difficult in regard to the ensemble, but the sonatas are more straightforward and classical in style. Enesco has the reputation of being a fine pianist as well as violinist. EDITOR.]

†**ENGEL**, CARL, b. 1883, American composer and musicologist.

Triptych, pf, v, g mi Boston Music Co., 1920.

Carl Engel, though European by birth, has played an important part in the encouragement and development of the higher musical endeavours in the United States, where he became a resident in 1905. In 1909 he accepted the post of editorial adviser to the Boston Music Co., and occupied this position until 1921, when he was appointed head of the music division of the Library of Congress at Washington, D. C.

Engel's single work in larger form—the *Triptych* for violin and piano—is his most significant utterance. Here is a work suffused with intimate charm, deep emotion, and mordant irony. From the first to the last bar one is impressed with the intensely subjective character of the expression. There is never the slightest truckling to academic expediency, and the work is typically modern in its harmonic and tonal freedom. There is notable plasticity of form, and much dissonance, the manipulation of which is both delicate and adroit. The technical difficulties are very considerable, and need not be minimized, since they present problems of a nature that will fascinate the mind and fingers and enthral the ear. Indeed, to performers on first acquaintance there may well seem to be too many fascinating details, but to listeners the expressive power and lyricism will finally predominate and linger in the memory.

A record of Engel's activities would be incomplete without mention of his important association with the splendid project of Mrs. F. S. COOLIDGE (*q.v.*), whose patronage has given a lively impetus to chamber music in the United States. The headquarters of Mrs. Coolidge's enterprise have recently been established in Washington, where the entire series of concerts is now under the direct supervision of Mr. Engel. ARTHUR SHEPHERD.

†**ENGELSMANN**, WALTER.

Trio, pf, v, vc, C	op. 6	Kahnt,	1915.
Sonata, pf, vc, a mi		,,	1911.

ENGLISH HORN. *v.* COR ANGLAIS.

ENTERTAINMENT TAX.

A British tax upon the endeavours of chamber music players to elevate the public taste without adequate pecuniary reward. A brake upon wheels labouring up-hill. EDITOR.

†**ERB**, MARIA JOSEF, b. 1860, Alsatian composer.

Quartet, str, F		Senart.
Sonata, pf, v, e mi	op. 21	U.E., 1901.
Suite, pf, v, B flat	,, 45	,, ,,

This composer's quartet has been spoken of in a French periodical as containing an impressive funeral march, an elegantly written minuet, and a fiery finale.

†**ERDMANN**, EDUARD, b. 1896, Latvian composer.

One of the most prominent modern composers in Germany, where he is now domiciled. He has written no chamber music in the strict sense, but a sonata for violin alone was played at one of the festivals of the International Society.

ERDMANNSDÖRFER, MAX VON, 1848–1905, German composer.

Trio, pf, v, vc, a mi	op. 27	Fürstner, 1880.
Sonata, pf, v, e mi	,, 25	Schott, 1877.

†ERHART, Dorothy, English composer.

Quintet, pf, 2 v, vla, vc, D	Chester, 1917.

v. article Women Composers.

†ERLANGER, Baron Frédéric d', b. 1868, French composer, naturalized British subject.

Quartet, str, F	Rouart, *c.* 1900.
Quintet, pf, 2 v, vla, vc, c mi	Simrock, *c.* 1901.
Sonata, pf, v, g mi	Rouart, 1910.

Baron Frédéric d'Erlanger is the son of Baron Émile d'Erlanger, of the famous banking house. Some of his early works appeared under the name of Frédéric Regnal, in order to avoid confusion with another composer of the same surname. It was about the same time that he first manifested his interest in chamber music, in a string quartet and a violin sonata, which, however, must be regarded as immature. Apart from these he is represented only by his quintet. It is a clear and sunny work, combining a certain French flavour in the lyrical themes and their harmonization, with close adherence to German formal tradition. Individuality is not aggressively shown, but the absence of any suggestion of the portentous leaves an engaging intimacy, which makes it more agreeable to play than many quintets of the same rank but greater pretensions. It is in the usual four movements, of which the andante and scherzo are the most attractive. The suavity of the former is relieved by an episode which verges on the dramatic, and the latter, though formal, is not lacking in vivacious phantasy. Edwin Evans.

[A brilliant performance of Baron d'Erlanger's quintet was given at the 'Pops' on March 1, 1902, with the composer at the piano. The artists were recalled three times to the platform. His string quartet is distinguished by grace and charm, and is well suited for performance in private circles. Editor.]

ERLANGER, Gustav, 1842–1908, German composer, pupil of Reinecke.

Sextet, v, vla, vc, cl, horn, fag, E flat	op. 41	Kistner, 1882.
Quintet, pf, 2 v, vla, vc	„ 39	„ 1880.
Sonata, pf, v, d mi	„ 44	Zimmermann, 1890.

ERLEBACH, Rupert O., b. 1894, English composer and pianist.

Folk-song sonata, pf, vc, C	op. 8	Curwen.

A rhapsody for flute, oboe (or cor anglais), violin, viola, and 'cello received a supplementary Carnegie Award (1922), MS. copies being provided in order to facilitate performance. The parts are obtainable from Stainer & Bell.

ERNST, Heinrich Wilhelm, 1814–1865, German violin virtuoso.

Quartet, str, B flat	op. 26	Cranz, 1864.

Two of Ernst's quartets were played at the 'Pops' in 1863–4, one of them, in A major, from manuscript. Their quality is of the poorest. Ernst, who was once himself a superb quartet leader, had fallen upon evil days, and one of these concerts was organized, at Joachim's instigation, for his benefit.

The *Pensées fugitives*, for pf and v, in which Ernst collaborated with Stephen Heller, are elegant pieces, each provided with a poetic motto—typical drawing-room music. Editor.

†ERTEL, Jean Paul, b. 1865, German pianist.

Quartet on Hebrew Melodies (*Hebraikon*), str, d mi	op. 14	Kistner, 1912.
Suite im alten Stil, pf, v, D	„ 38	Leuckart, 1912.

The Hebraic melodies treated in Ertel's three-movement quartet are to be heard in the synagogue to-day. The second movement, which stands out from the rest, consists of four variations on a 'Pessach' melody, of which Dr. Altmann writes as follows:

> 'I cannot conceive why the composer has dedicated these variations to the *manes* of Franz Schubert (who was not of Jewish birth), and linked them with the main theme of the great C major symphony.'

It may, however, be suggested that at the present moment the recent occurrence of the centenary of Schubert's death lends interest to Ertel's quartet. Editor.

ESCRICHE, E. Halffter. *v.* Halffter Escriche.

ESPLÁ, Oscar, b. 1886, Spanish composer.

Sonata, pf, v	Unión Musical (Madrid).

The thematic material (in the last three movements in particular) is derived from little-known folk melodies from the composer's native province, the so-called 'región levantina' in the east of Spain. For instance:

Ex. 1.

The lyrical character of the sonata in general may be exemplified by the following bars from the first movement (Ex. 2). This sonata, marked op. 9, is, both from the technical and aesthetic points of view, the most ambitious specimen of its kind as yet produced in Spain.

Ex. 2.

It is, at the same time, an early announcement of the characteristic sincerity and discretion of the composer as shown in subsequent and maturer works. O. Esplá has also composed a piano trio and a piano quintet, both unpublished. PEDRO G. MORALES.

[On the question of the peculiar scale employed by Esplá, the reader is referred to the article in *Dent* by the same author.]

†ESPOSITO, MICHELE, b. 1855, Italian composer and pianist.

		Composed	
Quartet, str, D (Feis Ceoil prize, 1899)	op. 33	1886	B. & H.
Quartet, str, c mi (Concorso Internazionale prize, 1908)	,, 60	1906	,, C. E. Ed. (Dublin).
Sonata, pf, v, G	,, 32	1885	Schott.
Sonata, pf, v, e mi (Concours International de Musique prize, 1907)	,, 46	1899	Astruc (Paris).
Sonata, pf, v, A	,, 67	1913	C. E. Ed. (Dublin).
Sonata, pf, vc, D (Incorp. Soc. of Musicians prize, 1898).	,, 43	1898	B. & H.

Esposito went to Dublin in 1882 as professor of piano playing at the Royal Irish Academy of Music. He was the pianist for many years at the concerts of classical chamber music organized by the Royal Dublin Society. He resigned his position in 1928, and returned to Florence.

THE FIRST SONATA is an unambitious work of considerable melodic beauty, with a finale based on a subject of Hungarian character.

THE STRING QUARTET IN D has an opening based on a quiet phrase announced by the viola and taken up in succession by the other instruments, leading to a more agitated section. An allegretto with the sub-title intermezzo is followed by an adagio which embodies much excellent part-writing. The finale has a fugal development.

THE 'CELLO SONATA in D opens with a lovely phrase for 'cello, answered by the piano, leading, after some development, to a more animated section. The second movement (lento) has a sustained melody with staccato moving bass.

VIOLIN SONATA IN E MINOR. A feature of this work is the second movement (andantino), which opens with pizzicato chords on the violin answered by short ritornelli on the piano. A contrasting passage occurs before a return to the opening phrases. The finale is founded upon an energetic subject with a brilliant piano part; an expressive second subject leads directly into a new theme of great beauty played in turn by each instrument.

THE QUARTET IN C MINOR is mainly in energetic and fiery mood, with a triumphant close in C major.

THE VIOLIN SONATA IN G opens *affettuosamente* with a lovely interrogative phrase for the violin, later taken up by the piano. The second movement consists chiefly of a short syncopated subject, with a graceful and fanciful accompaniment. The andante cantabile is constructed on a dignified melody with varied accompaniment. The allegretto grazioso, in rondo form, has a charming opening subject elaborated with contrasting themes; it is a movement of singular beauty, imbued with a spirit of serenity and happiness as rare in modern music as it is delightful.

Esposito's chamber music is classical in form, but the harmonic treatment shows modern tendencies. His work is dominated by an ordered sequence, imposing a restraint often lacking in modern music. His music displays the tenderness and fire of an Italian temperament, and this gives it great charm and beauty. EDITH BEST.

ESSER, HEINRICH, 1818–1872, German violinist.

Quartet, str, g mi	op. 5	Simrock.
Trio, pf, v, vc, E	op. 6	Schott, 1842.

'As a composer Esser was industrious and successful. His works contain scarcely a commonplace thought, and much earnest feeling, well and naturally expressed.' (*Grove.*)

EVERS, KARL, 1819–1875, German pianist.

Two quartets, str, G, E flat	opp. 52, 58	Kistner, 1854.
Trio, pf, v, vc, A flat	op. 99	Cranz, 1876.
Sonata, pf, v, D	„ 65	Kistner, 1854.

Evers was under Mendelssohn at Leipzig. Fétis says, 'As a composer Evers is distinguished by a feeling for beauty, serious thought, and purity of style, though his works are mostly in modern forms'. A reminder that modernism is a relative term.

†EVSEIEV, SERGE VASSILIEVITCH, b. 1894, Russian pianist.

Trio (*Heroic Poem*), pf, v, vc, G	op. 7	Mus. Sect. State Publ. Dept. 1923.

Evseiev is a young composer belonging to the Moscow group, a pupil of Goedicke and Miaskovsky. He entered the arena whilst still a student, and at first showed very brilliant promise as an extremely talented composer, possessed of a great melodic gift. His style shows no tendency towards the 'left', but on the contrary is rather reactionary and reminiscent of the early Scriabin and Rachmaninov. This is the key-note of the only chamber composition which he has so far produced—the *Heroic Trio*—a big work in a mixture of styles; it shows the influence of Rachmaninov and Scriabin, together with traces of Arensky and Grieg. It is written with much pathos and is not wanting in a broad lyricism, but the multiplicity of influences, the lack of independence, and the diffuseness are serious defects. Evseiev's chamber style is rather clumsy, and the heaviness of the piano part drowns the strings to a certain extent. These faults are of course explained by the composer's insufficient experience. Judging from his latest compositions, however, it seems improbable that his creative work will develop into anything independent. L. SABANEIEV.

†EWALD, VICTOR, b. 1860, Russian composer.

Quintet, 2 v, 2 vla, vc, A	op. 4	Belaiev, 1895.
Quintet, 2 horns, althorn, tenor horn (or baritone), tuba, b flat mi	„ 5	„ 1911.
Quartet, str, C	„ 1	„ 1894.

Like so many Russian composers, Ewald has another profession besides music, being professor at the High School of Civil Engineering at Petrograd. His music belongs to the school of Tchaikovsky. It is written with a developed sense for charming sound, though not with much polyphonic art, and is not difficult technically. HUGO LEICHTENTRITT.

†EYBLER, JOSEPH (EDLER VON), 1765–1846, Austrian composer. Pupil of Albrechtsberger.

Three quartets, str (dedicated to Haydn)	op. 1	Traeg (Vienna), *c.* 1794.
Three quartets, str	„ 10	„ „

A long and interesting notice of Eybler is in *Grove*. 'He played quartets regularly with the Emperor Francis II (of Austria), and was ennobled by him in 1834. His chamber music . . . was popular in its day. He was tenderly attached to Mozart, whom he nursed in his last illness.'

F

FACULTY OF ARTS, Golden Square, Regent Street, London, an association of workers engaged in every branch of art. Its musical section (Faculty of Music) has activities which lie along several separate roads, all, however, tending towards a common goal, i.e. the performance of interesting chamber music in the most favourable conditions. They may be enumerated as follows:

1. A music library assembled for the use of members and students.
2. A quartet of string players available for the trial of new works as opportunity offers.
3. Invitation concerts periodically arranged for the production of new works of composer members.
4. Concerts of chamber music (to which the general public is admitted), under the title of 'Concerts Spirituels'. The idea underlying the construction of the programmes of these concerts is that of contrasting contemporary music with that of the classical schools, by judicious juxtaposition in the same scheme, thus securing variety, to the mutual advantage of each type of music given.

The programmes, since January 1926, have included a number of contemporary chamber works, many of which have been given for the first or second time. HERBERT BEDFORD.

†**FÄHRMANN**, HANS [ERNST HANS], b. 1860, German organist.

Quartet, str, e mi	op. 42	Junne, 1913.
Trio, pf, v, vc, B	,, 37	,, 1907.
Trio, pf, v, vc, c sharp mi	,, 43	,, 1909.

†**FAIRCHILD**, BLAIR, b. 1877, American composer, pupil of Widor.

Quartet, str, d mi		Eschig (Demets).
Quartet, str, g mi	op. 27	,, ,, 1911.
Chamber concerto ('*Concert de Chambre*'), pf, v, str. quartet, cb ad lib.	,, 26	Augener, 1912.
Quintet, pf, 2 v, vla, vc		Hayet, *c.* 1920.
Rhapsody, pf, 2 v, vla, vc		,, *c.* 1920.
Trio, pf, v, vc	,, 24	Augener, 1919.
Sonata, pf, v, c mi		Durdilly, 1908.
Sonata, pf, v, e mi	,, 43	Durand, 1919.

Fairchild received his first music lessons in Boston, but in 1903 he settled in Paris, devoting himself thenceforth exclusively to musical composition. He is one of the most prolific of American chamber composers, having written eight works, ranging from the unpretentious two *Novelettes* for string quartet, op. 10, to the formal *Concert de chambre*. As the list of his compositions shows, the balance between these extremes is held by the more conventional forms of chamber music for two, three, or more instruments. Though he lived for a time in the East, his chamber music is free from oriental influence. Rather has it taken on a good deal of the colour of the purely French environment in which he has spent the most fruitful years of his musical labours. Perhaps in his eagerness to adopt a style, the clarity, polish, and refinement of which were congenial to his own nature, the composer has allowed it to become suffused with less personal tints, which rather efface the outlines of his own musical physiognomy. Thus the impeccable workmanship, studiously learnt from his French masters, has perhaps unfitted him to strike out more boldly. However, what Fairchild has to say is well expressed, competently presented, and singularly free from redundance. Beginning with the piano trio, the composer's methods gain in surety and effectiveness. His flow of ideas is unhampered, yet free from prolixity. A keenly disciplined mind and fastidious taste are apparent in all of his later chamber works. CARL ENGEL.

†**FAISST**, CLARA, German composer.

Sonata, pf, v, G	op. 14	Simrock, 1912.

This sonata had the honour of a favourable notice, rarely accorded to women composers, from the critic of *The Times* in 1913.

FALL, SIEGFRIED, b. 1877, pupil of Max Bruch.

		Composed	
Quartet, str, e mi	op. 9	1915	Stahl (Nuremberg), 1924.
Trio, pf, v, vc, a mi	,, 4		Kistner, 1900.

Dr. Altmann (*Handbuch*) gives high praise to Fall's quartet, which, he says, is written in true chamber music style, exception being made of the adagio, an elegiac movement evidently written to honour the memory of a friend who fell in the great war. It includes an attractive viola solo, somewhat operatic in style.

†**FALLA**, MANUEL DE, b. 1876, Spanish composer.

Psyche (French words by G. Jean Aubry), mezzo-soprano, fl, harp, v, vla, vc	Chester.
Concerto, clavicembalo (or piano), fl, ob, cl, v, vc	Eschig.

The latter composition, which is in three movements—allegro, lento, vivace—is wrongly described at times as a 'Concerto' for clavicembalo and small orchestra, but is in reality a concerto da camera for the six instruments mentioned, in which the clavicembalo predominates not as a solo in the accepted sense of the word, but as the leading part in a polyphonic ensemble.

The origin of its inspiration is to be found in old Spanish music, mainly liturgical. The writing in its ultra-modern retrospection may appear to many experimental, the composer relying for his effects on a sensitive handling of rhythm and harmony independent of melody, which is made use of only as an elusive element. Up to the present this strikingly original composition is the most advanced ever written by this distinguished artist, generally recognized as the outstanding figure of his profession in Spain. The work is dedicated to Madam Wanda Landowska, for whom it was composed, and was first performed in England by the composer in 1927. It appears on the programme of the festival of the International Society for Contemporary Music, Siena, 1928. *Psyche* was first performed in London, in 1926, with Anne Thursfield as vocalist.

PEDRO G. MORALES.

†FALTIS, EVELYN, b. (Trautenau, Bohemia) 1890.

Sonata, pf, v, d mi	op. 6	R. & E., 1923.

This woman composer has written a number of other chamber works.

FAMINZIN, ALEXANDER SERGEIVITCH, 1841–1896, Russian composer and historian.

Quartet, str, E flat	op 1	Kahnt, 1869.
Serenade, str. quartet, d mi	,, 7	Fürstner, 1877.

Faminzin received his musical education in Petersburg and Leipzig. This partly accounts for his attitude of hostility to the composers of the Russian National school. Dr. Altmann (*Handbuch*) has something to say in favour of the chamber works of Faminzin, who had a special preference for fugal form, and, in his quartet op. 1, makes frequent use of the old church modes. The unusually named 'Serenade' quartet has for its finale a set of variations on a smoothly written andantino: (1) canone, (2) valso, (3) andante, (4) scherzino. The third variation appears to Dr. Altmann to be the most original, but he warns the reader against possible disappointment!

EDITOR.

FANCY.

The English Fancy—or Fancie—was an improvement made by English musicians on the Italian instrumental music of their day, and constitutes a notable advance on the ricercari and fantazias of the Italians. This evolution from the fantazia to the fancy played an important part in the history of chamber music, and the fancies are worthy of more attention than they have yet received.

To quote from a lecture by the late Sir Frederick Bridge:

'The fancy was cultivated as an instrumental form of chamber music down to the Stuart period, and there are examples on record by Ferrabosco, Coperario, Lupo, William White, John Ward, Dr. Charles Coleman, John Jenkins, Matthew Locke, and in fact nearly every composer of instrumental music during about eighty years previous to 1670. The fancy was the counterpart of the chamber quartet and trio of the present day.'

In the days of the viols, then, chamber music was a real and living thing, and, were not the imperial aims and ends of the British people so opposed to its interests, it would probably have developed into a national art, being for so many reasons akin to the English nature.

Sir Frederick Bridge devoted one of his lectures to a consideration of the instrumental music of Orlando Gibbons. Personally I thought that Gibbons's three-part music, fine as it is, had more of the austerity of church music and less of the imaginative quality which becomes a writer of fancies than that of other composers, but at subsequent lectures I heard fancies by Ravenscroft, Deering, Ward, Lawes, Crawford, Locke, and others, which were a revelation to me. They contain striking little adumbrations of modern harmony and string effect which would not have shamed one of the great writers of a later century. That they were full of naïvetés of construction and tonality—rarely ending in the initial key—and that development was absent for the most part is not surprising, considering their date, but as centuries-old native productions they were so interesting that I was moved to commission a number of composers of the younger generation to write so-called *Phantasies* for various chamber combinations—works which may be described as the modern analogues of the fancies, conceived of course in modern idiom, and without their structural defects.

The fancies are not formless, though the form is not of the academic type; some may be described as being in abbreviated sonata form, all being in one movement, but in varying tempi.

I heard the fancies played on modern instruments, but with a second viola in place of a second violin: Sir Frederick had wished to have them played upon the viols for which they were originally written, but this was found to be impracticable. In the case of a short piece by Henry Purcell, the thickness of tone produced was especially noticeable, and a second experience of another piece by Purcell produced the same result.

Some of Purcell's pieces have recently been edited by André Mangeot and Peter Warlock for modern stringed instruments. One of these is a fantazia on one note, the viola holding middle C throughout. Others are written in the form called the *In Nomine*, which has a fixed melody in one of the parts, with imitation by the others.

EDITOR.

†FANELLI, ERNEST, 1860–1919, French composer.

A composer who was discovered too late, and died with many of his best works in MS. Among them is a string quintet.

FANO, GUIDO ALBERTO, b. 1875, Italian pianist.

Sonata, pf, vc, d mi	op. 7	B. & H., 1905.

The Milan Società del Quartetto awarded him a prize in 1898 for a violin sonata.

FANTASY. *v.* PHANTASY.

†FARJEON, HARRY, b. 1878, English composer.

4th quartet, str, C	op. 65	Paxton, *c.* 1927.

The quartet, which is in three movements, opens brightly with the main subject. The first bar contains an upward semiquaver figure which assumes considerable importance later, whilst the second theme, in G, is of a more cantabile character. Both themes are treated in the development, and the recapitulation is somewhat abbreviated.

The andante, which opens with a long solo for first violin, is mainly tranquil in mood, but grows more agitated in the quicker middle section (in A minor). A feature of this movement is the frequency of the 'French sixth'.

The finale opens with a theme in the style of a jolly country dance, and continues on normal lines. The quartet is not difficult, and is well written for the instruments. There is no research after modernity.

M. DRAKE-BROCKMAN.

†FARNABY, GILES, b. *c.* 1560.

Modern republication:

Suite of seven short pieces, pf, 2 v vla, vc	Novello.

A great Elizabethan composer whose work is becoming increasingly popular.

FARRAR, ERNEST BRISTOW, 1885–1918 (killed in action), English composer.

Celtic suite, pf, v (after Fiona Macleod)	op. 11	Novello.

A composer of strong nationalistic tendencies.

FARRENC, LOUISE [JEANNE-LOUISE], *née* DUMONT, 1804–1875, French composer and pianist.

Quintet, pf, v, vla, vc, cb, a mi	op. 30	Costallat, Hofmeister	1842.
Quintet, pf, v, vla, vc, cb, E	,, 31	Farrenc.	
Trio, pf, v, vc, E flat	,, 33	Leduc.	
Trio, pf, v, vc, d mi	,, 34	Farrenc.	
Trio, pf, fl or v, vc, e mi	,, 45	Leduc, *c.* 1850.	
Sonata, pf, v, c mi	op. 37	Leduc, *c.* 1848.	
Sonata, pf, v, A	,, 39	,,	
Sonata, pf, vc, B flat	,, 46	,, *c.* 1851.	

and several sets of variations for various combinations.

Madame Farrenc and her husband were both composers, she much the more famous. For her nonet, sextet, quintets, and sonatas she obtained in 1869 the prize of the Académie des Beaux-Arts, and shared with Ch. Dancla the first Prix Chartier (for chamber works) in 1861, the year of its inception. Voluminous notices of both Farrencs are in *Fétis* and *Pougin*. She is best known by the *Trésor des Pianistes*. See also article FRENCH CHAMBER MUSIC.

M. DRAKE-BROCKMAN.

FASCH, JOHANN FRIEDRICH, 1688–1758, German composer.

Modern republications include an 'orchestral' quartet and five trio sonatas, in H. Riemann's *Collegium Musicum* (B. & H.), details of which are given below.

Sonata, str. quartet, d mi	Coll. Mus. 13, B. & H., 1914.
Three trios, pf, 2 v, vc (ad lib.), a mi, F, G	Coll. Mus. 10–12, B. & H., 1903-4.
Two trios in canon, pf, v, vla, d mi, D	Coll. Mus. 8–9, B. & H., 1903.

Bach thought so highly of Fasch's music that he copied out five of his orchestral suites. The quartet is one of the earliest known.

†FAURÉ, GABRIEL URBAIN, 1845–1925, French composer, former Principal of the Paris Conservatoire.

	op.	Composed	
Quartet, str	121	1925	Durand.
Quintet, pf, 2 v, vla, vc, d mi	89	1906	Schirmer; Hamelle.
Quintet, pf, 2 v, vla, vc, c mi	115	1921	Durand.
Quartet, pf, v, vla, vc, c mi	15	1879	Hamelle.
Quartet, pf, v, vla, vc, g mi	45	1886	,,
Trio, pf, v, vc, d mi	120	[*c.* 1924]	Durand.
Sonata, pf, v, A	13	1876	B. & H.
Sonata, pf, v, e mi and E	108	1917	Durand.
Sonata, pf, vc, d mi	109	1918	,,
Sonata, pf, vc, g mi	117	1921	,,

NOTE.—Messrs. Durand publish a photographic reproduction of the original MS. of Fauré's string quartet in score.

Chamber music has an important place in Gabriel Fauré's list of compositions: it is most certainly more important than the piano works, and even than the collection of songs, which are, nevertheless, regarded by a superficial public as Fauré's principal work.

THE VIOLIN SONATA, op. 13, though a 'coup d'essai', is none the less a 'coup de maître'. It was performed for the first time by the composer and Paul Viardot, at the concerts of the

1878 Exhibition, in the Trocadéro. It is in the four traditional movements. The opening allegro molto begins with a splendid outburst on the piano—the first part of a noble melody which is completed by the violin. A short dialogue between the instruments leads to the second subject, in the dominant, a more peaceful and tender melody, followed by a prolonged repose on the new tonic, in accordance with a habit from which Fauré was rarely to depart. After the double-bar, quite in the classical style, comes a working-out of various rhythmic figures. But here the development is far from being a watertight compartment in which the working-out of the themes begins by opening the left-hand partition and ends by shutting the right-hand one—unfortunate but necessary, it would seem—a place whence the musician, entangled in his contrapuntal web, generally emerges worn out, with a sigh of relief at the reappearance of the theme in its entirety.

With Fauré there is nothing of this; the music flows on with the same unconstraint and the same graceful ease, yet never appears to lack invention.

The second movement, at first in D minor, then in the major, is an andante of admirable purity of line. Against a gently rocking 9/8 theme on the piano, the violin introduces a phrase of tender melancholy. Then the disposition of the instruments is inverted, and a brief coda in dialogue leads to the second subject, in the relative major. The first phrase modulates and expands. No further use is made of the second theme till it reappears in due course, after the recapitulation and in the tonic—D major—and provides a happy conclusion to this charming movement.

An allegro vivo follows, a scherzo of the lightness of thistledown, sparkling with swift darting passages and bounding pizzicati. By way of contrast, the middle section consists of an expressive melody accompanied at first in F sharp minor, then in A major, in a 3/4 time, three bars of which equal eighteen of the preceding. After this, the quick section is repeated almost note for note, the second part, of course, now in the tonic.

In the finale, allegro quasi presto, the piano announces a long and impassioned phrase in 6/8 time, repeated in part by the violin. Then, in the course of a dialogue with a vigorous syncopated figure, the phrase is dispersed, and vanishes, while the figure swells out and leads to the second subject, which bursts forth in octave double-stops. This, in its declamatory, almost barbaric violence, recalls some gipsy improvisation. The piano, sempre *ff*, takes up the theme, and the violin in its turn carries on the rhythmic figure. A tranquil and moving passage intervenes with a very Schumannesque incidental melody. But the agitation soon returns with the reappearance of the principal theme in the relative minor, which at first seems as if about to conclude. Then the principal theme appears in its own key, but only to escape swiftly to distant tonalities; in the course of an ingenious development it is treated in counterpoint with a most charming episodal theme. The recapitulation takes place, not in A, as expected, but in C, and the second theme, also transposed a minor third, appears in A; all is thus in order. But this reprise out of the principal key is singularly bold,[1] an infraction of the rules which must have incurred terrible censures from the Beckmessers of the day. It would be interesting to read the *Revue des Deux Mondes* of 1878! Here is an unintentional, an unwitting revolutionary, for many examples of a similar departure from the established order can be quoted in Gabriel Fauré's work.

The sonata in A appears, by its beauty and originality, on the one hand to continue a line of development which seemed to have ended with Schumann and Chopin, and, on the other hand, to foreshadow Franck's work of ten years later; and it marks a red-letter day in the history of chamber music. It is the first stage in the composer's splendid progress, and already foreshadows the two fine piano quartets and the second quintet which are the greatest of Fauré's works.

THE FIRST PIANO QUARTET, op. 15. Like the sonata, it is in four movements, with the slight difference that the andante follows the scherzo and immediately precedes the finale. This seems the more logical plan: the scherzo, with its fluid rhythms, tempers, as it were, the austerity of the allegro, and prepares for the meditation of the slow movement; then, after this peaceful oasis, the tumult begins again with renewed ardour. Without preamble—Fauré rarely has recourse to the rhetorical preliminaries of an introduction—the three strings, in their strongest register, sing aloud a bold and strongly rhythmic theme, of unusual range but admirably coherent, seconded by the sweeping syncopated chords of the piano. The song calms down momentarily, but only to burst out afresh and display itself in all its splendour. A succession of rich enharmonic changes leads to the relative major-E flat, in which key the extremely graceful and flexible second subject is announced in short phrases. The exposition concludes with an extended coda[2] in which the first theme appears in the new tonic. Then the various themes are developed in the happiest fashion, with skill and elegance; the different figures are presented now in direct, now in contrary motion, their rhythms gradually intertwining, and this with surprising ease, with no trace of scholasticism, the impression being of a con-

[1] There is an example of this in a piano sonatina of Mozart, composed 1788, no. 15, Peters Edn. The reprise is in F, and second subject in C.

[2] The French terminology is somewhat different; in England this is sometimes called the 'coda of the first part', but more frequently the 'final episode'. [ED.]

tinuous renewal. At length, in the classical recapitulation, each theme appears in its original state, the second in C major, according to tradition.

'For the master', says Roger Ducasse, 'has no thought of breaking the ancient moulds. He accommodates himself with the greatest ease to the simplest traditional forms. The development and the recapitulation are in the regular place. The four movements unreservedly obey the essential scholastic rules. His usual scheme has long been well known to us. How is it that, in this novelty-seeking age, he never disappoints us? The reason is that, with Gabriel Fauré, the one important thing is the music itself. The scheme he follows is well known? Granted; but he was endowed by the Muses with the gift of ideas full of youth and beauty. Be the flask of crystal, earth, or gold, what matters it if the imperishable scent be there? . . .'

The scherzo is a masterpiece of taste and vivacity. 'With a buzzing of fairy insects it starts off on a moonbeam, in a Shakespearian glade,' writes Louis Aquettant in his poetic sketch. Through the pizzicato of the strings there trips a breathless, hurrying phrase, interrupted by brief rests; this, when the rôles are exchanged, turns over its 6/8 rhythm to the strings, taking in exchange a more sustained and closely woven 2/4. After a dialogue between the two groups, in alternate 6/8 and 2/4 rhythm, the first section ends brilliantly on the tonic, E flat. Without other transition than a rapid accompaniment figure on the piano, the trio follows in the dominant. From the muted strings ascends a lovely song, with expressive harmonies which give it a wonderful sweetness, those Fauré harmonies which have the secret of passing through every key without modulating. The piano takes up both melody and harmony again, while the strings, each in turn, throw in their lightning runs. Then the first part is repeated note for note, quite in the classic style, except that the movement is slightly shortened by the omission of the incidental phrase which was interpolated between the two repetitions of the theme.

The adagio is one of Fauré's most typical and most justly celebrated conceptions. A solemn and deeply moving theme, at first on the 'cello alone, grows gradually more intense by the successive addition of viola and violin in unison. The piano completes the phrase with a brief and powerful crescendo. Without transition, on the fourth degree of the major scale, appears a central melody of more sensuous aspect. This is in dialogue between the strings, while the piano keeps up a rhythm in which triplets alternate with simple groups; it is developed extensively, mounts to a *ff*, leaving in its wake a series of bold and rapid figures, with which the piano accompanies the return of the first subject. On a tonic pedal, the sensuous phrase reappears as a coda, to end *pp*. Were this not very long movement—nine pages only—to be lost to us, an immeasurable void would be created in the music of the nineteenth century.

If the first subject of the finale has rather too much suggestion of the hopping rhythm of the mazurka—and a mazurka of a type which lacks the strange wildness of Chopin's masterpieces—this impression is, fortunately, not lasting. The rhythm, too, is broken by bars of 4 time, which to a certain extent save the situation, and, from page 4 onwards, a vigorous rhythmic figure restores that masculine energy which is, so to speak, the mainspring of the work. After a short episode, in which an abbreviated form of the opening theme appears, an adorably feminine second subject is displayed; this after a long ascent dies away on the tonic, in the invariable Fauré manner. On a rhythmic groundwork—an amplification of the figure announced during the exposition, but now in mysterious *pp*—a third subject is introduced, a subsidiary idea maybe, yet strangely expressive, beneath which, in the most unexpected and yet the most natural way, the melodic phrase insinuates itself. Here, as in the andante of the second quartet, is one of those discoveries peculiar to Fauré, with whom the development, far from being the rigorous dissertation admired by the Leipzig school, seems, on the contrary, to be a perpetual renewal. Into the parallel ascent of these two themes in combination there enter fragments of the principal theme, the rhythmic vigour of which leads, with a very rapid crescendo, to the recapitulation. But this last is no longer a simple transposition. A rhythmic theme, as yet merely outlined, materializes, and expands to lyric grandeur, and now, beneath this persistent theme, the second, the sensuous feminine subject, reappears, when least expected. Then the other themes, entering the lists in their turn, bring the work to a fiery conclusion.

The *Elegy* for piano and 'cello, op. 24, though eventually orchestrated, is none the less a chamber work; this is the more true as it is mostly played in its original form, and is a valuable stand-by in the virtuoso's repertory of modern music. It is only a short piece of seven pages, very simple in form, but it is a work of a very high order. The 'cello states the subject (a four-bar melody) three times, in C minor, first in a vibrant *f* on the second string, faithfully echoed by the same four bars *pp*, then, yet more mysteriously after the crescendo of an incidental phrase, which appears but this once, and so gives out straightway all its possibilities, dynamic and expressive. The piano now announces the second subject, a flexible and tender cantilena, partly syncopated and partly in triplets. This is supported by a persistent quaver-figure on the 'cello, now in its original rôle of bass, then it is taken up by the latter, leading, by a slow crescendo, to an explosion of rapid passages, which brings us to the reappearance of the opening phrase, *ff*, and at the upper limits of the A-string. On a tonic pedal, a reminiscence of the cantilena is outlined, and dies slowly and insensibly away into silence.

THE G MINOR QUARTET, op. 45, dedicated to Hans von Bülow, is separated from the C minor by an interval of seven years and some thirty works. The evolution which began with the sonata has slowly but surely continued. Individuality is more apparent, and the mastery becomes prodigious. This is the definitive Fauré: the ideas are grander, the harmony bolder, the sentiment yet deeper and more human. Never was phrase more impulsive than the impassioned opening of the allegro molto moderato; this phrase alone would have assured immortality to its composer. And this is not all. Twice announced, but interrupted by the insistence of the grandiose theme, which is hardly prevailed upon to abdicate, a tender and graceful melody appears and provides a subduing influence. A third theme, of peaceful nature, now makes its appearance. But in this feminine garb the dominating theme is readily recognized, for the present tamed and softened. The transformation of this imperious theme to an expressive melody, simply by change of mode and nuance, is undoubtedly the notable episode in this first phase of the drama. Slowly the theme gains ground, little by little its true nature is revealed. Then it is that the third theme bars the way, endeavouring in its turn to gain the upper hand. But suddenly, by way of an enharmonic change, the sovereign theme comes forward in its original key, more imperious than ever. The recapitulation is varied with a pacifying coda, in which all join hands at the final apotheosis.

The scherzo is a veritable moto perpetuo. But it is the tumult of the storm. 'The lighter material', says R. Ducasse again, 'is replaced by a stuff less elastic and closer in texture; it is no longer a transparent lace-work, the design is woven into the cloth.' And L. Aquettant: 'Wild and full of mocking laughter, it whirls in mad gyration, a round of demons or a giddy dance of Aïssanahs.' Against a pizzicato accompaniment figure, the piano starts with a swift rush, broken with syncopations which, far from checking its speed, give a suggestion of fevered haste. And this rushing motif persists, and forms the shifting foundation on which the various themes must hazard themselves. All without distinction are caught up in this frantic flight, and unity is achieved in this peculiar way. So there is no trio. But there is a second subject, which is none other than the feminine phrase of the allegro, changed from binary to ternary rhythm, the accompaniment remaining in 6/8; by this transformation it becomes singularly masculine and vigorous, delivered, as it is, full throated by the strings. Paradoxically, the dramatic opening theme—dragged in its turn into the maëlstrom—is changed into an expressive melody, which is developed with all the serenity possible in the contrasting atmosphere of storm.

'This'—my quotations are from Roger Ducasse—'is no borrowing from so-called cyclic-form, but simply a return of the two themes. Cyclic form requires, if I may venture to say so, a somewhat mechanical turn of mind, and is therefore entirely foreign to Gabriel Fauré. Already a little out of date, it has a somewhat cramping and restrictive effect on music; it has to do rather with reason than with feeling, rather with slavery to method than with free inspiration. It implies patient research, a trituration in the laboratory. To render it endurable, it simply needs ideas of genius, ideas which must not convey the impression of being the result of daily labour, but possess a freshness which gives the illusion of hearing them for the first time. Shall I name the masterpiece of cyclic form? I do not think it is to be found in Franck, nor in any of his school: this masterpiece is Debussy's quartet.'

Or rather, it *might have been* Debussy's quartet, but that the cyclism is here merely fantastic and dilettante, too much improvised to meet the needs of the moment to be suggested as the absolute and perfect model, a suggestion which, by the way, would have pained Debussy.

It is very difficult to convey in words the beauty of the third movement, adagio non troppo. From beginning to end one is overwhelmed with music of the rarest fragrance. At the very beginning, a kind of mysterious carillon on the piano alternates with a song of meditative character introduced by the viola. 'These successions of fifths, with the syncopated doubling of the tonic, sound all through this adagio like the deep tones of distant bells.'

The theme, at first elusive, has finally taken shape, and has become a phrase with ethereal accompaniment on the piano, a phrase repeated by the violin and decorated by the viola with discreet imitations. Here the piano outlines an incidental theme which, at the end of the movement, forms a moving coda. It expands, becomes impassioned, and mounts in vibrant crescendo. Again the carillon appears, heralding the second subject, in the dominant (B flat major), a long melody closely akin to the first. Materializing by degrees, it mounts, hovers, then finally descends on a tonic which here is merely suggested, the real bass, F, starting an ascending passage which ends with the chiming of bells once more.

Then follows a fugitive return of the theme. The composer did not see fit to reproduce the whole first part transposed, as in the C minor quartet, for he had in reserve a fresh scheme. After a long-held chord of the diminished fifth and sixth on F sharp, the muted 'cello draws out in longer notes the melody of the bells, this alternates with the fainter and fainter carillon of the piano, and then, on this dotted-crotchet rhythm—which is doubled by the viola in the octave—the violin, also muted, engrafts its tender cantilena in contrary motion in the most natural way. 'They all start in unison, then separate, but they separate as friends; soon they come back once more, meet, and embrace in fraternal unison.'

And the coda, with its note of plaintive resignation, lends variety to all these different beauties, and the distant effect of the mutes produces a conclusion of ethereal delicacy.

If the final allegro molto is less deeply emotional than the adagio, it at least arouses emotion of a new kind. It is instinct with extraordinary tempestuous ardour. Of joy? Not more than in the allegro or the scherzo. Almost tragic, on the contrary, is the slashing race of the triplets which rush as to the assault of some imaginary citadel. This almost brutal outburst was, so to speak, necessary, in order to break with the divine ecstasy of the adagio, a break which had to be; it is followed by a more flexible and human melody, which establishes the tonality of G minor. But while it flows on in graceful curves, the angry triplets dully rage at their threatened defeat. An incidental theme in strongly marked crotchets leads to the main second theme, in the relative major, a long phrase which in turn implores and shrieks like a chorus of lost souls, one of the most powerful and moving inspirations of the master, and one which seems absolutely inevitable in this work of genius above all. Again the triplets, in close order, attempt to break through, at first by stealth, then with open attack. But they are beaten back by the second part of the theme, on which, alone, almost the whole development is based.

After recapitulation *in extenso* of the rhythmic motif, the incidental crotchet-theme assumes unlooked-for importance: it passes to every instrument and into every key, with every shade of expression, leading finally to the second theme, in G major. The work ends with a furious rush, mingling in ever closer stretto the different themes; of these the opening triplets finally prevail, and their impetuous course ends only with the final chord.

After the second quartet Fauré seems to have given up chamber music for a time. But he was notably active in other fields. To this long period of twenty years between the G minor quartet and the D minor quintet belong a series of masterpieces, when the composer's genius was at its height.

The quintet in D minor, op. 89, impatiently awaited by the master's admirers, was completed in 1906, and first performed at the Salle Pleyel by the composer and the Ysaÿe Quartet, to whom it is dedicated. Space will not allow of a complete analysis of this perhaps rather hurriedly written work, which is inferior to the quartets in thematic invention. The D minor quintet is not one of Fauré's greatest works, but, none the less, it has sufficient merit to have established the fame of a lesser musician.

THE E MINOR VIOLIN SONATA did not appear until after another interval of twelve years. Without preamble—Fauré hated introductions—the piano, with a vigorously rhythmic theme, prepares the entry of the violin. The latter flies in octave leaps from the G to the E string, whence a tense impassioned phrase descends in irregular syncopations, i. e. on the second and the third quaver alternately in a 9/8 bar. A fiery passage in canon, derived from the principal theme, leads to the same syncopated descent in the dominant on the piano. Then the phrase becomes melodic, mounting by progressions of fourths and fifths to the dominant of G, the relative major. Then come a few peaceful bars; this is the serene and placid second subject, which, however, is but transitory. In a second exposition the first theme is developed, and the impassioned theme is in dialogue between the instruments, leading to a second, less furtive, appearance of the feminine theme, in E major. One may remark, in passing, how astonishing it is that an exaggerated respect for tonal unity should bring about two reappearances of the second theme in E major, before and after the development proper. It may be offered as some extenuation of this rather irritating redundancy, that in the recapitulation the feminine theme is changed from 9/8 to 12/8, and is freshened and altered in character by new harmonies. In the very brilliant ending, the two themes are ingeniously interwoven.

The andante is one of those wonderful inspirations into which Fauré was able to compress a whole world. Never was sweeter eloquence in the common chord of A major. And the second theme, wavering between E major and F minor, is indelibly stamped with Fauré's personality.

The finale is in E major, and goes on imperturbably in this key, with remote though brief modulations, which become irritating. The continual imitations and harmonic progressions by minor or major thirds also seem overdone. But the movement has fine unity, and the impulse never slackens.

THE 'CELLO SONATA IN D MINOR followed immediately on this second violin sonata, being written the following year. The opening allegro starts with a very rhythmic theme in triple time, set out by the 'cello in its middle register, while the piano throws in sharp chords in duple time. A second theme in the relative major is combined with the principal rhythm. In the recapitulation the theme is in the upper octave, in all the glory of the A-string, enriched with a new melodic element, which leads, in a very natural fashion, to the second subject.

The andante is in a form rather unusual with Fauré. First the principal subject is preceded by a subsidiary theme, a kind of introduction, which on its reappearance—in the subdominant—is treated more fully. Then the principal subject, which starts on the fifth degree of G minor, accompanied by the tonic chord, reappears on the first degree, accompanied by the same chord—in other words, the melody is changed, and not the key.

So in the finale, the first theme of which is a bold and extended phrase, the second seems to exhaust all its possibilities in a canon at the octave, so prolonged that the composer judged it best not to introduce it a second time. The first theme is therefore developed alone to the end.

THE SECOND QUINTET was written some years later, Fauré then being seventy-six. One would like to find as much freshness and youthful enthusiasm in the work of some of our precocious geniuses of to-day. In this work Fauré has reintroduced the scherzo, which had disappeared after op. 45. After one bar of accompaniment, the viola launches the theme. At the relative major the 'cello enters, then the second violin, and finally the first, which reproduces the whole theme. The second subject, in abrupt chords, is given out by the quartet alone, and is also interspersed with snatches of the first theme, then, becoming more flexible and melodic, it finally settles down into a long and animated colloquy between piano and strings. During the development it reappears with imitations at the fourth and the octave. A fragment of the bass accompaniment, here promoted to the rank of a new theme in an ascending progression of thirds, serves to reintroduce the first subject ingeniously at the end of a long crescendo.

The scherzo, though it has not the dramatic character of the scherzo in C minor, is clever and vivacious, and has features in common with the sonata in A. It displays an unbroken melodic line, with its rapid semiquaver figure which wanders into every group and hustles the indolent melodies aside, so that it is difficult to disentangle the themes. In any case, it would be hard to say whether the reminiscences of the first movement which seem recognizable in it are intentional or not. So many mares' nests have been discovered, notably in analysing Beethoven's sonatas, in the way of anticipations of cyclic form never dreamed of by the composer, that a decent reserve is best on this subject.

The andante moderato is full of deepest emotion. The sovereign beauty of the four-bar theme, sung by the strings in solemn grief, at once seizes the hearer. The violin and piano question and answer each other as if uncertain what they think. Their dialogue arises simply from the seeking of an inner thought, which then bursts forth, vibrant with passionate tenderness. Without other transition than a modulation from G to E minor by the shortest way, i.e. the change of the fifth, comes the second subject, with melancholy expression, on the piano, while the strings figure out a bass scale. The theme is taken up by violin and viola, the expression intensified. Soon the first subject reappears in its pride, unadorned, but slowly extends, exchanging grave confidences with the piano, and finally ends with a return of the second theme. For the third time the opening theme returns, like a kindly obsession, always on the same low strings, alternating with the second subject. After the final, supreme climax, the movement ends at last with far-away long-held notes from the quartet, and, while the piano gently whispers its final arpeggios, the souls of the listeners 'thrill with wonder'.

Then comes the finale, allegro molto, in C minor. On a triple-time bass, which the piano accents in duple rhythm, the viola gives out a short and rapid theme which mounts by degrees to the upper instruments, and is repeated in the dominant by the piano. An incidental theme, repeated in imitations, forms the transition to the second subject. This, which is more extended, is first announced by piano alone. But the strings, creeping in one by one, must make it their own to bring out its full expressiveness. After a brief reminiscence of the first subject, the opening rhythmic figure occupies the foreground, passes through the most unexpected reincarnations, and, under the caressing touch of the violin, becomes a sustained and expressive melody, which continues until the reprise. 'The changes in significance of which Fauré's themes are capable', says Louis Aubert, with perfect truth, 'are a characteristic feature of his work. Whereas, in most of the classics, each musical phrase has its own definite character—tender, passionate, mournful, joyous—which it preserves unchanged throughout, Fauré is able to invest his phrases continually with fresh interest and emotion.'

THE SECOND 'CELLO SONATA followed almost at once. Notable in the opening allegro is the unusual fusion of the development with the recapitulation, in which the composer, after a long crescendo on the first portion of the principal theme, juggles away, so to speak, the true return of this theme in its original key, and when it does reappear, the second portion only is presented. An ingenious trick, which is brought about by what had gone before. Notable, too, at the end is the delightfully 'Fauréan' coda, which modulates from G to D flat and back again in four bars.

The second movement is another example of the musician's profundity in his adagios. Its serenity and sobriety of line are even more marked than in the second violin sonata, the different themes following one another without the slightest transition. The same remark applies to the finale, allegro vivo (2/4), in which the persistent three-bar rhythm, making in reality a 3/4, gives an effect of great warmth.

THE PIANO TRIO was the next work. It is 'a little trio', as the master modestly said (and how mildly), in answer to the fatidical question, 'What are you working at?' or 'What have you on the stocks?' or 'What shall we have the pleasure of hearing this season?' &c. —a most irritating question, for people never listen to the answer—if, indeed, there is one.

Little? In dimensions, perhaps, but great in what it contains and suggests. After such numerous discoveries scattered through his immense mass of work, from the sonata in A to the second quintet, one might imagine that the great musician's invention would be somewhat exhausted. This is far from being the case. From end to end of its three movements there is always the same radiant youth, the same incomparable grace and elegance, which, unique as it may be, are the creators of vitality and longevity—a very comforting thought.

There is a minimum of ornamental trappings, and the absence of all artifice of virtuosity and empty decoration leaves the bare conception, a conception so lofty, so pure, and one which touches the heart so deeply, that the hearer's faculties are suspended and ask no further superficial subtleties. This is music, and nothing but music. It is thin as Rameau, serene and strong as Bach, tenderly persuasive as Fauré himself. To take a few examples only, in the melodic theme of the first movement, note how, in some miraculous way, the secret of which is gone for ever with him, the musician finds a way of remaining essentially tonal while passing through the paradoxical keys of D flat and A flat, in order to go from the dominant to the tonic of B flat. And this in such a way that, when done (like Columbus's egg), it seems the simplest thing imaginable. Note, too, the theme of the second movement, andantino, and the splendid phrase of the piano cantando espressivo, of such unspeakable charm! Admire the ease, the spontaneity with which they develop and blossom inexhaustibly.

The themes of the finale—by the way, it would be no surprise to hear that this was originally meant for a scherzo, as in the first quintet—are original and full of life, especially the first with its curious rhythmic breaks. Though technically not difficult, it is doubtful whether performers, however skilful, always rise to the heights of such a task. The work requires wider understanding and more refined sensibility than would at first appear from its infantile 'little trio' appearance. To the honour of the fellowship of virtuosi, let it be recorded that it was admirably played by Mlle de Sampigny and MM. Jean Witkowski and Gil-Marchex at the first performance at the Société Indépendante (S.M.I.).

THE STRING QUARTET ends the incomparable series all too soon. From the point of view of actual composition, the most successful movement is undoubtedly the opening allegro moderato. Yet the writer will always prefer the andante, with its profound and melancholy charm. And if the perfection of its lines is marred by certain slips, how touching they seem to us, these hurried syncopations or over-symmetrical progressions, set down perhaps with the feverish desire to complete it whatever happened, with an evident presentiment of the approaching end. Death surprised the artist before he could revise this last work with the master's final survey; let us none the less admire the work as a whole, and lament that the great musician was taken away in the full power of his immortal genius.

FLORENT SCHMITT.

†FAYE-JOZIN, FRED DE, French composer.

2nd sonata (*pittoresque*), pf, v	atonal	Mathot, 1909.

FEDERATION OF MUSIC CLUBS.

Founded 1921. The object of the society is to co-ordinate the work of various music clubs throughout the country, to assist them by giving information and advice, and to encourage the formation of fresh clubs. The Federation included in 1927 twenty-nine clubs with a total membership of 7,000. Chamber music, in which interest is growing, is a feature of the society's activities, the finest of the artists identified with this branch of music being engaged for the various club concerts. Mr. Evlyn Howard-Jones is president of the Central Council. EDITOR.

FENNEY, WILLIAM J., b. 1891, English composer, pupil of Granville Bantock.

1st trio, pf, v, vc, G	op. 20	Chester, 1916.

Fenney is to some extent influenced by Elgar, but if one may occasionally recognize the Elgarian flavour, one misses in the trio a correspondingly easy flow of expression. The impression conveyed is rather one of sincerity than of finished proficiency. It proceeds, however, from a genuine chamber music impulse, which the composer has no inclination to frustrate with the adventitious devices so often found in the early works of modern composers. A quality one could wish away, despite the Schumann precedent, is the occasional doubling of the violin in the piano part.

Several chamber works by this composer are still in MS. EDWIN EVANS.

†FERRATA, GIUSEPPE, b. 1866, Italian composer.

Quartet, str, G	op. 28	J. Fischer (N.Y.), 1913.

This quartet was awarded first prize by the Pittsburg (U.S.A.) Art Society. It is in the nature of effective drawing-room music.

FESCA, (1) FRIEDRICH ERNST, 1789–1826, German violinist and composer.

There is a complete edition of Fesca's twenty quartets and five quintets published by Rimbault, and a full list of his works is given in *Fétis*. Fesca had much chamber music experience from his youth upwards, and, like Mozart, was a performer on the piano at the age of four. In 1804 Spohr heard him play in a quartet of his own composition, and pronounced it to be 'bien travaillé et plein de talent' (from Spohr high praise indeed). Of Fesca's execution he spoke less favourably. In 1807 Fesca became solo violinist under Reichardt at Cassel; from Cassel passed to Vienna (1813), and thence to Carlsruhe (1815).

Later his quartets and quintets had considerable vogue in Vienna, and found a ready sale among the publishers in that city. One of the quartets began with the notes which form the composer's name:

Dr. Altmann (*Handbuch*) selects Fesca's quartet, op. 34, in D, for special praise, recommending it to amateurs as being extremely melodious and clearly constructed; and Vidal, in his *Instruments à archet*, says of him, 'c'est un des plus charmants génies qu'ait produit l'Allemagne'.

(2) ALEXANDER ERNST, 1820–1849, son of the above.

Two quartets, str, c mi, f mi	op. 42	Bachmann, 1845.
Quartet, str, C	posth.	Litolff, 1850.
Two septets, pf, v, ob, vla, vc, horn, cb, c mi, d mi	opp. 26, 28	,, 1843–4.
Sextet, pf, 2 v, vla, vc, cb, B flat	,, 8	(New ed.) Hofmeister, 1859.
Six trios (complete or separate), pf, v, vc	,, 11, 12, 23, 31, 46, 54	(New ed.) Hofmeister, 1876.
Sonata, pf, v, d mi	op. 40	(Rud. Niemann) Haake, 1884.

In his day Fesca's trios enjoyed much popularity among amateurs. Two of them may be selected for special mention: the early op. 12 (E minor), and the last (in F), composed in 1848, which has been played at South Place with success. Alex. Fesca's music is not without originality, and is characterized by extreme elegance. The two septets are also published as piano quartets. EDITOR.

FESTIVALS. *v.* BONN; BRADFORD; DONAUESCHINGEN; INTERNATIONAL SOCIETY FOR CONTEMPORARY MUSIC.

FÉTIS, FRANÇOIS JOSEPH, 1784–1871, Belgian musician and critic.

Three quintets 2 v, 2 vla, vc, A, D, e mi		Schott, 1861–62–69.
Sextet, pf (4 hands), str. quartet, E flat	(composed *c.* 1810)	,, 1864.

All his other chamber works were destroyed by Fétis, except some string quartets composed at the age of twelve, kept as a curiosity. The sextet went through two editions in Paris before being published by Schott.

'La musique est l'œuvre idéale de l'humanité.' It was thus that Fétis wrote of the art to which he devoted the whole of a long and laborious career. Composer, teacher, historian, theorist, and critic, he accomplished an amount which is equalled by few. It is mainly as historian, critic, and writer on music that he is remembered to-day, though many famous musicians studied under him during his thirty-nine years as director of the Brussels Conservatoire. As a composer he scarcely fulfilled his early promise, but he can have had little time for composition. The quintets are in the manner of Haydn and well-constructed, according to one of the great Leipzig papers, and this is endorsed by *Vidal*.

Two of his theoretical works have endured, and have passed through many editions and been translated into many languages: these are his *Traité complet de la théorie et de la pratique de l'harmonie* and his *Traité du contrepoint et de la fugue*. But his most important work was the monumental *Biographie universelle des Musiciens*, the first edition of which was published in 1834. A work of this kind is beyond the power of any single man to carry out effectively, but Fétis was peculiarly fitted for such a task by reason of his immense knowledge in every branch of music. The author sought, above everything, to be complete; hence for the purposes of those who require to study the music of the past it is still indispensable, and is an almost inexhaustible mine of information. Almost alone among biographers, Fétis took the pains, in nearly every case, to discover and supply the names of the publishers of each composer's works. The book is full of errors, especially of chronology; indeed, it almost seems sometimes as if he had a positive genius for wrong numbers, whether opus numbers or dates; yet, with due checking, his work is the most complete and useful of its kind that has yet appeared. The labour spent on it is almost incredible—twenty-five years to collect materials, and twenty-five more for the corrections and additions for the second edition of 1860–65, so greatly enlarged as to form almost a new work. Fétis was well aware of the defects of his method, and defended it on the doubtful ground of 'unity of judgement'. The work was that of a pioneer. He says, 'There were some fifteen hundred German musicians, of whom the greater number had real merit; these I endeavoured to rescue from oblivion'. He was also the first biographer to give due attention to Spanish musicians. He travelled about continually making his researches, in the course of which he amassed a very important library, now the property of the Brussels Bibliothèque Royale.

By his foundation of the *Revue Musicale* in 1827 Fétis gave the first impulse to musical criticism in France, for this was the first journal in French to be devoted exclusively to music.

As to the value of his work as critic and writer on music and subjects connected with music, there is no doubt that he held somewhat circumscribed views, and that he was dogmatic and arbitrary in his assertion of them.

For him the greatest of modern musicians was Mozart, almost equal to whom was Beethoven, until the period of his 'decline', i.e. the 'third period'. He judged all music in the light of certain theories; one of these may be stated in his own words as follows: 'One of the greatest obstacles to a just opinion of the value of a work lies in the doctrine of progress as applied to the arts. I have long opposed this doctrine, and have been fiercely attacked for saying that music is merely transformed; there is progress only on its material side.' Thus he says of Mozart, 'He was the greatest of modern musicians; he had what does not progress, genius, the richest and most varied, the most delicate and most impassioned, united with the most perfect taste'. He says that Mozart was the most original, the most complete of composers, and the model of perfection; since Beethoven's second period he sees only decadence, as an example of which he points to the habit of development for its own sake so common with contemporary writers. Another of his sayings was, 'It is easier to acquire habits than to have ideas'. He was strongly opposed to the tendencies of the romantics, in whose art he saw a dull uniformity, and whose lack of perfection of form was an offence to him.

But his judgements were frequently not without perspicacity. At a period when Mendelssohn was placed on a level with the great classics, Fétis puts his finger on this master's weaknesses. To Schumann he is less than just, yet he was able to admire the quintet, which has 'an order and clarity in its developments quite unusual with this composer, together with true poetic inspiration'. Note, too, his remarks on Bach, whom he describes as 'one of the greatest musicians of Germany, and perhaps the greatest of all', an opinion which was by no means universal at the time when the notice was written.

Of Beethoven's later works he held the opinions common to his day. Yet it is only just to say that even to-day these opinions are held by a number of cultivated musicians. Thus a writer in a modern periodical[1] speaks of the 'incoherence' of the master's late quartets 'after the mists had descended upon his mind'. And his criticisms on Schumann are frequently heard to-day, with, however, this difference, that though we are aware of this composer's defects, we realize the genius, the poetry, and the wonderful beauty which no defects could hide, though they sometimes mar his work. Yet again, according to his lights, he is not unjust, for at the end of his article he says, 'There is no doubt that Schumann is ranked too high by native musicians, *and too low in foreign countries*'. [The italics are the writer's.]

A notice of Fétis should contain some reference to the famous controversy over Mozart's much discussed C major quartet. Here his own words may be quoted.

'I was attacked concerning a correction proposed by me for a passage in the introduction of Mozart's quartet in C. It is admitted that this passage, painful to the ears, has always been a subject of astonishment to those who understand. My correction was highly approved by Cherubini, Reicha, Boieldieu, and other famous musicians; it has the advantage of simplicity and regularity, and leaves untouched the conception of the illustrious composer.' Elsewhere he says that Cherubini described this passage as a 'barbarism', and goes on to explain, 'The harshnesses arise from the lack of regularity in the imitations, and I showed that by placing the entry of the first violin a beat later, Mozart *would have produced sound harmony* without injuring his conception.'

Fétis was bitterly attacked for his temerity by Kiesewetter, under the pseudonym 'A. C. Leduc', and supported by Oulibichev in his book on Mozart, in which he wrote, 'I shall always play the Introduction as thus corrected: it is henceforth sublime throughout, thanks to M. Fétis's happy emendation'. [For further discussion of this vexed problem see *A Music Critic's Holiday* by Ernest Newman.]

But when all is said, Fétis rendered the most eminent services to the art he so passionately loved; and his work was both original and enduring.

A full list of his works is given in the *Biographie* and Pougin's *Supplément*. *Riemann* and *Grove* may also be consulted.

M. DRAKE-BROCKMAN.

[I take this opportunity gratefully to acknowledge my obligation to the *Biographie universelle* for many details concerning the less well-known musicians. There are many inaccuracies to forgive, but his self-sacrificing labours are almost without parallel in the history of musical research. EDITOR.]

1 *The Music Bulletin*, British Music Society's Journal. Editorial. March, 1927.

† FÉVRIER, HENRI, b. 1876, French composer.

Trio, pf, v, vc, A	Gregh, 1907.
Sonata, pf, v, a mi	„ 1899.

FIBICH, ZDENĚK, 1850–1900, Bohemian composer.

	op.	Composed	
Quartet, str, G	8	1878	Fr. A. Urbánek.
Theme and var^{ns}., str. quintet, B flat	—	1885	„ „

	op.	Comp.	
Quintet, pf, v, cl, horn, vc, also pf, 2 v, vla, vc, D	42	1894	Fr. A. Urbánek.
Quartet, pf, v, vla, vc, e mi	11	1874	,, ,,
Trio, pf, v, vc, f mi	—	1872	,, ,,

Fibich is usually placed next to Smetana and Dvořák as the third representative of the music of the country in its classic period. He devoted himself mainly to chamber music in the decade 1870–1880. In 1874 he wrote the quartet for strings in A major (still in MS.), in which was used for the first time in chamber music the national Czech dance known as the polka. Fibich published only one chamber work in each of the different instrumental categories for which he wrote. Thus, there is one piano trio, one string quartet, and one piano quintet with wind instruments.

THE TRIO IN F MINOR is a typical production of the author's youth, and the impression it gives is that of a composition with a good deal of movement in it, and with the least possible suggestion of repose. It consists of three movements, the first of which, molto con fuoco, is built up on the following motif:

Ex. 1.

The second movement, adagio ma non troppo, is significantly very short, most probably with the object of maintaining the character of the work. The third movement, vivacissimo, seems to continue the first movement, as indicated by its principal theme:

Ex. 2.

THE PIANO QUARTET, which followed the trio, may be called his chef d'oeuvre, and is written with the profound knowledge of technique indispensable for chamber music; the work won high praise from Hanslick and others. This quartet is remarkable for power and richness of invention, as well as for the closely woven character of the ensemble, there being only five themes in the entire work. Like the trio, it has three movements; but in this case there is not only rhythm, but also much of the lyrical element. The themes are thus distributed. The first movement, allegro moderato, is built on two themes; the second, tema con variazioni, on one; and the third, allegro energico, on two, the five being heard in combination at the close. Here are the five themes in question, *a* and *b* from the first movement, *c* from the second, and *d* and *e* from the third, while the fragment of *c* marked *a* is the form in which this theme appears at the end in combination with the others:

Ex. 3. (*a*)

(*b*)

(*c*)

(*d*)

(*e*) 1st Violin.

THE STRING QUARTET is a third chamber work written in the 'seventies. Here Fibich's musical speech approaches very near to Smetana and Dvořák, from whom ordinarily he remains far removed; in fact, the work strikes one as typical of the Czech race and of the Czech *Volkston*. Thus, there is a very gay, very melodious note not at all habitual with Fibich, and this may be attributed to the fact that the quartet was composed at a time when the composer was recovering from a somewhat serious illness. This is to be felt especially in the third and fourth movements. The work is in the usual four movements: (1) allegro, (2) adagio, (3) allegro scherzando (with a polka in the trio), and (4) allegro vivace, at the beginning of which the instruments imitate the bagpipes. Here is the theme of the scherzo:

Ex. 4.

This is the polka in the trio of the scherzo:

Ex. 5.

Ex. 6. gives the subjects of the finale.

THE PIANO QUINTET is the only remaining work to be considered, if the theme and variations for string quintet be excluded. It is in four movements, and is characterized by great wealth of colour. It can be performed with various combinations of instruments, of which, quite naturally, that which includes clarinet and horn is the most original and poetic. The idiom of the quintet differs, of course, from that employed in the compositions of the 'seventies. At the close of the adagio there appears a very characteristic hymn, which reappears at the end of the work, with additions,

Ex. 6. (*a*)

in the following form, which may serve as a musical illustration of this work.

Ex. 7.

JOSEF BARTOŠ.

[I have frequently played the arrangement of the quintet for piano and strings. Each instrument in turn has effective solos to play, more brilliant than serious in character. Fibich was an extremely prolific writer, though chamber music forms but a small proportion of his total output, which amounted to some 700 works. EDITOR.]

FIELD, JOHN, 1782–1837, Irish pianist.
Modern republication:

Quintet, pf, 2 v, vla, vc, A flat B. & H., 1880.

Field's reputation rests upon his piano works, chiefly the nocturnes, precursors of the more famous works of Chopin. Originally an apprentice and pupil of Clementi, he was afterwards expatriated in Russia, which became the main scene of his labours. The above work, with its clear four-part harmony, may be recommended to beginners.

FIÉVET, PAUL, b. 1892, French composer, pupil of Widor.

Quartet, str, d mi	Evette & Schaeffer,	1924.
Quintet, pf, 2 v, vla, vc, g mi	,, ,,	1923.
Suite Slave, pf, v, vc	,, ,,	1922.

Sonata, pf, v, d mi	Evette & Schaeffer, 1924.
Sonata, pf, vc, c mi	Philippi (Paris), 1921.

Fiévet's works have been frequently performed in France. The *Suite Slave* was played in 1928 at the Concerts Lamoureux. He comes of a musical family, both his father and his mother being professors at the Valenciennes Conservatoire, where Fiévet studied.

THE QUINTET is an important work in three movements. It opens with a broad introduction, giving the main lines of the first theme *ff*, followed by an allegro. The second subject, announced by viola, soon reinforced by 'cello, is a cantabile melody; the two subjects are later combined, and the movement ends quietly in G major.

The following movement (modéré), in E minor, is built on an expressive phrase announced by the first violin. The finale (animé) has a fiery first subject built on the minor scale with augmented fourth announced *unisono* by the strings. The second subject, again a cantabile melody, is announced by the viola, reinforced by the second violin and then taken up by the whole body of strings. The writing is mainly diatonic, and the style classical. The piano part is not overloaded; a notable feature is the frequency of unison passages for the strings.

The *Suite Slave* is a shorter work, in four movements in different keys—andante (G minor), lent (A major), allegretto (F minor), allegro (D major), very rhythmic in character.

The string quartet is in three movements: animé—andante—animé et décidé.

THE VIOLIN SONATA (three movements) is again an important work. The finale presents some curious features: it opens with a short andante recitativo, leading to the modéré 15/8 in D major, in the course of which the time-signature changes frequently, 5/4, 3/4, 15/8, 9/8, the greater part of the movement being, however, in 3/4. The harmony is very dissonant, but the slow movement has a beautiful opening. M. DRAKE-BROCKMAN.

FILTZ, ANTON, *c.* 1725/1730–1760, German 'cellist.

Modern republications:

Trio 2 v, vc, A	op. 3, no. 2	(H. Riemann) D.T.B., vol. 28, B. & H., 1915.
Trio, pf, 2 v, vc (ad lib.), E flat	,, 3, ,, 5	(H. Riemann) Coll. Mus. 17, B. & H., 1905.
Trio, pf, v, vc, C	,, 4, ,, 3	(H. Riemann) D.T.B., vol. 28, B. & H., 1915.

List of original publications in *Fétis*. 'As a composer Filtz ranks with the best of the Mannheim symphonists. He was a 'cellist of great renown.' (*Grove*.)

FINDEISEN, TH. ALBIN.

Romantic suite, pf, cb	C. F. Schmidt, 1922.

FINK, HANS.

Quartet, str, e mi	op. 20	Kistner, 1900.

* FINKE, FIDELIO, b. 1891, Bohemian composer, professor of theory and composition at the German Academy of Music, Prague.

Has written a number of chamber works, as yet unpublished, advanced in character, and including a lengthy string quartet in one movement lasting forty-five minutes! ERICH STEINHARD.

[Many prizes have been awarded to Finke's works, including a State prize early in 1928. His chamber works include eight string trios.]

FINNISH CHAMBER MUSIC.

In addition to the Finnish composers to whom a place is assigned in this book (Sibelius, Melartin, Kunla, Furuhjelm), the following names are cited (in *Dent*) as writers of chamber music: Raitio, Madetoja, Hanni Kainen, and Linko. Their works are, I believe, as yet unpublished. To these names may be added that of Selim Palmgren (b. 1878). EDITOR.

*† FINZI, GERALD.

A Severn Rhapsody, chamber orch. S. & B. (Carnegie Award.)

'A picturesque and imaginative composition, written with a genuine sense of style, and likely to be a welcome addition to our concert programmes.'—Carnegie Trust Report.

† FIORILLO, FEDERIGO, 1753–*c.* 1823, Italian violinist.

This musician, whose name is familiar to violinists, is best known by his studies and his duets for two violins; but he also composed a large number of chamber works. *Fétis* mentions three string quintets, twenty-four string quartets,[1] and eighteen trios for strings or flute and strings. These he himself described as 'des vieilleries'.

He settled in London in 1788, where he remained, playing viola in Salomon's Quartet. His last public appearance was in a viola concerto in the Hanover Square Rooms. A list of republished violin duets and sonatas is given in *Altmann*; for other works *v. Fétis* and the *Q.-L.*

FISCHER, JOHANN, 1646–1721, German virtuoso violinist.

Modern republication:

Quartet (*The Skilful Violist*), 2 v, vla, fig. bass (pf) (G. Beckmann, *Das Violinspiel*, H. 2), Simrock, 1921.

Fischer anticipated Paganini by many years in the device of special tunings (*scordatura*). They are even found in his compositions for viola, an instrument he sought to popularize. He was the Lionel Tertis of his day.

Among his works is to be found a primitive example of programme music. EDITOR.

[1] *Vidal* gives only fifteen published quartets, and twelve trios 2 v, vc.

FISCHER, Johann Christian, 1733–1800, famous German oboist in the service of Frederick the Great.

Fischer wrote some string quartets, as well as music for his own instrument. 'J. C. Bach wrote for him a quartet for two oboes, viola, and 'cello, which he frequently played' (*Grove*). His music was published by Hummel (Berlin).

FISCHER, Julius.

2nd sonata, pf, v, E flat op. 21 Robitschek, 1911.

†FITELBERG, Grigor (or Grzegorz), b. 1879, Polish composer and conductor.

Trio, pf, v, vc, f mi	op. 10	Gebethner & W., 1903.
Sonata, pf, v, F	„ 12	„ „ 1905. A. Stahl.

The first violin sonata, op. 2, is not published, but won first prize (the Paderewski prize) in the international competition at Leipzig in 1896. The trio won Count Zamoyski's prize for trios at Warsaw, 1901. *Dent* describes him as a 'pioneer of modern Polish music and a bold progressive'.

The trio in F minor is a fine work: the first movement has a bold, tragic theme; the second, an *Obertass* (Polish national dance), is very amusing, with a beautiful melody in the trio. The *Elegy* which follows has a remarkable 'cello solo. The finale swings joyously along, but near the end the bold theme of the first movement, now somewhat chastened, returns. E. W. Organ (*Musical Mirror*).

FLAGEOLET TONES. *v.* Harmonics.

†FLAMENT, Édouard, b. 1880, French pianist and bassoon virtuoso.

1st sonata, pf, vc, g mi	op. 14	C. Selva.
2nd sonata, pf, vc, A	„ 55	Senart, 1922.

Studied at the Paris Conservatoire, where he acquired an excellent technique. This together with an easily flowing style are the chief qualities of his work.

†FLÉGIER, Ange, b. 1846, French composer.

Dixtuor, str and wind	Grus (Paris), 1890.
Trio, ob, cl, fag, B	Gallet, 1897.

There is a notice of Flégier in *Pougin*, who says his work is clear and well constructed.

LE FLEM, Paul, b. 1881, professor at the Schola Cantorum, Paris.

	Composed	
Quintet, pf, 2 v, vla, vc, e mi	1910	Hérelle (Paris), 1911.
Sonata, pf, v, g mi	1905	„ „

A Breton by birth, Paul le Flem spent his youth in an atmosphere of legends.

The Violin Sonata. This poetic work has a classical first movement. In it is announced the 'generating-theme' of the work, a Lied-phrase[1] of tender melancholy, essentially Breton in spirit.

The second movement is an andante in two sections, built out of materials already employed. Beginning as a kind of elegy, the music grows more animated, with impulsive bursts of passion. The conclusion (muted) restores the tranquillity of the opening. In the finale, a rondo, the mother-theme, in 5-time, serves as groundwork for the accompaniment to a lively folk-song theme, which is derived from a fragment of the second subject of the first movement. The couplets[1] make happy use of the various materials of the sonata, and the entries of the refrain[1] are always piquant. At the end the instruments take up the theme of the refrain, unaccompanied, *très-vif*, and there is a powerful conclusion in 5-time rhythm.

The Quintet for piano and strings is in three movements. Two principal themes, announced in the slow introduction in E minor, dominate the work, and to these is due its essentially Breton character. The first, in octaves on the strings, is poised on the arpeggios of the piano, with an effect of distant bells heard through the mist, the second is tenderly serene. The first movement enters without break with the exposition, in E minor, of the first subject. A transition, developed at some length, leads to the second subject, the bold first element of which bursts out forcibly in B major. The second element follows with its suggestion of some old legend, in answering phrases on viola, violin, and 'cello. Then a third element, mysterious, haunted by the echo of bells, completes the exposition.

The development treats all these themes with great variety of combinations. The recapitulation begins with the reappearance, in E minor, of the slow introduction with the mother-theme *ff*, on all the strings in octaves. The movement quickens gradually, and the recapitulation proceeds normally. The bold second theme bursts forth, rather more animated than before, in E major, then a calmer third element links up with a slow conclusion founded on a reminiscence of the second theme and the mother-theme with its distant bells on the piano, sounding through the transparent mists of evening.

The second movement (lent D flat), in Lied-form with a short introduction, is a plaintive meditation, interwoven with evocations of nature, full of warmth and poetry. This reflective mood gradually gives place to an impassioned section with a climax of exaltation, then, by degrees, the calm of the opening is restored.

The finale, in E minor, makes use of strongly marked rhythms, diversified by bars of rapid 7-time. An inflexible ('sourd') and vehement theme, delivered by the whole quartet,

[1] See Foreword, art. Beethoven.

gives place to calmer ideas, and prepares the way for a frankly popular theme which conjures up the *ripailles* (feasting) of a Breton festivity.

In the conclusion, in E major, the principal themes of the work reappear; they are broken up and combined in all kinds of ways with an interweaving of rhythms which is full of life and colour.

It is noteworthy that the themes, even popular ones, are never borrowed from the provincial folk-songs, but are simply 'born of the spirit of Brittany', as were, originally, the folk-songs themselves.

Paul le Flem's quintet will hold a high place beside the great modern quintets which have enriched the literature of chamber music.

ADOLPHE PIRIOU.

FLONZALEY QUARTET.

The Flonzaley Quartet was organized in 1903 by Edward J. de Coppet of New York City, and took its name from the Villa Flonzaley, his summer home in Switzerland, where the Quartet first assembled. (The word 'Flonzaley' in the dialect of the Canton de Vaud means 'little river'.) The original personnel comprised Adolfo Betti, Alfred Pochon, Ugo Ara, and Ivan d'Archambeau. The only changes have been at the viola desk, which has since been occupied successively by Louis Bailly, Félicien d'Archambeau, and Nicolas Moldavan. For three years Betti and Pochon took alternately the first and second violin part.

The Flonzaley Quartet has been the outstanding chamber music organization in the United States for many years, and has to its credit great achievements in the development of taste for the highest type of chamber music. They have played in 450 cities in forty-five states. Important works by prominent living composers have been given first performance by the Flonzaley. They were the first quartet party to give a programme of all American chamber music composers.

Since E. J. de Coppet's death, his support of the organization has been continued by his son, André de Coppet. The Flonzaley is not only the legitimate successor of the Kneisel, and for the American people a national musical asset: it has now attained the rank of a World Quartet. They give concerts regularly in London, where it is a source of regret that their appearances are not more frequent.

It is on record that in the early days of the Quartet, Joachim was anxious that the inclusion of his pupil Klingler should be considered, but it transpired that Klingler's mother would not allow her son to go to America.

The question of joining the Quartet was also studied by other artists of eminence, including Pablo Casals, the brothers Thibaud, E. Bloch, and the Roumanian violinist Enesco, Carmen Sylva expressing the wish that the last mentioned should not go to the States. Eventually choice fell upon Pochon's fellow students in the class of César Thomson at Liége, Betti and Ara, with the addition of d'Archambeau, who was recommended by Victor Vreuls, as 'cellist. Ara volunteered for the war, at the conclusion of which his health broke down, and to the great chagrin of his colleagues he was obliged to resign. The news reaches us at the time of writing (April 1928) that this splendid organization will be disbanded after their forthcoming tour in America. Their last London concert was given on 14 April, 1928, *The Times* critic taking the opportunity of thanking them 'for the example of self-forgetfulness and joy in collaboration which they have so long set to artists and associated with the name of 'Flonzaley'.

EDITOR.

FLOTOW, FRIEDRICH VON, 1812–1883, operatic composer.

Sonata, pf, v, A	op. 14	Cranz, 1861.

In the nature of salon music.

FLÜGEL, ERNST PAUL, 1844–1912, German organist.

Trio, pf, v, vc, E flat	op. 25	R. & E., 1882.
Sonata, pf, vc, a mi	„ 41	Reinecke, 1893.

FLUTE.

(Down to the beginning of the present century.)

N.B.—This article only mentions selected typical works; all include a flute part. The key is given in circular brackets, thus (C). The majority of the works specifically mentioned can be obtained from B. & H.; in other cases, the firm from whom they can be obtained is named in square brackets, either in full or abbreviated as follows: R. & C. = Rudall, Carte & Co., London; Z. = Zimmermann, Leipzig; P. = Peters ed.; L. = Litolff ed.

The story is told of the conductor of an orchestra unprovided with a second flute player, who, lamenting the deficiency to Cherubini, exclaimed, 'What is worse than one flute?' Whereupon the latter replied, 'Two flutes!' This witticism was to a certain extent justified by the defects of the instrument of that time, upon which it was wellnigh impossible even for skilled performers to play in tune. Hence the flute—though much was written for it by minor and now forgotten composers—was seldom employed in chamber music by the great classical masters, who evidently preferred the oboe. Doubtless they would have written much more for the flute, had the improved instrument of to-day been available; some of them, however, did occasionally employ the flute in chamber works.

When writing for the flute with other instruments—wind or string—the early composers almost invariably confined it to the upper part, like the soprano voice in concerted vocal music. If used with strings, it generally merely doubled the first violin in unison (or an octave higher), or a passage would be played twice, first by the strings alone, then with the flute playing the tune to an accompaniment on the strings, e.g. the first allegro in J S. Bach's suite (or overture) in B minor, for flute and strings. The earliest style of writing for flute with piano, as exemplified in the sonatas of Jean-Baptiste Loeillet (*c.* 1700) recently republished (H. Lemoine, Paris), was extremely simple, devoid of any intricacies or subtleties, but sometimes showed considerable skill in development. These sonatas, like most writings of the period, consist of a number of short movements, chiefly old dance measures; the same form was adopted by Handel in his seven sonatas for flute and piano [P.]. In these latter the flute is very rarely employed above the first two octaves, and the lower notes (D below the stave was then the lowest) are used very sparingly, owing to their uncertainty. They are not distinctively flute music, and might equally well have been written for the violin or oboe. This is the case with many other early compositions, which are often marked 'flute or violin'. Haydn's sonata, no. 8 in G [L.], thus entitled, is, however, well suited to the flute; it is practically identical with one of the string quartets, op. 77. Haydn's excellent flute writing shows a considerable advance and greater understanding of the character of the instrument.

Some time previously J. J. QUANTZ (*q.v.*), the first flautist composer of note, had written a large number of flute sonatas and concertos, which display a thorough knowledge of the capacities of the one-keyed flute of the time. These works, though stereotyped in form, showed that the instrument was capable of rendering something more important than a series of dance tunes. It remained for J. S. Bach, in his six sonatas for flute and piano [P.] (written about 1747), to raise the flute to a position of dignity infinitely above that which it had hitherto occupied—a position equal to any in the music of subsequent times. These famous works, though still mainly written in the first two octaves of the instrument, show much more frequent use of the higher and also of the lower notes down to D. They are much more difficult than anything previously written for the instrument, and tax the powers of the most skilled flautists, even with the perfected flute of the present day. Mozart is said to have disliked the flute, but no one has written more gracefully for it. Like Haydn, he treats it as a melodic instrument, but his works for flute and strings are more concertante than those of Haydn. His three quartets for this combination, however, are hardly equal to those for strings alone. Beethoven, in his serenade (D.), op. 25 [L.], for flute, violin, and viola, shows a great advance in bold and skilful handling of the flute; e.g. the opening phrase on the flute alone, the characteristic short dialogues between the various instruments in the first movement, the highly effective writing for the flute in the second trio and in some of the variations in the andante. Mozart and Beethoven alike made little use of the lower notes, which were still weak and uncertain, but used the high notes up to A‴ comparatively freely. Neither, however, included the flute in their quintets for wind and piano.

Meanwhile, several improvements had been made in the flute: extra keys had been added to the mechanism, which not only improved the intonation, but also facilitated playing in rapid passages and in more remote keys; thus composers were no longer confined to the easier keys. With the exception of some very antiquated serenades for eight wind instruments and a double-bass by Hoffmeister and Pleyel [R. & C.], little or nothing had as yet been written for the flute in the larger combinations of instruments. Ere long several such works appeared, the most notable being Hummel's septets for wind, strings, and piano, op. 74 in D minor and op. 114 in C—which latter includes a trumpet—and G. Onslow's sextet, op. 30, for flute, clarinet, horn, bassoon, double-bass, and piano, and his septet, op. 79, for the same instruments with the addition of the oboe. All these works are too much in the nature of brilliant and diffuse piano solos, with accompaniments. The advisability of including the piano in large combinations of this kind is somewhat doubtful, for it seems frequently to lead to this result, as in Rubinstein's octet, op. 9, for flute, clarinet, horn, violin, viola, 'cello, double-bass, and piano, and, in a lesser degree, in his quintet, op 55 (F), for flute, clarinet, horn, bassoon, and piano. Spohr, in his quintet, op. 52 (C minor), for the same instruments, has not altogether avoided this error, but in his septet, op. 147 (A minor), for the same together with violin and 'cello, he has been more successful. Other important works for large combinations were F. Lachner's octet, op. 156, for flute, oboe, two clarinets, two horns, and two bassoons; Onslow's quintet, op. 81 (F), for wind, and his nonet, op. 77, for five wind instruments and four strings (including double-bass), for which combination Spohr wrote his op. 31 [L.], a work of considerable merit and importance. In all the above-mentioned works Spohr's treatment of the flute is masterly.

During Spohr's lifetime Böhm and Gordon revolutionized the flute, substituting a cylindrical for the old conical bore, and making various other improvements. Rudall, Rose & Carte of London, with the assistance of R. S. Rockstro, perfected the instrument, making it the most perfectly tuned wind instrument in existence.

In the earlier part of the nineteenth century the playing of duets and trios for flutes alone was highly popular, and between 1820 and 1870 a large amount of really high-class flute music was written, chiefly by the classical flautist composers, Kuhlau, Walckiers, Gabrielski, Kummer, and A. B. Fürstenau, and the lesser lights, Berbiguier and Tulou. These composers, being themselves skilful flautists, had thorough technical knowledge, and many of their compositions—especially those of Kuhlau—are masterly, evincing admirable contrapuntal skill combined with great originality. Their compositions are distinctively flute music. Much of it is little known outside the flute-playing world, being for two, three, or four flutes alone. Mention may incidentally be made here of two recent composers who have also written excellent quartets for four flutes, viz. E. Kohler, op. 92 in D [Z.], and A. Wouters, op. 77, in E flat [Oertel, Brussels]. Works for flutes alone soon pall upon the listeners, but four flutes playing sustained passages may be very effective, producing, so to speak, a treble organ effect.

About the same period much was written for flute and guitar, but the combination is feeble, and by no means so effective as flute and harp, for which Mozart wrote a concerto, and which was adopted by Berlioz in his solitary piece for a chamber combination—*Trio des Jeunes Israëlites* (*Enfance du Christ*). The combination has recently been used by B. Hilse in his suite, op. 6 [Z.], in very modern style, and by Bemberg, Gaubert, Mouquet, and Ingelbrecht in pieces descriptive of Greek dances, for which purpose both instruments are admirably suited.

Owing partly to the great improvements made in the instrument and partly to the higher standard of technique attained, the past half-century has seen a great increase in the number of chamber works for flute with other wind instruments, and, to a less extent, for flute and strings—works written for almost every conceivable combination with or without the addition of the piano. When wind instruments only are employed, the larger combinations are best, as each can produce but one note at a time. Small wind combinations necessarily suffer from a certain thinness and lightness, hence they are best adapted to light, dainty writing, such as P. de Wailly's *Aubade* for flute, oboe, and clarinet, and the quartets of Hugues (*q.v.*) and Goepfart, op. 93, for the same instruments with bassoon. The addition of the piano to such small combinations is advantageous, e.g. the last-named composer's trio (C minor), op. 74, for flute, oboe, and piano, and F. Amberg's suite in B flat for flute, oboe, clarinet, and piano, provided the work does not become a mere series of solos for the wind instruments. The piano is desirable even with four wind instruments, as in the quintets of E. Duncan, op. 38 [R. & C.], E. Taubert, op. 48, and Rimsky-Korsakov, a posthumous work, all for flute, clarinet, horn, bassoon, and piano. A noticeable point of difference between modern and earlier writers is that the flute no longer has a monopoly of the upper part, but often plays a subordinate rôle, the top voice being given to some other instrument. The flute is often used also for decorative purposes.

Many older composers wrote works for four or five wind instruments—A. Reicha composed no less than twenty-four such quintets [R. & C.]. Almost all were purely mechanical, and quite devoid of inspiration. The combination of flute, oboe, clarinet, horn, and bassoon affords great variety of tone colour, and has been largely adopted of late, with great success, in the lighter suites of Ch. Lefebvre, op. 57 [Hamelle], and P. Taffanel (G minor); and also in works of a more serious character by J. Sobeck, opp. 9, 11, 14, and 23; A. Klughardt, op. 79; C. Rorich, op. 58 [Z.]; and others. The addition of the piano to the wind quintet produces the best and most satisfactory of all these various combinations, and it has been admirably handled by L. Thuille, op. 6, and J. Rheinberger, op. 191 b.

Very large combinations have become quite popular. That such works, written for wind instruments only, may be exceedingly effective, has been demonstrated, especially by Raff's double quintet, sinfonietta, op. 188 [R. & C.]; also by Th. Gouvy's nonet, op. 90, and octet, op. 71, and R. Strauss's serenade (E flat), op. 7 [R. & C.], for thirteen wind instruments (including a double bassoon). But in such large combinations a fairly equal mixture of strings and wind is desirable, as it admits of the pleasing alternation of passages for strings or for wind alone with those for both combined, as in Th. Dubois's double quintet (F) for five wind and five strings. Works for such large mixed combinations, however, belong rather to the small orchestra than to chamber music.

The piccolo can hardly be considered a chamber instrument; still, it has been introduced into G. Schreck's wind nonet, op. 40, Dubois's *Au Jardin* suite for seven wind instruments, and also into light works by Liadov (op. 32) and Florent Schmitt (op. 54).

Flute and Piano. It is often alleged that there is hardly any really good concertante music for flute and piano. This erroneous idea is mainly due to the fact that almost every flautist of note has deemed it incumbent on him to compose especially for his instrument. The numerous effusions of Drouet, Demersseman, Briccialdi, Ciardi, Nicholson, Richardson, &c., are merely vehicles for the display of virtuosity and finger dexterity; whilst but few of the numerous compositions of more modern writers, such as Terschak, E. Köhler, F. Buchner, and Popp—excellent as many of them are—are entitled to be classed as chamber music. Even Schubert's introduction and variations on *Trockene Blumen*, op. 160 [L.], and Kalliwoda's concert rondo, op. 80 [Z.], must be excluded. But, besides the works of the great classical composers already mentioned, quite a number of concertante works of real musical value have been composed in recent times for flute and piano. Amongst these are the sonatas of G. A. Macfarren, E. Prout, op. 17, J. F. Barnett, op. 41, C. Reinecke, op. 167 [R. & C.], and Hamilton Clarke, all musicianly works in orthodox form. Several other works of this description have been written, chiefly by German composers, with conscientious diligence, but without inspiration and of inordinate length. Such heavy works are not suited to the character of the flute, which is much better adapted to shorter, lighter compositions, such as the suites of C. M. Widor, op. 34 [Heugel], B. Godard, op. 116 [Durand], E. German [R. & C.], and T. H. Verheiy, op. 60 [Z.], the concertino of Mme Chaminade, op. 107 [Enoch, London], and Reinecke's ballade, op. 288 [Z.].

The simple straightforward style of the older writers is extremely well suited to the flute, and it has been admirably reproduced by two modern flautist composers, viz. E. Kronke in his suites, opp. 81, 160, and 164 (two flutes), and *Kammer-Konzert*, op. 112, and H. Probost in his sonata, op. 17 [Z.].

In conclusion, it may be noted that many recent writers make frequent and effective use of the lower notes of the flute, the tone colour of which is quite unique, and also freely employ the extreme upper notes of its compass—occasionally even exceeding it. Moreover, they do not hesitate to write passages of extreme difficulty, such as the older composers would never have ventured to assign to the instrument. H. M. FITZGIBBON.

[The reader's attention is drawn to Prof. Tovey's mention of Haydn's flute writing in his article upon that composer. EDITOR.]

THE FLUTE IN MODERN CHAMBER MUSIC.

Before proceeding to any enumeration or analysis of modern chamber works which include the flute, it is necessary to state the causes of the reaction of the last quarter of a century in favour of an instrument much neglected by serious composers during the greater part of the nineteenth century. In the writer's opinion, the principal cause of this revival is the personal influence of several great flautists, who disdained to write works of pure virtuosity as their predecessors had done, and preferred to put their talents at the service of the great classical and contemporary masters.

Among these virtuosi Paul Taffanel may be considered as having the greatest influence. He followed immediately on a generation of flautist-composers who had deliberately neglected the rich harvest of the eighteenth century, and played little but their own productions. Although he had himself composed a certain number of pieces for the flute, Taffanel devoted himself chiefly to making known the masterpieces of the past. This he did as much by his own performances as by those of the Chamber Music Society for Wind Instruments, founded by him in 1878. It was he who started the movement which resulted in the revival of interest in the flute among composers.

Another cause of this revival is that the composers and virtuosi of our own times have, as a rule, abandoned the brilliant effects and pompous developments of the nineteenth century, demanding, as they do, from the flute a degree of power which it does not possess. This change is doubtless owing to the better knowledge of eighteenth-century music, in which the flute was so greatly favoured. Ceasing to regard the flute purely as an instrument for performing mere feats of skill, composers have been more willing to introduce it into chamber music—perhaps the highest form of the art.

It is proposed to examine one by one the different combinations in which the flute is employed in an interesting way in modern chamber music.

SONATAS FOR FLUTE AND PIANO. Few modern writers have cared to attempt a work in full sonata form, with its customary lengthy development, for an instrument whose range of power is restricted, and which, on this account, is either unable to express all kinds of sentiments or fails to express them fully. Yet the way had been shown them by the delightful work of a composer much neglected at present—Carl Reinecke. A sonata of his for flute and piano will remain, perhaps, as the sole enduring work of his immense output.

This sonata, which has the sub-title *Undine*, is of considerable length, and is in four movements: an allegro, a scherzo (interrupted by a graceful andantino), an andante, and a rapid and passionate finale. But Reinecke was clever enough to confine himself to a single root idea which accorded admirably with the character of the flute. His work is essentially graceful, charming, and flexible—with the exception of the finale, in which he demands of the flute a greater degree of passion than it is able to express—and the work, considered as a whole, is delightful. Ill-natured critics may perhaps discover more reminiscences of Schumann than are consistent with originality, but it is not the less true that this sonata, marking, as it does, an epoch in the history of the flute, was accepted by flautists from the moment of its appearance.

If the German Reinecke drew his inspiration from Schumann, the Englishman Barnett took Mendelssohn for his model. His sonata, also extremely well written for the flute, is a slavish imitation of this master. Somewhat nearer the present time (1926), the French composer Widor, in a suite which has all the characteristics of a sonata, has produced the happiest effect from the contrasting timbres of flute and piano. The first movement (moderato) might serve as a model of the judicious employment of the two qualities of tone. The arabesques for the flute and for the piano, both keeping to the same octave—the lowest octave of the flute—give a most graceful effect, most happily inspired by the same effects in J. S. Bach's sonata in E flat.

Ex. 1.

Ex. 2.

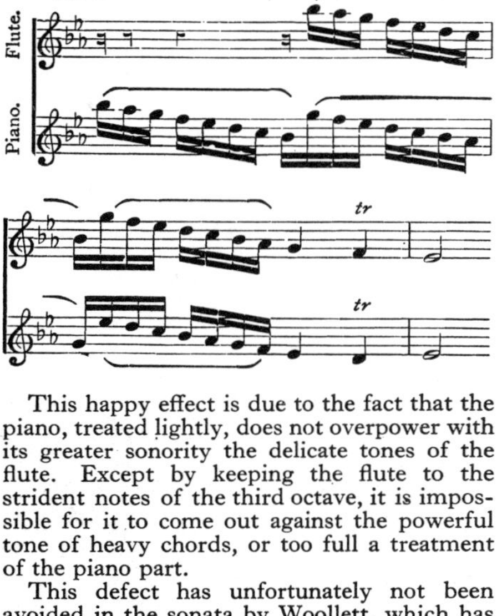

This happy effect is due to the fact that the piano, treated lightly, does not overpower with its greater sonority the delicate tones of the flute. Except by keeping the flute to the strident notes of the third octave, it is impossible for it to come out against the powerful tone of heavy chords, or too full a treatment of the piano part.

This defect has unfortunately not been avoided in the sonata by Woollett, which has great musical interest, but the finale of which, being extremely powerful, demands from the flautist a degree of physical effort which may mar the quality of the interpretation. And the composer, carried away by his ideas, has found himself somewhat hampered by the restricted range of the flute (three octaves and a note), and has multiplied the high C's

Ex. 3.

at the extreme limit of the instrument, which are rarely played in tune, especially in the louder passages.

The same observation applies to the finale of Koechlin's sonata, which is rather too orchestral in conception. Here the composer, also hampered by the lack of range of the instrument, has been forced to break the melodic lines in a very apparent manner—a common enough proceeding in the orchestra, where the details are lost in the mass of sound, but one which is displeasing in a single instrumental part.

Ex. 4.

These slight defects detract but little from the merit of these very remarkable works.

No such faults are to be found in the works of M. Philippe Gautier, himself a celebrated flautist, whose sonata for flute and piano is admirably written for the instrument. Somewhat less successful—for this composer, though beginning as a flautist, never became a virtuoso—are the works for flute of L. Mouquet. His *Flûte de Pan* is remarkably well written for the instrument. But its sub-title of 'sonata' seems rather arbitrary, the piano part (which was eventually orchestrated by the composer) being reduced to a mere accompaniment.

This section of the article will conclude by mentioning the sonata, recently written and still in MS., by the Belgian composer Joseph Jongen. This is by far the most important work for flute and piano which has been written since 1897, and its nobility of conception is worthy of the highest praise. Finally, the sonatas of Mel-Bonis (with a fine adagio), J. Pillois, F. Cools, and Francis Toye may be mentioned.

Several contemporary composers, less ambitious in their designs, have chosen the less fully developed form of the sonatina. The works which seem to the writer the most happily inspired in this type of composition are those of the French composer Darius Milhaud and the Germano-Spaniard Ph. Jarnach. Milhaud's sonata is full of poetry and vigour, and the rhythmic ingenuity of the second movement is remarkable. Lastly may be mentioned the very amusing sonatina of the Italian Vittorio Rieti (in three movements of a total duration of three and a half minutes), the humour of which is irresistible.

FLUTE AND STRINGS. The use of the flute in combination with stringed instruments is of frequent occurrence in the classics. This form of composition, which was completely abandoned for the best part of a century, has recently found favour again with several composers. One of the first of these was the French composer Bourgault-Ducoudray, who brought back from a journey in Wales the materials for a short piece for flute and string quartet, entitled *Abergavenny*. It is merely an air with no considerable development, but it is quite sufficient to show the charm of this harmonious combination.

Much more important is Ch. Bordes' *Suite Basque*, a work of exquisite freshness, founded on popular Basque airs. In both cases the instrumental combination is the string quartet with flute. The same instruments are used in D. F. Tovey's remarkable *Variations on a Theme of Gluck*, one of the most striking and original works of this learned English musician. The composer has used the charming theme of the Sicilienne from *Armida*—

Ex. 5.

and has drawn from it all that the ingenuity of an expert contrapuntist could suggest, with the addition of an emotion growing ever more intense to the end.

One of the most famous classical works for flute and strings is Beethoven's serenade for flute, violin, and viola. This perilous combination, in which the weak viola replaces the bass, tempted the German composer Max Reger, who unfortunately treated these three slender instruments with regrettable heaviness. On the other hand, mention should be made of the work of a young Franco-Polish composer, Rohozinski, a suite in four movements for flute and violin without accompaniment, which is worthy of notice by reason of its freshness of inspiration and its ingenuity. A serenade by Wailly for flute, violin, viola, and bass also deserves mention.

FLUTE, STRINGS, AND PIANO. The immortal sonatas for flute, violin, and bass of J. S. Bach, and those of Handel, should have found numerous imitators. This is not the case, and the modern composers who have availed themselves of this combination are few. It is extremely regrettable, for the highly individual timbre of the flute forms a happy contrast with that of the violin, and when the two instruments are supported by the solid foundation of the piano, they produce a richness of sound which may be observed in the above-mentioned classical works. A charming little piece, 'Andante and scherzo' by H. Rabaud, a dainty suite by Mel-Bonis, some quite short pieces by César Cui and Gaubert, form, as far as the writer knows, nearly the whole of this repertory, which deserves to be enlarged. The same may be said of the combination of flute, 'cello, and piano, which, however, Weber's happy example failed to popularize, though Eugene Goossens in his *Five Impressions of a Holiday* has used it with success.

FLUTE AND HARP (with or without other instruments). A fine example of this combination was left by Mozart in his concerto in C, written to the order of the Duc de Guines. Then, with the arrival of the Romantic period, the association of these two poetical instruments had a certain amount of success which has not been followed up. It is probably to Debussy that we owe the return to favour of this combination. His sonata for flute, viola, and harp, performances of which have been frequent in recent years, is a real masterpiece, if not in originality of ideas, at least in the manner in which the composer was able to turn to account this association of tone-qualities. The penetrating sweetness of the lower octave of the flute, the veiled and plaintive voice of the viola, the ethereal tones of the harp, produce, especially in the second movement, an ensemble which is unique in the effect obtained from the timbres of the instruments, and the restrained and, as it were, chaste emotion of the work. In this respect it is Debussy at his best.

About the same time (although it is not suggested that he was inspired by Debussy's work) Arnold Bax published, for the same combination, an *Elegiac Trio*, which is not without merit. It was not Debussy who first thought of this combination of instruments: the old French composer Théodore Dubois, whose artistic tendencies were at the opposite pole from those of his great fellow-countryman, had already published a terzetto for flute, viola, and harp, which was poor in invention, though written by the hand of a master.

Eugene Goossens wrote, almost at the same time, a pleasant trio for flute, violin, and harp, and there are at least two sonatas for flute and harp, one by the Dutch composer Sem Dresden, and one by the Frenchman D. E. Inghelbrecht.

The danger of this combination lies in the monotony resulting from the lack of power of the two instruments, and, above all, from the limited technique of the harp. Although good harpists of the present day are able to cope with great difficulties, and even to appropriate the repertory of the piano, it is none the less true that, in a work seriously written, the part of the harp must be restricted to what will 'come off' in performance—that is to say that the composer's inspiration will be confined within precise limits. In this respect Inghelbrecht's sonata is successful; but there results from it a wearying monotony. Sem Dresden's is much more varied and full of life, but the wider field over which it ranges renders its execution difficult.

FLUTE WITH WIND INSTRUMENTS. Modern music contributes largely to this class of compositions. Readers may be reminded that the classics (Beethoven, Haydn, Mozart) did not associate the flute very much with other wind instruments. They considered it as having quite a separate tone-quality. The moderns have thought otherwise, and to quote all the works which include a flute part would be to give a more or less complete catalogue of the whole of chamber music for wind instruments, which would exceed the limits of this article. The writer will confine himself to defining the role of the flute in these different combinations.

In contradistinction to what happened in the case of chamber music for stringed instruments (with or without piano), which is confined always within the strict limits of the quintet, quartet, or trio—with the same combinations of instruments—chamber music for wind instruments offers every variety of combination, according to the personal fancy of the composer. This refers to music written for from two to ten instruments. There exists, indeed, a certain number of quintets or double quintets for wind, and some sextets with piano, but the other combinations are legion.

The tendency of inexperienced composers is to treat flute and oboe alternately as a first violin, the clarinet as a second violin, the horn as a viola, the bassoon as a 'cello. In most cases the flute fails to fulfil its role. Too weak to show to advantage against the combined tones of the other instruments, it lacks the necessary 'bite', and as soon as the exigencies of the melodic line force it to use the lower octave it is overwhelmed. The real masters of the flute prefer to seek variety and the picturesque, and they write 'leggiero'.

The criterion of success is the feeling of ease of the flautist when not obliged to struggle against his fellow-players, and when he is able to make himself heard without effort. In this respect a work like the divertissement of Émile Bernard (a musician who lacks genius but who has an admirable technique), a suite in four movements for two flutes, two oboes, two clarinets, two horns, and two bassoons, is a model. The flute moves at ease in this heavy mass because the composer employs it only with thorough knowledge. On the contrary, in Enesco's Dixtet—a splendid piece of music, full of inspiration and originality, but extremely 'thick' in harmony—the flautist is frequently out of breath without being able to dominate the ensemble when he has the most important part.

In Vincent d'Indy's *Chanson et Danses* (flute, oboe, two clarinets, horn, and two bassoons) this drawback is again apparent, but less frequently and in a lesser degree. Nevertheless, the following passage

Ex. 6.

is an example of what to avoid. Magnard's quintet, which is full of beauties, also contains passages of this kind. It is noticeable that the works best written technically (referring more particularly to the manner of writing for the flute) have been produced by composers whose inspiration is not their greatest quality. Th. Dubois, Ch. Lefebvre, Gouvy—these are never mistaken in their use of the timbre of an instrument. The best example to follow in this path seems to be Saint-Saëns, a musician of the widest attainments, who has at the same time an impeccable technique. One might profitably study the score of his *Caprice on Danish and Russian Airs*, in which the flute (as well as the other instruments) is treated with incomparable mastery.

It would be interesting to compare this score with that of Darius Milhaud's sonata for flute, oboe, clarinet, and piano. Here the flute is just as effectively used, but in quite a different way. After the most blatant brutalities of harmony or tone, the composer brings in the gentle tone of the flute with a kind of soothing effect, like that of balm on a wound. What Milhaud has so perfectly understood is the power of the flute to express emotions of tender melancholy.

MUSIC FOR TWO FLUTES WITHOUT ACCOMPANIMENT. An interesting revival of a kind of composition highly popular in the eighteenth century—the sonata for two flutes without bass—has been successfully essayed by several composers, in particular by Ch. Koechlin, whose sonata is the earliest known to the writer. This skilful contrapuntist has carried his ideas to their logical extreme, and has been led to write asperities of marked audacity. It is interesting to note that these asperities—unbearable, for example, on the piano—acquire a certain charm of their own when played by two good flautists, who are able to grade their tones skilfully. The following example is very characteristic (Ex. 7).

A recent work by Hindemith, *Kanonische Sonatine für zwei Flöten*, goes much farther still. The first movement is a canon at the third, the second a canon at the second, and the third at the fifth.

Ex. 7.

Flute with other Combinations of Instruments. Their number is extending daily, and to include all would turn this article into a catalogue. Nevertheless, mention should be made of a charming concerto by R. de Castéra for flute, clarinet, 'cello, and piano, and, above all, of Vincent d'Indy's remarkable *Suite française*, for two flutes, trumpet, and string quartet. It is remarkable especially for the curious effect of timbre obtained by the combination of the two flutes coming like a prolongation of the trumpet, with striking effect, notably in the introduction.

This study of modern music will conclude with a reference to the use of the flute in one of the most daring productions of contemporary art: Schönberg's *Pierrot Lunaire*. The composer has reduced his tiny orchestra to the minimum (four instruments and a piano). The flautist has to play flute and piccolo alternately. One must give Schönberg credit for great skill, for he obtains from this slender combination the utmost it can give. One of the most happily inspired pages of the work is certainly no. 7, where the solo flute is left as the only accompaniment to the singer, a curious page with a nostalgic effect, which has overcome the distaste of audiences least inclined to like the work. Louis Fleury.

†FOERSTER, Adolph M., b. 1854, American composer.

Quartet, pf, v, vla, vc, E flat	op. 21, c. 1887	Kahnt, 1888.
Trio-serenade, pf, v, vc	c. 1907	Carl Fischer, 1915.
Trio, pf, v, vc, g mi	op. 29	Challier, 1890.
Trio, pf, v, vc, D	,, 83, c. 1919	{ Carl Fischer, F. Schuberth } 1922.
Suite, pf, v, G	op. 36	B. & H., 1895.

Foerster's chamber music reveals the gift of fluency without pronounced individuality. His themes are definite and broadly conceived, and their development is scholarly and logical. He attempts no harmonic innovations, finding the orthodox vocabulary of the German theorists sufficient for his purposes. His most widely performed work is the trio-serenade; the trio, op. 83, has also been frequently played. Other works are in MS.

A. L. Goldberg.

FOERSTER, Christoph, 1693–1745, German composer.

Modern republication:

Suite with overture, str. quartet, G (H. Riemann, Coll. Mus. 22), B. & H., 1906.

Dr. Altmann considers that Foerster's suite for chamber orchestra (all movements in the key of G), which can also be played with single instruments, may be considered as one of the earliest attempts at string quartet writing. The movements are for the most part little pieces of dance music, in which the bass part ('cello) has not the independent treatment to be found in quartets of a later period.

Other works may be found in *Fétis*, &c. C. P. E. Bach had a collection of Foerster's works in MS. Editor.

FOERSTER, Emanuel Aloys, *c.* 1748–1823, German composer.

In Sir W. H. Hadow's admirable book on Beethoven's op. 18 quartets, he writes:

'During this period Beethoven made friends with an old professor—twenty-two years his senior—named Emanuel Aloys Förster, who lived in Vienna and gave composition lessons. Förster, a competent teacher and an adventurous quartet writer, held twice a week at his house musical parties which were attended by some of the most famous virtuosi of the time: Schuppanzigh who became Beethoven's favourite first violin, Linke the 'cellist, Weiss, the greatest viola player in the city, and many others. Beethoven had free access to this house and was a constant visitor; it may be taken as positive that the six quartets were tried here in MS. and discussed between the composer and the performers. Indeed, we have on this point a tiny but illuminating piece of evidence. On June 25, 1799, Beethoven gave Amenda a copy of the quartet in F with an affectionate inscription on the first violin part. "Whenever you play it", he says, "recall the days that we have spent together." About a year later he wrote to Amenda: "Do not give your quartet to anybody, because I have greatly changed it, having learned how to write quartets properly." Whether this implies actual instruction from Förster is uncertain—Beethoven afterwards spoke of him as his "Alter Meister", and recommended pupils to go to him—in either case we may conclude that the quartets owe something of their present shape to the suggestions and criticisms of the players.'

Some interesting comments, which space will not allow me to quote, upon Foerster's quartets, are to be found in Dr. Altmann's *Handbuch*, and a long list of his compositions in *Fétis* and *Vidal*. Editor.

*†FOERSTER, Josef Bohuslav, b. 1859, Bohemian composer.

	op.	Composed	
Quintet, fl, ob, cl, horn, fag, D	95	—	Hudební Matice.
First quartet, str, E	15	1888	Junne, 1898.
Second quartet, str, D	39	—	Edition Sadlo, 1927.

	op.	Comp.	
Third quartet, str, C	61	1913	U.E., 1914.
Trio, pf, v, vc, f mi	8	1883	Fr. A. Urbánek.
Trio, pf, v, vc, B flat	38	1894	U.E., 1918.
Trio, pf, v, vc, a mi	105	—	Foerster Society, 1927.
Sonata, pf, v, b mi	10	—	U.E., 1910.
Suite (*Prinzessin Gänseblume*), pf, v	35	—	Fr. A. Urbánek, 1902.
Sonata, pf, vc, f mi	45	—	M. Urbánek, 1905; U.E.

If the above be placed in chronological order, it will be perceived that they symbolize, up to a certain point, the intellectual evolution of this interesting master. It is true that Foerster spent fifteen years of his life away from his own country. Yet his musical language has always retained the stamp of its birth.

The earliest of these works is the trio, op. 8, the first two movements of which were written during Foerster's studies at the Organ School at Prague, and the influence of the classic masters and of Schumann is still visible. One may also point to certain naïvetés in this important work which are not to be found in his later compositions. The instrumentation, moreover, is somewhat massive as compared with that of subsequent works, but the impression left by the whole trio is pleasing, thanks to the finale, which is the best movement. At the close of this movement, the leading theme of the adagio is heard.

Here is the subject of the first movement,

Ex. 1.

manifestly a theme of a type which lends itself readily to academic treatment.

The real Foerster shows himself in the middle of the second movement, with the following subject (Ex. 2).

The String Quartet, op. 15, is the next work. This composition won the praise of Dvořák, whose influence may be perceived in it, as well as that of Tchaikovsky. It is a real chamber work, in which every instrument plays its part, the middle voices being particularly well treated. This quartet also must be classed among the works of the master's first period. Other influences are still perceptible in it, but the advance on the trio is very great. It is less rhythmic than the latter, but there is more of the lyrical element, while

Ex. 2.

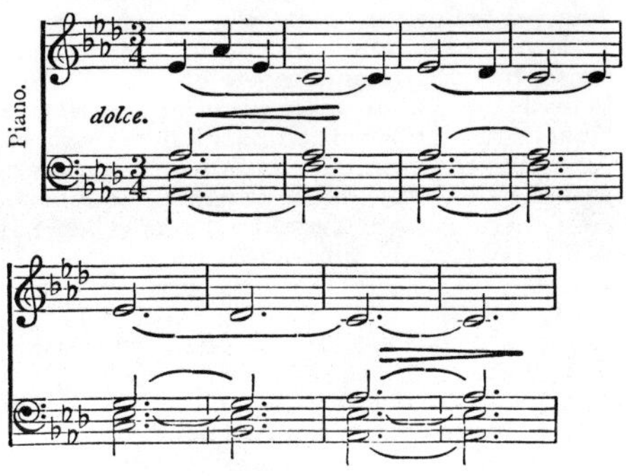

the musical language has become much more finely shaded. Here is the theme of the first movement (on the viola):

Ex. 3.

The composer's individuality is noticeable in the adagio.

Ex. 4.

In 1894 the composer had it in mind to replace the finale by another movement. He did not carry out his intention, but produced a new and independent work, an *allegro giocoso* for strings, which is at present unpublished.

The Second String Quartet is a quite original work, very characteristic of the happy period spent by the composer at Hamburg.

The circumstances of Foerster's life have always played their part in his compositions. What has been written by him has previously been lived by him; in fact, one must know the source of his musical inspiration in order to understand his music properly. Though his compositions may, of course, be judged by purely musical standards, yet one often discovers suddenly, while listening to them, that external influences have also been at work. It is not programme music in the ordinary sense, but programme music of a kind which is made clear by a single phrase indicating on what occasion a given composition was written. As a rule the composer indicates this also by a dedication, to which attention should be paid. The music, therefore, is of a kind in which life and art join hands; the ethical side, too, is inseparable from it, and cannot be disregarded.

THE PIANO TRIO, op. 38, offers an illustration of the foregoing remarks. It is in three movements, the last of which is an adagio. A slow movement is unusual as a conclusion, but the matter is explained by the fact that the trio was composed not long after the death of the composer's beloved sister Marie. This important work begins with much gaiety, but the end is melancholy and meditative. It is to be noted, too, that Foerster's musical speech has grown very fervent and very noble, as the leading themes exemplify. In the first movement we have:

Ex. 5.

then with much fervour:

Ex. 6.

while, in the third movement, we find at the start the following song for the 'cello:

Ex. 7.

and this meditation for the piano:

Ex. 8.

THE THIRD STRING QUARTET, op. 61, shows the later development of the kind of programme music already mentioned. This work is in one continuous movement, which may be divided into four contrasted sections. The original form of the principal theme, which is met with throughout the work, is as follows:

Ex. 9.

Subsequent variants of it are the following:

Ex. 10.

Ex. 11.

Ex. 12.

Very important is the dedication of this third quartet, 'To my beloved wife, September 1, 1913'. (The date was the twenty-fifth anniversary of the composer's marriage.)

THE PIANO TRIO IN A MINOR is a third composition of the same type. Yet it is one of Foerster's masterpieces, which, however, has only lately (1927) been published. The work was written in memory of the composer's only son, Alfred, who died at fifteen years of age, on March 11, 1921.

THE QUINTET, op. 95, for wind instruments is the only remaining work that requires mention here. This, by reason of its very lively character, forms an exception in the body of Foerster's work. It will be enough to quote here the beginning of the first movement (clarinet) (Ex. 13) and the capricious opening of the scherzo (Ex. 14). JOSEF BARTOŠ.

Ex. 13.

Ex. 14.

†FOGG, ERIC, b. 1903, English composer.

Quartet, str, A flat	Elkin.
Suite, harp (or pf), v, vc	London & Continental.
Poem, pf, vc	Elkin, 1923.
Phantasy, pf, vc	Bosworth, —

Eric Fogg's compositions belong to the new school of musical thought, but one in which clarity is not sacrificed to modernity. His quartet is far from easy to play, the scherzo, especially needing the co-operation of first-rate artists to make it effective. The composer, therefore, has been fortunate in securing performances at Manchester by the Catterall and Edith Robinson Quartets, who have placed this clever work in a favourable light. EDITOR.

FOLK-SONG IN CHAMBER MUSIC.

The significance of folk-song in chamber music is perhaps not generally realized. Its use is by no means confined to variations; on the other hand, we seldom find a whole work based on folk-tunes. When Schumann gave the designation 'Im Volkston' (in folk-song style) to his five pieces for 'cello and piano (which may reasonably be included in chamber music), he certainly intended them to be regarded as 'traditional' by association, although, as actually written, they proved to be the purest art music rather than true folk music. Bungert, again, gave the title 'In folk-song style' to the slow movement of his piano quartet, and many composers have more or less consciously fastened on a folk-song—as a basis for slow movements—in Lied form[1] particularly. Folk dances, too, which are in many cases accompanied by singing, and thus stand in close relation to folk-songs, are also found in chamber music from time to time. The greatest users of them are the Russian composers, who do not, however, think it necessary to announce the fact. Beethoven, however, did state that he had used Russian airs in the two string quartets, op. 59, nos. 1 and 2; and, but for the fact that he was wont to acknowledge the source of any borrowed theme, one might be inclined to assume a Russian folk-tune as the foundation of the *andante con moto quasi allegretto* in the third of the Rasoumovsky quartets.

But there is no reason to reproach the composers who suppress the source of their inspiration, so long as it is really inspiration, and the treatment is their own independent achievement. Conrat, in his essay on *Haydn and*

[1] *v.* Foreword, art. BEETHOVEN.

Croatian folk-songs (in *Die Musik*, vol. 14, p. 14 et seq., Berlin, 1905), points out that the beginning of the string quartet, op. 17, no. 6, and the last movement of op. 33, no. 3, are based on Croatian national airs, but one needs only to look more closely to see what Haydn made of them! He very possibly made use of many another folk-song in his quartets without thereby impairing the original quality of his work.

It is a matter of indifference, for instance, whether the theme in Beethoven's septet variations is, or is not, a Rhenish folk-song; all that matters is his manner of transforming it, which is truly admirable. Mozart does not appear to have exploited folk-song, but both Weber and Schubert did so. It is interesting that so thoroughly German a composer as Brahms should have been drawn to Hungarian gipsy tunes on different occasions in his chamber works. He calls attention to the fact himself, in the case of the last movement of the G minor piano quartet, by the words *alla zingara*; not so, however, in the finale of the string quintet in G, or the slow movement of the clarinet quintet. The last named, in particular, is the best proof of the fertilizing possibilities of folk music taken from an entirely different race. There have recently (1928) been attempts to introduce exotic music into European compositions, including chamber music; on the other hand, there are composers who see in their own national song the only means of furthering the 'culture music' of their country, e.g. Joseph Holbrooke, Swan Hennessy, and numerous others. It looks almost as if, in those countries where national feeling is strongly developed, composers are filled more and more with the desire to create an art music which can no longer be felt as international (in the sense in which many of the great masters' works are international), and for which they rely on their own distinctively national music. It must be admitted that such consciously national music has, as a rule, a much more powerful effect on the people of other nations than colourless universal products devoid of all originality.

A number of chamber works in which national airs are used are given among the string quartets and violin sonatas collected in the writer's *Kammermusik-Literatur* (3rd edition, 1923). WILHELM ALTMANN.

As a special subject, the influence of folk-song on chamber music is difficult to divide from that of folk-song on music in general. Chamber music is to be distinguished from other music chiefly in its scope and technique; an influence like that of the folk-song is likely to be felt by a composer equally whether he is writing symphonies, operas, or quartets.

Therefore, to trace the influence of folk-song on chamber music must, of necessity, be a rather arbitrary proceeding, consisting merely of tracing the folk influences on a composer's style generally and concentrating attention on those of his works which happen to fall under the head of chamber music.

There is, however, one class of such music which is particularly likely to be influenced by folk-song, namely, all that which is of melodic pattern and on a small and simple scale, written for a solo instrument or for two or three instruments in combination. This kind of chamber music has always been very susceptible to the influence of the folk-song.

There are two ways in which the music sprung from the people may be felt in a composer's work.

First: the idiom which is equally native to him and to the folk-songs of his own country may permeate his music as a whole. In this case we shall not be able necessarily to trace actual quotations from folk-song in his compositions, but we feel that his music is part of the national musical language which finds its simplest and most direct expression in his native folk-song. This is the case in all great music, which, to whatever heights it rises, always has its roots planted in its native soil.

Secondly (and this is not exclusive of the first way): composers often feel tempted to make use of actual quotations from folk music, especially that of their own country, as a basis for short pieces such as variations, fantasias, dance movements, and the like. This is partly due to the fascination which these primitive and beautiful melodies exercise over all musical minds, and partly because composers feel (unconsciously no doubt) that an occasional draught at the fountain-head will invigorate and refresh the stream of their own musical thought.

It is in this second case that folk-song has an influence over chamber music in particular; that kind of chamber music, especially, which takes the form of short piano pieces, solos for violin, and so on—pieces of a small and simple type, which are melodic in their nature or embody some striking rhythmic formula.

Among the earliest music which can properly be classified as 'chamber music' is the collection, edited by Fuller Maitland and the late W. Barclay Squire, known as the *Fitzwilliam Virginal Book*. This book consists of a number of small pieces composed for the virginals by various Elizabethan composers of note, among them being John Bull, Byrd, Dowland, Farnaby, and others. These pieces consist of fantasias and variations on tunes, most of them folk-tunes evidently popular in Elizabethan times. Such titles as *John, come kiss me now*, *My Robin is to the greenwood gone*, *Walsingham*, *Malt's come down*, *Greensleeves*, are frequent. Many of these tunes are well known to us through Chappell's great work, *Popular Music of the Olden Time*, and one of the tunes, at least, exists to this day as a Morris tune, which is even now played where Morris dancing is still a traditional art.

It is, I think, not straining a term too widely to include under the heading 'chamber music' the shorter, at all events, of J. S. Bach's choral preludes for the organ; many of these are on quite a small scale, and more suited for the chamber organ than for the great instruments of our cathedrals. In these preludes Bach has taken the hymn-tunes so beloved throughout Lutheran Germany and treated them with his own consummate art. There can be no doubt that many of these German *Choräle* are adapted from folk-tunes.

The indirect influence of the folk-song can be seen in the music of the Italian composers of the late seventeenth century—Scarlatti, Corelli, Tartini, and others—though it is the design more than the character of the folk-song whose influence is felt. The object of these early Italian composers was to produce melodic, simple and direct music, and in seeking for some easily grasped pattern on which to mould their ideas they hit (accidentally, no doubt) on the very pattern on which so many folk-tunes are built. This pattern they enlarged and developed, and left as a heritage to the classical school of Haydn, Mozart, and Beethoven; and it was from these slender beginnings that the whole scheme of sonata form sprang, so that a direct descent from the simple folk-song to the complexity of Beethoven's ninth symphony is traceable—a proof, if one were needed, that great music is not something abnormal and precious, but has its roots in the common needs of human nature.

There is hardly need to speak of the folk-song influence on Haydn—he was a countryman, and the subjects of his quartets and symphonies are full of the spirit, if not of the very shape, of his own national melodies—it was the spirit of the folk-song which gave his music that vitality, coupled with simplicity, which distinguished it from the vapid commonplace of his contemporaries.

Beethoven's music, saturated though it is with the spirit of German folk-song, has, as far as the writer knows, few actual quotations from folk music. However, as regards his chamber music, the theme of the variations in his septet is said to be a Rhine *Volkslied*, and one calls to mind the *Thème Russe* in his second *Rasoumovsky* quartet, which turns up unexpectedly, very differently treated, and under very different circumstances, in the Coronation scene of Moussorgsky's *Boris Godounov*.

Of more modern composers it is, perhaps, in certain of the works of Chopin that we find the folk-song element most strongly marked. There are two Chopins—the Parisian, the inventor of brilliant piano passages, the composer of the valses and impromptus; and the Polish, intensely national Chopin, the composer of the mazurkas and polonaises. Some of Chopin's mazurkas have a strong family likeness to actual Polish folk-songs, and his polonaises are directly founded on the national dance. In the case of Chopin there is, indeed, a special application of the folk-song influence to chamber music. The national spirit of Chopin could be expressed in no better way than in these slight forms, coupled with that intimacy of feeling which is found only in music designed for solo players.

It is hardly necessary to speak in detail of the national influences in the work of such eminently nationalist composers as Grieg, Dvořák, and Tchaikovsky. Grieg's small piano pieces are often hardly to be distinguished from Norwegian folk-songs; Dvořák's *dumky* and *furiants* are deliberately founded in form, if not in material, on the songs and dances of his native country; while Tchaikovsky has more than once used Russian folk-songs in his chamber music, notably in the theme of the variations in his piano trio and in the slow movement of his second string quartet.

One of the most interesting developments of modern English music has been the influence of the folk-song on the style of many of our younger composers, an influence shown chiefly in their chamber music. The younger composers, however, have not been without guidance in this matter from their older colleagues. Sir Hubert Parry's delightful piano duets on British airs are too little known; and both Sir Charles Stanford and Sir Alexander Mackenzie made fine use of their own national melodies, though in the case of these two composers it is in their orchestral and vocal music that the national influence is most apparent.

Among the younger composers one of the earliest to make use of English folk-tunes was Nicholas Gatty in his early string quartet, where the finale takes the form of a set of variations on a Worcestershire melody. Mention must be made also of the slow movement in J. B. McEwen's splendid second string quartet, where the influence of Scottish idiom is very strong.

The most conspicuous use of English and Irish folk-song has been made by Percy Grainger. Grainger's work, even in his orchestral and choral music, is small in scope, and it is in his chamber music that he is most characteristic, because it is in this style of music that he can concentrate vividly all he has to say in the most concise and direct manner. His use of folk-song sometimes takes the form of varied treatment of a tune, as in his *Molly on the Shore* and *Shepherd's Hey*—sometimes, as in his *Ramble, My Robin is to the greenwood gone,* he takes a folk-song as the basis of an instrumental piece, while in the *Mock Morris* he follows the example of Chopin in his mazurkas, and has composed original music suggested in its rhythm and general scheme by our own national dance, the Morris.

It is the younger composers especially that the English folk-song has influenced. It is about twenty-five years since, through the efforts of Miss Broadwood, the late Cecil Sharp, and others, the vast wealth of beautiful melody to which English musicians are the heirs was made accessible to the world at large. Naturally, then, the older composers, to whom they were new and strange, could hardly take to them quite naturally, however much they might admire them: their style was already formed, and to them their own folk-songs inevitably remained something external. But with the younger composers it is different; they have grown up with their own national music, it has become part of their system, they have assimilated it, and with the composers of the future this may be still more so. When every child is taught his mother music with his mother tongue, the two will be equally natural means of expression, and it will be as natural for an English musician to write English music as for an English author to write the English language. R. VAUGHAN WILLIAMS.

[How far composers have been influenced by folk-song may not be gauged by the actual quotation of themes. The point is that its spirit is felt in the work of all the best writers of chamber music. In some cases, of course, this is more marked than in others, in that of Grieg and Dvořák for instance. Such music *is* folk-song, and were chamber music to become as popular as it deserves to be, were it to enter into the people's life, it might all come to be considered in the end as belonging to the same category. But this will not happen if certain of the moderns have their way. One of them is reported to have said that 'Beethoven is not a musician but a melodist'. With the latter half of this aphorism most will agree, and as to the former, as to the word 'musician', its significance changes apparently at the will of *les jeunes*. I like to see these young colts kicking their heels on the slopes of Parnassus, but shall always adhere to my opinion that a man is not a musician *unless* he is a melodist, and therefore more or less influenced by folk-song.

Haydn came of humble parents, who loved the songs of the people, which in Austria and Germany approach nearer to the type of universal music than in any other country. The members of the family circle were accustomed to assemble at night and sing them together; so often that they 'slid into the soul' of the young musician and ended in forming part of his nature. There was no need for conscious striving on his part to find original themes; as a melodist he was what folk-song had made him, and it is clear that if every composer worked with the same freedom from self-consciousness, leaving his individuality to show itself in harmonic, rhythmic, and contrapuntal development, ugliness would much less frequently find a place in modern music.

Sir Henry Hadow was the first to point out that Haydn's *God Save the Emperor* was built upon a Croatian folk-song. A writer who attempted to trace every folk-tune to its lair in chamber music would find a lengthy spell of work before him. Most composers have been influenced by those of native origin, though Mozart came exceptionally under Italian influence. Beethoven, as Dr. Williams has pointed out, introduced Russian themes into his eighth quartet as a compliment to Count Rasoumovsky, to whom it was dedicated. One at least of these, which lends itself readily to musical treatment, has been frequently employed by various Russian composers. I have met with this old friend in Arensky's quartet for violin, viola, and two 'cellos, and in another Russian quartet, from *Les Vendredis*, have found some Breton melodies which had strayed into the score and become Russianized in the process, from which I infer that composers are upon safer ground when they seek for inspiration among the melodies of their own and kindred races. It leaves a choice that is wide enough.

It is obvious that Brahms was altogether German. His first appearance in public was made in a performance of some variations for piano upon a German folk-tune, whilst in his early trio in B, otherwise a rather austere work, a delightful popular melody appears, one used by Humperdinck in *Hänsel und Gretel*. Brahms was also much attracted by folk dance, by Austrian *Ländler*, Hungarian *Czardas*, and peasant dances generally. The few wonderful bars which form the trio of the scherzo written for his sextet in G form the finest imaginable piece of folk dance. One hears the heavy-footed peasants bounding around, uttering cries of joy, and can imagine that Brahms drew inspiration from his experience at some country merrymaking.

Of the innumerable composers influenced by folk-song and dance I will mention only two, Lekeu and Vreuls, not only because they have used the melodies and *Cramignons* of their native *pays Wallon*, but because they aptly illustrate an interesting phase of the subject. They have made use of the irregular rhythms which are found in their native songs, and which have become a fascinating feature of modern chamber music, though sometimes very much overdone. It will be an evil day for composers when the stream of inspiration ceases to flow towards them direct from the heart of the people. EDITOR.]

FOLK IDIOMS AND NATIONAL TRAITS IN CHAMBER MUSIC.

It has been customary to regard chamber music as a wholly abstract type of music, its forms as art forms pure and simple, and, latterly, since master-minds have developed the sonata, quartet, and other classical forms, as something quite apart from popular musical forms represented by popular songs and dances. A very cursory investigation goes far to prove this a false assumption. In the most highly organized classics folk elements emerge clearly, even when veiled by developed forms and sophisticated artifice.

CHAMBER MUSIC AND NATIONAL SOCIAL LIFE. What could be more natural? Chamber music is, *par excellence*, the music of intimate life, music originally domestic in origin and to-day essentially the most social in appeal. Society has only recently become so permeated with cosmopolitan influences as to differentiate it markedly from the mass of the people; hence many national features and folk traits maintained themselves in the social life of countries down to periods which cover the lives of many great classical composers. Musicians also, down to comparatively recent times, were invariably recruited from the people, not from the upper classes. The artists proper often remained servitors, as in the notable case of Haydn as retainer to the princely Esterhazy family, and in the institution of such offices as the Capellmeister in Germany, the more official development of the medieval minstrel or bard of the nobility. The family was a more intimate and domestic entity than at present, and the music made for such noble families partook of such domesticity. The great estate was merely the folk life in particular, as the country, viewed nationally, was the folk life in general. The lines of demarcation between aristocracy and people were scarcely those of type, but rather the natural boundaries between rich and poor, and were based on a common ground of national custom and tradition.

Before the rise of industrialism the people were direct natural growths from the soil; the aristocrats were the forced products of specialized hereditary functions. In art they stood for patronage; but creation and execution came, with rare exceptions, from the people, at least so far as music was concerned.

SOCIAL CUSTOMS IN CHAMBER MUSIC FORMS. The social characteristics of chamber music are clearly manifest in those forms essentially belonging to it. In the basic elements of these forms their folk origin is discernible. The suite, which was the generic origin of sonata and symphony alike, was a direct emanation from folk dance and song. The earliest suites, such as those of Sweelinck, were sequences of dances adopted from folk tradition and refined and formalized. The variation form, virtually originated by the Tudor masters of the virginal, was again a derivative of folk-lore, being almost invariably based on well-known popular airs or tunes of true folk character. Both variation and rondo assumed great importance in suite and sonata forms, the latter being a typical folk form in origin, based on the dance song with a round refrain danced to round figures, with fixed repetitions of given themes or cadences associated with repeated word refrains. The fantasia, as understood and developed by the Elizabethans and the early classical Italians, such as Frescobaldi, had much in common with the variation form, though it was more fully developed, with less rigid adherence to the central theme; but its form was almost invariably based upon popular dance measures. These forms, with the air and the prelude, a free and usually contrapuntal treatment of a given theme, provided almost the entire material from which the sonata, and later the symphony, derived their original substance. The domestic character of these forms is clearly indicated in such titles as sonata da camera, which differentiated them from the types not derived from popular sources. These include, on the one hand, the sonata da chiesa, which was a development of the early Italian classical instrumental form, the ricercata, a free contrapuntal development of the ecclesiastical chant, or chorale, treated along the lines of the later fantasia, though more akin to the vocal polyphony derived from the medieval French, or Gothic, schools typified in Franco de Paris, Berotin, and Franco de Cologne—the ars antiqua of early musical theorists and historians. On the other hand we have the freer development of this typified in de Vitry, de Muris, and de Machaut—the ars nova of their time—inherited by the Gallo-Belgians (Dufay, Binchois, Faugues, de Busnois), from which developed the Netherland school (comprising Okeghem, Josquin des Prés, Gombert, Willaert, Cyprian van Rore, Orlando Lasso, Holbrecht, Arcadelt, and Sweelinck in successive generations)—the source and inspiration, indeed the actual masters of the Roman composers whose glory culminated in Palestrina, and whose work played a part in the development of the early classical Venetian school. Here, since sonata da camera and sonata da chiesa contributed in varying degrees to modern sonata form, it is interesting to note that the Franco-Gothic—that is, the French—medieval schools incorporated into the motet such typical folk forms as the rondo, and that the Gallo-Belgians took a similar course in forsaking Gregorian plainsong for the free melodic characteristics of folk-song. Thus, in a manner of speaking, they created a musical medium for that phase of national aspiration which gave rise to the national churches. The earliest generators of the first classic chamber music forms were thus permeated by folk music elements and the folk idiom of various countries, the essential characteristics of which were subsequently overlaid, but never obliterated.

SUBCONSCIOUS AND CONSCIOUS INFLUENCES IN NATIONAL IDIOMS. Such elements, however, must have had an important subconscious influence on creative thought and the development of musical forms, once the initial stages of adapting folk forms to abstract musical construction were past. There are not lacking, however, tangible instances of conscious popular inspiration in the works of classic masters of the later period, even in cases where this music has hitherto been presented as purely abstract in conception. A notable instance is the use of acknowledged national dance forms in the suites of Bach, for these are specifically German chamber music, which was to attain so marvellous and exquisite a culmination in the genius of Mozart. In the equally important suites for clavichord of Domenico Scarlatti, conscious national popular inspiration is visible in the inclusion of such typically Italian dance measures as the Siciliano. And it is not only in the more defined formal types that such conscious preoccupation is evident. There are, apart from the typically folk-idiomatic nature of so many themes by Haydn and his use of local folk forms (such as the *All'ongarese* in the well-known trio), such direct presentation of folk types in chamber music form as the *Contretänze* of Mozart, which bear no trace of the alleged Italianization of the master's inspiration, while his Austro-Germanic impulses are definitely presented. The divertimenti continually revert to undisguised adaptations of Austro-Germanic folk-song and folk dance, thus introducing into what is essentially music for the chamber similar elements to those found in his symphonies, quartets, and other music which is classed as chamber music in its ordinary meaning. This ordinary meaning is accepted through long-existing Germanic associations of thought and practice, but is inadequate to express the wider and more varied conception of chamber music as held and expressed by the pre-Germanic classics—English composers from Elizabeth and James I to the Restoration, the Italians from the Gabriellis through Corelli to Scarlatti, the French from Chambonnières to Couperin and Rameau. Amongst the better-known and later classics and romantics there is even more positive conscious national and folk inspiration in chamber music. Beethoven, of course, found constant inspiration in themes and forms which, if not actually of authentic folk origin (though this is actually the case in some instances), have all the characteristics of German folk music, and especially of the German dance, and these occur so persistently that it is impossible to tabulate them adequately. With the romantics, the blend of poetic and literary inspiration with nationalistic tradition accentuated such conscious adoption of folk forms. To give one instance only, Schubert without the *Ländler* form would be inconceivable, and Germanic folk-song characteristics are almost invariably evident in his exquisite chamber works, those lyric poems in quartet, trio, and quintet form, which are amongst the happiest, most intimate and expressive things in music. Chopin, who was inspired by the songs of his native Poland, is another notable instance.

Turning to more modern times, one notes, as the epoch of German dominion declines, that the folk elements in chamber music become more definite and conscious, in some cases almost to the verge of mannerism. Here, also, it becomes necessary to differentiate between the perpetuation of these folk elements and the evolution of national consciousness in music, with ever more direct bearing upon the hitherto comparatively abstract forms of chamber music.

THE CHARACTER OF GERMAN CLASSICISM. It is the opinion of the present writer that the alleged universality claimed for the types and characteristics of German classical music is not sustained either by the internal evidence of German music or by that of other nations—pan-Germanic theories notwithstanding—and the clear fact emerges that, in spirit and substance, the more epic German masters were thoroughly German in inspiration and expression.

THE RISE OF NATIONALISTIC MUSICAL ASPIRATIONS. The Napoleonic wars revived national consciousness and stimulated revolt amongst those nations—virtually the whole of civilized Europe with the exception of Great Britain—which felt the weight of the French onslaughts. Russia was too little affected, and her music too little developed, for the Napoleonic march of conquest to touch her folk feeling as affecting art, or to produce the deep-seated sense of rebellion which followed on the humiliation of Austria and Prussia. Germanic romanticism, however, as exemplified in the initial poetic impulse of Uhland, Körner, and their like, was national feeling brought to white heat through the flame of political stress and revolution. Hence it follows that Germanic musical romanticism, in spite of its literary and poetically fanciful trappings, was by nature national to some degree in this sense also. Weber, essentially the first of the German romantics, consciously desired to incorporate German tradition and a German idiom in his operas. Beethoven, though an internationalist and republican, could not escape similar influences. These, however, expressed themselves comparatively subconsciously, through the bucolic leanings which are evident in so much of his music. But, except in the case of some German dances, his external form diverged widely from folk models, though the spirit of these is maintained to a very large degree. With Brahms, the Germanic ideal and the Germanic idiom became dominant, even in the most abstruse formal types of chamber music, while, on the other hand, he had undisguised interest in indigenous forms of dance.

THE ARTISTIC DEVELOPMENT OF NATIONAL TRAITS: DIALECTS AND IDIOM. It will therefore be realized that national traits in music can find dual expression, firstly, by the adoption and extension of the folk-song and dance, secondly by means of an abstract process of refinement which preserves the characteristic national types of melody, phrase, and rhythm underlying national folk music. It is, in effect, a stripping of popular and local mannerisms from a national musical vernacular, in order to free its spirit and substance for the evolution of forms in which only the essentials of national impulse and inspiration remain. Thus emerges a music as distinctively national as any folk music, and in the direct line of inheritance from it, but which is a cultured and developed idiom, not a crude or naïve dialect.

LOCAL CONDITIONS AS DETERMINING FOLK TRAITS. There are, however, less self-conscious sentimental and intimate factors also at work, and these inevitably bring national folk traits into chamber music. And this must be so, for each country has its special environment, with particular physical conditions, geographical and atmospheric, especially such countries as evolve a strongly typical national idiom in art of all kinds. The art does not develop by conscious mechanical processes; it evolves by subtle stages of circumstantial change and the influence of physical conditions. Mountainous countries tend to pipe-music, for stringed instruments have little chance when the life of the people is mainly in the open air. The life of the plains produces other instrumental types characteristic of the environment and the temperament of the inhabitants.

NATIONAL INSTRUMENTS AND NATIONAL MUSICAL TYPES. The characteristics of national melody are thus largely determined by the nature of the national instruments, for such characteristics imperceptibly affect the whole of the given national music, whatever instruments may actually be written for. No better example of this can be given than the music of Grieg, where one is at every turn confronted by the echoes of the mountain pipes of the composer's native Norway. And this is true, to a certain extent, even of his chamber music, for the familiar pipes sound in the musician's ear. The forms of Norwegian folk-song and dance also descend from such characteristic instrumental influences. So, in melodic line, in rhythm and form, Grieg, inspired by the folk music of the pipers, wrote under a dual stimulus which dominates even his abstract works.

The national Hungarian peculiarities, again, find their origin in the national instrument. The violin of the *tzigane* can be heard in every decorative configuration, every melodic turn, in the snap of its cadences. One finds these equally in the chamber music of Hubay and in the more modern works of Bartók and Kodály.

Vocal habits in countries such as the Germanic ones, where the domestic round song and the religious chorale are general, also affect the seemingly remote branch of chamber music. Consciously or subconsciously, a host of German slow movements, from Haydn to Hindemith, are based on the essential character of vocal part-singing, and this is particularly manifest in Beethoven, Brahms, and Schumann. In this sense, Germany may be said to be the true home of the four-part voice conception of music, and by reason of the dominance of the quartet in chamber music the influence of this vocal part-writing is strong.

NATIONAL TRAITS AND HISTORIC EXPERIENCE. The historic vicissitudes of nations and the instrumental habits resulting from them also exercise powerful influences on national musical forms. In France, where military feeling has been powerful since Charlemagne and reached a climax in Napoleon's campaigns, one is always aware of a martial trend in the national melody, excepting in music derived from pastoral sources, in which one can discern the influence of the musette, which, significantly, is the title given to several French chamber works of the early classic period, the seventeenth and early eighteenth centuries.

THE SLAV STIMULUS IN MUSICAL NATIONALISM. The true sense of national elements as a source of national style, in contradistinction to national manner, originated with the Slavs. The famous nationalist 'Five' of Russia—Borodin, Balakirev, Moussorgsky, Rimsky-Korsakov, and Cui—set a new ideal before the musicians of Russia and of all countries of nineteenth-century Europe, and it is in Russia that the most marked national influence on chamber music is found. It is seen, however, on investigating the lives of the 'Five', that the intimacy which gave an extremely individual touch to the co-operative creation peculiar to their national movement led naturally to a keen interest in, and a prolific production of, works of a chamber music type. To what aesthetic quality this attained is manifest, for instance, in the lovely Borodin works. The close relationship between the Russian nationalist movement in music and the intimate social life of Russia inevitably led to chamber music as a prominent medium of expression. It was the cause of collaborations impossible in the more epic or extended forms, e.g. the delightful co-operation of composers in the production of variations on folk themes for string quartet, to which each contributed his own variation, thus subscribing to the folk inspiration doctrine, while at the same time demonstrating its flexibility for the expression of personal preferences.

THE CZECH CONTRIBUTION. Similar to the Russian development of folk elements in chamber music was the nationalist movement of the closely related Czechs. This produced at least two masters of chamber music permeated with the Slav idiom of this people—Dvořák and Smetana—who made material contributions to the treasures of intimate music. The sense of racial intimacy and of music as an intimate feature of everyday life amongst the Czechs is also demonstrated in the works of later Czech composers, notably that fine chamber ensemble artist, Josef Suk. Here folk characteristics are used in a subjective sense, to conjure up the imagery of incidents, personal impulses, and traits of environment, as in *Experiences and Memories*, for string quartet—such music as corresponds rather to the elusive communion of intimate life than to the considered utterances of more public occasions.

FRENCH IDIOMATIC MUTATIONS OF CHAMBER MUSIC. Among the initiators of Russian and Czech musical nationalism, as among the Teutons, one finds chiefly the conventional combinations of sonata, trio, quartet, or quintet. It naturally follows on the national instrumental influences already mentioned, that other races will not so easily attune their musical expression to these comparatively stereotyped though immortal forms. Hence one discerns, from about the late eighties or early nineties of last century, a eaning towards combinations of wood-wind and strings in French chamber music, which is nationalistic inasmuch as it corresponds to such pastoral revivals as are manifest in modern French poetry. Especially notable is the idiomatically French use of the flute since the advent of Debussy, a use particularly developed to-day by Albert Roussel; and this marks another phase in the influence of race idiom on chamber music.

THE VERNACULAR NUANCE IN FRENCH MELODY. The cadence of French speech inspired Erik Satie's conception of an expressive continuous recitative in opera, which Claude Debussy carried out so memorably in *Pelléas et Mélisande*. Speech itself progresses from primitive utterance to subtle nuances, yet preserves the characteristic cadences of the given language. And so it is with national expression in music; the elusive phrases which so materially altered the prevalent conceptions of musical thematic matter in symphonic music also announced the adoption of certain phases of music into the idiom of the French vernacular. *Pelléas et Mélisande* epitomized this in its co-relation of speech and sound; but it is no less emphatically evident, though more abstractly so, in the exquisite Debussy quartet, as truly a moulding of music to the spirit and substance of essentially French expression as was *The Vision of Piers Plowman* in its shaping of language and poetic form to literary purposes and peculiarities purely English. There have been superficial analogies drawn between the chamber music of Ravel and Debussy; but in matter and treatment the two differ fundamentally, and in this difference race again plays its part. The Basque Ravel is not the Celto-Latin Debussy in thematic conception or expressive nuance. The impalpable shading of an almost verbal nuance in the music of Debussy is in sharp contrast to the often almost dialectic definiteness of Ravel's themes. The question of added colour is a thing apart; the main lines of expressive design are wholly foreign one to another. The art of Debussy is subjective, that of Ravel objective. The one is something of an introspective symbolist, the other a luxuriant stylist.

NATIONAL MANNER AND NATIONAL STYLE. The question of stylism brings us to the last phase of national idiom to be considered here. Traits are inherent in nature and impulsive in expression. Stylistic features, on the other hand, come into being only when thought and impulse have reached the stage of design which eliminates all save the essentials of form. The first—traits—are a natural product developed by natural processes; the second—styles—are purely products of art. Yet in such art production the psychological elements underlying predilection, taste, and selection, as well as the conception of design and construction, are fundamentally determined by racial tendencies. Hence it comes about that so sophisticated a composer as Stravinsky can achieve chamber music which is typically national in inspiration and substance and yet of an advanced style which concedes nothing to the most challenging innovations of international modernity, in his *Three Pieces for String Quartet*. Here Stravinsky, whether the work pleases one or not, has achieved something as undeniable and as eternally debatable as the underlying conception of a Byzantine ikon. Here, indeed, is the very essence of the matter. Stravinsky takes the characteristics of folk manner and matter just as Byzantine designers took physical form and its features.

THE NATIONAL ELEMENTS IN MODERN ITALIAN NEO-CLASSICISM. A folk tradition carries with it little of the sensational type of sentiment or the quaint appeal which such things make to the superficial alien mind. Hence, what is picturesque and novel for the foreigner is a commonplace for the native. The vogue of the so-called Italian opera is on the wane in the land of its origin, in spite of the commercial bribes which it offers to the creative conscience. So, as the more sensitive modern musical minds of Italy are aroused to wipe out the stigma of cheap melodrama attached to Italian music, one finds a renascence of classic forms of characteristically Italian nature, and, in particular, a natural and inevitable revival of Italian chamber music. Folk forms proper, which bring in decorative elements in formal fashion, are reappearing in the use of the siciliano, notably by Casella, as a definite basis for Italian chamber music movements. Malipiero, at first a colourist, tends ever towards chaste and almost ascetic forms directly traceable to the tradition of social music which attained its zenith with the chamber music of the Florentine Bardi coterie in the sixteenth and early seventeenth centuries. In these the courtly formal adaptations of the folk dances, with their typical rhythms and linear traits of Italian localities, play a great part. As Debussy and Ravel re-applied such forms as the gigue and the pavane to chamber music, so does Malipiero find modern developments for forms of the gracious period which gave us the exquisite *forlana*. Pizzetti, on the other hand, inclines to a modern resuscitation of the early fusions of folk form and religious types for a more architectonic Italian neo-classicism in chamber music. The vocal element, so characteristically Italian, is maintained in the approximation of musical forms to the classic poetic ones—of folk origin also—such as the *inno* and the *canzonetta*.

National Traits in Modern British Chamber Music. In Great Britain, national influences, like races, are mixed. The English, for the most part, content themselves with a rather literal adoption of the folk manner, as developed up to Georgian times. This tendency is interesting, when it is remembered that the English were the developers of the Comedy of Manners, and that foreigners are impressed rather by the English manner than the English mind or method. The whole tendency of English nationalism in music to-day is a somewhat sentimentalized reversion to the bucolic manner of rustic folk music. The strong elements of Tudor music, a direct growth from the British folk-lore of its day, are, however, becoming more influential since the researches of Dr. Fellowes, Sir Richard Terry, and others, which have rescued this national musical heritage from the obscurity of museums and libraries. The bucolic style is evident in Vaughan Williams, almost to the extent of a mannerism at times; Ireland, Moeran, and Armstrong Gibbs have given it more spontaneous expression, particularly the latter two; the former has not yet evolved a distinctively personal mode of expression, and is often inclined to submerge spirit in matter. Another, and less sentimentalized, influence which is penetrating chamber music is the characteristic breezy lilt of the traditional sea-shanty, again a revelation of Sir Richard Terry. The chamber music of Felix White has much of this lilt, though there are other elements which lessen its effect. Even with such advanced cosmopolitan composers as Bliss, the sea strain is evident in works such as *Madame Noy*, for voice and chamber orchestra. Folk-song rather than folk dance characterizes Gerrard Williams, whose work seems to suggest England as seen by a French impressionist. It is unfortunate that many modern British composers, while inspired by English patriotic ideals, should be unable to shake off the Germanized Victorian mode of thought. This, paradoxically enough, is characteristic of the more imperialistic composers, such as Elgar, whose work thus stands outside anything typically British in musical substance. Delius and Goossens are other composers who cannot truly be said to be typically British, although the latter has given us Scots impressions suggestive of a French vivandière in a Highland kilt, and a 'Folk-song' which seems to have its basis in a sort of musical Esperanto with a dominant Franco-Russian element.

The Celts in Modern British Chamber Music. Many of the distinctive features of British character and thought are traceable to the strong Celtic infusion in the nation. The introspective trend of Celtic thought, its mysticism and symbolism, tend naturally towards the more intimate and lyrical forms of expression. Clear design and translucency of tissue are peculiarly Celtic characteristics; hence it is natural that so essentially Celtic a composer as Arnold Bax should have written many lovely chamber works dominated by national or racial traits in a Celtic sense. Here a decorative conception of form and sound itself is manifest. It is the Celtic nature to see most things in terms of abstract decorative design. That phase of poetic abstraction and acute sense of the subjective influence of physical minutiae sometimes termed the 'Celtic Twilight' also tends to a definite idiom. In Bax these elements are combined. The design of his chamber music is invariably decorative and ornate; hence his predilection for the harp, with its delicate qualities of tracery and sound convolution, and the flute, with its lyric qualities of embroidery. Those characteristic traits of Celtic modes, with their Hellenic influences dating from the old associations of Celtica and Greece, have also left their mark. Greek also were the origins of Gregorian plainsong, with its kinship to Celtic modes and its influence on medieval folk music; hence all these elements converge in Bax to produce a kind of musical pre-Raphaelitism. The more rugged and ancient elements of Celtic folk chant have found modern development in chamber art since Granville Bantock returned to the Hebrides, and gave us works like the *Celtic Lament*, music which has spiritual affinity to that monumental sense evidenced in ancient Celtic cromlechs. In Wales a similar fervour to that which led to the preservation and maintenanace of the language has occasioned a recent revival of musical nationalism. Here a great part is played by poetic tradition, as well as by the ancient bardic forms. The characteristic national folk types of penillion singing provide unique kinds of improvised counterpoint, a singer taking up a theme given out by harp, and varying it according to strict traditional metric rules, thus creating a peculiar and extremely free type of rhythmic counterpoint. This element is developed by some contemporary Welsh composers in chamber music, the associated instruments taking the place of voice and harp, notable amongst such composers being Vaughan Thomas. Vaughan Thomas and Dafydd de Lloyd have also developed chamber music treatments of the metric characteristics of the traditional poetic forms of *cywydd* and *englyn*, used as elements of a typically Welsh musical form. Another Welsh tendency is directed towards the revival of the national instruments which influenced so many of the chief characteristics of Welsh folk melody—the *telyn* (harp), *pibgorn* (Welsh pipes or musette), and *crwth* (Welsh viol, the first evolved bowed instrument of Europe). Hence the appearance of what we may term a nationally conceived chamber orchestra—wood-wind, harp, and strings, which is unique in the world's national music.

NATIONAL INFLUENCES IN THE EVOLUTION OF CHAMBER MUSIC FORMS. The modern tendency is towards the chamber orchestra and chamber music, a tendency which has its roots in the spirit of nationalism. The part played by national instruments in folk idiom has been indicated, as well as its tendency to create new national chamber combinations which are also in the early classic spirit of the 'consort of musicke'.

In conclusion it may be said that national ideals and conceptions expressive of the diverse aspects of humanity maintain their stimulus, thus preserving to all types of chamber music that quality of vital interest and psychological revelation which must ever render it the type of music closest to the life of peoples, and most revelatory of the subtler aspects of the human heart. LEIGH HENRY.

†FOOTE, ARTHUR WILLIAM, b. 1853, American organist and composer.

	op.	
Quartet, str, g mi	4	Litolff.
Theme and var^{ns}., str. quartet, a mi	32	A. P. Schmidt.
Quartet, str, D	70	,,
Quintet, pf, 2 v, vla, vc, a mi	38	,,
Quartet, pf, v, vla, vc, C	23	,,
Trio, pf, v, vc, c mi	5	Schott.
Trio, pf, v, vc, B flat	65	A. P. Schmidt.
Sonata, pf, v, g mi	20	,,

Arthur Foote's name is much respected in the American musical world both as composer and pianist. In the course of three successive seasons he gave twenty-one recitals of trios for piano, violin, and 'cello. His trio in C minor was played at the 'Pops' Jan. 29, 1887.

FORKEL, JOHANN NICOLAUS, 1749–1818, German historian.

The celebrated biographer of Bach. He wrote three piano trios, op. 6, published in London in 1799.

FORNEROD, ALOYS, b. 1890, Swiss composer, pupil of the Lausanne Conservatorium.

Sonata, pf, v, B — Chester (Agent).

†FORRESTER, JAMES CLIFFE, b. 1860, English composer.

Folk-song Phantasy, pf, v, vc — Novello. (Cobbett Prize, 1917.)

A musicianly work of much melodious charm.

FÖRSTER, ALBAN, 1849–1916, born Reichenbach (Vogtland).

Five easy piano trios. List in Altmann's *Catalogue*, opp. 47, 61, 172, 174, and one without opus number. List of other chamber works in *Riemann*.

FORTERRE, H.

Sonata fantasque, pf, v — op. 29 — Jurgenson.

†FOURDRAIN, FÉLIX, b. 1880, well-known French song-writer.

Poème romantique, pf, v, vc — Deiss & Crépin (Paris), 1922.

†FOWLES, ERNEST, b. 1864, English pianist and lecturer.

The pioneer work of Ernest Fowles in the cause of British chamber music is deserving of cordial recognition. He initiated in 1894 a series of concerts, continued annually till 1899, with programmes which comprised the names of every prominent native composer of the period. Although all were not of conspicuous merit, they included not only the names of Parry and Stanford, foremost protagonists of that period, but also those of others known to fame to-day, among them Walford Davies, R. H. Walthew, Coleridge-Taylor, and William Hurlstone. The seed sown by Ernest Fowles has yielded a goodly harvest. EDITOR.

FRANCHOMME, AUGUSTE JOSEPH, 1808–1884, distinguished French 'cellist.

He wrote various chamber works, mostly for solo 'cello with chamber accompaniment, and collaborated with Chopin in the polonaise for 'cello and piano in C major, Chopin's op. 3.

FRANCK, CÉSAR AUGUSTE, b. Liége, 1822; d. Paris, 1890.

		Composed.	
Quartet, str, D		1889	Hamelle, 1898; Peters, 1922.
Quintet, pf, 2 v, vla, vc, f mi		1878–9	Hamelle; Peters, 1921; Eulenburg, 1922.
1st trio, pf, v, vc, f sharp mi	op. 1	1840	J. Schuberth & Co., 1843; Peters, 1922.
2nd trio, pf, v, vc, B flat	op. 1	,,	J. Schuberth & Co., 1884.
3rd trio, pf, v, vc, b mi	op. 1	,,	,, ,, 1845.
4th trio, pf, v, vc, B		1842	,, ,, 1846.

Sonata, pf, v, A	1886	Hamelle; Schott & Litolff, 1921; Cranz, 1922.
Andante quietoso, pf, v, A	1843.	

The *Prelude, Aria, and Final* for piano has been arranged for piano trio by Woollett (Hamelle, 1900).

In the history of music there is a phenomenon which is almost periodically recurrent throughout the ages, and which is an important factor in the progressive development of our art. This phenomenon may be thus described. An artist of genius, or even one of great talent, discovers—either in the domain of harmony or in that of form and construction—a path previously untrodden, some happy modification of the older symphonic scheme, in short, an innovation which revivifies and creates new resources for forms which seemed to be growing stereotyped through over-strict observance of conventional formulas. The artist's discovery, sometimes unwitting,[1] is, strange to say, rarely followed up either by his contemporaries or by his immediate successors, and it is only after a slumber of forty or fifty years that the new idea finds a soil suitable for its development, and reaches its full growth in the works of another artist of creative genius.

Thus the system of dramatic composition based on significant keys, first employed by Weber—in *Der Freischütz* and, more especially, in *Euryanthe* (1823)—was only taken up and carried to its fullest development forty years later by Richard Wagner and led, by a logical sequence, to the appearance of the Leitmotif.

Thus, too, Beethoven, having laid down the principle of cyclic composition in his op. 13, a principle so characteristic of the sonatas and quartets of his last period, was followed in this path neither by Weber, Schubert, nor Spohr, nor by the other German composers who followed him. It was left to a young French[2] artist of nineteen to attempt the revival of this principle in his first chamber work, more than ten years after the death of the composer of the ninth symphony. One might say that Beethoven's spirit 'brooded over the waters' of Art, as did the spirit of the Eternal over the Creation, and was reincarnated in the personality of César Franck, who, extending the discoveries of the mighty composer of the Mass in D, was later to give so powerful an impulse to the progress of music.

Trio in F sharp minor. It was in 1840 that young Franck—at that time a student at the Conservatoire of Paris, first under Reicha, then under Leborne—began the composition of the trio in F sharp minor (op. 1, no. 1). Though he had little experience of the constructive art known as 'musical composition'—abundant proof of this is to be found in the timidity, I might almost say the artlessness, of the modulations in this work—yet, with its budding genius, the trio marks an epoch in the history of musical evolution.

Was it intentional? was it caused merely by a keen instinct for novelty? This can never be decided with certainty, but the fact is there to prove to us that, alone at this period, the young composer ventured to plan his first important work according to data which Beethoven did little more than indicate in the last years of his life.

At the beginning of the trio in F sharp minor there appear in succession two themes, each of which is the completion of the other, one serving as counter-subject to its fellow:

Ex. 1 a.
Theme A.
'Cello.

Ex. 1 b.
Counter-subject A[1].
Piano.

These two themes seem at first to be purely academic and devoid of any element of expressiveness, but this impression is removed by acquaintance with the work as a whole. It would even seem that this counter-subject, so simple in appearance, may yet be regarded as one of the most characteristic manifestations of Franck's melodic genius, since we shall meet it, more than thirty years later, promoted, now, to the rank of an expressive cyclic theme, in the quintet for pianoforte and strings (Ex. 2).

A third theme, B, charming in its artlessness, in which is recognizable the influence of Méhul, a favourite composer of Franck's, appears during the second section of the move-

[1] Philipp Emanuel Bach, the first to venture on the introduction of a second melodic element in his so-called *Württemberg* sonatas (1745), seems not to have profited by this discovery in the sonatas written at Hamburg towards the end of his life, between 1782 and 1787.

[2] César Franck, though born at Liége, became French at the age of twelve, by the naturalization of his father, and all his life remained thoroughly French at heart as well as in his music.

Ex. 2.

ment, and it is from these three themes, A, A[1], B, that the whole melodic form of the movement is derived.

The first movement is in Lied form,[1] divided into five sections. It differs from the five-section andante-Lied, established by Haydn and frequently employed by Beethoven, in the following way The theme, A, A[1], is set out and treated in sections 1, 3, and 4, instead of being confined to the odd-numbered sections as in the classical adagio, the expressive theme, B, being merely stated (never developed) in sections 2 and 5.

The second movement of the trio is in the great scherzo form with double reprise as introduced by Beethoven, and later adopted by Schumann. But here, Franck appears to have forestalled the composer of the Rhenish symphony by the admission, as a fourth section, of a new element forming a trio, not the same as that set out in the second section. This arrangement is to be met with for the first time in Schumann's first symphony, op. 38, also written in 1840, and consequently unknown to Franck at this time.

The scherzo portion, then, which is in B minor, is followed by a first trio, the theme of which is derived from that of the scherzo itself. After the third section (a repetition of the first) there appears, as second trio, the expressive theme B, already heard at the beginning of the work; this time it is accompanied by a persistent rhythmic bass derived from the first element of the scherzo theme:

Ex. 3a.
Th. (B).

Ex. 3b.
Th. (A[2]) *of scherzo.*

[1] See Foreword, art. BEETHOVEN.

The fifth section follows; in this the cyclic theme, A[1], of the first movement is skilfully combined with that of the scherzo, and gives rise to a fine development. Finally, the sixth section brings back the trio, B, for the second time; this has no conclusion and is linked up with the finale.

This last movement, the only one in sonata form, is longer and more developed than the others. The melodic elements, though simple, have the peculiarities which characterize Franck at this period, and could be the work of no other musician. The opening phrase is an impassioned version of the cyclic theme A, while the second theme, in D flat (enharmonic C sharp), carries us away to those celestial regions whence the angelic choirs of *Rédemption* and the sanctified multitudes of the *Béatitudes* were later to descend upon the earth. The movement follows normal structural lines. The development, over which the composer has perhaps lingered unduly, moves ever towards the light, finally bringing back the cyclic theme, B, in a triumphant peroration, when this theme, invariable throughout, is enthroned as monarch over the entire work.

If I have dwelt at some length on this first trio, it is, as I said before, because it marks an epoch in the history of musical form, reducing to practice tendencies dimly perceived by Schumann and Liszt, but which they were unable fully to realize, and, more especially, because, by reason of its thoroughly French character, it may be considered as the starting-point of that splendid outburst of instrumental composition which took place in France at the end of the last century and the beginning of this.[2]

Second and Third Trios.

I shall not linger over an analysis of the second and third trios, which are greatly inferior to the first, alike in style of composition and in musical interest. Concerning this anomaly, I may be permitted to formulate a theory, which is extremely probable, though documentary proof of it cannot be given. It is evident that the young César Auguste conceived and wrote the F sharp minor trio for his own satisfaction, in the freshness and enthusiasm of his eighteen years. But it must not be forgotten that the young man was then under the strict rule of an authoritative father, who had fixed on a musical career for his two sons without consulting them, and who intended to employ their talents for the welfare of his family.

Perceiving the ease with which César had produced his first trio, this practical father resolved to turn it to account by offering the

[2] Certain not very clear-sighted critics have attempted to attribute Franck's art to German origins. A careful study of the works of a master who sums up in his own personality all the characteristics of our French spirit will suffice to correct this misunderstanding.

dedication to some important personage who might prove to be a useful patron for the dedicator. Observing, further, that dedications of this kind usually include several works of the same type (Beethoven dedicated six quartets to Prince Lobkowitz and three others to Count Rasoumovsky), he would seem to have required his son to add two more trios to the first.

And the dutiful son seems to have undertaken the task, but without joy in thus writing to order, and so were produced the trio in B flat, which he called a 'Drawing-room trio', and the third, in B minor. The three trios were dedicated to Leopold I, King of the Belgians, and it was with the object of personally presenting his work to its royal recipient that César Franck momentarily left Paris and gave up the chance of competing for the Prix de Rome. Did the King of the Belgians reward the young composer's homage with some gift? There is no trace of any in the family archives.

The Fourth Trio.

This discussion of the early works is the proper place to mention an occurrence which may throw light on the 'social state' (if it may be so expressed) of the fourth trio in B major. During his journey to Belgium César Franck had met Franz Liszt, then at the summit of his glory as virtuoso composer of fantasies, waltzes, caprices, and other works of technical display. With that ready welcome for young artists which distinguished him throughout his life, Liszt asked Franck to show him his first attempts, and, fired with enthusiasm by the perusal of the last movement of the third trio, he induced the young man to re-write this as a separate single-movement trio, to be dedicated to himself. Franck therefore wrote a new finale for the third trio, and, entirely recasting the old one, published this last with the title, 'Fourth Trio (op. 2), *dedicated to his friend Fr. Liszt*'.[1]

Was the opinion of the composer of *Christus* well founded? There is reason to doubt it, for this fourth trio, while it has fine moments and is original in form—the recapitulation beginning with the second subject—is far from equalling the first in musical interest.

Curiously enough, Franck, after such a promising beginning, wrote no more chamber works for more than thirty years. I shall attempt to give the reasons for this.

It is a well-known fact, which I have discussed elsewhere in this book,[2] that the work of great artists—painters, sculptors, musicians—whose career was sufficiently long, may be divided into three periods, which differ considerably in imagination and in style. In the first, a period of imitation and assimilation, the young artist only seeks his inspiration in the best works of his seniors or his contemporaries. In the second, certain of his talent and with assured technique, he seeks to 'externalize' his imagination and his impressions, thus disclosing, almost unconsciously, his personality in works characterized by solidity and originality. The third period is that of reflection, in which the artist creates for himself alone, and thus produces his finest masterpieces, direct and intimate impressions of the soul of a genius. In the case of all really great men, examples of these three styles, often strikingly different, can be found.

But there is another factor to be considered in the case of these great men. This is the adaptation of the style and of the nature of the work to the environment in which they are placed and to the musical resources at their disposal.

So long as Bach was simply doing the duties of organist or Capellmeister at Arnstadt, Mülhausen, and even at Weimar (1703 to 1712), his compositions were confined to organ works in the style of Pachelbel and Buxtehude, variations on chorales or fugues preceded by an extended prelude, and a few cantatas. When he became Capellmeister to the Duke of Anhalt, at Cöthen, and was thus entrusted with the direction of the instrumentalists of the ducal chapel (1712 to 1723), there came a profusion of instrumental works: suites for clavier, for violin, for violoncello, concerted pieces, concertos, &c. But when at Leipzig (1723 to 1750) he had the orchestra of the Thomasschule and the choirs of the University at his disposition, he conceived the 266 cantatas, the *Passions*, and the extraordinary Mass in B minor, certain parts of which surpass in originality of conception and novelty of execution all the discoveries of our modern music.

In Franck's case the three periods of composition and the influence of the environment upon the nature of the works are sharply defined.

As soloist and travelling virtuoso, he began by writing a large number of piano pieces: fantasies in the manner of Thalberg and Liszt, airs with variations and 'morceaux de genre'. The only really noteworthy works of this first period are the oratorio *Ruth et Booz* (greatly influenced by Méhul) and the Beethovenish trio in F sharp minor.

In 1860, appointed as organist of the church of Sainte-Clotilde, where he had been choirmaster for two years, the whole activity of the future composer of the *Béatitudes* was concentrated on church music as understood at that time: motets, offertories for soloists, mass with harp and double-bass, and other works, among which two productions stand out above the others: the first six organ pieces and the oratorio, *Rédemption*. So far it had not occurred

[1] 'His friend' Liszt did not fail to acknowledge the young composer's homage, and made his music known in Germany, even before it was known in France. An American doctor tells how he was present, at Weimar, in 1853, at the first performance of two trios by César Franck, with Laub, Cossmann, and Liszt himself as interpreters. [*Memoirs of a Musical Life*, by Dr. Mason, p. 122.]

[2] See art. Beethoven.

to the organist, delighted with the tonal qualities of his four manuals, to write pure instrumental music.

But in 1872, after the disasters of the Franco-German war, a galaxy of French musicians determined to found a Society whose aim should be to encourage a national school of composition in symphonic and chamber music, a field till then untouched by us. The little Société Nationale de Musique, then new-born, had no notion that it was to inspire the production of a great number of works, some of which are veritable masterpieces of the loftiest inspiration and the most undeniable beauty.

Saint-Saëns, Fauré, Henri Duparc, Alexis de Castillon, Ernest Chausson, Guy Ropartz, and the present writer laboured towards this end, and helped to produce a splendid awakening of instrumental music in our country. Franck was among the first to profit by this atmosphere and threw himself with ardour into the new paths opened up to French music. It is to the Société Nationale, then, that our art owes the evolution of the modest organist of Sainte-Clotilde towards absolute music and the conception of the three admirable masterpieces which we are now to study: the quintet, the violin sonata, and the quartet in D.

The Piano Quintet.

There is as great a distance, in the spirit of the works, between the trios composed by Franck in 1840 to 1842 and the quintet of 1878, as between the first works which Beethoven dedicated to his master Haydn and the B flat trio, in which the composer of the ninth symphony immortalized the name of his beloved pupil and friend, Archduke Rudolph of Austria, in 1811. But the change gradually taking place in Beethoven's spirit from his first attempts of 1793 to the loftiness of imagination which gave us the trio, op. 97, is shown in numerous examples in which the ascent towards Beauty is readily perceptible, from the septuor, op. 20 (of which the composer said that at this period he 'did not know how to compose'), onwards through the seventh, tenth, and eleventh quartets.

In Franck's case, on the other hand, the change of style was purely inward, and the prodigious leap forward, starting with three or four compositions which were merely good student works, and attaining complete mastery in a work of thirty-six years later, was effected all at once, a phenomenon almost without parallel in the history of music.

In the F minor quintet we find the application, now conscious, of the system of composition based on one or more cyclic themes, which go to make up the musical foundation of the structure and impart to it unity in variety, the undoubted aim envisaged by every creative artist.

A melody, in the highest degree expressive, hovers over the three movements of the work and gives to it the necessary cohesion. After several essays in rather adventurous keys, in which it seems to be seeking to express itself, this melody is at length definitely announced in the relative major, A flat,

Ex. 4.

and assumes the functions of a second subject from the exposition of the first movement onwards. It proceeds to play an important part in the development, and after the usual reappearance in the recapitulation, in the tonic (F major), at the end of the movement it takes on a new aspect, effected by a change of rhythm, and gradually brings with it peace and the union of the two melodic ideas, till now in rivalry, even in opposition.

It is this theme again which raises itself aloft, in the middle of the second movement (lento), like a peak towards which the character-theme of the movement has directed its toilsome march, and from which it then descends to breathe out its life at the end in a sigh of grief. Here the cyclic melody appears in the key of D flat major, very remote from that of the lento (A minor).

Ex. 5.

For this reason it is permissible to compare it to some holy mountain till now untrodden.

In the finale, this fine theme is called upon to fill the office of regulator and appears only at the end of the cycle, at first in D flat, then in the tonic key,

Ex. 6.

with the object of setting all in order and of bringing back to the fold such of the other themes as may have strayed from the path.

Besides the great cyclic theme, the important function of which has just been outlined, and the three fine melodies: A¹, A², A³, which constitute the first subject of each of the movements,

Ex. 7 a.

Derived from the opening introductory phrase.

Ex. 7 b.

Ex. 7 c.

other important constituent elements are to be met with in this work; first, a very captivating phrase,

Ex. 8.

employed in the first movement only, in order to mitigate, by its gentleness, the fury of the first theme A¹, in which task it succeeds, thanks to the intervention of the cyclic theme (B¹); then we have two figures, X and Z,

Ex. 9.

serving as bass for the second subject in the first movement.

Ex. 10.

This last figure, which appears only during the exposition of the lento, assumes, in the sequel, an importance sufficient to form the subject of the second idea of the finale.

Is it necessary to add that the beauty of the themes and the masterly skill with which Franck's architecture displays them make of the F minor quintet a monument of imperishable grandeur and strength?

An analysis of the work is here appended:

ALLEGRO: (F minor)
Exp. — A¹, derived from A, F minor, modulating.
Bridge, modulating.
B¹, cyclic theme; in various keys—D♭, E, G—then announced definitely in A♭, supported by fig. X.
Dev. — A¹, moving onwards;
A, E minor, (B¹), moving onwards;
A, F♯ minor, (B¹)—A and D♭; dev. of figure X.
Recapit. A¹, F minor.
Bridge, then Th. C, in F♯ minor alternating brokenly with (B¹).
(B¹), F minor.

Terminal Dev.[1] on (B¹) with change of rhythm.

Coda, on A¹ and A, growing calmer.

LENTO, in three sections:

(A minor) I. Th. A² (A minor, F minor, A minor), repeated with addition of figure Z.
II. — Dev. of Th. A², in D♭, moving onwards.
Cyclic theme, (B¹), repose.
Dev. of A², moving onwards in deep sorrow.
III. Th. A², A minor—short terminal dev. and conclusion.

ALLEGRO CON FUOCO: Introduction, on fragments of subject which follows.
(F major)
Exp. — A³, F minor, F.
Melodic *Bridge*, on fragments of A³.
B³, B major and minor, on figure Z.
Dev. — A³, moving towards *Bridge*—F♯ minor.
Rhythmic dev. of A³—B♭ minor, moving onwards.
Z, developed chromatically.

[1] For explanation of this and other technical terms see Foreword, art. BEETHOVEN.

Recapit. — A^3, figure z and Th. A^2 (from lento), superimposed, then:
A^3 alone, in F.
B^3 (z), F♯ minor.

Terminal Dev. — (B^I), cyclic th., by augmentation and change of rhythm.
Exposition of (B^I), D♭ minor, combined with A^3.
The same, in F minor.

Coda. F major.

The first performance of the quintet was given, at a concert of the Société Nationale de Musique, on 17 January, 1880, by the Marsick Quartet. Saint-Saëns, Franck's colleague on the committee of the Society, had consented, at the composer's desire, to undertake the piano part. The following odd incident is little known. At the end of the concert, good old Father Franck, in great delight (he was always pleased with any performance, however poor, of his works), went up to Saint-Saëns, and, handing him the manuscript of the quintet, exclaimed with generous warmth, 'Thank you, my friend! Since you have interpreted my work so wonderfully, it is yours; accept my dedication of it and keep my manuscript in memory of this delightful evening!' Saint-Saëns, with a wry smile ('grimaçant un sourire')—those who witnessed the scene can never forget it—twirled round and made off towards the exit, leaving the precious score on the piano. Long afterwards, an employé of the firm of Pleyel found it among a heap of waste paper.

THE VIOLIN SONATA.

Six years later, Franck, in his enthusiasm for the talent of the great violinist Ysaÿe, determined to write for him and Madame Bordes-Pène—the great pianist whose early death was a loss to our art—a work worthy of such first-rate interpreters. This work was the A major sonata for piano and violin.

Here, the cyclic type of construction, already employed in the quintet, finds a new and remarkable application; this sonata is, in fact, one of the first and most striking examples of this adaptation (foreshadowed by Beethoven) of the developmental variation to traditional forms.

The melodic framework is made up of three themes, the first of which, a 'germ-cell', presented at first as a simple neum,

Ex. 11.

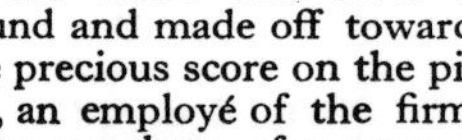

regulates, by means of multiple variations, the whole internal economy of the work.

To this figure, in its various incarnations, is allotted the task of forming the four first subjects of the four movements of the cycle. In the first movement (*sonata form*, *without development*) it provides the calm and happy opening theme:

Ex. 12.
Th. (x).

in the following allegro it is transformed into the impassioned theme which continues without intermission to the triumphant peroration:

Ex. 13.
Th. (x).

of it is then begotten the lovely and mournful lament of the fantasia in F sharp minor:

Ex. 14.
Th. (x).

and its influence is again felt in the charming melody in canon which sings so joyously through the final rondo:

Ex. 15.
Th. (x).

As for the other two cyclic themes,

Ex. 16.
Th. (Y)

Ex. 17.
Th. (z).

they appear successively, as required for the construction of the work, the first (Y) appearing with the allegro (second movement), the second, not until the fantasia, and they do not attain their full growth till the structural climax in the last movement of the sonata.

We shall not detain the reader with a description of the first two movements, difficult as it is to pass over the two splendid and glowing themes of the allegro in D minor, each of them in three phrases, like Beethoven's second subjects, and no whit inferior to their model in musical value, but the structure of the third movement, entitled 'Recitativo-fantasia', calls for fuller notice.

First of all, why fantasia for a movement which seems so orderly in construction? Those who were acquainted with the composer of the

Béatitudes can attest the fact that his intensely scrupulous respect for form would not have permitted him to apply a classical title to this transition-movement, beginning, as it does, in D minor and ending in F sharp minor. Hence the term 'Fantasia'—and it should be further remarked that the tonality of F sharp is not definitely established till the second cyclic theme, fragmentarily sketched in the preceding allegro, appears at last as a complete phrase. This phrase becomes, then, the guiding principle of the development of the work, and thus the last cyclic melody is unhesitatingly appended to it, to form the second constructive element of the finale.

For this last movement Franck evolved a new type of rondo, consisting in four expositions of the refrain[1] in canon, the first three being linked together without intervening couplets,[1] in three different keys—A, C sharp, and E, while the fourth, separated from the others by a development in which all the principal motifs appear, leads, by means of a greatly extended crescendo, to the splendidly brilliant conclusion.

Analysis of the sonata in A:

ALLEGRETTO—(Sonata form without development.)
(A major)

Exp.:
- A—Th. (x), modulating to the dominant.
- B—modulating and returning directly to

Recapit.:
- A—Th. (x) in the tonic.
- B—concluding in the tonic.

ALLEGRO—(First-movement form.)
(D minor)

Exp.:
- A, derived from Th. (x), in three phrases, A[1], A[2], A[3].
- *Bridge*, founded on (x).
- B, F major, in three phrases, B[1], B[2], B[3].

Dev.:
- 1st appearance of Th. (Y), in F minor.
- Dev. of B[3] with (x), in C♯ minor.
- Dev. of A[1] and A[3] with B[1]—G♭, E♭.

Recapit.:
- A, in the tonic.
- *Bridge*.
- B, in D major.

Conclusion, on A.

FANTASIA (D minor to F♯ minor)
- I. Th. (x) as a short figure; from D minor to F♯ minor.
- II. Th. (Y) in melodic form, giving rise to the appearance of Th. (z) in F♯ minor.
- III. Th. (x) as short figure. Dominant of F♯ minor, and conclusion in this key.

[1] See Foreword, art. BEETHOVEN.

ALLEGRETTO—(Rondo-form.)
(A major)

- 1st Refrain: A (derived from Th. (x)), then from Th. (z) modulating.
- 2nd Refrain: A, in C♯ major, then Th. (z) modulating.
- 3rd Refrain: A, in E, the dominant.

Dev.:
- On Th. (x) (figure-form) and subsidiary fragment of A.
- Continuation by same elements—in D♯ minor, A♯ minor, F minor, C.

- 4th Refrain: A, in the tonic, and conclusion.

If one who has witnessed the conception of this work may be permitted to offer a word of advice to future executants, I would have them guard against a tendency, which is apparently becoming the fashion, to play the first movement as a slow movement. This allegretto really expresses a gentle cheerfulness, and to treat it as a dramatic recitative is to fly in the face of the composer's intentions.

On the other hand, the final rondo requires to be taken at a moderate speed, and loses much when made to serve as a medium for a display of finger-dexterity by the virtuosi. Further, the peroration of the movement

Ex. 18.

must be very broadly interpreted, with power and nobility, and not in that *polka*-rhythm to which it is too often condemned by the vulgarity of mind of certain performers. Such were the composer's exact intentions.

The violin and piano sonata was performed for the first time in the winter of 1886, by Eugène Ysaÿe and Madame Bordes-Pène, at one of the concerts of the 'Twenty',[1] which at that time were given in one of the rooms of the 'Musée Moderne de Peinture' at Brussels. The séance, which began at three o'clock, had been very long, and it was rapidly growing dark. After the first allegretto of the sonata, the performers could scarcely read their music. Now the official regulations forbade any light whatever in rooms which contained paintings, even the striking of a match would have been matter for offence. The public was about to be requested to leave, but the audience, already full of enthusiasm, refused to budge. Then Ysaÿe was heard to strike his music-stand with his bow, exclaiming, 'Get on, get on'. And then, unheard-of marvel, the two artists, plunged in

[1] The Société des XX (les Vingt), founded by Octave Maus, a man of high intellectual endowments, played in Belgium as important a part in the propaganda for modern works—painting, sculpture, and music—as did our 'Société Nationale' for music alone.

gloom in which nothing could be distinguished, performed the last three movements from memory, with a fire and passion the more astounding to the listeners in that there was an absence of all externals which could enhance the performance. Music, wondrous and alone, held sovereign sway in the darkness of night. The miracle will never be forgotten by those present.

THE D MAJOR QUARTET.

With this last of César Franck's chamber compositions, we are surveying the most astonishing conception of the mind of this genius in tonal architecture.

Like the F minor quintet, the symphony, and the violin sonata, this quartet is based on a generating theme which supplies in itself the expressive origin of the whole musical cycle. This theme cost its author infinite toil before it attained its final form. Just as Beethoven five times re-wrote the refrain of the finale of the piano sonata, op. 53—a refrain which is yet so very simple in appearance—so Franck fought regular battles with himself over the 'mother-theme' of his quartet before he could reduce it to subjection.

For a long time he kept beginning again, nervously erasing with india-rubber what had seemed absolutely settled the day before. He even constructed a full third of the first movement on a melodic idea, the form of which he later entirely remodelled. He unhesitatingly crossed out everything already written out neatly, and began again on the very foundations, following a second version; with this, too, he was still dissatisfied, and it was also destroyed and replaced by the final version.[1]

The first movement presents absolutely new features, and is, to this day, unique in the history of music. The fundamental idea of the work is the intimate union of two separate pieces of music, each with its own individual life and its own complete organization, interpenetrating each other without the slightest confusion, thanks to the perfect manipulation of the structural materials, and thus is produced an admirably unified whole. No musician before Franck had ventured to attempt so marvellous a feat, none has since attempted it. If a mathematical symbol may be employed as an aid in the description of a musical work, we might say that this movement—presenting the elastic idea of a sonata movement *inscribed* in a Lied form[2]—could be represented by this figure:

Ex. 19.

[1] This labour is visible in the sketches for the quartet, belonging to Madame Ernest Chausson, widow of one of the master's favourite pupils. See also, on this subject, *César Franck*, by Vincent d'Indy, pp. 167–70. (Published by F. Alcan.)

[2] See Foreword, art. BEETHOVEN.

The exposition of the Lied, which is in slow time, is entirely constructed out of the 'mother-theme' of the cycle, Th. (x), in the key of D major.

Ex. 20.

Th. (x).

Immediately afterwards, in moderately quick time, enters the sonata exposition, with its two themes, the first in D minor,

Ex. 21.

Th. A.

the second in F major.

Ex. 22.

Th. B.

These two themes are linked by a cyclic figure (motif (c)) which assumes great importance in the finale.

Ex. 23.

Motif (c).

The exposition ends in F, the concluding figures being identical with those which conclude the Lied.

At this point, instead of the classical development of the two subjects, we have the Lied once more; this time, however, it appears in fugal entries, thus forming a central slow movement section, a mysterious meditation which unfolds as twilight falling at eventide, tinged with ever-deepening hues. But now the sonata allegro reasserts itself, and, shaking off the mantle of night just now assumed by the Lied, it strives, in an upward development, to attain brighter regions. But this is not to be, and the recapitulation lifts but for a moment the veil of gloom. Then the Lied, appearing for the third time, in accents of exquisite tenderness, brings, with the return to the tonic key, the light so earnestly desired.

The plan of this extraordinary movement can be better followed if it is carefully studied with the help of the elastic schema given below, referring to the foregoing musical examples.

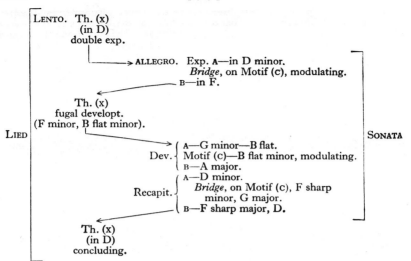

LENTO. Th. (x)
(in D)
double exp.

→ ALLEGRO. Exp. A—in D minor.
Bridge, on Motif (c), modulating.
B—in F.

Th. (x)
fugal developt.
(F minor, B flat minor).

LIED — SONATA

Dev. { A—G minor—B flat.
Motif (c)—B flat minor, modulating.
B—A major.

Recapit. { A—D minor.
Bridge, on Motif (c), F sharp minor, G major.
B—F sharp major, D.

Th. (x)
(in D)
concluding.

But—and so it always is with a masterpiece—the hearer has no idea of the unusual structure of this work of art, a structure to whose influence he must yet, perforce, yield, in the certainty attained that here is a mighty work which charms his very soul and raises him to the heights whereon eternal Beauty is enthroned.

The second movement of the quartet, scherzo-vivace, in F sharp minor, is simply a game, almost a dance of the tiny spirits of the night. In the middle of the gentle trio, with the full tone of the 'cello cutting across the muted voices of the other instruments, appears Theme (x)—a few bars only—in D major, looking in on its way, one might imagine, with the idea of bringing some degree of order into the mischievous pranks of the tiny dancers. Then, the scherzo resumes, and all vanishes. This charming movement was written in ten days, 29 October (when the first movement was finished) to 9 November 1889.

The third movement of the quartet, the larghetto in B major, is, again, a splendid monument of purity, grandeur, and artistic sincerity. Since the andantes of Beethoven's last quartets we do not think it possible to instance, in the whole range of music, anything so lofty, so perfectly beautiful in conception, in proportion, and in its total effect, than this prayer-like slow movement, the luminous result of long and painful toil.

The larghetto is in the form of an extended Lied, in five sections. The fourth, which is somewhat agitated, brings back one of the themes already heard in the trio of the scherzo, while the odd-numbered sections give three expositions without alteration of the admirable theme, so tranquil and serene.

The finale, though less strikingly original in structure than the first movement, still deserves close study. It is in sonata form and is preceded by an introduction in which the different themes of the earlier movements—larghetto, scherzo, trio—are brought before the hearer, and set out in order as if for him to choose. The choice finally falls on the great cyclic theme here entitled 'Theme (x)', and the finale begins, taking for its starting-point the opening bars of Theme (x), the first idea of the second subject being the cyclic Theme (c), already met with in the exposition of the first movement.

This motif (c):

Ex. 24.

c.

is first presented in the intermediate section in augmentation:

Ex. 25.

Motif c.

and is prepared by an agitated figure,

Ex. 26.

Fig. Y.

which serves as the active element throughout the finale.

When this motif (c), shortly afterwards, is transformed into a second subject it appears in double augmentation (𝅝 = ♩), and thus gives rise to a complete theme divided into three distinct phrases, after the manner of Beethoven.

Ex. 27.

The arrangement of the development offers a truly marvellous wealth of colour. Starting with an augmentation of figure Y

Ex. 28.

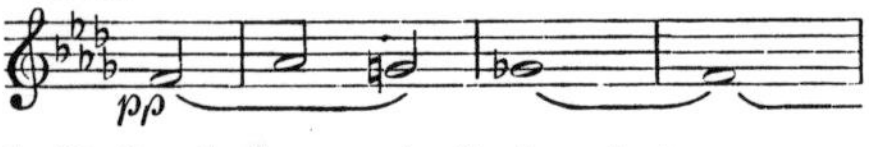

in D flat (enharmonic C sharp), it passes to F sharp minor, E flat, and comes to rest for a moment in B flat, a key intermediate between D major and minor; then its flight is resumed, ending with the recapitulation, which is followed by a terminal development. Here the persistent theme borrowed from the scherzo, ends by restoring, in longer notes, the luminous prayer of the larghetto,

Ex. 29.

which gives an almost religious conclusion to this magnificent whole.

We think it will be useful to give here a formal analysis of this wonderful finale, so that the perfect balance which governed its construction may be fully appreciated.

INTRODUCTION—Figure Y and successive reminiscences of the themes of the larghetto, the scherzo, and the first movement.

Exp.
- 1st subject—A—founded on Th. (x), in D major.
- *Bridge*—Motif (c) (from first movement) in augmentation.
- Second subject
  - B¹—Motif (c) in double augmentation and figure Y, in A minor.
  - B²—in A major.
  - B³—in A minor, combined with (c) and B².

Dev.
1. Figure Y, in augmentation in D flat; the figure here becomes a complete phrase, developed alternately with B¹.
2. Figure Y, developed with B², in F sharp major, then A (Th. (x)) in E flat.
3. Central section of repose, in B flat, founded on A combined with Y (in phrase form).
4. B¹, in B flat minor, development in shorter notes, leading to
5. A, treated as a recitative, on the dominant of E flat.

Recapit.
- A, in D major, then in A flat (for contrast with D).
- *Bridge*, modulating, on Y and (c).
  - B¹—D minor.
  - B²—D major and F sharp major.
  - B³—D minor.

Terminal Dev.
1. Y, in phrase form, alternating with scherzo theme.
2. A, in A minor, leading to
3. Th. of the larghetto in D major and minor.

Conclusion. A, as a recitative and figure Y to end.

The first performance of the quartet in D took place at a concert of the Société Nationale de Musique, on 19 April, 1890, and was greeted with warm and unanimous enthusiasm. Every one was standing up, shouting, and calling for the master who, with his usual modesty, never imagining such success possible for a simple quartet, persisted in believing that all this was meant for the performers.[1] However, he was obliged to yield to the evidence, and next day, full of pride in this first success (at sixty-eight!), he said naïvely to his pupils, 'Well, the public is actually beginning to understand me'.

For him, however, these joys were of short duration. Less than seven months later the noble spirit of this sincere and devout artist was called home to that God, the source of all Art and Beauty, whom he had so splendidly glorified in his *Béatitudes*.

Need we labour to draw from this study the conclusion which must be obvious?

[1] The executants at this first performance were: MM. L. Heymann, Gibier, Balbreck, and C. Liégeois.

César Franck, who may be said to be the real father of French chamber music, was also an innovator of genius, and especially in this branch of music. But, far from claiming to found his originality on a disdain for the principles laid down by his artistic forbears—principles evidently needing to be perfected but also to be respected—far, too, from seeking absurd elements of novelty in the cult of the ugly, he always desired and was able to base his audacities and build up his discoveries on the foundations of tradition. For these, alone, possess the strength accumulated through the ages which is needed for that eternal evolution which we call Progress.

So it has been with all those great and noble musicians who have subordinated the cult of the ego and of success at all costs to disinterested love of the Art which they worshipped. And of these was César Franck.

VINCENT D'INDY.

FRANCK, (1) EDUARD, 1817–1893, German composer.

	op.	
Sextet, 2 v, 2 vla, 2 vc, E flat	41	Schlesinger.
Sextet, 2 v, 2 vla, 2 vc, D	50	,,
Quintet, 2 v, 2 vla, vc, e mi	15	B. & B.
Quintet, 2 v, 2 vla, vc, C	51	Schlesinger.
Quartet, str, f mi	40	,,
Quartet, str, c mi	55	,,
Quintet, pf, 2 v, vla, vc, D	45	,,
Trio, pf, v, vc, e mi	11	Heinrichshofen.
Trio, pf, v, vc, E flat	22	R. & E.
Trio, pf, v, vc, D	58	Schlesinger.
Sonata, pf, v, c mi	19	R. & E.
Sonata, pf, v, A	23	,,
Sonata, pf, v, E	60 (posth.)	Stahl.
Sonata, pf, vc, D	6	Heinrichshofen.
Sonata, pf, vc, F	42	Schlesinger.

This excellent composer, who published some sixty chamber works, by no means deserves the neglect with which he has of late been treated. His mastery of form is shared with many other composers now forgotten, mainly because their melodic idiom makes no appeal to the younger generation. But Eduard Franck had also a lively imagination, amounting often to originality, which manifested itself in fine and attractive ideas, though he admittedly drew upon classical models.

THE STRING QUARTET IN F MINOR, though strongly influenced by Beethoven's op. 95, is nevertheless still worthy of public performance. The opening allegro is broadly designed throughout; the main theme has a well-defined incisive rhythm, the second has its emotion well under control, and the development is not overloaded with contrapuntal devices. A pleasing effect is achieved by the short and ingenious closing section. Deep and genuine emotion inspires the adagio, while the vigorous rhythm of the minuet is grateful, and the trio is refreshing with its natural flow of melody. The finale is passionate, though there is a graceful and soothing second subject, and the work ends with a most effective coda.

THE VIOLIN SONATA, op. 19, which affords many opportunities for display to both instruments, is of decided merit. The broadly constructed first movement begins with an introduction in the manner of a recitative, foreshadowing the flowing cantabile theme which follows; this is joined by a lighter subsidiary theme followed by the second subject, another expressive cantabile theme. The main section of the andante is distinguished by the nobility of its melody; the second theme owes its existence, it must be confessed, rather to necessity than to original inspiration. There is no scherzo. The flowing first subject of the finale is somewhat reminiscent of Mendelssohn, but a striking effect is achieved by the broad cantabile theme. The working out of the first theme is particularly successful; at one point it is fugally treated. Those who make the acquaintance of this sonata will find their time well spent.

† (2) RICHARD, b. 1858, son of Eduard, pianist and composer.

	op.	
Quartet, pf, v, vla, vc	33	Schlesinger.
Quartet, pf, v, vla, vc, E	41	,,
Trio, pf, v, vc, B	20	Hug.
Trio, pf, v, vc, E flat	32	Schlesinger.
Sonata, pf, v, D	14	,,
Sonata, pf, v, c mi	35	,,
Sonata, pf, vc, D	22	,,
Sonata, pf, vc, e flat mi	36	,,

Richard Franck's work has not the importance of his father's. His chamber compositions, besides being more derivative, are little more than pleasing drawing-room pieces. He is comparatively simple and natural in the violin sonata, op. 14; and in the sister sonata, op. 35, there is a vigorous opening movement and an adagio in song form, conceived in a somewhat lofty vein, but drifting later into insipidity. This composer's works do not call for extensive notice. WILHELM ALTMANN.

FRANCK, MELCHIOR, *c.* 1573–1639, German composer, famous in his day.

Two six-part *Intraden*, 3 v, 2 vla, vc (or cb) (A. Schering), composed 1608, C. F. Kahnt.

For original publications *v. Riemann.*

FRANCMESNIL, ROGER DE, b. 1884, French pianist.

Quartet, str, g mi		Mathot, 1921.
Sonata, pf, v, c mi	op. 25	,,

FRANCO-MENDES, (1) JACQUES, 1812–after 1860, Dutch 'cellist of Portuguese origin.

(2) JOSEPH. Two composers, brothers, who gave a series of quartet concerts in Paris in 1840–41. Joseph, the younger brother, won the Netherlands Music Society's prize, with two string quartets, in 1835. List of works in *Altmann*.

FRÄNZL, FERDINAND, 1770–1833, German violinist.

Nine quartets, str, (in 3 books)	op. 1, &c.	André.
Three trios, 2 v, bass	,, 17	Simrock.

Other works in *Fétis* and *Riemann*.

Fränzl, a Bavarian Capellmeister, the son of Ignaz (1736–1811), was a remarkable violinist and a composer of talent. His music is best described as 'Capellmeister-music', betraying the lack of originality which belongs to all of its kind.

†FREITAS BRANCO, LUIZ DE, b. 1890, Portuguese composer.

Sonata, pf, v, D Pabst (Leipzig), 1909.

FRENCH CHAMBER MUSIC SINCE THE REVOLUTION.

The whole of the eighteenth century was a period of splendour in chamber music. Thanks to the patronage of many a Maecenas, such as the famous La Pouplinière, it had been very popular in Parisian salons. A considerable literature of sonatas, trios, quartets, and pieces for wind instruments had come into being in Paris, and it was here, too, that very many celebrated composers of Italy or Germany sent their works to be printed. Nearly all the concerts were private ones; they were given in the salons of rich amateurs, and interested mainly the cultured few.

With the coming of the Revolution, wealth passed into other hands. The tastes of the new wealthy class—purchasers of national domains, or army contractors—were of a low order, and their musical culture was nil. They had their box at the Opéra, but cared little to listen to quartets. Chamber music kept its adepts, but it is a curious fact that, whereas before the Revolution amateurs prided themselves on their liking for novelties and on introducing budding talent to their friends, after the great crisis the adepts developed a spirit of narrow conservatism. In private gatherings little was now played but Haydn, Mozart, and, unfortunately, Pleyel. Contemporary writers were shut out, toleration being shown only to those who coldly copied the recognized masters. It was much the same with orchestral concerts, especially those given at the Conservatoire. Haydn, Mozart, and, somewhat later, Beethoven, had the field to themselves. It was no bad choice, but the ostracism of living composers imperilled the whole development of music. And this is what actually happened: for three-quarters of a century French composers ceased to write chamber music. It would, however, be an exaggeration to say, with Saint-Saëns, that until the formation of the Société Nationale in 1871 'the French composer who was foolish enough to try his hand at instrumental music had no other course open to him than to give a concert of his own works, and invite his friends and the Press'. The truth is—at least in Paris and in some of the great towns—that chamber music, although greatly neglected, was never completely abandoned.

Little information is available about chamber concerts in Paris during the Revolution and the Empire. What, for instance, was the ordinary repertory of the concerts at the Maison Wenzel, Rue l'Échiquier, where the celebrated violinist Baillot had trios of his own performed from 1795 onwards? It is not known. Not until the end of the Empire can any precise details be obtained of the musical life of the time, apart from the music of the stage.

In 1814 Baillot gave several chamber concerts which were very popular; the programmes of these were devoted mainly to Haydn and Mozart, a place being found for some trios and quartets of his own. Baillot's works are entirely forgotten to-day, but, in spite of the obvious influence of the German School, they are far from contemptible, and some of them might well be revived. They make little concession to the popular taste of the day for trivial and facile melody. There is a certain daring in the harmony, and its roughnesses and lack of correctness disturbed Fétis. The public found Baillot's music odd. Its difficulty terrified amateurs, who preferred at their meetings to play the quartets of Onslow.

The vogue of Reicha's quartets is not without justification. This Bohemian composer, who had known Beethoven and Haydn, came to live in France, and was appointed professor at the Conservatoire of Paris, where Berlioz was among his pupils. More than a hundred chamber works of his are known, quartets, quintets, &c., for strings and for wind instruments. He had one of the rarest gifts, a feeling for the combination of the timbres of different instruments, and amused himself by writing quintets for flute, oboe, clarinet, horn, and bassoon. These quintets were first played at the Salle Favart, from 1815 to 1818, with immense success. Published in series, they were soon played throughout France.

In these quintets, as well as in his string quartets and trios, Reicha shows himself to be a skilful composer, with an assured technique, and a power of writing original harmonies which are often daring and expressive.

Cherubini's six string quartets were never known or appreciated by more than a handful of amateurs. The dry and angular style and the scholarly writing of these works made them unattractive to a public whose taste was steadily deteriorating.

About 1830, however, the beginning of a reaction is evident. Classical music was beginning to be more widely appreciated. Numerous amateur societies were founded, in Paris as well as in the provinces. In 1835 the Gymnase Musical began its meetings, where Liszt and César Franck were to make their appearance. Here scarcely anything but the classics was played, the moderns being only admitted if not above 'an honourable mediocrity': a trio by the Viennese composer, Mayseder, for example, or a sextet of a slightly higher class by the French writer, Henri Bertini. Under Louis-Philippe an amateur society, the Cercle de Bèze, aroused a good deal of interest. At this society's concerts the first performance was given, in 1846, of a work by Gouvy, a pleasant trio which shows the influence of Mendelssohn.

Under the Second Empire, in 1860, Prince Poniatowski founded the Union Artistique, which gave alternate chamber and orchestral concerts. The Société des Jeunes Artistes gave quintets, sextets, or octets, sandwiched between orchestral items.

New names appear on these programmes. Reicha, Onslow, Baillot, &c., give place to men like Gouvy, H. Bertini, Litolff, Niedermayer, Fétis, Lefébure-Wély—who were soon to be followed by Deldevez, Kreutzer, Réber, Georges Mathias, and Louise Farrenc. The work of the last-named has a firmness of touch which is rarely to be met with among the French composers of this period, and her music shows evidence of fine artistic taste. She gave further proof of this artistic taste by forming that splendid collection known as *Le Trésor des Pianistes*, which brought within reach of the public the works of the old writers for the harpsichord, and of the great masters of the seventeenth and eighteenth centuries, at that time completely forgotten. Qualities of a high order are shown in her chamber music, especially in the nonet which was performed in 1850 at Erard's, under Joachim. These qualities are also to be found in her symphonies, which are too little remembered to-day.

However completely the symphonies and chamber music of such men as Gouvy and Réber seem to us to-day to have been forgotten, it is none the less true that France had her true pioneers like Madame Farrenc. Taking for their models the works of the classical masters, as well as those of the neo-classicist Mendelssohn, they showed French musicians that there are other paths than that of the theatre, and taught the public to make trial of new works from time to time. They were artists of the second rank who had the courage to brave the indifference of the many, and they brought abstract music once more into honour among composers.

The influence of Berlioz, considerable in orchestral music, was non-existent in chamber music. As for César Franck, although his trio dedicated to Liszt is dated 1841, he remained unknown to the general public. During the last years of the empire, chamber music was much in fashion. Eminent operatic composers did not disdain to write it; Félicien David wrote a trio, the simplicity of which assured its success; Saint-Saëns and Lalo began to make themselves known.

The taste of the public had been educated during the preceding years by more and more frequent performances of Mozart's and Beethoven's quartets. After 1850, performances of chamber music increased rapidly in number. At the Conservatoire, Alard and Franchomme gave matinée concerts, which were very well attended. At Erard's, in 1850, the youthful Joachim was the moving spirit in some very interesting concerts, where the names of Mendelssohn (quartet) and Madame Farrenc (quintet) were to be found cheek by jowl with those of Bach, Haydn, Mozart, and Beethoven.

Beethoven's last quartets were not included in these programmes. They seemed in France (as in Germany, for that matter) to be absolutely incomprehensible. Baillot alone had given a few private performances of them to friends. It was the Maurin Quartet which, not without struggles, introduced them to the Parisians, from 1849 onwards. In 1852 this Quartet, which had just been joined by the famous 'cellist Chevillard, performed Beethoven's last six quartets for the first time in public, thereby greatly fluttering the critics. These works had for some time been ardently and secretly worshipped by several musicians, who used to meet together to hear them, either at Maurin's house, or at Massart's—the latter a professor at the Conservatoire. The works soon forced themselves on the attention of the musical *élite*, and did a great deal to educate musical taste in France.

The members of the Maurin Quartet were: Maurin, Sabatier, Maas, and Chevillard. It had no rival till 1856, when there appeared the celebrated Quartet Armingaud, Lapret, Lalo, and Jacquard, who, besides the classics, included in their programmes all Mendelssohn's quartets, and occasionally played the works of their violist, Édouard Lalo.

It is worthy of note that, in 1856, the *Gazette Musicale* affirms the growing appreciation of the public for chamber music; performances, it says, 'are rapidly growing in number and in popularity; they have their dilettantes, even their fanatics; it is, in some sense, a new era, the era of the quartet which has arrived at last'. One clear-sighted critic, Henri Blanchard, even observed, 'Who can tell? Perhaps the time is come for France to take the lead in instrumental music.'

It must be recognized, however, that this infatuation of the public for chamber music did not extend to modern works. These continued to make only tentative appearances on the programmes.

In 1869 the Trompette was founded by an amateur who was passionately devoted to music, M. Lemoine, an old pupil of the École Polytechnique. This private society, which still exists after many vicissitudes, gives each year a certain number of invitation concerts to its members. The society has certainly contributed to the development and refinement of the taste of the *bourgeois* public, whose appreciation, up to this time, had scarcely extended beyond Meyerbeer's operas. But its influence on musical evolution has been practically nil, for modern composers were almost systemically excluded from its earlier programmes. Not till 1880 did the Trompette commission a septet from Saint-Saëns, and in 1887 another from Vincent d'Indy.

The popular classical concerts founded by Pasdeloup in 1861 gave a powerful stimulus to the education of the public, and thus exerted an indirect influence on chamber music.

But, in spite of all this, it remained very difficult for a composer to make his name known by means of chamber works, and many had to be content with giving a concert at their own expense. This is what Saint-Saëns did regularly, from 1860 onwards. In that year he gave a performance of his quintet, op. 14, at Erard's, and in 1865 his admirable trio in F, op. 18, a masterpiece which marks an epoch in the history of French music.

Now and then modern works would appear on the programmes, but, unfortunately, the executants did not turn to Saint-Saëns, César Franck, and Lalo, but to Réber, Gastinel, Vancorbeil, or Georges Mathias. Occasionally there timidly appears the name of Boëly—an organist, and an artist of real worth, who dared like César Franck to write in an austere and contrapuntal style, without any attempt to please the coarse tastes of the crowd.

In 1867 Édouard Colonne started a series of chamber concerts; in March 1870 the Schumann Society (founded somewhat earlier) introduced Castillon's quintet. The last-named was one of the earliest and most interesting of Franck's pupils. In the later years of the Empire chamber music associations abounded: in addition to the Société Classique, which consisted of Armingaud, Turban, Maas, and Jacquard, and the Quartet Lamoureux, Coblain, Adam, and Tolbecque, there appeared the Séances de Musique de Chambre—Delahaye, White, Hollander, Waefelghem, and Hollmann; the Marsick Quartet; the Trio—Delaborde, Hammer, and Jacquard, &c.

The war of 1870 interrupted all this musical activity. In a sudden fit of energy, French composers felt the need of a reaction against the crushing German predominance, and the need, too, of organizing concerts where they could have their works performed, without having to depend on the caprice of a more or less greedy impresario. The idea of concerts for purely French music had been in the air for some time. The critic Chouquet had declared in favour of them ever since 1867. Taking advantage of the patriotic uprising of France, musicians managed to come to an agreement, and to obtain the necessary support for the foundation of the Société Nationale de Musique, which was to exert so decisive an influence on the course of musical evolution in France, and to bring composers into continuous relations with the Parisian public.

The prime movers were Saint-Saëns and Romain Bussine, professor of singing at the Conservatoire. In February 1871 they brought together César Franck, Massenet, Gabriel Fauré, Guiraud, Henri Duparc, Théodore Dubois, Garcin, and Taffanel. It was decided that the Society should confine its energies to the performance of the works of living French musicians. The first meetings were interrupted by the Commune, but they were resumed from October 1871 onwards. The rules were drawn up by one of Franck's pupils, Alexis de Castillon, who died in 1873, at the age of 35, in consequence of the war. The Society took as its device ARS GALLICA, and for its title, Société Nationale de Musique.

Among the members of the first committee were Saint-Saëns, César Franck, Lalo, Gabriel Fauré, Guiraud, &c. The inaugural concert took place in the Salle Pleyel on November 25, 1871, the programme including a trio of Franck's. The chance of being able at last to have their chamber works performed was a powerful incentive to composers. They set to work, and a wonderful harvest was to result from their labours. It was at the Société Nationale that all César Franck's principal chamber works made their first appearance;—violin sonata, trios, quartet, quintet, preludes and fugues, as well as important orchestral works and church music.

This is not the place for a discussion of orchestral and dramatic works: this side of the Society's activities will therefore be disregarded. It was for the Society that Saint-Saëns wrote a quartet, several sonatas, and the *Mélodies Persanes*: for the Society, too, Vincent d'Indy wrote his quartet and quintet: Chausson, his quartet: Debussy, the quartet, piano pieces, and songs: Dukas, his piano sonata: Albéric Magnard his quartet, trio, and violin sonata: Ravel, his *Schéhérazade*, the *Histoires naturelles*, the string quartet, and piano pieces: Florent Schmitt, the piano quintet, &c., &c.

In 1886 Vincent d'Indy proposed to extend the scope of the programmes so as to include ancient, classical, or foreign works. The founders of the Society, Saint-Saëns and Bussine, protested strongly, and, as their opinion did not carry the day, they resigned from the committee. C. Franck refused the office of President, but he did, in fact, undertake it, and was succeeded in 1890 by his pupil, Vincent d'Indy.

In spite of the change in the rules, the Société Nationale did not throw its gates wide open to foreigners. With the exception of Richard Strauss's quartet, and a very limited number of works by Grieg, Borodin, Moussorgsky, Rimsky-Korsakov, Glazounov, Liadov, &c., the programmes may be said to have remained exclusively French. Ever since 1900 there had been complaints that the Society was becoming more and more a private preserve of the Franckist school. The discontent continued to grow with the strengthening of the new tendencies towards the work of Debussy, Fauré, and Ravel.

In 1909 the split came. A new society was founded, under the title of the Société Musicale Indépendante (S.M.I.), the committee of which was composed of the following members:—Gabriel Fauré, President; Louis Aubert, André Caplet, Roger Ducasse, Jean Huret, Ch. Koechlin, Maurice Ravel, Florent Schmitt, E. Vuillermoz. Foreign members were added to the committee, among the number being Stravinsky, Béla Bartók, and Cyril Scott.

During the war the two societies were amalgamated, under the presidency of Gabriel Fauré, but, after the armistice, they separated once more. It must further be recognized that their importance has greatly diminished, the Société Nationale remaining the stronghold of the Franckist school, while Ravel is the moving spirit of the S.M.I. As for the young composers, the greater part belong to both societies, and, with equal indifference, get their works performed by either; this is notably the case with Honegger, Milhaud, &c. Thus the aims of the two societies are now ceasing to conflict.

It must be admitted that the principal reason for their existence is gone now that the public has been educated and no longer fears first performances. Composers of chamber music have now no difficulty in obtaining a hearing. There are in Paris some fifteen Quartets, which dispute among themselves the honour of performing new works; also two societies for wind instruments, and numerous chamber music societies—in fact, now composers have an *embarras du choix*.

It would be wearisome to trace chronologically the history of all the chamber music societies now existing in Paris; this article must be confined to an enumeration of those that are best known.

The Société Philharmonique gives twelve concerts only each year, with the assistance of very distinguished executants. Its programmes give but a very limited place to modern music. The prestige of this society is justified by the high level of its performances, and its concerts attract large audiences. The Capet Quartet, whose ensemble was one of the finest, if not the finest, in the world, specialized in classical music, giving performances, in chronological order, of the Beethoven quartets. The death of the leader, Lucien Capet, in Dec. 1928, was an irreparable loss to French chamber music.

The concerts of the *Revue Musicale*, which were started in 1920, are an attempt to remedy an omission, by performing chamber works, ancient and modern, which are unknown, or little known, in France. Here were to be heard for the first time in Paris the works of Béla Bartók, Karol Szymanovsky, Ernest Bloch, Malipiero, Casella, Rieti, Bliss, Goossens, and also the works of modern French composers. There are, on an average, about thirty of these concerts each year, for which the most eminent artists are engaged:—Cortot, Thibaud, Kochansky, Arthur Rubinstein, Robert Casadesus, Wanda Landowska; and the following Quartets:—the Capet, Pro Arte (of Brussels), Rosé, Hungarian, Poulet, Crinière, &c.

A very interesting series of concerts was started by a young pianist-composer, Jean Wiener: at these he gives the most daring works of the advanced guard with an admixture of sonatas or works by J. S. Bach. To him is due the revelation of Schönberg's *Pierrot Lunaire*, and the interesting performances of the works of Satie, Milhaud, Stravinsky, Poulenc, Auric, &c. He gives, on an average, four performances a year.

It is impossible to give details of all the recitals and private concerts, which swarm in Paris, as in London. Each year there are several concerts of the Société Moderne des Instruments à Vent (conducted by the late Louis Fleury), the repertory containing a large number of new works; as also of the Société des Instruments à Vent (founded by Taffanel), which gives less modern than classical music, and is composed exclusively of virtuosi.

The Société des Instruments anciens (founder, Casadesus) and the Société Violes et Clavecin (conductor, Macon) devote themselves to old music. Finally there exist *cénacles* (a kind of club) like *Le Caméléon* and *L'Œuvre inédite*, where composers bring their own works before an audience of friends and habitués. At the Tuesday receptions of the *Revue Musicale* new works are also heard, played mostly by the composers, or by foreign artists on a visit to Paris.

So greatly has the appreciation of chamber music grown that the performances of the famous Trio, Cortot-Thibaud-Casals, had to be given in the huge hall of the Opéra, and, despite the very high prices, people were turned away! At Kreisler's concerts the same thing happened, but in this case it was due to the presence of a great virtuoso, and not a trio.

This ever-growing interest of the public in

chamber music explains the great attention paid to it by the younger school of composers. Darius Milhaud has already written seven quartets, as well as instrumental sonatas, &c.; Honegger, a quartet, and three sonatas for violin, viola, and 'cello respectively; Germaine Tailleferre, a quartet, and a violin sonata; Poulenc, numerous instrumental pieces. Chamber music, so neglected during the nineteenth century in France in favour of the theatre, is enjoying a period of great splendour now that composers turn to it from opera. Without taking into account the works of the younger school which are still open to discussion, the list of French chamber works is considerable, and has been augmented during the last quarter of a century by additions of the greatest importance: Gabriel Fauré's quintets, piano trio, and quartets; Debussy's sonatas, for violin, for 'cello, and for flute, viola, and harp (which, together with his quartet, his songs, and his piano pieces, form an artistic treasure of inestimable worth); Maurice Ravel's piano trio, and the sonata for violin and 'cello; Florent Schmitt's quintet, and sonata for violin and piano; Albert Roussel's divertimento for wind instruments, his *Flute-players*, and second violin sonata; Gabriel Pierné's trio and quintet; Guy Ropartz's trio; Vincent d'Indy's quintet, &c.

All these works, which have widely differing, and even opposite, tendencies, attest the vitality and creative force of the French school of chamber music—the fruits of the labour of those three splendid pioneers, Saint-Saëns, César Franck, and Lalo.

HENRY PRUNIÈRES.

[Ella writes in 1856 commenting on the fact that in Paris no less than six parties were giving séances of chamber music. The longest established, he says, was that led by Alard, his colleagues being Blanc, Ney, and Franchomme, with F. Planté, pianist. Other parties were led by Ernst, whose pianist was Madame Mattmann. Ella also mentions a 'Mendelssohn party' (Armingaud, Jacquard, Madame Massard), presumably performers of trios. And a private party met at the residence of Gouffé, the contrabassist, to play mainly new works.

In a notice of the society La Trompette, the *Strand Magazine* published in 1910 some amusing details relating to its early days. It sprang from Lemoine's private quartet, whose severest critic was a friend named Laurent, who, entering one day when the quartet was playing, exclaimed, 'Leave your *trumpets* and come with me to the library'. The name stuck and Lemoine gave all his care and attention to what he was pleased to call 'his daughter'.

At first amateur performers took part in the meetings at Lemoine's rooms, but when young artists of distinction displayed interest in the proceedings, the amateurs gave up their places to them, and from that moment the affair began to attract attention. Amongst these then comparatively unknown artists were Saint-Saëns, Diémer, Pugno, &c., and later, under the auspices of La Trompette, which moved in 1878 to commodious quarters in the Salle d'Horticulture, Rue de Grenelle, the names of artists visiting Paris, such as Rubinstein, Von Bülow, and Paderewski, appeared on the programmes. EDITOR.]

FRENCH PERFORMING ORGANIZATIONS.

The formation of permanent associations for chamber music is due, in France as elsewhere, to the creation and rapid development of a new form, the string quartet, which reached its full stature in the works of the great masters of the last third of the eighteenth century.

Before this time, however, there were occasional associations, sometimes of distinguished artists—François Couperin performed his CONCERTS ROYAUX (published in 1722) with Duval, Philidor, Alarius, and Dubois as partners. Under different circumstances the *Mercure de France* speaks of performances of chamber music by the flautist Blavet, the violinist Guignon, and the violists Edouard and Forqueray (1737), or Blavet, Morella, Forqueray, and Labbé (1745). But these séances were purely occasional in character. It was quite otherwise with the first Quartets of the modern type—two violins, viola, and 'cello.

The most notable of these, and the first of real importance, was that of BAILLOT (Pierre-Marie-François de Sales, 1771–1842), friend and pupil of Viotti, a remarkable virtuoso and one of the most renowned teachers of the last century. His first public performance was given on December 12, 1814: his partners in the string quartets, quintets, and sextets which he had undertaken to bring to a hearing were Guynemer, Tariot, Saint-Laurent, Lamare, Norblin, later replaced by Vidal, Sauzay, Urhan, Mialle, and Vaslin. He is remembered as one of the most accomplished interpreters of this type of music, as is seen by the praises bestowed on him by Fétis, Spohr, Mendelssohn, &c. To him is due the first performance in France of Beethoven's early quartets, but he never ventured to perform the late works in public. His other favourite masters were Boccherini (unjustly neglected by his contemporaries), Haydn, and Mozart.

In 1833, the violinist Théophile TILMANT (1799–1878), with the help of his brother Alexandre, violoncellist, founded an association similar to the foregoing, but much less notable. Their repertory was the same (Beethoven's late quartets still excluded), with, however, the addition of contemporary works, of no great merit, as a rule.

Then came the SOCIÉTÉ DE MUSIQUE DE CHAMBRE, founded by Delphin Alard

(1815–88) and the violoncellist A. Franchomme. Their first concert was given on January 1, 1835, and, after various rearrangements, an active career was resumed in 1847. The last occasion on which Alard and Franchomme were heard in quartets was in 1872.

But the most important organization since Baillot's is the society formed in 1850 by the violoncellist Pierre Alexandre CHEVILLARD (1811–77), father of the famous conductor, Camille C., for making the public acquainted with Beethoven's late quartets. He had already given the eighth and tenth quartets with Alard, Dancla, and Croisilles, with whom he had been associated since 1840. He now found in Jean Pierre Maurin (1822–94) a violinist capable of undertaking to lead the later ones. Their partners (second violin and viola) were repeatedly changed: the most distinguished were Viguier, Sabatier, and Maas. In 1867 Chevillard himself gave way to Valentin Müller.

In 1855 was formed the JULES ARMINGAUD QUARTET, with Armingaud (1829–1900) as first violin, Lapret second violin, Jacquard violoncellist, the viola being Édouard Lalo, who was soon to make his name as a composer.

In 1862 appeared the quartet CHARLES LAMOUREUX (1834–99), Colblain, Adam, Rignault, who called their concerts 'Popular Chamber Concerts', and did their best to popularize a form of art hitherto confined to the few.

In 1863 the SOCIÉTÉ DES QUATUORS FRANÇAIS was founded by Albert Ferrand, with Rhinc, Bernhardt, Rabaud as partners. This was devoted to native composers: the intention, at this period, was of greater value than the actual performance, the repertory being poor.

Since then similar organizations have continued to multiply, and it is impossible to give a full list of them. Some idea of their activities may be gathered by following the history of one Society, LA TROMPETTE, founded in 1860 by amateurs who were pupils at the École Polytechnique, the quartet forming the basis of their programmes.

The first professional Quartet to lend its assistance regularly was that formed in 1875 by Léon Reynier, Hollander, Benjamin Godard, and Delsart. This original nucleus was transformed again and again. Marsick soon became the leader. In 1878 the quartet was composed as follows:—Marsick, Colblain, Van Waefelghem, Delsart. In 1879 Colblain was replaced by Rémy, who was, some years later (1887), himself leader of a Quartet—Rémy, Parent, Van Waefelghem, Delsart.

In 1893 MAURICE HAYOT entered the MARSICK QUARTET as second violin, and was entrusted with the leadership during Marsick's tour in America. In 1900 he founded his own Quartet with Touche, Bailly, and Salmon: Bailly was replaced by Denayer in 1902, Touche by André in 1905.

Apart from LA TROMPETTE, to which almost all of them gave occasional assistance, the following Quartets should be mentioned:—Geloco, Tracol (replaced by Capet), Monteux, Schneklud, which began its career in 1889; Armand Parent, Loiseau, Brun, Fournier, who gave a considerable number of first performances of important works, while devoting several concerts annually to Beethoven; the Berthelier-Loeb Quartet; besides organizations of wider scope, like that founded in 1881 by Nadaud, Laforge, Pugno, Viardot, Philip, Cros-Saint-Ange, &c., for the performance of works for all combinations of instruments which come under the head of chamber music, or, on a still larger scale, the SOCIÉTÉ NATIONALE, where string trio, quartet, and quintet have a special place.

The most famous French Quartet to-day is certainly the CAPET QUARTET. Lucien Capet (1873–1928), who, on leaving the Conservatoire, had founded a youthful Quartet passionately devoted to the study of Beethoven, formed, in 1903, with André Tourret (since then also leader of a Quartet), Louis Bailly, and Louis Hasselmans, the body which was soon to acquire European celebrity. Dissolved in 1910, this first association was reorganized with Capet, Maurice Hewitt, Henri Casadesus, and Marcel Casadesus as members, continuing thus till 1914. Since 1919 the organization, stricken by the war, has been reconstituted with Lucien Capet, Maurice Hewitt, Henri Benoît, Camille Delobelle. If certain of its interpretations are open to criticism, yet in finish, in beauty of tone and homogeneity of conception it is incomparable.

The HEWITT QUARTET (Maurice Hewitt, Albert Locatelli, Henri Benoît, Camille Delobelle) is an offshoot of the Capet Quartet. They travel abroad, and make a speciality of discovering and performing new quartets in addition to the regular repertory of the Capet Quartet. The leader, Hewitt (second violin of the Capet), is French but of English origin, his grandfather having been English. All except Locatelli are regular members of the Capet.

In line with the Capet Quartet may be placed that formed by Gaston Poulet, Giraud, Le Guillard, Ruyssen, which has won renown by its interpretation of romantic (Schumann) and modern works. Its maximum activity lies in the period 1919–26. The following Quartets also deserve notice:

Argeo ANDOLFI (formed 1913) with V. Prat, Y. Englebert, E. de Bruyn (replaced in 1922 by A. Cruque).

Jean CALVET, Georges Mignot, Louis Pascal, Paul Mas.

Fernande CAPELLE, Alice Piantini, Marguérite Lutz, Marika Bernard.

Marcel CHAILLEY (formed 1905) with Gravrand, Jurgensen, Schidenhelm, several times changed; the latest (1922) being Chailley, Guilevitch, Pascal, Alexanian.

Georges CRINIÈRE (1918), Marcel Gonzalès, Jean Gay, M. Duchon-Doris.

KRETTLY (1919), G. Taine, P. Mayer, J. Patte: at present Krettly, R. Costard, G. Taine, Pierre-Fournier.

Léon ZIGHERA (1921), G. Palla, P. Jurgensen, A. Zighera.

Also the BASTIDE, CANTRELLE, CAREMBAT, LEJEUNE, LOISEAU, OBERDOERFER, and PASCAL-TOUCHE Quartets.

Trios. There have been few permanent Trios. We may note the SOCIÉTÉ DES TRIOS ANCIENS ET MODERNES formed in 1866 by White, Lasserre, and de la Nux. To-day there is a TRIO DE PARIS—Madeleine de Valmalète, Yvonne Astruc, Marguérite Caponsacchi; another highly talented women's Trio was founded in 1924 by Madeleine Grovlez, Françoise Monnier, and Madeleine Monnier; there is also the TRIO HISPANIA formed in 1913 by the pianist Costa (now replaced by Bonaterra), Louis Pichot (violin) and Ricardo Pichot, whose domicile is French. Lastly, each year sees the temporary reconstitution of the admirable Trio Alfred Cortot, Jacques Thibaud, and Pablo Casals.

Ancient Instruments. Two societies share the heritage of Diémer's SOCIÉTÉ DES INSTRUMENTS ANCIENS, one of which bears the same title. This was formed in 1901, with Saint-Saëns as president, by Henri Casadesus (viola d'amore), with Gabriel Grovlez, Mme Casadesus-Dellerba, Marcel Casadesus, and Édouard Nanny. After several changes it consists to-day of Marius Casadesus (quinton[1]), Henri Casadesus (viola d'amore), Lucette Casadesus (viola da gamba), Maurice Devilliers (basse de viole), Regina Patorni-Casadesus (clavier).

The SOCIÉTÉ VIOLES ET CLAVECIN formed in 1911 was completely reorganized in 1920 by Émile Macon, with G. Morel (pardessus de viole), E. Macon (dessus de viole),[2] Francis Thibaut (basse de viole), Germaine Portehaut (clavier). G. Morel was succeeded by André Bittar, then by Marcel Duran, F. Thibaut by Alfred Zighera, then by Victor Clerget, Germaine Portehaut by Mme Pauline Aubert.

Wind Instruments. In 1879 the famous flautist Paul Taffanel founded a chamber music society for wind instruments, since known as the SOCIÉTÉ TAFFANEL: his coadjutors were Diémer (for works with piano), Gillet Bas, Turban, Grisez, Brémond, Pénable, Letellier, and Bourdeau. Up to 1895 he gave very well attended performances at the Salle Pleyel. Philippe Gaubert succeeded him when, in 1917, he resigned in favour of his pupil René le Roy. The society is composed to-day of MM. René le Roy (flute), Louis Bas (oboe), Achille Grass (clarinet), Jules Vialet (horn), Édouard Hénon (bassoon).

A similar organization, whose activities, however, are more especially directed towards contemporary music, was formed in 1895 by Louis Fleury under the title of SOCIÉTÉ MODERNE D'INSTRUMENTS À VENT. The principal movers were the flautists Louis Fleury (d. 1926) and G. Barrère, the oboist Gaudard, the clarinettists Guyot and Cahuzac, the bassoon-player Flament, with the occasional help of the pianist Louis Aubert.

Finally, since 1921, the principal soloists of the wind-band of the Société des Concerts du Conservatoire have constituted a WIND DIXTET. This includes MM. Moyse, Bleuzet, L. Costes, Vuillermoz, Oubradous, Manouvrier, A. Gobert, J. Guyot, P. Delgrange, Guilloteau. MARC PINCHERLE.

[1] Quinton—a mean (medium) viol.

[2] Two discant viols. The pardessus de viole was a small treble viol with upper string tuned to G, a fourth higher than the dessus de viole. They continued in use in France very late, after the other viols were out of fashion and were much favoured by the ladies, who regarded the violin as an unfeminine instrument. They do not seem to have been used in England. They had sometimes five and sometimes six strings. [ARNOLD DOLMETSCH.]

†FREY, EMIL, b. 1889, Swiss pianist.

Sonata, pf, v, D	op. 22	Simrock, 1922.
Sonata, pf, vc, B	,, 8	,, 1911.

Frey is a composer of somewhat modern tendencies, while his music shows unmistakable traces of Brahms's influence. Freshness of invention, warm feeling, good technical work, and varied harmony make his compositions very attractive.

THE 'CELLO SONATA. Frey's talent is recognizable in the lyrical 'cello sonata, op. 8. The first subject of the opening movement is full of expression, and thoroughly suited to the character of the 'cello: the piano accompanies this with simple broken chords, and then takes over the theme. The second subject, however, is not equal to the first, while the development, though concise, is a little awkward. In the adagio the composer gives free rein to his lyricism, but successfully resists the temptation to become too diffuse. The finale, allegro molto, which is in keeping with the preceding movement is well constructed and less exacting for the instruments.

THE VIOLIN SONATA. The violin sonata shows great progress, both technically and artistically. The first movement, allegro, begins very spiritedly with a passionate first subject, which later appears in the bass of the piano, the right hand accompanying with animated broken chords. In this movement the second subject is again less satisfactory than the first, and is rather thought out than inspired: the development, however, is very good, and the coda highly effective. The andante con moto is, artistically, an advance upon the allegro: the harmony is richer, and the movement is more poetic. The hand of the pianist-composer is plainly seen in the complex but euphonious piano part. The scherzo is neither original in invention nor particularly effective, but it has, at least, the merit of brevity. In the finale, allegretto con fuoco, Frey again strengthens the good impression made by the opening: passionate feeling is here coupled with ample employment of artistic means, but the piano with its rich passage work is not infrequently too heavy for the violin: it is not till near the end that the latter becomes, in its turn, the predominant partner. The movement as a whole, however, is the most effective and artistic of the work. RUDOLF FELBER.

†FREY, MARTIN, b. 1872, German composer.

Sonata, pf, v, g mi op. 26 Steingräber, 1907.

A solidly built sonata of the Brahmsian type, which presents no unusual features.

FRICKE, RICHARD, b. 1877, German composer.

Quartet, str, F op. 1 Hofmeister, 1906.

Obtained the Mendelssohn prize of the Prussian Academy of Arts.

FRIEDBERGER, EMIL.

Quartet, str, D U.E., 1914.

†FRIEDMAN, IGNAZ (or IGNACY), b. 1882, Polish pianist and conductor.

Quintet, pf, 2 v, vla, vc, a mi Hansen, 1919. (Copenhagen.)

FRIEDMAN, SONIA C.

Sonata (*Ma première*), pf, v op. 12, no. 1 Maurice & Jane Vieu, 1913.

FRIEDRICH II (KING OF PRUSSIA), 1712–1786, flautist.

Modern republication:

Sonata, pf, vc, c mi (F. Grützmacher), Bosworth, 1903.

Twenty-five sonatas for piano, violin, and flute (arranged Ph. Spitta) by the royal composer were published by B. & H. in 1890. Frederick the Great was a keen flute-player and studied with Quantz. An amusing account of the king's chamber music meetings is to be found in Carlyle's *Frederick the Great*.

FRISKIN, JAMES, b. 1886, Scottish composer and pianist.

Phantasy quartet, str, D	—	Novello.
Quintet, pf, 2 v, vla, vc, c mi	op. 1	S. & B., 1909.
Phantasy quintet, pf, 2 v, vla, vc, f mi	—	,,
Phantasy trio, pf, v, vc, e mi	—	Novello.
Sonata, pf, v, G	,, 5	S. & B.

This composer, who at present lives in America, has made few but very valuable contributions to the chamber music repertory.

THE PIANO QUINTET, written in his twenty-first year, is one of the most brilliant op. 1's in existence. It is in the usual four movements, and is planned on a large scale. The significant subject which opens the quintet may be regarded as a kind of motto theme, for it is utilized throughout the work in a variety of ways, sometimes merely as a boisterous figure, sometimes transformed into a cantabile melody of great expressiveness. The second subject of the first movement has a folk-song flavour, and is suggestive of the composer's Scottish descent.

The scherzo is excellent, and as remarkable for its happy good humour and freakishness as for the ripe skill of its scholarly setting. There is a very quaint section in 2/4 time with an almost outrageously flippant subject for viola and 'cello in octaves, the piano supplying a drone accompaniment, which must always be greeted with a smile. The technique of the whole work is of the most finished order; although complex in texture it is never overladen with detail, and every point tells.

It should be recorded that the work was received on its first performance with the greatest enthusiasm, and a remarkable article by the music critic of *The Times* of that day did much to call attention to its merits. Sir Charles Stanford's declaration to the present writer that this was 'the *third* great piano quintet', though perhaps not a completely convincing statement, was at least a comprehensible view, and affords an indication of the great impression made by the work at the time of its production upon a master-mind in music.

If it can hardly be said that Friskin has succeeded in recapturing this 'first fine careless rapture' in his later chamber works, this is not to say that the successors to this work are unimportant. There is delicacy of feeling in his string quartet phantasy (which obtained an honourable place in one of W. W. Cobbett's early phantasy competitions) and serious intimacy of expression in his trio phantasy (which gained the second prize in a similar competition in 1908).

A greater degree of brilliancy as well as a more important message is conveyed in the phantasy for piano quintet, written to Mr. Cobbett's commission. This indeed is a fine and forceful work, ably designed and executed, and more mature in thought, if less immediately attractive, than his op. 1. It is to be regretted that the public has not had more opportunities of becoming acquainted with its many beauties. T. F. DUNHILL.

[The high opinion of the talent of his pupil, James Friskin, held by Sir Charles Stanford and recorded by Mr. Dunhill in the above article, was confirmed by remarks he made to me on more than one occasion. Once he sat by my side at Bechstein (now Wigmore) Hall listening to a performance of one of Friskin's phantasies, and said that he 'envied the young composer his gift of melody'—praise indeed from a 'master-mind of music'. There is no doubt of Friskin's affinity for chamber music, and all who wish him well must regret that since his departure to America, about 1913, he has made no further contribution to the repertory. Upon his gifts, however, one is justified in basing the hope that he is storing up energy, and that he will yet startle the world with an example of his mature period, combining piano (an instrument of which he is a master) and strings. His early sonata for piano and violin, by the way, is well worth the attention of amateurs.

Further references to his compositions in phantasy form will be found under COBBETT COMPETITIONS. EDITOR.]

†FROBERGER, JOHANN JAKOB, d. 1667, German composer.

Diverse ingegnosissime, rarissime e non mai più viste curiose *Partite* di Toccate, Canzone, Ricercate, Allemande, Correnti, Sarabande e Gigue di Cimbali, Organi e Instrumenti (1693).
Diverse Curiose e rare Partite musicali (1696).
10 Suites de Clavessin (Amsterdam).
New edition of works in the *D.D.T.*, vols. iv, vi, x, by G. Adler (Vienna). B. & H.

In his suites Froberger profited by the efforts of his predecessors, especially Frescobaldi (whose pupil he was), and finally evolved the sequence: allemande - courante - sarabande - gigue, which became the standardized form for those who succeeded him. Each suite is in the same key throughout; and considerable use is made of variation form. Certain suites have that characteristic feature of seventeenth-century song variations—the retention of a basic harmony throughout. As the composer's technique develops, the separate movements become more and more independent. He also makes use of chromatics, particularly in the sixth partita, *Die Mayerin*.

In the toccatas his art reached its summit, for the freer form gave fuller scope to his imagination, and he becomes really bold in handling the parts. According to his pupil the duchess Sibylla of Württemberg, however, the written notes are but an inadequate expression of his originality. 'It is difficult to realize it from the notes,' she writes, and no one who had not heard him play his pieces and learnt the interpretation at first hand could possibly render them 'with the correct discretion'. His art is on a level with that of a Chambonnières or a Louis Couperin; it is only François Couperin who puts him in the shade with his finer imaginative genius. EGON WELLESZ.

FRÖHLICH, C.

Quartet, str, G	Hoppe (Breslau), 1913.

†FRUGATTA, GIUSEPPE, b. 1860, Italian pianist.

Trio, pf, v, vc, a mi		B. & B., 1894.
Suite, pf, cl	op. 44	Ricordi, *c.* 1899.

Frugatta was awarded three prizes for his chamber works—the prize of the Florence Academy (1893) for the above trio; prize of the Academy of St. Cecilia, Rome (1898), for a string quartet (MS.); and a piano quintet with clarinet (MS.) won a prize in London (1899).

†FRÜHLING, KARL.

Quintet, pf, 2 v, vla, vc, f sharp mi	op. 30	Leuckart, 1894.

FUCHS, ALBERT, 1858–1910, Swiss composer.

Quartet, str, e mi	op. 40	Kahnt, 1904.
Three little sonatas (*all'antica*), pf, v, D, b mi	,, 36	Simon, 1898.
Sonata, pf, vc, D	,, 27	Siegel, 1894.
Suite *Mignonne*, pf, vc, d mi	,, 28	R. Forberg, 1896.
Suite (*Silhouetten*), pf (or harm), vc, G	,, 37	Simon, 1889.

In his string quartet Albert Fuchs appears in the role of a modern Mendelssohn. He knew how to make the instruments sound well, and handled his melodic ideas with skill and charm. The first movement is the most successful. The scherzo has piquancy apart from the fugato section, admirable on its own account. The andante sostenuto, lovely in itself, is not really in quartet style, being essentially a solo piece for the first violin. The finale, allegro assai, is a fiery movement and interesting rhythmically. WILHELM ALTMANN.

FUCHS, FERDINAND CARL, 1811–1848, Viennese composer.

Quartet, str, D	op. 36	Haslinger, 1844.

FUCHS, GEORG FRIEDRICH, 1752–1821, German clarinettist.

A list of his works, including some for unusual combinations of wind instruments, is given in *Fétis*.

FUCHS, ROBERT, 1847–1927, Viennese composer.

	op.	
Quintet, 2 v, vla, cl (or 2nd vla), vc	102	Robitschek.
Quartet, str, E	58	U.E.
Quartet, str, a mi	62	Schlesinger.
Two quartets, str, C, A	71,106	Robitschek.
Trio, v, vla, vc, A	94	,,
Two terzettos, 2 v, vla, E, D	61	Schlesinger.
Terzetto, 2 v, vla	104	Robitschek.
Quartet, pf, v, vla, vc, g mi	15	Kistner.

	op.	
Quartet, pf, v, vla, vc, b mi	75	Robitschek. U.E.
Trio, pf, v, vc, C	22	Kistner.
Trio, pf, v, vc, B flat	72	Robitschek. U.E.
Seven Phantasiestücke, pf, v, vla	57	Schlesinger.
Three sonatas, pf, v, f sharp mi, D, d mi	20, 33, 68	Kistner.
Sonata, pf, v, E	77	Robitschek. U.E.
Two sonatas, pf, v, A, g mi	95, 103	Robitschek.
Sonata, pf, vla, d mi	86	,,
Sonata, pf, vc, d mi	29	Kistner.
Sonata, pf, vc, e flat mi	83	Robitschek.
Sonata, pf, cb, g mi	97	,,

Fuchs was an extremely refined and cultured composer. He stood high in favour with Brahms, who continually gave him warm recommendations to publishers. Together with an excellent technical equipment, he possessed the gift for writing charming melodies, instinct with the friendliness and gaiety of his Austrian nature, and even in his old age he retained his freshness of invention. He definitely enriched the repertory available for the home circle, though he no longer holds his ground with concert-givers, by reason of his having modelled himself too closely on Schubert and Brahms.

The PIANO QUARTET, op. 75, is a finely inspired work of great formal merit. Of the two outer movements, the energetic, buoyant finale (allegro comodo) makes a more lasting impression than the first (allegro risoluto), which is reminiscent of Schubert's trio in E flat. There are many beautiful passages in the variations (andante, in D) and the scherzo (allegro vivace, in G)—particularly in the trio of the latter, which is in true Austrian vein and quite charming.

STRING QUARTETS, opp. 58, 71. These two deserve special mention. That in F major, op. 58, begins with a bold ascending phrase in the Bruckner manner; this serves as introduction to the lively first movement. The development, though containing pleasing details, is not on the composer's highest level. The second movement, allegro scherzando, is full of Fuchs's delightful humour; humour is evident, too, in the andante grazioso. The finale is particularly impressive, and gives an effective temperamental finish to a pleasing work.

The quartet in C, op. 71, shows constructive skill, and there is charm and real feeling in the themes. It has a piquant and original scherzo, a graceful slow movement, and a lively finale, which is splendid to play.

STRING TRIO, op. 94. Considering the dearth of good string trios, this work should be very welcome. The fresh unhackneyed main theme of the first movement is immediately attractive. The slow movement consists of very melodious variations on a Scottish folk-song, perfect in design and simple in character. The last movement contains a slow introduction, an allegretto piacevole with a fugato opening and a really thrilling allegro vivace.

VIOLIN SONATAS, opp. 68, 77. These are two of the most interesting of the violin sonatas. The D minor sonata, op. 68, has a spirited first movement, which leaves the best impression of the three; in the second, a theme with variations, the variations are more interesting than the theme. The finale has a modulatory diffuseness which is rather surprising, for Fuchs rarely sinned in this respect. The E major sonata, op. 77, has merit, even though it does follow the track of Brahms throughout.

The VIOLA SONATA, op. 86, is open to the same criticism, but will be very welcome to viola-players. The outer movements are spirited and attractively designed; the usual slow movement is replaced by a minuet, andante grazioso, in B flat, with a middle section in D major of great harmonic charm.

Fuchs is no modernist, but adheres to the older tried forms of composition. The foregoing notes will explain why acquaintance with his works is recommended, in spite of the fact that he is but the disciple of another.

WILHELM ALTMANN, with additions by RUDOLF FELBER.

FÜRSTENAU, ANTON BERNHARD, 1792–1852, German flautist.

Fürstenau was taught the flute by his father, Caspar (a flautist of some note, who composed duets for two flutes, of which six (op. 39) have been republished by Ricordi). He travelled with his father all over Europe, giving concerts, for which he probably wrote his various pieces for two flutes and piano. In 1820 he became first flute in the Chapel Royal at Dresden, under the direction of Carl Maria von Weber, who is supposed to have assisted him in some of his compositions, and with whom he in 1826 visited London, where Weber died in his arms. Fürstenau was a prolific composer for the flute. His compositions, formerly very popular, have been somewhat overrated. They are clever but lacking in soul or depth.. They number over eighty works in all and include a quintet, op. 28, for flute, two violins, viola, and 'cello (Simrock); four quartets for flute, violin, viola, and 'cello, op. 39 in E (Richault), op. 60 in A flat, op. 62 in F, and op. 74 in G minor (André); eight or nine trios for two flutes and piano, including a rondo brillant in D, op. 102—one of his best works, written in collaboration with Reissiger (Litolff).

Of his trios for three flutes, the best are op. 14 (3)—especially no. 2 in F (B. & H.); op. 118, a fine work in F, containing a beautiful andante (B. & B.); and op. 22 (3) containing some fugal writing (Hansen). He wrote at least seventeen sets of duets for two flutes, the favourites being op. 83 (3) and op. 112 (3); other good sets are opp. 36 and 89 (Richault) and op. 75 (Fürstner); and a fine quartet for four flutes is op. 88 in F (Ashdown). He also composed a duet for flute and harp, op. 67, and many pieces for flute and piano.

Kuhlau wrote many of his works for Fürstenau and played them with him.

H. M. FITZGIBBON.

[*Fétis* speaks very highly of his flute compositions.]

FURUHJELM, ERIK GUSTAF, b. 1883, Finnish composer.

Quintet, pf, 2 v, vla, vc, c mi Apostol, 1909.

FUX, JOHANN JOSEPH, 1660–1741, famous theorist.

The author of the *Gradus ad Parnassum* wrote some chamber works, of which a list is given in *Fétis*. His trios were much praised by Mattheson, the adversary of Handel (*v. Grove*).

G

† GABRIELI (1), ANDREA, *c.* 1510–1586, Venetian composer.

Sonatas a 5, *per i stromenti* Aug. Gardane, Venice, 1586. *Fétis.*

Andrea Gabrieli was a great contrapuntist (*v. Q.-L.*).

† (2), GIOVANNI, 1557–1613, Venetian composer, nephew of above.

Quartet, pf, 3 v, G (Hugo Riemann, *Old Chamber Mus.* I) Augener, 1896.

A remarkable composer of whom *Riemann* writes as 'epoch-making'. *Grove* remarks on the extreme boldness of his modulations. Instrumental music by both Gabrielis is in L. Toschi's *L'Arte Musicale*, vol. 3, &c. *Fétis* remarks on his novelty of form, and gives him the highest praise.

A complete edition of the works of the two Gabrielis is in preparation (1928), edited by Giacomo Benvenuti. EDITOR.

GABRIELLI, LADISLAV, contemporary Italian composer.

Suite, 4 v	G	Schott, 1901.
Three trios, 2 v, vla (or vc)	C, D, G	Carisch, 1900.
Two trios, 2 v, vc (or vla)	E flat, d mi	Schott, 1899.
Three trios, pf, 2 v	C, D, G	,, 1889.

† GABRIELSKI, JAN WILHELM (JOHANN WILH.), 1795–1846, flute virtuoso.

Became chamber musician to the King of Prussia (1816). He also played the oboe. He wrote over 120 works, many of which exhibit great taste and knowledge of the instrument. As a rule the harmonies are remarkably full. His fifteen sets of duets for two flutes are chiefly remarkable for their originality (almost amounting to eccentricity) and for the unexpected transitions in which they abound—with, however, occasional dull passages. The best set is op. 92: other good sets are opp. 59, 72, 84, 85 (B. & H.), and 100 (B. & B). The best of his many trios for three flutes are op. 10 (3) in A, E flat, and E minor (B. & H.); op. 31 in D (Schlesinger)—especially the fine opening movement; op. 33 in G; op. 34 in F; op. 41 in B flat; op. 78 (3) in E flat, A, and G minor (B. & H.); and op. 104 (3) in G, A, and D minor: nearly all have been edited by Clinton (Ashdown). His three quartets for four flutes, op. 53 (B. & H.), in G, A, and E minor, entitled *Hommage à Kuhlau*, are exceedingly well written and melodious, and abound in fine passages—especially no. 2. Gabrielski's chamber works include a quintet for flute and string quartet, op. 103 (Kistner); a couple of quartets for flute, violin, viola, and 'cello, opp. 60 in D (Probst, Leipzig) and 95; a trio for flute, violin, and viola, op. 45 in A; and a duet for flute and violin, op. 73 (B. & H.).

H. M. FITZGIBBON.

GADE, NIELS WILHELM, 1817–1890, Danish violinist and composer.

	op.	
Octet, 4 v, 2 vla, 2 vc, F	17	B. & H., 1849.
Sextet, 2 v, 2 vla, 2 vc, d mi	44	Kistner, 1865.
Quintet, 2 v, 2 vla, vc, e mi	8	B. & H., 1846.
Quartet, str, D	63	,, 1890.
Novelletten, pf, v, vc,	29	B. & H., 1855 & *c.* 1897; Costallat, 1855.
Trio, pf, v, vc, F	42	B. & H., 1864 & 1896.
Sonata, pf, v, A	6	B. & H., 1843 & 1891.
Sonata, pf, v, d mi	21	B. & H., 1850 & 1893.
Sonata, pf, v, B flat	59	B. & H., 1887 & 1907.
[Opp. 6, 21 also for pf, vla, & pf, vc; & op. 21 for pf, fl.]		
Fantasiestycker, pf, cl	43	B. & H., 1864; Hansen.

The most celebrated Danish composer of his time, Gade owed his introduction to the public to Mendelssohn, by whom he was much influenced, as well as by Schumann. He was the Scandinavian pioneer of the romantic school. *Riemann* says that his Scandinavian tendencies are shown chiefly in his musical colouring and an individual poetic touch, but he has not the characteristic harmonic and melodic peculiarities of Northern music. *Fétis* has little criticism to give and that is not complimentary; he finds in him a monotony due to the influence of Mendelssohn.

His trio in F, the *Novelletten*, and the sonata in D minor are prime favourites among amateurs seeking for pieces of moderate difficulty for public performances. I have myself frequently led the octet, to which I am much attached. It has not the stark virility which marks the companion work of his Scandinavian contemporary, Svendsen, but there is romantic charm in every page. For such an addition to the limited octet repertory musicians have reason to be grateful. Joachim occasionally played his music, the value of which is, I think, under-estimated in the musical world of to-day. It gives one the impression of being the expression of a poetic, and in the finer sense of the word feminine nature. He wrote well for the violin, the letters of his name being, appropriately enough, identical with the four open strings, G, A, D, E.

His string quartet and quintet are much to be recommended for practice to amateurs, especially the latter, many bars of which might have been signed Mendelssohn. EDITOR.

His son AXEL WILLI (1860–1921), pupil of Joachim, was also a composer.

GAGNEBIN, HENRI, b. 1886, Swiss composer born in Belgium.

	Composed	
1st quartet, str, F	1916–17	Hug.
2nd quartet, str, E	1924–25	Lemoine.
Sonata, pf, v, E	1914–15	Hug.
Sonata, pf, v	—	Senart, 1927.
Sonata, pf, vc	1922	,, ,,

This composer's characteristics are to be found rather in the intellectual development of his musical themes than in his inventive ability and imagination. The result is that many pages of Gagnebin's work, e.g. in his violin sonata, seem rather academic and lacking in feeling. He is better in his string quartet in F, which shows great polyphonic skill and interesting rhythms, and is also marked by greater depth of expression. In his later chamber music, Gagnebin is definitely modern (polytonal). His 3rd quartet (MS.) is also very interesting as regards form; he uses in the first movement the form of the old concerto grosso, treating the various members of the ensemble in turn as solo instruments. His style is classical, and free from all romantic elements; all his works demand technical ability and power of interpretation from the performers. FREDERICK HAY.

GAILLARD, MARIUS FRANÇOIS, b. 1900, French pianist.

Sonata, pf, v — Senart.

GÁL, HANS, b. 1890, pupil of Mandyczewsky.

	op.	Publ.
Quartet, str, f mi	16	1924.
Five intermezzi, str. quartet	10	1921.
Quartet, pf, v, vla, vc, B flat	13	1922.
Var^{ns}. on a Viennese melody, pf, v, vc	9	1921.
Trio, pf, v, vc, E	18	1928.
Sonata, pf, v, b flat mi	17	1928.
Suite, pf, vc, f sharp mi	6	1920.

All published by Simrock.

Won the Oesterreichischen Staatspreis for composition. He studied in Vienna and here received his degree as Philosophiae Doctor, his dissertation being 'On the peculiarities of style of the young Beethoven'.

Gál is one of the few young Viennese composers who belong to no definite group; he pursues his own way which has deviated greatly from that of the young radicals, but is without conservative tendencies. As a composer his inclination is chiefly towards chamber music, and in this field it is that his deep feeling finds its fullest expression.

THE VIOLIN SONATA. In the first movement (pateticc, molto moderato) the attention is at once arrested by the energetic first subject; this consists of two contrasting motifs to which the violin afterwards adds a new one. A somewhat agitated bridge-passage leads to the fervent second subject (dolce, tranquillo). The slowly beginning development deals at first with fragments of the first subject, then with the bridge-subject, and moves onward to a powerful climax; a transition to the principal key follows and the first subject again appears, although in greatly abbreviated form, complete. The second movement (vivace), in free scherzo form, contains two principal ideas, the first being delivered solo by the violin, while the second, in B flat minor, alternates between violin and piano. The trio in E major is built up on a broad, song-like basis.

Of the remainder of the work the chief feature is the melodious adagio, in C sharp minor. This movement has a coda in D flat major which introduces the first subject of the first movement, this being polyphonically interwoven with the original melody. The movement dies away delicately and dreamily with motifs from both themes.

THE PIANO TRIO is more interesting musically, and yet more so as regards its form. In the first movement the first subject has a 'cello theme as actual principal idea, to which the piano successively opposes two other themes. The second subject, in G major, is a lyric episode, complete in itself. The development is entirely founded on the group of ideas which constitutes the first subject, but the repetition is confined to those of the second subject; it is only in the coda that the first subject appears in its original form.

The scherzo, allegro violento, is constructed

on a single theme, delivered successively by violin, 'cello, and piano, while episodes are interspersed somewhat in the manner of development. The trio is developed from a five-bar theme, and is an aria in three sections.

The final movement is deeply felt. An eight-bar theme constitutes the chief material of the slow introduction, which is repeated in the middle section of the rondo-finale which follows. The form of this is very interesting, and especially remarkable is the coda, in which is a canonic development of the principal idea.

THE PIANO QUARTET, op. 13, deserves mention as one of Gál's important chamber music works. The effective introductory movement contains a concise exposition (which is repeated), a powerful, well constructed development and a modified recapitulation, beginning with the second subject. The second movement is somewhat inferior to the capriccio-like third movement, which is in concise sonata form with three principal ideas in its exposition. The rondo-finale is also very stimulating, with its three independent groups of themes, its middle section in B flat minor and spirited coda.

THE STRING QUARTET is also attractive, especially in regard to its form. This is particularly the case with the first movement, moderato ma con passione, which again contains an exposition with three groups of themes, a short development and an abbreviated recapitulation. The scherzo has two trios.

In his first chamber works Gál is still under the influence of Brahms; later he gradually frees himself from this, and in steadily growing measure discloses his own distinctive musical personality, but, like Brahms, he evinces always a strict regard for form and structure. Masterly technique, warm feeling, and great variety are the most prominent features of this sympathetic young composer's music.

RUDOLF FELBER.

[Gál's music is a pleasing surprise. The dissonances characteristic of the modern Austrian school are conspicuously absent. It is not difficult to play, the intermezzi especially being written for amateur performers, whilst the influence of Brahms is felt, but not the influence of Schönberg. In short, it is genuine Viennese music, though a little wanting in the gaiety and sensuous charm of pre-war days. How that comes about one understands only too well. EDITOR.]

GALLON, NOËL, b. 1891, French composer.

Suite, pf, fl — Rouhier, 1921.

†GANAYE, J. B.

Quartet, str, d mi — Hamelle, 1901.
Sonata, pf, v, C — op. 22 — Lemoine, 1906.

In 1901 the quartet was awarded the prize of the Société des Compositeurs.

†GARDINER, H. BALFOUR, b. 1877, English composer.

Quartet, str, B flat (one movement) — Novello.

A delightful short work, occupying about ten minutes in performance, and exhibiting much metrical and rhythmic variety. One of the earliest examples of the renaissance of interest in chamber music shown by English composers in recent times, and therefore of historic interest. EDITOR.

GARDINER, WILLIAM, 1770–1853.

A musical amateur, son of a Leicester manufacturer 'entangled', to use his own expression, 'in the toils of a factory' during most of his life, was able in his last years to retire, and review the past events of his career in three books entitled *The Music of Nature*, *Music and Friends*, and *Sights of Italy*. They contain much matter of interest to lovers of chamber music, though the author made no pretence to literary, or even to musical culture, his remarks alternately sagacious and naïve, being characterized in the main by sound common sense and a devotion to the musical art which was probably without a parallel in his day among the residents of provincial towns.

A quaint feature in his books is the interleaving in its pages of selections from his favourite composers arranged for the piano, and including several movements from various chamber compositions by Haydn, Beethoven, and Weber. A still more quaint feature of his life's work as a musician was his persevering attempt to popularize instrumental music of the abstract order by wedding it to words of his own choosing. One instance among many was his conversion of the andante of the *Kreutzer* sonata (slightly mangled) into 'Beethoven's prayer deploring his deafness'. He even perpetrated a whole oratorio constructed on this plan, and, it is to be hoped, never realized, poor man, that his efforts were only useful in a perverted sense. They served as a warning to musicians not to follow his example, or, vulgarly speaking, not to put the cart before the horse. A particularly irritating specimen of his amiable perversions is his setting of a comic dialogue to the andante of Beethoven's E flat string trio, though, strange to say, it was this very trio (in which he took part when it first reached England) which inoculated him with a taste for the music of Beethoven, of whom he became a life-long worshipper. Few Londoners had heard the composer's name at all, and those who had heard his works pronounced them the ravings of a Bedlamite. Gardiner had many opportunities later of making acquaintance under favourable circumstances with Beethoven's quartets, being apparently *persona grata* with many professional artists. He played all the op. 18 with Baillot in private and heard the *Rasoumovsky* and the posthumous, led in public by Bazzini and Eliason. His appreciations of chamber music in general were written in homely language, but their absolute sincerity is so apparent, and his judgement on the whole so sound, that even at the present day they make good reading. I quote a few of Gardiner's pen pictures of the famous Quartet leaders of his day, as affording some interesting glimpses into the musical past:

'Cramer, for firmness and fulness of tone, in the old school is without a rival.

Mori has extraordinary execution and beautiful articulation. He is quick and active, but too eager to be graceful.

Spagnoletti, though less forcible, is distinguished by a style chaste and delicate.

Vaccari, the Spaniard, is all gaiety and lightness, having none of the dark shades of the Germans; his notes are like the glitter of the diamond.

Spohr is full of ease and grace, and rather sings than plays. For so large a man, he has much grace and suppleness of bow.

The bow of Kiesewetter is swift and darting. At times he lays his ear upon the instrument, as if listening to the sounds inside it, pressing it upwards with apparent delight.

Yaniewitz is furious; his whole body partakes of the movement he is engaged in.

Baillot combines the Italian and German schools, and probably is the greatest master, having the greatest number of efforts (*sic*) at command. In him we have the Talma of the art—an inexhaustible mine of expression and emotion.'

EDITOR.

†GARDNER, SAMUEL, b. 1892 (in Russia), American composer.

Quintet, *To a Soldier*, f mi	op. 18	O. Ditson (Boston).

His compositions include several string quartets, one of which was awarded the Pulitzer prize.

†GASCO, ALBERTO, b. 1879.

Quartet, str, *The Sleeping Venus*	Leuckart.
Vision of St. Ursula, pf, v	Ed. Musica (Rome).
Virgin with the Cradle, pf, v	Ricordi.
Mary of Magdala, pf, v	Pizzi (Bologna).

In the above the composer seeks to translate into music the emotions evoked by paintings (those of Giorgione and Carpaccio) or by scenes of his own imagining. The music is at once descriptive and emotional, and though the writing is unequal the scoring is distinctly effective. The tone-poem, *Mary of Magdala*, is ambitious in intention but somewhat diffuse, and on the whole inferior to the *Sleeping Venus* quartet, inspired by Giorgione's well-known picture.

GUIDO M. GATTI.

GASTINEL, LOUIS-GUSTAVE-CYPRIEN, 1823–1906, French composer.

Quartet, str	E	op. 6	Costallat, 1850.
Quartet, str	—	—	Richault.
Quartet, str	—	—	Richault.
1st sextet, pf, 2 v, vla, vc, cb	—	—	Lemoine.
2nd sextet, pf, 2 v, vla, vc, cb	—	—	,,
Four sonatas, pf, v			Richault.
Sonata, pf, vc			,,

Pougin says that he was one of the first French composers to turn his attention to music other than opera, and, in consequence, was rather ahead of his time in France.

†GATTY, NICHOLAS, b. 1874, English operatic composer.

Sonata, pf, v, G	The Strad Library (formerly Novello).
Var^{ns}. pf, v	,, ,, ,,

MS. works include variations and fugue for string quartet and a piano trio (1927).

This sonata displays an unusual feature. The opening movement (prelude) is of feathery lightness and a foil to the more serious writing of the romantic larghetto which follows. The scherzo is animated by the true chamber music spirit, and the work is generally to be recommended to amateurs in search of sonatas of medium difficulty.

The variations are upon a tune found in *English County songs*, edited by J. A. Fuller Maitland and Lucy Broadwood. It was played with great success by the Spencer Dyke Quartet in 1926.

The late Mr. Wells Harrison, a writer on chamber music with an exceptional grasp of the intricacies of form, pointed out in one of his articles on British chamber music that in Nicholas Gatty's variations 'the actual theme is never lost sight of', a feature none too common in modern composition. 'The first two variations are practically richer presentations of the theme itself, whilst the following two concern themselves with variations over the same groundwork.' The analysis closes with a tribute to the inherent beauty of the music, which is an excellent specimen of the neo-British school of composition.

EDITOR.

†GAUBERT, PHILIPPE, b. 1879, French flautist.

Suite, pf, fl	Heugel, 1922.

Gaubert's music is 'neo-classic but tinged with modernism'. (*Dent*.)

GEBAUR, J., German composer.

Trio, pf, v, vla	op. 10, no. 3	Julius Weiss.

An unusual combination and useful for home practice, but uninspired.

GEBEL, FRANZ XAVER, 1787–1843, German composer and pianist.

	op.	
Double quintet, 2 groups, 2 v, vla, 2 vc, d mi	28	J. Schuberth & Co., 1863.

	op.	
2nd quintet, 2 v, vla, 2 vc, b mi	21	Hofmeister, Jurgenson.
3rd (*Antique*) quintet, 2 v, vla, 2 vc, F	22	Hofmeister.
4th quintet, 2 v, vla, 2 vc	23	Jurgenson.
5th quintet, 2 v, vla, 2 vc, F	24	Hofmeister, 1842; Jurgenson.
6th quintet, 2 v, vla, 2 vc, E flat	25	Hofmeister, 1842.
7th quintet, 2 v, vla, 2 vc, C	26	Hofmeister, 1842.
8th quintet, 2 v, vla, 2 vc, B flat	27	J. Schuberth & Co., 1862.
Quartet, str, D		Peters.

Gebel settled in Moscow, 1817, and died there. He organized chamber music séances, at which his works were played. The double quintet is, needless to say, a very rare combination.

GÉDALGE, André, 1856–1926, French composer and teacher.

Two sonatas, pf, v, G, a mi — opp. 12, 19 — Enoch.

Gédalge is the author of a remarkable *Traité de Fugue et de Contrepoint*, showing the close relationship of the art of Bach with modern writing, and revolutionizing the official system of education with the happiest results for most of the musicians of the present generation who studied under him.

The first sonata, in G major, opens with an allegro moderato e tranquillamente, a peaceful and poetic pastoral movement, notable for clarity and excellence of style. It is followed by a kind of rapid intermezzo in B flat (vivace), light and joyous, pleasing, and full of wit; and this again by a tranquil adagio non troppo (D major), in simple Lied form. The final presto con brio (G major) begins with a kind of popular dance, announced by the violin *solo*; it then passes to the piano, and after very varied but simple development the movement closes with a *saltarello*.

The second sonata has only three movements, but they are more fully developed and more complex than those of the preceding. The principal theme is announced in a slow introduction, which leads to a presto con fuoco, a most interesting and well balanced movement, with a strong rhythm reminiscent of Saint-Saëns. The second movement (E major) is a Lied, which is treated with distinction. The finale (molto vivace), in rondo form, has a refrain containing whirling semiquaver passages suggestive of a dance of dervishes. There is a certain unexpectedness in the returns of the refrain, while the couplets contain the most varied rhythmic devices, and the movement as a whole is full of life.

Gédalge was a skilled contrapuntist, with a real gift of rhythmic invention. Among French musicians his place is near that of Saint-Saëns.

Adolphe Piriou.

†GEISLER, Chr.

Sonata, pf, vla, d mi — op. 10 — Skandinavisk Musikförl., 1922.

GENARRO, Marcel.

Trio, fl, ob, cl, G — Evette & Schaeffer, 1922.

GENIN, T. (Junior).

Sextet, pf, fl, ob, cl, horn, fag — E flat — Eschig (Demets), 1906.

GENISCHTA, Joseph, b. 1810, Russian pianist and 'cellist.

Sonata, pf, vc (or v)	op. 7	Kistner.
Sonata, pf, vc	„ 9	„
Sonata, pf, vc, D	„ 13	Hofmeister, 1847.

Genischta's death date is uncertain, but he appears to have been living in 1860. (*Fétis*.) Schumann (*Gesammelte Schriften*) speaks of the sonata, op. 7, as 'lyrical and full of feeling', and deprecated its arrangement for violin, the work being originally composed exclusively for the 'cello.

GERBER, Julius.

2nd quartet, str, G — op. 19 — Kahnt, 1883.

* GERHARD, Roberto, b. 1896, composer of Swiss origin, born in Spain.

2nd trio, pf, v, vc — Senart, 1921.

Studied in Berlin and later with Felipe Pedrell, being the last pupil of the famous musicologist.

Gerhard has also written a string quartet (MS.).

†GERMAN, Sir Edward (E. G. Jones), b. 1862, English composer of light opera and incidental music for the theatre.

Suite, pf, v — Novello.

GERMAN AND AUSTRIAN CHAMBER MUSIC.

The beginning of German chamber music in the present sense of the term is generally dated back to about 1750, when Haydn made his first attempts in string quartet writing, and when the later sonata form began to be developed. In order, however, to understand the historic importance of Haydn's reforms, it is necessary to know something about the state of chamber music during the first half of the eighteenth century. Haydn did not by any means invent the new style of chamber music; the sonata da camera, for one, two, and three instruments with figured bass accompaniment had been cultivated by several generations of his predecessors. The suite or partita for several instruments, though generally orchestral in style, approaches chamber music in many cases, and is also to be considered as an ancestor of modern chamber music. The sonata da camera, with its serious musical style and its display of contrapuntal art, and the suite, with its popular dance melodies, are, to a certain extent, combined in Haydn's new sonata form, which also was foreshadowed in the works of the Mannheim school (Stamitz, Richter, Filtz, Cannabich, &c.), of the Viennese school (Monn, Wagenseil, Starzer, &c.), of C. P. E. Bach and others. Haydn was formerly also credited with the invention of the string quartet. Modern research, however, has shown that the *quadro* or string quartet, with or without basso continuo, is to be met with quite frequently as early as 1740 and even earlier. Dall' Abaco's *concerti a quattro da chiesa* (1712–14) are classical models of quartet writing in the form and style of the sonata da chiesa, though of course they were played more frequently in the chamber than in the church. Telemann's quadri are somewhat lighter in style. Tartini is one of the first composers to omit the basso continuo in his quadri.[1] Of late, string quartets of the Bavarian composer Placidus Camerloher (b. 1718) have been discovered, which are remarkably close to Haydn's style. Quartets of the Mannheim composers, Toëschi, Cannabich, of the Austrian composers, Zach and Wodiczka, and of C. P. E. Bach also show many traits similar to Haydn. Besides the sonata da camera and suite, the so-called 'cassation', the divertimento, the opera-sinfonia, and the concerto have also left their traces in the Haydn quartet. Many of Haydn's early quartets still bear names such as quadro, cassation, divertimento, and notturno, of which the last three are derived from the old orchestral suite. The cassation, with its predominance of minuet and march, is popular music, even more so than the suite, which in the hands of Bach, Handel, Couperin, and Rameau had reached too lofty a summit of art to appeal to simple folk. The same tendency towards simplicity and popular melody and the same reaction against artificial counterpoint are also to be perceived in the divertimento, serenata, and notturno.

The period about 1750 is a critical epoch in music. The great contrapuntal art of Bach and Handel had reached so sublime a height that progress in the same direction became impossible and a reaction was the natural consequence. In instrumental music this revolution took place slowly and gradually in many different places. Of all musicians participating in it Haydn was by far the greatest artist and, owing to his talent and the period in which he lived, the one best fitted to profit from all these new ideas. Thus he became the father of the classical Viennese style.

Following the new methods of the Mannheim school, especially of Carl Stamitz, Haydn did away with the basso continuo, and developed a new quartet style by individualizing the parts, instead of equalizing them as the contrapuntal style had done. He also adopted and improved the new sonata form, with its leading themes in the tonic and dominant, its working-out section in the middle, and its recapitulation. Though the chronology of Haydn's eighty-three quartets is not yet settled beyond dispute, one may nevertheless divide this great mass of them into two groups; the earlier group, consisting of thirty-eight quartets, embracing all those written before 1771, and the later group dating from 1781 till about 1800. In a letter to the prince of Oettingen-Wallerstein (quoted by Sandberger) Haydn remarks that his six new quartets (written in 1781, after a lapse of ten years in quartet composition) show an 'entirely new special style'.

The bulk of Haydn's trios for violin, 'cello, and piano is also to be attributed to the earlier epoch, before 1781; this is evident from the timid treatment of the 'cello part, which bears traces of the old basso continuo manner, and is hardly ever separated from the piano bass.

The most important German master of chamber music in the years 1760–80 (besides Haydn) was F. H. Richter of Mannheim, whose important string quartets (published by Riemann) appeared in the years 1767–71; two other composers of German origin, who influenced the young Mozart in London and in Paris, Johann Christian Bach and Schober, have also written remarkable chamber music in this epoch. J. C. Bach's op. 8 even clearly shows the modern type of quartet.

A new epoch of Haydn's chamber music is to be dated from the composition of his six quartets (1781) called *Jungfernquartette* or *Russian* or *Gli scherzi* by contemporaries. These quartets, Nos. 39–44, denote great progress, as compared with the earlier ones. They show a modern style in the thematic treatment, the dialogue, the peculiar mixture of popular melodic invention and contrapuntal writing, fully mastered new forms of the sonata, rondo, minuet, and song form.

About this time Mozart also becomes of prime importance in chamber music. His first string quartets were written in Italy in 1770, influenced by Italian models, perhaps Tartini, Sammartini, and others. But already, in 1773, he had produced in Vienna a set of quartets in contrapuntal style, which clearly reflect Haydn's six elaborate contrapuntal quartets of 1771 (Nos. 33–8). Haydn's new series of 1781 must also have excited Mozart's interest in the highest degree; this is proved by Mozart's quartets Nos. 14–19, written 1782–5 and dedicated to Haydn, with a celebrated preface (1 Sept., 1785) which expresses, in touching words, how much young Mozart feels himself indebted to father Haydn. From this time on Haydn's and Mozart's chamber compositions are inseparably intertwined. In subsequent years Mozart in his turn influenced his older friend, and Haydn's later quartets clearly show

[1] Prof. Adolf Sandberger: *Zur Geschichte des Haydn'schen Streichquartetts*, in *Gesammelte Aufsätze*, Munich, 1921.

how the refined art, the expressive tone, and romantic traits of Mozart gave him a new impetus, enriching his art without loss of any of its original freshness and individuality.

Mozart's quartets Nos. 14–19, though based on Haydn's manner, nevertheless contained so much new and unaccustomed musical matter that they were sharply criticized on their appearance, especially owing to the boldness of harmony and certain romantic traits of musical colour, as, for instance, the slow introduction to the C major quartet with its peculiar false relations. After these six quartets, which represent Mozart's climax of quartet writing, he produced only four more; three of these (Nos. 20–2), dedicated to Frederick William II, King of Prussia, are characterized by a concertante 'cello part, a compliment to the king, who was a talented 'cello player. Seven other quartets (Nos. 24–30) of the complete edition are partly divertimenti, partly written for flute or oboe solo with strings.

Mozart's nine quintets for strings, and the two for horn and strings and clarinet and strings (especially the former), are among the master's most mature compositions. They initiate a new species of chamber music, which was cultivated later all through the nineteenth century. The elegance and ease of Mozart's contrapuntal art is displayed in the quintets still more brilliantly than in the quartets. The celebrated quintet for clarinet and strings in A major is a worthy companion to this series. Two duos for violin and viola and the beautiful divertimento for violin, viola, and 'cello, complete the tale of Mozart's chamber music for strings alone.

Another important group is influenced in style and technical treatment by the employment of the piano. Forty-three sonatas, besides several sets of variations, for violin and piano, show that Mozart had a special predilection for this combination. The entire growth of Mozart's art is seen here, from the first attempts of the boy to the ultimate wisdom of the great master, from simple piano pieces with an almost superfluous violin part ad libitum, from piano duets with basso continuo for the left hand to an elaborate concertante technique, an enchanting romantic sound, and most refined harmonic treatment. The eight piano trios, two piano quartets, and the piano quintet with wind are the remaining compositions in this concertante style, in which the piano is often placed in opposition to the group of strings. This dialogue generally lacks the subtle contrapuntal treatment of the string quartet; but new charms are offered by the contrast of timbre between the piano and the body of strings or wind instruments. In style these compositions resemble Mozart's piano concertos, with those differences of style necessitated by the use of solo instruments instead of the orchestra.

In Haydn's later epoch, lasting more than a dozen years after Mozart's death, he was considerably influenced by Mozart. Haydn's historical and immortal merit has been to make the string quartet an exponent of the highest art, whereas formerly it had been rather light and popular, without special artistic pretensions. In this transmutation Haydn might not have reached his aim without the powerful impressions received from Mozart, in the refinement of writing, in the intensity and variety of expression and form. The quartets, opp. 50, 54, 55, 64, 71, 74, 76, 77, 103 (thirty-four in all), published between 1782 and 1806, bear witness to the truth of this statement. Unfortunately the complete edition of Haydn's works is still in course of preparation, and therefore it is very difficult to trace the hundreds of chamber music pieces, especially those of the earlier years. There are, for instance, no less than 125 trio divertimenti for baryton, viola, and 'cello, hardly accessible at all in modern editions. The eight violin sonatas, with piano accompaniment, are universally known; they do not, however, belong to Haydn's most representative works, in spite of their charming details.

Beethoven's earliest chamber music is written for wind instruments, in the manner of music for social entertainments—serenades and the like. The octet, op. 103, published by Beethoven in a string quintet arrangement as op. 4, the trio, op. 87, for 2 oboes and English horn, the sextets, opp. 71 and 81*b*, belong to this earliest group. A little later he favoured the combination of piano and wind instruments, found in the trio, op. 11, the quintet, op. 16, the horn sonata, op. 17, concluding with the famous septet, op. 20, for strings and wind, which may be considered as a precursor of the first symphony. More weighty, as regards musical contents, is another group of chamber compositions for piano and strings. In his earliest years he had several times attempted the piano quartet; later, however, he discarded all these and other juvenile efforts and turned definitely to the piano trio and violin sonata as being best adapted to his musical intentions. His op. 1, which marks the beginning of his mature works, consists of three trios of extraordinary musical value. Many years passed before he again took up trio writing in his middle period (1808–11) with the trios in D and E flat, op. 70, and the sublime B flat, op. 97, compositions which in their class have never been surpassed. The interval of fifteen years between the first and the last trios was filled out by many violin sonatas, in which Beethoven gives to both instruments a brilliant solo character foreign to the trios and quartets. Most of these ten sonatas were written between 1798 and 1803. They comprise three sonatas, op. 12, which in their contents and style belong to Beethoven's earliest efforts. The sonatas, opp. 23, 24, are more advanced in technical treatment, more mature; still more so the three sonatas, op. 30, and the climax is reached in the famous *Kreutzer* sonata, op. 47, which may be ranked among Beethoven's most powerful inspirations. The last violin sonata, op, 96, written in 1812, shows a very different style, less brilliant, more intimate, of a delicate poetic character akin to the style of the last epoch. Five 'cello sonatas, written in 1796, 1808, 1815, are widely different in style. The two sonatas, op. 5, are superior to the first violin sonatas, op. 12. Op. 69 is the most classical and finished of the series. The two fantasy sonatas, op. 102, are most interesting but also somewhat problematic specimens, on account of a certain discrepancy between constructive ideas and sound-effect.

Beethoven did not turn to the string quartet until he had tried his hand for a considerable time at the string trio, a combination little employed by Haydn and Mozart. Between 1792 and 1797 he wrote his op. 3, the serenade, op. 8, and the three trios, op. 9, all compositions of masterly skill and youthful freshness of melody. The six quartets, op. 18, which display Beethoven as a clearly defined personality, were not written until 1800. The next set, three quartets, op. 59, pass as much beyond his great predecessors as the piano sonatas, op. 53 and op. 57, written at the same time. In op. 59 everything is on a grander scale; the ideas shaped here have passed through a mind which has created the *Eroica* symphony, the opera *Fidelio*, &c. The string quartet has now assumed a different aspect for Beethoven, new possibilities have become manifest, rooted in the symphonic and concertante style of the violin sonatas. Op. 59 realizes these new problems with a magnificent power of invention, of construction, of emotion, while op. 74, the so-called 'harp quartet', is a somewhat modified companion to op. 59.

A new world again opens in the later quartets. The heroic and Dionysian accents of op. 59 are now abandoned. The quartet, op. 95, written in 1810, marks the close of the first period of quartet composition. This 'quartetto serioso', as Beethoven calls it, is a tragic poem of unheard-of vehemence and passion, at least in its first movement. Fifteen years separate this from the group of the last five quartets, opp. 127, 130, 131, 132, 135, and the fugue op. 133, in which Beethoven found new ways to express in music the mysteries of the world beyond the senses, and the metaphysical problems rooted in a profound though entirely unconventional religious feeling. The problems in form and expression evolved in these last quartets are of deepest interest now, a hundred years later, and these quartets are still the most modern music existing.

Chamber music in Vienna was, of course, not entirely monopolized by Haydn, Mozart, and Beethoven. Influenced by these great masters, there were talented composers who, though now forgotten, were famous and popular in their day. The most important of these was Karl von Dittersdorf (1739–99), a younger contemporary and intimate friend of Haydn, whose amiable string quartets are still played occasionally. He left string quintets, string quartets, trios for two violins and bass, and many sonatas for violin and piano. Ignaz Pleyel (1757–1831), Haydn's pupil, later settled in London and Paris, was perhaps the most popular orchestral and chamber music composer of his time, and wrote an enormous number of quartets, quintets, trios, sonatas, &c. His pleasing and smooth duos for two violins are used even now for the instruction of beginners. Leopold A. Koželuh (1752–1818), successor of Mozart as imperial chamber composer, an ill-reputed opponent to all three great masters of Vienna, was, nevertheless, a very successful composer, a specialist in trios, of which he wrote a great number. Emanuel Aloys Förster[1] (1748–1823) possessed higher artistic qualities than Pleyel and Koželuh. Mozart spoke with respect of Förster; Beethoven called him his 'old teacher' and sent him many pupils. His piano quartets and trios and his chamber music with wind instruments are not of special importance, but the string quartets and quintets are valuable compositions, influenced by Mozart and Beethoven, without being confined to mere imitation. The numerous sonatas, trios, quartets, &c., of J. N. Hummel, the celebrated pianist, Mozart's pupil, are also entirely forgotten now. J. L. Dussek (1760–1812), one of the best pianists of his age, also wrote chamber music of some importance about 1800. He also edited a number of trios, quartets, quintets, &c., of his talented pupil Prince Louis Ferdinand of Prussia, the admirer of Beethoven.

Franz Schubert, the great master of song, Beethoven's younger contemporary, is also of considerable importance in chamber music. Of his numerous trios, quartets, quintets, violin sonatas, &c., only a part has survived, whereas almost the entire work of Beethoven is even now of undiminished vitality. But the few surviving Schubert compositions have their place among the greatest productions of musical art. Schubert combines the intimate lyric beauty of Mozart with something of the monumental art of Beethoven, to which, for the first time in serious art, is added the popular Viennese note. Schubert's ideas of construction do not go beyond Beethoven's innovations, but in harmony he was a genial inventor of new charms who opened the way into a romantic wonderland, and his wealth of expressive and characteristic melody is unequalled. Two piano trios, opp. 99 and 100,

[1] Cp. the study on Förster by K. Weigl, *Sammelband der Internationalen Musik-Gesellschaft*, VI, 1904–5, p. 274.

the *Forellen* quintet, the octet, evidently an offspring of Beethoven's septet, about half a dozen string quartets, and the string quintet are Schubert's contributions of lasting value to chamber music.

The Romantic School.

In Schubert classical and romantic tendencies are fairly balanced. The romantic traits become more predominant in the chamber music of those masters who are considered the champions of romanticism.

Carl Maria von Weber, the creator of German romantic opera, is not of much significance in chamber music, though he left a number of trios, quartets, and variations. He favoured the combination of clarinet or flute with strings and piano, and, on account of this predilection for wind instruments, his trio for piano, flute, and 'cello, op. 63, and his clarinet quintet, op. 34, are occasionally heard.

Louis Spohr, the celebrated violinist, Weber's contemporary, is of greater importance in chamber music. His speciality is the double quartet, written for two quartets, as the old Venetian masters wrote for double chorus. His thirty-four string quartets (including six *Quatuors brillants* with a brilliant first violin part in the concerto style) are entirely forgotten now. But his nonet for strings and wind is sometimes played.

Mendelssohn and Schumann represent the full flower of romanticism in German chamber music. Mendelssohn is the more musicianly of the two, more skilful and better taught, Schumann more frequently inspired in his music. The present attitude towards these masters is that more has really survived of Schumann's chamber music than of Mendelssohn's much more numerous efforts. Mendelssohn's seven string quartets, written with admirable art both of form and sound, are nowadays very unjustly shelved. The Joachim Quartet occasionally played the first quartet in E flat, op. 12, and the fifth one in E minor, op. 44, No. 2. Two string quintets, opp. 18 and 87, share the fate of the quartets, in spite of their many masterly traits. The most genial composition of Mendelssohn, however, is his octet for strings, written when he was about seventeen years old, at the same time as the *Midsummer-Night's Dream* overture. The octet is not often played, because the chance of combining two quartets of high rank is of rare occurrence. But whenever the octet is heard it appears fresh, full of charming sound, fantastic, exuberant, and original in invention, of impeccable mastery in construction. Here Mendelssohn's individual note, the fairy scherzo, breezy, light, and fantastic, is heard in full perfection. Two piano trios, in D minor and C minor, and the second 'cello sonata, op. 58, are generally recognized standard works of lasting value.

Robert Schumann's technical inferiority to Mendelssohn is evident in his treatment of form, of polyphony in the string quartets, and in the dominating part of the piano in sonatas, trios, and other compositions, the strings being generally a mere doubling of the melodic line, a mere colouristic imprint, or the piano a mere accompaniment of the strings. In spite of this lack of the purest chamber music style, Schumann's music has survived by virtue of its powerful musical inspiration. The piano quintet and piano quartet, both in E flat, opp. 44 and 47, enjoy deserved popularity. The three string quartets, op. 41, also maintain, even now, a prominent place. Of the three piano trios, the one in D minor, op. 63, ranks highest, and must be counted among the best works of the type. The other trios, opp. 80 and 110, bear the signs of Schumann's declining powers and are rarely played. Two violin sonatas, opp. 105 and 121, are fine works, of striking originality. A somewhat lighter vein of invention and treatment prevails in the charming *Phantasiestücke*, op. 88, for piano, violin, 'cello; the *Märchenerzählungen*, op. 132, for clarinet, viola, piano; the *Märchenbilder*, op. 113, for piano and violin or viola. The remaining pieces are of less importance: adagio and allegro for horn and piano, op. 70; *Phantasiestücke* for clarinet and piano, op. 73; three romances for oboe and piano, op. 94; five *Stücke im Volkston* for 'cello and piano, op. 102.

Mendelssohn and Schumann have considerably influenced German chamber music, and from about 1840 to 1880 especially Leipzig became the centre of the Mendelssohn–Schumann school. Of this school the most important composer was Robert Volkmann, whose admirable B flat minor trio, op. 5, in particular has survived. Occasionally one or the other of his string quartets is heard, hardly ever any of his other chamber compositions. The Leipzig school is represented by composers like Ferdinand Hiller, Max Bruch, Carl Reinecke, and Salomon Jadassohn (the canon specialist). Since about 1890 the Brahms influence became more and more predominant in Leipzig, for instance, in the chamber music of composers like Julius Klengel, Hans Sitt, Julius Roentgen (now in Amsterdam), and Stephan Krehl.

Johannes Brahms is, in the writer's opinion, the greatest master of chamber music in modern times. His music, based on the art of the Viennese classics, of Schubert, Schumann, and Mendelssohn, is still thoroughly individual and in the highest degree masterly in form, construction, and style. To his age he has set the standard of what modern chamber music should be; he has given a model which has been imitated in Germany and many other countries, without losing its power, for the last half-century. Classical sonata form is the basis of Brahms's music, but the form in his hands is considerably modified by romantic tendencies and modern traits; but these tendencies are as distant from romantic vagueness of form as from modern impressionist, colouristic methods. Brahms's neo-romanticism reconciles plastic classical form with romantic expression. His strong, subtle sense of rhythm meant the rediscovery of an almost lost art of rhythm. Of his twenty-four chamber works not a single one has yet been forgotten. It is difficult to attribute to any of these works a higher rank than to the others. With the exception, perhaps, of the clarinet trio, op. 114, and the clarinet sonatas, op. 120 (which are also fine works, only somewhat less inspired), Brahms's chamber music is remarkably uniform in its high level, whether one considers the string quartets or the sextets, the quintets for strings alone or those with piano or clarinet, the piano quartets, the trios for piano, violin, and 'cello, the violin sonatas or the 'cello sonatas. There is everywhere a noble elevation of ideas, virile strength and profundity of expression, great variety of moods and perfect mastery of the art of composition. Brahms's chamber music is perhaps the most valuable part of the master's art, and one of the few glories of German music in the second half of the nineteenth century, maintaining almost alone, with high honours, the cause of absolute music against the gigantic Wagnerian art of musical drama. The work of Brahms's genial contemporaries, Bruckner and Hugo Wolf, became really effective only in the twentieth century. Brahms, born and educated in North Germany and finding his permanent home in Vienna, produced, especially in his chamber music, a synthesis of North and South German with Austrian mentality, which is unique.

From about 1880 all chamber music in Germany is in some way indebted to Brahms, who became the chief of a school no less extended than that of Schumann and Mendelssohn. Vienna and Berlin became the centres of the Brahms tradition.

In Vienna the two violent adversaries of Brahms, Bruckner and Wolf, do not really belong to the masters of chamber music. Nevertheless, Bruckner wrote, besides his monumental symphonies and masses, a solitary string quintet of extraordinary value, and Hugo Wolf, the master of modern song, has left an ambitious, though immature, string quartet and the graceful *Italian Serenade*, arranged by himself for string quartet from the original version for small orchestra.

Other notable composers around Brahms in Vienna were: Karl Goldmark (two suites for violin and piano, trio, quartet, quintet), Robert Fuchs, Ignaz Brüll.

In Berlin, Friedrich Kiel (1821–1885), now unjustly forgotten, was considered a real master. He wrote about as much chamber music as Brahms, to whom he may be compared in the mastery of his writing, though hardly in the power and individuality of his melodic invention. Joseph Joachim, though not himself a composer of chamber music, was for nearly forty years the champion of chamber music in Berlin, and all composers of importance in Berlin were in close contact with him. Here Max Bruch and Friedrich Gernsheim must be mentioned, Bruch with two string quartets and a trio, Gernsheim with about twenty works. Woldemar Bargiel, Clara Schumann's step-brother (three trios, four string quartets, octet), belongs to the Schumann school; Heinrich von Herzogenberg is closely allied to Brahms; Philipp Rüfer and Philipp and Xaver Scharwenka combine German traits with Belgian and Polish temperament; Wilhelm Berger and Robert Kahn are talented Brahms disciples;' Georg Schumann continues this line, also Hugo Kaun, the latter with a Wagnerian touch.

Two contemporaries of Brahms must be mentioned here. Joachim Raff (1822–1882), also a most prolific composer of chamber music, was famous in his time. In close connexion with Liszt in Weimar, he utilized the novel methods of the Liszt and Wagner school with discretion in chamber music, giving a modern surface to his works, which were otherwise solidly constructed on a classical basis. Hermann Goetz (1840–1876) was an artist of very considerable talent, not only as a symphonic and dramatic composer, but also in chamber music. A trio, quartet, and quintet give evidence of the exceptional faculties of this artist, who died young.

The MUNICH SCHOOL begins with Franz Lachner (1803–1893), Schubert's friend, also a most prolific composer of chamber music, endowed with a gift of popular melody and considerable contrapuntal skill. Joseph Rheinberger (1839–1901) was a famous organist and teacher of composition in Munich. His numerous sonatas, trios, quartets, &c., show romantic spirit and exceptional contrapuntal ability. His pupil, Louis Thuille (1861–1907), was likewise a teacher of great reputation and a composer of effective chamber music of fairly modern tendency. His sextet for piano and wind instruments, his piano quintet, violin and 'cello sonatas have been much played in Germany. The great master, Richard Strauss, also started as a member of the Munich School. His chamber music, which is early work, is effective, but not as characteristic as his more mature art. The 'cello sonata, op. 6, violin sonata, op. 18, and the piano quartet, op. 13, are still played, whereas the youthful string quartet, op. 2, is hardly ever heard nowadays.

GERMAN CHAMBER MUSIC IN THE TWENTIETH CENTURY.

Max Reger and Arnold Schönberg are the most important leaders with new tendencies in modern chamber music. Both artists have become the founders of schools. While the Reger school is already losing influence,

Schönberg is still very active, and his ideas are continually gaining ground with the youngest generation. Max Reger's chamber music is the continuation of Brahms's art, primarily by complexity in harmony and rhythm. Compared with Brahms's, Reger's music is less plastic in melody, less direct and distinct in expression. But it gains many new shades of colour and expression by its subtle, sometimes exaggerated, complexities of rhythm, and by its Wagnerian chromaticism, which produces vagueness of tonality, or rather extends the boundaries of tonality into regions formerly not accessible. Reger's chamber music covers a vast ground comprising about forty different compositions. Only a small part of these numerous works has, however, taken root in German musical life; in fact, only a selection of Reger's later compositions, starting with the violin sonata op. 72, is nowadays to be heard. Those works which are really a gain to the treasure of German chamber music are the string quartets, opp. 74, 109, 121, the violin sonata, op. 84, the little serenade and trio, opp. 77*a* and 77*b*, the *Suite im alten Stil* for violin and piano, op. 93, the piano quartets, opp. 113 and 133, the sextet, op. 118, the violin sonatas, opp. 122 and 139, the 'cello sonata, op. 116, and the clarinet sonata, op. 107.

Compared with Reger's immense activity, Arnold Schönberg's chamber compositions are few in number, but of great weight. Each new composition brings a change of style and new ideas of construction. Schönberg started with his string sextet *Verklärte Nacht*, op. 4, entirely under the influence of Wagner's *Tristan* style. The first string quartet, op. 7, takes its starting-point from Beethoven's last quartets, adding the chromatic Wagnerian harmony and a complicated plan of construction. The *Kammersinfonie*, op. 9, for fifteen solo instruments, adds a new kind of melodic invention, based on the interval of the fourth, on the whole-tone scale, a harmony tending towards what is generally misnamed 'atonality'. The second string quartet, op. 10, shows an extremely subtle art of thematic construction, new constructive ideas, and a further progress into 'atonal' harmony. *Pierrot Lunaire*, op. 21, for declamation and five instrumental players (eight instruments), combines all the novel effects of Schönberg's style with a contrapuntal complexity almost without parallel in modern times. *Pierrot Lunaire* is certainly Schönberg's most characteristic and also his most curious and fascinating composition. The latest phase in Schönberg's system, the so-called 'twelve-tone' technique, is applied with strictness in the quintet for wind instruments, op. 26, and in the third string quartet.

Chamber music in Vienna is at present somewhat influenced by the radical Schönberg tendencies. The direct pupils of Schönberg, Alban Berg, A. Webern, Egon Wellesz, have already acquired a reputation as composers of chamber music. Another Viennese group, less radical in its tendencies, is centred around the celebrated Vienna Conservatorium, where Franz Schreker and Joseph Marx have been teaching since about 1910. Schreker, primarily an opera composer, has contributed to chamber music a remarkable *Kammersymphonie*, full of strange and fascinating colouristic effects. Joseph Marx, a follower of Hugo Wolf, is a belated romanticist in his chamber music. Erich Korngold, celebrated years ago as a prodigy in composition, has written much chamber music, in the manner of the Viennese modern tradition (Brahms, Mahler, Strauss) rather than in the ultra-modern Schönberg style. Egon Kornauth is a talented new-comer, similar to Korngold in his tendencies. Julius Bittner, Felix Weingartner, Paul Pisk, Felix Petyrek, Karl Weigl, Bruno Weigl are some of the very many Viennese chamber music composers of talent.

Hans Pfitzner occupies a peculiar position in Germany. One might call him the last romanticist of weight. An adversary to all radical modern tendencies, he is a descendant of Schumann in his art, possessing a certain portion of Schumann's poetic tendencies, blended, however, with considerable dryness. Nevertheless, he is a master, and his chamber music is full of strong and remarkable episodes, though a flawless masterpiece is rarely to be found among his works. He stands midway between the romantic and the modern schools, combining a peculiar modern flavour essentially his own with a musical basis compounded of Schumannesque, Brahmsian, and Wagnerian traits. His chamber music comprises six works: 'cello sonata, op. 1, trio, op. 8, string quartet, op. 13, piano quintet, op. 20, violin sonata, op. 27, and second string quartet, op. 36.

Frankfort-on-the-Main has also been the centre of a remarkable school of chamber music in connexion with the excellent conservatorium. This school, founded by Joachim Raff, was continued by Bernhard Scholz, a composer of rather conservative tendencies, Ivan Knorr and his pupil Bernhard Sekles, a composer of refined and somewhat exotic taste, and Arnold Mendelssohn of Darmstadt, a cultivated musician of Brahmsian tendencies. Hermann Zilcher, closely related to Pfitzner as an artist, is also a prominent member of the Frankfort school.

The most successful composer of the youngest generation has been Paul Hindemith, pupil of Sekles and Mendelssohn in Frankfort. His sound musicianship, vivid temperament, sense of humour, and virtuosity of writing place him near Richard Strauss, but at the same time he approaches Stravinsky rather more than Schönberg in daring modernistic experiments. He is at his best in his four string quartets and the string trio, op. 34. But his several concertos and song-cycles with chamber music accompaniment and his sonatas and suites have also made the round of the concert halls. His writing is very unequal, an admirable score being found side by side with an eccentric composition abounding in bad taste.

Ernest Krenek, pupil of Schreker at the Berlin Hochschule, has for some years been Hindemith's rival as exponent of the advanced linear contrapuntal writing, of grotesque, parodistic tendencies, and of atonal harmony.

Berlin has of late become an important centre of modern chamber music. Ferruccio Busoni, though Italian by birth, passed the greater part of his life in Berlin, and his chamber music is rather German than Italian. His contributions to chamber music are several string quartets and violin sonatas. The second sonata in E minor, op. 36*a*, is, in particular, a masterpiece of lasting value. Of Busoni's pupils, Philipp Jarnach and Kurt Weill have been much noticed of late; also Max Butting, Heinz Tiessen, Erich Sternberg, and Hugo Leichtentritt are all more or less inclined towards modern problems; others like Paul Juon, Max Trapp, James Simon, and Edvard Moritz are somewhat more cautious in their treatment of these same problems.

Joseph Haas, Hermann Unger, Adolf Busch, and Siegfried Karg-Elert are more or less descendants of Max Reger. In southern Germany, Ernst Toch has been specially successful during the last few years as one of the strongest exponents of modern tendencies. Julius Weismann in Freiburg, August Reuss and Heinrich Kaspar Schmidt, both members of the Munich School, belong to the Pfitzner group in their tendencies. Ewald Straesser in Cologne and Friedrich E. Koch in Berlin maintain the Brahms ideal.

Paul Graener in Leipzig shows moderate modernism, Erwin Lendvai treats the linear style with mastery in his trios, quartet, and quintet.

Heinrich Kaminski, who is strongly influenced by Bach and Bruckner, strives towards a modernization of the old contrapuntal art.

A great number of other composers of talent might still be mentioned, as Germany has produced abundance of chamber music during the last 150 years. The main intention of this survey, however, must be kept in mind: to show the lines of development, the different tendencies, and the various schools. The result is that Beethoven remains by far the greatest master of chamber music, and that the problems set in his last works are still unexhausted, whereas the romantic epoch has left but few problems likely to be fertile for our age. Brahms, more than any other artist, has summed up the essential values of romantic chamber music; Schubert, Schumann, and Mendelssohn have left to the world the most fragrant and precious blossoms of romantic art, while Wagner's and Liszt's influence on German chamber music has been but slight. Modern French impressionism has gained little ground in German chamber music. As to the efforts of the younger generation, it is too early to pronounce a judgement on the lasting value of their radical experiments. It seems certain, however, that the extremely energetic labour of our contemporaries has shown many new possibilities of sound effect, that polyphony, harmonic treatment, rhythmical problems, and melodic theory have received a considerable impetus. A marvellous technical equipment lies ready for use for the modern genius able to express great, new, and powerful ideas.

Hugo Leichtentritt.

GERMAN AND AUSTRIAN PERFORMING ORGANIZATIONS.

(1) General Survey

For the last hundred years at least chamber music organizations have been a most important factor in the musical life of Germany, Austria, and Hungary. The number of quartet and trio organizations is consequently so great that it is hardly possible to give an exhaustive list. Up to about 1890 only the most important organizations can be enumerated here; it has, however, been the aim of the present article to give an approximately complete list of all societies of note since about 1900.

Professional chamber music organizations began to acquire importance in Germany only about 1800, in consequence of the production of the chamber works of the great classical masters and the development of public concerts. The earliest Quartet of high rank was perhaps the Rasoumovsky Quartet in Vienna, patronized by Count Rasoumovsky (well known from biographies of Beethoven), and before him by Prince Lichnowsky. Schuppanzigh, Mayseder, Weiss, Linke (later Kraft) were the members of this Quartet, famous from about 1805 to 1825 for its interpretation of Beethoven's, Haydn's, and Mozart's quartets. The most celebrated Quartet in Germany before 1850 was the Müller Quartet in Brunswick, consisting of the four brothers Müller: Karl Friedrich (1797–1873), Georg (1808–1855), Gustav (1799–1855), Theodor (1802–1875). From 1831 to 1855 the Müller Quartet had no serious rival in Europe and was heard in many countries. (Cf. L. Köhler, *Die Gebrüder Müller und das Streichquartett* (1858), and Ernst Stier, *Das Streichquartett der Gebrüder Müller*, in *Braunschweigisches Archiv*, July, 1913.) The Younger Müller Quartet was formed, in 1855, by the four sons of Karl Friedrich Müller: Karl Müller-Berghaus (1829–1907), Hugo (1832–1886), Bernhard (1825–1895), Wilhelm (1834–1907). This Younger Müller Quartet was resident in Meiningen, Wiesbaden, and Rostock, and was active from 1855 to 1873. During the later years Karl Müller, the first violin, was replaced by Leopold Auer (now living in America). Another Quartet of considerable reputation was the GEBRÜDER HERRMANN QUARTET, which, however, had neither a member by the name of Herrmann nor four brothers in its ranks. It consisted of Jakob Zeugheer, J. Wex (later Anton Popp), Karl Baader, Joseph Lidel. From 1824 to 1830 the Quartet was heard all over Germany and Western Europe. Zeugheer was from 1831 orchestral conductor and teacher in Manchester and Liverpool.

Louis Spohr, the great violinist and composer, was also a passionate devotee of quartet playing, though he hardly ever in his long public career travelled with a permanent quartet. His partners were generally chosen from the best musicians in the many cities where he gave concerts. At his permanent home in Cassel he gave public quartet rehearsals for many years until 1850; in private he continued his 'Quartettkränzchen' until much later.

One of the earliest Quartets was that of the BROTHERS BOHRER from Munich, who had sensational success in 1805 in Vienna, even as boys at the ages of from 9 to 14 years. Peter and Franz died in 1805; the two remaining brothers Anton, the violinist (b. 1791), and Max, the 'cellist (b. 1793), became soloists of European fame. Chamber music was, nevertheless, one of their chief interests, and with the assistance of their wives, the sisters Dülken from Munich, excellent pianists, and others they did much for classical chamber music, especially in Paris.

In Vienna the HELLMESBERGER QUARTET, founded in 1849 (Joseph Hellmesberger, Durst, Heissler, Schlesinger), acquired a great reputation. In 1870 Joseph Hellmesberger the younger entered his father's Quartet as 2nd violin; in 1883 his brother Ferdinand succeeded Schlesinger as 'cellist; Adolf Brodsky was for some time also a member.

The so-called FLORENTINE QUARTET, famous between 1866 and 1880, when it was disbanded, was founded in Florence by Jean BECKER (*q.v.*), who chose as his partners Enrico Masi, L. Chiostri, Fr. Hilpert (since 1875 L. Spitzer-Hegyesi).

The culture of German chamber music finds its centre in the JOACHIM QUARTET, which for nearly forty years was heard in almost all European countries, always led by Joachim until a few months before his death (1907), though the other members were changed several times during its long existence. In his earlier years Joachim for some time played the 2nd violin in the BEETHOVEN QUARTET SOCIETY, Ernst being the leader, Wieniawski and Piatti the other members. The permanent Joachim Quartet was founded in Berlin in 1869, with Schiever, de Ahna, W. Müller. In 1871 de Ahna, Rappoldi, W. Müller were Joachim's partners; in 1877 Wirth replaced Rappoldi at the viola desk; in 1897 Robert Hausmann the 'cellist replaced Müller; Johannes Kruse succeeded de Ahna 1892–1897, and was himself replaced by Carl Halir after 1897. Andreas Moser, Hugo Dechert, Percy Such were regular participants as 2nd viola and 2nd 'cellist in quintets and sextets; Heinrich Barth assisted at the piano for decades.

In Leipzig chamber music was cultivated with redoubled zeal after the foundation of the Conservatorium (1843) and during the activity of Mendelssohn as director of the *Gewandhaus Concerts*. Since 1836 Ferdinand DAVID was leader of an excellent Quartet; Uhlrich, Queisser, and Grenser were his partners during the first years.

The Quartet of the brothers SCHROEDER (founded in Sondershausen in 1871: Herrmann, Franz, Alwin, Karl) was well known in Germany for a number of years.

The last generation, from about 1890 to 1914, had arrived at a summit of chamber-music culture in Germany and Austria. Numerous organizations of high rank carried the message of classical and romantic chamber music from the big centres, like Berlin, Vienna, Leipzig, Dresden, Frankfort, &c., to the smaller towns. The most prominent of these flourishing organizations may be named here.

In Berlin the JOACHIM QUARTET was of course leading, but it did not by any means absorb the entire interest of the public. Next to it the HALIR QUARTET (Halir, Exner, Markees (later Müller), Dechert), the TRIO BARTH, Wirth, Hausmann, the TRIO SCHUMANN, Halir, Dechert, were highly esteemed. Other quartets and trios of note in Berlin were: the GUSTAV HOLLAENDER QUARTET; the DESSAU QUARTET; the brothers BOHRISCH QUARTET; the MARTEAU QUARTET (Marteau, Reymond (later van Laar), Pahnke (later Birkigt), Rehberg (later Becker); the DUTCH QUARTET (van Veen, Feltzer, Ruinen, van Lier); the DUTCH TRIO (van Bos, van Veen, van Lier); the LOEVENSOHN QUARTET (van Laar, Hait, Kutschka, Marix Loevensohn), which rendered such important services to the cause of modern music; the PHILHARMONIC TRIO (Gerhard, Witek, Malkin), the Trios LAMOND, WITTENBERG, MALKIN; SCHNABEL, WITTENBERG, HEKKING; SCHNABEL, FLESCH, BECKER; the WITTENBERG QUARTET; the WALDEMAR-MEYER QUARTET; the concerts ZAJIC, GRÜNFELD, fashionable for decades; the HESS QUARTET (Hess, Exner, Müller, Dechert); the KLINGLER QUARTET.

In Dresden the PETRI QUARTET (Petri, Warwas, Spitzner, Wille) was the leading organization, enjoying a great reputation all over Germany; the LEWINGER QUARTET had also a high reputation.

In Leipzig the GEWANDHAUS QUARTET (with varying members, for many years Wollgandt, Blümle, Herrmann, Klengel) must be ranked highest; next to it came the ARNO HILF

QUARTET, the ROESGEN-HAMAN QUARTET, and the BRODSKY QUARTET.

Frankfort had its celebrated HEERMANN QUARTET (Hugo Heermann, Bassermann, Naret-Koning, Hugo Becker), active from 1890 to 1906 (visited London); the MUSEUMS QUARTET; the REBNER QUARTET; the FRANKFORT TRIO (Friedberg, Rebner, Hegar).

In Munich the AHNER QUARTET and the KILIAN-KIEFER QUARTET, the BLÄSER-VEREIN (founded by Richard Strauss's father, the horn-player), were of local importance.

In Western Germany the GÜRZENICH QUARTET in Cologne (varying members) was famous.

In Vienna the ROSÉ QUARTET has, from about 1885 to the present time (1928), acquired a unique position, comparable only with the Joachim Quartet in Berlin. Two other Quartets of high rank represented Viennese chamber music up to the beginning of the war, 1914: the PRILL QUARTET and the Quartet FITZNER, WEISSGERBER, CZERNY, WALTER.

An important figure in the decade 1904–1914 in German chamber music was Max Reger, who played his own works many hundred times in concerts all over Germany and Austria. Reger was never a member of a particular ensemble; he has played as pianist with most of the Quartets of rank in Germany. Marteau was frequently his partner.

HUGO LEICHTENTRITT.

Some further organizations are mentioned in Bachmann's *Encyclopedia of the Violin.*

(2) PRESENT-DAY ORGANIZATIONS

GERMANY

1. BERLIN:

(*a*) *Quartets:*

ISSAY BARMAS: Willy Petereins, Otto Klust, Fritz Deckert. Founded 1920. Known for its fine performances of works by modern Russian composers.

BEATRICE BENTZ: Hilde Schirmer, Lissy Entchoven, Lena von Hippel. Devoted to modern music.

BRÜDER POST: Four brothers—Max, Willy, Arthur, Richard. Founded in 1907. Performs chiefly classical programmes. This Quartet is said to have the most valuable collection of stringed instruments.

AUGUST BRUNIER: Margarethe Schmiedt, Karla Hoeckér, Hans Helmut Chemin Petit. Restricts itself chiefly to modern music.

DAMECKE QUARTET.

RUDOLF DEMAN: Wilhelm Cavallery, Willibald Wagner, Carl Deckert. Chiefly classical music.

FIEDEMANN QUARTET.

GUARNERI QUARTET: David Karpilovsky, Mauritz Stromfeld, Hermann Spitz, Walther Lutz. Has travelled extensively. Performs both classical and modern works. This Quartet is one of the most successful of chamber music organizations, and is known for its ensemble playing.

GUSTAV HAVEMANN: Georg Kniestädt, Hans Mahlke, Adolf Steiner; Rudolf Schmidt (pf.). Founded in 1921. Has achieved fame through its excellent ensemble playing.

HEKKING QUARTET.

KLAVET QUARTET.

KARL KLINGLER: Richard Heber, Fridolin Klingler, Max Baldner (who succeeded von Mendelssohn). Founded in 1906. Original personnel: K. Klingler, Joseph Rywkine, F. Klingler, Arthur Williams. Has toured nearly all European countries and won international fame. Is chiefly devoted to the works of old masters.

LOUIS VAN LAAR: Hans Ortleb, Fritz Laur, Ernst Silberstein. Formed in 1925. Its chief aim is the rendering of works of the French Impressionistic School.

NICHOLAS LAMBINON: Adolf Weger, Frieda Mosheim, Gottfried Zeelander. Founded in 1920. Gave a first performance (1921) of Ernest Krenek's C major string quartet at the Deutsche Tonkünstler Fest in Nuremberg.

MEISEL QUARTET.

LEOPOLD PREMYSLAV: Johannes Lasovski, Karl Reitz, Eugenie Premyslav. Has toured the East—China, Japan, India—and now devotes itself to the performance of modern German composers.

RADNITZ QUARTET.

RESKE QUARTET.

CHARLOTTE ROSEN: Margarethe Rawack, Gertrud Walter Kurau, Ellen Drobatschevsky.

SANDER QUARTET.

THERESE PETZKO SCHUBERT: Jadwiga Elsner, Jaga Stein, Lore Winkler. A women's organization with a mixed programme of old and new music.

SEIFFERT QUARTET.

VELDEN QUARTET.

VLADYSLAV WAGHALTER: Emil Kornsand, Hans Kraus, Adolf Krips. Founded in 1918. Has toured most countries of Europe.

WIETROWETZ QUARTET.

(*b*) *Trios:*

DAHLKE TRIO.

HEKKING TRIO.

KREUTZER: Wolfsthal, Piatigorsky.

MAAS: Andrée, Peschel.

MAHLKE TRIO: the original form of the Havemann Quartet, with Rudolf Schmid as pianist, who also joins the Quartet on occasions.

MAYER-MAHR: Wittenberg, Grünfeld.

SCHUMANN: Hess, Wille.

JONAS STOCKHAUSEN: Voigtländer, Stoltz-Premyslav (women).

(*c*) *Miscellaneous:*

QUINTET OF WIND INSTRUMENTS OF THE BERLIN STATE OPERA: Luther (fl.), Schreiber (oboe), Conrad (clar.), Glass (bassoon), Böttcher (horn), J. Simon (pf.).

SEXTET OF WIND INSTRUMENTS OF THE BERLIN STATE OPERA: Prill (fl.), Flemming (oboe),

Kohl (clar.), Rembt (horn), Scheiwein (bassoon), Flemming-Horing (pf.).

WIND INSTRUMENTS ENSEMBLE OF THE MUNICIPAL OPERA HOUSE: consists of flute, oboe, clarinet, bassoon, horn, piano.

CHAMBER MUSIC SOCIETY OF THE BERLIN STATE ORCHESTRA: strings, woodwind, horn, piano. Eleven members.

CHAMBER MUSIC SOCIETY OF THE BERLIN MUNICIPAL OPERA: strings, woodwind, horn, piano. Ten members.

2. AIX-LA-CHAPELLE (AACHEN):

AACHEN STRING QUARTET: Kleeman, Goebel, Fischer, Bogner.

AACHEN TRIO: Schnitzler, Kleeman, Bogner.

3. ALTONA:

OTTO F. NIEMAND TRIO.

4. AUGSBURG:

BOTHE QUARTET.

PAEPKE QUARTET.

STRING QUARTET OF THE CONSERVATORIUM.

AUGSBURG CHAMBER MUSIC ASSOCIATION.

WIND ENSEMBLE.

5. BARMEN:

BARMEN STRING QUARTET.

ANTON SCHOENMAHER: Ludwig Goebel, Karl Wilke, Erich Wilke.

SIEWERT QUARTET.

WESTDEUTSCHES TRIO.

BLÄSERKAMMERMUSIK VEREINIGUNG (6 instr.).

6. BENTHEN:

KAMMERMUSIK VEREINIGUNG (Aug. Sauer).

7. BIELEFELD:

BENDA STRING QUARTET.

BIELEFELD STRING QUARTET.

BENDA TRIO.

BENDA STRING TRIO.

PÜTTBACH: Schaefer, Becker.

8. BOCHUM:

HOFMANN QUARTET.

STRING QUARTET ENSEMBLE.

TREICHLER QUARTET.

WIND ENSEMBLE.

9. BONN:

GRÜMMER QUARTET.

10. BRUNSWICK (Braunschweig):

WACHSMUTT QUARTET.

SCHACHT: Glemsa, Steinhage (Trio).

11. BREMEN:

BREMER STRING QUARTET: Plate, Schiffmann, Schutz, Beck.

12. BRESLAU:

MAXIMILIAN HENNIG: Bernhard Kunze, Bruno Janz, Fritz Binnovski.

SCHLESISCHES STRING QUARTET.

BECKER TRIO.

BRONISLAV POZNIAK: Carl Freund, Joseph Schuster.

13. CASSEL:

CASSEL STRING QUARTET.

14. CHEMNITZ:

STÄDTISCHE KAMMERMUSIK VEREINIGUNG (str. quartet and pf.: O. Malata).

HALKE TRIO.

BLÄSERVEREINIGUNG (5 wind instr. and pf.).

15. COBLENZ:

STRING QUARTET OF THE COBLENZ ORCHESTRA.

BLÄSERVEREINIGUNG.

16. COBURG:

BOCHRÖDER QUARTET.

17. COLOGNE:

(*a*) *Quartets:*

H. ANDERS: M. Topstädt, Focco Klimmerboon, Karl Schaeffer.

GÜRZENICH QUARTET: Bram-Elderling, C. Körner, H. Zitzmann, Karl Hesse. The oldest chamber music Quartet in the Rhineland. Performs exclusively classical music. Zimmermann and Feuermann have also taken part.

OPERA HOUSE QUARTET: Walter and Mme Bussin, M. Schulze-Prisca, Erich Kraack, M. Schneider.

(*b*) *Trios:*

FASSBENDER TRIO.

GÜRZENICH TRIO: Lazzaro Uzielli, Bram Elderling, Grümmer.

RAABE TRIO.

BLÄSERKAMMERMUSIK VEREINIGUNG (5 wind instr. and pf.).

ERSTE KÖLNER BLÄSERVEREINIGUNG (5 wind instr. and pf.).

18. DARMSTADT:

(*a*) *Quartets:*

ADOLF BUSCH: G. Andreasson, Doktor, Paul Grümmer. Founded in 1919. Herr Busch, an exceptionally fine violinist, was heard in London (1927).

OTTO DRUMM: Oskar Schneidhauser, Rudolf Sprenger, Franz Andrae.

PAUL SCHNURRBUSCH: Karl Jaeger, Wilhelm Horn, Konrad Klammer.

(*b*) *Trios:*

BUSCH TRIO: Rudolf Lerkin, Adolf Busch, H. Busch.

JOSEF ROSENSTOCK: Otto Drumm, Franz Andrae.

(*c*) *Wind:*

BLÄSERVEREINIGUNG (5 wind instr.).

19. DESSAU:

DONATH: Lux, Weber (Trio).

CHAMBER MUSIC SOCIETY OF THE FRIEDRICHS-THEATER.

20. DORTMUND:

DORTMUND STRING QUARTET.

VAN KEMPEN QUARTET.

SCHMIDT-REINECKE QUARTET.

DORTMUND TRIO.

21. DRESDEN:

BÄRTICH: Wunderlich, Rokohl, Schilling.

DRESDEN STRING QUARTET: Gustav Fritzsche, Fritz Schneider, Hans Riphahn, Alex. Kropholler. Founded in 1922. Performs regularly the entire chamber music works of Beethoven.

Has also given many first performances of modern works. Has toured all over Europe.

STRIEGLER-VEREINIGUNG FÜR KAMMERMUSIK: Johann Striegler, Dusedau, Seifert, Zenka, Kurt Striegler (pf.).

DRESDEN TRIO: F. Wagner, Bärtich, G. Wille. Chiefly modern works.

MODERN TRIO: Klingler, E. Warnas, Zenker. Chiefly modern works.

BLÄSERQUINTETT DER STAATSOPER (5 wind instr.).

ERSTES BLÄSERQUINTETT DER DRESDNER STAATSOPER (5 instr.).

22. DUISBURG:

DUISBURG STRING QUARTET: Grevesmühl, Spindler, Hilbert, Franke.

KOEHLER-HEDLER QUARTET.

NIEDERRHEINISCHES STREICHQUARTETT.

NIEDERRHEINISCHES TRIO.

23. DÜSSELDORF:

DÜSSELDORF STRING QUARTET.

GRETE EWELER QUARTET.

RHENISH STRING QUARTET.

STÄDTISCHES STREICHQUARTETT.

DÜSSELDORF TRIO.

RHENISH TRIO.

WESTDEUTSCHES TRIO.

24. ELBERFELD:

WUPPERTALER STRING QUARTET.

BLÄSERKAMMERMUSIK VEREINIGUNG (5 wind instr. and pf.).

SOCIETY FOR OLD MUSIC.

25. ERFURT:

ERFURT STRING QUARTET.

ERFURT TRIO.

26. ESSEN:

ESSEN STRING QUARTET.

KOSMAN QUARTET.

LEHMAN QUARTET.

BLÄSERQUARTETT (wind).

27. FLENSBURG:

FLENSBURG STRING QUARTET.

28. FRANKFORT:

(*a*) *Quartets:*

AMAR: Licco Amar, Walter Caspar, Paul and Rudolph Hindemith; also R. Frank. Came into prominence during the musical festivals in Donaueschingen and Salzburg in 1921 and 1922. Famous for its interpretations of modern music.

ANTON WITEK QUARTET (Frankfort Symphony Orchestra Quartet).

(*b*) *Trios:*

KAMMERMUSIK TRIO.

LAMPMANN: Herbert, Gawel.

MATOSI: Freund, Peters.

ROSENBAUM: Hock, Mehne.

BLÄSERKAMMERMUSIK VEREINIGUNG (4 instr.).

29. GERA:

ROSEN STRING TRIO.

BLÄSERVEREINIGUNG DER REUSSISCHEN KAPELLE (5 instr.).

30. GOTHA:

SCHWESER QUARTET.

31. GÖTTINGEN:

ACADEMIC ORCHESTRAL SOCIETY'S STRING QUARTET.

32. HAGEN:

HAUER-MEISSNER QUARTET.

BLÄSERVEREINIGUNG (5 instr.).

33. HALLE:

BOHNHARDT QUARTET.

BLÄSERVEREINIGUNG (5 wind instr. and pf.).

COLLEGIUM MUSICUM.

34. HAMBORN:

STRING QUARTET OF THE HAMBORN ORCHESTRA.

35. HAMBURG:

(*a*) *Quartets:*

HANS BANDLER: Lachmann, Möller, Engel. Founded in 1896, also known as the Society of Music Lovers.

HAMBURG STRING QUARTET: Ottoman Borwitzki, August Langbein, Willy Geyersbach, Paul Barth; with Elly Barth in piano works. Founded in 1922; an enlargement of the Hamburg Trio.

RATHJE QUARTET: Karl Grötsch, Siegmund Wolf, A. Grünfeld, Paul Moth.

(*b*) *Trios:*

HAMBURG TRIO. Founded in 1918.

SCHLESWIG-HOLSTEIN'SCHES TRIO.

(*c*) *Miscellaneous:*

WOODWIND QUINTET: Johannes Lorenz (fl.), August Gäbe (oboe), Bruno Wentzklaff (clar.), Carl Francke (bassoon), Otto Vollbrecht (horn).

WOODWIND ORGANIZATION OF THE HAMBURG PHILHARMONIC ORCHESTRA: H. Brinckmann (fl.), A. Reinhardt (oboe), R. Gräffe (clar.), E. Mayer (bassoon), A. Döscher (horn).

36. HANOVER:

HENDRIK PRINS: Karl Nothdwift, Franz Struckmeyer, Ernst Ackermann.

RILLER QUARTET.

KAMMERMUSIK VEREINIGUNG DER OPERNHAUS KAPELLE (wind and pf.).

37. KARLSRUHE:

KEHRMANN QUARTET.

VOIGT QUARTET.

BADISCHES TRIO.

KARLSRUHE BLÄSERVEREINIGUNG (5 instr.).

38. KIEL:

KIEL STRING QUARTET.

SCHLESWIG-HOLSTEIN STRING QUARTET.

DOEBEL-NISSEN: Bandler, Sakom (Trio).

KIELER BLÄSERKAMMERMUSIK VEREINIGUNG (5 instr.).

39. KÖNIGSBERG:

KÖNIGSBERG QUARTET.

SKALAK STRING QUARTET.

SCHUCHMANN: Hewers, Klemm (Trio).

40. KREFELD (Crefeld):

KREFELD STRING QUARTET.

PANZER QUARTET.

Peter Quartet.
Bläservereinigung (5 instr.).

41. Leipzig:
(*a*) *Quartets:*
Davisson Quartet.
Gewandhaus Quartet: Edgar Wollgandt, Karl Wolschke, Carl Hermann, Hans Münch-Holland. Founded in 1903 for the exclusive first performances of the chamber music works of Max Reger, on many occasions with the composer at the piano.
Häbler-Klengel Quartet.
Hungar Quartet.
Lange Quartet.
Heinrich Schachtebeck: Albert Patzack, Erich Wätzold, Alfred Patzack; Augusta Schachtebeck at the piano. Has given many modern piano works.
Leo Schwarz Quartet.
(*b*) *Trios:*
Leipzig Chamber Trio.
Leipzig Trio.
Leipzig Triovereinigung: von Bose, Davisson, Julius Klengel.
Liebermann-Rosswiese Trio.
Rosen Trio.
(*c*) *Miscellaneous:*
Gamben-quartett (for old music, 2 v, 2 viole da gamba).
Kammertrio für alte Musik (cembalo, v, viola da gamba).
Alb. Heinss Kammermusik Vereinigung.
Gewandhaus-Bläserquintett.
Erstes Leipziger Gewandhaus-Bläserquintett.
Leipziger Vereinigung für Kammermusik.
Leipziger Gewandhaus Cornet Quintet. Founded 1899. Has performed all the woodwind combinations of Theodor Blumer, with Anny Eisele at the piano.

42. Lübeck:
Kammermusik Vereinigung.
Lübeck String Quartet.

43. Magdeburg:
Kade Quartet.
Kobin Quartet.
Lambach Trio.

44. Mannheim:
(*a*) *Quartet:*
Max Kergl: Bernhard Conradi, Franz Neumeier, Karl Müller.
(*b*) *Trios:*
Badisches Trio.
Mannheim Trio: Hans Bruch, Max Kergl, Karl Müller.
Mannheim Trio: Hesse, Bernatz, Sinzheimer.
(*c*) *Wind:*
Bläservereinigung.

45. Mayence:
Kornely Trio.

46. Meiningen:
Bläservereinigung (5 instr.).

47. Munich:
(*a*) *Quartets:*
Felix Berber: Hans Weiner, Valentine Härtl, Johannes Hegar. Founded in 1916. Performs only classical music.
Hugo Birkigt: Placidus Morasch, Albin Hössl, Hans Fuchs. Founded in 1922.
Munich String Quartet: Jani Szántó, Felix Saupe, Haas, Dischez. Formed in 1920.
Petschiknoff Quartet.
Schuster-Woldan Quartet (women).
Herma Studeny: Lotte Hamburger, Alf. Beckmann, Karl List.
(*b*) *Trios:*
Chamber Trio: Michaelis, Menz, Dr. Schmidt.
Döbereiner Trio: for old chamber music.
Triovereinigung: Schmid-Lindner, Jani Szántó, Joseph Dischez.
(*c*) *Miscellaneous:*
Chamber Orchestra of Verein-Studentenhaus.
Munich Bläserquintett (5 instr.).
Munich Bläservereinigung (6 instr.).
Munich Vereinigung für alte Musik: leader, Christian Döbereiner (viola da gamba). Specializes in old chamber music played on the original instruments.

48. Nuremberg:
Nuremberg String Quartet.
Nuremberg Trio.
Nuremberg Bläservereinigung (5 wind instr. and pf.).

49. Potsdam:
Potsdam Trio.

50. Rostock:
Rostock String Quartet.

51. Saarbrücken:
Saarbrücker String Quartet.
Saarländische Bläservereinigung (5 instr.).

52. Sondershausen:
Quartettvereinigung.
Four different Trios.

53. Stettin:
Wiemann-Bautz Quartet.
Stettin Trio.

54. Stuttgart:
(*a*) *Quartets:*
Willy Kleemann: Hans Reichardt, Hermann Köhler, Ferdinand Merten.
Carl Wendling: Hans Michaelis, Ludwig Natterer (replacing Philip Neter), Alfred Saal. Founded in 1911. Has first performed many works of Reger.
(*b*) *Trios:*
Giesen: Kleeman, Merten.
Helene Lang: F. Doppler, W. Reichard.
(*c*) *Miscellaneous:*
Dreisbach Woodwind Ensemble: Franz Jungmitsch (fl.), Krümmling (oboe), Dreisbach (clar.), Bayer (bassoon), Fritz Karg (horn).

COLLEGIUM MUSICUM: R. Dittrich (fl.), Carl Riedel (oboe), Jakob Rauschert (clar.), Arthur Bartzsch (horn), Otto Bartholomaeus (bassoon).

55. WEIMAR:
NEW WEIMAR STRING QUARTET.
WEIMAR TRIO.
BLÄSERVEREINIGUNG (5 instr.).

56. WIESBADEN:
PEISCHER STRING QUARTET.
MANNSTAEDT TRIO: Brückner, Victor.
BLÄSERVEREINIGUNG (5 instr.).

57. WÜRZBURG:
ADOLF SCHIERING QUARTET: Karl Wyrott, Walter Kunkel, Ernst Cahnbley.

BLÄSERQUINTETT OF THE CONSERVATORIUM: Julius Mangold (fl.), E. Gugel (oboe), Gustav Steinkamp (clar.), Ernst Grossmann (bassoon), Rudolf Lindner (horn), Arthur Schreiber (pf.).

AUSTRIA

1. VIENNA:
(*a*) *Quartets:*

FRIEDRICH BUXBAUM: van den Berg, Marx Harkmann, Ernst Morametz, Buxbaum. An offspring of the Rosé Quartet. Original personnel: F. Mairecker, Starkmann, Morametz, Buxbaum. Later, Robert Pollak replaced Mairecker, who again was replaced by van den Berg, leader of the Berlin Philharmonic Orchestra until 1926. Has given many first performances. Has toured extensively and appeared several times in England.

RUDOLF FITZNER: Theodor Hess, Heinrich Graesser, Hugo Kreisler, brother of Fritz. Founded by Fitzner in 1894. Original personnel: Fitzner, Otto Zeit, Joseph Czerny, Buxbaum. In 1900 Otto Weissgarber replaced Zeit and Anton Watter took Buxbaum's place. The Quartet has given over a hundred first performances. It has toured widely, especially in the East and in Scandinavia.

HUGO GOTTESMANN: Wilhelm Müller, Max Weissgräber, Richard Krotschak. Founded in 1918. Chiefly modern music.

KOLBE (women): Kolbe, Hammerschlag, Kübler, Krause. Chiefly modern works. Has given several first performances.

KOLLMANN-BARTHOLOME: Kollmann, Scheberle, Domascho, Bartholome.

MILDNER: Kaufmann, Handl, Czegka.

FRANZ ONDŘIČEK: Silbiger, Junck, Jelinek.

PHILHARMONIC QUARTET: Knoll, Hess, Starkmann, Stieglitz.

KARL PRILL: August Siebert, Hugo von Steiner, Wilhelm Jeral.

REISNER QUARTET.

ROSÉ: Arnold Rosé, Paul Fischer, Anton Ruzitska, Anton Walter. Founded in 1882 by Rosé, 1st violin at the Court Opera House. Original personnel: Arnold Rosé, Julius Egghard, Anton Loh, Eduard Rosé. Various changes have occurred. Buxbaum joined as 'cellist in 1900 and Ružitska as viola in 1901 (Rosé, Fischer, Ruzitska, Buxbaum). In 1921 Walter replaced Buxbaum. Has toured all Europe. In Vienna alone gives about thirty concerts annually, the programmes consisting of both classical and modern works (many first performances). Many of Brahms's works had first performances from MS. Brahms's op. 8 was performed in 1884 by Rosé and Reinhold Hummer, with Brahms at the piano.

SEDLAK-WINKLER: Fritz Sedlak, Vittorio Borri, Gustav Gruber, Wilhelm Winkler. Founded 1922. Has performed all the string quartets of Haydn; also many modern works.

SWERTKA QUARTET.

WEISS QUARTET.

WIENER KONZERTHAUS QUARTET: August Jankovitz, Heinrich Graesser, Karl Doktor, Hugo Kreisler (brother of Fritz). This Quartet was soon dissolved.

VIENNA STRING QUARTET: Rudolf Kolisch, Felix Khuner, Eugen Lehner, Bemar Heifetz. Founded in 1924. Original personnel: Kolisch, Fritz Rothschild, Marcel Dick, Joachim Studschevski. Has appeared at all the great international musical festivals. Has given many first performances.

(*b*) *Trios:*

PROFESSOR DACHS: Kreisler, Brunner.

FUCHS: Langer, Zechner.

ROSENTHAL: Rodosi, Douat.

SIROTA: Pollak, Buxbaum.

EDUARD STEUERMANN: Franz Rothschild, Joachim Studschevski.

VIENNA TRIO: Friedrich Wührer, Karl Doktor, Hermann Busch.

ZINCKLER: Horwitz, Koller.

WOODWIND CHAMBER MUSIC ORGANIZATION: Composed of members of the Viennese Philharmonic Orchestra. Includes fourteen players: flute, oboe, clarinet, horn, bassoon, trumpet.

2. INNSBRUCK:
INNSBRUCK STRING QUARTET.

3. KLAGENFURT:
STRING QUARTET OF THE MUSIKVEREIN FÜR KÄRNTHEN.

4. SALZBURG:
SALZBURGER KAMMERMUSIK VEREINIGUNG.

GERNSHEIM, FRIEDRICH, 1839–1916, eminent German composer.

	op.	
Divertimento, fl, 2 v, vla, vc, cb, E	53	Augustin, 1888.
Quintet, 2 v, 2 vla, vc, D	9	Cranz, 1868.
Quartet, str, c mi	25	Simrock, 1872.
Quartet, str, a mi	31	„ 1875.
Quartet, str, F	51	Peters, 1866.
Quartet, str, e mi	66	B. & B., 1900.
Quartet, str, A	83	Simrock, 1911.
Quintet, pf, 2 v, vla, vc, d mi	35	„ 1877.
Quintet, pf, 2 v, vla, vc, b mi	63	„ 1897.

	op.	
Quartet, pf, v, vla, vc, E flat	6	B. & H., 1865.
Quartet, pf, v, vla, vc, c mi	20	Simrock, 1870.
Quartet, pf, v, vla, vc, F	47	Peters, 1883.
Trio, pf, v, vc, F	28	Schott, 1873.
Trio, pf, v, vc, B	37	Peters, 1879.
Sonata, pf, v, c mi	4	,, 1865.
Sonata, pf, v, C	50	,, 1885.
Sonata, pf, v, F	64	,, 1898.
Sonata, pf, v, G	85	Simrock, 1912.
Sonata, pf, vc (also v), d mi	12	Schott, 1868.

This composer, who was never given to writing for writing's sake, must not be regarded as a mere disciple of the classics. He advanced with the times, and became far more modern as regards harmony than his friend Max Bruch, with whom he had otherwise much in common. His aim, as he once told the writer, was to rise superior to the everyday level in the intellectual and emotional content of his compositions; they were to be works of art in which one bar followed the other inevitably, and the whole was to form a unity in which no phrase should be associated with another except of set purpose. In the development sections he strove to develop new material out of the themes without breaking them into minute fragments. He also allowed himself far more liberty in matters of pure form than the classics or the romantics, and was constantly trying to bring more variety and many-sidedness into his rhythms. His output—which includes, by the way, neither opera nor the type of choral work that fills a whole evening—is distinguished by nobility of aim, well-defined, beautiful and assured proportions, and complete mastery of form.

The divertimento, op. 53, for flute and strings is, as the title suggests, in the nature of a musical pastime; but thanks to its unconstrained and joyous character it is sure to please everywhere, while professional musicians will be enchanted by its delicate ingenuity. The string quintet is melodious and well-sounding, while the second piano quintet is undoubtedly an important work. Of the three piano quartets, the first is a particular favourite of the present writer, while the fourth string quartet is a work of outstanding interest as regards rhythm and harmony.

THE FIFTH STRING QUARTET is a really astonishing production in view of the composer's advanced years (72). The first movement, allegro non troppo, is built on two very melodious and engaging themes, in which, however, the element of contrast is lacking. A very original scherzo suggests programme music—to which Gernsheim was by no means averse, for example in his *Miriam* symphony—there are curious muted effects suggestive of spirits or the whispering of the breeze. It is followed by a trio, which takes the form of a vigorous march, and comes as a surprise. The andante (F major) is a fine movement, the themes of which have real distinction. Here and there it is reminiscent of Brahms, and certainly contains some of the most moving passages to be found in modern quartet music. The final allegro vivace is a dashing movement; the first subject resembles a gay arabesque, but the second, which is far more original, has notable effects of rhythm and timbre. This quartet, in the writer's opinion, ranks higher than the more generally admired no. 4.

THE PIANO TRIO in F is the better of the two, on account of its distinctive scherzo. As regards the other movements, it is obvious that Beethoven stood godfather to the first and Schubert (with the funeral march from the C major quintet) to the largo.

THE VIOLIN SONATAS. Of these, op. 50 may be recommended as a first choice. The fourth sonata, which demands some little virtuosity on the violinist's part, makes a strong appeal through its elegance and perfection of form. In the first movement, however, one is conscious of a certain academic chill. There are some quite uncommon effects of timbre in the andantino dolente, a sort of intermezzo with a quicker melodious middle section, which is happily inspired at the beginning, but falls off somewhat as the movement proceeds. The brilliant finale, allegro con brio, with its fugato opening is peculiarly attractive; its second subject, indeed, is the happiest inspiration of the whole sonata. WILHELM ALTMANN.

GÉZA, FRID, b. 1904, Hungarian pianist, pupil at the Hochschule in Budapest, of Kodály and, later, of Bartók. His works include string quartet in F (1926), string trio in A minor (1926), and duo for violin and 'cello (1925).

His chamber music, closely allied at first to the new Hungarian instrumental music of Kodály and Bartók, soon took on a personal note, both in melodic material and instrumental development.

THE DUO for violin and 'cello is in two movements. The first (lento), which is introductory in character and leads straight into the quick second movement, is in three-part Lied form and contains the following elements: a chromatic parlando motif on the violin, a sighing main theme and an agitato theme. The second movement, a quick dance-like allegro vivace, is in rondo form. A lyrical second theme joins on to the first quick dance motif, and ends with a motif made up of reiterated detached phrases. With the close of the exposition the main motif returns, and leads into the middle section (quasi trio), which works up to the recapitulation with some brilliant passages. The original motifs then reappear, abridged, and with the rôles of the instruments reversed. Finally the coda brings the movement to an end with the main subject.

THE STRING TRIO retains sonata form for the first movement. The first grotesquely sportive main theme is relieved by a chromatic 'call' motif. After an agitated development, the main motifs reappear, but are more sharply accentuated. In the second movement (F sharp mi.) the pensive cantabile melody of the violin is contrasted with a stormy chromatic middle section. A threefold development of the passionate parlando motif leads to the return of the main subject—now reduced to something in the nature of a violin cadenza —and the third movement then follows attacca. This is in rondo form, but its dance-like principal theme and introductory motif are combined with a cantabile subsidiary theme to form a development unit, to which a contrast is provided by the pastoral trio-motif of the middle section. The recapitulation concludes with a brilliant coda.

THE STRING QUARTET is in four movements. The first (tranquillo) opens with a quiet, rather melancholy theme built up on the chord F-A-C sharp-E; then comes a contrasting second theme of an agitated character, and the movement ends with a light and graceful coda. In the scherzo (presto) which follows, an insistent throbbing motif, played spiccato, is the principal feature. A middle section (meno mosso) introduces a trio motif, which moves in heavy strides above the glissando accompaniment of the lower instruments, the rôles being presently reversed; a 'cello fanfare then brings back the first part, and an echo of the trio motif is heard before the coda. The slow movement (lento rubato) has first a pensive monologue for the violin, then a middle section in which the same thematic material is worked up to a climax (agitato), and finally the recapitulation and a melancholy coda. The finale then follows without a break. This is in the form of a dance-rondo with a ringing fanfare-like motif; the second subject has a joyous cantabile theme which is worked up to a brilliant close, and leads to the first return of the main theme. In the trio the note is that of primitive folk-dances; and the return of the second theme is led up to by rubato pizzicato passages. The first theme now reappears, passing into a quick coda, which ends with a powerful stringendo after touching lightly upon the cantabile theme of the second subject.

E. WALDBAUER.

GHEBART, GIUSEPPE, 1796–1870, Italian violinist.

Two quintets, 2 v, 2 vla, vc, C, G	op. 56	Costallat (orig. Richault).
Two quartets, str, A, g mi	opp. 52, 53	,,
Quartet, str	op. 54	Richault.

Ghebart was the first player to introduce the chamber music of contemporary Germans (Mendelssohn, Spohr, &c.) at Turin, where he lived. According to Vidal three quintets were published as op. 56, by Richault.

GHENOVICI, CONSTANTIN, b. 1887, Roumanian composer, pupil of Juon, Humperdinck, and d'Indy.

Sonata, pf, vc, a mi	Senart.

The sonata is in four movements, with the scherzo in the middle of the andante.

GHEORGHIU, VICTOR L. *v.* ROUMANIAN COMPOSERS.

GIANTURCO, E., Italian composer.

Sonata, pf, v	Ricordi, *c.* 1900.

GIARDINI, FELICE DE, 1716–1796, famous Italian violinist.

Giardini wrote eighteen string quartets, opp. 22, 23, 29 (Hummel of Amsterdam, and Thompson of London), in some of which the first violin is replaced by oboe or flute. *Fétis* mentions six quintets, op. 11, for clavier and strings, and seven sets of trios for various combinations of strings, and some violin sonatas which have been republished. He wrote also some melodious duets for 2 violins (opp. 2, 13).

The quartets are unequal in merit, but there is unquestionable beauty in the harmonies. The six, op. 29, are exceptionally good, especially No. 4, which is to be republished by S. and B. (ed. James Brown). The violin parts are often brilliant. An interesting feature in No. 4 is that the first movement is made to lead into the second (grazioso e piano) by ending pianissimo on the dominant.

The statement made by William Gardiner that Giardini, who was a brilliant virtuoso, failed in reading a quartet by Pleyel at sight, is incredible.

EDITOR.

GIBBONS, ORLANDO, 1583–1625, English composer.

Modern republications:

Four fantasies of 3 parts, treble, mean, and bass viols.	(Dr. E. F. Rimbault) Musical Antiquarian Society, 1843.
Five fantasies of 3 parts, 2 treble, bass viol	(Dr. E. F. Rimbault) Musical Antiquarian Society, 1843.
Thirteen madrigals 'apt for Voyces or Viols'	Musical Antiq. Soc.

Further compositions have since been published, for which see article which follows.

As in the case of Byrd, Gibbons's fame as a composer will always rest upon his vocal work rather than on his instrumental music. But it has not generally been realized how much chamber music he wrote. A list of thirty-eight compositions for strings is given by the present writer in his *Orlando Gibbons, a short account of his life and work* (Clarendon Press). As many as twenty-five of these are for string trio. Nine of the fantasy trios were published about the year 1610 and fifteen more are in MS. in March's Library, Dublin. Two of the string quartets are among the most attractive of Gibbons's chamber works; they both open fugally and with some complexity of rhythm, but in each some melodies of a strong and regularly rhythmic character are introduced. These two quartets, together with a pavan and galliard for sextet, and the nine fantasy trios, are published in score and parts under the writer's editorship by Stainer & Bell, Ltd. About forty of Gibbons's keyboard works have survived; these have recently been collected and edited by Miss Glyn and published by Stainer & Bell, Ltd.

E. H. FELLOWES.

†GIBBS, CECIL ARMSTRONG, b. 1889, English composer.

3rd quartet, str, E	op. 18	Curwen, 1921.
Quartet (*Pastoral*), str	,, 41	,,
The Enchanted Wood, pf, solo v, str. quintet (Cobbett Prize, 1920)	,, 25	,,
Three pieces (*Country Magic*), pf, v, vc	,, 47	Goodwin, 1923.
Phantasy, pf, v		,, 1915.

Gibbs's string quartet in G received a supplementary Carnegie award, MS. copies being provided in order to facilitate performance.

For purposes of convenience Armstrong Gibbs may be considered as one of the younger school of British composers, but in point of fact his work shows no sign of national bias beyond a fondness for folk-song, which came to him naturally enough, one imagines, from his environment as an East-country man, and from the happy chance that his musical education at Cambridge coincided with the brilliant years when the folk-song movement was at its height in the University.

He has already tried his powers in many directions, but his songs and chamber music appear to be the channels in which, up to the present, his gifts have found their most congenial expression. He would seem to have a special leaning, moreover, towards the string quartet. He has composed five such works, besides a one-movement phantasy in G minor. Further, he has employed a string quartet and piano to accompany some of his best songs (*Nod*, *The Scarecrow*, *Five Eyes*, and *Mistletoe*), and has scored for string quartet his incidental music to *The White Devil*—composed for the Marlowe Society's production of the play at Cambridge in 1920.

Not all of his chamber works have been published. The selection in print does not correspond with the large part chamber music plays in his general output, nor does it indicate the accumulations of experience which have gone to mould his clear, easy style. These published works stand in the forefront, but close behind them are others, unpublished but equally meriting consideration. Behind these again are works which the composer has suppressed from motives of self-criticism.

Fortunately the published works are sufficiently representative to allow students to gain from them a clear idea of Armstrong Gibbs as a chamber-music writer.

THE STRING QUARTET, op. 18, is the most important, though it dates from 1918. It requires purity of style and intonation in the players, sympathy and vivacity in their interpretation, and while it never goes to extremes of technique or emotion, it does demand graceful accomplishment in performance to match the graceful music. The first movement—moderato e tranquillo—is coloured by a peculiar wavering between the minor and major forms of the tonic harmony—and this feature is cleverly reflected in the last movement. The second movement, allegro risoluto, is in 5/4 time. It takes the place of a scherzo but has a good deal of the English folk-dance about it, with vigorous tunes, stamping rhythms, and a general air of greensward jollity. The third movement really combines the functions of two, viz. a slow and a quick movement, for it begins as an air with variations marked 'andante e semplice', and the last variation is worked up into a lively little finale with a rhapsodic end.

Country Magic, op. 47, was composed in 1922 to meet the needs of amateurs for trio music of the better sort. More simple than the quartet and easier in every way, the music still exhibits pleasant touches of unexpectedness and the workmanship is good. Each movement has a title. *Siesta* contains some attractive invertible counterpoint between violin and 'cello. *The Open Road* and *An Old Song* are saturated with the English folk-song idiom.

Of other works published more recently, the *Pastoral Quartet* received its first performance from the Hungarian Quartet in 1924.

In these, as in his other works, Armstrong Gibbs is content with the clear forms that served the classical masters. His harmonic practice is that of a man aware of modern idioms who accepts them in a temper of well-bred tolerance. His clashes and arresting chords happen more often from the independent progression of individual parts than from premeditated compounds laid on with whole strokes. Sometimes these parts push forward so sturdily that they wring from one the same friendly appreciation won by characters in a play. He usually places his music well for his instruments and for the human hands that play upon them. Short points of imitation here and there imply, without inducing, the contrapuntal style. Each part is allotted an equitable share in the interest, the workmanship is neat, and the total effect well balanced. The tone is more often pure and singing than bold and sonorous, a quality which is characteristic both of his songs and chamber music. So, too, is the fairy streak in his thoughts, which has made him one of the best interpreters—or collaborators—of the poems of Walter de la Mare. That he frequently bestows titles on his instrumental pieces does not mean that he paints direct from natural objects. Unless definitely tied to words or drama, he says, he never has any physical image in his thoughts when composing.

Yet one of the best criticisms ever passed on his chamber music was made by evoking an image. A quartet by Armstrong Gibbs (said this acute critic) was like a water-colour drawing of an English landscape.

The Essex meadows possess no striking geographical features; and the chamber music of Armstrong Gibbs is free from the crudities and crises which have agitated contemporary evolution and art. But if his chamber music has not pioneer significance for progress in general, it is of interest and pleasure within its own bounds, for it is that rare thing—far more rare than some might suspect—true chamber music. MARION M. SCOTT.

[Armstrong Gibbs has rearranged his dance phantasy, *The Enchanted Wood*, which received a Cobbett prize in 1920, with ripieno parts, and it must be conceded that in its new form (as played by the Erhart chamber orchestra) it is more effective than as originally scored, especially the section written for muted strings. EDITOR.]

GIBBS, JOSEPH, 1699–1788, English organist.

Modern republication:

Sonata, v, fig. bass (pf), d mi — (Moffat) Novello, 1910.

Original publications:

Six quartets, 2 v, vla, fig. bass (vc or harpsic.), Thompson (London).

Eight solos for a Violin with a Bass for the Harpsicord (*sic*) or Bass Violin, publ. 1745–1748.

In his day Gibbs was the most active—and possibly the best—musician in East Anglia. His funeral was attended by the band of the Scots Greys; a curious fact, which is worth recording, is that the instruments were decked with crape.

The wording of the title-page of the quartets is given below as a specimen of the style used for these old works:

Six Quartettos For two Violins a Tenor and Violoncello or Harpsichord
Compos'd by
Joseph Gibbs,
Organist at Ipswich
Opera II
Humbly dedicated to Mrs. Mayne.
Price 10s. 6.
Engraved by T. Straight.

London. Printed for the Author, and sold by S: and A: Thompson, No. 75, St. Pauls church Yard, and at the Engravers, No. 138, St. Martins Lane near Charing Cross, and Thos Miller, Bookseller at Bungy [Bungay].

In these quartets the part for the viola is written in the alto clef, though the instrument is described as a tenor. Both alto and tenor were in use in the early eighteenth century.

†GIESEKING, WALTER, b. 1895, German pianist.

Quintet, pf, ob, cl, horn, fag	B flat	Fürstner, 1923.

Brought up in France and Italy, but studied in Germany.

GILBERT, HENRY, 1868–1928, American composer, pupil of MacDowell.

Gilbert wrote a string quartet, which was played at the Coolidge concerts in Venice, 1927, and elsewhere. He was an early champion of Indian and negro music; but his work was unaffected by contemporary tendencies.

†GILLES, CONSTANTIN, modern French composer.

Sonata, pf, v, d mi	Legouix, 1914.

†GILSON, PAUL, b. 1865, Belgian composer.

Studien, str. quartet	Cranz, 1923.
Little suite, pf, v	Maison Beethoven, *c.* 1905.
Suite in old style, pf, vc	Cranz, 1921.

Dent describes his music as essentially Flemish 'in the richness of his polyphony, and a certain reserve which distinguishes the Flemish musicians from their Walloon contemporaries . . .'

†GIORNI, AURELIO, b. Perugia, 1895, American composer (naturalized).

Sonata, pf, vc (or vla), d mi	S.P.A.M., 1925.

Pianist of the Elshuco Trio. He has written a violin sonata, still in MS.

GIOVANELLI, ALBERTO.

Trio, pf, v, vc, c mi	Carisch, 1909.

†GLASS, LOUIS CHRISTIAN AUGUST, b. 1864, Danish pianist.

	op.	
Sextet, 2 v, 2 vla, 2 vc, d mi	15	Hansen, 1896.
4th quartet, str, f sharp mi	—	,, 1907.
Trio, pf, v, vc, c mi	19	,, 1895.
Sonata, pf, v, E flat	7	Skandinavisk. Musikförlag. Hainauer, 1895.
Sonata, pf, v, C	29	Hansen, 1909.

Glass was a pupil of Gade. *Dent* says that he 'belongs to the conservative wing of the modern school, following Franck and Bruckner. His later works show strong and vigorous development.'

*† GLAZOUNOV, Alexander Constantinovitch, b. 1865, Russian composer.

	op.	Composed
Quintet, 2 v, vla, 2 vc, A	39	1892
Quartet, str, D	1	1882
Quartet, str, F	10	1883
Five novellettes, str. quartet	15	
Quartet (*Slavonic*), str, G	26	
Suite, str. quartet, C	35	
Quartet, str, a mi	64	1894
Quartet, str, d mi	70	1899
With Rimsky-Korsakov, Liadov, and Borodin:		
Quartet on name B-la-f, str		
With Liadov and Rimsky-Korsakov:		
Quartet (*Jour de Fête*), str		
Two pieces (Prelude and fugue; Courante), str. quartet		
Quartet (In modo religioso), Trpt (in B flat), horn, 2 trombones	op. 38	

All published by Belaiev.

Glazounov is a commanding figure among contemporary Russian composers. He was at one time a typical representative of the school, usually called 'national', which sprang up in the wake of Glinka and Dargomijsky, and whose musical idiom owed much to the influence of native and Eastern musical lore. His extraordinary precocity enabled him to work in close association with the leaders of this school, although he was by many years their junior. Some of his early orchestral works rank among the most representative examples of Russian 'national' music. And not a few of them (e. g. the tone-poem *Stenka Razin*) evince his interest in problems of pure form and development. After a period during which his individuality asserted itself in works which owed much to the influence of Liszt and of the older Russians, he took a prominent place among those who worked their way closer to Western tradition. The contrast between his early manner and his later is noticeable in his chamber music, but in order to appreciate it to the full, it is necessary to consider his orchestral music as well.

Glazounov is essentially an instrumental and chamber music composer. He has written but little for the piano or for the voice; and his only attempts at dramatic music consist of incidental music for Wilde's *Salome* and Grand Duke Constantine's *The King of the Jews*.

At the time when he entered the creative field, 'national' Russian music was just completing the most significant period of its evolution. Balakirev, the leader of the school, had already written the works that exercised the deepest influence on the composers around him. Moussorgsky's career was ended, and Borodin's was drawing to its close. Rimsky-Korsakov had already composed a good many of his most significant works, and already a desire to assimilate and utilize more of the traditional methods was asserting itself. Glazounov played an important part in the evolution which naturally followed.

From the outset his gifts and his power had been obvious to all who knew him. While still in his 'teens he was nicknamed 'our Samson' by Stassov, the critic; and Balakirev used to call him 'the little Glinka'. From 1880 onwards he studied theory with Rimsky-Korsakov, on Balakirev's advice, the latter continuing to take an active part in his education. As early as 1881 he had completed the sketches of his first symphony, which was performed in March 1882, Balakirev conducting. The seventeen-year-old composer of this truly delightful work attended the concert in the uniform of the professional school of which he was an industrious and successful pupil. His first string quartet, composed before the symphony, was first performed in November, 1882. At the age of twenty, Glazounov had written over a dozen important works. The total to-day amounts to about a hundred.

First String Quartet, op. 1. The introduction, andantino moderato, is entirely founded on the main subject—

Ex. 1.

which is given out fugato at the beginning of the allegro moderato, and immediately afterwards becomes the matter of light play. This mood of buoyancy and light-heartedness is maintained in the delightfully whimsical bridge-passage:

Ex. 2.

(Let it be noticed, by the way, that Glazounov does not always resort to the use of a definite transitional theme—or bridge—as he does here.) The second subject—

Ex. 3.

is in the character of a native dance tune. The bridge is frequently used as an accompaniment to it. A characteristic episode, of a kind which Glazounov often introduces elsewhere in the working-out, occurs when the viola accompanies the re-entry of the main subject with heavy fifths. The whole movement is bright, and skilfully carried out.

The coda is built upon the second subject. The scherzo is in the same light-hearted mood.

It is built upon two subjects, the first of which has a distinctly Schumannesque flavour.

Ex. 4.

A.

B.

There is no trio.

The second movement is a brief, expressive cantilena, andante, consisting of a melody repeated with slight changes, but without any attempt at working-out.

The finale is very Russian in character throughout. The vernacular and archaic quality of the main subject—

Ex. 5.

becomes even more obvious when this subject is repeated in crotchets.

The second subject—

Ex. 6.

is more lyrical. The second half is much used in the working-out.

There are, of course, certain defects in this work, but they are far fewer and far less serious than one would expect to find in an op. 1 by a seventeen-year-old composer. These defects are chiefly, that now and then the changes of key are abrupt and do not altogether carry their own justification; and that sometimes the development is a trifle meagre. But on the whole, the work lacks neither significance nor attractiveness.

Second String Quartet, op. 10. The main subject of the first movement, allegro non troppo, is in the same old Slavonic character as the main themes of the first quartet:

Ex. 7.

The second consists chiefly of one short motif—

Ex. 8.

which is repeated and prolonged by means of a sequence. The contrast between the rhythmical first subject and the more melodic second is turned to good purpose during the exposition, which continues with reappearances of the main subject in F minor, and immediately afterwards in E major (on the 'cello, the first violin accompanying with a variant of the same subject). Modulations lead up to the key of D flat major, in which the second subject reappears, *pp*, the contrast thus secured being most effective. The working-out section is short, and the recapitulation quite simple.

The scherzo is interesting in form and in substance. There is real piquancy in the subtle articulation of the main subject—

Ex. 9.

which reigns without challenge or contrast until a swift modulation to D flat major introduces the trio, which is founded on a quiet, persistent, melodic figure.

Ex. 10.

This reappears in the further course of the scherzo, and in the coda. The adagio is built on two themes, the first simple, calm, and meditative (A minor), the second more impassioned (D major). The contrast is emphasized by the more ornamental accompaniment, as well as by the change in key. When the first theme reappears—again in A minor—something of this richer colour persists in the accompaniment. In turn the second theme reappears, after the tone has become more dramatic. The conclusion is in A major.

The general character of both subjects of the finale, allegro moderato, is almost pastoral. The opening subject is an eight-bar phrase whose first half is remarkable for its graceful convolutions.

Ex. 11.

Its rhythm is that of a dance. Again one

notes the tendency to impart a more singing character to the second subject. This not unusual contrast is well utilized. So are the rhythmic possibilities of both subjects—e. g. at C, main subject; at D, second subject, much altered. At H an impressive transition, very characteristic of Glazounov, heralds the advent of a delightful episode (arabesques for first violin). At L the main subject reverts to its primitive aspect, but in a softer, more melodic form. The recapitulation begins animato, and is one big crescendo.

THE SLAVONIC QUARTET, op. 26, is one of Glazounov's most brilliant and attractive works; it presents features which are somewhat unusual in chamber music of this high order.

The first movement, moderato, is in perfectly regular sonata form.

The first subject is

Ex. 12.

and the second

Ex. 13.

The working-out is simple and effective.

The interludium is a sober, peaceful little movement founded upon an even, undulating motif, announced by the 'cello, with which a few episodic materials are combined.

The alla mazurka is bright, fairly developed, and the interest is well sustained. It introduces the festive atmosphere of the last movement.

The finale, *Une fête slave*, in all its characteristics, is the most orchestral thing written by Glazounov for a chamber combination. He is a born orchestrator, and his instrumental writing is always a delight both to listeners and to students. It makes for fullness of tone and richness of colour; the latter, however, plays a less prominent part in his later works. Here, without forfeiting any of the requirements of a small combination, he introduces (as he also does in part of the alla mazurka) much that is suggestive of a full orchestra. He keeps all four players busily engaged, and provides plenty of opportunities for brilliant playing.

The form is that of a rondo. The principal subject (or refrain) is:

Ex. 14.

and, naturally enough, most of the other materials used are likewise dance tunes. There are a great number of episodic subjects—some more or less worked out, others merely following one another, so that within the general form of the rondo there is really a kind of *suite de danses*—a form which is not generally resorted to in the more organized types of instrumental music, but which César Franck has not disdained to use in his tone-poem *Les Éolides.*

One of the episodic subjects may be quoted here in full as an instance of the 'orchestral' writing referred to:

Ex. 15.

Molto sostenuto. ♩ = 80.

THE SUITE FOR STRING QUARTET, op. 35, little known until lately, is an attractive work, in which a great variety of moods find adequate expression. The title 'suite' is used in its broadest sense. The work begins with a fine, impressive *Introduction et Fugue*, the main subject appearing first under this form—

Ex. 16.

and afterwards, suitably altered, as Dux and Comes in the fugue.

The next number is a bright and buoyant scherzo whose first subject is introduced in quintuplets—

Ex. 17.

(compare with the scherzo by Borodin in *Les Vendredis*), but soon takes the following sharper form:

Ex. 18.

The second subject is strikingly original in its simplicity:

Ex. 19.

By way of trio, there is a middle section (in A major, and later in E major) whose themes are very much in the character of dance tunes.

The third number, *Orientale*, is poetically melodic. The fourth is a theme with variations, all of which are full of interest and colour. They bear the titles *Tranquillo*, *Mistico*, *Scherzo*, *Pensieroso*, and *Alla Polacca*. Here, as in many other works by Glazounov and by other Russians, the Lisztian principle of theme transformation is applied with unerring skill.

The last number is a waltz—really a *suite de valses*, written very simply.

THE STRING QUINTET, op. 39, was written when the composer's conversion to altogether classical methods and colour schemes was an accomplished fact. His music is now characterized by greater deliberation and slower, more careful progress. The change is exemplified, as a rule, in the quality and build of the themes, which are now selected with a more definite view to their potentialities for working-out purposes.

In a way, Glazounov's actual achievement in this quintet may be said to constitute a kind of half-way house between his early methods and the more thorough formal methods of the later symphonies, chamber works, and piano sonatas. This is shown principally in the form and execution of the first movement, and likewise in the fact that whereas three movements out of the four are devoid of specifically Russian colour, the last retains an unmistakably vernacular tinge.

The form of the first allegro, although clearly apparent, is difficult to define. There are no two actual contrasting subjects; whatever contrasts exist originate in the treatment of one principal subject only, a treatment which is carried out partly in accordance with the principle of working-out, partly by variation, and partly by theme transformation. The attempt is interesting even if the execution is sometimes weak. Again, the tonal plan is curious. It consists mainly in modulations by thirds—a favourite device with Glazounov—and also with Rimsky-Korsakov—and recalls, after a fashion, the plan of Beethoven's variations, op. 34.

The main subject is a twelve-bar phrase

Ex. 20.

containing several motifs suitable for separate treatment. A first section, in A major, constitutes the exposition proper. A second section, in C major, introduces the following transformation, which gives birth to a new motif:

Ex. 21.

This motif will not be used further except in the coda. It is, of course, possible to consider this transformation as a second subject (the second subject in Schumann's piano concerto bears an even closer resemblance to the first than is the case here). But it does not play the part of an actual second subject in the sequel.

Two episodic motifs spring from it, the second of which, at D, is used in the coda, and a further transformation of motif II occurs at E, always in C major. The tempo changes to 9/8 (poco più sostenuto), and the following pattern is derived from motif III:

Ex. 22.

The characteristic motif I is constantly reappearing, and shortly afterwards a modulation to D flat major brings back the main subject. A further repetition of this subject contains an enharmonic modulation, the subject beginning in D flat and ending in A. The next modulation is to F major, in which key the transformation first heard in the second section (C major) reappears. This is further used in A major, and most of the patterns heard so far are utilized in the same key in order to lead up to the coda. Performers should consider the relations between the various patterns and sections very carefully. These, perhaps, may be interpreted in more ways than one, but a performance is likely to fall flat, unless based upon a very firm conception, not only of the fact that all parts of the movement are closely related, but of a definite scheme of relationship.

The scherzo is in no wise unusual in form. Thirteen introductory bars prepare the advent of the main subject.

Ex. 23.

There is a very effective trio, cantabile, in G minor, andante sostenuto, a long melodically sustained example of ternary form. The main subject is very similar, in general character, to that of the first movement, and is treated in somewhat similar fashion.

The finale is in rondo form. The main subject (or refrain) is purely Russian in rhythm and colour. Its treatment recalls Glazounov's earlier work. Its rhythm is that of a folk dance:

Ex. 24.

The first episodic subject to occur begins impressively, and ends with a sudden whimsical turn.

Ex. 25.

It is used further in slightly altered form.

The second episodic subject is

Ex. 26.

Its humorous ending will be noticed. It is also used to good purpose in the second couplet. As one instance among many of ingenuity in treatment, the combination, p. 52 (grazioso, A major), of both episodic motifs—the first in considerably altered form—may be adduced.

The Fourth String Quartet, op. 64, is largely cyclic, less rigorously so than the typical works of César Franck and his disciples, but far more extensively than, for example, certain of Brahms's works.

A large proportion of the materials used in

the various movements springs from the enigmatic notes with which the introduction to the first movement opens:

Ex. 27.
Andante. ♩ = 84.

Firstly, the first subject of the allegro,

Ex. 28.
Allegro. 𝅗𝅥 = 108.

Further, the opening of the slow movement (Ex. 29) and the opening of the finale (Ex. 30). The melody in the slow movement (Ex. 31) is obviously derived from that of the first movement, which in point of fact reappears, practically unaltered, a little later.

Another important cyclic subject is introduced in the exposition of the first movement (Ex. 32). It reappears in the finale (at F), and plays a great part from this point onwards.

The second subject of the first movement is given in Ex. 33 and an echo of it occurs in the trio of the scherzo (Ex. 34), while the materials of the scherzo further include the transformation of the above-mentioned second cyclic subject

Ex. 29.
Andante. ♩ = 66.

Ex. 30.
Allegro. 𝅗𝅥 = 76.

Ex. 31.

Ex. 32.

Ex. 33.

(Ex. 35). There are, of course, many other correspondences and analogies. The work is compact, and is interesting for its substantial quality as well as for its abstract logic. Its performance calls for constant alertness.

The Fifth Quartet, op. 70, is more lyrical and more dramatic. Its structure is simpler; and, on the whole, its spirit shows more affinities with Tchaikovsky's music than any other of Glazounov's chief chamber works.

The first movement opens with an introduction, andante, in which the main subject is given out fugato. Both here and in the allegro, which follows, it is announced by the viola—a favourite device with Glazounov—and the character and treatment of this subject in the allegro forthwith suggest a comparison with Tchaikovsky (Ex. 36). This lyrical quality and pathetic tone prevail throughout the movement, whose form is regular and clear.

Ex. 34.

Ex. 35.

Ex. 36.

The second subject is

Ex. 37.

which reappears at the end in exactly the same form, but with a slightly different harmonization (cadence in D minor instead of in F major).

The scherzo, allegretto, is equally simple, and ingenuous in character.

The first subject is:

Ex. 38.

and the trio

Ex. 39.

carries with it a distinct suggestion of Beethoven in a mood of quiet cheerfulness. These materials are used and combined to good purpose in the following section.

The adagio is carried out in a mood of tranquil, poetic reverie, and remains contemplative throughout.

The finale, allegro, is in regular sonata form.

There is a distinct touch of German *Gemüthlichkeit* in the first subject:

Ex. 40.

The second subject

Ex. 41.

is purely melodic; its evenness contrasts with the quaint little turns in the first—the middle of which is used in the final coda.

Of Glazounov's other chamber works, the *Cinq Novelettes*, for string quartet, consist of *Allegretto alla spagnuola*, *Orientale*, *Interludium in modo antico*, *Waltz* and *Allegretto all' ungherese*.

By way of conclusion, it may be pointed out that Glazounov in his chamber music, as in his other works, is essentially a master of instrumental music, and more especially a symphonist; a skilful, thoughtful craftsman, genuine throughout, not very lyrical by nature, but not lacking in melodic feeling, and endowed with a keen sense of rhythm and colour. At various times, various influences worked upon him strongly, but without ever overshadowing his individuality.

Professor A. Ossovsky, in an essay written in 1907, said that if indeed there are two main types of creative artists—those who strike out and those whose works represent the maturing of tendencies—then Glazounov is one of the latter.

'He effected the reconciliation between the Russian music of his time and Western music. In this respect his part was even more decisive than that of Tchaikovsky, who was in the thick of the struggle between Eastern and Western tendencies—wherefore it was psychologically impossible for him to fulfil the part of an actual peacemaker.'

M. D. Calvocoressi.

[The few additional words I am writing on the subject of Glazounov's wonderful quartets must be prefaced by a tribute to the memory of Belaiev, the public-spirited publisher and philanthropist. But for him they might never have seen the light.

It is true that some of the exquisite qualities in Glazounov's chamber music may be summed up in the word 'Russian idiom', and that there are harmonies in it common to all Russian composers. But the sonorities he gets out of four strings in his more inspired moments, and the rhythmic ecstasy which pervades his dance movements, are quite individual. An example of the former is the *Interludium in modo antico*, a serious movement found in his *Novelettes*, the other sections of which are quite different in character—to be described, perhaps, as a chamber music analogue of the Russian ballet. The last, richly sonorous bars of the *Interludium* could only have been written by a genius. Indeed, the whole work (the *Novelettes*) is, in its own peculiar way, a masterpiece. There is daemonic energy in the opening section (alla spagnuola), infinite charm in the valse and orientale, and gipsy music of the familiar corybantic type in the all' ungherese movement, which, though less distinguished than the rest, forms a brilliant finale.

The so-called orientales introduced by Russian composers into their chamber music form a most welcome variant to the inevitable scherzo. In the quartet suite, op. 35 (another remarkable work written in lighter vein), the weirdly conceived orientale was suggested to Glazounov when listening to wandering bands of Tartar musicians during a holiday in the Crimea. In the opening bars of this suite most exquisite use is made of muted strings. The valse which forms the concluding movement is frankly rollicking and banal, but it pulsates with life and is so brilliant in effect that one would not wish it different. I confess that I love that last galloping page.

The chef-d'œuvre among the quartets by Glazounov, written in conventional form, is no. 4 in A. I have had the unforgettable experience of playing second violin in this quartet to those magnificent Russian artists Heifetz and Zimbalist, both of whom revelled, of course, in the virtuoso passages of the moto perpetuo (scherzo), a mad race of semiquavers which leaves one breathless at the end.

Rumour says that Glazounov is at work on another string quartet. It would be welcomed by quartet players all over the world.

Editor.]

*†GLIÈRE, Reinhold Moritzovitch, 1875 N.S.–1926, Russian composer.

	op.	Composed	
Octet, 4 v, 2 vla, 2 vc, D	5	1900	Belaiev.
1st sextet (Prize work), 2 v, 2 vla, 2 vc, c mi	1	1900	,,
2nd sextet, 2 v, 2 vla, 2 vc, b mi	7	1904	,,
3rd sextet, 2 v, 2 vla, 2 vc, C	11		,,
1st quartet, str, A	2	1900	,,
2nd quartet, str, g mi	20		,,
Twelve duets, 2 v	49		Jurgenson.
Eight pieces, v, vc			,,
Ten pieces, vc, cb, or 2 vc	53		,,

Reinhold Glière, one of the most prolific and industrious workers in chamber music, was of Belgian nationality, but became completely Russianized, even to the extent of assimilating the Russian melos and applying it in his creative work. His chamber compositions show him to have been an absolute master of form, and a virtuoso in his control of the resources of musical composition and expression. Whilst he may not have had the gift of brilliant originality, nor be numbered amongst the composers who revealed new paths in art, Glière was skilful enough to follow those opened up by others, and in his time did not shun the newest influences. His chamber music, mainly written in the earlier part of his career, was principally affected by Borodin, Glazounov, Tchaikovsky, Rachmaninov, and later by Scriabin. Glière excelled as a melodist, and his themes often reveal the beautiful contours of the Russian style, which he loved and understood so well. He had a masterly knowledge of the instruments and of the conditions of their resonance; hence his chamber works are astonishingly rich and skilfully written. He is further interesting as one of the few composers who have written for the larger combinations—the sextet and the octet, for which he had a great liking.

His first chamber work was a sextet, which set forth all the merits of the young composer—mastery of form, fine and expressive melody, and excellent musical taste. At the same time this sextet, very skilfully written for the instruments, reveals Glière's fundamental defect—his eclecticism, his musical 'omnivorousness'. Everything he met on the way was taken into his work and converted to his own use. Tchaikovsky, Wagner, Glazounov, Scriabin, Rimsky-Korsakov—this ravenous composer swallowed them all, thereby ruining the clear outlines of his own physiognomy. But he had one unquestionable advantage in that his music is invariably good, though sometimes it has no pretensions to be independent.

The String Quartet, op. 2, shows Glière to be a great master of the old and strict form. Here he may have been chiefly influenced by S. Taneiev, the 'Russian Brahms', whose strict style of quartet writing made itself felt by every Russian composer. But Glière has none of Taneiev's academic dryness; he is more emotional, more passionate, though at the expense of independence. His first quartet is to this day one of the favourite works in the Russian quartet repertory, and there is no doubt that the sextet could lay claim to a similar success and popularity, were it not that the combination is unfortunately too rarely available in the present state of affairs in Russia. Russian chamber ensembles do not usually attain to the size of the sextet, and works of that type are doomed to an existence in the composer's study. [These remarks apply to other countries besides Russia. Ed.]

The Octet, op. 5, a fine work, proves that Glière was supremely qualified to deal with the larger chamber ensembles, which have found so few lovers amongst Russian composers. The octet amazes one by the fullness of the resonance and the masterly, semi-orchestral treatment of the instruments. Its style is tranquil, with a slightly academic touch, but never becomes dry. Glière's melodies are full of feeling and emotion, and the fine sonority and noble harmony are always sufficient guarantee against the academic aridity which so often overtakes chamber composers.

The Sextets. Faithful to his sympathy, which had already found expression, for big chamber ensembles, Glière then wrote a series of string sextets, of which the most successful and important from a musical point of view is the third, op. 11. Here the composer's mastery is expressed in all its power, with the maturity which his talent had now attained. His harmonic style had become more complex and solid and more emotional; the influence of Wagner's chromaticism definitely creeps into it, the tissue of the music is more contrapuntal and is manifestly affected by the teachings of his master, S. Taneiev. Nevertheless, the composer does not attain to independence of musical thought, but restricts himself to the skilful transformation of the tendencies of the past.

The Quartet, op. 20, completes the series of Glière's chamber compositions. The style of this work is mature and confident, but it does not introduce any new traits or characteristics.

Glière, who produced such an important collection of works, cannot but be regarded as one of the most popular of chamber composers; his works have often been performed, particularly during the pre-war period, and it is only in recent times, when interest had been transferred to the composers of a new generation, that the influence and diffusion of his creative work began to fail. Simultaneously with this, the composer's inspiration took another direction, and his latest work belongs to other branches of the musical art.

S. Taneiev and Glière are the representatives of a ripe mastery of academic chamber writing in the best sense of the term. Glière appears to be almost the last composer in this direction, marking the final stage, as it were, of an academic style which has had its day. The composers of his own generation began to depart from these norms of creation, and to be attracted by modernist tendencies, with which Glière's work has essentially no affinity. Even the insignificant influences of Scriabin scattered through his latest compositions are insufficiently shaped and little characteristic; moreover they are derived, not from the later Scriabin but from his middle and early periods, when that composer was not so much of an innovator.

L. Sabaneiev.

[Of Glière I have something to say which will surprise many readers. I am well acquainted with his quartets and sextets, and know them to be very valuable accessions to the repertory. But still more valuable, in my opinion, are his twelve short duets for two violins. They are quite unique. To my mind no other composer, with the exception of Spohr, with whom, needless to say, Glière's music has no affinity whatever, and perhaps Leclair, has written music for two violins unaccompanied, of real interest outside the class-room. But these duets please listeners almost as much as a string quartet. By what magic this is accomplished I know not, for it must be frankly admitted that duets for two violins are tedious things as a rule, and I am glad to have this opportunity of drawing attention to a feat so remarkable. Both parts are printed on the same page, which is convenient for teaching purposes. For private playing, however, it is pleasanter for each violinist to have a copy, and I suggest to the publisher that he would do well to see that the printer arranges his sheets alike in both copies, otherwise turning over becomes unnecessarily awkward. The duets for violin and 'cello are also to be recommended in a lesser degree.

Of Glière's two quartets, the earlier, in A major, is by far the more popular. The viola, to which the dignified opening theme is assigned, is prominent throughout. In the first section of the tema con variazioni (A minor), a movement of singular beauty, there is one of those effects which only a consummate craftsman can provide. After a series of bell-like sounds from all the instruments, the viola enters at the close with the following figure in double stops:

If this is played sotto voce and the viola is in perfect tune, the effect is magical. The second quartet is of coarser fibre. The finale is of excessive length, and not worthy of this extraordinarily gifted composer. His sextets, which are also of unequal merit, form a splendid contribution to a restricted repertory.

EDITOR.]

†GLINKA, MICHAEL IVANOVITCH, 1803–1857, Russian composer.

Quartet, str, F	Jurgenson (orig. Bernhard), 1830.
Sextet, pf, 2 v, vla, vc, cb	Jurgenson (orig. Bernhard), 1833.
Trio *Pathétique*, pf, cl, fag (or pf, v, vc)	Jurgenson (orig. Bernhard), 1827.

Glinka is justly regarded as the founder and father of Russian music. Prior to him it was either entirely amateur, or was too subject to powerful foreign influences (particularly Italian and German) and therefore not independent. Glinka was the first to give Russian music a language of its own, by basing his original creative work on Russian folk-songs, and endeavouring to divine the harmonic and contrapuntal style most suited to the specific peculiarities of the Russian melos.

These efforts and achievements of Glinka, which conferred on him so honourable a part in the history of Russian music, are chiefly evident in his riper and later compositions. His chamber music, to which he devoted a comparatively insignificant share of his genius, belongs pre-eminently to his early period, and it is therefore difficult to discover in it those qualities which made his name famous amongst the Russian public and in Europe. Glinka was one of the first Russian musicians to forsake the path of dilettantism and to study in earnest the art of music, its science and technique. He underwent quite a serious musical training under the guidance of the celebrated German theorist, Dehn, and hence his early work shows the predominating influence of German music, particularly of the great composers contemporary with him, amongst whom Haydn, Mozart, and to some extent the early Beethoven occupy the first places.

In these early productions of the great national genius of the future there are no traces of the musical independence and the qualities which afterwards made him a celebrity throughout the world, and which conditioned for a full century the development of Russian musical art. These compositions were written in accordance with the classical examples, and essentially are not much above the general level of the second-rate works of the time. On hearing them it is even difficult to foresee that their composer was destined in after-years to occupy one of the foremost places in the history of music. The turns of the themes and their harmonization, the form, the general structure—all this is most strongly inspired by the German musical school and particularly by the classics, but it also shows traces of the influence of the French music of the eighteenth century.

The characteristic qualities of Glinka, apart from his specific national tinge, are, however, present in these compositions. In them is found the striving for beauty of tone, the external refinement—a heritage of French culture which, as is well known, had an enormous influence on the aristocratic class in Russia, an influence so powerful that a considerable section of the Russian nobility did not converse in their own language but in French, and were nourished entirely on French literature. Characteristics of Glinka in these early compositions of his are the absence of real depth in the music, and this preference displayed for external refinement and outward polish. His chamber compositions, written easily and freely, already reveal considerable technical powers, and testify amongst other things to the composer's great mastery and taste in the matter of scoring for the chamber ensemble—a quality which later invariably distinguished the future father of Russian music.

To chamber music Glinka contributed but little. These compositions of his should be regarded solely as a tribute to his serious efforts to acquire musical mastery—and nothing more. From the very nature of his talent, from the make-up of his psychical and musical organism, Glinka was little inclined to an equipoised, profound, and serious style of chamber music. On the contrary, his genius attracted him preferably to opera and symphony. In general, absolute music did not appeal to him, and he preferred the realm of applied music, connected with song, speech, theatrical presentation, or at least with a poetic programme or subject. These qualities of Glinka's talent, thanks to his authority, for a long period strengthened in Russian music a certain aversion to absolute music—an aversion which lasted until the time of Tchaikovsky. In connexion with this, these chamber works of Glinka, though interesting as the productions of a composer who had so great a significance in the history of Russian art, cannot be considered sufficiently satisfactory from the point of view of chamber style alone, which has its norms and its restricted aesthetics. On account of these qualities, Glinka's chamber compositions are overshadowed by his operas, symphonies, and songs, and even in Russia are performed rarely and to a limited extent.

The majority of them were published some time after they first saw the light by one of the few Russian publishers of those days—Bernhard, whose rights in them subsequently passed to the firm of Jurgenson.

L. SABANEIEV.

GLUCK, CHRISTOPH WILLIBALD, 1714–1787, opera composer.

Seven trios, pf, 2 v, vc (ad lib.) (H. Riemann, Coll. Mus.), B. & H., 1904–7.

The above trios are also published by the Gluck-Gesellschaft.

The original publications were by Simpson (London), 1746. Gluck visited London in this year.

Riemann says these trios 'in abundance of ideas and attention to detail stand between those of Pergolesi and Joh. Stamitz'. A sonata for piano and two violins has recently been published for the first time. EDITOR.

†GNIESSIN, MICHAEL FABIANOVITCH, b. 1883, Russian composer.

	op.		Comp.
Var^ns. on a Hebrew theme, str. quartet	24		U.E.
Quintet (*Requiem*), pf, 2 v, vla, vc	11	1909	Jurgenson.
Sonata-ballade, pf, vc, c sharp mi	7		Jurgenson.

Gniessin is a composer who began his career by writing chamber music. His début was brilliant in every respect, the 'cello sonata being performed for the first time by Siloti and Casals. The opinions of the musical public were very much divided, but these conflicting views must in any case have been very flattering to the vanity of the young composer, who might easily see even in the disapproval of the crowd an admission of the significance of his talent. In this sonata Gniessin shows himself to be an adherent of the impressionist movement, which had just been originated on a grand scale. This was in 1910–11. Over the sonata hover the influences of Debussy and the later Rimsky-Korsakov; his manner of expressing himself is refined and intricate. The harmonic style is rather cumbrous, solid, and complicated; he uses complex chords of five or six notes, a type of deformed augmented harmonies, but on the whole, notwithstanding its monumental bulkiness, the harmony is always interesting, and is not lacking in a specific originality. In the matter of melody the sonata is rather weaker, and this may have been the reason for its want of success, in spite of the qualifications of its first performers. In the harmony, apart from Debussy and Rimsky-Korsakov, it is possible to read the influence of Scriabin—his cult of augmented chords and semitonal constructions—but the melodic line is not very striking and is lost in the harmonic mass. The 'cello is rather at a disadvantage; throughout the sonata it is confined almost entirely to the lower register—which is not very melodious nor lyrical—and is essentially merely decorative. The form of the sonata—it is in one movement and in a comparatively slow tempo—is somewhat disconnected, and a certain rhapsodical quality is noticeable, a compilation of a mass of forms from a number of fragments. Nevertheless it cannot be denied that, with all its defects, this work in its time was something of an event in the world of Russian musical composition.

Later on, Gniessin, who had come forward in other fields and whose powers as a composer had grown, wrote his *Requiem*, in which he showed himself to be more independent. The work was written on the death of Rimsky-Korsakov, which occurred in 1908. His style becomes brighter, the impressionistic influences give place to a more austere and rigid musical line. Gniessin, like Alexander Krein, afterwards became prominent as an adherent of the 'Hebrew national movement', but these compositions, which belong to the neutral period of his creative work, show hardly any trace of Hebrew influences, save, perhaps, those inherent in his creative organization. Surveying his chamber compositions now, from the height of his present-day evolution, one may detect in the sonata and quartet certain symptoms of the Hebrew melodism, certain methods which afterwards obtained importance in the light of his national revelation.

L. SABANEIEV.

GODARD, BENJAMIN LOUIS PAUL, 1849–1895, French violinist and composer.

	op.	
Quartet, str	33	Durand.
Quartet, str, A	37	B. & H.
Quartet, str, A	136	Durand.
Trio, pf, v, vc		Heugel.
Trio, pf, v, vc, F	72	Durand.
Six duets, 2 v, with pf	—	Schirmer.
Sonata, pf, v, c mi	1	Durand.
Sonata, pf, v, a mi	2	,,
Sonata, pf, v, g mi	9	,,
Sonata, pf, v, A flat	12	B. & B.
Suite, pf, v, d mi	78	Fürstner.
Sonata, pf, vc, d mi and D	104	Durand.

Godard studied at the Paris Conservatoire (1863) under Reber (for harmony). He began by writing chamber music, in the playing of which he had much experience as violist, and it is with this type of music that he is now mainly identified. His two piano trios are quite delightful, and unhesitatingly to be recommended to amateur performers. Also the six violin duets for two violins (with piano) are effective both for home and concert performance. In his string quartets there are sections filled with graceful turns of melody, but although moments of lapse into sentimental commonplace are occasionally evident, he proved himself capable of good fugal writing.

Bracketed with Dubois, Godard was awarded the prize offered by the Paris municipality in 1878.

EDITOR.

GODFREY, PERCY, b. 1859, English composer.

Quintet, pf, v, vla, vc, cb, E flat	op. 16	Donajowski.

Godfrey gained the Lesley Alexander Prize for his piano quintet, 1900.

†GOEDICKE, ALEXANDER FEDOROVITCH, b. 1877, Russian pianist.

Quartet, str, c mi	op. 33	Mus. Sect. Russ. State Publ. Dept., 1926.
Quintet, pf, 2 v, vla, vc, C	,, 21	Russ. Musik-Verein, 1911.
Trio, pf, v, vc, g mi	,, 14	Jurgenson, 1903.
Sonata, pf, v, A	,, 10	,, 1901.

The high value of Goedicke's compositions is inadequately acknowledged as yet. They have a classical tendency similar to that found in the music of S. Taneiev and Medtner, but are highly individual in character and style. Just as Taneiev's music traces its origin to Mozart's, and Medtner's leads us back to the renaissance of classical tradition combined with the romanticism whose first great exponent is Brahms, so does Goedicke's art find its roots in Reger's. Such comparisons, of course, should not be pushed too far.

Goedicke seeks depth of psychological expression rather than colour. His chief achievements are his three superb symphonies. Chamber music is another significant part of his output.

THE PIANO TRIO obviously shows the variety of influences undergone by the composer. The introductory phrase and a few other passages are suggestive of Rachmaninov. The whole exposition and recapitulation of the first movement show the influence of Schumann, but the movement is most effective. The slow movement displays more of the true, mature Goedicke. It is short and sparely worked out, but deep and earnest; it might be compared with the slow movements in the chamber works of Taneiev, whose music was then beginning to influence Goedicke. The scherzo is brief and dramatic. The finale (a rondo) is beautifully finished and classical in character, and expresses a light-hearted mood, with which a dramatic middle section stands in strong contrast.

THE PIANO QUINTET shows the composer in his full maturity. It is one of the finest things in Russian chamber music, and represents a new step forward. It stands apart for the sustained intensity of its suggestive power. The elaborate workmanship and fullness of tone suggest a comparison with Medtner's style.

This pathetic and lofty work consists of three ample movements. The first is remarkable for the beauty of its harmonic and contrapuntal tissue. The poetic, earnest, and sustained andante molto sostenuto, which follows, is a piece of extremely intricate writing, and seems to embody to the full the artistic expression of the moods suggested in the largo of the trio, op. 14. The finale is a splendid, highly effective fugue.

Goedicke has recently finished a string quartet whose performance in Russia (1925) created a profound impression.

V. M. BELAIEV.

[The sonata is a work of considerable charm, presenting great attractions to amateurs, to whom I recommend it. EDITOR.]

GOETZ, HERMANN, 1840–1876, German composer.

		Composed	
Quintet, pf, v, vla, vc, cb, c mi	op. 16	1874	Kistner, 1878.
Quartet, pf, v, vla, vc, E	,, 6	1867	B. & H., 1870; (H. Sitt), Peters, 1911.
Trio, pf, v, vc, g mi	,, 1	1863	B. & H., 1868.

Goetz, who wrote the fine comic opera, *The Taming of the Shrew*, also made three peculiarly charming contributions to chamber music.

THE QUINTET is not likely to become popular in amateur circles, owing to the employment of the double-bass. This is all the more regrettable as the composer has produced a work of real importance, especially in the first movement. In the MS. he quotes Goethe's lines, 'Und wenn der Mensch in seiner Qual verstummt, gab mir ein Gott zu sagen, was ich leide,' before pouring out his passionate grief in the music, and although the second theme of the opening allegro gives promise of brighter things to come, it cannot finally penetrate the darker mood. After the fighting strain of this movement, the andante con moto has a soothing effect; the allegro moderato quasi menuetto is also consolatory, particularly its trio, which is in the nature of a *Ländler*, and in the final rondo in C minor a note of positive cheerfulness is achieved by the melodious theme in E flat. But none of these movements is quite on a level with the first.

THE QUARTET, however, shows mastery of style throughout; this work has moments both of inspiring energy and profound sadness. The emotional theme of the variations and the painfully melancholy introduction to the finale reveal how essentially temperamental was the composer, while the three-part canon which forms the trio of the magnificent scherzo is an instance of his technical skill.

THE TRIO, Goetz's first published work, already gave evidence of his powers. This astonishingly mature opus 1, though undeniably influenced by Mendelssohn, Schumann, and even Brahms, can be recommended for home performance. It is also easier to play than the piano quartet, which latter, however, presents no great difficulties to good amateurs, and should receive serious consideration from those who wish to judge the composer fairly.

WILHELM ALTMANN.

GOETZE, ED. DIETERICH.

Sonata alla antica, pf, v, F op. 21 Hug, 1907.

†GOEYENS, FERNAND, b. 1892, Belgian composer.

Suite, pf, v	Senart.
Sonata, pf, v, a mi	Chester (agent).

GOLDMARK, CARL, 1830–1915, Austrian composer.

	op.	
Quintet, 2 v, vla, 2 vc, a mi	9	Doblinger.
Quartet, str, B flat	8	Cranz.
Quintet, pf, 2 v, vla, vc, B flat	30	Haake.
Quintet, pf, 2 v, vla, vc, D flat	54	Weinberger.
Trio, pf, v, vc, B flat	4	Kistner.
Trio, pf, v, vc, e mi	33	Haake.
Suite, pf, v, E	11	Schott.
Sonata, pf, v, D	25	Schott.
Suite, pf, v, E flat	43	Simrock.
Sonata, pf, vc, F	39	Schott.

At thirty-five years of age Goldmark wrote his first chamber work, a piano trio, op. 4, a product of his 'Sturm und Drang' period. Although somewhat lacking in inventive power and originality, this work already reveals a genuine artistic nature, and shows admirable technical facility in the development of the themes. Particularly effective is the adagio, with its introductory improvisation recalling Hungarian gipsy tunes.

THE QUARTET, op. 8, is already a mature work. It opens with a short andante, notable for its rich harmony, leading to an impetuous allegro moderato. The first subject is virile and broadly unfolded; the second, which is strongly contrasted, and full of gentle grace and lyric feeling, is accompanied by the viola with a lovely melody in counterpoint. In the development, the first violin and 'cello introduce the first subject at intervals, while the second is given, with modifications, to the second violin, all the possibilities of the two themes being most skilfully exploited. In the andante sostenuto, sorrow and gloom are worked up to a climax with a dramatic outburst. In the scherzo Goldmark's robust humour again breaks forth; the finale, however, shows some falling off.

THE STRING QUINTET is also a mature work of masterly construction, and may be regarded as one of Goldmark's finest chamber works. The opening allegro reveals fresh invention and wealth of imagination; here the composer's characteristic tendency to Oriental colouring already appears. First and second subject are happily contrasted; the former pathetic, the latter of a meditative nature; later, a third theme appears, and all three are further splendidly developed. The end of this movement is particularly beautiful, and the skilful interweaving of the parts makes a deep impression. The deeply emotional andante is greatly influenced by Mendelssohn, the chief fault being that there are too many sequences. In this movement the second 'cellist has to tune his C string down to B. The gay mood of the scherzo gives way in the next movement to tones of grief, but a spirited finale restores the balance.

Goldmark's best chamber works are the first suite for violin and piano, the violin sonata, and the piano trio, op. 33.

THE SUITE is a highly melodious composition, full of piquant harmony and delicate rhythms. Freshness and wealth of invention combined with skilled technical work make it one of Goldmark's most original compositions and also one of the most effective of its class. The first movement is opened by the piano with a few bars of strongly marked rhythm; the violin then enters with a strain full of fire and passion, culminating in an effective dramatic climax; the middle section brings a slight relaxation, and thus increases the effect of the succeeding recapitulation.

The second movement, an andante sostenuto, expresses a dreamy, twilight mood, and shows the lyricist Goldmark on his best and most imaginative side; and a similar high artistic level is reached in the scherzo-like third movement. The fourth movement is full of melodic charm, whilst the final presto may be described as of somewhat corybantic nature.

THE VIOLIN SONATA, op. 25, has an artistic finish of form not always to be met with in Goldmark's chamber music, and reveals the supremacy of a master-hand, particularly in the development of the themes. It is so full of youthful impetuosity and impulsive joy, that one hardly realizes that it is the work of a mature composer. This mood is felt in the first subject of the allegro moderato with its spirited triple rhythm (a well-known characteristic of Goldmark), but the second subject is more restrained. The andante which follows is introduced by a short motif, which appears several times in the bass later on. The third movement, an adagio con molto espressione, consists essentially of variations on a theme bearing eloquent witness to the composer's gift of invention. Once more the finale is much too long. It is characteristic of Goldmark that he occasionally composes more from outer than inner impulse, and loses the natural feeling for corresponding relation between form and contents. Thus technique triumphs over inspiration, and the composer indulges in unnecessary length.

THE PIANO TRIO, op. 33, is a fully mature work, and shows Goldmark at the height of his artistic and technical mastery. The first movement begins in simple but very noble manner; then follows a second subject, delicate in feeling and imaginative in development. The lively scherzo is impish, goblin music, while the middle section, andantino grazioso, pleasingly naïve in character, offers an effective contrast. A short andante sostenuto reveals a certain feminine grace, and after the mad whirl of the scherzo produces a doubly pleasing effect by its unpretentiousness. It leads, attacca, to the allegro, which is full of *joie de vivre*, but at the close passes into a more elegiac mood, and ends softly, in meditative and dreamy fashion.

THE PIANO QUINTET, op. 30, is also rich in interesting episodes and charming ideas. The first movement is good, but over-lengthy. The adagio attracts from the very beginning by the beautiful singing of the 'cello, which is accompanied by soft quaver beats on the piano. The scherzo is a very charming piece of music, full of original and witty ideas, and may be regarded as the best part of the work; but the finale is much too diffuse, and trickles along as if it would never stop. This explains why the quintet does not leave so strong an impression as Goldmark's other chamber works, and is so seldom played at concerts.

Goldmark's pronounced romanticism is clearly reflected in all his chamber music; and it is the lyrical sections of his works which are the most moving. His melody and harmony are spontaneous, and mainly diatonic. The operatic composer is visible now and then in certain themes of arioso type, and in his occasional disregard of chamber music intimacy and over-attention to mere effect. His abundant technical skill is evident in the conscientious development of all his works. The best proof of the artistic value of Goldmark's chamber music is the fact that it is still frequently heard in German concert halls, and produces the same pleasing effect as at the time of its first appearance. RUDOLF FELBER.

[The first violin suite in E is undeservedly neglected by concert players. I can say for myself that, often as I have played it, I have always returned to it with new zest. The impulsive opening allegro awakens keen interest, whilst the andante sostenuto sets one dreaming of Schubert and the *Erl King*, though plagiarism is not insinuated. After the graceful scherzo and the allegretto (a movement of infinite tranquillity) comes the brilliantly violinistic finale, with its fascinating cadenzas, and a coda of mingled spiccati and pizzicati that sparkle like points of light. What can concert artists who are out to please wish for more? When Sarasate played it the audience rose to him.

An amusing story is told of Goldmark, who travelled great distances to hear his suite played. On one occasion he wrote his name in an hotel book, and after it a humorist added, 'and his suite'. Much was the disappointment of mine host when he found that his guest was a diffident little man accompanied by—a hand-bag.

The second suite (E flat) is far less spontaneous than the first. It was, I believe, composed for, and played by, Sarasate.

Goldmark's beautiful piano quintet, op. 30, is kept out of the concert-room by the excessive development in which he indulges in the outer movements. There is a glorious solo for the 'cello in the adagio, a movement of singular beauty. EDITOR.]

†GOLDMARK, RUBIN, b. 1872, American composer. Nephew of Carl.

Quartet, pf, v, vla, vc, A	op. 12	Schirmer, 1912.
Trio, pf, v, vc, d mi	,, 1	B. & H., 1896.
Sonata, pf, v, b mi	,, 4	,, ,,

Goldmark studied composition under Dvořák when that composer was director of the National Conservatorium of Music at New York, and afterwards taught at the same institution.

The trio and the sonata may be viewed as works in the formative stage. The composer, in his twenties, is plainly in the process of assimilation, his work is romantic in content and classical in form, and exhibits vigorous inventiveness. His full characteristics were not revealed until the production of the quartet which won the Paderewski prize for chamber music in the competition of 1909, but which was not published until 1912. This work is one of ample proportions (four movements), skilfully written, idiomatic and grateful in every respect and very moderate in its technical demands. There is a particularly fine slow movement, while the piano part throughout is fluent and never too full. ARTHUR SHEPHERD.

GOLDSCHMIDT, OTTO, 1829–1907, German pianist.

Trio, pf, v, vc, B flat op. 12 B. & H., 1884.

Goldschmidt was a pupil of Mendelssohn and Chopin. About 1858 he settled in London, where he was best known as conductor of the Bach choir. He married the celebrated singer, Jenny Lind. The present writer has frequently enjoyed playing chamber music for piano and strings with him. EDITOR.

†GOLESTAN, STAN, b. 1876, Roumanian composer.

Quartet, str, c mi U.E.
Sonata, pf, v, E flat Gallet, Paris (1908).

Studied composition under Vincent d'Indy, Auguste Sérieyx, and Albert Roussel. Musical critic of the *Figaro* and Chevalier de la Légion d'honneur. F. LAZAR.

[The violin sonata is generally considered to belong to the French school, and is a very delightful work. EDITOR.]

GOLTERMANN, GEORG EDUARD, 1824–1898, German 'cellist.

Has written and published several ensemble works in which the 'cello has a prominent part. They are, however, of little interest to musicians in general. For list *v. Altmann.*

GOLYSCHEV, JEF, contemporary composer.

Trio, v, vla, vc (on 12-tone system) Schlesinger.

Golyschev is one of the many composers in Central Europe to-day who have elaborated new musical theories and written works to illustrate them. He has also adopted a twelve-degree notation which, however, for clarity, compares somewhat unfavourably with those which others, Schönberg among them, have at various times recommended as a means of escaping from the maze of accidentals in present-day music. From 'compositions down to 1925' he has published a trio consisting of three short movements for violin, viola, and 'cello inscribed simply *Mezzo-forte, Fortissimo,* and *Piano,* and containing no other dynamic indications. These he calls *Zwölftondauer-Musik.* Figures indicate the end of each *Zwölftondauer-Komplex,* which appears to be a section in which occur, vertically or horizontally, all the twelve notes of the scale, and, except for doublings in unison or octaves, only once each. Appended as example is one such 'complex', in ordinary notation.

At certain points his views appear to touch upon those of Hauer, but in a more elementary form. EDWIN EVANS.

†GOMPERTZ, RICHARD, b. 1859.

Sonata, pf, v, g mi Wernthal, 1899.

*GOOSSENS, EUGENE, b. 1893, composer and conductor.

	op.	Comp.	
Phantasy nonet, fl, ob, 2 cl, 2 fag, 2 horns, trpt	40	1924	Curwen.
Sextet, 3 v, vla, 2 vc	35	1923	Chester.
Three songs, med. voice, str. quartet	26	1920	,,
Phantasy quartet, str	12	1915	,,
Quartet, str	14	1915	,,
Two sketches (*By the Tarn, Jack o' Lantern*), str. quartet	15	1916	,,
Suite, fl, v, harp (or pf, 2 v)	6		,,
Quintet (one movt.), pf, 2 v, vla, vc	23*a*	1919	Rouart; Chester.
Five Impressions of a Holiday, pf, fl (or v), vc	7	1914	Chester.
Pastorale and Harlequinade, pf, fl, ob	41	1924	Curwen.
Sonata, pf, v	21	1918	Rouart; Chester.
Lyric Poem, pf, v	24	1919	Chester.
Rhapsody, pf, vc	13	1915	,,

Goossens is the son of a well-known conductor who, though belonging to a Bruges family, was born in France; but, as so often happens, environment has prevailed over heredity, and there is more than the accident of birth to classify Goossens with British composers. There survive, however, some fundamental traits in his character and general outlook that betray Latin leanings.

On completing his studies Goossens joined the Queen's Hall Orchestra under Sir Henry Wood, and, a little later, the Philharmonic String Quartet, in which he played second violin for several years. There can be little doubt that the experience and the intimate familiarity which he acquired with vast and varied quantities of music, by playing in both orchestra and quartet, contributed to his easy command of instrumental resources. Eventually the growing demand for his services as a conductor made it necessary for him to divide his abundant energy exclusively between these functions and composition. He therefore retired from the Philharmonic String Quartet, but not before having enriched the repertory with several works. As a composer he developed early, passing rapidly through a succession of phases, which, though a marked individuality could be discerned even in his earliest works, reflected his preferences of the time. At first he was attracted to the French composers, and he has retained permanently some of their best qualities; but he also had a German phase which, as was chronologically to be expected, took a Straussian form. Even an alleged Stravinsky influence has furnished a somewhat slender ground for comment, but at the most these elements were formative, and the idiom that grew from them is personal. It is characterized by a free use of the twelve-note tonality—that is to say chromaticism, often of an extreme kind, but without sacrifice of tonality; further, by a lavish use of parallels, which, when he colours the successive notes of two converging melodic lines with a three- or four-note chord, creates a deceptive effect of chromatic complexity, whereas his construction is usually very simple, and his texture rarely has more than two or three independent strands. Of greater importance than these technical details is the evolution of his musical thought. At first he became identified with the modern revolt against idealism and the reaction against the moribund romantic movement. He was credited with a love of cold glitter, and with being incapable of expressing emotion in music. This was, of course, nothing more than the accusation which it was the fashion for upholders of the dying romantic movement to level at the new régime, but in his case it was not even superficially justified, for in relatively early works such as the phantasy quartet and the 'cello rhapsody, and again later in the piano quintet and the slow movement of the violin sonata, there are pages of deep and tender emotion, though he does not wallow in sentiment as was apparently expected of him. But from the beginning his path was almost foreordained. The eighteenth-century elegance of his earliest works, even to the occasional chinoiseries, marked him out as an adherent of the 'back to Mozart' movement, in other words, a neo-classic, and when eventually the first movement of his sinfonietta performed a chromatic obeisance to Haydn, one felt that his destiny was accomplished, even though the succeeding movement belied it.

It is, of course, still far too early to speak of periods in his work, but his chamber music falls chronologically into four groups of works, each of which reveals a certain homogeneity of feeling and of idiom, though this may be chiefly due to the fact that a brief interval of comparative abstention from writing separates each group from the next.

The first group consists of early works, not all of which are published. The list opens with a phantasy octet for flute, clarinet, horn, harp, and string quartet (op. 3, 1911), produced at the Incorporated Society of Musicians conference, Christmas 1913, and *Four Sketches* for flute, violin, and piano, which are not accessible in print. The list of chamber music publications may be said to open with the remaining works of this group: the suite for flute, violin, and harp (or piano), and the *Five Impressions of a Holiday*, both of which first became known at the War Emergency concerts in 1915, when they made an immediate impression. The former consists of an impromptu, serenade and divertissement, and the *Impressions* are respectively entitled *In the Hills*, *By the Rivers*, *The Water-Wheel*, *The Village Church*, and *At the Fair*. All are rich-hued genre pictures, and if some of the harmonic pigments on the painter's palette correspond with those used by Debussy or Ravel, young as he was then Goossens knew how to make them subservient to his own designs.

Just as the early phase produced four works (an octet and three trios), the next is represented by opp. 12 to 15, four works, of which, however, three are for string quartet. All were written in the two years 1915–16, and reflect the composer's association with the Philharmonic String Quartet.

THE PHANTASY FOR STRING QUARTET, op. 12, dedicated 'to my friends the London String Quartet', is the earliest of the four. This is the first work which is really characteristic of the composer. Mr. Philip Heseltine records that it 'was sent in MS. to Frederick Delius, who pronounced it the best thing he had seen from an English pen; and it is not improbable that the new resources revealed and suggested by this work may have served to break down his apparent aversion to quartet writing, since his latest work (1916) has been cast in this form'. The phantasy is in three sections, of which the first two are interlaced with recurrent material, the whole preceded by a brief introduction which contains the motto theme of the entire work. The third (scherzo) section is thematically independent, but some earlier matter is heard again in the approach to the coda. If any influence were to be traced, it would probably be ascribed to Ravel, notably in

Ex. 1.

but the personal touches predominate on every page. The slow section, from which is quoted

Ex. 2.

has an emotional warmth which shows, even at this early date, how ill-considered was the criticism which ascribed Goossens' normal avoidance of sentimental expression to an absence of feeling.

The Rhapsody for 'Cello and Piano inscribed to Warwick Evans, the 'cellist of the 'London', came next. This is another characteristic work, conceived in a mood of passionate meditation which is perhaps less readily accessible than that of the phantasy. The declamatory quality of the instrument is employed in preference to executive brilliance. It is based upon two principal themes, with a brief introduction (andante 3/2) foreshadowing the first of these, which is given in full when the time changes (con amore ma tempo giusto 2/2). Later follows a slow section, the trend of which, however, soon returns to the restless mood of the opening. This leads to a climax, after which the rhapsody concludes with an impressive coda over a reiterated pedal-note E.

The String Quartet in C major is next in order, the three movements being severally dedicated to the composer's three colleagues in the Philharmonic String Quartet: Arthur Beckwith, the first violin, who has since visited America, Raymond Jeremy, the viola, and Cedric Sharpe, the 'cello. To what extent they may be regarded as musical portraits comparable with those of the Elgar variations is doubtful, though in each case certain intimate touches are there for the appreciation of those acquainted with the respective subjects. An interchange of melodic fragments between the three sections might, in the light of dedications, be held to symbolize the solidarity that should animate all quartet-players (and certainly did these); but it is more likely to have proceeded from the composer's instinctive craving to establish the musical unity of the work. The first movement, inscribed to Arthur Beckwith, opens with

Ex. 3.

which is extended to some length, with more than one melodic figure of which use is made later. From the opening phrase afterwards an effective fugato is derived. The movement concludes with a meditative passage for 'cello with the C string tuned down to B, accompanied by open fifths on the other instruments. In the second movement, which is inscribed to Raymond Jeremy, prominence is appropriately given to the viola. It is a quiet andante mostly played con sordino, but not without marked contrasts, provided by a somewhat whimsical second subject, and an extended con moto section, which occupies the centre and consists of a viola solo founded on the opening subject with a murmuring triplet accompaniment. It is related that Cedric Sharpe, the 'cellist, to whom the finale is inscribed, was temporarily obsessed with a music-hall ditty of the period running:

> 'You're here and I'm here,
> So what do we care?'

and especially with the four notes associated with 'What do we care?' These, accordingly, open the movement, which at the fifth bar plunges into a boisterous theme with strongly marked rhythms. A cantabile contrast is furnished by a reminiscence from the first movement, but before long the music-hall tune is played not by the 'cello but by the second violin, suggesting friendly badinage. The tempo then slackens and a long 'cello solo follows, based upon an augmentation of the first subject. Afterwards the animation is resumed, until this time the 'cello thunders out the obnoxious tune. Thereupon a wild fugato ensues. A brief return of Ex. 3 heralds the lively coda.

THE TWO SKETCHES FOR STRING QUARTET (op. 15), which have become perhaps the most popular of these compositions, complete this brilliant cycle of works. The first, which has since been arranged for stringed orchestra, is a subtle, pastel-like landscape entitled *By the Tarn*. The second is a piece of virtuosity in the form of a wild, elusively tantalizing, dance appropriately named *Jack o' Lantern* (*Ignis Fatuus*).

THE VIOLIN SONATA appeared after an interval of two years, mainly devoted to songs and piano pieces. It is the first of another group of four chamber works. In this work at once the emotional side of his temperament and the devices of his personal technique are found in full development. Except, however, in the lyrical slow movement, the sentiment is embedded in a context that harbours some contradiction, as if the voice of irony refused to be entirely silenced. The following,

Ex. 4.

from the development section of the first movement, is a characteristic example of the composer's chromaticism. The slow movement is

Ex. 5.

the most single-minded piece of tone poetry the composer has written. From its manifold beauties the preceding (Ex. 5) calls for quotation. In it two subjects are heard together and associated with suggestions of a third. The finale yields, in Ex. 6, a very characteristic example of the converging and diverging parallels to which, as we observe above, the composer is, or rather was at this time, so much addicted.

Ex. 6.

THE QUINTET FOR PIANO AND STRINGS is the next of this group. It is in one movement and founded upon one principal subject, which, however, is shown in such conflicting aspects as to become almost unrecognizable in its many transformations. One perplexing thing about it is that the composer, practically for the first time in five-and-twenty works, has had recourse to some of the devices sanctioned by usage in a more conventional form of romanticism. The form is that of a phantasy, comprising three movements in one, preceded by an introduction containing the theme from which the whole is constructed. It is a form which he has repeatedly adopted, before (phantasy-quartet) and since (string sextet and wind nonet).

THE LYRIC POEM for violin and piano, which is the next work of this group, is so richly coloured that, from the first, one suspected the composer of orchestral intentions in regard to it, though it was not until some years later that he actually began scoring it. Structurally it consists in the rhapsodical treatment of a single subject. The following is taken from the introduction:

Ex. 7.

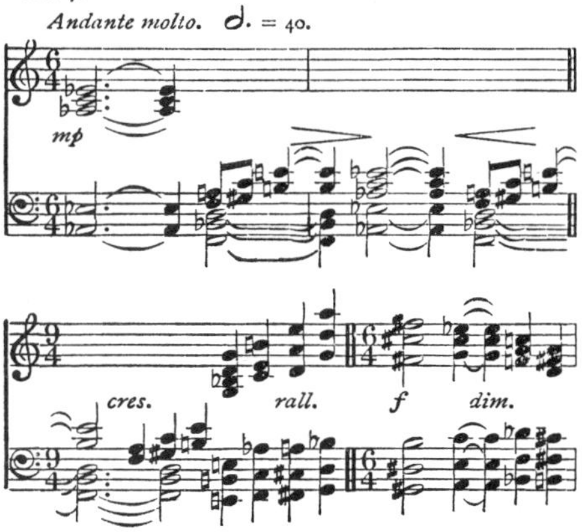

The Three Songs with string quartet form the fourth work of this group. They are settings of sixteenth and seventeenth century poems: *The Appeal* (Sir Thomas Wyatt, 1503–1542), *Melancholy* (John Fletcher, 1579–1625), and *Philomel* (Richard Barnefield, 1574–1627).

Again an interval passed during which he was engaged upon other work, chiefly orchestral. Eventually, on the initiative of Mrs. Coolidge, he reverted to chamber music, and composed, for the Berkshire Festival of 1923, a sextet for three violins, viola, and two 'cellos. This is another example, and perhaps the most complete, of the three movements in one type of phantasy, welded together by recurrent phrases derived from the chief thematic material. A characteristic example is this quotation from the slow section (Ex. 8). The upper stave gives a variant of the principal theme, the second a figure based upon an auxiliary theme from the first (allegro) section; a variant of this figure is given to the first 'cello, whilst the second supports the whole over a pedal bass.

Ex. 8.

About this time the composer's brother, Léon Goossens, a famous oboe player, joined with Albert Fransella (flute) and Francesco Ticciati (piano) to form the Philharmonic Trio, and naturally Eugene Goossens promised a contribution to their repertory. Thus originated the pastorale and harlequinade for flute, oboe, and piano. The title-page bears the indication that either the flute or the oboe part (but not both) may be played in case of need on the violin, but that is only a concession to practical considerations, for the two pieces are so essentially in the character of the instruments that any substitution is a poor expedient.

Perhaps it is the instrumental colouring that makes them recall in a curiously remote way the composer's two early trios (opp. 6 and 7), though that may also be the effect of French influences emerging once more on the surface, where they had not been so clearly discernible in the intervening works. Though not very important in themselves, the two pieces form a very attractive interlude in the survey of the composer's chamber music.

The third work of this latest group consists of a phantasy for nine wind instruments (flute, oboe, two clarinets, two bassoons, two horns, and trumpet), consisting of three movements in one—allegro, andante, and scherzo—preceded by an introduction based upon the motto theme. This exhausts the list for the present. During the last few years Goossens' activities as a conductor have absorbed so much time and necessitated such frequent displacements that it has become difficult for him to find opportunities for the concentration needed in composition. But though the fame he has earned as a conductor may prove a temporary impediment, his first inclination is to composition, and especially to chamber music, in which he has worked to such good purpose.

EDWIN EVANS.

[To Mr. Evans's appreciations I have a few words to add. Circulation of the string quartet in C major, written in dissonant vein, should in my opinion be confined to friends of the extremely talented artist to whom it is dedicated. It is little more than what in Germany is known as a *musikalischer Spass*. But the phantasy quartet is on an altogether higher plane; a work in which one discerns the quality of genius. Eugene Goossens is the perfect Fantasist (or Phantasist?), and of all the one-movement works written round the ideas promoted by the Phantasy Competition, this work realizes best my own conception of a short, concise, and essentially *fantastic* composition. It is not written for amateurs, the ensemble being somewhat intricate, but it richly repays the expenditure of time in extra rehearsals needed by professional quartet players who desire to add it to their repertory.

EDITOR.]

GOSSEC, FRANÇOIS JOSEPH, 1734–1829.

Modern republication:

Trio, 2 v, vc, E flat	op. 9, no. 1	(H. Riemann, Coll. Mus. 47), B. & H., 1909.

A list of other chamber works, string quartets, &c., is given in *Fétis* and *Vidal* (18 quartets, and 6 trios for 2 v, vc).

Gossec was a composer of much talent, whom Mozart described (April 5, 1778) as 'mein sehr guter Freund und sehr trockener Mann' (my very good friend and very dry man). See also BELGIAN CHAMBER MUSIC.

EDITOR.

GOTTHARD, JOHANN PETER (PÀZDIREK), 1839–1919, Moravian composer.

Andante ongarese, var^{ns}. and scherzo, str. quartet	op. 68	Doblinger, 1872.
Quintet, pf, 2 v, vla, vc, E flat	,, 60	R. Forberg, 1870.
Sonata, pf, v, C	,, 77	Haslinger, 1877.

†GOTTHELF, FELIX, b. 1867, German opera composer.

		Composed	
Quartet, str, C	op. 10	1891	R. & E., 1893.

Dr. Altmann (*Handbuch*) writes indulgently of Gotthelf's operatic proclivities, and suggests that 'one cannot be a theatrical Capellmeister for years with impunity'. There are both humour and charm in the above quartet, in which effective use is made of the folk-song 'Upon a tree a cuckoo sits'. EDITOR.

GÖTZE, HEINRICH, 1836–1906, German composer.

Trio, pf, v, vc, c mi	op. 25	B. & H., 1883.

GOUFFÉ, ACHILLE HENRY VICTOR, 1804–1874.

Patron of young chamber composers; he organized séances of chamber music for the performance of their works, and wrote a certain amount of music himself. See *Pougin*.

GOUNOD, CHARLES, 1818–1893, French operatic composer.

Petite Symphonie, fl, 2 ob, 2 cl, 2 horns, 2 fag, B flat	Costallat, 1904.
3rd quartet, str, a mi, posthumous	Choudens, 1895.

Dr. Altmann (*Handbuch*) speaks of Gounod's quartet as having charm, though not calculated to increase the composer's reputation, and considers that, regarded as 'house music', it has certain attractions. It presents no technical difficulties, and though it includes a fugal section, is in its nature salon music of an excellent kind.

The *Petite Symphonie* was written for Paul Taffanel's *Société de Musique de Chambre pour Instruments à Vent* (*vide* FRENCH CHAMBER MUSIC and FLUTE IN MODERN CHAMBER MUSIC). It was performed for the first time in 1885, the composer being present. The work represents Gounod at his best. EDITOR.

GOUVY, LOUIS THÉODORE, 1819–1898, Alsatian composer, of French parentage.

	op.	
Petite Suite Gauloise, fl, 2 ob, 2 cl, 2 horns, 2 fag	90	U.E.
Octet, fl, ob, 2 cl, 2 horns, 2 fag, E flat	71	Kistner.
1st serenade, fl, 2 v, vla, vc, cb, G	82	,,

	op.	
2nd serenade, fl, 2 v, vla, vc, cb, f mi	84	Rahter.
Quintet, 2 v, vla, 2 vc, G	55	Costallat.
Serenade, 2 v, vla, vc, cb	11	Richault.
Two quartets, str, B flat, C	16	Costallat.
Two quartets, str, D, a mi	56	Costallat.
Quartet, str, c mi	68	B. & H.
Quintet, pf, 2 v, vla, vc, A	24	Costallat.
Serenade, pf, v, vla, vc, E flat	31	„
Trio, pf, v, vc, E	8	B. & H.; Costallat.
Trio, pf, v, vc, a mi	18	Costallat.
Trio, pf, v, vc, B flat	19	„
Trio, pf, v, vc, F	22	„
Trio, pf, v, vc, G	33	„
Sonata, pf, v, g mi	61	B. & H.
Sonata, pf, cl (or v), g mi	67	Costallat.

and some duos pf, v, *vide Altmann.*

Fortunate in possessing means which enabled him to live entirely for his work, this composer is one of many whose compositions, once greatly esteemed, are now almost unknown to the public. Whether it be fair to regard him merely as a disciple of Mendelssohn is open to question. He certainly has in common with him that delicacy of sentiment which amounts almost to effeminacy in the melodic formation, but also, no less markedly, his perfection of form and extremely acute sense of timbre. An Alsatian by birth, Gouvy was undoubtedly more attracted by the artistic ideals of which the Leipzig Conservatorium was the centre, than by those which prevailed in Paris. At the same time, he was very much at home in that city, though he found in Leipzig on the whole a more congenial atmosphere. It is perhaps on account of his cosmopolitan bias—for he found life in Italy likewise to his taste—that his work lacks individuality, a fact which is apparent in his numerous chamber compositions. Credit is due to him for his use of wind instruments at a time when these were undeservedly ignored in chamber music. There is hardly one of his chamber works that will fail to give some satisfaction to players, but the inequality between individual movements will undoubtedly make itself felt. Gouvy's compositions might well survive in amateur circles to-day, were it not for the wealth of glorious music in this category supplied by the great classics and romantics. Only a few of his works can be dealt with in detail here.

There are, first, the duos for piano and violin. From the title one would suppose these to be pieces in several movements; they are, however, all single pieces, in the nature of 'songs without words' and similar to Molique's excellent melodies—now practically forgotten. Five of these duos are comprised in op. 34 (written 1865; pubd. Costallat 1866). The first number, allegro moderato, in G, is a very attractive piece, effective by reason of its rhythm. The second, moderato assai, in A, is soft and tender; the third, in E minor, broadly humorous and to be recommended as a really fine piece. No. 4, allegro non troppo, B flat, is simple in style and has a certain melodic charm. In the last, *Memories of the Past*, Gouvy experiments with the gavotte and the minuet, linking them together to preserve the one-movement form of duo. The six duos, op. 50, are published by Peters.

The Violin Sonata, first published in revised form, with a new middle movement, as op. 61, the writer would rate higher than does Otto Klauwell, Gouvy's excellent biographer. It is in three movements, entirely classical in style and of great transparency. The first movement, allegro moderato, opens restlessly in a manner somewhat reminiscent of Schubert's *Erl King*. The second movement has ingenious and, at times, virtuoso-like variations on a simple moving andante theme, which is well treated rhythmically. Gouvy was, indeed, a master of the art of variation. Considerable variety is provided by the energetic finale; the air given to the violin, with an accompaniment of broken chords, is a particularly happy inspiration.

The Third String Quartet, op. 56, no. 1, which, together with the fifth, most deserves attention, is in admirable classical style. A tender melody forms the opening theme of the allegro non troppo, but is less used subsequently than the more trifling second theme. The preference for dotted rhythms, particularly in transitions, gives this movement a distinctive character. Quite charming is the scherzo, which somewhat resembles Mendelssohn's *Elfin Music* in its delicate piquancy; the short trio is more or less pastoral in character. The larghetto con moto consists of clever variations, very effective and excellently contrasted, on the simple song-like theme of an alleged Swedish folk-song—hence the title 'Swedish' affixed to this work. One notes here and there an indebtedness to Schubert's D minor quartet. The finale is comparatively weak. It is related thematically and rhythmically to the first movement, and introduces the Swedish folk-song shortly before the close. The fine workmanship of this finale does not compensate for its paucity of invention. Its great length is characteristic of Gouvy, who tends to be long-winded.

The Fifth Quartet, in C minor, can be most warmly recommended to amateurs. The two outer movements in particular are quite admirable in style, and the invention is of a high order. The opening allegro undoubtedly recalls Beethoven's quartet in the same key, but is a model as regards ingenious working-out of motifs. Solemnity and pathos characterize the first theme; the second is more soothing, while the coda has a certain attractive breadth, which, indeed, is a distinguishing feature of this movement. The middle movement is a graceful intermezzo, which is, perhaps, a trifle long. Gouvy's mastery of the art of variation, to which attention has been drawn, is again demonstrated in the andante con moto, which has a smooth and pleasing theme. The finale is weightier than the first movement, which it resembles in dignified solemnity; the rhythm is not without distinction, and it closes with an effective climax.

WILHELM ALTMANN.

[*Fétis*, in his notice of Gouvy, mentions errors of writing, dissonances unresolved or badly resolved, and basses which are not always well placed. But these errors, he says, are redeemed by vitality of imagination and sentiment.]

†GRABERT, MARTIN, b. 1868, German organist.

Quintet, pf, 2 v, vla, vc, f mi	op. 22	Simrock, 1905.
Sonata, pf, ob, g mi	,, 52	,, 1921.

GRÄDENER, (1) CARL GEORG PETER, 1812–1883, German 'cellist and composer.

	op.	
Octet, 4 v, 2 vla, 2 vc, E flat	49	F. Schuberth, jnr.
Three quartets, str, B flat, a mi, E flat	12, 17, 29	Peters.
Trio, v, vla, vc, B flat	48	F. Schuberth, jnr.
Two quintets, pf, 2 v, vla, vc, g mi, c sharp mi	7, 57	B. & H.
Trio, pf, v, vc, E	22	F. Schuberth, jnr.
Trio, pf, v, vc, E flat	35	,, ,,
Sonata, pf, v, D	11	B. & H.
Two easy little sonatas, pf, v, B flat, D	41	F. Schuberth, jnr.
Sonata, pf, vc, C	59	Haake.

This composer, who was also a successful writer on musical subjects, is known principally by his clever Schumannesque piano pieces, several volumes of which appeared in succession, entitled *Fliegende Blätter* and *Fliegende Blättchen* (Flying leaves). He is a thoroughly sound and accomplished musician, though without marked originality. His chamber music is not without interest, even though it does not wear very well.

THE STRING QUARTET, op. 29, however, is quite admirable, and is by no means easy to play. It begins with a slow introduction; this recurs in the middle of the allegro di molto, and again, in abbreviated form, in the finale, and impresses the hearer as being the work of a serious artist unusually skilled in modulation. This allegro di molto is full of life, and its rhythm is anything but commonplace; the impassioned main theme is more interesting than the second subject. The largo rises to heights of genuine feeling, especially in the cantabile section. The broad and rhythmically effective main section of the scherzo is followed by two trios; the first of these, presto furioso (which also serves as coda), in spite of a vigorous display of strength, is not lacking in melodious charm, a quality present to a greater degree in the second. The finale restates—in the opening and again later—the beginning of the introduction to the first movement; the main body of the movement has a powerful swing, but there is also one graceful and charming theme.

THE TWO LITTLE SONATAS for piano and violin are of a lighter order. They are attractive and cleverly written pieces, not altogether easy for the violin in respect of intonation. The first has a transparently clear first movement; and a second based on the North German folk-song, *The dame, she would a-dancing go*, and the same air is used, in humorous guise, in the finale, which opens very gracefully. The second sonata has a cheerful first movement, which starts with a theme announced by the violin by way of prelude, and there is a charming cantilena for the same instrument later on. The scherzino has some delicate figure work. The mournful Lower Rhenish folk-song, *Sister mine, sister mine, when shall we go home?* well known through Brahms's transcription, provides the andantino with a theme for some very clever and attractive variations. It is introduced once more, unvaried, towards the end of the final rondino, and brings a note of serious reflection into an otherwise joyous movement.

† (2) HERMANN THEODOR OTTO, b. 1844, violinist, son of Carl Georg Peter.

	op.	
Octet, 4 v, 2 vla, 2 vc, C	12	Brockhaus.
Quintet, 2 v, vla, 2 vc, C	23	,,
Quartet, str, d mi	33	Weinberger; U.E.
Quartet, str, D	39	U.E.
Two quintets, pf, 2 v, vla, vc, b mi, c mi	6, 19	Kistner.
Trio, pf, v, vc, F	1	F. Schuberth, jnr.
Trio, pf, v, vc, d mi	15	Kistner.
Sonata, pf, v, c mi	35	Doblinger.

In addition to his fruitful work as a teacher of theory and conductor, Hermann Grädener has produced fifty compositions worthy of notice, a few of which are chamber works.

THE STRING QUARTET, op. 39, is a very thorough piece of work. The somewhat long drawn-out first movement, non troppo allegro, which is buoyant, if not precisely original in conception, has a finely-treated melodious main theme. In the andante, a delicate emotional picture is formed out of tasteful melodic material. The scherzo, which begins in B minor and ends in D major, has a charmingly sketched principal subject and an ingratiating second theme; there is no trio, but the coda has some very well sounding effects. The most important movement is probably the final allegro energico, which is in D minor;

the tersely rhythmic main theme is admirable, and there is, further, a noble cantabile melody and a well worked-up coda in the major key, in which new material is used.

THE VIOLIN SONATA, Grädener's only work of the kind, is of undoubted merit and distinction, and shows that the composer had in more than one respect followed in Brahms's tracks, and was, moreover, a skilled contrapuntist. The two outer movements, the allegro appassionato, with a deeply emotional second theme, and the rhythmically interesting finale, allegro non troppo, are, with their plastic themes, admittedly on a higher level than the slow movement, the interest of which is too slight for its excessive length. With regard to rhythm and harmony, too, this sonata—which makes great demands on both players—affords many points of interest. It may be recommended for concert performance. WILHELM ALTMANN.

[The sonata in C minor was played in 1902 by Borwick and Kruse at the 'Pops'.]

†GRAENER, PAUL, b. 1872, German composer and conductor.

	op.	
1st quartet, str	33	U.E.
2nd quartet, str	54	B. & B.
3rd quartet, str	65	Simrock.
Rhapsody, pf, alto voice, str. quartet	53	B. & B.
Suite, pf, v, vc	19	Cecilia Mus. Pub. Co. (London).
Kammermusikdichtung (no. 2), pf, v, vc, f mi	20	Kistner.
Trio, pf, v, vc	61	Peters.
Sonata, pf, v	56	B. & B.
Suite, pf, v	64	,, ,,
Petite suite italienne, pf, v		Donajowski.
Suite, pf, vc	66	Simrock.
Suite, pf, fl, A	63	Zimmermann.

Graener's chamber music has a character of its own, and is remarkable from the fact that it differs essentially from other types of German chamber music. It is not monumental nor pathetic, not complicated in construction nor learned in counterpoint; it is neither a part of the Brahms succession nor does it follow modern radical tendencies. Its positive qualities, in the mature works, starting with op. 33, are genuine lyricism, slender, graceful form, and abundance of fine sound-effects. Probably Graener's long residence in England and the example of Debussy's art have helped him to overcome the characteristic Teutonic complexity and heaviness, though one can hardly call him an imitator of Debussy. The naïve expression and simple charm of folk-song has been deeply felt by Graener, and has been the source of some of his finest inspirations.

THE TRIO, op. 20, shows Brahmsian traits, especially in the first, passionate movement. Graener's own characteristics are more evident in the slow intermezzo, with its tenderly expressive melody.

THE FIRST QUARTET, based on a Swedish folk-song, is one of Graener's purest and most valuable works, the first movement, a lyric prelude (andante), of melancholy character, presenting a simple folk-tune in the middle. The motif of this song serves as thematic material for the two following allegros, which are rather phantasies with varying moods, than strictly worked-out sonata movements. A short adagio, an elegy of peculiar and refined sound-effect, serves as an unconventional finale.

THE SECOND QUARTET has similar rhapsodic, lyrical traits, and a delicate, pastoral ring, with great transparency of writing and many changes of character and tempo in each of the three movements. It is a quiet, beautifully sounding piece.

THE VIOLIN SONATA, consisting of one long movement in three sections, is also rhapsodic but darker in colouring, and more complex in harmony.

The same disregard for traditional classical sonata form is noticeable in the third quartet, op. 65. Contrasting themes are lacking, the first movement being developed from one main theme only, with considerable art of variation.

Variation plays a conspicuous part also in the interesting trio, op. 61. This masterly and quite individual use of variation form demands special attention.

THE SUITES, opp. 63, 64, 66, may be described as a modernized version of Bach. They show Graener's art of part-writing and agreeable melodic invention in a very pleasing manner. HUGO LEICHTENTRITT.

[Those who possess Dr. Altmann's *Handbuch* will find in it exhaustive analyses of Graener's string quartets, the first of which is based upon the Swedish folk-song, *Spin, spin, dear little daughter*. Long ago I played it, and remember that it is difficult, especially the 'cello part. The second quartet, op. 54, consists of three short movements, the interest of which is so well sustained that Dr. Altmann strongly recommends it for public performance; whilst of the third, op. 65, one of Graener's latest works, unknown to me, he speaks with real enthusiasm. A fiery, temperamental work, rich in invention.

Graener spent some years in London as conductor of the Haymarket Theatre orchestra. EDITOR.]

†GRAINGER, PERCY ALDRIDGE (George P.), b. 1882, Australian pianist.

Octet, *The Twa Corbies*, tenor voice, 2 v, 2 vla, 2 vc, cb	Schott.
Quintet, *Walking Tune*, fl, ob, cl, horn, fag	,,
Irish reel, *Molly on the Shore*, str. quartet	,,
Suite (Scandinavian), pf, vc	,,

There are also various arrangements, three in Chester's Library for piano trio.

It is a fact, and one with which psychologists might profitably occupy themselves, that some composers of great eminence—Schumann, Chopin, Mendelssohn—have exhibited a marked style at the beginning of their career, while others, for instance Wagner, have taken years to approach creative maturity. Of the first type is Grainger, whose works are gaining an ever-widening recognition.

One notable point he has in common with Schumann, namely, that his earliest inspirations were derived, not from a fellow musician, but from a novelist-poet. In Schumann's case it was 'Jean Paul', in Grainger's it was Rudyard Kipling. Already around his sixteenth year Grainger discovered what one might call his artistic affinity, and from that time onward he began to translate Kipling's literary characteristics into terms of music. There was to be found in his work the same ruggedness, the same poetic treatment of vulgarity, the same spirit of nationalism, the same sporadic appearance of the folk element. Whether he actually set Kipling's verses in the form of songs, or whether he wrote purely instrumental music, the Kipling atmosphere was the inspiring factor. It was the foundation on which Grainger built his musical edifice, whatever developments and complexities may have since been added.

There are instances in musical biography where it is possible to divorce the man from his music, but in the case of Grainger not only does he present a highly interesting psychological study in himself, but an understanding of his idiosyncrasies affords a greater insight into his work. Thus, one is not surprised to find in him a love of virility, of athleticism, of primitive races and peoples—in fact, of all that goes contrary to accepted artistic traditions. His dislike of the conventionally artistic is so pronounced that he even carries it into domains where it is out of place—as witness the many slangy expressions with which he interlards his scores. Nevertheless, these excrescences—for so they must be termed—are the defects of his qualities rather than pure affectations. But Grainger has yet other idiosyncrasies, one of which, at any rate, has exercised a marked influence on his output.

Quite unlike most composers, he loves his early work, and loves it with a sentimental love which prompts him to dress it up in various guises. A glance at the catalogue of his works reveals a remarkable array of arrangements, all undertaken by Grainger himself. For instance, *Molly on the Shore* was originally written for string quartet, and therefore comes under the heading of chamber music proper; but it is also arranged for orchestra, for violin and piano, for piano solo, and, with embellishments, for pianola. Again, the charmingly poetic *My Robin is to the greenwood gone* was originally composed for flute, English horn, and six strings, but later it appeared for piano, violin, and 'cello, and for piano solo. Grainger has also arranged the *Walking Tune*, the original edition being for flute, oboe, clarinet, horn and bassoon; also the *Mock Morris*, the *Clog Dance*, *Handel in the Strand*, *Irish Tune from County Derry*, *Shepherd's Hey*, *Colonial Song*, and the *Sussex Mummers' Christmas Carol*.

But although Grainger has occupied himself with so many arrangements, the result—because carried out with so much love—has not been detrimental to the compositions in question. They do not savour of the makeshift, and, to give one example, *My Robin*, for trio, is a perfect little gem of chamber music writing with novel harmonies and effects.

It will be noticed that all Grainger's chamber works or 'Room music Tit-bits', as he naïvely calls them, are based on some folk-tune, either original or simulated. The *Walking Tune*, for instance, savours distinctly of a quick version of the *Minstrel Boy*, the first bars in fact being identical. Grainger's treatment, however, is always novel and ingenious, alike in harmony, form, and instrumentation. He possesses a marked aptitude for using all instruments and combinations to their best advantage, and it is difficult to imagine more effective quartet-writing than his well-known *Molly on the Shore*. The breeziness of this Irish reel is stimulating both to players and listeners, and it is not extravagant to term it, *à la* Chesterton, a 'Tremendous Trifle'. But then Grainger, with laudable courage, does not fear the obvious. To him well defined melody and phrase are an absolute primary condition of musical enjoyment. They are the framework on which he builds his structure. Polyphony and harmony play an important rôle, but never at the expense of melody. Furthermore, Grainger is never ponderous, long-drawn-out or complex in form; he believes in brevity and conciseness of effect. For the conventionally fashioned quartet or trio he has no predilection; sonata form does not appeal to him.

It is safe to assume that Grainger's production of chamber music is far from complete, for he has many unfinished early compositions which from time to time he unearths, works at, and finally publishes. They are the inspirations of his youth, dear to him because for him they reflect the past. He believes that the days of his inspiration are over, and that he has merely to continue and complete those numerous works he began years ago. In this respect, as in many others, he differs from most composers, but this again is no doubt because he discovered his individuality while young.

Herein is also to be found a partial explanation (for an intense love of detail is likewise one of his characteristics) of many indications of the time when certain works were begun, continued, and ended during intervals of several years; yet who knows but that it is just owing to this method of work that his creations combine the most finished workmanship with the wonderful freshness of youth?

Looking at Grainger's personality as a whole, he will be seen as one of the first composers to break away from formal traditions and give to the world a new type of chamber music, yet one that is withal not over-dissonant nor obscure and heavy, like that of certain of his contemporaries. This does not imply that Grainger cannot be dissonant and intensely modern when he so wishes, for there are moments in his orchestral works quite as 'modern' as any in those of other composers. But so far such moments have not appeared in his chamber works, the reason being best known to Grainger himself. CYRIL SCOTT.

GRAMMANN, KARL, 1842–1897, German composer.

Quintet, pf, 2 v, vla, vc, g mi	op. 19	Cranz, 1876.
Trio, pf, v, vc, c mi	„ 27	J Schubert & Co., 1883.
Sonata, pf, v, D	„ 45	„ „ 1884.

A composer of romantic tendency, and mainly an operatic writer, Karl Grammann is now unjustly forgotten. His chamber music is distinguished by richness of invention, beauty of sound, and perfection of form, though, naturally enough, it is overshadowed by the greater works of his contemporaries. A string quartet, op. 11, dating from his Conservatorium days at Leipzig, he held to be unworthy of publication, but his piano quintet made a sensation on its appearance. The slow movement of this piece works up near the end to a fine fervour of emotion, and there is more than the mere good music of a highly trained composer in the other movements too; for instance, the second theme of the first movement, the trio of the scherzo with its overflowing energy, and the rapid, joyous finale.

THE PIANO TRIO, however, is yet more arresting. Here is the happiest combination of buoyant energy and tender lyricism, the finale, the second theme of which is of so sunny an inspiration, being the finest movement of the trio.

THE VIOLIN SONATA is a truly poetic work. The sorrowful introduction to the first movement betrays the influence of *Tristan*, but this should not weigh against the stimulating vigour of the principal theme and the elegance and beauty of the second, which may rank with Schumann's best. The movement ends with a return to the grief-laden introduction, which becomes gradually quieter and finally dies away. Two elements are successfully combined in the second movement—a fiery virile scherzo, and an exquisitely dreamy and satisfying slow section. The words 'Mit tiefer Empfindung' (with deep feeling), which head this slow part in B major, are no empty ones. The brilliant rhythmical finale is full of real fire, while a quieter middle section contains another melody which pleases the ear without loss of distinction. Before the exuberant coda there is a reminder of the *Weltschmerz* which pervades the introduction, but it soon passes away, leaving joy triumphant. This sonata will be found very effective by both players; the violinist, in particular, must be able to give adequate expression to its charm and vitality. WILHELM ALTMANN.

GRAMOPHONE AND CHAMBER MUSIC, THE.

Robert Louis Stevenson decided that the freedom it conferred upon a man to have his own string quartet and his own yacht was the chief, in fact the only real advantage attached to the possession of great wealth. Without claiming that the gramophone will soon discredit the utility of riches, it may be argued that with all the recent improvement on the technical side of recording and in the quality of the music recorded the gramophone is already a kind of rival of the private string quartet, and is likely in the near future to become an almost completely adequate substitute. Of course, it will never be quite the same thing as the actual presence of the players, because not even with the aid of any cinematographic device that the future may provide could the purely external decorativeness of a string quartet be conveyed. Even should the gramophone ultimately succeed in deceiving the finest ear, it will always cheat the eye, for whether it be a woman seated at the piano or whether it be a full orchestra on the platform of a concert hall, the sight of instruments being played must surely add, even for the most austere lovers of music, some further magic to the sound. To watch a violin concerto and be reminded of a bird singing in a wood, to watch a piano concerto and perceive a boat at one with the waters on which it rides: I hope that these are not just the pictorial impressions of a literary temperament spoiling music with a pathetic fallacy, dishonest though it would be not to admit that some of these pictorial impressions are so vivid that I can recall the visual effect of music of which I should less easily recall the sound, as, for instance, the sight of the strings in the slow movement of Brahms's B flat concerto lapping against the piano and seeming almost to be rocking it gently beneath the green-shaded lamps of Queen's Hall.

Now, the outward effect of a string quartet on my fancy is that I am perceiving a sublimation of all the domestic tasks that were ever undertaken, from that of the spider in weaving her web to those of spinsters knitting in the sun or old wives at their embroidery. In watching the combination of instruments I discern a pattern wrought in visible silver on the air, a pattern of not less exquisite complication and simplicity than that with which the frost may pattern a window-pane. Contrariwise, if I watch a spider at her task in the sunlight, I must always be straining my ears to hear the fine pattern of sound that seems to be directing her intricate path. All this external beauty of played music is denied us by the gramophone. Indeed, one of the great reproaches deservedly levelled against it is the utter lack of the reposeful beauty of sound in motion. The winding of it, the hiss of the needle, the interruptions caused by changing or turning the discs, these would still be a detestable handicap, even if the reproduction of the music were perfect and the variety of it unlimited. Yet were the choice to lie between hearing all my chamber music in a concert-room and being entirely dependent upon the gramophone, I should elect to rely upon the latter. I find the contact of strangers repulsive when I am listening to chamber music, and even if I sit between friends, with friends in front of me and with friends behind me, the discomfort of a concert-room stall and the odious system of sitting in rows combine to destroy the intimate delight of such music. I am not conscious of this malaise during the performance of an orchestra. Indeed, the presence of hundreds of other people adds much to my enjoyment, and were I rich enough to command the greatest orchestra in the world to perform for my solitary pleasure I should never claim the privilege. But chamber music for my contentment ought to be not so much something that is being performed as something that is happening, and if I cast my mind back to seek for an illustration of the extreme pleasure that chamber music has given, I find it in old days at the Oxford and Cambridge Musical Club, when, coming in about six o'clock of a foggy November evening from the murk and clatter of Leicester Square, one lounged in Joshua Reynolds's old studio and listened in the quiet, then contrived by double windows, to quartets of Haydn and Mozart, triumphing over time as one smoked and dreamed.

Thus to insist upon the sensuous and the sentimental appeal of chamber music may appear to be treating it like a drug, and the danger of treating music as a drug should be kept in mind. I should be inclined to dread the perfect gramophone which never required winding, whose fibre needles were durable as teak, whose steel needles were velvet as cats' paws, whose discs changed themselves and never warped. In such circumstances, music for me might come to serve as poppies and mandragora indeed, for I believe that I should never listen to anything else except the first thrushes in February. Yet, without becoming slaves to music, we might make a better use of it than we do, now that we have the gramophone. In these days music always seems to partake too much of a ceremony. People sit down to enjoy it as they might sit down to eat dinner. In fact, the only occasional use that is made of music is to accompany a meal. And this inappropriate service has begotten a form of its own, so that we speak contemptuously of restaurant music where the clatter of dishes and the jingle of forks have entered into the very texture of the orchestration. But what occasions there are for music of which few avail themselves! It is easy to believe that he who has not heard a Mozart quartet played in the freshness of dawn has never enjoyed his music to the full, and since it might puzzle even a millionaire to rouse his private quartet at such an hour and make the players sit in the dews beneath his bedroom window, the gramophone becomes indispensable for such an occasion. The fatigue of turning the discs may be more than usually tiresome when one has to cross a cold floor to get at them; but for compensation one hardly misses the visible grace of the players, because the changing sky above the tree-tops or the chimney-stacks is enough for the eye, and in so many of Mozart's quartets the pattern of the music is the pattern of the dayspring itself. Nor must Brahms be forgotten for this hour: particularly those two quartets of opus 51, both of which we possess in recorded form. There are times when they seem to express better than anything else the business of the new day, for there is nobody like Brahms for meditating deliberately upon what seems at first such a commonplace little phrase until patiently and lovingly, as some old weaver of the Middle Ages, he has decorated it with the grave and gay design of his romantic common sense. There is nobody who can more gently clarify a mind made turbid by the stir of worry or darkened by the shadow of looming complications. His music has the dignity of a trusted family doctor, who by his confidence not merely drives away our physical ills, but in doing so affects us with his own spiritual calm. Brahms has that perfect sanity which touches holiness, and the more often I listen to his chamber music the more profound becomes my reverence for him. One may turn to Mozart or Haydn for relief, gaining from their music an illusion that care will be as easily overcome as the sweet sadness of their own andantes by minuets and tripping measures. We may take refuge in Beethoven and feel that our small displeasures are much ado about nothing; but Brahms is able to seize our pettiest moods and direct them as wisely as he will use his first violin. There is nobody like him for suppressing the individual instrument in his chamber music except when he writes for the clarinet, to which he allows the freedom of a spoilt child. Where did I read of Brahms at table emptying the oil out of the bottom of a tin of sardines into his mouth? Almost one feels sometimes that he is allowing his favourite instrument to behave as greedily. No other composer has allowed the clarinet to gobble quite so lusciously, and no other composer, not even Weber, has with those gobbles rivalled the nightingale herself.

There are two composers whose chamber music is unworthily represented on the gramophone, and it happens that these two composers—Schumann and Mendelssohn—are sadly out of favour all round at the moment. That being so, it would be impertinent to occupy space with an argument which would neither correct those who suppose that they have outlived such falsifiers of what a fashion chooses to call reality nor edify those who feel themselves secure against the ebb and flow of taste. I cannot refrain, however, from expressing a fervent wish that young people could be given a chance to know and love as much of Mendelssohn and Schumann as, thanks to the gramophone, they can know and love of Haydn and Mozart. Distrusting as I do the short cuts to perfect taste which are a feature of this 'get rich quick' age, I feel convinced that the owl-eyed young man of the moment who has never been thrilled by Tennyson's *Maud* has missed as authentic an emotion of youth as if he had never loved before he was twenty; equally I am sure that to pass in one jump from a self-conscious and literary enjoyment of Mozart to horn-spectacles and Stravinsky leaves that young man as callow in taste and as aesthetically raw as if because he had always travelled by aeroplane he should claim to despise the beauty of meadows and forests and the sound of bees in small gardens. Among my letters from strangers I receive many musical confidences, but none was ever more welcome than a letter from an Eton boy who wrote to beg my influence for the recording of a complete work of chamber music by Mendelssohn. This request filled me with hope that the generation now on the road to manhood was turning back to the more familiar ways of youth and to 'such sights as youthful poets dream on summer eves by haunted stream'. I heard, faintly indeed and dim as Oberon's horn, the first tremulous fanfare of a romantic revival. At any rate, whether it portends a change in fashion or not, it is reassuring to know that young people still exist who can enjoy sweets without being ashamed of their taste. However, in wanting more Mendelssohn to be recorded for the gramophone I am equally concerned for those thousands who can enjoy so much of music but who are still cut off by a wide gulf from the pleasures of chamber music. We want more bridges, and Mendelssohn is one of the bridges. Knowing as I do how many people cross the gulf by means of Schubert and turn back because Brahms repels them, I want more Schumann, because it seems to me that Brahms is most easily reached by way of Schumann. Yet beyond two mutilated versions of the piano quintet, a mutilated and badly recorded version of the quartet in A, two snippets from the quartets in A minor and F, and a snippet from the *Phantasiestücke*, we have nothing in England. I had hoped that members of the National Gramophonic Society would have voted for the recording of some of Schumann's chamber music that has been proposed; but the response was cold. I suppose he is paying the penalty for allowing cerebration to interfere with simple emotion, for every period has its peculiar cerebration which is often apt to seem superficial or insincere to other periods. Moreover, the mixture of it with intense emotion, as in the case of Schumann, may produce an effect of sentimentality just because the artist is well aware of the danger and is trying to avoid it. Schumann sought too much inspiration from art instead of life. Did he not lock himself up for a year to study Beethoven's quartets before he wrote his own? Perhaps nothing dates an artist so mercilessly as self-consciousness, because that self being what he supposes himself to be rather than what he genuinely is, he will reflect for the future only the illusions of his period and personality. Schumann thought too much about what he was doing. He was one of the precursors of the present self-conscious age and he has paid the penalty, for the present age is too profoundly occupied with itself to listen to him. Without suggesting the least parallel between him and R. L. Stevenson, I could use the latter as an example of what I mean in literature. Had Stevenson never written a word about his craft, he would probably have avoided the disrepute into which he has fallen among our contemporary intellectuals.

Schubert, who, as far as I know, was never hampered by theories, has survived the malice of time as a piece of natural scenery might survive new main-roads and the traffic of charabancs. Of his chamber music we already have recorded the octet, two quintets, two quartets, two trios, and a number of snippets, and I can safely assert that just as the *Unfinished Symphony* is the most popular of all symphonies, possibly of all orchestral works, so by one or other of his compositions in chamber music more people have entered that charmed highway of art than by any other; for chamber music is a highway, though, like the Via Appia, it may have all the amenities of a byway. I find that I am always inclined to play Schubert's chamber music at twilight; and that not because he appeals to the sentimental mood which arrives so easily when the day's work is done, for to say truth my day is lazier than my night, so that about twilight I am more likely to be feeling tense than relaxed. But Schubert suits the twilight, distilling his melodies as the flowers their scents at such an hour. His tunes come in successive gusts of perfume as when one passes from border to border of the garden at the shutting-in of a long June day. Now it is a cluster of stocks, now the 'homely cottage smell' of sweet-williams, then suddenly a melody rich as lilies, but threaded by a brief and exquisite poignancy as of crushed thyme or sprig of rosemary plucked in passing and lightly tossed away.

It may be objected that to surrender oneself to such a purely sensuous enjoyment of music is in fact to become its slave. That is the difficulty of trying to communicate in words what except by music is incommunicable. It would appear from reading what I have just written that I deliberately set myself to procure from music a series of sensations; but that is not so. With the aid of the gramophone I obtain for myself as much music as from a Medici print of the *Primavera* I can obtain of painting. What, after all, is the reason of hanging any picture upon our walls? Not that we should sit down and deliberately use it to evoke a sensation, but that it should beautifully haunt the background of our minds. In these days the man of most fastidious taste is a prey to ugliness. However earnestly he may strive to preserve his immediate surroundings from any taint of that ugliness, he will hardly resist the temptation of reading the daily paper. That is quite enough to corrupt his style, even should he forswear all but the noblest literature for the rest of his reading. I cannot help feeling that to read one's daily paper in the presence of a great picture, even though that picture be present only in the form of a reproduction, and to the accompaniment of great music, even though that music be played only on a mechanical instrument like the gramophone, is to provide oneself with a prophylactic against some of the ugliness that is perpetually being pumped into the mind. Were the gramophone a much less efficient machine than it is, the privilege of putting one's mind in order by what surely at its best is the most orderly medium of art in existence—a string quartet—would be of inestimable value. The reason why I have made a habit of working to the accompaniment of chamber music is not due to any desire on my side to procure an appropriate state of emotion; but every writer, whatever his capacity for concentration, is peculiarly exposed to attacks of the irrelevant and trivial when he is most fain to be free of them. And these petty assaults are somehow warded off much more successfully when the background of my mind is occupied by great music. I do not intend to convey by that phrase the subconscious mind. It is more imperative that the subconscious mind should be concentrated on the business in hand than any other function, because finally it will be the subconscious mind which will produce the material. It is the background of the conscious mind for which I crave an occupation. The music is playing the same part as the beads of a rosary. Usually, in spite of working I am able to follow the music intelligently enough to know when the wrong side of a disc has been placed on the turn-table, but there are times—rare, alas, but all the more wonderful for their rarity—when the determination to hammer some sentence into shape is so tremendous that a long quartet can be played from beginning to end without my being consciously aware of it. And this is really a surprising and delicious experience, because I shall have heard the whole composition as it were in a moment of time, so swiftly will time have swept past, and the impression of the whole work on my imagination will have been faintly comparable to the original conception of the composer, since I shall have heard the essence of his inspiration as he must have heard it in a moment of time. I should be inclined to make a positive claim that the only way for the average man to listen to music for more than a very short while is as an accompaniment to some occupation. All honest people will admit that the trivial and irrelevant are most aggressive when they are deliberately listening to music, and one of my objections to programme music has always been that perpetual intervention of the trivial and irrelevant between myself and the composer's mood. Moreover, I am inclined to resent his assumption that he is capable of inducing in me the state of mind and the experience round which he is writing, just as, were I a musician, I should resent being told by a poet that words strung meaninglessly but musically together were a substitute for music itself. I am so jealous of music's potency that I hate to see it shackled with fetters of which poets and painters would only be too happy to disembarrass themselves, could they but do so. Nothing is more hostile to programme music than the gramophone, because, as it seems to me, the possibility of frequent repetition is fatal to such a convention; for either the composer's programme is so realistically conveyed that the composition becomes a short story, in which case, however subtly wrought, familiarity must breed contempt at last, or the programme is so vaguely conveyed that it was not worth affixing. Take, for instance, Schönberg's sextet, *Verklärte Nacht*, to which is attached a tiresome and sentimental piece of Teutonic narrative. By all the rules of the game, frequent repetition should gradually inure us to its beauties. Does this follow? On the contrary, the frequent repetition of what is only saved from complete amorphousness by the illustrations in words that accompany it, may become finally more exasperating than the first performance might have seemed to the most conservative ear. And here is a problem for the gramophone to solve. One is so continually hearing it asserted that modern music only fails to attract because it is unfamiliar, that one is anxious to take advantage of the gramophone as one might take advantage of the printing press to remove this handicap. An important object of the National Gramophonic Society was to give modern works of chamber music a chance to compete with the classics. Yet since the society was founded, the majority of the members have voted more and more emphatically every time against modern works. This may be only a very small straw, but it may be taken as a good enough indication of the wind's direction; because among the members of such a society we might expect to find a large proportion of modernists. The older lovers of chamber music, most of whom for a long time regarded the gramophone as a vulgar and inadequate machine to supply them with music, are in fact a small minority. Moreover, contemporary composers, who have taken the existence of the gramophone for granted, surely ought not to be more heavily handicapped by it than Haydn and Mozart.

Yet there are times when one is grateful for a label. A case in point is the *Spring* sonata of Beethoven, which, perhaps because the name was not affixed by the composer himself, seems to possess a better descriptive value, for inasmuch as we are not obliged to accept it, we can accept it more easily. I never hear it played but I become aware beyond the music of the sharp young green of the budding quickset, of deep and luminous April dusks in which lingers the frore breath of Winter, the bitter-sweet perfume of primroses and the waking fern. It is not Spring as we look forward to Spring in Winter, thinking to stand again in the sun's eye, but the shy Spring we remember in the plenitude of July, such a Spring as Keats wrote of on St. Mark's Eve. There is a sonata of Mozart's for violin and piano which we are lucky enough to possess in recorded form also —op. 18, no. 1, in A—to give it the only title it ever had—and this does suggest the Spring to which we look forward, poignant indeed, but only as all youth is poignant and as every Spring is poignant with a delicate and faint apprehension of what might be, but pure of all regret for what might have been.

There is a further charm which the so frequent playing of chamber music to oneself can cast, and that is the way snatches of melody and brief phrases will come unbidden to provide the music that some exquisite moment demands. It is easy enough at such times to beguile oneself with the fancy that the secret meaning of that andante of Mozart's or that rondo of Beethoven's has been revealed, or why should it return thus as free of one's bidding as a butterfly? Nor is it necessarily one's own mind that is illuminated by the echo of a tune. Sometimes a companion by whistling or humming it will make the revelation. The fourth movement of César Franck's sonata, so beautifully played and recorded for the gramophone by Cortot and Thibaud, will always be associated in my memory with going downhill through thickets of broom and myrtle, past crimson cyclamens in the glinting shade of the big arbutus bushes that overhung the fragrant path; for once, when by such a path I was descending a gorge to the blue Tyrrhenian sea fifteen hundred feet below, my companions a few yards ahead were whistling the melody of that fourth movement. If for nothing else, I should hold the gramophone justified by making us free of César Franck's sonata and quartet and sublime quintet. He, perhaps, more than any other composer, requires the right mood for his music, and how seldom shall we find it in a concert hall! I do not care to hear that quartet in a crowd, but in my own room with my own books and pictures round me, I am beside him in his organ loft, and I have heard the 'seraphim whose footfalls tinkled on the tufted floor'. Surely, if ever the Holy Angels walked beside a human being, they walked beside César Franck up there in the organ loft of Ste. Clotilde. Like Blake, he never lost his childish vision; and of all sublunary delights I know of few that can compare with reading to oneself the *Songs of Innocence* late on a winter night and then playing to oneself the quartet. That, indeed, is to hold eternity in an hour. I am not forgetting Palestrina when I lament that the age of faith never really expressed itself in music. When we hear what a César Franck with the vision of a Van Eyck can do in music, we look, but in vain, for a composer who might be set beside Dante. Not even to Beethoven can we grant that eminence of the human mind. When I heard the later quartets occasionally I used to think that Beethoven had passed beyond the reach of a mortal, but now that I have been able to play these quartets over and over again, and listen to the ninth symphony over and over again, I have realized that he never for an instant transcended mortality as in the *Paradiso* Dante transcended it. The finale of the ninth symphony is a descent to earth from those flutterings in the first movement on the brink of life's secret. Not that I would have Beethoven shed one trace of his common humanity with ourselves. I glory in his sublime failure to voice the ineffable, and I love him as I could never love Dante; but there are moments when I long for him to be able to soar undismayed and never to groan, as he inevitably will somewhere in his greatest compositions, that life is after all naught but a wry joke. Prometheus bound was a greater poetic conception than Prometheus unbound, and it is significant that since Shelley we have had no cosmic great poet. Prometheus was unbound and poetry died. And now, though we know that it was nothing but a titanic delusion from which Shelley and Beethoven suffered, and though we have proved its falsity on many battle-fields, poetry does not come to life again, and even music gasps. This is one of the pleasures of the gramophone, this continual company of music which enables one to speculate upon it in various moods, which makes one independent of other people's programmes, and which turns half one's library into records of music. Those gifted and fortunate beings who can take a miniature score to bed with them as I might take a volume of Propertius are often too musical to be able to convey even to themselves what music means to them. In any case it must be a very long while before the average intelligent man will be able to read a score as he will read a book. Although we owners of gramophones possess the privilege of familiarity hitherto denied to all but the most musical, it would be unduly sanguine to expect from us any aesthetic speculations of much value. People like myself, who find music an illustration of life rather than life an illustration of music, are so apt to attach an undue importance to those illustrations. Still, in being able to listen with all our attention to music on the gramophone, as we can in the solitude and comfort of our own rooms, we are gaining more from music than by listening to it in a concert hall with a mind distracted by the impertinence of the surroundings or buzzing with the trivialities of everyday existence. Yet perhaps it is too much to claim that we do actually listen with a more genuine concentration. Perhaps the habit of thinking about music is set up by the sheer amount of it that percolates through the mind when, as by the aid of the gramophone, it becomes the normal accompaniment of one's daily life. The old way of educating by endless repetition had more to be said for it than most people in these days are ready to admit. The abandonment of that system for what seems a more enlightened way of teaching Latin and Greek is only what the Americans did many years ago, with what some of us may consider disastrous results. Knowingness does not entirely take the place of knowledge, and the knowledge that directs taste can only be acquired by a process of exhaustion. Repetition effects a kind of catalysis of the mind, and no substance demonstrates this more clearly than music. Habituated as we are to the chemical action of reading a book over and over again, we take for granted that only the best books, as we call them, will bear frequent re-reading. I do not find, however, that the ability to be often re-read necessarily endows a book with 'goodness' as a work of art. Some of the worst books ever written will sustain repetition more easily than some of the best, and I find this even more definitely the case with music. The early and middle period quartets of Beethoven bear reiteration—I mean extensive reiteration, not a mere half a dozen performances—more satisfactorily than the late quartets. The chamber music of Haydn and Mozart can be played night after night without the least wearisomeness. In the earlier days of the gramophone, when some fifty records making a total of six hours' music were all that I could collect, I have played the same isolated and often much shortened movement every night for two months at a stretch without even a momentary desire for a change. Indeed, nowadays when my shelves are crammed with a variety of chamber music that makes it unnecessary to repeat a whole quartet more than once in three months, I sometimes find myself looking back with something very near regret to those restricted programmes. And asking myself now what was the precise quality in the music that made it not merely endurable but equally delightful every time it was repeated, I have come to the conclusion that it was the predominant gaiety of the excerpts to which we were treated. Mirth set out in a pattern eases the heart more surely than any other kind, and I believe it is fair to say of all chamber music that the outstanding quality is its allegria:

> Thou Goddess fair and free,
> In heaven yclept Euphrosyne,
> And by men, heart-easing Mirth,
> Whom lovely Venus at a birth,
> With two sister graces more,
> To ivy-crowned Bacchus bore.

So much does this tradition persist that even Tchaikovsky allowed himself a happy ending in his D major quartet, and it is not until we reach contemporary writers that we are liable to find a complete elimination of allegria from their chamber music. We are inclined to talk about the externality of Haydn's and Mozart's music, and by that epithet impute to them a lack of depth. I think we assume too easily their innocence of life's profundities. It is true that progress has added so much to the complication of existence that numbers of people have sought from music the expression of an inward emotion and an assurance of something permanent behind the rapid shifting of external circumstance; but really it is the contemporary composer of chamber music who scarcely ever does reach beyond external circumstances. His music, in fact, is far more truly external than that of Haydn. It is far more the illustration of a state of affairs than the expression of a mental or emotional attitude. Ugliness is nothing new; but the self-consciousness of the modern artist causes him to be overwhelmed by it, and with a desperate optimism he strives to perceive beauty in that ugliness and to extract beauty from it. His art is a kind of homoeopathy or inoculation; the art of Haydn and Mozart was an antidote. Not that I would suggest for a moment any deliberate attempt to uplift poor humanity or soothe its ills. Such an express determination would have appeared presumptuous to composers whose music glows and blushes with a beautiful modesty. It is a commonplace of criticism to say that Mozart's music reflects none of the trials of his workaday existence; and if this means that his music is never a defiant exploitation of himself it may pass unchallenged. Yet I cannot believe that anybody like myself, who has rarely allowed a day to pass without turning to trio or quartet of Mozart as he might turn to a crystalline spring for refreshment, could be content to perceive no more in that music than the bright hours of a sun-dial. It is true that the pointer marks only the sunny hours, but it marks them with a moving shadow. And for me Mozart's music is like that shadow travelling over the dial of our life. As I have been writing these words and thinking about Mozart, the gramophone has been playing the G minor quintet. I happen to know that these three discs were recorded by the players during one of the daylight air-raids of the war. They played the quintet under the stress of the nervous tension that such conditions would naturally create, and the music, turning all that tension to the service of beauty, is so compact of grace and courage that all the debonair sacrifice of youth flowers in that quintet as a world may flower in four lines from the Greek anthology. The least imaginative creature could hardly fail to respond to these old-fashioned discs which perpetuate, in the guise of sounds emitted according to a pattern of two violins, two violas, and a 'cello, yet hardly recognizable as such and almost drowned by the hiss of the needle, half an hour in the emotion of our national life. No doubt with improved methods of recording we shall soon have another version of the quintet, but some of these early discs of chamber music will have a charm quite independent of any adventitious help from air-raids, a charm that greater realism will never succeed in dispelling. The fluty tones of the strings may sound grotesquely false, the scratch may exacerbate a sensitive ear; but if these discs are played with a fibre needle on a good machine in the intimacy of their own rooms, all who are not the slaves of realism will surrender to the spell this elfin music casts upon the firelit air—surrender so completely, perhaps, as not to miss the outward beauty of the players about their business and to accept the motion of the shadows on the walls and ceiling as a perfect substitute for the flickering bows and the way the 'cello seems to be reading with its master the music. There are two trios of Mozart arranged for piano, violin, and viola which make the very books on my shelves appear to dance. There is a quartet in E flat by Haydn (op. 64, no. 6) which, played to the accompaniment of Siamese cats and kittens at their sport, confounds sorrow. Purists may object, and reasonably, that the antics of kittens have nothing to do with Haydn's chamber music. I can but reply that with the help of the gramophone I have convinced myself that everything which enhances the beauty of the interior scene gains something from the performance of chamber music and in its turn adds something to it. Sweet peas in a bowl look more beautiful if looked at through an invisible web of sweet sounds. So much, indeed, is my library impregnated with music that I have almost reached the stage of believing that the music is made by the room itself, and I can hardly listen to the gramophone in a strange interior without being discouraged by its mechanical aspect. But then I am quite unable even to read a borrowed book with the least pleasure, and I have denied myself a sight of many of the earth's beautiful places merely because I should have to stay in an hotel to enjoy them. Yes, I suppose I were wise to admit that my chamber music on the gramophone is nothing but self-indulgence. Let it be. I shall not defend myself, but find my justification in Milton:

> Lap me in soft Lydian airs,
> Married to immortal verse,
> Such as the meeting soul may pierce,
> In notes, with many a winding bout
> Of linkéd sweetness long drawn out,
> With wanton heed and giddy cunning,
> The melting voice through mazes running,
> Untwisting all the chains that tie
> The hidden soul of harmony.
>
> . . . .
>
> These delights if thou canst give,
> Mirth, with thee I mean to live.

Addendum.

Since the above was written, electric recording has brought the gramophone much nearer to perfect reproduction. We are not actually near it yet, but we can imagine the possibility which with old methods had ceased to be even a dream. The first electrical recordings of chamber music were a great disappointment. What was gained in balance and spatial sense was lost in tone. The violins sounded metallic, the viola watery, and though the 'cello played its part more conspicuously, it seemed sometimes to be performing a solo accompanied by Jews' harps. By the use of fibre needles some of this metallic effect was damped down, but such early electrical recordings as that of the Debussy quartet by H.M.V. or the Mendelssohn trio in C minor by Columbia are already as much out of date in a couple of years as old acoustical recordings became in ten. The improvement, indeed, was astonishingly rapid, and within a few months the recorders showed a realization of their new powers that deserves the highest praise. The Beethoven centenary in 1927 gave the recording companies an opportunity to publish a large amount of chamber music, and the twelve quartets of Beethoven played by the Lener Quartet and published by Columbia did more to familiarize the ordinary public with chamber music than any musical enterprise yet undertaken. It would be tedious to enumerate the additions made lately to the gramophone's repertory of chamber music, and if special attention be called to such performances as that of Casals, Thibaud, and Cortôt in Schubert's trio in B flat major or Mendelssohn's trio in D minor published by H.M.V., it is not merely because of the unusual splendour of the ensemble, but also because of the really remarkable technical triumph of the recorders. Nor should the publications of the N.G.S. from 58 Frith Street, Soho, be passed over. Many works of chamber music for which the popular demand would have been too small have been published for a limited and appreciative public of amateurs, and among these works have been several of contemporary British composers.

The next few years are likely to see even greater improvements both in recording and in methods of reproduction, and with the repertory being steadily enlarged almost every month, the future for lovers of chamber music is debonair. COMPTON MACKENZIE.

[I am no gramophone expert, but my experiences enable me to speak definitely of its value in spreading wide a knowledge of the beauties of chamber music. Speaking of my own early experiences as a listener, I was once in a country place, amid romantic surroundings, enjoying for an evening the company of a friend who happened to be at once a gramophone enthusiast and a man of unexceptionable musical taste. To my great delight he switched on for me record after record of familiar chamber music, and, as the delicate strains impinged on the quiet of a summer's evening, it dawned upon me that here was a new source of happiness for that not very numerous section of the community whose ears are attuned to grades of sound of the finer sort. Though a string quartet on the gramophone is subdued in tone, though it has not the intensity of the original, though the dynamics are not felt to the same extent, there is compensation. The music has a delicate beauty, an individual quality of its own which is infinitely touching. And what an opportunity these records afford to score readers for the *aural* study of musical structure. There is a body of gramophone lovers springing up amongst us who have picked up more knowledge of form in a year or two than the average amateur acquires in a lifetime. I know not to what extent the teacher of harmony and counterpoint has exploited the possibilities of the gramophone, but I do know that here is an instrument of priceless educative value ready to his hand.

Speaking as a player, the members of my home Quartet have from time to time joined me in making records. On one occasion we played for the N.G.S. movements from string quartets written in lighter vein by Raff (*Schöne Müllerin*) and Rubinstein, and sent them to subscribers as a new year's gift. Although this was before the days of electric recording, they came out well, and I received seventy letters from various parts of the world expressing the gratification of the recipients, some of whom lived in *remote districts*. Therein lies the crowning triumph of the gramophone. Mr. Adolfo Betti, leader of the famous Flonzaley Quartet, tells me that on their concert tours in the States phonographic records act as *avant-coureurs* among audiences in small towns, to whom their repertory has already become familiar through the records of H.M.V. and Columbia. They are winged sounds finding their way to the earth's lonely places. And to one who lives in a crowded city the gramophone presents this advantage. He may chance to see announced for performance a favourite work, but may be unable to attend. The gramophone, his devoted slave, is always at hand, ready for him in moments of leisure, ready to give him some at least of the pabulum for which his soul hungers, with as many da capos as he desires. EDITOR.]

†GRASSE, EDWIN, American composer.

Sonata, pf, v, C op. 14 Schirmer, 1912.

†GRAUN, JOHANN GOTTLIEB, 1698–1771, German composer, brother of Carl Heinrich Graun, composer of the passion-cantata, the *Death of Jesus*.

Modern republication:

Three trio-sonatas, F, G, c mi (H. Riemann, Coll. Mus. 24/26), B. & H., 1906.

No. 1, pf, ob, v, vc, or pf, 2 v, vc

Nos. 2, 3, pf, 2 v, vc

†GRAY, ALAN, b. 1855, English organist.

Sonata, pf, v Laudy.

Dr. Gray's compositions include several unpublished chamber works (*v. Grove*).

GREEK CHAMBER MUSIC.

Modern Greek music is still in the earliest stages of the making—naturally enough, considering that the country lacked both tradition and incentives, remaining, until a very recent date, bereft of almost all elements of musical culture. On the other hand, genuine Greek church music is of great beauty; and throughout continental Greece and the islands there exists an incredible wealth of folk-tunes which testify to the keenness and soundness of the people's musical instinct.

The few composers who have appeared so far are more or less under the influence of church music and folk music, but were compelled to derive their technique from western sources.

Whether the Greek school, in proportion as it develops, will prove strongly national is a matter for conjecture. Among the few available works by Greek composers, some are decidedly Eastern in character—e.g. the septet *The Song of the Exile* (for voice, clarinet, piano, and string quartet) by Poniridy, a composer who has solved the problem of adapting his technique to the materials he uses, and who displays a fine sense of colour and poetry.

Petrides is essentially a symphonist, but has composed, so far, a flute sonata and a 'cello sonata in which he displays ease, restraint, and genuine purpose.

These two composers are the most worthy of attention among the younger generation.

Of the older composers of to-day, two, M. Kalomiris and D. Levidis, have written chamber music. The output of the former comprises a piano trio in four movements, in which the influence of native tunes is discernible. Levidis has written a *Divertimento* for the following combination: two violins, viola, 'cello, double-bass, celesta, two harps, percussion, and principal cor anglais.

M. D. CALVOCORESSI.

GREENE, DR. MAURICE, 1695–1755, Organist of St. Paul's, and Master of the King's Music.

A famous English composer, and contemporary of Handel. He wrote a quartet for stringed instruments and a sonata for clavier and violin, published by Preston (London).

*† GRETCHANINOV, ALEXANDER TIKHONOVITCH, b. 1864, Russian composer, pupil of Rimsky-Korsakov.

	op.	Composed	
Quartet, str, G	2	1892	Belaiev.
Quartet, str, d mi	70	1913	Gutheil.
Quartet, str, c mi	75	1915	U.E.; Gutheil.
Trio, pf, v, vc, c mi	38	1906	,, ,,
Sonata, pf, v, D	87	1918	,, ,,

Gretchaninov must be regarded as one of the most fruitful Russian composers of chamber music. Chamber music, indeed, forms a considerable portion of his output, and he has constantly returned to it throughout his career.

THE STRING QUARTET, op. 2. In his first chamber work the composer, then a young man, adheres to the manner of the most prominent musical authorities of the day—Tchaikovsky and Rubinstein. Gretchaninov, who is conservative in spirit and has never displayed any innovating tendencies in the chamber style, follows classical models.

This first experiment cannot be considered successful from every point of view; in the music there is a very great deal of straightforward melody; it is naïve and beautiful, but it does not as yet reveal mastery, and still less originality. Notwithstanding this, it was awarded the prize at the quartet competition organized in 1894 by the Petersburg Chamber Music Society, and in the same year it was performed for the first time, and it was this work which established Gretchaninov's renown as a composer.

THE PIANO TRIO marks the composer's return to chamber music after an interval of many years, during which his experience in the art of composition had matured and his style had been formed. By this time he was well known as a composer, chiefly of operas and songs, in which he had adopted a style akin to that of the Russian national school with its insistence on folk melody, and in general reminiscent of Borodin and to some extent of Tchaikovsky. But in the trio none of these qualities is displayed; it may be described as academic music, and comes nearest to S. Taneiev. It is confidently written, and has melodies which are fine but not original; the musical tissue is generally very simple in form, and the style comparatively sustained and homophonic; in this respect it differs from Taneiev, who is inclined to polyphony. In his subsequent chamber works Gretchaninov has added no essentially new features. His second trio, written about 1913, is still unpublished.

THE SECOND QUARTET, written the same year, shows a marked advance on the first. It is a beautiful and very melodious composition, in which clearness and unpretentiousness are combined with modesty of style and simplicity. Written in masterly fashion and with knowledge of the instruments, this quartet may be said to continue the quartet traditions of Tchaikovsky and Borodin, who introduced melodism and homophonic lucidity into the chamber ensemble, and abandoned—at least in part—the contrapuntal style and academic complexity. This work also gained the prize in a competition of the same society (which in 1913 bore the title of 'The M. Belaiev Chamber Music Society'), and was then performed for the first time.

Gretchaninov's third quartet appeared in 1915, but the war and the revolution delayed its publication for nine years. A comparison with the second quartet will not reveal any important change in the style; like its predecessors it is a fine and lucid work, well written, sustained, pre-eminently melodious, and without any pretensions to originality or modernity—though in this quartet the composer permits himself a somewhat freer use of harmonic colours than hitherto.

THE VIOLIN SONATA is an interesting work; its publication was delayed owing to the same causes which delayed the third quartet. Here Gretchaninov manifests himself more as a lyricist, and the violin becomes almost a voice, to which he entrusts a melody which is simple and spontaneous, but beautiful and extraordinarily sincere—as is always the case with him. The sonata style is not entirely sustained in this work—as a general rule the composer is not entirely a master of this form—but it is a grateful composition for the players and attractive to the public, thanks to its clear and straightforward melodiousness. Though a contemporary creation, it stands aloof from the fashionable quest for novelty, nor does it set or solve any problems, but in spite of this it is always very well received.

L. SABANEIEV.

[It is the voice of an amateur speaking, an amateur with long experience, when I say that although I agree with every word that Mr. Sabaneiev writes on the subject of Gretchaninov's first quartet, I know that it will be more often played than the more mature second and third, whose appeal is to the expert musician. The opening movement and the scherzo of this quartet are instinct with life and youth, the latter being extraordinarily effective, thanks to some deft touches of craftsmanship. The andante is rather in song than quartet style, and the finale is frankly popular in character. Such works are of the greatest use to concert-givers who are willing to consider the claims of the semi-musical layman, especially when they are from the pen of so accomplished a musician as Gretchaninov. The first piano trio is good from every point of view, and may be recommended to all who are in search of fine playable works for piano, violin, and 'cello. The second and third quartets are packed with thought and likely to grow on acquaintance. EDITOR.]

GRÉTRY, ANDRÉ ERNEST MODESTE, 1741–1813, Belgian operatic composer.

Although Grétry is not considered as a chamber composer, his op. 1 consisted of two quartets for piano, flute, violin, and 'cello (André), and his op. 3 of six string quartets. *Fétis* states that the themes of these works are given in B. & H.'s list for 1774. A complete edition of his works (issued by the same firm) was undertaken by the commission for the publication of the works of Belgian masters.

GRIEG, EDVARD HAGERUP, 1843–1907, Norwegian composer.

Quartet, str, g mi	op. 27	Peters, 1879.
Unfinished quartet, str, F	posth.	„ 1908.
Sonata, pf, v, F	op. 8	„ 1866.
Sonata, pf, v, G	„ 13	B. & H., 1869 and 1895.
Sonata, pf, v, c mi	„ 45	Peters, 1887.
Sonata, pf, vc (or v), a mi	„ 36	„ 1885.

and a few unfinished posthumous works.

After the 'Forty-five', which ended with the English victory at Culloden in 1746, many Scottish business men left their country. Alexander Greig from Aberdeen emigrated in 1779 to Bergen, where he afterwards took the name Grieg and became English consul. From him is descended Edvard Grieg.

Ole Bull discovered Grieg's talent and persuaded his parents to send the boy to the Leipzig Conservatorium (1858–62). Here he took as his models the most distinguished composers of the time: Schumann, Chopin, and Wagner. Afterwards, under the influence of Richard Nordraak, he devoted himself to the study of Norwegian folk music, and became the great interpreter of genuine Norwegian melody, rhythm, and modes.

His rhythmic models were the cadences of the folk dance, the *springer* and the *halling*. His melodic model was the Norwegian folk music with its dominant leading note, its modal scales, and its melodic ending on the dominant instead of on the tonic.

Grieg was a true child of nature, with a fondness for the stirring rhythm of the dance and for the folk music's passion for nature and its underlying note of plaintive sadness. His harmony varies between the note of medieval mysticism, in which the choral tone prevails, and the nervous rhythms and dissonances of later times.

THE FIRST VIOLIN SONATA, ostensibly in F major, begins in E minor. The first theme flows smoothly in the Mendelssohn–Schumann style. The second movement opens with a theme in A minor, in the style of Norwegian folk music. The trio is in A major, and is a genuine Norwegian *springer*, carried forward to a grand crescendo. This passage is the best in the sonata, and among the most characteristic music that Grieg has written. The third movement is a loosely arranged mosaic, but is fresh and pulsating with life.

THE SECOND VIOLIN SONATA is also called the dance sonata. Here Grieg reveals himself as a true Norwegian. He breaks with the old form of sonata and writes a passage with a dance motif as the main theme and a ballade motif as the secondary theme, and gives the whole piece a rhapsodic form, so that the passage is really a symphonic poem full of life and dramatic climaxes. The second movement contains a beautiful song theme, which he has used and developed in the romanza in the third sonata. The third movement is a genuine *springer*, full of youthful enthusiasm, vigour, and joy of life. This sonata was composed in the finest and most vigorous period of his life.

THE THIRD VIOLIN SONATA may be described as a dramatic sonata. It is classical in form, and with its simple lines and clearly defined formation, imbued with the spirit of conflict and melancholy, it stands as a monumental work in the sonata literature of the North.

The main theme of the first movement is wild and defiant, leading up to great emotional outbursts. A beautiful, calm, minor theme sings of consolation, but the theme of conflict prevails and the movement ends on the tragic note.

The second movement, a romanza, is among the most beautiful things Grieg has written. The melody begins on the piano, continues on the violin, and the whole passage is built on grand lines yet with supreme delicacy.

The third movement is full of energy, and the subject, which recalls the minor theme in the first movement of Schubert's symphony in C major, is carried forward in its development to a proud hymn of triumph.

THE 'CELLO SONATA has affinity with the violin sonata in C minor. The first movement recalls the concerto in A minor, the second movement reminds one of the *Homage March*, and the third of *Solveig's Song*. The finale contains a very effective coda. The whole sonata is extremely well written for both instruments. Its subject, sombre and impassioned, is intended to portray the moods of his deceased brother, to whom it is dedicated.

THE STRING QUARTET begins with a slow and powerful introduction. It has been said that the quartet is unique in that all its themes are derived from that of the opening. The work has thereby acquired an outward unity, but, on studying the contents, so many breaks are found in its main lines that the composition might well be described as a suite or four lyrical pictures. In spite of these intrinsic weaknesses, the quartet possesses so many beauties and so intense an inner life that it is one of those works that arouse enthusiasm.

The first movement is an elaborate mosaic, but fresh and effective, the second a romanza of calm beauty with a lively interlude. The third is an intermezzo, powerful and temperamental. The finale, like the first movement, begins with a slow introduction, but is interrupted by a wild rhythmic dance, which sweeps along in exuberant life and youthful freshness.

After Grieg's death there was found an incomplete quartet in F major, which was published by Julius Röntgen. The second movement, with its lively *springer* dance and a trio, in which the theme of his *Albumblatt* (op. 28, no. 4) is met with again, is of great beauty. Further, there exists a sketch for a piano quintet in B major and an andante for trio.

Grieg is often criticized for his form and choice of themes. But these critics forget that Grieg belonged to a race living in a remote and peculiar land with rugged mountains and romantic valleys, and a climate varying from the fierce winter storms of the Atlantic to the bright summer nights when the sun is in the sky the whole night long. He was one with his people. When other nations abandon themselves to the joy of life they play a scherzo, a rondo, &c. Grieg played a Norwegian *springer*, or a *halling*, as was the custom of the ancient inhabitants of Norway. And a Norwegian *springer* compares well with the merry and inspiriting dances of any other country. He has been severely criticized for his choice of this as main subject of the first movement of a sonata. But he sought to give expression to the spirit of conflict and courage in life, and what could then be more natural than to employ Norwegian symbolic music for the purpose? On these national foundations laid by Grieg later Norwegian composers will build, for an artist must be true to his race and his fatherland. M. M. ULFRSTAD.

[The chamber music of Grieg has been much criticized for the shortness of its phrases and their illogical treatment. Grieg was not a logician but a poet, one of a new school of Scandinavian poets which arose in his time; and he happened to choose music as his medium of expression in preference to literature. His native mountains, fjords, and pine woods, the joys and sorrows of the Norwegian peasants, echoes of the sagas, as well as of the folk-songs of his country, and finally his own romantic self, had all to be, and were, pictured in his music, which, therefore, did not lend itself to academic treatment. Such a unique personality as Grieg's has rarely been seen in the world of art. Frail in physique, with ultra-delicate sensibilities, he yet was able to vent his emotions with volcanic energy. The introduction, for example, of the string quartet expresses the rugged strength of the Norse nature, and the finale of the C minor sonata for piano and violin the violence of human passion. My impression has always been that musicians are more moved by Grieg's music than they are willing to admit. They are subconsciously aware of his power, not as a musician but as a tone poet, which is not quite the same thing.

One word on the subject of the orchestral nature of the string quartet, so often deplored by critics. They contend with reason that, speaking generally, there should be a prevailing atmosphere of refinement and delicacy in chamber music, but the storm and stress of an orchestrally conceived work are welcome on occasion, and by way of contrast. Music-lovers are, after all, human beings, not aestheticians.

Some years ago a contributor to a New York paper wrote as follows: 'The last time the Kneisels played the Grieg quartet the enthusiasm of the audience exceeded anything I have witnessed at any of their concerts.' This report is not without significance, for it is well known that the appeal of the Kneisel concerts was always to the cream of the musical intellectuals of the city. There must be exceptional magnetism in a work which, manifestly open to adverse criticism from more than one standpoint, is yet able to rouse the enthusiasm of such an audience.

The two movements from Grieg's second quartet, the only two he left completed, have been played in London. Julius Röntgen completed the rest from the composer's notes. The Grieg idiom is more than usually pronounced in this posthumous work. EDITOR.]

GRIFFES, CHARLES TOMLINSON, 1884–1920, American composer.

Two Sketches (based on Indian themes), str. quartet — Schirmer, 1922.

Griffes gave promise of a most hopeful future, and his early death was a severe loss to American music. The chamber music he left forms only a slender part of his musical estate. Perhaps he had intended to leave this form of composition until he had reached a further stage of development. The *Two Sketches based on Indian Themes* were first played by the Flonzaleys in 1918. The two movements are contrasted, the first a lento e mesto, the second an allegro giocoso. The Indian themes are well chosen and adroitly handled. The first movement has a touch of the eerie and fantastic, while the allegro teems with the primitive enjoyment of sharply accentuated rhythms. The ending is typical of a strenuous Indian dance. Owing to its comparative brevity, this composition serves admirably as a middle number on the usual programme of chamber works, in which it should so happen that the first and third are over-bounteous in 'heavenly length'. CARL ENGEL.

GRIFFIN, GEORGE EUGENE, 1781–1863, English pianist.

Three quartets, str	op. 8	Imbault (Janet), (Paris).

Griffin was one of the founders of the Philharmonic Society, who gave performances at their concerts of one of his string quartets (1814) and of his MS. piano quartet (1814), the composer taking the piano part.

GRILL, LEO, b. 1846, at Pest (Hungary).

1st quartet, str, E flat	op. 9	Kistner, 1875.
2nd quartet, str, a mi	,, 11	Peters, 1887.

Grill was a pupil of Franz Lachner, and taught for many years at the Leipzig Conservatorium. Dr. Altmann analyses his first quartet sympathetically in his *Handbuch*.

GRIMM, KARL, German composer.

Kammermusikdichtung, pf, v	op. 22	Kistner.

The foundation of this piece is some lines from Dante, and the title reads 'for violin and piano with a foreword and an epilogue for spoken voice and song'.

GROMIS, CHARLES.

Quartet, str, A	Eulenburg, 1902.

GROPP, HELMUT, German composer.

Sonata, pf, horn, a mi	op. 5	B. & H., 1922.

GROSS, JOHANN BENJAMIN, 1809–1848, German 'cellist.

2nd quartet, str, F	op. 16	Hofmeister.
3rd ,, ,, F	,, 37	B. & B., 1844.
4th ,, ,, E flat	,, 39	Schlesinger, 1845.

Gross was in Count Liphart's Quartet, led by Ferdinand David, from 1833 to 1835. Notices in *Fétis* and *Riemann*.

†GROSZ, WILHELM, b. 1894, Viennese composer.

Sonata, pf, v	op. 6	U.E.

There is also a smaller work entitled *Jazzband* for violin and piano (U.E.).

†GROVLEZ, GABRIEL, b. 1879, French composer, pupil of Fauré.

	Composed	
Sonata, pf, v, d mi, and D	1904	Durand, 1908.

The already considerable output of this composer includes numerous works which are outside the scope of this book, chamber music being represented by a solitary violin sonata. It is in two sections and four movements—animé and adagio linked together, as are also the allegretto scherzando and the final allegro.

The opening theme is anticipated in a few slow bars, wherein the theme is 'filmed in slow motion'. Then it straightway appears at its proper speed, on the same notes of the scale of D minor; the whole theme occupies but four bars of a quick 3/4, and is announced several times to show it in all its aspects. The sprightly rhythm of this bright and smiling exposition breathes life and good humour.

A second theme in 2/4, in the relative major—tenderer and less stormy—is given out in syncopations by the violin, while the piano marks the strong beats. Between two periods of the syncopated phrase, a condensed and epitomized version is given, *f*, in quavers. The phrase, too, is short enough, for the first theme soon returns, and is developed *in extenso*, together with an incidental melodic idea, which was merely outlined in the exposition, but here has room to expand.

The rhythm gradually slackens; anguished themes in long-drawn notes come suddenly surging up, then, after a short transition to A major, the lovely melody of the adagio in 12/8 makes its entry, decked with all the graces and virtues. No less attractive is the second subject with its touch of melancholy, especially when, later, it is wedded to the first in delicate polyphony. Very musical and as free as possible from all scholasticism is the canon at the octave in the recapitulation. The elegance of the details and the avoidance of all pedantry of style give the feeling that Gabriel Grovlez's polyphony is rather one of sentiment than of contrapuntal combination.

The scherzo is an example of strength of wing in a 5/8. The composer who ventures on these ticklish rhythms is usually soon wearied, loses his thread, and, leaving this thorny path at the first cross-roads, wanders down the flowery glade of a 3/4, and this, whether intentional or otherwise, is observable in the greatest musicians since the coming of quintuple time, from Lalo to Rimsky-Korsakov, from Borodin to Debussy. Here Grovlez holds bravely on, as naturally as he started and with no ungainly contortions, during the whole of the first part of the movement, and, for once, one feels quite comfortable with this exceptional rhythm, without fear of gaping seams or failure of invention. This part of the sonata occupies some of the happiest of the twenty-nine minutes occupied by the work.

A short melodic interlude follows, in 3/8, then a brief resumption of the 5/8, catching up the theme of the interlude into its own rhythm, and dying gradually away at the end to a dominant pedal. But the finale dashes off again with a boldly rhythmic theme, in D major, parading its brand-new four-in-a-bar. This has an expressive ending which introduces the melodic theme, on the E string, in B minor, whose unchanging serenity contrasts with the first. All ideas are not equally susceptible of dynamic changes. So it remains *p* till the return of the principal subject. This gives rise to ingenious developments, during which it furtively annexes the first movement themes. Then comes the recapitulation, with a brief reminiscence of the second theme of the opening, and a final stretto rising from a *pp* to the *ff* of the final chord.

The work is not without defects, e.g. rather frequent repetitions due to the extreme brevity of the themes, over-use of arpeggio accompaniments, lack of emphasis in the re-entries of the themes, and a persistent dominant bass in the transitions between the movements. But these reservations are far outweighed by the virtues. It should not be forgotten, too, that the sonata is the work of a youth, and it would be unfair to complain that feeling and expression matter more than style,—were it otherwise at his age it would be regrettable. The great thing is the music; style will come. Nowadays there are only too many young musicians who think more of the style than of the music. Space will not allow me to enlarge further upon Grovlez's gifts, but the reader may take it that in no work is there to be found more grace and youthful freedom than in this clear and restful sonata.

FLORENT SCHMITT.

GROZ, ALBERT, b. 1873, French composer, pupil of Vincent d'Indy at the Schola Cantorum.

Sonata, pf, v, B	Rouart, 1910.

†GRUENBERG, LOUIS T., b. 1882 (in Russia), pupil of Busoni.

	op.	
The Daniel Jazz (Poem by Vachel Lindsay), tenor voice, pf, 2 v, vla, vc, cl, trpt	21	U.E.
Four Indiscretions, str. quartet	20	,,
1st sonata, pf, v (1922)	9	Composers' Mus. Corp. (Agent, Carl Fischer, N.Y.).
2nd sonata, pf, v (1924)	18	,, ,,
Suite, pf, v (1914)	3	Schirmer.
Poème, pf, vc	19	U.E.

Gruenberg was brought to America by his parents when he was two years old. The above are his only published chamber works, but in 1914 he destroyed about fifty unpublished works with which he had become dissatisfied. With that year began a new epoch in his creative development. Hence the suite may be regarded as a forerunner in the new style, rather than as the product of one who, past his thirtieth year, had arrived at some settled mode of expression. The suite, then, is still new wine, heady and effervescent, but not altogether clear and transparent, although much simpler than the two later works. Gruenberg's sonatas have retained some of the tartness of the suite, but on the whole their 'bouquet' is fuller, and their 'bite' that of an older vintage. Thoroughly modern, the sonatas betray an orderly sense of construction and a vivid imagination. The second is a few steps in advance of the first, as regards harmonic detachment and boldness. Robust and vigorous are most of the themes, and their employment is deft and concise. Gruenberg leans towards rhythmic squareness, relieved now and again by impish and capricious moments of a most delightful turn. His scherzos have verve and abandon, and humour is among his qualities as a composer.

CARL ENGEL.

†GRÜTZMACHER, FRIEDRICH WILHELM LUDWIG, 1832–1900, celebrated German 'cellist.

Quartet, str, E	op. 15	Peters, 1855.
Trio, pf, v, vc, c mi	,, 6	Litolff, 1853.

Grützmacher, besides writing very copiously for his own instrument, has revived many forgotten works of interest.

GUARNIERI, FRANCESCO DE, 1867–1927, Italian violinist.

Quartet, str, F	Pizzi, 1922.
Sonata, pf, v	Rouhier, 1908.
Sonata, pf, v, A	Eschig (Demets), 1911; Hug.

Guarnieri was a chamber music player, and founded the International Society for Chamber Music in Paris. As a composer he is far more influenced by the French school (d'Indy, Fauré) than by his compatriots. This quartet is a work of fine sensibility. GUIDO M. GATTI.

GUERRINI, GUIDO, b. 1890, Italian composer.

Quartet, str, C	Pizzi (Bologna).
Trio, pf, v, vc, b mi	,, ,, 1922.

Guerrini, a teacher of composition at the Conservatorium in Parma, is a musician of eclectic taste.

GUILD OF SINGERS AND PLAYERS. A society concerned with the giving of chamber concerts at the People's Palace in the East End of London (Mile End Road). Since 1923 concerts have been given every Sunday afternoon between October and Easter, attended by large audiences.

GUILHAUD, Henry, French composer.

Trio, pf, v, vc, c mi	op. 54	Hamelle, 1913.

GUILLARD, Albert Le, b. 1887, French composer.

Quartet, str	Senart, 1919.
Sonata, pf, v, g mi	„ 1922.

Le Guillard's sonata is a violinistically inspired work, bearing the impress of the writers of the modern French school (Debussy-Fauré). He has been described as writing in a 'discreetly cyclic form'.

The quartet contains many of the features of the modern school, the use of the whole-tone scale, of consecutive fifths, frequent change of metre, &c., and is by no means easy to play. Editor.

†GUILLOUX, Ph.

Sonata, pf, v, g sharp mi	Vieu.

GUITAR. At the beginning of the nineteenth century the guitar was a much favoured instrument in fashionable circles on the Continent and in England, where it was brought into notice by Ferdinand Sor, a Spaniard, who took part in a 'concertante' for Spanish guitar and strings at a concert of the old Philharmonic Society. In the catalogue printed in Stuttgart of a lending library of that period, of which I have had a sight, the number of ensemble works in which the guitar figures is remarkable. Most of them are operatic selections and dances, but two composers appear as writers of quartets for piano, flute, viola, and guitar: Louis Carulli of Naples, b. 1754, and Leonard von Call, b. 1779. These have been considered worthy of republication under the editorship of Hans Schmidt-Kayser. Von Call wrote also about 150 serenades and other pieces for guitar, flute, and string instruments, all in the nature of salon music. Paganini, who was a guitarist as well as violinist, wrote several ensemble works in which the instrument has a part; and his contemporary, Mauro Giuliani, also wrote some duets with flute, but the only really classical work of the kind appears to be Schubert's little-known quartet for guitar and strings (Drei Marken-Verlag, Munich).

Grove has an informing article on the various types of guitar, with illustrations, mentioning *inter alia* that Berlioz, who was a guitarist, betrays in his composition the influence of the instrument, 'as may be seen in his spacing of chords'. Editor.

GUND (or GOUND), Robert, b. 1865, German pianist.

Quartet, pf, v, vla, vc, b mi	op. 35	U.E., 1912.
Trio, pf, v, vc, a mi	„ 6	Karczag & W., 1893.
Romantic suite, pf, v, e mi	op. 18	Kistner, 1893.
Sonata, pf, v, d mi	„ 33	U.E., 1922.
Sonata, pf, v, a mi	„ 44	Doblinger, *c.* 1925.

GUNKEL, Adolf.

Suite, pf, vc, G	op. 8	Kahnt, 1892.

GURLITT, Cornelius, 1820–1901, German composer.

Quartet, str, e mi	op. 25	Cranz, 1861.
Trio, pf, v, vc, C	„ 10	J. Schuberth & Co., *c.* 1846.
Miniature trio, pf, v, vc, G	„ 181	Augener-Schott (New ed.) 1912.
Two miniature trios, pf, v, vc, F, G	„ 200	Litolff, 1893.
Sonata, pf, v, D	„ 4	J. Schuberth & Co., 1847.
Sonata, pf, vc (also v), D	„ 3	J. Schuberth & Co., 1844.

A mass of other work (easy sonatas, duets, and trios) is given in *Altmann*. Gurlitt's output was prodigious, including 241 opus numbers, and immense quantities of educational music. The importance of his work lies entirely in his appeal to elementary students. Editor.

†GURNEY, Ivor Bertie, b. 1890, English composer.

Song-cycle (*The Western Playland*), voice, str. quartet (Carnegie Award, 1924.)	S. & B.
Song-cycle (*Ludlow and Teme*), voice, pf, str. quartet (Carnegie Award, 1921.)	S. & B.

Ivor Gurney is best known by a series of song-cycles on words by A. E. Housman, with string quartet accompaniment. 'The melodies, sensitive and poetic, are admirably suited to the lyric quality of the verse, and cover a wide range of emotional expression' (Report of the Carnegie Trust).

GYROWETZ, Adalbert, 1763–1850, immensely prolific German composer.

Sixty quartets for strings; also quintets for strings, and quartets for flute and strings; about forty sonatas for piano and violin. List in *Fétis* with publishers. Many of his works were published by André. Of a symphony of Gyrowetz, Berlioz wrote one of the most scathing criticisms on record: 'Je ne crois pas que jamais chaudronnier, marchand de peaux de lapins, épicier romain ou barbier napolitain ait rêvé des platitudes pareilles.' Yet both his symphonies and quartets were accounted in his time successful imitations of Haydn.

Editor.

H

†HAARKLOU, Johannes, 1847–1926, Norwegian organist and musical critic.

Sonata, pf, v, g mi	op. 21	Norsk. Verlag; Reinecke, 1922.

'Shows sureness of form and technical skill' (M. M. Ulfrstad).

[*Dent* mentions his 'rare polyphonic endowment', and says that his works 'bridge the romantic and classical, while emphasizing the national element'.]

†HAAS, Joseph, b. 1879, Bavarian composer, pupil of Max Reger.

Quartet, str, A	op. 50	Tischer, 1919.
Divertimento, str. quartet, C	,, 32	Leuckart.
Kammer-Trio, pf, 2 v, a mi	,, 38	Tischer, 1912.
Sonata, pf, v, b mi	,, 21	Rahter, 1908.
Suite (*Grillen*), pf, v	,, 40	Tischer, 1913.
Suite, pf, ob	—	,,
Sonata, pf, horn, F	,, 29	,, 1910.

In Haas's music there is much that is typical of the German spirit expressed attractively in music with contrapuntal skill, and, in his later days, with a sense of humour.

* HABA, Alois, b. 1893, Moravian composer.

Quartet, str	op. 4	U.E., 1922.
Quartet, str (in quarter-tones)	,, 7	,, 1921.
Quartet, str (in quarter-tones)	,, 12	,, —

Alois Haba studied composition at Prague Conservatorium under Novák, then at Vienna and Berlin under Schreker, whose influence predominates in his early works, overlaying the memories of Moravian and Slovakian folk-song which have since reasserted themselves. His early period includes a string quartet, op. 4, of which the variations in the slow movement have been much admired.

One of Haba's most striking idiosyncrasies in the later works is the fashioning of extended melodies without the aid of symmetry, and without recourse to the traditional devices tending to create the feeling of symmetry, such as repetition, transposition, inversion, sequence, &c. Already, in the first movement of op. 4, we have Ex. 1, which is asymmetrical, and in which the only repetitions, *a* and *b*, are exceptions destined soon to disappear altogether from Haba's idiom.

The most important feature of his work is, however, the introduction of smaller subdivisions of the scale than the twelve degrees sanctioned by usage. As a boy, Haba became intimately acquainted with peasant music through the practical experience of taking part in a village band. To this experience he traces

Ex. 1.

his first interest in quarter-tones, for he found in the folk-songs of his native Moravia intervals difficult to reconcile with the tempered scale, and observed that they became more pronounced as his wanderings took him eastwards, until in Eastern Slovakia he found himself definitely confronted with quarter-tones, which he endeavoured to reproduce on his violin. Afterwards, when a pupil at the Berlin Hochschule, he took a course of acoustics at the University, and became well grounded in the investigations of Helmholtz and his successors. Thus his interest in quarter-tones passed from the empirical to the scientific stage. Before he employed them in actual composition, he had not only probed their relations to the scale, but investigated their harmonic and contrapuntal possibilities. It was no mere desire to be different or to startle the musical world, but honest conviction, that led him to introduce, first the scale of twenty-four quarter-tones, and subsequently other systems of eighteen, thirty-six, and seventy-two degrees. The technical corollaries of the new intervals are embodied in a treatise, *Neue Harmonielehre des Diatonischen, Chromatischen, Viertel-, Drittel-, Sechstel-, und Zwölftel-Tonsystems* (Siegel, Leipzig, 1927). This is a systematic survey of the material (scales and chords) existing within each of these systems, and it is worthy of note that even within the twelve accepted semitones he tabulates far greater possibilities than have ever been applied.

Apart from a couple of short works for violin, op. 9, and one for 'cello, op. 18, all unaccompanied, his chamber music in the new systems consists of three string quartets in quarter-tones, opp. 7, 12, and 13, a string quartet in sixth-tones, op. 15, a phantasy for violin and quarter-tone piano, op. 21, and a suite for quarter-tone clarinet and piano. Of these the violin pieces, op. 9, and the string quartets, opp. 7 and 12, are published.

The first point that calls for attention is the important question of notation. In 1920 he adopted for his string quartet, op. 7, a system which retains the accepted accidentals (sharps, flats, naturals) and adds to them two others, the effect of which is to raise or lower by a quarter-tone the note to which they are prefixed. These are:

Ex. 2.

 = a quarter-tone higher.

 = a quarter-tone lower.

Their application is shown in the following example of a scale:

Ex. 3.

By the time the second quartet was ready for publication two further signs had been found necessary. These are:

Ex. 4.

 = three quarter-tones higher.

 = three quarter-tones lower.

Haba being himself a violinist, the problem of fingering has also had his close attention, as may be seen from a study of the parts (not the score) of op. 7. In short, there is nothing of theoretical abstraction about Haba's work, either in the quarter-tone system or in his later study of still smaller intervals. His point of view is that all tone values and tone relations which are capable of being apprehended are also available for the composer's use. His ear perceives these intervals, therefore they are material for composition, and it only remains to establish the principles of technical procedure.

The first string quartet in the quarter-tone system, op. 7, not unnaturally aroused a considerable degree of interest in the musical world. It is in four connected sections: allegro non troppo, scherzando, largo, allegro agitato. The following occurs in the first movement:

Ex. 5.

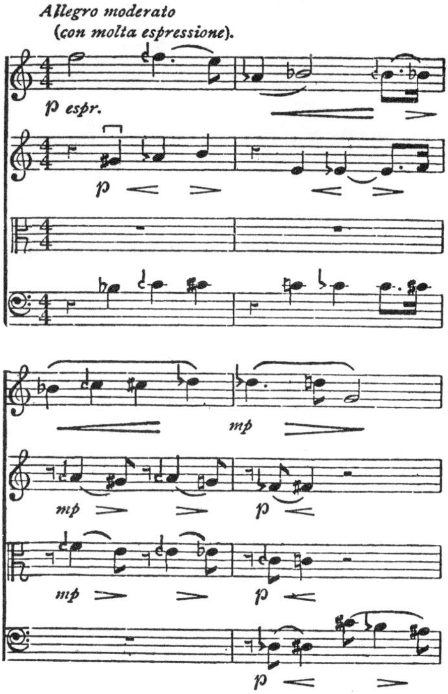

This work still belongs, however, to Haba's earlier phase, before his formal tendencies had been subjected to the same self-discipline as the results of his adventures among the smaller intervals. It is in the second quarter-tone quartet, op. 12, that we find formal principles of construction as definite as those he applies to his tonal systems. Here he has entirely broken away from thematic development. It is said that the element in Slovakian folk-song by which he was most influenced was its extraordinarily abundant outpouring of melodic phrases. Certain it is that in extending a melody he now rigidly avoids all the familiar devices mentioned above, particularly the sequence, and constantly has recourse to new material to prolong the musical thought. Thus the first movement (moderato) of this quartet consists of five extended melodic sentences without repetition, development, or recapitulation. They are entrusted in turn to the viola, first violin, 'cello, second violin, and again the viola. The first of them begins as in Ex. 6.

It extends through sixty-two bars, and employs the whole of the twenty-four quarter-tones. During its progress the three other instruments have equally independent, but

Ex. 6.
Andante.

otherwise articulated, melodies which neither echo nor imitate, nor comment upon anything in the leading part, with which they maintain a kind of equilibrium in motion. The first three sections represent the 'forward' march of the movement; the fourth is relatively clearer and may stand for the node of the movement, and the fifth is the conclusion.

Similarly, the livelier second movement consists of six sections, in two groups of three, corresponding to a rise and fall. In the first section the first violin leads; the second is of rhythmic-harmonic character; in the third the viola leads; the fourth is a point of repose; in the fifth the 'cello leads, reinforced afterwards by the viola in octaves; the sixth is again rhythmic-harmonic, and leads to the conclusion.

On Haba's initiative the first quarter-tone pianos have been manufactured by the firm of August Förster. Apart from numerous solo phantasies and suites, the composer has written one phantasy, op. 21, for violin and quarter-tone piano, and has introduced the new instrument in a combination designed for theatre and cinema use, and including also a string quartet, two quarter-tone clarinets, and two harps tuned a quarter-tone apart.

Only one string quartet in sixth-tones, op. 15, figures as yet in Haba's list of works to represent the theories of the smaller intervals so elaborately worked out in his treatise. Here, again, one of the first problems to be faced is that of notation. The system Haba employs, and recommends for general adoption, is as follows:

Ex. 7.

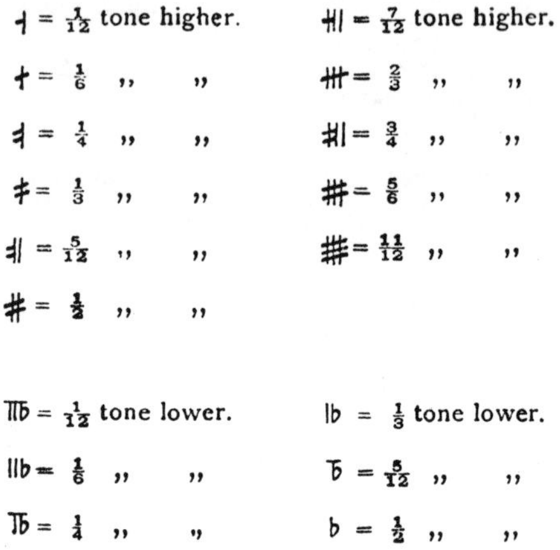

It might be concluded from the foregoing that Haba is to be classed with doctrinaire composers, such as Hauer, or the Schönberg of the third period (opp. 23 to 26, and on), but this is far from being a complete statement of the case. He asserts that theory has always preceded practice in composition—that all the great composers of the past wrote to a system, though they may have left others to codify their doctrines—whereas the commoner view is that the art of composition has developed in defiance of theory, which has limped painfully in the rear, never adequate, and never up to date. In his case the extension of the actual note-material necessitated preliminary codification, which was less urgent where the note-material was the same and only the procedure was affected. Therefore he stood committed to work which another composer would have left to succeeding scholiasts. That, at least, is the impression one gathers from his copious writings and lectures. But, in the main, his mode of composition is far more spontaneous than one might imagine. He does not write to illustrate his theories. He has devised his theories to assist him in expressing himself, and, within their operation, he writes as fluently as another—occasionally even too fluently. It is far from being a case of mathematics applied to music, but, finding smaller intervals conducive to his task as a composer, he has taken the precaution of justifying them mathematically whilst putting them to practical use. As a composer he stands to be judged, not by his quarter-tones, but by the freedom of his fancy and the fertility of his musical invention.

As to the actual effect of these smaller intervals, there are probably few musicians whose ears, however accurate and sensitive, are capable of adapting themselves quickly and automatically to a first hearing of quarter-tone music, whether Haba's or another's. The great majority of listeners pass, at a speed which varies with the individual, through three successive and well defined stages.

During the first stage the music seems very little different from that to which they are accustomed. They have a vague feeling that something is wrong with the intonation, but, except for those who have 'absolute pitch', the impression is so indefinite that if asked to point out a passage that sounded out of tune, they would be almost as likely to hit upon one in which no quarter-tones occurred as one which bristled with them. The reason is obvious: intermediate quarter-tones are in the same relation to each other as semitones, and a passage written in them, or in which they predominate, sounds more or less like a normal passage at a pitch a quarter-tone higher (or lower). Where they occur only occasionally as accidentals, the first effect at this stage is that some notes are 'out of tune', but that impression passes very quickly.

During the second stage the listener hears the quarter-tones as definite degrees of the scale, a kind of secondary chromatics, or chromatics of chromatics. As the basis of Haba's musical thought is already chromatic to begin with, the quarter-tones quickly become the sharps and flats of his chromatic scale, and from this to realizing the presence of a twenty-four-note scale is merely a matter of time, which will be short or long according to whether the listener has previously accustomed himself to the modern use of the twelve-note scale, or is still dependent upon diatonic relations to make the music clear to him. Obviously a listener to whom atonal music is familiar has a shorter road to travel than one to whom it is unintelligible, but in the end the average ear is quite capable of adjusting itself to a twenty-four-note scale and apprehending a musical idea of which it is the vehicle.

The third and final stage is when the listener himself begins to think, with the composer, in quarter-tones with the same ease as his thought encompasses the part-writing of a Beethoven or a Brahms quartet. Full musical intercourse between composer and listener is not a monologue of the former. It is a dialogue in which the latter's part is unspoken. It therefore needs a common vocabulary, and, until the listener who has learned to hear quarter-tones has also acquired the faculty of thinking in them, Haba's music will still, metaphorically speaking, drive him to the dictionary. To pass quickly through those three stages is, however, by no means difficult if the listener is willing to make the effort.

Whether the twenty-four-note scale is a vital necessity of the immediate future is another matter. Haba himself, in company with numerous other modern theorists, has pointed out that, so far from being exhausted, the possibilities of the twelve-note scale are only beginning to be explored, owing to its age-long domination by two systems (major and minor) to the practical exclusion of all others. Long ago Busoni wrote of 133 diatonic scale-systems. Haba's examples, based on the chromatic scale, include 581 scale-systems containing from five to twelve degrees, all logically constructed in accordance with definite principles, and all capable of being put to practical use, and he does not pretend that the list is complete. Though individual composers like Haba and Bloch may be attracted to the use of quarter-tones, generations may pass before the above-named possibilities have been exploited to a point where the musical community as a body will declare them insufficient for its purposes.

It is, however, likely that quarter-tones will play an important part in establishing music on a world-wide basis. At present, when one speaks of music, it is generally understood to mean exclusively Western music. Oriental music is a different art, which has hitherto defied absorption into the general *materia musica*. It is always within range of possibility that some Hindu or Japanese musician may bring together the ingenuity of an Oriental mind and the resources of Western technique, and then the Haba system should prove invaluable in welding the divergent traditions.

Meanwhile the value of the quarter-tone is that of the music in which it is employed—for the present chiefly that of Haba himself. The hearer's impressions of Haba's works are so intimately linked with the technical preoccupations involved that it is difficult to come to an objective appreciation of the music itself. As a purely personal impression it seems to the writer that Haba has at present a corresponding difficulty in keeping his technical preoccupations in their right, subordinate place. His music flows freely and conveys an impression of fertile fancy and invention, but this is sometimes canalized, so to speak, by too rigid observance of self-imposed principles. This is by no means limited to the question of quarter-tones. For instance his rejection, on principle, of sequential repetition may favour the efflorescence of his melodic line, but it is also, at the same time, a curtailment of his freedom, inasmuch as he would not permit himself such a repetition even at a point where his natural inclination suggested it. That is the inherent danger of all musical doctrine. But, within these restrictions, Haba has already displayed so much genuine musical fancy, that we may confidently expect great things from him when he has learned to take them less seriously. EDWIN EVANS.

[It may be of interest to record that Nigitti, organist of Florence Cathedral in the early eighteenth century, commissioned the construction of a keyboard instrument (clavecin) with four manuals and all the quarter-tones, on which he himself performed.]

HABENECK, FRANÇOIS ANTOINE, 1781–1849, French violinist and conductor.

Variations, v, str. quartet Frey (Paris).
Grande Fantaisie, pf, v, (with Schunke) Schlesinger (Paris).

Habeneck, a pupil of Baillot, was himself a successful teacher of the violin, for whom a special class was formed (1825–1848) at the Paris Conservatoire. In the list of his pupils the names of several famous violinists appear, amongst them Alard and Léonard. As a conductor he is an historical figure, owing to his persevering and successful efforts to introduce Beethoven's symphonies into France at the Société des Concerts du Conservatoire.

His two brothers, Joseph and Corentin, were both violinists of some distinction. EDITOR.

HABERT, JOHANNES EVANGELISTA, 1833–1896, Bohemian organist.

		Composed	
Quartet, str, e mi	op. 77	1866	B. & H., 1908.
Quartet, str, E flat	,, 80	1889	,, 1918.
Quartet, str, D	,, 81	1890	,, 1908.

Habert was chiefly a church composer of importance. For further information *vide Riemann.*

† HADLEY, HENRY KIMBALL, b. 1871, American composer.

Quintet, pf, 2 v, vla, vc, a mi op. 50 Schirmer.

Hadley is one of the most versatile of American composers, his output including six chamber works. Of these the only one published is the above quintet, a work in every way typical of a composer who is never concerned with profundity, nor with tonal and atonal experiments. Spontaneity, verve, and expert craftsmanship are the characteristic features of his work. All of these qualities are present in abundance in the quintet, the idyllic slow movement and the piquant scherzo being especially happy in conception.

ARTHUR SHEPHERD.

† HADOW, SIR WILLIAM HENRY, b. 1859, English writer and lecturer on musical subjects, Vice-Chancellor of Sheffield University.

Quartet, str, E flat Novello.

There is to be found in the pages of *Grove* a full account of the work of Sir Henry Hadow, who besides being an attractive writer is a deep philosophical thinker. His qualities give him a position of great influence in the musical and academic worlds. His acquisition of technical mastery was partly gained by the composition of a number of concerted chamber works, including the above quartet (1885) and a piano trio in G minor (1887), both of which have been performed in public with success. EDITOR.

† HÄGG, GUSTAF W., b. 1867, Swedish composer.

Trio, pf, v, vc, g mi op. 15 Leuckart, 1897.

Other important chamber works mentioned by *Riemann* and *Dent.*

HAHN, ALFREDO, German composer.

Sonata, pf, v, E flat C. F. Schmidt, 1903.

† HAHN, REYNALDO, b. Caracas, S. America, 1875, naturalized French composer.

Quintet, pf, 2 v, vla, vc	f sharp mi	Heugel, 1923.
Sonata, pf, v	C	,, 1927.

and some smaller works for pf, fl; pf, cl, &c. (Heugel).

Reynaldo Hahn has a complete knowledge of the technique of his art. His writing is flexible and light, his harmony clear and never overloaded with unnecessary detail, and he has an abundant and easy flow of melody.

In his quintet the first movement, molto agitato, with its principal theme, in F sharp minor, in unison on the strings, hurrying on breathlessly over the trembling semiquavers of the piano, is developed on a solid plan of construction. The second, andante (C sharp minor), is a moving and gravely expressive Lied.[1] This has a middle section in F major, full of tenderness; then the two themes are combined, with modulation, and the movement ends with a gleam of brightness in C sharp major.

The third, allegretto (F sharp major), is a sprightly and cleverly written rondo, in which strength and vigour are united with grace and elegance. It forms a joyous conclusion to the work.

Hahn, who has the French love of clarity, successfully carries on the traditions of Saint-Saëns, but with a touch of the sensitiveness of a Massenet, whose brilliant pupil he was.

ADOLPHE PIRIOU.

† HALFFTER ESCRICHE, ERNESTO, contemporary Spanish composer, pupil of de Falla.

Quartet, str, C Eschig (in the press).

Other chamber works by this young composer, still in MS., have been performed by the Quintetto Hispania, and have awakened much interest. The above quartet has been played by the Flonzaleys. PEDRO G. MORALES.

HALL, MADAME BEATRICE MARY, English composer.

Sonata, pf, v Senart.

[1] See Foreword, art. BEETHOVEN.

† HALL, G. W. L., MARSHALL, b. 1862, Anglo-Australian composer, professor at Melbourne University.

A well-known figure in Australian musical life. He has written string quartets.

HALM, ANTON, 1789–1872, Austrian composer.

Halm wrote three string quartets and other chamber music, a list of which is given in *Fétis* and *Altmann.*

It is said that Beethoven thought a good deal of him; and it was by his wish that Halm made a piano arrangement of the Grand Fugue, which was not, however, published, and was afterwards replaced by an arrangement of Beethoven's own. See Thayer, *Life of Beethoven*, v. The account which Schumann gives (*Gesammelte Schriften*)) of Halm's trio, op. 57, gives the reader the impression that his music is unimaginative, and without a trace of the discipline of good taste. That such music could have interested Beethoven is almost incredible. EDITOR.

† HALM, AUGUST, b. 1869, German composer, and writer on musical subjects.

Quartet, str	B flat	B. & B., 1903.
Prelude; Fugue, str. quartet	E flat; f mi	Zumsteeg, 1916.

Suite, pf, v, vc		Grüninger, 1910–20.
Two suites, pf, v, vc	D, C	Zwissler, 1922.

† HALVORSEN, JOHAN, b. 1864, Norwegian composer and conductor, pupil of César Thomson.

Suite, pf, v, g mi		Nordisk. Musikförlag, 1890.
Kleine Tanzsuite, pf, v	op. 22	Edition Wilhelm.

The suite in G minor is a technically exacting work in four movements, much played in Scandinavia. It is based on the Norwegian *halling* and *springer* with nationally coloured melody. The *Kleine Tanzsuite* is composed of the following: gavotte, tarantelle, Spanish spring dance, and Hungarian dance.

M. M. ULFRSTAD.

[Halvorsen's arrangement of a passacaglia of Handel for violin and viola or 'cello (Hansen, Copenhagen) has won a great reputation among violinists. It is superbly written for the strings, and has taken a permanent place in the repertory. EDITOR.]

HAMERIK (HAMMERICH), ASGER, 1843–1923, Danish composer.

A prominent figure in Danish music. He has written a piano quartet.

HANDEL, GEORGE FREDERICK, 1685–1759.

1st concerto grosso	2 ob, 4 v, vla, 2 vc, continuo	B flat	B. & H.
2nd „ „	ob, 2 fl, 2 v, 2 vla, 2 fag, vc, continuo	g mi	„
3rd „ „	4 v, vla, vc, continuo	F	„
4th „ „	4 v, vla, vc, continuo	b mi	„

Nos. 5, 6 (d mi, D), obtainable in pf arrangement only. Instrumentation not given.

Nine trio sonatas 2 ob (2 fl or 2 v), vc (fag) ad lib., fig. bass (pf) op. 2.

No. 1. c mi	No. 2. g mi	(Emil Krause)	Schott.
3. F	4. B flat	„ „	„
5. F	6. g mi	„ „	„
7. g mi		„ „	„
8. g mi		(Hans Sitt)	Peters.
9. E		(Emil Krause)	Schott.

Six trio-sonatas 2 ob (2 v), fig. bass (pf) (Emil Krause) (vc or fag ad lib.)

No. 1. B flat	No. 2. d mi	Schott.
3. E flat	4. F	„
5. G	6. D	„

Seven trio-sonatas 2 v, fig. bass (pf) (Emil Krause) (vc or fag ad lib.)

No. 1. A	No. 2. D		Rühle
3. e mi	4. g mi		„
5. G	6. F	7. B flat.	„

Sonatas for one instr. and fig. bass. op. 1 (Max Seiffert). B. & H.

No. 1*a*.	fl, fig. bass (pf)	e mi	No. 8.	ob, fig. bass (pf)	c mi
1*b*.	„ „ „ „	e mi	9.	fl, „ „ „	b mi
2.	„ „ „ „	g mi	10.	v, „ „ „	g mi
3.	v, „ „ „	A	11.	fl, „ „ „	F
4.	fl, „ „ „	a mi	12.	v, „ „ „	F
5.	fl, „ „ „	G	13.	v, „ „ „	D
6.	ob, „ „ „	g mi	14.	v, „ „ „	A
7.	fl, „ „ „	C	15.	v, „ „ „	E

Three sonatas for fl, fig. bass (pf) without opus no. a mi, e mi, b mi.
Also a sonata, viola da gamba and cembalo concertato.

Handel's complete works are published by the *Händel-Gesellschaft* in 97 volumes. The chamber music is to be found in vols. 21, 27, and 48.

There are very numerous other publications of most of the works given above; these may be found in *Altmann*. M. D. B.

Apart from the viola da gamba sonata, all Handel's chamber works are designed, not (like most of Bach's contemporary chamber music) with obbligato clavier, but with a plain continuo bass, from which the keyboard performer (perhaps doubled by a bass stringed instrument) filled in the indispensable harmonic support. The flute sonatas are marked sometimes for 'flauto', sometimes for 'traverso', but this is a merely verbal difference of no practical significance. The G major trio has, in one of the MSS., an additional viola part, but this is in another handwriting, and is not authenticated.

Three of the flute sonatas and that for viola da gamba (all four early works) are to be found in the miscellaneous 48th volume of the *Händel-Gesellschaft*; the 27th volume is the authoritative modern edition of the remainder. There are four main sets. The *Six sonatas or trios for two hoboys, with a thorough bass for the harpsicord* date from their composer's tenth or eleventh year, and were not published in his lifetime. The *Fifteen solos for a German flute, hoboy, or violin, with a thorough bass for the harpsicord or bass violin* were (for the most part) first published in 1724, in Amsterdam, as were the *Nine sonatas or trios for two violins, flutes, or hoboys, with a thorough bass for the harpsicord or violoncello*; both sets were soon reprinted in London. Finally comes the set of *Seven sonatas or trios for two violins or German flutes, with a thorough bass for the harpsicord or violoncello*, published in London in 1739. The varying titles show the accommodating methods of the time, but it is plain that some of the works were specifically designed for certain instruments, and for those only. A good deal of the material was utilized by Handel himself for other purposes; apart from various cross-references within the limits of the chamber works, we find many borrowings in clavier music, in orchestral concerti, in operas, and oratorios[1]—the chamber music version being sometimes earlier, sometimes later.

The violin sonatas are in the keys of A major (2), D major, E major, F major, and G minor; all of them are designed on the same four-movement plan of alternating slow and quick sections—the second of the slow sections (no. 3 in the scheme) being sometimes very short, as in the most familiar (and perhaps the finest) of the set, the first of the two A major sonatas. The same structure is found in the sonata for viola da gamba and cembalo concertato (a work of simple texture that was very possibly decorated in performance), but the sonatas for wind instruments show more diverse organizations. Of the two oboe sonatas that in G minor is indeed on the ordinary four-movement plan, but the other in C minor, though still in four movements, is differentiated by the fact that the fourth—a regular little bourrée, though not so entitled—is exceptionally short in comparison with the others.

In the flute sonatas we find many structural methods. The three early sonatas (in A minor, E minor, and B minor) and, in the later set, the G minor, the A minor, and one of the two versions of the E minor, have the normal four movements; the alternative version of the E minor has five (one of them practically identical with the opening movement of the D major violin sonata). The F major also has four movements, but the third is definitely entitled a siciliana, and we find similarly explicit dance measures in the five-movement sonatas in C major (a gavotte) and in G major (a bourrée and a minuet), with a final minuet also in the B minor sonata, a work of exceptional length in seven full-scale movements.

Of the trios, the six for two oboes and continuo, and eight of the set of nine published in 1724, all have the customary four movements (the F major trio for flute, violin, and continuo has five—the no. 4 allegro being succeeded by another in contrasting rhythm), but in the seven trios of 1739 it is seen that the sonata has very markedly shifted towards the suite. The movements vary from five to seven, and in all the works there are definite suite forms; there are altogether four gavottes, three minuets, a musette, a march, a gigue, a (very extended) passacaille, a sarabande, an allemande, a rondeau, a bourrée, and an air.

Musically, all these works are, as a rule, of singularly equable quality. Even the 1696 trios are very deft and firm in texture, and there is practically none of the later sonatas and trios that might not be chosen as very fairly representative. Influences from Italy are no doubt strong; but many of the delightful dance measures look back not a little to such typically English work as the *Airs for the Theatre* of Purcell, and it is not perhaps paradoxical to trace the fusion of the two types of melodic and rhythmic charm in such movements as the 12/8 finale of the familiar A major violin sonata.

ERNEST WALKER.

[One thinks of Handel as a musical giant—a giant with a tender heart, but always a giant. Superficially regarded, his chamber works are but miniatures compared with those with which he scaled the heavens, and which made him an object of worship to the world's greatest musicians, Beethoven amongst the number; yet they are no less perfect. Such is their lyric charm that the choice of a concert violinist in search of a suitable opening

[1] Romain Rolland's *Handel* (English translation, pp. 157, 158) gives a list of some of the more noteworthy of these transferences.

number more often falls upon a Handel sonata than upon any of the other numerous pieces included in his extensive repertory. And if a second violinist is perchance available, the lovely G minor trio (two violins and bass) is a sure card to play, if he seeks to awaken the enthusiasm of a really musical audience.

By a singular coincidence both Schubert and Beethoven are reported to have expressed themselves similarly upon reception of a gift of Handel's works. These were Schubert's words: 'To-day a great joy has come into my life; I have received as a present some publications of Handel, and now I see for the first time how much I have yet to learn.' And Beethoven in his last days, receiving from London the edition, in forty volumes, of Handel's works, said to von Breuning, 'See what I have received to-day; of all musicians Handel is the greatest; from him I can still learn something.' EDITOR.]

HANNIVOORT, HENDRIK WILLEM, b. 1871, Dutch amateur composer.

Quartet, str, G — Senart.

Hannivoort is a functionary in the Government service. The above is his only published chamber work.

HÄNSEL, PETER, 1770–1831, German violinist.

Works include:

Quintet, 2 v, 2 vla, vc	op. 9		Schott.
Quartet, fl, v, vla, vc	„ 17		„
Three trios, 2 v, vc	„ 30	(New edn.),	„ 1876.

One of the most productive of chamber composers. *Fétis* says, 'His works are little known outside Germany'. They include four string quintets, fifty-five string quartets, three wind quartets, six trios, 2 v, vc. The still existing publishers of some of these works are: Haslinger, André, and Simrock. Others by Artaria and by Cappi, who joined Artaria. His violin duets are still played. For list see *Vidal* (also *Fétis*).

† HANSEN, ROBERT EMIL, b. 1860, Danish 'cellist.

Trio, fl, v, vc — op. 13 — Zimmermann.

Hansen has also written a string quartet, a piano quintet, &c.

HANSEN, TH.

Sonata, pf, cornet (or trpt), E flat — op. 18 — Hansen, 1903.

*† HANSON, HOWARD, contemporary American composer, winner of a Coolidge prize. See art. EASTMAN SCHOOL OF MUSIC.

HARDER, KNUD, b. 1885, Danish organist.

Quartet, str, B flat — op. 4 — Haake, 1908.

As Dr. Altmann (*Handbuch*) remarks, this composer 'may be an excellent organist, but his acquaintance with the technique of stringed instruments is limited. What is he thinking of when he asks the first violin, who has had two bars' rest in which to tune the G string down to F, to retune later to G whilst playing?' And in the finale, the C string of the viola is tuned down to B. These abnormal tunings (scordatura) are risky experiments. Knud Harder shows good musicianship in the writing of an excellent fugue. EDITOR.

HÄRING, PAUL.

Trio, pf, v, vc, e mi — op. 4 — Aurora, 1923.

HARMONICS (FLAGEOLET TONES). Spohr's manly denunciation of artificial harmonics, which, he thought, 'degraded a noble instrument,' is little heeded to-day. Not satisfied with the use of natural harmonics, introduced with so much quaint effect by Borodin in his first quartet in A, modern composers of chamber music use the artificial kind with undesirable frequency. They are emulous of the success of certain French composers, notably Debussy and Ravel, in producing ethereal effects by their aid, but it would appear that all have not studied sufficiently the technique of the violin, and do not realize the dangers which attend the use of the shortened string. Artificial harmonics are of such feeble volume that the balance of tone is often disturbed; they do not always 'come off' in a hot room; when suddenly introduced in single notes the tone approximates to that of a penny whistle; and, in fine, one is reminded that the use of falsetto is always dangerous and that from the poetic to the ridiculous there is but one step. EDITOR.

HARP (PEDAL AND CHROMATIC).

Down to the beginning of the nineteenth century the harp was a diatonic instrument, which could be used only in a certain very limited number of keys; thus it was only natural that the classical composers of the eighteenth century made little use of this instrument in their chamber music.

OLD WORKS. A sonata for flute, harp, and double-bass by Haydn, anda few works by the distinguished harpist Johannes Baptist Krumpholz (1745–1790)—one string and harp quartet and two so-called symphonies for harp, flute, two horns, two violins, and 'cello—appear to be the only chamber works of this period which have any real value.

THE NINETEENTH CENTURY. The first quarter of the nineteenth century gave the harp its new construction, since when it has remained practically without alteration. This reconstruction enabled it to take its part in polyphonic music with scarcely any restriction except in respect of rapid chromatic runs.

But the harp still remained in the background, owing to the rise of the piano, and, in spite of the fact that since Berlioz and Wagner the harp had become a necessity in the orchestra, it was hardly ever used in chamber music and became practically a drawing-room instrument, whose repertory consisted of a vast number of solo pieces without pretence to serious musical value. Just one or two exceptions to the rule may be noted. Spohr, whose wife was a distinguished harpist, wrote a few works in which the harp was used as a chamber music instrument, and these all have the usual merits and defects of his period and style. Among them the three sonatas for harp and violin and a fantasia for the same instruments are, perhaps, the most important. Saint-Saëns's fantaisie for violin and harp may also be mentioned, but it is a work of little value, in which the harp has not been employed by any means to the best advantage.

THE TWENTIETH CENTURY FRENCH WORKS. So things stood till well into the twentieth century, when a notable change came about in the attitude of cultivated musicians towards the harp, a change which is of good augury for the future of this long-neglected instrument. It was to the influence of the impressionist movement that this change may be primarily ascribed, and to the leader of that school, Claude Debussy, must be credited one of its most valuable firstfruits in the shape of his sonata for flute, viola, and harp, which is one of the most important of his chamber works, and unsurpassed in its melodic beauty, its admirable blending of tone colours, and its formal perfection.

A few years earlier had appeared Florent Schmitt's quintet in one movement for string quartet and harp, likewise a very distinguished work, in which the new chromatic harp was first used in a chamber work, although the music written for it can also be played on the pedal harp and with rather more effective tone.

P. T. Ingelbrecht comes next with his clever and very delightful sonatina in three movements for flute and harp and the very important quintet for strings and harp, both of which show a perfect understanding of the qualities of the instrument. Albert Roussel's serenade, op. 30, in three movements, for flute, violin, viola, 'cello, and harp, must be considered as one of the composer's most important achievements in chamber music, the andante especially being of an inspiration which shows this remarkable musician at his very best. The harp part is written with admirable skill, and does full justice to the instrument.

Interesting and effective combinations of instruments are used in the *Légende* for flute, oboe, and harp by Marcelle Soulage; the first of the *Pièces Dialoguées* by Paul Dupin, scored for flute, 'cello, and harp; and the quartet for flute, clarinet, violin, and harp by Ch. Migot.

Ravel's introduction and allegro for harp accompanied by strings, flute, and clarinet, should of course not be overlooked. This charming work, though scored for string orchestra, is often played as a septet, and in this form a more individual and intimate rendering of it is possible.

To the same order belongs André Caplet's *Conte Fantastique d'après le Masque de la Mort Rouge d'E. A. Poe* for harp and string quartet or orchestra. This is an extremely dramatic piece of descriptive music, very original both in conception and in execution, and, though very difficult, it successfully displays the musical qualities of the harp and its possibilities in a manner never, it seems, attempted before.

SEM DRESDEN'S SONATA. One of the most fascinating of modern chamber works with harp, and one in which the instrument is used in a way both new and impressive, is the sonata in three movements for flute and harp by the Dutch composer, Sem Dresden. This is a thoughtful, thoroughly musicianly, and highly imaginative work, such as could only be produced by a composer possessed of quite exceptional creative power; and it deserves to be much more widely known than it is at present.

RUSSIAN WORKS. Another notable sonata, for flute and harp, also in three movements, was contributed in 1924 by a composer of the modern Russian school, Adrian Schaposhnikov, who is closely related in his methods and sympathies to the group of Nicolas Miaskovsky, the leading Russian symphonist. This sonata shows undoubted talent and a high degree of skill; it is, however, uneven in inspiration, the first movement being far superior to the others. But all through the work, both instruments are used with great mastery, and the harp part in the third movement affords a perfect example of the unexpected resources of the instrument, though it undoubtedly presents great technical difficulties.

Two other recent chamber works introducing the harp by Russian composers are a quintet for harp, oboe, two violas, and 'cello by N. A. Roslavetz, and a nonet for string quartet, harp, piano, violin solo, dance and light, by V. V. Stcherbachev. In both works attention is attracted by the unusual combination of instruments, and in the second, moreover, by the obbligato parts of dance and light. As both composers belong to the Extreme Left of the modern Russian school, the merits of their creations have still to stand the test of time.

AMERICAN WORKS. The suite by the American composer, D. G. Mason, for flute, violin, viola, 'cello, and harp (1923) is an interesting work, which shows its author's thorough mastery of his subject. The last movement especially, with its quaint use of the 7/8 rhythm, bears all the marks of true inspiration.

Another delightful American work is T. M. Spelman's *Poème* after Th. Gautier's *Pavillon sur l'eau*, for violin, viola, 'cello, flute, and harp, in which this combination of instruments is handled with uncommon skill. The influence of the modern Italian school is noticeable.

ENGLISH WORKS. No modern composer has written more and to better purpose for the harp in chamber music than Arnold Bax; in fact his compositions mark a new stage in the evolution of our instrument in chamber music. They comprise an early elegiac trio for flute, viola, and harp in one movement, the quintet for string and harp also in one movement (1922), the very important sonata in four movements for harp and viola (1927), the sonata in three movements for flute and harp (1928), and an earlier work in one movement for cor anglais, string quartet, and harp—the last two still in MS. The following representative works of the modern English school also deserve mention: Eugene Goossens' suite for flute, violin, and harp, written in the composer's usual attractive style; and Keith Douglas's recent *Sea Wrack* for string quartet, flute, and harp.

The forerunner of German 'expressionism', the late Rudi Stephan has used the harp in his *Musik für sieben Saiteninstrumente*; but the part is not important, and seems to serve mainly to complete the full number of stringed instruments used in modern music. The work itself is, however, of considerable musical interest.

HARP WITH VOICE. An interesting group of works is that consisting of the songs with chamber music accompaniment, in which the harp, in several instances, takes an important place. Prominent in this class are Dame Ethel Smyth's four de Régnier songs—a work in which the harp is given the most important part of the accompaniment, and de Falla's *Psyche* for voice, flute, string trio, and harp.

In conclusion, an extremely interesting work by Schönberg's disciple, A. von Webern, may be mentioned, namely, *Fünf Geistliche Lieder* for voice, flute, clarinet, trumpet, harp, and violin. This, which is a work of extreme modern tendencies, is remarkable for the unusual use of the several instruments, constituting in effect quite a new development of this type of chamber music.

M. KORCHINSKA and C. KONY.

[Further comments on works in which flute and harp collaborate will be found in Fleury's article, THE FLUTE IN MODERN CHAMBER MUSIC.]

* HARRIS, ROY, b. 1898, American composer, half English by parentage.

His output of chamber music consists of two string quartets and a sextet for string quartet, clarinet in B flat, and pianoforte, of which the last is shortly intended for publication. He belongs to a group of American composers —Copland, Sessions, Grunberg, and Varèse— whose aim to found a school of American music is meeting with growing recognition. It is not surprising to find them turn instinctively to the rich store of negro spirituals and to jazz-rhythms for their inspiration and embody them in their art as their folk-music.

The sextet, performed in Paris and New York, is the most recent of his chamber works. The occasional influence of César Franck and a somewhat unctious conception of 'romanticism', noticeable in his early works, are here eliminated. Few composers at Harris's stage of evolution give such a satisfying impression of form as in the first movement. The second, an effective scherzo, and the third, a well-contrasted adagio, are achievements of a musician to be reckoned with. The finale is in a very free fugal form: wild and impetuous in spirit, one cannot help feeling that a more rigorous technical training would enable him all the better to cope with such a free handling of his subject. But the work as a whole bears the hall-mark of sincerity and is the product of one who completely disregards the groups of artists who periodically attract the attention of society in the capitals of Europe. As a musician of no mean calibre he is one of the most promising among present-day American composers.

EDWARD LOCKSPEISER.

HARRISON, JULIUS, b. 1885, English composer.

		Composed	
Prelude music, 2 v, vla, vc, harp (or pf), G flat		1912	Curwen.
Humoresque, *Widdicombe Fair*, str. quartet	op. 22		Hawkes.
Quartet, str			,,

*† HARSÁNYI, TIBOR, b. 1898, Hungarian composer, pupil of Kodály.

	Composed	
Nonet, fl, ob, cl, fag, horn, str. quartet	1927	In the press.
Quartet, str	1925	La Sirène (Paris).
Trio, pf, v, vc	1926	Heugel.
Sonata, pf, v	1926	In the press (U.E.)
Sonatina, pf, v	1918	Deiss.

His first chamber work is a sonatina for violin and piano. The four important chamber works available at the time of writing are thoroughly representative; all of them are atttractive, though difficult to play.

THE VIOLIN SONATA (1926) is in three movements, the first of which is in sonata form, the third being a dance.

THE PIANO TRIO (1926) is in four movements. Both the first and the last movement are in sonata form, each with three subjects. The work is ingeniously written, and straightforward and clear throughout.

THE STRING QUARTET (1925) shows interesting peculiarities of structure. The first allegro is in sonata form; there are three subjects with a 'bridge' between. The second movement is a lento, with a middle section (allegro) occupying the place of the trio. The third consists of an introduction, allegretto, and presto, the introduction being repeated by way of conclusion. And the fourth consists of a slow introduction and a brisk dance.

THE NONET is in four movements, the last of which (allegro giocoso) is a dance whose second subject is a fox-trot tune in 7/8 time.

Harsányi is a composer endowed with a strong, decidedly optimistic individuality and with vivid, sparkling fancy. Both classical and national influences are felt, though neither dominates his work, nor is there any very strong German influence. His technique is fluent and versatile. He is not an uncompromising exponent of atonality, though most of his bigger works are so very nearly atonal that it is impossible to assign a definite key to most of their movements. However elusive the tonal foundation may appear in theory, it invariably proves, in practice, to be firm; and the expression is never indefinite, whether the mood be lyrical (e.g. the beautiful slow movement of the trio) or dramatic (as in the finale of the same work). M. D. CALVOCORESSI.

[Harsányi's string quartet was broadcast on April 2, 1928, from Savoy Hill.]

HARTLEB, G.

Carnival quartet, str	R. & E., 1881.

† HARTMANN, ARTHUR, b. 1882, American violinist.

Suite in ancient style, pf, v	op. 27	Carl Fischer, N.Y., *c.* 1926.

HARTMANN, (1) JOHANN PETER EMILIUS, 1805–1900, Danish composer.

Suite, pf, v, g mi	op. 8	Hansen (orig. Löhse).
Sonata, pf, v, C	„ 39	Hansen, 1846; J. Schuberth & Co.
Suite, pf, v, a mi	„ 66	Hansen, 1870; Kistner.
Sonata, pf, v, g mi	„ 83	Hansen, 1888.
„ pf, fl, B flat	„ 1	(P. Hagemann) Hansen, 1913.

Hartmann, who was of German descent, was once considered during his long life one of Denmark's chief composers. One of his violin sonatas was crowned by the Institute of the North German Musical Union in Hamburg. Of this work Schumann (*Gesammelte Schriften*) speaks highly, especially of the first movement. He finds in Hartmann 'an artist who at once propitiates by the harmonious development of his powers, and who, a master of form and no slave to his own feelings, understands how to touch and to fetter our interest throughout'.
EDITOR.

(2) EMIL, 1836–1898, son of the above, Danish composer, pupil of Gade.

Serenade, fl, ob, 2 cl, 2 fag, 2 horns, vc, cb	op. 43	R. & E., 1890.
Quartet, str, c mi	„ 37	Rühle, 1887.
Trio, pf, v, vc, B flat	„ 10	Kistner, 1869.
Serenade, pf, cl (or v), vc	„ 24	Simon, 1890; Hansen, 1878.

† HARTY, SIR HAMILTON, b. 1879, Irish composer.

Suite, pf, v	Schott.

Other chamber works still in MS., among them a string quartet (in A, op. 5) which was awarded a prize at the Irish musical festival, Feis Ceoil, in 1902, and a piano quintet (in F, op. 12).

HASLINGER, (1) TOBIAS, 1787–1842.

Quartet, pf, fl, vla, vc, G		Haslinger.
Sonata, pf, vc, C	op. 17	„

Tobias Haslinger was Beethoven's friend and publisher, and the subject of some of his many jokes (see Canon in *Grove*, ii. 337). He wrote other chamber works, see *Fétis*.

(2) KARL, 1816–1868, Viennese pianist and publisher, son of the above.

His works include a piano trio, two violin sonatas, and a 'cello sonata, published by his own firm.

HATTON, JOHN LIPTROT, 1809–1886, popular English song-writer.

Two trios, pf, v, vla, g mi, a mi	Zumsteeg, 1883, 1885.

The composer was almost entirely self-taught.

† HAUER, JOSEPH MATTHIAS, b. 1883, Austrian composer.

4th quartet, str	op. 47	U.E.
Five pieces, str. quartet	„ 30	Schlesinger.
Quintet, pf, cl, v, vla, vc	„ 26	„

Hauer's theories of atonal music are elaborated in a number of books and pamphlets which should be consulted by those desiring to understand the significance of his music, and its relation to other currents of musical development. In the order in which they appeared they are: *Über die Klangfarbe* (Waldheim & Eberle, Vienna, 1920); *Vom Wesen des Musikalischen, ein Lehrbuch der Zwölfton-Musik* (Schlesinger, Berlin); *Deutung des Melos* (Tal, Vienna, 1923); *Von Melos zur Pauke, eine Einführung in die Zwölftonmusik* (Univ. Ed., Vienna, 1925); *Zwölftontechnik, die Lehre von den Tropen* (Univ. Ed., Vienna, 1926).

The starting-point of his speculations was Goethe's *Farbenlehre*, and he is also believed to have been influenced by Kandinsky. Just as the latter recognizes only 'colour for its own sake', so Hauer carries to extreme lengths his exclusion of all but abstract music. Hauer's atonal system is based on the twelve-degree scale, and was at first limited to tempered instruments, though he has since written for others with the strict injunction that tempered intonation is to be observed. According to him the twelve notes permit of 479,001,600 possible 'Melos' formations, divided into groups which he terms 'tropes'. Within each of these reside latent forces which it is the composer's province to liberate. At first Hauer admitted only homophony, but as his method grew he began to develop polyphonic combinations of sound. Despite these rapprochements, Hauer remains in opposition to the whole development of Western music, and has, philosophically at least, much more in common with the musical traditions of some Eastern races. His intense earnestness and sincerity have earned for him a deep and general respect. Even Schönberg, who, generally speaking, dislikes the atonal label and rarely ventures from his own furrow, has bestowed a blessing upon this lonely and austere prophet. The effect of Hauer's method is, in the main, pattern-weaving. This effect is made even more apparent by his avoidance of accepted amenities of horizontal writing, such as the rise from the leading note to the octave, and, in general, all sentimental or 'graceful' inflexions. For a long time his music was regarded as of more theoretical than practical interest, but a succession of performances has considerably modified this view. The most successful of these was that of his seventh orchestral suite at the Frankfort festival (1927) of the International Society for Contemporary Music. This work, like its predecessors, was a succession of patterns, but their sonorous effect, considered as patterns, was almost unanimously regarded as beautiful, and many who were sceptical of Hauer's theory went away declaring that there 'must be something in it' if its results were so euphonious. It is to be expected that this success will lead to a closer study of Hauer's principles. Meanwhile, owing to his own former inhibition against instruments which do not use the tempered scale, his contributions to chamber music represent a relatively small portion of his output as a composer. Apart from pieces for various solo instruments with piano, they consist of a quintet for clarinet, violin, viola, 'cello, and piano, and four string quartets (opp. 30, 34, 38, 47), which are mostly suites of short movements. As a simple example a quotation is given from op. 30.

It should be noted that, even within the same bar, accidentals hold good only for the note to which they are prefixed.

EDWIN EVANS.

HAUPTMANN, MORITZ, 1792–1868, German composer and theorist.

Two quartets, str	op. 7	Artaria, Vienna.
Sonatas, pf, v, g mi, E flat, D	,, 5	Litolff, 1899; Peters.
Sonatas, pf, v, B flat, G, d mi	,, 23	Litolff, 1899; Peters.

Altmann gives a list of duets for 2 v, and sonatinas for pf and v.

Hauptmann, originally intended for the profession of an architect, is chiefly remembered for his remarkable faculty for teaching the theory of music. Among his many distinguished pupils may be mentioned Joachim, Kiel, Bülow, and Sullivan. As violinist he played at Cassel (1822) in the band conducted by Spohr, whose lifelong friend he became, and whose influence is felt in his chamber music.

His quartets were well spoken of by the German press (*Leipzig Gazette*, 1829), but they are less attractive than the sonatas for piano and violin, which are still played in private circles. During the latter part of his life Hauptmann wrote exclusively for the voice.

EDITOR.

HAWORTH, HERBERT.

Sonata, pf, v — Augener, 1921.

† HAY, EDWARD NORMAN, b. 1889, Irish composer and organist.

Quartet, str, A — S. & B., 1922.

The quartet received the Carnegie Award, 1918, and was spoken of as 'a work of remarkable originality, large conception, and high achievement'. A folk-song phantasy, for string quartet, won a supplementary Cobbett prize two years earlier.

HAYDN, FRANZ JOSEPH, 1732–1809.

Octet	2 ob, 2 cl, 2 fag, 2 horns	F	(F. Grützmacher) Kahnt, 1901.
The Echo	4 v, 2 vc (or pf, 2 v, vc) [to be performed in two separate rooms]		Heinrichshofen, 1841.
Quintet	2 v, 2 vla, vc [Doubtful]	G	(New ed.) Simrock, 1874.

Seventy-six (or eighty-three) quartets, str, published by various houses as follows:

		Number	
Six quartets	B flat, E flat, D, G, B flat, C	1–6	op. 1.
Six quartets	A, E, E flat, F, D, B flat	7–12	,, 2.
Six quartets	E, C, G (with bagpipe minuet), B flat, F (with serenade), A	13–18	,, 3.
Six quartets	C, E flat, G, d mi, B flat, A	19–24	,, 9.
Six quartets	E, F, E flat, c mi, G (with recitative in adagio), D	25–30	,, 17.
Six quartets	E flat, C, g mi, D, f mi, A	31–36	,, 20.
Six quartets	(The 'Russian' quartets), b mi (D), E flat, C (*Bird*), B flat, G, C	37–42	,, 33.
Quartet	d mi	43	,, 42.
Six quartets (ded. to Fredk. Wm. II)	B flat, C, E flat, f sharp mi, F (with adagio *The Dream*), D (*Frog*)	44–49	,, 50.

		Number	Alternatively.	
Seven quartets (*The Seven Last Words*), arranged from Good Friday music composed for Cadiz Cathedral, 1785			(50–56)	,, 51.
Three quartets	G, C, E	50–52	(57–59)	,, 54.
Three quartets	A, f mi (*Razor*), B flat	53–55	(60–62)	,, 55.
Six quartets	C, b mi, B flat, G, D (*Lark*), E flat	56–61	(63–68)	,, 64.
Three quartets	B flat, D, E flat	62–64	(69–71)	,, 71.
Three quartets	C, F, g mi (*Rider*)	65–67	(72–74)	,, 74.
Six quartets	G, d mi (*Quinten*), C (*Kaiser*), B flat (*Sunrise*), With largo in F sharp, E flat	68–73	(75–80)	,, 76.
Two quartets	G, F	74–75	(81–82)	,, 77.
Quartet (unfinished)	B flat	76	(83)	,, 103.

Thirty trios for strings, and other combinations:

Six divertimentos	v, vla, vc	G, A, C, D, G, A		Zumsteeg, 1864 (1st 3). 1869 (2nd 3).
Two divertimentos	v, vla, vc (arranged from movts. of several trios, baryton, vla, vc)			U.E., 1902.
Three trios	v, vla, vc	G, B flat, D	op. 53	André, 1855.
Twelve easy trios	2 v, vc (or vla)	G, D, A, G, B flat, E flat, D, G, A, D, A, D.	,, 21	C. F. Schmidt, 1898.
Trio	v solo, vla (concertante), bass			—
Two trios	fl, v, bass			—
Three trios	3 fl			—
Trio	cor di caccia, v, vc			—

Three duets	2 v		,, 99	André, 1851.
Three sonatas	v, vla		,, 93	(New ed.) André, 1860.
Duet	v, vc	D		(F. Bennat) and (F. Grützmacher), R. Forberg, 1888 and 1903.

Trios, pf, v, vc B. & H. publish thirty-one trios, complete or separate, as follows:

No. 1. G	No. 12. E flat	No. 23. F
2. f sharp mi	13. B flat	24. A flat
3. C	14. g mi	25. F
4. E	15. e flat mi	26. C
5. E flat	16. g mi	27. F
6. D	17. E flat	28. G
7. A	18. C	29. F, also with fl for v.
8. c mi	19. d mi	30. D, ,, ,, ,,
9. A	20. E flat	31. G, ,, ,, ,,
10. e mi	21. D	
11. E flat	22. B flat	

Other trios:

Trio-sonata (divertimento)	pf, 2 v	B flat	(B. Engelke)	Eos, 1913.
Two trios	lute, v, vc			
Sonata	fl, harp, bass			

Violin Sonatas. I possess an old edition containing eight sonatas, of which the last two are arrangements of the quartets, op. 77, nos. 1 and 2, without minuet (Holle, Wolfenbüttel, probably out of print). *Riemann* mentions twelve. A list of twelve arrangements of the string quartets is given in *Altmann*. Many of the quartets have been arranged for both violin and 'cello with piano, and issued by various publishers.

Works for baryton: Haydn wrote 175 of these, for two barytons or for baryton with other instruments. For these *vide Grove*.

Spurious works: There are several of these, notably the string quintet, op. 88, still attributed to Joseph Haydn in *Altmann*, but in reality the work of his brother Michael.

Note.—As no complete edition of Haydn's works exists as yet, the above list does not contain the whole of his chamber compositions, some of which are still unpublished. A complete edition was begun by B. & H. in 1908, estimated to run into eighty volumes. Up to 1928 the chamber works had not been begun.

Editor.

In the history of music no chapter is more important than that filled by the life-work of Joseph Haydn. He effected a revolution in musical thought hardly less far-reaching than that effected at the close of the sixteenth century by the monodists who wrote the earliest operas, and supplanted the pure vocal polyphony of Palestrina by the new art of supporting solo voices on instrumental chords. But, whereas the monodic revolution destroyed a great art so effectively that there is a gap of a century between Palestrina and the new polyphony of Bach and Handel, the revolution effected by Haydn has its only immature phases in unpretending tuneful efforts within the lifetime of Handel, whose art-forms Haydn supplants, not by destruction, but by reabsorption into his own new musical life as soon as this has firmly established its independent basis.

Before it is possible to measure Haydn's achievement it must be realized that his conscious musical culture rested on a music much older than that of the generation before him; and that, except in so far as his music is derived literally from the streets, its foundations are not in Bach and Handel, but in Palestrina. When the young Haydn came to Vienna, Fux, the court organist, had not long been dead, and Fux's *Gradus ad Parnassum* was more important to him than victuals for his body and fuel for his garret in mid-winter. Fux's church music, which is still drawn upon by serious Roman Catholic choir-masters, is genuinely masterly work by an eighteenth-century composer who prefers to write in pure sixteenth-century style. To Fux, if to nobody else at the time, that style was still a living language; and even if it could be proved that Haydn knew nothing nearer to Palestrina than Fux, the fact would remain that he educated himself with a sixteenth-century musical culture. In his old age he even lent his name to a project for publishing the archaic works of Obrecht.

Now the pure polyphony of the Golden Age had solved for all time the central problems of vocal harmony. Its medium was the unaccompanied chorus of voices producing a mass of harmony by singing independent melodies; and its grammatical laws (surviving for the vexation of students to-day in the form of garbled and arbitrary rules for exercises that exist only on paper and represent no musical language) were essentially practical rules of instrumentation. For not only was the chorus the only instrument seriously cultivated, but no other instrument had familiarized the ear with any complete ideas that the voice could not spontaneously express. The great monodic revolution at the beginning of the seventeenth century is far too complex a process to sum up in a phrase, or even in a volume; into the world of Palestrina it opened out the aspirations of Wagner, and provided no technical experience for the equipment of its pioneers. After Bach and Handel had closed their epoch, the latter half of the eighteenth century still found need for a fuller solution of what might be supposed to be the simplest musical problem of the seventeenth century—that of producing an instrumental harmony not less complete and satisfactory than a purely polyphonic chorus.

It is vain to regard viol-music as in any line of ancestry to the string quartet. The viols merely played vocal music which was enjoyed for the sake of the vocal sense, and hardly, if at all, for the tone of the viols. As the word 'monody' implies, the revolutionary composers of the early seventeenth century directed their attention to the solo voice; and their first urgent practical question was how to organize a harmonic accompaniment for the supporting instruments. Within a surprisingly short time they developed the art of playing a semi-extempore accompaniment from a figured-bass on a keyboard instrument. At the same time the violin and its family were ousting the flat-backed husky-toned viols, and were raising more important new issues by flying and diving into regions far beyond the compass of human voices.

Thus at the outset of the seventeenth century the two problems of the solo performer and the instrumental accompaniment were already defined. Uncharted difficulties remained in the special techniques of the various instruments, and contrasting and blending their tones in a mass of harmony. A full century passed before these difficulties were artistically solved; and the solution as achieved by Bach and Handel is so remote from the aesthetic system of even Haydn's and Mozart's orchestra that it is only now beginning to be realized that it is a genuine solution, and that to dismiss Bach's and Handel's orchestral intentions as primitive is as Philistine as to modernize Palestrina's modal harmony. The life-work of Haydn effected the whole transition from the aesthetic system of Bach to that which is common to all instrumental music from Haydn to Brahms; and it effected it by no destructive revolution, but in an orderly progress of works full of promise at the outset and culminating in a long series of masterpieces.

Haydn's culture in the Palestrina style remained a fundamental, though undisplayed, element throughout his art; but the hypothesis of Bach's and Handel's instrumentation was immediately and irretrievably abolished by him in his earliest instrumental works. Yet on that hypothesis every musician in Haydn's young days was trained, and there was no definite period in Haydn's long life at which the hypothesis was consciously abandoned. The hypothesis still depended on the monodists' device of the continuo. Carl Philipp Emanuel Bach, the most famous of Bach's sons, and the master whose clavier-works and treatise on clavier-playing were appearing as a revelation to the boy Haydn in his Vienna garret, protested bitterly against the growing neglect to provide a continuo for performances of oratorios and orchestral music. The hypothesis of the continuo is based on a truth which is as important to-day as it was in the time of Bach; for neither practically nor ideally does the orchestra produce a homogeneous mass of harmony like a chorus endowed with instrumental powers. The contrast between background and foreground is involved in the nature of all instrumental combinations, and is only artificially imported into pure vocal polyphony. If a composer writes choral harmony according to certain old grammatical rules, without troubling to imagine the effect, he will never be disappointed with the result, for the rules are absolutely safe, and the composer who writes correctly, without using his mental ear, is unlikely to appreciate anything better even when he hears it. But with all instrumental combinations the limits within which vocal rules apply are soon reached; and the composer who writes concerted music without using his mental ear is quickly brought to his senses by defects obvious to everybody as soon as he ventures beyond vocal idioms. The pioneers of instrumental music in the years 1600–1620 showed an accurate instinct by promptly treating all groups of instruments as consisting of a firm bass and a florid treble, held together by an unobtrusive mass of harmony in the middle. Up to the death of Handel and beyond, throughout Haydn's boyhood, this harmonic welding was entrusted to the continuo player, and nobody ever supposed that the polyphony of the 'real' orchestral parts could, except accidentally or by way of relief, sound well without this supplement. The written instrumental parts are an aristocracy for whom the problems of domestic service are perfectly solved by that most learned and most modest of artists, the continuo player, who was, in the best performances, generally the composer himself.

It is not too much to say that one-half of the problems of instrumentation, both in chamber music and in the orchestra, since Haydn began to work, up to the present day, lies in the distribution of the continuo-function among all the instruments. But, for Haydn, most of the other half of the problem arose from a feature in early eighteenth-century music which concerns only the keyboard instruments and which leaves no trace in the written record of compositions. Hence its existence is often overlooked, though the modern art of instrumentation has to replace it besides the continuo. In the early eighteenth century, everybody who played upon keyboard instruments (that is to say, every educated musician) was brought into constant contact with the power of the organ and the harpsichord to double in higher or lower octaves whatever was played upon them. One obvious result of this is that good counterpoint in two or three parts need never sound thin, for, by merely pulling out a stop, it becomes a mass of sounds which would require four or six vocal parts to produce, but which adds nothing more than a quality of timbre, much as if the upper partials of each 'clang' were heard through a set of Helmholtz resonators. And there is no more striking illustration of the correct instincts of medieval musicians than the fact that one of the most ancient devices of the organ is the use of 'mixtures' extending to the whole first six overtones, thus anticipating Helmholtz's theory of timbre by half a millennium.

With these facts in mind it is more easily understood that, when Haydn began his work, his auditory imagination was fed on experiences fundamentally opposed to the whole hypothesis of future chamber music—the hypothesis that the written notes completely define the composition. How could the string quartet develop in a musical world where necessary harmonic filling-out was always left to be extemporized, and where a single written note might sound in three different octaves at once? There were string quartets before Haydn, but nobody troubles to revive them. In his later years Haydn was indignant at the suggestion that he owed anything to the quartets of Gluck's master Sammartini, saying that he had indeed heard them in his youth but that 'Sammartini was a dauber' (*Schmierer* or 'greaser'). Haydn's own first quartets were commissioned by a patron in whose house quartet-playing was an established custom. The date given by early accounts is 1750, the year of Bach's death; but Pohl assigns Haydn's first quartets to 1755, partly for vague biographical reasons and partly because he considers the technique too advanced to have been achieved without long study and leisure. The growth of ideas and style in Haydn's first eighteen quartets (opp. 1, 2, 3) is so fascinating that Pohl may be forgiven for overrating their artistic value; but there is really nothing in the first eighteen quartets which is technically beyond the power of a talented young musician between 1750 and 1760; some features (e.g. the structure of the finale of op. 1, no. 6) could hardly have survived any study at all; and the merits of the works are not accountable for by study, for the whole significance of Haydn's development is that it took a direction which no other composer before Mozart ever suspected or even recognized when it became manifest.

There was, at the outset, no clear distinction between a string quartet and a string orchestra. The fifth quartet is undoubtedly Haydn's first symphony, though it is at least four (if not more) years earlier than the work that has been catalogued as such by all authorities, including Haydn himself. Authentic wind-parts have been found for this 'quartet'; and here the point is not merely that it is indistinguishable from orchestral music, but that Haydn never objected to its inclusion among his published quartets, though he omits it in his own MS. catalogue. In external form it differs from the quartets, and conforms to the first two acknowledged symphonies, inasmuch as it has no minuets and its three movements are occupied with formulae and argumentative sequences to the exclusion of anything like a tune. The first eleven real quartets, on the other hand, have five movements, including two minuets, one on each side of the middle movement; and the other three movements often combine tunefulness with a certain tendency at first hardly distinguishable from awkward irregularity, but already urging towards the quality by which Haydn's life-work was to effect a Copernican revolution in musical form.

Though all the important chamber music before Haydn was designed on the continuo hypothesis, it would be a mistake to suppose that Haydn started without experience of what could be done by instruments unsupported by keyboard harmony. Such experience was familiar to him in the music of—the streets. Serenading was a favourite pastime, enjoyed as much by listeners as by players. One of Haydn's boyish practical jokes consisted in arranging for several serenade parties to perform different music in earshot of each other, to the annoyance, not only of a respectable neighbourhood, but of an adjoining police station. Serenade music consisted naturally of dance tunes, marches, and lyric ariosos. By the time of Mozart it had developed into works longer, if lighter, than symphonies, the typical serenade becoming in fact a cheerful six-movement symphony, with two slow movements alternating with two minuets. If the combination of instruments was solo rather than orchestral, the composition would be called a divertimento; and the remaining name for such works, 'cassation', is a corruption of *Gassaden*, which means music of the *Gassen* or back-streets. And just as Hans Sachs was accused by Beckmesser (or by more historical persons) of writing *Gassenhauer*, so Haydn, whose first quartets became rapidly and widely popular, was frowned upon by this and that preserver of the official dignity of music who could predict no good from such vulgar beginnings; nor was Haydn ever spared the charge of rowdiness even in his ripest works.

For the purposes of a catalogue it may be important to distinguish between quartets, divertimenti, and symphonies; but for aesthetic purposes the distinction emerges only gradually as the works improve, each in their own direction. Haydn's first twelve quartets are moving cautiously from the style of the *Gassaden* to that of the future symphonic sonata forms. The movement towards a genuine quartet style can be traced only with reference to what was present to Haydn's auditory imagination at the time. Of street music one thing is certain, that it never sounds well. The sound may be romantically suggestive, the occasion gratifying to the listener, and the performance perfect; but suggestiveness is almost all that is left of the actual body of sound, the finer nuances of performance are lost, and the rest is all moonshine. The development of Haydn's auditory imagination will depend upon the use he makes of the experience of hearing, writing, and playing music unsupported by the continuo, within four walls and a ceiling. And for pioneer work, a fastidious taste in performance is both an obstacle to enterprise and a necessity to progress. On the whole it is more of a necessity than an obstacle.

Haydn himself knew the technique of several different instruments, but was, he confesses, 'no conjurer on any of them'. Composers' playing is proverbially bad; since not only is the composer unlikely to devote his time to acquiring the technique of a conjurer, but he is of all persons the most capable of imagining desirable qualities without needing to supply them himself. Only when he takes up the conductor's baton do conditions naturally awaken in him a present sense of what a performance should be. It is accordingly significant that Haydn's achievement in his first twelve, or even his first eighteen quartets is no fruit of his experience under the stimulating conditions as conductor of Prince Esterhazy's private orchestra, but is rather a demonstration of his eminent fitness for that post four or perhaps nine years before it was offered him. It is significant that there is no sign of the need for a continuo in the general conception of these earliest quartets. Here and there one finds Haydn insensitive to the baldness of a progression which long habit of reliance on the continuo had completely submerged below the composer's consciousness; and thus, even as late as 1769, in a quartet otherwise astonishingly mature (op. 9, no 4), Haydn not only leaves a blank space for a cadenza at the end of a slow movement, but represents its conventional 6/4 chord by a bare fourth.

Ex. 1.

Even in his old age, Haydn's pen is liable to small habitual slips, which, like all such lapses, should reveal to the psychologist how far the mind has travelled, instead of suggesting dismal broodings on squalid origins. It will save space to deal with these lapses here. The fact that Haydn's fifth quartet was actually a symphony raises the question whether throughout opp. 1 and 2 his 'cello part was not supported, or even (as many years later in Mozart's ripest divertimenti for strings and horns) replaced by a double-bass. Aesthetically the question is more open than it might appear to a fastidious taste in mature chamber music. Long after Haydn's and Mozart's quartets had set the standard of style for all educated musicians, Onslow, having found the double-bass an unexpectedly good substitute for a missing 'cello, proceeded to write several very decent quintets for strings with double-bass.

The double-bass is unthinkable in Haydn's quartets, from op. 9 onwards; and yet he is never quite sure of his octave when, without using the tenor clef, he writes his 'cello above the viola. Even after Mozart's artistic debt to Haydn appears repaid with compound interest, there is an astonishing miscalculation throughout six bars of the development of one of Haydn's greatest first movements, that of the quartet in E flat, op. 71, no. 3 (bars 20–26 from the double-bar).

Ex. 2.

The passage is not, like other accidents of the kind, to be remedied by putting the 'cello part an octave lower (as with an incident in one of the last six quartets, op. 76, no. 4, where the use of the treble clef at its proper pitch may have caused confusion), for Haydn is evidently thinking of the tone of the A string. And in a later passage of the same movement the viola and 'cello are found crossing each other with exquisite adroitness, the lowest note at each moment being the real bass.

Ex. 3.

&c.

Where Haydn miscalculates in these mature works, the error really lies in the viola part. Thus, in Ex. 2, the one possible and perfectly satisfactory correction consists in substituting a rest for the first quaver in each bar of the viola part. There is a more special significance of such oversights in Haydn's viola parts; but for the present it is important to realize that they originated in the habit of thinking of the 'cello as supported by a double-bass.

The double-bass was not the only cause of ambiguity as to the octave in which passages of early chamber music are conceived; and Haydn's first quartets, no less than his symphonies, show certain uses of octaves which suggest the mutation-stops of the organ and harpsichord. It is possible to watch the process by which these uses, beginning in habit, awakened Haydn's consciousness to their actual sound when transferred from the automatic action of a stop on the organ or harpsichord to the efforts of four living players on four instruments. In orchestral music the young Haydn agreed with his contemporaries in finding two-part harmony more satisfactory to the ear when merely 'registered' in several octaves than when filled out with a viola part which, like those of Bach and Handel, makes no attempt to usurp the function of the continuo. Where Haydn from the outset differed from almost all his contemporaries was just in the excellence of his two parts. And in his quartets he startled his listeners by doubling the melody in octaves as well as the bass. Accurate discrimination is needed in comparing his early procedure in quartets with that in his orchestral music; it must suffice here to summarize the result by stating that Haydn's use of octaves in his first quartets is far more a matter of conscious art than in any but his ripest symphonies. He can hardly have needed to wait for practical experience to tell him how successfully he had imagined the effect of the second minuet in the quartet, op. 1, no. 1.

Ex. 4.

Menuetto.

&c.

There is nothing in the scoring of this spirited little movement which Haydn would have thought necessary to alter at any period of his life, though the viola has only four bars in which it is not in octaves with the 'cello. The fact that this bold and bleak doubled two-part harmony is common in the first eighteen quartets and rare in the later ones must not be allowed to hide the more important facts that it startled his contemporaries and that it is an effect as genuinely imagined in op. 1 as in the wonderful canonic *Hexen-Menuett* in op. 76, no. 2.

Ex. 5.

Menuetto. Allegro ma non troppo.

His imagination has promptly grasped the vital difference between octaves produced by a mechanical coupler and octaves played by two living players on separate instruments. Moreover, it has grasped the more delicate but equally vital difference between octaves in the orchestra and octaves in the string quartet. In spite of all ambiguities, Haydn's earliest efforts are distinctly more effective as the string quartets they purport to be, than as the semi-orchestral works with which publishers continued to confuse them as late as 1784.

Haydn's chamber music may now be profitably surveyed in approximate chronological order from the first quartet, op. 1, no. 1, to the unfinished quartet, op. 103, his last composition. As to the chronology of the quartets, the order of opus numbers given in the familiar *Payne's Miniature Scores* is fairly accurate; though Haydn's opus numbers were in an unholy muddle in the editions of his lifetime. The whole extant collection will thus consist of the following sets, six quartets in each opus: opp. 1, 2, 3, 9, 17, 20, 33; a single quartet, op. 42; six in op. 50; three each in opp. 54, 55; six in op. 64; three each in opp. 71, 74; six in op. 76; two in op. 77; and the unfinished last quartet, op. 103. The quartet arrangement of that curious work, *The Seven Last Words* (a series of orchestral adagios composed for a Good Friday service in the Cathedral of Cadiz, and afterwards expanded into a choral work), shows no technical detail beyond the capacity of a copyist, though it was, strange to say, admitted into the collection of quartets as op. 51 by Haydn himself. This collection of seventy-six quartets, equal in bulk to quite a large proportion of the most experienced quartet party's classical and modern repertory, is probably nearly complete. Quite complete it certainly is not, but it contains no spurious works. At the time of writing, the great critical edition of Haydn's complete works (B. & H.) has not yet sorted out the chamber music, and a survey of what is commonly known must therefore suffice. But in Haydn's lifetime Breitkopf & Härtel used to publish an annual catalogue of works in stock, both manuscript and printed, and by good luck the Reid Library in the University of Edinburgh possesses this catalogue from the year 1762 to 1784. Here are found sporadic evidences of what was attracting attention among lovers of orchestral and chamber music and solos, from Haydn's op. 1 (which first appears in 1765) to some *Variations da Louis van Betthoven* (sic), *âgé de dix ans*, in the single part dated 1782–1783–1784. The Haydn entries include all the quartets from op. 1 to op. 33, besides four unpublished works, one of which is vouched for by Haydn's mention of it in a catalogue drawn up by himself. Most of the quartets in opp. 1 and 2 are first announced as divertimenti; two of these, op. 2, no. 3 (E flat) and op. 2, no. 5, appear as sextets with two horns. Throughout the catalogue, B (for basso) stands for double-bass or continuo as well as for 'cello, which seldom appears in its own name. The mature set of quartets, op. 33, also appears under the alternative title of divertimenti; and the quartets are outnumbered by the scherzandi, cassations, or notturni for all manner of semi-orchestral and solo combinations. The symphony, op. 1, no. 5, does not appear among the first quartet entries, but is incorporated later. According to Pohl, the sextet versions of the quartets, op. 2, nos. 3 and 5, are original, and Haydn afterwards reduced them to quartets. Pohl further tells us that in the D major quartet, op. 3, no. 5, the viola and second violin represent the original horns in the trio of the second minuet. This awakens attention to several horn passages traceable in op. 2, no. 3; especially the so-called 'variation 1' in the second minuet, where again it is the viola that chiefly represents the horn.

Ex. 6.

The old Breitkopf catalogue bristles with evidences of Haydn's early and growing popularity. Early works, like the quartet-sextet-divertimento, op. 2, no. 3, continue to appear when the mature styles of Haydn and Mozart were already in favour, in spite of controversy. There is no means of distinguishing the genuine chamber music from the orchestral; or from that in which 'basso' implies the continuo hypothesis. Pohl sums up the situation by remarking that the term 'symphony' was freely applied to compositions for any number of instruments exceeding three. Many of the divertimenti and scherzandi may, for all we can tell, be as valuable as the quartets in op. 33, and may have become neglected because of the extreme difficulty of Haydn's horn writing, or the obsolescence of certain instruments. Trios for two violins (or other soprano instruments) with 'basso' may be suspected of being a survival of the continuo hypothesis; and into his piano trios Haydn poured a stream of his finest music—early, middle, and late—without once justifying the use of the 'cello or scrupling to make the piano double the violin part during whole sections. But trios for violin, viola, and 'cello are a serious matter; and in 1772 the catalogue announces the six quartets of op. 17, and a set of six genuine string trios by Haydn. If these trios can be supposed to be of anything like the calibre of his quartets in opp. 9 and 17, the set would be an achievement even more important than these quartets. Haydn is, however, known to have written trios at the earliest period; and the themes here quoted do not (as such quotations once in a while may do) happen to indicate whether the works are early or not.

A divertimento in A seems to be a string quintet (2 violas); though it has been denied that Joseph Haydn wrote any quintets, the one in C, ascribed to him as op. 88, being by Michael Haydn. The appearance of a set of six unknown quartets by Giorgio Hayden, op. xviii, in Paris, is thrilling, but the name Giorgio (unknown in Haydn's family) is a warning against disappointment. The persistent spelling of the surname with an E is probably right for the first time in the catalogue; in which case the author of these quartets will be George Hayden, organist of St. Mary Magdalen, Bermondsey, and composer of the two-part song, 'As I saw fair Clara walk alone'. Other confusions are suggested by the statement that certain of Haydn's duets for two violins '*laufen im MS. unter dem Namen* KAMMEL' (*q.v.*). The critical edition of Haydn's works now in progress has already disentangled Haydn's symphonies from the divertimenti and from spurious works, with the result that 104 symphonies are known to be genuine; thirty-eight known to be spurious; and thirty-six are doubtful. The chamber music is probably in no better case. Haydn and Mozart were popular enough for erroneous attributions to be profitable, in one direction; and it may be doubted whether the error would be so readily acknowledged if Kammel's works were to '*laufen im MS. unter dem Namen*' HAYDEN.

No doubt later volumes of the catalogue would give further matter for thought; but it seems likely that, after the appearance of op. 33, Haydn's published works were settling down into more or less the condition in which they are known. Evidently the quartets have survived in a far more complete and orderly *corpus* than the rest of Haydn's works; and this fact is itself a proof of the early and permanent ascendancy which they attained over the minds of musicians.

In the five-movement divertimenti which constitute opp. 1 and 2 of Haydn's quartets, the first movements and finales seem hardly more developed than what may aptly be termed the *melodic* range of form such as is found in a good-sized allemande or gigue in a Bach suite. But the development of Haydn's sonata style is a matter neither of length nor of diversity of theme; and its dramatic tendency asserted itself in his earliest works.

On comparing the first movement of Haydn's op. 1, no. 1, with a typical Bach gigue, the first observation will probably be that, whereas Bach's texture is polyphonic, Haydn's is not, and the second 'observation' (if the observer ceases to observe and begins to quote books) will be that Bach has only one theme whereas Haydn has a definite second subject. This term 'second subject' is the most misleading in the whole of musical terminology; the German term *Seitensatz* is correct enough, for *Satz* may mean clause, sentence, paragraph, or a whole musical movement; but the wretched word 'subject' is always taken to mean 'theme', with results equally confusing both to criticism and musical education. If the practice of Haydn, Mozart, and Beethoven be taken as a guide (and who shall be preferred to them?) the discoverable rules of sonata form are definite as to distribution of keys, and utterly indefinite as to the number and distribution of themes in these keys.

The matter may be tested by comparing the first movement of Haydn's op. 1, no. 1, with the gigue of Bach's C major 'cello suite, which, being unaccompanied, cannot be polyphonic, and which happens to have a very distinct second subject, if by that term is meant a second theme. That feature is by no means rare in Bach; dance movements with four themes might be cited from his partitas. Whatever progress Haydn's first movement shows is not on text-book lines. As to themes, it has either none, or as many as it has two-bar phrases, omitting repetitions; the second part contains no more development than the second part of Bach's gigue; and, though the substance that was in the dominant at the end of the first part is faithfully recapitulated in the tonic at the end of the second part, the formal effect is less enjoyable than in Bach's gigue in proportion to the insignificance of the material. Artistically Bach's gigue is obviously of the highest order, while Haydn's present effort is negligible. Yet within the first four bars Haydn shows that his work is of a new epoch, anticipated in Bach's time only by the harpsichord music of that elvish freak, Domenico Scarlatti. Bach's C major gigue, in spite of its contrasted second theme and its enforced lack of polyphony, is of uniform texture. Its limits are those of an idealized dance tune, which actually does nothing which would throw a troupe of dancers out of step. Within such limits Bach's art depends on the distinction of his melodic invention. But to Haydn it is permissible to use the merest fanfare for his first theme, because his essential idea is to alternate the fanfare with a figure equally commonplace but of contrasted texture, throwing the four instruments at once into dialogue, *p*, after the *f* opening. And he is not going to keep up this alternation as a pattern throughout the movement. As soon as it has made its point, other changes of texture appear; and the phrases, apart from their texture, soon show an irregularity which in these earliest works appears like an expression of class prejudice against the imperturbable aristocratic symmetry of older music.

Before Haydn there is nothing like this irregularity, nor in any of his contemporaries. The only approach to it was a single recipe made fashionable all over Europe by composers of the Neapolitan school. It consisted in making a four-bar or two-bar phrase repeat itself or its latter half, and then, as it were, tie a knot by making a firmer cadence of the last echo. A careful note must be made of this Neapolitan rhythmic formula, which will be illustrated by Ex. 13. It is a *cliché* for producing irregular rhythm without accepting the responsibility of making the music genuinely dramatic; and its presence in anything of Haydn's is a mark of early date. Otherwise, in these first quartets, Haydn, alone in a crowd, cares not what awkwardness or abruptness he admits in his first movements and finales, if only he can prevent the music from settling down to the comfortable ambling gait with which the best chamber music of the rising generation was rocking the listener to sleep. The comic opening of the finale of op. 1, no. 1 is already worlds away from such decorum.

Ex. 7.

Its six-bar opening would already sound irregular, even if it played out the sixth bar instead of stopping in the middle. And there is no intention of making this opening a pattern for the rest. The hearer's sense of design must be satisfied with its return in the recapitulatory part of the movement, with all or most of the other bits of coloured glass in Haydn's kaleidoscope; the only pattern and the only congruity lies in the whole. In virtue of this it is still felt that the dramatic style has not exceeded the limits of melodic form; the listener has merely enjoyed a certain bulk of lyric melody distributed in witty dialogue and stated more in terms of fiddles and fingers than of song.

The slow movement of op. 1, no. 1 has four bars of solemn sustained harmonies by way of prelude, which are expanded into six bars as a postlude. This is all that gives distinction to a poor and pompous specimen of a Neapolitan aria in which the first violin is a tragedy queen singing an appeal to generations of ancestral Caesars, and accompanying with superb gestures her famous display of *Treffsicherheit* in leaping from deep contralto notes to high soprano and back. The other instruments devoutly accompany, in humble throbbing chords which are allowed to be heard in solemn approving cadence when her tragic majesty has paused for breath. From this type of slow movement Haydn advances in three directions, of which only two are distinctly seen in the first twelve quartets. First, then, he can improve the type of melody, in which case he will underline its form by drawing a double-bar with repeat marks after its main close in the dominant, so that his slow movement becomes formally identifiable with a first movement. This is the case with op. 1, nos. 2, 4, and 6; and with op. 2, nos. 1, 3, 4, and 5. Secondly, he can improve the accompaniment; and in this respect no two of these early slow movements are exactly alike. But though this arioso type of adagio may become a duet, as in op. 1, no. 3 (which begins with the slow movement), and op. 1, no. 4, and though all manner of colour-schemes may be used in the accompaniment, e.g. pizzicato as a background to the muted first violin, as in op. 1, no. 6, and in the famous serenade in op. 3, no. 5; yet none of these devices will carry him a step forward in the direction of the true quartet style; for they are merely decorative, and, far from contributing to dramatic motion, fix the pattern and metre throughout the whole movement in which they are used.

Chronology is better in disproof than in constructive argument, otherwise it might be tempting to draw *a priori* conclusions from the fact that Haydn's early work coincides with the full influence of Gluck's reform of opera. But, strange to say, the peculiar dramatic force of Haydn's mature style owed nothing to Gluck, and was, indeed, hopelessly paralysed when he wrote for the stage. For Haydn's dramatic movement is the tersest thing in the fine arts; it is the movement of the short story. Gluck's reform of opera did, as he claimed for it, sweep away nuisances; but he was not more careful to avoid interrupting the action than to avoid hurrying it, and to impress upon his librettist the necessity of reducing it to the simplest and broadest issues. The finale of any of Haydn's greatest symphonies would explode its whole three-act comedy of manners in the listener's face before Gluck's Admetus could, in a single heart-rending scene, wring from Alceste the admission that she was the victim who had offered her life for his. The only part of Gluck's reforms which touches Haydn's art is that which Gluck expressed when, in his famous preface to *Alceste,* he wrote, 'I conceived . . . that the grouping (*concerto*) of instruments should be managed with regard to [dramatic] interests and passions'. It was this sentence that meant death to the old art of scoring decoratively and architecturally; and its implications have little dependence on the material resources of the orchestra. Many luxurious possibilities of texture in the string quartet would have been an actual danger to Haydn's progress if he had developed them. The warning is exemplified by Haydn's enthusiastic admirer Boccherini, who wrote literally hundreds of quartets and quintets. The quintet published in *Payne's Miniature Scores* will do for an example; it was made more famous than the rest by its celebrated minuet, which, though extraordinarily pretty in scoring, is by no means its only remarkable feature. As regards string-colour, this quintet is a casket of jewels more gorgeous than anything Haydn ever aspired to. But a casket of jewels will have to be stolen before it contributes anything to the progress of a drama. The listener may be surprised at the brilliance of the inner parts in Boccherini's quintet. But, alas! this is an illusion fatal to Boccherini's own progress. It means merely that he played the 'cello himself and that his innumerable quintets are accordingly written with two 'cellos, who take it in turns to supply the bass and to warble in high positions. We shall find more and more reason to admire Haydn's concentration on the essentials of quartet style and his rejection of all tempting hindrances.

In the slow movement of the symphony-quartet, op. 1, no. 5, Haydn abandons the arioso style, and works on the lines of his first movements and finales. Poor and blustering as the whole of this primitive symphony is, its peculiarities show that in the rest of opp. 1 and 2 Haydn was deliberately confining himself to the style of the divertimento, and was actually trying to restrain his first movements and finales from seriously outweighing his minuets. Otherwise, no doubt, passages like that hereafter quoted from op. 2, no. 4 would have been less exceptional.

It is natural that by far the ripest things in these quartets should be the minuets. They already show Haydn's boundless capacity for inventing tunes and for making the most irregular rhythms convincing by sheer effrontery. While the minuets of opp. 1 and 2 are distinctly what the naïve listener would call tunes, and never more tuneful than where the rhythm is irregular, the tendency of the trios is to build themselves up into regular structures by means of sequences. The trios of Haydn's later works tell a very different tale. But it would be rash to assert of many of his earliest minuet tunes that they could not have been written with zest at any later period of his art.

What has been said of op. 1, no. 1 will cover the remaining ground of opp. 1 and 2. Two quartets begin with slow movements; op. 1, no. 3, in D (beginning with an arioso duet), and op. 2, no. 6, in B flat (beginning with an air and variations). These accordingly have a presto middle movement, of the same size as a minuet and trio, instead of another slow movement. In later works Haydn finds no difficulty in making his third movement slow when he has opened with an andante con variazioni.

Though the quartets of op. 2 show no general advance on op. 1, they contain significant features. The second minuet of op. 2, no. 3 (E flat) is mysterious inasmuch as its trio is followed by three sections called variations. But variations these sections are certainly not, for they follow the lines neither of the minuet nor of the trio. They do not even follow one another's lines. Perhaps Haydn has simply strung a row of actual dances together, and the publisher has tried to explain them by calling them variations. The fact that they and the trio happen, unlike the minuet, to be in regular four-bar rhythm, would fit with their being practical dance music. A sight of the original divertimento version with its two horns might explain much. The slow movement of op. 2, no. 4 (F minor) is Haydn's first sustained effort in a minor key, and it achieves a tragic note which would have enhanced and prolonged the reputation of any of Haydn's contemporaries. But the most significant thing in this quartet is the development of its first movement, where, perhaps for the first time in musical history (except for some Arabian-night incidents in Domenico Scarlatti), the true dramatic notion of sonata-development is realized. A short quotation can show the first dramatic stroke, but the consequences are followed up in a series of better and better strokes for another twenty-four bars, right into the heart of the recapitulation.

Ex. 8.

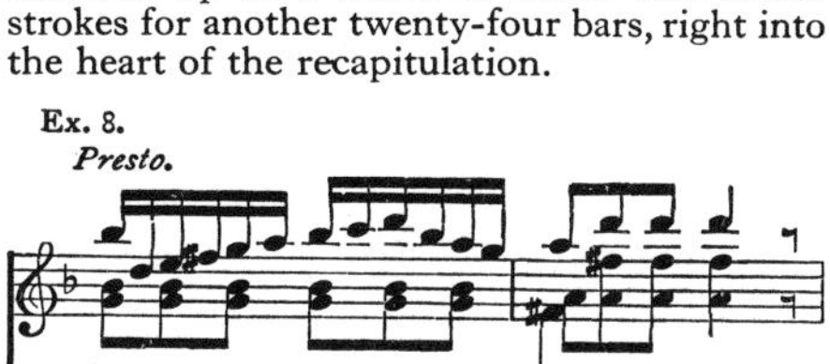

In op. 2, no. 5, there is another incident of historical importance, the interrupted cadence into B flat where the hearer would expect D major, in the slow movement (bars 17–21).

Ex. 9.

Largo cantabile alla breve.

Regard these bars with reverence; they are the source of all the purple patches in Mozart's, Haydn's, and Beethoven's 'second subjects', of all Beethoven's wonderful themes that pack two profoundly contrasted keys into one clause, and of all Schubert's enormous digressions in this part of a movement. How such modulations bulked in the imagination of Haydn's best contemporaries may be realized by looking at the change from B flat to G flat in Dittersdorf's quartet in E flat, a work not unknown to modern quartet players, and easily accessible, with five others of its set, in *Payne's Miniature Scores* (Ex. 10). In the recapitulation Dittersdorf shows further insight by making the foreign key C major instead of C flat; and his quartets show in other positive merits that it was not by accident that he became a successful composer of comic operas. But nowhere is he like Haydn in the capacity, predicated of genius by Keats, to 'walk the empyrean and not be intoxicated'.

Ex. 10.

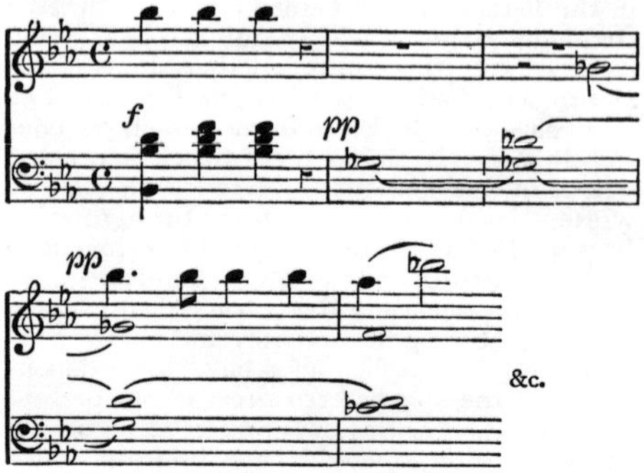

In op. 2, no. 6, it is surprising to find Haydn's technique in ornamental melodic variations already so ripe. Trivial as the problem seems, and poor as is some of Haydn's and much of Mozart's later work in this fashionable eighteenth-century form, it is needful to look carefully at contemporary examples before one can realize the boundless opportunities of going pointlessly wrong where Haydn and Mozart know of nothing but what is inevitably right. And the very composers who have gone farthest in the basing of variations on deeper rhythmic and harmonic factors have shown an unexhausted interest in the simplest melodic embroidery. Beethoven's purely melodic variations in the slow movement and choral finale of the Ninth Symphony are to him as important as the deepest mysteries of the Diabelli Variations; and Brahms's views on this matter were equally shocking to the Superior Person.

If Pohl demands a post-dating of five years for study preparatory to Haydn's op. 1, it is strange that he should not demand another five years to account for the great progress made between op. 2 and op. 3; a progress which makes it impossible to put the first eighteen quartets into one group. The difference is obvious to practical musicians and the general public; for, with op. 3, Haydn enters into the public repertory of modern quartet players. Pohl cites the case of a famous quartet party that used to substitute the delightful *Dudelsack* minuet of op. 3, no. 3 for the minuet of one of the finest later quartets; and the whole of op. 3, no. 5, with its well-known and irresistible serenade (a title applied to its andante), has recently been chosen by the Busch Quartet for a gramophone record. The *Dudelsack* minuet, the serenade, and its twin-brother the andante of op. 3, no. 1, are examples of luxury-scoring, contributing, with all their charm, no more than the art of Boccherini to the development of quartet style and dramatic sonata-activity. They are not out of place in the works as wholes, for everything that enlarges the range of contrast between the middle and outer movements is a contribution to sonata style. And, in the four normal cases, the outer movements of op. 3 are firmly established on Haydn's early symphonic scale. Haydn no longer finds it necessary, though he may still find it amusing, to use irregular rhythms in order to enforce dramatic movement; and so op. 3, no. 1 (E major) can afford to begin by trotting along in four-bar phrases without fear that the motion may degenerate into somnolent carriage-exercise. Before the double-bar the crescendo in syncopated crotchets and dotted quavers will have roused the hearer's mental muscles quite satisfactorily, without spoiling the placid character of the whole. With the minuet it may be noted that the trio is not a sequential structure, but a specially tuneful contrast, enhanced by its being in the same key. The andantino grazioso is not inferior to its twin brother, the famous serenade in op. 3, no. 5. In fact we are emerging from the regions of progressive musical history into those of permanent beauty, though we are not yet under its full sway. The finale is a freak; Haydn marks it *presto*; begins with twelve introductory bars of minims and crotchets, then proceeds to give a binary dance tune, 16+32 bars, writing the repeats in full in order to change the scoring, which does not become lively till the repetition of the last sixteen bars. Then the finale concludes with its twelve introductory bars. As for any sense of pace, Haydn might just as well have used bars of double length with quavers and semiquavers and called it andante. This is the first and perhaps the last occasion when his sense of tempo fails him.

Op. 3, no. 2 (C major) begins with an excellent little set of variations on a theme which it is extremely unlikely that Clara Wieck knew when she invented the similar tune on which Schumann wrote his impromptus, op. 5. With the ensuing minuet it is certain that beauty has dawned: it pervades the sound as well as the sense; and the beauty of sound is not achieved by anything like luxury-scoring. The finale (there are only three movements) is another freak, a genuine presto this time, but sprawling in long, loose phrases which unfold themselves in a symphonic sonata form without repeat marks. When this is finished in 228 bars (twice the length of Haydn's largest earlier finales), there is a sort of trio consisting of a decidedly sentimental binary tune, mainly in crotchets, eighteen bars plus thirty-four, with repeats. After which the listener is asked to hear the former 228 bars da capo! Perhaps the movement (and hence the rest of the quartet) might be presentable if the da capo were started from its recapitulation at bar 135.

Op. 3, no. 3 (G major) is remarkable chiefly for the *Dudelsack* minuet. In its largo Haydn fully replaced the lyric arioso manner by a genuine symphonic sonata-style. This largo would pass muster, with less suspicion than the *Dudelsack* minuet, in a much later quartet, though it would not be its most attractive feature. The finale is also an advanced specimen of sonata form.

Of all Haydn's accessible works, op. 3, no. 4 is the most unaccountable. It consists of two movements which not only fail to make a whole, but which manifestly cannot belong to the same work. Both are sprawling, long-limbed sonata-form movements, with some half a dozen agreeable themes, and a perfunctory and primitive passage of goose-step on the dominant to serve for development. One movement is in B flat; the other, a shorter movement with a recurring slow introduction, is in E flat. It is a mystery how anybody could suppose that they belonged together.

Op. 3, no. 5 (F major) has been proved to be a work of art acceptable to the general public. The first movement carries the hearer along in full tide, and as to development, nothing could be more convincing than the imbroglio Haydn produces from an episodic figure which he then drops for some fifteen bars, in order that it may then clinch matters by leading back to the recapitulation. Then comes the famous serenade. The minuet and the finale (called scherzando) show no falling off.

The quick movements of op. 3, no. 6 (A major) are equally successful; but the slow movement relapses heavily and at great length into the old arioso style, with elaborations and dramatic pauses in the accompaniment which contribute historical interest without achieving permanent artistic power. Haydn was loth to part company with the arioso slow movement; which indeed has continued to be rediscovered by great composers, from Mozart to Dvořák, whenever luxury-scoring and homogeneous textures are admissible.

Then comes a great gap. This interval, between opp. 3 and 9, is approximately filled by the first forty symphonies, and Pohl knows how many cassations, divertimenti, sonatas; trios for two violins and bass (i.e. continuo) and for two flutes and bass; pieces for Prince Esterhazy's queer kind of gamba, the baryton; and operatic and vocal works galore. Of the divertimenti, the writer has seen the autograph of one in the possession of Mr. Edward Speyer, a trio for horn, violin, and 'cello. It consists of three tiny movements, of which one is a set of variations containing horn-passages which make Bach's most appalling flights appear almost easy. There are other evidences that the principal horn-players at Esterhazy had a technique that was demoralizing to the composer's artistic economy. Among the divertimenti advertised in that old Breitkopf & Härtel catalogue, I suspect, and Pohl confirms me, that one of those for two oboes, two horns, three bassoons, and serpent contains one of the greatest melodies in the world, the theme entitled *Corale St. Antoni*, on which Brahms wrote his orchestral variations. If a contrafagotto be used for the third bassoon and serpent, the instruments given in the catalogue correspond to the scoring of most of that theme.

One of Haydn's works for wind instruments is accessible in a modern score, the little octet in F published by C. F. Kahnt, Leipzig. In his old age Haydn expressed regret that he must soon die, just as he had found out how to write for wind instruments. Slight as this octet is, it shows that by the time Haydn wrote it he could die in peace, if the handling of wind instruments was his only anxiety. While the definitive edition of Haydn's complete works remains in its present merely initial stage (1928), no systematic discussion of his less-known chamber music is possible; and it will save interruption at a less opportune point if his treatment of wind instruments is dealt with here. This octet shows the profound influence of Mozart's finest wind band serenades, with the addition of Haydn's independent thought. Mozart's technique is shown first in the deliberate choice of chord-formulas and other severely schematic types of theme which may serve to concentrate the listener's attention on the tone-colours for their own sake; secondly, in the sympathetic treatment of the clarinets; thirdly, in the absence of the flute, which, as Mozart realized, stands to the rest of the band as water-colour to oil paint; and lastly, in the perfect and normal balance of the chords, a matter in which Haydn in all his music often attains perfection, but seldom achieves it by normality. (Even here the bassoon occasionally shows Haydn's inveterate confusion between bass and double-bass.) His independent thought is shown in several features, notably the difficult but not reckless G minor horn solo in the third variation of the slow movement; the fourth variation, with the melody as bass for the two bassoons in unison; and the effective way in which, near the end of the finale, the first oboe is screwed up to its top F, a detail Haydn may have learnt from Mozart's masterly little quartet for oboe and strings (K. 370). The maturity of this tiny octet shows, by comparison with Haydn's treatment of wind instruments elsewhere, that in saying that he had only just learnt in old age how to write for them there was no more affectation in his modesty than boastfulness in his claim. It would be interesting to obtain sight of the early works for wind instruments mentioned in old catalogues; e.g. trios for clarinet, violin, and bassoon: for Haydn's treatment of the clarinet in the orchestra is primitive until those crowning works *The Creation* and *The Seasons*. The oboe and bassoon Haydn always understood. The 'Great Bassoon Joke' is the smallest, though the most obvious item in his exhaustive knowledge of the capacities, poetic more than comic, of that important and long-suffering bass of the woodwind. The flute represents one of the most curious problems in Haydn's aesthetic system. It is very important in his mature orchestral works; and at all periods he was ready to write for it in chamber music. Three of the thirty-one piano trios now in print (Edition Peters, Nos. 29, in F; 30, in D; and 31, in G) are with flute, and cannot be early works—they would fall into line soon after the quartets of op. 33. The writer does not find them, and did not expect to find them, in the old Breitkopf catalogue of works in stock up to 1782. Then there is a musically very great sonata with piano in G, which, with the addition of a minuet as large and powerful as a mid-Beethoven scherzo, was afterwards re-written as one of the last and greatest of the string quartets. Haydn seems in sympathy with the soul of the flute, or with its Undine-like aspirations towards a soul, and he appreciates its April-rain translucency. But he never seems to realize that its lower octave, which was excellent under the conditions of the continuo period, is powerless under those of his own art; and in an orchestral tutti or the final tonic-and-dominant scrimmage of a sonata he will set the flute to puff its low notes away in a futile nominal fortissimo calculated rather to damage the dignity of the performer than to attract the ear of the listener.

A more important moral is pointed by Haydn's treatment of the horn. During his long tenure of office at Esterhazy he took full advantage of the presence of horn-players who must have had the most enormous technique ever achieved on that acoustically interesting but most hazardous instrument. But sharp disillusionment evidently awaited him when he left the shelter of Esterhazy and came to deal with European orchestras at large. He promptly ceased to take risks; and when in a mature symphony some exceptional high or low note for the horn is found, it is always so covered that failure will not be noticed. More important is the occasional prominence of some passage which text-books will assert to be impossible; e.g. the low staccato rapid quaver octaves in the finale of the *Oxford Symphony*; but—*solvitur ambulando*, for it proves to be a knack. Apart from knacks, however, the moral is that a composer cannot learn much from generous young virtuoso-players with a formidable technique. Generous veterans have learnt fastidiousness as part of their wisdom; and they demand that all technical difficulties shall serve two purposes only, to reveal the nature of the instrument and the ideas of the composer. The young virtuoso is apt to make it a point of honour to prove that nothing can be difficult for him. Thus it is by no means clear that Haydn's duties at Esterhazy were stimulating to his own line of progress, in either orchestral or chamber music. We should be glad of an opportunity for studying his music for Prince Esterhazy's favourite instrument, the baryton. But when one is told, first that it was considered impossible to use it in more than one key; secondly, that Haydn set about learning it in order to prove that it could be used in various keys; thirdly, that Prince Esterhazy did not relish Haydn's success, but merely said 'Well, it's your business to play better than I'; and lastly, that Haydn saw that such efforts were a waste of his time—it is hardly necessary to study the actual baryton music before risking the guess that it belongs to the region of *tours de force*; and this may be suspected of some proportion of the chamber music for curious combinations. With the first forty symphonies the facts can be measured by observation. Their many interesting features disguise the fact that the fortieth symphony is on the same plane of orchestral thought as the first; for most of the special orchestral effects consist essentially of solo combinations and *tours de force* against a background of primitive orchestration. In form and range of contrast there are significant events; and the first symphony (not counting op. 1, no. 5) represents more nearly the level of the quartets in op. 3 than that of opp. 1 and 2. But the advance from op. 2 to op. 3 is far more decided than the subsequent advance from symphony no. 1 to symphony no. 40. And, with all their interest, there is no such progress in these forty symphonies as can explain or illustrate the advance made from the quartets of op. 3 to those of op. 9, which now claim attention. While none of the first forty symphonies are known to the public of to-day, the quartets of op. 9, written in the same year as the fortieth symphony, belong to the presentable Haydn repertory. Haydn himself requested the publisher, Artaria, to put them forward as the first quartets, and to ignore all his earlier ones. Beauty, which was dawning in op. 3, shines in full daylight here. They are not yet among the infinities of art where comparisons are meaningless; but they are beyond the regions of historical patronage. What is right for one work is irrelevant and therefore wrong for another, and there is seldom anything wrong in the particular work in hand. The technique is not that of later works. Enormous progress remained for Haydn yet to accomplish, if by progress is meant a process of enlarging the range of ideas in successive works of art. But if 'progress towards perfection' is meant, we are chasing rainbows, and the centre of the rainbow is perfection and is here: here as the quality of the artist's mind, not as the actual finished execution of his designs; here as in Shakespeare and Handel, not as in Milton and Bach. We shall find inequalities, such as the bad lapse already quoted (in Ex. 1). And the style of op. 9 is perhaps better suited to an audience of connoisseurs than to the general public; though the writer well remembers the impression made by the D minor quartet, op. 9, no. 4, at the 'Pops' in 1887, at a time when Wagnerians tolerated Haydn and Mozart mainly from charity towards the feelings of children and dotards.

In four of these quartets the first movement is in a tempo of peculiar significance, a moderato or allegro moderato distinctly slow for counting four in a bar, and consequently with plenty of room for triplet semiquavers or even for demisemiquavers. This indicates an ornate style, and is Boccherini's favourite tempo. But it also permits of a thoughtful style, and Haydn knows how to prevent it from ambling monotonously. It is no imperfection in the style that the part of the first violin is full of brilliant features which the other instruments cannot share. The other instruments are perfectly happy in their place, and there is not a dull or useless note. In the presence of such art it seems as unmannerly to point out lapses like Ex. 1, or places where the 'cello has forgotten that it is not a double-bass, as to call attention to a cough or a sneeze. History and progress are forgotten while one listens and enjoys.

Of the six quartets in op. 9, no. 1 in C major has a noble first movement very sonorously scored; a graceful minuet with a sly abrupt end (the eternal joke of ending with one's initial phrase), and a glum little trio, the second part of which does not finish, but leads back to the minuet; an indolently sweet and simple slow movement in sonata form; and a finale which is reminiscent of earlier examples in its nervous abruptness. But the quartet writing throughout is such as can only be heard with the ears and fed on by the imagination. Even such a simple-seeming melody as the theme of the slow movement can express the most intimate secrets of the violin, with its legato rising tenth at the end of the first bar. No. 2, in E flat, less attractive in appearance, is well in step with its companions; and the development of the first movement might serve as a *locus classicus* for its function. The minuet is one of Haydn's loveliest melodies, and he liked it well enough to write a pretty little set of piano variations on it; which, however, are no such work of art as it makes with its trio (in the same key) in this quartet. With the slow movement we encounter the only art-form Haydn owes to Bach (C. P. E.). The movement (in C minor) has a slow recitative-like introduction in common time, seven bars long; after which it proceeds in an arioso in 3/4 time. When this has come to the close of its first part in the relative major, the first part is repeated; but the repeat is written out in full, in order that the ornaments of the melody may be varied. The second part, which Haydn cuts down to perfunctoriness, is not repeated, but a blank space is left (over the usual 6/4 chord) for a cadenza before the end.

Now this idea of writing out a repeat in full (instead of using repeat-marks), in order to vary or add to the ornaments, was the special invention of Philipp Emanuel Bach's later years, and was highly prized by him. Not only had he a great and inspiring influence on the young Haydn (clearly discernible in Haydn's piano style), but, when Haydn's early piano sonatas appeared, Bach sent him a message to say that nobody else had understood him so completely. In the face of such testimony it must seem unreasonable to dispute the accepted opinion that C. P. E. Bach is the founder of the sonata style, and the man to whom Haydn owed the possibility of his own work. And yet the very facts before us point to a different conclusion. Without claiming a knowledge of C. P. E. Bach's complete works, one may be justified in drawing one's own inferences from the study of some eighty sonatas, besides many rondos and fantasias, ranging from the year in which Sebastian Bach wrote the B minor mass to the year in which Mozart produced *Don Giovanni*. After perusing these sonatas with a zest that would cheerfully burn all the 'progressive' matter in all the fine arts for the sake of preserving one example of permanent beauty, one is forced to conclude that C. P. E. Bach never shows an inkling of the special idea of 'development' in sonata style. As an art-form apart from the sonata he invented a special type of rondo, utterly unlike anything in earlier music. In these rondos he digresses wildly and at absurd length, bringing his beautiful main theme back in the most unexpected keys and expanding it in passionate modulating sequences. It is in these rondos alone that he shows the idea of development; but the only trace of their influence upon Haydn is to be found in two splendid and obviously late piano pieces, Haydn's fantasia in C and capriccio in G. In both of these Haydn enjoys all the sense of adventure in C. P. E. Bach's rondos; but the quality which he emphatically does not owe to them is that by which these two pieces live, a sense of climax and finality. The long passages of unsupported runs and light arpeggios, which are a common feature in Haydn's ripest sonatas and are freely translated into the language of the violin in his quartets, may again, together with the whole range of his piano style, be traced to C. P. E. Bach. Not so, however, the fact that from the outset (e.g. in the quartets of op. 17, where, *mutatis mutandis*, they first appear) Haydn presents in them a perfect study in the psychology of dramatic suspense, whereas the immediate effect of nearly all C. P. E. Bach's digressions is to cause the friendliest critic to exclaim 'This won't do!'

Not only is the notion of development absent from C. P. E. Bach's sonatas, but this late and highly prized invention of the *Veränderte Reprise* (repeat with alterations), which Haydn now adopted, is radically hostile to it. Can anything be conceived more incompatible with the dramatic activities of a true sonata-development than that the repetition of both parts of a binary movement should be written out in full, in order that the *ornaments* should be varied? This can imply nothing else than that the whole attention is fixed on an uninterrupted flow of lyric melody: which is precisely C. P. E. Bach's intention, and which is Haydn's reason for confining the device to slow movements.

What, then, is Haydn's real debt to C. P. E. Bach? It is a pity that the word 'rhetoric' has been degraded to a term of abuse, for it means an art the perfection of which is as noble as the noblest cause in which it can be used. Rhetoric is what Haydn learnt from C. P. E. Bach: a singularly beautiful and pure rhetoric, tender, romantic, anything but severe, yet never inflated. This great and comprehensive gift is independent of all reform or progress. The example of Bach's chaotically wild rondos and fantasias may have been necessary in order to stimulate Haydn's far more realistic sense of adventure. But of art forms, the only thing that Haydn adopted from C. P. E. Bach was this device of the *Veränderte Reprise*. Its original motive arose from the fact that in any movement, sections marked to be repeated were in fact often varied by the performer on repetition, the repeats being, indeed, supposed to be prescribed for that purpose. The real aesthetic function of repeats lies deeper than this hypothesis; and the view taken of it by Haydn, Mozart, and Beethoven is, of all points in their art, the most remote from the habits of modern listeners. It is evident, from the way in which C. P. E. Bach carries out his invention, that, with or without variation, the repeats were actually executed wherever they were marked. And while unwritten variation is unthinkable with Haydn, Mozart, and Beethoven, the juncture of the repeat is, as late as Beethoven's last quartet (op. 135), often so subtle that a fine point is missed when the repeat is omitted, though the length of the section to be repeated is formidable.

Now, how does Haydn treat Bach's reprise-device? Besides restricting its use to lyric slow movements, he shows none of the patience which enabled C. P. E. Bach to write out an ornamental repeat of both parts. In the final recapitulatory stage of his movement the ornaments will combine both versions of the exposition or will otherwise throw appropriate light on it. The reprise-movements in Haydn's quartets are the slow movements of op. 9, no. 2; op. 9, no. 4; op. 20, no. 6; and op. 33, no. 3: with which the history of this art-form closes, to be reopened only once, many years later, in the most original and exquisite masterpiece of orchestration Haydn ever achieved, the slow movement of the ninth *London Symphony*, in B flat, in which the repeat of the first part is written out, in order to alter, not the ornaments, but the scoring. There is another version of this movement in a piano trio in

F sharp minor. As Haydn's trios give no scope for changes of scoring, this version has no repeat at all.

The survey of the individual quartets can now be resumed. To an audience of connoisseurs, op. 9, no. 3 (G major) should prove a convincing masterpiece. The first movement is spirited and sonorous, and the minuet epigrammatic and witty. One should make no hasty judgement about the slow movement. The sight of two blank spaces for cadenzas, one at the end of each part, is apt to provoke a comment on the lines of Dr. Johnson's summary of the effect of mythological machinery in English poetry. 'The attention retires from the transactions of' the virtuoso violinist when the fatal 6/4 chord has wound him up and released the clutch. But if the attention will consent to fix itself on the largo of op. 9, no. 3, from the outset of a devout performance in adequately broad tempo, it will find itself rewarded by music too great to be destroyed even by bad cadenzas, and quite unharmed by suitable ones. The resemblance of the opening, with its broken rhythms and long measured pauses, to that of the largo of Beethoven's sonata, op. 7, is probably accidental, but is not superficial. Haydn is ornate where Beethoven is laconic; Haydn's gravity is meditative, and grows upon one as the music settles into a long sustained flow, whereas Beethoven instantly inspires awe, and allows his largo only just as much uninterrupted flow as will carry the listener across its many abrupt unfathomable depths. But if there is any earlier movement in Haydn that so comprehensively foreshadows Beethoven's most solemn moods, it has not yet been printed.

The finale is, as usual, lively and witty, the wittiest device being a surprising joint across the dividing line at the repeats.

Op. 9, no. 4, in D minor, is, as we have seen, a work that is sometimes heard in public. One effect of making its acquaintance is that Mozart's great D minor quartet becomes inseparably associated with its sombre first movement. The minuet is one of Haydn's largest, and is full of vehement passion, though its tempo is, if anything, slower than his minuets have hitherto been. Up to this point the tempo of a Haydn minuet is the same as with Sebastian Bach; a three-in-the-bar at a smart stride, too fast for the stately dance of the *Don Giovanni* minuet, but making no approach to the one-in-a-bar rhythm of a scherzo. The trio of this D minor minuet is a suave melody in the major, and is literally a trio in the long-forgotten sense of being in three-part harmony. But Haydn has amused himself and the leader of the quartet by writing it as a duet for the violins, the first violin playing in double stops.

The slow movement is on the reprise lines, but the alterations in the ornaments are much slighter than those in the accompaniment, which is extensively re-written. Could anything better indicate Haydn's tendency towards the deeper issues of whatever art-form he presses into the service of instrumental music? Yet it is in this beautiful movement that the lapse quoted in Ex. 1 occurs.

The finale is a masterpiece so concentrated on the idea of development that it would be an ideal example to set beside the largest possible polyphonic gigue. It makes a spirited end to a work unquestionably great as a whole.

Op. 9, no. 5 (B flat) begins with an andante theme with variations; a form in which, as we have seen, Haydn already knew in op. 2, no. 6, all that was as yet to be known. It is not until the middle of his whole series of quartets that he enlarged the scope of his variations by inventing a new form on a pair of alternating themes. The minuet is a little faster than previous examples, and is as gracefully witty as usual. The slow movement is a fine, serious, and mature composition in sonata form with repeats (not *veränderte Reprisen*), and without pauses or cadenzas. The finale is a presto with long-limbed slightly sprawling phrase-rhythms, the successful handling of which contributes to the progress of Haydn's technique.

Op. 9, no. 6 (A major) begins with a first-rate presto, full of picturesque passages and lively (not luxurious) scoring. The freedom of its recapitulation shows a tendency which will eventually necessitate a discussion of the vast subject of Haydn's mature sonata form. The minuet is in the old tempo, and has a pensive trio in the minor. The slow movement is an arioso with repeats, and, but for a certain breadth and simplicity, would have attracted little notice if it had occurred in op. 2. It has a blank space for a cadenza at the end. The finale begins as if it were going to be an energetic rondo (a thing that has not yet appeared in these quartets). After its first phrase, one listens with interest to an expanding middle phrase and a return, and to several cumulative afterthoughts, tapering away to an emphatic close. This is repeated from the middle phrase onwards. But that is all! Though inadequate, its effect is not as absurd as the description sounds; but this quartet undeniably collapses after two movements well worthy of the rest of the set in which Haydn first knew himself. There is only one more such collapse in the whole series.

The quartets of op. 17 are on a larger scale. The first movement of no. 1 (E major) is a moderato (the characteristic tempo of this period) with a grass-green theme that is already the quintessence of Haydn. The rhetoric is highly strung, and the first violin begins to display itself more extensively than in op. 9. A remarkable feature in the development section is the return of the main theme in the tonic a little before it seems due, whereupon, however, its second bar expands into a fine vista of sequences before the theme is allowed to return again and follow its normal course. The minuet is very fine, and on a large scale. The slow movement, in E minor, is in broad sonata form without repeats; flowing, symmetrical, and pleasantly pathetic. One interesting turn of harmony, in the recapitulation (bar 68) is actually Wagnerian in principle.

Ex. 11.

It is by no means out of place, though the style of the movement no more resembles Wagner than lemonade resembles wine. The finale is the subtlest part of the work, the final results of a passage in the subdominant near the beginning being a stroke of genius at the end. The development section begins with no less than the first eighteen bars of the movement in the tonic before it strikes out elsewhither. The effect will be excellent if Haydn's repeat marks are disregarded, and disastrous if the repeats are played. The tempo must be very fast to bring out the coherence of Haydn's lanky phrasing. He is in about the stage of experience in handling form that Mozart reached in his *Paris* symphony. He wants plenty of elbow-room.

Op. 17, no. 2 (F) begins with a fine specimen of Haydn's early ornate rhetoric. The short minuet (distinctly faster than Bach's tempo, but not hasty) is splendid both in sound and in sense. Its quiet trio in the relative minor does not finish, but pauses on its dominant in order that the minuet may re-enter more splendidly than ever. The slow movement is a placid adagio in sonata form, bordering on the arioso style. With the aid of op. 2, no. 5, it enables us to clear up a point that sometimes mystifies players, viz. the use of alla breve time signature ₵ for slow movements, as here. It obviously cannot mean two in a bar. But Haydn actually entitled the slow movement of op. 2, no. 5, 'largo alla breve'; and it happens that in both these movements the eye is not distracted by any demisemiquaver passages that would make them look like other slow movements. Thus the ₵ signature means 'take your time at about half the value you would give to most adagios'.

The finale of op. 17, no. 2 is a sprawling allegro di molto. The effect of the joint from the end of the second part to the beginning of the development is the best stroke in the movement, and, if this quartet is to be heard at all, leisure and patience will be needed for once to listen to what perhaps no living concert-goer has ever heard, the repeat of the second part of a long binary movement.

Op. 17, no. 3 (E flat) begins with a set of variations. Advance is shown in the ripe Haydnesque beauty of the second part of the theme, a thing he could not have achieved earlier. But the main advance in this quartet is shown by the minuet, which would be thought remarkable if met with in op. 76. Its trio is an intensely original tune, scored in a way that would be as surprising in a quartet of Dvořák as it is here.

Ex. 12.

The slow movement, in A flat, is nobly serious, mellow in sound, and has a rich digression of harmonies in its broad transition passage to the dominant. There are several pauses, but they are for reflection, not for cadenzas. The finale is terse, and more in the best style of op. 9.

Op. 17, no. 4 (C minor) is full of subtle points. Its first two notes (E flat G/C) being unaccompanied, the key of C minor is revealed only when the other instruments enter in the second bar. The two notes can accordingly modulate in other contexts to E flat and elsewhere. They pervade the inner parts, and seem prophetic of a renascence of polyphony. The movement, and indeed the whole quartet, is in a passionate vein not far from tragedy. In this context we first experience the most heavenly type of Haydn's favourite contrasts. The minuet is in the major (distinctly faster than hitherto), and begins with childlike consolation. Its trio is plaintive and thoughtful in the minor mode. Here, again, it would be impossible to rule out the latest date for this movement, if we did not know when it was written. The slow movement is in the reprise form. In spite of fine points, its length weighs the quartet down. One is glad that C. P. E.

Bach's procedure did not impel Haydn to carry out the reprise of both parts. The finale is in a blustering temper, and has a theme suggestive of more polyphonic treatment than it actually receives. The first violin has many rather difficult double stops and other brilliant features. After the recapitulation there is a fine coda, short but dramatic. With consummate playing this quartet might make a considerable impression on connoisseurs.

Op. 17, no. 5 (G major) has established itself in concert repertories. The first theme gives an opportunity of seeing how Haydn's brother Michael handles it; for he used it in one of his four duets for violin and viola, to which Mozart added two to complete the contract for six which illness prevented Michael from finishing. Michael's four have recently been republished, and are quite pretty; but he shows no more capacity than Boccherini to vary the pace of whatever amble his first theme sets. And so it happens that where he and Joseph hit upon the same theme, five bars of the one against eight of the other will show that Joseph is an inveterate comedian whose first eight bars are no multiple of two, but already contain rhythmic contrasts that will have unpredictable but inevitable consequences throughout the movement; whereas Michael would feel that the smallest deviation into the unexpected created a situation beyond the resources of his tact, his five bars owing their irregularity to their fashionable Neapolitan 'quite so' cadence.

Ex. 13.

Every phrase, taken in its context, in this thoroughly normal example of Joseph Haydn's sonata form, is a lesson in the highest art of composition.

Ex. 14.

Perhaps the *locus classicus* is to be found at the end of the development.

Ex. 15.

Brilliance is the last word to apply to so meditative a passage, but its function of dramatic suspense is essentially that of the most brilliant fireworks in Haydn's piano music; and it is fair to remind oneself that these were suggested by those in the rondos and fantasias of C. P. E. Bach. But discoveries must not be transferred from those who achieve them to those who did not understand the drift of their own suggestions. The slow movement of this quartet is a test of the musical historian's sense of proportion. It is a scena in operatic recitative, such as may suggest to one kind of enthusiast a prophecy of Beethoven's arioso dolente in the sonata, op. 110; while another kind of enthusiast will trace it back to sonatas written by C. P. E. Bach before Sebastian Bach had begun the *Christmas Oratorio*. Which of the three recitatives will have the most wonderful modulations—the recitative of 1740, of 1770, or of 1822? The modulations of C. P. E. Bach are beyond all comparison the most remarkable.

Those in Beethoven's op. 110 are within the simplest harmonic range of Corelli or Handel, but the key of A flat happens to be so situated that the familiar modulation to its flat submediant (F♭=E♮) seems to require a complicated change of notation.

Now there is no disputing that C. P. E. Bach's modulations are wonderful flights of imagination. There is high art in them, as there is in the *Arabian Nights*; conscious art, as there is in the *Shaving of Shagpat*. But to plan a voyage in a seaworthy vessel demands not less but more imagination than to describe a journey by magic carpet. This favourite composer of Haydn and Beethoven can no more persuade these adventurous spirits to emulate his imaginative flights than the legends of alchemy can induce the man of science to publish his conclusions prematurely. Haydn and Beethoven have the self-discipline which produces an art truthful beyond the dreams of what is commonly called idealism, and unrealistic only in being universal. Why is so unique an incident as the Wagnerian progression quoted in Ex. 11 not disturbing to Haydn's aesthetic system? Precisely because the progression is actually Wagnerian; that is to say, a typically rationalistic device by which a couple of passing-notes are dwelt upon long enough to suggest to the ear that they are a complete chord in some impossibly remote key, after which suggestion they explain themselves away. Thus the incident is within the range of that sense of probability which governs Haydn's pathos and humour from first to last; and his self-discipline is even more strikingly shown in his not founding upon this highly convincing effect a style which would have been (*pace* Reger) irrelevant to the key-system of sonata form, than in his abstention from the higher imaginative flights of his beloved C. P. E. Bach. As to the recitative movement in op. 17, no. 5, it proves that the sonata style has little more difficulty in digesting operatic recitative than in digesting the operatic aria. The movement is thus merely an extreme case of the arioso-adagio, and, *mutatis mutandis*, foreshadows the discovery, made by Spohr in 1820, that a violin concerto could be designed on the lines of an operatic scena. On the other hand, there is no warrant for connecting Haydn's instrumental recitatives in any such way with Beethoven's, even though, as will be found in Haydn's op. 20, the operatic impulse coincides (as in Beethoven) with a reaction to the other extreme, the style and form of the fugue. Beethoven, it is true, retained to the last his early love of C. P. E. Bach; but his instrumental recitatives are no echo of his childhood. Haydn's recitative in op. 17, no. 5, and the dramatic fantasia (not in recitative but nearly allied thereto) in op. 20, no. 2, are the last of their line because to him they are already becoming old-fashioned. They belong to a music which has not yet risen beyond the scope of the stage: whereas Beethoven can at a sublime crisis recall the ancient dramatic tropes and gestures as things heard and seen in an ecstasy.

The finale of Haydn's op. 17, no. 5 is, like the minuet (which precedes the slow movement), worthy of its position. Its device of ending comically with its initial phrase is on the way to becoming standardized for larger movements in both Haydn and Mozart. One more point of historical and aesthetic importance in op. 17, no. 5 is the brilliant passage of double stops for the first violin in the 'second subject' of the first movement.

Ex. 16.

This brings to a crisis a tendency which if carried farther would have threatened one of the vital criteria of quartet style. Only a killjoy criticism could object to it here, for no unbiased listener can find the passage less enjoyable to hear than the violinist finds it to master and to play. Dangerous shoals await the critic who sails rashly into the channels of these early quartets, secure in his two criteria, that a string quartet must not be orchestral, and that it must not be a 'first-violin' quartet. Every individual work of art exists in its own right, and has nothing to fear from any developments except those within its own form and matter. Now these two criteria of quartet style involve an evolutionary process; they are applicable only in the degree suited to the development attained by each individual work. There is, of course, a primitive stage below which a quartet style cannot exist; and with Haydn opp. 1 and 2 are evidently below the line, and op. 3 is evidently rising above it. But the health of his work depends on its progress in all directions; and a developed quartet style with an undeveloped sonata form would be a monstrosity. As to orchestral style, Haydn's quartets have already completely parted from it in the first bars of op. 9, no. 1, if not already in op. 3, no. 5. This criterion is, even then, not easy to handle; for each practical way of organizing musical instruments will aim straightforwardly at producing music, and will not deviate to avoid resemblances to other musical organizations. A string quartet is to blame, not when it sounds like orchestral music, but when it fails in an effort to do so. It has a right to succeed in that effort if it can; and its best condition for success is that it shall remain the music of four players. Haydn's illusions with double stops in opp. 9 and 17 are carried far enough to enhance instead of destroying our sense and his own that we are listening to a string quartet and not to organ music cleverly spread over sixteen fiddle strings. As to the brilliance of the first violin, Spohr himself hardly carries it as far as Haydn in op. 17, and actually writes more interesting parts than Haydn's for the other instruments on the whole. But his point of view is fatally wrong; his work reveals a later stage of development; the positive merits of his accessory parts condemn him for leaving them as they are while his first violin has all the melody; and the whole scale of his work purports to be as large as that of Beethoven's, while his form cautiously follows one single procedure generalized from the inexhaustibly various Mozart. Spohr actually told Joachim that he wished some day to produce 'a set of quartets in the true strict form—i.e. with the cadences ending with a trill'. This inculcates as a criterion of string quartet style that the first violin shall sit upon the safety-valve! Turn from this to Haydn's indiscreet fireworks in op. 17, and see how efficiently they contribute to open up the texture. Why does he give them to the first violin? Because he is writing music in which the normal place for melody is on the top. Had he been a 'cellist like Boccherini, he might have been tempted to give the fireworks to the 'cello. Meanwhile, whether the violin rule or not, music is not, even in string quartets, going to reconcile its dramatic growth with the cultivation of quadruple counterpoint until Beethoven has attained his last phase. (And yet quadruple counterpoint appears in Haydn's next opus!)

Haydn's criteria, though evolutionary, are already positive and severe in op. 17. That a work of art belongs to an early stage of evolution is not an excuse for its failing to satisfy its own implications. Op. 17, no. 6, in D major, opens with a presto which puts to admirable use a theme feebly treated in variation form (perhaps about the same date or earlier) in one of Haydn's queer violin sonatas, about which a word must be said hereafter. In this quartet the plunging of the 'second subject' into C major where A major is expected is a Beethoven-Schubert device executed quite broadly. The minuet contrasts well with this lively hunting-scene, and should be taken at a statelier moderato than is by this time usual in Haydn. Now comes a disconcerting surprise. The largo is an arioso of the most archaic type, and would produce no comment in a quartet from op. 1. In times and places where classical revivals are matters of fashion rather than of popularity, it is impossible to say what styles may be thought interesting so long as they are at least partially unconvincing to the naïve listener; and so perhaps Haydn's op. 17, no. 6 might now be revived as it stands without anybody noticing that its largo is a relapse into an obsolete style, and a dull specimen at that. The distinguished quartet party mentioned by Pohl that rescued the *Dudelsackmenuett* from op. 3, no. 3 at the expense of the minuet of a later quartet committed an outrage not justified by the rescue, for no minuet of Haydn, early or late, is without its proper effect in its own place. But it would be a real charity to replace the largo of op. 17, no. 6 by one of the best of the slow movements buried in the archaic quartets. Two keys are possible, without violating the limits of Haydn's range in op. 17: the present subdominant key of G, and A major, the dominant. In G we could use Pohl's favourite movement from op. 1, no. 6 ('a serenade such as the rosiest child could not wish more beautiful'), or the less attractive largo cantabile alla breve from op. 2, no. 5, which, otherwise nearly as archaic as the present largo, has the modulation quoted in Ex. 9, which would bring it into line with the harmonic range of op. 17, while its archaic language would exactly carry out Haydn's present intention without dullness. In A major one might enjoy the exquisite andante of op. 3, no. 1, a quartet which, unlike op. 3, no. 5, with its famous serenade, has failed to live as a whole. If one of these experiments be tried on op. 17, no. 6, a first-rate and flawless work will be obtained, with a witty finale surpassing all Haydn's earlier finales as an intellectual masterpiece of concentrated development of a single theme, admirable in sound and sense.

The next set of quartets was known to contemporaries by two titles: *die Grossen Quartette* and *die Sonnen-Quartette*. Great they are and, even after op. 17, a sunrise over the domain of sonata style as well as of quartets in particular. Every page of the six quartets of op. 20 is of historic and aesthetic importance; and though the total result still leaves Haydn with a long road to travel, there is perhaps no single or sextuple opus in the history of instrumental music which has achieved so much or achieved it so quietly. Imagine that one has listened with attention, keen and duly rested and refreshed, to all the quartets from op. 1, no. 1 to this point. A deep, quiet chuckle from the 'cello at the end of the fourth bar of op. 20, no. 1 then comes as a warning that a new element is entering into Haydn's quartet style; and eight bars have not passed before the 'cello is singing in its tenor regions, not as a solo, nor with any new technique, but nevertheless with an effect which instantly shows that Haydn's imagination has now awakened to the tone of the 'cello as something more than a mere amenable bass to the harmony. This awakening, which freshens the tone-colour of all four instruments from now onwards, leaves Haydn as liable as ever to his habitual quasi-clerical errors as to the octave of his bass notes. But perhaps another explanation of these errors may now be found. The startling example already quoted (Ex. 2) from op. 71, no. 3 showed that the fault and its easy correction lay in the viola part, and not in the 'cello. And after studying all Haydn's quartets from op. 1 to op. 103, the surprising fact emerges that his imagination hardly ever awoke to the sound of the viola as it is found in op. 20 awakening to the sound of the 'cello. Of course there is no passage in which, except in these slips of the pen, the viola sounds bad; nor is Haydn ignorant of its peculiar tone; it has already been seen that in op. 2, nos. 3 and 5 he recognizes that it is better suited than the violin to replace a melody originally conceived for the horn. But he shows no further interest in its quality; and there are few passages in his later quartets where the sound of his viola is as characteristic as it already is in the little-known quartets which Mozart at the age of seventeen was writing, at about the period of Haydn's opp. 20 and 33. Haydn's quartet style, then, attains maturity without asserting the special character of the viola, but by no means without giving it a satisfactory place in the scheme.

Taking the quartets of op. 20 in order, we find in no. 1 a quiet first movement admirable in every respect of its technique, with a peculiarly Haydnesque piece of audacity in form at the beginning of the development, where the first theme calmly returns in the tonic before three bars have elapsed, of course only to strike out in vigorous real development immediately afterwards. The full effect is felt only if the previous repeat has been played, as otherwise the first false start of the development will sound merely like a prolonged lead-back to the beginning. The next movement fulfils, as always, Haydn's wish that 'somebody would write a new minuet'; and its thoughtful abruptly broken-off trio returns to the minuet in an unexpected way. The slow movement (affettuoso e sostenuto) is an utterance of such quiet gravity that consummate playing is needed to do it justice. Unquestionably it must have been in Mozart's mind when he wrote the andante of his E flat quartet (K. 428) in the set dedicated to Haydn as the master from whom he had learnt quartet-writing. The finale glides quickly along, with lively moments, but on the whole as quietly as the rest of the quartet. Perhaps there are not more people who can appreciate this work than there are connoisseurs of T'ang china. Music of this quality would draw crowds if it could be priced like ceramic art.

Op. 20, no. 2 is also unknown to concert-goers, but it is one of Haydn's finest works. It begins with a cantabile for the 'cello, which tersely achieves a fine spaciousness by the way in which it repeats its figures and adds a 'dying fall', which latter strain, repeated, gains energy to move to the dominant, in which key the violin takes up the theme. But for the translucent string quartet tone such an opening might not have been inconceivable in the old Neapolitan music; yet here there is no reversion to an old style, but the rediscovery of ancient truth in a modern light. And this opening is no mere case of a 'cello solo: the discovery that the instrument can warble away in the tenor clef is not more important than the discovery that its fourth string can, with good economy, sound unfathomably deep, and that a not too rapid arpeggio ranging over all four strings *pesante* is one of the most sonorous possibilities of quartet style. Note the significant fact that Haydn, Mozart, and Beethoven refrained from the more brilliant kinds of arpeggio, long known to string players and usually indicated by abbreviations, as in J. S. Bach's *Chaconne*. In the classical quartet style there is no place for a technique that is not, as it were, pure draughtsmanship. This restraint is unknown to Boccherini, as the rondo of his E major quintet (with the celebrated minuet) shows; and the coda of the first movement of Beethoven's *Harp* quartet, op. 74, gloriously approaches without violating the limit. Severe critics who scruple to enjoy the brilliant violin passage in op. 17, no. 5, would find less danger in the not less rich and sonorous violin arpeggio at the beginning of the development of the first movement of op. 20, no. 2, inasmuch as the figure is not only an accompaniment to a dialogue on the main theme, but is given to the second violin. Among all these luxurious effects, the quieter passages stand out in exquisite relief, especially the purple patch of the modulation from G to its flat submediant (E flat) in the course of the 'second subject', an effect which has been traced from its dawn in the slow movement of op. 2, no. 5, and which is now fairly on the way to becoming standardized. It is treated here exactly as it would be treated by Beethoven. In this wonderful piece of quartet-writing even the viola, besides having a vote (as it has had from op. 9, no. 1 onwards), actually achieves a maiden speech in the parliament of four, at bar 61, a single bar in which one feels that Haydn's imagination has for once heard the querulous tone of the high-lying viola as he now hears the cantabile of the 'cello. Yet, as will be seen, this movement, so rich and so uniquely romantic in sound, does not represent Haydn's final solution of the quartet problem. Perfect in itself, it is not normal; it is a striking success, and one can imagine how, under modern commercial conditions, strong pressure might have been brought on the artist to devote the rest of his days to making imitations of it; just as, under good business management, Beethoven ought to have written nothing but Kreutzer sonatas from op. 47 to op. 135, and Mr. Arnold Bennett's Priam Farll ought to have painted nothing but policemen. Haydn teaches a stern lesson; this movement is without sin or blemish; yet he never scored so gorgeously for string quartet again! With the slow movement of op. 20, no. 2, Haydn takes a lingering farewell of all operatic idioms in a grand fantasia beginning with a noble, tragic unison theme which moves in vast sequences, expanding now and then into ruminating and declamatory passages for the first violin, shared in due course by the other instruments. This plan is nobly conceived, and executed with accurate dramatic sense; with the result that when eventually a pause on the dominant, *pp*, is reached, one is prepared for some such event as the opening of a lively or impassioned finale. What happens instead is a continuation of the adagio in a stream of consoling melody in the relative major. Familiar in its Neapolitan style, the simple pathos need not fear comparison with that of Gluck's Elysian music in *Orfeo*. As to form, Haydn shows here that he has clearly grasped the principles of composition on a larger scale than sonata form permits: it is manifestly inconceivable that this cantabile should behave as a 'second subject', or that the first theme ever had any intention of confining itself to the function of a 'first subject'. It would take twenty minutes to work the material out in that way, and then there would be no sense of freedom and expansion. But Haydn is here able to make his melody ruminate and rhapsodize, to interpolate several ominous interruptions in the former tragic style, and finally to drift, in three solemn steps of gigantic sequence, down once more to the dominant of C. And now, in C major, the minuet begins, in a hesitating syncopated rhythm, like an awakening gaze dazzled by the daylight—after which all is sunshine, with just the right shadow in the trio. Haydn shows in this pair of movements what Mozart showed later in his C minor fantasia (K. 475), that if composition within the time-scale of the sonata had not absorbed his interest, he could easily have produced a music that moved like a modern symphonic poem. His art of composition is a general power which creates art-forms, not a routine derived from the practice of *a priori* schemes.

Not even in this unique fantasia is his freedom better shown than in the finales of four quartets: viz. of this one, of op. 20, nos. 5 and 6, and op. 50, no. 4. These four finales are fugues, and nothing but fugues. Now it was not from J. S. Bach that Haydn derived his ideas of fugue. His traditions in this art were Italian, and the old text-books will not help one to understand his fugue forms; while later treatises, from Cherubini onwards, bewilder us by flying in the face of every fact in Bach's works (including his didactic last opus *Die Kunst der Fuge*) without throwing light on any other composer. The fact is that the later text-books are trying to lay down laws of form for an art whose rules define nothing but a texture. It would be a correct use of language to speak of certain kinds of music being 'written in fugue', as certain kinds of poetry are written in blank verse; and Cherubini's rules for compositions written entirely in fugue are true only in so far as they concern matters of texture. Their authority on matters of form may be gauged by the fact that though J. S. Bach's last work, *Die Kunst der Fuge*, is an explicit demonstration of all kinds of fugue in the abstract, classified in a progressive system and all written on the same subject, yet Bach shows the same shocking ignorance of the rules here as he showed in fugues written at large. Now the mystery is, where Cherubini found his rules of fugue form. Cherubini, though out of favour at present, was near enough to greatness as a composer for us to find Beethoven's enormous admiration of him not inexplicable, in the light of Beethoven's reverence for all that was austerely firm of purpose. Now, one of the formative events in Cherubini's career was the occasion when he first heard a Haydn symphony. It moved him to tears. Perhaps this fact becomes easier to reconcile with the sour martinet portrayed even by friendlier witnesses than Berlioz, when we note that the only classical fugues that faintly adumbrate Cherubini's scheme of fugue form are these quartet fugues of Haydn, and a few in Mozart's masses, together with two in some early quartets he wrote possibly already under the influence of Haydn's op. 20. The point in which they agree with Cherubini's rules is that they tend to save up the stretto (where subject and answer are to overlap in closer and closer combination) until the end, actually separating it off by a pause on the dominant. As a fixed rule this notion is, on the face of it, unclassical. It implies that the devices of a fugue stretto are inherently surprising; whereas they were matters of course to any composer to whom fugue texture was a normal language. A more serious objection to such a rule is that it excludes all fugue subjects that are not capable of stretto, thus extinguishing some ninety per cent. of Bach's fugues at large, besides thirty-five of the 'Forty-eight' and (as to treatment of subject) at least six of the *Kunst der Fuge*.

But if a fugue is going to be a rare and conscious essay in a form romantically or solemnly imported from an older world, it will tend to include everything that is characteristic of all the most brilliant ancient examples taken together, and will, moreover, choose old subjects markedly unlike those of more modern art forms. Now a school of criticism may or may not like the fugues of Haydn, Mozart, and Beethoven; but whether it likes any fugues or none, it cannot dismiss these examples with facile man-of-the-world patronage as deviations into scholasticism. The aesthetics of sonata fugues are no more scholastic than the aesthetics of a play within a play, such as the *Murder of Gonzago* in *Hamlet*. Here are dramatic conditions in which common sense demands the use of an evidently old-world language; and it is no accident that even Haydn has, in the quartets of op. 20, a hint of the emotional and dramatic impulse which became so volcanic in Beethoven's fugues.

Of Haydn's four quartet fugues, two represent a sublimation of an emotion of almost tragic pathos, the F minor in op. 20, no. 5, and the F sharp minor in op. 54, no. 3. The C major in op. 20, no. 2 is, as we have seen, the finale of an extraordinarily romantic work. Only the A major fugue in op. 20, no. 6 can be said to be written for pure fun. All four fugues are directed to be played *sotto voce* until, at or near the end, a sudden *forte* winds them up in a coda which more or less abandons fugal polyphony so as to end the work in sonata style. The counterpoint is of the highest and smoothest order, a fact all the more remarkable as Haydn is elsewhere anything but an academic writer, far less scrupulous about grammatical purity than Beethoven, to say nothing of the immaculate Mozart. Haydn calls his fugues 'a quattro soggetti'—'a tre soggetti'—as the case may be, according to the number of permanent counter-subjects accompanying his main subject, whether one or more of these is announced simultaneously with the main subject or introduced only as accompaniment to its answer. Cherubini would have called all except the main theme counter-subjects. The fugue in op. 20, no. 2 is 'a quattro soggetti', two of which are announced together; as in the case of the fugue 'a tre soggetti' in op. 20, no. 6. That in op. 20, no. 5 is 'a due soggetti', announced simultaneously, and both consisting of well-known ancient formulas. The fugue in op. 50 in F sharp minor, though it has a not negligible counter-subject, is not labelled by Haydn as double. It is one of his most deeply-felt utterances, and will demand quotation in due course.

Enormous importance lies in these fugues. Besides achieving in themselves the violent reconquest of the ancient kingdom of polyphony for the string quartet, they effectively establish fugue texture from henceforth as a normal resource of sonata style. Here and hereafter Haydn knows not only how to write a whole fugue for instruments, but how to let a fugue passage break out in a sonata movement and boil over quickly enough to accomplish dramatic action instead of obstructing it. A mere revival of the old polyphony would have been as wide of the purpose as the introduction of Greek choruses, even in Miltonic verse, into *Hamlet* instead of the *Murder of Gonzago*. But, apart from its value as a means of development, fugue texture is a most important resource as a type of instrumentation. Obviously it solves the problem of equality in quartet-writing by a drastic return to Nature, and puts the four instruments where four voices were when all harmony was counterpoint. But the very nature of contrapuntal harmony is impartially friendly to all instruments that can sing. And all instruments try to sing as well as they can, except those whose normal functions are thrumming and drumming. Hence, when the texture of the music is contrapuntal, the listener's attention is no longer concentrated on the instruments in themselves; within reasonable limits good counterpoint sounds well whatever group of instruments plays it. An endless variety of new tone-colours becomes possible, simply because the admissible range is no longer restricted to those effects on which the ear would dwell for their own sake. The interplay between the polyphonically interesting and the acoustically euphonious puts an end to monotony and to the temptation to develop luxury-scoring at the expense of dramatic vigour. We must not be misled by the common allegation that the fugue style lends itself to silly ingenuity; what is wrong with bad fugue passages is what is wrong with all bad composition and bad scoring. Contrapuntal combinations as such are not very difficult; the materials will either combine or not. The only effect of ingenuity is to make the combinations smooth, or, if smoothness be not desired, to give a convincing meaning to harshness, as is Beethoven's intention in his rough-hewn counterpoint, and Mozart's indisputable achievement in the introduction to his C major quartet (K. 465). At first one is inclined to say that Haydn is never harsh; but the exceptions are even more remarkable than in Mozart, for they are in passages which are not contrapuntal at all. In the peaceful slow movement of the F minor quartet, op. 20, no. 5, a ruminating passage at the end of the development (compare the similar incident cited from the first movement of op. 17, no. 5) is inscribed by Haydn '*per figuram retardationis*'.

Ex. 17.

The writer well remembers Joachim's answer when, in 1888, a bewildered small boy asked him about this passage. 'It means that the figures of the violin are always a step behind the chords; it must be played dreamily and tenderly, not stiffly and coldly.' With this passage Haydn completes his resources of harmony.

Op. 20, no. 3, in G minor, begins with a fiery and passionate first movement, with several of Haydn's most spirited themes. A certain agitated passage in the 'second subject' is expanded in the recapitulation to a climax with a freedom which anticipates Haydn's later treatment of sonata form. The note is almost tragic, and is well maintained in the minuet with its trio that leads so romantically back to the da capo. This minuet and the still more impassioned and sombre minuet of the F minor quartet, op. 20, no. 5, are probably the sources of Mozart's inspiration in the most passionate of all his minuets, that in the great G minor quintet. The finale of op. 20, no. 3 is in sonata form, but with a polyphony as close as any fugue. With all its liveliness and energy its quiet end is nearer to tragedy than to comedy. The whole work would certainly have found a position in concert programmes but for its slow movement, which has a breadth not easily distinguished from length by spoilt modern audiences; and Haydn almost admits this when he calls it *poco adagio*, which shows that it will not bear dragging. The grand possibilities revealed by the largo of op. 9, no. 3 are not easy even for Haydn to follow up, and of the four sonata-form slow movements in op. 20, only that undiscovered little violet in op. 20, no. 1 is terse enough to achieve breadth without length. Perhaps this explains how the D major quartet, op. 20, no. 4, has met with more public recognition than the other five; for not only are its first movement and finale in Haydn's most comic vein, but its only melancholy part, the slow movement, consists of a pathetic theme (un poco adagio affettuoso) with four variations ending with an admirable coda, and thus avoiding the difficulties of designing a big adagio in sonata form on the scale of these quartets.

No. 5, in F minor, is the most nearly tragic work Haydn ever wrote; its first movement being of astonishing depth of thought, with quite a big coda containing a new *ff* climax of its own, followed by a pathetic collapse. The other movements have already been described.

No. 6, in A major, is a graceful comedy, in which the adagio cantabile, in C. P. E. Bach's reprise form, is the only part that can be said by severe criticism to drag. The neglect of this quartet can hardly be due to any other cause; and perhaps, as with the rest of op. 20, we may nowadays expect a public appreciation of Haydn less patronizingly fastidious and more appreciative of subtleties than that which has dictated the survival of the more brilliant and comic works at the expense of the more reflective.

It is interesting to compare the remarkable modulating opening of the 'second subject' in the first movement of op. 20, no. 6,

Ex. 18.

with that in the first movement of Beethoven's sonata, op. 2, no. 1.

Ex. 19.

What Haydn thought of a young man who could have the effrontery to dedicate to him a work in which a 'second subject' starting in E minor modulates to B flat, has not been recorded; but he was presumably clever enough to see that Beethoven's modulations are the by-products of an irresistible steady upward movement of his bass, whereas Haydn's, in op. 20, no. 6, are an improvisatorial adventure undertaken for relaxation, and controlled by the unaided power of its melody.

With op. 20 the historical development of Haydn's quartets reaches its goal; and further progress is not progress in any historical sense, but simply the difference between one masterpiece and the next. Not all the later works are equally valuable; inequalities of value are relatively more rather than less noticeable, and no later set of six quartets, not even op. 76, is, on its own plane, so uniformly weighty and so varied in substance as op. 20. If Haydn's career had ended there, nobody could have guessed which of some half-dozen different lines he would have followed up: the line of Beethovenish tragedy foreshadowed in the F minor quartet; the Wilhelm Rust line suggested by the fantasia in the C major; a return to fugal polyphony as the main interest; the further development of the comic vein of the D major; the higher and non-farcical comedy of the A major; and the development of (or subsidence into) luxury scoring.

Something different happened. The 'Russian' quartets, op. 33, are the lightest of all Haydn's mature comedies. In one place in the old Breitkopf catalogue the opus appears with the alternative title of Divertimenti; and it is also known as *Gli Scherzi*, from the fact that its minuet movements (which are in a quicker tempo than hitherto) are entitled by Haydn himself either scherzo or scherzando. This title Beethoven borrowed for his great satyric movements; but these little scherzi of Haydn's are, except in their quick tempo, nothing like as near to Beethoven's scherzi as the larger minuets, sometimes even marked presto, in which Haydn was in later works to encroach upon the style and scale of Beethoven's second period.

Op. 33, no. 1 often figures in catalogues as in D major. But though it begins with a D major chord, it is really in B minor, and half the point of the opening consists in its effect when resumed in repeating the exposition which, of course, has closed in D. In Haydn's only other quartet in B minor, the same point is made. Haydn got it from a sonata by C. P. E. Bach, also in B minor. In the same key the same idea, elevated from wit to sublime pathos, inspires the opening of Brahms's clarinet quintet, the point here also fully revealing itself only when the repeat is begun. (See article BRAHMS.) Other instances of this device, with bolder key-relations, are to be found in C. P. E. Bach and in works of this date by the eighteen-year-old Mozart. The musicians who were shocked at Beethoven's beginning his first symphony in the subdominant must have been of an uncultured class if they did not know that the composers whom they already revered as classics had gone much farther in this matter.

The slow movement of op. 33, no. 1 conceals behind its formal opening a wealth of quaint beauty, notably its 'second subject' (Ex. 20), and contributes perhaps more than the slow movement of op. 20, no. 1 to the andante of Mozart's E flat quartet. The finale is full of energy, and is the only sonata-form finale in

Ex. 20.

this set. For in the other quartets of op. 33 we encounter not only the new title of scherzo for the otherwise unchanged minuet and trio, but the essentially new element of finales in lighter rondo and variation forms. All the six first movements of op. 33 steadily maintain a high level of thought; and of the slow movements it may be affirmed that Haydn has now completely solved the problems of all kinds of form in a slow tempo. The principle of his solution is well seen in the 'second subject' of the slow movement of op. 33, no. 3, an adagio in which Haydn manages to make the reprise device compatible with a sense of sonata activity.

Ex. 21.

The secret (which may also be found in the largo sostenuto of op. 33, no. 2) lies in the composer's realizing that a bar of slow music is not a bar of quick music played slowly, but an altogether bigger thing. In music slowness either means bigness, or it means emptiness. And to express action in a slow tempo demands the power of executing a plan in less than a quarter of the number of notes reasonably required in a quick tempo. Nor does it make any difference if any part of an adagio breaks out in demisemiquavers; a run can effect no more dramatic action than the changes of its underlying harmonies. From op. 33 onwards we may be certain that no slow movement of Haydn, however unimportant, will stagnate.

In the largo cantabile of op. 33, no. 5, Haydn shows us what can be done with the old arioso, punctuated by an ominous figure.

Ex. 22.

For the middle section he deliberately uses a cliché which is found in Gluck's *Orfeo*; while the cadenza is the finest climax of a highly organized composition, and all the instruments take part in it. The result is a fine movement, contrasted on one side with one of Haydn's largest and most humorous first movements, and on the other with the most comic of the six little scherzi. The finale, however, shows that the revival of the divertimento style, though adding important new resources to the string quartet, has its dangers. Three melodic variations and a runaway coda do not make an adequate finale to a quartet with so important a first movement; and the prettiness of Haydn's Siciliana theme is extinguished by comparison with the poetry of that of the finale of Mozart's D minor quartet, a comparison it has the misfortune to suggest. Another variation finale, in op. 33, no. 6, is more fortunate, and introduces us to a form peculiar to Haydn and already used by him in piano works. Whether or not he was anticipated by some other composer is a matter for statisticians; the solitary specimen the writer has found in C. P. E. Bach might possibly be later than Haydn's first example. Anyhow, in the record of permanent works of art, Haydn is the master who created delightful sets of variations on a pair of themes, one in the major and the other in the minor; and nobody has followed up this idea except Beethoven, at the height of his second period, with the solitary example of the Haydnesque allegretto in C major and minor in his great E flat trio, op. 70, no. 2. The examples of this form in Haydn's quartets are the finale of op. 33, no. 6; the first movement of the *Rasirmesser* quartet, op. 55, no. 2 (F minor); and the slow movements of the quartets, op. 50, no. 3 (E flat), op. 50, no. 4 (F sharp minor), and op. 71, no. 3 (E flat). Except in the *Rasirmesser* quartet and in op. 71, no. 3, the form is not seen at its best in Haydn's string quartets; his full enjoyment of it is shown in piano music, especially in the later trios where he pours out some of his greatest themes, using the alternating variation form without scruple for a first movement, a middle movement, or a finale.

The remaining three finales in op. 33 are rondos; a form which, with rare exceptions, is wholly different in Haydn from the form standardized by Mozart. In op. 33, no. 4 (B flat) it is a mere dance, the main theme alternating with several square-cut other tunes, and facetiously varied whenever it returns. The final pizzicato joke is good, and is introduced with just enough composition to provide a *locus in quo dulce desipere sit*. The finale of the otherwise meditative and mellow quartet in E flat, op. 33, no. 2, is known *par excellence* as 'The Joke'. It is a rondo with one episode, and a trailing coda to do duty for the other episodes; and the joke consists in Haydn's winning, by grossly sharp practice, his wager that 'the ladies will always begin talking before the music is finished'. His ridiculous theme consists, as to its first strain, of four two-bar clauses. At the end of the work, after a solemn adagio warning, the strain is played with two-bar pauses between its clauses. When the fourth clause has been played, the music is morally over; and if Haydn chooses to indicate another four bars' rest and repeat the first clause again, he ought to lose his wager.

The rondo of op. 33, no. 3 (C major) is one of Haydn's most comic utterances, but is (like the first movement of op. 33, no. 5) none the less a vital item in the record of his art, and well worthy of its place in the only quartet in this opus that has been often taken up by concert-players. One would like to think that the delicious effect of its opening on a six-four chord was not a consequence of the usual oversight about the octave of the 'cello.

All six quartets are important in their first movements. In the smallest of the six quartets (no. 6, in D) the first movement is important as in the other five, but the unpretending arioso slow movement, while turning the long *messa di voce* of the first violin into an occasion for fine polyphonic organization of the other parts, actually leaves a blank space for a cadenza at the end; for the last time in Haydn's works.

The whole opus gravitates round Joachim's favourite C major quartet (no. 3), which remains one of Haydn's profoundest studies in childhood, trailing clouds of glory at any and every moment. Its tiny scherzando, with the contrast between its tenderly grave melody on the fourth string and the bird-like duet which does duty for trio (whence the title 'Vogelquartett'), has always been a popular feature. The first movement is at once the quietest and the greatest Haydn had so far achieved, and it sounds most spacious if played without either repeat. It is time that musicians and music-lovers paid attention to the B minor quartet, a not less thoughtful work and equally perfect in every way. Nor is there more gain than loss in refinement of taste by neglect of the rest of this opus.

The isolated quartet in D minor, op. 42, occupies a central position in Haydn's art. Pohl, puzzled by its astonishing terseness, and faced with the undoubted fact that it was published after op. 33, conjectures, on no ground whatever but his failure to see anything in it, that it was written about the same time as opp. 1, 2, and 3. This is even more absurd than to suppose that Beethoven's F sharp major sonata, op. 78, might have been written before he left Bonn because it is so short. Haydn's D minor quartet, op. 42, is to his art very much what the F sharp major sonata is to Beethoven's. The slow movement is, as Pohl says, *anspruchslos*; and this unpretentious movement will do as well as any other part of the quartet to prove that Haydn could not have written it any earlier than the date of its publication. If he had only had the luck or cunning to call it a cavatina, nobody would have failed to see the point of this melody without development, without a contrasting second theme or middle section, without sign of dramatic action, extending itself before us till we note, first, that it is not going to be a mere theme for variations; secondly, that it is becoming broader than any melody that we have ever heard worked into larger designs with other themes; finally, that it is rounding itself towards a conclusion, and is sufficient in itself, and justified by sheer contrast for its position in a work of dramatic action. The rest of the quartet (even the tiny four-bar-rhythmed minuet) is a lesson in composition such as would have puzzled the Haydn of 1765 almost as much as it puzzled Pohl, and for very different reasons. In 1765 Haydn could not have written eight bars of andante or adagio without more ornament than suffices for the whole of op. 42. Even in opp. 9, 17, and 20, the moderato tempo of his first movements is not the same thing as the andante ed innocente of op. 42, which is a real andante moving with such economy of action as to accomplish without haste all that sonata form can do, both architecturally and dramatically. The moderato tempo in his earlier first movements has the purpose of crowding as much movement as possible into comfortably long bars; the slow tempo in the first movement of op. 42 has the purpose of spreading few notes over a large space. Finally, Haydn here follows up a point already noticed in the first movement of op. 20, no. 3, and works up part of his recapitulation to a passionate climax in no way anticipated by the original statement. This climax brings to maturity the peculiar freedom of form which is to be a leading feature in Haydn's works from now onwards. In conclusion, if there were any doubt about the date of op. 42, no date within Haydn's lifetime would be too late, and the actual date of publication is the earliest which is technically possible.

From this point onwards Haydn and Mozart converge; they were soon to meet in person, and Haydn's quartets of opp. 20 and 33 were probably among those that had inspired Mozart in his own great set of six dedicated to Haydn. At this point it will be convenient to consider how Haydn's art forms, after influencing those of Mozart, diverge in spite of the obvious returning influence of Mozart's style.

Up to op. 42 Haydn's treatment of sonata form, though urgently dramatic, lays a decided stress upon symmetry. A normal first movement (and up till now the same form is adopted for slow movements, with the rare exception of themes with variations) consists of a group of material clearly in the main key, leading in a well organized transition passage to another group of material in the complementary key (the dominant in a major movement, the mediant major, or rarely the dominant minor, in a minor movement). This second group (so misleadingly called 'second subject') comes to a definite end, and leads back to the repetition of the whole exposition, and, after repetition, forward to a development which travels, unlike the exposition, freely through many keys until its course brings it back to the tonic. Here the whole material of the exposition is recapitulated, the second group being now in the tonic as well as the first; and its end often suffices for the end of the whole movement. This description has avoided all assertions as to how many themes there are, and how they are distributed; and by this reticence it contrives to be true of Haydn's procedure so far, and of Mozart's and Beethoven's *passim.* But we have now reached the point where it will no longer be a trustworthy guide to Haydn's first movements. His recapitulations have already begun to expand conspicuously: the term 'second subject' as implying a different theme opposed to a single 'first subject' never was applicable to Haydn except in cases which, counted up statistically, are as individual as the cases of many unclassified procedures; nothing could be clearer than the 'second subjects' of op. 33, nos. 3 and 5; and nothing could be more parenthetic than the only discoverable new figures in the corresponding regions of op. 33, nos. 1, 2, and 4. But as to the recapitulation, the very idea utterly breaks down already in op. 33, no. 4; there is instead a brilliant peroration, and this is also the case in op. 33, no. 5, in spite of its clear 'second subject'. From the earliest works to the latest, nothing can be firmer than Haydn's distribution of keys; and nothing can be more dramatic than his later indications of return to his tonic: but beyond this all *a priori* assertion must cease. Pitiful will be the subterfuges of the teacher or student who succeeds in making out that the first movement of our next quartet, op. 50, no. 1 (B flat), has a 'second subject' and a recapitulation; nor will orthodoxy be saved by saying 'this is form in the making, before these things were differentiated'. It is form in the highest state of efficiency, freedom, and terseness, long after every element has been differentiated. From op. 50 onwards there is no dealing with Haydn's first movements except by individual analysis.

His finales remain more often amenable to rule; a symmetrical recapitulation is a useful thing in finales because the end of a work requires more perspicuity than the beginning, and (even in sonatas, where the necessity is not that of the logic of concrete events) its function is to satisfy expectation rather than to raise doubt. Though an individual analysis of each case is the only means of obtaining even a roughly correct idea of Haydn's mature sonata forms, it is fortunately possible to sum up his main resources by the single general statement that *Haydn invented a brilliant type of coda à la Beethoven, and used fully developed codas instead of recapitulations.* From op. 33 onwards one of his strongest impulses was towards terseness, and it was balanced by an equally strong impulse towards expansion. Outward symmetry was for him an obstacle to the reconciling of these two opposite impulses; and the reconciliation of such opposites is a fundamental condition of art. Mozart reconciled them by working on a larger scale, where outward symmetry was a necessity. Hence Mozart lays stress on his recapitulation, is usually terse and mono-thematic in his developments, and seldom has a large coda. The freedom of his form, vital as Haydn's, is to be sought in fine detail; and in fact the entasis of the Parthenon is not more suitable and accurate than Mozart's handling of his apparently so symmetrical recapitulations. Beethoven, writing on a scale initially larger than Mozart's, and expanding to a totally different order and range, adopted as a matter of course the recapitulation of Mozart together with the peroration of Haydn. And Haydn himself, in the first movement of one of his most famous quartets (*The Lark*), op. 64, no. 5, has casually tucked a fairly complete recapitulation of his complementary-key material into one of his most brilliant perorations, with an effect neither like Mozart's nor like Beethoven's forms. With this conception of the procedure of the three masters, we can trace the forms of Haydn's later works without difficulty; with the commonly accepted doctrine of sonata form the task is hopeless.

Before following Haydn to the end of the various threads he has now gathered up, we must note a detail of instrumentation which raises general principles, and gives occasion to discuss Haydn's other chamber music as far as it is in print to-day. Note the case of the adagio cantabile of one of the greatest quartets, op. 64, no. 5 (A major).

Ex. 23.

Here there is unmistakable evidence that the piano was more of a hindrance than a help to the formation of Haydn's chamber music style, even when he was already a veteran. It is, of course, pedantic to object to a simple musical formula that it can be played as well by a piano as by two violins; and the critic would forget that instruments were made for music and not vice versa, if he sought to damage Haydn's last and greatest complete quartets (the two in op. 77) by pointing out that they were first written as sonatas for piano and violin (or flute). So elaborate an instrument as the piano would be a strange ineptitude if, with the aid of another instrument, it could not give a tolerable account of most things likely to happen in a string quartet in Haydn's musical language. This, however, does not justify Haydn in condemning a violin and viola to spend two-thirds of an adagio in playing an accompaniment which is actually better on a piano, since half the notes of one of the two stringed instruments are redundant where they meet between the beats. It is a forlorn hope to call this a special effect; it is nothing but a lapse in Haydn's imagination, more serious as such than as a sacrifice of the inner parts to mere accompaniment. Contrast the sound of this with that of the accompaniment to a similar but less inspired melody in the curious adagio finale of Haydn's C major quartet, op. 54, no. 2, where the slow creeping arpeggios of the 'cello rise from the depths right into the region of the melody, combining with the simple repeated chords of the accompaniment in one of the finest tone-colours in any quartet. ('Da hab' ich mir Mühe gegeben,' said Hausmann, when the effect was admired.) (Ex. 24.)

Haydn used to compose at the piano; and the example from op. 64 is the only passage in all his string quartets where we may trace any harm to this habit. It evidently did not limit

Ex. 24.

his powers of phrasing, as it does with weaker musical heads. What it did unequivocally ruin for him was all possibility of working out the combination of the piano with other instruments. Haydn, enjoying himself on the piano with C. P. E. Bach's technique (filled out where necessary), simply 'could not keep a dog without doing the barking himself'; with the result that all his magnificent piano trios are just what his favourite pupil Pleyel called them when, having gone into business as a publisher in Paris, he produced a *Collection complette des Sonates d'Haydn pour Forte-Piano*. You may play unsuspectingly through a magnificent sonata in this edition until you are brought to a stand by a long passage of mere accompaniment, with no melody; and then you will find, on looking at the index, that the work is '*avec accompagnement de Violon et Basse*'. You will never have suspected the slightest need for the *basse*, though when you try the work with the violin you will see that where it is playing an inner part Haydn wants 'cello tone to complete it, though the piano is already playing the necessary notes. But you may play many of these sonatas without missing anything at all, even though the index tells you that they are '*avec accompagnement de Violon*'. Some of these are known nowadays as piano sonatas; and, though the new critical edition of Haydn's complete works has not as yet (1928) begun to clear up the chamber music, it has already eliminated all but three of the so-called violin sonatas by publishing them as the piano solo sonatas which Haydn intended them to be.

The trios are in a different case. All the thirty-one now in print require the violin (or, in three cases, the flute) to play important themes; and in accompanying passages they further require the 'cello to support the violin, though hardly for a dozen notes in the whole collection is it allowed to diverge from the bass of the piano. The only movement in real trio writing in the whole thirty-one works is the adagio at the beginning of the two-movement work in A major, no. xv in B. & H.'s edition. For the rest, the musical contents of these trios are, with a few early exceptions, glorious; and the works cover Haydn's whole career, and are far richer than the quartets in fine specimens of his smaller forms, such as alternating variations, sectional rondos, lyric 'A, B, A' slow movements, and, above all, movements breaking off and leading into finales, a dramatic event that only twice happens in the quartets, but always coincides with Haydn's finest imagination in these smaller works. It is not difficult to place the trios in approximate chronological order among the quartets. The main thing to bear in mind is that Haydn takes the view that a quartet is a symphony, whereas a piano trio is an accompanied solo. Consequently a slight finale, such as a merely sectional rondo, or an unpretending movement in any position, is no evidence of early date. The famous *Gipsy* rondo, for instance, belongs to one of the last trios (which of course figures as no. 1 in current editions; they always put the ripest works first)—and that trio begins with a set of rondo variations (i.e. variations with divers episodes instead of a second theme), and has a middle movement in simple A, B, A form; so that this most famous among Haydn's trios contains no sonata form at all. It is none the less mature for that. No trio contains four movements; the presto that follows the splendid alternating variations in the G minor trio, no. 17, is itself an expanded variation of the second theme. Some of the sonata-form first movements are in Haydn's greatest style, e.g. trios nos. 3 (a work to which occasionally 'cellists have sacrificed themselves in public), 6, 8, 13, and 23, and so are some of the finales, whether developed rondos or sonata movements; e.g. in trios nos. 3, 5, 8, 13, 17, and 23. All the double-variation and rondo-variation movements are great; and some of the smaller finales are intensely poetic; e.g. the gentle consolatory allegro ma dolce, which, after a deeply pathetic fragmentary andante intermezzo, brings the great D major trio no. 6 to an abrupt end; and perhaps most of all the melancholy tempo di menuetto of the quite late trio in F sharp minor. One of the earliest trios, in G minor, in the style of op. 9 or earlier, is as beautiful as any. Two other early works (no. 12 in C and no. 27 in F) sprawl with a gawkiness compared with which that queer couple of fragments known as the quartet op. 3, no. 4 is graceful and terse. Trio no. 27, however, is the more presentable of the two. The flute trios, nos. 29, 30, and 31, are easy-going, early-middle Haydn. Trio 18, in E flat minor, is one of Haydn's last compositions, and consists of the most pathetic of all sets of rondo variations, followed by a subtle and pensive finale in the major, allegro ben moderato. Many other trios claim attention; but we must now deal with the remaining quartets.

Op. 50 consists of six quartets (B flat, C, E flat, F sharp minor, F, and D). The F sharp minor quartet is a great work. It shows for the first time Haydn's definite renunciation of tragic ends to sonata movements, and his now typical association of the minor mode with a passionate, somewhat blustering temper, ending with a recapitulation (in these circumstances regular) in the tonic major, so that everything turns out well. As he said of himself, 'Anybody can see that I'm a good-natured fellow'. It is a pity that he did not think fit to provide the variations of his andante with at least a few bars of coda; the contrast between the two themes is grand, but the impression left by the unexpanded end of the whole is perfunctory. In striking contrast to the happy end of the first movement, the final fugue, quietest and deepest of all the few instrumental fugues since Bach, strikes a note so tragic that Beethoven's C sharp minor quartet is the first thing that one can connect with it (Ex. 25). Op. 50, no. 5, F major, in exquisite childlike happiness from beginning to end, is one of the most perfect and subtly proportioned of all Haydn's works. Its poco adagio is known as *Le Rêve*.

Op. 50, no. 6 (D major) begins as if in the middle of a sentence, and is broadly designed. It is known as *Der Frosch*, from the frog-like effect of the theme of its finale, which plays across open strings and their unisons. Op. 54 contains three of the most brilliant quartets. Brilliance is the note of the opening of no. 1

Ex. 25.

(G major), which has for slow movement a wonderful quiet allegretto in sonata form with profound modulations. No. 2 (C), a great favourite with Joachim, has the biggest and most symphonic first movement so far. The astonishing adagio consists of a sepulchral melody with a wild, florid counterpoint for the first violin, all *per figuram retardationis*, as we saw in op. 20, no. 5 (Ex. 17). It leads into the minuet, which has a very remarkable trio. The finale is a freak, already cited for its scoring. It is a lyric adagio, with an introduction and one short presto episode. No. 3 (E) is one of Haydn's greatest works, and should be better known. Equally great is the first of the three quartets of op. 55; in A major, with an adagio in rondo form (a very difficult thing to handle with Haydnesque breadth), a remarkable use of the extreme heights of the violin in the trio of the minuet, again exploited in op. 64, no. 6, and a finale which begins like a rondo, and runs away in an excellent (unofficial) double fugue.

Op. 55, no. 2 is the *Rasirmesser* quartet, so called because Haydn's host overheard him exclaiming, under the torture of shaving, 'I'd give my best quartet for a new razor'. The wish was fulfilled, and the vow redeemed with this F minor quartet. In its opening double variations Haydn wallows in the sentiment evoked by the heavenly contrast between its passionate minor and consolatory major theme. A proved personal friend of Haydn's whole family of a thousand sonata movements might venture to ask Haydn's permission, at the second (i.e. last) variation of the major theme, to omit the unvaried first statement of its first eight bars, and begin it immediately with the fresh tone of the 'cello. This would lose nothing, and would save the movement from dragging. The rest of the quartet is among Haydn's most intellectual works, and its neglect is due to the fact that, besides being subtle, it is by no means easy. Let no musician call it ineffective if he would escape the shame of the fox in that affair of the grapes.

Now that we are sure of Haydn's methods and mastery, op. 55, no. 3 need not detain us; nor need op. 64, no. 1. But the other five of op. 64 are of the highest importance. The thoughtful B minor, no. 2, with its replica of the D major ambiguity of op. 33, no. 1, and its humorous ethereal end in B major, is a great work unduly neglected. Not so the remaining four (B flat, G, D, and E flat), which are among the most constantly played of Haydn's works, nos. 5 and 6 being specially popular. The common new feature in these four quartets is the appearance of lyric slow movements in the form of a broad melody, a minor middle section, and an ornamental da capo. This form had already appeared in the great E major quartet, op. 54, no. 3, but in a more ornate and less idyllic style. Op. 64, no. 5, called *The Lark*, from the entry of the first violin warbling in the heights after a staccato opening theme by the other instruments, is famous for its little *perpetuum mobile* finale. Op. 64 as a group has some resemblance to op. 33. On the basis of longer experience, it gloriously develops the lighter side of Haydn's art forms.

The remaining complete quartets (opp. 71 (3), 74 (3), 76 (6), and 72 (2)) are all on the largest symphonic scale, and so doubtless would the wonderful fragment, op. 103, have been if Haydn had had the strength to write a first movement and finale for it. Of the three neglected masterpieces in op. 71 (B flat, D, E flat), the third is the greatest and most perfect. Two passages have already been quoted in connexion with the viola-below-'cello problem (Exx. 2 and 3); another quotation from the exquisite rondo-variation slow movement will show a new tone-colour.

Ex. 26.

Andante con moto.

The D major quartet (no. 2) is the only quartet with a slow introduction; a fact curiously in contrast with the custom Haydn had long since come to establish in his symphonies. The finale of that neglected quartet has one of the loveliest themes of his special later kittenish type.

Op. 74 begins with a glorious work in C major, taken up with enthusiasm by Joachim in his last years. For the first time we encounter a feature by which a work of Haydn's may be surely recognized as a work of his latest period. The trio of the minuet is in A, a key only remotely connected (through its tonic minor) with C, the key of the movement. The choice of these keys for sections not continuously linked up in a flowing structure (e.g. in trios of minuets and as keys for middle movements) is Haydn's contribution to the scheme of tonality which Beethoven, Schubert, Brahms, and (*mutatis mutandis* for the conditions of the music drama) Wagner were to develop into so mighty a resource. Haydn's insight is shown in his abstention from explanatory or miraculous modulations where these key-relations are concerned. His beloved C. P. E. Bach was always treating remote modulations as things to declaim upon; Haydn puts the contrasted keys in plain juxtaposition; for which he would assuredly get no marks in our Mus. Bac. modulation questions. And so his key contrasts shine out like the colours of a sunset. You will find them in most of the later trios (Breitkopf nos. 1, 3, 5, 8, 9, 11, and 23); though of course their absence will not prove an earlier date.

Op. 74, no. 2, F major, is another neglected masterpiece. No. 3, in G minor, on the other hand (called 'Rittquartett' from the prancing rhythm that pervades its first movement), is a great favourite, with its blustering tragic first movement and finale, both ending happily 'like the good-natured fellow I am', and its specially solemn largo in the remote key of E major.

The six quartets in opp. 71 and 74 have, with op. 76, no. 1, the common feature of beginning with some introductory gesture or phrase.

In op. 76, nos. 1 and 3, Haydn presents a feature imitated only by Mendelssohn in his Italian symphony and Brahms in his B major trio and F major symphony. Although each of these works is in a major key, the finale is in the minor. The reverse relation is, of course, not uncommon. As usual, Haydn's two blustering finales end happily in the major; but not without some downright solemn thoughts in their development. The intellectual depths and the freedom of form in the last twenty quartets are among the inexhaustible experiences of art; and Brahms's friends need never have been surprised to find him absorbed in the study of a Haydn quartet. Only once, towards the end, does the work seem a little too easy; the graceful ingenuities of op. 76, no. 6 (E flat) roll away like the process of peeling an onion; the fantasia, which is the slow movement, seems more arbitrary than free; and actually the most beautiful part of the quartet is the trio of the minuet, which consists wholly of the scale of E flat in iambic rhythm, descending and ascending with counterpoints as multitudinous and heavenly as the angels on Jacob's ladder.

But the rest of op. 76 is beyond description. No. 2, in D minor, with a powerful first movement unique in its concentration on its first theme of four notes, has the most imaginative minuet (the *Hexen-Menuett*) before Schubert. No. 3, in C major, nearly as great, is famous for its variations on Haydn's Austrian Hymn. These, which simply pass the unadorned melody from one instrument to the other, are not as great as their tune, but can be made to sound very spiritual. No. 4, in B flat, is known as *The Sunrise*, from its remarkable sustained opening. One of the most glorious of Haydn's tunes is that of the anomalous first movement of op. 76, no. 5, which is followed by the great largo in F sharp major which has given this quartet its title in the catalogues. Beside these melodies we may place the theme of the andante of the last complete quartet, op. 77, no. 2 (the whole quartet is perhaps Haydn's greatest instrumental composition, with two of the last symphonies to bracket with it); and, finally, the deeply touching andante theme of his last composition, the fragment, op. 103. With this Haydn bids us farewell, not in terms of the quotation from his part-song, *Der Greis*, which he issued as a visiting-card, complaining of age and weakness, but rather in terms of the end of that song, which says, 'Thanks to Heaven, a harmonious song was the course of my life'. Power and eternal youth remained in these last and gentlest strains that the venerable creator of the sonata style allowed his pen to record. That power we can feel; in that eternal youth we can rejoice; and we may be satisfied to seek out what Haydn has done for us without more than a mystic notion of how he did it. DONALD F. TOVEY.

[There are instances when, within the bounds of a single word, there stands portrayed the genius of a great man. Browning writes of 'Euripides the Human', and in a flash the fidelity of the characterization is apparent. Similarly, the word 'genial' in its English sense, warm and friendly, in its Latin sense indicative of the quality of genius, epitomizes the life as well as the music of Haydn. Can one wonder at the deep affection in which the memory of such a musician and such a man is held by every amateur quartet player the world over? The sobriquets associated with so many of his quartets reflect the humorous sallies they contain, and if they lack in dignity, ample compensation is to be found in their usefulness both in ordinary conversation and in literary reference. It is so much less ponderous to speak of the 'Sunrise' or the 'Bird' quartet than to quote the opus number and the key. Unfortunately, some of them have more than one pet-name which is less convincing. To these quartets I shall have occasion to refer in the course of the following informal notes.

Haydn's connexion with an Austrian nobleman, Karl Joseph von Fürnberg, was, to quote Michel Brenet, 'of great importance to his career'. This personage, who shared the general taste of the Viennese aristocracy for chamber music, engaged the young musician as violinist and took him to his residence at Weinzierl, near Vienna, where every day he played instrumental music with amateurs or paid musicians. For the musical evenings at Weinzierl, Haydn composed eighteen string quartets. Thus it was through Fürnberg, as he recalled in his old age to Griesinger, that he made his first experiments in a form of composition in which he attained his greatest success.

The six quartets, op. 1, and six, op. 2, are seldom played, except by parties of enthusiastic amateurs, some of whom are impelled to work with exemplary patience throughout the whole eighty-three numbers without the omission of a single note or repeat, and are richly rewarded for their pains. All were performed in Vienna (1926) by the admirable Sedlak-Winkler Quartet, in a series of concerts which awakened great interest in Austrian chamber music circles. A feature of these twelve short quartets is the inclusion of two minuets in each (op. 1, no. 5 excepted), one before and one after the slow movement. The two are always in the same key, but the tonality of the trios varies. A writer has observed that Haydn's minuets were in these days occasionally omitted both in symphony and quartet playing. It may be that, as there was little or no development in the first and last movements, a supplement was thought desirable, to provide additional length rather than as an essential part of the scheme.

In the adagio of op. 1, no. 6, and op. 2, no. 3, and in the andantino to op. 3, no. 1, the mute is used with charming effect. The serenade in op. 3, no. 5 is also marked 'con sordino', and though extremely pretty and popular, scarcely represents Haydn at his best. There is no further instance in Haydn's quartets of the use of the mute,[1] which was little favoured by any of the classical composers.

Professor Tovey has dwelt in his article on the attractiveness of the early quartets. Of one of these I am moved to speak, as it happens to be the first I ever played, and now, after sixty years interval, it has equal power to charm. I allude to op. 9, no. 1, which, like the rest of the quartets of that period, is not thickly scored, though the two violin parts are fairly interesting; but there is a wistful beauty in it which pictures the mind of a youth to whom new vistas of art are beginning to open out. The finale, an energetic, all too short presto, forms a striking contrast to the rest.

Op. 9, no. 2 is less interesting though more elaborate; nos. 3 and 4, the latter played by Lady Hallé at the 'Pops', are both full of interesting matter. No. 5 starts with an adagio with variations, one of which is a bustling encounter between viola and 'cello. Op. 17, no. 3 also starts with variations in which, as so often happens in Haydn's early quartets, the first violin takes the leading part throughout. No. 5 contains the famous recitative for violin which Joachim always played con amore, quite in the mood of a singer appealing to a crowded audience at the Opera. Beethoven may have had this passage in mind when he wrote the recitative for violin in the great A minor quartet.

Haydn has used the initial theme of no. 6, marked 'presto', in his first sonata for piano and violin, but in another key and another tempo; also provided with sforzandi on the weak part of the bar—embryo, it may be, of similar effects produced by Beethoven in after days.

The six quartets, op. 20, are known in Germany as the *Sonnenquartetten*, for a reason no more romantic than the appearance of the sun on the title-page of the original edition, that luminary serving as the publisher's trade-mark. No. 1 contains a slow movement marked 'affettuoso', in which the part-writing is exceptionally fine, and to which I draw the attention of organists in search of short voluntaries. No. 2 opens with a bold solo for the 'cello, and contains in the minuet some of the 'Dudelsack' droning of which Haydn was very fond, and which makes frequent and most effective appearance in his quartets. The finale is one of the fugues said to be written in response to the doubts expressed by a critic as to his ability to write a good fugal movement. It is a four-subject fugue, part of it written *al rovescio*. No. 4 of this opus was much played by the Joachim Quartet. The adagio varié gives fine opportunities to all the instruments, but more especially to the 'cello, which has also a jolly solo in the trio of the *Gipsy* minuet, a little masterpiece in its way, containing, once more, effective sforzandi on the up-beat. No. 5 is in F minor, a key which predisposes even Haydn to sombre thoughts. The music in this quartet is certainly more introspective than is usual with Haydn, but we have a glimpse of his sunny nature in the adagio. In the finale he again writes a fugue (with two subjects), the predominant theme of which, introduced by the second violin, has proved attractive to so many composers. It is even found in the adagio of Corelli's third violin sonata, and the way in which it is worked up by Haydn, from a sotto voce to a splendid fortissimo climax in canon, affords yet another proof of the versatility of his genius. But such a climax needs more volume of sound than is afforded by the four voices of a string quartet, and would find more fitting and fuller expression as an organ piece. In no. 6 there is also a fugato (with three subjects), full of learned devices.

After op. 20, composed in 1771, there elapsed ten blank years as far as quartet composition is concerned. The six quartets, op. 33 (1781), are famous for many reasons. They were sometimes known, through the dedication to Prince Paul, as the *Russian* quartets, and sometimes—I know not why—as the *Jungfer* or *Virgin* quartets, but more often as 'Gli Scherzi', owing to the use of the word 'scherzo' by Haydn in lieu of 'minuetto'. This may have suggested the use of the word to Beethoven, with whose scherzi it has little affinity. Haydn's scherzi are perhaps more lyrical than his minuets, but that is all one can say about them.

The last bars of the finale give to no. 2 the name of the *Joke*, and indeed it is impossible to hear them and keep a serious countenance. No. 3, the *Bird*, is unique; not because of the numerous charming bird-like effects it contains, but because, though it presents no difficulties of technique, and is therefore accessible to every amateur, the effect, when well played, is full and satisfying, as in a work written in the grand style. Even the scherzo, given on the G string by the leader, is grave and moving, and is followed in the trio by a fascinating, twittering dialogue between the two violins. The lovely andante is followed by one of the

[1] The *Seven Last Words* excepted.

composer's most humorous finales, the call of the cuckoo being heard in every corner of the score. The music of this quartet gives the impression that at this period of his life Haydn must have felt exceptionally happy. No. 4 of the same opus contains, in the slow movement, some pizzicato passages of a kind in which children at every stage of growth rejoice, and no. 5 opens with a greeting which has suggested words to the frivolously inclined—

Ex. 27.

This delightful quartet contains matter of which Mozart took heed, whilst Haydn repaid the compliment later on by assimilating some of the methods of the younger man, whom he regarded with so much affection and ungrudging admiration. Op. 50, no. 4 opens with a Beethovenish phrase, and finishes with another fugue, the last of the entirely fugal movements, and strangely sad in character. To no. 6 I have heard many titles given, for which the eccentric finale is responsible. Haydn uses BARIOLAGE (*q.v.*) bowing on a small scale in many of his quartets, but in this movement he indulges in an orgy of it. The local nicknames I have heard given to this quartet include *The Frog*, *The House on Fire*, *The Row in Vienna*, and they all seem to fit, but are inconveniently numerous.

Op. 54, no. 1 is remarkable for the beauty of the allegretto. The descending passage of the two violins, vocalizing in thirds, dwells in the memory. No. 2 was a favourite of Hausmann, the 'cellist in the Joachim Quartet. In the final adagio, which contains a fragment of a theme afterwards used in the *Creation*, he had a great opportunity for displaying his fine tone production in the upper register of his Strad 'cello. Of no. 3, as well as of op. 55, no. 1, Professor Tovey has written. In the minuet of the former, the Scotch snap makes its appearance, possibly suggested by Haydn's experience in writing accompaniments to Scottish melodies. Nos. 1 and 2, op. 55, have each been quoted as the *Razor* quartet, but it matters not which is authentic, as the familiar story has no bearing on the music. Op. 55, no. 2, which opens with an andante varié in which all the instruments are kept busy, strikes a more serious note than most of Haydn's quartets. The key in which it is written, F minor, predisposes to sadness, but it finishes brightly enough in the major. Incidentally, it is worth remark that the major mode prevails in sixty-seven out of seventy-six of his quartets (the *Seven Last Words* excluded). This is significant of the composer's optimistic mentality.

In this connexion it may be interesting to note that six quartets, all in minor keys, are said to have been written by Haydn, and, unfortunately, lost. The story is told in *Fétis* of how the master, who at this time had private troubles, wrote six quartets in minor keys, and, as was his habit, left them on the piano, intending to revise them later. Some time afterwards, when he came to do this, the quartets had disappeared, and, from that day to this, no trace of them has been discovered. The only person who had access to the room was his pupil, Pleyel, who lived with him and was very affectionately regarded by his master. For a long time Haydn believed Pleyel to be guilty of the theft, but owing to the boy's evident affection for him, he eventually appears to have been convinced of his innocence. Whatever may be the truth, no use of the lost quartets was ever made by Pleyel in his own music.

With op. 64 begins Haydn's finest period. Professor Tovey points out the greatness of no. 2, whilst nos. 4, 5, 6 are among those most played. No. 5 is the most popular, including as it does the brilliant *perpetuum mobile* known as the *Hornpipe*, heard sometimes in the concert-room transcribed as a violin solo, and invariably played much too fast. These fast tempi exalt the virtuoso and kill the music. Thanks to the opening movement, in which the violin soars upwards with a trill, this quartet is sometimes also known as the *Lark*. In the andante of no. 6 there is a powerful declamatory passage in the minor, with some delicious modulations ushering in the major.

Of op. 71 Professor Tovey has written. The op. 74 quartets were, I am told, favourites of Joachim, which alone stamps them as things of worth. The opening jog-trot, three crotchets in a bar, of no. 3 gives to it the suitable name of the *Rider* (*Rittquartett*), but it is the largo whose Miltonic grandeur dwells in the memory and gives it rank among the finest and most serious things Haydn ever wrote. The six works comprising op. 76 are of outstanding beauty, and if Haydn had never written another quartet they would have served to immortalize his name. They are wider in their appeal than those preceding them, richer in the inner parts, and consequently more suitable for public performance. The andante of no. 1 is intensely dramatic, and the last movement very lively. The final bars suggest the joyous close of an operatic number—in the Papageno vein.

The broad opening passages in fifths have given to no. 2 the name of the *Quinten*, whilst the canonical minuet, picturing a set of brawling clowns stamping their feet tempestuously, one of them finishing after the rest, is at once a fine example of canonical writing and a priceless piece of fooling. It is, I suppose, the melodramatic whispering of the opening bars that has given to the trio in Germany the name of *Hexentrio* (Witches' trio). The story goes that while writing the finale to this quartet

Haydn was disturbed by the hee-haw of a donkey and incorporated it in the music—truly a most euphonious bray.

Of the *Emperor*, no. 3, what can one say that has not been said before? In the variations each instrument has a solo in turn, and then, all blending, there is heard one of the most beautiful bursts of pure diatonic harmony in all chamber music. It is of course much hackneyed, but the interest it inspires never flags. In no. 5 there is Mozartian inspiration in the opening movement, but the largo in F sharp major is profoundly original; nothing he ever wrote is more romantically youthful, and it is not surprising that the quartet is a favourite with the Flonzaley Quartet. I suspect that it was also a favourite of Franz Kneisel, for at his funeral it was played by four of his pupils, who, it may be supposed, knew what were his predilections. A resemblance to an air in the *Stabat Mater* of Rossini, who notoriously owed much to Haydn, has been traced in this movement by reminiscence hunters, but it is very slight. No. 6 is less remarkable than the rest of op. 76, but the alternativo to the minuet stands out as a flowing piece of contrapuntal writing.

Op. 77, nos. 1 and 2, written in his last days, are full of strength and vivacity, a tremendous effort to a man of Haydn's advanced age, and they form a magnificent finish to this long series of masterpieces. To match the virility found in the minuet and trio of no. 1, one must turn to the F minor quartet of Beethoven. I remember the way in which Joachim attacked the opening of the trio on the G string; it was like a tiger seizing its prey. Of the pianistic origin of the op. 77 quartets, Professor Tovey has written.

Looking back upon my notes, I find that in a series of experimental and short-lived stages, from each of which the composer learned his lesson, he used successively and then rejected the double minuet, the mute, the (entirely) fugal finale and the scherzo, arriving at the apogee of his art in the opp. 76 and 77 quartets. I have not taken into consideration the suite of seven sonatas known as the *Seven Last Words*, as they are not quartets properly so called. This work was composed for and performed by various groupings of instruments and voices, and frequently conducted by Haydn himself, the original combination being flute, oboe, horns, clarinets, timpani, and contra-basso with string quartet. Arranged for string instruments it may be less impressive; the 'terremoto' at the end certainly verges on the burlesque; but the solemn grandeur of the music is not all lost in the arrangement for string quartet.

Postscriptum. Since writing the above I have had the privilege of hearing a remarkable, and in some respects unique, series of performances of Haydn's quartets given by four young lady members of Lionel Tertis's ensemble class at the R.A.M. Each week three quartets were played, occupying about an hour in performance. The final session took place on June 28, 1928, the artists receiving public acknowledgement from the Principal (*v.* McDonald). They afforded evidence of what can be done by youthful performers who, unlike artists in the full tide of professional work, are able to find time for daily rehearsal, and who enjoy the advantage of guidance by a supremely gifted coach. Mr. Tertis had thrown himself into the task with unexampled enthusiasm and with startling results.

Professor Tovey has written so much on the quartets that I am almost ashamed to add more, but it seems worth while for an old stager like myself to say that I never before realized to the full the beauty of the early quartets of Haydn. The absence of polyphony is to some extent compensated by the beauty of the figures of accompaniment when played, as they were on these occasions, with meticulous care. They will never be so popular as the later quartets among performers, who very naturally crave for full inner parts, but really, for listeners of unsophisticated taste, no greater musical treat can be conceived.

One impression I had which is almost eerie. The music seems haunted throughout by the spirit of Beethoven, whose spiritual birthplace resides, most evidently, in these quartets. It is with an overpowering sense of gratitude to the father of the string quartet that I bring these notes to a close. Editor.]

(2) Johann Michael, 1737–1806, brother of Joseph, violinist and organist.

Modern republications:

Quintet, 2 v, 2 vla, vc, G	(G. de Saint-Foix) Senart, 1922.
,, ,, ,, ,, C (attributed to Joseph as op. 88)	New ed., André, 1861.
Quartet, str, A	(L. H. Perger) D.T.Ö. B. & H., 1907.
Four sonatas, v, vla, C, D, F, E	(Wilh. Altmann) U.E. and B. & H., 1911.

Michael Haydn is chiefly known to-day by his quintet and its attribution to Joseph. His quartet has been played by the Rosé Quartet. According to *Fétis* he refused to allow his works to be published in his lifetime, despite the fact that Breitkopf had asked for them.

Besides the above, *Altmann* gives two divertimenti (B. & H.), one for str. quintet, the other for wind and strings.

It is perhaps of interest to mention that Leopold Mozart, who disliked his manners, wrote to Wolfgang, 'Herr Haydn is a man whose merit you will be forced to acknowledge'. Schubert also held him in high esteem (*vide Grove*, ii. 348). Full list of his works in *Q.-L.*

Editor.

HAYNES, WALTER BATTISON, 1859–1900, English pianist and composer, educated partly at the Leipzig Conservatorium, where he gained the Mozart scholarship. Among his chamber works are a piano trio, a sonata for piano and violin, and some clever scholastic pieces for two violins and piano. EDITOR.

HEAP, CHARLES SWINNERTON, 1847–1900, English composer.

Sonata, pf, cl, B flat	B. & H., 1880.

Further publications in *British Musical Biography* include a quintet for piano and wind.

HEATH, JOHN RIPPINER, b. 1887, English composer.

The Lamp (a chamber music drama)	3 solo voices, chorus, str. quartet, fl, cl, fag, horn
Quartet (*Serbian*)	str
Poem (*In the Heart of the Country*)	pf, v
Three Macedonian Sketches	pf, v

All published by Chester.

Heath is one of the few musicians who follow another profession, combining medical practice with musical composition. His outlook is, above all, imaginative; he is attracted less by the external manifestations than by the feelings arising from contemplation of nature (e. g. in *The Heart of the Country*, for violin and piano), yet his harmonic fabric is intensely personal. Both the *Serbian* string quartet and the *Three Macedonian Sketches*, which record impressions from the Macedonian front during the war, form conspicuous examples of this.

Space will not allow of a full description of the last-named interesting work, which contains some remarkable impressionistic effects. The pieces are founded on folk-song—one picked up from an old native priest—and on dance tunes collected from players of native-made fiddles, flutes, bagpipes, and a kind of rudimentary oboe. ADOLPH MANN.

[Heath's most important chamber work is the *Serbian* quartet (four movements). The first, in F sharp minor, opens with a slow introduction in 5/4 time, followed by an allegro giocoso. The second, andante, is in D minor; the third, presto, a very short, strongly rhythmic movement, is in A minor. The finale, rather unexpectedly in D minor, opens with a short adagio, followed by an allegro with a slower middle section. There is a great climax at the end, followed by the repetition of the adagio with which the movement began. I have derived much enjoyment from the playing of this interesting work. EDITOR.]

HEGAR, FRIEDRICH, 1841–1927, Swiss violinist and conductor.

Quartet, str, f sharp mi	op. 46	Simrock, 1920.
Ballade, pf, v	,, 45	,,

Hegar was a friend of Brahms, whose influence is apparent in his quartet, of which Dr. Altmann (*Handbuch*) speaks as being difficult to play, and at times more intellectual than inspired, yet breathing at other moments a deeply religious spirit. A feature of the finale (allegro agitato) is the moving chorale with which it concludes. EDITOR.

HEGER, ROBERT, b. 1886, Alsatian composer and conductor.

Trio, pf, v, vc, f mi	op. 14	Leuckart, 1910.

A composer whose work shows traces of the influence of Brahms and Reger. This composition follows the tendencies of his time, but not to an extreme extent.

HEGGE, ODD GRÜNER, b. 1899, Norwegian pianist.

Trio, pf, v, vc, b mi	op. 4	Norsk. Musikförl.

A youthful work, showing good technique and sense of form.

†**HEGNER**, ANTON, b. 1861, Danish 'cellist.

Quartet, str, B flat	op. 13	B. & H., 1905.
Suite, pf, vc, D	,, 20	,, 1903.

HEIDRICH, MAXIMILIAN, 1864–1909, German composer.

Quartet, str, e mi	op. 24	C. F. Schmidt, 1911.
Quartet, str, g mi	,, 29	,, ,,
Trio, cl (or v), vla, vc, a mi	,, 31	,, 1912.
Trio, pf, cl, horn, c mi	,, 25	Kistner, 1894.
Sonata, pf, v, g mi	,, 12	C. F. Schmidt, 1888.
Sonata, pf, vc, f sharp mi	,, 4	,, 1887.

Vide Riemann, who singles out the clarinet trio, op. 33, for especial notice.

†**HEILMAN**, WILLIAM CLIFFORD, b. 1877, American composer.

Trio, pf, v, vc, C	op. 7	S.P.A.M., 1923.

Like that of many American composers, Heilman's musical training was begun in his native land, at Harvard, and finished in Europe—under Rheinberger in Germany and Widor in France. Although he has published but one chamber work, it bears the sponsorship of S.P.A.M., which testifies to its merits.

The trio is an ingratiating work which reveals its composer as one who is concerned first and last with euphony; his music 'sounds'. Throughout the three movements there is a minimum of dissonance, and the harmonic dispersions, particularly in the piano part, recall the Brahmsian sonorities that proved so adaptable to the chamber music style. The blandness of Heilman's rhythms is wholly in keeping with the smoothness of his harmonic texture. An attractive feature of the work is the sonorous slow movement—poco adagio—a well sustained song of no more than four pages, which keeps a thoroughly unified mood of tranquillity and has a finely wrought climax. The work is of moderate difficulty, and grateful to players and hearers alike.

ARTHUR SHEPHERD.

HEIM, MAX.

Quintet, wind instr, E flat C. F. Schmidt, 1903.

HEINE, AXEL, Scandinavian composer.

Melodic suite, pf, v, vc, a mi op. 9 Hansen, 1909.

HEINRICH XXIV, PRINCE VON REUSS. *v.* REUSS.

HEISE, PETER ARNOLD, 1830–1879, Danish composer.

Trio, pf, v, vc, E flat Hansen, 1908.
Fantaisie-sonata, pf, vc, a mi ,, 1902.

HEITSCH. *v.* HUMOUR IN CHAMBER MUSIC.

†HELLER, STEPHEN, 1815–1888, Hungarian pianist.

Wrote, in collaboration with Ernst, two books of *Pensées fugitives* for piano and violin (Augener). Each number of these essentially drawing-room pieces is prefaced by an excerpt from one of the French poets. The music is amiable and agreeable, and well written for both instruments.

EDITOR.

HELLMESBERGER, (1) GEORG (senior), 1800–1873, Austrian violinist and conductor.

Quartet, str op. 1 Artaria.

The Hellmesbergers have been a famous family of violinists for several generations. Georg was a celebrated teacher; Joachim and Ernst were among his pupils, as also Leopold Auer and Miska Hauser. His son Joseph (1829–1893) was the leader of the celebrated quartet, being succeeded by his own son Joseph junior (1855–1907), previously second violin.

Moser relates that Georg Hellmesberger had, as pupils, a quartet of infant prodigies, all at the same time—Joachim, his two sons Joseph and Georg, and young Simon, afterwards Concertmeister at the Hague.

EDITOR.

(2) GEORG (junior), 1830–1852, Austrian violinist, son of Georg senior.

Sonata, pf, v, A flat op. 3 Cranz, 1848.

†HELSTED, GUSTAV CARL, b. 1857, Danish composer.

Trio, pf, v, vc, e mi	op. 6	Hansen,	1888.
Sonata, pf, v, A	,, 13	,,	1910.
,, ,, ,, G	,, 20	,,	1899.

Helsted wrote much chamber music that still remains in MS.

HENDRICHS, C. F.

Sonata, pf, v, g mi Leduc, *c.* 1913.

HENLEY, WILLIAM, b. 1876, English violinist.

1st sonata, pf, v, g mi op. 56 Joseph Williams.

Among his unpublished works are a second violin sonata in D minor, op. 71, and two string quartets in G minor and D minor. William Henley has an amazing record, not only as soloist but as a writer of violin studies, elementary and advanced, particulars of which would fill pages of this book; and he is engaged in the compilation of an Encyclopedia of the violin, in which everything connected with the violin family will be treated, including, of course, chamber music.

The late Mr. Wells Harrison, a writer on chamber music, spoke of the slow movement of the above sonata as a gem of 'deep poetic beauty . . . a work as difficult to assimilate as it is to perform, depending on an understanding of every shade of tonal colouring employed in its structure'.

The Henley Quartet, organized in 1907, consisting of himself, Gertrude Crompton, James Lockyer, and Gertrude Ess, introduced several new works in 1908 during their continental tours.

EDITOR.

†HENNESSY, SWAN, b. 1886, Irish composer.

Suite, str. quartet	op. 46	Eschig.
2nd quartet, str	,, 49	,,
Serenade, str. quartet	,, 65	,,
Variations on theme of six notes, fl, v, vla, vc	,, 58	,,
Trio, 2 cl, fag	,, 54	,,
Petit trio celtique, v, vla, vc	,, 52	,,
Sonata (in Irish style), pf, v, F	,, 14	Schott.
Rapsodie celtique, pf, v,	,, 63	Eschig.
Sonate celtique, pf, vla, E flat	,, 62	,,
Rapsodie gaëlique, pf, vc	,, 50	,,

Hennessy is Irish by birth. He studied music at Stuttgart, and is now settled in France. The influence of Irish folk music and the modes peculiar to it is noticeable in most of his work.

THE SONATA IN IRISH STYLE is easy to play, rather slight in construction, very academic, and with very obvious developments. Without employing actual folk-tunes, the composer is evidently influenced by the style of melody and the intervals peculiar to Irish folk music.

THE SUITE, op. 46, FOR QUARTET is elegant in style, the writing is contrapuntal, not very full, and not always very correct. Successions of fifths and octaves are numerous, and, no doubt, intentional. Certain attempts at modernism are noticeable, and contrast with purely classical passages. The composer is especially happy in the treatment of his native folk-tunes, with simple harmonies and numerous pedals.

THE STRING QUARTET, op. 49, is a mixture of classical and modern styles. The counterpoint is fairly flexible; with regard to form, simplicity is carried to excess. The finale shows ingenuity; it is in the form of variations on a popular air.

THE PETIT TRIO CELTIQUE is classical in style,

and the counterpoint very strict. The work consists of little movements in which the instruments converse pleasantly, but the form has nothing of the traditional about it. The finale is treated in canon, in flowing style.

Ex. 1.

The variations, op. 58, are very ingenious, and skilfully worked out.

THE SONATE CELTIQUE, op. 62, is rather a fantasy than a sonata. The construction is simple but elegant, and there are no complexities. The plan is as follows:—First movement: Principal subject A in C minor, expressive theme B in E flat, and a little subsidiary theme C in F. Allegro molto, 6/8, in E flat major. It is the popular air, *St. Patrick's Day in the Morning*, with a charming counterpoint. Return of A in C minor, in the bass, with C above. Then B in C major and coda in C minor with a suggestion of C and four blatant bars of A. The second movement is merely a simple folk-song. The finale is composed of two alternating themes, one (Celtic) syncopated, in 2/4, the other in 6/8.

Ex. 2.

Ex. 3.

Ex. 4.

H. WOOLLETT.

[It is difficult in a few words to assess Hennessy's talents as a composer, which have received more recognition on the Continent than in the land of his birth. He is an excellent musician, who, without writing down to his audiences, yet provides them with decidedly popular, melodious music, in which the Irish idiom is plainly heard—a rare and very useful gift. EDITOR.]

†HENRIQUES, FINI VALDEMAR, b. 1867, Danish violinist, pupil of Joachim.

Sonata, pf, v, g mi op. 10 Hansen, 1893.

He also wrote a violin suite (MS.).

†HENSCHEL, SIR GEORGE (ISIDOR GEORG), b. 1850, Polish-German (naturalized English) singer, conductor, composer, and author.

Quartet, str, E flat op. 55 Schlesinger, 1897.

The above is the essay of a prominent vocalist and musician in a difficult form of composition, made in his younger days. A grave opening in E flat minor introduces a movement which reveals solid qualities and good part-writing. The air varié which follows includes an unusual but effective variation for all the instruments, played pizzicato. The scherzo is full of youthful vigour, but the finale (andante con moto) leaves one in doubt whether it is wise, from the public performer's point of view, to conclude a work of this kind with a slow movement. It is, however, pleasant to play, and shows no tendency to drag.

A concert consisting entirely of Henschel's compositions has been given at South Place. EDITOR.

HENSEL, FANNY CÄCILIA (*née* Mendelssohn), 1805–1847.

Trio, pf, v, vc, D op. 11 (posth.) B. & H., 1850.

Mendelssohn's elder sister, an excellent pianist and fine musician.

HENSELT, ADOLF VON, 1814–1889, famous Bavarian pianist.

Trio, pf, v, vc, a mi op. 24 J. Schuberth & Co., 1851.
Duet, pf, vc (or v, or horn), b mi ,, 14 Cranz, 1842.

Henselt's not very numerous compositions are mostly for piano solo. *Grove* describes the trio as 'stillborn'!

HEPWORTH, WILLIAM, 1846–1916, organist and composer.

Quartet, str, D op. 10 Klemm, 1882.

Hepworth's father (b. 1825) was an Englishman, but went to Germany in 1841, and remained there. His son was born and educated in Germany.

HERBECK, JOHANN VON, 1831–1877, Austrian composer and conductor.

Second quartet, str, F op. 9 Haslinger, 1864.

Herbeck has distinguished himself as propagandist for the works of Schubert. His quartet, which is fairly easy to play, is remarkably melodious, and shows, in the finale, a partiality for gipsy music.

HÉRITTE-VIARDOT, LOUISE (*née* Viardot), 1841–1918, French teacher of singing.

Quartet (*Im Sommer*), pf, v, vla, vc, A op. 9 B. & H., 1883.
Quartet (*Spanisches*), pf, v, vla, vc ,, 11 Peters, 1883.
Sonata, pf, vc, d mi ,, 40 Hofmeister, 1909.

This composer's mother, a celebrated singer, was sister of Malibran. They were of Spanish descent, Madame Viardot being the daughter of Manuel Garcia.

†HERMANN, E. HANS G., b. 1870, German double-bass player.

Quartet, str, g mi op. 47 Simrock, 1900.
Suite in sonata form, pf, v, F ,, 8 Heinrichshofen, 1897.

Hermann makes use of the letters in the name of his friend and patron, Professor Reinhold Begas (BEGAS-es), as a theme in the first and third movement of his quartet, op. 47. W. Altmann (*Handbuch*) speaks of this work as of minor importance but attractive.

HERMANN, FRIEDRICH, 1828–1907, German violinist.

Besides some not very important chamber works (*v. Altmann*), Hermann published sets of movements to assist in the practice of chamber music for wind instrument players.

HERMANN, ROBERT, 1869–1912, Swiss composer.

Quartet, pf, v, vla, vc, f mi op. 9 Hofmeister, 1901.
Trio, pf, v, vc, d mi ,, 6 ,, 1895.
Sonata, pf, v, c sharp mi ,, 13 ,, 1905.

Hermann started as a medical student, and except for a short time under Humperdinck was self-taught. His compositions show remarkable independence, according to *Riemann*.

HÉROLD, LOUIS JOSEPH FERDINAND, 1791–1833, opera-composer.

Three unpublished quartets, written in 1814, are in the library of the Conservatoire de Musique, Paris. They were sent by Hérold from Rome, while he was staying there after winning the Prix de Rome.

Grove says, 'These quartets contain much

that might even now be heard with pleasure ... and show that Hérold might have shone in this branch of composition'.

† HERRMANN, Eduard, contemporary German composer.

Sextet, ob, cl, 2 v, vla, vc, g mi	op. 33	Raabe & Plothow, 1916.
Quintet, 2 v, vla, 2 vc, G	,, 31	,, ,, 1912.
1st quartet, str, F	,, 32	,, 1918–19.
2nd ,, ,, C	,, 36	,, ,,
Serenade, 3 v, vla (or vc)	,, 14	Augener-Schott, 1895.

Herrmann, who is now advanced in years, is a violin teacher in New York.

HERSCHEL, (1) Sir William, 1738–1822, famous astronomer, originally a professional musician.

It is recorded that he wrote two considerable chamber works, which were published at London in 1768. In 1792 he was visited by Haydn at Slough.

His brother (2) Jacobus (*c.* 1734–1792) was also a composer of string quartets and trios, published by Hummel (Amsterdam) and Bremner (London).

HERZOGENBERG, Heinrich, Baron von, 1843–1900, Austrian composer.

Quintet, 2 v, 2 vla, vc, c mi	op. 77	Peters.
Quartet, str, d mi	,, 18	Siegel.
Three quartets, str, g mi, d mi, G	,, 42	Peters.
Quartet, str, f mi	,, 63	,,
Two trios, v, vla, vc, A, F	,, 27	,,
Quintet, pf, 2 v, vla, vc, C	,, 17	B. & H.
Quintet, pf, ob, cl, horn, fag, E flat	,, 43	Peters.
Two quartets, pf, v, vla, vc, e mi, B flat	opp. 75, 95	,,
Two trios, pf, v, vc, c mi, d mi	,, 24, 36	,,
Trio, pf, ob (or v), horn (vla, or vc), D	op. 61	,,
Phantasie, pf, v, B flat	,, 14	Siegel.
Three sonatas, pf, v, A, E flat, d mi	opp. 32, 54, 78	Peters.
Duet, pf, vc, d mi	op. 12	Siegel.
Three sonatas, pf, vc, a mi, D, E flat	opp. 52, 64, 94	Peters.

Herzogenberg was a pupil of the Vienna Conservatorium; he eventually settled in Berlin, where he did excellent work as professor of composition at the Hochschule and at the Academy of Arts. A composer of great refinement, he unfortunately gained the reputation of a dry contrapuntist, which was far from being deserved. He was, in his way, an original thinker, and a musician whose genuine emotional and poetic qualities should endear him particularly to all Brahms lovers, once they become acquainted with his work. His chamber compositions in particular stand out among his hundred or more published works, for they are not only masterly from the technical point of view, but interesting on the intellectual side. The present writer has had occasion to write about them three times: in an essay for the publication *Die Musik*; in a pamphlet entitled *Heinrich v. Herzogenberg, sein Leben und sein Schaffen* (1903, an amplification of the essay); and in a longer article written for the periodical *Der Musiksalon* in 1909. Only a few works will be discussed here, namely those in which the composer, originally a disciple of Wagner and Schumann, shows himself an adherent of the classical school.

The String Quintet is distinguished by breadth of conception, serenity, and skilful utilization of the tone colour of the instruments. The first movement is an impetuous piece of character painting, the second a folk-song theme with delicately wrought variations, and the scherzo a ghostly whispering, with a middle section in C major of reassuring daylight. The broad, march-like melody—also in folk-song character—of the finale is thrown into relief by a slow, passionate introduction, which reappears in the course of the movement.

The quintet for piano and wind has clever tonal effects, and displays a fine quality of humour. The adagio has an ethereal beauty of its own.

The string quartet in G, the third of the group dedicated to Brahms, is a concise and transparently clear piece of writing, distinguished by a full and spontaneous flow of invention and a certain appealing, unassuming simplicity.

The string trios. The first of these, in A major, is marked by freshness and originality. The second, in F major, has some effective passage writing, and not a few harmonic peculiarities.

The trio for piano, oboe, and horn, with its suggestion of sunny Arcadian fields, is a charming idyll.

The piano trio, op. 36, is innocent of all artificiality; it is unaffectedly natural, both in inspiration and in character.

The Violin Sonata, op. 54, deserves rather more than a passing glance. The opening theme of the first allegro makes an instant appeal to the ear, while the bridge passage leading to the second subject has a charm worthy of Bach himself; on the other hand, the development errs on the side of over-elaboration; but the little coda that follows the recapitulation is quite delightful. The scherzo is quite Spanish in character, and begins with a seductive serenade, a guitar effect being achieved, in the usual way, by the pizzicato of the violin. This is interrupted by a solemn and stately melody assigned to the violin; the serenade then recurs, gives place once more to a broad flow of melody, and finally returns to end the movement with much charm and ingenuity. The adagio begins with an impressive, richly inspired melody; a change of mood comes with the quicker middle section, which is of an agitated and passionate character. The movement closes with an embellished version of the original melody, around which accompanying arabesques are woven with charming effect. The finale is cheerful throughout; in its general plan it might well stand for a work taken from the end of Beethoven's first period.

WILHELM ALTMANN.

[The sonata for piano and violin in A, dedicated to his friend Joachim, was introduced by him at the 'Pops'. It fully confirms Dr. Altmann's judgement. So far from being 'dry', it has an opening movement which is fresh as a spring morning, and a finale best to be described as rollicking. The adagio, however, is a little laboured. His string quartet in G, op. 42, in which the influence of Brahms is strongly felt, was also played at the 'Pops'.

Von Herzogenberg was friend and fervent admirer of Brahms, who, strange to say, showed but little appreciation of his merits as a composer. EDITOR.]

*†HESELTINE, PHILIP (Peter Warlock), b. 1894, English composer.

The Curlew (song cycle), tenor voice, fl, cor angl, str. quartet (Carnegie Award, 1923)	S. & B.
Sorrow's Lullaby, sopr. and barit. voices, str. quartet	O.U.P.

Heseltine has also written *An Old Song*, for chamber orchestra, (Chester) and *Corpus Christi Carol* arranged for chamber orchestra (Curwen).

The Curlew is an original impressive work, for an unusual combination, which has been performed with much success.

In making the award the Carnegie Trustees wrote: 'A most imaginative setting of Mr. Yeats's poems, of which, indeed, it may be regarded as the musical counterpart. It is pervaded by a keen feeling for harmonic colour, which is here used to most appropriate effect.'

HESSE, ALEXANDER FRIEDRICH, Landgrave of. *v.* ALEXANDER FRIEDRICH.

HEUBNER, KONRAD, 1860–1905, German composer.

Quartet, str, a mi	op. 1	Peters, 1883.
,, ,, e mi	—	Kahnt, 1903.
Quintet, pf, 2 v, vla, vc, g mi	—	Siegel, 1904.
Trio, pf, v, vc, D	,, 9	,, 1895.
Sonata, pf, v, G	,, 8	,, 1895.

At the time of his death, Heubner occupied the post of director of the Conservatorium at Coblenz.

The quality of good-heartedness, which was among his personal characteristics, shines through his chamber compositions.

Taking the violin sonata as a typical example, there is a significance in its very dedication, 'to the memory of his dear Robert Heckmann'.

The opening allegro is persuasive in mood, and throughout its course, which runs on accepted lines, breathes a definitely lyrical quality. An andante con variazioni follows, conspicuous by its well-pointed and dexterous allusions to the original theme. In such an otherwise well-turned-out work, especially rich in thematic material, the only flaw consists in a slight falling-off in interest in the final rondo. This promises well at the outset, but becomes a trifle burdensome when the material eventually begins to sag. This is the only reservation to be made regarding an otherwise capable work, which has the additional merit of being enjoyably written for both instruments. ADOLPH MANN.

†HILL, ALFRED, b. 1869, Australian composer.

1st quartet (*Maori*), str, B flat		B. & H., 1913.
2nd quartet (*Maori*), str		,, ,,
Schottische sonata, pf, v, f mi	op. 6	Wild (Leipzig), 1892.
Sonatina, pf, v	,, 5	,, ,, ,,

Interesting examples of Antipodean chamber music by a professor at the State Conservatorium at Sydney.

†HILL, EDWARD BURLINGAME, b. 1872, American composer and writer on music.

Sonata, pf, cl (or v), A	op. 32	S.P.A.M., 1927.

A melodious work written in a placid and reserved style.

HILL, HENRY, 1808–1856, violist of outstanding ability, specializing in the performance of chamber music. Was associated with the founders of the Beethoven Quartet Society. Played the solo viola part in Berlioz's *Harold in Italy* when first performed in London, 1848.

EDITOR.

HILL, WILHELM, 1838–1902, German pianist.

Posthumous publication:

Quartet, str, D (Karl Schmidt) B. & H., 1915.

Altmann gives a list of original publications, including two trios and a piano quartet.

HILLEMACHER, PAUL, b. 1852, French composer.

Suite dans le style ancien, pf, vc.

'P. L. Hillemacher' is the pen-name of Paul and Lucien (1860–1909) Hillemacher, who wrote their works in collaboration. The above work, however, appears to be by Paul alone.

Grove says 'The Hillemachers are among the most distinguished of modern French composers, but the complete development of their originality has been somewhat retarded by the undue influence upon them of Wagner's music'.

HILLER, Ferdinand von, 1811–1885, German composer.

Two quartets, str, G, b mi	opp. 12, 13	Hofmeister.
Quartet, str, D	op. 105	Kistner.
and two other quartets.		
Capriccio fugato, 4 v, C	,, 203	Hofmeister.
Quintet, pf, 2 v, vla, vc, G	,, 156	Siegel.
Quartet, pf, v, vla, vc, b mi	,, 1	Lemoine.
Quartet, pf, v, vla, vc, f mi	,, 3	Simrock.
Quartet, pf, v, vla, vc, a mi	,, 133	Kistner.
and two other piano quartets.		
Three trios, pf, v, vc, B flat, f sharp mi, E	opp. 6, 7, 8	Simrock.
4th (serenade), pf, v, vc, a mi	op. 64	Kistner.
5th trio, pf, v, vc, E	,, 74	,,
6th (serenade), pf, v, vc, c mi	,, 186	,,
Duo concertant, pf, v	,, 2	Lemoine.
Duo appassionato, pf, v, C	,, 58	Schott.
Suite in canon-form, pf, v	,, 86	B. & H.
Sonata, pf, vc	,, 22	Simrock.
Serenade, pf, vc, E	,, 109	Cranz.
Serenade, pf, vc, d mi	,, 140	Kistner.
Serenade, pf, vc, a mi	,, 172	Cranz.

Hiller was an all-round musician of the highest rank, and an extremely versatile composer. His most valuable work was, perhaps, in chamber music, which offered rich possibilities to his bright nature, his love of form, and his uncommon gift of easy invention.

His very first composition was the piano quartet, op. 1. It is a 'Sturm und Drang' product, which in plan, development of ideas, and treatment of the instruments still shows the pupil's unskilled hand and plainly exhibits his teacher's influence; but there are signs that the young composer will later have something better to say.

In his second string quartet, op. 3, Hiller's skill has increased, and his growing technical ability admits of greater economy of ideas and more effective development.

The Quintet, op. 156, is a rather difficult work, being written somewhat in concerto style. The first movement, allegro con anima, is particularly interesting by its harmonic colouring, its bold modulations, and the equal prominence given to all the instruments. The adagio also has plenty of variety, and great attention is paid to careful shading both in rhythm and harmony; the piano is here given greater prominence, and is treated in virtuoso style. The third movement, an intermezzo, is less vivid in colour, a staccato motif being kept up too long, and there is only one brief interruption by a contrasting cantabile theme. There is much brilliance in the finale, which assures the fine effect of the whole work.

Violin Sonata in D. The great concerto sonata for piano and violin, op. 122, is also very effective. It is rather long, and makes considerable demands on the technical ability of the performers. The first movement, allegro energico, has probably the highest artistic value, and contains many passages of harmonic interest. There are original passages in the finale, which sparkles with wit and humour, but, like most of Hiller's works, it aims only at outward effect.

The Serenade, op. 109, which consists of five movements, is also very lengthy. The first two movements, an allegro quasi andante and a minuet, which are linked together, do not impress very favourably. The third movement, a capriccietto, contains more interesting ideas, and reflects much of the composer's cheerful spirit. In the theme with variations he becomes more emotional, returning in the finale to the more brilliant style.

In conclusion, praise is due to the trio in F sharp minor, the two quartets, opp. 12, 13, and the 'cello sonata, but it must be admitted that his work, on the whole, lacks originality and depth. Rudolf Felber.

[A full list of Hiller's works is given here as tribute to the memory of an admirable musician who was intimately associated with all the distinguished artists of his day, but they are now little played. Schumann, always kind, had a good word for his three trios (*Gesammelte Schriften*): 'The first', he wrote, 'seems to me to have been written in a happy mood, and with great pleasure and freshness, so much so that we can regard the oddity and unripeness that has crept in amid the haste of composition with exceptional indulgence . . . both the others seem more insipid and forced, as if he had determined to write three trios.'

Hiller, who was a fine pianist, gave chamber concerts with Baillot and others. Max Bruch was one of his pupils. Editor.]

HILLER (or HÜLLER), Friedrich Adam, 1768–1812, German composer.

A very famous musician in his day, but his instrumental works are of little account. He wrote six string quartets, published by Spehr of Brunswick.

HILLMANN, Karl.

Sonata (*pathétique*), pf, v, g mi	op. 59	André, 1915.

HILSE, B.

Suite, harp (or pf), fl, e mi	op. 6	Zimmermann, 1911.

HIMMEL, Friedrich Heinrich, 1765–1814, German composer.

Three sonatas, pf, v, vc, C, G, A flat	op. 16	B. & H.
Six sonatas, pf, v, vc (in 2 sets) { C, f mi, D / E flat, B flat, D }	—	,,

Fétis includes a sextet for pf, 2 vla, vc, 2 horns, op. 19 (Erard & Pleyel)—a curiosity from the absence of violins.

Fétis criticizes Himmel thus: 'He has had considerable success in northern Germany owing to his pleasant vein of melody. . . . But he lacks breadth and elevation, his harmony is generally feeble, and finally he lacks variety. Thus his work is forgotten.'

The above works are still obtainable from B. & H.

† HINDEMITH, Paul, b. 1895, German violist and composer.

Six poems (*Die junge Magd*), contralto voice, fl, cl, str. quartet	op. 23, no. 2	Schott.
Kleine Kammermusik, fl, ob, cl, horn, fag	,, 24, no. 2	,,
1st quartet, str, f mi	,, 10	,,
2nd quartet, str, C	,, 16	,,
3rd quartet, str, atonal	,, 22	,,
4th quartet, str, atonal	,, 32	,,
Die Serenaden, a cantata on Romantic texts, sopr. voice, ob, vla, vc	,, 35	,,
Trio, v, vla, vc	,, 34	,,
Sonatina in canon-form, 2 fl	,, 31, no. 3	,,
Two sonatas, pf, v, E flat, D	,, 11, nos. 1, 2	,,
Sonata, pf, vla, F	,, 11, no. 4	,,
Sonata, pf, vc, a mi	,, 11 ,, 3	,,

Also a MS. quintet, cl, str, op. 30 (performed at Salzburg). There are concertos with chamber orchestra for piano, violin, viola, 'cello, and four sets of instructive pieces for ensemble players: (1) 9 pieces in first position, 2 v, (2) 8 canons in first position for elementary pupils, 2 v with accompaniment of 3rd v, or vla, (3) 8 pieces in first position for more advanced pupils, 2 v, vla, vc. The fourth set is for orchestra. These are published by Schott (op. 44) and serve as an introduction to modern methods of composition.

Hindemith entered Hoch's Conservatorium at Frankfort, and studied composition under Arnold Mendelssohn and Bernhard Sekles. To the former may be ascribed his solid grounding in all the constituents of technique, to the latter the fostering of a congenital inclination to the quest of musical adventure along new paths. His own most characteristic contribution to his musical equipment is a sense of humour more buoyant than is common among his countrymen. From 1915 to 1923 he first led and then conducted the Frankfort opera. He plays the viola in the Amar Quartet, sometimes known as the Amar-Hindemith, and devotes the rest of his time to composition. A stroke of luck enabled him to purchase the Kuhhirtenturm, an old tower on the Sachsenhäuser Ufer at Frankfort, where he resides when not touring with the Quartet. The foundation of his fame was laid at Donaueschingen in 1921, and his compositions have become an annual feature of the festival held there. His communicated opus-list bears a note to the effect that the composer gives no information concerning unpublished works. New manuscripts do not leave his possession; old ones do not call for performance. This may be taken to imply that those of his early works which still remain unpublished are definitely shelved, but of his present work little is likely to remain in manuscript, now that he is recognized as one of the outstanding figures in modern German music. It is safe to assume at least that the two sonatas for piano with viola and viola d'amore respectively (op. 25), and the clarinet quintet (op. 30), will duly appear in print.

Hindemith is a many-sided musician. He began professional life as a violinist, and is one of the best viola players in Germany. He is a good pianist, and is competent to play the clarinet part—no mean feat—in his own quintet. Latterly it has even been rumoured that he has acquired proficiency on the saxophone. In his early days he claims to have 'done' everything from opera to cinema and jazz. Those who know him personally go farther, and assert that he has brought to each sphere the same resilient spirit, extracting from each whatever exhilaration his ingenuity could devise. He is, for instance, a master of parody, but his efforts in this direction are reserved for the private delectation of his friends.

This variegated experience has naturally intensified the facility in performance which he acquired in early youth, and his intimate knowledge of instrumental possibilities constantly reacts upon his mode of composition until he almost appears a throw-back to those days when player and composer were one. Whatever the instrument for which he is writing, his identity becomes, for the time being, merged in it. As Paul Becker has said of him: 'Er komponiert überhaupt nicht, er musiziert'. This is not an unmixed blessing to a composer, for, if on the one side the merging of means and expression eliminates the need of consciously reconciling them, on the other it creates an unconscious trend to instrumental formulas of the type which may be heard in any orchestra before the conductor steps onto the platform. Germany abounds in composers to whom these preludial *clichés* represent thematic material. They constitute what is commonly termed 'Musikantentum'. But Hindemith's ingenuity and his fondness for giving it free play have preserved him from this pitfall. He uses nothing that is threadbare. He is constantly inventive. His invention sometimes, however, takes a form which indicates the player rather than the composer as the originator.

His earliest published work (op. 8) consists of three pieces for 'cello and piano—capriccio, Phantasiestück, and scherzo—well conceived but not particularly significant, testifying as they do to his successful studies and his admiration of certain masters rather than to originality of outlook. But the quartet in F minor (op. 10), which followed, represents him as well on the road to maturity and independence, albeit he has not yet burned his boats. As he has numbered his quartets from this one, we may take it that an earlier work (op. 2) is definitely discarded. The F minor quartet is in three movements, of which the first is an allegro in sonata form with two well contrasted subjects. In lieu of development there is a short fugato with an effective, if somewhat conventional, crescendo leading to the recapitulation. The second section is the most characteristic of the three. It consists of a theme and five free variations, one of which takes the form of a slow march as heard in the distance. The third movement, which combines the functions of scherzo and finale, is comparatively diffuse, not so much in a formal sense as in proportion to the importance of its material, but it is effectively written and proceeds with so much spirit that the interest is nevertheless sustained, and one readily condones a post-romantic divagation. For a hundred bars (220 to 320) the 'cello is tuned down to B flat. The recapitulation is again approached by a fugato over a pedal note repeated for thirty-three bars. The work abounds in points of executive interest, and although it may not be considered representative of Hindemith to-day, it remains one of the most satisfactory of his numerous chamber works.

At this point it is expedient to leave his quartets and turn to his sonatas, of which there are, published and unpublished, no fewer than fourteen, including one for piano solo. The others are:

with piano: 2 v, 2 vla, 1 viola d'amour, 1 vc.
unaccompanied: 3 v, 2 vla, 1 vc, 1 two fl.

The unaccompanied sonatas are not well known, and scarcely suitable for concert performance. They were designed for the enjoyment of the player in intimate surroundings. Of the sonatas with piano, only those belonging to op. 11 are published. These are two for violin, one for viola, and one for 'cello. All four are in definite tonalities, but Hindemith frequently dispenses with a key-signature.

The First Violin Sonata, in E flat, is a short work in two movements, one quick, the other a slow and stately dance of a somewhat exotic character involving chromatic harmony. Otherwise the composer shows already here the disposition to rebel against the harmonic despotism of the later romantic movement, and to rely more upon melodic development.

The Second Violin Sonata, in D, is more extended. It has three sections, the third being a rapid dance-movement combining the functions of scherzo and finale. The most personal movement is the first. Afterwards there is a distinct throw-back to Brahmsian influences. But the opening theme of the sonata

Ex. 1.

foreshadows the composer's later linear development, and even suggests the atonality to follow. As a whole, the sonata is unequal and lacks uniformity of style and outlook, but nevertheless represents a higher level of achievement than was attained in its predecessor.

The 'Cello Sonata in A minor followed next, and is a striking and important work, representing a marked progress along the lines which the composer has marked out for himself. It is in four real movements, which are, however, linked to make two sections. The latter half of the first section will repay examination from this point of view, for it contains many relatively simple but characteristic examples of the use of the twelve-note scale for thematic progress without allegiance to a harmonic background. The effect is often uncompromisingly harsh, but, at this early stage of the road which leads to linear atonal polyphony, it is comparatively easy to feel the underlying logic of the writing. The second section comprises slow movement and finale, the former with a central march-like theme whose diatonic character gives it a startling effectiveness in its environment. The finale is dominated by the interval of the augmented fourth, which has been heralded in the slow movement. It is, in fact, a not infrequent device of Hindemith's to impart a special character to a movement by insistent use of a selected interval.

The Viola Sonata is a work of different character, consisting of a fantasie followed by a theme with seven variations, which are divided so as to give the sonata three movements. Despite constant restless and subversive modulations, the feeling is distinctly tonal, and the progressions occasionally suggest modal influences. The variations begin in G flat and end in the relative minor, but only after an eventful tonal journey which embraces one variation, the fourth, with the signature of two sharps against F and G (instead of F and C). This however is not so alarming as it looks, being simply a convenient notation of that portion of the tonal scale which is comprised by the tritone D—G sharp. Elsewhere, also, for instance in the second variation, there is a tendency to coquet with the tonal scale. The theme itself is simple, like a folk-song, but its innocence of chromatics does not even outlast its first statement. Of less exciting interest than the 'cello sonata, this work does more to ingratiate the listener.

The next work is the first to reconcile within itself in some measure the conflicting tendencies displayed in its predecessors.

THE SECOND STRING QUARTET was played in 1922 at Salzburg at the preliminary meeting which led to the creation of the International Society for Contemporary Music, and was afterwards the first of Hindemith's works to be heard in England, at a concert of the Contemporary Music Centre. It is in three movements: an energetic allegro, a lento, and a vertiginous vivace. Except that it still avoids the direct issue of atonality, it might be regarded as the inaugural work of the composer's later manner. But his allegiance to tonality is now precarious, as may be seen from the opening subject of the first movement—

Ex. 2.

which also indicates the remarkable vigour of the conception. It is this quality which makes the complexity of the work palatable to the listener, who is irresistibly carried along past happenings which, without such energetic persuasiveness, might prove disconcerting. There is a certain remote kinship between the idiom of the slow movement and that of the variations in the first quartet. Both tend to show that *Tristan* is not yet forgotten. But this does not prevent the thematic line, especially in the middle section, from proceeding with a freedom equal to that of the first movement. The finale is comparatively less chromatic, except in its modulations and its use of the tonal scale. The second subject is in fact so diatonic that on its first appearance there are six lines of score without a single accidental, a rare phenomenon in Hindemith's music. The movement wears, in fact, a plausible garb of simplicity, which contributes greatly to its magnetic effect. Towards the end there is an unusual type of cadenza, in which the second violin holds A on one string, and reiterates ad lib. a rapid three-note figure on another, regardless of the fluctuations of tempo affecting the dialogue of the other instruments. The main weakness of this otherwise brilliant composition is one it shares with so many modern German works; the four instruments are constantly employed, with the result that there is a certain uniformity of tone-power which would benefit considerably by a more liberal distribution of rests.

THE THIRD STRING QUARTET suggests that Hindemith himself realized this, for here the defect largely disappears, and the result is a marked increase in clarity. This quartet made its appearance soon after the second, and was performed for the first time at Donaueschingen, November 4, 1922. It is in five movements:

I. A fugato (atonal) of which this is the main theme:

Ex. 3.

Ex. 4.
Rondo. Gemächlich und mit Grazie.

This movement, which contains hints of polytonality, leads without interruption to:

II. A singularly dynamic scherzo with an irregular rhythm, opening (5/8, 3/4, 3/8 &c.), much emphasized (*am Frosch*). It has a more flowing middle section.

III. A slow movement proceeding evenly (6/4) in sharp contrast to the preceding section.

IV. A short prefatory movement of a type suggesting a toccata or prelude, leading to:

V. A rondo which opens polyphonically (see Ex. 4) but subsequently assumes a more homophonous character except towards the end, where the above is briefly resumed.

A perusal of the score shows a still more marked tendency towards horizontal independence, whether in one or several melodic lines. There are apparent contradictions in method, suggesting that even at this stage the composer was undecided what to retain and what to discard, but a strong desire for clarity seems to be exerting itself. The idiom itself may have its difficulties for the listener, but the latter is given every opportunity of hearing it unencumbered with accretions.

Next follows op. 23, consisting of two song-cycles, of which the first, *Des Todes Tod* (Eduard Reinacher), is for soprano with two violas and two 'cellos. Of this only one song, for voice and viola, has been published, as a supplement to *Melos*. The second cycle, *Die junge Magd* (Georg Trakl), consists of six songs for contralto with flute, clarinet, and string quartet. The work is a characteristic example of melodic declamation. The first and last songs have a harmonic background, but in the others the parts maintain the independence that has latterly become frequent in compositions of this kind.

Op. 24 comprises two works with the title *Kammermusik*, the first of which employs a chamber orchestra numbering eleven players, and is therefore beyond the scope of this Cyclopedia. The second, *Kleine Kammermusik*, is a wind quintet (flute, oboe, clarinet, horn, and bassoon) in four movements: Lustig, Walzer, Ruhig und Einfach, Schnell. It is an interesting work, full of ironic humour, with an occasional suggestion even of parody. The quotation, from the first movement, may serve to illustrate the composer's handling of the tone-colours (Ex. 5).

Hindemith's next chamber work was a quintet for clarinet and strings, op. 30, which was performed at the 1923 festival of the International Society for Contemporary Music at Salzburg, but has not yet been published. This was followed by two sonatas for violin alone and a *Kanonische Sonatine* for two flutes, which are grouped together as op. 31.

THE FOURTH STRING QUARTET, op. 32, followed. It is here and in the string trio, op. 34, that one sees the outcome of the irresolution apparent in some of Hindemith's earlier works. He seems definitely to have decided upon the relative merits of different modes of expression, and some have been uncompromisingly discarded. There is, for instance, no turgid weaving of parts. So far as the idiom itself permits, with its independence of movement, all is clearly exhibited, without subterfuge, without horizontal or vertical redundance. Hitherto the listener was given a composite impression, in which he might be responsive to one feature and not to another. Henceforth, to use a colloquialism, it becomes a case of 'take it or leave it'—of appreciating the blend of qualities that constitutes Hindemith's musical physiognomy, or of breaking off the acquaintance, for these two works show the man as he intends to be seen. Naturally, whatever their executive difficulties may be, they are much less complex in thought and statement, for his whole progress has been a process of winnowing. Also they are almost consistently contrapuntal, for that, too, has been a constant preoccupation with him, the only diversion being caused by the search for the right method. The result is, in a certain qualified sense, a step backwards, at least for those who associate modern music with esoteric mysteries.

Ex. 5.

The quartet is in four movements: allegro, lento, a *little march*, and an extended passacaglia. Both the principal subjects of the allegro make their entrance fugally, the second consisting itself of the two subjects of a double fugue. Later, all three are combined as in the passage in Ex. 6, which leads to some interesting contrapuntal weaving. The opening of the slow movement has the middle parts in canon at the interval of the major seventh. The *little march* offers a welcome but incomplete respite from this polyphonic spate, which is, of course, fully resumed in the passacaglia.

Ex. 6.

This concludes with a fugal stretto, played prestissimo.

THE STRING TRIO, op. 34, as already indicated, belongs to the same order of ideas, but now that Hindemith has found his own particular solution to the problems of composition, he seems to give more freedom to his natural exuberance, especially in the opening movement, a brilliant toccata which, after a few introductory bars in which the theme is stated in octaves, proceeds thus:

Ex. 7.

There follow a pensive, flowing, slow movement, an exhilarating pizzicato movement, and a fugue of extraordinary complexity and ingenuity, with inversions, rhythmic transformations, and devices which trick the listener into forgetting that it is only in three parts. There occurs in it a quiet episode (sehr ruhige Achtel) which presents some difficulties of ensemble. At one point of it the viola and 'cello are barred differently, whilst the violin is told to go straight ahead (vorangehen). And after all the contrapuntal turmoil the trio ends peacefully with a very original cadence which emits a quiet charm if one is not disconcerted by its strangeness.

Ex. 8.

Hindemith's last published chamber work is *Die Serenaden*, op. 35, described as a small cantata on romantic texts for soprano, viola, and 'cello; unless one includes the two new compositions described as *Kammermusik*, nos. 2 and 3, op. 36 (the *Kleine Kammermusik*, op. 24, no. 2, is evidently not included in this numbering of the larger works). These are in reality concertos, respectively for piano with twelve solo instruments, and for 'cello with ten, so that they lie beyond the definition of chamber music adopted by the Editor of this Cyclopedia.

This ends the survey of the present output of a composer whose fertility is startling in proportion to his thirty odd years, especially considering that, first his connexion with the Frankfort opera, and subsequently the constant engagements of the Amar Quartet, have occupied most of his time. It is even said that many of his later works have actually been partly composed on his numerous railway journeys. This sketch would not be complete without a reference to compositions not intended for publication, such as the *Militär-Musik*, for string quartet, of which no score exists, since it was written direct into the parts. It was inspired by the well-intentioned performances of the military band outside the little Kurhaus at Donaueschingen. There are six numbers, burlesques of familiar musical phenomena, such as *Abendempfindung* with an effect of trumpets in the distance, the usual piccolo solo imitating a song-bird, the *Poet and Peasant* overture, the inevitable Viennese waltz, and a *Parade-March* in which every now and then somebody misses a step which is, however, retrieved before any mischief is done. These exploits may not be of great musical value or importance, but they somehow help to explain a personality of a type which has not abounded in German music, and which is, with all the reservations individual taste may desire to make in regard to the musical idiom of his choice, singularly attractive.

EDWIN EVANS.

†HINTON, ARTHUR, b. 1869, English composer.

Quintet, pf, 2 v, vla, vc, g mi	op. 30	Elkin.
Trio, pf, v, vc, d mi	,, 21	Rahter, 1905.
Sonata, pf, v, B flat		B. & H., *c.* 1910.
Suite, pf, v, D	,, 20	Novello, 1903.

Studied at the R.A.M., and afterwards at Munich under Rheinberger.

The first of Hinton's chamber works is the violin sonata in B flat. It is hardly surprising, in such an early work, written at the end of his student days, that the composer is under some outside influence, more particularly that of Brahms, but perhaps this is hardly so evident as the opening bars and certain rhythmical features of the first and last movements lead one to expect. The first movement is on classical lines, and the finale, while showing more freedom of design, is also in sonata form. In the slow movement, however, there is some breaking away from tradition. The structure, while perfectly clear and well balanced, is unusual, an entirely new section (più mosso) appearing after a concisely developed treatment of the two principal themes. This new matter introduces an atmosphere of strenuousness—what one might almost call a fighting element—into surroundings of gloom which are only relieved by the peaceful second theme, seemingly significant of resignation to the inevitable. The whole movement seems to have been written under the stress of some definite emotion.

THE SUITE IN D MAJOR is in a much lighter vein than the sonata, but the interest is nevertheless equally divided. It is in four movements, the scherzo preceding the slow movement. The opening allegro begins with a brilliant violinistic theme, which lends itself equally well to pianistic treatment. A contrasted subject in F major (lusinghevole) containing a charming canonic effect, and the reappearance of the first subject with an amplified piano part completes the material, which is developed with much variety. The scherzo is of great delicacy. The main theme is followed by a well contrasted moderato section in a more contemplative mood, a reminiscence of which appears in the recitativo opening of the slow movement. This part of the suite is full of melodic interest. The finale opens with a bright and lively subject, which lends itself to some very effective treatment; after being carried out at some length, it rushes into an appassionato which is a transformation of the second subject of the first movement, portraying, as it were, the same character in an entirely new guise; some reference to the middle section of the scherzo is also noticeable. This bringing together of the themes in the various movements gives a sense of unity to the whole, which concludes very effectively in that gay vein which predominates throughout the work.

THE TRIO IN D MINOR has the usual four movements. Without going into a detailed analysis of each, it may be said that the opening allegro appassionato is of a strenuous and impassioned character, with some strong and impelling rhythms: while the contrapuntal treatment is very free, the combinations being such as to give a roundness of contour and a fullness of intermelodic weaving which result in the obtaining of many rich and broad effects in the instrumentation. Particularly effective is the double-stopping passage for strings alone in the middle section, the calm of which greatly relieves the effect of the impetuosity of the context. The scherzo, with its 2/4 rhythm in the strings against the 3/4 of the theme in the piano, is a movement of marked originality. The adagio has a deeply felt and expressive subject, while the piano part is here very free and elaborate; it is marked by some points of climax which are almost dramatic in their significance, but concludes with a coda which sounds but a deeper note of the tender sorrowfulness of the opening. With the finale, a return is made to the somewhat strenuous mood of the opening movement. Conciseness of treatment and the clothing of the subject-matter in a variety of garbs, both rhythmic and melodic, hold the interest, which is well sustained to the end, where, in the coda, there is some brilliant work for all the instruments.

THE QUINTET is of larger dimensions than the trio. Of this work A. W. Kramer, the New York critic, wrote as follows:

'The opening movement, allegro giusto, is begun by a theme on the four stringed instruments in unison with an accompanying passage on the piano. There is a sweep in this melody which draws the listener into the mood of the movement at once. A second theme on the viola is emotionally full, and treated with lovely harmonic taste. The composer makes much of this theme, and it is handled in a varied manner, with richness of harmonization. On the recapitulation, the main theme is heroically set for the piano, and the second subject is treated with fine polyphonic work in the strings. The coda is built on the opening theme in diminution, a happy idea which in its working-out proves of great effect.

The scherzo. For piquant, ingenious mood pictures one has to go far to surpass this movement. There are in it both great variety of thematic material and of rhythms. That of the theme in 6/8 time is captivating.

The finale opens with an andante con moto in D flat. The composer has actually succeeded in giving us his slow movement as an introduction to his last, and has constructed it on a motto theme which leads to the closing allegro as naturally as, and far more effectively than, he could have made it by separating them. The 'cello announces the same theme with which the work begins, giving us in the major the same intervals which have gone to make up the majestic and opening theme of the first movement. The passage is for strings alone. While the violins and viola give forth a fine sequence, the 'cello keeps this motto in ostinato fashion, and the result is an excellent one. Leading through a series of questions and answers between the piano and strings, the final allegro appassionato is reached.

The opening singing theme is well worked out, and after a sub-theme productive of much imitation in the strings, we reach the second subject, a melody of rare beauty. The development section is firmly and closely knit, and the return and summing-up of the thematic materials masterly. The work stands high among the newer quintets.'

Taking a general view of Hinton's chamber music, the notable characteristics of it may be said to be a natural spontaneity of ideas and a keen musical sense in their development.

H. W. RICHARDS.

HIRSCHBACH, HERMANN, 1812–1888, German composer.

Four quintets	2 v, 2 vla, vc	Siegel.
Two ,,	v, vla, vc, cl, horn	,,
Thirteen quartets	str	,,

He also wrote an octet and a septet for strings and wind. For full list of works with opus numbers and keys *v. Altmann*, *Fétis*, and *Vidal*.

Hirschbach gave to his quartets the name of *Pictures of Life*, and inscribed op. 1 with a motto from Goethe's *Faust*, though this was only done after the work was finished. One of the most interesting comments on chamber music written by Schumann was apropos of Hirschbach's quartet writing.

'One sees', he writes, 'that the composer would fain be styled a poet, and that he desires to escape as far as possible from all stereotyped forms. Beethoven's last quartets he evidently views as but the beginnings of a new poetical era, in which he wishes to continue working. Haydn and Mozart lie far away in the background. Thus he has a good deal in common with Berlioz's creative lust, with his preference for the larger forms, poetic tendencies, to some extent contempt of the old, and he has had, furthermore, a similar life experience. He was in his youth a student of medicine, devoting himself only in his twentieth year to music. This is worthy of mention, and accounts for the defective musical culture which is here and there apparent in his music.'

It also, no doubt, accounts for Schumann's loss of interest in Hirschbach in later days.

Dr. Altmann deals in his *Handbuch* only with the tenth quartet, op. 38. He says that it is not a string quartet in the real sense of the word.

'The elegant conversation of four instruments is not there, the first fiddle, who is responsible for a very difficult part, predominates, the other instruments having only occasionally the parole. The music is arresting, but it is not strong in invention ... and for public performance it can no longer be considered eligible.' EDITOR.

† HOBOKEN, A. VAN.

Public-spirited originator of a scheme for photographing the original MSS. of works by great composers in order to correct numerous errors which have crept into the editions in use. The scheme is to be carried out (1928) by a board of directors in Vienna with van Hoboken as chairman, and among the works selected to be dealt with first are Beethoven's quartet, op. 95, and six of Haydn's quartets. EDITOR.

HOCHBERG, BOLKO, GRAF VON. [Pseudonym: Franz, J. H.], 1843–1926.

Quartet, str, E flat	op. 22	André, 1874.
Two quartets, str, D, a mi	„ 27	B. & B., 1894.
Quartet, pf, v, vla, vc, b flat mi	„ 37	Eulenburg, 1908.
Trio, pf, v, vc, A	„ 34	B. & H., 1899.
„ „ „ „ B flat	„ 35	Eulenburg, 1904.

Count von Hochberg, a pupil of Kiel, was the founder of the Silesian music festivals (1876). His chamber music, greatly influenced by Beethoven, has many good qualities. His quartets are strongly recommended to Quartet organizations by Albert Tottmann in his *Führer*. EDITOR.

HÖEBERG, GEORG, b. 1872, Danish violinist, pupil of Gade.

Sonata, pf, v, G	op. 1	Hansen, 1905.

† HOÉRÉE, ARTHUR, b. 1897, Belgian composer, pupil of Vincent d'Indy.

Septet, pf, mezzo soprano voice, fl, str. quartet	op. 3	
Pastorale et Danse, str. quartet	„ 2	Senart.

Hoérée's septet was performed at the 1926 festival of the International Society for Contemporary Music. The second movement contains a song on happiness by Paul Fort.

The *Pastorale et Danse* was awarded the *Prix Lepaule* in 1923. Hoérée is attached to the Institut International de Coopération Intellectuelle (Société des Nations) for musical questions, and writes for many leading musical reviews as music critic.

† HOESSLIN, FRANZ VON, b. 1885, German composer and conductor, pupil of Max Reger and Felix Mottl.

Quintet, cl, 2 v, vla, vc	c sharp mi	Simrock.

This clarinet quintet is an ambitious, contrapuntally rather complex work, influenced by Reger. It is well spoken of in the German press as being rhythmic and warmly inspired.

HOFFMANN, ERNST THEODOR WILHELM, 1776–1822, German writer and composer.

An eccentric genius of remarkable versatility, much of whose music has been lost. He is known, however, to have written a quintet for harp and strings and a piano trio. Beethoven wrote a canon on his name.

HOFFMEISTER, FRANZ ANTON, 1754–1812, German composer and publisher.

Modern republication:

Quartet, fl, v, vla, vc	Schott.
Six duos concertants, 2 v	André, 1870.

A long list in *Vidal* and *Fétis* includes forty-eight published string quartets, eight string quintets, five piano quartets, nineteen string trios, eleven piano trios, &c. *Vidal* states that he wrote no less than 340 works for flute, from concertos and quintets to duos. His chief interest to-day is that he had important relations with both Haydn and Mozart.

We might have had a long series of piano quartets from Mozart, had not Hoffmeister, writing of those in G minor and E flat, complained that they were too obscure for the public.. Mozart promptly cancelled the contract. His relations with Beethoven are shown by the latter addressing him as 'geliebtesten Herrn Bruder' [best-beloved brother] *(Grove)*. M. DRAKE-BROCKMAN.

HOFMANN, HEINRICH KARL JOHANN, 1842–1902, German composer.

Hofmann enjoyed very wide popularity in his time, but his vogue ceased before his death. Those interested in his works may hear of them at the publishers, B. & H., Hainauer, and R. & E. They include an octet for strings and wind, and a string sextet.

HOFMANN, RICHARD, 1844–1918, German violinist.

Quartet, 4 v, C	op. 98	Hug, 1896.
Serenade, pf, v, vc	„ 73	A. P. Schmidt, 1908.
Sonata, pf, vla (or fl), F	„ 46	Siegel, 1885.

Altmann gives a lengthy list of educational music, among which may be noticed an easy string quartet, op. 116 (Zimmermann), and six easy pieces for string quartet, op. 97 (Hug). Richard Hofmann also arranged, for teaching purposes, fourteen four-part Bach fugues from the *Wohltemperirtes Klavier* for string quartet. EDITOR.

*† HOLBROOKE, Joseph, b. 1878, English composer.

Sextet (*Henry Vaughan*)	2 v, 2 vla, 2 vc		op. 43	Chester, *c.* 1915.
Cavatina and var^{ns}.	cl, 2 v, vla, vc	D	,, 27*a*	,, 1914.
Quintet	,, ,, ,, ,,	G	,, 27*b*	,, 1914.
Miniature suite	fl, ob, cl, horn, fag		,, 33*b*	Rudall Carte.
Phantasy quartet	str	d mi	,, 17*b*	Chester.
2nd quartet (*Impressions of Belgium, Russia*, &c.)	,,		,, 59*a*	Chester, 1916.
3rd quartet (*The Pickwick Club*)	,,		,, 68	Chester.
4th quartet (*Suite on National songs and dances*)	,,	d mi	,, 71	,,
5th quartet (*Suite on Folk-songs of Great Britain*)			,, 72	,, 1920.
Sextet (*In Memoriam*)	pf, 2 v, vla, vc, cb	f mi	,, 46	Chester.
Four dances	pf, cl, str. quartet		,, 20	Ricordi.
Sextet	pf, fl, ob, cl, horn, fag (or pf, str)	f mi	,, 33*a*	Chester.
Symphonic quintet (*Diabolique*)	pf, 2 v, vla, vc	g mi	,, 44	,, 1910.
Symphonic quartet	pf, v, vla, vc	g mi	,, 21	,, 1910.
Symphonic quartet (*Byron*)	,, ,, ,, ,,	d mi	,, 31	,, 1915.
Trio (*Fairyland*)	pf, ob d'amore (fl or cl), vla		,, 57	Chester.
Trio	pf, v, horn (vla)		,, 28	Rudall Carte.
Sonata (or sonatina)	pf, v		,, 6	Larway.
Sonata	pf, v	F	,, 59*b*	Ricordi, 1918.
3rd sonata (*Oriental*)	,, ,,			Chester, 1926.
Phantasy sonata	pf, vc	g mi	,, 19	,, 1914.

Holbrooke studied at the R.A.M. in 1893, winning the Sterndale Bennett scholarship.

For some years after leaving the Academy he lived a hard-working professional life in London, diversified by occasional concert tours, but found time to write many elaborate works; in fact, his industry and persistence have always been extraordinary.

His name has been more frequently connected with orchestral music and opera than with chamber music, and it may surprise many people to know that his work in this field is so copious and interesting. He is fond of big effects, of a mass of sound, of imposing climaxes. He is a master of orchestral colour, and has a flair for the picturesque. Moreover, his music is generally direct and outspoken, without subtlety or suggestion. These qualities of themselves do not make for great success in chamber music; yet there is no doubt that in this domain Holbrooke has accomplished far more than could have been expected, and that his works for small instrumental combinations rank with the best of the English school. His music is sincere, spontaneous, and unaffected by prevailing fashions. He has dallied with the folk-song cult without giving evidence of any particular enthusiasm for it. Without being impeccable, he is, at least, never anaemic, and the unforced flow and swing of his music do not leave one time to be much disturbed by an occasional lack of refinement.

Some of Holbrooke's works appear at different times in different forms. Thus the sextet (op. 33 *a*) was originally written as a quintet for wind instruments and piano; subsequently an oboe part was added, converting it into a sextet; and its final stage is that of a sextet for piano and strings. Again, the G minor trio (op. 21) subsequently became a quartet for piano and strings, in which form it is published; two of the sextets were originally written as quintets, and there are other examples of rearrangement and revision.

One of his most successful works is the string quartet in D minor, which was called into being by the phantasy scheme of W. W. Cobbett. Like nearly all Holbrooke's more important works, it is in three movements only; in this instance they are connected, and named *Departure, Absence*, and *Return*. The themes are fine, and (unlike some works of the composer) there is no falling-off in the last movement.

The piano quartet in G minor (op. 21) has an expressive *Lament* for its slow movement, and is interesting throughout, if somewhat immature in style.

A particularly charming work written in true chamber style is the trio in D minor for piano, violin, and horn. It is unusual to find Holbrooke in such a genial and placid mood as that of the first movement. The second movement has more passion, but is conceived in much the same admirably restrained style. Unfortunately the third movement is not on the same high level, and contains one of Holbrooke's occasional lapses into the commonplace; its second theme is not worthy of inclusion in a work such as this. Holbrooke is fond of revision, and it would be well if he had re-written this movement. With a fitting finale, this trio would rank among the composer's best works.

The *Byron* piano quartet was first performed in 1903. It is full of youthful vigour and impetuosity, but it is perhaps, of all the composer's chamber works, the most orchestral in conception and treatment. It is not divided into separate movements, but runs on without a break.

The string sextet, op. 43, is headed *Henry Vaughan*, and was partly inspired by a passage from one of the works of that poet. It is complex in detail, yet sounds perfectly spontaneous in performance. Like much of Holbrooke's work, it gives the impression of having been written with great rapidity. It is, as usual, in three movements only, for the scherzo element is generally to be found in the finales. The short adagio introduction to this sextet is as expressive as anything Holbrooke has written. The subsequent 5/4 allegro is also perfectly unforced; it is, in a sense, a genuine 5/4 in that it does not consist of bars of 3/4 followed by 2/4 or vice versa. In the slow movement (*Unhappy boyhood*) the hearer is reminded of the luxurious melancholy of Tchaikovsky, but there is a melodious and consolatory middle section (poco allegro). The last movement is inspiriting, and contains a complete fugal exposition founded on the principal subject. Holbrooke is fond of this method of treatment, though it is regarded in some quarters as old-fashioned.

The quintet for piano and strings, op. 44, is called *Diabolique*, the third movement being a *Valse Diabolique*, from which the work takes its title. It is not easy to see why this particular movement should have been so described; it is elegant and easy-moving, and the theme is given out by the four stringed instruments in regular succession. Perhaps its curt conclusion smacked of *diablerie* to the composer. This work contains in the slow movement one of Holbrooke's most sumptuous cantilenas, and has the usual fugal exposition in the last movement.

The *In Memoriam* sextet in F minor (with double-bass) was written before the quintet, although it has a later opus number. It is a genuinely emotional and sincere piece of music obviously written under the influence of Tchaikovsky, although the opening theme reminds one strangely of the *Egmont* overture. The last movement contains a curious melody, distinctly Scottish in character. The piano-writing in this work is straightforward and effective, if a little lacking in distinction.

The Pickwick Club is the title of the string quartet, op. 68, and it is further described as a *Humoreske*. It is in two sections; each movement deals with some episode or personality in the novel: *A Field Day*, *The Amorous Tupman*, *The Picnic*, *Mr. Pickwick and Mrs. Bardell* are some of the headings of the movements (there are thirteen in all).

It is a very difficult and intricate work, and one may be doubtful of its complete success. Holbrooke has a keen and individual sense of humour, but it is not Pickwickian humour, and the spacious geniality of the subject is hardly reflected in the music, although there is much cleverness and fantasy. It may be mentioned that at the first performance of this quartet, in 1916, the first violin part was taken by John Saunders, to whom English lovers of chamber music owe so much, and who was connected with the first performances of many of Holbrooke's works.

Other works that should be mentioned are a 'romantic' sonata for violin and piano, in which the themes are of excellent lyrical quality, but which is rather an accompanied violin solo than a duet; a sonatina for violin and piano; song and dance suites for string quartet, in which the composer does homage to the present-day enthusiasm for folk music; *Belgium* and *Russia*, written in the early days of the war and described as 'impressions' for string quartet; a clarinet quintet; a very graceful little suite (op. 32*b*) for five instruments, including a minuet in fugal style; and an early sextet, *The Dances*.

It should be remembered that when Holbrooke was writing most of his chamber music there was no such interest and enthusiasm for native music as is now displayed (1928). It required some courage in a struggling professional musician to sit down and compose works for which there was no adequate monetary return, and which could never even become widely known. Holbrooke may be regarded in some sort as a pioneer, and though fashions have changed many times even in the comparatively short period since he began to write, it is difficult to believe that work so spontaneous, full-blooded, and sincere will ever lack admirers. And he has been fortunate enough to get it nearly all published.

R. H. Walthew.

[After reading a favourable account of Joseph Holbrooke's chamber music from the pen of so competent a musician as Mr. Walthew, the question naturally arises: why are these clever works so seldom heard in the concert-room? That his music is difficult to play is not an insuperable barrier. The trouble is that his string passages do not lie as well as those of the great masters in the tracks of the fingers; thus they do not yield as readily to strenuous practice, and demand more time for preliminary study than artists can spare. The *Pickwick* quartet is an instance of this peculiarity.

Given the exercise of a little more self-criticism, Joseph Holbrooke might have won a still higher place in the estimation of chamber music lovers. Editor.]

† HOLLÄNDER, Alexis, b. 1840, German pianist and conductor.

Quintet, pf, 2 v, vla, vc, g mi	op. 24	Schlesinger, 1881.
Six characteristic pieces in canon-form, pf, v, vc (or pf, cl, vla)	,, 53	,, 1898.
Suite, pf, v, G	,, 40	,, 1891.

† HOLLANDER, Benoît, b. 1853, Dutch violinist.

1st quartet, str, b flat mi	op. 20	Phillips & Oliver.
2nd quartet, str, c sharp mi	,, 30	Durand.
Fantasie trio, 2 v, vla		Schott.
Septet, pf, str. quartet, 2 horns, E flat	,, 28	Phillips & Oliver.
Trio, pf, v, vc		,, ,,
Sonata, pf, v	,, 19	,, ,,
Sonata, pf, v, g mi	,, 35	Graham & Black.
Suite, pf, v, D	,, 6	André.

Hollander is described as a Dutch violinist, but was taught at the Paris Conservatoire, and has passed the greater part of his life in England. He has undoubtedly a flair for the composition of chamber music, for less than half of his chamber works have been published. He was for some time a member of Auer's Quartet at the Musical Union, and played the viola (and also occasionally the violin) at the 'Pops'.

That he is entitled to respect as a composer is evidenced by the fact that occasionally whole evenings have been devoted to his music at South Place. His septet (dedicated to Saint-Saëns) is a great favourite with the audiences there, and has been given seven performances. In writing for the piano he has recourse rather more often than is desirable to arpeggio accompaniment, but his scoring for strings is, as might be expected, exemplary.

While for the most part he has been content to work on conventional lines, his music is occasionally interesting from the point of view of construction. The slow movement of the septet, for instance, is unusual in form. A short rhapsodical melody is given to the viola, accompanied by chords on the piano; this is followed in turn by (1) a few bars for strings—allegro; (2) a very short andante; and (3) a further few bars of allegro. The whole of this matter is then treated in variation form. Following a cadenza on the piano, the music takes on the character of a slow movement, and proceeds without further interruptions to the end. His earlier string quartet is also unusual in character. After the usual opening and development sections, the subject-matter of what appears to be the recapitulation is considerably quickened, and leads straight into the slow movement. The quick section is then referred to again, and leads to an unexpected close in the minor.

The second violin sonata is a work of considerable charm, particularly as regards the second movement. An unusual feature is that all the movements are in minor keys. The works, as a rule, are not difficult, and are within the powers of amateurs.

W. J. Mitson.

[The circumstance that Benoît Hollander has lived for the greater part of his life in England has been much to the advantage of British concert-goers. The velvety tone which he produced on the viola when playing at the 'Pops' I have never heard surpassed. As a teacher of the violin, chiefly at the Guildhall School of Music, he has had much success. Among his pupils was that admirable chamber music player, John Saunders. Editor.]

HOLLÄNDER, Gustav, 1855–1915, German violinist, pupil of F. David.

Suite, pf, v, e mi	op. 21	R. & E., 1885.
Sonata, pf, v, d mi	,, 59	Simrock, 1903.

Gustav Holländer was director of the Sternsches Konservatorium in Berlin. His music is well written for the strings in the manner of Schumann and Brahms, but is somewhat antiquated. He was a pupil of Joachim, and was favourably known as a chamber music player, leading for a time the Cologne String Quartet. He also gave trio concerts with Grünfeld and Scharwenka.

Hugo Leichtentritt.

HOLMES, (1) Alfred, 1837–1876, English violinist.

Chiefly noted for his fine playing of duets for two violins in conjunction with his brother Henry. Spohr dedicated his three duets, opp. 148, 150, 153, to the two brothers, and speaks in his autobiography of their 'highly finished and surprising performances' at a concert given at Cassel.

In 1864 he established a Quartet in Paris, and gave a series of chamber concerts. These were patronized by the Minister of Public Instruction 'to encourage a taste for classical art among the numerous scholars of public institutions'. This sufficiently rare instance of encouragement given to an English performer in a continental city is worthy of chronicle.

Editor.

(2) Henry, 1839–1905, English violinist and composer, brother of the above.

Grand concert duet, 2 v, E flat	op. 9	Peters, 1858.

Henry Holmes was an artist of high rank, professor of the violin at the R.C.M. from its foundation till his enforced resignation in 1894, and was in his time a prominent figure in the chamber music life of London. He made, in early days, several tours on the Continent with his brother Alfred, and later on gave a series of concerts in London under the title of 'Musical Evenings', at which several chamber works (MS.) of his own composition were performed, including an octet for strings and two horns. He edited a selection of solo sonatas of the old masters in 1879 (Augener-Schott).

EDITOR.

*† HOLST, GUSTAV THEODORE, b. 1874, one of England's most important composers, has unfortunately given little attention to chamber music.

His only published work of the kind consists of *Seven Scottish Airs* (1908) for strings and piano, but, being written for school purposes, it is more properly classified as educational. A string quartet projected some years ago was not divulged, and a terzetto (1925) remains at present in MS. Before, however, discussing this work, it is expedient, for completeness, to mention two others which indirectly come under the heading of chamber music. The first is the very beautiful opera di camera *Savitri*, op. 25 (1908). The second consists of four songs for voice and violin, op. 35 (1916), a series of lovely dialogues in an atmosphere of medieval mysticism. Despite the apparent freedom of the melodic declamation, they are models of a form in which it is a feat of craftsmanship to excel.

The terzetto, op. 44 (1925), is for flute, oboe, and viola, and comprises two movements, allegretto and scherzo. Throughout the first movement, and the greater portion of the second, the flute part is written in A major, the oboe in A flat, and the viola in C. In the remainder of the scherzo the flute is in E, the oboe in D flat, and the viola in E flat—that is to say, not only the keys are changed, but the key-relationships. The work is thus an interesting example of polytonality, but of a kind that is more apparent than real, for the composer makes much use of enharmonics, and generally resolves his bitonal or tritonal effects at the cadences, sometimes with great ingenuity. Owing to the exceptional nature of the part-writing, examples will be of more service than description. The following is taken from the allegretto:

Ex. 1.

An interesting point is the recapitulation of the first group of subjects, which begins thus:

Ex. 2.

The scherzo is, in the main, a fugato beginning thus:

Ex. 3.

with a lyrical episode for contrast.

EDWIN EVANS.

HOLSTEIN, FRANZ VON, 1826–1878, German composer. Began life as an army officer.

Quartet, str, e mi	op. 49	Peters, 1899.
Trio, pf, v, vc, g mi	,, 18	Siegel, 1870.
Sonata, pf, v, F	,, 40	Peters, 1899.

'Hardly strong enough to defy the action of time' (*Riemann*).

†HOLTER, IVER PAUL FREDRIK, b. 1850, Norwegian composer and conductor.

Quartet, str, E flat	op. 1	André, 1879.
,, ,, G	,, 18	Reinecke, 1914.

HOLY, J.

Reisebilder—Four pieces, str. quartet	op. 56	Blosfeld, 1911.

HOLZBAUER, IGNAZ JAKOB, 1711–1783.

Modern republication:

Quintet (divertimento), 2 v, 2 vla, vc, E flat	(Riemann) D.T.B. Vol. 27, 1914.

Holzbauer was a prolific composer. An interesting account of him is in *Grove*, with quotations from letters of Mozart which show appreciation of his music. He wrote eighteen string quartets, according to *Fétis*, but *Vidal* was unable to trace them and supposes them to have remained in MS.

HOMBERG, JOSEPH, contemporary French composer, pupil of d'Indy.

Trio, pf, v, vc, D	Senart, 1922.
Sonata, pf, vc	,,

HOMILIUS, KONST.

Quartet, 4 horns, B flat	op. 38	Merseburger, 1893.

*†HONEGGER, ARTHUR, b. 1892, of German-Swiss parentage, born in France.

		Composed	
1st quartet, str	c mi	1916–17	Senart.
2nd ,, ,,			Sirène.
Sonatina, 2 v		1920	,,
Rhapsody, pf, 2 fl, cl (or 2 v, vla)		1917	Senart.
1st sonata, pf, v		1918	,,
2nd ,, ,, ,,		1919	,,
Sonata, pf, vla			Sirène.
,, pf, vc			,,
Sonatina, pf, cl (in A)		1921–22	Rouart-Lerolle.

Honegger's earliest steps in composition were guided by the sonatas of Beethoven; even before he had fully understood the method of notation, he was able to grasp their general plan, and endeavoured to reproduce it. Then the instinct of the future quartet writer was early awakened in him by chamber music meetings with friends, and he soon enriched their repertory with the firstfruits of his muse; compositions which were original at least in the method of writing, for the composer—having learnt the violin early—was none too sure of any clef but that of G, and employed it for all the instruments, with many an '8va' above or below.

Honegger entered the Paris Conservatoire in 1912, in Professor Gédalge's class. This great contrapuntist, so notoriously hostile to the mechanical developments of the Franckist school, submitted him to a discipline, fertile in its results, which doubtless contributed to his formation at least as much as did the lessons of d'Indy and Widor. He left the class perfectly equipped for his task, and with aims which he defined in a letter to M. Paul Landormy (*Revue de Genève*, Sept. 1921):

'I attach great importance to musical construction, which I would not see sacrificed to literary or pictorial considerations. My great model is J. S. Bach—I do not seek a return to harmonic simplicity, as do some of the anti-impressionists. I think, on the contrary, that we should make use of the harmonic materials created by our predecessors, but in a different way—as a basis for our melodic lines and for our rhythms. Bach uses the elements of tonal harmony as I should like to use modern polytonal combinations of notes.'

As Honegger himself invokes the name of Bach, and as his affinity with the Master of masters is in constant evidence in his works, it should be added that he, among contemporary composers, does really play a part comparable to that played in the eighteenth century by the first musical genius of European range. Just as Bach succeeded in blending the ancient German art with the charm of the French clavecinists, so, in Honegger's essentially polymorphic style, there is an instinctive, yet paradoxical agreement, which but yesterday must have seemed inconceivable, the paradox of the German spirit born and nurtured on foreign soil. This agreement is the uniting of a spirit imbued with Claude Debussy's harmonic atmosphere, and coloured by his magic, with an intellect aroused by Wagner to the conquest of virgin peaks of pure melody. The aim is a reconciliation between two traditions which, since that time, have reached, in opposition, their highest point of beauty.

This being so, the new-comer must not be reproached for a wealth which he abuses no more than did the old master. Indeed, whether Honegger withdraws himself in a contemplative and somewhat Debussyesque manner to form his impressions of the world, or whether he records the experiences of his inner life with a passionate ardour reminiscent of Wagner, the exact manner of his thought never interferes with his abundant flow of original harmony and melody. The strongly personal character of his work appears all the more significant, stamped, as it were, with an individuality which renders it like to no other. For there is to-day scarcely a musician (especially among the 'Six' to which Honegger attached himself, both by his friendships and his doctrines) who has not proclaimed the bankruptcy of Debussyism, or of Wagnerism, or of both.

Unless the writer is mistaken in this short analysis of the elements which go to form the groundwork of Honegger's art, there is only the more reason, once the combination is effected, to admire an art which proves itself ever living and personal. He has a hundred ways of being himself, in the plasticity of his melodies and the strictness of his counterpoint, in the fullness of his harmony or the agility of his rhythms, but it is always in a way which enables one to identify him at a glance. Observe those networks of lines in contrary motion, the patterns woven by conjunct steps which give a geometrical foundation to his freest designs, the decorative elements being at the same time woven into the unity of the concept.

Examples of this are found in the first and second movements of the sonata for viola and piano, and in the scintillating conclusion at the end of the development.

There is a similar procedure in the 'cello sonata, where a figure seems to spring up spontaneously, and to support and embellish the second theme, itself so expressive, in the second movement; and again, there is a brilliant explosion at the summit of the ascent. There appears, even in the smallest details, that unbroken clarity which is the mark of the well-schooled artist. For inspiration he frequently turns to impressions of nature, which he is careful to suit to his idiom before they are transformed into sound, so that they seem to spring direct from these inexhaustible sources of poetic suggestion: sea, sky, mountain, &c.

And such glimpse as he affords of his inner life shows depth of soul—a soul simple in its rhythms, but complex in its alternations of gravity and gaiety, and excellently well fitted, in whatever manner he may write, for the lyrical strain.

With regard to the themes best suited to this lyricism, whether tender or lofty, it is impossible to speak fully without digressing from the subject of chamber music. But there is one distinguishing feature in Honegger's work which must be emphasized. Many of his contemporaries excel in the treatment of sonata form, but one is inclined to think that Honegger is one of the very few who move in it as in their native element. His music never gives the impression of being worked out by laboratory experiments, in which attempts are made to infuse new life into a worn-out tradition. The tradition he is carrying on is instinctive, and lives anew with him, ready for present needs and directly applicable to his own personal talent. Herein lies the value, in his chamber music, of the sonatas and sonatinas which form an important and significant part of it, not only because they are models of constructive skill, but also because they show throughout, in the arrangement of the parts and in the structure of the whole, the harmony existing between sonata form and the dramatic factors inherent in this musician-soul.

Whatever variety of 'schema' may modify the order of the factors, these latter remain as guiding principles associated by a law of contrasts, which sets on each work his personal seal. There is passion unrestrained in an allegro or an agitato—more often than not harsh and gloomy—passion sometimes so fierce as to suggest a storm at sea in the background of his inspiration; a slow movement may bring to mind the spiritual reaction in which he withdraws, to seek in solitude and meditation the key to the enigmas of passion; there is thirdly—as a finale, or in some cases an interlude—deliverance by flight, in movements essentially rhythmic, and it may also be (as in Beethoven) the way of escape through action (as in *Faust*—action instead of useless words) with a song of triumph for the deed of heroism.

The String Quartet. An analysis of the quartet reveals the presence of these psychic factors in the construction: heartfelt passion, a spirit of meditation, and a will to unite the two in spirit and in substance, the whole effort being consummated by a hymn of peace. But one would prefer to take it as an illustration of the dual influence (Wagner and Debussy) which has gone to the formation of the composer's genius. Here, then, in the meditative adagio, between the appassionato which opens the work ('violent et tourmenté') and the final allegro ('rude et rhythmique'), are the two 'atmospheres' which from the outset are in opposition—to the detriment of neither, in fact, quite the reverse:

Ex. 1.

—music evidently of the nature of a Tristanesque rêverie on the mysteries of the world—and (Ex. 2) music with an evident flavour of the nostalgia of Debussy, which consoles itself for not cursing the dawn, by smiling at it.

At the time when the quartet was written, these influences, formerly unconsciously re-

Ex. 2.

ceived, had been so completely assimilated as to produce only an added wealth of ideas. Moreover, no trace of them is to be found in the leading ideas of the work, from its wild opening, which is purely his own,

Ex. 3.

to the conclusion with its accents of profound serenity, a serenity won only by fierce struggles against the imprisoning forces.

Ex. 4.

And if this heir of J. S. Bach has abated nothing of his worship for this master, while freeing himself from others, in order the better to reconcile them; if the last ten years have only served to strengthen his predilection for fugue, canon, and every kind of artifice of this school, yet his own originality shines only the brighter, since it partly consists in an adaptation of the contrapuntal polyphony of the great ages to the conditions of the polytonality of his own day. But this technical merit, however interesting, is the least of the merits of Arthur Honegger's genius.

ROBERT GODET.

HÖNIG, HEINRICH.

Quartet, 4 v, G	op. 53	Zierfuss, 1896.

HOPFE, JUL.

	op.	
Trio, v, vla, vc, C	41	Challier.
Trio, v, vla, vc, g mi	69	Schlesinger.
Quintet, pf, 2 v, vla, vc, e mi	44	Challier.
Quartet, pf, v, vla, vc	48	,,
Trio, pf, v, vc, D	40	,,
Trio, pf, v, vc, A	43	,,
Easy trio, pf, v, vc, F	46	,,
Easy trio (*Pastoral*), pf, v, vc	49	,,
Trio on German folk-songs, pf, v, vc	59	Heinrichshofen.
Easy trios, pf, v, vc	75*a*	Simon.
Sonata, pf, vc, G	47	Challier.

Some easy piano trios are also mentioned in *Altmann*. The quartet op. 48 is entitled *Ein Frühlingsmärchen in Jörren.*

HORN. Because of the beautiful quality of its tone and its ability to blend with a small group of other instruments, the horn is the only brass instrument used to any extent in chamber music. There is no need here to expatiate upon the wide range of its compass and nuances. While its tone has great power, it can, nevertheless, be made unobtrusive in the softest passages. For all these reasons the horn has always been associated with the wood-wind instruments as well as the brass, and is frequently a member of the wind quartet or quintet in chamber music.

Special attention should be drawn to the horn in combination with the strings or piano, for in these groupings is found the most musically interesting chamber music for the instrument. Greatest of all is the Brahms trio, op. 40, for piano, violin, and horn, bringing out all that is loveliest in the cantilena, gayest in the staccato, and deepest in the sustaining qualities of the horn. One can hear or play this work again and again only to discover new beauties and carry the themes more lovingly in mind.

Jos. Holbrooke and Donald Tovey have also written trios for the same combination, and Reinecke composed two satisfactory trios for piano and horn, one with oboe, the other with clarinet.

Of horn sonatas with piano, thirteen are known to exist, of which the Beethoven, op. 17, easily heads the list. Those by Rheinberger, op. 178, Setaccioli, and Kamillo Horn also deserve mention, likewise the Lied and scherzo by Florent Schmitt.

In the larger combinations the horn is more often represented. Mozart was very fond of the instrument, and the quintet for horn, violin, two violas, and 'cello is delightful. There are also divertimenti for strings and two horns, including the famous *Dorfmusikanten* sextet, where the musicians are occasionally required to play out of tune, and Beethoven has written a sextet for this combination.

There is a melodic and playable serenade by Sinigaglia for horn and string quartet, and (for the same combination) quintets by Dauprat, op. 6, Kreuz, op. 49, and Reicha, op. 106. Hirschbach substitutes a clarinet for the second violin in his quintet.

The combination of horn, clarinet, violin, 'cello, and piano has attracted von Baussern, Zdenko Fibich, and Robert Kahn, who have written musical but unimportant works. A quintet by Draeseke includes a viola in place of the clarinet. The quartet by Karg-Elert for piano, flute, clarinet, and horn is very modern in style, and difficult.

There are many quartets for four horns, including a group of six by the Russian Tcherepnin. BURNET C. TUTHILL.

[The reader's attention is drawn to Professor Tovey's mention of Haydn's treatment of the horn in his article on that composer's music.]

HORN, EDUARD.

Quartet, str, A	op. 10	Kahnt, 1878.
Trio, pf, v, vc, b mi	,, 19	Doblinger, *c.* 1885.

†HORN, KAMILLO, b. 1860, Bohemian composer.

Quintet, 3 v, vla, vc, G	op. 50	Kahnt, 1915.
Trio-Fantasy, pf, v, vc, E		,,
Fantasy, pf, v, G	,, 42	,, 1908.
Sonata, pf, v, b mi		,,
,, pf, horn, c mi	,, 58	,, 1912.

Horn has gained distinction chiefly as a song composer, and his chamber music gives evidence of his lyrical spirit. Emotion is its dominant characteristic, yet there is vigour and an inner cheerfulness which renders his work very attractive.

THE HORN SONATA. These qualities are revealed in his sonatas, one for violin and one for horn, the latter of which is particularly pleasing. It opens with a sharply defined theme, followed by a second very lyrical subject in G major and a modulation into E flat. Both themes are effectively treated in the development; the recapitulation follows, closing tempestuously with the first subject. The second movement opens with soft syncopated chords on the piano, then follows the beautiful dreamy first subject in A flat, modulating to the bright key of A major. A second idea is treated in counterpoint at the octave, and closes *pp* in A flat major. The movement now grows more lively till the melodious middle section is reached, whereupon a powerful crescendo leads back to the principal theme, and the movement closes quietly with a suggestion of distant bells. After this harmonious close follows the gay rondo finale in C major, in which the simplicity of the second subject contrasts admirably with the fresh rhythms of the principal theme, while the third exhibits a more masculine character, and this melodious work ends with a merry stretto.

THE VIOLIN SONATA is a much more passionate work. The first subject is tempestuous, the second, which is in canon, expresses a more contemplative mood. Both themes are employed in the development, where the composer's contrapuntal skill is displayed, but without pedantry. A melody on a pedal F sharp follows, and leads to the recapitulation, which ends with a dramatic climax. The second movement, consisting of variations on an original theme, gives a favourable idea of the composer's imaginative gift. The third variation, with its gloomy chorale strain, and the sixth, in the manner of a country dance, are particularly charming. The last movement is again in rondo form, and though at first rather stormy, it calms down, and the work has a joyous ending.

THE TRIO FANTASY, which is in the form of a sonata movement, likewise makes a very good impression. The opening is full of spirit, the second subject is gently emotional, and the ending, in which the two main themes are artistically interwoven, is fascinating.

THE QUINTET. Horn's most important chamber work is the quintet, a work full of grace and pleasing melody, of which the lovely second subject of the opening movement is an attractive example. The scherzo is marked by its careless gaiety, especially noteworthy being the trio, in which the singing of the viola is particularly striking. In the third movement, which contains some good part-writing, there appears to be an echo of painful experiences, but in the finale cheerfulness resumes its sway.

Horn's chamber music is classical in form; his subject-matter, however, emulates the romanticists. The form is clear, unambiguous, and distinctly outlined throughout; he shows complete technical mastery, and his idiom has the genuine chamber music spirit, pleasing, unforced, and full of intrinsic gaiety.

RUDOLF FELBER.

HORSLEY, CHARLES EDWARD, 1822–1876, English composer.

Trio, pf, v, vc, A	op. 7	Cranz, 1845.	
,, ,, ,, ,, b mi	,, 13	B. & H., 1849.	
Sonata, pf, v, F	,, 14	Kistner, 1848.	
,, pf, vc, A	,, 3	,, 1843.	

Horsley, the son of the celebrated glee-writer (William, 1774–1858), was a pupil of Mendelssohn and Moritz Hauptmann.

HORTON, J. R., English composer.

Suite, 2 vc (or vc, cb), d mi	Schlesinger, 1922.

One of the outstanding works for this combination.

HORVATH, ATTILA, 1862–1920, Hungarian composer.

Sonata, pf, v, G	op. 26	Rózsavölgyi, 1902.

†HOUFFLACK, A.

Sonata, pf, v	Michel, 1902.

HOWELL, DOROTHY, b. 1898, English pianist.

Phantasy, pf, v	Augener.

The work was a Cobbett commission, and was played at the Contemporary Music Centre in May, 1925.

†HOWELLS, HERBERT, b. 1892, English composer.

Rhapsodic quintet, cl, 2 v, vla, vc	op. 31	S. & B.
Lady Audrey's Suite, str. quartet	,, 19	Curwen.
Phantasy quartet, str, C	,, 25	,,
Quartet, pf, v, vla, vc, a mi	,, 21	S. & B.
Sonata, pf, v, E	,, 18	Hawkes.
3rd sonata, pf, v, e mi	,, 38	O.U.P.

Though Howells' chamber works represent but a fourth of his total output, they form an integral part of it, and embody ideas which, in all probability, would not have been otherwise expressed. The influences which have affected his work include the associations of his native Gloucestershire, national folk-songs (especially the English and Welsh), modal Tudor counterpoint, and his studies under Sir Charles Stanford. To his early maturity belong some of his happiest and most successful chamber works.

Lady Audrey's Suite for string quartet, published under the auspices of the Patrons' Fund, is first in date. In *The Four Sleepy Golliwogs' Dance* the colouring is modal: such changes as there are depend more on chord than key. In the following movement—*The Little Girl and the Old Shepherd*—much of the beauty turns on the subtle arrangement of key, particularly the delicate poising of E flat major at the beginning against G major at the close. The third movement, *Prayer Time*, is a fine set of variations, and *The Old Shepherd's Tale* winds up the whole in a cheery rhythmic mood.

THE PIANO QUARTET won an award in the first competition of the Carnegie Trust (*vide* CARNEGIE FUND). It is distinguished by its classic contours, modern contents, and its complete reliance on music to explain music. No hint of a programme is given, yet it had a poetic basis. The three movements are three different aspects of the Hill of Chosen (Churchdown, near Gloucester), and the country of Cotswold and Severn. The movements might be described as *Dawn*, *Midsummer*, and *March Winds*. The first movement is in sonata form, and the folktune-like second subject, with its splendid 'lift', is the very core of the work. The moment at which it is quoted in the second movement is singularly beautiful. This lento has a rich texture, partly due to the constant use of the interval of the fifth, with added sixths or sevenths; and the modulation scheme is striking. The finale is a compound of scherzo and last movement, enigmatic to analyse unless the student understands that the real first subject does not appear till no. 33 in the score.

THE PHANTASY STRING QUARTET, op. 25, was written for the Cobbett Folk-song Phantasy competition, in which it won a prize. The fine modal tunes on which it is built are not traditional, but are by Howells himself; their treatment is in keeping with folk-song characteristics. Modal colouring persists throughout, and the themes are subjected to a process of permutation, rather than direct development, which is analogous to the process which tunes undergo when transmitted orally. Howells has succeeded in the hard task of constructing a large work out of purely melodic material; the form he has evolved combines the spontaneity of a phantasy with the logical design which intelligence demands. He contrives in the single movement of a phantasy to let his themes pass through a series of moods which are equivalent, in miniature, to the fully expressed phrases of a four-movement work in sonata form, and he has met dramatic needs by working towards one big climax near the end. Almost every page displays the close relevance of subsidiary to thematic matter which gives to some of his works an appearance of complexity, but which is in reality simple and self-explanatory. Other noteworthy points are the clever use of tone colour, and the poetic nature of the harmonies. For these it is as if Howells had been unconsciously influenced by that most English sound of the countryside, the beautiful tangle and hum of bell overtones.

A string quartet, 'In Gloucestershire', is still unpublished. It is Howells' most advanced and mature work in this form.

THE VIOLIN SONATAS. The first and third sonatas only are obtainable, the second having been withdrawn by the composer. The first sonata, in E major, owes its character to the impression made upon the composer by the playing and personality of Albert Sammons. The third sonata, in E minor, drew its inspiration from the Canadian Rockies and their savagery and grandeur.

In both, the violin part is melodic and declamatory, with ornamental passages used at times for emotional intensification, but more frequently as a species of intellectual filigree.

The first sonata embodies a clever structural experiment. The four linked movements are an exposition *in extenso* of the sonata form, which is usually confined to one movement. The first movement represents the first subject, the slow movement the second subject, the scherzo the development section, and the finale the recapitulation.

The E minor sonata is also unusual in design. The strongly contrasted subjects of the first movement are introduced in reversed order as the climax and coda of the final movement. In between are the most individual second movement (with its light tripping pizzicato passages for the violin, alternating with a swinging tune played arco), and the remainder of the restlessly energetic finale.

THE RHAPSODIC QUINTET for clarinet and strings is written with sensitive appreciation of instrumental needs. But the work is difficult to interpret because the characteristic traits of several styles of writing are combined closely. Written as a continuous movement, the texture is polyphonic rather than harmonic, while the subjects themselves are treated with the permutations typical of harmonic variation form. The equivalent effect of several short contrasting movements is given by diversified moulding of the same thematic material, and the parts all move with great vitality and independence, even with apparent rhythmic contradiction. The passages between nos. 11 and 21 seem bewildering until related to the steady beats of the 'cello part. The quintet is hardest to play of all Howells' chamber works, and requires fine players, first-rate ensemble, and devoted study. It repays the effort, for it is beautiful in an unusual and unworldly way.

As regards the other works, *Lady Audrey's Suite* and the phantasy quartet are of medium difficulty and very approachable. The piano quartet is also grateful to play, though more difficult—particularly the piano part—and the sonatas are hard, but not to a prohibitive degree.

In performance, all Howells' works demand players who can present the intellectual as well as the emotional contents. When interpreting them, it is useful to apply the method of rendering *pianissimos* and *crescendos* that obtains in the best performances of plain-song. To some degree the same thing applies to his rhythms; their frequent changes of time-signature indicate their relationship to the freedom of folk-song and plain-song.

Howells' chamber compositions are notable for their architectural strength, interesting texture, close masonry, and original imagination. But the later works have been slower to find acceptance. It is possible that their appeal turns a good deal upon the unconscious acceptance or refusal by hearers of the interval of the second as a concord. To Howells, as to many advanced musicians, the second *has* all the restful properties of a concord, but to many hearers it is still a discord. Moreover, his complexity of detail is difficult to disentangle, but his chamber music is full of beauty of an

unusual and elevated order. It is true chamber music, and truly English in the best sense.
MARION M. SCOTT.

† HOYER, KARL, b. 1891, German composer and organist.

Serenade, fl, ob, cl, horn, fag, F — op. 29 — Simrock.

See *Riemann* and *Dent*.

† HUBAY, JENÖ (originally Eugene Huber), b. 1858, Hungarian violinist.

Sonate romantique, pf, v, D — op. 22 — Hamelle, 1871.

Supported by a Hungarian state stipend, Hubay studied for five years at the Hochschule under Joachim. He was principal professor at the Brussels Conservatoire from 1882 to 1886. His music may be described as purely violinistic, and his connexion with chamber music as that of a performer: at Brussels with Servais as 'cellist and at Budapest with Hegyesy and Popper. His Quartet (Hubay, Herzfeld, Waldbauer, Popper) was highly praised by Brahms. Among his many distinguished pupils are Jelly d'Aranyi, Szigeti, and von Vecsey.
EDITOR.

HUBER, HANS, 1852–1921, Swiss composer, pupil of Reinecke.

				Composed	
Quartet	str		posth.	1873	
1st quintet	pf, 2 v, vla, vc	g mi	op. 111		Kistner, 1896.
2nd ,, (divertimento)	,, ,, ,, ,,	G	,, 125		Simrock, 1908.
Quintet	pf, fl, cl, horn, fag		,, 136		Hug, 1920.
Quartet	pf, v, vla, vc	B flat	,, 110		,, 1893.
,,	,, ,, ,, ,,	E	,, 117		,, 1902.
1st trio	pf, v, vc	E flat	,, 20		B. & H., 1877.
2nd ,,	,, ,, ,,	E	,, 65		,, 1917.
Trio-phantasie	,, ,, ,,		,, 83		Siegel, 1885.
3rd trio	,, ,, ,,	F	,, 105		Hainauer, 1890.
4th trio (*Eine Berg-novelle*)	,, ,, ,,	B flat	,, 120		Kistner, 1903.
Sonata	pf, 2 v	B flat	,, 135	1913	Leuckart, 1913.
Phantasie	pf, v	g mi	,, 17		B. & H., 1877.
1st sonata	,, ,,	c mi	,, 18		R. & E., 1877.
2nd ,,	,, ,,	B flat	,, 42		B. & H., 1877, 1898.
3rd ,,	,, ,,	b mi	,, 67		Siegel, 1883.
Suite	,, ,,	G	,, 82		R. Forberg, 1884.
4th sonata	,, ,,	G	,, 102		B. & H., 1888.
5th ,,	,, ,,	E	,, 112		Kistner, 1897.
6th ,, (appassionata)	,, ,,	d mi	,, 116	1901	B. & H., 1901.
7th sonata (graziosa)	,, ,,	G	,, 119		Kistner, 1903.
8th sonata (lirica)	,, ,,	A	,, 123		Simrock, 1907.
9th sonata (quasi fantasia)	,, ,,	g mi	,, 132	1901	Steingräber, 1901 and 1915.
Sonata	pf, vc	D	,, 33		Schott, 1876.
,,	,, ,,	A	,, 84		Rahter, 1885.
Suite	,, ,,	d mi	,, 89		Peters, 1886.
Sonata	,, ,,	c sharp mi	,, 114		Kistner, 1900.
,,	,, ,,	B flat	,, 130		Hug, 1909.

Huber, who was one of the most distinguished of Swiss musicians and a composer of sterling worth, wrote some 150 works, among which quite a number have made more than a fleeting impression. Although his latter years were given up mainly to symphonic and church music, he did not neglect chamber music, for which he had from his youth cherished a certain affection. It is remarkable that a single quartet is all he wrote for strings alone. This was published posthumously, though written in his student days at Leipzig, and he thought enough of it to re-write it in extended form as his eighth symphony. Evidently he was too much of a pianist to write chamber music that did not include his own instrument, but he sometimes combined wind instruments with it, and had a special predilection for piano and violin sonatas.

THE SIXTH VIOLIN SONATA (appassionata) was written in 1901, but according to Refardt, Huber's first biographer, the first movement was adapted from a violin sonata written in 1885 and transformed later into a concerto which was never published. This first movement, consisting of an introduction and allegro, is as long as an ordinary sonata; nevertheless it grips one, and is truly great in conception. The adagio non troppo, 'in tender, yearning mood', is predominantly poetical, even in the fugued and unnecessarily difficult middle section—a further relic of the said violin concerto. The comparatively short finale is inferior to the two preceding movements as regards invention, and is a new creation of 1901. It is a really valuable work, one of the best among modern sonatas, and repays performance by skilled and experienced players.

THE SONATA QUASI FANTASIA, op. 132, written and published in the same year as the other, should probably be rated even higher. As the title indicates, there is here no strict sonata form to fetter the composer's fancy, which is thus able to soar to greater heights. It may be added that the piano part is excellently written throughout, with full appreciation of tone gradations and sound effects generally, while the violin part is handled with equal skill. It is thoroughly modern in effect, and there is often originality in the harmonies. The first movement, an adagio, is tender, poetical, even bewitching at times. A piquant scherzo forms the second movement; here the slower middle section is particularly successful. The spirited finale has some insistent and rhythmically interesting melodies. This sonata is equally suited for private or public performance, but requires thorough practice on account of its difficulty.

SONATA FOR TWO VIOLINS AND PIANO. Sonatas for this combination are so rarely written now that Huber's op. 135 should be very welcome. According to Refardt, the work is an adaptation of six short concert pieces for violin and piano. The writer does not consider their musical content to be on the level of their technical form, which is beyond all praise. In the first movement, maestoso, especially, the melody is not sufficiently flowing; there is, too, a certain aridity of invention, and too great a tendency to change the key, but the tempo di menuetto is decidedly graceful, and not without originality. As regards melody the all too short romance is by far the most pleasing. The work is rounded off by a very dashing finale, notable for its rhythmic swing. Experienced ensemble players are needed for this sonata.

THE SECOND PIANO QUARTET, op. 117, is inspired by Gottfried Keller's fine poem:

'Arm in arm and tree to tree stand the oaks in th' ancient wood.
This day to me their old, old song they sang in kindly mood.'

There is a real breath of the forest in the opening andante, which, despite its kinship with the forest murmurings in *Siegfried*, is very impressive and quite the best part of the work. The succeeding allegro con fuoco is evidently intended to suggest a storm in the forest, in contrast to the peace of the first movement. The main theme is well worked out. The short adagio espressivo is less pleasing. It leads directly into the finale, a vigorous allegro inspired by the ending of the poem. The introduction of an old-time melody gives it a homely charm, but the short fugato seems rather far-fetched. At the close, the main theme of the first movement is recalled. Although this quartet cannot be called an outstanding work, it is, on any showing, worthy of notice, and can be recommended for performance at home and in public. WILHELM ALTMANN.

[The present writer has played a great many of Huber's sonatas for violin and piano, from time to time, and would like to draw the attention of amateurs who do not already know them, to the works of a genuine romantic amongst chamber music writers.

In his early sonatas there runs a vein of tenderness which may ill consort with post-war feelings, but which appeals to those who remain young in heart. These sonatas are strongly influenced by his compatriot Raff (b. 1822), and of both composers it may be said that they came under the spell of Liszt. Huber's latest sonatas, however, give evidence of development in other directions. An added strength is apparent and they are of more interest to musicians, but there is less of the romantic element which was natural to him in earlier days, and which then formed his chief charm. EDITOR.]

HUDSON, J. W., contemporary composer.

Trio, pf, v, vc, D — Augener-Schott.

† HUGHES, HERBERT, b. 1882, Irish composer and critic.

Three Satirical Songs, voice, fl, v, cl, fag — Enoch.

This proves to be a very effective combination.

HUGUENIN, CHR.

Two suites (nos. 1, 2), pf, v — Huguenin, *c.* 1906.

HUGUES, LUIGI, 1836–1913, Italian flautist.

Works include:

Quartet, fl, ob, cl, fag, g mi	op. 72		Ricordi.
,, ,, ,, ,, ,, B flat	,, 76		,,

Hugues, though an amateur (an engineer by profession), was head of the music school at Casale. The above two quartets are very concertante in character. Other works include an attractive allegro scherzoso, intermezzo, op. 92 (taken from a quintet in D, which was apparently never published), for the same with two flutes; numerous studies for flute alone; duets for two flutes—almost equal to those of Kuhlau but more modern in style—op. 109; several trios for two flutes and piano; a sonata romantica, op. 57; and numerous other pieces for flute and piano, distinctly original in style. All Hugues's published works were issued by Ricordi. H. M. FITZGIBBON.

†HUMISTON, W. H.

Suite, pf, v, f sharp mi		B. & H., 1913.

†HUMMEL, Ferdinand, b. 1855, German pianist and harpist.

Quintet, pf, 2 v, vla, vc, a mi	op. 47	Siegel, 1887.
Quartet, pf, v, vla, vc, c sharp mi	„ 19	Schott, 1879.
Sonata, pf, v, c mi	op. 24	Brockhaus, 1881.
„ pf, vc, a mi	„ 2	Junne, 1877.
„ „ „ A flat	„ 9	Simrock, 1877.
„ „ „ A	„ 12	Peters, 1879.
„ pf, vc (or vla), e mi	„ 38	Siegel, 1885.
Duo, pf, horn	„ 20	Schott, 1880.
Sonata, pf, horn	„ 117	Protze, 1914.

HUMMEL, Johann Nepomuk, 1778–1837, famous composer and pianist.

Works include:

Three quartets	str	C, G, E flat	op. 30	Haslinger.
Septet	pf, fl, ob, vla, vc, cb, horn, (also as string quintet)	d mi	„ 74	Schott, 1869; André, 1870.
Septet 'militaire'	pf, fl, v, cl, vc, cb, trpt	C	„ 114	Haslinger, 1878.
Quintet	pf, v, vla, vc, cb	E flat	„ 87	Litolff, 1875; Peters, 1874.
Quartet	pf, v, vla, vc	G	Posth.	B. & H.

Seven trios, pf, v, vc, of which the following are obtainable:

Trio	E flat	op. 12	U.E., 1911.
„	E	„ 83	Peters, 1856.
„	E flat	„ 93	U.E., 1911.
„	E flat	„ 96	J. Schuberth & Co., 1852.

The remaining trios are opp. 22, 35, 65.

Five sonatas, pf, v (or alternative instr.), opp. 5, 19, 25, 28, 37, various publishers.

also:

Sonata	pf, vc (or cl, or v)	A	op. 104	Peters, 1872 and 1880.
„	pf, fl (or v)	D	„ 50	B. & H.; B. & B., 1920.
„	„ „ „	A	„ 64	B. & H.

also two serenades, opp. 63, 66 (pf, v, guitar, cl, fag), a viola sonata, and some smaller pieces.

Hummel's chamber music undoubtedly represents the best fruit of his activities; it not only enjoyed the greatest appreciation in its own time, but has retained much of its significance up to the present day. His violin sonatas have for the most part been forgotten, although some of them are distinguished by interesting features, especially fine harmonic details and the gift of invention. There is not much depth of feeling, however, and they contain so much that is trifling and superficial that they cannot be regarded as wholly artistic. The same holds good of the quartets, albeit in less degree. But credit is due to Hummel for having written the first sonata for viola and piano, a work which is worthy of republication.

The Trios have greater importance. The first, op. 12, contains original ideas moulded into a pleasing form by a skilled hand, and shows understanding of the instruments and their use, the piano being particularly favoured. The opening allegro is passionate in character, and the andante, which reflects the sensitive nature of the composer, is striking because of the unique treatment of the 'cello, while the finale, if rather shallow, is at least superficially effective.

The Second Trio, op. 22, is more notable for technique than for artistry. It owes its existence, apparently, more to a strong desire to compose than to inner motives. In this work, also, the unusual treatment of the 'cello strikes the hearer. Form and development are satisfactory throughout, but inventive power is less in evidence. The trio contains some pleasing variations on an original theme, and the work ends with a gay and brief alla turca movement.

Third and Fifth Trios. The third trio, op. 35, occupies a middle position between the two just mentioned, but is more clearly influenced by Mozart, whilst the fifth, op. 83, is extremely well written, and not only shows surprising skill in regard to form, but bears eloquent witness to Hummel's progress in technical ability. In the finale, a carefully worked-out rondo, the composer's virtuosity, long held in check, breaks forth and indulges itself to the full with brilliant passage work.

The Sixth Trio, op. 93, also has praiseworthy technical and artistic qualities. Though it exhibits Hummel's characteristically preferential treatment of the piano, there is much to admire in the bright opening movement, the emotional larghetto, and the whirling rhythms of the final rondo.

The Seventh Trio, op. 96, does not show Hummel's inventive power at his best. But he would not be the master that he really is if he did not understand how to use his technical skill to hide artistic defects, thereby throwing dust in the eyes of the general public and preventing the recognition of the real shallowness of this composition. The first allegro speedily captures the hearer with its rhythm and spirit; the andante is conceived somewhat in the manner of Haydn, but the defects are not so well disguised as in the other movements. The piquant dance finale *à la russe* (allegro vivo) is very delightful, and the hearer is left with pleasant though not permanent impressions.

THE QUINTET, op. 87, is a masterpiece; the first movement at once captivates and impresses the hearer with its power and passion. The peculiar principal theme, of a somewhat martial character, begins in E flat minor, and offers good material for development. In the second part the theme appears in D major, with fine imitations. The recapitulation is introduced by retarded progressions, the motif being altered and abbreviated, and an intermediate period inserted. This period forms a fine contrast to the following fiery flow in triplets, and to the gently expiring close. After this passionate utterance follows the minuet, allegro con fuoco, a mixture of animation and exuberance with a melancholy strain. Original modulations and chromatic progressions then lead to the sunny trio in which gloomy thoughts are dispelled for the time, until, finally, the opening mood returns. A short largo, which modulates to no more distant key than the dominant (B flat major), is full of pleasing melody and deep feeling, and is followed, *attacca subito*, by the final allegro agitato. Here light-hearted merriment reigns, and the movement ends with a brilliant and effective close.

THE SEPTET, op. 74, is Hummel's best-known work, and though the enthusiasm it once aroused can no longer be reawakened, its high artistic value remains undisputed, and it must be assigned a place of honour in the literature of chamber music. Its many good qualities—harmony of form, grandeur of conception, wealth and noble expressiveness—outweigh the defects due to the composer's virtuosity, more than is the case with any of his other works. It was first performed in England at a Philharmonic concert in 1818.

In the opening allegro the piano indulges in florid passage work, with occasional pauses to allow the other instruments to speak more impressively. The melodic line is taken chiefly by the flute. The F horn is also employed with particular skill; it sometimes has to deal with very difficult passages, but is extraordinarily effective. There are some original turns of harmony; for instance, in the second part, the modulation from F to F sharp, then the deviation to C major through B major and E minor, the piano playing soft arpeggios at the same time, while the contrabass provides the foundation, and the other instruments accompany with sustained notes.

The capricious second movement forms an excellent contrast. The piano is here treated with far more reticence than in the first movement, remaining at first in the background with but little to say; but later it accompanies the other instruments in modest passages and runs. It takes a more important part again in the lovely trio (alternativo, D major) with dancing quaver passages and many grace-notes. The D horn prepares the resumption of the theme with an F sharp marked < > sounding through several bars, after which it continues alone for four bars, and then assumes the upper voice of the motif. The movement ends with a coda following the trio.

In the third movement, andante con variazioni, the piano begins with a folk-like theme of noble simplicity. The other instruments gradually join in, flute and oboe alternately playing the principal parts. By way of epilogue, a cadenza connects the theme with the variations. In the first variation the quavers of the theme are accelerated to semiquavers, which fall principally to the share of the piano, while flute, oboe, and horn in turn take up the theme. In the second variation the theme is given chiefly to the pianist's left hand, the right accompanying in demisemiquavers, which later appear in the bass also, whilst flute and oboe take up the somewhat varied theme. In the third variation (in F minor) the theme is at first varied by 'cello and contrabass, with sustained notes on viola and horn; later, flute and oboe take an important part. The piano accompanies chiefly in triplet semiquavers, and in a prolonged finale accomplishes the transition to the last variation. In this (again in F major) the piano part is full of strange and interesting harmonies, the other instruments acting chiefly as accompanists; but before the close they resume the theme, in five parts at first. They then drop off one by one towards the end. This last variation may be regarded as the most effective, while the third is the most artistic.

In originality of invention and finish of form the finale, vivace, is on a level with the other movements, and its passion is the more impressive after the preceding quiet movement. In a surprising way the viola leads off with a short fugue subject, answered by the oboe at the octave, the contrabass at the fourth below, and the 'cello at the second. A pleasing intermediate part in A major follows, whereupon the theme unexpectedly returns, with sustained notes from the other instruments and a tremolo on the bass. The fugue motif appears again on the viola, this time in B minor, the other instruments answering in the same manner as before. After chromatic modulations, the intermediate section in A major is resumed in D major, at first by the 'cello, afterwards by the wind instruments, to which the violin replies with soft pizzicato, while the piano moves in broken chords. Here the D horn is employed particularly skilfully, with few, but significant notes. The theme appears once more in a minor key, played *ff* by the left hand, the right accompanying in triplets, while the other instruments march forward in stately measures, and then all hasten tempestuously to the end.

SEPTET MILITAIRE, op. 114. The second septet is not equal in importance to the famous work just described, though it has many attractive features—imagination, skilled technical treatment of the instruments, and sound structure. The title 'militaire' is derived from the use of the trumpet, an instrument not formerly used in chamber music, except in Bach's second Brandenburg concerto. Hummel's work obviously inspired Saint-Saëns to employ the trumpet in his septet, op. 65.

The opening allegro con brio is full of youthful fire, and the instruments are employed to the best advantage. In the calm second movement the trumpet is not employed, but in the third, allegro, it is indemnified for its long absence by free use in the production of surprising effects, and it ends the movement in vigorous fashion. The finale, vivace, in spite of its simplicity and economical employment of means, has many and various moods, but joyousness is its most prominent characteristic. This attractive, though not in every respect perfect, work ends in softly expiring notes like a passing dream.

In his time Hummel played a very prominent part, and was considered by his followers as a rival to Beethoven, a comparison which to-day appears incomprehensible. Hummel's chamber music is the product of a highly gifted musician, who skilfully applied Mozart's suggestions to this type of music. He is a composer who, true to tradition, opened no new paths, a task which remained for Beethoven. Hummel's tendency to virtuosity, which induced him to seek effect rather than emotion, is kept in the background in his principal works. But even these are in no way comparable with those of Beethoven, who revolutionized music in form as well as in contents. Beethoven's music proceeded from his inmost soul; Hummel's was rather of the sensuous kind, such as formed a school of its own, further developed by his pupils and followers, and, after Beethoven's principles of art had been generally accepted, this type of music lost greatly in estimation. RUDOLF FELBER.

[At the age of seven, Hummel's musical ability attracted Mozart's attention. The latter took him as a pupil, on condition that Hummel should live with him, so that he could superintend his studies. Hummel became a great pianist, with a special gift for improvisation. The story of his quarrels with Beethoven and the death-bed reconciliation with the master is told in *Grove* and *Fétis*.

There is difficulty in giving an accurate list of his works. Many are no longer played, and the scores of concerted works in some cases do not exist; further, there is confusion with regard to opus numbers. In my youth Hummel's piano trios were among the household gods of the British chamber music player; and the first of the famous MUSICAL UNION CONCERTS (*q.v.*) included one of them (op. 83, written for John Cramer, and perhaps for that reason favouring the piano more than the strings). At the same concerts his septet, op. 74 (also published as a string quintet), was played every year side by side with Beethoven's septet, and invariably received by an audience of connoisseurs with enthusiastic applause. The piano part is exceptionally brilliant, and though in some respects the work is old-fashioned, its melodies are of the kind that never dies. They are full of charm, and treated in a way which appeals to musicians. There is reason to think that a revival of this septet would be attended with more than a success of curiosity. Ella, the founder of the Musical Union concerts, wrote of this work as 'preserving its stability and duration throughout Europe for more than a century—not suspended on the slender thread of fashion and caprice, but bound to the human heart by every tie of sympathetic approbation'. One objection to its inclusion in modern programmes may be the absence of a violin part.

Liszt took the piano part in Hummel's septet at a concert of the old Philharmonic Society, and introduced so many embellishments that (so writes Myles Birket Foster) the composer's music was unrecognizable. And Ella, writing in 1854, states that the septet was played during ten years with ten misprints.

EDITOR.]

HUMOUR IN CHAMBER MUSIC.

If I were asked to define the mental quality known as musical humour, I would straightway refer the inquirer to the finales of Haydn's quartets, in which is to be found humour of the inimitable kind which holds the sense of the ludicrous and the sense of beauty in one. In the course of my researches I have been surprised to find how many composers have made humour a feature of their musical programme. Here is a list of *soi-disant* humorous works which I submit in the hope that they may be found amusing, but without pretence that anything beyond the title-page is known to me. Frankly, to play them all through might prove anything but a joke.

Graf (or Graaf), Carl Friedrich: *Economical duet for two performers on one violin*, op. 27 (Hummel, Berlin).

Haensel, A.: *Plaisanterie musicale*, str. quartet, op. 79 (Bauer, Dresden, 1860–67).

Heitsch, Alfred: *Humoristisches Dilettanten-Quartett* (Klemm).

Hermann, A.: Duet, 2 v, *Duo comique*; No. 1 starts at the beginning and No. 2 at the same time at the end, playing the same part reversed. (Carl Fischer, N.Y., 1926.)

HOLBROOKE, J. (*q.v.*): *Pickwick Quartet.*

KASSMAYER, M. (*q.v.*), spoken of by *Riemann* as a musical humorist of the first order. Thirteen humorous settings in counterpoint for string quartet of folk-songs of various nations. H. 1–13 (Schlesinger, 1870–1885). One similar setting, v, vla, vc, op. 40 (Schlesinger, 1855).

Neumann, A.: Comic quartet, 3 v, vc (C. F. Schmidt, 1884).

Piber, J.: *Musikal. Humorist. Szene: Gastspiel des Streich-Terzetts Paganini*, v, vla, vc, op. 40. (Schott, 1904.)

Richter, Aug.: Humorous string quartet. (Seeling, 1887.)

Schenk, Joh.: *Oddities of the Gout*, viola da gamba and bass.

Sechter, Simon: *Les quatre tempéraments*; Musical Pleasantry for string quartet, op. 6. (Coppi, Vienna.)

Thiele, Richard: Three quartets in comic style.

WERNER, Gregorius Jos. (*q.v.*): *The Election of the Village Judge*, 5 voices, 2 v, fig. bass. *The March of the Vienna Old Clothes Men*, 4 voices, 2 v, fig. bass.

WETZEL, Hermann (*q.v.*): Humorous Serenade.

There is a plentiful supply of humour of the purely literary kind in Robert Haven Schauffler's two clever books—*Fiddler's Luck* and *The Musical Amateur, A Book on the Human Side of Music* (Houghton Mifflin Co., Boston and New York). These vivacious chronicles of musical life in America do not lend themselves well to quotation, and I suggest that every chamber music 'fan' should acquire for himself and peruse both of them from cover to cover. To readers who take my advice I promise a good time, for Mr. Schauffler is the Artemus Ward of amateur music.

I find the following *jeux d'esprit* in my commonplace book. They may be old stories, but they are good ones.

'At our musical parties we played Haydn's symphonies compressed as quintets. Our leader, who attacked every piece as a bulldog would a badger, set off at a furious rate, and being a corpulent man soon fiddled himself into such a heat that he took off his coat. The 'cello player was not behind him in fervour, for on coming to a difficult passage he screwed up his muscular powers till his mouth had a shape not unlike that of a water-bottle, which, with a goggling stare, would have charmed Cruikshank himself. Our leader, disdaining anything like a halt, jumped over all the rests, dashed out of one movement into the other, keeping the same helter-skelter pace, so that it was difficult to come in with any sort of grace at the death.'

'A HAYDN QUARTET. An intelligent lady said that when she heard a Haydn quartet she fancied herself present at the conversation of four agreeable persons. She thought the first violin had the air of an eloquent man of genius of middle age, who supported a conversation the subject of which he suggested. In the second violin she recognized a friend of the first, who sought by all possible means to display him to advantage, seldom thought of himself, and kept up the conversation rather by assenting to what was said by others than by advancing any ideas of his own. The alto was a grave, learned, and sententious man. He supported the discourse of the first violin by laconic maxims, striking for their truth. The bass was a worthy old lady, rather inclined to chatter, who said nothing of much consequence and yet was always desirous of putting in a word. But she gave an additional grace to the conversation, and, while she was talking, the other interlocutors had time to breathe. It was, however, evident that she had a secret inclination for the alto, which she preferred to the other instruments.'

It is related of the Austrian composer Weigl that he played quartets with the Emperor Frederick. On one occasion the august violinist felt called upon to lead, but played without slavish regard for accidentals, whereupon the composer, nearly on his knees, advanced and most reverentially said, 'Would your Majesty grant my humble prayer for a gracious F sharp?'

My budget concludes with some curiosities of performances at the 'Pops' communicated to me by that fine artist Benoît Hollander. They are perhaps in style not quite suited to the main body of the Cyclopedia, but under the heading Humour they pass and are of no little interest, as every one likes to take a peep behind the scenes.

'On a certain Monday morning we rehearsed a new quartet. After a long spell of it we were too tired to go through the Haydn quartet which was the last item on the programme, but we knew these works so well that there was no need of rehearsal. It must be noted that the celebrated eighty-three were bound together in thick folios. On the platform at night an unfortunate (?) remark of Ries brought to light the fact that each player had a different quartet before him—all being, of course, in the same key. I say 'unfortunate' as, being fond of a joke, I was very sorry Ries had discovered it, for the effect on the audience would have been delightful!

The first time I played viola in the Schumann piano quartet the audience applauded three bars before the end of the slow movement (*v.* art. PIANOFORTE AND STRINGS); after the applause had subsided I quietly played the remaining bars solo, as the viola virtually finishes the movement. Years later Sir Charles Stanford, who had been present, reminded me of the incident, and said how delighted he had been.

The following will give an idea of the life of a member of the 'Pops' Quartet in those days:

Saturday: 'Pops'—London.

Sunday: Four hours' rehearsal for Schubert's wind octet.

Monday: Schumann quartet rehearsal.

Evening concert ('Pops').

Tuesday: 10 o'clock train to Liverpool. Concert at night.

Wednesday: 'Gentlemen's Concert', Manchester.

Thursday: Hallé Concert, Manchester.

Friday: Bradford.

The cold at Bradford was intense. After my solos, I came into the green-room shivering. Sir Charles Hallé, seeing this, made me swallow a tumbler of port wine—in those days I was almost a total abstainer. The result may be left to the imagination. As Hallé had had no time for rehearsal, I had to play Beethoven's 'variation-trio' at sight. My one thought on the platform was how to keep awake. To this day I have no idea what these variations are like, and no wish to investigate further.

On the Saturday we returned to town for the Saturday 'Pop', a Beethoven concert, the last item on the programme being the great B flat trio.

Towards the end of the finale I noticed Piatti, who sat facing me, looking worried. Thinking he was unwell, for we had had no time to get any food, I waited on the steps to assist him, when he told me that the trouble was that the last page of the trio was missing and he had played a large part of the movement from memory.

I myself had a similar experience while playing Beethoven's C major quartet, op. 59, Joachim being the leader. I was troubled with a stye in the left eye, and during the opening of the fugue I went suddenly blind and for thirty bars played from memory. Next day the offending stye was removed by a doctor who insisted on discussing the concerts throughout the operation. I did not enjoy that conversation in the least.' EDITOR.

HUNGAR, PAUL.

Sonata, pf, v, G	op. 10	Kistner & Siegel, 1925.

HUNGARIAN PERFORMING ORGANIZATIONS.

BUDAPEST:

(a) *Quartets:*

BUDAPEST STRING QUARTET: Emil Hauser, Roismann (replacing Imre Poganyi), Istvan Ipolyi, Harry Son—all members of the Royal Opera House Orchestra. First public recital in 1921, after three years of rehearsal. Has given over five hundred public recitals. Has toured Europe and visited the Canary Islands. In addition to its programmes of classical works, has given many first performances of modern compositions.

HERZL QUARTET.

HUNGARIAN STRING QUARTET: Emerich Waldbauer, Tivadar Orszagh, Jean de Temesvary, Eugène de Kerpely. These artists have specialized in the interpretation of Hungarian chamber music. The quartets of Bartók and Kodály were introduced by them to the English public. The distinguishing feature of their style is its extreme vitality.

LADIES' QUARTET: Barany, Szeremy, Zipernovsky, Ulbrich.

JENO LEHNER[1] or LENER QUARTET: Joseph Smilovits, Sandor Roth, Imre Hartman. After two years of rehearsal this Quartet made its first appearance in Vienna (1920) before an international gathering of musicians. Has toured Europe. Famous for its historical programmes. Has given first performances of many modern works, and has included in its programmes quartets of the Mannheim school. But its greatest success in London has been in the performance of accepted works by the great masters.

MELLES-KARPATHY QUARTET.

FERI ROTH STRING QUARTET: Jenno Antal, Ferenc Molnar, Albert van Doorn.

(b) *Trios:*

BUDAPEST TRIO: Endré Petri, Nicholas Roth, Georg Roth. A body of artists giving modern programmes and excelling in unanimity of expression.

In Budapest there formerly existed the *Keméṅy* and *Grünfeld* Quartets, predecessors of the younger Hungarian Quartets, which to-day (1928) have acquired universal fame.
HUGO LEICHTENTRITT.

HÜNTEN, FRANZ [OR FRANÇOIS], 1793–1878, German composer.

Trio, pf, v, vc, E flat	op. 14	Farrenc (Paris); Schott (portions only).
Trio, pf, v, vc, d mi	,, 91	Schott.
Trio, pf, fl, vc, d mi	,, 91 bis	,,
Terzetto, pf, v (or cl), vc	,, 175	,,

Hünten had an enormous vogue in the early years of the nineteenth century, 'though his works (with the exception of a trio concertant for pf, v, vc) were of little value' (*Grove*).

†HURÉ, JEAN, b. 1877, French composer, founder of the Paris École Normale de Musique.

	Composed		
1st quartet, str	1916	Mathot.	
2nd ,, ,, atonal	1920	Senart.	
Quintet, pf, 2 v, vla, vc, D	1908	Mathot.	
Petite suite en trio, pf, v, vc	1898	,,	
Serenade, pf, v, vc, atonal		,,	1920.
Sonata, pf, v, c mi	1900	,,	1920.
Sonatina, pf, v, G	1906	,,	
1st sonata, pf, vc, f sharp mi	1901–2	,,	
2nd sonata, pf, vc, F	1906	,,	
3rd sonata, pf, vc, F sharp	1909	,,	

[1] As originally spelt.

Huré's *Petite Suite* is founded on Breton folk-songs, developed in very simple form, with piquant harmonic and contrapuntal resource. The last but one is a moving cantilena, without accompaniment, which has the serene beauty of a Gregorian chant.

THE C MINOR VIOLIN SONATA is in four movements: prelude and allegro, of solidly classical structure; intermezzo, in A flat, changing to E major in the middle, with a very slow conclusion in which is to be found the second theme of the preceding movement and a sketch of a fresh theme to be treated in the following movements: scherzo (C minor) enclosing a Lied[1] in G flat, a key intentionally remote, which forms a parenthesis as it were, containing various subsidiary themes. After the repeat of the scherzo, in C major, the Lied returns (also in C major), and the conclusion is built on the rhythm of the scherzo.

In the finale, after an exposition in slow tempo of the opening theme transformed, in C minor, followed by a phrase in E flat—derived from the second theme of the first movement—there begins a fugato which leads to the recapitulation in C minor, with conclusion in C major, recalling the principal themes.

THE VIOLIN SONATINA in G major has the peculiarity that the principal subjects of its three rather short movements are formed of the three essential notes E-G-D, the D being the lowest note.

THE THREE 'CELLO SONATAS present original structural features. The first, in F sharp minor, is in four movements, all linked together. It is preceded by a prelude and followed by a postlude, and is played without a break. The second, in F major, also in four movements, marks an original return to suite-form combined with sonata-form. A single motif gives rise to the whole of the themes. The first movement (F major) is an allegretto on a single theme; the second a bourrée in suite-form; and the third, an andante in triple time (A minor), is set out as a Lied-phrase evolved from the various transformations of the principal subject, now hardly recognizable. This links up with the last movement, also in triple time, but 'assez-vif' (rather lively), with a trochaic rhythm, in rondo-form, the couplets[1] being full of spirit. This ends with a brilliant conclusion in F major.

The third sonata, in F sharp major, in three movements without break (like the first sonata), is a remarkable work. The first movement, a rather short allegretto on a single theme (F sharp major), has a very pure type of melody, and is structurally analogous to the foregoing sonata. In the concluding section a new fiercely rhythmic motif appears. This is to become the counter subject of a fugue in the second movement.

This second movement, in G minor, is an allegro with a wild rhythm, but quite classical in form. The recapitulation is turned into a fugue, in G minor, the subject being the principal motif of the first subject, and the counter-subject the fiercely rhythmic motif of the opening. With the second subject, now in G major, the fugue reappears in stretto and by contrary motion, with ever-growing rhythmic and polyphonic life. Gradually all this subsides, and leads straight into a very tranquil andante. The principal melody of this is derived from a new theme, and the intermediate portions recall former themes. This postlude, ending peacefully in F sharp major, concludes a fine work, in which the robust style of a Bach is coupled with the grand manner of a Beethoven.

THE QUINTET for piano and strings is in four linked movements, a favourite arrangement with this composer. The first movement, allegretto in Lied-form with two themes, begins with a poetic carillon which runs all through the work; it serves as accompaniment to a pastoral theme full of freshness, which soon brightens up into a brilliant *Kermesse*. To this theme, superimposed on the carillon, is added a *vieille chanson*, rudely rhythmic, borrowed from Breton folk-song. The music grows gradually calmer, and the viola sings a dreamy phrase which leads to a long voluptuous passage, in B major, sung by the violin and accompanied by various snatches of former themes. The Lied ends with a return of the *Kermesse* (in D major) and a coda in which the violin sings as a recitative—in jubilant rhythm, unbarred—the melody of the second section of the Lied, ornamented now with numerous *melismata* over atonal harmonies. A development of the carillon on 'cello and viola serves as link with the second movement. This is an allegro *tumultueux*, in classical sonata form. A vigorous new theme, in D minor, appears in the exposition. A transition leads to a calmer section, in which the elastic and tenderly melodic second theme appears in F major, at first broken up among the different instruments. After reminiscences of the opening carillon and the first-movement themes, the development starts, in F minor, with a prolonged melody derived from the breaking up of the various themes already employed. This is then combined with the actual themes themselves in richly varied polyphony. The recapitulation proceeds normally, in D minor; the second theme, this time, is in G flat, and, with a reminiscence of several previous themes, links up with the third movement. This leads into an andante, in D major, which serves as postlude. This work, so full of life, draws to a serene close with this deeply emotional meditation, in which is developed the second subject of the second movement, with a reminiscence of the pastoral theme and the carillon; the movement then dies quietly away.

The two string quartets are admirably written, and here is found a return to the true spirit of chamber music.

[1] See Foreword, art. BEETHOVEN.

THE FIRST QUARTET (dedicated to Armand Parent) is in three movements, the first preceded by a short introduction, in which the principal themes are set out, one grave and mournful, the other, in slower tempo, haunting and mysterious. This last runs all through the work.

THE SECOND QUARTET is in four linked movements: allegro with two themes, joyous *Kermesse*, full of spirit and variety, and a charming *villanelle* rhythm; a second movement consists of a fugato followed by a second theme, which leads to an andante, a kind of deeply emotional elegy, which ends with a reappearance of the fugato, first in contrary motion, then in stretto. The finale is a reproduction of the first allegro, *pp* and pizzicato almost throughout, with numerous melodic and harmonic transformations.

With keen sensibility, a marked leaning towards the dramatic, and a vivid and healthy imagination, Jean Huré possesses wide culture and a robust technique. He has sought to restore to health the musical mentality of his day with draughts from the life-giving springs of the past. While respecting cyclic unity, his inventive mind is ceaselessly discovering happy modifications of the structural framework of the ancient classical forms. Jean Huré's music suggests a lofty and glorious ancestry. It will be his pride to have returned to absolute music at a period when the tendency is to wander away from it, and to have given all his strength, with a continual sacrifice of vital force, to restore the muse of France to perfect health.

ADOLPHE PIRIOU.

HURLSTONE, WILLIAM YEATES, 1876–1906, English pianist and composer.

Phantasy quartet, str, a minor and A	Novello.
Quartet, pf, v, vla, vc, e mi, op. 43 (posth.)	Curwen.
Trio, pf, v, vc, G and g mi	Cary (Avison ed.); Novello.
Sonata, pf, v, d mi	Augener, 1897; Schott, 1911.
,, pf, vc	Curwen.
,, pf, fag, F	Novello, 1909.
Four characteristic pieces, pf, cl	Cary (Avison ed.).

By the early death of this most accomplished and promising musician native chamber music suffered a great loss. Some musicians take to music of this type because they have no time to write a symphony and no prospect of getting it played, or because a friend asks for a sonata, or because they want a change. But Hurlstone was a born writer of chamber music; he had great constructive ability, and the themes of his larger works are admirably designed for the interesting treatment that they invariably receive; his sense of balance was extraordinarily keen, and he never allowed his music to get out of hand; the hearer is always conscious of a calm, directing intelligence. This is not to say that his work is unimpassioned or mechanical—far from it. It is the expression of a nature serene and wholesome, but capable of deep feeling which is never ostentatiously paraded. Hurlstone's music is never affected and never morbid, and there is an intimate feeling about his work which marks him out as an ideal composer for the small circle to which true chamber music appeals.

At the age of eighteen Hurlstone gained a composition scholarship at the R.C.M., where he studied under Sir Charles Stanford, the teacher and mentor of so many brilliant musicians. Hurlstone was always in delicate health and suffered much, but, unlike many other artists in a like condition, neither his work nor his personality tended to decadence or morbidity; he was always manly and cheerful, and his music is an accurate reflection of his honest and straightforward nature.

His chamber compositions are few, but, apart from a few *juvenilia*, they are full of interest. The works which stand out as being most completely characteristic of him are, perhaps, the phantasy string quartet, the piano quartet, and the piano trio; and it may be interesting to treat these with a certain particularity.

THE STRING QUARTET won the first prize in the first of W. W. Cobbett's now famous competitions, and it may be considered a lucky happening that the series of phantasies should be inaugurated with a work so truly representative of genuine chamber music. This phantasy is really in four short movements, but the whole work is built up on a few themes which appear in different forms throughout. This is the plan on which Liszt worked in many of his big compositions, and it is rather curious that a prominent phrase in Hurlstone's quartet strongly recalls one in Liszt's B minor sonata for piano:

Ex. 1.

But the general character and spirit of the two works are, of course, entirely different. Hurlstone was a classicist, and it is obvious that Brahms was a powerful influence with him, as with most Royal College students of his time.

In the course of this phantasy a very fine climax is worked up, from which a few bars are quoted.

Ex. 2.

(The viola part, filling up the harmony with a persistent rhythm of two quavers, followed by a crotchet and a crotchet rest, is omitted.)

In this extract the 'cello part is founded upon the first theme of the work, and the first and second violins in canon play about with the leap of a seventh, which is a characteristic feature of the first theme in a major key. A few bars later the viola takes up the seventh leaps, and the whole passage culminates in a pause on a high 'cello note—

Ex. 3.

which, sinking a minor seventh, leads into a repetition of the major theme mentioned above. This is a masterly and powerful piece of writing, and is the real climax of the work. The finale seems a little scrappy, as if the composer had not space enough for the leisurely development of material to which he naturally leant. The string quartet writing is perfect throughout.

The Piano Quartet is Hurlstone's most elaborately written chamber work, and, in some respects, the finest. This is the striking opening subject of the first movement, given out by the strings in octaves:

Ex. 4.

It will be seen that Hurlstone has here caught Brahms's well-known trick of writing arpeggio passages with one note omitted. There are other instances of this in his work. Interesting points in the construction of this movement are the appearance of the second subject in the very unusual key of E flat major (in the recapitulation it is in G major), the return to the original key via a dominant seventh chord on B flat, and the treatment of the first theme in canon. The slow movement is simple and flowing, with a charming principal melody. The second theme seems at first hardly so attractive, and perhaps a little square, but its treatment is masterly, and he leads up with great art to the return of the first theme, which now appears *f* on a dominant bass.

The scherzo is hardly jovial, but moves along with a fine swing. The theme of the 'trio' has something of a Scottish flavour, and one forceful passage towards the end recalls the scherzo in Brahms's piano quintet. Perhaps to atone for the lack of geniality in the scherzo, the finale is a singularly cheerful movement. It is preceded by an introduction founded on the first theme of the quartet, which makes another appearance in its canonic attire towards the end of the work. In general mood and style this movement reminds one of the finale of Brahms's second symphony, and, at times, of the last movement of the same master's piano quartet in A. But in judging Hurlstone's work as a whole, these reminiscences must not be taken too seriously. Every young man is, and must be, influenced by what he admires. It is not now the fashion to write in the Brahms manner; our young composers now go farther back and affect the medieval and primitive, or even the barbaric, but the urbane and civilized art of chamber music does not easily assimilate such peculiarities.

The Piano Trio is an altogether delightful work. The themes are fresh and attractive, the workmanship is on the same high level as that of the piano quartet, and it is far less influenced by Brahms. It is happy and genial throughout. The easy flow of the opening movement, the unforced lyricism of the slow movement, the charming rhythms of the scherzo, and the capital finale with its clever treatment of the leading theme and the attractive Scotch tune which serves as a second subject;—all go to make a work as enjoyable to play as it is to listen to. One must again note the entire absence of any kind of affectation in this, as in Hurlstone's other works.

Sonatas. An early violin and piano sonata is technically interesting if not characteristic, but the sonata for 'cello and piano is a fine work, and so is the sonata for bassoon and piano, with which it has been sometimes confused. This last work deals very effectively with a difficult medium; Hurlstone was fond of wind instruments, and a performer on the clarinet (besides being, of course, a fine pianist). Some of the material of the piano quartet was taken from an early quintet for piano and wind, and the four *Characteristic pieces* for clarinet and piano contain some admirable clarinet writing.

In the bassoon sonata the piano is treated very discreetly, and never allowed to overpower the wind instrument; perhaps the most striking movement is the second, a *Ballade* which is entirely based on the rather bleak opening melody; its subsequent treatment in the style of a fugal exposition is both novel and effective.

In reviewing Hurlstone's brief career, one cannot help recalling the celebrated epitaph on Schubert: 'Music has here entombed a rich treasure but much fairer hopes.' What Hurlstone's attitude would have been to the various tendencies of modern music can hardly be guessed. It is not likely that he would have been influenced by Stravinsky or the new French school, but a few passages in his work suggest that he might have developed his folk-song tendencies in sympathy with the ideas of a section of modern English musicians. One thing, however, may be regarded as certain—that his work would be innocent of any kind of pose or insincerity. R. H. WALTHEW.

[Hurlstone, besides being a composer, was, as pianist, greatly skilled as an interpreter of chamber music, though his technique was of an unconventional order. He was a personal friend of my own, and it is of painful interest to me to recall that I took part in Tchaikovsky's piano trio with him a fortnight before his death, at a concert of the King Cole Chamber Music Club, and that the first performance of his piano quartet was given on the day of his funeral. Mention should be made of the help given to Hurlstone at a critical moment of his career by Capt. Alex. Beaumont, himself an amateur composer, and a generous patron of music. EDITOR.]

HURUM, ALFONSE b. 1882, Norwegian composer.

Quartet, str, a mi	op. 6	Hurum, 1915.	
Sonata, pf, v, d mi	,, 2	,,	
,, ,, ,, a mi	,, 8	,,	1915.
Eksotisk suite, pf, v	,, 9	,,	1916.

Hurum's works possess lyric qualities and show national tendencies.

HUS-DESFORGES, PIERRE LOUIS, 1773–1838, French 'cellist.

Was in his day considered a composer of distinction. A list of his works, which included no less than nine quintets for 2 v, vla, vc, and cb (also 2 vc), is to be found in *Vidal* and *Fétis*. F. A. Hadland (in the *Strad*) mentions three sonatas for 'cello and cb dedicated to Napoleon I, and sold in London by the firm of R. Cocks & Co.

HUSS, HENRY HOLDEN, b. 1862, American composer and pianist.

Quartet, str	op. 31	S.P.A.M. Schirmer, 1921.
Sonata, pf, v, g mi	,, 19	Schirmer, 1903 and 1920.

These two works by no means represent the whole of Huss's chamber music, but they are all that have at present been published.

THE VIOLIN SONATA has had frequent public performances. The hand of a skilled technician is evident throughout, and it is distinguished by personal charm. This is particularly in evidence in the second movement—a blend of minuet and scherzo—almost Ravelian in its continence and clarity.

THE QUARTET for strings was selected for publication by the S.P.A.M. As an expression of the composer's ripe maturity, this work gives clear evidence that the hazardous methods of modernist experimentation hold no allurements for him. The harmonic weavings of Franck may have left their impress here and there, but the energy and charm of the first movement bear clear token of an artistic personality capable of fully articulate expression. The work is of excellent proportions; there is no striving after effect, no faltering in the handling of the medium. A work of direct and warm appeal, sincerity of purpose, and sureness of effect. ARTHUR SHEPHERD.

†HUTCHENRUYTER, WOUTER, Dutch composer.

Sonata, pf, vc	op. 4	Cranz.

†HUYBRECHTS, ALBERT, b. 1899, Belgian composer, pupil of Jongen.

Huybrechts was awarded the Elizabeth Sprague Coolidge prize of the Library of Congress, Washington, D.C., for a violin and piano sonata; also the Ojai Valley prize offered by Frank Jefferson Frost, for a string quartet. This quartet was played at the Ojai Valley festival of chamber music, in 1926, a festival arranged jointly by Mr. Frost and Mrs. Coolidge.

REPRINTED LITHOGRAPHICALLY IN GREAT BRITAIN
AT THE UNIVERSITY PRESS, OXFORD
BY VIVIAN RIDLER
PRINTER TO THE UNIVERSITY